A PRACTITIONER'S GUIDE TO THE EUROPEAN CONVENTION ON HUMAN RIGHTS

A PRACTITIONER'S GUIDE TO THE EUROPEAN CONVENTION ON HUMAN RIGHTS

BY

KAREN REID

SWEET & MAXWELL

THOMSON REUTERS

First Edition	1998
Reprinted	2003
Second Edition	2004
Third Edition	2007
Fourth Edition	2011

Published in 2011 by Sweet & Maxwell, 100 Avenue Road, London NW3 3PF part of Thomson Reuters (Professional) UK Limited (Registered in England & Wales, Company No 1679046 Registered Office and address for service, Aldgate House, 33 Aldgate High Street, London EC3N 1DL)

For further information on our products and service, visit *www.sweetandmaxwell.co.uk*

Typeset by LBJ Typesetting Ltd, Kingsclere

Printed and bound by CPI Group (UK) Ltd, Croydon, CR0 4YY.

No natural forests were destroyed to make this product; only farmed timber was used and replanted.

A CIP catalogue record for this book is available from The British Library

ISBN 978–0–41404–242–1

ACKNOWLEDGMENTS

To my family, friends and fellow toilers in the Registry.

DISCLAIMER

The views expressed in this book are solely those of the author and do not represent those of any institution.

CONTENTS

TABLE OF CASES BEFORE THE EUROPEAN COURT OF HUMAN RIGHTS

TABLE OF CASES BEFORE THE EUROPEAN COURT OF HUMAN RIGHTS

TABLE OF CASES BEFORE THE EUROPEAN COURT OF HUMAN RIGHTS

TABLE OF CASES BEFORE THE EUROPEAN COMMISSION OF HUMAN RIGHTS

TABLE OF LEGISLATION

Table of Rules of Court of the European Court of Human Rights

Table of National Legislation

INTRODUCTION

PURPOSE OF THIS BOOK

This is intended to be a practical book. It will not offer solutions or theories or an exhaustive study. It will, hopefully, indicate the range of situations and legal problems which may fall within the scope of the European Convention of Human Rights ("the Convention") and its Protocols. And it aims to explain the what, when, how and why of a particular procedure, that of introducing applications before the European Court of Human Rights ("the Court").

WHAT

The basic subject-matter of this procedure is human rights. This is a concept which is trammelled with popular misconceptions, false expectations and knee-jerk prejudices. In this book, the term means solely those rights and freedoms expressly guaranteed under the Convention and its Protocols. The competence of the Court is defined by the Convention. Every complaint must base itself squarely on the Convention's provisions and comply with its requirements. Essentially, the provisions of the Convention cover classic civil and political rights: economic and social rights are only covered indirectly, if at all. Pt IIA: Problem Areas highlights the situations and disputes, which fall, or may fall, within the ambit of Convention rights.

HOW

An application begins, simply, with a letter to the Court setting out the substance of the complaint.

The procedures which follow do require some explanation (see Pt IA: Practice and Procedure). However, there are a minimum of formalities and no fees which reflects the fact the system is meant to be open to everyone, legally represented or not, and that a significant number of applications are pursued by individuals who have no access to, no means to pay or no inclination to use, lawyers.

WHEN

A strict time-limit applies. An application must be made within six months of the final decision relating to the subject-matter of the complaint where domestic remedies exist or within six months of the act or event complained of where no domestic remedies exist. Limited exception arises where there can be said to be a continuing situation (see Pt IB: Admissibility Checklist).

WHY

The responsibility of Governments to adhere to minimum standards of fair and proper conduct in exercising their powers in respect of their own citizens and any others within their jurisdiction is acknowledged on domestic and international level. In ratifying the Convention, the Government of the United Kingdom has expressly pledged, by way of treaty obligation, to ensure the observance of fundamental rights and freedoms guaranteed in that instrument. It has, as a result, accepted the rights of individuals, groups of individuals, non-governmental organisations and private companies to introduce complaints against it (and all public authorities under its responsibility) under the implementation system provided in Strasbourg. Since this is a supranational instance, it offers the possibility of remedies where a domestic system cannot. No national legal system is free from *lacunae*, historical anomalies, cultural biases or blindspots. While the United Kingdom seems, sometimes unfairly, to be subject to unfavourable scrutiny in Strasbourg, it is a compliment to the Government, which allows free, unhindered access to the system and co-operates fully and fairly in the procedures; to the applicants who are prepared to fight for justice against the weight of the State; and to the lawyers who bring a common law approach and British trained legal expertise to the process.

In the proceedings, applicants can obtain a limited but not negligible range of remedies. It is possible that the Government will offer to settle the case: providing specific reparation (for example, right of entry to the United Kingdom, grant of planning permission); or a change of legislation or administrative practice; ex gratia payment of compensation; and reasonable legal costs. A binding judgment may make public declaration of the State's breach accompanied by a monetary award of just satisfaction and the payment of legal costs (Pt III). Following such a judgment, the State is required to comply with the Court's findings which may also lead to a specific result such as legislative change or other steps necessary to remedy whatever failing has been identified.

Besides rendering a successful outcome for a particular individual, an application can be seen in a wider context. It is a method of achieving law reform and improving or maintaining civil rights standards. It participates in furnishing a system of model standards contributing to worldwide developments. In that context, practitioners prepared to represent applicants play a significant and creative role in identifying those cases which can usefully be dealt with in Strasbourg and in developing the case-law under the Convention by the arguments and principles which they advocate in pleading.

YES, BUT. . .

There are drawbacks. The admissibility threshold is high: at most one in ten cases succeeds in crossing it (see Pt IB: Admissibility Checklist). But it is possible to be selective and successful. Some practitioners from the United Kingdom have a high success rate in reaching the admissibility stage, and subsequent friendly settlement or findings of violation by the Court.

There is delay. Ironically, for an institution which sits in judgment on allegations that domestic courts have failed to decide cases within a reasonable time, it may take more than three years for a successful case to conclude before the Court. (Less successful cases are generally disposed of more summarily and sometimes as quickly as within three to six months.) The reasons for the delay are several: the backlog of applications which increases with every new country that joins the system, long series of cases generated by systemic problems, the inherent openness of the system which allows, and requires decisions in, large numbers of unmeritorious or hopeless complaints; and shortage of staff and resources. The Court is sensitive to the problem, constantly reviewing its procedures and introducing such modifications as are compatible with its powers, but the situation has long been unsatisfactory. Further fundamental reforms, following Protocol No.11 in 1998 and the latest Protocol No.14, are under discussion; yet another new inadmissibility criterion may be added and alterations made to the system of filtering incoming applications to enable the Court to cope with the tide of incoming complaints.

There are also inequalities as regards the position of the applicant. Governments enjoy certain procedural advantages in addition to obvious superiority of resources.

No international system can be perfect or immune to error. All who have worked with the Court have had experience of cases that were, in their view, disappointing, regrettable, if not worse. But these are, on the whole, outweighed by the successes. The Convention system is a tool of remarkable possibilities. While the continuing rise in the volume of cases has practical disadvantages, it has also contributed to dynamic trends in interpretation as the case-law extends into new areas and adapts to changing climates and perceptions. As a final and hopefully persuasive illustration, the following changes in UK legislation and practice resulted from, or were contributed to by, cases dealt with in Strasbourg: the Security Service Act 1989; Interception of Communications Act 1985; end of blanket censorship of prisoners' letters; change in practice regarding the grant of legal aid on appeal in Scotland; the Children Act 1989; end of criminalisation of homosexual relationships between consenting adults over 16; regular review by a tribunal of the continued detention of mental health patients and life sentence prisoners; end of corporal punishment in schools and birching on the Isle of Man; revision of the court martial system; the Special Immigration Appeals Commission Act 1997, providing for legal representation of applicants to be deported in the interests of national security and review by the special tribunal of the evidence basing the decision; an introduction of a new code of conduct lifting the ban on gays serving in the military; an independent tribunal to consider complaints about covert surveillance by the police; measures taken concerning independence of investigations into police involvement in the lethal use of force, the giving of reasons for not prosecuting and the use of sensitive security materials in evidence; and providing widowers with benefits on an equal footing with widows.

PART I: PRACTICE AND PROCEDURE

A. PROCEDURE BEFORE THE EUROPEAN COURT OF HUMAN RIGHTS

1. The Court

On November 1, 1998 pursuant to Protocol No.11, the single permanent Court replaced the previous Convention organs, the European Commission of Human Rights ("the Commission") and the old Court. Both bodies had sat on a part-time basis. The Commission had acted as a quasi-judicial, fact-finding and filter mechanism, its files and hearings not open to the public. It had dealt with the bulk of applications, applying the admissibility criteria to decide which cases could eventually be referred to the Court which held public hearings and issued binding judgments, monitored by the Committee of Ministers of the Council of Europe.[1] The new Court now examines both admissibility and merits. I–001

Membership of the Court

The qualifications for the new Court remain the same as the old Court, namely, that the judges must be of high moral character and possess the qualifications required for appointment to high judicial office or be jurisconsults of recognised competence.[2] Protocol No.11 added an age-limit of 70, after which a judge can no longer sit. The judges are also under an obligation not to engage in any activity incompatible with full-time office, the intention being that the judges should live in Strasbourg and sit on a permanent basis. Ad hoc judges may be appointed by a Contracting State in particular cases where the national judge withdraws.[3] I–002

The appointment procedure, in brief, is that each Member State nominates three suitable candidates for their national seat. They are encouraged to find women candidates. They may or may not indicate their order of preference. A committee of the Parliamentary Assembly of the Council of Europe (made up of representatives of the legislatures of Member States) interviews all candidates and reports to the Assembly which elects the judge for each seat by majority vote. There is an also an advisory group which issues opinions as to whether the candidates on a list fulfil the required qualifications, as part of an initiative to ensure that elected judges fully match the requirements of the Convention.

The Court is headed by a President, two Vice-Presidents (who act also as Presidents of Sections) and three additional Presidents of Sections, each elected for a

[1] The Committee of Ministers consists formally of the Foreign Ministers of the member States of the Council of Europe, but generally its functions are carried out by deputies attached to the various embassies and representations in Strasbourg.

[2] Currently, amongst the Court, there are figure members of the judiciary from their home countries, ex-practising lawyers, ex-ambassadors or Government Agents and a fair sprinkling of academics specialising in international law.

[3] r.28 of the Rules of Court, e.g. where a judge has or had a connection with a case on the domestic level.

three-year period. They may be re-elected once to the same level of office.[4] The President of the Court has the power to issue practice directions (Art.32).[5]

Organisation of the Court

I–003 There are five types of composition: Single Judge, committees of three, Chambers (Sections), the Grand Chamber and the Plenary Court.

The **Plenary** Court has a primarily internal administrative function.

Single Judges may reject as inadmissible or strike out cases which are clearly inadmissible. The vast majority of cases are rejected in this manner (in 2011, some 90 per cent of decisions taken on admissibility were reached in Single Judge formation). Single Judges are assisted by non-judicial *rapporteurs*, members of the Registry.[6]

Committees of three may reject as inadmissible or strike out cases by unanimous vote. They may also adopt judgments in cases concerning well-established case-law by unanimous vote.

Chambers consist of seven judges. There is no quorum and substitute judges sit to maintain the numbers. There are at the moment five Sections from which the Chambers are composed. Two are headed by Vice-Presidents and the others by Presidents of Section. Cases not dealt with by Single Judges or committee are examined in Chambers. Where a Chamber considers that the case raises a serious question affecting the interpretation of the Convention or protocols, or where the resolution of a question might have a result inconsistent with a judgment previously delivered by the Court (Art.30), it may relinquish jurisdiction to the Grand Chamber, unless within one month one of the parties to the case objects.[7] After the Chamber gives judgment on the merits, the parties may within three months in exceptional cases request that the case be referred to the Grand Chamber (Art.44). A panel of the Grand Chamber (five judges including the President, the Presidents/Vice-Presidents of the Sections not previously involved in the case and a judge designated in rotation) may accept the request if the case raises a serious question affecting the interpretation and application of the Convention or a serious issue of general importance (Art.43).

The **Grand Chamber** (17 judges including the President, Vice-Presidents and Presidents of the Sections and the national judge for any respondent State) examines cases where the Chambers have relinquished jurisdiction or those referred by the Panel after request by one of the parties following a Chamber judgment. It may also issue advisory opinions (Arts 47–49) at the request of the Committee of Ministers concerning legal questions on the interpretation of the Convention. To date it has

[4] r.8.

[5] r.32. Four practice directions have issued: on interim measures, the institution of proceedings, written pleadings and just satisfaction. See Annex 6 for the first three.

[6] Arts 26 and 27: Single Judges are in operation since June 1, 2010, when Protocol No.14 came into force.

[7] r.72(2) refers to a "duly reasoned objection" and stipulates that an objection which does not fulfil the criteria will be considered invalid. This perhaps leaves scope for discounting objections which do not contain sound objections, as well as those containing no reasons at all.

received three requests, the first of which it declined as outside its competence[8]; two opinions have been issued to date.[9]

2. Outline of procedure

Traditional procedure

- Lodging of application I–004
- Preliminary contacts with the Court's Registry
- Registration in the list of cases awaiting judicial decision.
- Case allocated to Single Judge if clearly inadmissible; if not, case listed for examination in a Chamber of a Section, *Judge Rapporteur* appointed.
- Case rejected *de plano* in a Section, if inadmissible. If not, communication of the case by a Chamber or Chamber President to the respondent Government in a joint procedure of admissibility and merits (Art.29–3).
- Filing of observations on admissibility and merits.
- Friendly settlement proposals.
- Examination before the Chamber in the light of parties' observations;
  - — rejection of case as inadmissible (Art.29 disapplied); on occasion adoption of a separate decision on admissibility;
  - — oral hearing on admissibility and merits (rare);
  - — relinquishment to the Grand Chamber;
  - — in most cases, adoption of judgment on the merits incorporating admissibility.
- Where judgment adopted, possibility of referral to Grand Chamber (subject to grant of leave by the Panel).

1. Lodging of application

Introduction of an application[10] may be done by letter or fax. To stop time running for the purposes of the six-month rule, any preliminary letter, pending submission of a detailed application, must contain a brief outline of the facts and complaints sufficient to convey the substance of the application.[11] I–005

A full application must be made on the application form provided by the Registry and include the information specified in r.47–principally, details identifying the applicant (name, date of birth, nationality, sex, occupation and address); the Contracting Party/Parties; a succinct statement of facts; a succinct statement of alleged violations; an explanation as to compliance with the six-month rule and rule of exhaustion of domestic remedies; the object of the application; accompanied by any relevant supporting documents, in particular the decisions, whether judicial or

[8] Decision on the competence of the Court to give an advisory opinion, June 2, 2004: concerning possible conflict between the European Convention system and the human rights treaty drawn up by the Commonwealth of Independent States.

[9] *Advisory Opinion*, February 12, 2008 concerning the composition of lists of candidates for election as judges of the Court (in particular whether a list could be rejected for failure to include a woman); *Advisory Opinion (No. 2)* January 22, 2010 concerning whether, and within what time-limit, a Contracting State may withdraw a list of candidate judges for the Court submitted to the Parliamentary Assembly.

[10] See Practice Direction on Institution of Proceedings, Appendix 6.

[11] r.47(5).

not, relating to the complaints. Failure to comply with these requirements may result in the application not being examined by the Court, namely it will not be included on the list of pending cases.[12]

An applicant's name is public, unless, on request and supported by adequate reasons, the President authorises anonymity. This is commonly done in cases involving children or sexual abuse victims or asylum seekers who fear reprisals. The President may, in such cases, order anonymity of his or her own motion.[13]

A period of eight weeks is usually indicated in the first letter from the Registry as the time within which an application form should be returned. This is not a formal rule derived from the Convention but a practice to prevent long lapses in time in registering a case for examination by the Court: it is possible, if necessary and not unreasonable in the circumstances, for longer time to be taken (see s.B: sub-s.1: Admissibility, Six months). A gap of more than six months in correspondence will now result in the file being destroyed.[14]

A legal representative must provide a letter of authority signed by the applicant authorising the lawyer to represent him before the Court.

2. Preliminary contacts with the Registry

I–006 The Registry, staffed by lawyers from Contracting States, manages applications as follows. A file is opened with each new complaint/letter. It is allotted to a case lawyer within an applications division who has the relevant linguistic and legal expertise. The Registry will send the application form and may inform an applicant whether he has omitted any necessary information or supporting documentation. As a general rule, it will not register a case for examination until all information or documents have been provided. The Registry is authorised to draw to applicants' attention any apparent problems as to admissibility, though due to the increasing work load of the Court this is no longer done as a matter of course. However, any points raised by the Registry, even if disagreed with, should be answered. Since clearly inadmissible cases can be rejected in summary fashion (Single Judge), it is advisable to establish that the case does not fall into that category.

Admissibility stage

3. Registration of the application

I–007 Once the case file is ready, the application is included in the list of cases awaiting examination by the Court. The speed with which it receives its first examination will depend on the pressure of work and complexity of the case (varying from three to 18 months in UK cases, up to four years or even longer for countries with a massive backlog of cases such as Russia and Turkey). Cases may be given priority under r.41 by a Chamber or a President (e.g. where an applicant has serious health problems[15] or children are involved). Other cases are also ranked in order of priority to ensure urgent cases, cases of systemic importance and those concerning Arts 2, 3, 4 and 5

[12] r.47(4).
[13] r.47(3).
[14] See Practice Direction on Institution of Proceedings, para.11, Appendix 6.
[15] *Pretty v UK* April 29, 2002, ECHR 2002–III.

do not languish too long unexamined. A case identified as raising a Convention issue is generally allotted to a Section in which the national judge sits).

4. Appointment of a *judge rapporteur*

Save in Single Judge cases, the President of the Section appoints in each case a *judge rapporteur* a judge charged with presenting the case to the Court.[16] The identity of the *rapporteur* is never disclosed and it cannot be assumed that it is the national judge. It is the *rapporteur*, with the assistance of the case lawyer from the Registry, who makes proposals to the Court as to the procedure, decisions and texts to be adopted in respect of a case. Before presenting a case to the Court, a *rapporteur* may request factual information or documentation from one or more of the parties.[17] I–008

5. Initial examination

(a) Examination by Single Judge

Cases which are clearly inadmissible or appropriate to be struck out are listed for examination by Single Judges, who work with non-judicial *rapporteurs* appointed by the President from amongst the experienced lawyers in the Registry.[18] A one-page decision letter is sent to the applicant. This procedure, which enables the Court to reject large numbers of cases swiftly, is a key means for dealing with its huge work load. Single Judge procedure is used not only to reject hopeless or misconceived applications but also cases which, albeit factually or procedurally complex, interesting or well-argued, can nonetheless be rejected under the admissibility criteria.[19] If the Single Judge does not take a decision rejecting the case, it is forwarded to a Committee of three judges or a Chamber.[20] I–009

(b) Examination by Committee of Three Judges

A Committee may, if unanimous, reject as inadmissible or strike out cases referred to it by Single Judges.[21] It would appear to act, in this capacity, as a mechanism whereby Single Judges seek confirmation by a panel of peers as to the correctness of the assessment of inadmissibility. If the Committee does not consider the case inadmissible, it will be sent to the Chamber for examination. I–010

(c) Examination in a Chamber

Cases may be referred to a Chamber following initial examination by a Single Judge or a Committee of three judges. It may be examined for the first time in a Chamber if the issues are considered sufficiently important.[22] The Chamber may, on occasion, I–011

[16] r.49 (concerning individual applications under Art.34). However, in inter-State cases under Art.35, it is the Chamber that appoints one or more *rapporteur(s)* (r.48).
[17] r.49(3)(a).
[18] Art.27, r.52A para. 2—a Single Judge cannot decide cases from his or her own country.
[19] In first nine months of 2011, of 33,693 decisions on admissibility or striking out, 30,779 were rejected by Single Judges.
[20] r.52A(3).
[21] Art.28, para.1(a).
[22] Art.29, para.1.

request further information (e.g. issues of fact or domestic law or particular documents).[23] Where, however, a Convention issue is considered to arise requiring examination, the complaint is communicated to the respondent Government for observations on admissibility and merits (see further below). It may reject as inadmissible part of the application, communicating only the part with live issues.

The Chamber will not declare a case admissible without first inviting the Government's comments.

A Chamber may, at any stage, relinquish jurisdiction of a case to the Grand Chamber (Art.30). It must consult the parties first and where a party objects it must continue the examination of the case.[24] An objection must, however, comply with Art.30 and r.72 of the Rules of Court. In particular, it must be lodged within one month of notification of the Chamber's intention to relinquish and constitute "a duly reasoned objection". An objection which does not comply with these conditions is invalid. For the moment, there is no indication of the grounds on which a Chamber could discount an objection as invalid or lacking due reasoning . Chambers will often wait until after admissibility to pass a case to the Grand Chamber and have so far not shown themselves overzealous in giving up jurisdiction themselves.[25]

6. Communication by a Chamber or Chamber President

I–012 Where a Convention issue is considered to arise requiring further examination, the respondent Government is invited to submit observations on admissibility and merits. Questions are put indicating the areas of concern. The parties may also be directed that no submissions are required on other points, which is generally an indication that they are regarded as inadmissible. The questions put to the parties should be addressed or risk going by default.

The Government is generally given three months to reply, then a copy of the reply is sent to the applicant for his response, for which a shorter time-limit of a month is standard. However, applications can be made for an extension in the time-limit, which should be received by the Court before the expiry of the time-limit. Submissions sent after the expiry of the time-limit may not be accepted.[26] An applicant is advised to reply to any arguments raised by the Government on inadmissibility, whether non-exhaustion, six-months or manifestly ill-founded. While the Court is perfectly capable of rejecting Government arguments on its own knowledge of domestic and Convention case-law, well-prepared argument by applicants is of valuable assistance to a thorough and accurate examination of the issues. The form and contents of pleadings, including the requirement where submissions are over 30 pages for a short summary to be provided, are subject to a practice direction.[27]

In the majority of cases, the President of a Chamber decides on communication of a case to the respondent Government.[28] This possibility was instituted to allow for

[23] r.54(2)a.

[24] e.g. *Pellegrini v Italy*, July 20, 2001 ECHR 2001–VIII, where the applicant objected.

[25] e.g. *Pretty*, fn.15 above, which raised new points of interpretation of Convention law, was kept in a Chamber, perhaps with a view to the more expeditious procedures available. The Grand Chamber, made up of 17 judges and extra substitutes, tends to attract problems of timetabling and involve more cumbersome procedures.

[26] r.38 is formulated in strict terms—it is necessary for the President to decide to accept late submissions.

[27] Practice Direction on Written Pleadings, see Annex 6.

[28] r.54(2)b as amended.

more expeditious treatment of applications which are clearly communicable, in particular, as they are part of a series of cases.[29] The President cannot, for the moment, declare any part of the application inadmissible. Partial decisions (e.g. partly inadmissible or partly adjourned for observations) continue to be decided by the Chamber.

It is not excluded in the Convention that a three-judge committee can communicate a case. For the moment it is not envisaged in the Rules of Court.

6a. Communication by joint or disjoined procedure

Traditionally, applications which resulted in a judgment went through a two-stage examination—admissibility and merits—with the opportunity for two rounds of observations. Article 29, para.3 of the Convention was introduced to allow the Court to decide both stages together and this is the method which now predominates as a means of fighting the backlog of cases. In this abbreviated or joined procedure, the Chamber, or President, on communicating to the respondent Government, puts the parties on notice that it may proceed to determine admissibility and merits together in a judgment and to that end require the parties to put forward their submissions on just satisfaction and any proposals for friendly settlement.[30] The Chamber may at any time disapply Art.29, para. 3 and issue a separate decision on admissibility and a subsequent judgment on the merits.[31] I–013

7. Oral hearings

Before declaring a case admissible or issuing a judgment in the joint procedure, the Court may, in exceptional cases, hold an oral hearing on admissibility and merits. A hearing may also be held on the merits alone after a decision on admissibility. Hearings only tend to occur where a novel or complex point of law arises on which oral argument may provide assistance or, on occasion, where a case may, in the view of the Government, have fundamental effects on an important area of domestic law or practice. The vast majority of cases are decided without an oral hearing. I–014

When a oral hearing is decided, the Court sends the parties a list of questions to be addressed. This indicates its primary concerns and other issues are addressed at the risk of being regarded as irrelevant. An opportunity is provided to supplement any oral observations with further written materials submitted by a fixed time-limit shortly before the hearing. This may be useful for providing relevant background information, further factual developments or subsidiary arguments.

Parties are also requested to provide a copy of their speech at least one day in advance. This is solely to assist the interpreters (English-French, the two official languages of the Court). Adjustments may be made to the speech as required. Speakers should bear in mind the interpretation process and avoid talking fast. Court hearings are in public, unless, in exceptional circumstances, the Chamber decides otherwise.[32]

[29] e.g. length of civil or criminal proceedings, or, from the United Kingdom, cases dealing with court martials, discrimination in allowances/pensions payable to widowers, etc.

[30] r.54A(1). While this rule refers only to the Chamber, in practice the Presidents of Sections, presumably acting by way of delegated powers, communicate cases and apply the joint procedure at the same time.

[31] r.54A(1).

[32] r.63. Press and public may be excluded in the interest inter alia of the protection of private life or juveniles, or in special circumstances where publicity would prejudice the interests of justice (r.63(2)). Very few hearings have been held even partly in camera, mostly involving children.

The procedure for the hearing is notified to the parties beforehand, the timing being subject to strict regulation. The standard hearing held in a morning, or in an afternoon, consists of 30 minutes each for the Government and the applicant, questions put by the judges, a 20–30 minute adjournment, a final round of 15 minutes each for Government and applicant to address the questions and make final points (including response to the other side's oral pleadings). The average hearing is over in two hours. Exceptionally complex cases, or cases joined and being heard together, will be allocated further time, but this generally does not exceed 90 minutes total for each party.

Lawyers make their submissions standing and are not required to, and generally do not, wear robes.

After the hearing is closed, the Court proceeds to deliberate and will generally reach a decision on admissibility or merits the same day. However, no advance notice is given and the parties must wait until the adoption of the relevant written decision or judgment.

8. Decisions on admissibility

I–015 Where the Court declares a case inadmissible, there is no provision for appeal. The text of the decision indicates whether the decision was unanimous or by a majority, without specifying the exact votes. No dissenting opinions by judges are given on admissibility.

Cases communicated by the President or Chamber may, instead of being examined by the Chamber, be referred to Committees of three judges where it may be determined on the basis of well-established case-law (the so-called "WECL" procedure).[33] The parties are generally notified in advance and given the opportunity to object. An inadmissibility decision or judgment on the merits is issued where the three-judge committee is unanimous (see further below). The Committee may instead refer the case to the Chamber of seven judges if it thinks it appropriate.

Where a separate decision declaring a case admissible is taken, the friendly settlement and merits stages follow.

A case may be restored to the list (Art.37, para.2 of the Convention, r.43(5)). This is not the same thing as an appeal and only occurs in the most exceptional circumstances, such as the Court's clear mistaken reliance on an erroneous fact (for example the wrong date of introduction).

9. Establishment of the facts

I–016 The Court has power to take evidence and hear witnesses (see Annex to the Rules of Court concerning investigations).

It is rare that the Court is unable sufficiently to determine the factual basis of an application on the documentary material provided by the parties. Where a matter has been adjudicated in a domestic system, at first instance and on appeal, it is likely that the crucial facts have become common ground between the parties or that the differences between them are unlikely to be resolved further. The Court, as the

[33] Art.28, para.1(b), r.53, para.3: the national judge is not automatically part of the formation. It appears that they may be invited if, for example, the respondent State has contested that the case is suitable for WECL treatment

Commission before it, occasionally carries out fact-finding missions where the location is of particular relevance, for example, conditions of detention cases.[34] Where there are no apparent effective investigations at the domestic level, and there exists disagreement between the parties as to the basic facts, the Court has also been forced to take on the role of hearing witnesses, following the practice of fact-finding missions conducted by the Commission from 1995–1999 in cases from the state of emergency region in south-east Turkey.

On such missions, hearings are generally conducted before a delegation of three judges. Witnesses are heard on oath and the parties are present and able to put questions after the judges have done so. An inquisitorial, rather than adversarial, approach is adopted.[35]

10. Friendly settlement procedure and striking out[36]

The Court informs the parties when it sends the decision on admissibility, or on instigating the joint procedure, that it is at their disposal to assist a friendly settlement. It does not however follow the previous practice of the Commission in giving an indication of its provisional opinion of the merits with a view to encouraging settlements. The Registrar of the relevant section will, however, consult with the parties in appropriate cases concerning the possibility of settlement and may make proposals to the parties in standard cases. I–017

Friendly settlement negotiations are confidential and not referred to in the judgment. Nor are the documents concerning settlement accessible to the public.[37] The Court is not bound to strike a case out where the parties agree to settle. It is required to continue the examination of the case where human rights so require.[38] However, it has accepted the vast majority of settlements or requests from the applicant to withdraw.[39] In a system of individual applications, it would take very exceptional circumstances for the Court to continue a case where the individual claiming to be a victim of the breach no longer wished, of his free will, to pursue it further.

Where agreement is reached, the parties are generally required to make declarations to that effect and undertake not to seek to refer the case to the Grand Chamber. The Court adopts a decision or judgment striking the case out, which is public and sent to the Committee of Ministers. The parties are generally left to arrange payment of compensation and reasonable costs between themselves.

The Convention organs, struggling under an ever-increasing workload, have always been favourable towards settlements. Where a lead case has established the Convention position on an issue, or a breach is acknowledged and appropriate redress is offered, it might be considered an ineffective use of the Court's time and resources to proceed to a judgment on the merits. Some applicants, understandably,

[34] e.g. *Valasinas v Lithuania*, July 24, 2001, ECHR 2001–VIII.

[35] See Annex to the Rules of Court concerning investigations.

[36] See also sub-s.2(7) of this section: Striking out.

[37] r.33(1). See *R.R. v Poland*, May 24, 2011, where the Court rejected the Government's attempt to take the applicant's refusal to accept a settlement into account in the contentious proceedings.

[38] Art.37(1).

[39] The few exceptions include *Tyrer v UK*, April 25, 1978, Series A, No.26, paras 24–27; *Karner v Austria* (40016/98) July 24, 2003, ECHR 2003–IX, where the applicant died and the next-of-kin declined to continue the case; and *Ukrainian Media Group v Ukraine*, March 29, 2005.

look more to the principle of their cause and prefer to obtain a public, binding judgment against the Government. Settlement cannot be compelled, but the use of unilateral declarations (see further below) may end cases in which the Court considers the matter has been resolved.

The applicable provisions for striking out are found in Art.37, para.1. Paragraph 1(a) applies where the applicant expresses an intention to withdraw his application. The applicant's consent has not been held necessary when striking out under the other limbs of Art.37. In an expulsion case, where the extradition order against the applicant could no longer be enforced, the new Court proceeded to strike the case out under Art.37, para.1(b) on the basis that the matter had been resolved, notwithstanding the applicant's objections.[40]

The Court has also developed a practice of striking an application out under Art.37, para.1(c) (circumstances rendering it no longer justified to examine the case) where the Government makes a unilateral declaration which acknowledges the breach and provides redress. This will depend on whether, in the circumstances, the Court considers that the unilateral declaration offers a sufficient basis for finding that respect for human rights does not require the continued examination of the case. In *Akman v Turkey*[41], where the applicant's son had been shot by security forces, the case was struck out on the basis of the unilateral declaration by the Government which expressed regret at the use of excessive force in the case and accepted that this disclosed a breach of Art.2, undertaking to issue appropriate instructions and take necessary measures in future (including effective investigations) as well as to pay the applicant £85,000. The Grand Chamber has since clarified in *Tahsin Acar v Turkey*[42] that in cases of disappearance and killings by unknown perpetrators, where the facts are disputed by the parties, there must as a minimum be an acknowledgement by the Government of a failure to furnish an effective investigation and an undertaking to provide a Convention compliant investigation as redress. Applicants, who in future reject a Government proposal to settle a case on the basis of a concession of a breach and compensation or other form of adequate redress, therefore run the risk of having the case struck out on the basis of a unilateral declaration to the same effect.[43]

Where the Court strikes out a case under any of the above heads, it may award costs to the applicant under r.43, para.4.[44] As with awards of just satisfaction under Art.41, the costs must relate to the alleged violation or violations and be reasonable as to quantum.[45]

[40] *Bilasi-Ashri v Austria*, (3314/02) (Dec.) November 26, 2002, ECHR 2002–X; see also *Perna v Italy (Striking Out)*, October 24, 2002, paras 42–50, where the applicant's conviction had been quashed after hearing a witness not previously heard.

[41] *Akman v Turkey,* June 26, 2001, ECHR 2001–VI.

[42] *Tahsin Acar v Turkey,* May 6, 2003, ECHR 2003–VI.

[43] See, e.g. *Swedish Transport Workers Union v Sweden*, (53507/99) July 18, 2006, where the Government's unequivocal acceptance of a breach of Art.6 (access to court), an ongoing legislative review and offer of compensation and costs was found adequate despite objections by the applicant.

[44] Previously r.44(4), e.g. *Kalantari v Germany*, October 11, 2001, paras 61–64; *J.M. v UK* (41518/98) (Dec.) September 28, 2000, ECHR 2000–X; *Pilato v Italy*, (18995/06) (Dec.) September 2, 2008; *JN v UK*, (58043/08) (Dec.) November 24, 2009; contrast *Sisojeva v Latvia* (GC), January 15, 2007, para.134 where the applicants had received legal aid from the Court, no other sums were awarded.

[45] *Sisojeva*, fn.44 above, para.133.

11. Judgment on the merits

The Chambers may put specific questions for written observations on the merits or hold an oral hearing on the merits (see Oral Hearings above) before proceeding to adopt a judgment. The procedure at any hearing is largely identical to hearings prior to admissibility, save that in hearings on the merits the applicant addresses the Court first. I–018

The applicant is invited at this stage (if this did not occur on communication of the application to the respondent Government in the joint procedure) to submit his claims for just satisfaction at the same time as any further submissions on the merits. The heads of claim–pecuniary, non-pecuniary and costs and expenses–must be covered and details given. A failure to submit claims within the time-limit may result in no award being made.[46] A failure properly to quantify claims may also lead to no award.[47] Occasionally, in cases involving complex financial or property claims, the question of just satisfaction is adjourned and the matter addressed in a separate judgment. Judges who vote against the majority may, and generally do, give dissenting opinions. Concurring and separate opinions also occur where a judge agrees with the result but not necessarily the reasoning.

Few judgments are delivered in public in Strasbourg, though important Grand Chamber judgments are read out in extract by the President. It is considered sufficient to deliver them in writing and to have them available the same day on the Court's website.

Chamber judgments become final within three months of delivery, unless one of the parties before the expiry of this time period have requested referral to the Grand Chamber (Art.43, para.1). A panel of five judges of the Grand Chamber examines the referral request and are required by Art.43, para.2 to grant it where the case raises a serious question affecting the interpretation or application of the Convention or a serious issue of general importance. To date they have not given published reasons showing how they approach this assessment. The panel is however showing extreme restraint in granting requests from interests of legal certainty and to prevent the referral system becoming an automatic appeal system.[48] No appeal lies to the Grand Chamber from the decision of the panel.[49] Once a case is referred, the Grand Chamber enjoys the full range of judicial powers conferred on the Court and its examination is not necessarily confined to the points of concern raised by the referring party.[50] It is thus open to the Grand Chamber to recharacterise complaints under a provision of the Convention not relied upon by the parties or to decide that it is more appropriate to deal with an issue under one particular Article, as long as the same facts, declared admissible, are in issue throughout.[51]

[46] *Ferrantelli and Santangelo v Italy*, August 7, 1996, 1996–III, No.12.

[47] *Ausiello v Italy*, May 25, 1996, Reports, 1996–III, No.10.

[48] For recent examples of referred cases, e.g. *Hirst v UK (No.2)* October 6, 2005, ECHR 2005–IX; *Evans v UK*, April 10, 2007.

[49] *Pisano v Italy (Striking Out)*, October 24, 2002, paras 26–27.

[50] *Pisano v Italy (Striking Out)*, October 24, 2002, paras 27–28. This includes admissibility points.

[51] See e.g *Serife Yigit v Turkey*, November 2, 2010, paras 51–51, where the Chamber had considered the complaints of the applicant about refusal of a widow's pension due to her religious-only marriage under Art.8, the Grand Chamber instead invited the parties to make submissions under Art.14 in conjunction with Art.1 of Protocol No.1. This includes admissibility points; *Scoppola v Italy (No.2)*, September 17, 2009, paras 48–57, where complaints under Art.6 had been rejected as inadmissible, but complaints under Art.7 were admissible, the Grand Chamber considered it was still legitimate to extend examination of those facts admissible under Art.7 to Art.6 also.

A party may within one year from delivery of the judgment request interpretation of the judgment (r.79).[52] The request must state precisely the point or points in the operative part of the judgment (the conclusion of the judgment setting out the Court's votes on each part of the case) on which interpretation is required. Where the Chamber accepts the request, the other party is invited to make written submissions. A hearing may be held.

A party can also request revision of a judgment in the event of discovery of a fact which might have a decisive influence but was not known to the Court at the time and could not reasonably have been known to that party (r.80).[53] Examples of such circumstances have been the death of the applicant before the adoption of the judgment,[54] where documents have been overlooked in the Court case-file,[55] where the Government uncovers new information as to when property in issue in the judgment had been transferred out of the applicant's ownership[56] and where a party was not given an opportunity to comment on another party's pleadings.[57] Such request must be lodged within six months of discovery of the fact. Where the Chamber accepts the request, the other party is invited to make written submissions. A hearing may be held. Strict scrutiny is applied to such requests, the Court taking the view that legal certainty weighs against granting revision requests on anything but an exceptional basis.[58]

12. Pilot judgment procedure

I–019 The pilot judgment procedure[59] is initiated by the Court as the optimal method of dealing with a systemic problem in a Contracting State. Rather than examine the large numbers of similar applications individually, one or several cases are identified and communicated to the respondent Government. The parties' views as to the systemic nature of the problem and the suitability of the procedure are invited. In giving judgment, the Court will seek to identify the nature of the problem and the type of remedial measures required and may impose a time-limit on the Government to implement those measures.[60] Other similar applications may be adjourned

[52] e.g. *Ringeisen v Austria (No.3)*, June 23, 1973, Series A, No.16, para.13; *Allenet de Ribemont v France (interpretation)*, August 7, 1998, R.J.D., 1996–III, No.12, where the Commission asked the Court whether any sum awarded as just satisfaction should be paid without attachment, the Court found that this was an abstract point of interpretation and outside the rule. As regarded the second question as to how the global figure awarded for pecuniary and non-pecuniary damage should be distinguished, it stated that it had not distinguished any percentage, did not need to do so and had no intention of so doing—its judgment was clear and to hold otherwise was modification, not clarification.

[53] Revision was granted in *Pardo v France (revision)*, July 10, 1996, Reports, 1996–III, No.11, where the applicant had produced two letters, previously unobtainable, one of which had been referred to expressly by the Court in the context of lack of substantiation of his complaint. See also *Gustafsson v Sweden (revision)*, R.J.D. 1998–V, No.84.

[54] Revision was granted in *Pardo v France (revision)*, July 10, 1996, Reports 1996–III, No.11, where the applicant had produced two letters, previously unobtainable, one of which had been referred to expressly by the Court in the context of lack of substantiation of his complaint. See also *Gustafsson v Sweden (revision)*, R.J.D. 1998–V, No.84.

[55] *Fonyodi v Hungary (revision)*, April 7, 2009, invoice relevant to award of costs overlooked.

[56] *Nicola v Turkey (revision)*, October 26, 2010.

[57] *Adamczuk v Poland (revision)*, June 15, 2010.

[58] e.g. *Bajrami v Albania (revision)*, December 18, 2007, Court ordered award to be paid to the applicants' heirs.

[59] r.61.

[60] e.g. *Burdov v Russia (No.2)*, January 15, 2009.

meanwhile and once a remedy is provided on a national level, those cases may be settled or struck off for non-exhaustion, the applicants being required to resort to the new remedy.

13. Intervenors

The Contracting State of which the applicant is a national (if not the respondent State) may intervene as party in the proceedings as a matter of right (Art.36, para.1).[61] The State is informed of its right to intervene in a particular case when the case is communicated to the respondent State and is given twelve weeks to inform the Court of its intentions. It may submit written observations and participate in an oral hearing. I–020

The Commissioner of Human Rights of the Council of Europe has recently been given the right to intervene, through written submissions and participation in an oral hearing, subject to similar procedural conditions as Contracting States.[62]

Others require the leave of the President, or the invitation of the Court (Art.37, para.2).[63] Requests should be lodged within twelve weeks of the communication to the respondent State, although the President may exceptionally fix different time-limits.[64] Generally, leave is limited to the submission of written observations of a specified maximum length which deal with domestic and international law issues or statistical and factual information, without arguing the facts and merits of the case. It is very much rarer for non-State intervenors to be given leave to participate in an oral hearing.[65]

14. Length of court proceedings

Time taken depends on the current state of the Court's work load, the number of applications pending from a particular country, the complexity of the case and any requirements for gathering further evidence. Cases to which priority have been given have been known to take under a year to reach judgment, under six months in the case of *Pretty v UK*. On average, cases fall within the following range for the United Kingdom: I–021

Single judge 12–24 months

Decision to communicate 12–24 months

Case rejected as inadmissible after communication 15–30 months

[61] See r.44. For example, Turkey intervened in *Sen v Netherlands*, December 21, 2001.

[62] Art.36, para.3; r.44 para.2.

[63] See r.44 paras 3–5. The Voluntary Euthanasia Society and the Catholic Bishops' Conference of England and Wales were permitted to intervene in *Pretty*, fn.15 above, while Liberty made submissions, inter alia, in *Christine Goodwin v UK* (GC), July 11, 2002, ECHR 2002–VI. In *TI v UK*, (43844/98) (Dec.) March 7, 2000 ECHR 2000–III, concerning the safety of deporting the Tamil applicant from the UK to Germany where a previous asylum application had been refused, the Court invited both the German Government and the UNHCR to make written submissions before deciding on admissibility. The UNHCR participated in *M.S.S. v Greece and Belgium*, January 21, 2011.

[64] r.44(3)a.

[65] See *V v UK*, December 12, 1999, ECHR 1999–X, where permission was given for the lawyers of the parents of the victim, murdered by the applicant, to address the Court briefly.

Case decided on the merits in a judgment 24–36 months

15. Monitoring compliance

I–022 Pursuant to Art.46, para.2, the Committee of Ministers[66] supervises execution of Court judgments. Its role is to oversee what action is taken by Governments in response to a finding of a violation. When the case is placed on its agenda, it invites the State to inform it of the measures taken, and the matter is automatically recalled on the agenda at intervals of not less than six months. When it is satisfied that a Government has complied, it issues a resolution recording the position and declaring that it has exercised its function. Since the Court rarely hints at what steps would remedy a violation,[67] the Committee of Ministers operates largely independently. It has received criticism not only for the length of time taken to issue a resolution and complete the monitoring process but also in respect of its position in, on occasion, accepting a lack of positive action by a Government as sufficient response.[68] Thus in *Brogan v UK*, the Committee of Ministers accepted the Government's derogation under Art.15 as complying with the judgment finding a breach of Art.5, para.3.[69] In other cases, it has found it enough for the State to publicise the judgment and draw it to the attention of the relevant authorities.

Under the Committee of Ministers' rules, an applicant may make communications about failure to receive compensation awarded by the Court or any other matter relating to execution.

3. Interim relief

I–023 Under r.39, the Court may indicate that a measure be taken in the interests of the parties or the proper conduct of the proceedings. Though the equivalent measure previously applied by the Commission was not regarded as binding,[70] the Court found in *Mamatkulov and Askarov v Turkey* that a failure by a Contracting State to comply with interim measures is to be regarded as preventing the Court from effectively examining the applicant's complaint and as hindering the effective exercise of his or her right of individual petition in violation of Art.34 of the Convention.[71] Notwithstanding the Chamber's indication under r.39, Turkey had extradited to Uzbekistan two men who had claimed that they would be at risk of torture or inhuman treatment there. The Court found that it had thereby been prevented from carrying out a proper assessment of the applicants' complaints under Art.3 and, ultimately, from protecting them.

As the Court nonetheless relies on the good will and co-operation of the Contracting States, it was in the past careful not to abuse this procedure by intervening in domestic affairs without pressing reason. In more recent times, due to

[66] See fn.1 above.

[67] It considers that this is outside its role—see, e.g. *Akdivar v Turkey (Art.50)*, April 1, 1998, R.J.D. 1998–II, No.69, para.57; *Finucane v UK*, July 1, 2003, para.89.

[68] See, e.g. "The Committee of Ministers" by Adam Tomkins, E.H.R.L.R., Launch issue.

[69] *Brogan v UK,* November 29, 1988, Series A, No.145, B E.H.R.R. 117, Resolution DH (90) 23.

[70] *Cruz Varas v Sweden*, March 20, 1991, Series A, No.201, para.102.

[71] Judgment of February 4, 2005 (Grand Chamber), ECHR 2005–I. The Court had regard to international practice, inter alia, the International Court of Justice, the Inter-American Court and the UN Committee against torture.

the mounting number of asylum cases, complaints have arisen from Governments that the measure is applied too readily. The President of the Court has issued a practice statement emphasising that the Court cannot act as an appeal court for the immigration and asylum tribunals in Europe and calling on both applicants' lawyers and Governments to co-operate fully with the Court and to adhere to procedures.[72]

As a general practice, measures are applied only where there is an apparent real and imminent risk of irreparable harm to life and limb (cases under Arts 2 or 3).[73] There is generally a very high compliance rate by Contracting States. Most typically, the interim measure requested is the suspension of expulsion of an applicant to a country where there is a risk of serious ill-treatment, for example, a Tamil to Sri Lanka,[74] a deserter to Iran,[75] a girl to Tanzania where she claimed to be at risk of female genital mutilation,[76] and suspected Chechen terrorists from Georgia to Russia.[77] The Court has also indicated measures to be taken where prisoners' health was at apparent serious risk due to lack of appropriate treatment or conditions or in order to obtain medical examinations in respect of alleged ill-treatment or ill-health[78]; on occasion it has been applied to allow a lawyer to gain access to a detainee alleging Art.3 treatment.[79] While there is a certain presumption that Contracting States provide the necessary guarantees against ill-treatment, the Court has applied r.39 to Turkish Kurds threatened with return to Turkey and to an Afghan being sent to Greece where the asylum procedures were dysfunctional and conditions for asylum seekers, whether in detention or at liberty, were problematic.[80] The Court may also request information from the Contracting State, for example, regarding guarantees available or request, as in *Ocalan v Turkey*, that the applicant's lawyers be given full access to a detainee.[81]

Rule 39 has also been applied where the risk derives from the effect on health of the measure per se, for example where the applicant facing expulsion was in the later stages of a difficult pregnancy with a history of miscarriages[82] or where the applicant was an AIDS sufferer who was very ill and would have no access to treatment on deportation from the United Kingdom to St Kitts.[83]

While the procedure has been invoked in respect of other types of cases, e.g. adoption of children, which may arguably be of an irreparable nature, r.39 has not

[72] Statement of February11, 2011.

[73] Although *Evans v UK*, see fn.48 above, was principally an Art.8 case (private and family life issues) the Court indicated that the Government should take appropriate measures to safeguard the stored embryos, the destruction of which formed the subject-matter of the applicant's complaints: there was also an Art.2 complaint and as the applicant's ovaries had been removed due to cancer, any opportunity of having a child of her own would have been removed meanwhile.

[74] *Venkadajalasarma v Netherlands*, (58510/00) (Dec.) July 9, 2002.

[75] *Amrollahi v Denmark*, July 11, 2002.

[76] *Lunguli v Sweden*, (33692/02), (Dec.) July 1, 2003.

[77] *Shamayev v Georgia and Russia*, April 12, 2005, ECHR 2005–III.

[78] e.g. *Diri v Turkey*, July 31, 2007, the Court indicated that the prisoner, who complained of *falaka* (beating on the soles of the feet) should receive an MRI scan or bone scintigraphy; *Aleksanyan v Russia*, December 12, 2008, paras 230–231, request that the applicant suffering from advanced AIDS and lymph cancer, be transferred from prison to a specialist facility due to his critical condition and later that he be examined by a medical commission to obtain uptodate report on his condition.

[79] e.g. *Shtukaturov v Russia*, March 27, 2008, para. 4.

[80] e.g. *Avcisoy v UK*, (49277/99) (Dec.) February 19, 2002; *M.S.S. v Belgium and Greece*, January 21, 2011.

[81] *Ocalan v Turkey*, May 12, 2005, paras 197–202.

[82] (26985/95) (Dec.) May 15, 1996.

[83] *D v UK*, May 2, 1997, Reports, 1997–III, No.37.

been applied save in a few highly exceptional cases.[84] Matters of detention or interference with property, for example, are not regarded as necessitating interim measures.[85]

If an applicant intends to request a measure, it is necessary to submit the facts of the case in an outline application, detailing the complaints. It should be shown that domestic remedies have been exhausted (r.39 may not be applied if there are any pending procedures unless these do not have suspensive effect)–copies of the decisions should be provided.[86] The expulsion must also be imminent–the date should be provided or it should be pointed out that removal can lawfully take place without further warning. Any materials substantiating the alleged risk to life or of ill-treatment should be provided, such as medical reports concerning past incidents of torture, up-to-date reports on conditions in the receiving country (Amnesty International, UNHCR, US State Department country reports, etc).

Rule 39 requests are dealt with urgently and the decision is taken by an Acting President. However, as much time as possible should be given to allow the necessary procedure to be instituted by the Registry. It is wise to fax the request, with "Rule 39–Urgent" prominently on the first page, and to telephone the Registry either to warn of the arrival of the request or to verify its receipt. If the request is granted, the Government is informed immediately. The matter may be put before the Chamber for review at an early opportunity. If the request is refused, the case may nonetheless proceed for examination on admissibility and merits in the normal manner. The Practice Direction on Requests for Interim Measures[87] warns that a failure to make a request with the appropriate expedition or to supply relevant documents, in particular domestic court decisions and any material substantiating the applicant's allegations, may result in the Court being unable to examine the request. It also specifies that, in cases of expulsion or extradition, details should be given of the expected date and time of removal as well as the applicant's place of detention and case or reference number.

Measures are generally applied for limited, but renewable, periods. Since they rely on the continued existence of the risk, they will not be renewed if that risk disappears.[88]

Rule 39 may also be applied to the applicant. This is rare but has occurred in hunger strikes where the Commission or Court requested an applicant to give up the strike until the proceedings have been resolved.[89]

[84] See *Neulinger and Shuruk v Switzerland*, July 6, 2010, para.5. Cases concerning the welfare of children presumably attract particular concern.

[85] See, however, (25849/94) (Dec.) November 16, 1994, where the Commission applied interim measures to a woman allegedly faced with the risk of strict house arrest and other ill-treatment from her husband's family on return to Lebanon.

[86] In UK cases, this generally means the decision of the Secretary of State refusing asylum, the decision of the Immigration and Asylum Tribunal, and its rejection of further review and the decisions of any available courts (High Court/Court of Appeal or, in Scotland, the Court of Session) on judicial/statutory review application.

[87] See Annex 6.

[88] For example, due to steps taken by the Government or due to the receipt of guarantees against the alleged risk, as in the *Shameyev* case, fn.77 above, where the Russian Government gave guarantees of unhindered access to medical treatment, legal advice and to the Court and undertook not to apply the death penalty and to protect the applicants' health and safety.

[89] e.g. *Ertürk and Ertürk v Turkey*, (49683/99) (Dec.) August 24, 1999; *Ilascu v Moldova and Russia*, July 8, 2004, ECHR 2004–VII, para.11.

4. Legal Aid and Representation

Procedure

Legal aid only becomes available when a case is communicated by the Court to the respondent Government.[90] At that stage, declaration of means forms are sent to applicants who have either requested legal aid or it is considered appropriate. Other applicants may be informed of the opportunity to apply. The declaration of means must be certified by the relevant domestic authority. This is a formality required by the Rules of Court and insisted on rigidly by some Contracting States. Currently, the certifying body in the United Kingdom is the Legal Services Commission, which applies the standard of eligibility for domestic civil legal aid–which is not strictly relevant to Convention proceedings in Strasbourg. I–024

When the Court receives the means form and certification, it is no longer the rule that the Government be requested to comment; the President of the Section may so request when it is considered appropriate.[91] Once the Government's comments have been received, or the time-limit expired, and the observations from the Government on admissibility have also been received or the time-limit expired, the President proceeds to decide the application. If granted, offers of legal aid are sent at each stage of the procedure. The applicant's lawyer must sign and return them. When the work covered by the offer has been done, a claim form is sent to the lawyer, requiring bank details. On its return, the Registry forwards the paperwork to the Council of Europe finance division, which has the amounts sent by bank transfer.

The conditions for the grant of legal aid

The Rules of Court impose a condition of financial necessity (i.e. the applicant has insufficient means to meet all or part of the costs: r.101(b)). Though there is another criterion, that it is necessary for the proper conduct of the case before the Chamber (r.92(b)), provision of legal aid to needy applicants is generally regarded as axiomatic. However, in cases which form part of a repetitive series on identical issues, legal aid may not be granted at all. There are no written guidelines as to what insufficient means are and the Court takes a flexible approach. It is aware that the cost of legal representation is likely to be prohibitive to any person of moderate income and that, where an applicant is pursing a human rights issue, it is in the general interest that it be facilitated. A person on income support or a prisoner with no income is certainly covered. Low to middling salaries may also attract legal aid, as in the case of *Goodwin*, a working journalist. The extent to which other family members' income and means are taken into account is not subject to guidelines. It is only likely to be relevant where a parent/spouse is wealthy and can be reasonably be expected to contribute. I–025

In practice, it is rare for the UK Government to comment negatively on applications and rare for the Court to refuse.

Level of legal aid

In the vast majority of cases a standard grant of legal aid is made by way of set contributions for specified items of work or costs incurred (see Annex 5: Legal Aid Rates). The rate awarded is generally the maximum amount allowable but may be I–026

[90] r.100.
[91] r.100(2).

reduced for submissions which are of particular brevity or concern cases based on an established precedent. The amounts are not generous compared with the level of UK professional fees and are intended rather to be a contribution towards costs and expenses.

Hearings

I–027 For representation at oral hearings, generally a fee for pleading and expenses for one lawyer are paid. Exceptionally, for the United Kingdom, expenses for two lawyers, counsel and solicitor, are paid, though only one fee. Applicants will generally be granted expenses for attending. Additional counsel/legal advisers may attend if given leave, but, needless to say, this will be uncovered by legal aid.

Additional items

I–028 Legal aid is not given in respect of any work done without specific request from the Court. Any specific additional items, e.g. costs of obtaining transcripts, fees for translations, medical opinions must obtain prior approval.

Legal representation

I–029 The Rules of Court require that an applicant must be represented by an appropriate lawyer once the case has been communicated to the Government and at any stage where there is an oral hearing (r.36(2) and (3)). Generally, a legal representative must be a lawyer resident and qualified to practise in one of the Contracting States.[92] This covers barristers and solicitors from the United Kingdom. Anyone else purporting to represent an applicant, for example, an academic or legal officer or a lawyer resident outside the Contracting States, must obtain leave from the President. A lawyer who fails to comply with Court procedures or who is otherwise regarded as unsuitable can be refused permission to act in Court proceedings.[93]

While an applicant may introduce his own application therefore, he must generally obtain a lawyer once the case is communicated. He may apply for leave to represent himself or to obtain authorisation for assistance from another person. However, leave is unlikely to be granted by the President where an oral hearing is held, or where the case is considered complex; failure to obtain legal representation may in those circumstances lead to the case being struck off.[94] The rule is less rigidly applied in cases following a lead judgment where arguably no further legal argument is required. The Court does not recommend lawyers. Nor does it have any list of approved firms or representatives. An applicant who does not have a lawyer and wishes to instruct one will be generally directed to contact the domestic bar association or its equivalent.

[92] There is no bar on an applicant from one contracting State using a lawyer from another, e.g. UK lawyers represented Turkish applicants in many of the fact-finding cases conducted 1996–2000, despite the objections of the Turkish Government that this inflated the amount of legal costs (e.g. *Kurt v Turkey*, May 25, 1998, R.J.D, 1998–III, No.74, para.179).

[93] e.g. *Manoussos v Czech Republic*, (46488/99) (Dec.) September 7, 2002.

[94] e.g. *Grimaylo v Ukraine*, (69364/01) (Dec.) February 7, 2006, where the Court considered that it could not continue an examination of the case, which included complaints under Arts 3, 5 and 6, without appropriate legal representation.

Lawyers should be able to address oral or written submissions to the Court in one of the official languages, French or English. Leave is required to use another language. Applicants applying in person may use an official language of a Contracting State until the case is communicated and thereafter must also obtain leave if they are unable to switch to English or French.[95]

Unrepresented applicants

Applicants who obtain leave to represent themselves will only be reimbursed expenses. No claim can be made for hours worked by analogy to legal fees. I–030

[95] r.36(5).

I–031 Cases must comply with the grounds of admissibility identified below. A case may also be struck out before or after admissibility under Art.37 (see below).

Governments are required to raise objections before the decision declaring a case admissible and will be estopped from raising them afterwards. Rule 55 provides "[a]ny plea of inadmissibility must, in so far as its character and the circumstances permit, be raised by the respondent Contracting Party in its written or oral observations on the admissibility of the application . . ." It is not sufficient that the Government pleaded non-exhaustion before admissibility; it must have done so on the specific ground later relied on.[1] Where, however, an applicant changes the nature of the application or complaint after the decision on admissibility, or where a new legally relevant procedural event subsequently occurs, estoppel may not apply.[2] Grounds of incompatibility, which concern the Court's jurisdiction under the Convention or the six-month time-limit, may be raised at any stage.[3]

Governments are also barred from raising before the Court arguments inconsistent with those run in the domestic court proceedings. [4]

1. Six months[5]

Principle of rule: legal certainty and avoidance of stale complaints[6]

I–032 The rule cannot be waived, either by the Court or a respondent Government.[7] Even if a Government does not raise it, the Court will do so of its own motion.[8]

The Court has stated, however, that it will not apply the rule with undue formalism which would run counter to the purpose of the Convention as a mechanism for providing effective protection of human rights.[9]

[1] *Mooren v Germany* (GC), July 9, 2009, paras 57–59.

[2] *Malama v Greece*, March 1, 2001, ECHR 2001–II, para.40; *NC v Italy*, December 18, 2002, ECHR 2002–X, paras 44–47; *Sejdovic v Italy*, March 1, 2006, ECHR 2006–II, para.41.

[3] *Blecic v Croatia*, March 8, 2006, ECHR 2006–III, the Government did not raise incompatibility *ratione temporis* until referral to the Grand Chamber.

[4] *A v UK*, March 8, 2006, paras 153–159, the Government had reserved their position; it was unusual, not inconsistent, for the Government to argue that their highest court had been wrong in its conclusions; *Al-Skeini v UK*, July 7, 2011, paras 99–100, the Government was estopped from arguing that the killings by British soldiers in Iraq were attributable to the UN, as this had not been raised in the national proceedings.

[5] Art.35, para.1 (formerly Art.26).

[6] e.g. (10626/83) (Dec.) May 7, 1985, 42 D.R. 205; *Karabardak v Cyprus*, (76575/01) (Dec.) October 22, 2002; *Bulut and Yavuz v Turkey*, (73065/01) (Dec.) May 18, 2002.

[7] e.g. (10416/83) (Dec.) January 9, 1995, 38 D.R. 158; *Hay v UK*, (41894/98) (Dec.) October 17, 2000, ECHR 2000–XI, where the Government had settled a case in domestic proceedings "without prejudice" to an application to Strasbourg); *Ipek v Turkey*, (39706/98) (Dec.) November 1, 2000.

[8] *Walker v UK*, (34979/97) (Dec.) January 25, 2000, ECHR 2000–I; and *Belaousof v Greece*, May 27, 2004, where the Government made no objection on six months, the Court dismissed complaints on that basis nonetheless.

[9] e.g. *Fernandez-Molina Gonzalez v Spain*, (64359/01) (Dec.) October 8, 2002, where the applicants could only invoke Art.14 in their *amparo* appeal, it would have been artificial to require them to bring their Art.1 of Protocol No.1 complaints based on the same facts before these proceedings had ended; *Ahtinen v Finland*, (48907/99) (Dec.) May 31, 2005, where the applicant made prompt use of a remedy normally regarded as extraordinary but which could have arguably provided redress and then brought his case directly to Strasbourg afterwards, it was not consonant with the purpose of Art.35 to reject his case as out of time.

1. When time runs from

(a) Where there are domestic remedies

- Time begins running from the day after the final decision in the process of exhaustion of domestic remedies in respect of each complaint (see below). Only normal, effective domestic remedies are taken into account, since an applicant cannot extend the strict time-limit by misguided applications to bodies with no power or competence to offer effective redress[10] or by use of undefined and open-ended avenues of redress which have no precise time-limits, thus creating uncertainty and rendering nugatory the purpose of the six-month rule.[11] However, while applications to re-open or similar extraordinary remedies are not generally regarded as part of the normal exhaustion process, where in fact an applicant succeeds in obtaining the re-opening of the proceedings or review of a final decision, the six month period will run from the date of the outcome of those extraordinary proceedings only in relation to those Convention issues which were in issue and examined.[12] I–033

The date of the final decision is that when the judgment is rendered orally in public.[13] Where, pursuant to domestic law and practice, the applicant is entitled to be served ex officio with a written copy of the judgment, time starts to run from the date the judgment is received.[14] Where it is not announced in public and there is no provision for service, the relevant date is that when the applicant or his lawyer are informed of the final decision.[15] The date is taken from the earliest notification—the date at which the lawyer is informed is taken as the relevant date, even where the applicant becomes aware later.[16] As another variant, in some jurisdictions where decisions are lodged or registered within a court or court office, that date may be taken[17]; or since applicants cannot be expected to check day after day for any eventual lodging, the date may be taken from when they in fact pick it up,[18] as long as they have not allowed too long a time to lapse without taking reasonable steps to keep themselves informed.[19]

[10] e.g. *Fernie v UK*, (14881/04) (Dec.) January 5, 2006, where despite not appealing to the House of Lords, the applicant nonetheless made an application.

[11] e.g. *Denisov v Russia*, (33408/03) (Dec.) May 6, 2004, concerning unrestrained supervisory review; *Williams v UK*, (32567/06) February 17, 2009, Attorney-General's power to order fresh inquest, *Tucka v UK (No.1)*, (34586/10) (Dec.) January 18, 2011, concerning a request to the CCRC for referral to the Court of Appeal.

[12] *Sapeyan v Armenia*, January 13, 2009, paras 23–27, if the re-opening concerns matters not relevant to the complaints before the Court, it will not have effect on the normal operation of the six-month rule.

[13] e.g. *Loveridge v UK*, (39641/98) (Dec.) October 23, 2001.

[14] *Worm v Austria*, August 29, 1997, Reports, 1997–V, No.45, para.33.

[15] e.g. (21034/92) (Dec.) January 9, 1995, 80–A D.R. 87. See also *Haralambidis v Greece*, (36706/97) March 29, 2001, para.38, where the date ran from the finalisation and signature of the judgment as in Greece there was no provision for service of the judgment.

[16] e.g. *Keskin v Turkey*, (36091/97) (Dec.) September 7, 1999; *Celik v Turkey*, (52991/99) (Dec.) September 23, 2004, ECHR 2004–X.

[17] e.g. *Muresan v Romania*, (31530/05) June 22, 2010, paras 13–14.

[18] e.g. *Muresan v Romania*, fn.17 above, para.17; *N.T. Giannousis & Kliafas Brothers SA v Greece*, (2898/03) (Dec.) September 29, 2005; *Tahsin Ipek v Turkey*, (39706/98) (Dec.) November 7, 2000; *Yavuz v Turkey*, (48064/99) (Dec.) February 1, 2005.

[19] *Tahsin Ipek v Turkey*, fn.18 above.

Where the reasons for the decision are relevant for the application to the Court, time runs from the date on which the full text is received, rather than the serving of the operative parts of the decision.[20]

(b) Where there are no domestic remedies

I–034

- Where the complaint relates to a specific act or omission: from the date of the act or omission, or from the date of knowledge of that act or its effect or prejudice on the applicant.[21]
- Where there is a sequence of events linked in time and place: from the end of the episode, depending on whether it is practical to expect complaint earlier.[22]
- Where the applicant makes use of a remedy which later proves to be ineffective for the purposes of exhaustion of domestic remedies: from the moment that he becomes aware or should reasonably have become aware of this situation.[23]

2. When time stops running

I–035

- Date of introduction of the application before the Court—this is, in general, that communication[24] which sets out, even summarily, the object of the application,[25] or as is sometimes said, the substance of the complaint.[26] In practice, to introduce an application a qualifying communication must identify the applicant, the factual basis of each complaint and the violations of the Convention alleged to result.[27] Applicants are not obliged to specify

[20] e.g. (34728/97) (Dec.) October 20, 1997; *Andorka and Vavra v Hungary*, (25694/03) and (28338/03) (Dec.) September 12, 2006. See also cases where decisions only become final at a later date, e.g. (12077/86) (Dec.) December 9, 1991, 71 D.R. 13.

[21] e.g. (8440/78) (Dec.) July 16, 1980, 21 D.R. 138 (actual effect of measure); (12015/86) (Dec.) July 6, 1988, 57 D.R. 108 (date of knowledge); *Finucane v UK*, (29178/95) (Dec.) July 2, 2002 (date of knowledge of new information about alleged security force collusion); *Dennis v UK*, (76573/01) (Dec.) July 2, 2002 (date of knowledge of relatives of victims of the Marchioness tragedy that the bodies had been mutilated).

[22] (22280/93) (Dec.) January 9, 1995, where the six-month time-limit ran from the end of the raid of the village (which took place over a three-day period). See also *Solmaz v Turkey*, January 16, 2007, for pre-trial detention, time runs from the end of consecutive periods taken as a whole; *Seleznev v Russia*, June 26, 2008, paras 35–36, complaints about general prison conditions where the applicant has been transferred from place to place, time runs from end of the consecutive period (save where specific incidents of ill-treatment are alleged).

[23] (23654/94) (Dec.) May 15, 1995, 81–A D.R. 76, while the applicant applied to the public prosecutor in May 1993, he had received advice that this remedy was ineffective and he should have introduced his complaints when he became aware of this situation. See, conversely, *Paul and Aubrey Edwards v UK*, (46477/99) (Dec.) June 7, 2001, the applicants became aware of the non-availability of remedies after publication of the inquiry report into their son's death.

[24] Although the word used in r.47, para.5 is "communication", the Convention organs have not held in any decision that an application may be introduced by telephone. It is unlikely that this would be the case, save in an extreme emergency excluding the possibility of written notification. See (34728/97) (Dec.) October 20, 1997, 91–A D.R. 85, where a purported introduction of an application by telephone was not accepted.

[25] r.47(5), e.g. *Baumann v Austria*, (39917/98) (Dec.) September 4, 2001.

[26] e.g. *Paroisse Greco Catholique Sambata Bihor v Romania*, (48107/99) (Dec.) May 25, 2004.

[27] There is a certain flexibility, e.g. a reference to interference with freedom of expression is enough without mentioning Art.10. See, however, *Latif v UK*, (72819/01) (Dec.) January 29, 2004, where a bald reference to a trial and appeal was not sufficient to indicate the object of the application under the Convention.

which Article, paragraph or sub-paragraph, or even which right, they are praying in aid as any greater strictness would lead to unjust consequences; for the vast majority of "individual" petitions are received from laymen applying to the Court without the assistance of a lawyer.[28] Failure to specify all complaints in the introductory communication may lead to application of the six-month time-limit to those raised at a later stage.[29]

The date taken is, according to the practice in UK cases:

- the date written on the letter (an undue gap between this date and arrival will be regarded with caution)[30];
- where the letter is undated, from the post mark on the envelope;
- if post mark illegible, date of arrival at the Court (stamped in Registry);
- the date of arrival of the fax version at the Court.

3. Calculation of the six-month period

The six-month period does not take into account domestic rules of calculation of time-limits or domestic public holidays or weekends. If it happens to expire on such a day, there is no extension to the next postal date.[31] **I–036**

4. Effect of undue delay in subsequent communications

- An unreasonable or unexplained delay in communications after the original introductory letter may result in the first letter ceasing to be regarded as introducing the application.[32] The date of introduction is then taken from the later communication in which the applicant re-affirms his intention to revive or continue the case. **I–037**

[28] See *Soluvey and Zozuya v Ukraine*, November 28, 2008, para.51, a complaint about unlawful detention of over 35 months; sufficient for a length of pre-trial detention issue to arise as well as issues of unlawfulness.

[29] See *Allan v UK*, (48539/99) (Dec.) August 28, 2001, where the first communications raising specific allegations under Art.6 did not mention the drawing of inferences from silence under police questioning, a general reference to unfairness did not introduce this aspect; *Bozinovski v FYROM*, (68368/01) (Dec.) February 1, 2005, merely sending documents concerning domestic proceedings did not introduce complaints about those proceedings.

[30] See *Arslan v Turkey*, (36747/02) (Dec.) November 11, 2002, ECHR 2002–X, the letter was dated April 12 and postmarked April 19, whereas the six-month time-limit expired on April 13, the Court dismissed the complaint as out of time, there being no explanation for the delay in submitting the letter to the post office.

[31] *Otto v Germany*, (21425/06) (Dec.) November 10, 2009. See anomalous decision in *Sabri Gunes v Turkey*, May 24, 2011, paras 39–44, where a Chamber discounted the last day which was a Sunday as this did not count in assessing domestic time-limits. This case has been referred to the Grand Chamber.

[32] r.47, para.5 *in fine* referring to "good cause" for changing the date of introduction: this practice is to prevent an application lying dormant and thus bypassing the spirit and purpose of the six-month rule. See (10626/83), fn.6 above; *Chalkley v UK*, (63831/00) (Dec.) September 26, 2002, where the Government objected to the long periods of delay in the applicant's communications but the Court did not find that the applicant's representatives had acted in an abusive or unreasonable manner overall and considered that they kept in touch with the Court with sufficient regularity to prevent any appearance of the matter lying dormant; *Gaillard v France*, (47337/99) (Dec.) July 11, 2000, where a 10-month lapse in returning the application form led to a change in the introduction date; *Nee v Ireland*, (52787/99) (Dec.) January 30, 2003, a gap of one year in returning the application form led to a later date being taken as the date of introduction.

A holding introductory letter will only serve its purpose if the application is pursued actively. If there are intervening domestic events which render the case premature, it is only possible to keep the file active in the Court for a limited period. It will either have to be pursued regardless or where effective domestic remedies are being exhausted, be re-introduced within six months of the final effective decision in those proceedings.

In addition, new rules have come into operation to encourage promptness in submitting a full application. Applicants are informed, on receipt of their first letter, that the full, completed application form must be submitted within eight weeks. Where an applicant failed to submit the original form within the eight weeks, the introduction date was taken from the posting of the form, not the first communication or faxed application form, leading to the case being rejected as out of time.[33]

5. Special circumstances suspending the period

I–038 Only very limited circumstances of force majeure are regarded as suspending the running of the period:

- illness and mental incapacity have not been accepted in any case[34];
- detention is not sufficient in itself, unless it is proved that outside contact with others was totally barred;
- ignorance of the Convention or its case-law is not enough. In particular, time is not suspended by applications to non-effective remedies such as the Parliamentary Commissioner of Administration or applications for discretionary or exceptional remedies (e.g. requests to the Home Secretary for a reference to the Court of Appeal, applications to ex gratia criminal injuries compensation funds or supervisory review procedures instigated after a "final" decision).[35]

6. Continuing situations

I–039 Where there is a continuing situation, act or omission or state of affairs, e.g. a state of legislation which continuously affects the exercise of a guaranteed right or freedom, the six-month time-limit does not apply.[36] The primary examples are the situations of ongoing uncertainty and failure to account for the whereabouts and fate of disappeared persons[37]; situations of non-enforcement of domestic judgments[38];

[33] *Kevualko v Netherlands*, (65938/09) (Dec.) June 1, 2010, paras 20–25.

[34] (6317/73) July 10, 1975, 2 D.R. 87, mere reference to a bad state of health was insufficient; (25435/94) (Dec.) February 20, 1995, where the applicants both suffered mental illness, this did not prevent them from complying with the six-month time-limit given that they were able to pursue domestic proceedings at that time.

[35] e.g. concerning supervisory review, *Sardin v Russia*, (69582/01) (Dec.) February 12, 2004; *Sitokhova v Russia*, (55609/00) (Dec.) September 2, 2004.

[36] e.g. *Dudgeon v UK*, October 22, 1981, Series A, No.45, 4 E.H.R.R. 149, legislation banning adult consensual homosexual acts; *Malama*, fn.2 above, para.35, ongoing failure to pay compensation; *Ülke v Turkey*, (39437/98) (Dec.) June 1, 2004, a series of prosecutions and convictions for conscientious objection amounted to an "ongoing state of affairs" against which the applicant had had no remedy in domestic law; *Iordache v Romania*, October 14, 2008, paras 63–64, ongoing parental restrictions in child custody procedures.

[37] *Varnava v Turkey*, September 18, 2009, paras 145–149, distinguishing the procedural obligation to investigate an incident of killing or death which is not a continuing situation.

[38] *Tarverdiyev v Armenia*, July 26, 2007, para.52.

situations where expropriation of land is carried out by an occupying power not recognised under international law, leaving the title owner of land unable to access or enjoy his property[39]; and situations of electoral disabilities or restrictions.[40]

A distinction must be drawn between a situation disclosing a situation of ongoing violation and the after-effect or consequence of a breach which occurred and ended at a particular point in time.[41]

This exception—judge-made—is of rare application. Also, continuing situations will not hold off the application of the six-month rule indefinitely. Applicants should nonetheless bring their cases to Strasbourg with due expedition, once it is apparent that there is no realistic prospect of any favourable outcome or progress for their complaints on a domestic or international level.[42] In non-enforcement cases, where the enforcement becomes impossible on a domestic level, due to the bankruptcy of the private debtor or destruction of the property at stake for example, the six-month time-limit will run from when this impossibility became known, or should reasonably have become known, to the applicant.[43]

2. Exhaustion of domestic remedies[44]

1. Principle of the rule

Before an international jurisdiction decides whether a State has violated a human right, the State should have the opportunity to remedy the matter itself. The Strasbourg organs should primarily be a supervisory last resort and the main business of enforcing human rights should be done by domestic authorities who are in the best position to do so.[45] I–040

2. Application of the rule

- The burden is on the Government invoking the rule to prove the existence in theory and practice of available and sufficient remedies at the relevant time.[46] However, once this burden of proof has been satisfied it falls to the I–041

[39] e.g. *Loizidou v Turkey*, March 23, 1995, Series A, No.310, 23 E.H.R.R. 513; see *Preussiche Treuhand GMBH & Co, KG.A.A. v Poland*, (47550/06) (Dec.) October 7, 2008, holding that acts of expropriation within a State are generally regarded as instantaneous for the purposes of the six-month rule.
[40] e.g. *Paksas v Lithuania*, January 6, 2011, paras 83–84, concerning ineligibility of an impeached President to stand for Parliament; see also *Tete v France*, (11123/84) (Dec.) December 9, 1987, concerning regulations on voting, deposits, publicity and access to media.
[41] e.g. (25681/94) (Dec.) April 1, 1996, 85–A D.R. 134, where the traumatic personal suffering of the families of the victims of "Bloody Sunday" did not constitute a continuing situation; *Posti and Rahko v Finland*, September 24, 2002, para.40; *Malhous v Czech Republic*, (33701/96) (Dec.) December 12, 2000, where deprivation of ownership rights was regarded as an instantaneous act.
[42] e.g. *Varnava*, fn.37, paras 160–172, concerning ongoing disappearances.
[43] e.g. *Cone v Romania*, October 14, 2008, paras 25–26, where the order to reinstate the applicant in his post in a firm became impossible due to its winding up.
[44] Art.35, para.1.
[45] e.g. *Akdivar v Turkey*, September 16, R.J.D. 1996–IV, No.15, para.65; *Azinas v Cyprus*, March 28, ECHR 2004–IV, para.41; *Demopoulos v Turkey*, (46113/99) (Dec.) March 1, 2010, para.69.
[46] e.g. *Deweer v Belgium*, February 27, 1980, Series A, No.35, para.26; *Horvat v Croatia*, July 26, 2002, ECHR 2002–VIII, para.45, where a constitutional remedy relied on by the Government was not sufficiently certain; *Zhu v UK*, (36790/97) (Dec.) September 12, 2000, where there was no established

applicant to establish that the remedy was in fact exhausted, was for some reason not effective or adequate in the circumstances of the case,[47] or there existed special circumstances absolving him from the requirement.[48] A Government may not use arguments which are incompatible with those which they relied on in domestic court proceedings.[49] Where the highest national court stated that it was not necessary to use a particular remedy, the Court was not prepared to find otherwise.[50]

- A Government must generally invoke the rule prior to the Court's decision on admissibility.[51] Failure by the Government to respond to communication of complaints may result in the matter going by default and any issues as to effectiveness of remedies being dealt with on the merits where relevant.[52] The Convention organs have nonetheless, on occasion, relied on an argument of non-exhaustion which has not been raised by the Government.[53]
- The applicant is generally required to raise in substance in the domestic proceedings the complaints made in Strasbourg and in compliance with the

authority indicating damages for breach of duty in such a case, the mere possibility of such a remedy was "too speculative"; *Merit v Ukraine*, March 30, 2004, practical application of a law allegedly remedying delays not sufficiently established by Government; *Sergey Smirnov v Russia*, (14085/04) (Dec.) July 6, 2006, where the Constitutional Court could only examine constitutionality, not whether a law had been correctly applied in an individual case; *Saoud v France*, October 9, 2007, paras 78–79, case-law interpretation providing that the remedy was not sufficiently established, the Government only furnishing one decision. Contrast with the approach where the contracting State has introduced a remedy expressly aimed at redressing a particular problem, where the Court gives leeway for case-law to develop the remedy and "mere doubt" as to effectiveness in practice is not a ground for exemption: *Daddi v Italy*, (15476/09) (Dec.) June 2, 2009; "Pinto law" remedying delay in proceedings: *Robert Lesjak v Slovenia*, July 21, 2009, para.50, "certain level of flexibility" as long as the legislative provisions sufficiently clear; and not showing "ambiguity", e.g. *Parizov v FYROM*, February 7, 2008, paras 44–45.

47 *Grisankova and Grisankovs v Latvia*, (36117/02) (Dec.) February 13, 2003, ECHR 2003–II; *Caldas Ramirez de Arrellano v Spain*, (68874/01) (Dec.) January 28, 2003, ECHR 2003–I; *Pütün v Turkey*, (31734/96) (Dec.) November 18, 2004, ECHR 2004–XII.

48 *Akdivar*, fn.45 above, para.68, where the total passivity of the national authorities in the face of serious allegations of misconduct by State agents was given as such a factor and shifted the burden of proof rendering it incumbent on the Government to show what they had done in response to the scale and seriousness of the matters complained of. See also *Aksoy v Turkey*, December 18, 1996, R.J.D. 1996–IV, No.26, 23 E.H.R.R. 553, where the applicant was exempted in view of the failure by the State prosecutor to react to his injuries incurred during custody; *Selmouni v France*, July 28, 1999, ECHR 1999–V, paras 78–81, where delays and inaction in the investigation rendered the alleged remedy ineffective.

49 e.g. (23892/94) (Dec.) October 16, 1995, 83–A D.R. 57 citing *Kolompar v Belgium*, September 24, 1992, Series A, No.235, 16 E.H.R.R. 197.

50 *DH v Czech Republic*, November 13, 2007, para.118.

51 See r.55; *Malama*, fn.2 above; *NC v Italy*, fn.2 above, where the Government were estopped from raising a non-exhaustion point based on a fact arising after the decision on admissibility due to undue delay in bringing it to the attention of the Court.

52 e.g. *Ergi v Turkey*, (23818/94) (Dec.) March 2, 1995, 80–A D.R. 157.

53 (20946/92) (Dec.) August 8, 1994, where the applicant had not applied for judicial review in respect of complaints of opening of his letters from his solicitor by a Scottish prison, following the English Court of Appeal decision holding ultra vires a prison rule allowing such interference on wider grounds than merely to ascertain if they were bona fide communications. Also on the first examination of applications, clear cases of non-exhaustion will be rejected by the Court of its own motion.

formal requirements and time-limits imposed by domestic law.[54] This includes any procedural means which might have prevented a breach of the Convention.[55] It is sufficient for the substance of the Convention complaint to be put before the domestic courts, even if it is not formulated expressly.[56] However, it is not sufficient that the applicant may have, unsuccessfully, exercised another remedy which could have overturned the impugned measure on other grounds not unconnected with the complaint of violation of a Convention right: it is the Convention complaint which must have been aired at national level for there to have been exhaustion of "effective remedies".[57] On the same basis, an applicant's failure to utilise the proper formalities will not be held against him if the domestic court nonetheless looks at the substance of his complaint of its own motion.[58]

- The rule does not apply to administrative practice of violation, since in the face of State connivance or acquiescence the system will be considered globally ineffective.[59]

3. Convention approach

- Remedies must be real and practical and not theoretical or illusory,[60] e.g. genuine fear of reprisals or intimidation.[61] I–042
- Account will be taken not only of the personal circumstances of the applicant, but the general legal and political context in which the alleged remedies operate.[62]
- An unduly formalistic approach is not to be taken by the Convention organs which will apply a certain degree of flexibility.[63]

[54] *Cardot v France*, March 3, 1991, Series A, No.200, 13 E.H.R.R. 853; *Augusto v France*, (71665/01) January 11, 2007, paras 42–45; *Doliner and Maitenez v France*, (24113/04) (Dec.) May 31, 2007, failure to raise all Convention complaints on appeal. Concerning procedural mistakes, e.g. (18079/91) (Dec.) December 4, 1991, 72 D.R. 263; *MPP Golub v Ukraine*, (6778/05) (Dec.) October 18, 2005. The shortness of time-limits for submitting evidence could, arguably, render compliance with procedural rules unrealistic, e.g. in asylum cases (see *Bahaddar v Netherlands*, February 19, R.J.D. 1998–I, para.45). See *Merger et Cros v France*, (68864/01) (Dec.) March 11, 2004, applicants raised Convention complaints out of time on appeal but as this was because the court judgment relied on was delivered after the time-limit expired, this showed no negligence and they had duly exhausted.

[55] e.g. *Barbera, Messegue and Jabardo v Spain*, December 6, 1988, Series A, No.146, 11 E.H.R.R. 360.

[56] *Gasus Dosier und Fordertechnick GmbH v Netherlands*, February 23, 1995, Series A, No.306–B, 20 E.H.R.R. 403, where the applicant had not relied on Art.1 of Protocol No.1 expressly before Dutch courts, relying rather on Art.6. The Court was not impressed by the fact that the applicant had not invoked Art.1 of Protocol No.1 since, in any event, it did provide the courts with the opportunity of preventing or putting right the alleged violation of that provision. The purpose of the rule is to allow the contracting States the opportunity of putting right violations (para.48).

[57] *Azinas*, fn.45 above, para.38.

[58] e.g. *Vladimir Romanov v Russia*, July 24, 2008, para.52.

[59] e.g. *Donnelly v UK*, (5577–5583/72) (Dec.) December 15, 1975, 4 D.R. 4. See Pt IIB, s.46: Torture, inhuman and degrading treatment.

[60] *Akdivar*, (Dec.) October 19, 1994, fn.45 above; *Icyer v Turkey*, (8888/02) (Dec.) January 12, 2006, compensation law effective in practice as shown by 170,000 users.

[61] Cf *Siddik Aslan v Turkey*, October 18, 2005, where the Court was not persuaded of the well-foundedness of the applicants' fears to share information about their relatives with the investigating authorities.

[62] *Akdivar*, fn.45 above, para.69.

[63] *Cardot*, fn.54 above, para.34.

Remedies must:

I–043

- be effective, i.e. capable of providing redress for the complaint (e.g. power to recommend is not enough as in the Board of Visitors, ombudsmen)[64]; the speed of the procedure may also be relevant to its effectiveness[65]; the remedy must be capable of directly remedying the state of affairs[66];
- form part of the normal process of redress involving normal use of the remedy, e.g. not cover exceptional or discretionary remedies such as requests for ex gratia compensation or for re-opening of judicial proceedings[67]; where an applicant is involved in extraordinary proceedings, this will not provide grounds of non-exhaustion but may be relevant in Art.41 if he obtains, or has the prospect of obtaining compensation[68];
- be accessible[69]: it may be relevant if an applicant is barred from taking action due, for example, to lack of money or legal representation, where these are practically essential[70]; automatic imposition of fines for using an appeal unsuccessfully, even if not abusive, penalised the use of the remedy and did not satisfy the requirements of Art.35[71]; in principle where complaints are against another State, an applicant is required to exhaust in that jurisdiction, difficulties notwithstanding[72];
- offer reasonable prospects of success[73]; a mere doubt as to the prospect of success in going to court does not exempt from exhaustion. Where case-law

[64] e.g. (11192/84) (Dec.) May 14, 1987, 52 D.R. 227; *Lehtinen v Finland*, (39076/97) (Dec.) October 14, 1999.

[65] (15530–1/89) (Dec.) October 10, 1992, 72 D.R. 169; *Tomé de Mota v Portugal*, (32082/96) (Dec.) December 2, 1999, ECHR 1999–IX; *Pallanich v Austria*, January 30, 2001, para.30; *McFarlane v Ireland*, September 10, 2010, para.123; *Bellizzi v Malta*, June 21, 2011, paras 38–55.

[66] (12724/87) (Dec.) May 3, 1989, 61 D.R. 206; (15404/89) (Dec.) April 16, 1991, 70 D.R. 262; *Civet v France*, September 28, 1999, ECHR 1999–VI, para.43; *Khashiyev and Akiyeva v Russia*, February 24, 2005, civil remedies incapable of giving redress without the benefit of the conclusions of a criminal investigation.

[67] (14545/89) (Dec.) October 9, 1990, 66 D.R. 238, request for exercise of ministerial discretion to award compensation not included; (20348/92) (Dec.) March 3, 1994, power of Secretary of State shown to have been rarely exercised; *Assanidze v Georgia*, April 8, 2004, ECHR 2004–IV, paras 127–128, Parliamentary scrutiny was an extraordinary procedure; *Roserio Bento v Portugal*, November 30, 2004, ECHR 2004–XII, request to Court to reconsider not an effective remedy; *Tucka v UK (No.1)*, fn.11, application to Criminal Case Review Commission ("CCRC") for referral to Court of Appeal was not an effective remedy as it was discretionary, was open-ended as an application could be made at any time, and there was no limit to the number of applications, thus rendering nugatory the application of the six month rule to criminal cases; contrast, however, *Reilly v UK*, (53731/00) (Dec.) June 26, 2003, where exceptionally the applicant had not appealed after his trial and the Court of Appeal had subsequently clarified domestic law and reviewed similar cases, it was expected that the applicant apply to the CCRC for referral to the Court of Appeal. Normal use of remedies, e.g. (16278/90) (Dec.) May 3, 1993, 74 D.R. 93; (19092/91) (Dec.) October 11, 1993, 75 D.R. 207.

[68] e.g. *Salah v Netherlands*, July 6, 2006.

[69] e.g. (14545/89), fn.67 above; (12604/86) (Dec.) July 10, 1991, 70 D.R. 125; (14986/89) (Dec.) July 3, 1991, 70 D.R. 240, where remedies were brought to the attention of a foreign detainee in a language she did not understand.

[70] The Convention organs have generally expected applicants to take proceedings themselves where they have been refused legal aid; in very complex proceedings, as in *Airey v Ireland*, October 9, 1979, Series A, No.32, (1979–80) 2 E.H.R.R. 305, lack of legal aid could conceivably form a ground of exemption; *Gnahore v France*, September 9, 2000, ECHR 2000–IX, where the applicant was refused legal aid for an appeal by the president of the court due to lack of any arguable ground, his failure to continue the appeal did not show non-exhaustion.

[71] *Prencipe v Monaco,* July 16, 2009, paras 95–97.

[72] *Demopoulos v Turkey*, fn.45 above, paras 101, 124–126; *Pad v Turkey*, (60617/00) (Dec.) June 28, 2007.

[73] *Akdivar*, fn.45 above, para.68.

is unclear, contradictory or in the process of ongoing interpretation, an applicant may be expected to pursue an action or appeal which allows the courts to rule on the issues.[74] Where a statute provides new provisions, it may be necessary to put them to the test even where their scope or application is untried and unknown. Counsel's opinion that there is no prospect of success may be enough to indicate that a remedy or appeal would not be effective.[75] The fact that an identical claim has been dismissed may be sufficient to indicate that there is no prospect of success.[76]

Also:

- if there is more than one remedy available, an individual is not required to try more than one[77];
- an applicant is generally not required to try the same body again by way of a repeated request or application[78]; and
- an applicant is generally only required to exhaust those remedies available at the date at which the application was lodged; exceptions arise where a remedy has been introduced after that date specifically with a view to giving redress in a series of cases.[79] Nor can an applicant generally be expected to use a new remedy flowing from a court judgment which is subsequent to the introduction of the complaint.[80]

(a) Particular remedies in the United Kingdom

Note: these are generally required but will always be subject to the principles above and to the provisions or practice of domestic law as they develop. As concerns the Human Rights Act 1998, the possibility of applying under s.4 to the courts for a **I–044**

[74] (20357/92) (Dec.) March 7, 1994, 76–A D.R. 80; concerning the importance of constitutional testing, e.g. *D v Ireland*, (26499/02) (Dec.) June 27, 2006, where the applicant should have taken certain legal steps to clarify further the uncertainties about the effectiveness of a constitutional challenge to obtain a lawful abortion; contrast *Roseiro Bento*, fn.67 above; *Sejdovic v Italy*, March 1, 2006, ECHR 2006–II, paras 45–56 (remedy bound to fail).

[75] e.g. *Selvanayagam v UK*, (57981/00) (Dec.) December 12, 2002, where four counsel (three senior) advised no hopes of success indicating "settled legal opinion" that appeal to the House of Lords would not have succeeded; see, however, (10789/84) (Dec.) October 11, 1984, 40 D.R. 298, where counsel's doubts did not absolve the applicant from applying to the House of Lords, especially where the Court of Appeal gave leave in a similar case shortly afterwards; *Mogos v Germany*, (78084/01) (Dec.) March 27, 2003.

[76] e.g. *DH*, fn.50 above, paras 119–122.

[77] *McCann v UK*, (Dec.) September 3, 1993; (19092/91), fn.67 above; *Sargin and Yagci v Turkey*, (14116–7/88) (Dec.) May 11, 1989, 61 D.R. 250; (14838/89) (Dec.) March 5, 1991, 69 D.R. 286. Where there is a choice of remedies, the selection of the appropriate one is primarily for the applicant: *Airey*, fn.70 above, para.23; *Hilal v UK*, (45276/99) (Dec.) February 8, 2000, the applicant's decision to pursue one avenue of appeal rather than another was not unreasonable and did not exclude the courts from examining the relevant issues.

[78] *Granger v UK*, (Dec.) May 9, 1988.

[79] *Demopoulos v Turkey*, fn.45, para.87, remedy introduced to deal with thousands of property complaints of owners of land in the occupied north of Cyprus; see also remedies introduced to deal with systemic length of proceedings problems cited therein.

[80] *Depauw v Belgium*, (2115/04) (Dec.) May 15, 2007, the Court considered that the new development in case-law could not be regarded as established or known by applicants until some six months after the judgment which reversed a previous line of jurisprudence. See also *Provide SRL v Italy*, July 5, 2007, para.18, applicants not regarded as being effectively aware of new case-law until six months after judgment deposited with registry.

declaration of incompatibility to the effect that a particular legislative provision infringed the Convention has, so far, been held not to furnish an effective remedy as the minister exercises a power, not a duty, to amend the offending legislation.[81] However, where it is arguably possible for the courts to interpret domestic law in a manner compatible with the Convention without applying for a declaration, an applicant must make use of the Human Rights Act 1998.[82]

(I) CRIMINAL

I–045 Application for permission to appeal against conviction and/or sentence to the Court of Appeal, renewing application from single judge to the full court[83]; it is generally assumed that appeal to the House of Lords is an exceptional remedy though there might be, in a particular case, a point of law of general public importance which might be reasonably be expected to be pursued.[84]

(II) CIVIL

I–046 Generally in a civil case, the highest avenue of appeal where there is a prospect of success is the Court of Appeal; whether it is necessary to go to the House of Lords may depend on the nature of the claims and the existing state of case-law.[85]

Childcare cases:

- appeal may not be required to the Court of Appeal due to its limited intervention on the assessment of facts, but will depend, inter alia, on the nature of the complaints about the proceedings, counsel's opinion as to the existence of grounds of appeal, and whether the Court of Appeal has intervened in the exercise of the particular type of discretion by a first instance judge before.

Prisoners:

- for matters of internal discipline and regulation, petition to the prison authorities/Secretary of State in relation to the application of norms is expected, though not in respect of the content of those norms[86]; the Board of Visitors generally is not effective as it is without binding powers of decision; judicial review may not be effective due to its limited scope of review but this may depend on the nature of the claims made and the existence of case-law showing a prospect that a court will examine them in substance[87]; in respect of assault, ill-treatment, and negligence, the appropriate civil proceedings are generally expected.

[81] e.g. *Hobbs v UK*, (633684/00) (Dec.) June 18, 2002. See, however, indications that declarations may earn recognition as effective remedies due to practice: *Burden v UK*, April 29, 2008, para.43.

[82] e.g. *Upton v UK*, (29800/04) (Dec.) April 11, 2006.

[83] e.g. *Reilly*, fn.67 above.

[84] e.g. (10789/84), fn.75 above.

[85] e.g. (20075/92) (Dec.) August 31, 1994, there were conflicting decisions of the Court of Sessions and Court of Appeal, which could have been ruled on by the House of Lords on appeal.

[86] *Silver v UK*, March 25, 1983, Series A, No.61, 5 E.H.R.R. 347.

[87] e.g. (13669/88) (Dec.) March 7, 1990, 65 D.R. 245; (20946/92), fn.53 above.

Planning:

- appeal is from inspectors and decisions of the Secretary of State to the High Court, notwithstanding the limited scope of review, where the matters of complaint may arguably be considered by the court in some manner.[88]

Immigration and expulsion:

- appeals to immigration judges, appeal tribunal where such lie; judicial or statutory review may be required where risk to life or limb is concerned (see Pt IIB, s.29: Immigration and expulsion) or in other cases, depending on whether the nature of the complaints falls within the scope of the limited review and having regard to previous precedents.[89]

3. Manifestly ill-founded[90]

- Complaint unsubstantiated or unsupported by the material submitted; I–047
- the facts complained of do not disclose an interference in the enjoyment of the right invoked[91];
- act or decision complained of discloses prima facie an interference but justified on grounds contained in the provisions of the Convention, e.g. child removed from parents but circumstances support the view that it is necessary to protect the rights of the child;
- loss of victim status:
    - an individual may no longer claim to be a victim of a violation of the Convention where the national authorities have acknowledged, either expressly or in substance,[92] the breach of the Convention and afforded redress.[93] What is appropriate redress will depend on the circumstances, compensation is not, in principle, a prerequisite[94]; an apology

[88] e.g. *Bryan v UK*, November 22, 1995, Series A, No.335–A, 21 E.H.R.R. 342.

[89] e.g. (14507/89) (Dec.) April 2, 1990, 65 D.R. 296, judicial review ineffective for discretionary decision refusing entry of non-national wife.

[90] Art.35, para.3(a) (formerly Art.27, para.2).

[91] e.g. (24875/94) (Dec.) September 6, 1996, 86–A D.R. 74, where the operation of child support legislation was not such as to disclose any lack of respect for family life.

[92] The acknowledgement must be sufficiently clear, e.g. *Jensen v Denmark*, (Dec.) September 20, 2001, ECHR 2001–X, where the court reduced the applicant's sentence to reflect the delay in proceedings but refused to acknowledge any breach of Art.6. In *Labita v Italy*, April 6, 2000, ECHR 2000–IV, para.143, the Court referred to lack of any acknowledgment, express or implied, by the court, when awarding compensation, that the pre-trial detention was excessive; while reduction of sentence must be express and measurable to remove victim status in a criminal trial length case, this does not have to be spelt out: see *Beck v Norway*, June 26, 2001, where although the sentencing court did not specify what discount in sentence flowed from the excessive delay factor, the reduction was measurable in comparative terms (a two-year sentence instead of the nine-year maximum) and having regard to comparative sentencing practices.

[93] *Eckle v Germany*, July 15, 1982, Series A, No.51, para.66; *Dalban v Romania*, ECHR 1999–VI, para.44; *Posokhov v Russia*, March 4, 2003, ECHR 2003–IV; *Rechachi and Abdelhafid v UK*, (Dec.) June 10, 2003, ECHR 2003–IV, where the applicants received substantial ex gratia payments for detention without proper legal basis; no victim status in *Achour v France*, (67335/01) (Dec.) March 11, 2004, annulment of expulsion order; *Grasser v Germany*, October 5, 2006, still a victim as although the domestic court acknowledged the delay, no compensation or other redress was forthcoming.

[94] e.g. *DJ and A-KR v Romania*, (34175/05) (Dec.) October 20, 2009, para.79, decision forbidding the applicants from leaving the country was revoked swiftly and there was sufficient redress.

may be sufficient where no issue of damages or other reparation arises.[95] However, increasingly, the Court has found victim status remains notwithstanding a decision by a domestic court in the applicant's favour awarding compensation, purely on the basis that the amount of compensation was not sufficient.[96] Given that the Court expressly compares awards with what it would itself give in such cases, albeit with an apparent but undisclosed discount rate, its statement that there is a margin of appreciation left to domestic authorities as to the appropriate redress is a tad disingenuous.[97] It has refrained from publishing its internal tables or scales, apparently considering that these can be deduced from previous cases.[98]

Also, where, for example, an applicant accepts a sum of compensation in settlement of the civil claim before the domestic courts and thereby renounces further use of local remedies, he or she can no longer claim to be a victim.[99]

Examples of victim status lost:

— in respect of excessive length of proceedings, acknowledgment of violation and payment of compensation of a reasonable or not manifestly inadequate amount/[100] or discontinuation of proceedings, together with payment of some legal costs/[101] or exemption from significant legal costs[102];

— in respect of a death of a family member, establishment of the facts, identification and conviction of those responsible and payment of compensation.[103]

Example of victim status retained:

— where the alleged violation is delayed enforcement of a State judgment debt, belated payment does not remedy the authorities' failures[104]; nor payment with an inadequate amount of compensation for the delay[105];

[95] e.g. *MA v UK*, (35242/04) (Dec.) April 26, 2005, where the family judge apologised for the failures in the childcare system and made recommendations for the future to avoid repetition.

[96] e.g. *Armoniene v Lithuania*, November 25, 2008, paras 46–47, the domestic courts found that there had been a breach of privacy and awarded compensation; the Court considered the ceiling on sums payable under domestic law were too paltry to reflect the seriousness of what was in issue.

[97] *Simaldone v Italy*, March 31, 2009, para.30.

[98] The Italian Government, involved in many of these cases, has argued that the Court's approach is incoherent, inconsistent and unfair; the Court has found these arguments without substance, e.g. *Aragosa v Italy*, December 18, 2007, paras 18–24; *Simaldone*, fn.97, para.32.

[99] e.g. *Caraher v UK*, (41894/98) (Dec.) January 11, 2000, ECHR 2000–IX; *Hay v UK*, (41894/98) (Dec.) October 17, 2000, ECHR 2000–XI.

[100] *Cataldo v Italy*, (45656/99) (Dec.) June 3, 2004, ECHR 2004–VI; *Bako v Slovakia*, (60227/00) (Dec.) March 15, 2005; *Kalajzic v Croatia*, (15382/04) (Dec.) September 8, 2006, in assessing the reasonableness of compensation the Court takes into the local standard of living, the fact that domestic authorities pay more quickly etc; *Esposito v Italy*, November 27, 2007, para.26, sufficient where for delay the domestic court gave 70 per cent of what the Court would have awarded; contrast *Tomasic v Croatia*, October 19, 2006, still a victim for access to court complaint where the compensation given was significantly less (15 per cent) of what the Court would have awarded.

[101] *Sprotte v Germany*, (72438/01) (Dec.) November 17, 2005 (criminal).

[102] *Hansen v Denmark*, (26194/03) (Dec.) May 29, 2006 (civil).

[103] *Göktepe v Turkey*, (64731/01) (Dec.) April 26, 2005.

[104] e.g. *Metaxas v Greece*, May 27, 2004.

[105] e.g. *Kudic v Bosnia-Herzegovina*, December 9, 2008, paras 17–19.

— where the domestic court award for unreasonable length of proceedings is too low in comparison to Court awards and/or is paid after still further unreasonable delay[106];
— refusal by an applicant of a friendly settlement proposal by the Government has no effect on victim status.[107]

Special considerations apply as regards Arts 2 and 3, where there is an interplay of substantive and procedural obligations. Recent case-law indicates that payment of compensation, without an effective investigation, does not affect the applicants' victim status under both heads where intentional killing or torture are concerned. Where positive obligations are concerned, such as medical or other negligence, payment of compensation may still be enough. See further Pt IIB, s.43: Right to life, s.(2)(c): Victim status and s.46: Torture, inhuman and degrading treatment, s.(2)(a): Victim status.

4. Incompatibility

These grounds concern the Court's competence, or jurisdiction, in temporal and geographical terms, as well as the subject-matter and respondent party. The Court will therefore examine these issues of its own motion, even where not raised by the parties or if the parties are estopped from raising them.[108] Where a Contracting State is involved in acts outside its own territory, in its own name or participating under the umbrella of an international organisation, jurisdictional issues sometimes arise in a broad sense and the complaints are rejected as incompatible without specifying a particular ground.[109] I–048

1. Incompatibility *ratione temporis*[110]

Where the complaint relates to events which occurred before a Contracting State's acceptance of the right of individual petition under Art.34 (former Art.25 for cases introduced before the Commission before November 1, 1998 or former Art.46 for the acceptance of the old Court's jurisdiction) it must be rejected as incompatible *ratione temporis* where the State has specified that its ratification is prospective only.[111] Without such stipulation it will be regarded as retrospective and the Convention organs will be competent to examine the complaints, subject to the other admissibility criteria.[112] Temporal jurisdiction depends on the date of the facts constitutive of the alleged interference[113]; where interference predates ratification I–049

[106] e.g. *Simaldone*, fn.97, paras 27–33, the award was only 7.8 per cent of the equivalent Court award, and was paid after a year's delay.

[107] e.g. *RR v Poland,* May 26, 2011, para.96, friendly settlement matters are confidential and cannot be taken into account in contentious proceedings.

[108] e.g. *Medvedyev v France* (GC), March 29, 2010, paras 68–72.

[109] e.g. *Bankovic v Seventeen European States*, (52207/99) (Dec.) December 12, 2001, ECHR 2001–XII.

[110] Art.35, para.3(a) (former Art.27, para.2).

[111] e.g. *Veeber v Estonia (No.1)*, July 11, 2000, paras 54–55, the Court would still retain jurisdiction in situations of continuous breach extending beyond the relevant date.

[112] e.g. (9559/81) (Dec.) May 9, 1983, 33 D.R. 158.

[113] *Ilascu v Moldova and Russia*, July 8, 2004, ECHR 2004–VII, paras 395–408, no jurisdiction under Art.6 for a trial before ratification; however, as detention continued after ratification and a death sentence imposed before ratification had not been set aside afterwards, jurisdiction remained under Arts 2 and 5.

and a refusal of domestic courts to provide a remedy is post-ratification, the latter proceedings cannot bring the matter within the jurisdiction.[114]

There are special situations of continuing violation which may persist over a period of time and thus, even if first arising before the relevant date of ratification, persist into the period within the Court's temporal jurisdiction. The phenomenon of enforced disappearances falls into this category. The act or event of the substantive disappearance will be incompatible *ratione temporis* if it occurred before the relevant date; the procedural obligation to account for the whereabouts and fate of the person, for which the ongoing uncertainty may drag on for years, may well continue to exist after the relevant date and a violation under Arts 2 and 5 can arise for any State failure to investigate in that regard.[115] Situations of continued denial of access to property, where the taking of property was by an entity not recognised in international law and not capable of validly disposing of ownership, must be distinguished from the general situation in which deprivation or confiscation of property takes place within a State and is an instantaneous act which, if occurring before the relevant date, is outside the Court's temporal jurisdiction.[116]

The situation is somewhat different as concerns deaths under Art.2. The event or fatality which took place on a date before the relevant date cannot be examined under the substantive head. However, it may well be that there were ongoing domestic procedures concerning the death after the relevant date. This possibility led the Court to specify that in some circumstances the procedural obligation could apply to proceedings into the death where there was a "genuine connection between the death and the entry into force of the Convention," in particular where the investigative steps mostly occurred, or would have been expected mostly to occur, after that date.[117] The meaning or application of this test is not very clear. If it was intended to cover situations where, as in *Silih*, the death occurred so shortly before the date as to make it artificial to exclude the investigation that took place in the aftermath, this restrictive interpretation has not been applied in practice. In a number of cases in which the Court has assumed temporal jurisdiction, the deaths preceded the date of ratification by many years, the test in those cases apparently requiring only that most of the investigation took place within the temporal jurisdiction, notwithstanding how much of a lapse of inactivity there has been meanwhile.[118] In *Silih*, the Court also stated that, in any event, it did not exclude that in certain circumstances the "genuine connection" could also be based on the need to ensure that the guarantees and the underlying values of the Convention are protected in a real and effective manner. The meaning of this exempting formula, potentially extending temporal jurisdiction without limit, is unexplored for the moment.[119] Some paragraphs in *Silih* seem to imply that the same considerations would apply in Art.3 as regarded investigations into ill-treatment that occurred before the relevant date.[120]

[114] *Blecic v Croatia*, March 8, 2006, ECHR 2006–III, paras 77–82; *Meltex Ltd v Armenia*, (37780/02) (Dec.) May 27, 2008.
[115] *Varnava v Turkey*, fn.37, 147–150.
[116] *Preussiche Treuhand GMBH & Co, KGA.A. v Poland*, (47550/06) (Dec.) October 7, 2008, paras 58–62, distinguishing *Loizidou v Turkey (Preliminary Objections)*, March 23, 1995, para.41.
[117] *Silih v Slovenia*, April 9, 2009, paras 153–163.
[118] e.g. *Sandru v Romania*, December 8, 2009, paras 55–59, death occurred in 1989; ratification in 1994.
[119] *Silih v Slovenia*, April 9, 2009, para.63. Complaints arising out of the murder of large numbers of Polish officers in 1940 have been declared admissible in *Janowiec v Russia*, (55508/07) and (29520/09) (Dec.) July 5, 2011, where the Government's objection on temporal jurisdiction has been joined to the merits. Judgment on the merits not likely to issue before 2012.
[120] See fn.117 above, paras 147–148.

For the moment, procedural complaints under Art.5 do not fall within temporal competence if the deprivation of liberty occurred before the Convention entered into force.[121] On the other hand, as regards the new Art.3 of Protocol No.7, concerning the right to compensation for wrongful conviction, it does not matter if the original conviction predated entry into force of the Convention, as long as the date of quashing post-dated it.[122]

Note: where a complaint is about the length of proceedings covering a period before and after acceptance of the right of individual petition, the prior period may be taken into account in assessing the reasonableness of the later period (see Pt IIA, s.17: Length of proceedings). The same applies to periods of pre-trial detention and conditions of detention.[123]

2. Incompatibility *ratione loci*[124]

This applies where complaints are based on events in a territory outside the Contracting State and there is no sufficient link between those events and any authority within the jurisdiction of the Contracting State. I–050

This is likely to arise only where an applicant complains of matters within an overseas territory for which the Contracting State has not extended its acceptance of the right of individual petition under Art.56 (former Art.63).[125] A declaration under Art.56 is required to extend the Convention to a Contracting State's overseas territories.[126]

Where Russia claimed complaints about the death of a Russian girl in Cyprus were incompatible *ratione loci* as the events took place outside its territory, the Court considered that it could still examine complaints as to whether Russia complied with any obligation to protect the girl from trafficking on its own territory and to carry out an investigation into whether the girl was victim of any trafficking activity under its jurisdiction.[127]

Most issues of a State's jurisdiction tend to be examined under the heading "ratione *personae*" as concerns the other ways in which, besides the basic territorial aspect, the Contracting State can exert jurisdiction.

3. Incompatibility *ratione personae*[128]

There are two aspects, the first concerning the responsibility of the State and the second relating to the applicant's own status as a complainant. I–051

[121] *Korizno v Latvia*, (68163/01) (Dec.) September 28, 2006.
[122] *Matveyev v Russia*, July 3, 2008, para.38.
[123] *Kalashnikov v Russia*, July 15, 2002, paras 96 and 111.
[124] Art.35, para.3(a) (former Art.27, para.2).
[125] e.g. *Yonghong v Portugal*, (50887/99) (Dec.) November 25, 1999, ECHR 1999–IX, concerning Macao.
[126] *Quark Fishing v UK*, (15305/06) (Dec.) September 19, 2006, no jurisdiction to deal with fishing licence dispute in the Falklands; the Court rejected arguments that there should be a presumption of application in overseas territories or that an alternative basis of jurisdiction flowing from "effective control" could be relied on.
[127] *Rantsev v Cyprus and Russia*, January 7, 2010, paras 206–208.
[128] Art.35, para.3(a) (former Art.27, para.2).

(i) Responsibility of the Contracting State

- An application must be directed against a Contracting State[129] or a public official or body for which such a State may be held responsible.[130] A State cannot escape responsibility where it delegates its obligations to a body operating under private law.[131] Where a State is the effective controller of a company or municipal enterprise, it may be held responsible for its failings, having regard to the public nature of its functions and management.[132]

Jurisdiction is primarily a territorial notion. Extra-territorial acts only constitute an exercise of jurisdiction in exceptional cases.[133] A State is presumed to have control within its own jurisdiction and, even where no longer in effective control, may remain responsible to take what steps it can to safeguard fundamental rights within its territory.[134] Where a State bound by the Convention later splits into different parts which continue to adhere to the Convention in their new State form, the Court considers that the new State takes responsibility, by way of State succession, for any violations occurring in the period beforehand.[135] Jurisdiction applies extra-territorially on two principal bases:

- by exercise of authority and control of a State agent.[136] Examples include acts of diplomatic and consular agents[137]; exercise of public powers, by consent, invitation or acquiescence on the territory of another[138]; use of force by a State's agents operating outside its territory, as in carrying out arrest, taking control of a ship in international waters and holding persons in detention[139]; and by exercising authority and control through acts carried

[129] e.g. the respondent must have ratified the Convention and any Protocol that has been invoked.

[130] e.g. lawyers (unless there is an issue that a State-appointed lawyer failed to assure the defence of an accused in circumstances for the which the domestic courts should have taken responsibility: see Pt IIA: Legal representation in criminal proceedings) or, commonly, neighbours or private employers (assuming no positive obligation arose on the State to prevent the interference by the private person or body).

[131] *Wos v Poland*, (22860/02) (Dec.) March 1, 2005, where the Polish State, under agreement with Germany, was to provide financial assistance to victims of Nazi persecution from funds supplied by the latter and established a Foundation for that purpose.

[132] e.g. *Yershova v Russia*, April 4, 2010, paras 53–63. See also *Mykhaylenky v Ukraine*, November 30, 2004, para.44, indicating that the test is whether the company shows sufficient institutional and operational independence from the State to absolve the latter from responsibility for its acts and omissions.

[133] e.g. *Bankovic*, fn.109 above, paras 79–80; *Al-Skeini*, fn.4 above, paras 131–132.

[134] e.g. *Ilascu v Moldova and Russia*, July 8, 2004, ECHR 2004–VII, Moldova remained under a positive obligation to use diplomatic, economic, judicial or other measures within its power concerning the detention of the applicants in the Transdniestrian region, under separatist regime.

[135] *Bijelic v Serbia and Montegro*, April 28, 2009 paras 67–70, concerning the secession of Montegro from Serbia; *Koneüný v Czech Republic*, October 26, 2004, para.62, concerning the split of Czechoslovakia into two entities.

[136] *Al-Skeini*, fn.4 above, paras 133–137.

[137] *Bankovic*, fn.109 above, para.73.

[138] e.g. *Drozd and Janousek v Spain and France*, June 26, 1992, para.91.

[139] *Ocalan v Turkey*, May 12, 2005, para.91, handover of person on Kenyan soil by Kenyan officials for arrest by Turkish officials; *Al-Saadoon and Mufdhi v UK*, (61498/08) June 30, 2009 and *Al-Jedda v UK*, July 7, 2011, detention in British-controlled military prison in Iraq; *Issa v Turkey*, November 16, 2008, seizure by Turkish army of suspects in Iraq and execution therein would have been within Turkish juridiction; *Loizidou v Turkey (preliminary objections)*, Series A, No.310 and *Medvedyev v France*, March 29, 2010, para.67, seizure by French navy of ship on high seas and detention of the crew.

out in security operations in an area in which the State had assumed the exercise of public powers, including responsibility for security[140]; or

- by effective control of a territory by military action. Where a State exercises effective control of an area outside its territory through military action, lawful or unlawful, there will be an obligation to secure the entire range of Convention rights in the area under its control. This obligation has arisen in two situations to date, both where a Contracting Party has intervened on the territory of another state within the Convention system (Russia in Moldova, Turkey in northern Cyprus).[141] Control may be exerted by the military or by a local administration under its aegis.[142] The fact that the Court was concerned to prevent a legal vacuum within its own regional space played an important role. No "effective control" was found sufficient to base jurisdiction where Member States were involved in NATO operations in the airspace over the Federal Republic of Yugoslavia.[143] This head does not cover territories for whose international relations a Contracting State is responsible, to which the Convention may be extended by a declaration under Art.56, which is a separate and distinct category of situation.

As concerns international organisations:

- States are not liable for actions/omissions which did not take place on their soil or by virtue of a decision of their authorities which are part of operations attributable to the United Nations which has a legal personality separate from Member States.[144]
- Nor is there responsibility where an applicant complains essentially of a decision or measure directly issuing from the international organ, rather than of a lack of protection of rights by the Contracting State[145]—a rather fine distinction as shown by subsequent cases which examined both aspects to be on the safe side.[146]
- Where a State carries out acts within its own territory or jurisdiction in pursuance of international legal obligations undertaken with an international body, it does not escape responsibility but its actions will be justified as long as the relevant organisation protects fundamental rights, substantively and procedurally, in a manner equivalent to the Convention itself although there

[140] *Al-Skeini*, fn.4 above.

[141] *Ilascu*, fn.134 above; *Loizidou v Turkey (preliminary objections)*, Series A, No.310.

[142] *Cyprus v Turkey*, May 25, 2001, ECHR 2001–IV, para.77.

[143] *Bankovic*, fn.109 above, concerning the bombing of a radio station and killing of civilians.

[144] *Behrami v France, Saramati v France, Germany and Norway*, (71412/01) and (78166/01) (Dec.) May 2, 2007, complaints about the acts/omissions of soldiers helping UN missions in Kosovo; see also *Beric v Bosnia-Herzegovina,* (36357/04) (Dec.) October 16, 2007, acts of UN High Representative attributable to UN and outside the responsibility of the State; *Stephens v Cyprus, Turkey and the United Nations,* (45267/06) (Dec.) December 11, 2008, UNFICYP's actions attributable to UN.

[145] *Boivin v 34 Member States of the Council of Europe*, (73250/01) (Dec.) September 9, 2008, concerning the decision by Eurocontrol not to employ the applicant.

[146] *Rambus v Germany*, (40382/04) (Dec.) June 16, 2009, concerning the applicant's complaints about the European Patent Office, the Court noted this did not involve any act or decision by the German authorities but even if their responsibility was somehow engaged, there was equivalent protection not shown to be manifestly deficient: see the *Bosphorus* line of cases below. See also *Beygo v 46 Member States*, (36099/06) (Dec.) June 16, 2009, complaints against the administrative tribunal of the Council of Europe, both strands of reasoning adopted.

will be a presumption of compliance unless the protection is shown to be "manifestly deficient".[147] It is on this equivalence of protection that implementation of European Union directives and procedures before the European Court of Justice, for example, has been found not to offend the Convention.[148] The mere fact an international tribunal has its headquarters in a State, with whom it has a "Headquarters Agreement", does not bring its activities within the State's responsibility.[149]

(ii) The status of the applicants themselves:

I–052 • The applicant must be able to show that he or she is a victim of the events or measures which base the allegations. No *actio popularis* will be entertained.[150] A person may claim to be a victim where he is directly affected by a measure—it is not necessary to show damage.[151]

Particular examples:

- Shareholders cannot claim to be victims of interferences with the rights of the company save in exceptional circumstances,[152] e.g. where it is clearly established that it is impossible for the company to apply to the Court through the organs set up under its articles of incorporation or, in the event of liquidation or bankruptcy, through its liquidators or trustees in bankruptcy[153]; where there is direct effect on the property rights in the shares or where the applicant can show that he is the sole shareholder or that the

[147] See equivalence of protection found as regarded the NATO internal adjudication body in *Gasparini v Italy and Belgium*, (10750/03) (Dec.) May 12, 2009. Contrast *Beric*, fn.144 above, measure of the UN High Representative had not required any further procedural steps of implementation by the domestic authorities; no State responsibility to consider.

[148] *Bosphorus Airways v Ireland*, June 30, 2005, ECHR 2005–VI, paras 152–156; *Connolly v 15 EU Member States*, (73274/01) (Dec.) December 9, 2008, concerning the applicant's complaints as employee against internal EU disciplinary bodies and appeals to the Tribunal of First Instance and ECJ; *Cooperatieve Producentenoganisatie van de Nederlandse Kokkelvisserij UA v Netherlands*, (13645/05) (Dec.) January 20, 2009, where the domestic courts sought the involvement of the ECJ in the Art.234 procedure.

[149] *Galic v Netherlands,* (22617/07) and *Blagojevic v Netherlands*, (49032/07) (Decs.) June 9, 2009, concerning the international criminal tribunal for former Yugoslavia set up by the UN Security Council; *Lopez Cifuentes v Spain*, (18574/06) (Dec.) July 7, 2009, concerning the International Olive Oil Council.

[150] e.g. *Skender v FYROM*, (62059/00) (Dec.) March 10, 2005; *Rossi v Italy*, (55185/08) (Dec.) December 16, 2008; *Ouardiri v Switzerland*, (65840/09) (Dec.) June 28, 2011.

[151] e.g. *Dudgeon*, fn.36 above, para.41, referring to continuous and direct effect on private life from legislation prohibiting adult homosexual acts irrespective of the fact that the applicant had not been subject to a measure of implementation; *Wassink v Netherlands*, September 27, 1990, Series A, No.185–A, status of "victim" may exist even where there is no damage, which is relevant to the application of Art.41 (just satisfaction for pecuniary or non-pecuniary damage). See also interception of communications and surveillance cases where applicants may complain of being a victim from the existence of legislation permitting secret and covert measures due to overly broad definitions and insufficient safeguards without showing that any surveillance measures were applied to them: e.g. *Association of European Integration and Human Rights and Ekimdzhiev v Bulgaria*, June 28, 2007, paras 58–63.

[152] *Agrotexim v Greece*, October 24, 1995, Series A, No.330, 21 E.H.R.R. 250; *Amat G Ltd and Mebaghishili v Georgia*, September 27, 2005, para.33. See also *Družstevní-záložna Pria v Czech Republic*, July 31, 2008, paras 99–101, individual members of a credit union with separate legal personality could not complain about the union being put into receivership; it had acted itself through its supervisory board.

[153] *Agrotexim*, fn.152 above, para.66.

company is the means by which he runs his own affairs.[154] Nor can company officers claim to be victims of violations against the company.[155]

- Where organisations bring applications in their own name, their own rights have to be affected, not only their members.[156]
- Where a lawyer representing an applicant fails to provide a letter of authority signed by the latter within the requisite time-limit, there will be no "applicant" for the purposes of Art.34.[157]
- A person who is acquitted at the end of criminal proceedings may not claim to be a victim of any aspects of lack of fairness under Art.6, paras 1 and 3 (save, for example, as regards length, breach of presumption of innocence, and free interpretation, the effects of which may not be cancelled out by the acquittal).[158] Similarly, while generally a complaint (save length again) may be regarded as premature if brought before the final culmination of the proceedings, in some circumstances victim status may be disclosed due to intervening effects.[159]
- In limited circumstances it may be sufficient for an applicant to show potential future victim status but this requires reasonable and convincing evidence of the likelihood that a violation affecting him personally will occur; mere suspicion or conjecture of possibility is insufficient.[160]

[154] *Ankarcrona v Sweden*, June 29, 2000, ECHR 2000–VI; *Nosov v Russia*, (30877/02) (Dec.) October 20, 2005; *Pokis v Latvia*, (528/02) (Dec.) October 5, 2006.

[155] *Meltex Ltd and Movsesyan v Armenia*, June 7, 2009, paras 66–68.

[156] e.g. (15404/89), fn.66 above, the trade union was not affected by the broadcasting restrictions though its members were, *Rossi v Italy*, fn.150 above, applicant associations protecting the interests of patients in a vegetative state could not claim to be victims themselves of a measure allowing life support to be withdrawn in a high profile case; contrast *Izmir Savas Karsitlari Dernegi v Turkey*, (46257/99) (Dec.) September 23, 2004, where the applicant association was allowed to be a victim where its members were subject to penalties for exercising their rights of association abroad; *Grande Oriente d'Italia di Palazzo Giustiniani v Italy (No.2)*, May 31, 2007, para.21, the association could claim to be victim of measures infringing the rights of its members as these affected its image and could diminish its membership; *Georgian Labour Party v Georgia*, July 8, 2008, paras 72–73, when electoral legislation or measures restrict individual candidates' right to stand for election through a party list, the relevant party, as a corporate entity, can claim to be a victim under Art.3 of Protocol No.1 independently of its candidates.

[157] *Post v Netherlands*, (21727/08) (Dec.) January 20, 2009.

[158] e.g. *Sapan v Turkey*, (36075/03) (Dec.) May 3, 2007; *Doubtfire v UK*, (31825/96) (Dec.) April 23, 2002, where the applicant had the possibility of applying for compensation for the conviction and detention served.

[159] e.g. *Dink v Turkey*, September 14, 2010, paras 107–109, the applicant died before the criminal trial for denigrating Turkishness had ended; however, the fact that he had been convicted, albeit not finally, had rendered him a target for ultra-nationalists who had assassinated him.

[160] e.g. *Senator Lines GMBH v Austria and other European Union States*, (56672/00) (Dec.) March 10, 2004, referring, inter alia, to secret or covert measures or expulsion measures; no such risk was shown in the case where the fine, although not suspended, was not enforced and was, finally, quashed. See references in *Rossi v Italy*, fn.150 above, no potential victim status established where applicants complained of a court decision allowing a father to have life support removed from his daughter; or in *Ouardiri v Switzerland*, fn.150 above, no potential victim status for a Muslim from the constitutional amendment banning minarets, where there was no indication that he would be involved in any action to which the amendment might apply.

4. Incompatibility *ratione materiae*[161]

I–053 This includes:

- where a person invokes a right not included in the Convention[162];
- where the person's complaints fall outside the scope of particular rights invoked[163];
- where a person invokes another international instrument or general principle of international law as a ground of violation, rather than an aid to interpretation.[164]

5. Substantially the same[165]

I–054 Complaints are substantially the same as a matter where they:

- are identical as to parties,[166] complaints,[167] and facts in issue. Any such application will be rejected if it has already been examined:
  - — by the Court; or

[161] Art.35, para.3(a) (former Art.27, para.2).

[162] e.g. right to a job, or to minimum wage, or certain standard of living: (6807/75) (Dec.) December 10, 1975, 3 D.R. 153; (11776/85) (Dec.) March 4, 1986, 46 D.R. 251; right to driving licence: (7462/76) (Dec.) March 7, 1977, 9 D.R. 112; to obtain a prosecution against another person, right to political asylum: (21808/93) (Dec.) September 8, 1993, 75 D.R. 264; free choice of doctor: (19898/92) (Dec.) August 30, 1993, 75 D.R. 223; right to conscientious objection: (17086/90) (Dec.) December 6, 1991, 72 D.R. 245; right to use the local language in the regional assembly: *Birk-Levy v France*, (39426/06) (Dec.) September 2010.

[163] e.g. where the applicant complains of the fairness of proceedings under Art.6 which do not involve the determination of a criminal charge or civil rights: *Maaouia v France*, October 5, 2000, ECHR 2000–X, Art.6 not applicable to asylum or expulsion proceedings; no right to adopt contained in Art.12: *Frette v France*, (36515/97) (Dec.) June 12, 2001; refusal of re-opening of a case after the Court's finding of a breach of Art. 6: *Steck-Risch v Liechtenstein*, (29061/08) (Dec.) May 11, 2010.

[164] *Calheiros Lopes v Portugal*, (69338/01) (Dec.) June 3, 2004.

[165] Art.35, para.2(b) (former Art.27, para.1(b)).

[166] e.g. (11603/85) (Dec.) January 20, 1987, 50 D.R. 228, where it was not the applicants who had brought the complaints before the ILO); *Varnava v Turkey* (GC), fn.37, para.118, even if in an inter-State case all the disappeared persons from 1974 were part of the complaints, including the applicants' relatives, the cases had not been introduced by the same applicants; *Folgero v Norway*, (15472/02) (Dec.) February 14, 2006, this ground did not apply even where the parents had run domestic proceedings jointly and then some had applied to the Court and others to the UN Human Rights Committee, making identical complaints through the same lawyer, in a nifty piece of co-ordinated forum shopping; even if the case essentially was the same in both fora, the Court held to the criterion that the individual applicants had to be identical in both; *Illiu v Belgium*, (14301/08) (Dec.) May 19, 2009, the case before the Working Group on Enforced Disappearances had been brought by an NGO, not the applicants.

[167] *Smirnova v Russia*, (46133/99) and (48183/99) (Dec.) October 3, 2002, where the complaint before the Court was wider in scope than that brought by one applicant before the HRC.

— by another procedure of international[168] investigation or settlement[169] which is independent, judicial or quasi-judicial[170] in proceedings which are adversarial, deliver public reasoned decisions on the individual case, making findings and dealing with, even in recommendatory form, the attribution of responsibility and the award of redress[171]; and

- if they contain no new, relevant information.

New, relevant facts may include: further lapse of time in the length of proceedings already examined by the Court[172]; continuation of a period in remand[173]; where an application was rejected for non-exhaustion and the applicant has terminated the domestic proceedings; the discovery of new evidence relevant to the previous complaints[174]; and complaints about facts subsequent to those examined in another international procedure.[175] They do not include legal arguments concerning the interpretation of the Convention that the applicant did not submit in the prior application.[176]

6. Abuse of petition[177]

It may be applied in cases of: I–055

[168] e.g. the Human Rights Chamber, although set up by an international treaty, was an internal domestic body: see *Jelicic v Bosnia-Herzegovina*, (41183/02) (Dec.) November 15, 2005. This also is interpreted as excluding NGOs, applying only to bodies set up by States: see *Lukanov v Bulgaria*, (21915/93) (Dec.) January 12, 1995.

[169] e.g. (16358/90) (Dec.) December 10, 1990, 73 D.R. 214, an organ of the ILO qualified; (17512/90) (Dec.) July 6, 1992, 73 D.R. 214, UN Human Rights Committee 'HRC' qualified; *Peraldi v France*, (2096/05) (Dec.) April 7, 2009, UN Working Group on Arbitrary Detention qualified.

[170] e.g. *Zagaria v Italy*, (24408/03) (Dec.) June 3, 2008, the CPT was not judicial, but a preventive body; *Karoussiotis v Portugal*, February 1, 2011, paras 62–77, infraction procedure before the European Commission was geared not to adjudicating and giving redress to individual claims but ensuring the compliance with EU norms by contracting States.

[171] e.g. *Peraldi*, fn.169 above, the UN Working Group on Arbitrary Detention qualified although it could only make recommendations as to State responsibility and redress; *Varnava v Turkey*, (16064/90) et al, (Dec.) April 14, 1998, the Committee for Missing Persons in Cyprus did not qualify as it was limited to discovery of bodies, it was not able to make findings as to the cause of death or to attribute responsibility for events; *Mikolenko v Estonia*, (16944/03) (Dec.) January 5, 2006, the "1503 procedure" before the UN Commission for Human Rights did not qualify as it examined situations, not individual cases and did not offer redress to individuals (its procedure was also confidential: *Celniku v Greece*, June 5, 2007, para.40); *Zagaria v Italy*, (24408/03) (Dec.) June 3, 2008, the CPT was not judicial, but a preventive body, its procedure was confidential, not adversarial; *Yagmurderli v Turkey*, (29590/96) (Dec.) February 13, 2011, even if the UN Special *Rapporteur* had interviewed the applicant, he drew up a general report on a particular type of human rights problem, not individual cases; *Malsagova v Russia*, (27244/03) (Dec.) March 6, 2008, the UN Working Group on Enforced and Involuntary Disappearances did not investigate individual cases, attribute responsibility for any deaths, make findings as to causes of death or give redress to applicants.

[172] (8233/78) (Dec.) October 3, 1979, 17 D.R. 122.

[173] (9621/81) (Dec.) October 13, 1983, 33 D.R. 217.

[174] e.g. (23956/94) (Dec.) November 28, 1994, concerning new information about the applicant prisoner's security status relevant to his previous complaints about transfer/visiting restrictions.

[175] *Patera v Czech Republic*, (25326/03) (Dec.) April 26, 2007.

[176] (8206/78) (Dec.) July 10, 1981, 25 D.R. 147; *Previti v Italy*, (45291/06) (Dec.) December 8, 2009, paras 292–294.

[177] Art.35, para.3 (former Art.27, para.2).

- forgery; fraud; or deliberate misrepresentation[178];
- failure to inform the Court during the proceedings of significant developments, relevant to its ruling on the case in full knowledge of the facts[179];
- vexatious and repeated applications of a similar nature[180];
- claim based on facts for which the applicant is himself responsible[181];
- deliberate, flagrant breach of procedural rules[182];
- persistent use of insulting and provocative language[183] (emotive, exaggerated critical language does not count)[184]; or
- complaints of a trivial, *de minimis* nature.[185]

It may not be necessary for the Court to establish who was responsible or had knowledge of a forged document, whether the lawyer, applicant or other. If the Court was misled by the document as to an essential element of the application, that may be sufficient for the application to be rejected for abuse.[186] In other cases, the Court has referred to the intentional nature of the abusive conduct.[187] Where breach of confidentiality is concerned, the applicant must be directly linked to the leak; a suspicion is not enough.[188]

178 e.g. *Bagheri and Maliki v Netherlands*, (30164/06) (Dec.) May 15, 2007, documents forged; *Poznanski v Germany*, (25101/05) (Dec.) July 3, 2007, signature forged on letter of authority (purported applicant already dead at that date).

179 *Kerechashvili v Georgia*, (5667/02) May 2, 2006, in a non-enforcement case, the applicant failed to inform the Court that authorities had partially honoured their obligations; *Pederescu v Romania*, December 2, 2008, paras 24–27, an heir seeking to join the application failed to inform the Court that the original applicant and owner of the property in question had died.

180 e.g. (13284/87) (Dec.) October 15, 1987, 54 D.R. 214, abuse found on the fifth application; the Commission held that it was not its function to deal with a succession of ill-founded and querulous complaints, which created unnecessary work incompatible with its function of ensuring the implementation of the Convention and which hindered it in that function; *Mirolubovs v Latvia*, September 15, 2009, para.65.

181 e.g. where the applicant complained of the length of extradition proceedings, the Commission considered that this was the result of the applicant going into hiding to avoid arrest (Ireland, (9742/82) (Dec.) March 2, 1982, 32 D.R. 251)

182 e.g. revealing to the press or others confidential documents. Minor inadvertent breaches are likely to attract a warning, e.g. concerning disclosure of friendly settlement documents, see *Hadrabova v Czech Republic*, (42165/02) et al (Dec.) September 25, 2007, abuse from disclosure of such documents in a domestic claim for compensation and *Mirolubovs*, fn.180, paras 66–71, disclosure not linked to applicants.

183 *Duringer v France*, (61164/00) (Dec.) February 4, 2002 and *Rehak v Czech Republic*, (67208/01) (Dec.) May 18, 2004, where the applicants made repeated insulting accusations against, variously, Court judges, Registry lawyers and State officials; *Di Salvo v Italy*, (16098/05) (Dec.) January 11, 2007, abusive attack on Government's representative. See *Georgian Labour Party v Georgia*, (9103/04) (Dec.) May 22, 2007, where the applicant's apologies and non-repetition of provocative statements were taken into account; *Chernitsyn v Russia*, April 6, 2006, paras 27–28, no abuse where the applicant withdrew attack on the Government's representative's good faith and issued an apology.

184 *Aleksanyan v Russia,* December 22, 2008, paras 117–118, the applicant's lawyer's florid criticism of the Government, e.g. "unseemly haste", "breathtakingly irresponsible statements".

185 *Bock v Germany*, (22051/07) (Dec.) January 19, 2010, the length of proceedings complaint concerned a claim for reimbursement of a product of €7; noting the applicant was a well-paid civil servant, the Court said, exceptionally, that as this type of complaint congested domestic and European instances and no principle was at stake, this was abusive; *Dudek v Germany*, (12977/09) (Dec.) November 23, 2010, petty claims congesting the domestic courts and Strasbourg.

186 e.g. *Poznanski v Germany*, fn.178 above.

187 *Mirolubovs*, fn.180, paras 63 and 66.

188 *Mirolubovs*, fn.180, para.66, the applicants denied leaking the confidential friendly settlement correspondence with the Court's registry to F who had used them in contacts with the Government; the Court gave them the benefit of the doubt.

It is not for the Government to bring action against an abusive applicant; it should inform the Court who has sole competence to act. Threat of criminal or disciplinary sanction by the authorities in such a case might raise an issue of hindrance of the right of individual petition under Art.34.[189]

Political motivations

The fact that applicants may be pursuing a political goal or purpose of some kind is generally not sufficient to disclose abuse. The Convention organs have not found it abusive for applicants to use the Strasbourg procedure as part of a pressure campaign or as publicity to put pressure on a State or to influence public opinion subject to the proviso that the complaints are based on true facts, not unsupported by the evidence or concerning matters outside the scope of the Convention.[190]

7. Striking out

The Court may proceed to strike a case from its list under Art.37 (former Art.30) where: I–056

- the applicant does not intend to pursue his application.[191] This includes withdrawal by the applicant, where there has been an informal settlement with the Government[192] or where the applicant has lost interest in pursuing the case[193]; in case of doubt about the genuineness of a withdrawal or the mental state of the applicant, the Court has considered that respect for human rights required a continued examination[194];
- where the matter has been resolved, for example, by a settlement between the parties[195]; or the situation about which the applicant is complaining has ceased to place him at risk of a violation[196]—in the latter circumstance, it is not relevant that the applicant wishes to continue with his complaints, as the Court will examine whether there remains any objective justification for pursuing the application, namely whether the circumstances complained of directly by the applicant still obtain and whether the effects of a possible

[189] *Mirolubovs*, fn.180, para.70.

[190] e.g. *Akdivar*, fn.45 above, para.54, where the Government alleged applications by Kurds were abusive as part of a PKK propaganda campaign to undermine the State; *Georgian Labour Party*, fn.183 above.

[191] Art.37, para.1(a).

[192] *Swaby v UK*, (65822/01) (Dec.) May 23, 2002, where the applicant withdrew on ex gratia award from the Government.

[193] e.g. failure to respond to requests for information, observe time-limits without reasonable explanation, notify a change of address or keep in contact with lawyer (e.g. *Feal-Martinez and Pearson v UK*, (1309/02) (Dec.) July 1, 2003).

[194] *Tehrani v Turkey*, April 13, 2010, paras 55–57.

[195] Art.37, para.1(b), *e.g. Hutten-Czapska v Poland*, April 28, 2008.

[196] Art.37, para.1(b), e.g. *Tsavachidis v Greece*, January 21, 1999, where a friendly settlement was reached on the basis of compensation and an assurance of no further surveillance of Jehovahs' Witnesses on grounds of their religion; *Kovacic v Slovenia*, October 3, 2008, paras 258–269, where the applicants' claims for foreign currency deposits had either been paid in full with interest or were pending in other *fora*; *Abdouni v France*, February 27, 2001, where the applicant was no longer at risk of expulsion; contrast *Salah Sheekh v Netherlands*, January 11, 2007, paras 115–118, the applicant asylum seeker had only been given temporary asylum pending a final decision on the merits and thus a strike out by the Court would have left the matter unresolved.

violation of the Convention on account of those circumstances have been redressed[197]; where a systemic problem has been addressed by general and individual measures after a pilot judgment procedure, giving the applicants an avenue of adequate redress[198];

- where for any other reason the Court finds it no longer justified to continue the examination of the application[199]; where, for example, the applicant has died[200] without heir or relative wishing to pursue the complaint[201]; where there has been a unilateral declaration by a Government acknowledging the breach in some form (including the expression of regret or apology) and providing adequate redress[202]; where the circumstances are such that the Court is unable to continue an effective examination[203]; where there has been deliberate and manipulative breach of confidentiality rules;[204] or where the applicant has failed to keep the Court informed of relevant circumstances.[205]

The Court may nonetheless continue the examination of a case in any of the above situations where "respect for Human Rights" requires such a course. A unilateral declaration by a State may not be accepted, for example, if the case concerns issues of human rights importance on which there is little established jurisprudence[206] or

[197] *Pisano v Italy*, October 24, 2002, para.42, pending the Court's examination of complaints about an unfair trial, including failure to hear a witness (B), the applicant's conviction was quashed following a retrial at which B was heard and he could apply for compensation for the wrongful conviction; *Kaftailova v Latvia*, December 7, 2007, where no attempt was made to enforce the deportation order and the authorities had contacted the applicant giving details of how she could regularise her situation, no other redress was needed; *El Majjaoui & Stichtung Touba Moskee v Netherlands*, December 20, 2007, the applicant imam was given a work permit to remain at the applicant mosque and was no longer subject to threat of expulsion; *Stojanovic v Serbia*, April 28, 2009, paras 76–81, the applicant prisoner was given the lacking dentures free of charge, that was sufficient to resolve the matter (no physical damage in the interim; non-pecuniary or moral damages not mentioned, or presumably required).

[198] See *e.g Wolkenberg v Poland*, (25525/03) (Dec.) December 4, 2007, paras 72–77; *Association of Real Property Owners in Lodz v Poland*, (3485/02) (Dec.) March 8, 2011.

[199] Art.37, para.1(c).

[200] e.g. *Skoutaridou v Turkey*, December 17, 1999, where the Court noted that there were numerous other pending cases raising similar issues; *Gladkowski v Poland*, March 14, 2000.

[201] *Benazet v France*, (47/03) (Dec.) January 4, 2007, where the case was struck off when the applicant died and the guardian of his heir declined to continue; *Leger v France*, March 30, 2009, where the applicant died and the purported relation signing the lawyer's letter of authority had not given proof of a family relationship or other legitimate interest.

[202] *Akman v Turkey*, June 26, 2001, ECHR 2001–VI; *Kalanyos v Romania*, April 26, 2007; *Facondis v Cyprus*, (9095/08) (Dec.) May 27, 2010; cf. *Tahsin Acar v Turkey*, May 6, 2003, concerning inadequate unilateral declarations; also *Prencipe v Monaco*, July 16, 2009, paras 62–64, declaration did not acknowledge the breach in any form; *Hakimi v Belgium*, June 29, 2010, para.29, redress offered insufficient as the applicant required a Court judgment to be able to obtain a re-opening of his case; for a UK example: *MacDonald v UK*, (301/04) (Dec.) February 6, 2007.

[203] e.g. (22057/93) (Dec.) January 13, 1997, 88–A D.R. 17; *Sevgi Erdogan v Turkey*, April 29, 2003, para.38.

[204] e.g. (20915/92) (Rep.) March 3, 1995, where the lawyer of the applicant company had submitted to the Supreme Court in support of his appeal a confidential Commission letter informing him of the provisional opinion on the merits, which was a serious breach of its rules for which there was no justification.

[205] e.g. *Oya Ataman v Turkey*, (47738/99) (Dec.) May 22, 2007.

[206] *Rantsev*, fn.127, paras 198–202, the Cyprus Government had acknowledged the breaches, taken investigative steps and offered sufficient money; however, the case concerned trafficking, a subject little explored and of current European concern.

the compensation offered is not equitable.[207] Moreover, even where the applicant announces withdrawal, it is not always the end of the story; in theory, an applicant cannot be allowed to be bought off by a Government leaving a situation where similar violations may continue to occur.[208]

There have been very few cases where the Convention organs have continued a case in the absence of an applicant. Where the Commission was not satisfied that the applicant's expression of intention to withdraw was genuine, it rejected the Government's objections on this ground.[209] Where there was doubt about the applicant's intentions to pursue the application in an expulsion case, the Court put weight on the complaints concerning risk to life and risk of torture and did not strike out the application as this would remove protection of the Convention from the applicant.[210]

In *Tyrer v UK*, the Court continued examination of complaints under Art.3 about birching of a juvenile, even though the applicant himself had withdrawn on reaching his majority.[211] More recently, in *Karner v Austria*,[212] even though the applicant had died and no relative wished to continue the application, the Court proceeded to find a violation of Art.14 in conjunction with Art.8 in respect of the applicant's inability, as the homosexual partner of a deceased tenant, to succeed to the tenancy. It observed that, while Art.34 required the existence of a victim to engage the protection mechanism of the Convention, this criterion did not apply rigidly during the proceedings. As human rights cases had a moral importance transcending the individual applicant, it was in accordance with the purpose of the Convention to continue with the case in the absence of the applicant where, as in this case, an important question of general interest arose not only for Austria but for Contracting States generally. Unlike other cases struck out on the death of the applicant, it may be noted that the principal issue at stake had not been resolved or examined in other similar, recent cases and it was possible to carry out an effective examination of the case without the participation of the applicant, e.g. no questions of factual dispute or credibility.

The above principles were also applied where, following lodging of the application through its lawyer, a company was wound up by the State. The Court rejected the Government's objection to the lawyer continuing the case in the name of the defunct company, noting that to hold otherwise would undermine Convention protection by allowing States to bring applications to an end through their own unilateral actions.[213]

[207] *Megadat.com SRL v Moldova,* May 17, 2011, paras 12–15, the amount was equitable, given that the applicant's claims were excessive and concerned conjectural income which was not a legally protected interest of sufficient certainty.

[208] e.g. *Tsavachidis*, fn.196 above, para.25, where the Court noted that it had already clarified the nature and extent of the contracting States' obligations in similar surveillance situations.

[209] e.g. *Kurt v Turkey*, (24276/94) (Dec.) May 22, 1993, 81–A D.R. 112.

[210] *Tehrani v Turkey*, April 13, 2010, paras 53–57.

[211] *Tyrer v UK*, April 25, 1978, Series A, No.26, paras 24–27.

[212] *Karner v Austria,* July 24, 2003, ECHR 2003–IX. See also *Ukrainian Media Group v Ukraine*, March 29, 2006, para.36, where the Court continued the case despite the parties' settlement. Contrast *Benazet v France*, (47/03) (Dec.) January 4, 2007, where the case was struck off when the applicant died and the guardian of his heir declined to continue; *Leger v France*, March 30, 2009, where the applicant died and the purported relation signing the new lawyer's letter of authority had not given proof of the close family relationship or any other legitimate interest.

[213] *OAO Neftyanaya Kompaniya Yukos v Russia*, (14902/04) (Dec.) January 29, 2009, this leaves open the somewhat knotty question to whom any subsequent, and potentially enormous just satisfaction award would be payable after any finding of violation.

8. Appeal against admissibility decisions or re-opening

I–057 There is no appeal by an applicant against a decision declaring his application or part of his application inadmissible.[214] Pursuant to Art.37, para.2, the Court may restore an application to the list. The practice is only do so where the Court has made a factual error in the decision which is of relevance to its conclusions, for example, where it overlooked a letter introducing the application which affected the calculation of the six-month time-limit or where it relied in its reasoning on a fact which was not correct. It might also be possible that re-opening might occur where it appears that the Government has failed to comply with a settlement[215]; or where new circumstances arose enabling the Court to resume its examination.[216]

9. Standing

I–058 An individual, group of individuals or non-governmental organisation claiming to be a victim of a violation of the Convention or other person (friend, relative, etc. as well as lawyer or NGO representative) who has authority to act (by means of signed letter of authority specifying that the applicant wishes him/her to act in the proceedings before the Court) may present an application. The fact that an applicant has a guardian appointed under domestic law and the guardian's permission is required in domestic law for any action does not prevent an applicant having standing to introduce an application.[217] Domestic rules on standing are not decisive.[218] Parents may generally bring applications on behalf of their children, even if they have no custody rights; however, foster-parents who applied to adopt a child have no biological or legal links entitling them to bring a case on her behalf.[219]

Municipal bodies or public law corporations performing official duties, running a public service under governmental control or participating in the exercise of governmental powers cannot bring an application,[220] nor any local authority, collectivity or commune.[221] Account is taken of legal status and the rights that status gives the body, the nature of the activity carried out and its context and the

[214] Governments, however, may raise fresh admissibility objections even after the case is declared admissible. See para.I–030 on estoppel at the beginning of this section.

[215] e.g. (16266/90) (Dec.) May 22, 1993, 65 D.R. 337. See e.g. *Katic v Serbia*, (13920/04) (Dec.) July 7, 2009, application restored to role where applicants, under mental incapacity, complained that the settlement money was not being released to them.

[216] e.g. an applicant who failed to make contact with his lawyer renewed his complaints with a convincing reason for the lapse (e.g. intimidation).

[217] *Zehentner v Austria*, July 16, 2009, paras 39–41, the Court noted that guardianship served the function of preventing an incapable person from disposing of their rights or assets to their disadvantage; this consideration did not apply in proceedings before the Court.

[218] e.g. *Scozzari and Giunta v Italy*, July 13, 2000, ECHR 2000–VIII, paras 138–139, concerning representation of children.

[219] *Moretti and Benedetti v Italy*, April 27, 2004, paras 33–34.

[220] e.g. (25978/94) (Dec.) January 18, 1996, 84–A D.R.129, the status of the BBC has been left open; *Ayuntamiento de Mula v Spain*, (55346/00) (Dec.) February 1, 2001, ECHR 2001–I. See also *Pasa and Erkan Erol v Turkey*, December 12, 2006, where the applicant father could not complain of his son's injury as his own administrative responsibility as local mayor was engaged.

[221] e.g. *Dösemealti Belediyesi v Turkey*, (50108/06) (Dec.) March 23, 2010, irrespective of whether the commune was able to carry out "private law acts".

degree of independence from the political authorities.[222] The fact that a commercial corporation is wholly owned by a State is not decisive of its status, if it is sufficiently independent in its running and not involved in exercise of public power.[223] The exclusion extends to public entities of non-Contracting States.[224]

An application cannot be brought in the name of a deceased person.[225] A live victim of a breach of a right is required to set in motion the protection mechanism under the Convention, although once the application is validly introduced there is more flexibility.[226] Where an applicant dies during the proceedings, it may continue where a spouse or appropriate close relative with a legitimate interest adopts it. This has been permitted in most cases.[227] However, cases have been struck out where the persons seeking to continue the application were not close relatives or heirs.[228] There is also reference to certain rights being personal and non-transferable.[229] In cases introduced under Art.2, where most of the victims are, unfortunately, dead, the cases may, exceptionally, be introduced by a relative with the requisite standing as next-of-kin, close relative or as heir of the estate.[230]

In even more exceptional circumstances, apart from Art.2 cases, applications may be introduced by relatives of the deceased primary victim. This has occurred where the victim's heir had standing in the domestic proceedings to continue the claims domestically and where the relative or heir could claim a patrimonial interest, or

[222] *Radio France v France*, (53984/00) September 23, 2003, ECHR 2003–IX, the broadcasting company was owned by the State, set up by decree and carried out a public mission, but its editorial independence was guaranteed and it was not controlled by the State or under its aegis; *Unedic v France*, December 18, 2008, even though it had public duties bestowed on it, the organisation was independent of government control.

[223] *Islamic Republic of Iran Shipping Lines v Turkey*, December 13, 2007, para.80, in other words, States can be involved in private, commercial enterprises.

[224] *Islamic Republic of Iran Shipping Lines*, fn.223, para.81.

[225] *Dupin v Croatia*, (36868/03) (Dec.) July 7, 2009; *Dvoracek and Dvoracekova v Slovakia*, July 28, 2009, para.41.

[226] *Fairfield v UK*, (24790/04) (Dec.) March 8, 2005, ECHR 2005–VI, where a daughter unsuccessfully sought to bring complaints under Art.10 concerning her dead father.

[227] e.g. *Lukanov v Bulgaria*, March 20, 1997, R.J.D. 1997–II, No.34, wife of deceased applicant continued complaints of unlawful arrest and detention; *Laskey, Jaggard and Brown v UK*, February 19, 1997, R.J.D. 1997–I, No.29, father of deceased continued complaints about private life interference; *Stretch v UK*, June 24, 2003, son continued complaints about deprivation of property.

[228] *Scherer v Switzerland*, March 25, 1994, Series A, No.287, 18 E.H.R.R. 276 (concerning an executor); *Thevenon v France*, (2476/02) (Dec.) February 28, 2006 (concerning a friend of the deceased). See, exceptionally, *Gagiu v Romania*, February 24, 2009, para.103, where the applicant prisoner, complaining of lack of medical treatment, died during the proceedings and the Court, relying on the criterion of ensuring respect for human rights (Art.37, para.1 *in fine*), continued the examination in the absence of any member of the family or lawyer.

[229] *Thevenon*, fn.228 above, concerning rights under Arts 3 and 8; *Sanles v Spain*, (48335/99) (Dec.) October 26, 2000, ECHR 2000–XI, where the sister-in-law of a person who had died while taking action in the courts to obtain the right to die with dignity sought to continue complaints in respect of those proceedings; *Vaari v Estonia*, (8702/04) (Dec.) July 8, 2008, mother's rights, Art.5, paras 1 and 4, closely linked to her person, son not allowed to continue them; *Gakiyev and Gakiyeva v Russia*, paras 161–165, while the applicant parents were able to invoke Art.2 in respect of the disappearance of their son, their complaint that he was deprived of his electoral rights was not admitted: these were personal and non-transferable rights and the complainants had no legitimate interest in pursuing the matter on his behalf.

[230] e.g. *Yasa v Turkey*, September 2, 1998, R.J.D. 1998–VI, No.88, paras 63–66, where the Court rejected the Government's objection to a nephew bringing a complaint about the killing of his uncle; see statement of principle in *Fairfield*, fn.226 above; see also violations under Art.3 where applicants brought complaints about persons whose death occurred in circumstances closely connected with the ill-treatment, e.g. *Keenan v UK*, April 3, 2001, ECHR 2001–III.

effect on their own pecuniary[231] or other rights.[232] Such cases must also concern an issue of general interest, in particular relative to legislation, policy or practice.[233]

10. Anonymous applicants

I–059 Perhaps unsurprisingly, there are few reported decisions rejecting complaints under Art.34, para.2(a). It would be hard to establish the facts, or receive meaningful observations from the respondent Government as concerns an applicant who remains anonymous even from the Court itself. The concern of principle behind the rule, as applied in the few relevant cases, would seem to be verifying that there is a genuine applicant and genuine application. In one case an applicant sought to introduce a case under an alias; it was rejected as there was nothing in the documents submitted by which he could be identified.[234] Where an association introduced an application on behalf of unidentified members, not itself claiming to be a victim, the case was rejected as being anonymous.[235] It seems that as long as some identifying information is contained in the application and there is no real doubt that the persons applying to the Court are those concerned in the alleged violations, the Court will accept pseudonyms or simple surnames as tactics adopted, for example, to protect family members in the context of an armed conflict.[236]

[231] See *Marie-Louise Loyen and Bruneel v France*, July 5, 2005, para.29, applicants were heirs of the deceased (patrimonial interest); *Micallef v Malta* (GC), October 15, 2009, paras 44–51, where Mrs M died during proceedings which raised an impartiality issue, and her brother, the applicant, continued as plaintiff (patrimonial interest), being held liable for costs at the end. The Court also considered it relevant that Mrs M had been involved in proceedings which exhausted domestic remedies, although it seems somewhat speculative to assume that this showed she intended to bring an application to Strasbourg as opposed to merely vindicating her rights at a domestic level; intention to lodge an application would be a strange, and nebulous, condition to import into this area. See the dissenting minority judges who disagreed that the applicant had any sufficient interest in the subject-matter of the application. Contrast, however, cases where no legitimate interest in pursuing Art.6 complaints for a deceased relative was found: *Direkci v Turkey*, (47826/99) (Dec.) October 3, 2006, where a father was unable to raise complaints about unfair criminal proceedings and interference with right to assembly concerning his deceased son.

[232] See *Armoniene v Lithuania*, November 25, 2008, paras 24–30, the widow of the deceased victim of an egregious breach of privacy by the press could introduce a case under Art.8 as the circumstances of the case showed the family had been adversely affected by the incident and had an interest in vindicating the deceased's reputation on behalf of the family; *Gradinar v Moldova*, April 8, 2008, paras 90–101, the applicant was a widow who continued to represent her husband after his death during criminal proceedings, with a view to vindicating his innocence; the Court considered that domestic law acknowledged that her own rights were in issue and thus she had victim status of her own in seeking to bring complaints about unfair proceedings.

[233] See *Micallef*, fn.231, para.46.

[234] *"Blondje" v Netherlands*, (7245/09) (Dec.) September 15, 2009, the applicant had already refused to identify himself to the Dutch authorities who treated him as an illegal immigrant and locked him up, pending expulsion.

[235] *Federation of French Medical Trade Unions and the National Federation of Nurses v France*, (10983/84) (Dec.) May 12, 1984. Contrast cases introduced by religious or similar bodies, where the Convention organs take the view that to distinguish between church and members is artificial: effectively, the church stands both as victim and representative, it not being necessary for all members to be identified individually: e.g. *Omkarananda and the Divine Light Zentrum v Switzerland*, (8118/77) (Dec.) March 19, 1981; a Church or ecclesiastical body may, as such, exercise on behalf of its adherents the rights guaranteed by Art.9 of the Convention (see *Cha'are Shalom Ve Tsedek v France* (GC), June 27, 2000, para.72).

[236] *Shamayev v Georgia and Russia*, (36378/02) (Dec.) September 16, 2003, see also judgment of April 12, 2005, para.275, the Court was satisfied, notwithstanding any initial concealment of real names, the applicants were "real, specific and identifiable individuals".

This ground does not apply merely because an application form is unsigned.[237]

11. No significant disadvantage

This criterion, added by Protocol No.14 on June 1, 2010, has little case-law for the moment. There are three elements to fulfil: I–060

- No significant disadvantage has been suffered by the applicant. This has applied mostly to the amount of money at stake for the applicants[238]; in one case, the procedural irregularity in the court proceedings was regarded as having no effect on the outcome of the case[239]; the subjective perceptions of the applicant, as well as what is objectively at stake are taken into account such that the criterion did not apply to complaints about theft of possessions which were of sentimental, if not much monetary, value, and questions of principle arose as to right to respect for possessions and home.[240] The Government argument that the applicant suffered no disadvantage concerning his complaints under Art.5, para.4, as his detention in remand had been deducted from his sentence, was rejected.[241]
- Respect for human rights does not require examination by the Court. This appears to cover situations where the Court has examined similar cases[242] or ruled on similar issues[243]; where the Court has addressed the systemic problem[244]; or where no further general measures are necessary in light of domestic developments.[245] It would appear unlikely, therefore, to cover a case identifying a new structural deficiency or with compelling reasons of public order.
- The case has been "duly" considered by a domestic court. This means that the applicant's case at the domestic level has been before at least one court in adversarial proceedings, even if his complaints under the Convention have not been ruled upon by the domestic court; "duly" considered is not the same as "fairly" considered (less than the Art.6 standard).[246]

[237] *Kuznetsova v Russia*, (67579/01) (Dec.) January 19, 2006, the Court referred to the application containing sufficient personal information as to erase any doubt as to the applicant's identity.

[238] *Adrian Mihai Ionescu v Romania*, (36659/04) (Dec.) June 1, 2010 (€90); *Korolev v Russia*, (25551/05) (Dec.) July 1, 2010, (less than €1); *Vasilchenko v Russia*, (34784/02) September 23, 2010 (€12); *Rinck v France*, (18774/09) (Dec.) October 19, 2010 (€150); *Gaftoniuc v Romania*, (30394/05) (Dec.) February 22, 2011 (€25); *Stefanescu v Romania*, (11774/04) (Dec.) April 12, 2011 (€125). Ground not fulfilled where sums €200–€13,000 at stake and delays in payment of 9–49 months (*Gaglione v Italy*, December 21, 2010).

[239] *Holub v Czech Republic*, (24880/05) (Dec.) December 14, 2010, complaint concerning the failure of higher court to provide applicant with copy of submissions from other party and lower court, but it rejected his claims on technical grounds without regard to those submissions; *Stefanescu*, fn.238, applicant had not explained how the failure of the energy authority to give him the required information had affected him. See also *Micallef*, fn.231, dissenting opinion of Costa, Jungwiert, Kovler, Fura who considered the case, concerning a dispute between neighbours over dripping laundry, trivial and taking up a disproportionate amount of court time, domestic and international.

[240] *Giuran v Romania*, June 21, 2011, paras 17–25.

[241] *Van der Velden v Netherlands*, July 19, 2011, paras 38–39.

[242] *Gaftoniuc*, fn.238.

[243] *Stefanescu*, fn.238, paras 40–44.

[244] *Vasilchenko*, fn.238.

[245] *Holub*, fn.239.

[246] *Holub*, fn.239.

12. Inter-State cases

I–061 The vast majority of cases are brought by individuals or non-governmental bodies. There have been only a handful of applications brought by Contracting States against another State, and a significant number of those were generated by the ongoing Cyprus problem.

The admissibility criteria operate in a slightly modified manner in such cases. Exhaustion of domestic remedies applies to the extent that a State makes a complaint effectively on behalf of a specific individual or individuals; if it is complaining about a general situation which constitutes an administrative practice, exhaustion of remedies is not required (on the basis of the principle that States should not "buy" their way out of persistent and deliberate flouting of the Convention), although proof of the practice must be established.[247] While it is open to individual applicants to allege an administrative practice, this may not be practicable for an individual applicant, given the range of evidence that would have to be provided. As a matter of Convention principle however, it is excluded that the Court reject any inter-State case as manifestly ill-founded[248]; although there is apparently the possibility of rejecting the case if the complaints can be regarded as so wholly without substance as not to constitute a genuine application at all.[249] Any examination of the merits must take place after admissibility.

[247] *Georgia v Russia*, (13255/07) (Dec.) June 30, 2009, paras 41–42, with cases cited therein.
[248] Art.35, para.3 applies only to individual applications.
[249] *Georgia v Russia*, fn.247 above, paras 43–45, with cases cited therein.

C. CONVENTION PRINCIPLES AND APPROACH

Applying the Convention involves a special perspective distinct from national law. There is a set of interlocking principles governed by its international and human rights context. The Court intends to lay down certain minimum international standards.[1] I–062

It is not seeking to identify the most appropriate way to protect human rights, recognising the diversity in the Contracting States. It identifies, at most, the minimum which a particular legal system should attain.

It must also be noted that, as a treaty, the Convention falls to be interpreted in light of the rules of the Vienna Convention of May 23, 1969 on the Law of Treaties. Accordingly, the Court must take account of any relevant rules of international law applicable in the relations between the parties and the Convention must be interpreted as far as possible in harmony with the other rules of international law of which it forms a part. That said, the Court places precedence on the special character of the Convention as a human rights treaty and has not owned itself necessarily bound by other international law norms.[2]

1. Subsidiarity

The Court is primarily a supervisory body and subsidiary to the national systems safeguarding human rights.[3] Pursuant to Art.1 of the Convention the Contracting States have undertaken to "secure to everyone within their jurisdiction the rights and freedoms" set out in the Convention. It is therefore first and foremost the role of the State to protect human rights. Article 13 imposes the obligation on the State to provide a remedy to all those who claim, arguably, that their rights under the Convention have been violated, while Art.35, para.1 requires the exhaustion of domestic remedies as a precondition which reflects the fact that coming to Strasbourg is meant to be very much the last resort.[4] I–063

[1] *Belgian Linguistics Case (No.1)*, February 9, 1967, Series A, No.5, 1 E.H.R.R. 241.

[2] See *Al-Adsani v UK*, November 21, 2001, ECHR 2001–XI, para.55, concerning State immunity and access to court; *Bankovic v Belgium and 16 other Contracting States*, (52207/99) (Dec.) December 12, 2001, ECHR 2001–XII, paras 55–58, concerning "within Contracting State's jurisdiction" in Art.1; and *Witold Litwa v Poland*, April 4, 2000, ECHR 2000–III, paras 57–59, concerning the meaning of "alcoholics" in Art.5, para.1(e).

[3] e.g. *Handyside v UK*, December 7, 1996, Series A, No.24, 1 E.H.R.R 737, para.48; *Eckle v Germany*, July 15, 1982, Series A, No.51, 5 E.H.R.R. 1, para.61; *Akdivar v Turkey*, September 16, 1996, R.J.D. 1996–IV, No.15, para.65; *Z v UK*, May 10, 2001, ECHR 2001–V, para.103.

[4] There is also the practical consideration that the Court has neither the time nor resources to decide on the merits all human rights cases in Europe. It is not particularly geared to do the fact-finding tasks commonly fulfilled by domestic courts, with no compellable powers over witnesses or discovery of documents.

2. Fourth instance

I–064 The Convention organs are not, as the Commission was fond of saying, a court of appeal for domestic courts and cannot intervene on the basis that a domestic court has come to the "wrong" decision or made a mistake. Their role is to ensure compliance with the provisions of the Convention by the Contracting States.

The Court will, generally, not rehear cases, except to the extent that factual or legal issues arise under the Convention similar to those in domestic proceedings; its fact-finding function is limited. While the Court may be required to make findings of fact in disputed cases, its examination is almost entirely limited to the written submissions of the parties and the documents provided. Its hearings are generally on points of applicable domestic law and the scope of Convention rights: it only rarely hears witnesses or even sees the applicant, its procedures being largely in writing. In the vast majority of cases, where a case has been thoroughly examined on the domestic level, the facts have been thrashed out and the Court cannot hope to do any better in resolving disputed elements.[5] In most cases, the essential facts are not in dispute or do not have to be resolved since the examination undertaken under the Convention often focusses on the procedural safeguards, the decision-making procedure, and the applicable standards.[6] If it is alleged that the Court relies too heavily on domestic courts' findings, this is a reflection of the nature of the exercise that is being undertaken. The Court will not redecide whether or not a decision to remove children was in fact the correct decision, but will assess whether the manner of decision-making and implementation failed in some way to protect the parents' rights. In a case of suspicious killing by an unknown assassin, the Court cannot seriously attempt to identify the culprit and thereby whether the State was directly responsible as alleged. What it can do is examine whether the victim was sufficiently protected beforehand—by the standards imposed by law, or, if applicable, by the necessary safeguards—and whether, afterwards, the incident was properly investigated in such a way as to indicate the rule of law is in force. Consequently, much of Convention case-law turns on procedural considerations.[7]

That said, there is a general overview of the merits taken in the Court's requirement that decisions and measures taken are supported by "relevant and sufficient" reasons[8] and, in the context of Art.14, by objective and reasonable justification. This is a means both of verifying that decisions are in fact in pursuit of the alleged aims and that they are not arbitrary or in abuse of power.

[5] *Stocke v Germany*, March 19, 1991, Series A, No.199, 13 E.H.R.R. 839, where the applicant alleged connivance by police officers with an informer who tricked him onto a plane to Germany where he was arrested. The Commission heard witnesses but was unable to come to any different conclusion than the domestic courts.

[6] There is also the frequently used technique of reaching conclusions "even assuming" a particular state of affairs, to avoid the necessity of settling doubtful factual matters.

[7] e.g. *Yasa v Turkey*, September 2, 1998, R.J.D. 1998–VI, No.88.

[8] In the context of the necessity for measures, e.g. *Olsson v Sweden*, March 24, 1988, Series A, No.130, 11 E.H.R.R. 259 (Art.8), the reason must be pertinent to the interference and justify the extent or nature of the interference; *Lingens v Austria*, July 8, 1986, Series A, No.103, 8 E.H.R.R. 407 (Art.10).

3. Margin of appreciation

The domestic authorities have always been recognised by the Convention organs as generally being in the best position to reach a decision, interpret domestic law, or assess the facts in a particular case,[9] or to decide on the measures necessary in a particular area, whether it concerns expropriation of property to build a new road, banning blasphemous videos or the distribution of sex education books.[10] The Court has stated it should not rush to substitute its view for that of the authorities who are best placed to assess the needs of their society.[11] Where complaints concerned the way in which domestic courts interpreted and applied the law to a testamentary dispute, the Court considered an issue could only arise where their assessment of the facts or domestic law were manifestly unreasonable or arbitrary or blatantly inconsistent with the fundamental principles of the Convention.[12] **I–065**

In this context frequent reference is made to the "margin of appreciation" to be accorded to Contracting States. This is a term which is not subject to, or perhaps capable of, precise definition and smacks somewhat of a "let out" to Governments, particularly in those cases where there is a prima facie interference with a right, arguments either way as to whether such interference is necessary, followed by the case being resolved by pulling the term "margin of appreciation" out of the hat.[13]

The fact that customs, policies and practices vary considerably between Contracting States is sometimes used to support the existence of a margin of appreciation, but is not of itself determinative.[14] Where there is no uniform conception, for example, of morals, there is accepted to be a number of possible solutions or approaches.[15] In *Dudgeon v UK*,[16] the Court referred to different moral and social conditions which can apply in different areas and commented that because a restriction was not seen as necessary elsewhere did not mean it was unacceptable in one particular area. However, in that case the Court considered that, notwithstanding the margin of appreciation, it was for the Convention organs to make the final evaluation and it came to the conclusion that the prohibition of adult homosexual activities was not necessitated in the conditions of Northern Ireland to maintain moral standards or protect vulnerable members of society. The cost was dispropor-

[9] e.g. *Van der Graaf v Netherlands*, (8704/03) (Dec.) June 1, 2004, where the Court declined to take the place of the competent national authorities in the exercise of their responsibilities when determining factual reasons for imposing permanent camera surveillance on a remand prisoner; *Pla and Pucernau v Andorra*, July 13, 2004, ECHR 2004–VIII para.46, concerning application of domestic law to a will.

[10] e.g. *Muller v Switzerland*, May 24, 1988, Series A, No.133, 13 E.H.R.R. 212, para.35, as being in direct and continuous contact with the vital forces of their countries; *Schalk and Kopf v Austria*, June 24, 2010, para.62, the Court should not rush to substitute its own view for that of the authorities in gay marriage. For the special weight given to the legislature in policy matters, see sub-s.9 of this section: Democratic values and institutions.

[11] e.g. *Schalk and Kopf v Austria*, fn.10 above, para.62, concerning whether gay marriage should be recognised.

[12] *Pla and Pucernau*, fn.9 above, para.46.

[13] e.g. *Handyside v UK*, fn.3 above, paras 48, 54 and 57, seizure and forfeiture and conviction in relation to "Little Red Schoolbook"; *Stubbings v UK*, October 22, 1996, R.J.D. 1996–IV, No.18, para.74, different time-limits imposed on persons claiming injuries; *Buckley v UK*, September 25, 1996, para.84, refusal of planning permission to gypsy family; *Wingrove v UK*, November 25, 1996, R.J.D. 1996–V, No.23, para.64, banning of a video film as blasphemous.

[14] *Hirst v UK (No.2)* (GC), October 5, 2005, ECHR 2005–IX, para.81, where it was the fact that it was a minority of States that prohibited convicted prisoners from voting which was emphasized.

[15] *Handyside*, fn.3 above, para.48.

[16] *Dudgeon v UK*, October 22, 1981, Series A, No.45.

tionately high on the individual with correspondingly little concrete gain for the community.

In other controversial areas, the Court has relied on the lack of consensus or common ground as indicating that it cannot impose obligations on Contracting States.[17] This shows a more cautious approach, since it might be argued that it is in such difficult areas that the Convention should assist a consensus to emerge. On the other hand, where there is a wide agreement in Member States as to particular standards to apply, this will generally be a material consideration, as in the case of judicial corporal punishment in *Tyrer v UK*[18] and concerning the legal recognition of gender re-assignment for transsexuals in *Christine Goodwin v UK*.[19]

The scope of the margin of appreciation will differ according to the context.[20] It has been held by the Court to be particularly wide in the areas of national security[21]; planning policies[22]; matters perceived as raising sensitive moral or ethical issues such as transsexualism or artificial insemination by donor (AID)[23]; and where the State has to strike a balance between competing private and public interests or Convention rights.[24]

Great diversity in culture and history in Europe also means that a margin of appreciation applies to decisions whether or not to continue traditions.[25]

As regards the area of the protection of morals, the Court in *Dudgeon*[26] did not accept that the margin was wide as a general proposition, stating that it was not only the aim of the measures which affected the scope of the margin of appreciation but the nature of the activities involved. Since *Dudgeon* concerned interference with an intimate area of private life, the balance tipped towards the applicants in requiring "particularly serious reasons" for interferences.

In practice, the margin of appreciation operates as a means of leaving a State freedom of manoeuvre in assessing what its society needs and the best way to achieve those needs and the timing of policies.[27] There is not only one way of

[17] See the early transsexual cases, e.g. *Rees v UK*, January 24, 1986, Series A, No.106, 9 E.H.R.R. 56, para.37; *Cossey v UK*, September 27, 1990, Series A, No.184, 13 E.H.R.R. 622, para.40; *B v France*, March 25, 1992, 16 E.H.R.R., Series A, No.232–C, para.48, where there was reference to insufficient scientific, medical, legal and social consensus on the phenomenon. More recently, *Benito v Spain*, (36150/03) (Dec.) November 13, 2006, lack of consensus on passive smoking in prisons.

[18] *Tyrer v UK*, April 25, 1978, Series A, No.26, 2 E.H.R.R. 1, paras 31 and 38, vast majority of States had not used such methods for years; reference to "commonly accepted standards". See also *Dudgeon*, fn.16 above, para.60, where the majority of States no longer considered it appropriate to apply criminal sanctions to consensual adult homosexual acts.

[19] *Christine Goodwin v UK*, July 11, 2002, ECHR 2002–VI.

[20] *Sunday Times v UK*, April 26, 1979, Series A, No.30, para.59; *Dudgeon*, fn.16 above, para.52.

[21] *Leander v Sweden*, March 26, 1987, Series A, No.116, 9 E.H.R.R. 433.

[22] *Buckley*, fn.13 above, para.75, in the planning area, the authorities have to exercise a discretion involving a multitude of factors.

[23] *X, Y and Z v UK*, April 22, 1997, R.J.D. 1997–II, No.35, where there was no common ground as to parental and family rights in relation to children born by AID; *Evans v UK*, April 10, 2007, 2006, para.77, use of stored embryos.

[24] *Evans*, fn.23 above, para.77; *Frette v France*, February 26, 2002, ECHR 2002–I, para.42; *Odievre v France*, February 13, 2003, ECHR 2003–III; see also where the State has to juggle religious and other interests, *Leyla Sahin v Turkey*, November 10, 2005, ECHR 2005–XI, para.109.

[25] *Lautsi v Italy*, March 18, 2011, para.68, concerning crucifixes in State-run classrooms.

[26] See fn.16 above, para.52.

[27] e.g. (11089/84) (Dec.) November 11, 1986, 49 D.R. 181, where the Commission noted that the margin of appreciation applies to when a State decides to change a system. The fact that the UK modified its tax system did not indicate a previous lack of objective and reasonable justification since

protecting children from abuse or of fighting drug trafficking. In multicultural Europe, with its morasse of local traditions, the Convention cannot, and should not, attempt to impose uniformity or detailed and specific requirements.[28] In its supervisory capacity however, the Court can require legitimate aims and ensure that the State does not step beyond certain boundaries. For example, in the field of nationalisation and expropriation, where issues of the national economy may be in play, the Court gives the general and public interest a wide meaning and will respect the State legislature's assessment unless manifestly without reasonable foundation.[29] Nonetheless, generally, provision should be made to compensate the persons affected. In the field of education, though without express mention of the margin of appreciation, the Court referred to limits which should not be exceeded. Thus, while the setting and planning of a school curriculum falls in the first place for the State to settle and the State is not prevented from imparting information or knowledge of a religious or philosophical kind, it cannot step over the line into indoctrination.[30]

Procedural safeguards available to the individual will be especially material in determining whether the respondent State has, when fixing the regulatory framework, remained within its margin of appreciation. In areas where there is a wide margin of appreciation, the Court's examination tends to focus on whether the decision-making process leading to measures of interference was fair and such as to afford due respect to the interests safeguarded to the individual by Art.8.[31]

Governments cannot pray in aid of the margin of appreciation in the context of executive-judicial relations on the domestic level, namely, seeking to persuade the Court not to give weight to decisions of their own courts for lack of due reverence to other organs of the State.[32]

4. Autonomous concepts

When it comes to interpreting the extent or application of the substantive rights and freedoms under the Convention, the Court looks very much to the substance of the right protected. It is not to be distracted by how a Contracting State chooses in domestic law to interpret a term or principle, which is, at most, a starting point.[33] Whatever the domestic label, it will examine the matter in form, substance and procedure before reaching its own decision. I–066

The Court thus maintains that the terms contained in the Convention are autonomous concepts and that it is free to assess their application to particular

goals could legitimately change from time to time. Also *Petrovic v Austria*, March 27, 1998, R.J.D. 1998–II, No.67, paras 41–43, gradual evolution of entitlement to paternity leave; *Schalk and Kopf v Austria*, fn.11, para.105, margin of timing for legislative recognition of same-sex relationships.

[28] e.g. *Sunday Times*, fn.20, para.61.

[29] e.g. *Lithgow v UK*, July 8, 1986, Series A, No.102 (nationalisation); *James v UK*, February 21, 1986, Series A, No.98 (sweeping leasehold reform); *Pressos Compania v Belgium*, November 20, 1995, Series A, No.332 (legislative intervention in pending tort claims).

[30] *Kjeldsen, Madsen and Pedersen v Denmark*, December 7, 1976, Series A, No.23, 1 E.H.R.R. 711, para.53.

[31] e.g. *Buckley*, fn.13 above, pp.1292–93, para.76; *Chapman v UK* (GC), January 18, 2001, ECHR 2001–I, para.92.

[32] *A and Others v UK*, February 19, 2009, para.184.

[33] e.g. *Chassagnou v France*, April 29, 1999, ECHR 1999–III, para.100, concerning the term "association" under Art.11.

situations in domestic systems. This covers the concepts of "civil rights and obligations", "criminal charge", "witness", etc. It will determine the scope of the rights guaranteed under the Convention and Contracting States cannot limit or redefine them by formal classifications and definitions in their own domestic law. But even where the Court does not refer to autonomous concepts, it approaches notions of "family" and "private life" by looking at the substance of what is at stake without being governed by the meaning given to the term in the particular State.

5. Effectiveness

I–067 The Convention is a system for the protection of human rights. This renders it of crucial importance that it is interpreted and applied in a manner which renders these rights practical and effective, not theoretical and illusory.[34] A State cannot therefore escape its obligations by protecting a right in a superficial or self-defeating manner. For example, it is not enough to appoint a lawyer for a trial, the assistance given must be effective[35]; a State cannot disclaim responsibility in expelling an individual to a country where he faces a real risk of treatment contrary to Art.3[36]; the use of deliberate lethal force by State agents must be subject to the most careful scrutiny, and attract some form of effective official investigation[37]; the protection provided to associations under Art.11 must cover not only their founding but extend to their entire life[38]; and the rules governing the eligibility of candidates for election to the legislature must conform with criteria framed to prevent arbitrary decisions and abuse of power.[39]

6. Strict limitations

I–068 Exceptions to the rights guaranteed under the Convention are to be strictly construed.[40] Thus, case-law indicates the importance of physical freedom or liberty and emphasises that exceptions are exhaustively limited to those set out in the sub-paragraphs of Art.5, para.1. If the detention does not fall within any of these categories then it cannot be justified under Art.5, para.1, however useful the aim might be.[41]

7. Essence of the right

I–069 In assessing the impact of restrictions or interferences the Convention organs sometimes have regard to the "essence" of the right, whether it has been effectively destroyed or an acceptable scope for its exercise remains. This originated in cases of

[34] *Artico v Italy*, May 13, 1980, Series A, No.37, 3 E.H.R.R. 1, para.33.

[35] *Artico*, fn.34 above, para.33; *Campbell and Fell v UK*, June 28, 1984, Series A, No.80, 7 E.H.R.R. 165, access by a prisoner to a lawyer was not effective where conducted within hearing of prison officers.

[36] *Soering v UK*, July 7, 1989, Series A, No.161, 11 E.H.R.R. 439.

[37] *McCann v UK*, September 27, 1995, Series A, No.324, 21 E.H.R.R. 97.

[38] *United Communist Party v Turkey*, January 30, 1998, ECHR R.J.D. 1998–I, No.62, para.33.

[39] *Podkolzina v Latvia*, April 9, 2002, ECHR 2002–II, para.35. See also *Matthews v UK*, February 18, 1999, ECHR 1999–I, para.33, concerning Government responsibility for European, as well as domestic, elections under Art.3 of Protocol No.1; *Conka v Belgium*, February 5, 2002, ECHR 2002–I, para.46, concerning the realistic possibility of using remedies against arbitrary detention.

[40] e.g. *Van Mechelen v Netherlands*, April 23, 1997, R.J.D. 1997–III, No.36, para.58, limits to defence rights must be restricted to those "strictly necessary".

[41] e.g. *Ciulla v Italy*, February 22, 1989, Series A, No.148, para.41, arrest and detention pending the order of preventive measures fell outside the permitted exceptions of Art.5, despite the acknowledged importance of the fight against the mafia. See also *Engel v Netherlands*, June 8, 1976, Series A, No.22, para.57, where the claim of special exclusion for military discipline was not accepted.

access to court where limitations, even if proportionate and pursuing reasonable aims, must not impair the essence of the right,[42] but has also been used in other contexts.[43] In the cases of *CR and SW v UK*, where the applicants challenged the decision of the House of Lords as retrospectively abolishing the marital immunity to rape, the Court found that the decisions, having regard to the manifestly debasing character of rape, could not be said to be at variance with the object and purpose of Art.7, which was to prevent arbitrary prosecution, conviction and punishment.[44]

8. Rule of law

The rule of law is one of the key principles underlying the Convention and part of the common heritage of Contracting States.[45] It implies that an interference by the authorities with an individual's rights should be subject to effective control, especially so where the law bestows on the executive wide discretionary powers.[46] Where in *Stran Greek Refineries v Greece* there was legislative interference with judicial process, the Court emphasised several times the idea of the rule of law which Greece undertook to respect in joining the Council of Europe and ratifying the Convention.[47] In *Al-Nashif v Bulgaria*, the concepts of lawfulness and the rule of law in a democratic society required that measures affecting fundamental human rights, even in the sensitive area of national security, must be subject to some form of adversarial proceedings before an independent body competent to review the reasons for the decision.[48] As a corollary of that, where a court has issued a final judicial decision, the principle of legal certainty, an aspect of the rule of law, requires that where the courts have finally determined an issue, their ruling should not be called into question, save in very limited circumstances.[49] I–070

A State may interfere with citizens' rights or regulate their freedom to act for specified legitimate aims but only if it does so by law, and a norm cannot be classified as a law unless it is accessible and also foreseeable to a reasonable degree in its application and consequences.[50] This is the approach generally taken wherever the word "law" or "lawful" appears as a requirement.[51] In addition, Art.2 makes

[42] *Ashingdane v UK*, May 28, 1985, Series A, No.93, para.57.

[43] Under Art.12, the essence of the right should not be hampered by national laws (see Pt IIB, s.31: Marriage and founding a family); under Art.3 of Protocol No.1, see *Matthews*, fn.39 above, paras 63–65; concerning positive obligations under Art.10, see *Appleby v UK*, May 6, 2003, ECHR 2003–VI, para.47; delays in executions of judgment, see *Burdov v Russia*, May 7, 2002, ECHR 2002–III, paras 34–35.

[44] *CR and SW v UK*, November 22, 1995, Series A, Nos 335–B and C.

[45] e.g. *Lenskaya v Russia*, January 19, 2009, para.30.

[46] e.g. *Silver v UK*, March 25, 1983, Series A, No.61, 5 E.H.R.R. 347, para.90; *Rotaru v Romania*, May 4, 2000, ECHR 2000–V, para.59; *Bitayeva and X v Russia*, June 21, 2006, para.118.

[47] See also *Hornsby v Greece*, March 19, 1997, R.J.D. 1997–II, para.40, where the Court emphasised the rule of law in the effective implementation of judicial decisions by the authorities; *Ekholm v Finland*, July 24, 2007, para.73, importance of administrative authorities complying with judgments.

[48] *Al-Nashif v Bulgaria*, June 20, 2002, para.123, although appropriate procedural limitations on the use of classified information might be conceivable.

[49] e.g. *Brumărescu v Romania*, October 28, 1999, para.61. See also on principle of legal certainty, Pt IIA, s.1(2): Aspects of fairness.

[50] e.g. *Sunday Times*, fn.20 above.

[51] See "in accordance with law" (Art.8); "prescribed by law" (Arts 9, 10 and 11); procedure prescribed by law (Art.5, para.1); "lawful" as a precondition for every sub-paragraph of Art.5; conditions provided for by law (Art.1, Protocol 1).

reference to protection by law,[52] while Art.6 deals with a detailed procedural code for the operation of courts of law, and Art.7 expressly prohibits retrospective imposition of criminal offences and heavier penalties. The requirement of effective access to court, and the scrutiny of any attempt to remove court jurisdiction over claims, can be said to derive from this fundamental concept.[53]

Lawfulness has been interpreted to refer to two elements. First, the measure in issue must have some basis in domestic law[54]; secondly, it must possess the quality of law, namely, that it is accessible and enables the individual to foresee, with a reasonable degree of certainty, the consequences of his actions or the circumstances in which authorities may take certain steps.[55] These elements are applied with a view principally to ensuring that safeguards against arbitrary abuse of power are in place in the domestic law itself. Powers to interfere with the rights of individuals must be subject to defined limitations as to their subject-matter, duration, methods of implementation, and having regard to the practical consideration that absolute certainty is neither possible or desirable and that many laws are inevitably couched in terms which are to some extent vague and whose interpretation and application are questions of practice.[56] The Court is interested in ensuring certain minimum standards; a wide discretion, and partially defined concepts will not necessarily offend.[57]

Matters of interpretation and application of domestic law itself are primarily for the national courts, and the Court is not likely to contradict their findings.[58] Nonetheless since compliance with domestic law is an integral part of the obligations of Contracting States, the Court has stated its competence to satisfy itself of such compliance where relevant, subject to its inherent limits in the European system of protection.[59] In particular, where deprivation of liberty is concerned, it may verify that domestic law is not interpreted or applied in an arbitrary manner, since no arbitrary detention can ever be regarded as "lawful".[60] In practice, this gives a certain leeway to domestic systems but might also be said to avoid breaches which are technical and lacking in merit.[61]

The Court has also referred to the fundamental principle of the separation of powers, in particular where the executive enjoys a decision-making power in a procedure to which judicial guarantees should apply.[62] The Court has stated that this

[52] See *McCann*, fn.37 above, (Rep.) para.92, reference to rule of law requiring effective oversight of the use of force by agents of the State to avoid the arbitrary abuse of power; *Avsar v Turkey*, July 10, 2001, ECHR 2001–VII, paras 393–395 and 404, concerning the importance of accountability and maintaining public confidence in the maintenance of the rule of law.

[53] *Fayed v UK*, September 21, 1994, Series A, No.294–B, 18 E.H.R.R. 393.

[54] e.g. *Malone v UK*, August 2, 1984, Series A, No.82, 7 E.H.R.R. 14.

[55] For general principles, see *Sunday Times*, fn.20 above, para.9; *Malone*, fn.54 above, paras 67–68; also findings of violation, *Kruslin v France*, April 24, 1990, Series A, No.176–B, 12 E.H.R.R. 547; *Amuur v France*, June 25, 1996, R.J.D. 1996–III, No.11; *Rotaru*, fn.46 above; *Sud Fondi Srl v Italy*, January 20, 2009, paras 111–118.

[56] *Sunday Times*, fn.20 above, para.49. Changes in case-law through judicial development are compatible with "lawfulness" criteria where reasonably foreseeable, if necessary with the assistance of a lawyer (see Pt IIA, s.22: Retrospectivity).

[57] See, e.g. cases concerning Surveillance and Interception of Communications (Pt IIB, s.44).

[58] e.g. *Casada Coca v Spain*, February 24, 1994, Series A, No.285, 18 E.H.R.R. 1, para.43.

[59] *Lukanov v Bulgaria*, March 3, 1997, R.J.D. 1997–II, No.34, paras 41–43, where the Court found that the applicant ex-minister's participation in a collective decision to send aid to the Third World did not constitute a criminal offence under Bulgarian law at the time.

[60] *Winterwerp v Netherlands*, October 24, 1979, Series A, No.33, 2 E.H.R.R. 387, paras 39 and 45.

[61] e.g. (9997/82) (Dec.) December 7, 1982, 31 D.R. 145.

[62] *Stafford v UK*, May 28, 2002, ECHR 2002–IV, para.78; *Easterbrook v UK*, June 12, 2003, para.28.

is not a matter of form but detracts from a necessary guarantee against the possibility of abuse.[63] This notion has also been accepted as a reason justifying the immunity of Members of Parliament from being sued in the courts in relation to their functions in Parliament.[64] However, the principle is to be applied in the context of the requirements of the Convention and does not require States to adopt any particular constitutional arrangements.[65]

9. Democratic values and institutions

In addition to the rule of law, reliance in interpretation and application of Convention rights is placed on "democratic values".[66] These involve recognition of the importance of rights to a fair trial[67] and the fundamental rights guaranteed by Arts 2 (right to life) and 3 (prohibition of torture and inhuman and degrading treatment).[68] States are required to adopt a certain tolerance and broad-mindedness and to accept a certain pluralism and diversity.[69] A democracy does not mean that the majority always prevails: a balance must be achieved which ensures the fair and proper treatment of minorities and avoids abuse of a dominant position.[70] States must also afford protection to the media, which acts in democratic society as a "watchdog" (see Pt IIB, s.22: Freedom of expression) and governments must expect to bear more criticism than others and react with restraint.[71] The link between the protection of human rights and democracy is such, however, that a State may, where necessary, take steps to defend its democratic order and institutions which limit the exercise of fundamental rights.[72] Corruption has been recognised as one of the ways in which democratic institutions may be undermined.[73] I–071

Pluralism has received emphasis where freedom of expression and monopolies in the media are concerned. The Court has said that there is no democracy without pluralism; and underlined that openness of debate in the public arena is crucial to solving problems through dialogue rather than violence. Dominance of any person or grouping, and any curtailing of editorial freedom in the media is regarded as a threat, against which States may be required to take positive measures.[74] Pluralism is

[63] *Benjamin and Wilson v UK*, September 26, 2002, para.36.

[64] *A v UK*, December 17, 2002, ECHR 2002–X, para.73.

[65] *Kleyn v Netherlands*, May 6, 2003, ECHR 2003–VI, para.193, where the Court was sensitive to the existence of bodies in a number of countries, which can play a judicial and legislative role.

[66] e.g. *Soering*, fn.36 above, para.87, "any interpretation of the rights and freedoms guaranteed had to be consistent with the general spirit of the Convention, an instrument designed to maintain and promote the ideals and values of a democratic society" citing *Kjeldsen*, fn.30 above, para.53; *Yumak and Sadak v Turkey*, July 8, 2008, para.105. "Democracy constitutes a fundamental element of the 'European public order. . .'"

[67] e.g. *Ait-Mouhoub v France*, October 28, 1998, R.J.D. 1998–VIII, No.96, para.52.

[68] *Soering*, fn.36 above, para.88; *McCann*, fn.37 above, para.147.

[69] *Dudgeon*, fn.16 above, para.53, concerning homosexual acts, but see *Laskey, Jaggard and Brown v UK*, February 19, 1997, R.J.D. 1997–I, No.29, where the applicants' plea for toleration and broad-mindedness was not successful in relation to group sado-masochistic activities of a certain severity.

[70] *Young, James and Webster v UK*, August 13, 1981, Series A, No.44, 4 E.H.R.R. 38, para.63.

[71] e.g. *Castells v Spain*, April 23, 1992, Series A, No.236, 14 E.H.R.R. 445, para.46.

[72] e.g. *Refah Partisi v Turkey*, February 13, 2003, ECHR 2003–III, paras 102–103; *Zdanoka v Latvia*, March 16, 2006, ECHR 2006–. . . , paras 98–101.

[73] e.g. *Dragotoniu and Militaru-Pidhorni v Romania*, May 24, 2007, para.41.

[74] e.g. *Manole v Moldova*, September 17, 2009, paras 95–102.

also mentioned in the educational context, where sensitive issues concerning exposure of children to a particular dominant religion is examined for any hint of indoctrination or undue influence.[75]

Special weight is given to the role of democratic institutions, in particular, the legislature, in cases where views on matters of general policy may reasonably differ.[76] Considerable weight is given concerning social and economic policies.[77] However, the legislature's views may enjoy less authority where it is not apparent that the issues at stake were thoroughly debated.[78]

Conduct of an applicant which attacks fundamental underlying values of tolerence, non-violence and non-discrimination may lead to applications being rejected under Art.17, which prevents the Convention being used as a means to destroy rights.[79]

10. Necessity

I–072 Where interferences under the Convention may be justified in pursuit of specified legitimate aims, the requirement that these interferences nonetheless be "necessary" appears to place a burden on the State. The Court has laid down the element that an interference with a right has to be justified by "a pressing social need".[80] However, in practice, this is not applied in such a manner as to require a Government to establish, for example, that the measure is of any particular urgency or is unavoidable, or that there is no other way of achieving the goal with lesser impact on individual rights. The findings of the Convention organs are phrased less demandingly in terms that, having regard to the various relevant factors, the interference may be considered as necessary in a democratic society.[81] The principle of proportionality is more decisive (see below).

Occasional reliance on this principle nonetheless occurs as in a case where a Government had made an international pledge to introduce reforms allowing alternative service to military conscription and was taking steps to implement reforms, but nonetheless continued to prosecute and imprison conscientious objectors for the time being. The Court took this into account in finding that there was

[75] e.g. *Lautsi*, fn.25, para.62.

[76] e.g. *Hatton v UK* (GC), August 7, 2003, ECHR 2003–VIII, para.97; *ASLEF v UK*, February 27, 2007, ECHR 2007–. . . , para.46.

[77] e.g. *James*, fn.29 above, para.46, where the Court stated that it would respect the legislature's judgment as to what is "in the public interest" unless that judgment was manifestly without reasonable foundation.

[78] e.g. *Hirst v UK (No.2)* (GC), October 5, 2005, ECHR 2005–IX, para.79. Contrast *Sukhovetskyy v Ukraine*, March 28, 2006, para.67, where electoral measures were subject to "careful consideration" by the legislature and courts.

[79] e.g. *Ivanov v Russia*, (35222/04) (Dec.) February 20, 2007, where the applicant invoked Art.10 in respect of a conviction for anti-Semitic articles which disclosed an attack on an entire ethnic group, inciting hatred and denying their dignity. See cases cited in Pt IIB, s.22(2).

[80] *Handyside*, fn.3 above, para.48; *Sunday Times*, fn.20 above, para.59, "necessary" identified as less than "indispensable" but not as flexible as "useful", "reasonable" or "desirable".

[81] e.g. *Laskey*, fn.69 above, para.50, "the national authorities were entitled to consider that the prosecution and conviction of the applicants were necessary in a democratic society for the protection of health. . ."

no "pressing social need" for convicting and detaining a Jehovah's Witness for draft evasion prior to the legislative introduction of alternative service.[82]

11. Proportionality

Proportionality is a dominant theme underlying the whole of the Convention. It is an ingredient of the necessity of the measure under Arts 2 and 8—11, and has been imported into other provisions: in the context of objective and reasonable justification for difference in treatment under Art.14; as regards restrictions on access to court under Art.6; and the framework of property rights under Art.1 of Protocol No.1, as well as part of the basis in finding States under a positive obligation to act. It requires a reasonable relation between the goal pursued and the means used.[83] It is also used in the sense of finding a balance between the applicant's interests and those of the community.[84] Many issues centre on the conflict between an individual and the good of the general amorphous mass of society: things like roads; taxes; airports; preservation of the countryside are arguably to everyone's benefit. Proportionality examines whether providing them places too much of a burden on certain individuals. Whether this burden has been mitigated by procedures or forms of relief will be relevant to whether the State has struck the right balance. I–073

The consideration of whether the State could achieve the goal in another way may be asked under proportionality but can only go so far.[85] Since the Convention is not setting ideal standards, it is not enough to establish a violation that, for example, other methods could be used or are used in another State.[86] The method used must fail the proportionality test and fall outside the margin of appreciation having regard to the particular circumstances of the case.

The Court has stated that where a mistake has been caused by the authorities themselves, without any fault of a third party, a different proportionality approach must be taken in determining whether the burden borne by an applicant was excessive.[87]

In some contexts, particularly the electoral, the Court has found blanket measures depriving categories of persons of rights as disproportionate. As some groups have

[82] *Bayatyan v Armenia*, July 7, 2011, para.128. This reasoning does not sit happily with the Court's general approach that the timing of implementation of reforms is generally left to the State and the mere fact that the law later changes does not remove the previous "necessity" of the measure beforehand (see fn.27 above). The dissenting judge noted that the Government had in fact complied with its undertaking to introduce the reform within three years of accession.

[83] *James v UK*, fn.29 above.

[84] *Sporrong and Llonroth v Sweden*, September 23, 1982, Series A, No.52, 5 E.H.R.R. 35, para.69.

[85] In *Inze v Austria*, October 28, 1987, Series A, No.126, 10 E.H.R.R. 394, the fact that the law about inheritance changed did not show that there had been a violation, but did indicate that there were other ways of achieving the Government's aim of maintaining farms.

[86] e.g. *Mellacher v Austria*, December 19, 1989, Series A, No.169, para.53; see, however, *Chahal v UK*, November 15, 1996, R.J.D. 1996–V, No.22, para.131, where in finding a violation of Art.5, para.4, the Court attached significance to the method applied in Canada to permit courts to review sensitive security material; see *Sejdic and Finci v Bosnia-Herzegovina*, December 12, 2009, para.48, electoral case where possibility of alternative means of achieving the same end without restricting the applicants' rights was an "important factor", it cites *Glor v Switzerland*, April 30, 2009, para.94, which stated that an alternative means *must* be excluded, a statement which contradicts decades of case-law and may be regarded as impliedly overruled in being restated by the Grand Chamber in the classical way.

[87] *Moskal v Poland*, September 15, 2009, para.73.

been subject historically to prejudice, continued legislative stereotyping may be struck down.[88]

In this area, reference has been made to the need for an "individualised evaluation" of applicants' situations and a "tailor-made " response by legislature and courts to individuals.[89]

12. Positive obligations

I–074 The provisions of the Convention impose primarily negative obligations on States, namely, to refrain from taking steps infringing fundamental rights and freedoms. Increasingly however, rights are being interpreted in such a manner as to impose positive obligations on States to take steps to protect the enjoyment of rights from interferences from other sources.[90] In this area, limitations on the imposition of obligations derive from the consideration of the factors identified above in the context of the margin of appreciation dominated by the perception that this trespasses more acutely in matters of State policy, priorities and allocation of resources.[91] In assessing whether the State is under an obligation to take a particular step, the Court examines whether a fair balance has been struck between the interests of the individual and those of the community. It has also referred to examining whether the essence of the right is destroyed or effective exercise of the right barred in the absence of positive measures.[92] In striking the balance, where Art.8 is concerned for example, the legitimate aims adverted to in the second paragraph may be relevant. The interests of the general community perhaps start out heavier in the balance, with a certain burden on the individual to establish that his interests clearly predominate.[93] The cases indicate that where an important individual right is at stake, the applicant suffering significant effects, a positive obligation may arise.[94] However, where the individual interest is not perceived as suffering material prejudice, or an important State interest is at stake, this is less likely.[95]

[88] *Alajos Kiss v Hungary*, May 20, 2010, para.42, concerning disenfranchisement of a person with mental disability under partial guardianship, citing *Hirst v UK (No.2),* fn.78, blanket ban on prisoners' voting struck down.

[89] *Shtukaturov v Russia*, March 27, 2008, para.95, concerning placing applicant under regime of total legal capacity which did not reflect his situation; *Kyutin v Russia*, March 10, 2011, para.73.

[90] Obligations found first, and most commonly, under Art.8; now also under Arts 2, 3, 10 and 11.

[91] *Abdulaziz v UK*, May 28, 1985, Series A, No.94, 7 E.H.R.R. 471, para.67; *Osman v UK*, October 28, 1998, R.J.D. 1998–VIII, No.95, para.91.

[92] *Appleby*, fn.43 above, para.47.

[93] See, e.g. *X, Y and Z*, fn.23 above, para.47, where the Court stated that, while it had not been shown that recognition of the filiation of a child born by AID was contrary to the interests of the community, it had not been established as necessary to the welfare of the child either.

[94] e.g. *B v France*, fn.17 above, transsexual applicant suffered daily humiliation and the civil register system did not require radical alteration; *Gaskin v UK*, July 7, 1987, Series A, No.160, vital interest of the applicant, in care almost all his childhood, to have access to information about his past in social security files).

[95] e.g. *Abdulaziz*, fn.91 above, (immigration policy); *Rees* and *Cossey*, fn.17 above, UK transsexuals not considered to suffer significant hardship such as would require the State to change its entire registration system; *Appleby*, fn.43 above, where the applicants, barred from a shopping centre, could exercise their freedom of expression elsewhere.

13. Individual rights

The Convention is based on the right of individual petition. An applicant must claim to be a victim of a violation of one of the guaranteed rights. The Court will not entertain complaints by way of *actio popularis* or *in abstracto*; its examination will generally be restricted to the measures as they affect the individual in his situation. The Court does not respond with enthusiasm to an invitation to look at the global position, as in the case of gypsies, who may well be suffering from unfavourable social and legal trends over the last 50 years, but can only complain with any hope of success to Strasbourg of measures which can be shown to effect them directly and concretely or, in the case of indirect discrimination, where measures can be shown to impact on particular groups in a disproportionate manner.[96] I–075

Arguments which focus on the general injustice or unfairness of a policy or measure will be of limited assistance unless relevant to explaining or setting in context the impact on the individual applicant.

14. Living instrument

The Convention is seen as a living instrument, to be interpreted in light of present day conditions.[97] As a result, notwithstanding the possible intentions of the drafters of the Convention over fifty years ago, the Court will have regard to developments in Contracting States in applying the rights guaranteed in the Convention. Thus changing attitudes to homosexuality,[98] children born out of wedlock,[99] equality of the sexes,[100] transsexuals,[101] the acknowledged priority of eradicating racism[102] and the acceptance of conscientious objection as ground for exemption from military service[103] have all played a role in decision-making. There must, however, be a general acceptance of the changing conditions before this can be decisive, as shown by the transsexual cases, where the Court kept the matter under review for a number of years and noted the evolving consensus.[104] The almost complete abandonment of the death penalty in peace time by Contracting States (through the ratification of Protocol No.6) led the Court to express the view that Art.2 had thereby been modified to exclude capital punishment in peace time as an exception and that its imposition would also be inhuman punishment contrary to Art.3.[105] I–076

[96] See Pt IIB, s.24: Gypsies and minorities.

[97] e.g. *Tyrer v UK*, April 25, 1978, Series A, No.26, 2 E.H.R.R. 1, para.31; *Johnston v Ireland*, December 18, 1986, Series A, No.112, 9 E.H.R.R. 203, para.53; *Inze*, fn.85 above, para.41.

[98] e.g. *Dudgeon*, fn.16 above; *Schalk and Kopf*, fn.11 above, para.93, recognition of "family life" for gay couples.

[99] e.g. *Johnston*, fn.97 above; *Inze*, fn.854 above.

[100] e.g. *Schuler-Zgraggen v Switzerland*, June 24, 1993, Series A, No.263, 16 E.H.R.R. 405, para.67; *CR v UK*, fn.44 above, para.60.

[101] *Christine Goodwin*, fn.19 above, para.75, where the Court stated that it was examining the case in light of present-day conditions.

[102] *Sander v UK*, May 9, 2000, ECHR 2000–V, para.23. See also emphasis in *Menson v UK*, (47916/99) (Dec.) May 6, 2003, ECHR 2003–V, concerning particular need for vigour in investigating racially-motivated attacks.

[103] *Bayatyan v Armenia*, July 7, 2011, paras 98–109.

[104] See also *L and V v Austria*, January 9, 2003, ECHR 2003–I, para.47, noting consensus on equality of ages of consent between girls and boys.

[105] *Ocalan v Turkey*, May 12, 2005, ECHR 2005–V, paras 163–165, though it did not express a firm opinion as it decided the case on other grounds.

The contents of domestic and constitutional law, Council of Europe texts, other international treaties and human rights jurisprudence may be of relevance in establishing developments or evolving principles. This can be in relation to specific changes or more general trends, as in *Selmouni v France*, where the Court considered that the increasingly high standard being required in the area of the protection of human rights and fundamental liberties correspondingly required greater firmness in assessing breaches of the fundamental values of democratic societies.[106] Thus, it is not decisive that a Contracting State has not ratified a particular international treaty, if the relevant international instruments denote a continuous evolution in the norms and principles applied in international law or in the domestic law of the majority of Member States of the Council of Europe and show, in a precise area, that there is common ground in modern societies.[107]

As part of this theme, the notion of flexibility can be identified. The Court's case-law develops progressively and has overruled earlier decisions.[108] In the area, particularly, of domestic remedies, it intends to apply the Convention flexibly, avoiding excessive formalism.[109] A failure to evolve case-law in light of changing conditions might, it has noted, render the Court a bar to progress within Contracting States.[110] Dynamic interpretation cannot, however, in principle extend so far as to create rights not intended to be included in the Convention.[111]

15. Legitimate expectations

I–077 The principle of legitimate expectation has been relied on in a variety of contexts. In property cases, it plays a significant role in establishing whether a claim to property can constitute a possession for the purposes of Art.1 of Protocol No.1 (see Pt IIB, s.38: Property). It was also used in cases concerning prison disciplinary proceedings, where the legitimate expectation of release on a particular date meant that loss of remission was equated to a deprivation of liberty, bringing Art.6, para.1 into play due to the seriousness of what was at stake.[112] There may also be a legitimate expectation that legislative measures or constitutional reforms are not applied

[106] *Selmouni v France* July 28, 1999, ECHR 1999–V, para.101, where the Court lowered the threshold for treatment falling within the prohibition of torture in Art.3.

[107] *Demir and Baykara v Turkey*, November 12, 2008, para.86, see general considerations at paras 60–86.

[108] e.g. *Borgers v Belgium*, October 30, 1991, Series A, No.214, 15 E.H.R.R 92, para.24, overruling *Delcourt v Belgium*, January 17, 1970, Series A, No.11, 1 E.H.R.R. 355, in light of the growing importance of public confidence in administration of justice.

[109] *Akdivar*, fn.3 above, para.69.

[110] *Stafford v UK*, May 28, ECHR 2002–IV, paras 67–68, noting developments in domestic and Convention case-law since the previous judgment on similar complaints, the Court found Art.5, paras 1 and 4 could now apply to mandatory life prisoners' detention after expiry of tariff. See also *Mamatkulov and Askarov v Turkey*, February 4, 2005, para.105, evolving interpretation of Court's power to issue interim measures; and *Société Colas Est v France*, April 16, 2002, ECHR 2002–III, para.41, extending Art.8 protection to the head office and agencies of a company; *Rantsev v Cyprus and Russia*, January 7, 2010, paras 272–282, interpreting Art.4 to cover trafficking in women.

[111] Where provided in the later Convention protocols (*ne bis in idem*; freedom of movement) or otherwise, e.g. *Johnston*, fn.85 above, para.53, concerning the Court's refusal to evolve interpretation of Art.12 to include a right to divorce clearly not intended by the drafters. There is therefore a distinction to be drawn, possibly fine, between the creation of new rights and the extension by interpretation of existing ones. See *Scoppola v Italy (No.2)*, September 17, 2009, where the minority considered that the majority, in interpreting Art.7 to include the principle, found in other international instruments, that an accused should benefit retrospectively from a favourable change in the law, had crossed the line.

[112] *Ezeh and Connors v UK*, July 15, 2002, ECHR 2002–X, para.93.

retrospectively to an applicant's detriment.[113] Where protection of private life is concerned under Art.8 of the Convention, the Court also takes into account whether in certain circumstances the applicant can claim a legitimate expectation of privacy.[114] The principle also makes an occasional appearance in the immigration and expulsion context where legitimate expectations of being allowed to establish or continue family or private life in the host state have been taken into account.[115]

16. Convention approach to evidence and burdens of proof

There are no rules of admissibility of evidence. Parties may present such documentary evidence as they think appropriate and are not bound to comply with required domestic forms of presentation or content.[116] In the hearing of witnesses, there is no prohibition of hearsay. Nor is there any formalised theory of burden and standard of proof. The Convention organs take the approach of a free assessment of the available evidence, including matters taken *proprio motu*.[117] I–078

In practice however, an applicant must present an application which provides prima facie substantiation of an interference with his rights and an arguable basis for an eventual violation. It will only be in exceptional cases, complaints raising serious issues against a background that provides justification for failure to present factual substantiation, that the application will be considered as meriting further examination by communication to the respondent Government.[118] Applicants will not be penalised where they do not have access to the relevant documents or information which are in the possession of the Government.[119] Benefit of the doubt is given in assessing the credibility of the statements of asylum seekers due to the difficulty facing them in substantiating their allegations, but where there are strong reasons to question the veracity of an asylum seeker's submissions, a satisfactory explanation must be provided.[120] Similarly, in the area of prison conditions, where the information lies in the hands of the authorities, the Court has said it will not make rigorous application of the principle "*affirmanti incumbit probatio*" (he who alleges something must prove that allegation).[121]

As regards admissibility criteria, the Government bears the burden of establishing the existence of available and effective remedies for the purpose of the exhaustion of

[113] *Lykouresoz v Greece*, June 15, 2006, para.57; *Paschalidis v Greece*, April 10, 2008, para.33; see also *Mursel Eren v Turkey*, February 13, 2006, para.48, where a student who obtained the necessary marks had a legitimate expectation to obtain a university place in the context of Art.2 of Protocol No.1.

[114] *Von Hannover v Germany*, June 24, 2004, ECHR 2004–VI, para.51.

[115] *Dorochenko v Estonia*, (10507/03) (Dec.) January 5, 2006.

[116] Though it is not infrequent for parties to submit statements by way of affidavit, and this may be taken into account as part of the weighing of the credibility of the evidence.

[117] *Timishev v Russia*, December 13, 2005, ECHR 2005–VII, para.39.

[118] e.g. the cases brought by villagers from southeast Turkey, where serious allegations were made and no documentary substantiation was allegedly possible due to the ineffective nature of domestic remedies. There was independent confirmation of village destruction in other international texts and NGO reports.

[119] *Akkum v Turkey*, March 25, 2005, ECHR 2005–II, paras 208–209. See also *Makhmudov v Russia*, July 26, 2007, para.68, information as to reasons for the banning of a meeting lay in the authorities' hands.

[120] e.g. *Elezaj v Sweden*, (17654/05) (Dec.) September 20, 2009 citing *Collins and Akasiebie v Sweden*, (23944/05) (Dec.) March 8, 2007 and *Matsiukhina and Matsiukhin v Sweden,* (31260/04) (Dec.) June 21, 2005.

[121] e.g. *Khudoyorov v Russia,* February 22, 2005, para.113, where the Government failed to provide specifications/occupancy details of prison transport vans; *Ogica v Romania*, May 27, 2010, para.45, where the Government failed to provide documents on occupancy, hygiene and conditions in the cells.

domestic remedies under Art.35, para.1 (see Pt IB: Admissibility Checklist). In other contexts, it may be seen that once an interference with rights is established, the burden shifts practically onto the Government to provide convincing justification.[122] However, where public and individual interests are more finely balanced, due either to the nature of the claims or the fact that it is a positive obligation in issue, it appears that the applicant faces the onus of substantiating the degree of prejudice alleged.

In relation to disputed factual situations, where there are allegations of unjustified killing or torture, or inhuman and degrading treatment contrary to Arts 2 and 3, the Court has used the standard of proof beyond a reasonable doubt. The first judgment in which it appeared was in an inter-State case, where dozens of witnesses were heard concerning practices used in interrogation in Northern Ireland.[123] It was rarely used again until the Convention organs undertook witness hearings in Turkey concerning allegations, under Arts 2 and 3, about ill-treatment and deaths at the hands of security forces.[124] The Court has recently said that it has never been its purpose to borrow the approach of the national legal systems that use a reasonable doubt test, which, in its practice, has an autonomous meaning, distinct from any notions of criminal responsibility. In its approach, the level of persuasion necessary for reaching a particular conclusion and the distribution of the burden of proof are intrinsically linked to the specificity of the facts, the nature of the allegation made and the Convention right at stake. There is also a hint that the stigma attached to a ruling that a Contracting State has violated fundamental rights may also affect the burden of proof.[125]

Outside the above context, the establishment of the facts is generally carried out without any reference to standards and burden of proof. Where it was alleged that security forces had acted unlawfully in arresting an applicant on foreign soil, the Court, rejecting the application of a reasonable doubt test, required the applicant only to provide proof in the form of concordant inferences that the authorities had acted extra-territorially in a manner that was inconsistent with the sovereignty of the host State and therefore contrary to international law; then the burden shifted to the Government to show that the arrest had been lawful.[126]

Presumptions, or inferences, of fact may be made where a Government has hindered the fact-finding process or failed to provide any, or any satisfactory, explanation concerning a situation within their particular knowledge, e.g. injuries or deaths in custody.[127] A failure by the Government to provide information or documents, in its possession, which are capable of corroborating or refuting an applicant's allegations may also lead to the drawing of inferences as to their well-foundedness.[128]

It is perhaps worth mentioning that there is a certain presumption in practice that Governments act in good faith, that the authorities comply with important domestic

[122] e.g. *Dudgeon*, fn.16 above; freedom of expression cases.

[123] *Ireland v UK*, January 18, 1978, Series A, No.25.

[124] e.g. *Aydin v Turkey*, September 25, 1997, R.J.D. 1997–VI, Nȯ.50, para.73; see also *Poltoratskiy v Ukraine*, April 29, 2003, ECHR 2003–V, paras 122–123.

[125] *Mathew v Netherlands*, September 29, 2005, para.156; *Nachova v Bulgaria* (GC), July 6, 2005, ECHR 2005–VII, para.147.

[126] *Ocalan*, fn.105 above, para.90.

[127] e.g. *Salman v Turkey*, June 27, 2000, ECHR 2000–VII, para.100. See Pt IIB, s.25: Hindrance in the exercise of the right of individual petition.

[128] e.g. *Akkum*, fn.119 above.

rules and that legal processes work in the way laid down by law.[129] For example, judges are presumed very strongly to abide by their oaths and duties[130] and statutory systems of protection to function as intended.[131] Any allegations alleging abuse or misuse of power tend to require a certain level of substantiation.

17. Structured approach

In any complaint of substance, the Convention organs analyse the application of the invoked provision with regard to each ingredient. This involves generally an examination of whether the complaint falls within the scope of the right claimed (applicability) and whether any interference with the right conforms with its conditions (compliance). While this may vary concerning the subject-matter, the general approach for the most commonly-invoked provisions is set out below. I–079

Article 5, para.1

- Is there a deprivation of liberty? I–080
- Is it in conformity with lawfulness considerations?
- Is it for a ground permitted under para.1? Does it comply with its conditions?

Article 6

Criminal: I–081

- Do the proceedings relate to a criminal charge? (see Pt IIA, s.1a: Criminal charge)
- If so, have the guarantees been complied with?

Civil:

Do the proceedings relate to:
- A right or obligation recognised in domestic law?
- Is there a genuine and serious dispute ("contestation") about the right or obligation (which includes the consideration whether the proceedings are directly decisive for that right or obligation)?
- Is the right or obligation "civil" in character?
- Have the guarantees under para.1 been complied with?

Articles 8–11

First paragraph: I–082

- Applicability: whether the complaint falls within the scope of the right.

[129] See *Kraska v Switzerland*, April 19, 1993, Series A, No.254–B, where a judge announced that he had not read the applicant's documents.

[130] See *Khordorkovskiy v Russia*, paras 255–261, high standard of proof applies to allegations that the authorities have acted for improper reasons to undermine Convention rights (Art.18).

[131] See, e.g. Pt IIB, ss.30: Interception of communications and 44: Surveillance and secret files; also *Goddi v Italy*, April 9, 1984, Series A, No.76, 6 E.H.R.R. 457, para.76, where, in the absence of substantiation of a factual point from either side, the Court was not prepared to find the Government at fault.

- Existence of an interference: whether the matters complained of infringe the right.

Second paragraph—justification for any interference:

- lawfulness criteria;
- legitimate aim;
- necessity, including considerations of "pressing social need", margin of appreciation, proportionality, procedural safeguards and relevant and sufficient reasons for any decisions involved.[132]

Where positive obligations are concerned the examination does not extend into the second paragraph but the considerations of aim and proportionality are transposed into a general balancing exercise as to the existence of the obligation.

Article 13

I–083

- Is the claim in relation to an alleged violation of a substantive provision?
- Is it arguable?
- Is there any effective remedy?

Article 14

I–084

- Is there a substantive right in issue?
- Is there a difference in treatment, direct or indirect?
  - — Between persons in relevantly similar positions;
  - — Based on grounds of personal status.
  - — Without objective and reasonable justification (including consideration of legitimate aim, proportionality and margin of appreciation)?

Article 1 of Protocol No.1

I–085

- Are "possessions" involved which fall within this provision?
- If so, does the measure constitute a deprivation, a control of use or an interference with peaceful enjoyment?
- Compliance: legitimate aim (whether specified as general or public interest), lawfulness, margin of appreciation and proportionality (including procedural safeguards, compensation) are relevant to all heads in some degree.

[132] So far the latter criterion has been almost wholly applied in cases under Arts 8 and 10, although it has also been applied to Art.9, e.g. *Svyato-Mykhaylivska Parafiya v Ukraine*, June 14, 2007, paras 144, 149, and 151 and Art.11, e.g. *Sidiropoulos v Greece*, July 19, 1998, R.J.D. 1998–IV, No.79, para.40.

D. SOURCES OF CASE-LAW AND INFORMATION

1. Court judgments and decisions

Available:

On the internet—*http://www.echr.coe.int*: I–086

- The site includes monthly information notes on judgments and decisions delivered, press releases on recent hearings and judgments, factsheets collecting case-law on numerous topics (such as new technologies, reproductive rights, terrorism, violence against women, etc) and a searchable database, "HUDOC", giving access to all Court judgments and decisions, most of which are issued in either English or French. Only judgments and decisions chosen for publication in the official series are translated into both of the Court's working languages.[1]

Official series—texts of judgments:

- until 1996, Series A Nos 1–338;
- 1996–1998, yearly volumes of Reports, published as *Reports of Judgments and Decisions* (cited by the Court as *Reports* 1997–. . .);
- from 1999, yearly volumes of Reports of the new Court's judgments and decisions (cited by the Court as ECHR 2000–. . .).

These contain the entire text of the court judgment in English and French including any separate opinions. In respect of cases sent to the Court before November 1, 1998, save where the length was prohibitive, the texts also contain the "Opinion" part of the Commission report on the merits, again with separate opinions.[2]

There is no formal doctrine of precedent binding the Court. The Court obviously pays attention to relevant or similar cases decided by itself, but may choose, if it considers it appropriate or timely, to depart expressly or impliedly from previous positions.[3] Therefore authority from the Court in support of a proposition is one of the most convincing arguments, although not necessarily conclusive.

2. Commission cases

Principal sources:

On the internet—*http://www.echr.coe.int*: I–087

[1] There is some delay before the translation is placed on the site.

[2] There is no official index for Series A or the subsequent Report series.

[3] Procedurally, however, any change in case-law should be conducted by a Grand Chamber. A Chamber should not depart from the previous cases since this is a ground on which the case should be relinquished to a Grand Chamber (r.72). See, e.g. *Stafford v UK*, May 28, 2000, ECHR 2002–IV, paras 68–69, where the Court departed from its reasoning in *Wynne v UK*, July 18, 1994, Series A, No.294–A.

- Commission decisions on admissibility and reports on the merits from 1986 which have been made public are accessible in the HUDOC database.

Decisions and reports:

- From 1974 Commission cases were principally published in numerical volumes D.R 1—94. Volumes 1—75 contained each extract in both English and French. To diminish the time taken for publication, there were subsequently two versions of vols 76—94: vol.A contains the text in the original language, and vol.B contains the translation into the other official language. Indexes by name and case number, and summaries by article and keyword, were produced at intervals of every 15—20 volumes.

Supplementary sources:

Collection of Decisions:

- Consists of 46 volumes covering 1955—74, including selected decisions, with indexes for 1—30 and 32—43 only. These include cases of interesting historical significance, e.g. Commission decisions in the *Ireland v UK* inter-State case.

Yearbook of the European Convention of Human Rights:

- Published annually, containing general institutional information and statistics and cases which tended to reproduce those in D.R., although some material may be included which is not published elsewhere. There is no complete index to the Yearbook.

Digest of Strasbourg case-law (1982):

- Arranged by chunks of relevant texts of decisions and reports under each Article of the Convention in five volumes). It is not regarded as an official source of published case-law and it is not cited as a source as a matter of practice. Looseleaf supplements have brought it up to 1990 for decisions and reports and up to 1992 for judgments.

The Court has openly given weight to Commission precedent as well as silently adopting it. It is, therefore, not irrelevant to refer the Court to Commission case-law which is particularly persuasive or was based on its special expertise on issues of admissibility. As the Court has been building up its own bank of precedents, however, references to Commission cases are diminishing.

3. Procedure

I–088 The Rules of Court, which govern Court procedure, are annexed (latest version, April 1, 2011). They are also available on the Court website.

Until recently, there was no equivalent of practice notes, with the result that there is no official published source of authority for Court practice over the years in various procedural matters such as legal aid, rights of audience or effects of delays in submitting written pleadings. The Rules of Court however do now provide, in r.32, for the President to issue Practice Directions. At the date of writing, the six Practice Directions (concerning interim measures under r.39, instituting proceedings, written pleadings, just satisfaction, secured electronic filing and requests for anonymity) have been issued. However, these deal more with technical detail about lodging of various requests and documents rather than giving any explanation as to how the Court exercises its discretion.

Basic notes are given for guidance to parties before oral hearings and brief explanatory letters sent by the Registry with each procedural step. Enquiry by letter or telephone to the Registry is possible but should not be abused.

4. Institutional and statistical information

The Court publishes annual surveys of statistical information which are available on the website. Information about judges and formations of the Court are also on the website. See also the Yearbooks for historic details of the old Court and Commission (sub-s.2 above). **I–089**

5. International and national law materials

The Court has frequent and serious regard to international law and comparative law, as well as information and reports from well-reputed NGOs. See in particular Pt C, s.(14): Living Instrument, concerning interpretation of the Convention; and Pt IIA, s.29: Immigration, sub-s.4(c): Factors and materials taken into account, concerning asylum and expulsion cases. **I–090**

PART II: PROBLEM AREAS

A. FAIR TRIAL GUARANTEES

1. General principles: fairness

Key provision:

Article 6, para.1 (fair and public hearing in the determination of criminal charges and civil rights and obligations, within a reasonable time, before an independent and impartial tribunal); para.2 (presumption of innocence); para.3(a) (information about the charge); para.3(b) (adequate time and facilities for preparation); para.3(c) (right to be present and represented); para.3(d) (right to call and examine witnesses); para.3(e) (right to interpretation). II–001

Key case-law:

Albert and Le Compte v Belgium, February 10, 1982, No.58, 5 E.H.R.R. 533; *Artico v Italy*, May 13, 1980, Series A, No.37, 3 E.H.R.R. 1; *Barbera, Massegué and Jabardo v Spain*, December 6, 1988, Series A, No.146, 11 E.H.R.R. 360; *Kamasinski v Austria*, December 19, 1989, Series A, No.168, 13 E.H.R.R. 36; *Kraska v Switzerland*, April 19, 1993, Series A, No.254–B, 18 E.H.R.R. 188; *V v UK*, December 16, 1999, ECHR 1999–IX; *Scoppola v Italy (No.2)*, September 17, 2009, ECHR 2009–. . .

1. General principles

Complaints about court proceedings form a major percentage of the cases before the Convention organs, reflecting that it is in court that most people are likely to come into contact, in a significant manner, with the power and authority of the State as it administers civil and criminal justice. However, justice is not the word that is highlighted by the Convention or the Convention organs. The key principle governing Art.6 is fairness.[1] Paragraphs 2 and 3 are constituent elements, or specific aspects of the fair trial guaranteed in para.1. Further, while sub-paras 3(a)—(e) exemplify the notion of fair trial in typical procedural situations, their intrinsic aim is always to ensure or contribute to ensuring the fairness of the proceedings as a whole.[2] Though they are expressed as applying to criminal proceedings, they have also been considered by the Court to be implicit requirements in fairness outside the criminal sphere, applying mutatis mutandis in civil proceedings.[3] While the "fairness" principle applies to both criminal and civil proceedings, a special II–002

[1] *Kamasinski v Austria*, December 19, 1989, Series A, No.168, 13 E.H.R.R. 36, para.62; *Hadjianastassiou v Greece*, December 16, 1992, Series A, No.252–A, 16 E.H.R.R. 219, para.31; *Vacher v France*, December 17, 1996, R.J.D. 1996–VI.

[2] The sub-paragraphs are often considered in conjunction with para.1, e.g. *Can v Austria*, (Rep.) July 12, 1984, Series A, No.96, 8 E.H.R.R. 121.

[3] *Albert and Le Compte v Belgium*, February 10, 1982, No.58, 5 E.H.R.R. 533, para.39.

importance is attached to the rights of the defence in criminal proceedings and, where civil litigation is involved, national authorities enjoy greater latitude.[4] Nonetheless, in general the same principles of equality of arms, adversarial proceedings, etc. described below apply, if not with the same force, in civil cases.

The right to a fair trial is seen as holding so prominent a place in democratic society that the Court has stated that there is no justification for interpreting Art.6, para.1 restrictively.[5] Whatever the importance of the public interest in, for example, fighting organised crime, the fair administration of justice cannot be sacrificed to expedience.[6] Nonetheless, in the area of regulatory offences or technical subject-matter outside the hard core of criminal law, the Court has found that, even if Art. 6 applies, it may not require the full range and rigour of guarantees, such as an oral or public hearing[7] or legal representation.[8]

As to fairness, it is perhaps simpler to say what it does not mean. The Commission frequently stated, and the Court continues to emphasise, that the Convention organs are not courts of appeal from domestic courts and cannot examine complaints that a court has made errors of fact or law, or reached the wrong decision, or that a person was, for example, wrongly convicted.[9] They will not enter into the merits of decisions. For this reason, complaints concerning miscarriages of justice are unlikely to succeed before them.[10]

Domestic courts are in the best position to assess the evidence before them, to decide what is relevant or admissible. Matters of appreciation of domestic law and the categorisation of claims in domestic law are also primarily for the appreciation of domestic courts.[11] In this area the Convention organs exercise only a limited supervisory jurisdiction, guided by the overriding principle of fairness. While more recently developments have indicated that the Court will require that reasons be given and that a lack of reasons on key points may disclose unfairness, it is unlikely that it will intervene on substantive matters, i.e. the decision itself, unless there is some gross unreasonableness or arbitrariness. This would appear to mean that there is something striking and palpable on the face of the decision.[12] Complete failure to

[4] e.g. *Niderost-Huber v Switzerland*, February 18, 1997, R.J.D. 1997–I, No.29, para.28.

[5] *Moreira de Azevedo v Portugal*, October 23, 1990, Series A, No.189, para.66.

[6] *Teixeira de Castro v Portugal*, June 9, 1998, Reports 1998–IV, para.36.

[7] *Jussila v Finland*, November 23, 2006, ECHR 2006–XIII (tax surcharge proceedings); *Suhadolc v Slovenia*, (57655/08) (Dec.) May 17, 2011 (driving offence).

[8] *Barsom and Varli v Sweden*, (407766/06) and (40831/06) (Dec.) December 4, 2008 (tax surcharge proceedings).

[9] e.g. *Sawoniuk v UK*, (63716/00) (Dec.) May 29, 2001, ECHR 2001–VI, where the trial procedures examining offences committed some 50 years earlier were fair, notwithstanding the lapse of time.

[10] e.g. (14739/89) (Dec.) May 9, 1989, 69 D.R. 296, where the Birmingham Six, alleging wrongful conviction, focussed on the failure to hold a jury trial to rehear the new evidence instead of the Court of Appeal, these matters did not reveal unfairness—juries are not standard features of criminal trials in Europe as a whole and no right to a re trial is contained in the Convention.

[11] e.g. (10153/82) (Dec.) October 13, 1986, 49 D.R. 67; more recently *Nejdet Şahin and Perihan Şahin v Turkey* (GC), October 20, 2011, para.49.

[12] e.g. *Canela Santiago v Spain*, (60350/00) (Dec.) October 4, 2001, the Court did not exclude that a domestic court refusal to make an Art.177 reference to the European Court of Justice might raise fairness issues if tainted by arbitrariness; *Van Kuck v Germany*, June 12, 2003, para.46, where the Court would not substitute its interpretation of domestic law for that of the domestic courts "in the absence of arbitrariness", and paras 53–57, where it found that their interpretation of "medical necessity" and evaluation of evidence was "not reasonable"; *Blûcher v Czech Republic*, January 11, 2005, paras 55–57, nothing arbitrary or illogical in the Constitutional Court's ruling to fill a legal *lacuna*.

address crucial complaints, arbitary findings of fact based on disregard of undisputed evidence and the setting of unattainable burdens of proof are examples.[13]

From the Convention point of view it is not so much the result that is in question but the process of "hearing". An applicant should be "heard", given an adequate and effective opportunity to present his case. Domestic courts are under a duty to conduct a proper examination of the submissions, arguments and evidence adduced by the parties, without prejudice to their assessment of whether they are relevant to its decision.[14] Basing a decision on a clearly inaccurate finding may disclose a failure by the court to ensure an applicant receives a fair hearing,[15] as may an oversight or omission that means an applicant's pleadings are not taken into account,[16] a failure to answer the applicant's main arguments[17] or an overly-formalistic approach which excludes a proper examination of the applicant's Convention complaints.[18]

2. Aspects of fairness

A number of subsidiary principles have been identified. *Equality of arms* between the parties, or a "fair balance", must be achieved. This means that each party must be afforded a reasonable opportunity to present his case—including his evidence—under conditions which do not place him at a substantial disadvantage vis-à-vis his opponent.[19] As the primary purpose of procedural rules is to provide the accused with *protection against abuse of authority*, they should be laid down by law with sufficient clarity and certainty.[20] II–003

Proceedings should also be *adversarial* in character, with an opportunity for the parties to a criminal or civil trial to have knowledge of and comment on all evidence adduced or observations filed, even by an independent member of the national legal service, with a view to influencing the court's decision,[21] including notes sent by the lower instance judge to the higher instance court[22] or material obtained at the court's own motion.[23] Since what is at stake is litigants' confidence in the system, it

[13] See *e.g. Khamidov v Russia*, November 15, 2007, paras 170–175, where the Court was "perplexed" by the domestic courts' inexplicable disregard of evidence that the applicant's property had been occupied and damaged by the security services and their findings of fact that flew in the face of the available evidence. See further, Pt IIA, s.21: Reasons for decisions.

[14] e.g. *Barbera, Massegue and Jabardo v Spain*, December 6, 1988, Series A, No.146, 11 E.H.R.R. 360, para.68; *Kraska v Switzerland*, April 19, 1993, Series A, No.254–B, 18 E.H.R.R. 188, para.30.

[15] *Fouquet v France*, (Rep.) October 12, 1994, R.J.D. 1996–I (settled before the Court), where the *Cour de Cassation* based itself, erroneously, on the finding that the applicants had admitted fault in their pleadings.

[16] *Quadrelli v Italy*, January 11, 2000, where the Court of Cassation made no reference to the applicant's submissions in its decision and no copy was later found in the file.

[17] *Buzescu v Romania*, May 24, 2005, para.67.

[18] *Perlala v Greece*, February 22, 2007, para.27, where the Court of Cassation rejected an applicant's complaints under Art.6 as inadmissible for failure to combine them with formal cassation grounds.

[19] e.g. *Dombo Beheer BV v Netherlands*, October 27, 1993, Series A, No.274, para.33.

[20] *Coeme v Belgium*, June 22, 2000, ECHR 2000–VII, paras 102–103.

[21] e.g. *Ruiz-Mateos v Spain*, June 23, 1993, Series A, No.262, para.63; *Belziuk v Poland*, March 25, 1998, R.J.D. 1998–II, No.67, para.37(iii). It may apply to proceedings ancillary to the main proceedings, e.g. in *Mantovanelli v France*, March 18, 1997, R.J.D. 1997–II, No.32, and *Augusto v France*, January 11, 2007, paras 51–52, concerning the expert report procedure. See also Pt IIA, s.8: Equality of arms.

[22] e.g. *Ferreira Alves v Portugal (No.3)*, June 21, 2007, paras 40–43.

[23] *Krcmar v Czech Republic*, March 3, 2000, paras 40–46. It was sufficient in the ECJ procedure where the applicant organisation had been unable to comment on the Advocate-General's opinion, that there was the opportunity to apply for re-opening, which application would be decided on the merits: *Cooperatieve Producentenorganisatie van de Nederlandse Kokkelvisserij UA v Netherlands*, (13645/05) (Dec.) January 20, 2009.

is irrelevant whether the submission concerned added anything new, it being for the party to assess for themselves whether it called for their comment; nor is it relevant whether it in fact influenced the tribunal.[24] Where the prosecution is present at an appeal, the principle of adversariality requires that the court ensure the presence of the applicant, or at the very least his lawyer, irrespective of the type of issues which might be at stake.[25]

Proceedings should also respect the *principle of immediacy*, namely, that witnesses be heard in the presence of the judges who ultimately decide the case,[26] although, where it is no longer possible for a judge to sit in a case, measures can be taken to ensure that the judges who continue to hear the case have the appropriate understanding of the evidence and arguments, for example, by making transcripts available where the credibility of the witness concerned is not in issue or by providing for a rehearing of the relevant arguments before the newly composed court.[27]

The importance of ensuring the *appearance of the fair administration of justice* is adverted to in a number of contexts. Foremost, there are the objective requirements of independence and impartiality but there is also the importance of public hearings which allows for public scrutiny of the processes of justice and maintains confidence in the administration of justice.[28]

The accused, and in civil proceedings the parties, must be able *to participate effectively in proceedings*.[29] While it is not, per se, incompatible to try a child in an adult court, he or she must have a broad measure of understanding of the nature of the proceedings and what is at stake.[30] It is also essential that not only those charged with an offence but also their counsel should be able to follow the proceedings, answer questions and make their submissions without suffering from excessive tiredness, and that judges and jurors should be in full control of their faculties of concentration and attention in order to follow the proceedings and to be able to give an informed judgment. Accordingly, unfairness was disclosed when a court sat for seventeen hours on one day of the trial.[31] In proceedings not involving complex legal issues, individuals may be regarded as able to effectively participate in the proceedings without legal representation.[32]

[24] e.g. *Ferreira Alves v Portugal (No.3)*, June 21, 2007, para.41. Contrast *Verdu Verdu v Spain*, February 2, 2007, paras 27–29, where the complainant had submitted a memorial agreeing with the public prosecutor's appeal and adding nothing new, it was not fatal that the former had not been communicated to the defendant.

[25] e.g. *Maksimov v Azerbaijan*, October 8, 2009, paras 40–43.

[26] *Pitkanen v Finland*, March 9, 2004, para.58, normally a change in composition of the court after the hearing of an important witness should lead to the rehearing of the witness.

[27] *Mellors v UK*, (57836/00) (Dec.) January 30, 2003.

[28] *Bulut v Austria*, February 22, 1996, R.J.D. 1996–III, No.5, para.47; *Borgers v Belgium*, October 30, 1991, Series A, No.214–B, para.24; *Krcmar*, fn.23 above, para.43.

[29] e.g. *V v UK*, December 16, 1999, ECHR 1999–IX, paras 85–91, where the child accused was unable to participate effectively in the public and formal criminal trial procedures in a case attracting intense media attention and public emotion; *Guvec v Turkey*, January 20, 2009, where a boy, aged 13, tried on serious charges was not represented by a lawyer until late in the proceedings and that lawyer failed to attend many hearings, the authorities failed to ensure that he was able to participate effectively in the trial.

[30] *SC v UK*, June 15, 2004, where the Court said that the 11–year-old should have been tried in a specialised and informal tribunal; see, however, strong dissent from the President and Vice-President of the Section, distinguishing this case from *V*, fn.29 above, as the child was not subject to a traumatic atmosphere and the court had properly considered whether he was able to participate.

[31] *Makhfi v France*, October 19, 2004.

[32] *Barsom and Varli v Sweden*, fn.8 above.

Measures taken in the conduct of a criminal trial must be reconcilable with *an adequate and effective exercise of the rights of the defence*.[33] The importance of securing defence rights in criminal proceedings has been identified as a fundamental principle of democratic society and, in this respect, Art.6 must be interpreted to render them practical and effective rather than theoretical and illusory.[34] States are expected to exercise diligence in ensuring defence rights[35] and any measures restricting them should be strictly necessary.[36] Thus while an applicant's own conduct will be relevant, domestic courts must still ensure that the requirements of Art.6, para.1 are met.[37]

The standard applied, however, is not one of perfection. The proceedings are looked at as a whole and one restriction on the defence may be insufficient to render the proceedings as a whole unfair. The Court will examine whether any other opportunities were offered to remedy or make up for some shortcoming. Defects in a trial may be remedied by subsequent procedures before appeal courts.[38] The Convention organs have also had a pragmatic approach to difficulties of criminal justice, in particular concerning drug-trafficking, organised mafia-type crime and terrorism, and where good reasons exist to keep witnesses anonymous or where circumstances make it impossible for the authorities to act otherwise, allowance is generally made notwithstanding the undesirable effects on defence rights.[39] Recognition has also effectively been given to the practical importance of enforcing traffic regulations to prevent road accidents, the Court considering that the owners of motor vehicles must be regarded as accepting certain responsibilities, including the obligation to inform the authorities of who was driving when a suspected offence was committed.[40]

Whether or not the "unfairness" alleged had an effect on the outcome of the proceedings is a factor which generally is not, or should not be of relevance.[41] However, occasionally it is taken into account whether some factor had the possibility of effecting the course of proceedings or outcome and whether the

[33] e.g. *Ludi v Switzerland*, June 15, 1992, Series A, No.238, 15 E.H.R.R. 173.

[34] *Artico v Italy*, May 13, 1980, Series A, No.37, 3 E.H.R.R. 1, para.33.

[35] See, e.g. *Colozza v Italy*, February 12, 1985, Series A, No.89, 7 E.H.R.R. 516, para.28; *Vacher v France*, fn.1 above, para.28, where the Court objected to the appeal system putting the onus on convicted appellants to find out when an allotted period of time expired; *Vaudelle v France*, January 30, 2001, ECHR 2001–I, paras 52–66, where the courts should have taken additional steps to ensure the attendance of the applicant, who had mental disabilities, at a psychiatric examination and at the hearing; *Fretté v France*, February 26, 2002, ECHR 2002–I, para.49, where the burden should not have been on the applicant to contact the *Conseil d'Etat* constantly to discover when his case was listed.

[36] *Van Mechelen v Netherlands*, April 23, 1997, R.J.D. 1997–III, No.36, para.58, if a less restrictive measure can suffice then that measure should be applied.

[37] *Barbera*, fn.14 above, para.75, lack of fair trial notwithstanding the applicants' lawyers' failure to make an objection to documents not being read out which led to a drastically brief trial; *Kerojärvi v Finland*, July 19, 1995, Series A, No.322, para.42, it was irrelevant that the unassisted applicant made no complaint about non-communication of documents—the Supreme Court should have made them available itself.

[38] e.g. *Edwards v UK*, December 16, 1992, Series A, No.247–B, 15 E.H.R.R. 417. See Pt IIA, s.4: Appeals.

[39] e.g. *Ferrantelli and Santangelo v Italy*, August 7, 1996, R.J.D. 1996–III, No.12, where the applicants were unable to question a key witness who had died before an opportunity had been given; *Baegen v Netherlands*, October 27, 1995, Series A, No.327–B (inability to question abuse victim); *Doorson v Netherlands*, March 26, 1996, R.J.D. 1996–II, No.6 (drug trafficking).

[40] *O'Halloran and Francis v UK*, June 29, 2007, ECHR 2007–III, paras 57–62, no breach of the right to silence contrary to Art.6 was disclosed.

[41] e.g. *Artico*, fn.34 above, para.35.

applicant has shown whether it was capable of such effect to distinguish material factors from extraneous or trivial ones.[42]

More recently, the Court has started to emphasise that one of the fundamental aspects of the rule of law is *legal certainty*. This requires that where courts' judgments have become final their rulings should not be called into question. Higher courts' power of review of final decisions should be exercised to correct fundamental judicial errors and miscarriages of justice, but not to carry out a fresh examination or appeal in disguise, since the mere possibility of there being two views on the subject is not a ground for re-examination. A departure from that principle is justified only when made necessary by circumstances of a substantial and compelling character.[43] Supervisory review powers, however, may be regarded as a link in the chain of appellate remedy rather than an extraordinary re-opening procedure where they are strictly limited in time and defined in scope, attended by due adversarial procedures and open to the parties equally.[44]

Another aspect of this principle is seen in cases where domestic courts produce conflicting decisions in similar cases. While it is acknowledged that individual, independent courts may well reach different results on particular issues, a situation where such conflicts are not resolved by the operation of appellate or superior courts,[45] and where the nature or degree of inconsistency produces an atmosphere of uncertainty, may threaten to undermine confidence in the legal system. Thus, where there was inconsistent adjudication of claims brought by many persons in identical situations to the applicants even after the adoption of the purported definitive ruling on the payment of a particular benefit, the Court found that the judicial uncertainty deprived the applicants of a fair hearing.[46] Nonetheless, the Court does not intend to act as a mechanism for reviewing internal case conflicts and inconsistencies: divergences will largely be acceptable as part of the inevitable evolution of case-law and the off-shoot of overlapping jurisdictions, as long as the proceedings in issue before the Court itself disclose no arbitrariness.[47]

[42] e.g. *John Murray v UK*, February 2, 1996, para.66; see also Pt IIA, s.26(2): Use of anonymous witnesses.

[43] *Brumărescu v Romania*, October 28, 1999, ECHR 199–VII, para.61; *Ryabykh v Russia*, July 24, 2003, ECHR 2003–IX; *Salov v Ukraine*, September 6, 2005. Cf. *Bratyakin v Russia*, (72776/01) (Dec.) March 9, 2006, where the applicant himself asked for review and there were serious grounds for quashing the judgment; *Protsenko v Russia*, July 31, 2008, where the quashing was justified by breach of the procedural rights of another interested party; *Lenskaya v Russia*, January 29, 2009, paras 36–44, quashing justified to rectify a miscarriage of criminal justice, where gross errors denied a fair trial; contrast *Bujnita v Moldova*, January 16, 2007, para.23, where the acquittal was annulled in re-opened proceedings instituted not due to discovery of new facts or serious procedural defect, but because the prosecutor disagreed with the courts' assessment of the evidence.

[44] *OOO Link Oil SPB v Russia*, (42600/05) (Dec.) June 25, 2009.

[45] See e.g. *Schwarzkopf and Taussik v Czech Republic*, (42162/02) (Dec.) December 2, 2008, the short-term divergences were settled by the Supreme Court, no issue merely because the ruling came after the applicants' unsuccessful case.

[46] *Vincic v Serbia*, December 1, 2009; see also *Beian v Romania (No.1)*, December 6, 2007, paras 34–40, persistent, contradictory rulings on the eligibility of military conscripts to claim particular indemnities, violation for lack of legal certainty in the vindication of rights; *Tudor Tudor v Romania*, March 24, 2009, paras 29–32, profound, longstanding differences by an appellate court in taking into account, or not in restitution cases, the good faith of buyers of nationalised properties (violation); *Iordan Iordanov v Bulgaria*, July 2, 2009, profound and longstanding divergence in the application of law in similar redundancy cases given by the Supreme Administrative Court, where the available mechanism of obtaining an interpretative ruling to settle the problem was not activated by those with the competence to do so.

[47] *Nejdet Şahin and Perihan Şahin v Turkey*, fn.11 above, paras 49–58 and 68–96.

3. Aspects of conduct of the proceedings

(a) Conduct of the judge

Besides the requirements of independence and impartiality, the conduct of the judges in the proceedings must, in principle, comply with the standard of fairness. However, the cases have so far revealed a certain reluctance to find judges at fault. In *Colak v Germany*, the Court found no unfairness in an alleged assurance to defence counsel from the President of the Assize Court that the only basis for conviction would be grievous bodily harm, although subsequently his client was convicted of attempted murder.[48] While in *Kraska v Switzerland*, where in appeal proceedings in a fraud case one of the five judges had stated in open court that he had been unable to read the file, the Court, even while noting the importance of appearances in the administration of justice, found that the applicant's standpoint was not decisive and any misgivings must also be objectively justified. It found that there was no evidence to suggest that the members of the court failed to examine the appeal with due care before taking their decision and, though the judge's comments were open to criticism, it did not give rise to any reasonable misgivings.[49] In *CG v UK*, the judge's interruptions of defence counsel's examination of witnesses were "excessive and unduly blunt", but since the applicant's counsel was never prevented from continuing his line of defence and his closing speech lasted 45 minutes, with only one brief interruption, the Court assessed that the interruptions were not such as to render the trial, viewed as a whole, unfair.[50] II–004

A failure by a court to comply with domestic procedural rules will not necessarily be fatal either. Where a judge failed as required by law to record his comments to the jury, the Commission noted that Art.6 did not lay down any requirements regarding internal court procedures which were primarily a matter for the domestic courts, although it did not exclude that non-observance of such national rules could raise an issue.[51]

(b) Appearances and incidents in the conduct of the proceedings

While the conformity of a trial with the requirements of Art.6 must be assessed on the basis of the trial as a whole, a particular incident may assume such importance as to constitute a decisive factor in the general appraisal of the trial overall. In this context there have been occasional incidents where witnesses have been arrested in open court, a dramatic intervention which might be considered to influence the views of juries in particular.[52] Where the applicant's main witness was arrested as an II–005

[48] *Colak v Germany*, December 6, 1988, Series A, No.147, 11 E.H.R.R. 513, the Court noted that the formal position was clear as to the charge before the court and counsel should have known that the Court would only rule after its deliberations.

[49] See the minority which stressed that in a democratic society the courts must inspire confidence in the public and above all the parties: the judge had indicated that he wanted to read the memorial which he regarded as pertinent and there was accordingly a doubt, which should have been decisive, that the applicant's observations had been not been properly considered by one member of the court.

[50] *CG v UK*, December 19, 2001.

[51] (13926/88) (Dec.) October 4, 1990, 66 D.R. 209, though the Commission noted sound reasons for the rule, having regard to proceedings as a whole, it concluded that they were not conducted so as to place the applicant at any disadvantage vis-à-vis the prosecution.

[52] See Pt IIA, s.13: Juries. See also *GB v France*, October 2, 2001, ECHR 2001–X, paras 69–70, where there was a dramatic "*volte face*" by an expert witness during the trial which the applicant was not given opportunity to counter and which could have lent the evidence particular weight with the jury.

accomplice during the hearing, the Commission noted that the matter of the arrest had been debated before the jury, which considered that it did not feel influenced and was able to continue, and that the applicant had not been prevented from questioning the witness by the action taken.[53]

As regards the potentially adverse effect of the handcuffing of defendants during criminal trials, the Commission criticised the practice as undesirable in public but never found the issue decisive. Where an applicant was handcuffed during his appeal, no problem of appearances arose and the Commission did not consider that it prevented him presenting his own appeal adequately.[54] Where a defendant sat in a glass cage, the Commission did not accept this stigmatised him before the court and jury as it was a permanent security feature; nor did it place him at a disadvantage as he was able to communicate with his lawyer freely.[55] In *Welch v UK*, where there was a heavy security presence at the applicant's trial, which was alleged to overdramatise his dangerousness, the Commission considered that the security arrangements had not been shown to be unnecessary or to have been stage-managed and, referring to the practical view that otherwise no trial could be held in security-risk cases, held that the precautions may have led a jury to deduce that the police considered the accused to be dangerous but that this was not the same as a presumption of guilt.[56]

Similarly, in theory, a virulent press campaign may adversely affect the fairness of a trial by influencing public opinion and consequently a jury, although to date it has yet to be shown that a campaign was likely to sway the outcome of a trial.[57]

(c) Types of trial

II–006 There is no right as such to summary trial, with whatever advantages that bestows; but where such a procedure is available, the Court will examine whether it has been arbitrarily excluded from the applicant.[58] A change in applicable procedures, which unilaterally removed the benefit of an election for summary trial which the applicant had opted for, disclosed a lack of fairness.[59] Assurances or promises by prosecutors

[53] (9000/80) (Dec.) March 11, 1982, 28 D.R. 27.
[54] (12323/86) (Dec.) July 13, 1988, 57 D.R. 148.
[55] (11837/85) (Rep.) June 7, 1990, 69 D.R. 126. See also *Ashot Harutyunyan v Armenia,* June 15, 2010, paras 136–140, where the use of the "metal cage" was found degrading under Art.3 but did not prevent the applicant from participating in the trial, as he was represented by two lawyers and able to communicate with them freely.
[56] See also security precautions strapping accused to a stretcher in *Meerbrey v Germany*, (37998/97) (Dec.) January 12, 1998, which were not considered to suggest that he was guilty.
[57] e.g. *Wloch v Poland*, (27785/95) (Dec.) March 30, 2000; *Pullicino v Malta*, (45441/99) (Dec.) June 15, 2000; *Papon v France (No.2)*, (34896/97) (Dec.) November 15, 2001, ECHR 2001–XII, where the Court noted the role of the press in contributing to the publicity of proceedings, etc, although they should not overstep the bounds imposed in the interests of the administration of justice; *Craxi v Italy (No.2)*, (34896/97) (Dec.) December 5, 2002, severe press criticism of the morality of senior government figures was accepted as inevitable, but professional judges could be expected not to be unduly influenced by the debate.
[58] *Hany v Italy*, (17543/05) (Dec.) November 6, 2007, no unfairness where summary trial was not granted as the applicant had not been present at the preliminary hearing, and had not taken proper steps to ensure he could be contacted in due form by the authorities (a telephone number in Egypt with an acquaintance was not sufficient). See also *Scoppola v Italy (No.2)*, fn.58 below.
[59] *Scoppola v Italy (No 2)*, September 17, 2009, ECHR 2009–. . .

during the proceedings which an applicant relies on and which are not kept may raise issues of fairness.[60]

4. Extent of the applicability of fairness

Fairness applies not only to the immediate conduct of proceedings before the domestic courts inter partes, but to the proceedings as a whole. Thus the intervention of the legislature to determine the outcome of pending proceedings by passing a law may violate the principle of equality of arms,[61] while intervention by other State authorities in obtaining the overturning of final judgments violates the principle of legal certainty which is part of the rule of law.[62] Execution of judgments also falls within the notion of "trial".[63] **II–007**

[60] *Mustafa (Abu Hamza) v UK*, (31411/07) (Dec.) January 18, 2011, alleged assurance of non-prosecution not made out on the facts; *Buijen v Germany*, April 1, 2010, where the prosecutor had given an assurance during the trial that the applicant could serve his sentence in the Netherlands, unfairness arose where the applicant was later unable to challenge the prosecutor's reneguing on the promise.
[61] *Stran Greek Refineries v Greece*, December 9, 1994, Series A, No.301–B, para.49.
[62] e.g. *Brumarescu v Romania*, October 28, 1999, ECHR 1999–VIII. See Pt IIA, s.2: Access to Court, sub-s.3(j): Problems of legal certainty.
[63] *Hornsby v Greece*, March 19, 1997, R.J.D. 1997–II, No.33. See Pt IIA, s.2: Access to Court, sub-s.3(h): Lack of enforcement.

1a. Criminal charge

Key provision:

II–008 Article 6, paras 1—3.

Key case-law:

Engel v Netherlands, July 8, 1976, Series A, No.22, 1 E.H.R.R 706; *Öztürk v Germany*, February 21, 1984, Series A, No.73, 6 E.H.R.R. 409; *Campbell and Fell v UK*, June 28, 1984, Series A, No.80, 7 E.H.R.R. 165; *Agosi v UK*, October 24, 1996, Series A, No.108, 9 E.H.R.R. 1; *Weber v Switzerland*, May 22, 1990, Series A, No.177, 12 E.H.R.R. 508; *Demicoli v Malta*, August 27, 1991, Series A, No.210, 14 E.H.R.R. 909; *Société Stenuit v France*, February 27, 1992, Series A, No.232–A, 14 E.H.R.R. 509; *Ravnsborg v Sweden*, March 23, 1994, Series A, No.283–B, 18 E.H.R.R. 38; *Raimondo v Italy*, February 22, 1994, Series A, No.281–A, 18 E.H.R.R. 237; *Bendenoun v France*, February 24, 1994, Series A, No.284, 18 E.H.R.R. 54; *Air Canada v UK*, May 5, 1995, Series A, No.316–A, 20 E.H.R.R. 150; *Gradinger v Austria*, October 23, 1995, Series A, No.328–C; *Putz v Austria*, February 22, 1996, R.J.D. 1996–I; *Garyfallou AEBE v Greece*, September 24, 1997, R.J.D. 1997–V, No.49; *Pierre-Bloch v France*, October 22, 1997, R.J.D. 1997–VI, No.53; *Malige v France*, September 23, 1998, R.J.D. 1998–VII, No.93; *Janosevic v Sweden*, July 23, 2002. ECHR 2002–VII; *Ezeh and Connors v UK*, October 9, 2003, ECHR 2003–X; *Jussila v Finland*, November 23, 2006, ECHR 2006–XIII; *Zolotukhin v Russia*, February 10, 2009, ECHR 2009–. . .

1. General considerations

II–009 In determining the existence of a "criminal charge" for the purposes of applying Art.6, paras 1—3, *Engel v Netherlands* established the three criteria to be read in light of the autonomy of the concept under the Convention: the classification of the offence in domestic law, the nature of the offence and the severity of the penalty. It suffices that the offence in question is "criminal" by its nature from the Convention perspective or that the offence renders the person liable to a penalty which, by its nature and degree of severity, belongs in the general criminal sphere.[1] However, where the separate analysis of each criterion does not make it possible to reach a clear conclusion, the Court may adopt a cumulative approach.[2]

The Court has begun to distinguish between charges which belong to the hard core of criminal law and those, such as tax surcharges, which do not. The criminal-head guarantees will not necessarily apply with their full stringency to the latter.[3]

2. Autonomous concept

II–010 The Court will not allow the Contracting States to re-categorise offences at will to avoid the application of Art.6 guarantees. It reserves supervisory jurisdiction over whether an offence is properly designated as disciplinary, but has commented that a

[1] The *Engel* criteria were confirmed by the Grand Chamber in *Ezeh and Connors v UK*, October 9, 2003, ECHR 2003–X, para.82 and in *Jussila v Finland*, November 23, 2006, ECHR 2006–XIII, para.30.

[2] *Bendenoun v France*, February 24, 1994, Series A, No.284, 18 E.H.R.R. 54, para.47; *Garyfallou AEBE v Greece*, September 24, 1997, R.J.D. 1997–V, No.49, para.33.

[3] *Jussila*, fn.1 above, para.43, where the proceedings involving the imposition of tax surcharges fell under the criminal head, but could be dealt with fairly without an oral hearing; *Barsom and Varli v Sweden*, (40766/06) and (40831/06) (Dec.) December 4, 2008, where legal aid for representation was not required where businessmen were challenging the imposition of a tax surcharge.

State would be free to designate as a criminal offence an act or omission not constituting the normal exercise of one of the rights that the Convention protects since such a choice renders applicable Arts 6 and 7.[4] Although in *Öztürk v Germany* the Court was not in theory opposed to decriminalisation of traffic offences to "regulatory" matters, it considered that it must nonetheless ensure that States do not act against the object and purpose of Art.6. Similarly, notwithstanding the special context of military or prison discipline, the guarantee of a fair hearing under Art.6 is one of the fundamental principles of a democratic society and any dividing line between the "disciplinary" and "criminal" sphere has to be consistent with that provision.[5]

3. The *Engel* criteria

(a) *Classification of the offence in domestic law*

This has not proved an important criterion in practice and is only a starting point.[6] It is also subject to comparison with the applicable legislation in other Contracting States. II–011

(b) *Nature of the offence*

This is a factor of "greater import".[7] The Court has regard to factors such as how the offence is regarded in other Contracting States, the procedures applied, their connection or similarity to criminal offences and procedures,[8] and whether the subject-matter constitutes an offence because of its context or because of general prohibition in the public interest.[9] However, the imposition of liability on objective grounds without the need to establish any criminal intent or neglect does not deprive an offence of its criminal character.[10] II–012

[4] *Engel v Netherlands*, July 8, 1976, Series A, No.22, 1 E.H.R.R. 706, para.81; *Société Stenuit v France*, February 27, 1992, Series A, No.232–A, 14 E.H.R.R. 509, paras 60–61, where domestic law was alleged to exclude fines on corporate bodies from being criminal.

[5] *Engel*, fn.4 above, paras 81–82; *Campbell and Fell v UK*, June 28, 1984, Series A, No.80, 7 E.H.R.R. 165, para.69; *Ezeh and Connors v UK*, fn.1 above, para.88.

[6] e.g. taxation surcharge cases such as *Janosevic v Sweden*, July 23, 2002, ECHR 2002–VII, para.66; "preventive" detention in *M v Germany*, December 17, 2009, paras 125–126, where it was noted that in some countries this was regarded as penal.

[7] *Engel*, fn.4 above, para.82; *Ezeh and Connors v UK*, fn.1 above, para.91.

[8] e.g. *Gradinger v Austria*, October 23, 1995, Series A, No.328–C, where the terminology of administrative "criminal" offences was noted; *Steel v UK*, September 23, 1998, R.J.D. 1998–VII, No.91, para.48, where breach of the peace was not classed as criminal but the nature of the proceedings, with the applicable penalties, rendered it such.

[9] In *Campbell and Fell*, fn.5 above, the Court examined whether the conduct was only an offence because it was committed in prison, or whether it was also prohibited by the criminal law (e.g. mutiny and incitement was akin to conspiracy), which could give a "certain colouring" beyond that of a purely disciplinary matter; *Société Stenuit*, fn.4 above, (Rep.) para.62, where the ministerial imposition of a heavy fine on a company was for infringement of economic legislation which affected the general interests of society normally protected by criminal law; *Bendenoun*, fn.2 above, where tax penalties applied to all citizens under a general rule. Conversely see (7341/76) (Dec.) March 4, 1978, 15 D.R. 35, a refusal to obey an order (fatigues) was clearly a disciplinary matter, based on internal operating rules of the armed forces as was five days' isolation as punishment of a soldier for late return in (7754/77) (Dec.) May 9, 1977, 11 D.R. 216.

[10] *Janosevic*, fn.6 above, para.68.

Offences which serve by their nature to guarantee the protection of human dignity and public order normally fall within the sphere of protection of criminal law.[11]

A distinction is often drawn between offences applicable to persons under a specific regime or group with a special status and those affecting potentially the whole population. For example, criminal offences were at stake in *Weber v Switzerland*, where contempt of court, applied to a journalist unconnected with the trial, was not regarded as part of the internal functioning of the court, and in *Demicoli v Malta*, where breach of privilege, applied to a journalist's external publication about a member of the legislature, was not a matter of internal parliamentary discipline. In *Ravnsborg v Sweden*, however, the Court noted that the applicant was fined as a party in domestic proceedings, which contempt provisions did not apply to persons making statements outside those proceedings. Sanctions imposed on persons participating in proceedings pursuant to court powers to ensure the orderly conduct of the proceedings are therefore likely to fall outside the criminal sphere[12] unless the penalty is severe enough to attract the guarantees of Art.6.[13] Disciplinary proceedings against lawyers and doctors accordingly will not become criminal where confined to an essentially disciplinary context, even where the fine can be described as punitive in size.[14] Where an official was fined for failures in safety procedures in his job in the railway and then tried for causing damage by fire, the Court found it was a disciplinary offence applying only to those fulfilling particular functions.[15]

Where tax surcharges are not intended as pecuniary compensation for any costs incurred as a result of the taxpayer's conduct but are predominantly punitive and deterrent, they have been found to disclose a criminal character.[16]

As concerns detention for recidivism or where the person is regarded as dangerous and bound to re-offend, the fact that the primary intended purpose of the detention is preventive does not deprive it of a punitive character, as both preventive and punitive detention had overlapping aims of prevention and rehabilitation. The Court noted that the unlimited nature of the detention was a deterrent and that it had been imposed, and was supervised, by courts in the criminal justice system.[17]

The lack of seriousness of minor offences, as in careless driving in *Öztürk*, may not divest offences of their criminal character.[18] In *Öztürk*, the Court had regard to the character of the rule, noting that it was still criminal in other countries and aimed at the public generally.[19]

[11] *Zolotukhin v Russia*, February 10, 2009, ECHR 2009–. . ., para.55, "minor disorderly acts" were criminal despite their domestic "administrative" label.

[12] *Putz v Austria*, February 22, 1996, R.J.D. 1996–I, para.33, concerning fines imposed on the applicant by a court for disrupting the proceedings, which fell outside Art.6.

[13] *Zaicevs v Latvia*, July 31, 2007, para.33, imposition of three days' administrative detention for contempt of court was "penal" by nature, not disciplinary.

[14] e.g. *Irving Brown v UK*, (38644/97) (Dec.) November 24, 1998, where a solicitor was fined £10,000.

[15] *Kurdov and Ivanov v Bulgaria*, May 31, 2011, paras 38–46.

[16] *Janosevic*, fn.6 above, para.68.

[17] *M v Germany*, fn.6 above, paras 127–131.

[18] See also *Ezeh and Connors v UK*, fn.1 above, para.104, the criminal nature of the offence does not necessarily require a certain degree of seriousness, while the severity of the penalty falls under the third criteria.

[19] See also *Schmautzer v Austria*, October 23, 1995, Series A, No.328–A (fine for not wearing seatbelt); *Umlauft v Austria*, October 23, 1995, Series A, No.328–B (refusal to give breath sample); *Malige v France*, September 23, 1998, R.J.D. 1998–VII, No.93 (loss of points on driving licence).

(c) Severity of the penalty

The Court looks at the nature and purpose of the penalty "liable to be imposed" on the applicant. While the actual penalty imposed is stated to be relevant, this is not seen as diminishing the importance of what was initially at stake.[20] Regard is had to the nature and purpose of the penalty, in particular whether it is intended to be deterrent and punitive.[21] Deprivation of liberty as a penalty (excepting measures which by length or nature are not appreciably detrimental)[22] generally belongs to the criminal sphere, bearing in mind the seriousness of what is at stake and the importance attached to physical liberty.[23] Indeed, where the penalty liable to be, and is actually, imposed on an applicant involves the loss of liberty, there is a presumption that the charges against the applicant are "criminal", a presumption which can be rebutted entirely exceptionally.[24] The threat of imprisonment may also be decisive. In *Engel*, the fact an applicant received a penalty not occasioning deprivation of liberty did not affect the Court's assessment since the final outcome of the appeal could not diminish the importance of what was initially at stake.[25] In *Campbell and Fell v UK*, loss of remission of almost three years, even though remission was a privilege rather than a right, was taken into account since it had the effect of extending the expected period of detention and came close to deprivation of liberty. The Court found that the object and purpose of the Convention required that imposition of a measure of such severity attracts guarantees of Art.6. This approach has been reinforced in *Ezeh and Connors v UK*, where the imposition of additional days on prisoners for punitive reasons after a finding of culpability was found to be a criminal penalty in nature and degree, notwithstanding that it did not increase a prisoner's sentence as a matter of law but affected the calculation of the release date. It referred to the test of whether the effective deprivation of liberty was "appreciably detrimental" in nature and found that the maximum period of 42 days imposable, and the actual penalty of 40 and seven days, respectively, crossed this threshold. Three days' so-called administrative detention has qualified also.[26] **II–013**

Where fines are concerned, consideration is given to whether they are intended as pecuniary compensation for damage or essentially as a punishment to deter re-

[20] *Ezeh and Connors v UK*, fn.1 above, para.120.

[21] *Öztürk v Germany*, February 21, 1984, Series A, No.73, 6 E.H.R.R. 409, para.53; *Steel* (Rep.), fn.8 above, para.67, where proceedings for breach of the peace leading to binding over were criminal in nature, as deterrent (requiring the person to keep the peace) and punitive (since if person did not agree he was imprisoned).

[22] *Engel v Netherlands*, where for one applicant a risk of two days' strict arrest for absence without leave was considered too short a duration and for another, four days' light arrest did not constitute deprivation of liberty; *Brandao Ferreira v Portugal*, (41921/98) (Dec.) September 28, 2000, ECHR 2000–X, five days' simple arrest where the applicant continued to discharge most of his duties was considered not severe enough.

[23] *Engel*, fn.4 above, para.82; *Campbell and Fell*, fn.5 above, para.72.

[24] *Zolotukhin v Russia,* para.56.

[25] *Engel*, where three applicants faced risk of three to four months committal to disciplinary unit; *Demicoli*, where the applicant, though only fined for breach of privilege, risked imprisonment of 60 days; *Weber*, where the applicant was at risk of a fine of 500 Swiss Francs for contempt, convertible in certain circumstances into a period of imprisonment; *Gradinger*, a fine for drink driving with prison in default.

[26] *Zolotukhin v Russia*, fn.11 above, paras 56–57, three days' administrative detention imposed, a fifteen day maximum at stake; *Zaicevs*, fn.13, paras 34–36, three days' administrative detention.

offending.[27] In *Öztürk*, where the applicant was only fined 60 DM, the Court referred to the purpose of the penalty being to deter and punish. In other cases, where considerations as to the non-criminal nature of the offence weighed more heavily, larger fines have not been decisive.[28] Further, the minor nature of the penalty cannot be decisive in removing an offence, otherwise criminal by nature, from the scope of Art.6.[29] Forfeiture measures have not been regarded as criminal penalties[30] nor have preventive measures or the application of personal security measures.[31] Confiscation orders, which are conditional on criminal convictions, and are deterrent in nature and purpose, rather than preventive, have been found to constitute "penalties" under Art.6, as well as Art.7 which prohibits retrospective criminal penalties.[32] A payment order imposed on an electoral candidate for exceeding the limit on campaign expenses was found by the Court to be a payment to the community of the sum by which the applicant improperly took advantage to seek votes and thus not a criminal penalty akin to a fine.[33]

The docking of points from a licence imposed in the context of, and as the outcome of criminal proceedings, was seen as punitive and deterrent in character and also, impliedly, serious as it could lead in time to the invalidation of the licence. Art.6 therefore applied to the procedure.[34]

Educational measures imposed on drivers, involving costs and loss of licence in case of failure to comply, were not criminal where imposed separately from criminal

[27] e.g. *Benedoun*, fn.2 above, para.47, where tax penalties were not intended as compensation for pecuniary damage but as punishment to deter re-offending; *Société Stenuit*, para.64, where sanctions were imposable on a company equal to up to 5 per cent of its turnover, it indicated that it was intended to be deterrent; cf. *Shirley Porter v UK*, (15814/02) (Dec.) April 8, 2003, where the surcharge imposed on the applicant for wilful misconduct as leader of a council reflected the loss suffered by the local authority.

[28] *Ravnsborg v Sweden*, March 23, 1994, Series A, No.283–B, 18 E.H.R.R. 38, which involved three fines of 1000 Kroner for contempt, convertible to imprisonment by the court in limited circumstances when the applicant would be summoned to an oral hearing in separate proceedings—also the fines were not registered on police files as other criminal "fines" were; *Putz*, fn.12 above, fines were convertible but only up to 10 days, not entered on the record and appeals were possible; *Bendenoun*, fn.2 above, where the substantial fines of 400,000–500,000 FRF were not decisive in themselves; *Shirley Porter*, fn.27 above, where the sheer size of the surcharge (millions of pounds) did not render it criminal.

[29] *Jussila*, fn.1 above, para.35, overruling *Morel v France*, (54559/00) (Dec.) June 3, 2003, ECHR 2003–IX, concerning a minor tax surcharge of some €300.

[30] *Butler v UK*, (41661/98) (Dec.) June 27, 2002, ECHR 2002–VI, forfeiture of large amounts of cash under drug trafficking legislation was preventive in nature; *Agosi v UK*, October 24, 1996, Series A, No.108, 9 E.H.R.R. 1, (seizure and forfeiture of kruegerrands by Customs); *Air Canada v UK*, May 5, 1995, Series A, No.316–A, 20 E.H.R.R. (Customs seizure of an aircraft, released on payment of £50,000). Where property or pecuniary rights are concerned, however, Art.6 in its civil aspect is likely to apply.

[31] e.g. *Raimondo v Italy*, February 22, 1994, Series A, No.281–A, 18 E.H.R.R. 237, para.43, special supervision, including confiscation of property of the applicant on grounds of suspicion of membership in a mafia-type organisation; *Riela v Italy*, (52349/99) (Dec.) September 4, 2001 (preventive and confiscatory measures); *Guzzardi v Italy*, November 6, 1980, Series A, No.39, para.108 (compulsory residence requirements).

[32] *Welch v UK*, February 9, 1995, Series A, No.307–A, 20 E.H.R.R. 247 (Art.7); *Phillips v UK*, July 5, 2001, ECHR 2001–VII, (Art.6); contrast *Walsh v UK*, (43384/05) (Dec.) November 21, 2006, where assets were recovered as the proceeds of crime outside any criminal procedure; and *Saccoccia v Austria*, (69917/01) (Dec.) July 5, 2007, where forfeiture proceedings in Austria following criminal proceedings in the US were found not to involve a "criminal charge" themselves.

[33] *Pierre-Bloch v France*, October 22, 1997, R.J.D. 1997–VI, No.53, para.58.

[34] *Malige*, fn.19 above, paras 38–40; contrast *Escoubet v Belgium*, October 28, 1999, ECHR 1999–VII, where Art.6 was not applicable to the short-term provisional withdrawal of a driving licence prior to the applicant being charged with an offence.

proceedings and independently of any conviction.[35] A bar on holding certain legal, public or political office for ten years was found at least to be partly punitive and deterrent in character, as it could have a very serious impact on a person, depriving him or her of the possibility of continuing professional life.[36] Where proceedings for an infraction, through building of a holiday home without permission, resulted in a finding of guilt and an order to restore the site to its previous condition (demolition in otherwords), the Court was not persuaded that the measure was "reparative", finding that the classification, nature and penalty disclosed the criminal character of the proceedings.[37]

4. Proceedings excluded from Art.6: "criminal aspect"

The following have not been found "criminal": II–014

- proceedings which relate to issues of lawfulness of detention where the *lex specialis* is Art.5[38] or to the execution of sentences[39];
- decisions to deport an alien[40] or to exclude an alien, even where imposed in the context of criminal proceedings, are regarded as special preventive measures of the purposes of immigration control[41];
- extradition proceedings, since these do not involve the full process of determining guilt of a criminal offence themselves[42];
- proceedings in execution of a European arrest warrant[43];
- proceedings for transfer of a prisoner to serve his sentence in another country[44];
- decisions by courts on extradition requests, even where there is an assessment as to whether there is a case to answer[45];
- restrictions placed by the Secretary of State on activities in running insurance companies[46];
- proceedings ancillary or associated with criminal proceedings which are not decisive for the determination of the criminal charge, e.g. applications for legal aid[47] or Constitutional Court proceedings which are not capable of affecting the outcome[48];

[35] *Blokker v Netherlands*, (45282/99) (Dec.) November 7, 2000.
[36] *Matyjek v Poland*, (38184/03) (Dec.) May 30, 2006, concerning lustration proceedings.
[37] *Hamer v Belgium*, November 27, 2007, paras 59–63.
[38] e.g. (6541/74) (Dec.) December 18, 1974, 1 D.R. 82; *Reinprecht v Austria*, November 15, 2005, para.48, review of lawfulness of pre-trial detention.
[39] *Aydin v Turkey*, (41954/98) (Dec.) September 14, 2000.
[40] e.g. *Agee v UK*, (7729/76) (Dec.) December. 17, 1976, 7 D.R. 64.
[41] *Maaouia v France*, October 5, 2000, ECHR 2000–X, para.39.
[42] *Al-Moayad v Germany*, (35865/03) (Dec.) February 20, 2007, paras 93–94.
[43] *Monedero Angora v Spain*, (41138/05) (Dec.) October 7, 2008.
[44] *Erno Szabo v Sweden*, (28578/03) (Dec.) June 27, 2006; contrast *Buijen v Germany*, April 1, 2010, where the prosecutor had given an assurance during the actual trial that the applicant could serve his sentence in the Netherlands, the subsequent proceedings concerning the transfer in which the prosecutor renegued on his undertaking were regarded as so closely linked to the trial proceedings as, exceptionally, to attract the application of Art.6.
[45] (10479/83) (Dec.) March 12, 1984, 37 D.R. 158; *Penafiel Salgado v Spain*, (65964/01) (Dec.) April 16, 2002.
[46] (7598/76) (Dec.) July 17, 1980 21 D.R. 5.
[47] *Gutfreund v France*, June 12, 2003, the procedure was separate from the criminal trial and did not involve the establishment of guilt, the fixing of sentence or establishment of facts.
[48] *Gast and Popp v Germany*, February 25, 2000, ECHR 2000–II, paras 63–68.

- applications for re-opening of proceedings, retrial, nullity or amnesty[49]; complaints concerning refusal by a court of a re-opening after a judgment of the Court finding a breach of Art.6[50];
- proceedings under s.4A of the Criminal Procedure (Insanity) Act 1964 where the applicant has been found unfit to plead and the procedure, aimed at establishing the facts, cannot result in a conviction[51];
- imposition of a warning on a juvenile under the Crime and Disorder Act 1998[52];
- proceedings under the Local Government Finance Act 1982, reclaiming as surcharges the amount of money lost by the local authority due to an officer's wilful misconduct[53];
- imposition of interest for late tax payments[54];
- administrative fines for carrying out work on a house without planning permission[55]; and
- publication of information in the press given by the police about the applicant's suspect status in a murder enquiry.[56]

Cross-reference

Part IIA, s.17: Length of proceedings (duration of "criminal charge").
Part IIA, s.22: Retrospectivity (penalties).
Part IIB, s.3: Armed forces, sub-s.2: Military discipline.

[49] e.g. *Fischer v Austria*, (27569/02) (Dec.) May 6, 2003 (retrial or plea of nullity); *Montcornet de Caumont v France*, (59290/00) (Dec.) May 13, 20000 (amnesty).
[50] *Ocalan v Turkey*, (5980/07) (Dec.) July 6, 2010.
[51] *Antoine v UK*, (62960/00) (Dec.) May 13, 2003.
[52] *R v UK*, (33506/05) (Dec.) January 4, 2007.
[53] *Shirley Porter*, fn.27 above.
[54] *Boofzheim v France*, (52938/99) ECHR 2002–X.
[55] *Inocencio v Portugal*, (43862/98) (Dec.) January 11, 2001; contrast *Hamer*, fn.37 above.
[56] *A v Norway*, April 9, 2009, paras 46–47.

1b. Civil rights and obligations

Key provision:

Article 6, para.1. II–015

Key case-law:

Lecompte, Van Leuven and De Meyere v Belgium, June 23, 1981, Series A, No.43, 4 E.H.R.R. 1; *Sporrong and Llönnroth v Sweden*, September 23, 1982, Series A, No.52, 5 E.H.R.R. 35; *Benthem v Netherlands*, October 23, 1985, Series A, No.97, 8 E.H.R.R. 1; *Feldbrugge v Netherlands*, May 29, 1986, Series A, No.99, 8 E.H.R.R. 425; *Deumeland v Germany*, May 29, 1986, Series A, No.100, 8 E.H.R.R. 448; *Van Marle v Netherlands*, June 26, 1986, Series A, No.101, 8 E.H.R.R. 483; *W v UK*, July 8, 1987, Series A, No.121, 10 E.H.R.R. 29; *Pudas v Sweden*, October 27, 1987, Series A, No.125, 10 E.H.R.R. 380; *H v Belgium*, November 30, 1987, Series A, No.127, 10 E.H.R.R. 339; *Tre Traktorer v Sweden*, July 7, 1989, Series A, No.159, 13 E.H.R.R. 309; *Allan Jacobsson v Sweden (No.1)*, October 25, 1989, Series A, No.163, 12 E.H.R.R 56; *Fredin v Sweden (No.1)*, February 18, 1991, Series A, No.192, 13 E.H.R.R. 784; *Kraska v Switzerland*, April 19, 1993, Series A, No.254–B, 18 E.H.R.R. 188; *Ruiz-Mateos v Spain*, June 23, 1993, Series A, No.262, 16 E.H.R.R. 505; *Schuler-Zraggen v Switzerland*, June 24, 1993, Series A, No.263, 16 E.H.R.R. 405; *Schouten and Meldrum v Netherlands*, December 9, 1994, Series A, No.304, 19 E.H.R.R. 432; *Procola v Luxembourg*, September 28, 1995, Series A, No.326, 22 E.H.R.R. 193; *Masson and Van Zon v Netherlands*, September 28, 1995, Series A, No.327–A, 22 E.H.R.R. 491; *Süssman v Germany*, September 16, 1996, R.J.D. 1996–IV, No.15; *Georgiadis v Greece*, May 29, R.J.D. 1997–III, No.38; *Rolf Gustafsson v Sweden*, August 1, 1997, R.J.D. 1997–IV, No.41; *Pierre-Bloch v France*, October 22, 1997, R.J.D. 1997–VI, No.53; *Maaouia v France*, October 5, 2000, ECHR 2000–X; *Z v UK*, May 10, 2001, ECHR 2001–V; *Ferrazzini v Italy*, July 12, 2001, ECHR 2001–VII; *Roche v UK*, October 19, 2005, ECHR 2005–X; *Eskelinen v Finland*, April 19, 2007, ECHR 2007–II; *Enea v Italy*, September 17, 2009, ECHR 2009. . . ; *Micallef v Malta*, October 15, 2009, ECHR 2009–. . .

1. General considerations

Outside the criminal sphere, the guarantees of fair trial under Art.6, para.1 apply only to proceedings which involve the determination of "civil rights and obligations". This includes a number of considerations: the rights or obligations must at least, on arguable grounds, exist in domestic law; there must be a dispute or "contestation" about those rights and obligations of a "genuine and of a serious nature" and which is decisive for those rights; and the rights claimed must be "civil" in nature. II–016

Interpretation has been progressive in this area. Matters which once were considered as outside the scope of Art.6, para.1, such as welfare benefits, now generally fall inside the notion of "civil rights and obligations". The concepts applied are wide and capable of application to almost any type of significant dispute.

2. Basis in domestic law

II–017 Article 6 does not guarantee any particular content for "rights and obligations" in the substantive law of Contracting States. There must at least, on arguable grounds, be a basis for the right in domestic law,[1] while matters at the total discretion of the authorities may not disclose a "right".[2] In assessing whether a "right" is at stake, the Court has stated that the starting point must be the provisions of the relevant domestic law and their interpretation by the domestic courts and that where superior national courts have conducted a comprehensive and convincing analysis on the basis of relevant Convention case-law and principles, it would need strong reasons to differ from the conclusion reached by those courts on a question of interpretation of domestic law.[3] The existence of an unfettered discretion may be indicative of the absence of a right, in particular where the needs or situation of the claimant is irrelevant to the outcome of the evaluation of the authorities.[4]

Where legislative provisions on tendering for public contracts expressly excluded that they extended a right and specified that there was no obligation on the authorities to accept the lowest bid, the Court considered that the evaluation of tenders was an "administrative act"; the fact that it had economic consequences for the applicant company was not enough to bestow any right.[5] In the context of religious organisations, the Court has recognised that internal matters of churches may well be kept independent from the State; rules whereby a priest could be transferred without his consent indicated that there was no "right" at stake when he contested the transfer. The availability of an extraordinary appeal to the Supreme Administrative Court did not alter this position.[6]

Where in childcare cases the Government claimed that parental rights resolutions had the effect in domestic law of extinguishing parental rights of access, the Court noted that the effect of the measures did not extinguish all parental rights in respect of a child, which in any event would hardly have been compatible with fundamental rights of family life under Art.8. Having regard to statutory recognition that parental access was desirable, it found that there was at least, on arguable grounds, a right of access in domestic law. It would seem that, where parent-child relationships are concerned, the Convention organs will be reluctant to find no right existing in domestic law on an underlying assumption that such matters are of

[1] e.g. *Z v UK*, May 10, 2001, ECHR 2001–V, paras 87 and 98; *Roche v UK*, October 19, 2005, ECHR 2005–X, para.119.

[2] e.g. *Masson and Van Zon v Netherlands*, September 28, 1995, Series A, No.327–A, 22 E.H.R.R. 491, where compensation for costs in criminal proceedings ending in an acquittal were at the discretion of the courts; (16484/90) (Dec.) January 17, 1991, where the applicant could not claim a right to obtain a licence in Gibraltar to operate a fast launch; (11098/84) (Dec.) July 1, 1985, 43 D.R. 198, where compensation for criminal injuries was ex gratia.

[3] *Roche*, fn.1 above, para.120. See e.g. *Oao Poldovaya Komaniya v Russia*, June 7, 2007, para.35, no civil right where the applicant company claimed a right of corporate succession without any basis in domestic law.

[4] *Ladbrokes Worldwide Betting v Sweden*, (27968/05) (Dec.) May 6, 2008, no right to be granted a permit to carry out gambling activities under domestic law.

[5] *I.T.C. v Malta*, (2629/06) (Dec.) December 11, 2007, nor was it relevant that a tenderer had a right to object to the award of the contract at a public hearing; this was a right of a public nature; contrast *Arac v Turkey*, September 21, 2006, para.21, a right was at stake where an applicant was excluded totally from the public tender market due to alleged discimination.

[6] *Ahtinen v Finland*, September 23, 2008, paras 39–43, citing also *Duda and Dudová v Czech Republic*, (40224/98) (Dec.) January 30, 2001.

fundamental importance.[7] Similar considerations might apply where proceedings concern serious interferences with other fundamental rights guaranteed under the Convention.

The nature of compensation claims is such that, regardless of their characterisation under domestic law, they are likely to be regarded as creating rights for the victims where they have complied with the eligibility conditions and in those circumstances their claims cannot be regarded as ex gratia.[8]

Merely because a claim is not found to concern legitimate expectation of enjoyment of a property right for the purposes of Art.1 of Protocol No.1 does not mean automatically that there is no arguable basis for a "right" under Art.6.[9]

3. Dispute or "contestation" concerning rights and obligations

This element which is derived from the French text of Art.6, is not to be construed too technically, and to be given a substantive, rather than formal, meaning.[10] A tenuous connection or remote consequences between the dispute and the right does not suffice.[11] Civil rights or obligations must be the object, or one of the objects, of the dispute and the result of the proceedings must be directly decisive for such a right[12] or, as is sometimes stated, involve the determination of the right. For that reason, interim orders which do not substantially affect the legal position of the applicant are not considered as covered.[13] Where the legal position of the applicant is substantially affected, or the interim measure requested disposes of the main issues to a considerable degree, Art.6, para.1 may well apply, as in *Micallef v Malta* where the interim injunction procedure determined the same right as was being contested in the main proceedings and was immediately enforceable.[14] Non-contentious proceedings may also attract Art.6 where they are decisive for the effective exercise of rights.[15] Application to a public prosecutor for him to exercise an appeal may be II–018

[7] See however *Price v UK*, (12402/86) (Dec.) July 14, 1988, 55 D.R. 224, no rights in domestic law were found in favour of grandparental access to children.

[8] *Rolf Gustafsson v Sweden*, August 1, 1997, R.J.D. 1997–IV, where the Court found domestic law conferred a right to compensation where certain conditions were fulfilled; see also *Wos v Poland*, June 8, 2006, ECHR 2006–IV, concerning a claim for compensation for forced labour during the Second World War; and *CB v UK*, (35512/04) (Dec.) August 25, 2005, finding Art.6 applicable to the Criminal Injuries Compensation Scheme in the UK; contrast *Associazione Nazionale Reduci Dalla Prigionia dall'Internamento e dalla Guerra di Liberazione v Italy*, (45563/04) (Dec.) September 4, 2007, applicants were not within any category to which compensation for forced labour was granted.

[9] *JS and AS v Poland*, May 24, 2005, para.51; *Kopecky v Slovakia*, September 28, 2004, para.52.

[10] *Lecompte, Van Leuven and De Meyere v Belgium*, June 23, 1981, Series A, No.43; 4 E.H.R.R. 1, para.45.

[11] *Lecompte*, fn.10 above, para.47.

[12] *Lecompte*, fn.10 above, para.47; *Balmer-Schafroth v Switzerland*, August 26, 1997, R.J.D. 1997–IV, No.43, para.32.

[13] e.g. the procedure for the designation of experts adopted prior to the proceedings on the merits was not covered: *Kress v France*, (39594/98) (Dec.) February 29, 2000; attachment of assets to safeguard the position of possible claimants: *Dogmoch v Germany*, (26315/03) (Dec.) August 9, 2006; contrast *Markass Car Hire Ltd v Cyprus*, (51591/99) (Dec.) October 23, 2001, where the interim order (requiring the applicant to hand over most of his fleet of lorries to the claimant) was regarded as drastic, causing irreversible prejudice to the applicant's interests and substantially draining the final outcome of the proceedings of significance: Art.6 applied.

[14] See also *Mercieca v Malta*, June 14, 2011, para.34, Art.6 applied to an interlocutory appeal since the issues at stake could have determined the dispute.

[15] *Buj v Croatia*, June 1, 2006, where there had been delay in the Land Registry inscribing the applicant's inheritance rights.

regarded, in light of the realities of a particular legal system, as being an integral part of the proceedings and related to a "dispute" for the purposes of Art.6.[16]

A dispute can for these purposes concern not only the actual existence of the right but the scope of the right or its manner of exercise.[17] It may concern both questions of fact and law.[18]

The dispute must also be of a "genuine and serious nature".[19] For example, where an applicant complained about the amount of child maintenance imposed by the Child Support Agency, the Commission noted that there was no provision for the costs of access visits to be taken into account as the applicant claimed and that he did not deny that the assessment had been correctly made under the legislation. Thus there was no dispute, or any dispute of a genuine or serious nature, about any civil right or obligation.[20] In *Van Marle v Netherlands*, the Court found no dispute where the applicants had been refused registration as certified accountants following an examination of their competence. It considered that there were no claims of irregularity in the procedure and that assessments involving the evaluation of knowledge and experience for carrying on a profession were akin to school or university examinations and as such were removed from normal judicial functions. Conversely, in *H v Belgium*, where the applicant had been struck off from the Bar and refused reinstatement, the Court found a dispute capable of judicial assessment, having regard to the terms of the regulations which allowed reinstatement in "exceptional circumstances" which left scope for a variety of interpretations and under which the applicant could arguably claim the right to practise at the Bar since he fulfilled the conditions.

The Court has stated that Art.6, para.1 can be relied on where an applicant claims that an interference with the exercise of a civil right is unlawful.[21] Thus in cases where, notwithstanding the wide discretion imposed on public authorities in the imposition of measures, applicants were able to challenge the lawfulness of the measures in the most general sense, a "dispute" arose. Although it may be noted that the authorities' discretion was not totally unfettered since they were bound by generally recognised legal and administrative principles.[22] However, allegations of unlawfulness will not in themselves be sufficient if the applicant fails to show the requisite personal prejudice or interference with his individual rights which could, at least on arguable grounds, call for an award of compensation under the applicable domestic law: in those circumstances there may be no serious or genuine dispute.[23]

Recognition is now apparent of the legitimate interests of associations and concerned citizens in bringing actions challenging decisions with environmental

[16] *Gorou v Greece (No.2)*, March 20, 2009, paras 32–36.

[17] e.g. *Lecompte*, fn.10 above, para.47, thus Art.6 applied even though the right to practise medicine was not removed but only briefly suspended.

[18] e.g. *Pudas v Sweden*, October 27, 1987, Series A, No.125, 10 E.H.R.R. 380, para.31.

[19] *Benthem v Netherlands*, October 23, 1985, Series A, No.97, 8 E.H.R.R. 1, para.32.

[20] (24875/94) (Dec.) September 9, 1996, 86–A D.R. 74.

[21] *Lecompte*, fn.10 above, para.44.

[22] *Pudas*, fn.18 above, para.34; *Allan Jacobsson v Sweden (No.1)*, October 25, 1989, Series A, No.163, 12 E.H.R.R. 56, para.69; *Tre Traktorer v Sweden*, July 7, 1989, Series A, No.159, 13 E.H.R.R. 309, paras 39–40: e.g. where applicants alleged improper motives by the authorities, departure from long-standing practice, failure to take their interests into account, discrimination, abuse of power, which was regarded as raising issues of lawfulness; *Mendel v Sweden*, April 7, 2009, paras 44–46, a Board's discretion to include or reject jobseekers from an employment programme was not unfettered, governed by tangible criteria: thus, a dispute of a "right" existed where the applicant's participation was revoked; it was also closely linked to allowances and subsistence, with serious economic consequences for the applicant.

[23] *Skorbogatykh v Russia*, (37966/02) (Dec.) June 8, 2006.

impact. Thus, there was a dispute about rights where a local association challenged planning permission to extend a large rubbish dump; the Court distinguished claims based on the "general interest" from an "*actio popularis*"; in that particular case, the members of the association lived locally and thus had a personal stake in the issues raised.[24]

4. Civil nature of the right or obligation

The concept of "civil rights and obligations" is not to be interpreted solely by reference to the respondent State's domestic law but is an autonomous notion based on the character of the right.[25] Article 6, para.1 also applies irrespective of the status of the parties, the character of the legislation which governs how the dispute is to be determined and the character of the authority which is invested with jurisdiction in the matter, the key point being whether the outcome of the proceedings is decisive for private rights and obligations.[26] **II–019**

The Court has regard to the private and personal nature of the right, whether it is connected with contractual relationships,[27] connected with the exercise or enjoyment of property rights[28] or the exercise of commercial, business or professional activities,[29] or whether the subject-matter of the action is pecuniary in nature and founded on infringement of rights of a pecuniary nature[30] or employment contracts.[31] For example, in *Pudas v Sweden*, where the applicant taxi-driver's taxi

[24] *L"Erablière ASBL v Belgium*, February 24, 2009, paras 24–30.

[25] e.g. *Konig v Germany*, June 28, 1978, Series A, No.27, paras 88–89; *Baraona v Portugal*, July 8, 1987, Series A, No.122, paras 42–43, it was not decisive that Portuguese law distinguished between acts of private and public administration, where the right in issue was a personal property right.

[26] *Ringeisen v Austria*, July 16, 1971, Series A, No.13, 1 E.H.R.R. 455, para.94; *Editions Periscope v France*, March 26, 1992, Series A, No.234, para.40, where it was not decisive that the dispute originated in the State's role in levying tax and fell under the administrative courts; *Martinie v France*, (58675/00) (Dec.) January 13, 2004, ECHR 2004–II, where liability of public accountants for repaying losses to State institutions was found akin to tort although under the jurisdiction of special administrative courts.

[27] *Lecompte*, fn.10 above, para.48, concerning where a profession is conducted by means of private relationships with clients on a contractual or quasi-contractual nature, even if exercised in the public interest with special duties, e.g. medical profession.

[28] e.g. *Baraona*, fn.25 above, para.44; property cases, e.g. *Sporrong and Llonroth v Sweden*, September 23, 1982, Series A, No.52, 5 E.H.R.R. 35, para.79 (imposition of expropriation permit); *Fredin v Sweden (No.1)*, February 18, 1991, Series A, No.192, 13 E.H.R.R. 784, para.63 (revocation of permit to exploit gravel pit); *Ortenberg v Austria*, November 25, 1994, Series A, No.295–B, 19 E.H.R.R. 193 (public law objections to planning permission granted by authorities to owners of neighbouring land); *Alatulkkila v Finland*, July 28, 2005 (fishing rights attached to ownership of waters).

[29] *Benthem*, fn.19 above, para.36, concerning the refusal to the owner of a garage of a licence to install a LPG storage tank to supply motor vehicles; *Tre Traktorer*, fn.22 above, para.43, finding that revocation of a restaurant licence to serve alcohol had adverse effects on the goodwill and value of the business and that the serving of alcohol was a private commercial activity based on the earning of profits and contractual relationships; *H v Belgium*, November 30, 1987, Series A, No.127, 10 E.H.R.R. 339, right to practise as an advocate; *Voggenreiter v Germany*, January 8, 2004, occupation in freight traffic.

[30] e.g. *Editions Periscope*, fn.26 above. However, this is to be distinguished from proceedings which merely have an economic aspect, e.g. *Pierre-Bloch v France*, October 22, 1997, R.J.D. 1997–VI, No.53, para.51, or which involve tax or normal civic obligations: *Martinie*, cited above, fn.26, citing *Ferrazzini v Italy*, July 12, 2001, ECHR 2001–VII, para.25 and *Shouten and Meldrum v Netherlands*, December 9, 1994, Series A, No.304, 19 E.H.R.R. 432, para.50.

[31] e.g. *Cudak v Lithuania*, March 23, 2010, paras 45–46, claims for wrongful dismissal covered. Proceedings even indirectly linked with employment appear to be covered e.g. *Koottummel v Austria*, December 10, 2009, concerning refusal of an employer's application for an employment permit for an overseas worker.

licence was revoked, this was clearly civil, having regard to its connection with his business activities, carried out with the object of earning profits and based on contractual relationships with customers. State regulation of certain activities in the public interest, e.g. transport or sale of alcohol or the practice of law, may bestow features of public law but will not suffice to exclude private commercial activities from the category of civil rights.[32] While there is no right to revenge, where an applicant lodged a criminal complaint of defamation with a civil party claim of a nominal €3, the Court considered that this claim vindicated her civil right to reputation and involved a pecuniary element, even if symbolic.[33]

Proceedings for compensation generally have a private law character even where derived from public law or criminal proceedings.[34] Where the outcome of constitutional or public law proceedings may be decisive for civil rights and obligations, such proceedings, even if before the Constitutional Court, will fall within the scope of Art.6, para.1. In *Ruiz-Mateos v Spain*, the Court noted that the constitutional proceedings challenging a law were the sole means available to the applicants to complain of an interference with their property rights by an expropriation decree. Application to the *Conseil d'Etat* for the annulment of orders fixing milk quotas in *Procola v Luxembourg* was closely connected by its possible outcome to the pecuniary rights and economic activities of the applicant agricultural association.[35]

In the areas of social security or State benefits, the Court's examination previously centred on whether the private law or public law features were of greater significance.[36] Particular weight has been given to the similarity between social security schemes and private insurance as lending a private law character. Links with contracts of employment have also been emphasised. In the cases so far considered by the Court these private law features have outweighed the public law elements present, such as the character of the legislation, assumption of responsibility by public authorities, and the compulsory nature of the schemes.[37] In *Schuler-Zgraggen v Switzerland* the Court stated that as a general rule Art.6, para.1 applied in the field of social insurance and that the most important consideration militating in favour of applicability was that the applicant had suffered an interference with her means of subsistence and was claiming "an individual, economic right flowing from the specific rules laid down in domestic law".[38] While this approach was stated not to

[32] e.g. *Pudas*, fn.18 above, para.37; *Tre Traktorer*, fn.22 above, para.43; *H v Belgium*, fn.29 above, where advocates were part of the judicial system and subject to public law regulation, they still exercised an independent profession and their chambers and clientèle constituted property interests.

[33] *Gorou v Greece (No.2)*, fn.16 above, paras 24–26.

[34] e.g. *Georgiadis v Greece*, May 29, R.J.D. 1997–III, No.38, para.35, claims for compensation for detention following acquittal; *Beaumartin v France*, November 24, 1994, Series A, No.296–B, 19 E.H.R.R. 485, where the compensation claim for expropriated property in Morocco derived from an international agreement between France and Morocco—notwithstanding the treaty and State prerogative aspects, French nationals could claim a share pursuant to a decree and the right was pecuniary in nature based on property rights.

[35] See also *Kraska v Switzerland*, April 19, 1993, Series A, No.254–B, 18 E.H.R.R. 188 (public law proceedings concerning practice of the medical profession); *Süssman v Germany*, September 16, 1996, R.J.D. 1996–IV, No.15 (Constitutional Court proceedings concerning amendments to civil servant pension schemes); *Voggenreiter*, fn.29 above, (Constitutional Court proceedings concerning the alleged unconstitutionality of tariff abolition legislation).

[36] e.g. *Schouten and Meldrum v Netherlands*, December 9, 1994, Series A, No.304, 19 E.H.R.R. 432, paras 40–60.

[37] e.g. *Feldbrugge*, *Deumeland*, *Salesi v Italy*, February 26, 1993, Series A, No.257–E.

[38] *Schuler-Zraggen v Switzerland*, June 24, 1993, Series A, No.263, 16 E.H.R.R. 405, para.46.

apply automatically to obligations to pay contributions, as opposed to claims to entitlements, Art.6 was still found to apply to disputes about the amount of contributions to be paid in *Schouten and Meldrum v Netherlands* (See Pt IIB, s.48: Welfare benefits). The right to compensation from a Foundation set up concerning forced labour during the Second World War was also regarded as civil by analogy to social security cases, as the claim related to subsistence and damage to health.[39]

The Court has also stated in wide terms that where a State confers rights which can be enforced by means of a judicial remedy, these can, in principle, be regarded as civil rights within the meaning of Art.6, para.1. Thus, even broad spectrum rights enforceable under the domestic constitution through the courts such as the right not to be discriminated against will be regarded as civil rights.[40] Fundamental rights, such as the right to education, will do so also.[41] Restrictions on the exercise by prisoners of their rights, in a very general sense, to keep in contact with their families by correspondence and by telephone, have also been found to be "civil rights" which must be protected in judicial proceedings.[42] Proceedings challenging the lawfulness of a fiscal search and seizure were found to be "civil" in nature as they concerned the right to respect for home which was protected in domestic law in both the civil code and in the incorporated European Convention of Human Rights.[43] A recent case left open whether proceedings challenging the interception of communications, an area falling under Art.8, concerned civil rights.[44] As to whether the "right to liberty" is a civil right, this is clearly the case for such an important freedom; however, care must be taken with regard to the operation of Arts 5 and 6 in its criminal head which are the *leges specialis*, in particular for review of the lawfulness of pre-trial detention and continued detention under Art.5, paras 3 and 4.[45]

The status of European community "rights" for the purposes of Art.6, para.1 has been considered in a few cases. The Commission found that "civil rights" included rights arising under directly applicable European community law,[46] but where the character of the right was perceived to be public Art.6 was excluded.[47]

[39] *Wos*, fn.8 above, para.76.

[40] *Orsus v Croatia,* March 16, 2010, para.105.

[41] *Orsus,* fn.40 above, para.106; *Emine Araç v Turkey*, (9907/02) September 23, 2008, paras 23–24 (university level).

[42] *Enea v Italy*, September 17, 2009, ECHR 2009 . . . paras 99–107. See also *Boulois v Luxembourg*, December 14, 2010, paras 60–61, application for temporary leave from prison to prepare for release was considered sufficiently connected to private life issues, reference also made to such rights being contained in the European Prison Rules. Pending before the Grand Chamber.

[43] *Ravon v France,* February 21, 2008, para.24. See *Uzukauskas v Lithuania*, July 6, 2010, paras 35–40, proceedings concerning entry of the applicant's name in a police risk register which required him to hand in his firearms concerned civil rights as it was relevant to his right to reputation and concerned personal data within the scope of "private life" and enjoyment of possessions.

[44] *Kennedy v UK*, May 18, 2010, paras 177–179, the domestic tribunal considered it was dealing with civil rights; see earlier authorities cited where complaints about access to court were held not to attract Art.6.

[45] *Reinprecht v Austria*, November 15, 2005, paras 49–55, identifying a limited role for Art.6 in its civil head in a handful of previously-decided mental health cases where the person challenging lawfulness of detention and seeking compensation had no longer been detained.

[46] (24960/94) (Dec.) January 11, 1995, where nonetheless the applicant *avocat stagiaire* in Rome did not enjoy the status under EEC provisions to claim the right to practise law in Greece.

[47] (28979/95) and (30343/96) (Dec.) January 13, 1997, where the applicants claimed freedom of movement within the European Union, the Commission noted the origin and general nature of the Maastricht provision, and the lack of personal, economic or individual aspects characteristic to the private law sphere.

The following have been found to be covered: the proceedings relating to the costs of proceedings[48]; measures confiscating property of suspected organised crime members[49]; proceedings enforcing a foreign court's forfeiture order[50]; procedures for changing surnames[51]; civil-party interventions in criminal proceedings[52]; private prosecutions for defamation[53]; the right to a healthy environment, where such was guaranteed under domestic law and the procedure to protect the local inhabitants' physical integrity could lead to compensation[54]; procedure challenging the limitations on personal liberty imposed on a prisoner under a special restrictive regime[55]; disciplinary procedure in prison leading to a restriction in visiting rights[56]; and a dispute as to whether a period of medical study abroad should be taken into account as qualifying for domestic specialisation.[57] Where a widow was able in domestic law to continue in a criminal retrial involving her husband who died with a view to seeking his acquittal and rehabilitation, the Court considered that the right to vindicate his good reputation was of a civil nature.[58]

Areas falling outside Art.6 are principally matters relating to deprivation of liberty which fall to be dealt with under the *lex specialis* of Art.5[59]; proceedings relating to asylum, expulsion and nationality[60] or extradition,[61] or concerning entries in the Schengen database.[62] The Court also decided in *Eskelinen v Finland*, that matters relating to the employment or dismissal of public officials or civil servants who exercise the authority of the State and enjoy a special bond of trust and loyalty fall outside Art.6, where domestic law so identifies and excludes them from access to court and where the subject-matter of the dispute is related to their special role.[63]

[48] See Pt IIA, s.5: Costs in court.
[49] e.g. *Riela v Italy*, (52439/99) (Dec.) September 4, 2001.
[50] *Saccoccia v Austria*, (69917/01) (Dec.) July 5, 2007.
[51] *Mustafa v France*, June 17, 2003.
[52] *Perez v France*, February 12, 2004, ECHR 2004–I, where a claim was made for compensation. Where participation of the victim is exclusively punitive in purpose, no civil rights are involved: *Garimpo v Portugal*, (66752/01) (Dec.) June 10, 2004.
[53] *Kusmierek v Poland*, (10675/02) September 21, 2004; *Irena Pieniazek v Poland*, (62179/00) September 28, 2004, as they concerned the right to enjoy a good reputation.
[54] *Taskin and Others v Turkey*, November 10, 2004, ECHR 2004–X.
[55] *Musumeci v Italy*, January 11, 2005.
[56] *Gülmez v Turkey*, May 20, 2008, para.30.
[57] *Kök v Turkey*, October 19, 2006.
[58] *Gradinar v Moldova*, April 8, 2008, paras 92–104.
[59] e.g. (6541/74) (Dec.) December 18, 1974, 1 D.R. 82; *Reinprecht v Austria*, November 15, 2005, paras 51–55, while Art.6 may apply to proceedings concerning the lawfulness of detention, even without an issue of pecuniary compensation, it will not do so during the currency of criminal proceedings or where there is ongoing detention which is protected under the specific guarantees of Art.5.
[60] e.g. *Maaouia v France*, October 5, 2000, ECHR 2000–X, paras 36–41, where Art.6 was held not to be applicable to decisions concerning the entry, stay and deportation of aliens; *Katani v Germany*, (67679/01) (Dec.) May 31, 2001, where Art.6 was held to not be applicable to asylum procedures.
[61] *Salgado v Spain*, (65964/01) (Dec.) April 16, 2002 (extradition proceedings).
[62] *Dalea v France*, (964/07) (Dec.) February 2, 2010, due to the register's close connection with visa and entry issues.
[63] *Eskelinen v Finland*, April 19, 2007, ECHR 2007–II, para.62, developing *Pellegrin v France*, December 8, 1999, ECHR 1999–VIII. It is likely that the exclusionary category will continue not to cover nursery school, secondary school or university teachers (*Volkmer v Germany*, (39799/98), *Petersen v Germany*, (39793/98) and *Knauth v Germany*, (41111/98) (Decs.) November 11, 2001, ECHR 2001–XII); low-level civil servants (*Devlin v UK*, October 30, 2001); school caretakers (*Procaccini v Italy*, March 30, 2000); director of a district medical-pedagogical centre (*Satonnet v France*, August 2, 2000); or a ministry technical adviser sent under contract to work overseas (*Frydlender v France*, June 27, 2000, ECHR 2000–VII). Contrast *Savino v Italy*, April 28, 2009, paras 63–79, where Art.6 did apply to salary disputes of staff of the legislative chambers.

This may still continue to cover the armed forces and the police[64] and also senior judges,[65] senior diplomats and Foreign Ministry officials.[66] It is possible, however, that disputes about salaries, privileges and pension rights which are not directly related to the special bond of trust could still fall within Art.6.[67]

Matters relating to the obligation to pay tax will generally fall outside the scope of civil rights,[68] save where relating to pecuniary claims with a foundation in private law[69] (see Pt IIB, s.45: Tax). Claims relating to electoral or political matters will be excluded (See Pt IIB, s.14: Electoral rights). Nor is there any right to have other persons prosecuted or sentenced for a criminal offence[70] or any right to vengeance, including any right to intervene in plea bargaining between an accused and the prosecution to obtain a higher sentence.[71]

Cases have also held Art.6, para.1 inapplicable to the right to report on a public trial[72]; refusal to issue a passport[73]; unilateral decision of the State to compensate the victims of a natural disaster[74]; and proceedings before a Parliamentary Commission.[75]

Cross-reference

Part IIA, s.2: Access to court.
Part IIA, s.5: Costs in court.
Part IIB, s.14: Electoral rights.
Part IIB, s.33: Pensions.
Part IIB, s.45: Tax.
Part IIB, s.48: Welfare benefits.

[64] *Batur v Turkey*, (38604/97) (Dec.) July 4, 2000; *Sukut v Turkey*, (59773/00) (Dec.) September 11, 2007, dismissal of army officers.

[65] *Pitkevich v Russia*, (47936/99) (Dec.) February 8, 2001; contrast *Olujic v Croatia*, Feburary 5, 2009, the *Esklinen* exclusion did not apply as domestic law in fact did grant access to court to the senior judge who was subject to disciplinary measures.

[66] *Pellegrin*, fn.63 above, concerning a senior civil servant exercising considerable responsibilities in public finances which entailed participating directly in the exercise of powers conferred by public law and designed to safeguard State interests.

[67] See *Massa v Italy*, August 24, 1993, Series A, No.265–B, 18 E.H.R.R. 266, a claim for pension provision by a surviving spouse and, mutatis mutandis, *Martinez Caro*, (42646/98) (Dec.) March 7, 2000, concerning salaries and special allowances.

[68] *Ferrazzini*; *Vidacar and Obergrup SL v Spain*, (41601/98) and (41775/98) (Dec.) April 20, 1999, ECHR 1999–V.

[69] *O.B. Heller A.S. and FCeskoslovenska Obchodnibanka A.S. v Czech Republic*, (55631/00) and (55728/00) (Dec.) November 9, 2004, where the applicants were under a contractual obligation, not a fiscal duty, to reimburse the customs duties of another company.

[70] *Perez*, fn.52 above, para.70.

[71] *Mihova v Italy*, (25000/07) (Dec.) March 30, 2010.

[72] (23868–23869/94) (Dec.) February 24, 1995, 80 D.R. 162.

[73] (19583/92) (Dec.) February 20, 1995, 80 D.R. 38.

[74] (14225/88) (Dec.) December 3, 1990, 69 D.R. 223.

[75] *Montera v Italy*, (64713/01) (Dec.) July 9, 2002.

2. Access to court

Key provision:

II–020 Article 6, para.1.

Key case-law:

Golder v UK, February 21, 1975, Series A, No.18, 1 E.H.R.R. 524; *Campbell and Fell v UK*, June 28, 1984, Series A, No.80; *Ashingdane v UK*, May 28, 1985, Series A, No.93, 7 E.H.R.R. 528; *Powell and Rayner v UK*, February 21, 1990, Series A, No.172, 12 E.H.R.R. 355; *Philis v Greece (No.1)*, August 27, 1991, Series A, No.209, 13 E.H.R.R. 741; *Hennings v Germany*, December 16, 1992, Series A, No.251–A, 16 E.H.R.R. 83; *De Geouffre de la Pradelle v France*, December 16, 1992, Series A, No.253; *Zumtobel v Austria*, September 21, 1993, Series A, No.268–A, 17 E.H.R.R. 116; *Fayed v UK*, September 21, 1994, Series A, No.294–B, 18 E.H.R.R. 116; *Air Canada v UK*, May 5, 1995, Series A, No.316–A, 20 E.H.R.R. 150; *Bellet v France*, December 4, 1995, Series A, No.333–B; *Bryan v UK*, November 22, 1995, Series A, No.335–A, 21 E.H.R.R. 342; *Stubbings v UK*, October 22, 1996, R.J.D. 1996–IV, No.18; *Hornsby v Greece*, March 19, 1997, R.J.D. 1997–II, No.33; *Canea Catholic Church v Greece*, December 16, 1997, R.J.D. 1997–VIII, No.60; *Tinnelly and McElduff v UK*, July 10, 1998, R.J.D. 1998–IV, No.79; *Osman v UK*, October 28, 1998, R.J.D. 1998–VIII, No.95; *Brumarescu v Romania*, October 28, 1999, ECHR 1999–VIII; *Z v UK*, May 10, 2001, ECHR 2001–V; *Al-Adsani v UK*, November 21, 2001, ECHR 2001–I; *A v UK*, December 12, 2002, ECHR 2002–X; *Ryabykh v Russia*, July 24, 2003, ECHR 2003–IX; *Markovic v Italy*, December 14, 2006, ECHR 2006–XIV; *Cudak v Lithuania*, March 23, 2010, ECHR 2010–. . . ; *Sabeh El Leil v France*, June 29, 2011, ECHR 2011–. . .; *Nejdet Şahin and Perihan Şahin v Turkey*, October 20, 2011, ECHR 2011-. . .

1. General considerations

II–021 The interpretation of Art.6, para.1 to confer an effective right of access to court in the determination of civil rights and obligations is one of the most significant and creative steps taken by the Convention organs. In *Golder v UK*, where a prisoner had been refused permission to contact his solicitor with a view to bringing a civil action for libel against a prison officer, the Court, faced with the question as to whether Art.6, para.1 was limited to guaranteeing the right to a fair trial to pending legal proceedings, or whether it also secured a right of access to court for persons wishing to bring an action concerning their civil rights and obligations, found in favour of the latter. The Court noted that otherwise a Contracting State would be free to abolish its courts or remove jurisdiction over particular classes of action, which would bring in the danger of arbitrary power and the denial of the principles of justice.[1]

[1] Reiterated since, e.g. *Fayed v UK*, September 21, 1994, Series A, No.294–B, 18 E.H.R.R. 116, para.63 and *A v UK*, December 12, 2002, ECHR 2002–X, para.63, to the effect that it would not be consistent with the rule of law if States could, without restraint or control by the Convention organs, remove from the jurisdiction of the courts a whole range of civil claims or confer immunities from civil liability on large groups or categories of persons.

The right of access to court is not absolute, however, but subject to limitations. By its very nature, the Court has said, it calls for regulation by the State, which may vary in time and place according to the needs and resources of the community and individuals.[2] The State has a margin of appreciation in making such regulations but the limitations applied must not restrict or reduce the access left to the individual in such a way or to such an extent that the very essence of the right is impaired. In addition, a limitation will not be compatible with Art.6 if it does not pursue a legitimate aim and if there is not a reasonable proportionality between the means employed and the aim sought to be achieved. These criteria are sometimes referred to as the "*Ashingdane* principles".[3]

There is a very limited domain in which the issue of right of access to court in criminal matters may arise, in particular in those jurisdictions where persons seek to have a trial against them in order to clear a perceived stain on their reputation from unfounded accusations. As there is, however, no absolute right to obtain a prosecution, whether against another person or oneself, restrictions may be justified by strong public interest, such as immunity enjoyed by Parliamentarians.[4] An issue may also arise in specific circumstances where there is lack of access to court to challenge an aspect of criminal procedure[5] or where civil party claims are closely connected to the criminal complaint which has been lodged.[6]

2. Applicability

Access to court can only apply in respect of *contestations* (disputes) over civil rights and obligations which can be said, at least on arguable grounds, to be recognised under domestic law; it cannot in itself guarantee any particular content for those rights.[7] II–022

An applicant's complaint of denial of access must relate to a right which has a basis in domestic law. In *Powell and Rayner v UK*, where a statute provided that nuisance and trespass would not lie in respect of the ordinary incidents of flights of aircraft which conformed with reasonable height requirements and navigation regulations, the Court found that as a result of this exclusion of liability the applicant houseowners could not claim to have a substantive right under English law to obtain relief for exposure to aircraft noise in those circumstances.[8]

Whether a limitation on a claim constitutes a procedural bar restricting access to court, or forms part of the substantive definition of the right in domestic law, may

[2] *Golder v UK*, February 21, 1975, Series A, No.18, 1 E.H.R.R. 524, para.38.

[3] *Ashingdane v UK*, May 28, 1985, Series A, No.93, 7 E.H.R.R. 528, para.57.

[4] *Kart v Turkey*, December 3, 2009, paras 85–114, where the MP's application to have his immunity lifted in order for the trial to proceed against him was refused by Parliament; no violation.

[5] *Buijen v Germany*, April 1, 2010, paras 60–65, where the applicant had no means of challenging the refusal of a prosecutor for transfer to serve his sentence in a prison in his own country, in circumstances where those proceedings were linked to the fairness of his criminal trial due to the assurance of the prosecutor that transfer would be allowed.

[6] *Ligue du monde islamique et Organisation islamique mondiale du secours islamique v France*, January 15, 2009, paras 53–58, the two organisations' complaints of criminal defamation, with accompanying compensation claims were not admitted to court on insufficiently foreseeable provisions relevant to residence requirements.

[7] e.g. *W v UK*, July 8, 1987, Series A, No.121, 10 E.H.R.R. 29; *Z v UK*, May 10, 2001, ECHR 2001–V, para.98.

[8] See also (12810/87) (Dec.) January 18, 1989, 59 D.R. 172; (14324/88) (Dec.) April 19, 1991, 69 D.R. 227.

in some cases be difficult to distinguish and the matter has been left open by the Court in a number of cases. Difficulties have arisen particularly as the operation of special defences, privileges and immunities (see sub-s.4 of this section: Defences, privileges and immunities, below).

3. Procedural and practical restrictions

II–023 Procedural and practical impediments may contravene the Convention where they operate to bar effective access to court.[9]

(a) Obstacles in obtaining access

II–024 Refusal of permission to a prisoner to contact his solicitor with a view to suing a prison officer in libel deprived him of access to court: it was not for the Secretary of State to take the role of determining whether or not such a claim had prospects of success.[10] Inability for a prisoner to have confidential out-of-hearing consultations with a solicitor was also considered to deny effective access to court.[11]

If the authorities, without cause, prevented applicants from gaining access to documents in their possession which would assist them in their claims, or falsely denied the existence of such documents, the Court stated, in *McGinley and Egan v UK*,[12] that problems of fairness or effective access to court could arise. In that case, however, there was a procedure available for applying for access to relevant records and it had not been shown that the State had prevented access to any relevant evidence.

A breakdown of State control which results in the courts ceasing to operate for a significant period in a particular area may disclose a violation, as in Chechnya where the courts were closed from 1999 to 2001 and the Government made no provision for civil litigants to bring their claims in another region of Russia.[13]

Where domestic law makes provision for the electronic filing of claims and documentation, a refusal by a court to admit them may deny access to court. The Government was not able to rely on the fact that courts were not yet equipped with electronic registration systems where the civil code provided for the filing of materials on DVDs and the applicants' claims were such that this was not an abusive or inappropriate way of doing so.[14]

Where the criminal complaints, and associated civil claims, of two Arabic organisations concerning defamation were not admitted by the French courts on purported but inconsistent grounds relating to their lack of an office on French soil, the Court found that this was not an issue of non-compliance with a domestic

[9] *Golder*, fn.2 above, para.26.
[10] *Golder*, fn.2 above, para.26.
[11] *Campbell and Fell v UK*, June 28, 1984, Series A, No.80. See also *McComb v UK*, (10621/83) (Dec.) March 11, 1985, complaints of opening of legal correspondence between a prisoner and solicitor were declared admissible under Art.6 but settled on change of practice; *Hodgson v UK*, (11392/85) (Dec.) March 4, 1987, restrictions on prisoners' direct correspondence with domestic courts.
[12] *McGinley and Egan v UK*, June 9, 1998, R.J.D. 1998–III, No.76.
[13] *Khamidov v Russia*, November 15, 2007, paras 154–157, the applicant wished to bring claims for damage to property which had been occupied by State forces.
[14] *Lawyer Partners A.S. v Slovak Republic*, June 16, 2009, paras 51–56, the applicants' claims concerned tens of thousands of persons and millions of pages of supporting documents.

procedural formality but a restriction on access to court which had not been sufficiently foreseeable in its scope.[15]

Lack of physical access to court by a handicapped person could potentially raise an issue. However, the Court left it undecided in one case whether, in fact, the applicant could not enter the court building since in any event it was not persuaded that the applicant was unable to raise his claims effectively before the courts using electronic and postal means, and by using family or friends as "*mandataires*" as he had on other occasions.[16]

(b) *Limitations on categories of litigant and legal standing*

Where an applicant enjoys a right, the inability to have a dispute about that right determined in the courts due to a lack of standing is a procedural bar to access to court which must be justified in terms of the *Ashingdane* principles.[17] Limitations on access as regards minors and persons of unsound mind, bankrupts and vexatious litigants have been acknowledged as pursuing legitimate aims and so far restrictions examined have generally not been found incompatible with them.[18] Where vexatious litigants had complained about being fined for using a statutory legal remedy, the Court noted that the fines nonetheless had not prevented their claims being heard at two instances.[19] II–025

In *Luordo v Italy*, the bar on a bankrupt's ability to litigate was considered to pursue the aim of protecting the rights of others, including the creditors, and only fell foul of Art.6 due to the disproportionate length of time (over 14 years) that the incapacity had lasted.[20] However, other restrictions on standing, which are less justified, may offend. For example, the inability of the managing director and sole shareholder of a company to challenge its liquidation was regarded as a disproportionate bar on access to court[21] as was the inability of minority shareholders to challenge a decision to wind-up a company and transfer assets to the majority shareholder after the resolution had been recorded in the commercial register.[22]

Where a claim belonging to an individual may only be pursued by another person or body, in the absence of any incapacitating feature as those above, it may be harder for the restriction to be justified. In *Philis v Greece (No.1)*, the applicant engineer's claim for remuneration for work done could only be pursued by the Technical Chamber of Greece pursuant to decree. While this might have provided engineers with the benefit of experienced legal representation for little expense, the Court found it insufficient to justify removing the applicant's capacity to pursue and act in his own claim.

[15] *Ligue du monde islamique et Organisation islamique mondiale du secours islamique*, fn.6 above, paras 53–58.

[16] *Farcas v Romania*, (32596/04) (Dec.) September 14, 2010, the Court seems to have regarded the applicant's complaints as exaggerated; if perhaps the applicant had gone so far as he could in his claim by postal and electronic means and then had been unable to attend a court hearing, the reasoning might have differed: although, of course, if the State can rely on disabled persons receiving help from others, no doubt friends and relatives could have tried to carry him into the building.

[17] e.g. *Jurisic and Collegium Mehrerau v Austria*, July 27, 2006, paras 69–70.

[18] cf. *Winterwerp v Netherlands*, October 24, 1979, Series A, No.33, paras 73–76, where there was a breach of Art.6, para.1, where proceedings by which a person committed to mental detention had the automatic effect of divesting him of all capacity to administer his property but did not afford him the opportunity to appear or be represented.

[19] *Toyaksi v Turkey*, (43569/08) et al (Dec.) October 20, 2010.

[20] *Luordo v Italy*, July 17, 2001.

[21] *Arma v France*, March 8, 2007.

[22] *Kohlhofer and Minarik v Czech Republic*, October 15, 2009.

The removal or denial of legal capacity to take proceedings may also impair the substance of the right to a court, as in *Canea Catholic Church v Greece*, where a court ruling that the applicant church did not have legal personality led to the dismissal of actions brought to assert its property rights. The general bar on property claims being brought before the courts by non-Orthodox churches was found to be a disproportionate bar on access to court.[23]

(c) *Time-bars and prescription periods*

II–026 Time-limits imposed on the bringing of claims are acceptable in the interests of good administration of justice, pursuing the legitimate aims of preventing stale claims and injustice to defendants faced with evidential difficulties in contesting allegations relating to distant events and of promoting legal certainty.[24] The Convention organs have accepted final time-limits which cannot be waived, even when new facts have arisen after the expiry of the time-limit,[25] or where knowledge of the cause of action only arose after the time-limit.[26] A three-year time-limit was found to be reasonable for paternity proceedings[27] and six years for assault and trespass to the person, including sexual abuse.[28] However, where a new law widened paternity challenges, the Court found a lack of access to court arising from inflexible application of a six-month time-limit from birth to an applicant who had never been able to contest paternity of a child born many years before.[29] Lack of suspension of a time-limit during the claimant's minority, leading to prescription before adulthood, has also been found to be a disproportionate restriction on access to court.[30]

Where a time-limit is so short as to render it practically impossible to act within time it may effectively deprive the applicant of access to court.[31] In *Hennings v Germany*, where the applicant claimed such of the one-week notice given by the prosecution summons, the Court found that his main excuse for not reacting to the notice was the claim that he had no key to his mailbox, which he could reasonably have been expected to obtain and for which the authorities were not responsible. Retrospective application of a shorter time-limit for appealing, which meant that the applicant would have had to appeal before the amending law was passed, offended the principle of legal certainty, notwithstanding the legitimate aim of speeding up civil procedures.[32]

[23] *Sambata Bihor Greek Catholic Parish v Romania*, January 12, 2010, the provision for disputes to be settled by a special commission did not suffice.
[24] *Stubbings v UK*, October 22, 1996, R.J.D. 1996–IV, No.18, para.51.
[25] (9707/82) (Rep.) October 6, 1982, 31 D.R. 223, where the applicant had three years from the birth of the child to contest paternity but did not discover that he could not be the father until 24 years later.
[26] In *Stubbings*, fn.24 above, the applicants (sexual abuse victims) complained that it was not possible to comply with an inflexible time-limit (suppressed memories, etc.). The Court found that a six-year time-limit from the age of majority did not impair the essence of right of access to court, noting no general principle of flexibility in time-limits (i.e. from date of knowledge) in Contracting States.
[27] (9707/82), fn.25 above.
[28] *Stubbings v UK*, fn.24 above.
[29] *Mizzi v Malta*, January 12, 2006.
[30] *Stagno v Belgium*, July 7, 2009, paras 29–35.
[31] See *Perez de Rada Cavanilles v Spain*, October 28, 1998, R.J.D. 1998–VIII, No.96, where the applicant sent his appeal by recorded delivery within the three-day time-limit but it was rejected as received outside that time—he could not have reasonably been expected to act more quickly.
[32] *Melnyk v Ukraine*, March 28, 2006.

Conversely, there is no obligation that prescription periods be imposed; the lack of such a period applied to the challenge of certain administrative acts did not disclose a lack of legal certainty.[33]

Where a prescription period expires due to the fault of the authorities, this may impinge on the right of effective access to court. The extinction of a criminal procedure, which had dragged out so long that the offence became time-barred, had the effect that the applicant, who had joined the proceedings as a civil party claiming damages, could no longer have her claim determined. The Court did not consider that the applicant should be required to start again in civil proceedings.[34]

(d) Coherent procedures

Although leeway is given to domestic courts in applying and interpreting procedural rules, applicants may claim a right to procedures which are "coherent" and afford a clear, practical and effective opportunity to challenge administrative acts which affect their rights.[35] Thus where the law was considered to be extremely complex, and an applicant could not be expected to realise time for appealing ran from the official publication of the decree rather than the serving of the notice, there was a denial of effective access to court.[36] A court rejection of an applicant's claim for damages for HIV infection from a blood bank, on the basis that he had accepted compensation from a special fund, was found to constitute a restriction on access to court since the applicant reasonably relied on the wording of the applicable legislation in bringing his claim; the system was not sufficiently clear or sufficiently attended by safeguards to prevent misunderstanding as to the procedures for making use of available remedies and the restrictions stemming from the simultaneous use of them.[37] Overly strict or arbitrary interpretation of procedural rules in rejecting claims, in particular for errors for which the applicants are not to blame, has also disclosed a disproportionate hindrance on access to court,[38] as well as **II–027**

[33] *Millon v France*, (6051/06) (Dec.) August 30, 2007, the applicant regional politician's allocation of an official residence and grant of an allowance was challenged more than ten years later by another politician.

[34] *Atanasova v Bulgaria*, October 2, 2008, paras 41–47.

[35] *De Geouffre de la Pradelle v France*, December 16, 1992, Series A, No.253, para.34.

[36] *De Geouffre de la Pradelle*, fn.35 above, i.e. the time-limit expired the day before the Prefect served the notice of the decree. Also *Miragall Escalano v Spain*, (38366/97) etc. (Dec.) January 25, 2000, ECHR 2000–I, overly strict interpretation of a procedural rule where the one-year time-limit ran from a decision not served on the applicants; mutatis mutandis, *Geffre v France*, (51307/99) (Dec.) January 23, 2003, where the system of publishing a decree in several ways gave sufficient opportunity to make appropriate applications. See also *Saoud v France*, September 13, 2007, paras 132–136, where the applicants' court-appointed lawyer was unable to lodge observations as the date of appointment was subsequent to a procedural step after which the rules said no further pleadings could be submitted.

[37] *Bellet v France*, December 4, 1995, Series A, No.333–B; *FE v France*, October 30, 1998, R.J.D. 1998–VIII, No.97. See also *Hajiyev v Azerbaijan*, November 16, 2006, where it was not apparent to which court the applicant should appeal and the courts did not act to put him right.

[38] *Garcia Manibardo v Spain*, (38695/97) (Dec.) February 15, 2000, ECHR 2000–II, refusal of an applicant's appeal for failure to pay into court the damages awarded at the first instance, where persons granted legal aid were exempt but the applicant's application for legal aid was granted too late for her to make use of it; *Leoni v Italy*, October 26, 2000, where it was the fault of the lower court that the appeal documents were not transmitted within the time-limit; *Sotiris and Nikos Koutras Attee v Greece*, November 16, 2000, ECHR 2000–XII, where a claim was dismissed for a procedural error committed on lodging the application by public officials; *Platakou v Greece*, January 11, 2001, ECHR 2001–I, para.39, failure of

formalistic insistence on requirements not necessary for an examination of the issues.[39]

Failure to give plausible explanation for procedural decisions impinging on access to court may also cause problems. Where an applicant, given one week's notice of an appeal hearing, tried unsuccessfully to lodge detailed submissions both before and at the hearing, the Court noted that no reason had been put forward for the refusal, finding that this was a restriction on the applicant's effective access to court.[40]

Rejection of an appeal on the procedural grounds of failure of the defendant to execute the lower court judgment is not, per se, an unacceptable bar on access since requiring payment of an order of damages or compensation pursues the legitimate aims of safeguarding the creditor's interests, preventing vexatious appeals and the congestion of the appellate instances. However, where there is a manifest disproportion between the judgment debt and the means of the appellant, the Court has found that this is a restriction on access in breach of Art.6.[41]

Refusal, without explanation, by a court to give a decision in a case may deny effective access to court. Where in Albania, the Constitutional Court refused to rule on an appeal, claiming that there was a tied vote, the Court noted that this was inexplicable given that there were seven judges and it was not possible for a judge to abstain. The lack of coherence and legal certainty in this situation breached Art.6.[42]

(e) *Costs*

II–028 Prohibitive levels of court costs may raise issues of denial of access to court. See Pt IIA, s.5: Costs in court.

(f) *Arbitration*

II–029 While it is compatible with Art.6 for parties to regulate their civil disputes by submitting them to arbitration proceedings in place of the courts—this pursues the aim of encouraging non-judicial settlements and relieving the courts of an excessive

the court bailiff to serve a notice within time, and paras 43–44, concerning the Court of Cassation's overly rigid application of rules on the contents of the appeal notice; *Zvolsky and Zvolska v Czech Republic*, November 12, 2002, concerning an overly strict, and little known requirement that applicants should lodge appeals simultaneously with the Supreme Court and Constitutional Court. Mutatis mutandis, *Canete de Goni v Spain*, October 15, 2002, where it was not considered arbitrary to apply constructive notice of proceedings to a third party, where the applicable case-law was published, accessible and sufficiently precise that the applicant, if necessary with skilled legal advice, could have determined what steps she should have taken to join the case; *Ivanova v Finland*, (53054/99) (Dec.) May 2002, not arbitrary to require claims in an official language; *Grof v Austria*, (25046/94) (Dec.) April 4, 1998, not overly formalistic to reject appeal for failure of the lawyer to provide signed copies of documents for service.

[39] *L'Erablière ASBL v Belgium*, (48230/07) February 24, 2009, paras 39–44, the *Conseil d'Etat* refused to accept the notice of appeal as it did not set out the facts, whereas the notice had appended the administrative decision in issue which had set out the facts comprehensively; see also *Wagner and J.M.W.L. v Luxembourg*, June 28, 2007, paras 94–98, refusal to reply to ground of appeal invoking Art.8, as allegedly too vague, without however asking the applicants to provide further specifications.

[40] *Dunayev v Russia*, May 24, 2007, paras 35–38; see also *Blumberga v Latvia*, October 14, 2008, paras 77–79, the Court found an unwarranted refusal to look at the merits on the ground that the applicant had failed to provide the documents necessary but without specifying which.

[41] See *Annoni di Gussola v France*, November 14, 2000, the sum exceeded the applicant's means 42 to 1; *Chatellier v France*, March 31, 2011, paras 34–44, the applicant had means of some €2,500, the judgment required payment of over €600,000.

[42] *Marini v Albania*, December 18, 2007, paras 118–123.

burden—issues may arise where the procedure is not voluntary or part of a contractual arrangement to which the applicant can be considered to have agreed.[43] While some degree of court supervision of arbitration procedures may be required, Contracting States enjoy considerable discretion in regulating the grounds on which an arbitral award should be quashed.[44]

A system whereby claimants were required to submit to arbitration due to agreements reached by other parties, and the arbitrators were chosen from a list of a private company, effectively denied access to a proper tribunal.[45]

(g) *Denial of legal aid*

Lack of legal aid may constitute a denial of access to court. See Pt IIA, s.14: Legal aid in civil cases. II–030

(h) *Lack of enforcement*

Execution of a judgment is an integral part of the "trial" for the purposes of Art.6, para.1, the guarantees of which would become illusory if a domestic legal system allowed a final, binding judicial decision to remain inoperative to the detriment of one party. Failure by the authorities for more than five years to take the necessary steps to comply with a final enforceable decision was therefore found, in *Hornsby v Greece,* to deprive Art.6, para.1 of all useful effect and disclose a violation. II–031

Subsequent case-law establishes that decisions taken by the authorities which effectively prevent, invalidate or unduly delay the enforcement of a judicial decision, whether civil or criminal, may be regarded as depriving the applicant of the right to have the dispute decided by a court and Art.6 of all useful effect.[46] Lack of funds for honouring a judgment debt is not a sufficient excuse by the authorities[47] and even if staggering payments may pursue the public interest, a situation of continued uncertainty as to date of actual payment will offend.[48] Nor is it an excuse that a third party has obstructed enforcement, since the Court will examine whether the authorities have taken available measures to obtain compliance, for example enabling bailiffs to carry out their assigned tasks, if necessary by the participation of other authorities that may assist enforcement.[49] The State cannot transfer the

[43] e.g. (11960/86) July 13, 1990, concerning a private contractual relationship providing for arbitration.

[44] (23173/94) (Dec.) October 22, 1996; (28101/95) (Dec.) November 27, 1996, where the Commission implied that some court review of arbitration was required but that arbitral bodies did not need to comply with Art.6, para.1 and strict conditions could be imposed for the quashing of an arbitral award; *Suovaniemi v Finland*, (31737/96) (Dec.) February 23, 1999, where the applicants were found to have waived their right to a court and the arbitration was attended by sufficient guarantees.

[45] *Suda v Czech Republic*, October 28, 2010.

[46] e.g. *Immobiliare Saffi v Italy*, July 28, 1999, ECHR 1999–V, a prefectoral stay of enforcement for more than six years of order for possession in landlord-tenant dispute; *Antonakopoulos v Greece*, December 14, 1999, refusal of the State Treasurer to comply with the judgment of the Audit Court; *Taskin and Others v Turkey*, November 10, 2004, ECHR 2004–IX, where the authorities did not comply with a court order to suspend operation of an experimental mine; *Assanidze v Georgia*, April 8, 2004, where the decision acquitting the applicant was ignored and he remained in detention for several years.

[47] *Burdov v Russia*, May 7, 2002, ECHR 2002–III, para.35, some delay in payment may be justified but not such as to render Art.6 devoid of purpose (some four years in this case); see also *Qufaj Co. Sh.P.K. v Albania*, November 8, 2003, lack of budget provision not a justification.

[48] e.g., mutatis mutandis, *Karchuk v Ukraine*, June 12, 2008, paras 24–26, a violation under Art.1 of Protocol No.1.

[49] *Pini v Romania*, June 22, 2004, ECHR 2004–V, where a private children's home refused to hand over children under a final adoption order.

burden of enforcement onto the applicant, either through additional obligations to fulfil[50] or additional costs to pay.[51]

Whether difficulties or complicated circumstances can excuse non-enforcement depends on the nature and degree of the obstacles. The Court found that the occupation of a building by the US Peace Corps did not prevent the authorities transferring title to the applicant in compliance with a court judgment.[52] Where a former serviceman had a court order allotting him an apartment in a particular building, the authorities were not to blame for delay in enforcement where the building had not yet been built due to financial problems.[53] The Government's claim that repaying foreign currency deposits would lead to financial disaster did not furnish an excuse where it appeared that only a handful of people, such as the applicant, had obtained a judgment in their favour, the enforcement of which would not beggar the Treasury.[54] Nor does the fact that the State body which owed the debt has become bankrupt or ceases to exist: absolve non-enforcement the State is under an obligation to provide for the outstanding debts.[55]

Delays of periods of a year or more are generally sufficient to disclose a problem of non-enforcement; under a year generally do not. Where the enforcement concerns compensation for proceedings which have already been found to be excessively lengthy however, the Court has said that no more than six months should elapse before payment.[56]

(i) Other delays in proceedings

II–032 Where a court delays in acting on applications so that any eventual ruling becomes void of practical effect or diminishes significantly the benefit of the ruling, this may remove the effectiveness of access to court and infringe the right to a court.[57]

(j) Problems of legal certainty

II–033 The principle of legal certainty first arose in cases involving the setting aside of final judgments.

[50] *Jasiuniene v Lithuania*, March 6, 2003, where the Government contested the judgment and imposed additional obligations on the applicant to obtain enforcement; *Beshiri v Albania*, August 22, 2006, para.54, a person who has obtained an enforceable judgment against the State as a result of successful litigation cannot be required to resort to enforcement proceedings in order to have it executed.

[51] *Apostol v Georgia*, November 28, 2006, the applicant had to pay 7 per cent of the judgment debt for enforcement.

[52] *Hirschhorn v Romania*, July 26, 2007, the Court was not persuaded that there was diplomatic immunity, such not having been pleaded in the proceedings. Contrast *Manoilescu and Dobrescu v Romania*, (60861/00) (Dec.) March 3, 2005, paras 70–82, where the property and title had been transferred to the Russian State and was used as embassy premises, to which diplomatic immunity clearly attached: lack of enforcement measures justified in the circumstances.

[53] *Volnykh v Russia*, December 17, 2009.

[54] *Jelicic v Bosnia-Herzegovina*, October 31, 2006, paras 40–46. *Colic v Bosnia-Herzegovina*, November 11, 2009, para.15, while the creation of a general compensation scheme may be a legitimate way of solving the problem of mass claims, it could not provide a reason not to enforce final judgments already issued.

[55] *Shlepkin v Russia*, February 1, 2007, para.24.

[56] *Simaldone v Italy*, March 31, 2009, para.48.

[57] *Musemeci v Italy*, January 11, 2005, where the court's failure to comply with the ten-day period for the challenges to repeated special detention measures deprived the applicant of much of the benefit of the belated quashing orders and his appeals to the Court of Cassation had no legal interest due to the lapse of time.

There was a denial of access to court in *Brumarescu v Romania*, where after final judgment had been given and executed in a property case, the Procurator-General, who was not a party to the proceedings, exercised a power to bring the case before the Supreme Court which held that the courts had no jurisdiction to decide civil disputes such as the applicant's. The procedure allowing the quashing of a final judgment was also found to infringe the principle of legal certainty and deprive the applicant of a fair hearing. The procedure of supervisory review was found in *Ryabykh v Russia* to deprive the applicant of the right to a court and infringe legal certainty. The Court commented that the right to a court would be illusory if the Contracting State's legal system allowed a judicial decision which had become final and binding to be quashed by a higher court on an application made by a State official or through a procedure instituted by a judge. While there may be circumstances in which cases may be re-opened, these have to be clearly circumscribed, with time-limits to prevent delayed or recurrent procedures, access given to the parties, and the grounds confined such as newly discovered circumstances, serious procedural errors or breach of fundamental rights; not merely an appeal in disguise.[58]

The principle has since arisen in other contexts, in particular as concerns apparent inconsistency in the way in which courts examine similar cases. Where a higher court changes case-law, this fact in itself does not disclose a problem—there is no right to unchanging case-law—even though the litigant might be aggrieved that the change has had an impact on the determination of his claim.[59] It is one of the normal functions of appellate instances to review and adapt the development of case-law and the application of legislative provisions; the retroactive application of a reversal of case-law to ongoing proceedings is thus not regarded as a problem of access to court.[60] However, where the superior instance produces persistent and serious divergences itself, this is regarded as sowing uncertainty and depriving an applicant of effective adjudication of his rights.[61]

The Court looks poorly on courts reaching conflicting decisions on essentially the same issues arising in one case in different proceedings; it is the State's responsibility to organise the legal system in such a way as to identify related proceedings and, where necessary to join them or prohibit the further institution of new proceedings related to the same matter, in order to circumvent the review of final adjudications and disguised appeals.[62] That also holds where there is inconsistent adjudication of claims brought by many persons in similar situations which leads to a state of uncertainty.[63] It is relevant in this context whether there is a mechanism at a higher level for resolving inconsistencies,[64] and whether it works in practice: an extraordinary remedy is not good enough apparently.[65] Nonetheless, inconsistencies between separate jurisdictions within a State are regarded as inevitable and the Court does

[58] *Marian Nita v Romania*, December 7, 2010, paras 30–39; *OOO Link Oil SPB v Russia*, (42600/05) (Dec.) June 25, 2009, and authorities cited therein.

[59] *Unedic v France*, December 18, 2008, paras 72–78, the Court noted that the change did not wipe out the applicant's claims but impacted only on the amount of liability; it perceived no comparison with cases concerning the setting aside of final judgments.

[60] *Legrand v France*, May 26, 2011, paras 33–43.

[61] *Beian v Romania*, December 6, 2007, paras 36–40.

[62] *Driza v Albania*, November 13, 2007, paras 65–71.

[63] *Stefanica v Romania*, November 2, 2010, para.38; *Vincic v Serbia*, December 1, 2010, para.56.

[64] *Tudor Tudor v Romania*, March 24, 2009, paras 29–31.

[65] *Stefanica*, fn.63 above, para.37.

not see itself as a review mechanism for complaints: the existence of arbitrariness is the element which causes it concern.[66]

4. Exclusion of court review: defences, privileges and immunities

II–034 Where the courts decline, or for other reasons are unable, to examine a case where the applicant has, arguably, a civil right at stake, this will disclose a bar on access to court which requires justification. Violations have arisen where the Polish Supreme Court decided that under new legislation the courts could not examine claims against the State treasury for compensation payable for building works on land returned to religious associations[67]; or where both administrative and civil courts declined jurisdiction to the other in a claim for return of unused expropriated land.[68] Summary refusal of a Russian court to deal with a case on largely unreasoned grounds due to the claim that it fell within a foreign jurisdiction was considered a denial of justice contrary to the essence of effective access.[69] On the same basis, if a court does not decide a case submitted to it at all, for example, due to apparent loss of the case-file, this will deprive access to court of any usefulness in breach of Art.6.[70]

Potential problems also arise where an immunity or special defence has the effect of bringing court proceedings to an end, without consideration of the applicant's substantive claims.

In *Ashingdane* (concerning an immunity in statute barring civil actions by mental patients against staff or health authorities without leave on grounds of bad faith or lack of reasonable care) and in *Fayed v UK* (concerning the privilege of Department of Trade inspectors from suit in defamation) the Court found it unnecessary to decide whether these limitations defined the content of the right or imposed a restriction on access, since in any event the essence of the right to a court was not impaired nor the principle of proportionality transgressed. In *Ashingdane*, it found that the applicant could nonetheless take proceedings for negligence, whereas in *Fayed*, it found that any restriction pursued a legitimate aim (ensuring the proper conduct of the affairs of public companies) in a proportionate manner and that in producing their report the Inspectors were bound by a duty to act fairly and were subject to judicial review where they exceeded the bounds of their function.

This distinction, between elements that relate to the existence of a right in domestic law or which act as procedural bars to obtaining determination of a right, has proved difficult to apply in practice in UK cases. In *Osman v UK*, which concerned the public policy immunity from suit in negligence for the police acting in an investigative or preventative capacity, the Court considered that there was a common law right to sue in negligence and that the domestic law approach in excluding a duty of care on public interest considerations acted as an automatic immunity from suit that was a disproportionate restriction on access to court. Where a similar exclusion of a duty of care for suing social services for negligence

[66] *Nejdet Şahin and Perihan Şahin v Turkey*, October 20, 2011, paras 89–96.
[67] *Zwiazek Nauczycielstwa Polksiego v Poland*, September 21, 2004, ECHR 2004–IX, where the decision meant the applicant had no other means of vindicating its rights and the Court was not persuaded that the financial interests of the State in avoiding paying compensation justified removing access to court.
[68] *Beneficio Cappella Paolini v San Marino*, July 13, 2004.
[69] *Zylkov v Russia*, June 21, 2011, paras 28–29.
[70] *Dubinskaya v Russia*, July 13, 2006.

regarding their duties in child protection arose later in *Z v UK*, the Court acceded to the Government's arguments that the domestic court ruling that no duty of care arose in such circumstances could not be regarded as either an exclusionary rule or an immunity which deprived the child applicants of access to court. While a novel point of interpretation of negligence law arose for determination attracting the application of Art.6, the striking out procedure, in which the applicants were represented and able fully to argue their claims for extending a duty of care, did not therefore disclose a restriction on access to court.[71] Similarly, in *Markovic v Italy*, where the Court of Cassation ruled that it did not have jurisdiction where claims for damages were based on acts of war by the Government, this was not regarded as disclosing an immunity but as flowing from the principles governing the substantive right of action in domestic law: the applicants had access to court for the point to be decided, albeit against them.

Privileges and immunities in other contexts have been treated as acting as bars on access to court which require justification under the *Ashingdane* principles. Privilege from suit in defamation attaching to documents produced in criminal proceedings or investigations,[72] immunity from suit of the official receiver for alleged misstatements made in the exercise of his functions[73] and the application of the ex turpi causa rule to strike out the applicant's claims in tort[74] have been found to pursue legitimate aims in a proportionate manner. In the context of the privilege preventing members of Parliament from being sued in defamation, the Court found it unnecessary, in *A v UK*, to settle whether the privilege was a matter of substantive content or procedural bar, although it noted that Art.9 of the Bill of Rights was framed not in terms of a substantive defence to civil claims, but rather as a procedural bar to the determination of the court. In any event, it found the restriction on access justified by the fundamental importance of protecting free debate in Parliament.[75] The immunity is to be strictly confined to a connection with legislative duties however.[76] Immunity given to a magistrate from civil claims in damages was found justified in *Ernst v Belgium*, although in that case the Court appeared to place particular weight on the existence of other means by which the applicants could protect their interests.[77] The immunity from suit in defamation of members of the Judicial

[71] The Court took the view that the problem was one of effective remedies rather than access to court, finding a violation of Art.13 instead. Similar approach in *TP and KM v UK*, May 10, 2001, ECHR 2001–V; *DP and JC v UK*, October 10, 2002, namely to the extent a dispute about the existence of a right arose and the applicants had adequate access to court to put their claims.

[72] *Taylor v UK*, (49589/99) (Dec.) June 10, 2003 (statements by Serious Fraud Office officials); *Mahon and Kent v UK*, (70434/01) (Dec.) July 8, 2003 (documents submitted to The Securities Association concerning share fraud).

[73] *Mond v UK*, (49606/99) (Dec.) June 10, 2003, accepting that fear of vexatious actions would seriously impede performance of duties and the administration of justice.

[74] *Clunis v UK*, (45049/98) (Dec.) September 11, 2001.

[75] Immunities were disproportionate in *Cordova v Italy (No.1)*, January 30, 2003, ECHR 2003–1, where it was not appropriately linked to the ongoing performance of legislative functions (i.e. it applied for life to certain politicians); *Cordova v Italy (No.2)*, January 30, 2003, ECHR 2003–1, where it applied to speech outside Parliament or parliamentary duties.

[76] *C.G.I.L. and Cofferati v Italy (No.2)*, April 6, 2010, paras 45–54, violation where it applied to MP's statements at a press conference outside the legislature; it was irrelevant that it was the same subject as a recent debate within the legislature.

[77] *Ernst v Belgium*, July 15, 2003, paras 53–56, the applicants could have sued anyone else involved in the allegedly abusive search and seizure and were able to lodge a claim for damages against the State. Mutatis mutandis *C.G.I.L. and Cofferati v Italy*, February 24, 2009, para.76, the Court gave weight in finding the MP's immunity disproportionate to the applicants' lack of other means to vindicate their rights.

Services Commission in Italy, although absolute, was justified as it protected the interests of the institution in carrying out its important public functions, not those of individual members.[78]

In the context of international law and international organisations, immunities preventing the litigation of issues in domestic courts have also been characterised as restrictions on access to court. Initially, they were justified as pursuing legitimate aims in a proportionate manner, with decisive weight being placed on the vital public or international law interests.[79] In *Al-Adsani v UK*, where the applicant sought to sue the Government of Kuwait for torture in English courts, the Court noted that the applicant was claiming damages for personal injury, a cause of action well known to English law, and that the action against Kuwait was not barred *in limine* since if the defendant State waived immunity it would proceed to hearing and judgment—Art.6 therefore applied. It found, however, that the principle of sovereign immunity pursed the legitimate aim of complying with international law to promote comity and noting that the Convention had to be interpreted as far as possible to harmonise with other rules of international law, considered that measures taken by a High Contracting Party reflecting generally-recognised rules of public international law could not be, in principle, regarded as imposing disproportionate restriction on access to court.[80] The evolving tendency in international law to limit state immunity has since come to the fore, in particular as regards employment contracts by embassies with non-diplomatic staff. In *Cudak v Lithuania*, the refusal of the courts to entertain the sexual harassment and unlawful dismissal claim of the applicant who worked as telephone operator in the Polish embassy was found disproportionate, given her functions did not fall within the exceptions set out in the ILC Draft Articles.[81] Where the French courts upheld a claim of state immunity raised by Kuwait in an action brought by their embassy's chief accountant for dismissal, the Court noted that they had not taken into account the relevant international law provisions, now set out in the 2004 UN Convention on Jurisdictional Immunities of States and their Property, which required strict interpretation and had not given relevant and sufficient reasons for holding that the immunity applied in the case of an accountant who had not exercised any governmental authority.[82]

[78] *Esposito v Italy*, April 5, 2007.

[79] See, e.g. *Waite and Kennedy v Germany*, February 18, 1999, ECHR 1999–I, immunity from suit enjoyed by the European Space Agency in an employment case pursued the legitimate aim of ensuring the proper functioning of such organisations free from government interference; *Prince Hans-Adam II of Liechtenstein v Germany*, July 12, 2001, ECHR 2001–VIII, where the German courts declared inadmissible a claim for restitution of a painting confiscated in 1946 in former Czechoslovakia, the Court emphasised the vital public interest in Germany regaining sovereignty which was behind the post-war Settlement Convention.

[80] See also *McElhinney v Ireland*, November 21, 2001 (state immunity applied in Irish courts in a claim for damages for assault by a British soldier); *Fogarty v UK*, November 21, 2001 (state immunity applied to US Government in a labour dispute with an embassy employee); *Kalogeropoulou v Greece and Germany*, (59021/00) December 12, 2002, ECHR 2002–X (state immunity applying to enforcement of judgment against German property in Greece); *Grosz v France*, (14717/06) (Dec.) June 16, 2009 (state immunity for Germany against claims for forced labour of Frenchman during WW2).

[81] *Cudak v Lithuania*, March 23, 2010, ECHR 2010–. . . , paras 62–75, the Court did not consider that the Polish States' security or other relevant interests were at stake. *Fogarty v UK* (fn.79 above) was distinguished as concerning a dispute abour recruitment, not dismissal.

[82] *Sabeh El Leil v France*, June 29, 2011, ECHR 2011–. . ., paras 57–67.

5. Limitations in the scope of review of the court

Where claims may only be put before a court which does not have full jurisdiction over the facts and legal issues in the case, there may be a denial of access to court.[83] Relevant factors here relate to the subject-matter of the dispute; whether the court may, even with limited competence, adequately review the disputed issues; the manner in which that decision was arrived at; and the content of the dispute, including the desired and actual grounds of the action or appeal.[84] For example, where the only appeal against the lawfulness of a search under fiscal powers was to the Court of Cassation which had no competence to review the facts, a lack of access to court was found.[85] The failure of a domestic court to examine whether the measure of receivership imposed on the applicant company had been justified, and to rely, without verifying, on factual assumptions, disclosed a lack of proper judicial scrutiny.[86] **II–035**

In childcare cases, where parents sought access to or custody of their children in local authority care, judicial review, which was confined to issues of illegality, unfairness or irrationality, was not sufficient, the Court finding that Art.6, para.1 required that local authority decisions be reviewed by a tribunal having jurisdiction to examine the merits.[87]

Where executive certificates remove a court's jurisdiction to examine the applicant's claims on a particular point, this may render access to court ineffective. In *Tinnelly and McElduff v UK*, where statutory provisions against discrimination in employment did not apply where an act was done, inter alia, to safeguard national security, the Court found that the serving of a certificate by the Secretary of State as conclusive evidence that national security applied was a disproportionate restriction on access to court. The applicants should have been able to argue and present evidence to show that the act did not pursue national security purposes and the court was able to assess the issue freely.

In administrative areas of a more technical nature, restricted review of decisions by the courts has been accepted as a common feature in Contracting States. In *Zumtobel v Austria* where there was dispute over expropriation of property and the appropriate compensation, with expert assessments of property values, etc, the Court referred to a notion of expediency, i.e. that courts may legitimately restrict their review of decisions by the administrative authorities on grounds of expediency. In *Bryan v UK*, concerning enforcement proceedings for breach of planning controls in respect of the applicant's "barns", appeal to the High Court restricted to points of law was not a problem even though its jurisdiction over the facts was limited. The Court stressed the specialised character of planning, considered to be a typical example of the exercise of discretionary judgment in the regulation of citizens' conduct, and this was found to render it reasonable to restrict the intervention of courts vis-à-vis the factual application of this discretion, the realm of the executive. The manner in which the decision was reached, in particular that the planning

[83] See in an employment context, *Koskinas v Greece*, June 20, 2002 (no power of assessment of facts).

[84] *Bryan v UK*, November 22, 1995, Series A, No.335–A, 21 E.H.R.R. 342, para.45.

[85] *Ravon v France*, February 21, 2008, paras 28–35, this was not remedied by the fact a judge had ordered the search as this had not been adversarial, the person concerned not being informed or present at this stage.

[86] *Družstevní záložna Pria v Czech Republic*, July 31, 2008, paras 109–114.

[87] *W v UK*, fn.7 above, para.82.

enquiry beforehand was run on fair, adversarial lines, was also a relevant factor in finding the limited review compatible with Art.6.[88] In *Alattulkila v Finland*, where the Supreme Administrative Court provided an extraordinary remedy with limited scope of review in a fishing restriction case, the Court talked of having to accord a certain respect to decisions taken by administrative authorities in the field of environmental protection, where there were important conflicting considerations and interests and, in this case, a wider international context in the form of an inter-State co-operation agreement. As the court had considered the lawfulness of the fishing prohibition and its conformity with the Constitution as well as Art.6 of the Convention, giving the applicants an adequate opportunity to put their objections in the procedures and on no point declining jurisdiction, the scope of review was found adequate.[89]

Where a court effectively limits the scope of its powers by deferring to the view of an external authority, or otherwise deprives itself of jurisdiction over a crucial aspect of the case, the problem may also be viewed as a lack of independence or status as a "tribunal", satisfying the requirements of Art.6 as having jurisdiction to all questions of fact and law relevant to the dispute before it.[90]

Cross-reference

Part IIA, s.5: Costs in court.
Part IIA, s.10: Independence and impartiality.
Part IIA, s.14: Legal aid in civil cases.
Part IIA, s.16: Legislative interference in judicial process.
Part IIA, s.25: Tribunal established by law.

[88] e.g. *Air Canada v UK*, May 5, 1995, Series A, No.316–A, 20 E.H.R.R. 150, where H.M. Customs confiscated an aircraft and released it on payment of a sum of money, the Court rejected the applicant's arguments that the scope of judicial review would have been too narrow to allow any meaningful challenge of the very broad discretion bestowed on the customs by statute; (32788/96) (Dec.) April 9, 1997 where, having regard to the special statutory context, judicial review satisfied the requirements of Art.6 for the complaints of a foster carer about deregistration by a social services fostering panel; *X v UK*, (28530/95) (Dec.) January 19, 1998, the scope of review of the Secretary of State's decision declaring the applicant unfit to be chief executive of an insurance company was adequate; *Chapman v UK*, January 18, 2001, ECHR 2001–I, applying the *Bryan* approach to applications for judicial review of decisions refusing gypsies planning permission to station caravans on their own land; *Potocka v Poland*, October 4, 2001, ECHR 2001–X, adequate scope of review by the Supreme Administrative Court of lawfulness of an administrative decision on land ownership.

[89] *Alattulkila v Finland*, July 28, 2005

[90] e.g. *Van de Hurk v Netherlands*, April 19, 1994, Series A, No.288, 18 E.H.R.R. 481 (lack of independence); *Terra Woningen BV v Netherlands*, December 17, 1996, R.J.D. 1996–VI, No.25 (lack of "tribunal" status).

3. Adequate time and facilities

Key provision:

Article 6, para.3(b) (adequate time and facilities for preparation of defence). II–036

Key case-law:

Campbell and Fell v UK, June 28, 1984, Series A, No.80, 7 E.H.R.R. 165; *Bricmont v Belgium*, July 7, 1989, Series A, No.158, 12 E.H.R.R. 217; *Hadjianastassiou v Greece*, December 16, 1992, Series A, No.252–A, 16 E.H.R.R. 219; *Melin v France*, June 22, 1993, Series A, No.261–B, 17 E.H.R.R. 1; *Kremzow v Austria*, September 21, 1993, Series A, No.268–B, 17 E.H.R.R. 322; *Domenchini v Italy*, November 15, 1996, R.J.D. 1996–V, No.22, 32 E.H.R.R. 68; *Vacher v France*, December 17, 1996, R.J.D. 1996–V, No.25, 24 E.H.R.R. 482; *Foucher v France*, March 18, 1997, R.J.D. 1997–II, No.33, 25 E.H.R.R. 234; *Pelissier and Sassi v France*, March 25, 1999, ECHR 1999–II, 30 E.H.R.R. 715; *Fitt v UK*, February 16, 2000, ECHR 2000–II, 30 E.H.R.R. 480; *Rowe and Davies v UK*, February 16, 2000, ECHR 2000–II, 30 E.H.R.R. 1; *Zoon v Netherlands*, December 7, 2000, ECHR 2000–XII; *Sadak v Turkey*, July 2, 2001, ECHR 2001–VII; *GB v France*, October 2, 2001, ECHR 2001–X; *Ocalan v Turkey*, May 12, 2005, ECHR 2005–IV.

1. General considerations

II–037 The provisions of Art.6, para.3 depend on a criminal charge having been brought, though the Court has commented that these elements are implicit in the notion of fair trial in civil matters mutatis mutandis.[1] The case-law indicates that they are aspects of the general principle of fairness guaranteed in the first paragraph, to be assessed not on the basis of an isolated incident or element, but having regard to the proceedings as a whole. Thus while the sub-paragraphs of Art.6, para.3 exemplify the notion of fair trial in typical procedural situations, their intrinsic aim is always to ensure or contribute to ensuring the fairness of the proceedings as a whole.[2] Frequently, therefore, complaints under Art.6, para.3 are considered in conjunction with Art.6, para.1.

Where non-criminal cases are concerned, questions of adequate time and facilities are dealt with under Art.6, para.1, having regard to fairness and other applicable principles such as equality of arms, adversariality and the ability to participate effectively in the proceedings.[3]

In criminal cases, applicants' access to evidence, facilities and lawyers is restricted to what is necessary for the defence.[4] In *Lamy v Belgium*, the applicant's inability to consult the investigation file in the first 30 days did not affect the preparation of his defence and the Commission found that Art.6, para.3(b) was not applicable.[5]

[1] *Albert and Le Compte v Belgium*, February 10, 1983, Series A, No.58, 5 E.H.R.R. 533, para.39.
[2] *Can v Italy*, (9300/81) (Rep.) July 12, 1984, Series A, No.96 (settled before the Court).
[3] See Pt IIA, s.1: General principles: fairness.
[4] e.g. (8463/78) (Dec.) July 9, 1981, 26 D.R. 24, no right to unrestricted access to lawyer; (11396/85) (Dec.) December 11, 1986, 50 D.R. 179, where there were practical limits to the legal research materials prison authorities could be expected to provide.
[5] *Lamy v Belgium*, (Rep.) October 8, 1987, Series A, No.151.

2. Victim status

II–038 A person acquitted in criminal proceedings may not complain of alleged difficulties in preparing his defence.[6] An accused who declares that he will not take any further part of the proceedings cannot complain either.[7]

3. Adequate time

II–039 Where time for preparation of trial is concerned, short periods have been found acceptable. Counsel are expected to be able to arrange their work to respond in some degree to the special urgency of a case.[8] It is also expected that applications for adjournment are made where there is an alleged problem. Thus, in *Campbell and Fell v UK*, concerning prison disciplinary proceedings, five days notice of charges and notice of the report given the day before were found by the Court to be sufficient in the circumstances, noting that no request was made for an adjournment.[9] On that basis, the Commission appeared to accept the UK practice of briefing counsel at short notice, presuming that by training they were able to cope and that if they could not, they had the possibility to apply for an adjournment.[10] However, there may be circumstances where a court may be required to intervene and impose an adjournment of its own motion, e.g. where it is plain that the accused has not had enough time to discuss the case with freshly-appointed counsel.[11]

Although expedited criminal hearings are not, per se, contrary to Art.6, the Court considered that where an accused, who was not represented, was tried a few hours after his arrest on public order charges, this did not give him sufficient time to assess the charge and prepare a defence.[12]

As regards preparation times, in *Kremzow*, the Court found a period of three weeks was sufficient for counsel to draft a reply to a 49–page document.[13] However in *Ocalan v Turkey*, a period of two weeks before a trial given to defence lawyers to

[6] (8083/77) (Dec.) March 13, 1980, 19 D.R. 223, applicant no longer a victim as the Court of Appeal quashed the charge of contempt.

[7] (8386/78) (Dec.) October 9, 1980, 21 D.R. 126, where counsel withdrew from the trial, embarassed by statements made by the applicant contradicting his not guilty plea, the applicant refused offer of help from solicitors or to pursue questions himself or to call witnesses.

[8] *Mattick v Germany*, (62116/00) (Dec.) March 31, 2005, where it was adequate for counsel to receive the case-file one month before the trial and an expert opinion three days before. Time between various hearings was also regarded as preparatory time as regarded other materials submitted three days before the first hearing date.

[9] Also *Kremzow v Austria*, September 21, 1993, Series A, No.268–B, 17 E.H.R.R. 322 where the Attorney General served documents three weeks before an appeal hearing, and the applicant could also have consulted the file beforehand, no violation; *Craxi v Italy (No.2)*, December 20, 2002, where no complaint was made by the applicants' representatives at the time about the alleged difficulties arising from the close proximity of various hearing dates.

[10] Also *Twalib v Greece*, June 9, 1998, R.J.D. 1998–IV, No.77, paras 40–43, where counsel was given a "short interval" to prepare at the commencement of the trial but no complaint about lack of preparation time was made then or on appeal.

[11] *Sakhnovskiy v Russia*, November 2, 2010, paras 103–107, only 15 minutes contact before the hearing: violation from the point of view of lack of effective legal assistance, Art.6, paras 1 and (3)c.

[12] *Galstyan v Armenia*, November 15, 2007, paras 85–88, the applicant could not be faulted for not asking for an adjournment, as he was not informed of this possibility.

[13] *Kremzow*, fn.9 above, para.48. See also *GB v France*, October 2, 2001, ECHR 2001–X paras 60–63, where it was acceptable for the prosecution to file new evidence at the beginning of the trial, with the defence having three days until the conclusion of the proceedings to assimilate it.

prepare from a 17,000–page file was not sufficient time, together with other restrictions, rendering it difficult for the applicant to exercise the defence rights guaranteed under Art.6.

Where time-limits are imposed which, either by their brevity or vagueness, render the right of any appeal ineffective, violations have been found.[14] The rules by which the courts function must be "sufficiently coherent and clear".[15] The Court has emphasised that States must ensure that everyone charged with a criminal offence benefits from the safeguards of Art.6, para.3. Putting the onus on convicted defendants to find out when an allotted time started to run or expired was not compatible with the diligence which the Contracting States must exercise to ensure that rights are enjoyed in an effective manner.[16] Where, however, a full judgment was not made available to an accused before the expiry of the period for appeal, this did not unduly affect defence rights as an abridged version had been served and the appeal process was not directed against the first instance judgment but against the charges and would involve a completely new assessment of facts and law.[17]

4. Facilities: access to evidence

The Court has held that the right to an adversarial trial, with equality between prosecution and defendant, means that the defence must be given the opportunity to have knowledge of and comment on the observations filed and evidence adduced by the prosecution. This requires that the prosecution should disclose to the defence all material evidence in their possession for or against the accused.[18] II–040

There is no absolute right of access, however, with acknowledgment to potentially superceding public interests such as national security, witness protection,[19] risk of reprisals, or safeguarding police working methods.[20] The general principle that only restrictions on the rights of the defence which are strictly necessary are permissible tends to cede to the public interest as the Court leaves it to the domestic courts to assess the evidence in such cases but verifies instead whether the procedure followed by the judicial authorities sufficiently counter-balanced the limitations on the

[14] *Hadjianastassiou v Greece*, December 16, 1992, Series A, No.252–A, 16 E.H.R.R. 219 where the time-limit for lodging grounds of appeal expired before the applicant knew the substance of the court's decision convicting him, there was a violation since he was thus unable usefully to exercise his right of appeal. It was not enough, as the Government argued, for parts to be orally pronounced and for him to deduce the rest from the previous proceedings. See also *Vacher v France*, December 17, 1996, R.J.D. 1996–V, No.25, 24 E.H.R.R. 482.

[15] *Melin v France*, June 22, 1993, Series A, No.261–B, 17 E.H.R.R. 1, para.24; *Vacher*, fn.14 above, para.26.

[16] *Colozza v Italy*, February 12, 1985, Series A, No.89, 7 E.H.R.R. 516, para.28. See *Melin* and *Vacher*, fnn.14 and 15 above, concerning the practice of the Court of Cassation not to inform appellants in person when the hearing of the appeal was listed or set time-limits for submissions. There was a violation where, in *Vacher*, the appeal was dismissed eight days before lodging of the grounds of appeal; no violation in *Melin*, by a narrow majority: *Melin* was a lawyer who had worked at the bar and there was over a four-month delay before the dismissal of the appeal, whereas in *Vacher* the period was two months shorter than the average time usually taken.

[17] *Zoon v Netherlands*, December 7, 2000, ECHR 2000–XII, paras 45–51.

[18] *Fitt v UK*, February 16, 2000, ECHR 2000–II, 30 E.H.R.R. 480, para.44; *Rowe and Davis v UK*, February 16, 2000, ECHR 2000–II, 30 E.H.R.R. 1, para.60.

[19] (11219/84) (Dec.) July 10, 1985, 42 D.R. 287, where a defence lawyer was barred from discussing with the applicant the statements of anonymous witnesses which would allow him to identify them.

[20] e.g. (29335/95) (Dec.) January 17, 1997, where evidence was not disclosed since it would uncover details of police informers.

defence with appropriate safeguards.[21] It was therefore compatible with Art.6 for evidence to be withheld at trial on public interest grounds where the judge reviewed the evidence himself in light of the principle of ordering disclosure if it might further the defence[22]; it was not compatible where the material was withheld at trial by the prosecution and only reviewed on appeal by the Court of Appeal ex parte.[23]

The right has also been stated to be restricted to those facilities which assist or may assist in defence, which may in some cases appear to put the burden on applicants to prove the relevance of material they have not seen.[24] The Commission also appeared to take the view that where information was available elsewhere or within means of an applicant and lawyer to obtain, that this was sufficient by way of facilities, even if it might have been reasonably expected (as well as quicker and more efficient) for the prosecution to provide the information.[25] Lack of access to a file for a part of the period before the trial will not raise issues, if nonetheless access was possible for a sufficient time to prepare the defence.[26] Where there was a more fundamental lack of access to the file, however, and no opportunity to make copies of documents at first instance, then the possibility to make application for access at the appeal stage did not prevent a violation of Art.6, para.3(b).[27]

An accused does not have to be given direct access to the case file. It may be sufficient for him to be informed of the material in the file by his representatives, as long as the limitations on access by an accused to the court file do not prevent the evidence being made available to the accused before the trial and the accused has an effective opportunity to comment on it through his lawyer in oral submissions.[28] However, there was a violation in *Ocalan v Turkey* where the applicant did not obtain access to the investigation file and evidence produced by the prosecution until almost the end of his trial,[29] and also in *Matyjek v Poland*, where in lustration proceedings access to the file was severely restricted, no copies of documents or notes being allowed to leave the secret registry.[30]

In the context of expert evidence, circumstances may require that courts accede to an accused's requests for expert opinion on a particular matter. In *GB v France*, the

[21] *Fitt*, fn.18 above. paras 45–46; *Rowe and Davis*, fn.18 above, paras 61–62.

[22] *Fitt*, fn.18 above, paras 47–49.

[23] *Rowe and Davis*, fn.18 above, paras 65–66, the procedure in the Court of Appeal could not remedy the defect at trial, as the appellate body was not in the same position as the trial judge to assess and monitor through the trial the relevance of the withheld material; *Dowsett v UK*, June 24, 2003, nor was it enough that the applicant could apply to the Court of Appeal for it to order disclosure to the defence as it would reach its decision without assistance from the defence or first-hand knowledge of the trial. In effect the onus is on the prosecution to obtain a judicial ruling on non-disclosure of potentially relevant material (see Sir Nicolas Bratza's concurring opinion).

[24] (8403/78) (Rep.) December 14, 1981, 27 D.R. 61.

[25] (8403/78), fn.24 above. Also *Bricmont v Belgium*, July 7, 1989, Series A, No.158, 12 E.H.R.R. 217, no violation for the authorities' failure to produce an exhibit which the applicants said would have enabled them to rebut the charge, since they did not give details supporting this, nor was there a violation from failure to obtain a special audit of accounts since they had never asked for one.

[26] *Padin Gestoso v Spain*, (39519/98) (Dec.) December 8, 1998, ECHR 1999–II.

[27] *Foucher v France*, March 18, 1997, R.J.D. 1997–II, No.33, 25 E.H.R.R. 234, para.32.

[28] *Kremzow*, fn.9 above, para.63.

[29] *Kremzow*, fn.9 above, para.63; *Ocalan v Turkey*, May 12, 2005, ECHR 2005–IV, paras 139–144, finding a violation where the accused was not permitted to inspect the evidence produced by the prosecution personally before the hearings and when the applicant's lawyers made their comments on that evidence, they had yet to obtain the accused's observations following a direct inspection of the documentation.

[30] *Matyjek v Poland*, April 24, 2007.

refusal to order a second expert opinion where a psychiatrist changed his opinion in a very adverse manner during questioning at trial violated Art.6, paras 1 and 3(b), though the Court emphasised that the mere fact that an expert changes an opinion would not, per se, infringe the principles of fairness (see further Pt IIA, s.9(6): Refusal to call expert evidence or take other investigative measures).

5. Facilities: overlap with access to legal advice

There is overlap with the right of access to a lawyer, since representation by a lawyer is often meaningless unless some prior consultation is included in the "facilities" provided to the defendant.[31] In *Domenchini v Italy*, monitoring of a prisoner's correspondence with his defence lawyer was a violation of Art.6, para.3(b) since the delay in forwarding a letter led to the filing of grounds after the statutory time-limit. Similarly, the restriction on the number and length of the applicant's meetings with his lawyers in *Ocalan v Turkey* was one of the factors rendering the preparation of his defence difficult.[32] **II–041**

6. Article 6, para.3(a): information about the charge

Where an applicant has not been promptly informed of the charge, this may prevent him from properly preparing his defence at the same time.[33] The provision of information that an offence has been reclassified, or that the material facts at the base of the charge have been modified, is not enough since it has to be in good time and allow the opportunity to organise the defence in a practical and effective manner on the basis of the changes.[34] **II–042**

Cross-reference

Part IIA, s.1: General principles: fairness.
Part IIA, s.11: Information about the charge.
Part IIA, s.15: Legal representation in criminal proceedings.

[31] *Campbell and Fell v UK*, June 28, 1984, Series A, No.80, 7 E.H.R.R. 165.
[32] *Ocalan v Turkey*, fn.29 above, paras 134–137.
[33] e.g. *Chichlian and Ekindjian v France*, November 28, 1989, Series A, No.162–B.
[34] *Pelissier and Sassi v France*, March 23, 1999, ECHR 1999–II, 30 E.H.R.R. 715, para.62; *Mattocia v Italy*, July 25, 2000, ECHR 2000–IX, paras 71–72; *Sadak v Turkey*, July 2, 2001, ECHR 2001–VII, paras 56–58; (24751/94) (Dec.) June 28, 1995, 82–A D.R. 85.

4. Appeals

Key provision:

II–043 Article 6, paras 1–3 (fair trial).

Key case-law:

Delcourt v Belgium, January 17, 1970, Series A, No.11, 1 E.H.R.R. 355; *Pretto v Italy*, December 8, 1983, Series A, No.71, 6 E.H.R.R. 182; *Axen v Germany*, February 22, 1983, Series A, No.72, 6 E.H.R.R. 195; *Sutter v Switzerland*, February 22, 1984, Series A, No.74, 6 E.H.R.R. 272; *Monnell and Morris v UK*, March 2, 1987, Series A, No.115, 10 E.H.R.R. 205; *Ekbatani v Sweden*, May 26, 1988, Series A, No.134, 13 E.H.R.R. 504; *Kremzow v Austria*, September 21, 1993, Series A, No.268–B, 17 E.H.R.R. 322; *Brualla Gomez de la Torre v Spain*, December 19, 1997, R.J.D. 1997–VIII, No.61.

1. General considerations

II–044 There is no right to appeal contained in the Convention itself (as opposed to the right provided for in Art.2 of Protocol No.7). However, where a judicial system provides for appeals, the Court has held, since *Delcourt v Belgium*,[1] that the fundamental guarantees provided in Art.6 will apply. Having regard, however, to the fact that in many Contracting States higher instances take differing forms, this is subject to the rider that the way in which Art.6 applies will depend on the special features of the proceedings. This includes consideration of the functions, in law and practice, of the appellate body, its powers and the manner in which the interests of the parties are presented and protected.[2]

There can, therefore, be no right either to provision of any particular kind of appeal procedure or manner of dealing with appeals. For example, Art.6 does not require that matters of new evidence raised on appeal should be remitted by the Court of Appeal for rehearing by a jury.[3] Access to a final instance may be regulated and include conditions such as the requirement to be represented by a lawyer or the imposition of fines for abusive appeals.[4]

2. Application of Art.6 guarantees

II–045 Where an appeal lies, the provisions of Art.6 generally will apply. However, there may be special features of the appellate body or its procedure which will affect the way in which the guarantees apply.

One important distinction has been found to exist between appeal proceedings proper and leave to appeal proceedings. In *Monnell and Morris v UK*, the Court found it was not incompatible with fairness that the applicants were not present or

[1] *Delcourt v Belgium*, January 17, 1970, Series A, No.11, 1 E.H.R.R. 355, paras 25–26.
[2] *Monnell and Morris v UK*, March 2, 1987, Series A, No.115, 10 E.H.R.R. 205, para.56.
[3] e.g. (14739/89) (Dec.) May 9, 1989, 60 D.R. 296.
[4] (16598/90) (Dec.) November 16, 1990, 66 D.R. 260; (15384/89) (Dec.) May 9, 1994, 77–A D.R. 5.

represented in leave to appeal applications as they did not involve the rehearing of witnesses or re-examination of the facts, the issue being whether there were arguable grounds which would justify the hearing of an appeal. The principle of equality of arms was respected since the prosecution did not appear and the applicants had advice as to their prospects of appeal and the opportunity to submit written submissions. Where applicants had already been represented by counsel at trial, this was considered sufficient to safeguard their interests. In contrast, in *Granger v UK*, where full appeal proceedings were in issue, the failure to provide the accused with legal representation did disclose a violation of Art.6, para.3(c). The prosecution was present and the applicant could not be expected to present his case effectively.

Where appeal proceedings involve points of law only or a limited cassation procedure, the approach has been taken that lack of an oral hearing at second or third instances may be justified by these special features.[5] Where, however, as in *Ekbatani v Sweden*, a court of appeal has to examine both facts and law and cannot fairly or properly determine the issues without hearing the applicant or other witnesses in person, the denial of an oral hearing or right to be heard in person may disclose a violation. Similarly, where an appeal raises issues as to the personality of the applicant, he may claim a right to be present and participate.[6] The Court has stated, however, that the personal attendance of the accused does not take on the same crucial significance for an appeal hearing as it does for trial.[7]

The requirement for higher instance courts to render judgments publicly has also been interpreted in light of their role. Where their function is to confirm lower instances' judgments or give brief decisions, it has been considered sufficient if the lower instances' judgments are rendered publicly and "public" access to the superior court's decision is provided for by way of, for example, access to court registry records.[8]

Presumption of innocence may also cease to apply in appeal proceedings, due to the nature of those proceedings, after an accused has been convicted at first instance. It has therefore not been successfully argued that the Court of Appeal in England fails to comply with this requirement in the test which it applies in deciding whether or not to quash a conviction in light of new evidence.[9]

The Court has also found that conditions of access to superior appeal courts, in particular Supreme Courts, may be stricter and more formal. It found no deprivation of access to court in *Brualla Gomez de la Torre v Spain*, where an applicant's appeal to the Supreme Court was rejected due to an intervening change in the criteria for cases which it could deal with.[10] The applicant had, it noted, received two full hearings in lower instance courts. Where appeal lies however, procedural rules

[5] *Axen v Germany*, February 22, 1983, Series A, No.72, 6 E.H.R.R. 195; *Sutter v Switzerland*, February 22, 1984, Series A, No.74, 6 E.H.R.R. 272.

[6] *Kremzow v Austria*, September 21, 1993, Series A, No.268–B, 17 E.H.R.R. 322.

[7] *Kamasinski v Austria*, December 19, 1989, Series A, No.168, 13 E.H.R.R. 36, para.107, where the Court also noted the difficulties that attach to the attendance of prisoners.

[8] *Pretto v Italy*, December 8, 1983, Series A, No.71, 6 E.H.R.R. 182; *Axen*; and *Sutter*, fn.5 above.

[9] (14739/89), fn.3 above.

[10] See also *KDB v Netherlands*, March 27, 1998, R.J.D. 1998–II, No.68, where the Supreme Court gave the applicant no warning as to when it would consider his case, but he had not shown that he had not had the opportunity to file his written grounds; *Berger v France*, December 3, 2002, ECHR 2002–X, acceptable limitations on access to higher instance by a "*partie civile*"; *De Ponte Nascimento v UK*, (55331/00) (Dec.) January 31, 2002, concerning the grounds on which the Court of Appeal should grant leave. See also Pt IIA, s.2: Access to court.

should not operate or be interpreted so strictly so as to block effective access.[11] An overly-formalistic approach which prevents the substance of the applicant's Convention complaints being examined may also be incompatible with fairness requirements.[12]

The requirement to pay a fine before being permitted to appeal is not seen as unduly onerous, being regarded as a measure pursuing the effective administration of justice and dissuading abusive and dilatory appeals.[13] Nor is the obligation to pay the award ordered by the lower court as a precondition to an appeal, per se, a restriction on access to court. However, where there has been a manifest disproportion between the sum payable and the appellant's means, the Court has found an unreasonable restriction on access to court.[14]

A lawyer cannot be required to lodge appeal grounds if of the view that none arise. Nonetheless the procedure must be so arranged that the applicant is not denied the opportunity to pursue his appeal by other means. Thus, where the applicant was only notified by the lawyer that no appeal would be lodged three days before the expiry of the time-limit to appeal, the applicant was deprived of any real opportunity of appealing.[15] Even where the time-limit ran from the date of notification to the applicant of the lawyer's refusal to lodge grounds of appeal, there was a failure to secure his access to court in a concrete or effective manner as the court failed to inform him that he had a month to seek a replacement lawyer.[16]

If, however, an appeal is doomed to fail on technical grounds, procedural inequalities may not raise problems as the Court has stated that Art.6 did not operate to protect purely theoretical rights.[17]

3. Curing defects at first instance

II–046 In criminal proceedings, the extent to which a higher court can cure defects in the trial is limited, though the possibility exists where the nature of the defect permits the effect of the shortcoming to be rectified.[18] An accused has a right to a fair trial

[11] See, e.g. *Miragall Escolano v Spain*, January 25, ECHR 2000–I, concerning running of a time-limit from an event of which the applicants had no knowledge; *Sotiris and Nikos Koutras Attee v Greece*, November 16, 2000, ECHR 2000–XII, where the applicant company's appeal to the Supreme Administrative Court was struck out for an excessively formalistic approach to a clerical error for which it was not responsible; *Beles v Czech Republic*, November 12, 2002, ECHR 2002–IX, application of procedural rule blocking effective access to Constitutional Court; *Mercieca v Malta*, June 14, 2011, concerning refusal to annul a wrongful application of a time-limit which prevented access to an appeal.

[12] *Perlala v Greece*, February 22, 2007.

[13] *Schneider v France*, (49852/06) (Dec.) June 30, 2009, the Court rejected the applicant's claim that her financial means were too low to allow her to pay: see Pt IIA, s.5: Costs in court, concerning issues of access to court from impecuniosity.

[14] *Annoni di Gussola v France*, November 14, 2000, ECHR 2000–XI, sum exceeded the applicant's means by 42 to 1; *Chatellier v France*, March 31, 2011, paras 34–44, disproportion of 240 to 1.

[15] *Sialkowska v Poland*, March 22, 2007, paras 108–117.

[16] *Kulikowski v Poland*, May 19, 2009, paras 60–71.

[17] e.g. *Sale v France*, March 21, 2006.

[18] *De Cubber v Belgium*, October 26, 1984, Series A, No.86, para.33; *Adolf v Austria*, March 26, 1982, Series A, No.49, paras 38–41, where the Supreme Court cleared of any finding of guilt an applicant in respect of whom the lower court had breached the presumption of innocence; *Edwards v UK*, December 16, 1992, Series A, No.247–B, 15 E.H.R.R. 417, where it was found that the review of a conviction by the Court of Appeal in light of material undisclosed to the defence by the police at the trial remedied the defects in the original trial. See other cases cited Pt IIA, s.9(5): Failure to disclose evidence.

at first instance with all the guarantees and it is no argument to state that, for example, the appellate body offers the independence lacking below.[19]

In civil proceedings however, proceedings lacking in conformity with Art.6, para.1 may be cured by subsequent review of the case by a tribunal offering the necessary guarantees and appropriate scope of review.[20]

However, it is not always an answer to refusing access on an interlocutory appeal that the applicant may appeal later in the substantive procedure on the merits. A defect in civil interim proceedings may not necessarily be remedied at a later stage since any prejudice suffered in the meantime might by then have become irreversible.[21] Also where the interim appeal could have determined the issues, the access to the appeal at the merits stage did not counter the wrongful annulment of that appeal where the applicants had meanwhile to suffer the anxiety and costs of the further proceedings.[22]

[19] *Findlay v UK*, February 25, 1997, 1997 R.J.D. 1997–I, No.30, para.79, lack of independent and impartial tribunal at first instance court martial; *Foucher v France*, March 18, 1997, R.J.D. 1997–II, No.33, denial of access to the file at first instance not cured by the possibility of applying for access on appeal; *Rowe and Davis v UK*, February 16, 2000, ECHR 2000–II, para.65, where the trial judge should have assessed whether evidence should not be disclosed on public interest grounds and review by the Court of Appeal was not sufficient to remedy this; *Condron v UK*, May 2, 2000, ECHR 2000–V, para.63, where the review by the Court of Appeal of the safety of the conviction did not remedy the trial judge's failure to direct the jury not to draw any inference from the applicants' failure to answer police questions.

[20] *Le Compte, Van Leuven and De Meyere v Belgium*, June 23, 1981, Series A, No.43, 4 E.H.R.R. 1, where the proceedings before the Appeals Council were not in public and not cured by a public hearing before the Court of Cassation since it could not take cognisance of the merits of cases. See, however, in special contexts, e.g. *Bryan v UK*, November 22, 1995, Series A, No.335–A, 21 E.H.R.R. 342; and *Zumtobel v Austria*, September 21, 1993, Series A, No.268–A, 17 E.H.R.R. 116, where restricted scope of review was accepted; (18874/91) (Dec.) January 12, 1994, 76–A D.R. 44.

[21] *Micallef v Malta*, October 15, 2009, para.80.

[22] *Mercieca v Malta*, fn.11 above, para.50.

5. Costs in court

Key provisions:

II–047 Article 6, paras 1 (access to court for fair trial) and 2 (presumption of innocence), and Art.1 of Protocol No.1 (peaceful enjoyment of possessions).

Key case-law:

Airey v Ireland, October 9, 1979, Series A, No.32, 2 E.H.R.R. 305; *Tolstoy v UK*, July 7, 1995, Series A, No.316, 20 E.H.R.R. 442; *Masson and Van Zon v Netherlands*, September 28, 1995, Series A, No.327, 22 E.H.R.R. 491; *Robins v UK*, September 23, 1997, R.J.D. 1997–V, No.49, 26 E.H.R.R. 527; *Ait-Mouhoub v France*, October 28, 1998, R.J.D. 1998–VIII, No.96, 30 E.H.R.R. 382; *Kreuz v Poland*, June 19, 2001, ECHR 2001–VI.

1. General considerations

II–048 Principally problems have arisen as to the compatibility with the presumption of innocence of costs orders against acquitted accused; the extent to which the guarantees of Art.6, para.1 apply to the costs proceedings following substantive litigation; and the impact which costs may have on effective access to court.

The obligation to pay "litigation costs" as such does not appear to involve any right under substantive provisions since they are "contributions" within the meaning of the second paragraph of Art.1 of Protocol No.1 and escape detailed supervision.[1] The Commission found that the basic rule that costs follow the event in civil litigation was reasonable, acting as a disincentive to unnecessary litigation and providing for at least the recovery of some of the successful litigant's costs.[2]

2. Costs orders against acquitted accused

II–049 See Pt IIA, s.19: Presumption of innocence.

3. Applicability of Art.6, para.1 to costs procedures

(a) Criminal proceedings

II–050 Whether the guarantees of Art.6 apply to proceedings concerning reimbursement of legal costs incurred in a criminal trial in which an applicant has been acquitted depends principally on whether there is a "right" to costs in domestic law. The grant to a public authority of a considerable measure of discretion may indicate that no right is recognised in domestic law, as in *Masson and Van Zon v Netherlands*, where the courts made awards where "reasons in equity" existed.

(b) Civil proceedings

II–051 Cost procedures following substantive proceedings were generally held by the Commission not to involve the civil rights of the individual.[3] This view was overruled by the Court in *Robins v UK*. It now appears established that, where the

[1] (15434/89) (Dec.) February 15, 1990, 64 D.R. 232.

[2] See fn.1 above.

[3] (8569/79) (Dec.) May 8, 1985, 42 D.R. 23, where the substantive action concerned public law; (21775/93) (Dec.) May 25, 1995, 81 D.R. 48, where the Commission found the question of costs was a subsidiary issue to the main civil proceedings and did not concern civil rights and obligations; majority Commission opinion in *Robins v UK* September 23, 1997, R.J.D. 1997–V, No.49, 26 E.H.R.R. 527.

substantive proceedings involve civil rights and obligations, the cost proceedings, even if separately decided, must be seen as a continuation of the substantive litigation, therefore falling within the scope of Art.6, para.1. Thus, four years taken in the costs proceedings in the *Robins* case disclosed a violation of the reasonable time requirement of that provision.[4] Considering the limited or technical nature of the issues arising in costs proceedings, it is perhaps doubtful that the guarantees of Art.6 will apply with full vigour, for example as regards the requirement for public hearings or the public rendering of decisions.

Any unfair advantage enjoyed by a party in proceedings as regards costs may raise issues of equality of arms. In *Stankiewicz v Poland*, where, contrary to the normal rule, the public prosecutor could not be held liable for litigation costs in civil proceedings brought unsuccessfully against the applicant concerning allegedly overpaid land compensation, the Court noted that while such a privilege may be justified for the protection of the legal order, it should not be applied so as to put a party to civil proceedings at an undue disadvantage vis-à-vis the prosecuting authorities, and the court should have used their powers to mitigate the costs implications for the applicant.[5] Conversely, although comment was made that it was perhaps surprising that a judge ordered an environmental NGO to pay the costs of a third party, a multinational intervenor, this was not found unfair in the circumstances where the intervenor had a legitimate interest to defend and the amount of costs was moderate.[6]

4. Access to court

The requirement to pay fees or costs in advance in connection with civil claims is not, in itself, incompatible with Art.6, para.1.[7] However, although there is no right to free proceedings nor a right to repayment of costs and fees,[8] the high cost of proceedings could raise a problem with respect to right of access to court, if it can be shown to have a prohibitive effect depriving an applicant of the essence of the right having regard to the *Ashingdane* principles.[9] II–052

For example, there was lack of effective access to court in *Airey v Ireland*, where the costs for representation (legal aid not available) in a separation application were "very high", the procedure so complex, and the subject matter entailing an emotional involvement such that the applicant could not be expected effectively to present her own case.

Where a precondition for appeal is the payment into court of security for costs or fees, the cases indicate that such orders which pursue the legitimate aim of protecting one party from being faced with an irrecoverable bill for legal costs if the party appealing is unsuccessful, will disclose no problem if there has been a full and fair hearing at first instance and the court gives a fair chance to the applicant to

[4] See also *Beer v Austria*, February 6, 2001, para.13, affirming the *Robins* approach.

[5] *Stankiewicz v Poland*, April 6, 2006.

[6] *Collectif Stop Melox and Mox v France*, June 12, 2007, the Court noted the risk that this might deter the NGO from pursuing its aims; impliedly it might have decided differently if the costs had been higher.

[7] *Kreuz v Poland*, June 19, 2001, ECHR 2001–VI, para.60.

[8] e.g. (6202/73) (Dec.) March 16, 1975, 1 D.R. 66; (15488/89) (Dec.) February 27, 1995, 80–A D.R. 14.

[9] e.g. whether the essence of the right is impaired and whether the restriction pursues a legitimate aim in a proportionate manner, having regard to the proceedings as a whole. See Pt IIA, s.2: Access to court.

argue that the interests of justice require an appeal to go on.[10] Where such an order is unrelated to an assessment of the merits of the case or prospects of success, the Court stated in *Podbielski and PPU Polpure v Poland* that there should be a particularly rigorous scrutiny from the point of view of the interests of justice. It found that an order for costs which was too high for the applicant company, which was on the verge of insolvency, and which was unrelated to protecting the other party but geared instead to providing funds to the Government, did not strike the right balance.[11] The Court has given weight to the importance of what is at stake for the applicant, as in *Kniat v Poland* where the applicant was appealing in a divorce case and found it unreasonable to require her to pay fees in such an action, particularly where it would have to come out of the award which was going to be her only asset.[12] Similarly, where the Supreme Court refused to examine the applicant prisoner's appeal about force-feeding due to failure to pay the court fee, the Court found that it should have considered his application for fee waiver in light of the seriousness of his complaint, particularly since this was a ground for waiver: further, the court should have considered this ground even though it had not been raised by the applicant himself.[13]

The Court has been even stricter where significant costs orders have been imposed as condition for the claim being processed at first instance, emphasising the prominent place held by the right to a court in a democratic society.[14] In *Ait-Mouhoub v France*, where 80,000 franc orders were imposed on an applicant without financial resources, seeking to bring civil actions against police officers for misconduct, the Court found that the sum was disproportionate and deprived him of access to court.[15] The merits of the complaints were apparently irrelevant, the Court not accepting the Government's claims that the orders were necessary to prevent wrongful claims being brought. A lack of adequate procedural safeguards has also been found where the court refused to grant assistance for costs on merits grounds in a written procedure, without hearing the applicants and without any appeal possible.[16]

[10] See *Tolstoy v UK*, July 13, 1995, Series A, No.316, 20 E.H.R.R. 442, where the applicant, the unsuccessful defendant in defamation proceedings (£1.5 million award) was required to pay £124,000 as security in costs in order to pursue his appeal. However, the applicant had had a full hearing at first instance; there was no indication that the sum was not a fair reflection of the likely costs and the Court of Appeal considered the merits of the case in deciding whether or not the measure would amount to a denial of justice, thereby showing no arbitrariness but basing itself on a full and thorough evaluation of the relevant factors. If the matter had been decided purely by the registrar of the court, the result might not be so obvious.

[11] *Podbielski and PPU Polpure v Poland*, July 26, 2005, paras 65–69.

[12] *Kniat v Poland*, July 26, 2005.

[13] *Ciorap v Moldova*, June 19, 2007, para.95. See also *Iordache v Romania*, October 14, 2008, para.42, the Court emphasised the importance of the appeal, concerning the applicant's right of access to his son and the best interests of the child; it also noted that the courts had not explained the stamp duty procedure or the possibility of applying for exoneration.

[14] e.g. *Ait-Mouhoub v France*, October 28, 1998, R.J.D. 1998–VIII, No.96, 30 E.H.R.R. 382, para.52; *Kreuz*, fn.7 above, paras 57 and 66; *Weissman v Romania*, May 24, 2006, para.42.

[15] See also *Kreuz v Poland*, fn.7 above, where a requirement to pay 100 million PLZ for lodging an action was considered excessive—the Court found the domestic court's view that the applicant could pay that amount was based on assumptions and that they rejected his assertion of inability to pay without obtaining or considering any evidence on the point. See, conversely, *Sinko v Slovakia*, (33466/96) (Dec.) May 20, 1998, where the court fees were not considered excessively high and the applicant had been offered the chance to make instalments and had not shown that he could not afford them; *Reuther v Germany*, (74789/01) (Dec.) June 5, 2003, where fees (about €750) for the Bavarian Constitutional Court were not considered excessive.

[16] *Bakan v Turkey*, June 12, 2007.

On the other hand, where court fees are levied on a percentage basis in respect of pecuniary claims, the Court has noted that there is a direct relationship between the object of the proceedings and the court fee, since that fee depends on the amount that the person concerned has chosen to claim.[17] In *Jankauskas v Lithuania*, it did not find fees of 5 per cent of a pecuniary claim in a defamation case problematic where the applicant had failed to justify the high amount claimed.[18] Where continuation of the proceedings was not dependent on payment of the fees and there was flexibility in the system allowing for exemption, total or partial, the Court found no problem of access to court in a system requiring, in an insolvency case, payment of a percentage of total debts claimed rather than the percentage recoverable.[19] Conversely in *Weissman v Romania*, where the applicant's claim for loss of profits from a building confiscated by the State was not unreasonable given the value of the property, the requirement to pay stamp duty of some €300,000 at first instance was found to be disproportionate and impairing the essence of the right of access to court.[20]

Where claims for compensation are against the State, the Court has emphasised that costs systems should not work in such a way that what the State gives with one hand it takes back with the other. A levy of 4 per cent by way of court costs on the unsuccessful monetary amount of a claim, even where the applicant won on the legal issue of wrongful pre-trial detention, was found to be unduly disproportionate. The Court did not think the applicant was to blame in putting a high price on his loss of liberty and noted that non-pecuniary damage was notoriously difficult to assess in advance. Since in this case he lost 90 per cent of his compensation award to costs, the Court found a denial of access to court, remarking that in other jurisdictions this situation was avoided by either not levying fees, imposing a low flat rate or giving the courts a discretion.[21]

The manner in which the domestic court decides whether the applicant is able to pay court fees is a relevant factor. If the court gives reasons and shows due regard to the personal situation of the applicant, there may be no problem.[22] However, an assessment based on hypothetical considerations without proper enquiry into the applicants' means disclosed a violation in *Jedamski and Jedamska v Poland*.[23] Reliance on an assumption of ability to pay due to the fact that the applicants had legal representation was found arbitrary.[24]

[17] *Kniat v Poland*, fn.12 cited above, para.41.

[18] *Jankauskas v Lithuania*, December 16, 2003.

[19] *Urbanek v Austria*, December 9, 2010, paras 55–65, the applicant had not shown that this system necessarily would result in fees higher than the amount recovered.

[20] Cited fn.14 above.

[21] *Stankov v Bulgaria*, July 12, 2007, paras 58–66.

[22] *VM v Bulgaria*, June 8, 2006. See also *Rylski v Poland*, July 4, 2006, where the Court's decision was not arbitrary, the applicant having failed to provide supporting documents.

[23] *Jedamski and Jedamska v Poland*, July 26, 2005. See also *Telcatronic CATV v Poland*, January 10, 2006, where the domestic court was unreasonable to assume that a small company in a precarious situation could obtain a loan or to expect it to sell assets.

[24] *Bakan*, fn.16 above. See also *Mehmet and Sunna Yigit v Turkey*, July 17, 2007, paras 33–39, the applicants were refused exemption from court fees as they had a lawyer, the domestic court not taking into account that he was hired on a contingency fee agreement and that the applicants had no means to pay the court fees.

5. Penalty costs orders against lawyers

II–053 Wasted costs orders against lawyers in courts do not concern the determination of civil rights or obligations and thus do not attract guarantees of Art.6. Nor have they been found to involve the determination of a criminal charge.[25] Such orders are regarded as "contributions" within the meaning of the second paragraph of Art.1 of Protocol No.1, and not an interference with possessions.[26]

6. Success costs

II–054 A system which resulted in the imposition of exorbitant costs fees against a losing newspaper in an action for breach of confidence was found to have a disproportionate and unjustified chilling effect on press freedom of expression.[27]

[25] (10615/83) (Dec.) July 3, 1984, 38 D.R. 213; *Tormala v Finland*, (41528/98) (Dec.) March 16, 2004.
[26] (7544/76) (Dec.) July 12, 1978, 14 D.R. 60; (7909/74) (Dec.) October 12, 1994, 15 D.R. 160.
[27] *MGN Ltd v UK*, January 18, 2011, paras 198–220, where the model, Naomi Campbell, had successfully sued a newspaper for publishing details of her attendance at Narcotics Anonymous, the newspaper only had to pay her £3,500 in damages but a massive £500,000 to her lawyers in success fees and base costs.

6. Double jeopardy

Key provisions:

Article 6, para.1 (fair trial); Art.4 of Protocol No.7 (no trial or punishment in same State for offence for which already acquitted or convicted). II–055

Key case-law:

Gradinger v Austria, October 23, 1995, Series A, No.328–C; *Oliveira v Switzerland*, July 30, 1998, R.J.D. 1998–V, No.83, 28 E.H.R.R. 289; *Franz Fischer v Austria*, May 29, 2001; *Nikitin v Russia*, July 20, 2004, ECHR 2004–VIII; *Zolotukhin v Russia*, February 10, 2009, ECHR 2009–. . .

1. General considerations

The principle of "double jeopardy" or *non bis in idem* which prohibits that a person be tried twice for the same offence is not expressly contained in the Convention itself but subject to specific provision in Art.4 of Protocol No.7, which only came into force relatively recently for a number of Contracting States.[1] II–056

2. Fairness

While it has not been clearly excluded that the trial of a person for the same offence in the same State could not raise separate issues of fairness under Art.6, para.1,[2] which would be of relevance where a State has not ratified Protocol No.7, such a possibility would be difficult to reconcile with the existence of the specific right in Protocol No.7, notwithstanding arguments as to the widespread recognition of the fundamental principle. II–057

The Commission stated that, in interpreting the provisions of the Convention, it might be useful to take into account provisions contained in other international legal instruments, including the Brussels Convention which barred prosecution of a person in one State in respect of whom a trial had been finally disposed of in another State concerning the same facts. However, there was no question of lending provisions of the Convention a scope which the contracting parties expressly intended to exclude by means of a Protocol which applied only to prosecution of a person twice within the same State. Article 6 could not, therefore, be interpreted to imply a more extended right applying between States.[3]

The re-opening of criminal trials is to be distinguished from separate proceedings concerning the same offence (see below). Even if permitted under Art.4 of Protocol No.7, the manner in which the power to re-open is exercised may raise issues of fairness under Art.6. The authorities must strike a fair balance between the interests of the acquitted individual and the effectiveness of the criminal justice system.[4]

[1] The UK and Ireland have not ratified.
[2] (9433/81) (Dec.) December 11, 1981, 27 D.R. 233; (8945/80) (Dec.) December 13, 1983, 39 D.R. 43.
[3] 2(1072/92) (Dec.) January 1, 1995, 80–B D.R. 89, where the applicant had allegedly been tried in Denmark and Italy in respect of the same matters.
[4] *Nikitin v Russia*, July 20, 2004, ECHR 2004–VIII, paras 47 and 54–57, no violation as the application for re-opening was in fact decided in the applicant's favour.

Violations have arisen where the grounds for re-opening the proceedings were not based on new facts, nor on serious procedural defects, but rather on disagreement with the assessment of the facts and the classification of the applicant's actions by the lower instances.[5]

3. The prohibition against trial or punishment for an offence already subject to an acquittal or conviction

II–058 The first paragraph of this provision establishes the principle that no one shall be liable to be tried or punished in criminal proceedings under the jurisdiction of the same State for an offence for which he has already been finally acquitted or convicted. Both sets of proceedings must be criminal; where an applicant was sanctioned administratively for safety failings in a disciplinary context and later tried on a criminal charge, Art.4 of Protocol 7 did not apply.[6]

The Court has taken a pragmatic view on one point, holding that where a court closes a second set of criminal proceedings on recognition of fact of an earlier decision on the matter, no issue arises.[7] However, the fact that a person is acquitted in the second proceedings, on grounds not relevant to the *non bis in idem* principle, does not prevent a violation as the prohibition covers prosecution and trial as well as punishment.[8] An acquittal on substantive grounds does not therefore remove victim status; acquittal or other termination of the subsequent proceedings which later acknowledge a violation of the *non bis in idem* principle and offer appropriate redress by way of effacing its effects would do so.[9]

Nor did the provision apply where a public prosecutor had earlier discontinued proceedings, such not amounting to a conviction or an acquittal, or other form of final decision, first time round.[10] Where in one set of proceedings the court does not in fact rule one way or another on an element specified in the indictment, a second trial concerning a similar offence containing that element will not offend as the defendant will not have already been convicted or acquitted in that regard.[11] Nor does the prohibition cover imposition of several penalties flowing from one conviction, e.g. a prison sentence and fine by a court and withdrawal of the driving licence by an administrative body in respect of a drunken driving offence.[12] Measures which are not criminal in nature, such as the withdrawal of a residence permit, do not count.[13]

[5] e.g. *Savinsky v Ukraine*, February 28, 2006, para.25.

[6] *Kurdov and Ivanov v Bulgaria*, May 31, 2011, paras 35–46.

[7] See *Zigarella v Italy*, (48154/99) (Dec.) October 3, 2002, ECHR 2002–IX.

[8] See *Zolutukhin v Russia*, February 10, 2009, ECHR 2009–. . ., paras 110–111.

[9] See *Zolutukhin v Russia*, paras 115–118, citing as an example *Ščiukina v Lithuania*, (19251/02) (Dec.) December 5, 2006, where the Supreme Court had found a breach of the *ne bis in idem* principle and there was provision for repealing the effects.

[10] See *Smirnova v Russia*, (46133/99) and (48183/99) (Dec.) October 3, 2002. Similarly in *Sundqvist v Finland*, (75602/01) (Dec.) November 22, 2005, as the decision of the public prosecutor not to prosecute was not final in domestic law, the review by the Prosecutor General reversing that decision did not lead to a second, separate trial.

[11] *Bachmaier v Austria*, (77413/01) (Dec.) September 2, 2004. See also *Marcello Viola v Italy*, October 5, 2006, same offence in two trials, but covering different time periods.

[12] *RT v Switzerland*, (31982/96) (Dec.) May 30, 2000; see also *Nilson v Sweden*, (73661/01) (Dec.) December 13, 2005, where the suspension of a licence was sufficiently linked in substance and time to the earlier criminal conviction.

[13] *Davydov v Estonia*, (16387/03) (Dec.) May 31, 2003. See also *Storbraten and Mjelde v Norway*, (12277/04) and (11143/04) (Dec.) February 1, 2007, where the disqualification from holding company directorships or forming companies was a preventive, civil measure and did not bar subsequent prosecutions for insolvency offences.

There have been few significant cases in this area. Those there are mainly establish that administrative proceedings which penalise the same conduct in issue in a criminal trial will offend the prohibition, notwithstanding the differing designations and the allegedly different purpose of the proceedings. In *Gradinger v Austria*, the applicant, who killed a cyclist while driving, was convicted of causing death by negligence rather than the more serious crime of being under influence of alcohol since his level was below the prescribed limit. The administrative authorities proceeded to fine him for driving under the influence of drink on the basis of a medical report which deduced that in fact he was over the limit. Since both decisions were based on the same conduct, there was a violation of Art.4 of Protocol No.7.[14]

However, the fact that a person is convicted of separate offences arising out of a particular event was not found incompatible with this provision where, as in *Oliveira v Switzerland*, the applicant was convicted first of failing to adapt her speed to road conditions and then, in a separate procedure relating to the same road traffic accident, of negligently causing injury. The Court commented, however, that it would have been more consistent with the principles governing the proper administration of justice for a sentence in respect of the two offences to be passed by the same court in a single set of proceedings. In later cases, this was distinguished from the situation where the essential elements of two offences based on one act are the same, for example where one offence encompasses all the elements of the other plus an additional one, in which case two prosecutions will in fact concern the same essential elements and a violation will arise.[15]

In *Zolotukhin v Russia*, the Grand Chamber sought to harmonise the varying approaches summarised above. It held that the focus should not be on "the essential elements" of the respective offences or the legal characterisation of the different offences, which it regarded as too restrictive an interpretation of a fundamental right. Instead, the focus should be on whether the offences are based on the same facts, the existence of which must be demonstrated in order to secure a conviction or institute criminal proceedings. Thus where the applicant was sanctioned administratively for minor disorderly acts (swearing at a public employee and breach of public order in a police station by pushing an official) and then convicted for the same incident of swearing and misbehaviour in the police station, substantially the same facts were at the base of both offences, disclosing a violation. It was not relevant that the later offence also took into account the element of threatening violence.[16]

[14] The Commission commented strongly that it would render Art.4 of Protocol No.7 ineffective if States could prosecute an individual under nominally different offences.

[15] *Franz Fischer v Austria*, May 29, 2001, violation where the applicant was fined by an administrative authority for drunken driving and convicted by a court for causing death by negligence while intoxicated—the problem was not resolved by reduction of his prison term to take into account the administrative fine; contrast *Ponsetti and Chesnil v France*, (36855/97) and (41731/98) (Dec.) September 14, 1999, ECHR 1999–VI, where the constitutive elements of the two offences (the fiscal penalties imposed for failure to make tax returns and the criminal offence of wilful tax evasion) were considered to be different, incompatible *ratione materiae*; *Goktan v France*, July 2, 2002, where the applicant was fined by customs for importation of contraband and convicted and imprisoned for drug trafficking offences, the Court found no violation, albeit with some reluctance.

[16] *Zolotukhin v Russia*, February 10, 2009, ECHR 2009–. . . , paras 78–87. See also *Tsonyo Tsonev v Bulgaria (No.2)*, January 14, 2010, paras 51–52, fine for breach of by-law in breaking down a door and assaulting a person concerned substantially the same facts as the criminal charge for inflicting bodily harm; and *Ruotsilainen v Finland*, June 16, 2009, paras 56–57, where the applicant was subject to a penal order and fuel fee debit based on substantially the same facts, namely, his use of fuel subject to a lesser tax rating.

4. The re-opening exception

II–059 The second paragraph excludes from the prohibition the situation where criminal proceedings are re-opened, according to domestic law, because of evidence of new or newly-discovered facts or if there has been a fundamental defect in the proceedings which could affect the outcome of the case. In *Nikitin v Russia*, the Procurator's request for supervisory review of an acquittal was regarded as a form of re-opening since, if the review occurred, it would have the effect of annulling decisions previously taken by courts and to determine the criminal charge anew. The applicant was therefore not "liable to be tried again" for the purposes of Art.4 of Protocol No.7.

7. Entrapment and agents provocateurs

Key provisions:

Article 6, para.1 (fair trial), and Art.8 (private life). II–060

Key case-law:

Ludi v Switzerland, June 15, 1992, Series A, No.238, 15 E.H.R.R. 173; *Teixeira de Castro v Portugal*, June 9, 1998, 1998–IV, No.77; *Ramanauskas v Lithuania*, February 5, 2008.

1. General considerations

The fine line between entrapment, incitement and legitimate undercover investigation is a well-known problem. There has been a growing body of cases in Strasbourg dealing with exactly this. In the leading case to date, *Teixeira de Castro v Portugal*, the Court emphasised the need to limit the use of undercover agents and to put safeguards in place, holding that, notwithstanding difficulties of fighting crime, the public interest could not justify the use of evidence of an offence obtained at the instigation of the police.[1] Issues principally arise as to the fairness of proceedings where a person becomes involved in a crime which would otherwise not have been contemplated but for the suggestion of the agent provocateur, as to whether the use of evidence gathered undercover is compatible with the rights of the defence, and potentially respect for private life. II–061

2. Relevance to fairness of trial

(a) Instigation of offences

The essential question appears to be whether the role played by the police officer concerned went beyond that of an undercover agent investigating in an essentially passive role and could therefore be considered as instigating the offence. In *Teixeira de Castro v Portugal*, the Court noted that there had been no investigation or suspicion previously against the applicant and that there was nothing to suggest that without police intervention the applicant would have committed the offence of obtaining drugs for them. Similarly in *Vanyan v Russia*,[2] where there was nothing to suggest that the offence would have been committed without the instigation of the informant acting for the police, the conviction of the applicant, mainly on evidence from the tainted police operation, undermined the fairness of the trial. Nor may the police proceed to a "test buy", sending out informants to buy drugs at random.[3] Where a police officer was in frequent contact with the applicant at the former's initiative disclosing a "blatant prompting" to commit the offence of taking bribes and there was no evidence of previous corruption offences, the Court found no II–062

[1] *Teixeira de Castro v Portugal*, June 9, 1998, 1998–IV, No.77, para.36.
[2] *Vanyan v Russia*, December 15, 2005.
[3] *Khudobin v Russia*, October 26, 2006, para.134.

indication that the applicant would have committed the offence without the police action, which had therefore gone beyond investigation.[4]

In contrast, in *Radermacher and Pferrer*,[5] where the Commission found on the facts that the police informer had not initiated the offence but that a third person had come to him, bringing one of the applicants, there was no violation, notwithstanding the active and important role of the police informer in the events leading to the delivery of counterfeit money. The Court has drawn a distinction between infiltration and instigation; where police officers had reason to suspect that a company was involved in offering prostitution services it was not contrary to Art.6 for the police, in investigating undercover, to go online to incite offers of prostitution.[6] Similarly, where a private individual came to the police alleging the applicant had requested a bribe, the Court considered that the police had "joined" rather than instigated the criminal offence when they gave the private individual money and continued in an officially-authorised operation with a view to catching the applicant in the act.[7]

In its assessment, the Court also has regard to the extent to which the police operation was under judicial supervision and the existence of procedural safeguards in the proceedings, namely, the possibility of challenging the use of evidence or the conviction and the seriousness with which the domestic court investigate any element of alleged entrapment.[8] While the Court will not query the findings of domestic courts that there was no entrapment, where such are not arbitrary or manifestly wrong, it may find a lack of fairness where the defence is restricted in access to information and therefore prevented from arguing its case effectively on the issue of entrapment.[9] It has specified that the ordinary safeguards of equality of arms and adversariality are not sufficient to satisfy fairness once a not wholly improbable allegation of entrapment is raised; it has gone so far as to state that the prosecution should prove that no entrapment has occurred and, in the absence of such proof, the domestic court should investigate thoroughly the issue, including the respective roles of the protagonists and the nature of any pressure or incitement.[10]

4 *Ramanauskas v Lithuania*, February 5, 2008, paras 66–68. See also *Malininas v Lithuania*, July 1, 2008, para.38, where, without having any good reason to suspect the applicant of criminal activity, the police officer approached the applicant offering money to buy drugs, playing a "determinative" part in the offence.

5 (12811/87) (Rep.) October 11, 1990, Yearbook of the ECHR, p.274.

6 *Eurafinacom v France*, (58753/00) (Dec.) September 7, 2004, ECHR 2004–VII. See also *Calabro v Italy*, (59895/00) (Dec.) March 21, 2002, where the undercover agent had not provoked the offence—the applicant had contacted him and shown that he was part of a trafficking network—and it was also noted that the conviction was not conclusively based on the agent's testimony, unlike *Teixeira de Castro*, fn.1 above similar reasoning in *Sequiera v Italy*, (73557/01) (Dec.) May 6, 2003.

7 *Miliniene v Lithuania*, June 24, 2008, paras 37–38. See also *Bannikova v Russia*, November 4, 2011, para.69, the drugs deal was underway before the police agent joined in.

8 In *Vanyan*, fn.2 above, the Court commented adversely on the trial court's lack of scrutiny of the police claim that they had information that the applicant had been previously involved in drugs and in *Khudobin*, fn.3 above, where the court did not carry out any factual or legal analysis and there was no judicial or independent supervision of the operation; contrast *Rajcoomar v UK*, (53203/99) (Dec.) December 15, 2005, inadmissible—the judge examined the allegations at length and been "entirely satisfied" the applicant had not been pressurised to commit the offence.

9 *V v Finland*, April 24, 2007, paras 72–81. See also *Edwards and Lewis v UK*, October 27, 2004, ECHR 2004–X, lack of disclosure of evidence relevant to entrapment.

10 *Ramanauskas*, fn.4 above, paras 70–73, the courts failed to examine the issue adequately, violation from the use of the evidence at trial obtained by the police through their incitement. Contrast *Miliniene*, fn.7 above, paras 39–41, the applicant had full opportunity to challenge the evidence against her and the courts examined thoroughly the applicant's allegations, giving a reasoned response for rejecting them.

The Court has also noted with approval the thorough examination of a plea of incitement in which the domestic court took all necessary steps to establish the truth and eradicate doubts as to whether the applicant had been incited by an agent provocateur.[11]

It is no defence for the Government to assert that a police officer was acting on private initiative as distinct from a reported and authorised investigation.[12]

Where an applicant was victim of "private entrapment" by a journalist who obtained evidence against him of drug dealing, the Court considered that the State's role was limited to the prosecution and it restricted its examination to the fairness of the use of evidence at trial.[13]

(b) Use of evidence from undercover agents

The principal consideration is whether the evidence in a trial is put forward in such a way that the proceedings are fair as a whole, including an adequate opportunity for the defence to challenge any evidence before the court. In *Ludi v Switzerland*, where evidence against the applicant included an undercover agent's report, the inability to challenge the agent's evidence in oral proceedings breached Art.6, para.3(d) taken together with para.1, as the rights of the defence had been limited to an extent depriving him of a fair trial. The Court was not satisfied that a need for anonymity excluded all defence challenge of the agent, since matters could have been arranged so as to protect the legitimate police interest in using their agent again.[14] **II–063**

Using informers to trick suspects into making confessions may raise problems of oppression and unfairness, if the methods used sidestep procedural safeguards and are not sufficiently respectful of the privilege against self-incrimination.[15]

3. Invasion of privacy complaints

Deliberate intervention in the affairs of suspects, involving the striking up of relationships and personal contact, might appear to involve an invasion of privacy and to raise problems of respect for private life under Art.8. **II–064**

In *Ludi*, where an applicant was convicted on drugs charges on the basis of evidence of an undercover agent and telephone tapping, the Commission found an interference with private life from the involvement of the undercover officer together with telephone tapping, since the words intercepted had resulted wholly or in part from the relationship which the officer established with the suspect, gaining entry by subterfuge to the suspect's private life. That aspect was not in accordance with law as required by Art.8, para.2, there being insufficient safeguards against arbitrariness, in particular, the legislation did not specify in which cases undercover work was allowed, on whose authority, for what duration or using which methods. The Court did not rule on this aspect, however, since it found that the use of an undercover agent alone or in connection with the telephone interception did not affect private

[11] *Bannikova,* fn.7 above, paras 73–78.

[12] *Ramanauskas*, fn.4 above, paras 63–65, the Government is responsible for police action in carrying out their duties whether on their own or their superiors' initiative.

[13] *Shannon v UK*, (67537/01) (Dec.) April 6, 2004.

[14] See also *Sequiera*, fn.6 above, proceedings found fair where the two undercover agents were heard in court and the applicant was able to question them.

[15] See Part IIA, s.23: Right to silence.

life. It observed that the undercover agent's actions took place within the context of a large cocaine deal, that the applicant must have been aware that he was engaged in a criminal act and that he ran the risk of encountering an undercover police officer. There was apparently no interference with a protected right on the basis that the conduct concerned related to criminal activities, which was perhaps an overly restrictive approach. This old case should be contrasted with the more recent *Bykov v Russia* in which, without discussion, the Grand Chamber stated that it was without dispute that there was interference with private life where a police informer wearing a wire was sent onto the suspect's property (a guest house) in order to record incriminating conversations about an assassination contract. It is not, however, apparent whether the new Court would have considered Art.8 to apply if there had not been a mechanical recording of the conversations, which in the telephone tapping and surveillance cases has long been within the scope of Art.8.[16]

While the conformity with the "law" of telephone tapping and secret surveillance has been subject to review by the Convention organs, the only challenge to "lawfulness" of undercover activities has been *Ludi*. The nature of undercover work would however appear to render it less amenable than telephone tapping to detailed statutory regulation and it is arguable that the minimum would suffice.

Cross-reference

Part IIA, s.9: Evidence.
Part IIA, s.26: Witnesses.
Part IIB, s.30: Interception of communications.
Part IIB, s.44: Surveillance and secret files.

[16] *Bykov v* Russia, March 10, 2009, para.72, a so-called "operational experiment" in Russian terms.

8. Equality of arms

Key provision:

Article 6, para.1 (fair trial). II–065

Key case-law:

Delcourt v Belgium, January 17, 1970, Series A, No.11, 1 E.H.R.R 355; *Bonisch v Austria*, May 6, 1985, Series A, No.92, 9 E.H.R.R. 191; *Monnell and Morris v UK*, March 2, 1987 Series A, No.115, 10 E.H.R.R. 205; *Brandstetter v Austria*, August 26, 1991, Series A, No.211, 15 E.H.R.R. 378; *Borgers v Belgium*, October 30, 1991, Series A, No.214, 15 E.H.R.R. 92; *Ruiz-Mateos v Spain*, June 23, 1993, Series A, No.262, 16 E.H.R.R. 505; *Schuler-Zgraggen v Switzerland*, June 24, 1993, Series A, No.263, 16 E.H.R.R. 405; *Dombo Beheer BV v Netherlands*, October 27, 1993, Series A, No.274, 18 E.H.R.R. 213; *Bendenoun v France*, February 24, 1994, Series A, No.284, 18 E.H.R.R. 54; *Van de Hurk v Netherlands*, April 19, 1994, Series A, No.288, 18 E.H.R.R. 481; *Hentrich v France*, September 22, 1994, Series A, No.296, 18 E.H.R.R. 440; *Stran Greek Refineries v Greece*, December 9, 1994, Series A, No.301–B, 19 E.H.R.R. 293; *Schouten and Meldrum v Netherlands*, December 9, 1994, Series A, No.304, 19 E.H.R.R. 432; *Lobo Machado v Portugal*, February 20, 1996, R.J.D. 1996–I, No.3, 23 E.H.R.R. 79; *Bulut v Austria*, February 22, 1996, R.J.D. 1996–II, No.5, 24 E.H.R.R. 84; *Vermeulen v Belgium*, February 20, 1996, R.J.D. 1996–I, No.3, 32 E.H.R.R. 513; *Ankerl v Switzerland*, October 23, 1996, R.J.D. 1996–V, No.19, 32 E.H.R.R. 1; *Mantovanelli v France*, March 18, 1997, R.J.D. 1997–II, No.32, 24 E.H.R.R. 370; *Kress v France*, June 7, 2001, ECHR 2001–VI.

1. General considerations

Equality of arms, as in the sense of "fair balance", is one of the long-established elements of fairness.[1] It is sometimes linked to considerations that proceedings must be adversarial. It implies that each party must be afforded a reasonable opportunity to present his case—including his evidence—under conditions which do not place him at a substantial disadvantage vis-à-vis his opponent.[2] This means, in principle, the opportunity for the parties to a criminal or civil trial to have knowledge of and comment on all evidence adduced or observations filed.[3] Particular importance is to be attached in this context to the appearance of the fair administration of justice.[4] II–066

It generally goes without saying that if one party is present during a hearing, the other party should also be given the opportunity.[5] Most cases concern the

[1] *Delcourt v Belgium*, January 17, 1970, Series A, No.11, 1 E.H.R.R 355, para.28.

[2] *Dombo Beheer BV v Netherlands*, October 27, 1993, Series A, No.274, 18 E.H.R.R. 213, para.33; *Kress v France*, June 7, 2001, ECHR 2001–VI, para.72.

[3] *Ruiz-Mateos v Spain*, June 23, 1993, Series A, No.262, 16 E.H.R.R. 505, para.63; *Lobo Machado v Portugal*, February 20, 1996, R.J.D. 1996–I, No.3, 23 E.H.R.R. 79, *Borgers v Belgium*, October 30, 1991, Series A, No.214, 15 E.H.R.R. 92, and *Vermeulen v Belgium*, February 20, 1996, R.J.D. 1996–I, No.3, 32 E.H.R.R. 513; *KDB v Netherlands*, March 27, 1998, para.31.

[4] *Bulut v Austria*, February 22, 1996, R.J.D. 1996–II, No.5, 24 E.H.R.R. 84, para.47; *Borgers v Belgium*, fn.3 above, para.24.

[5] *Zhuk v Ukraine*, October 21, 2010, paras 32–35.

participation or role of other persons or officials in the proceedings or inequalities flowing from the priviliged position of the State.

2. Aspects of equality of arms

(a) *Opportunity to receive and respond to submissions*

II–067 The right to an adversarial trial has also been held to mean that in a criminal case both prosecution and defence must be given the opportunity to have knowledge of and comment on the observations filed and the evidence adduced by the other party. While there are various ways by which national law may seek to achieve this, whatever method is chosen should ensure that the other party will know if observations are filed and will get a real opportunity to comment.[6] Where civil rights and obligations are concerned, even in the context of the special nature of Constitutional Court proceedings, parties must as a rule be granted free access to the observations of other participants and a genuine opportunity to comment on them.[7] This extends also to ancillary matters such as cost applications, where even if for reasons of judicial economy and efficiency the possibility to present factual and legal argument may be limited, as litigants' confidence in the workings of justice, which is based, inter alia, on the knowledge that they have had the opportunity to express their views on every document in the file, remains at stake.[8]

Where State legal officers, such as *procureurs-général*, participated in proceedings, the Court initially accepted that they could be regarded as neutral or impartial and therefore no breach of equality resulted from failure to give parties or an accused the opportunity to know the content of or respond to their interventions.[9] However the Court has since found that where a legal officer has recommended that an application be rejected or accepted, such an officer can no longer be regarded as neutral and the applicant should have the possibility of commenting on the officer's

[6] *Brandstetter v Austria*, August 26, 1991, Series A, No.211, 15 E.H.R.R. 378, para.67, violation where the prosecutor's submissions were not communicated to the applicant: it was not enough that in the Austrian system the applicant could have anticipated something might have been submitted and applied to see the complete file, nor that there was an indirect opportunity to answer prosecutor's points which had been adopted in the appeal court's judgment; *Kuopila v Finland*, April 27, 2000, where the prosecutor submitted an additional police report to the Court of Appeal on which the applicant had no opportunity to comment—it was irrelevant that the court did not refer to the report in its decision; *Milatova v Czech Republic*, June 21, 2005, para.65; *Augusto v France*, January 11, 2007, non-communication of the opinion of the court's medical expert.

[7] *Ruiz-Mateos*, see fn.3 above, violation where State Counsel had filed observations on the validity of the impugned law and the applicants were not given the opportunity to reply; conversely, in *Van de Hurk v Netherlands*, April 19, 1994, Series A, No.288, 18 E.H.R.R. 481, no violation where the minister changed his ground of objection before the tribunal, since the applicant had a genuine opportunity to respond; and in *Gorraiz Lizarraga v Spain*, April 27, 2004, ECHR 2004–III, in a special preliminary ruling procedure in which no exchange of documents took place, it was sufficient that the Constitutional Court had in the file all the applicants' submissions from the lower instances and that the applicants had not requested leave to take part in the procedure.

[8] *Beer v Austria*, February 6, 2001, para.18.

[9] *Delcourt*, see fn.1 above.

submissions.[10] The presence of such judicial officers during court deliberations has also disclosed inequality of arms, since even if their role is limited to neutral points of law, which may be doubted, an accused may legitimately fear that the opportunity is used to bolster arguments to obtain a particular result.[11] It is not necessary for identifiable prejudice to flow from a procedural inequality. In *Bulut v Austria*, the Government's argument that the observations lodged by the Attorney General with the Supreme Court (but not served on the applicant) merely recommended the court to deal with the case in a particular manner were rejected. It was for the defence to assess whether a submission deserved a reaction and it was therefore unfair for the prosecution to make submissions to a court without the knowledge of the defence. Appearances may be significant; the mere presence of a Government Commissioner as a "silent witness" during deliberations of the court was also found to disclose a violation.[12]

However, in *Kress v France*, sufficient procedural safeguards were in place in respect of the submissions of the government commissioner made orally during the proceedings, as the parties' lawyers could ask in advance for an indication of the tenor of those submissions and put in a memorandum in reply for the deliberations.[13] No problem arose where State Counsel's submissions were first made orally as no party or judge had prior knowledge of their contents and the applicant could respond at the hearing or request an adjournment to prepare a reply.[14]

Non-communication to all parties of the report of a *judge rapporteur*, setting out a summary of the facts for the use of the tribunal in drawing up its judgment, is not regarded as placing any party at a substantial disadvantage vis-à-vis any other.[15]

(b) Opportunity to present or give evidence

Where a party is permitted to confine its submissions in a summary fashion which deprives the other party of an effective opportunity to counter them, there may be a breach.[16] Generally, a party may claim the right to give evidence in his own behalf, **II–068**

[10] e.g *Bulut*, see fn.4 above; *Borgers*, see fn.3 above, while the Court still accepted the independence and impartiality of the *procureurs*' department, it referred to the evolution in its case-law concerning the importance to be attached to appearances and to the increased sensitivity of the public to the administration of justice. Inequality disclosed by role of similar officers in criminal cases: *JJ v Netherlands*, March 27, 1998, R.J.D. 1998–II, No.68; *Reinhardt and Slimane-Kaid*, March 31, 1998, R.J.D. 1998–II, No.68, imbalance in procedure where the reporting judge's report and draft judgment was seen by the advocate-general before the hearing, whereas only part was disclosed to applicant during the hearing and the applicant also did not receive the advocate-general's submissions.

[11] e.g. *Lobo Machado*, *Borgers*, and *Vermeulen*, fn.3 above; *KDB v Netherlands*, fn.3 above, paras 42–44; *Kress v France*, fn.2 above, paras 83–87, concerning the government commissioner in administrative court proceedings who attended the deliberations; *Tedesco v France*, May 10, 2007, paras 63–65, presence of *commissaire du gouvernement* during the deliberations of the *Conseil d'Etat*.

[12] e.g. *Martinie v France*, April 12, 2006, ECHR 2006–. . .

[13] *Kress v France*, see fn.2 above, para.76.

[14] *Wynen v Belgium*, November 5, 2002, 2002–VIII.

[15] *Houdart and Vincent v France*, (28807/04) (Dec.) June 6, 2006. Contrast *Martinie v France*, fn.12 above, para.50, where inequality was disclosed as State Counsel, unlike the accountant applicant, was able to attend and participate in the hearing before the Court of Audit and had had sight of the *judge rapporteur's* report and heard the latter's submissions.

[16] e.g. *Hentrich v France*, September 22, 1994, Series A, No.296, 18 E.H.R.R. 440, where in the proceedings to challenge the pre-emption by the Revenue of the applicant's purchase of property, she was unable to challenge the Revenue's assessment by adducing evidence to show that she had acted in good faith and that the proper market price had been paid. In addition, the tribunals allowed the Revenue to confine its reasons for pre-emption to a summary and general statement.

despite technical domestic rules.[17] It was compatible with fairness for an accused to be prevented from consulting his reference notes while giving evidence at his trial, where he was represented by experienced counsel and no apparent difficulty in giving his testimony resulted.[18]

Refusal to hear witnesses on behalf of a party generally requires a reason to be given. Where that reason was inconsistent with the court's hearing of witnesses for the other party a breach of the equality of arms principle arose.[19]

(c) *Unequal status of witnesses*

II–069 The position of experts must be attended by a fair balance between the parties. The mere fact that official experts in expropriation proceedings worked for the administrative authority was not a ground in itself for justifying fears that they did not act with neutrality. Otherwise it would place unacceptable limits on the possibility to obtain expert advice.[20] In respect of court-appointed experts, potential problems may arise where the expert has been involved in the prosecution, but whether a violation arises will depend on whether he in fact exercised a privileged role.[21]

Technical differences may be discounted, as in *Ankerl v Switzerland*, where the wife was not allowed to take an oath, but her evidence was nonetheless before the court.

(d) *Procedural inequalities*

II–070 Potentially, issues might arise where one party enjoys, by their position, advantages over the conduct of the proceedings or access to material.[22] However, these may to some extent be unavoidable where State authorities are concerned and the Court seems to take a pragmatic approach as to whether the applicant has in fact been disadvantaged. For example, there was no prejudice from the fact that a time-limit

[17] *Dombo Beheer*, see fn.2 above, violation found where the applicant company was in a civil dispute with a bank over an oral agreement, but the applicant company director was barred from being a witness since he was identified with a party to the proceedings; whereas the representative of the bank, who was involved in the transaction, could be a witness.

[18] *Pullicino v Malta*, (45441/99) (Dec.) June 15, 2000.

[19] *Peric v Croatia*, March 27, 2008, paras 21–26, the court refused the applicant's witnesses stating that the facts were established on the evidence submitted by the parties, yet then went on to hear four witnesses requested by the defendants.

[20] *Zumtobel v Austria*, September 21, 1993, Series A, No.268–A, 17 E.H.R.R. 116, para.86, the applicants were free to submit their own expert opinions, which if disregarded, could be subject to appeal.

[21] *Bonisch v Austria*, May 6, 1985, Series A, No.92, 9 E.H.R.R. 191, violation of Art.6, para.1, since the expert whose report had led to the applicant's prosecution was appointed court expert with powers to question, whereas the applicant's expert was only a witnesss and had limited attendance; *Brandstetter*, see fn.6 above, no inequality since, even though the expert who initiated the proceedings was appointed court expert, he did not question anyone and the defence, largely agreeing with the court expert, relied on matters on which he had made no submissions.

[22] e.g. *Mantovanelli v France*, March 18, 1997, R.J.D. 1997–II, No.32, 24 E.H.R.R. 370, violation as regarded the applicants' lack of effective involvement in the preparation of the court expert report, whereas the defendant hospital staff were involved (framed as infringement of the adversarial principle); *Sara Lind Eggertsdottir v Iceland*, July 5, 2007, paras 48–52, where the court appointed as experts a board whose members also worked for the hospital which was defendant, thus favouring the position of the hospital.

was not imposed on the submission by the Attorney General of his position paper to the Supreme Court[23]; there was no inequality of arms where the applicant complained of not being given copies of the contents of the file held by tax authorities in tax evasion proceedings, where the Court found that those documents were not among those relied on by the tax authorities and he did not put forward any reasons for seeking disclosure[24]; and a specially extended period for appeal enjoyed by a *procureur* was not found to place the applicants at a substantial disadvantage as, although the 10–day time-limit they enjoyed was much shorter, it did not deprive them of a meaningful use of the same remedy.[25] As to an alleged ability by a State authority to delay the proceedings, the Court found no substance in the allegations that the authority could choose the order of cases, since no preceding case prejudged his or prevented him putting his arguments.[26]

However, where there was a procedural rule that time ceased to run against the State during judicial vacation, the Court found that the applicant had suffered inequality of arms since her application, rejected as out of time, would not have been deemed outside the time-limit if the same rule had applied to her.[27] Where the presciption periods for debts were vastly longer for the State than for a private party who lost their claim while the State maintained its counter-claim, the Court considered that this could not be justified either by vague reference to the interests of the Treasury in enforcing its debts or the position of the administration.[28]

When in expropriation proceedings the government commissioner played both role of party and expert, and enjoyed a dominant position with significant influence over the judge's assessment of value, this was also incompatible with the principle of equality of arms.[29] Power of the prosecution to decide whether or not to disclose evidence to the accused at trial on public interest grounds disclosed unfairness and lack of equality of arms in a series of UK cases,[30] while in lustration proceedings, drastic limitations on the applicant's access to the file, together with a prohibition on taking copies of documents or notes from the registry, which restrictions did not apply to the commissioner who instituted the proceedings, similarly offended.[31]

Availability of exemption for court fees for magistrates who are sued did not raise an issue. The Court found that this advantage did not distort the balance of the proceedings any more than the grant of legal aid to only one party to any other proceedings would.[32] Nor did the joinder as party to proceedings between the applicant NGOs and the State of a multinational corporation who had interests at stake. Even if this meant that the environmental organisations were faced with two

[23] *Kremzow v Austria*, September 21, 1993, Series A, No.268–B, 17 E.H.R.R. 322, para.75.

[24] *Bendenoun v France*, February 24, 1994, Series A, No.284, 18 E.H.R.R. 54; *Schuler-Zgraggen v Switzerland*, June 24, 1993, Series A, No.263, 16 E.H.R.R. 405, where there was no inequality of arms in access to material—the applicant had access to the file and could make copies, while the report which she did not see was not part of the file, but was summarised in another available document and the courts did not have the full report either.

[25] *De Guigue & SGEN-CFDT v France*, (59821/00) (Dec.) January 6, 2004, ECHR 2004–I.

[26] *Schouten and Meldrum v Netherlands*, December 9, 1994, Series A, No.304, 19 E.H.R.R. 432.

[27] *Platakou v Greece*, January 11, 2001, paras 47–48.

[28] *Varnima Corporation International SA v Greece*, May 28, 2009, paras 30–35.

[29] *Yvon v France*, April 24, 2003, the judge was required by law to keep within the limits of the valuation proposed by the commissioner in certain circumstances and had to give express reasons for not following the commissioner's conclusions.

[30] See Pt IIA, s.9(5): Failure to disclose evidence, and the cases cited therein.

[31] *Matyjek v Poland*, See Pt IIA, s.9(5): Failure to disclose evidence, and the cases cited therein.

[32] *Gouveia Gomes Fernandes and Freitas e Costa v Portugal*, (1529/08) (Dec.) May 26, 2009.

giant opponents, this was not seen as posing such a problem of procedural fairness, although issues could have arisen if the costs imposed, at the application of the corporation, had been excessive.[33]

No inequality arose where the prosecutor was present, and addressed the jury, during an information session with newly-inducted jurors presided over by a senior judge. The issues raised were technical and general; the interests of the accused were safeguarded from any improper influence by the presence of a legal aid lawyer and the judge.[34]

(e) Legislative interference

II–071 Where a State intervenes by passing a law to ensure the favourable outcome of pending proceedings in which it is a party, there may be a striking inequality of arms. In those circumstances, it is not enough that in the proceedings before the domestic court a party is able to present all the arguments they wish, since fairness applies to the proceedings in their entirety, not merely the hearing inter partes. Such intervention infringes the principle that each party must be afforded a reasonable opportunity to present his case under conditions that do not place him at a substantial disadvantage vis-à-vis his opponent.[35]

Cross-reference

Part IIA, s.1: General principles: fairness.
Part IIA, s.9: Evidence.
Part IIA, s.16: Legislative interference in judicial process.
Part IIA, s.26: Witnesses.
Part IIB, s.42: Review of detention, equality of arms (Art.5, para.4).

[33] *Collectif National d'Information et d'opposition a l'usine Melox-Collectif Stop Melox et Mox v France*, (75218/01) (Dec.) June 12, 2007.
[34] *Corcuff v France*, October 4, 2007, paras 32–33.
[35] e.g. *Stran Greek Refineries v Greece*, December 9, 1994, Series A, No.301–B, 19 E.H.R.R. 293, para.46.

9. Evidence

Key provision:

Article 6, paras 1—3 (fair hearing guarantees). II–072

Key case-law:

Barbera, Messegué and Jabardo v Spain, December 6, 1988, Series A, No.146, 11 E.H.R.R. 360; *Schenk v Switzerland*, July 12, 1988, Series A, No.140, 13 E.H.R.R. 242; *H v France*, October 24, 1989, Series A, No.162, 12 E.H.R.R. 74; *Edwards v UK*, December 16, 1992, Series A, No.247–B, 15 E.H.R.R. 417; *Dombo Beheer BV v Netherlands*, October 27, 1993, Series A, No.274–A, 18 E.H.R.R. 213; *Ferrantelli and Santangelo v Italy*, August 7, 1996, R.J.D. 1996–III, No. 12; *Fitt v UK*, February 16, 2000, ECHR 2000–II, 30 E.H.R.R. 480; *Rowe and Davies v UK*, February 16, 2000, ECHR 2000–II, 30 E.H.R.R. 1; *Khan v UK*, May 12, 2000, ECHR 2000–V, 31 E.H.R.R. 1016; *GB v France*, October 2, 2001, ECHR 2001–X; *Allan v UK*, November 5, 2002, ECHR 2002–IX; *Edwards and Lewis v UK*, October 27, 2004, ECHR 2004–X; *Papageorgiou v Greece*, May 9, 2003; *Jalloh v Germany*, July 11, 2006, ECHR 2006–IX; *Gäfgen v Germany*, June 1, 2010, ECHR 2010–. . .

1. General considerations

The admissibility and assessment of evidence is, primarily, a matter for the domestic courts. Whether or not the courts have correctly assessed the evidence is largely outside the competence of the Court.[1] There has only been a limited supervision by the Convention organs, having regard to their position that they are not a fourth instance, nor in an appropriate position to overrule the opinion of the local courts who have first-hand knowledge and experience. II–073

The Court examines, in terms of the Convention, whether the requirements of Art.6, para.1 as to fairness have been complied with, including the way in which evidence was submitted.[2] This means, generally, that any alleged evidential imbalance or unfairness will be looked at in light of the proceedings as a whole and as to whether an applicant has been deprived of an ability to participate effectively in the proceedings or whether the position of the defence was significantly impaired.[3] In criminal cases, the whole matter of the taking and presentation of evidence must also be looked at in light of the guarantees of paras 2 and 3. For example, in light of the presumption of innocence, when carrying out their duties, the members of a court should not start with the preconceived idea that the accused has committed the offence and the burden of proof is on the prosecution, thus any doubt should benefit the accused. It also follows that the prosecution must inform the accused of the case against him, so that he may prepare and present his defence, and adduce evidence sufficient to convict him.[4]

[1] (6172/73) (Dec.) July 7, 1975, 3 D.R. 77.
[2] *Barbera Messegué and Jabardo v Spain*, December 6, 1988, Series A, No.146, 11 E.H.R.R. 360, para.68.
[3] e.g. *Dombo Beheer BV v Netherlands*, October 27, 1993, Series A, No.274–A, 18 E.H.R.R. 213, para.33 (equality of arms), a party must have a reasonable opportunity to present his case, including evidence, under conditions not placing him at a substantial disadvantage vis-à-vis his opponent.
[4] *Barbera*, see fn.2 above, paras 76–77.

2. Presentation of evidence at trial

II–074 In principle, the evidence against the accused should be presented in court publicly, subject to an adversarial procedure. In *Barbera, Messegué and Jabardo v Spain*, where a case of robbery and murder resulting in sentences of up to 36 years was examined in a trial lasting one day, the Court found a violation cumulatively on a number of defects but, particularly, in that very important pieces of evidence were not adequately adduced and discussed at the trial in the applicants' presence and under the public eye. This included material evidence such as weapons relied on by the prosecution but not produced in court; confessions which the applicants stated were given under duress and in which respect the Court had reservations since they were obtained during a long period of incommunicado custody; and lack of attendance at the trial of witnesses whose statements incriminated the applicants and whom the applicants had no prior possibility of examining. In *Papageorgiou v Greece*, the failure to produce key evidence in court for examination in the presence of the accused, namely the originals of the allegedly forged cheques, rendered the applicant's trial and appeal unfair, where the first instance court had in fact ordered their destruction and relied on photocopies. Destruction or loss of evidence may not impinge on fairness, however, where the defence is not unduly handicapped as a result.[5]

There is a duty on courts to ensure evidence is properly and fairly presented. Thus in *Barbera*, the Court held that, even though the prosecution and defence had agreed to waive the oral presentation of documentary evidence at trial, this did not dispense the court from complying with the requirements of Art.6, para.1.

Regarding methods of presentation of evidence, the Commission criticised the practice where, before an appeal court, the statement of the witness was read out and he was asked if he maintained it, noting that it may reduce the value of the statements of a witness if he is reminded of what he previously said. However, since the parties were able to put further questions to the witnesses and to challenge the correctness of the evidence, the method was not of such a character that it rendered the hearing unfair.[6]

3. Admissibility of evidence

II–075 Article 6, para.1 does not lay down any rules as to the admissibility of evidence which is primarily a matter for the regulation under national law.[7] A failure by the applicant or his counsel to object to any evidence is an important, if not necessarily decisive factor, bearing in mind the courts' general duty to ensure the fairness of the proceedings of their own motion.[8] Also relevant are any aspects which might remedy or mitigate the alleged unfairness and whether the matter was subject to careful scrutiny by the appeal courts.

[5] *Sofri v Italy*, (37235/97) (Dec.) May 27, 2003, the Court regretted that administrative error had led to the destruction of evidence (clothing, car and bullets) in a murder case; however, the applicants had not shown that the lost clothing of the victim could have assisted the defence, reports existed on the state of the car and on bullets and the prosecution faced the same problems in carrying out further expert examinations.

[6] (10486/83) (Dec.) October 9, 1986, 49 D.R. 86.

[7] e.g. (12505/86) (Dec.) October 11, 1988, 58 D.R. 106.

[8] e.g. (7306/75) (Dec.) October 6, 1976, 7 D.R. 155; (8876/80) (Dec.) October 16, 1980, 23 D.R. 233.

(a) *Accomplices*

Issues of fairness may arise where an accomplice, who has been granted immunity, gives evidence against an applicant. However, where that fact was known to the defence and the court, and the accomplice extensively examined as to his reliability and credibility, no unfairness was found.[9] Where a guilty plea of a co-accused to tax evasion charges was admitted as evidence at the applicant's trial, this did not render the proceedings unfair, given, inter alia, the judge's warning to the jury of its limited relevance.[10] II–076

(b) *Indirect or documentary evidence*

The Commission held that use of indirect evidence is not prohibited by the Convention. It had regard, however, to whether it was the sole evidence. In a German case where the applicant complained that the evidence before the court was largely written statements of alleged witnesses, it noted that the conviction was based primarily on the accused's own statements made before the first instance court.[11] Also relevant is whether an applicant has had an opportunity to challenge, at some stage, a witness whose written evidence was used against him.[12] II–077

(c) *Hearsay*

The Commission considered that the rule excluding hearsay evidence was legitimately based on the aim of ensuring the best evidence before the jury, who can evaluate the credibility of witnesses before them, and to avoid reliance on evidence untested by cross-examination. It is not, in principle, contrary to Art.6, para.1.[13] However, in *Al-Khawaja and Tahery v UK*, the Court dealt with complaints that documentary hearsay evidence was admitted in evidence from an assault victim who had committed suicide before trial and from a witness who would not appear at trial due to fear of retaliation. The Chamber found that there was a breach of Art.6 in both cases, primarily as the hearsay statement had been the only direct evidence against both accused; in those circumstances, a warning from the judge as to the untested nature of the statement was not enough to counterract the prejudicial effect. The case-law concerning anonymous witnesses was relied upon (see Pt IIA, s.26(2): Use of anonymous witnesses or written evidence from unexamined witnesses). This case was pending before the Grand Chamber at the date of publication.[14] II–078

(d) *Confessions and coercion*

In early cases, the Commission had put significant weight on the existence of a procedure whereby the validity of evidence, allegedly obtained by coercion, could be examined. It found the process in English courts of a *voire dire* (adversarial trial- II–079

[9] *Cornelis v Netherlands*, (994/03) (Dec.) May 25, 2004, ECHR 2004–V; see also (73605/75) (Dec.) October 6, 1976, 7 D.R. 115, the defence knew, the terms of the agreement explained to the jury, who were warned by the judge and the matter examined on appeal, so no problem arose; and (17265/90) (Dec.) October 21, 1993, 75 D.R. 76.

[10] (28572/95) (Dec.) January 17, 1997.

[11] (8945/80) (Dec.) December 13, 1983, 39 D.R. 43.

[12] See Pt IIA, s.26: Witnesses.

[13] 12045/86, (Dec.) May 7, 1987, 52 D.R. 273.

[14] *Al-Khawaja and Tahery v UK*, January 20, 2009.

within-a-trial, including evidence and argument, before a judge in the absence of jury) which issued a ruling on admissibility and left the probative value to the jury was a sufficient safeguard and provided a fair trial.[15] Similarly, in *Ferrantelli and Santangelo v Italy*, where the applicants complained that they had been convicted on the basis of confessions obtained by coercion, the Court, noting that the question of ill-treatment was subject to specific investigation by the judicial authorities, who ruled no case to answer against the alleged perpetrators, found insufficient material before it to depart from the domestic findings. Since then the Court has applied particularly rigorous scrutiny to claims that evidence has been obtained by ill-treatment.

Where it is established that confessions have been obtained by torture or other forms of proscribed Art.3 treatment, and used later in some way in the trial, this is likely to disclose issues of unfairness. Use of statements taken from the accused, subjected to inhuman treatment by the police contrary to Art.3, has founded a number of violations of Art.6, para.1, in conjunction with Art.6, para.3(c) due to the absence of a legal representative when signing the statement and lack of access to a lawyer's advice beforehand.[16]

Recently, in *Jalloh v Germany*, the Court has emphasised the fundamental importance of the guarantee under Art.3 of the Convention, which cannot be subject to derogation. Accordingly, it has held that incriminating evidence, whether in the form of a confession or real evidence, obtained as a result of acts of violence or brutality or other forms of treatment which can be characterised as "torture", should never be relied on as proof of the victim's guilt, irrespective of its probative value. Any other conclusion would only serve to legitimate indirectly the morally reprehensible conduct which Art.3 sought to proscribe. The fact that a statement obtained by torture was later confirmed to another investigator did not necessarily justify reliance on its contents, particularly where there was ample evidence of continued threats of torture and retaliation.[17] In *Jalloh* the Court left open whether use of evidence obtained by lesser forms of "inhuman and degrading treatment" automatically rendered a trial unfair as concerned real evidence, considering that in any event the use in that case of drugs evidence obtained by the forcible administration of emetics was unfair in the circumstances: namely, there was no discretion to exclude the evidence which was lawfully obtained in domestic terms, the evidence had been obtained by breach of a core right, it had been decisive in the conviction and the public interest in securing the conviction was not of weight as the applicant was a street dealer selling on a small scale.

Where in *Gäfgen v Germany*, in a tragic child kidnapping case, real evidence was obtained from the suspect due to police threats categorised as inhuman treatment, the Court noted the conflicting interests, in particular, the crucial interest in finding the child and that Art.6 was not absolute and seemed to tend, although in ambiguous terms, towards finding that the use of such evidence should also, as a

[15] (9370/81) (Dec.) October 13, 1983, 35 D.R. 75.

[16] e.g *Soylemez v Turkey*, September 21, 2006, the statement, although relied on by the court in convicting, was not apparently the sole or decisive evidence; *Haci Özen v Turkey*, April 12, 2007, the statements were the "main evidence". In neither case was the admissibility of the disputed statements subject to a ruling by the courts who attached no consequence to the issue; in *Göcmen v Turkey*, October 17, 2006 and *Yusuf Gezer v Turkey*, December 1, 2009, there was no need to decide if the impugned confessions were decisive as the procedures failed to provide any protection against the use of material obtained in breach of Art.3.

[17] *Harutyunyan v Armenia*, June 28, 2007, para.65.

rule, be excluded due to the requirement to protect individuals and to prevent police use of such methods.[18] In the circumstances however, as the evidence, although before the courts, did not have a bearing or an impact on his conviction and sentence, no problem of fairness arose.[19] Thus, in such cases, the role played by the evidence at trial will be the key issue.

In the absence of a finding, domestically or in Strasbourg, of a violation of Art.3, the existence of adequate procedural safeguards in the domestic courts allowing examination of any claims of ill-treatment and unfairness allegedly flowing from use of evidence obtained thereby is also likely to continue to be of significance.[20] Where a court relied on a confession made by the applicant without access to a lawyer, and which he alleged to have been obtained by coercion, the Court found that the lack of an adequate investigation by the court into how the confession had been obtained rendered the use of the material at trial unfair.[21]

Methods of obtaining admissions from suspects may raise fairness issues even where involving subterfuge short of direct physical or mental ill-treatment in interrogation. In *Allan v UK*, where there were elements of oppression and entrapment in coaching an informer as a cell-mate to obtain admissions from a detained applicant placed under deliberate pressure, the Court found use of the evidence effectively deprived the applicant of his right to silence to police questions. In contrast, in *Bykov v Russia*, where V, lying about having carried out a killing, taped an incriminating conversation with the applicant, the Court rejected complaints that there had been oppressive trickery, noting that in the circumstances the applicant had been under no pressure, the conversation taking place on his own premises and with no element of subordination of role.[22]

(e) Unlawfully-obtained evidence

The use of unlawfully-obtained evidence is not excluded as a matter of principle (save as regards that obtained by torture, see sub.s.(d) above: Confessions and coercion). However, the way the evidence was obtained and the role played at the trial will be examined in the context of ascertaining whether the trial as a whole was fair.[23] In practice, alleged unlawful elements have not been found to disclose unfairness, where the evidence was not obtained by means of oppression, entrapment or coercion and has been examined in adversarial proceedings, subject to the challenge of the applicant.[24] Thus in *Schenk v Switzerland*, the Court found that **II–080**

[18] *Gäfgen v Germany*, June 1, 2010, ECHR 2010–. . . , paras 169–178.

[19] *Gäfgen v Germany*, see fn.18 above, paras 179–188. The majority considered the domestic court based itself exclusively on a later confession at trial; a minority lead by Judge Rozakis thought that this must also have been regarded as flowing organically from the earlier episode of coercion, since once the real evidence had linked him to the crime, confessing to obtain a lesser sentence was the only effective defence left open to him.

[20] *Latimer v UK*, (12141/04) (Dec.) May 31, 2005.

[21] *Yaremenko v Ukraine*, June 12, 2008, paras 78–81.

[22] *Bykov v Russia*, March 10, 2009, paras 100–105, the Court also had regard to the limited role the evidence played in the conviction.

[23] (12505/86) (Dec.) October 11, 1988, 58 D.R. 106.

[24] (12505/86), fn.23 above; *PG and JH v UK*, September 25, 2001, ECHR 2001–IX, para.78; *Perry v UK*, (63737/00) and *Chalkley v UK*, (63831/00) (Decs.) September 26, 2002; *Lee Davies v Belgium*, July 28, 2009, paras 46–54, no violation of Art.6 concerning evidence obtained by illegal search; *Heglas v Czech Republic*, March 1, 2007, concerning inadequate lawful basis for tapping mobile phone, breach of Art.8, but no violation of Art.6.

the use of a recording, unlawful insofar as it was not ordered by the investigating judge, did not render the trial automatically unfair or furnish a ground for violation per se. It examined the fairness factors, and it was sufficient that the applicant had knowledge of the tape and the circumstances in which it was recorded and was able to challenge its use. Although the Court also attached weight to the fact, in that case, it was not the only evidence on which the conviction was based, in *Khan v UK* where the taped telephone conversations obtained without any legal basis were the only evidence, the Court still found its use at trial was not unfair as procedures provided at two instances for the applicant to challenge its reliability and the fairness of its admission. The lack of proper legal authority for inventive police methods of obtaining evidence is considered by the Court rather as raising issues under the Art.8 right to respect for private life than as a fairness problem under Art.6.

(f) Identity parades

II–081 Irregularities in the conduct of identity parades may undermine the overall fairness of a trial. Where during several identity parades, the two applicant suspects were made to wear blue and white balaclavas similar to the robbers and the others in the line-up wore black, the Court considered that this was tantamount to prompting the witnesses to point "the finger of guilt" at the applicants. The Court also criticised the fact that the applicants' lawyer was not present to defend their interests at this stage. These defects could not be cured by legal representation or adversarial procedure later in the proceedings.[25]

(g) Effect of passage of time on evidence

II–082 Mere passage of time, even decades, will not automatically render a trial unfair. The Court has not been persuaded that this renders it unduly difficult for an accused to present a defence, obtaining evidence in his favour or countering evidence against him. It was in particular noted that lack of prescription for crimes against humanity as part of international law was not against the Convention.[26]

4. Weight given to evidence

II–083 The probative value of evidence also falls essentially for the domestic instances to determine.[27] Thus in an Italian case, where the applicant, accused of instigating a murder, complained the conviction was based only on circumstantial evidence and presumptions, the Commission found it sufficient that the charges against him were presented and debated adversarially before the trial judges and the Court of Cassation. It did list the elements of indirect proof presumably implying that the

[25] *Laska and Lika v Albania*, April 20, 2010, paras 63–67.
[26] *Sommer v Italy*, (36586/08) (Dec.) March 23, 2010, the accused, being tried some fifty years after World War II for war crimes, was represented and the proceedings showed that evidence had been presented on his behalf; the Court emphasised that he had also been able to give evidence himself about alleged events. See also *Sawoniuk v UK*, (63716/00) (Dec.) May 29, 2001, the jury could reasonably be left to decide how credible and reliable evidence was after such a lapse of time.
[27] e.g. (12013/86) (Dec.) March 10, 1989, 59 D.R. 100.

"whole body of indirect evidence" on which the judges based their finding that the applicant ordered the execution was not unfair.[28]

5. Failure to disclose evidence

There is a requirement for the prosecution to disclose to the defence all the material evidence for or against the accused.[29] Whether or not a failure to do so discloses objectionable unfairness will depend on an assessment of the proceedings as a whole. In *Edwards v UK*, the failure to disclose that one of the witnesses had not identified the applicant from a police photograph album and the existence of fingerprints, not the applicant's, at the scene of the burglary, was a defect, but the Court found it was cured since when this was discovered there was an independent enquiry and the case was referred to the Court of Appeal where counsel had every opportunity to persuade the Court to overturn the conviction, including the possibility to apply for police officers to be called as witnesses. II–084

The entitlement to disclosure of relevant evidence is not, however, absolute. The Court has acknowledged that it may be necessary to withhold certain evidence, for example to protect the fundamental rights of another individual or to safeguard an important public interest, e.g. to protect national security or witnesses, or to keep secret police methods of investigation.[30] Restrictions must, in those situations, be limited to what is strictly necessary and the impact on the defence must be sufficiently counterbalanced by procedures. Thus, in *Rowe and Davis v UK*, the procedure whereby it was the prosecution which decided that public interest required non-disclosure of relevant evidence and the material was not reviewed by the first instance judge, did not provide the necessary safeguards. In those circumstances, the review of the material ex parte by the Court of Appeal did not remedy the unfairness at first instance.[31] In *Fitt v UK*, where the judge assessed whether the material should be disclosed in the interests of the defence and the matter was kept under review during the trial, there were sufficient safeguards. Similarly, where there had been no deliberate concealment of evidence, an inter partes hearing by the Court of Appeal which ordered disclosure of at least part of the sensitive information remedied the non-disclosure at trial in circumstances where there was a proper examination, with argument from counsel as to the effect on the safety of the convictions, and a finding that the material added nothing of significance to the evidence available at trial.[32]

Where, however, the undisclosed material may be of potential relevance to another issue decided during the trial, the fact that the judge has reviewed the material may not sufficiently protect the position of the defence, which will not have

[28] (12013/86), see fn.27 above.

[29] *Jespers v Belgium*, (8403/78) (Rep.) December 14, 1981, 27 D.R. 61; *Edwards v UK*, December 16, 1992, Series A, No.247–B, 15 E.H.R.R. 417, para.36; *Rowe and Davis v UK*, February 16, 2000, ECHR 2000–II, 30 E.H.R.R. 1, para.60.

[30] *Rowe and Davis v UK*, fn.29 above, para.61; *Fitt v UK*, February 16, 2000, ECHR 2000–II, 30 E.H.R.R. 480, para.45.

[31] See also *Dowsett v UK*, June 24, 2003, para.50, where the material had not been disclosed to the trial judge by the prosecution, it was not sufficient that the defence could have applied for the Court of Appeal to review the material—this was not an adequate safeguard as the appellate court did not have the advantage of the trial judge in seeing and hearing the witnesses and would not be assisted by defence counsel's arguments as to relevance; *Atlan v UK*, June 19, 2001.

[32] *Botmeh and Alami v UK*, June 7, 2007, paras 38–44.

been able to make effective submissions on the point. In *Edwards and Lewis v UK*, the judge reviewed and then upheld non-disclosure of material on public interest grounds which material seemingly might have had bearing on the later ruling rejecting the applicants' applications on alleged police entrapment. The Court distinguished the *Fitt* line of cases by stating that in those the undisclosed evidence did not relate to an issue of fact decided by the trial judge.

Similar principles apply in civil proceedings. Thus, where the applicant was challenging the inclusion of his name in a police risk register and the courts examined the undisclosed operational activities file in chambers before reaching its decision on the facts, the Court found a lack of adversariality since the applicant and his lawyer had had no opportunity to make any submissions on the facts crucial to his claims.[33]

6. Refusal to call expert evidence or take other investigative measures

II–085 The Commission did not exclude that the refusal by a court to order an expert, hear a witness or to accept other types of evidence might in certain circumstances render the proceedings unfair. Since, however, it was for the national courts to decide what was necessary or essential to decide a case, it commented that only in exceptional circumstances would it conclude that a decision of a national court in such a matter violated the right to a fair hearing. It gave the example of where an applicant adduced some evidence which the court rejected outright, refusing to allow verification of it and without giving sufficient reasons for its refusal.[34] Although in *Elsholz v Germany*, the Court did find a violation arose where the domestic courts in child contact proceedings refused the applicant father's request for a psychological report on the five to six-year-old child's views on contact, the Grand Chamber has since reiterated that, as a general rule, it is for domestic courts to assess the evidence before them, including the means to ascertain relevant facts; having regard in particular to the age and maturity of the child who was heard in the proceedings in that case, it found the courts well able to reach a reasoned decision on the issues without the expert evidence requested by the applicant.[35] Where in *Accardi v Italy* the decision of a domestic court not to order a psychologist's report or to call the expert requested by the defence was based on logical and pertinent arguments and the conclusion that such evidential measures were of no relevance to the proceedings, there was no infringement of the rights of the defence or the fairness principle.[36] However, where a court refused to hear the applicant transsexual's

[33] *Uzukauskas v Lithuania*, July 6, 2010, paras 45–51.

[34] *H v France*, where the courts refused the applicant's application for a medical opinion for the purpose of proving the causal link between his medical treatment and his injury. The Commission noted, inter alia, that there had been medical expert evidence in the file and it was evident that the decision was reached after fairly detailed examination of the causation issue. The Court agreed, commenting adversely on the applicant's dilatoriness in taking proceedings. See, however, *Vidal v Belgium*, April 22, 1992, Series A, No.235, violation where the appeal court overturned an acquittal without hearing witnesses requested by the applicant and without giving reasons.

[35] *Sommerfeld v Germany*, July 8, 2003, ECHR 2003–VIII, concerning failure to order expert opinion on the negative views to contact expressed by a 13–year-old, where the Court's reasoning was under the procedural aspect of Art.8, with no separate issue arising under Art.6. Similar reasoning regarding the failure of the court to hear a five-year-old concerning contact, where there was expert evidence as to the undesirability of direct questioning: *Sahin v Germany*, July 8, 2003, ECHR 2003–VIII.

[36] (30598/02) (Dec.) January 20, 2005, ECHR 2005–II.

expert evidence as to the genuineness and established nature of her condition, relying purely on the failure to fulfil the formal requirement of a two-year observation period, the Court considered that the domestic courts had failed to address themselves to the appropriate evidence in reaching its decision on a crucial medical issue and thus deprived the applicant of a fair hearing.[37]

Although the mere fact that an expert changes his views during proceedings does not, impinge on the fairness of a trial and require an opportunity for the defence to seek a second opinion, issues may also arise where this threatens to have undue influence on the jury.[38] In *GB v France*, where in oral examination an expert reacted to new evidence by abruptly changing his own opinion in a highly adverse manner to the accused, the Court could not exclude that this might have given the opinion particular weight in the eyes of the jury; fairness thus required that the defence have the opportunity to seek another expert opinion on the issue.

7. Admission of new evidence

Where new evidence following conviction appears, there is no right to retrial.[39] Nor where a case is re-opened, is there a requirement for a complete rehearing. In the *Birmingham Six* case, the Commission rejected the argument that the new evidence should have been put in front of a jury rather than reviewed by the Court of Appeal. The Commission noted that a jury trial was not essential to fairness[40] and it found the proceedings before the Court of Appeal fair, the Court of Appeal having stated that, if there had been the least doubt that the verdicts were safe or satisfactory, it would quash the convictions.[41] II–086

8. Judicial notice

The Commission accepted that the German courts were able to take cognisance of established historical fact. Thus, there was no problem in a refusal to admit evidence concerning the existence of the gas chambers and extermination of the Jews since this was established fact.[42] II–087

9. Assessment of evidence

Notwithstanding the general statements above, the Commission stated that it would intervene where the assessment of evidence disclosed gross unfairness or arbitrariness.[43] What this means in practice has not been explored. It seems to indicate that II–088

[37] *Schlumpf v Switzerland*, January 8, 2009, paras 51–58.

[38] *GB v France*, October 2, 2001, ECHR 2001–X, paras 68–70.

[39] (7761/77) (Dec.) May 8, 1978, 14 D.R. 171.

[40] Not all Contracting States rely on or admire the institution.

[41] (14739/89) (Dec.) May 9, 1989, 60 D.R. 296; see also *Edwards*, see fn.29 above, and *Oyston v UK*, (42011/98) (Dec.) January 22, 2002, where it was compatible with fairness for the Court of Appeal to assess the relevance of new evidence and decide whether the conviction should stand.

[42] (25096/94) (Dec.) September 6, 1995, 82–A D.R. 117.

[43] e.g. (7987/77) (Dec.) December 13, 1979, 18 D.R. 31, where an applicant company complained of the assessment of compensation for expropriated property, the Commission found that evaluation of the evidence could not be reviewed by it unless the judge had drawn grossly unfair or arbitrary conclusions from the facts before him; however, the judge's findings of fact were supported by the higher court and the reasons on which the decisions were based were sufficient to exclude any arbitrariness; (22909/93) (Dec.) September 6, 1995, 82–B D.R. 25.

there will be verification that there is some evidence to support the decision. The fact that a judge prefers the evidence of particular witnesses is unlikely to be sufficient, unless his stated reasons for doing so disclose a fundamental unsoundness.[44] Where an applicant was convicted on the basis of a statement given in his absence by a witness who later retracted it, the Court considered it sufficient that the court had the opportunity to observe the demeanour of the witness first-hand and, as it gave detailed reasons for its decision to attach weight to the accusatory statement, the verdict could not be deemed "arbitrary or manifestly unreasonable".[45]

Cross-reference

Part IIA, s.7: Entrapment and agents provacateurs.
Part IIA, s.19(2): Burden of proof: evidential assumptions.
Part IIA, s.26: Witnesses.
Part IIB, s.30: Interception of communications.

[44] e.g. mutatis mutandis, *Schuler-Zgraggen v Switzerland*, June 24, 1993, Series A, No.263, where the court relied on factors discriminatory on grounds of sex.
[45] *Camilleri v Malta*, (51760/99) (Dec.) March 16, 2000.

10. Independence and impartiality

Key provision:

Article 6, para.1 (fair trial by "independent and impartial tribunal"). II–089

Key case-law:

Ringeisen v Austria, July 16, 1971, Series A, No.13, 1 E.H.R.R. 455; *Le Compte v Belgium*, June 23, 1981, Series A, No.43, 4 E.H.R.R. 1; *Piersack v Belgium*, October 1, 1982, Series A, No.53, 5 E.H.R.R. 169; *Sramek v Austria*, October 22, 1984, Series A, No.84; *Campbell and Fell v UK*, June 28, 1984, Series A, No.80, 7 E.H.R.R. 165; *Belilos v Switzerland*, April 29, 1988, Series A, No.132, 10 E.H.R.R. 466; *De Cubber v Belgium*, October 26, 1984, Series A, No.86, 7 E.H.R.R. 236; *Hauschildt v Denmark*, May 24, 1989, Series A, No.155, 12 E.H.R.R. 266; *Langborger v Sweden*, June 22, 1989, Series A, No.155, 12 E.H.R.R. 416; *Oberschlick v Austria (No.1)*, May 23, 1991, Series A, No.204, 19 E.H.R.R. 389; *Demicoli v Malta,* August 27, 1991, Series A, No.210, 14 E.H.R.R. 47; *Pfeiffer and Plankl v Austria*, February 25, 1992, Series A, No.227, 14 E.H.R.R. 692; *Nortier v Netherlands*, August 24, 1993, Series A, No.267, 17 E.H.R.R. 273; *Saraivo de Carvalho v Portugal*, April 22, 1994, Series A, No.286, 18 E.H.R.R. 534; *Van de Hurk v Netherlands*, April 19, 1994, Series A, No.288, 18 E.H.R.R. 481; *Debled v Belgium*, September 22, 1994, Series A, No.292–B, 19 E.H.R.R. 506; *Diennet v France*, September 26, 1995, Series A, No.325, 21 E.H.R.R. 544; *Procola v Luxembourg*, September 28, 1995, Series A, No.326, 22 E.H.R.R. 193; *Thomann v Switzerland*, June 10, 1996, R.J.D. 1996–III, No.11, 24 E.H.R.R. 553; *Ferrantelli and Santangelo v Italy*, August 7, 1996, R.J.D. 1997–I, No.30, 23 E.H.R.R. 288; *Findlay v UK*, February 25, 1997, R.J.D. 1997–I, No.30, 24 E.H.R.R. 221; *McGonnell v UK*, February 8, 2000, 30 E.H.R.R. 289; *Kingsley v UK*, November 7, 2000; *Kleyn v Netherlands*, May 6, 2003, ECHR 2003–VI; *Kyprianou v Cyprus*, December 15, 2005, ECHR 2005–VIII; *Micallef v Malta*, October 15, 2009 , ECHR 2009–. . .

1. General considerations

This core element of the notion of a fair trial has generated many cases. The two aspects are often interlocked, a lack of independence coinciding with a lack of objective impartiality; thus the two notions are frequently treated together. The basic principles were established early. The cases tend merely to illustrate their application to a diverse number of factual and procedural circumstances. II–090

2. Independence

The tribunal or court must be independent of the executive and the parties,[1] and also of the legislature or Parliament.[2] As to whether it satisfies the condition of independence, regard is had to the manner of appointment of the members, the II–091

[1] *Ringeisen v Austria*, July 16, 1971, Series A, No.13, 1 E.H.R.R. 455, para.95.

[2] e.g. (8603/79) (Dec.) December 18, 1980, 22 D.R. 220; *Demicoli v Malta*, August 27, 1991, Series A, No.210, 14 E.H.R.R. 47, breach of privilege proceedings before the Maltese House of Representatives against a journalist for defamatory articles—the Commission found lack of independence, the Court found a lack of impartiality.

duration of their office, the existence of guarantees against outside pressure and the question whether the body presents an appearance of independence.[3]

3. Aspects and guarantees

(a) Composition

II–092 The presence of legally-qualified or judicial members is a strong indicator of independence, as in *LeCompte v Belgium* where on the Appeals Council the members were made up equally of medical practitioners acting in personal capacity and members of the judiciary, being chaired by one of latter.[4] Where, in *Sramek v Austria*, the regional authority in land disputes included three civil servants from the local government, which was a party in the proceedings; thus there was a legitimate doubt about their independence since, even though there was no indication that they were subject to instructions, they were subordinate to the officer acting for the local government in the proceedings. Where patents bodies were entirely made up of civil servants, who had no guarantees of irremovability and were appointed from a pool to act at first instance and on appeal, the Commission found problems of structural independence.[5]

(b) Appointment and term of office

II–093 The mere fact that a minister appoints members does not pose a problem since in many systems judges are appointed on approval by ministers of justice.[6] Nor can exception be taken to appointment by Parliament either.[7] However, the irremovability of judges is in general a corollary of their independence. Where members of a maritime disputes divisions (the president and vice-president) were appointed and removed from office by the Minister of Justice, and in a position of hierarchical subordination, there was a violation.[8] The lack of this guarantee is not necessarily fatal if it is not apparent that a problem arises in practice. For example, though there were no regulations or guarantees concerning Board of Visitors' members, it was accepted that, although the Home Secretary could require a member to resign, this would be done in only the most exceptional circumstances.[9] Similarly, although the Lord Chancellor could remove district and circuit judges, there had practically been no precedent for such a step which would have been subject to judicial review.[10] Where in Slovakian special courts for fraud and corruption the judges' security clearance could be removed preventing them from sitting, the Court looked

[3] *Piersack v Belgium*, October 1, 1982, Series A, No.53, 5 E.H.R.R. 169, para.27.
[4] *Campbell and Fell v UK*, June 28, 1984, Series A, No.80, 7 E.H.R.R. 165, where the Board of Visitors' membership was generally half magistrates.
[5] *British American Tobacco v Netherlands*, November 20, 1995, Series A, No.331–A, 21 E.H.R.R. 409, the Court found it unnecessary to decide as in any event appeal lay to a normal court.
[6] (18781/91) (Dec.) July 6, 1998.
[7] *Filippini v San Marino*, (10526/02) (Dec.) August 26, 2003.
[8] *Brudnicka v Poland*, March 3, 2005.
[9] *Campbell and Fell*, see fn.4 above, para.80; *McMichael v UK*, (Rep.) Series A, No.307–B, paras 61 and 114, where the Commission had doubts concerning removability of members of the Children's Panel by the Secretary of State.
[10] *Clarke v UK*, (23695/02) (Dec.) August 25, 2005.

at the system in practice and found no instance of removal occurring; the courts were found suitably independent.[11]

However, in *Henryk and Ryszard Urban v Poland*, the fact that in practice the Minister did not use his power to remove assessors (trainee judges) who sat in criminal cases, did not play any role in the reasoning; the Court lent decisive weight to the findings of the Constitutional Court which had held that there was a problem as there were no substantive or procedural safeguards setting out when an assessor could be removed and excluding removal due to his judicial decision-making.[12] The drastic impact of this finding—assessors were a key part of the justice system—was mitigated by the consideration that the violation could not be considered to vitiate all decisions taken and that retrials would not be necessary; it was left open, however, that this might be different if there was any ground to suspect that the Minister had, or could reasonably be taken to have had, an interest in a particular case.[13]

Fixed terms also tend to be regarded as a guarantee, if long enough. In *Le Compte*, six-year terms for Appeals Council members furnished a safeguard. Three-year terms for Board of Visitor members in *Campbell and Fell v UK* were considered rather short but it was acknowledged that the posts were unpaid and it was difficult to get volunteers. Four-year terms for military judges on the National Security Court in Turkey was questionable.[14]

(c) *Appearances*

While weight is given to the proper appearance of independence, suspicions have to be, to some extent, objectively justified. In *Campbell* and *Fell*, the Commission thought that the Board of Visitors did not give an appearance of institutional independence, since it fulfilled a number of administrative roles in prison and was associated by prisoners with prison management. The Court, however, found that the fact the Board had administrative roles was not decisive and it could still be independent. It also took the view that in a custodial setting certain sentiments by prisoners were inevitable, but there was no indication that they would be reasonably entitled to think that the Board was dependent on the prison. II–094

Where a police board acting in a judicial capacity was concerned however, appearances were found to be decisive in the context of determining whether it acted as a "tribunal" for the purposes of Art.6, para.1. In *Belilos v Switzerland*, a member of the police sat in his personal capacity on the Police Board, was not subject to orders, took an oath and could not be dismissed. Since, however, he was a civil servant who returned to other departmental duties and would tend to be seen as member of the police force subordinate to superiors and loyal to colleagues, this disclosed a situation which could undermine the confidence which courts should inspire.

Where a court privileges in some way the evidence of an official body which cannot be regarded as neutral to the proceedings, it may itself lose the appearance of

[11] *Fruni v Slovakia*, June 21, 2011, paras 143–149, the Court also took into account that a judge could challenge the removal of clearance before a parliamentary committee and then the superior courts.

[12] *Henryk and Ryszard Urban v Poland*, November 11, 2010, paras 49–55.

[13] *Henryk*, see fn.12 above, para.56.

[14] *Incal v Turkey*, June 9, 1998, R.J.D. 1998–IV, No.78, para.68, where a military judge sat in a court judging civilians. See, however, *Yavuz v Turkey*, (29870/96) (Dec.) May 25, 2000, four-year terms for military courts dealing with military discipline were considered favourably.

independence and impartiality. Thus, when the Supreme Court appointed a medical board ,whose members worked for the hospital defendant, to give expert evidence, it was found that the court's objective impartiality was compromised by the board's composition, procedural position and role in the proceedings before it.[15]

(d) Subordination to other authorities

II–095 The tribunal must not be subject to instructions in its adjudicatory role, although it may be compatible for a minister to issue general guidelines.[16] Where, in *Van de Hurk v Netherlands*, a minister had the power to set aside the decisions issued by the tribunal deciding on milk quota disputes, the Court found that the tribunal lacked the quality of independence, even though it seemed that the power was not exercised in practice. The power to give a binding decision which could not be altered by a non-judicial authority was identified as inherent in the guarantees of Art.6, as confirmed by the use of the term "determination".[17]

Where executive authorities intervened in judicial proceedings, obtaining annulment of decisions and the setting aside of final judgments, the Court has found that the applicants have been deprived of hearing by "an independent and impartial tribunal".[18]

Subordination of an inferior court to a higher court may also pose problems, where the latter had power to give binding instructions and had effective control of the careers of the judges in the former.[19]

4. Impartiality

II–096 The Court distinguishes between subjective impartiality—the existence of actual prejudice on the part of a judge or tribunal—and objective impartiality—whether a judge offers guarantees sufficient to exclude any legitimate doubt in this matter.[20] Personal impartiality of a judge is to be presumed until there is proof to the contrary.[21] In practice, this is a very strong presumption. The Court has commented that the fact that a judge takes a strongly negative view of an applicant's case or even of its character is not sufficient to disclose bias, and that unduly harsh or oppressive behaviour is not necessarily a reflection of personal prejudice.[22] The intemperate reaction of judges in imprisoning a lawyer for contempt of court was a rare example giving rise to a finding under the subjective element.[23]

[15] *Sara Lind Eggertsdottir v Iceland*, July 5, 2007, paras 48–52. See also *Hirschhorn v Romania*, July 26, 2007, paras 66–84, where a Court of Appeal president relied on an inspecting judge's opinion as to the unenforceability of a judgment, the latter being subordinate to the Ministry of Justice.

[16] *Campbell and Fell*, see fn.4 above, concerning the Board of Visitors.

[17] e.g. *Findlay v UK*, February 25, 1997, R.J.D. 1997–I, No.30, 24 E.H.R.R. 221, where the convening officer had power to confirm the court martial decision.

[18] e.g. *Sovtransavto Holding v Ukraine*, July 25, 2002, where the Court found resulting infringements of the basic principles of the rule of law and legal certainty.

[19] *Salov v Ukraine*, September 6, 2005. The Court also had problems with the way the Regional Court overruled the lower court's acquittal of the applicant.

[20] *Piersack*, see fn.3 above, para.30.

[21] *Le Compte v Belgium*, June 23, 1981, Series A, No.43, 4 E.H.R.R. 1, para.58.

[22] e.g. *Ranson v UK*, (14180/03) (Dec.) September 2, 2003.

[23] *Kyprianou v Cyprus*, December 15, 2005, ECHR 2005–VIII, paras 129–133, where the judges had felt personally insulted by the lawyer's comments. See also fn.26 below for cases where judges made comments in the press or elsewhere appearing to show prejudgment of issues: this was treated as undermining the impartiality of the tribunal.

In the context of objective impartiality, appearances are of importance having regard to the confidence which the courts must inspire in the public in a democratic society, and above all in criminal proceedings, in the accused. The latter aspect was later qualified when the Court noted that the standpoint of the accused was important but not decisive. What was determinant was whether the fear could be considered as objectively justified.[24] The Court has also commented that any judge in respect of whom there is a legitimate reason to fear a lack of impartiality must withdraw.[25] Judges are also expected to exercise maximum discretion with regard to their cases in order to preserve their image as impartial judges, in particular refraining from using the press for comment even when provoked.[26] However, leaks to the press of court deliberations and decision before delivery of judgment, even if presumed to have a judge as the source and however regrettable, have not cast doubt on the court's independence or impartiality.[27] On the other hand, there is a strong presumption that professional judges by their training are not influenced by adverse media coverage or hostile public opinion against an accused.[28] They cannot, however, be presumed to be neutral as regards alleged contempts of court carried out in their presence when they combine roles of complainant, witness, prosecutor and judge.[29]

Major problems can arise where a judge plays different procedural roles in the course of the proceedings; where the composition of a court coincides with another court which has been involved in some related aspect of the case; or where the tribunal is not, as the traditional court, made up of trained legal or judicial members.

(a) *Differing roles of a judge*

A conflict of roles commonly arises where judges have an investigating role or there is overlap between the prosecution (e.g. *procureur*) and the trial court. The mere fact that a judge has been involved in decisions before the trial is not sufficient to render him lacking in objective impartiality, special features being required beyond the judge's knowledge of the case file, the fact that he has looked at questions of risk on remand decisions or made assessment of the existence of a prima facie case.[30] It is necessary for the judge to have been squarely involved in deciding issues relevant to II–097

[24] *Piersack*, see fn.3 above, para.30; *Morel v France*, June 6, 2000, ECHR 2000–VI, para.44; *Nortier v Netherlands*, August 24, 1993, Series A, No.267, 17 E.H.R.R. 273, para.33, objective test even where the applicant's apprehensions may be understandable.

[25] *Hauschildt v Denmark*, May 24, 1989, Series A, No.155, 12 E.H.R.R. 266, para.48.

[26] See findings of lack of impartiality in *Buscemi v Italy*, September 16, 1999, ECHR 1999–VI, where a judge responded to the applicant's comments in the press in a manner implying that he already held an unfavourable view of the applicant's case; *Lavents v Latvia*, November 28, 2002, paras 118–121, where a judge expressed views critical of the defence; *Olujic v Croatia*, February 5, 2009, paras 61–68, three members of the National Judicial Council either made prejudicial and unfavourable statements about the applicant or agreed that they were disqualified (violation).

[27] *Saiz Oceja v Spain*, (74182/01) (Dec.) May 2, 2007.

[28] *Craxi v Italy*, (34896/97) (Dec.) December 5, 2002.

[29] *Kyprianou*, see fn.23 above, para.127.

[30] *Nortier*, see fn.24 above; *Saraivo de Carvalho*; *Morel v France*, see fn.24 above, concerning commercial court proceedings; *Jasinski v Poland*, December 20, 2005. See also *Chesne v France*, April 22, 2010, paras 37–40, where two appeal court judges had previously made rulings containing statements going beyond findings of suspicion but appearing to prejudge the guilt of the accused, their participation in later proceedings raised doubts as to impartiality of the tribunal.

those in the trial,[31] or to have been involved in a prosecution capacity or as a party to the proceedings.[32] The fact that a judge has detailed prior knowledge of the case is not sufficient, attention being given to the scope and nature of any measures taken before the trial.[33] No problem arose where the judge had merely been head of the prosecution service at the time the applicant was being questioned by police about a different offence.[34] Nor is there any objection to participation in court deliberations of a *judge rapporteur* who is member of the composition, unless he or she has been involved in the "*instruction*" or drawing up of the charges.[35]

At higher levels, judges should not be involved in hearing appeals against themselves or have been involved in ruling on the same issues in a different forum.[36] As admissibility of appeal issues may be procedural and unconnected with the merits, it may not offend for a judge, who has already issued a substantive decision, to sit on the panel deciding leave to appeal.[37] However, where most of the members of the appellate or cassation body appear to be redeciding on essentially the same

[31] *Hauschildt*, fn.25 above, where the presiding judge, taking decisions on pre-trial detention, had on nine occasions referred to a "particularly confirmed suspicion" that the accused committed the offence (i.e. the judge had to be convinced of a very high degree of clarity as to guilt), the difference with the issue to be settled at trial was tenuous; *Castillo Algar v Spain*, October 28, 1998, R.J.D. 1998–VIII, No.95, where two judges in the trial court had previously rejected an appeal against the issuing of the criminal charge on the basis of "sufficient evidence" that an offence had been committed; *Tierce v San Marino*, July 25, 2000, ECHR 2000–IX, violation found in successive role of the *commissario della Legge* as investigating judge and trial judge; *Perote Pellon v Spain*, July 25, 2002, violation where military court judges had taken decisions to detain on the basis of findings of "solid" proof of guilt; *Cianetti v Italy*, April 24, 2004, where judges on the trial court had issued preventive measures in terms suggesting that there had been sufficient evidence to conclude that an offence had been committed; *Adamkiewicz v Poland*, March 2, 2010, paras 102–108, a juvenile judge assembled the evidence, assessed that the applicant was the author of the impugned acts, and also sat in the trial court judging the same issues; *Cardona Serrat v Spain*, October 26, 2010, two members of the appeal court had also sat on the bench which had overruled an order of release pending trial and found, on its own motion, the existence of a risk that the applicant might intimidate witnesses.

[32] See *Piersack*, fn.3 above, where a judge had previously been the head of the public prosecutor's section which instituted the prosecution; *Svetlana Naumenko v Ukraine*, November 9, 2004, where a judge lodged a "protest" against a decision and was on the tribunal which ruled on the protest; *Kyprianou*, see fn.23 above, para.127, where the judges, in taking action for contempt against themselves, effectively prosecuted, convicted and sentenced; *Meznaric v Croatia*, July 15, 2005, where a judge had earlier acted as lawyer for the other party.

[33] e.g. no violation concerning an insolvency judge's varying interventions in *Morel v France*, fn.24 above, and in *Delage and Magistrello v France*, (40028/98) (Dec.) January 24, 2002, ECHR 2002–II, or concerning cassation judges sitting on different applications in *Depiets v France*, February 10, 2004, ECHR 2004–I. Contrast violation in *Werner v Poland*, November 15, 2001, where the insolvency judge's ruling on a motion prejudged the final decision.

[34] *Mellors v UK*, (57386/00) (Dec.) January 30, 2003, the situation might have differed if the judge had not left the prosecution post before the applicant was charged, remanded or indicted on the murder charge on which the judge later sat in an appellate role.

[35] e.g. *Tedesco v France*, May 10, 2007.

[36] e.g. *Ferrantelli and Santangelo v Italy*, August 7, 1996, R.J.D. 1997–I, No.30, 23 E.H.R.R. 288, where the presiding appeal judge had convicted the co-accused in a judgment referring to the applicants' participation in events and the appeal judgment cited extracts from that earlier judgment when convicting the applicants; *Oberschlick v Austria (No.1)*, where a judge who participated in the first instance judgment sat in the appeal hearing against that judgment; contrast *Lindon-Otchakovsky-Laurens and July v France*, October 22, 2007, paras 75–82, no problem where two appellate judges ruling on the defamatory nature of a publication which cited passages from a book already found defamatory by a court on which they had sat, as there were different defendants and different issues and there was no prejudging of the case despite a factual connection between the two.

[37] *Warsicka v Poland*, January 16, 2007.

factual issues as they did on an earlier occasion, a problem may arise; this appears to be a very fine line.[38]

No problem arises, per se, where a judge plays a role in a criminal case and then sits in an associated civil compensation claim.[39] As different evidential standards may apply, the finding of criminal liability will not always prejudge civil liability or vice versa. However, where civil and criminal defamation proceedings based on the same statements were ruled upon consecutively by the same judge, the identical nature of a key issue as to whether the statements were defamatory of the subjects led to the conclusion that there was a legitimate ground to doubt the judge's impartiality.[40]

(b) Judges' connections or affiliations

While there is no problem as such arising from a judge acting as a lawyer, the Court found an applicant could legitimately fear that a judge, who was acting as lawyer for another party in proceedings involving the applicant, continued to view him as the opposing party.[41] Previous links by a higher court judge with the opposing party in an expert capacity at the lower instance has also raised doubt as to impartiality.[42] Similarly, the fact that a judge had regular, close and financially lucrative links as a professor with the university sued by the applicant justified fears that he might lack impartiality.[43] Involvement of a judge in a financial agreement between her husband and a bank which was a party in proceedings in which she sat was considered to disclose links of "such a nature and amplitude", and was so close in time to the hearing of the case that the applicant could entertain reasonable fears that the court lacked the requisite impartiality.[44] Family connections between a judge and a party in the proceedings have also disclosed a problem.[45] Where an investigating judge was appointed to a case shortly after being an officer within a ministry implicated in the background to the criminal proceedings, the Court considered the shortness of II–098

[38] *Mancel and Branquart v France*, June 24, 2010., narrow majority; minority warning about the tyranny of "appearances".

[39] *Lie and Bernstenn v Norway*, (25130/94) (Dec.) December 16, 1999, where separate issues arose for determination; also *Kalogeropoulou v Greece*, (59021/00) (Dec.) December 12, 2002, where a judge acted on the merits and then in the execution procedure.

[40] *Fatullayev v Azerbaijan*, April 22, 2010, paras 136–140.

[41] *Wettstein v Switzerland*, December 12, 2000, ECHR 2000–XII, there was no material link between the two cases. It was the contemporaneous overlap of the proceedings that gave rise to objectionable appearances. The fact that an office colleague of two judges had also been a lawyer opposing the applicant would further confirm fears, though was of minor relevance by itself. See also *Puolitaival and Pirttiaho v Finland*, November 23, 2004, where a Court of Appeal judge's involvement in a law firm acting against the applicant in an earlier case was too remote to raise issues.

[42] *Svarc and Kavnik v Slovenia*, January 8, 2007, paras 41–44, appearances were at risk, even though the judge had acted many years previously, his earlier expert opinion had not been in issue in the higher instance and the questions before the court were different.

[43] *Pescador Valero v Spain*, June 17, 2003. See also *Belukha v Ukraine*, November 9, 2006, where the judge had demanded and accepted assets for free from the other party (e.g. a computer for the court).

[44] *Sigurdsson v Iceland*, April 10, 2003, para.45; see *also Tocono and Profesorii Prometeiti v Moldova*, June 26, 2007, paras 31–32, violation where in proceedings concerning registration of a private school, there sat a Supreme Court judge whose son had earlier been expelled from the school, with threats of retaliation having been issued by the judge; *Academy Trading v Greece*, April 4, 2000, para.46, where the fact that two judges' daughters worked for the friend of the head of the bank in proceedings did not affect impartiality.

[45] *Micallef v Malta*, October 15, 2009 , ECHR 2009–. . . , paras 100–105, where the Chief Justice sitting in the case was uncle of the other party's counsel and brother of that party's counsel at first instance whose conduct was in issue on appeal.

time was such that the accused could legitimately fear that the judge had inside knowledge or pre-formed views about the case from the executive point of view.[46]

The fact that a judge may have known political views opposite to those of an accused will not, of itself, disclose a problem. Nor will the fact that magistrates or a group of magistrates has expressed critical views of a legislative initiative give doubts as to their impartiality when later adjudicating on the resulting laws.[47]

A situation where a judge in a civil case had privately instructed the firm which also was representing one of the parties did not give rise to suspicion, when it concerned a will and a partner outside the litigation department.[48] The mere fact that a judge is a freemason is insufficient to cast doubt on his impartiality, even where a party or witness in the proceedings is also a freemason, at least in the United Kingdom. In *Salaman v UK*, the Court noted the Parliamentary inquiry into the matter and considered that there was no reason to doubt that a judge would regard his judicial oath as taking precedence over other obligations. Whether a judge should withdraw due to personal acquaintance with another freemason or due to the interests of a freemason being in issue would depend on the circumstances of the case.[49]

Where a court president with a connection to a party does not sit in the formation that decides the case, the issue of independence and impartiality will depend essentially on the degree of influence the president can wield over the disposal of the case and the pressure, direct or indirect, that could be exerted by him on the other judges of the court. The Court found no risk of a lack of objective impartiality where the president who had previously lodged a criminal complaint against the applicant had no legal power over assignment of cases and only limited hierarchical authority over the other judges, any promotions or disciplinary action being ultimately decided by other bodies.[50]

There is some indication that a judge against whom doubts have arisen may be able to dispel them by making an appropriate statement which is sufficient to allay any legitimate fears.[51]

(c) Specialist tribunals

II–099 It is accepted that there may be good reasons in technical areas for opting for special adjudicatory bodies.[52] The mere existence of professional connections between an applicant and members of a tribunal is generally not sufficient to cast doubt on their impartiality, even if it may be assumed there is a potential for a conflict of

[46] *Vera Fernandez Huidobro v Spain*, January 6, 2010, paras 119–125.
[47] *Previti v Italy*, (45291/06) (Dec.) December 8, 2009, paras 249–269.
[48] *Lawrence v UK*, (74660/01) (Dec.) January 24, 2002; no grounds for doubt in *Sofianopoulos v Greece*, (1988/02) (Dec.) December 12, 2002, where a magistrates' association expressed public views on an issue in a case but the individual judges had not.
[49] (43505/98) (Dec.) June 15, 2000; see *Kiiskinen v Finland*, (26323/95) (Dec.) June 1, 1998.
[50] *Parlov-Tkalcic v Croatia*, December 22, 2009, paras 82–97.
[51] *Chmelir v Czech Republic*, June 7, 2005, para.62, citing *Puolitaival and Pirttiaho v Finland*, fn.41 above, para.53.
[52] *British American Tobacco*, fn.5 above, concerning patents.

interests.[53] More direct links between members and a party may be required to raise issues and once a legitimate doubt is raised, it may not be enough to point to the presence of judicial members or a judicial casting vote.[54] In *Gautrin v France*, for example, medical members of the tribunal could be regarded as having a connection with competitors of the applicant doctors "*SOS Medecins*" and with bodies who had lodged complaints against their alleged advertising infringements.[55]

In the military area, hierarchical dependence between court martial members and superior officers has caused problems and the Convention organs have required guarantees against any appearance of control or influence.[56] The Court considers that the use of military tribunals over civilians in itself raises problems of independence and impartiality, in particular where the army could be seen as a party to the proceedings and its interests were at stake.[57] In cases from Turkey, the Court has also found that the inclusion of a military judge on the National Security Court, which sat on civilian criminal cases concerning State security issues, cast legitimate doubts on the court's independence and impartiality as the military judge belonged to the army which took orders from the executive and remained subject to military discipline and assessment reports. The applicants tried before the court, whether on security or drugs offences, could legitimately fear that it might allow itself to be unduly influenced by considerations which had nothing to do with the case.[58] Even where the military member of a court is replaced by a civilian judge, there may still be legitimate doubts about the independence and impartiality of the tribunal where the military judge participated in interlocutory decisions which continued to affect the proceedings and which were not revisited by an independent bench.[59]

(d) Dual functions

Where an institution has various functions which overlap, independence and impartiality as an adjudicating body may be undermined. In *Procola v Luxembourg*, concerning a milk quota dispute, four members of the *Conseil d'Etat* had performed **II–100**

[53] Where, in *Le Compte*, fn.21 above, the medical appeals council was made up equally from doctors and members of the judiciary, the Commission found that the former could not be deemed neutral since their interests were close to those of the parties. The Court disagreed, finding that the composition and a judicial chairman with casting vote was a definite assurance of impartiality (contrast *Langborger*, fn.54 below). In *Debled v Belgium*, September 22, 1994, Series A, No.292–B, 19 E.H.R.R. 506, where the applicant doctor made numerous complaints concerning members of the medical appeals structure, the Court was pragmatic, finding the system generally acceptable as regarded structural objectivity; that the applicant threatened to paralyse the whole system if challenged members were excluded from decisions; and that his complaints were general and abstract and not based on any material facts showing any member was hostile towards him.

[54] *Langborger v Sweden*, June 22, 1989, Series A, No.155, 12 E.H.R.R. 416, concerning the Housing and Tenancy Court, made up of two professional judges and two lay assessors nominated by property owners and tenants' associations, where the lay assessors had close links with the two associations which sought to maintain a clause the applicant was challenging—there being a legitimate fear that their interests were contrary to his own, it was not sufficient that the judicial president had the casting vote. Cf. *Kurt Kellerman AB v Sweden*, October 26, 2004, where the lay assessors on the Labour Court had no links with or direct interest in the case.

[55] *Gautrin v France*, May 20, 1998, R.J.D. 1998–III, No.72.

[56] See, e.g. *Findlay*, fn.17 above, and *Yavuz*, fn.14 above. See Pt IIB, s.3(3): Military justice.

[57] *Ergin v Turkey*, May 4, 2006, the Court stated that only in exceptional circumstances would it be compatible for a civilian to be tried by the military.

[58] e.g. *Incal*, fn.14 above, paras 72 and 78; *Sadak v Turkey (No.1)*, July 17, 2001, ECHR 2001–VIII; *Canevi v Turkey*, November 10, 2004, concerning drugs offences.

[59] *Ocalan v Turkey*, May 12, 2005, paras 114–118.

successive advisory and judicial roles in the case. This was capable of casting doubt on the structural impartiality of the judicial committee, giving rise to fears which were objectively justified and a legitimate doubt, however slight, that members might feel bound by their previous opinion.[60] In *McGonnell v UK*, the mere fact that the Deputy Bailiff who presided in the Royal Court in the determination of the applicant's planning appeal also presided over the States of Deliberation in adopting the development plan, allegedly breached, was enough to vitiate the impartiality of the Court even though the doubt was perceived as slight.

The Court subsequently took a more cautious and nuanced approach. In *Kleyn v Netherlands*, it expressly refrained from criticising constitutional frameworks that provided for dual roles of particular bodies in conflict with the notion of separation of powers and applied the approach of examining whether on the facts of the particular case the successive legislative advisory and judicial roles of the Council of State gave the requisite appearances of independence and impartiality. As the advisory opinions given in that case on the general transport infrastructure and the subsequent appeals on a particular routing decision could not be regarded as involving the "same case" or "the same decision" fears of lack of independence and impartiality were not objectively justified.[61]

Similarly, where a member of Parliament sat as an expert member of the court of appeal, there was no violation as he had no connection with any party or the subject-matter of the case, his mere status as a member of the legislature not in itself sufficient to cast doubt on his impartiality or independence.[62]

However, where the body, which has the potential for conflict of roles, does not specify which members sat on a decision, the Court found a problem; no possibility of challenge of members would have been possible in such circumstances.[63]

(e) *Rehearings*

II–101 Where a first instance decision is quashed on appeal and returned for a fresh decision, the fact that the same body, with or without the same membership, decides the matter again does not disclose legitimate fears of lack of impartiality.[64] Thus in *Diennet v France*, where the decision of a medical appeal tribunal was quashed by the Court of Cassation for a procedural error, the inclusion of three of

[60] Four out of five had been involved in the advisory panel giving an opinion on the draft regulation under judicial challenge. See also *Dubus SA v France*, June 11, 2009, paras 53–62, where the varying investigative, prosecutorial and disciplinary roles exercised by the Banking Commission were not clearly demarcated, giving the applicant company the reasonably-held view that the same officers were involved throughout the various stages of the procedure; *Savino v Italy*, April 29, 2009, where the internal appellate body for employment disputes for the department of the Chamber of Deputies included the members of the "Bureau" who had the running of the department, including financial, salarial and administrative competence, which had an overlap with the dispute about employee allowances.

[61] *Kleyn v Netherlands*, May 6, 2003, ECHR 2003–VI, para.200, this was the element identified, perhaps not very convincingly, as distinguishing the *Procola* and *McGonnell* judgments. See also *GL and SL v France*, (58811/00) (Dec.) March 6, 2003, where general complaints about the legislative and adjudicative roles of the *Conseil d'Etat* were insufficient to cast doubt on independence in that particular case, and *Sacilor-Lormines v France*, November 9, 2006, where the advisory and adjudicatory functions of the *Conseil d'Etat*, while related, did not concern "the same case".

[62] *Pabla Ky v Finland*, September 16, 2003, paras 33–35, the MP had not exercised any prior legislative, executive or advisory function in respect of the subject matter or legal issues.

[63] *Vernes v France*, January 20, 2011, paras 42–44.

[64] *Ringeisen*, see fn.1 above, para.97.

the same members in the second hearing which reached the same conclusion, raised no ground for legitimate suspicion. Where in *Thomann v Switzerland*, an applicant was retried by the court which had convicted him *in absentia*, the Court considered that the judges would be aware that they had reached their first decision on limited evidence and would undertake fresh consideration of the case on a comprehensive, adversarial basis. However, an appeal court sitting to reconsider whether it had itself made errors of law in its previous decision did give rise to legitimate fears of a lack of impartiality.[65] The Court has also commented that, if a case was sent back to be reheard by a first instance court where a substantive defect had irreversibly vitiated that judgment, as opposed to a procedural error, there might be objective ground to fear bias.[66]

(f) Juries

These principles apply equally to juries (see Pt IIA, s.13: Juries). II–102

(g) Court clerks and legal officers

Where legal officers such as advocates-general, *procureurs* and government commissioners play a role in proceedings, acting in the public interest or to ensure coherence of case-law, the Court has found that, although their independence and impartiality are not in doubt as such, they cannot be regarded as part of the tribunal and since they issue opinions on the outcome of the case, they can no longer be regarded as neutral. Thus considerations of equality of arms apply, requiring that the applicant be afforded the opportunity to comment on any submissions made by them for example and giving rise to problems where the officer retires with the judges.[67] II–103

Court clerks and judicial assistants, such as magistrates' clerks for example, may be regarded as part of the tribunal, however, and where they assist the court on points of law and evidence, and do not have any duty with regard to influencing the decision one way or another, no problem arises where they retire with the court. However, as a result such clerks must observe the requirements of impartiality and independence and should not, for example, exhibit bias when questioning an accused on behalf of the tribunal.[68] Where applicants in Consitutional Court proceedings challenged the fact that the Chief Justice's judicial assistant had six years earlier been a lawyer for the other party, the Court noted that the role of such an assistant in writing opinions for the judges and taking evidence was important to the judicial process and could raise issues of independence or impartiality of the tribunal. However, in the particular case, the Chief Justice had stated that she had not been involved in the particular case, the veracity of which statement had not been put in doubt by the applicants or any other element in the case: no legitimate doubt as to impartiality arose in the circumstances.[69]

[65] *San Leonard Band Club v Malta*, July 29, 2004, ECHR 2004–IX.
[66] *Stow and Gai v Portugal*, (18306/04) (Dec.) October 4, 2005.
[67] See, e.g. *Reinhardt and Slimane-Kaid*, March 31, 1998, R.J.D. 1998–II, No.68; see Pt IIA, s.8: Equality of arms.
[68] *Agnes Mort v UK*, (44564/98) (Dec.) September 6, 2001, ECHR 2001–IX.
[69] *Bellizzi v Malta,* June 21, 2011,

(h) Investigating judges

II–104 While investigating judges on the continent do not, as such, determine cases and are not part of the "tribunal", the Court nonetheless considers that their crucial role in assembling the evidence and preparing the case is such that the guarantee of impartiality must also attach to their part in the proceedings.[70]

5. Curing defects on appeal

II–105 Problems of independence and impartiality may be curable where a higher instance body provides a hearing with the necessary guarantees and adequate rehearing of the issues in civil cases.[71] In *Le Compte* and *Belilos*, the higher instances did not have jurisdiction to re-examine the facts or merits and therefore their undoubted independence and impartiality was not sufficient. The review by the Court of Appeal of civil proceedings where the judge had descended into the arena to harry the applicant was sufficient, where the Court of Appeal exercised full jurisdiction and re-assessed the lower court's findings thoroughly.[72] However, where, regardless of its overall competence, a superior court had power to quash a decision for lack of impartiality and declined to do so, the Court found that the defect had not been cured.[73]

Where investigating judges are concerned, any lack of impartiality may be cured if the court later reviews and carries out afresh the examination of witnesses and assembling of the evidence.[74]

In specialist administrative areas, less appears to be required by way of review by the judicial instances on grounds of expediency and the exercise of discretionary powers.[75] Thus, in *Kingsley v UK*, a full court hearing on both facts and law on appeal from the Gaming Board, which carried out a regulatory function in a classic exercise of administrative discretion, was not required, though the inability of the reviewing courts to quash and refer to an impartial tribunal deprived it of the requisite jurisdiction.

In criminal cases, it appears that an accused can claim to have the full guarantees of independence and impartiality at first instance.[76]

6. Waiver

II–106 The extent to which an accused may waive his right to an impartial tribunal by failing to challenge judges has not been clearly decided. To the extent that waiver may be possible, the Court has stated that this must be limited and minimum

[70] *Vera Fernandez Huidobro v Spain*, fn.46, paras 111–114.

[71] *De Cubber v Belgium*, October 26, 1984, Series A, No.86, 7 E.H.R.R. 236, para.33.

[72] *Ranson v UK*, fn.22 above; see also *Shirley Porter v UK*, (15184/02) (Dec.) April 8, 2002, where the Divisional Court's review of a local authority auditor's procedure cured any defect arising from his roles as investigator, prosecutor and judge.

[73] *Kyprianou*, see fn.23 above, para.134. See also *Henryk and Ryszard Urban v Poland*, fn.12 above, where the first instance lacked independence, the appellate level had no power to quash on that ground, so failed to remedy the defect. It may be noted that both these cases do not consider whether there was effectively a rehearing of the facts and legal issues which provided the applicant with a fair determination by an independent and impartial tribunal of the issues which had been at stake at first instance and thus replaced the potentially flawed proceedings with proceedings which were Art.6–compliant. Arguably the complaint about lack of impartiality appears to have been the principal issue in both cases.

[74] *Vera Fernandez Huidobro v Spain*, fn.46, paras 131–136.

[75] *Zumtobel v Austria*, September 21, 1993, Series A, No.268–A, 17 E.H.R.R. 116; *Bryan v UK*, November 22, 1995, Series A, No.335–A, 21 E.H.R.R. 342.

[76] *Findlay*, see fn.17 above, para.179, subsequent review powers did not compensate.

guarantees remain which cannot depend on the parties alone. In any event, the waiver must be established in an unequivocal manner. A failure to object, in *Pfeifer and Plankl v Austria*, to two court judges who had been investigating judges and were disqualified was not sufficient. The waiver argument also failed in *Oberschlick v Austria (No.1)*, where the judge presiding over the appeal had participated in previous proceedings and was disqualified under the Code of Criminal Procedure. Though the applicant did not challenge his presence, he was not regarded as waiving his right to impartial tribunal. The Court appeared to give weight in both these cases to the failure of the courts to abide by the domestic rules aimed at eradicating reasonable doubts as to impartiality.

Cross-reference

Part IIA, s.1: General principles: fairness.
Part IIA, s.4: Appeals.
Part IIA, s.13: Juries.
Part IIA, s.25: Tribunal established by law.

11. Information about the charge

Key provision:

II–107 Article 6, para.3(a).

Key case-law:

Albert and Le Compte v Belgium, February 10, 1983, Series A, No.58, 5 E.H.R.R. 533; *Campbell and Fell v UK*, June 28, 1984, Series A, No.80, 7 E.H.R.R. 165; *Brozicek v Italy*, December 19, 1989, Series A, No.167, 12 E.H.R.R. 371; *Gea Catalan v Spain*, February 10, 1995, Series A, No.309, 20 E.H.R.R. 266; *De Salvador Torres v Spain*, October 24, 1996, R.J.D. 1996–V, No.19, 23 E.H.R.R. 601; *Pelissier and Sassi v France*, March 25, 1999, ECHR 1999–II, 30 E.H.R.R. 715; *Mattocia v Italy*, July 25, 2000, ECHR 2000–IX; *Dallos v Hungary*, March 1, 2001, ECHR 2001–II; *Sadak v Turkey*, July 2, 2001, ECHR 2001–VII.

1. Applicability

II–108 The context of Art.6, para.3(a) is criminal and it is to be seen as a particular aspect of the right to fair trial.[1] Nonetheless in *Albert and Le Compte v Belgium*, concerning disciplinary proceedings against doctors, the Court commented that the civil and criminal aspects of Art.6, para.1 were not mutually exclusive and that Art.6, paras 2 and 3 were aspects of the notion of fair trial contained within para.1 of the civil context.

2. Information about the charge

II–109 This includes not only the cause of the accusation (the material facts which form the basis of the accusation), but the nature of the accusation (the legal classification of these material facts).[2] Full, detailed information concerning the charges are considered an essential prerequisite for ensuring the proceedings are fair. This involves sufficient information as is necessary for the accused to understand fully the extent of the charges against him with a view to preparing an adequate defence.[3] Thus, any changes in the accusation, including changes in the material facts must be duly and fully communicated to the accused who must be provided with adequate time and facilities to adapt his defence to them.[4]

[1] *FCB v Italy*, August 28, 1991, Series A, No.208–B, 14 E.H.R.R. 909, para.29; *Can v Austria*, (9300/81) (Rep.) July 12, 1984, Series A, No.96 (settled before the Court).

[2] *Pelissier and Sassi v France*, March 25, 1999, ECHR 1999–II, 30 E.H.R.R. 715, para.51; the information should be detailed: *Gea Catalan v Spain*, February 10, 1995, Series A, No.309, 20 E.H.R.R. 266; and following Commission case-law, e.g. *Chichlian and Ekindjian v France*, (Rep.) March 16, 1989, para.65, Series A, No.162–B, 13 E.H.R.R. 553.

[3] e.g. *Mattocia v Italy*, July 25, 2000, ECHR 2000–IX, paras 59–60.

[4] e.g. *Mattocia*, fn.3 above, para.61, the Court found a violation as changes in key facts about the alleged rape were communicated when it was no longer possible for the accused to react and no allowances were made by the Court for the difficulties caused to the defence confronted by another version of events. Cf. *Backstrom and Sundstrom v Sweden*, (67930/01) (Dec.) September 5, 2006, where a possible change in the legal classification of the offence was drawn to the attention of the defence on the penultimate day of the hearing, the Court was concerned at the shortness of time given but noted that defence counsel addressed the issues on the last day and made no request for an adjournment.

Information must in fact be received by the person: a legal presumption of receipt is not enough.[5] No particular form of notification is required.[6]

Common sense and practicality are to be applied in determining whether there has been a change in the offence under consideration. Though the Commission in *Gea Catalan v Spain* found a violation where the prosecution referred in its submissions to aggravating factor "one" and the domestic court convicted on aggravating factor "seven", the Court agreed with the domestic courts that it was a mere clerical error. The material facts relied on by the prosecution were the same relied on by the domestic court and factor seven was referred to expressly by the investigating judge on committal. In *De Salvador Torres v Spain*, though the offence of simple embezzlement had been in issue in the lower courts, the application by the Supreme Court of the aggravating factor of abuse of public office did not disclose a violation since it had been an underlying factual element throughout, the relevance of which the applicant could not claim to be unaware.[7]

Where, however, an offence has been reclassified in a substantive sense and this possibility has not been brought to the attention of the accused, a violation is likely to arise. In *Chichlian and Ekindjian v France*, the two applicants were acquitted of a currency offence charged under s.7 of a decree and then convicted on appeal of the offence under s.1. The Commission noted that the material facts had always been known to the applicants, but there was no evidence that the applicants had been informed by the relevant authority of the proposal to reclassify the offence before the appeal hearing.[8] Similarly, where in *Pélissier and Sassi v France* the appeal court convicted the applicants of aiding and abetting criminal bankruptcy, rather than criminal bankruptcy itself, and neither the prosecutor or the first instance court had ever made reference to that possibility, the Court found a violation as different ingredients made up the offence of aiding and abetting under the Criminal Code and it could not be considered an intrinsic element of the initial accusation known to the accused from the beginning of the proceedings.[9] It did not matter that the appellate court might, at the same time, lower the sentence imposed since it could not be excluded that the sentencing could have been affected also if the applicant had had the opportunity to address the requalified offence.[10]

[5] (10889/84) (Dec.) May 11, 1988, 56 D.R. 40, where notification by the investigating judge was delivered to the address, signed by someone else and the applicant claimed that he did not receive it.

[6] e.g. *Pelissier and Sassi*, see fn.2 above, para.53; *Erdogan v Turkey*, (14723/89) July 9, 1992, 73 D.R. 81, the applicant complained that he was not formally served with the arrest warrant or indictment but the Commission considered that he was aware of the terms of the arrest warrant and the fact that he did not get the indictment was attributable to his own conduct.

[7] Also *Campbell and Fell v UK*, June 28, 1984, Series A, No.80, 7 E.H.R.R. 165, where the applicant Campbell knew that he was accused of "mutiny" following disturbances in prison, the Court rejected his claim that he was not able to understand precisely what this term meant; *Garner v UK*, (38330/97) (Dec.) January 26, 1999, where the substituted conviction was based on the identical facts and misconduct, the applicant could not claim to be unaware of the nature and cause of the action against him.

[8] See fn.2 above.

[9] Although the counsel of the *partie civile* had made reference to the possibility, it had never been referred to by the judges or prosecutor; similar reasoning in *Mattei v France*, December 19, 2006. See also *Sadak v Turkey*, July 2, 2001, ECHR 2001–VII, paras 56–58, where the modified charge of membership of an illegal organisation could not be considered as an element intrinsic to the original charge of treason against the integrity of the State; *Miraux v France*, September 26, 2006, where after the closing of pleadings concerning a charge of attempted rape, the court put the charge of rape proper to the jury and *IH v Austria*, April 20, 2006, where the rape charge was reclassified by the trial court under a different provision than that on the indictment.

[10] *Mattei v France*, December 19, 2006, the court had also been influenced by her health, not offence-based considerations.

Subsequent proceedings in which the applicant is given the opportunity to advance his defence to a reformulated charge may cure defects in earlier procedures if he is able to contest all relevant and factual aspects.[11]

3. Language

II–110 The information about the charge must be in a language the applicant understands. In *Brozicek v Italy*, where the applicant was not Italian or resident in Italy and had clearly expressed his language difficulties to the domestic court, the Court found that the authorities should have had the notification translated unless they were in a position to establish that he knew adequate Italian.[12]

4. Promptly

II–111 Though the requirement is for information to be provided promptly, the Convention organs have not been particularly demanding. Thus in one case, where there was a delay in notification of proceedings, the Commission noted that the applicant was not affected immediately. Also, he was served with a notice four months before trial which was in good time for the preparation of his defence, which was the principal underlying purpose of the safeguard.[13] Similarly, in *Padin Gestoso v Spain*, no issue arose for the Court where the applicant had not been immediately informed of the investigations conducted by the investigating judge as he had not been directly affected by them and was informed in good time of the charges later preferred against him.[14] On the other hand, where an applicant had been under investigation in relation to an alleged banking fraud and his funds frozen, there was a violation as for almost ten years he had not been properly informed of the accusations against him, having been neither charged or brought before the investigating judge.[15]

5. Relationship with Art.6, para.3(b): adequate time and facilities for the preparation of the defence

II–112 Where an applicant has not been promptly informed of the charge, it may well be that this has prevented him from properly preparing his defence at the same time, there being a logical connection between the two provisions.[16] Information about the nature and cause of the accusation must be adequate to enable a suspect to prepare his defence. In *Chichlian and Ekindjian*, the Commission commented that notification of the mere fact of reclassification of the offence is not enough, it has to be in good time and allow the opportunity to organise the defence on the basis of that reclassification.

[11] *Dallos v Hungary*, March 1, 2001, ECHR 2001–II, para.52, where the applicant could put forward his defence to the reformulated charge before the Supreme Court; *IH v Austria*, see fn.9 above, para.37, where the Supreme Court could not review the facts, its proceedings did not give the applicants a real opportunity to argue their case.

[12] The Government submitted that in the context it was clear he knew Italian.

[13] (10889/84), see fn.5 above.

[14] (39519/98) (Dec.) December 8, 1999, ECHR 1999–II; also *Ines v France*, (28145/95) (Dec.) May 25, 1998, it was not necessary for the applicant to be told at the earliest possible moment of the judgments *in absentia* against him, the moment of the extradition was enough.

[15] *Casse v Luxembourg*, April 27, 2006.

[16] *Pelissier and Sassi*, see fn.2, para.54; *Sadak*, see fn.9, paras 58–59.

6. Relationship with Art.5, para.2

Article 5, para.2, concerning reasons for arrest and detention, generally requires less detail and is not as rigorous as Art.6, para.3(a). II–113

Cross-reference

Part IIA, s.3: Adequate time and facilities.
Part IIB, s.39: Reasons for arrest and detention.

12. Interpretation

Key provision:

II–114 Article 6, para.3(e) (free assistance of an interpreter).

Key case-law:

Luedicke, Belkacem and Koç v Germany, November 28, 1978, Series A, No.29, 2 E.H.R.R. 149; *Kamasinski v Austria*, February 21, 1984, Series A, No.73, 13 E.H.R.R. 36; *Cuscani v UK*, September 24, 2002.

1. General considerations

II–115 The ability to comprehend the proceedings in a criminal trial, guaranteed in Art.6, para.3(e), may be seen as another aspect of the importance for an accused to participate effectively in the proceedings. Further, while rules concerning the language of submissions, oral or written in court, are accepted as necessary for the administration of justice, they should not be applied in such a manner as to prevent the defendant using an available appeal or remedy.[1]

For the right to be effective, the obligation of the authorities is not limited to the provision of an interpreter but may also extend to a degree of control over the adequacy of the interpretation provided.[2] Issues as to the standard of the interpretation might arise if it could be established as damaging to the accused's effective participation in the proceedings. Although a failure to complain at the time may be fatal to claims before the Court, as generally domestic courts must be given an opportunity to remedy any inadequacy, the onus is nonetheless on the trial judge to treat an accused's interests with "scrupulous care" and take steps to ensure his ability to participate where problems are drawn to his attention.[3]

As the interpreter is not part of the court or tribunal, there is no formal requirement of independence or impartiality as such, the key requirement being that the services of the interpreter provide the accused with effective assistance in conducting his defence and that his conduct not be of such a nature as to impinge on the fairness of the proceedings.[4]

2. Absolute nature of the right

II–116 The right is absolute, with no expressed qualifications and none implied.[5] Interpretation costs cannot be reclaimed from defendants after conviction as the Government argued in *Luedicke, Belkacem and Koç v Germany*. Similarly, the Commission found a

[1] *Bocos-Cuesta v Netherlands*, (54789/00) (Dec.) March 11, 2003.

[2] *Kamasinski*, para.74; *Ucak v UK*, (44234/98) (Dec.) January 24, 2000.

[3] *Cuscani v UK*, September 24, 2002, para.39, the judge, informed of the need for interpretation before the hearing, should have acted, notwithstanding the applicant's counsel's readiness to do without proper interpretation; conversely, see findings of inadmissibility in *Ucak*, see fn.2 above,where the applicant made no complaint about the interpretation during trial or appeal, even when invited to inform the court if he did not understand what was being said, and in *Husein v Italy*, (18913/03) (Dec.) February 24, 2005, where the applicant did not complain of the Arab interpreter who translated the enforcement notice and led the authorities to believe that he understood the contents.

[4] e.g. *Ucak*, fn.2 above, where the applicant complained that the interpreter came from a police list.

[5] See, however, *Fedele v Germany*, (11311/84) (Dec.) December 9, 1987, where the applicant failed to attend two hearings and was later charged the interpreter's fees: the Commission found that "assistance" must refer to an accused who is present and that only someone who is present and cannot understand or speak the language used in court can be "assisted" by the interpreter; since the applicant was not present he could not claim free assistance of an interpreter.

violation even where an applicant who was required to pay costs of interpretation after conviction was covered by his legal insurance.[6]

The requirement for interpretation must, however, be genuine and necessary to the fair conduct of the proceedings. It applies in the early investigative stages of the proceedings which can be crucial.[7]

Where an applicant has sufficient understanding of the language of the proceedings, he cannot claim a cultural or political preference for another.[8] Once it is apparent that the applicant requires interpretation assistance, it is unlikely that informal and unprofessional assistance will be sufficient.[9] However, where there is some verification by the domestic court of the level of language skill, questioning in the accused's own language by the investigating officer over a short period of time may not disclose a problem.[10]

3. Translation of documents

The wording of the provision refers to an "interpreter" rather than a "translator" and oral linguistic assistance in understanding documents may, in some circumstances, be enough to satisfy the Convention's requirements.[11] Nevertheless, Art.6, para.3(e) has been held to cover some documentary material and pre-trial matters; it does not extend to requiring translations of all documents in the proceedings.[12] It is sufficient if the applicant is assisted by interpreters, translations and the help of his lawyers so that he has knowledge of the case which enables him to defend himself, in particular by being able to put forward his version of events. If this standard is reached, a failure to provide all the translations an applicant might have wanted is not a problem.[13] An applicant would presumably have to indicate that the untranslated documents were material to his ability to defend himself and that he was refused or not permitted the necessary facilities. **II–117**

Cross-reference

Part IIA, s.3: Adequate time and facilities.
Part IIA, s.11: Information about the charge.

[6] (11394/85) (Rep.) July 5, 1988. See more recently *Isyar v Bulgaria*, November 20, 2008, paras 45–49, accused held liable to pay costs of interpretation: violation.

[7] *Diallo v Sweden*, (13205/07) (Dec.) January 5, 2010.

[8] e.g. *Lagerblom v Sweden*, January 14, 2003, the applicant, whose mother-tongue was Finnish, had sufficient street Swedish and could not claim that his counsel should be Finnish-speaking.

[9] *Cuscani*, see fn.3, where in the absence of the interpreter the court made do with the "untested language skills" of the accused's brother.

[10] *Diallo v Sweden*, see fn.7 above, no convincing indication of mistranslation.

[11] *Husein v Italy*, see fn.3 above.

[12] *Kamasinski v Austria*, February 21, 1984, Series A, No.73, 13 E.H.R.R. 36, para.74.

[13] See (14170/88) (Dec.) November 13, 1987; (14106/88) (Dec.) December 6, 1991, where a British applicant tried in Sweden complained that the documents were in Swedish, the Commission noted that his lawyer understood English and that an interpreter was not refused when requested; *Bocos-Cuesta*, see fn.1 above, where the rejection of a note by the court of an untranslated note written by the applicant did not impinge on his access to the appeal process as other submissions were translated and counsel made oral submissions on his behalf; *Seraffedin Akbingöl v Germany*, (74235/01) (Dec.) November 18, 2004, where the applicant's complaints that he had to pay for translations of telephone conversations were rejected as he knew their contents and translation was not necessary for his defence.

13. Juries

Key provision:

II–118 Article 6 (fair trial by an independent and impartial tribunal).

Key case-law:

Holm v Sweden, November 25, 1993, Series A, No.279–A, 18 E.H.R.R. 79; *Remli v France*, April 23, 1996, R.J.D 1996–II, No.8, 22 E.H.R.R. 253; *Pullar v UK*, June 10, 1996, R.J.D. 1996–III, No.11, 22 E.H.R.R. 391; *Gregory v UK*, February 25, 1997, R.J.D. 1997–I, No.31, 25 E.H.R.R. 577; *Sander v UK*, May 9, 2000, ECHR 2000–V, 31 E.H.R.R. 1003; *Taxquet v Belgium*, November 16, 2010, ECHR 2010– . . .

1. Right to a jury

II–119 There is no right contained within Art.6, para.1 to trial by jury, not surprisingly since some Contracting States do not use juries. The Commission accordingly dismissed an Irish case in which the applicant complained of the special courts presided over by judges without a jury which were introduced for terrorist-related offences.[1] Similarly, when the Birmingham Six argued that new evidence should not have been considered by the Court of Appeal, submitting that they could not receive a fair trial unless the evidence in its entirety was heard by a jury, the Commission found no reason why new evidence could not be fairly and properly assessed by an appellate body of professional judges.[2] Nor, conversely, can it be said that a lay jury is per se in violation of Art.6 due to the absence of a reasoned judgment (see further below).

2. Undue influence on the jury

II–120 Concerns are sometimes raised as to the susceptibility of untrained, lay jurors to suggestions or inferences that an accused person is guilty contrary to the presumption of innocence as well as impinging on the fairness of the trial.

A virulent press campaign may, the Court accepts, adversely affect the fairness of trial through its effect on the jury.[3] No finding of unfair trial has yet been found on this ground, press interest and sometimes critical commentary being accepted as inevitable in a democratic society and a corollary of freedom of the press.[4] It would take more than close media interest in a case to raise a serious issue and the fact that the jurors took oaths and were warned to discount news coverage would generally be regarded as sufficient to offset prejudice.[5] Even in a controversial case of a

[1] (8299/78) (Dec.) October 10, 1980, 22 D.R. 51.
[2] (14739/89) (Dec.) May 9, 1989, 60 D.R. 296.
[3] e.g. (8403/78) (Dec.) October 15, 1980, 22 D.R. 100; (10486/83) (Dec.) October 9, 1986, 49 D.R. 86; *Wloch v Poland*, (27785/95) (Dec.) March 30, 2000; *Priebke v Italy*, (48799/99) (Dec.) April 5, 2001.
[4] e.g. *Priebke v Italy*, see fn.3 above.
[5] e.g. *Noye v UK*, (4491/02) (Dec.) January 21, 2003, press coverage some time in the past and dealt with by adequate direction.

terrorist suspect, the Court considered that the intervening events of 9/11 and the massive and sensationalist press reaction were not sufficient to cast doubts on the jury, who had been given a careful and skilful direction by the judge, reviewed on appeal.[6]

Other aspects of the proceedings, relating to security measures which appear to label the accused as "guilty" in advance, have also been examined. However, even where the Commission had expressed reservations, it had taken the attitude that juries can distinguish between security measures based on assessments of "dangerousness" and the examination of the merits in the trial.[7]

Offensive comments made during the proceedings by prosecuting counsel may not necessarily cause problems, where not adopted by the court and where assessed as not having deprived the applicant of a fair trial.[8]

3. Independence and impartiality

This requirement of a fair trial applies equally to lay jurors as to professional and lay judges (see Pt IIA, s.10: Independence and impartiality). In view of the fundamental importance that the courts inspire confidence in the public and, in criminal cases, the accused, the Court has stressed that a tribunal, including a jury, must be impartial from a subjective and objective view.[9] II–121

Convention organs will presume the subjective impartiality of a judge and also that of unprofessional, untrained jurors.[10] The Commission in *Holm v Sweden* noted, however, that the unreasoned nature of a jury's verdict leads to a particular need for objective guarantees of impartiality and independence.

Objective independence and impartiality may be called in doubt by an exterior feature, for example the connection between a juror and a party to a civil case or a juror and prosecution witnesses. Regard is had to the nature of the connection and the safeguards in the system. In *Holm*, where five jurors out of nine were members of the political party which was the dominant shareholder in the defendant company and political overtones were of relevance since the alleged libel related to the applicant's activities in an organisation hostile to that party, the connection was of such a nature as to allow the applicant legitimately to fear that the jurors would be influenced by their political opinions. There was also the factor that there were no procedural means to cure any defect in this case, the appeal court having limited jurisdiction where, as in this case, the jury acquitted. Where an expert juror sitting on a court withdrew after it transpired that his employer had contractual connections with the parent company of a party, the Court considered that the short duration and nature of his involvement in the case, and the manner in which the court reviewed whether it could continue to hear the case, did not lead to any legitimate doubts of impartiality of the tribunal through any possible influence of the juror.[11]

6 *Mustafa (Abu Hamza) v UK*, (31411/07) (Dec.) January 18, 2011.

7 e.g. (12323/86) (Dec.) July 13, 1988, 57 D.R. 148, concerning use of handcuffs before juries; glass cages for accused did not "stigmatise" in (11837/85) (Rep.) June 7, 1990, 69 D.R. 126; also (17440/90) (Dec.) February 12, 1993, where the intense security at trial was found necessary (one trial had been abandoned due an attempt to influence a juror), not stage-managed, and the effect on the jury was not such as to violate the presumption of innocence.

8 *Elias v UK*, (48905/99) (Dec.) January 16, 2001, where the prosecutor compared a Jewish defendant to Fagin without intending any offensive racial slur.

9 e.g. *Sander v UK*, May 9, 2000, ECHR 2000–V, 31 E.H.R.R. 1003, para.22.

10 *Sander*, see fn.9 above, para.25.

11 *Procedo Capital Corporation v Norway*, September 24, 2009, paras 59–72.

However, in *Pullar v UK*, where the doubt arose from the discovery that one juror was an employee of a key Crown witness, the Court discounted the fact that the juror was disqualified in domestic law.[12] In its view, it did not follow that because a member of a tribunal had personal knowledge of a witness he would be prejudiced in favour of that person's testimony. It was necessary, rather, to assess whether the familiarity was of such nature and degree to indicate lack of impartiality. Since the juror was a junior employee, unconnected with the events, and had been given notice of redundancy, it was not certain that he would be inclined to believe his employer rather than defence witnesses. It also noted other safeguards in the system, including the number of jurors (15), the sheriff's directions, and the oaths taken. This approach seemed to confuse considerations of the existence of actual bias with whether there were objective grounds for the applicant having doubts as to the impartiality of the jurors. The Commission had found that it could legitimately be feared that the juror, even if ignorant of the facts of the case, would bring his own personal views of the Crown witness to bear on his own and the other jurors' assessment of the case.

Since then, the Court has stated, concerning links between a juror and other individuals connected with the trial, that it will depend on the facts of each case whether the familiarity in question is of such a nature or degree as to indicate a lack of impartiality. In *Simsek v UK*,[13] the fact that a juror was sister-in-law of a prison officer in the Category A block where the accused was detained disclosed no real doubts, the accused's misgivings being based on a number of weak suppositions. Since the Court of Appeal looked into the matter and it appeared that the prison officer had reported the connection himself to his superiors, maintained that he had not talked with his sister-in-law and withdrawn from any contact with the accused, no further enquiry or measures had been necessary.[14]

Where racial bias has arisen, the Convention organs have had regard to the steps taken by domestic courts to counteract its influence. Given the importance attached to the eradication of racism as a priority amongst Contracting States, courts are required to react in a firm manner, and if necessary, question or discharge the jury.

In *Remli v France*, where a juror was overheard outside the courtroom saying "*En plus je suis raciste*", the applicant's lawyers brought it to the attention of the presiding judge who refused to take cognisance of it. Since domestic courts are under an obligation to verify their impartiality when a ground arises not manifestly without merit, the failure to take any steps disclosed a violation. Similarly, where during an appeal defence counsel complained that the *ministère public* had had a prohibited exchange with the jury in the absence of the court, the Court found a violation on the procedural basis that the court, which had heard addresses from counsel, had not questioned the jury itself as to any undue influence that might have been exerted nor placed the matter on court record thus enabling the Court of Cassation to review the matter on appeal.[15]

[12] See however *Oberschlick v Austria*, May 23, 1991, Series A, No.204, 19 E.H.R.R. 389, where it took a different view when a disqualified judge sat on a case, finding that the failure to abide by the domestic rules aimed at eradicating reasonable doubts as to impartiality left the proceedings open to doubt.

[13] (43471/98) (Dec.) July 9, 2002.

[14] See also *Ekeberg v Sweden*, July 31, 2007, paras 45–49, where a juror, W, was removed following discovery shortly after the start of the trial that she had made a statement to the police concerning the case. The Court considered that the timing, nature and short duration of her participation in the trial along with the directions of the presiding judge was sufficient to remove any doubt as to the impartiality of the jury.

[15] *Fahri v France*, January 16, 2007.

In *Gregory v UK* however, where a note was received from the jury, "jury showing racial overtones 1 member to be excused", the judge consulted counsel and addressed the jury directing them as to their obligation to decide the case according to the evidence without prejudice. The Court admitted that there might be circumstances where a judge might have to discharge a jury, but found that in this case a firmly-worded direction by an experienced judge who had observed the jury during the trial was sufficient to dispel doubts as to the impartiality of the tribunal. Conversely, in *Sander v UK*, where a note from a juror indicated that racist jokes were being made and that he or she feared a verdict based on the ethnic origin of the accused, the Court, by a narrow majority, considered that a firm redirection by the judge and the submission of a collective letter by the jury with an assurance that they would reach a verdict on the evidence alone was insufficient to take away a legitimate doubt as to the jury's impartiality. The majority distinguished *Gregory* as in this case the juror had, in a letter to the judge, admitted that he had made racist comments and they were not satisfied that the judge's direction, however forceful, could change racist views overnight. The minority placed more weight on the role of the judge, who was experienced and had observed the jury throughout and chosen to give a clear, detailed and forceful direction in place of discharging them.

In *Holm*, the fact that jurors take oaths to acquit their duties impartially was not considered a sufficient guarantee to outweigh the doubt on their impartiality deriving from their political affiliations, yet it was mentioned as a guarantee in *Gregory*, which concerned apparent racial bias, and in *Pullar* and *Simsek*, concerning personal connections. It was not mentioned at all in *Sander*. That the jury should be trusted to a degree to take their oaths seriously was also relied upon in a case where a police officer, technically a witness, had been left alone with the jury in order to replay for them CCTV footage. The jury had been directed to raise any concerns with the judge and none had done so. The mere fact the appeal court later issued guidelines to prevent such a re-occurrence did not mean that the situation had breached Art.6.[16]

4. Secrecy of jury deliberations

The prohibition on publishing details of jury deliberations was found compatible with Art.10 of the Convention, where a newspaper and two editors were fined for contempt of court for revelations about a controversial trial.[17] The Commission noted that secrecy was the basis of the jury system in the United Kingdom and that the absolute nature of the offence could be regarded as necessary to protect jurors and prevent undue influence on their decisions by factors outside the jury room. While research into juries in fraud cases had been recommended by the Royal Commission on Criminal Justice, the Commission observed that research was not in issue in the case, which solely concerned revelations in a high profile trial. II–122

5. Fairness of jury decisions

Even though the use of a lay jury which does not give a reasoned judgment is not a problem as such,[18] the accused and the public must be able to understand the verdict that has been given as a safeguard against arbitrariness.[19] For example, II–123

[16] *Szypusz v UK*, September 21, 2010.
[17] (24770/94) (Dec.) November 30, 1994.
[18] *Saric v Denmark*, (31913/96) (Dec.) February 2, 1999.
[19] *Taxquet v Belgium*, November 16, 2010, ECHR 2010–. . . , para. 90.

sufficient understanding may be derived from directions or guidance provided by the presiding judge to the jurors on the legal issues arising or the evidence adduced or precise, unequivocal questions put to the jury by the judge, forming a framework on which the verdict is based or sufficiently offsetting the fact that no reasons are given for the jury's answers.[20] Where only a few succinct questions were put to a jury, which were identical for all the defendants and did not refer to any specific circumstances that could have enabled the applicant to understand why he was found guilty, the Court concluded that he had not received a fair trial.[21] In contrast, sufficient safeguards were in place in the Scottish jury system, where the jury's unreasoned verdict was given in a framework including addresses by the prosecution, defence and presiding judge, with a clear demarcation of roles between judge and jury, the former having the duty to ensure the fairness of proceedings and to explain the law to the latter. Further, while the jurors were masters of the facts, the presiding judge was required to direct that there was no case to answer if the prosecution's evidence did not justify a conviction and, unlike the Belgian system, an appeal could remedy any improper verdict by the jury, and the appeal court was able to quash any conviction amounting to a miscarriage of justice or which was logically inconsistent or lacking in rationality.[22]

[20] *Taxquet v Belgium*, see fn.19 above, para.91 and authorities cited therein.
[21] *Taxquet v Belgium*, see fn.19 above, paras 94–100.
[22] *Judge v UK*, (35863/10) (Dec.) February 8, 2011.

14. Legal aid in civil cases

Key provision:

Article 6, para.1 (access to court). II–124

Key case-law:

Airey v Ireland, October 9, 1979, Series A, No.32, 2 E.H.R.R. 305; *Aerts v Belgium*, July 30, 1998, R.J.D. 1998–V, No.83, 29 E.H.R.R. 50; *Gnahoré v France*, September 9, 2000, 2000–IX; *McVicar v UK*, May 7, 2002, ECHR 2002–III; *Bertuzzi v France*, February 13, 2003; *Steel and Morris v UK*, February 15, 2005, ECHR 2005–II.

1. General considerations

There is no right as such in the Convention to receive legal aid in cases concerning civil rights and obligations. Issues may arise where lack of legal aid has the effect of depriving an applicant of effective access to court. The right of access to court, however, is not unlimited. Limitations may be compatible where they do not restrict or reduce access to the extent that the very essence of the right is impaired, where they pursue a legitimate aim and disclose a reasonable relationship of proportionality between the means employed and the aim sought to be achieved.[1] II–125

2. Lack of access to court

Whether legal aid may be required for effective access to court will depend on the particular circumstances of each case, in particular, upon the importance of what is at stake for the applicant in the proceedings, the complexity of the relevant law and procedure and the applicant's capacity to represent him or herself effectively.[2] II–126

The leading case was, until recently, *Airey v Ireland*. A denial of access to court in violation of Art.6, para.1 was found where, in the absence of legal aid for separation proceedings in the High Court, the applicant could not be expected to pursue proceedings herself. The procedure was complex, raising complicated points of law and necessitating proof of adultery, unnatural practices, or cruelty; it might have involved expert evidence and the examining of witnesses; and the subject-matter entailed an emotional involvement scarcely compatible with the degree of objectivity required by advocacy in court.

Following *Airey* the Commission, in practice, confined its application, giving weight to the reasons adduced by the authorities for refusal of legal aid. It considered that due to limited resources States could legitimately restrict the grant of legal aid, imposing contributions or requiring a case to be well-founded, not vexatious or frivolous. In such a case an applicant would bear the burden to bring the case some other way (by himself or obtaining assistance from another source), although the Commission would have regard to whether the assessment by the authorities was arbitrary.[3] The Commission generally found that unrepresented

[1] e.g. *Ashingdane v UK*, May 28, 1985, Series A, No.93, 7 E.H.R.R. 528, para.57.

[2] *Steel and Morris v UK*, February 15, 2005, ECHR 2005–II, para.61.

[3] e.g. (8158/78) (Dec.) July 10, 1978, 21 D.R. 95, refusal of legal aid to a prisoner was not arbitrary, the Commission finding the allegations unsubstantiated.

applicants still enjoyed reasonable access to court where they had the opportunity to be heard in person under the proper and effective control of the fairness and conduct of the proceedings by the court.[4]

The Court has effectively adopted this approach since, finding, for example, no violation in *Gnahoré v France* for refusal of legal aid for an appeal due to lack of any arguable ground where the procedure offered substantial guarantees against arbitrariness in the decision-making procedure.[5] However, there may nonetheless be cases where the exceptional complexity of the proceedings requires that the applicant receives assistance, as in *Steel and Morris*, where two members of Greenpeace were sued by McDonald's in the longest trial in English legal history with numerous interlocutory applications. Weight was also given to the fact that as defendants they had no choice and were defending their freedom of expression and it was found in the circumstances that the piecemeal assistance received pro bono was not sufficient to overcome the unfair disparity between the parties.

More recently, the Court has looked more closely at the procedures for granting legal aid in civil cases. It found the court's refusal of legal aid unjustified in a case concerning damages for a death at the hands of the security forces, for which the ground was that the fact the applicants were represented by a lawyer meant they were not financially needy. The Court did not consider that this consideration was relevant without inquiring properly into the applicants' means. Insofar as the court also ruled against legal aid due to its view that the case was ill-founded, the Court considered that to effectively reach an unequivocal finding on the merits of the case without hearing the applicants and, without any avenue of appeal, deprived them of access to court.[6]

Even where legal aid is granted, however, the responsibility of the Government does not necessarily come to an end. In *Bertuzzi v France*, where the applicant fulfilled the conditions for legal aid which was accorded by the legal aid office of the first instance court, there was a violation where three lawyers in turn declined to act for him because of their personal connections with the lawyer that the applicant was suing. The Court considered that the authorities were under an obligation to ensure the appointment of replacement counsel. This can be contrasted with the situation where the applicant's own conduct is to blame for the withdrawal of the legal aid lawyers.[7]

While legal aid counsel should not be compelled to lodge claims or appeals that are unmeritorious, there should be guarantees against arbitrariness in the procedure, namely, that written reasons for the refusal be given and their content leave the applicant in no doubt or uncertainty as to the legal grounds relied on.[8] Any refusal

[4] e.g. (9353/81) (Dec.) May 11, 1983, 33 D.R. 133.

[5] e.g. the Legal Aid Office was presided over by a judge of the Court of Cassation and an appeal lay to the President of the Court; similar reasoning in *Del Sol v France*, February 26, 2002, ECHR 2002–II; *Nicholas v Cyprus*, (37371/97) (Dec.) March 14, 2000, where the Court relied on Commission case-law that refusal of legal aid was not a denial of access to court where the proceedings had no prospects of success and the costs of funding was disproportionate to any likely damages. It also noted that the applicant had had "*pro bono*" assistance for some time and he had not attempted to find similar assistance later.

[6] *Bakan v Turkey*, June 12, 2007, paras 72–79.

[7] *Renda Martins v Portugal*, (50085/99) (Dec.) January 10, 2002, the applicant had gone through seven counsel and it was his lack of co-operation that based the decision not to provide any further replacement and to suspend the proceedings generally.

[8] *Staroszcyk v Poland*, March 22, 2007, para.135, oral explanation was not enough, nor that time remained in which the applicants could have sought replacement counsel to file an appeal.

to act should also be notified to the applicant within a time-frame giving a realistic opportunity of continuing and arguing the case.[9]

As regards circumstances where legal representation is rendered compulsory, this is not, in itself, a problem. However, where legal aid is made available for such proceedings, the authorities must ensure that access to court is secured in a "concrete and effective manner" and that there are substantial guarantees against arbitrariness.[10] The Court found a violation of Art.6, para.1 in *Aerts v Belgium* where the applicant was refused legal aid in proceedings concerning his right to liberty and compensation for unlawful detention before the Court of Cassation. Domestic law required representation by counsel and thus the Legal Aid Board's refusal of legal aid impaired the very essence of the right to a tribunal.[11] It was not relevant in that context that the Board had considered the appeal was not well-founded as the Court considered it was for the Court of Cassation to determine that issue.

Grounds for refusal of legal aid linked to abuse of process may also be acceptable, as in a case where the Commission found that even though the applicant had prospects of success in suing for divorce it was compatible to refuse her legal aid in view of court findings that she had not intended to set up married life with her husband (marriage was to obtain him an entry permit) and that she had divorced before in similar circumstances. The Commission did not find unreasonable the court's view that she knew the position and did not require legal protection.[12]

The mere fact that the other side is legally aided does not render the refusal of legal aid incompatible with Art.6, para.1.[13]

3. Defamation

When defamation, even in meritorious cases, could not be subject to a grant of legal aid in the United Kingdom, the Commission did not find the blanket prohibition to disclose any violation of Art.6, para.1, considering that it could be legitimate to exclude certain categories of legal proceedings altogether from legal aid and that it had not been shown to be arbitrary to do so in that case (having regard to the fact that the applicant secured a settlement and an apology by himself).[14] In *McVicar v UK*, the Court considered that the defamation action was not so complex as to require legal assistance and found in the circumstances that the applicant was well able to present his case effectively, obtaining some legal assistance by other means and that his emotional involvement was not incompatible with the degree of objectivity required by advocacy in court. Conversely, in *Steel and Morris*, where the defamation case was "exceptionally demanding", the Court held that it was unfair that the defendants, who were of very limited resources, had to defend themselves, with only sporadic help, against onerous claims for damages. II–127

[9] *Sialkowska v Poland*, March 22, 2007, para.114, the applicant and lawyer met some three days before the expiry of the time-limit for appealing.

[10] *Staroszcyk*, fn.8 above, paras 128–129, 138.

[11] In *Gnahoré*, the Court commented that it was the requirement of legal representation that was decisive in *Aerts* (para.41).

[12] (11564/85) (Dec.) December 4, 1985, 45 D.R. 291.

[13] (9353/81) fn.4 above.

[14] (10871/84) (Dec.) July 10, 1986, 48 D.R. 154; see also (10594/83) (Dec.) July 14, 1987, 52 D.R. 158; (27436/95) etc. (Dec.) July 2, 1997, 90–A D.R. 45.

4. Prohibition orders

II–128 The Commission found it compatible for a prohibition order to be used to prevent applications for civil legal aid where an applicant had made numerous applications. This is comparable to regulation of access for bankrupts, persons of unsound mind and vexatious litigants, where the aim is to prevent abuse of legal aid authorities.[15]

Cross-reference

Part IIA,s.2: Access to court.
Part IIA, s.15: Legal representation in criminal proceedings.

[15] (27788/95) (Dec.) January 27, 1996, the applicant could apply for the five-year ban to be lifted.

15. Legal representation in criminal proceedings

Key provision:

Article 6, para.3(c) (right to legal assistance of one's own choosing or, where insufficient means, assistance to be given free when the interests of justice require). II–129

Key case-law:

Artico v Italy, May 13, 1980, Series A, No.37, 3 E.H.R.R. 1; *Pakelli v Germany*, April 25, 1983, Series A, No.64, 6 E.H.R.R. 1; *Goddi v Italy*, April 9, 1984, Series A, No.76; *Kamasinski v Austria*, December 19, 1989, Series A, No.168, 13 E.H.R.R. 36; *Monnell and Morris v UK,* March 2, 1987, Series A, No.115, 10 E.H.R.R. 205; *Granger v UK*, March 28, 1990, Series A, No.174, 12 E.H.R.R. 469; *Quaranta v Switzerland*, May 24, 1991, Series A, No.205; *S v Switzerland*, November 28, 1991, Series A, No.220; *Croissant v Germany*, September 25, 1992, Series A, No.237–B, 16 E.H.R.R. 135; *Imbroscia v Switzerland*, November 24, 1993, Series A, No.275; *Maxwell v UK*, October 28, 1994, Series A, No.300–C, 19 E.H.R.R. 97; *Boner v UK*, October 28, 1994, Series A, No.300–B, 19 E.H.R.R 246; *Poitrimol v France*, November 23, 1993, Series A, No.277, 18 E.H.R.R. 295; *Tripodi v Italy*, April 22, 1994, Series A, No.281–B, 18 E.H.R.R. 130; *Lala v Netherlands*, September 22, 1994, Series A, No.297–A, 18 E.H.R.R. 587; *John Murray v UK*, February 8, 1996, R.J.D. 1996–I, No.1, 22 E.H.R.R. 29; *Daud v Portugal*, April 21, 1998, R.J.D. 1998–II, No.69, 30 E.H.R.R. 400; *Twalib v Greece*, June 9, 1998, R.J.D. 1998–IV, No.77; *Brennan v UK*, October 16, 2001, ECHR 2001–IX; *Meftah v France*, July 26, 2002, ECHR 2002–VII; *Czekalla v Portugal*, October 10, 2002, ECHR 2002–VIII; *Ocalan v Turkey*, May 12, 2005, ECHR 2005–IV; *Salduz v Turkey*, November 27, 2008, ECHR 2008–. . . ; *Sakhnovskiy v Russia*, November 2, 2010, ECHR 2010–. . .

1. General considerations

The provisions of Art.6, para.3 depend on a criminal charge having been brought. The case-law indicates that they are aspects of the general principle of fairness guaranteed in the para.1. As with the para.1, they are not to be assessed on the basis of an isolated incident or element, but having regard to the proceedings as a whole.[1] II–130

Article 6, para.3(c) guarantees three rights: the right to defend oneself; where one does not wish to defend oneself, the right to appoint a lawyer of one's own choosing; or where certain conditions are met, the right to free legal assistance.[2] These apply not only in the ordinary criminal trial context but also where criminal charges are elsewhere determined, such as in prison disciplinary proceedings.[3]

2. Pre-trial representation

The right to legal representation applies not only to the trial, but to the pre-trial stages.[4] It does not, however, confer unlimited access to legal representation. II–131

[1] e.g. *Can v Austria*, (Rep.), July 12, 1984, Series A, No.96, 8 E.H.R.R. 121, their intrinsic aim is always to ensure or contribute to ensuring the fairness of the proceedings as a whole; thus often the sub-paragraphs are considered in conjunction with para.1.

[2] *Pakelli v Italy*, April 25, 1983, Series A, No.64, 6 E.H.R.R. 1, para.31.

[3] *Ezeh and Connors v UK*, October 9, 2003, ECHR 2003–X, paras 131 and 134, where the applicants were denied the right to be legally represented at disciplinary proceedings in breach of Art.6(3)c.

[4] *Can*, fn.1 above, citing ICCPR and r.93 of Standard Minimum Rules for the Treatment of Prisoners (Council of Europe Res. CM(73)5).

While in earlier case-law there was no right to immediate contact with a lawyer, the Court's position has considerably evolved in the last few years. It emphasises that the early stages of the arrest and investigation can be crucial and have lasting impact on the course of the trial. This is particularly true where evidence is being obtained, including statements from the suspect. Where, in *John Murray v UK*, the applicant, arrested for terrorist offences, was refused access to a solicitor for 48 hours, there was a violation having regard to the special features of the procedures in the early interrogation stage in Northern Ireland where inferences could be drawn from silence or responses to police questions. Since the accused was in a position where his defence could be irretrievably prejudiced, restriction on access to legal advice was incompatible with Art.6, para.3(c) without it being necessary to show the applicant would have acted differently if he had seen his solicitor.[5] Violations of Art.6 paras 1 and 3(c) also arose in cases where accused were ill-treated by the police contrary to Art.3 and their statements admitted in evidence despite their lack of access to legal advice during the custody period and the absence of their lawyer when the statement was signed.[6]

The Court has also given weight to the vulnerability of the accused at this juncture, which in most cases can only be compensated for by the assistance of a lawyer who can inter alia advise as to the right of an accused not to incriminate himself.[7] Thus where the police questioned a minor (17 years old) in the absence of his father, obtaining a confession and without informing him of his right to legal advice, the Court doubted that in any event the minor would have understood the importance of obtaining legal representation: therefore there was a violation for failure to ensure that a minor was provided with a lawyer at the pre-trial stage.[8] Similarly, where a 15–year-old confessed participation in a murder to the police and to a family court judge, without having been able to consult a lawyer or be advised of his right not to incriminate himself, the Court found a breach.[9]

In *Salduz v Turkey*, the Court established the general principle that, save in exceptional circumstances, an accused must be provided with legal assistance from the first interrogation.[10] Exceptional reasons are required to justify departure from this principle.[11] It is not apparent that the applicant has to request legal assistance or that any identifiable prejudice, such as an incriminating confession, must flow from the lack of a lawyer.[12] However, even where the refusal of a lawyer is suitably

[5] See also *Magee v UK*, June 6, 2000, ECHR 2000–VI, where there was a 48–hour bar on access to a solicitor, during which period the applicant confessed, irretrievably prejudicing the defence, the Court found the restriction was incompatible with the rights of the accused; *Averill v UK*, June 6, 2000, ECHR 2000–VI, violation for 24–hour period where the applicant's silence was held against him.

[6] e.g *Söylemez v Turkey*, September 21, 2006; *Haciözen v Turkey*, April 12, 2007; *Göcmen v Turkey*, October 17, 2006.

[7] *Salduz v Turkey*, November 27, 2008, ECHR 2008–. . . , para.54.

[8] *Panovits v Cyprus*, December 11, 2008, paras 71–77, the ability to challenge the confession later in the trial was not sufficient to remedy this failing, the very existence of the confession raising credibility issues as regarded the applicant's later testimony in court.

[9] *Adamkiewicz v Poland*, December 11, 2008, paras 86–92, the lawyer was also refused access to the applicant for six weeks, was not present during further sessions before the family judge and was unable to see the file for three months.

[10] *Salduz*, see fn.7 above, para.55, see Judge Bratza's separate opinion that to be practical and effective, the accused should benefit from legal advice from the moment of being taken into custody.

[11] See fn.7 above, para.55.

[12] *Dayanan v Turkey*, October 13, 2009, para.33, violation for lack of a lawyer in the first days after arrest, even though the accused maintained silence and no confession was used during his trial.

justified, there will be a breach if the accused's defence has been unduly prejudiced: irremediable prejudice will be present if a confession was obtained when no access to legal advice was made available.[13]

No right to consult a lawyer arose where the applicant was stopped and questioned at a roadside check, the applicant having not been arrested.[14]

Legal representation is so important that the Court will look suspiciously at circumstances in which an applicant is effectively deprived of a lawyer at a time when it is crucial. Where an applicant was suspected of murder but charged with a lesser offence which allowed the police to question him without the presence of a lawyer and, after the applicant confessed, his lawyer was removed from the case by the prosecutor because he had advised the applicant to revoke his confession on grounds of coercion, the Court noted the notional value of the minimal legal assistance which the applicant managed to obtain during this early stage and found a breach.[15]

While an applicant can waive his right to see a lawyer, it must be a free and unequivocal choice. Where an applicant signed the waiver in police custody after his rights had been explained, a copy being given to him, and he did not raise any complaint until considerably later, the Court found that the waiver had been valid.[16] Mere signing by an accused of a form which stated that he had been informed of his rights did not disclose that the accused had waived his privilege against self-incrimination,[17] nor did the applicant's lack of protest or maintenance of silence when, despite a request for a lawyer, the police continued with the interrogation and obtained a confession.[18] However, where an applicant expressly wrote on a form that he did not wish to have a lawyer and continued to refuse a lawyer during the criminal proceedings, the Court found an express waiver, without any indication of coercion or trickery.[19]

The case-law indicates that any restrictions on free contact with defence counsel must remain an exception and must be justified by special circumstances, the accused's right to communicate with his advocate out of hearing of a third person being a basic requirement of a fair trial in democratic society.[20] Where a lawyer is bound by professional obligations, the Court is unlikely to be persuaded in the absence of objective justification that restrictions are necessary to prevent the risk of collusion through or with the lawyer.[21] A reasonable suspicion that the consultation

[13] *Salduz*, see fn.7 above, paras 56–62, where the applicant was subject to an automatic lack of access to a lawyer under anti-terrorist legislation. Although on the wording of the applicable principles, this was sufficient in itself to disclose a violation, the Court went on to note that the applicant's confession, obtained before he received legal advice, was used during the trial to found a conviction and that this affected his defence.

[14] *Aleksandr Zaichenko v Russia*, February 18, 2010, paras 46–51.

[15] *Yaremenko v Ukraine*, June 12, 2008, paras 85–91.

[16] *Yoldas v Turkey*, February 23, 2010, paras 52–55.

[17] *Salduz*, see fn.7 above, para.59.

[18] *Pishchalnikov v Russia*, September 24, 2009, paras 76–80.

[19] *Galstyan v Armenia*, November 15, 2007, paras 89–92.

[20] *S v Switzerland*, November 28, 1991, Series A, No.220, para.48; *Ocalan v Turkey*, May 12, 2005, ECHR 2005–IV, para.133, inability to confer with defence counsel out of hearing of security officers; *Brennan v UK*, October 16, 2001, ECHR 2001–IX; *Meftah v France*, July 26, 2002, ECHR 2002–VII, the Court found no compelling reason for the presence of a police officer during the important first interview of the applicant with his lawyer, where there was no allegation that the solicitor was likely to collaborate in passing information to other suspects.

[21] e.g. *Can*, fn.1 above; *S v Switzerland*, where there were vague unsubstantiated doubts of collusion.

is under covert surveillance may be sufficient to disclose a problem, as will the use of a glass screen that prevents an applicant detainee, without a history of violence, and his lawyer from consulting on documents together.[22] Casual overhearing and reporting of telephone conversations between an accused and his lawyer will also offend as it will create a failure to ensure confidentiality risks undermining the accused's confidence in being able to talk freely to his lawyer.[23]

Significant restrictions on consultations in the period leading up to trial are likely to raise issues. Restriction of three months on free unsupervised contact during the crucial investigation stage disclosed a violation in *Can*. Seven-month surveillance of defence counsel visits in *S v Switzerland* disclosed a violation even though there was a two-year period without restrictions before trial, indicating that it is not necessary to show damage to the presentation of the defence at trial from the restrictions and the right is to effective representation throughout the proceedings. In a highly complex and important criminal trial, provision of two one-hour visits per week to lawyers was not considered sufficient to allow preparation for the trial.[24] Delay of more than one year in appointing counsel, during which a number of procedural acts were carried out, including questioning of the applicants and their medical examination, also disclosed a violation.[25] Short periods of several days have been found not to infringe defence rights.[26] A period of eleven days after arrest without access to a lawyer was not regarded as depriving the applicant of a fair trial where he was not interrogated by the police during that period, and although he was questioned by the *procureur* and a judge, he made no statements which were later used against him.[27]

In the absence of any features of oppression or consequent risk to the fairness of the later trial, lack of access in circumstances not at the fault of the authorities does not always appear to raise issues, for example where the police tried to contact the solicitor, who was unavailable before the interview took place, or where the solicitor delayed a day in coming to see the applicant.[28] However, it may be noted that, in a more recent case, where the police were unable to contact the applicant's lawyer, the Court appears to have taken the view that they should have arranged for another lawyer before proceeding with an interrogation.[29]

[22] *Castravet v Moldova*, March 13, 2007, this was against a background of concerns about the possible bugging of the meeting room which had caused the Bar Association to take action.

[23] *Zagaria v Italy*, November 27, 2007, paras 32–36.

[24] *Ocalan v Turkey*, fn.20 above, para.135.

[25] *Berlinski v Poland*, June 26, 2002.

[26] (11526/84) (Dec.) September 5, 1988, 57 D.R. 47, where an applicant's inability to consult for three days prior to appearing before the investigating judge did not infringe defence rights, as there was free consultation afterwards and the applicant was able to make full use of procedures and remedies; (12391/86) (Dec.) April 13, 1989, 60 D.R. 182, concerning two and a half days without access to a lawyer, where the reason to deny access was potential prejudice to enquiries (the solicitor's premises were being searched), there was no indication that he had made any confessions or been unable to prepare his defence over the following year or to apply for bail.

[27] *Yurttas v Turkey*, May 27, 2004.

[28] *Brennan*, fn.20 above, paras 44–48, the applicant did not make any confessions during the period in which access was barred and no inferences were drawn from his silence during that period; *Harpur v UK*, (33222/96) (Dec.) September 14, 1999, the applicant's confessions were made after the 24–hour denial of access.

[29] *Pishchalnikov v Russia*, September 24, 2009, paras 74–75.

Actual presence of a solicitor during police interviews has not as yet been held essential: in the cases so far there were other sufficient guarantees concerning the reliability or use of statements recorded.[30]

3. Right to defend oneself in person

An accused can choose to defend himself, as long as the choice is free from coercion and is not contrary to the interests of justice. Where an applicant, who freely and expressly waived legal representation, was charged with a minor offence and only faced a maximum of 15 days' imprisonment, the Court considered that mandatory legal representation had not been required by Art.6, paras 1 and 3(c).[31] II–132

4. Legal representation of own choosing

Generally, problems will arise where, in proceedings which determine a criminal charge, the applicant is denied the right to be legally represented.[32] II–133

The right to legal assistance, free or otherwise, does not confer an absolute right to choose counsel. Domestic courts may override even the choice of a counsel paid for by the applicant where there are relevant and sufficient grounds.[33] Potentially issues could arise where a court barred counsel for lack of qualifications, but the Court would be likely to accept domestic rules on eligibility which were not totally unreasonable or arbitrary. In *Meftah v France*, the Court accepted the system whereby applicants could only use members of the *Conseil d'Etat* or Cassation bar and were prevented from using other lawyers or representing themselves. It noted the nature of the proceedings, which concerned points of law and were largely written and took account of European Union law providing that Member States could lay down specific rules of access to supreme courts to ensure the smooth administration of justice.[34]

Courts may also appoint defence counsel which an accused considers unnecessary or objectionable. Where in *Croissant v Germany*, the applicant had appointed two counsel and objected to the third appointed by the courts, the Court found that the domestic court's reasons were relevant and sufficient, namely serving the interests of justice by avoiding interruptions or adjournments. It was also found legitimate to appoint official counsel for a defendant company where its legal representative was also implicated in events and could not act.[35]

Where a court bars counsel from appearing on grounds that the accused has failed to surrender to custody, the Court has not been convinced that this is a proportionate response having regard to the importance of assuring an accused's defence.[36] It is for the domestic courts to ensure that an accused is properly

[30] *Brennan v UK*, October 16, 2001, ECHR 2001–IX, paras 51–55, reference to thorough examination of possible oppression at the trial: presence of a lawyer or tape recording were safeguards against misconduct but not indispensable preconditions of fairness.

[31] *Galystan*, fn.19 above, paras 89–92.

[32] e.g. *Ezeh and Connors v UK*, October 9, 2003, ECHR 2003–X, paras 131 and 134.

[33] *Croissant v Germany*, September 25, 1992, Series A, No.237–B, 16 E.H.R.R. 135, para.29.

[34] *Meftah v France*, July 26, 2002, ECHR 2002–VII, para.45.

[35] *Eurofinacom v France*, (58753/00) (Dec.) September 7, 2004, where official counsel was assessed as competent and on appeal the company was then allowed to choose their own counsel.

[36] e.g. *Poitrimol v France*, November 23, 1993, Series A, No.277, 18 E.H.R.R. 295, para.38; *Lala v Netherlands*, September 22, 1994, Series A, No.297–A, 18 E.H.R.R. 587, para.33.

defended and that the counsel who appears is afforded the opportunity to act. In *Poitrimol*, where the applicant had appealed against his conviction for child kidnapping but did not appear, the appeal court refused to hear his counsel on the grounds of appeal as a convicted person who failed to surrender was not entitled to instruct counsel. While it was important for an accused to be present, the Court held that it was more important for him to be adequately defended. Even if properly summoned, this does not, in absence of excuse for failure to appear, justify depriving him of the right to be defended by counsel.[37] Rigid application of a rule barring hearing of the applicant's lawyer in the absence of the applicant himself is likely to disclose a breach, the Court considering it a heavy sanction in circumstances where it cannot be said that the applicant's presence is indispensable to the proceedings.[38]

Where in *Tripodi v Italy*, however, a lawyer appointed by the applicant failed to attend a hearing in cassation proceedings because he was ill, the Court appeared to find that the State could not be responsible for the shortcomings of a lawyer appointed by the accused, bearing in mind code provisions indicating that lawyers should provide replacements.[39] President Ryssdal, dissenting, noted that the lawyer was required to rest completely so could not be expected to act, while the Commission had found that courts are not allowed to remain passive but must take steps to ensure an accused is properly defended. There seems no reason why the obligation by a court to ensure a proper defence should depend on the method of appointment of the accused's lawyer (see sub-s.5 below). Where a minor facing serious charges was represented by his own lawyer, who failed to turn up to many hearings, the Court considered that in light of the manifest failure of his lawyer to represent him properly the trial court should have ensured that he obtain adequate legal representation.[40]

5. Free legal assistance

II–134 Free legal assistance does not exclude liability to repay the fees later. It only has to be free at the time of trial and while the applicant's insufficiency of means continues. In *Croissant v Germany*, the German system, whereby convicted accused may be required to reimburse fees after trial, was not found to be incompatible per se with the Convention, where the lawyers appointed by the court could be regarded as necessary and the amounts charged not excessive. According to Commission case-law, a problem only arose if liability was enforced regardless of financial position.[41]

There are two conditions to qualify an applicant for free legal assistance:

[37] See also *Van Geyseghem v Belgium*, January 21, 1999, ECHR 1999–I, paras 33–35, counsel would have raised a crucial statutory limitation and even if the appeal court had looked at the point of its own motion, counsel's assistance was still regarded as indispensable for resolving conflicts and for the exercise of the rights of the defence; *Van Pelt v France*, May 23, 2000, violation where the appeal court refused to hear the applicant's counsel when the applicant was absent in hospital; *Krombach v France*, February 13, 2001, ECHR 2001–II, violation where the applicant failed to appear at trial and his counsel were prevented from raising legal objections, e.g. estoppel.

[38] *Kari-Pekka Pietilainen v Finland*, September 22, 2009, paras 33–35.

[39] See also *Milone v Italy*, (37477/97) (Dec.) March 23, 1999, where the applicant's lawyer failed to appear due to participation in a strike and the Court of Cassation refused to adjourn, the Court found that the lawyer should have notified the Court earlier of his absence and taken steps to obtain a replacement—the Government was therefore not responsible for the shortcomings of the applicant's chosen lawyer.

[40] *Guvec v Turkey*, January 20, 2009, paras 131–133.

[41] e.g. (9365/81) (Dec.) May 6, 1982, 28 D.R. 229.

(a) Financial eligibility

This aspect has been rarely disputed. Generally, it is for the domestic authorities to evaluate the applicant's financial circumstances. The Court will, however, review their decisions for arbitrariness or lack of adequate foundation. In *Pakelli v Germany*, where the Government contested that the applicant was indigent at the time of the appeal, though the ground for refusal of legal aid concerned the class of offence, the Court was satisfied by the documentary materials put forward by the applicant and the fact that he had been found to qualify for legal aid from the Commission. In *RD v Poland*, the Court, noting that the applicant had initially been found eligible for legal assistance and that the subsequent refusal did not indicate that his financial situation had in fact improved, found there were strong indications that he did not have sufficient means.[42] II–135

(b) Interests of justice

This condition does not require it to be proved that legal assistance, if provided, would have altered the course of the proceedings, as the Government argued in *Artico v Italy*, for example, by pleading a statutory limitation.[43] This was impossible to prove and would render the guarantee ineffective. However, this does not necessarily exclude the need to establish that the interests of justice require representation by pointing to reasons why, at a particular stage in proceedings, the accused required the assistance of a lawyer, namely that there was potentially something of material value which a lawyer could contribute. II–136

Generally, the seriousness of the offence and the severity of the sentence at stake are the crucial issues in the assessment of whether the interests of justice require legal representation.[44] The Court has also had regard on occasion to additional factors such as the complexity of the court procedure and any difficulties of language or comprehension of the accused.[45] In tax surcharge proceedings, not involving complex legal issues, the applicant businessmen were considered as capable of representing themselves, the interests of justice not requiring free legal representation.[46]

(I) First instance

In deciding whether interests of justice require legal representation, the Court looks at the seriousness of the offences and the potential sentence imposable; complexity of the case is an additional factor, lack of which is not decisive. In *Quaranta v Switzerland*, for example, where there were no special difficulties in establishing facts, II–137

[42] *RD v Poland*, December 18, 2001, para.46; see also *Twalib v Greece*, June 9, 1998, R.J.D. 1998–IV, No.77, para.51, where the applicant had been assisted by legal aid counsel at first instance, and pro bono on appeal, the Government's claim that the applicant could have paid for counsel at the cassation level was unsubstantiated.

[43] *Artico v Italy*, May 13, 1980, Series A, No.37, 3 E.H.R.R. 1, para.35.

[44] e.g. *Twalib*, see fn.42 above, para.52.

[45] e.g. *Twalib*, see fn.42 above, para.53, difficulties of cassation procedure for which a lawyer is obligatory at any hearing and the fact that the applicant, a foreigner, was unfamiliar with the Greek language or legal system.

[46] *Barsom and Varli v Sweden*, (407766/06) and (40831/06) (Dec.) December 4, 2008.

the Court considered that issues arose concerning applicable measures as well as matters relating to the applicant's personal situation, foreign origin, underprivileged background and long criminal record, which appeared more relevant to sentencing. It found his appearance before court on minor drugs charges facing up to eighteen months did not enable him to present his case in an adequate manner.

(II) Leave to appeal versus appeal proceedings

II–138 The Court rejected the argument that the guarantees of Art.6, para.3(c) ceased to apply after the first instance proceedings or the stage at which, in domestic terms, the applicant is regarded as "convicted".[47] Appeal, leave to appeal and continental cassation proceedings on conviction and/or sentence concern the determination of a criminal charge and the guarantees of Art.6, paras 1 and 3 continue to apply though the manner of that application will depend on the nature and significance of the proceedings, taking into account the powers of the court and the manner in which the applicant's interests were presented and protected.[48]

Leave to appeal and appeal hearings may be distinguished. Leave to appeal proceedings where the prosecution are not present may not require free legal assistance. In *Monnell and Morris v UK*, the applicants had representation at first instance and advice on the merits of an appeal with the possibility to put in written submissions. The Court found that they were able fairly and effectively to present their application and interests of justice were met in their ability to make written submissions, taking into account the fact that counsel had advised there were no grounds of appeal.

Conversely, in the Scottish system where there was a general right to appeal, without leave, and applicants appeared in person in oral proceeedings at which the prosecution was represented and could address the court, it was found that the nature of the proceedings would, where there was a serious matter at stake, require legal representation to be fair. This was found to be the case in *Granger v UK* where difficult legal issues were at stake on which there was oral argument before the court by the Solicitor General in which the applicant was unable to play an effective part.[49] But subsequent cases have showed that where substantial sentences are at stake, that alone will render matters sufficiently serious for the interests of justice to require legal representation at the appeal hearing.[50] In these cases, the applicants had presented arguments on their own behalf, perhaps not inexpertly in some instances, but there has been no question of considering that this rendered the

[47] *Meftah*, see fn.34 above, para.40.

[48] e.g. *Monnell and Morris v UK*, March 2, 1987, Series A, No.115, 10 E.H.R.R. 205, para.58; *Meftah*, see fn.34 above, paras 41–42.

[49] See also *Pham Hoang v France*, September 25, 1991, Series A, No.243, where the applicant, fined several million francs for drugs offences, was refused legal aid counsel for cassation appeal—interests of justice required legal representation having regard to the serious consequences at stake, the complexity of issues and his inability to present and develop the appropriate arguments (e.g. only experienced counsel could seek to persuade the court to depart from its previous case-law); *Pakelli*, see fn.2 above, where the applicant could not respond to the *judge rapporteur* or contribute to case-law development.

[50] Violations in UK cases: *Maxwell v UK*, October 28, 1994, Series A, No.300–C, 19 E.H.R.R. 97 (five years, no complex issues in the case); *Boner v UK*, October 28, 1994, Series A, No.300–B, 19 E.H.R.R 246 (eight years); *Wotherspoon*, (22112/93) (Rep.) October 16, 1996 (life imprisonment; relatively complex issues); *Murdoch*, (25523/94) (Rep.) October 16, 1996 (two years; relatively complex); *Robson*, (25648/94) (Rep.) October 16, 1996 (appeal against sentence only; concurrent sentences of over 12 years: still need lawyer even if sentencing issues less complex).

provision of legal assistance unnecessary in the interests of justice. Where legal aid for an appeal was not available, the fact that the applicant made no effort to lodge his own grounds or ask for assistance did not prevent a violation being found.[51]

The Commission rejected some cases concerning minor offences with low sentences where it considered that the interests of justice did not require legal representation on appeal, for example, in cases concerning a nine-month sentence for assault where it considered that there were no complex legal issues requiring assistance[52]; 60 days for failure to give a breath specimen, taking a car, etc.[53]; conviction for breach of peace, one-year suspended sentence.[54] The Court has not yet confirmed this case-law.

6. Scope of the obligation to provide legal assistance

The appointment of a legal aid lawyer does not exhaust the obligations of the State. II–139
Legal assistance provided must be practical and effective,[55] and if the authorities are on notice that a legal aid lawyer is unable to fulfil his duties they are under an obligation to replace him.[56] Once they are, or should be aware, of a problem, they cannot remain passive.[57] Where appointment of a lawyer is made in circumstances that affect the effectiveness of his participation, issues may arise, as in *Goddi v Italy*, where the court did not inform the applicant's lawyer of the hearing and the lawyer appointed as a replacement knew neither the client or the file. It was also considered inadequate where the applicant met his lawyer for the first time by videolink fifteen minutes before the proceedings in the Supreme Court began. Even if geographic distances would have rendered onerous the transport of the applicant to meet his lawyer in person at the court, there was no explanation as to why his original lawyer had not been re-appointed, or longer time and facilities made available for the accused to talk to the new lawyer.[58] Failure to ensure the effective defence of an accused was found by the Commission in *Biondi v Italy*, where a lawyer failed to appear at an appeal though notified and the interests of justice required the defence be represented to answer the prosecution and expand the grounds of appeal. Failure of a legal aid lawyer appointed shortly before the trial to request an adjournment to prepare does not relieve the court of its responsibility to ensure an adequate defence; it should adjourn of its own motion.[59] Ensuring the presence of a lawyer at an appeal took on particular importance where the applicant had a hearing defect, the interests of justice requiring that he had the benefit of legal assistance during the proceedings to ensure fairness and his effective participation.[60]

[51] *Biba v Greece*, September 26, 2000, para.30.

[52] (17120/90) (Dec.) December 3, 1990.

[53] (14001/88) (Dec.) January 19, 1989.

[54] (13098/87) (Dec.) May 6, 1988.

[55] *Daud v Portugal*, April 21, 1998, R.J.D. 1998–II, No.69, 30 E.H.R.R. 400, para.39.

[56] e.g. *Artico*, see fn.43 above, where a legal aid lawyer refused the appointment because of other commitments and the authorities failed to appoint a substitute.

[57] *Daud*, see fn.55 above, para.42, where the applicant had applied to the court for an interview with his lawyer who had done nothing in eight months, the court should have verified whether the lawyer was fulfilling his duty, possibly replacing him earlier and should have adjourned when new counsel was appointed three days before the trial and needed time to prepare; *Sannino v Italy*, April 27, 2006, where official counsel never appeared, the court was aware that the applicant was represented by a series of ad hoc court-appointed lawyers who never asked for an adjournment or called for any steps to be taken for the defence—the applicant's own passivity did not excuse the court's inaction.

[58] *Sakhnnovskiy v Russia*, November 2, 2010, ECHR 2010–. . . , paras 103–107.

[59] *Bogumil v Portugal*, October 7, 2008, paras 47–50.

[60] *Timergaliyev v Russia*, October 14, 2008, paras 59–60.

The State is not, however, liable for every shortcoming of a legal aid lawyer.[61] The conduct of the defence is essentially a matter between the lawyer and defendant[62]; an accused is not entitled to require counsel to adopt a particular defence strategy.[63] The competent authorities are only required to intervene if failure by legal aid counsel to provide effective representation is manifest or sufficiently brought to their attention in some other way.[64] The Court will have regard to the proceedings in their entirety and the mere fact that counsel in some respects acted against what applicants consider to be their best interests will not be sufficient to render the representation below the required standard,[65] for example, where counsel refused to draft grounds of appeal as the file did not disclose any statutory grounds.[66] Where, however, an appeal is declared inadmissible as a result of the failure of official counsel to comply with a formal requirement, this may be distinguished from tactical error or shortcoming in argument. In *Czekalla v Portugal*, the failure of the legal aid lawyer to complete the grounds of appeal with the necessary formal conclusions, which led to the rejection of the appeal, was found to deprive the applicant, a foreigner ignorant of the language, of a practical and effective defence.[67] Elsewhere the Court has noted that generally litigants had to expect procedural rules to apply in the interests of legal certainty and, where the applicant had the opportunity to lodge grounds in time himself, no problem of access to court arose.[68] Leeway is given to the domestic courts as regards their assessment of the appropriate qualifications of legal aid counsel.[69]

An applicant cannot claim a right to choose who is appointed as his legal aid counsel. The Court has stated that domestic courts must have regard to the applicant's wishes, but these could be overridden where there were relevant and sufficient grounds for holding this necessary in the interests of justice.[70]

The Commission had little sympathy for accused who have dismissed counsel during proceedings or, failing to obtain an adjournment or fresh counsel, continued

[61] *Artico*, fn.43, *Kamasinski v Austria*, December 19, 1989, Series A, No.168, 13 E.H.R.R. 36; *Imbroscia v Switzerland*, November 24, 1993, Series A, No.275, where the applicant's counsel was absent during interrogations with the prosecutor, the Court noted the short period, lack of complaint by the applicant and the provision of replacements by the authorities.

[62] e.g. *Czekalla v Portugal*, October 10, 2002, ECHR 2002–VIII, para.60. See also *Alvarez Sanchez v Spain*, (50720/99) (Dec.) October 23, 2001, ECHR 2001–XI, where the Court observed that direct interference by a judge with a counsel's conduct of a case would be incompatible with the independence of the profession from the state.

[63] (9127/80) (Dec.) October 6, 1981, where the court-appointed counsel refused to maintain the applicant's not guilty plea, the Commission noted that the lawyer found the plea impossible to maintain and that the applicant could have addressed the court himself.

[64] *Kamasinski*, fn.61 above, para.65; *Daud*, fn.55 above, para.38; *Czekalla*, fn.62 above, para.60.

[65] e.g. *Kamasinski*, fn.61 above, where the applicant criticised the brevity of counsel's visits, counsel's failure to inform him of prosecution evidence etc; (9728/82) (Dec.) July 7, 1983, 6 D.R. 155, no problem where legal aid counsel limited unnecessary consultations to save costs to the legal aid fund.

[66] *Rutkowski v Poland*, (45995/99) (Dec.) October 19, 2000, ECHR 2000–XI.

[67] Contrast *Alvarez Sanchez*, fn.60 above, the failure of the counsel to lodge an appeal in time to the Constitutional Court in an *amparo* appeal which did not involve a review of conviction or sentence was not so serious a shortcoming as to render his defence rights ineffective.

[68] *Freixas v Spain*, November 21, 2000, ECHR 2000–X.

[69] *Freixas*, fn.68 above, where in the absence of concrete indications of incompetence, the fact counsel specialised in labour, not criminal, law was not a problem under Art.6, para.3(c).

[70] *Croissant*, fn.33 above, para.29; *Lagerblom v Sweden*, January 14, 2003, para.54, where there was no violation in failing to appoint the applicant's preferred Finnish-speaking lawyer, where he had sufficient knowledge of Swedish himself.

the proceedings unrepresented.[71] Where the person has sacked numerous solicitors already, it is perhaps more obvious that the situation is of his own making and the domestic court may reasonably regard it as delaying tactics.[72] Where a person faces serious charges and loses confidence in inexperienced counsel, it would perhaps be harder to dismiss a complaint lightly. However, it would require gross or obvious failure on the part of the defence counsel, beyond mere exercise of tactical judgment that might be disagreed with, before the Court would be likely to find an obligation on the authorities to replace counsel.

The Court will not be quick to reach a finding that an accused has waived his right to a lawyer. The lack of legal knowledge of the accused was found to excuse his failure, on rejecting his legal aid lawyer, either to request another lawyer or an adjournment and did not count as a waiver.[73] Nor was there a valid waiver of a lawyer by an applicant who was illiterate and knew little Turkish and who was not provided with an interpreter.[74]

Provision of video conferencing means by which an applicant can participate in a trial at a distance is not, per se, contrary to Art.6 where pursuing legitimate aims and attended by requisite safeguards including confidential communication with his lawyer.[75]

Cross-reference

Part IIA, s.14: Legal aid in civil proceedings.

[71] e.g. (8386/78) (Dec.) October 9, 1980, 21 D.R. 126, where counsel withdrew but the judge refused to adjourn for new counsel, the Commission considered that the judge's view that other counsel would be similarly embarrassed was not unreasonable in light of the applicant's admissions in court and noted that he was given the opportunity to defend himself but chose not to; (13572/88) (Dec.) March 1, 1991, 69 D.R. 198, where a Sámi was unrepresented on appeal, due to his rejection of the court-appointed lawyer whom the court found had not failed to fulfil his functions, the Commission held that Art.6 para.3(c) did not give a right to choose, or change, official counsel—regard was had to the minor sentence imposed (one month).

[72] (24667/94) (Dec.) May 20, 1996, 85–B D.R. 103, where the applicant dismissed the lawyer towards the end of the trial.

[73] *Sakhnovskiy v Russia*, November 2, 2010, ECHR 2010–. . ., paras 89–93.

[74] *Saman v Turkey*, April 5, 2011, paras 30–37.

[75] *Zagaria v Italy*, fn.23 above, para.49; *Sakhnovskiy v Russia*, fn.73 above, para.98; *Marcello Viola v Italy*, October 5, 2006, paras 72–77; *Golubev v Russia*, (26260/02) (Dec.) November 9, 2006.

16. Legislative interference in judicial process

Key provision:

II–140 Article 6, para.1 (fair trial).

Key case-law:

Stran Greek Refineries v Greece, December 9, 1994, Series A, No.301–B, 19 E.H.R.R. 293; *Pressos Compania Naviera v Belgium*, November 20, 1995, Series A, No.332, 21 E.H.R.R. 301; *Papageorgiou v Greece*, October 22, 1997, R.J.D. 1997–IV, No.54; *National & Provincial Building Society v UK*, October 23, 1997, R.J.D. 1997–VII, No.55, 25 E.H.R.R. 127; *Zielinski and Pradal & Gonzalez v France*, October 28, 1999, ECHR 1999–VII.

1. General considerations

II–141 Where the legislature passes a law which has direct and significant effect on the adjudication of pending civil claims, issues will generally arise under Art.6, para.1. In *Stran Greek Refineries v Greece*, the Court rejected the Government argument that the legislative action was outside the court proceedings, emphasising that fairness applied to the proceedings in their entirety. While there was no doubt that the appearances of justice before the courts was preserved, the principle of the rule of law and the notion of fair trial precluded any interference by the legislature with the administration of justice designed to influence the judicial determination of the dispute.[1] Such interference could only be justified on compelling grounds of general interest.[2] Where, however, the legislation is introduced after the conclusion of civil proceedings, and therefore without influencing the outcome of the case, no problem may arise under Art.6 which does not go so far as to provide that the effects of final judgments in civil proceedings may not subsequently be overridden by the legislature.[3]

2. Effect on the proceedings

II–142 Violations of Art.6 have arisen where the State's intervention through legislative acts has intended either to influence the outcome of pending judicial proceedings, to prevent proceedings being opened, or to render void final and enforceable decisions which recognised personal rights to receive payment.[4]

In *Stran Greek Refineries*, the law which was passed effectively excluded any meaningful examination since it took away the enforceability of the court's findings. The Court in finding a violation also referred to the case-law on equality of arms.

[1] *Stran Greek Refineries v Greece*, December 9, 1994, Series A, No.301–B, 19 E.H.R.R. 293, para.49, violations were found under Art.6, para.1 and Art.1 of Protocol No.1 (interference with property rights).
[2] *e.g. Zielinski and Pradal & Gonzalez v France*, October 28, 1999, ECHR 1999–VII, para.57.
[3] *Preda and Dardari v Italy*, (28160/95) and (28382/95) (Dec.) February 23, 1999, ECHR 1999–II, the Court considered the statute was aimed not at interfering with the applicants' case but at ensuring equal treatment of all those in the applicants' position.
[4] *Gorraiz Lizarraga v Spain*, April 27, 2004, ECHR 2004–III, para.70.

Where the State is a party in proceedings, use of its legislative powers may clearly place an opponent at a substantial disadvantage. Where the effect of a legislative measure, in conjunction with the method and timing of its enactment, is effectively to extinguish a pending claim, a violation of Art.6, para.1 is likely to arise in that the applicant is thereby deprived of a fair hearing.[5]

The aspect of access to court, combined with lack of equality of arms, was the basis for the violation of Art.6, para.1 in the Commission's report in *Pressos Compania Naviera*, where the applicant ship-owners with claims pending before the courts, complained of legislation which was passed to exempt the State and its pilots from liability for negligent acts. The intervention was an interference in access to court, which was not proportionate and deprived the applicants of the right to obtain a decision on their civil rights following a fair trial before a tribunal. In *Zielinski and Pradal & Gonzalez v France*, the Court found a violation where a statute was passed endorsing the position taken by the public authorities in pending disputes and thereby determining the substance of the dispute in place of the courts. Though the case-law often refers to the legislative intervention being decisive for the outcome of the proceedings in favour of a State party,[6] it has also been considered sufficient where a court decision was based only subsidiarily on the statute concerned.[7] An intervening legislative measure which had the effect of staying indefinitely ongoing civil cases for compensation for war damage deprived the applicants of access to court,[8] as did subsequent legislation which prevented enforcement of a final judgment ordering the applicant's bank to repay her foreign savings.[9]

Where domestic courts were reaching conflicting decisions on entitlements to special employee allowances, the Court rejected the Government's argument that intervention by the legislature was necessary to impose uniformity in pending proceedings, considering that divergences were an inherent consequence of any judicial system based on a network of trial and appellate courts and that the role of the Court of Cassation was precisely to resolve such conflicts.[10]

Legislative intervention offends not only when it affects the disposal of cases pending before the courts, but also cases where administrative procedures, which are a precondition to lodging cases in the courts, have been taken.[11] It is also a problem where the State intervenes, even where it is not, directly, a party, since this destroys equality of arms between the litigants.[12] There is no problem under Art.6 where the applicant has not yet lodged his claim in the courts before the legislation intervenes.[13]

[5] *Papageorgiou v Greece*, October 22, 1997, R.J.D. 1997–IV, No.54, paras 34–40; see also *Anagnastopoulos v Greece*, November 7, 2000, ECHR 2000–XI, paras 19–20.

[6] *Stran Greek Refineries v Greece*, fn.1 above, para.50; *Preda and Dardari*, fn.3 above; *Agoudimos and Cefallonian Sky Shipping Co v Greece*, June 28, 2001, para.35.

[7] *Anagnostopoulos*, see fn.5 above, para.21.

[8] *Kutic v Croatia*, March 1, 2002, paras 28–33, the Court rejected the Government argument that the measure was only temporary as it had already lasted more than six years.

[9] *Jelicic v Bosnia-Herzegovina*, October 31, 2006.

[10] *Zielinski*, see fn.2 above, para.59.

[11] *SCM Scanner de l'Ouest Lyonnais v France*, June 21, 2007, para.29.

[12] *Arnolin v France*, January 9, 2007, para.74, although the authorities did stand to benefit due to their financing responsibility for the defendant organisations.

[13] *Phocas v France*, (15638/06) September 13, 2007.

3. Compatible interventions

II–143 Legislative interference may, even if retrospective, be compatible with Art.6 in certain limited and compelling circumstances. The financial interests of the Government do not appear, by themselves, to provide compelling grounds of public interest,[14] at least without convincing proof, for example, that the health and social security system would be placed in jeopardy.[15] Nor were such aims as to restore equilibrium to the pensions system or to prevent persons obtaining advantage from lower contributions rates sufficient to justify the dangers of retrospective legislation interfering in judicial process.[16] Where, however, legislative intervention is foreseeable, and to put right frustrated intentions, or where the purpose of the legislation is not intended to remove the jurisdiction of the courts, the effect on pending disputes may not offend Art.6.

In *National & Provincial Building Society v UK*, where retrospective legislation intervened with the building societies' prospects of obtaining restitution of tax paid under invalid regulations, the Commission followed, by a narrow majority, the *Stran Greek Refineries* approach that intervention by the legislature influencing proceedings in the State's favour was objectionable. However, the Court held that Art.6, para.1 could not be interpreted as preventing any interference with pending legal proceedings to which the State was a party, though respect for the rule of law and a fair trial required the use of retrospective legislation to be regarded with great circumspection. While in *Stran Greek Refineries* there was a nine-year-old private law dispute with the Government as a party to a contract where an arbitration award had been given and there was an inconsistency in the State position since the Government had originally requested arbitration, in this case there were special circumstances, namely, a clear intention of Parliament to tax the money from the beginning, the legislation had been swiftly introduced to prevent windfalls and the frustration of the legislative purpose caused by the fortuitous exploitation of technical defects in the original regulations. Similarly, where legislation was passed during the applicants' pending claims for reimbursement of social security benefits, the Court found that this intervention, to fill a regulatory loophole, had been foreseeable and compellingly in the public interest.[17]

In the area of regional planning, where issues are "evolutive" in nature and a wider margin of appreciation accorded, the Court did not consider that the introduction of legislation on protective zones which had the effect of undermining the applicants' pending challenge to the building of a dam was in conflict with Art.6. It considered that the legislation had not been passed to remove the jurisdiction of the courts which retained power to assess the merits and constitutionality of any measures.[18]

Retrospective changes in interest rates payable on judgment debts which do not affect the substance of the claims have also been found compatible.[19]

[14] *Zielinski*, see fn.2 above, para.59; *SCM Scanner de l'Ouest*, fn.11 above, para.31, prospective legislative intervention could have served to safeguard financial interests for the future without affecting pending disputes.

[15] *Arnolin*, fn.12 above, para.76, such a case not made out.

[16] *Maggio v Italy*, May 31, 2011, para.49.

[17] *OGIS-Institut Stanislas v France*, May 27, 2004; see also, on the same lines, *EEG-slachthuis verbist v Belgium*, (60559/00) (Dec.) November 10, 2005.

[18] *Gorraiz Lizarraga*, see fn.4 above.

[19] *Sud Parisienne de Construction v France*, February 11, 2010, no violation under Art.1 of Protocol No.1 and no separate issue under Art.6.

Cross-reference

Part IIA, s.2: Access to court.
Part IIA, s.7: Equality of arms.
Part IIB, s.38: Property.

17. Length of proceedings

Key provision:

II–144 Article 6, para.1.

1. General considerations

II–145 The requirement that proceedings do not exceed a "reasonable time" applies to both the determination of criminal charges and civil rights and obligations. The principles are well-established in a series of cases dominated by Italy. The reasonableness of the length of proceedings is to be assessed in the light of the particular circumstances of the case, regard being had in particular to three heads, the complexity of the case, the conduct of the applicant and the conduct of the authorities. On the latter point, what is at stake for the applicant is taken into account. Thus, criminal proceedings will generally be expected to be pursued more expeditiously than civil.[1] Where time may play a role in determining the merits, such as childcare and custody cases,[2] or where time is pressing for other reasons there may be special need for diligence on the part of the authorities.[3] Serious impact on the applicants may also be disclosed by factors of age, health and prejudice to professional and business interests.[4]

The Court has emphasised the importance of administration of justice without delays which might jeopardise its effectiveness and credibility. The accumulation of breaches, which show a continuing situation that has not been remedied, may, as in the case of Italy, lead to a finding of a practice incompatible with the Convention.[5]

[1] e.g. *Kalashnikov v Russia*, July 15, 2002, ECHR 2002–VI, para.132, "particular diligence" required.

[2] The child may bond with new carers, e.g. *H v UK*, July 8, 1987, Series, A No.120–B; need for "exceptional diligence" in *Johansen v Norway*, August 7, 1996, R.J.D. 1996–III, No.13, para.88 and *Paulsen-Medalen and Svensson v Sweden*, February 19, 1998, R.J.D. 1998–I, No.63, para.42. See also *Schaal v Luxembourg*, February 18, 2003, where the six years of criminal proceedings for alleged child abuse had an effect on the applicant's applications for contact and residence in care proceedings—exceptional diligence was required (para.35); *Boca v Belgium*, November 15, 2002, ECHR 2002–IX, para.29, where one year and two months' delay in setting down custody appeal was excessive.

[3] e.g. *De Clerck v Belgium,* September 25, 2007, paras 69–70, one applicant, of advanced age, was prejudiced in his defence by the lapse of time due to his deteriorating memory, while the 16–year criminal proceedings had consequences for the applicants' other companies and business interests, with numerous fiscal procedures being frozen.

[4] e.g. claims by AIDS victims for compensation for contaminated blood banks in *X v France*, March 31, 1992, Series A, No.234–C, 14 E.H.R.R. 483, a period over two years was excessive; and *Pailot v France*, April 22, 1998 R.J.D., 1998–II, No.69, 1 year and 10 months was too long; where the applicant is seriously ill, e.g. *Gheorghe v Romania*, March 15, 2007; where the applicant has suffered injuries, special, even exceptional diligence, has been required, e.g. *Silva Pontes v Portugal*, March 23, 1994, Series A, No.286–A, 18 E.H.R.R. 156, para.39 and *Martins Moreira v Portugal*, October 26, 1988, Series A, No.143; diligence has also been required in employment disputes, e.g. *Nibbio v Italy*, February 26, 1992, Series A, No.228–A; *Svetlana Orlova v Russia*, July 30, 2009, para.51, employment matter where the applicant, dismissed while on maternity leave, was in a vulnerable position; and in criminal cases, where the applicant is in detention, e.g. *Motsnik v Estonia*, April 29, 2003, para.40.

[5] *Botazzi v Italy*, July 28, 1999, ECHR 1999–V. Following a finding of administrative practice, subsequent violations of Art.6 in that respect disclose aggravating circumstances, e.g. *Rotondi v Italy*, April 27, 2000, para.15.

2. Period to be taken into consideration

Civil proceedings generally commence from the institution of the relevant court procedure which concerns the determination of a dispute relating to civil rights and obligations.[6] However, where under the national legislation an applicant has to exhaust a preliminary administrative procedure before having recourse to a court, the proceedings before the administrative body are included when calculating the length of the civil proceedings.[7] The proceedings terminate on the date of giving judgment in the final instance or, where later, the issuing of the written judgment to the applicant.[8] Where a court decision only became final after a year, the Court took that date.[9] Subsequent costs and enforcement proceedings may be taken into account where related to substantive proceedings concerning civil rights and obligations.[10] II–146

Criminal proceedings commence from the moment that a formal charge is brought against the applicant[11] or where the person has otherwise been substantially affected by actions taken by the prosecuting authorities as a result of the suspicion against him.[12] Even where no formal charge is brought for years, the fact that an applicant has been questioned as a suspect and confessed is sufficient to render him subject to a charge during the intervening period.[13] The charge may be defined as the "official notification given to an individual by the competent authority of an allegation that he has committed a criminal offence" which also corresponds to the test whether the situation of the suspect has been affected.[14] This may be the date of arrest,[15] the date the applicant was officially notified that he was to be prosecuted,

[6] *Darnell v UK*, (Rep.) October 26, 1993, Series A, No.272, 18 E.H.R.R., despite lengthy internal disciplinary enquiries, until the applicant was dismissed, there was no "dispute" as to civil rights or obligations. See, however, *Selmouni v France*, July 28, 1999, ECHR 1999–V, para.111, taking the starting point for the applicant's compensation claim from the date of his express complaint about serious police ill-treatment rather than the formal lodging of proceedings before the investigating judge.

[7] *Kiurkchian v Bulgaria*, March 24, 2005, para.51.

[8] e.g. *Soares Fernandes v Portugal*, April 8, 2004, para.17.

[9] *Trevisan v Italy*, February 26, 1993, Series A, No.257–F.

[10] *Robins v UK*, September 23, 1997, R.J.D. 1997–V, No.49 (costs); *Di Pede and Zappia v Italy*, September 26, 1996, R.J.D. 1996–IV, No.17 (enforcement).

[11] *Pedersen and Baadsgaard v Denmark*, December 17, 2004, para.44, date taken from the charging of the applicants—the initial reporting of the applicants to the police was not enough without any enforcement measures of criminal procedure.

[12] e.g. (9132/80) (Rep.) December 12, 1983, 41 D.R. 13, where the applicant was implicated in proceedings against another person, the date was taken from the moment that the authorities searched his premises, when it became clear that a suspicion existed that he was an accomplice and this measure severely affected his position; *Marpa Zeeland BV and Metal Welding BV v Netherlands*, November 9, 2004, date of search and seizure of documents; *Ewing v UK*, (11224/84) (Rep.) October 6, 1987, 56 D.R. 71, date of arrest; *Hozee v Netherlands*, May 22, 1998, R.J.D. 1998–III, No.73, when the applicant was first questioned and informed officially that he was under suspicion of having committed a criminal offence; *Aleksander Zaichenko v Russia*, February 18, 2010, paras 42–43, where the applicant was stopped in his van, questioned by a police officer, made incriminating statements and signed an inspection record, even though he was not formally charged at that point, given the record and admissions were the heart of the criminal proceedings, he could claim to be substantially affected from the encounter with the police officer.

[13] *Yankov and Manchev v Bulgaria*, October 22, 2009, para.18, where there was a lapse of over six years between the confession and the prosecutor formally charging the applicant. See also *Aleksander Zaichenko v Russia*, see fn.12 above, paras 42–43.

[14] e.g. *Eckle v Germany*, July 15, 1982, Series A, No.51, para.73.

[15] (9559/81) (Dec.) May 9, 1983, 33 D.R. 158.

the date preliminary investigations were opened, the date of opening of a criminal investigation,[16] the request for an investigation following initial questioning of the applicant,[17] the date of police interrogation where the applicants became aware of the existence of an investigation concerning them,[18] or the date of execution of search warrants on the applicants' business premises.[19]

Measures taken unknown to the applicant with no repercussions do not start time running,[20] nor did a preliminary investigation into an incident which did not involve any act of accusation or charge against the applicant.[21] Where specific separate counts are added later, the dates are taken from those occurrences as relevant.[22] Parliamentary immunity in suspending a prosecution or trial against an MP left the charges pending and the time which lapsed was taken into account in assessing the reasonableness of length of proceedings.[23]

Criminal proceedings end when the charges are finally determined or the sentence imposed becomes final.[24] This may be the date of the conclusion of last appeal or the issuing of the judgment. Where the imposition of confiscation orders is part of the criminal proceedings, the length of this procedure is taken into account as being part of the sentencing.[25]

Where civil proceedings are held in abeyance pending a criminal investigation, the period may well run from the beginning of the latter, particularly where the criminal procedure was crucial for the establishment of responsibility for the damage concerned.[26]

Length complaints may be examined where the proceedings have not terminated if it is alleged that there has already been unreasonable delay.[27] Where the Convention organs only become competent *ratione temporis* during the course of proceedings, the time already elapsed is taken into account in assessing the reasonableness of length of proceedings after that date.[28] Where a violation has already been found by Convention organs in respect of pending proceedings, the delay already elapsed is also taken into account in assessing the reasonableness of time taken in the later part of the proceedings.[29] Also, in cases where an applicant absconds or is a fugitive during the proceedings (criminal) that period is deducted.[30]

[16] *Mylnek v Austria*, (11688/85) (Rep.) March 10, 1988, 62 D.R. 120; see *Löffler v Austria*, October 3, 2000, para.19, where an applicant was convicted and the proceedings re-opened, the start date was the re-opening, not earlier proceedings which had resulted in a final decision.

[17] (13017/87) (Rep.) July 4, 1989, 71 D.R. 52.

[18] *Martins and Garcia Alves v Portugal*, November 16, 2000, the Court rejected the Government argument that the date ran from the appearance before the investigating judge.

[19] *De Clerck v Belgium*, fn.3, para.50.

[20] *Guisset v France*, September 26, 2000, ECHR 2000–IX, para.519; *Echeveste and Bidart v France*, March 21, 2002, paras 77–78, where the applicants were not aware of the arrest warrants issued against them, the date taken was their notification, while in custody on other charges, of the court orders against them.

[21] *Sommer v Italy*, (36586/08) (Dec.) March 23, 2010, concerning a massacre of villagers by the SS in 1944, there was an investigation in 1947 which did not lead to any proceedings; it was only in 1992 that the applicant was informed that he was the subject of an investigation; the Court found that he had not been affected by any investigative measure before that date.

[22] *Jesso v Austria*, (9315/81) (Rep.) May 7, 1986, 50 D.R. 44.

[23] *Kart v Turkey*, December 3, 2009, paras 68–70.

[24] *Eckle*, fn.14 above, para.77.

[25] *Crowther v UK*, February 1, 2005, paras 24–25.

[26] *e.g. Iribarren Pinillos v Spain*, January 8, 2009, para.65.

[27] e.g. *Mylnek v Austria*, (settled before the Court) (Rep.) December 9, 1991, Series A, No.242–C, period of three years, nine months and still pending in the domestic court at the date of judgment.

[28] *Mitap and Muftuoglu v Turkey*, March 25, 1996, R.J.D. 1996–II, No.6.

[29] *Rotondi v Italy*, see fn.5 above, para.14.

[30] e.g. *Girolami v Italy*, February 19, 1991, Series A, No.196–E; *Vayic v Turkey*, June 20, 2006, para.44.

3. Victim status

The fact that an applicant is acquitted does not deprive him of victim status for the purpose of a length complaint.[31] Where, however, national authorities have acknowledged the breach of the Convention expressly or in substance and afforded redress for the breach in circumstances where it would duplicate the domestic process to bring complaints to Strasbourg the applicant ceases to be a victim for purposes of an application.[32] This requires an acknowledgement in a sufficiently clear manner of the failure to observe the reasonable time requirement and redress is required, such as reducing the sentence in an express and measurable manner (in criminal cases),[33] payment of compensation of a reasonable or not manifestly inadequate amount,[34] discontinuation of proceedings together with payment of some legal costs,[35] or exemption from significant legal costs.[36] Where a domestic court examines complaints about the length of proceedings it must be competent to review the whole period under consideration.[37] While domestic courts do not have to award compensation on the same basis as that applicable in Strasbourg, the applicant will retain victim status if the amount is manifestly unreasonable when compared to the amount that the Court would have awarded for non-pecuniary damage.[38] A lesser amount of compensation is apparently acceptable if the redress offered also had an accelerating effect on proceedings.[39] Further undue delay in the payment of the damages may retain victim status also.[40] II–147

The Commission found that where a court failed to find, or expressly denied, a violation of the Convention, the applicant still could claim to be a victim but any action taken by the court in reducing the sentence in view of the length was to be taken into account in the assessment of the reasonableness of the delay.[41] The Court has also taken reduction of sentence into account in finding no violation.[42] The logic of this approach is not readily apparent since the applicant had suffered the delay whatever the result and without an express acknowledgment of the breach.

[31] (13156/87) (Dec.) July 1, 1992, 76 D.R. 5.

[32] *Eckle*, see fn.14 above, para.66.

[33] *Eckle*, fn.14 above; (9299/81) (Rep.) July 12, 1985, 46 D.R. 5, where the Swiss authorities implicitly acknowledged the breach, finding that there had been considerable delays and reduced 2 and a half years to 18 months and decided not to enforce the expulsion order; (17669/91) (Dec.) March 31, 1993, 74 D.R. 156, reduction from 2 and a half years to 8 months half-suspended in light of excessive delay; *Neubeck v Germany*, (9132/80) (Rep.) December 12, 1983, 41 D.R. 13, where the applicant remained a victim as the courts only referred to part of the excessive delay without quantifying the reduction, the Commission finding a vague reference to the fact that the sentence would have been longer was insufficiently clear. See, however, *Beck v Norway*, June 26, 2006, para.28, where the sentence reduction, although not specified, was sufficiently measurable.

[34] *Cataldo v Italy*, (45656/99) (Dec.) June 3, 2004, ECHR 2004–VI; *Bako v Slovakia*, (60227/00) (Dec.) March 15, 2005; *Kalajzic v Croatia*, (15382/04) (Dec.) September 8, 2006.

[35] *Sprotte v Germany*, (72438/01) (Dec.) November 17, 2005 (criminal).

[36] *Hansen v Denmark*, (26194/03) (Dec.) May 29, 2006 (civil).

[37] *Bako v Slovakia*, (60227/00) ('Dec.) March 15, 2005, where the Constitutional Court's review was globally adequate even though it examined different periods separately.

[38] *Cocchiarella v Italy*, March 29, 2006, para.106 (14 per cent was inadequate); *Musci v Italy*, March 29, 2006, para.107 (27 per cent was inadequate); *Kalajzic v Croatia*, (15382/04) (Dec.) September 8, 2006, amount adequate; *Simaldone v Italy*, March 31, 2009, para.30, 7.8 per cent of Court rate not inadequate.

[39] *Scordino v Italy (No.1)*, March 29, 2006, para.206.

[40] *Simaldone v Italy*, see fn.38 above, paras 31 and 37.

[41] e.g. *RB v Switzerland*, (18905/91) (Rep.) May 24, 1995, no violation in light of the complexity of the case and the fact that the domestic court reduced the sentence from 24 to 16 months.

[42] e.g. *Hozee*, see fn.12 above, para.54.

4. Complexity of the case

II–148 All aspects of the case may be relevant to the assessment of complexity of the proceedings, including the subject-matter, whether there are disputed facts, the number of accused, international elements, the number of witnesses, and the volume of written evidence. The economic nature of offences will not render proceedings especially complex per se, the Court looking more to the procedural aspects, as well as factual and legal issues in each case.[43]

The complexity of the case, balanced with the general principle of securing the proper administration of justice may justify a not inconsiderable length of time. In *Boddaert v Belgium*,[44] the Court found that six years and almost three months was not unreasonable since the case concerned a difficult murder enquiry and the parallel progression of two cases. Nor did seven years and ten months disclose a violation in *CP v France* where the criminal proceedings concerned complex company fraud investigations.[45] In a civil case, *Katte Klitsche v Italy*,[46] the Court found that eight years disclosed no violation, notwithstanding three identified periods of abnormal delay, since the case, a land developmental planning matter, was complex on facts and law and having regard to the importance of environmental interests and the importance for Italian case-law.

However, even where a case is complex there is a point where this ceases to suffice as justification for the lapse of time. In *Ferrantelli and Santangelo v Italy*, where the applicants were convicted finally after 16 years, the Court agreed that the case concerned a complex murder trial and involved sensitive problems of dealing with juveniles. The Court acknowledged that the proceedings were generally active, but when the case was looked at as a whole the only possible conclusion was unreasonable delay.[47] Similarly, where a colossal money laundering case took over 16 years, even though there were numerous international complications, the Court considered complexity by itself could not justify the length.[48]

5. Conduct of the applicant

II–149 Only delays attributable to the State may justify a finding of failure to comply with the "reasonable time" requirement.[49]

An applicant who stays outside the jurisdiction, for example failing to answer to an arrest warrant or who flees, cannot complain about length, even though the criminal proceedings remain pending indefinitely as a result.[50] Delays resulting from the impossibility of the applicant appearing due to his incarceration in another country likewise cannot be placed at the responsibility of the State.[51]

[43] *Pelissier and Sassi*, March 25, 1999, ECHR 1999–II, para.71.
[44] *Boddaert v Belgium*, October 12, 1992, Series A, No.235.
[45] *CP v France*, August 1, 2000. See also *Debbasch v France*, December 3, 2002, no violation for almost eight years in a complex international art fraud case, with numerous letters rogatory; nor in *Hozee*, see fn.12 above, for more than eight years in complex fraudulent tax case concerning a network of interlocking companies.
[46] *Katte Klitsche v Italy*, October 27, 1994, Series A, No.293–B.
[47] *Ferrantelli and Santangelo v Italy*, August 7, 1996, R.J.D. 1996–III, No.12; see also *Pafitis v Greece*, February 26, 1998, R.J.D. 1998–I, No.66, para.91.
[48] *De Clerck*, fn.3 above, paras 55–57.
[49] e.g. *Proszak v Poland*, December 16, 1997, R.J.D. 1997–VIII, No.59.
[50] e.g. *AP v Italy*, (27679/95) (Dec.) June 24, 1996; *Erdogan v Turkey*, (14723/89) (Dec.) July 9, 1992, 73 D.R. 81; *JA, RA and PM v Italy*, (37658/97) (Dec.) October 27, 1998.
[51] e.g. *Passaris v Greece*, (53344/07) (Dec.) September 24, 2009.

An applicant, in principle, cannot have it held against him that he has made full use of the procedures available to him under domestic law to pursue his defence.[52] An applicant is not required actively to co-operate with the judicial authorities, but nonetheless his conduct may be taken into account as an objective factor for which the Government are not responsible.[53] The fact that an applicant has applied for expedition is often a factor in his favour but failure to do so is not necessarily crucial, particularly where the Government have not shown that the possibility of speeding up the proceedings is a real one.[54] Some time-wasting or dilatory conduct will not create a violation where it does not contribute substantially to the overall length of proceedings.[55]

The factor of the applicant's conduct was significant in *Monnet v France*[56] (contested judicial separation lasting seven years, one month), where the applicant contributed considerably to prolonging the proceedings by two requests for deferment, delay in submitting documents and in setting down for the hearing of the appeal. In *Ciricosta and Viola v Italy*,[57] concerning an application to suspend works likely to interfere with property rights and where the applicants had requested at least 17 adjournments and not objected to six others requested by the other party, the Court held that, although 15 years on its face appeared unreasonable and the courts were responsible for some delay, they did not bear the primary responsibility and it did not accept that the judge was negligent in not putting an end to the applicants' dilatory conduct. Similarly, in *Patrianakos v Greece*, the Court considered that the delays were caused by the inactivity of the parties and their failure to attend the hearings for which the courts did not bear responsibility.[58]

A party to civil proceedings may be expected to show diligence in carrying out the procedural steps relevant to him and to avail himself of the scope afforded by domestic law for shortening proceedings. Thus, by failing to apply to the court to lift a stay imposed due to the lack of availability of another party, the subsequent

[52] *Eckle*, fn.14 above, para.82; *CP v France*, fn.45 above, para.31, applicants were not penalised for making use of procedures offered by domestic law.

[53] e.g. *Eckle*, fn.14 above, there were allegations of deliberate obstruction but, though the applicants slowed matters by numerous applications and appeals, the Court still found one of the main causes of the length of the proceedings to be the conduct of the judicial authorities, *Barfuss v Czech Republic*, July 31, 2000, para.74, the Court took into account the fact that the applicant changed his defence by submitting new facts deliberately not mentioned during the investigation; *Debbasch v France*, fn.45 above, the applicant's excessive applications were regarded as significantly contributing to the overall length; *Humen v Poland*, October 15, 1999, para.66, the applicant's failure to submit to a brain scan, plus the delaying effect of his inaccurate account of facts.

[54] e.g. *Ceteroni v Italy*, November 15, 1996, R.J.D. 1996–V, No.21, where the judge had never refused any adjournments by liquidator and the Court accepted that applications by the applicant would have had no effect; *Horvat v Croatia*, July 26, 2001, ECHR 2001–VIII, para.57. Contrast *M v UK*, (13228/87) (Dec.) February 13, 1990, where the Commission took into account that the applicant consented to the steps which delayed proceedings; *Ewing v UK*, fn.12 above, where the Commission noted that the applicant could have applied for an expedited hearing before the House of Lords and found the overall period (3 years, 10 months) was not unreasonable overall; *Pedersen and Baadsgaard*, fn.11 above, para.49, where the Court noted that the applicant had not objected to any adjournments.

[55] e.g. *Kudla v Poland*, October 26, 2000, ECHR 2000–XI, para.130. See also *Beaumartin v France*, November 24, 1994, Series A, No.296–B, where the applicants caused delay by bringing the case in the wrong court but the authorities were more at fault, e.g. inter alia the court taking over five years to hold the first hearing.

[56] *Monnet v France*, October 27, 1993, Series A, No.273–B.

[57] *Ciricosta and Viola v Italy*, December 4, 1995, Series A, No.337.

[58] *Patrianakos v Greece*, July 15, 2004, distinguishing situations where the domestic court bore responsibility for timetabling, obtaining evidence or granting of adjournments, etc.

lapse of five years was not seen as the fault of the authorities.[59] Generally applicants are not required to utilise extraordinary, as opposed to ordinary, procedures which could shorten the length of proceedings.[60]

6. Conduct of the authorities

II–150 Even in legal systems applying the principle that the procedural initiative lies with the parties, the courts have an obligation to ensure trials progress with sufficient expedition and will not necessarily escape responsibility where the parties are themselves largely responsible for dragging out proceedings unnecessarily.[61] In extreme cases their passivity in allowing such conduct can call into doubt the credibility of the legal system.[62]

The Court also has regard to the principle of proper administration of justice, namely, that domestic courts are under a duty to deal properly with the cases before them.[63] Domestic court decisions concerning the taking of evidence, to join cases, and adjourn for particular reasons, are therefore likely to be given some weight and justify the length of proceedings, at least up to a certain point. For example in *Ewing v UK*,[64] the joining of three cases, which delayed the trial, was not shown to be arbitrary or unreasonable, or as causing undue delay giving account to the due administration of justice. However, the Commission in *Reilly v Ireland*[65] noted that the decision taken to separate murder and burglary proceedings meant that the responsibility to ensure a speedy determination of the charges was more onerous given the potential impact on length of the proceedings. Further, while it may be important for the proper administration of justice to ensure that criminal proceedings are concluded before related civil matters are litigated, the national authorities must organise their legal systems to ensure that any resulting adjournment does not lead to delay which is a priori excessive.[66] Where delay is caused by the repeated remittal of a case within one set of proceedings, the Court has found a serious deficiency in the judicial system for which the State bears responsibility.[67] Mistakes by courts, for example, concerning jurisdiction can also cause delay in breach of requirements.[68]

Excuses as regards backlog or administrative difficulties are not accepted since States are under an obligation to organise their judicial systems in such a way that their courts can meet the Convention's requirements.[69] A temporary backlog before a court will not entail liability provided the authorities take reasonably prompt

[59] *Antyushina v Russia*, September 23, 2010, paras 54–57.
[60] *Union Alimentaria SA v Spain*, July 7, 1989, para.35.
[61] e.g. *Pafitis,* fn.47 above, para.93.
[62] *Berlin v Luxembourg*, July 15, 2003, 17 years for disputed divorce proceedings; see also *Papageorgiou v Greece*, October 22, 1997, 1997–VI, No.54, para.48; *Van Vlimmeren v Netherlands*, September 26, 2000, para.35.
[63] *Boddaert v Belgium*, fn.44 above, para.39.
[64] See fn.53 above.
[65] *Reilly v Ireland*, (21624/93) (Rep.) February 22, 1995.
[66] *Rezette v Luxembourg*, July 13, 2004.
[67] *Wierciszewska v Poland*, November 25, 2003, para.46. See also *Svetlana Orlova*, fn.4 above, paras 48–50, deficiencies disclosed by repeated referrals for supervisory review and failure to ensure the case was properly examined before an independent and impartial tribunal.
[68] *Gheorghe*, fn.4 above, para.58.
[69] e.g. *Pelissier and Sassi v France*, fn.35 above, para.74.

remedial action to deal with the exceptional situation.[70] Where the state of affairs becomes prolonged or a matter of structural organisation, provisional methods, such as giving priorities, are no longer sufficient and the State cannot postpone further the adoption of effective measures.[71] However, the obligation on States to organise judicial systems to comply with the requirements of Art.6 does not apply in the same way to a Constitutional Court which has a role of guardian that may render it necessary to take other considerations into account, e.g. the importance of cases in political and social terms rather than chronological order.[72] However, that factor will not always justify the dragging out of proceedings, in particular where time is of some significance as in a case relevant to Roma childrens' education.[73]

Matters outside the authorities' control will not be held against them where they do what is within their power to progress the proceedings, for example, delays arising from the execution of letters rogatory in another jurisdiction[74] or difficulties arising from a strike by the Bar.[75] The Court has not taken into account any delaying effect of a reference to Art.177 to the European Court of Justice, since this would adversely affect the system introduced by the EEC Treaty and offset its aim.[76]

Where specific periods of delay are attributable to courts, e.g. delay in the transmission of a file or documents from one instance to another or delay in issuing judgment, violations may be found where the rest of the proceedings were otherwise not lacking in diligence.[77] Delay during the investigation stage alone may be enough, where there are identifiable lapses in any activity, to disclose a violation.[78] The Court has also referred to the failure of the Government to provide convincing

[70] e.g. *Bucholz v Germany*, May 6, 1981, Series A, No.42, 3 E.H.R.R. 597, alleged economic recession causing backlog in labour courts: five years over three instances disclosed no violation since the authorities showed consciousness of responsibilities and had made efforts; *Foti v Italy*, December 10, 1982, Series A, No.56, troubles in Reggio causing unusual political and social climate taken into account but violation still disclosed; *Lynch v UK*, (9504/06) (Dec.) October 6, 2009, temporary backlog and legitimate prioritising of prisoners' applications under a new procedure did not lead to unreasonable delay.

[71] *Zimmerman and Steiner v Switzerland*, July 13, 1983, Series A, No.66, 6 E.H.R.R. 17, where there had been a steady increase in volume of administrative litigation since 1969, such that there was no temporary excess of work but a question of structural organisation to which the authorities had not given a satisfactory response. Since there were three and a half years during which the case was largely stationary, there was a violation.

[72] *Süssman v Germany*, September 16, 1996, R.J.D. 1996–IV, No.15, given the unique circumstances of reunification and the serious social implications of the disputes, the Constitutional Court was entitled to give priority to 300,000 employment cases—no violation for proceedings lasting three years, four months. Similar reasoning in *Gast and Popp v Germany*, February 25, 2000, ECHR 2000–II, grouping of cases to obtain comprehensive view of espionage and treason issues, no violation for two years, and ten months; and in *Maltzan and Others v Germany*, (71916/01), (71917/01) and (10260/02) (Dec.) March 2, 2005, ECHR 2005–V, no violation for over five years, five months; *Jankovic v Croatia*, (43440/98) (Dec.) October 12, 2000, ECHR 2000–X, reasonable for Constitutional Court to group cases to obtain comprehensive view of pension rights problems.

[73] *Orsus v Croatia*, March 16, 2010, paras 108–109, violation for over four years and one month.

[74] *Wloch v Poland*, October 19, 2000, ECHR 2000–XI, paras 149–150, that, together with the complexity of the case, justified six years of criminal proceedings.

[75] *Pafitis*, fn.47 above, para.96, the Athens Bar was regarded as an independent professional association.

[76] *Pafitis*, fn.47 above, para.95.

[77] e.g. in *Reilly*, fn.65 above, the Commission commented adversely on 12 months for the Supreme Court to render judgment and 14 months for the trial judge to approve the transcript of evidence; in *Bunkate v Netherlands*, May 26, 1993, Series A, No.248–B, the Court singled out 15 and a half months for the court of appeal to send the case file to the Supreme Court; *Kudla*, fn.55 above, para.130, a delay of nearly one year and eight months in holding a retrial after the original conviction was quashed.

[78] *Marpa Zeeland*, see fn.12 above.

explanations for periods of delay.[79] In some cases, the Court has found no violation on the basis that there has been steady and regular judicial activity in a case, without any substantial period of inactivity.[80] Some tardiness at a particular stage may also be acceptable where overall, taking into account the number of levels of jurisdiction, the time taken is not unreasonable.[81] Conversely, in cases of particularly excessive delay the time taken may, per se, appear too long and the burden will weigh particularly heavily on the Government to provide an explanation.[82]

UK length cases

Civil:
Bullerwell[83] (disablement benefit proceedings) under seven years: manifestly-ill founded.
Robins[84] (costs) over four years: violation.
Davies[85] (company director disqualification) over four years: violation.
Somjee[86] (industrial tribunal/racial harassment) over eight years for longest of three sets of interlocking proceedings: violation.
Foley[87] (contract) over 14 years: violation.
Price and Lowe[88] (property) over 12 years: violation.
Blake[89] (State claim for profits from breach of Official Secrets) over nine years: violation.
Richard Anderson[90] (challenge to statutory notices) Six years, eight months: violation.

Criminal:
Howarth[91] over two years for an Attorney General's reference on sentence: violation.
Mellors[92]: over three years, eight months.
Massey[93]: four years, nine months: violation.
Henworth[94]: six years (including two retrials): violation.
Crowther[95]: eight years, five months (including confiscation procedure): violation.
Bullen and Soneji[96]: five years, six months (including confiscation procedure): violation.

79 e.g. *Barfuss*, see fn.53, paras 82–83, violation for criminal proceedings taking three years, ten months and seven days.
80 e.g. *Humen*, fn.53 above, para.69; *Punzelt v Czech Republic*, April 25, 2000, para.96.
81 *Nuutinen v Finland*, June 27, 2000, ECHR 2000–VIII, para.110; *Motsnik*, fn.4 above, para.42.
82 e.g. *Schaal v Luxembourg*, fn.2 above, six years for one criminal instance; *Comingersoll SA v Portugal*, April 6, 2000, ECHR 2000–IV, 17 years for enforcement of bills of exchange.
83 (48013/99) (Dec.) December 12, 2002.
84 See fn.10 above.
85 *Davies v UK*, July 16, 2002.
86 *Somjee v UK*, October 15, 2002.
87 *Foley v UK*, October 22, 2002.
88 *Price and Lowe v UK*, July 29, 2003.
89 *Blake v UK*, September 26, 2006.
90 *Richard Anderson v UK*, February 9, 2010.
91 *Howarth v UK*, September 21, 2000.
92 *Mellors v UK*, July 17, 2003.
93 *Massey v UK*, November 16, 2004.
94 *Henworth v UK*, November 2, 2004.
95 *Crowther*, fn.25 above, paras 48–59.
96 *Bullen and Soneji v UK*, January 8, 2009, paras 48–59.

18. Presence in court

Key provision:

Article 6, paras 1 (right to a fair trial) and 3(c) (right to defend oneself in person). II–151

Key case-law:

Goddi v Italy, April 9, 1984, Series A, No.76, 6 E.H.R.R. 457; *Colozza v Italy*, February 12, 1985, Series A, No.89, 7 E.H.R.R. 516; *Monnell and Morris v UK*, March 2, 1987, Series A, No.115, 10 E.H.R.R. 205; *Kamasinki v Austria*, December 19, 1989, Series A, No.168, 13 E.H.R.R. 36; *FCB v Italy*, August 28, 1991, Series A, No.208–B, 14 E.H.R.R. 909; *Kremsow v Austria*, September 21, 1993, Series A, No.268, 17 E.H.R.R. 322; *Poitrimol v France*, November 23, 1993, Series A, No.277, 18 E.H.R.R. 130; *Zana v Turkey*, November 25, 1997, R.J.D. 1997–VII, No.57, 27 E.H.R.R. 667; *Sejdovic v Italy*, March 1, 2006, ECHR 2006–II; *Hermi v Italy*, October 18, 2006, ECHR 2006–. . .

1. General considerations

The applicant, generally, has a right to be present during criminal proceedings. The object and purpose of Art.6, paras 1 and 3(c)–(e) presuppose the accused's presence. It is considered to be of capital importance that a defendant appear, both because of his right to a hearing and the need to verify the accuracy of his statements and compare them with those of the witnesses.[1] This is not an absolute right, as in special circumstances where witnesses have to be heard anonymously or where the accused is unruly.[2] Nor will claimed ill-health necessarily require an adjournment.[3] The Commission in *Colozza* stated, however, that the rights of the defence could not be said to have been respected if the applicant had not been given the "possibility" of attending. In this context, the authorities must show requisite diligence in ensuring the accused's right to be present in an effective manner, having regard to the prominent place which the right to a fair trial enjoys in a democratic society.[4] Furthermore, the right to defend oneself in person is the basis of the principle that an accused should be able to participate effectively in the proceedings and this might not be satisfied by mere presence, as in cases where the person is labouring under a disability or difficulty of some kind. II–152

The most difficult problems have arisen in conviction *in absentia* cases where States retain the right to continue proceedings where an accused absconds or fails to appear. The refusal to re-open such proceedings, without any indication that the accused has waived his or her right to be present during the trial, has been characterised as a "flagrant denial of justice".[5]

[1] *Poitrimol v France*, November 23, 1993, Series A, No.277, 18 E.H.R.R. 130, para.35; *Ninn-Hansen v Denmark*, (28972/95) (Dec.) May 18, 1999, ECHR 1999–V.

[2] *Colozza v Italy*, (Rep.) February 12, 1985, Series A, No.89, 7 E.H.R.R. 516, para.17. See also (31066/96) (Dec.) January 14, 1998, where the applicant, through his own deliberate conduct, failed to appear at first instance and appeal and it was not unreasonable for the courts to continue without him.

[3] See *Ninn-Hansen*, fn.1 above, where the court held on the basis of medical evidence that, after a stroke, the applicant's state of health did not preclude his presence at the remainder of the trial and continued the final oral pleadings in his absence.

[4] *FCB v Italy* August 28, 1991, Series A, No.208–B, 14 E.H.R.R. 909, para.35.

[5] *Sejdovic v Italy*, March 1, 2006, ECHR 2006–II, para.84.

2. Waiver

II–153 Waiver by an accused of his right to be present may be possible but must be unequivocal and attended by the minimum safeguards commensurate to the importance of the right.[6] Where an applicant, represented by two counsel, had been informed of the appeal hearing but did not apply to attend by the deadline of five days beforehand, the court was entitled to take his conduct as a tacit but unequivocal waiver, in particular as there were no excessive procedural formalities involved in making the requisite application.[7] However, in *Zana v Turkey*, where the applicant was not present before the National Security Court which convicted him, the Court found that the procedural objection raised by the applicant on previous appearance in the Assize Court and his refusal to speak Turkish did not give rise to any implicit waiver of his right to appear.

Nor is mere failure to appear sufficient for waiver. In *FCB*, where the applicant was detained in the Netherlands, the Milan Court of Appeal held a retrial in his absence although informed by his counsel that he was detained abroad. The Court considered that the applicant had not expressed the wish to waive attendance and was not impressed by the argument that he had used deliberate delaying tactics in not providing the Italian authorities with his address. The crucial consideration was that the Italian authorities were aware that the applicant was subject to proceedings and it was hardly compatible with the diligence required in ensuring defence rights were effectively exercised to continue the trial without taking further steps to clarify the position.[8] Failure to attend after a notification which has not made clear what the hearing is about will not amount to waiver.[9]

3. Opportunity for rehearing on the merits

II–154 Proceedings *in absentia* may not be incompatible with the Convention if the person concerned has the possibility of obtaining a new hearing complying with Art.6, namely which provides a fresh determination of the merits of the charge, both factual and legal elements included.[10] Remedies which put the burden on the applicant to show that he had not tried to evade justice, been prevented from attending by force majeure, or that the authorities had not complied with applicable rules of service have been found insufficient.[11] However, although the burden must not be on the applicant to prove that he was not seeking to evade justice or that his

[6] e.g. *Poitrimol v France*, fn.1 above, para.31.

[7] *Hermi v Italy*, October 18, 2006, ECHR 2006–. . . , paras 89–103. See also *Battisti v France*, (2888796/05) (Dec.) December 12, 2006, where the applicant was convicted and sentenced to life imprisonment *in absentia* after he had fled, he had knowledge of the proceedings in which he instructed counsel throughout and could be regarded as unequivocally waiving his right to be present.

[8] Also *Kremzow v Austria*, September 21, 1993, Series A, No.268, 17 E.H.R.R. 322, a failure by the applicant to apply to attend the appeal hearing did not constitute a waiver, particularly as domestic procedures provided that, even without a request, the accused should attend where necessary in the interests of justice and there was a positive duty on the State to ensure his attendance; *Jones v UK*, (30900/02) (Dec.) September 9, 2003, no waiver from failure of accused to attend trial where there was no established practice of trials *in absentia*.

[9] *Sibgatullin v Russia*, April 23, 2009, paras 48–52.

[10] *Medenica v Switzerland*, (20491/92) (Dec.) June 14, 2001, ECHR 2001–VI; *Jones*, fn.8 above; *Sejdovic*, fn.5 above, para.85.

[11] *Colozza v Italy*, fn.2 above, para.29; *Stamoulakatos v Greece*, (Rep.) May 20, 1992, Series A, No.271.

absence was due to force majeure, the domestic courts are entitled to assess whether the accused showed good cause for his absence or whether there was anything in the case file to warrant finding that he had been absent for reasons beyond his control.[12] Where an applicant, by his own deliberate conduct, was unable to attend the trial, the Court found that his conviction *in absentia* and the refusal to grant him a retrial did not amount to a disproportionate penalty.[13]

Domestic procedures must provide, with sufficient certainty, that the applicant would have the opportunity of appearing at a new trial to present his defence. In *Sejdovic v Italy*, the time-limit for applying for a re-opening was ten days, which was too short given the obstacles facing the applicant, who was arrested overseas with no immediate access to an Italian lawyer.[14]

4. Exclusion or absence from the hearing

Where proceedings concern only points of law, no issue may arise from the refusal to allow an accused to attend in addition to his lawyer. The Court considers that personal attendance of an accused at the appeal hearing does not take on the same crucial significance as it does for trial. In *Kremzow v Austria*, where the applicant was excluded from a hearing on points of nullity (law), the Court found his presence was not required by Art.6, paras 1 or 3(c), his lawyer being able to attend and make points on his behalf.[15] There was a breach, however, where the applicant was excluded from the hearing of the appeal on sentence, which involved an increase in sentence to life imprisonment, committal to special prison and a ruling on the motive for the crime which the jury had been unable to establish. Since the assessment of the applicant's character, state of mind and motivation were significant to the proceedings, and there was much at stake for the applicant, fairness required that he, as well as his lawyer, be present and able to participate.[16] It is not decisive, where domestic law requires an accused to be present at the appeal, that the accused fails to make a request to attend as the State may then be under a positive duty to enable him to attend to "defend himself in person".[17] This may be contrasted with *Hermi v Italy*, where the detained applicant was informed of the appeal hearing but took no step to contact his lawyers or make the necessary II–155

[12] *Sejdovic*, see fn.5 above, para.88.

[13] *Medenica*, fn.10 above, reference to the margin of appreciation to be accorded to the State authorities—the Swiss court found that the applicant had made inaccurate and equivocal statements to the US court deliberately to secure a decision (a restraining order) rendering his attendance at trial impossible. This assessment was not found to be arbitrary or based on manifestly erroneous premises.

[14] *Sejdovic*, see fn.5 above, para.104.

[15] See also *Kamasinski v Austria*, December 19, 1989, Series A, No.168, 13 E.H.R.R. 36, para.106; *Pobornikoff v Austria*, October 3, 2000, para.27; concerning the special nature of the proceedings before the Court of Cassation in France, see *Meftah v France*, July 26, 2002, ECHR 2002–VII, where the inability of the applicants to attend an oral hearing was not a problem in a system where only specialised counsel were allowed to appear; *Hermi*, see fn.7 above, para.60.

[16] Similar violation in *Pobornikoff*, fn.15 above, para.32; *Belziuk v Poland*, March 25, 1998, Reports 1998–II, paras 38–40; *Sobolewski v Poland (No.2)* June 9, 2009, paras 37–44, presence required at appeal against conviction, where facts and evidential issues were in dispute. Contrast *Hermi*, fn.7 above, paras 85–88, where the applicant had not put any factual elements into dispute and the court could not increase the sentence, his absence at the appeal hearing did not disclose a violation.

[17] *Pobornikoff*, fn.15 above, para.32, citing *Kremzow*, fn.8 above, para.68, where in Austrian law a court should have an appellant brought before it if his personal presence appears necessary in the interest of justice.

request under domestic law to be present and was accordingly found to have waived his right to appear.

However, where the prosecution is present at an appeal, the principle of adversariality and equality of arms requires that the court ensure the presence of the applicant, or at the very least his lawyer, irrespective of the type of issues which might be at stake.[18]

In leave to appeal proceedings, absence of the accused and his lawyer may be compatible where the nature of the issues is not such as to require presence and having regard to the prior proceedings (in particular previous legal representation and legal advice as to the prospects of appeal). In these circumstances the interests of justice and fairness may be met by the possibility of presenting written submissions to the court.[19]

In *Kamasinski v Austria*, in rejecting a complaint of discrimination in that accused persons at liberty were not excluded from appeal hearings, the Court appeared to give weight to the difficulties that attach to the attendance of prisoners which do not apply to accused persons at liberty or civil parties. It was also found acceptable under Art.6 for an applicant prisoner to participate in the proceedings for leave to appeal against conviction via videolink. This was where the procedure followed the legitimate aims of the prevention of crime and protection of witnesses and was compatible with the effective exercise of defence rights.[20]

As concerns civil proceedings, Art.6 does not guarantee the right to personal presence before a civil court; there is only the general right to present one's case effectively before the court and to enjoy equality of arms with the opposing side. In general, representation by a lawyer may be sufficient in the absence of a detained plaintiff.[21] However, where the claim concerned allegations of ill-treatment, the prisoner's evidence was an important part of his case and his presence was necessary to ensure adversariality.[22] Where the case concerned entitlement to reside in particular housing and did not require any personal testimony, no violation arose when the accused was unable to attend.[23]

Where proceedings involve a decision affecting a large number of individuals, particularly those conducted before constitutional courts following a challenge to legislation, it is not always required or even possible that every individual concerned is heard before the court, and no breach of Art.6, para.1 arises from the inability of an individual applicant to be present.[24]

[18] e.g. *Maksimov v Azerbaijan,* October 8, 2009, paras 40–43; *Zhuk v Ukraine*, October 21, 2010, paras 32–35.

[19] *Monnell and Morris v UK*, March 2, 1987, Series A, No.115, 10 E.H.R.R. 205.

[20] *Marcello Viola v Italy*, October 5, 2006.

[21] *Khuzhin v Russia*, October 23, 2008, para.105, violation since after the applicants' lawyer walked out in protest against their absence, the court took no steps to allow the applicants to give instructions to their lawyer or to obtain another lawyer so that they could effectively participate in the hearing (paras 103–109).

[22] *Kovalev v Russia*, May 10, 2007, paras 33–38.

[23] *Kozlov v Russia*, September 17, 2009, paras 39–49.

[24] *Wendenburg v Germany*, February 6, 2003, ECHR 2003–II, where it was sufficient that associations were present to represent professional interests; *Gavella v Croatia*, (33244/02) (Dec.) July 11, 2006.

5. Effective participation in the proceedings

Where children are concerned, the Court frowns upon subjecting them to the full rigour and formality of an adult-style criminal trial. Adjustments should be made to facilitate their understanding of what is going on; the mere fact that they might be represented by a lawyer not being sufficient.[25] II–156

Conversely, where an adult has difficulties in following court proceedings, this has not always infringed the fairness of the proceedings. In *Stanford v UK*, where the applicant complained of poor acoustics in the court room, it was sufficient that the applicant's lawyer was able to inform him what was being said.[26] Where an applicant was on anti-depressant medication, the Court noted that the trial court had verified that he was fit to plead and that he was represented by a lawyer.[27] Thus, there appears to be an obligation on domestic courts to ensure that an accused is able to follow the proceedings sufficiently, although it is not altogether clear how far, for an adult, the presence of a lawyer makes up for any difficulties. Where an appeal court was notified of an accused's hearing impairment but did not take any steps such as obtaining a medical certificate or obtaining a hearing aid and the accused's lawyers failed to turn up, the Court put emphasis in its finding of a violation on the court's failure in those circumstances to ensure that a lawyer had been present.[28] Use of metal cages for the accused in court has not posed a problem of fairness where he could still communicate freely with his lawyers.[29]

Even where it is sufficient at an appeal hearing that a lawyer represents the absent accused, this will be nullified if the accused has had no opportunity to communicate with the lawyer or to give him instructions.[30]

Cross-reference

Part IIA, s.15: Legal representation in criminal proceedings.
Part IIA, s.20: Public hearing and judgment.

[25] e.g. *V v UK*, paras 85–91, where the child accused was unable to participate effectively in the public and formal criminal trial procedures in a case attracting intense media attention and public emotion. *SC v UK*, June 15, 2004, where the majority held that the 11–year-old should have been tried in a specialised and informal tribunal (see, however, strong dissent from the President and Vice-President of the Section, distinguishing this case from *V* as the child was not subject to a traumatic atmosphere and the court had properly assessed whether he was able to participate).

[26] *Stanford v UK*, February 24, 1994, Series A, No.282–A.

[27] *Liebreich v Germany*, (30443/03) (Dec.) January 8, 2008.

[28] *Timergaliyev v Russia*, October 14, 2008, paras 50–60.

[29] *Ashot Harutyunyan v Armenia*, June 15, 2010, paras 136–40.

[30] *Seliwiak v Poland*, July 21, 2009, paras 58–64.

19. Presumption of innocence

Key provision:

II–157 Article 6, para.2 (presumption of innocence).

Key case-law:

Minelli v Switzerland, March 25, 1983, Series A, No.62, 5 E.H.R.R. 554; *Lutz v Germany*, August 25, 1987, Series A, No.123; *Schenk v Switzerland*, July 12, 1988, Series A, No.140, 13 E.H.R.R. 242; *Salabiaku v France*, October 7, 1988, Series A, No.141–A, 13 E.H.R.R. 379; *Sekanina v Austria*, August 25, 1993, Series A, No.266–A, 10 E.H.R.R. 182; *Allenet de Ribemont v France*, February 10, 1995, Series A, No.308, 20 E.H.R.R. 557; *John Murray v UK*, February 8, 1996, R.J.D. 1996–I, No.1, 22 E.H.R.R. 29; *Leutscher v Netherlands*, March 26, 1996, R.J.D., 1996–II, No.6, 24 E.H.R.R. 181; *Heaney and McGuinness v Ireland,* December 21, 2000, ECHR 2000–XII; *Daktaras v Lithuania*, October 10, 2000, ECHR 2000–X; *Phillips v UK*, July 5, 2001, ECHR 2001–VII; *Butkevicius v Lithuania*, March 26, 2002, ECHR 2002–II; *O v Norway, Ringvold v Norway, Y v Norway* and *Hammern v Norway*, February 11, 2003, ECHR 2003–II.

1. General considerations

II–158 The presumption of innocence applies to persons charged with criminal offences.[1] The principle has primarily had relevance in regard to the different ways domestic systems deal with factual presumptions and the evidentiary burden of proof; the way in which courts penalise defendants in costs or issue qualified acquittals; and the prohibition of public statements of guilt by officials.

It is construed quite narrowly in its application. It does not cover the detention of remand prisoners in the same regime as convicted prisoners[2] or the obligation to surrender to detention prior to the hearing of an appeal.[3] The Court has commented that while it is not per se contrary to Art.6, para.2 for the authorities to enforce a monetary penalty before the decisions become final, such measures must be confined within reasonable limits, leaving it open as to whether issues could arise in a situation where an applicant suffered serious detriment disproportionate to the interests pursued.[4]

[1] However, in *Albert and Le Compte v Belgium*, February 10, 1983, Series A, No.58, 5 E.H.R.R. 533, the Court held that the presumption of innocence applied to disciplinary proceedings against doctors, whether they were civil or criminal, the principles set out Art.6, paras 2 and 3 being implicit in para.1. See also *A v Norway*, April 9, 2009, paras 46–47, information given by the police and published by the press about the applicant's suspect status did not disclose a situation of "criminal charge under Art. 6" but considerations as to presumption of innocence were taken into account in determining whether the defamation proceedings complied with Art.8.

[2] *Peers v Greece*, April 19, 2001, ECHR 2001–III, para.78.

[3] *Cuvillers and Da Luz v France*, (55052/00) (Dec.) September 16, 2003.

[4] *Janosevic v Sweden*, July 23, 2002, ECHR 2002–VII, paras 106–110, where the enforcement of substantial tax surcharges could have had serious implications notwithstanding the ability to obtain repayment on appeal, the Court noted that the State's financial interests weighed less heavily as it did not concern payment of due taxes but on the facts of the case no adverse enforcement had in fact taken place.

Presumption of innocence has been held to apply after conviction while there are pending appeal proceedings. Authorities may refer to the fact of conviction but should take care not to make statements that might appear to approve of the conviction, prejudge the appeal verdict or encourage the appeal court to confirm it.[5]

2. Burden of proof: evidential presumptions

Rules which impose presumptions of law and fact which act to place the burden on the defendant to rebut them are not contrary to Art.6, para.2. They must, however, be confined within reasonable limits which take into account the importance of what is at stake and the rights of the defence. In particular, the operation of presumptions must not strip a trial court of any effective power of assessment of the facts or guilt. **II–159**

Thus, in *Salabiaku v France*, where the applicant took delivery of a locked trunk which proved to contain drugs, he was subject to a presumption of responsibility. Since, however, the domestic courts maintained a freedom of assessment and gave attention to the facts of the case, quashing one conviction, the Court found no violation.[6] Where, in *Pham Hoang v France*, a presumption was applied to the driver of the car involved in a drugs deal who was convicted of possession, the Court found that it was not irrebuttable nor prevented the driver from raising a defence (e.g. force majeure, unavoidable mistake or necessity). Since the court refrained from any automatic reliance on the presumption, basing its finding of guilt on a cumulation of factors (the circumstances of the arrest and his earlier involvement in the gang's activities), the presumption was not applied in a matter incompatible with Art.6, para.2.

Similarly in a Maltese case, the Commission found that it was acceptable to impose liability on a company director for customs offences committed by the company unless he could show that the offence was committed without his knowledge and that he exercised all due diligence to prevent the commission of the offence. This was not an irrebuttable or self-contradictory presumption and the courts retained a genuine freedom of assessment in determining whether an offence had been committed by the applicant.[7] In cases where the owners of pitbull terriers and other specified breeds were faced with a presumption that the dog was dangerous unless proved otherwise, the Commission found no violation since there was the opportunity to disprove the assumption and the courts retained an area of assessment, albeit limited, where the matter was put in issue.[8]

However difficult presumptions are to rebut, as long as the applicant is left with some means of defence, it is likely that no violation will arise, as in the Dutch imposition of strict liability on a car owner for traffic offences involving the car.[9] The Court has talked of balancing the rights of the defence against the importance of

[5] *Konstas v Greece*, May 24, 2011.

[6] There was a defence of "unavoidable error" and the court gave weight to the fact that he had been warned by an official not to take the trunk unless he was sure it was his and therefore he had been put on notice and could have checked the contents.

[7] (16641/90) (Dec.) December 10, 1991. See also *Radio France v France*, March 30, 2004, ECHR 2004–X, where the presumption of responsibility of the editorial director for defamatory remarks made on the air was within reasonable limits.

[8] e.g. *Bates v UK*, (26280/95), *Foster v UK*, (28846/95) and *Brock v UK*, (26279/95) (Decs.) January 16, 1996.

[9] *Falk v Netherlands*, (66273/01) (Dec.) October 19, 2004, where the car owner could show that the car had been used against his will or that the police could have stopped the driver.

what is at stake, indicating that context may also be of relevance, as in taxation, fundamental to State's financial interests, where sanctions to ensure submission of correct information may be regarded as essential to the functioning of the system.[10]

In contrast, where an applicant was convicted of malicious prosecution because her criminal complaint alleging sexual harassment by her employer had been subject to a decision of "non-lieu" (lack of evidence to go to trial), the Court found that she had been subject to a double presumption of guilt significantly undermining the guarantees of Art.6; as the fact of the "non-lieu" and an assumption that she must have known that her complaints had no foundation removed from the court any role in assessing the facts and issues.[11]

Presumptions drawn as to the illicit source of income during proceedings after conviction for drugs offences for the purposes of imposing a confiscation order did not offend Art.6, para.2 as they were part of the sentencing process and assessment of the applicant's character and conduct after he had been found guilty of the charge.[12] If allegations were made of a nature or degree as to amount to the bringing of a new charge however, Art.6, para.2 might become applicable.[13] It is also a different matter where confiscation orders are based on offences for which the applicant was acquitted, since where it had not been found that the person had committed the crime, any measure based on the alleged advantage derived from the crime could only be based on a presumption of guilt.[14]

Even without any formal presumptions of fact or law, the way in which the courts approach the evidence may raise issues. A breach of the presumption of innocence was found where an Austrian court proceeded to convict the owner of a car for causing injury by negligence on the basis of assumptions that it was mainly the applicant who drove the car, even though other family members drove the car on occasion and there was no evidence to identify him as the driver. The way in which the courts approached the evidence, asserting that it was for the applicant to put forward a contrary version of events to the prosecution case, was perceived as going too far and giving the impression of a preconceived view of the applicant's guilt.[15]

3. Statements made by judges or courts

(a) *Comments or incidents during the proceedings*

II–160 The principle of presumption of innocence requires that when carrying out their duties the members of a court should not have any preconceived idea that the applicant has committed the offence charged.[16] A distinction is drawn between

[10] *Janosevic*, fn.4 above; also *Radio France*, fn.7 above, concerning the importance of preventing defamatory publications.

[11] *Klouvi v France*, June 21, 2011, paras 44–52.

[12] *Phillips v UK*, July 5, 2001, ECHR 2001–VII, para.35. See, however, the dissenting opinion of Sir Nicolas Bratza finding that Art.6, para.2 clearly could extend beyond conviction into the confiscation proceedings but found that the operation of the statutory presumptions in the applicant's case did not exceed reasonable and fair limits. See also *Grayson and Barnham v UK*, September 23, 2008, concerning the burden of proof placed on convicted drug traffickers to show the source of their assets was honest; the issue was examined under Art.6, para.1, but not found to disclose any unfairness.

[13] *Geerings v Netherlands*, March 1, 2007. Contrast *Walsh v UK*, (43384/05) (Dec.) November 21, 2006, where separate civil recovery proceedings for unlawfully obtained assets did not bring the criminal guarantees into play as there was no specific finding of guilt of offences and the judge was careful not to rely on any conduct for which the applicant had been acquitted.

[14] e.g. *Phillips*, fn.12 above, para.35

[15] *Telfner v Austria*, March 20, 2001.

[16] e.g. *Barbera, Messegué and Jabardo v Spain*, December 6, 1988, Series A, No.146, para.77.

statements made reflecting the opinion that the person is guilty and statements which merely describe a "state of suspicion", the latter being unobjectionable prior to the final determination by the court.[17] Where a judge, at a press conference before the conclusion of the trial, made the comment that she had not decided whether to convict or partially acquit, this disclosed a preconceived view of the applicant's partial guilt and infringed Art.6, para.2, as did her suggestion that the accused prove their innocence.[18]

Statements made by a judge in issuing provisional measures of seizure pending criminal proceedings thus did not fall foul of the presumption of innocence, where they referred to the existence of suspicion and not a finding of guilt.[19] Nor did a report by a prosecutor giving the opinion that grounds existed for imposing pre-trial detention.[20]

The presumption of innocence excludes a finding of guilt outside the criminal proceedings before the competent trial court and it is irrelevant to a finding of breach that procedural safeguards apply in parallel proceedings which prejudge the matters at trial.[21]

Presentation of the accused in court in prison dress has been held contrary to the presumption of innocence as giving the public an impression of guilt.[22]

(b) Orders on acquittal or termination of proceedings

Article 6, para.2 applies to criminal proceedings in their entirety, not solely the part dealing with the merits. Thus comments made by judges on the termination of proceedings or following acquittal which reflect the opinion that the applicant is guilty will violate the presumption of innocence.[23] Thus in *Minelli v Switzerland*, where a court, in declining to follow the normal rule of awarding costs to the accused, remarked that he "very probably" would have been convicted but for the termination of the proceedings due to rules of prescription, a violation was found. Where an applicant was acquitted by one court and refused costs by a different court, the presumption of innocence guarantee still applied to the second proceedings and was violated where the second court found that serious grounds for suspecting him still existed. Some voicing of suspicion regarding an accused might be conceivable before the conclusion of the proceedings but it was not permissible to rely on such suspicions after an acquittal became final.[24] This may be contrasted with cases, which are terminated or discontinued without an acquittal, where some **II–161**

[17] e.g. *Lutz v Germany*, August 25, 1987, Series A, No.123, para.62; *Leutscher v Netherlands*, March 26, 1996, R.J.D. 1996–II, No.6, 24 E.H.R.R. 181, para.31. See also *Daktaras v Lithuania*, (42905/98) (Dec.) January 11, 2000, where a comment by the Regional Court to the accused as "one of the leaders of the underworld" reflected the witnesses' testimony so far and did not suggest that the applicant was guilty.

[18] *Lavents v Latvia*, November 28, 2002, paras 126–127.

[19] *Gokceli v Turkey*, March 4, 2003, para.46, the Court appeared to give weight to the legal context rather than the actual terms used by the judge which on their face appeared to refer to the offence having been committed.

[20] *Marchiani v France*, (30392/03) (Dec.) May 27, 2008.

[21] *Bohmer v Germany*, October 3, 2002, para.67, revocation of suspended sentence proceedings which found that an offence had been committed on probation before the actual trial of the charges had been concluded.

[22] *Samoila and Coinca v Romania*, March 4, 2008, paras 99–100, it may be noted that the violation was also based on various prejudicial statements made by officials during the proceedings.

[23] e.g. *Minelli v Switzerland*, March 25, 1983, Series A, No.62, 5 E.H.R.R. 554, para.37.

[24] *Sekanina v Austria*, August 25, 1993, Series A, No.266–A, 10 E.H.R.R. 182, para.30.

comment on the existence of suspicion may be allowable, as long as this does not amount in substance to a determination of guilt.[25]

Where, therefore, a judge makes remarks which expressly or by clear implication attribute guilt to the acquitted defendant, there is likely to be a violation. In *Moody v UK*[26] and *Lochrie v UK*,[27] the judge's comments on disallowing the costs for a failed prosecution for sale of obscene material, which were to the effect that material was obscene and that the applicants should nonetheless be penalised for dealing with it, were incompatible with the presumption of innocence. Conversely, in *DF v UK*, where the judge refused a full costs order on acquittal commenting that the case stank of greed and that the applicant had brought the case upon himself by not saying anything to clear himself during the investigation, the Commission found that that the refusal of costs was not made on the basis of any continuing suspicion being harboured and that, though the judge referred to greed, his comments could not be interpreted as implying any finding of dishonesty which was an element of many criminal offences.[28]

(c) Findings or comments in other proceedings

II–162 Whether Art.6, para.2 applies to proceedings following an acquittal depends on whether there is a link with the prior criminal proceedings. Such a link will be disclosed where the facts or conduct in issue is essentially the same as that in the criminal proceedings.[29]

Where issues related to criminal charges on which a person has been acquitted arise in civil cases, courts may deal with the aspect of civil responsibility arising from the same facts but must regard themselves as bound by the finding of the criminal court with regard to criminal responsibility. Therefore no violation was found where labour courts dismissed a teacher who had been acquitted of the charge of supplying drugs to a boy who committed suicide under their influence. The domestic court referred to the surrounding circumstances in which the teacher failed to help the boy in appropriate ways rather than contradicting the finding of the criminal court in its acquittal.[30] A violation arose where courts, in rejecting defamation claims by the applicant who had been acquitted of some charges and was pending trial on others, made statements clearly giving their opinion that he had committed the criminal acts concerned.[31] Where the applicant was subject to compulsory retirement in disciplinary proceedings, the Court found that this procedure was not dependent on or linked to the criminal proceedings in which the charges had been dropped due to

[25] *Baars v Netherlands*, October 28, 2003, where in refusing costs for a prosecution terminated due to delay before a verdict, the court stated that the applicant had forged the document, thus going beyond a mere reference to the existence of a state of suspicion.

[26] (22613/93) (Rep.) January 16, 1996.

[27] (22614/93) (Rep.) January 18, 1996.

[28] (22401/93) (Dec.) October 24, 1995; see also, e.g. *Byrne v UK*, (37107/97) (Dec.) April 16, 1998; *Fashanu v UK*, (38440/97) (Dec.) July 1, 1998, where comments in refusing costs concerning a defendant's conduct bringing suspicion on himself and misleading the prosecution by giving no explanations, etc have not posed a problem.

[29] *Vassilios Stravopoulos v Greece*, September 27, 2007, paras 28–32, where the administrative tribunal was considering whether the applicant had made a false declaration about his property, which was the same issue previously before the criimnal court.

[30] (9295/81) (Dec.) October 6, 1982, 30 D.R. 227; also (11882/85) (Dec.) October 7, 1987, 54 D.R. 162, where a janitor of a school was acquitted of theft but his dismissal upheld by an industrial tribunal.

[31] *Diamantides v Greece (No.2)*, May 19, 2005.

a time-bar and that the administrative tribunal had restricted itself to issues relevant to his professional conduct without erring into assessment of guilt on the dropped charges.[32]

Refusal of damages for pre-trial detention of an acquitted accused based on findings that a necessary reasonable suspicion existed at the time before the acquittal did not infringe the presumption of innocence.[33] Statements made in refusing compensation which express or imply the continuing existence of suspicion, or otherwise call into doubt the correctness of the acquittal, have disclosed violations,[34] as did the refusal of compensation due to the applicant's failure to prove his innocence of charges in discontinued proceedings.[35] However, if in the proceedings for compensation, the applicant is required to show that the absence of a reasonable suspicion justifying the criminal proceedings, the finding by the civil courts that such a suspicion existed at the time is not a problem.[36]

An acquittal in criminal proceedings does not, as such, preclude the establishment of civil liability to pay compensation to the victims arising out of the same facts on the basis of a less strict burden of proof. However, breach of the presumption of innocence will arise if the decision on compensation acted in such a way or used such language in its reasoning as to create a clear link between the two sets of proceedings as could bring Art.6, para.2 into play.[37]

There is no difference as concerns the presumption of innocence between an acquittal due to lack of evidence and an acquittal due to established innocence. Thus, where an administrative court interpreted a criminal court acquittal as indicating that the applicant had only escaped due to the benefit of the doubt and reached the conclusion, contrary to the acquittal, that he had intentionally made a false statement, the Court found this breached Art.6, para.2.[38]

Issues may also arise where a court prejudges the issues which are to be determined by a criminal court in proceedings not yet completed. A violation was found where an appeal court, in revoking a suspended sentence, assumed the role of the trial court and unequivocally declared that the applicant had committed an offence during probation.[39]

[32] *Moullet v France*, (27521/04) (Dec.) September 13, 2007, no problem arose from the fact the disciplinary administrative bodies made reference to adverse findings of fact made by the criminal chamber.

[33] *Hibbert v Netherlands*, (38087/97) (Dec.) January 26, 1999.

[34] *Asan Rushiti v Austria*, March 21, 2000; *Lamanna v Austria*, July 10, 2001. The Court commented in those cases that it was irrelevant whether it was the trial court or another later court which made the remarks or whether they were allegedly based on the terms of the jury's verdict; see the Norwegian cases, *O* and *Hammern*, February 11, 2003, ECHR 2003–II, comments by the High Court refusing compensation on the basis that the applicants had probably committed sexual abuse were considered as voicing suspicion incompatible with the presumption of innocence.

[35] *Capeau v Belgium*, January 13, 2005.

[36] *Bok v Netherlands*, January 18, 2011, paras 40–48, the Court did note the use of inappropriate terms in the court decisions referring to the absence of disculpatory evidence and lack of appearance of "innocence", but in the context of the decision as a whole this did not offend.

[37] *Y v Norway*, February 11, 2003, ECHR 2003–II, violation where in a compensation decision the High Court stated that the applicant had probably committed the offences; conversely, *Ringvold v Norway*, February 11, 2003, ECHR 2003–II, no violation where the findings did not expressly or in substance hold that the conditions for criminal liability were fulfilled.

[38] *Vassilios Stravopoulos v Greece*, fn.29 above, paras 37–41. See also *Tendam v Spain*, July 13, 2010, paras 38–41.

[39] *Bohmer v Germany*, October 3, 2002, para.55.

4. Statements implying guilt by other State authorities

II–163 The presumption of innocence is binding not only on the court before which a person charged is brought, but on other State organs. "Public officials" is a wide and flexible term in this respect, extending to a well-known public and political figure who made statements about an accused person on television at a time shortly before he was elected as a governor.[40] It also seems that an investigator carrying out a pre-trial investigation into alleged offences may also activate the application of Art.6, para.2, as shown in a case where the investigator was found to have conducted a blatantly partial and one-sided inquiry with preconceived opinions of those under investigation.[41]

A distinction may be drawn between statements made to the effect that an applicant has committed an offence and in the assessments of risk.[42]

Objective information, including photographs, may be given to the public about the arrest of suspects, if done with discretion and prudence, avoiding any assessment or prejudgment of guilt[43] or any prejudgment of the facts to be assessed by the court.[44] In *Allenet de Ribemont v France*, where the applicant, while in police custody, was described at a press conference by senior police officers as being the instigator of the murder under investigation, the Court rejected the Government argument that Art.6, para.2 only applied to the judicial authority in the context of criminal proceedings ending in a conviction, but held that it applied to other public authorities where an applicant was "charged with a criminal offence". Since the declaration of guilt was made without any qualification or reservation and encouraged the public to believe the applicant guilty in prejudgment of the assessment of the facts by the competent judicial authority, there was a violation, which was not cured by the fact that the applicant was later released by a judge for lack of evidence. The Court emphasises, however, that statements must be taken in their context, giving some allowance for infelicitous phrasing. In *Daktaras v Lithuania*, where it was "unfortunate" that the prosecutor referred to the applicant's

[40] *Kouzmin v Russia*, March 18, 2010, paras 60–65, violation for statements that the applicant was a criminal and promising that he would soon be locked up as one.

[41] *Poncelet v Belgium*, March 18, 2010, paras 60–65, the violation arose where an appellate court quashed a lower court decision quashing criminal proceedings, inter alia, for breach of presumption of innocence by the investigator and made comments leaving the impression that the applicant had only escaped due to prescription.

[42] (20755/92) (Dec.) October 10, 1994, where the Commission found that the Parole Board was bound by the applicant's acquittal of rape and incest not to treat him guilty of these offences but was not precluded, in refusing release, from examining the circumstances leading up to the prosecution in its overall assessment of the applicant's risk to the public; similarly, *Murati v Switzerland*, (37285/97) (Dec.) July 1, 1998, where the authorities refused a residence permit on grounds of the risk of the applicant's future offending; *Daktaras v Lithuania*, October 10, 2000, ECHR 2000–X, where remarks by State officials aimed at describing the circumstances of the applicant's arrest and referring to his dangerous character were not found to be formal declarations of guilt which could encourage the public to believe him guilty.

[43] *YB v Turkey*, October 28, 2004, violation: the press release stated that the suspects were members of an illegal organisation and that it had been established that they had committed offences; *Samoila and Coinca*, fn.22 above, paras 91–98, statements by the prosecutor and police chief concerning the accuseds' intimidation of witnesses and wrongdoing.

[44] *Fatullayev v Azerbaijan*, October 28, 2004, paras 159–163, the Prosecutor-General announced to the press that the applicant's website had contained threats to commit terrorist acts, the central issue to be determined at trial. The Court here mentioned duties of caution and circumspection in informing the public about arrests and pending criminal trials.

guilt having been "proved' by the evidence, the Court noted that he was using the same term as the applicant in his application for a discontinuance and it was evident, in the context, that both were referring to the existence or not of sufficient evidence to justify the continuance of the proceedings.[45] Statements made by a minister concerning deprivation of citizenship due to promotion of anti-Western sentiment and violence were not found to offend, although perhaps lacking the required degree of circumspection, since they did not refer to any of the applicant's declarations that were in issue in the subsequent criminal proceedings.[46] In contrast, where, during pending appeals against fraud convictions, government ministers made statements in Parliament impugning the accused as crooks who had stolen, the Court found these remarks offended the presumption of innocence and underlined the need for discretion and restraint, particularly by a minister of justice.[47]

However, it appears that statements made implying involvement in criminal acts will not offend where no criminal proceedings are pending or anticipated. Where in the House of Commons a Minister named two Belgian applicants as involved in sanction busting in Namibia, the Court noted that there was no suspicion that the applicants had committed any offence within UK jurisdiction and no proceedings intended. In those circumstances the applicants could not be regarded as "charged with a criminal offence" for the purposes of Art.6, para.2.[48]

Where extradition proceedings are concerned, Art.6, para.2 will apply even though there is no "criminal charge" in the country concerned as there will generally be a close link with pending criminal proceedings in the requesting country. Thus, while an extradition decision per se does not offend, statements by officials stating guilt in unequivocal terms will raise issues. Thus, where in issuing an extradition decision, a chief public prosecutor stated that the applicants had committed the offences, a violation was disclosed.[49]

Where adverse comments appear in the press, this may adversely affect the fairness of the trial under Art.6, para.1, in particular through their effect on the jury. Issues might still arise under Art.6, para.2 where the press coverage could be regarded as inspired by, and thus under the responsibility of, the authorities.[50]

[45] See also *Butkevicius v Lithuania*, March 26, 2002, ECHR 2002–II, where comments by the Prosecutor-General could be regarded, in context, as referring not to guilt but to the existence of sufficient evidence to justify proceedings, but the comment by the Chairman of the Seimas (Parliament) amounted to a declaration of guilt, prejudging the assessment by the competent judicial authority; *Kouzmin*, fn.40 above, paras 65–69, statements by a prosecutor applying for the applicant's removal from office on the basis of evidence from the criminal investigation were regarded as setting out "a state of suspicion", not an affirmation of guilt, even if stringently expressed.

[46] *Mustafa (Abu Hamza) v UK*, (31411/07) (Dec.) January 18, 2011.

[47] *Konstas v Greece*, fn.5, in contrast, mere reference by the Prime Minister to "an unprecedented scandal" was not a prejudgment.

[48] *Zollman v UK*, (62902/00) (Dec.) November 27, 2002. Cf. *Montera v Italy*, (64713/01) (Dec.) July 9, 2002, comments in a Parliamentary report concerning links between magistrates and the mafia did not offend Art.6, para.2 as they referred to a state of suspicion against the applicant and did not disclose a finding of guilt.

[49] *Ismoilov v Russia*, April 24, 2008, paras 160–170.

[50] *Wloch v Poland*, (27785/95) (Dec.) March 30, 2000, where the Court left it open whether the press were inspired by public authorities' remarks and found that the coverage was not such as to affect the impartiality of the trial court and amount to a breach of the presumption of innocence. See Part IIA, s.13: Juries.

5. Penalties for failure to give information

II–164 In a number of contexts, liability involving fines or imprisonment may be imposed where a person fails to comply with a requirement to provide information. The Commission did not find a problem where an owner of the car was liable for traffic offences if he did not give the name of the person driving at the time of the offence; such a presumption was considered acceptable.[51] The Court initially cast doubt on this case-law as failing to take into account the right to silence, but in *Weh v Austria* considered that the imposition of a fine on the owner of a car for giving inaccurate information about the driver at the time of a purported speeding incident was not sufficiently connected with a pending criminal charge against the owner as to offend against the privilege against self-incrimination.[52] It has since found no unfairness arising from the requirement imposed on car owners to identify, under pain of a fine, the driver at the time of a suspected offence or from the use in evidence of any admission obtained thereby.[53]

Imposition of penalties for failure to provide breath specimens or material independent of the will of the accused person, even if the material is likely to be incriminating, has not ordinarily been found either to infringe the presumption of innocence or the privilege against self-incrimination.[54]

Where the question of the right to silence or privilege against self-incrimination has been in serious issue however, the Convention organs have tended to treat the issue as one of fairness under Art.6, para.1 rather than the presumption of innocence.[55]

Yet, in *Heaney and McGuinness v Ireland*, the conviction and imprisonment for six months of the applicants for failure to account for their movements at the time of an attack on a security checkpoint was found to infringe both the privilege against self-incrimination and the presumption of innocence. The Court laid emphasis on the degree of compulsion imposed on the applicants to incriminate themselves in serious offences which extinguished the very essence of their right to silence and also contravened the basic principle that the prosecution have to prove their case without resorting to evidence obtained by coercion or oppression in defiance of the will of the accused, which aspect was closely linked to the guarantee of presumption of innocence until proof of guilt according to law.

[51] (23681/94) (Dec.) May 17, 1995, car caught by radar for speeding; owner refused to say who drove and was fined 50,000 pesetas.

[52] *Weh v Austria*, April 8, 2004. See also *Rieg v Austria*, March 24, 2005, where the car owner was fined for not giving full details of the driver, but was never prosecuted for speeding herself.

[53] *O'Halloran and Francis v UK*, June 29, 2007.

[54] e.g. *Tirado Ortiz and Lozano v Spain*, (43486/98) (Dec.) June 15, 1999. See also Pt IIA, s.23: Right to silence, and the reference to *Jalloh v Germany*, July 11, 2006, ECHR 2006–IX, where the use in evidence of drugs obtained from the applicant by the forcible administration of an emetic was in breach of the privilege against self-incrimination.

[55] See Pt IIA, s.23: Right to silence, e.g. *Condron v UK*, May 2, 2000, ECHR 2000–V, the direction by the judge concerning the drawing of inferences from the applicants' failure to answer police questions breached Art.6, para.1, with no separate issue arising under Art.6, para.2.

6. Cure on appeal

It may be possible for a breach of presumption of innocence to be cured by a superior court making the matter clear where the person was acquitted or the proceedings terminated.[56] This occurred in *Adolf v Austria*,[57] where, in discontinuing the proceedings for triviality, the Austrian court made ambiguous statements which the applicant claimed were capable of suggesting that he had inflicted bodily harm on the complainant. However, the Supreme Court clearly stated that discontinuance was not to include anything in the nature of a verdict of guilt and it would have been preferable if the lower court had stated this more explicitly. The Court found that the lower court judgment had to be read in light of the Supreme Court ruling and therefore the applicant was cleared of any finding of guilt and the presumption of innocence was no longer called into question. II–165

Similarly, when during pending proceedings, the Prime Minister of Malta made statements prejudging the applicants' case, the ruling by the Constitutional Court that this was in breach of their presumption of innocence and directing their judgment to lie on the file before the first instance court was considered as providing redress and assurance of compliance at trial with the requisite safeguards.[58]

Where an applicant was found guilty and the breach occurred during the proceedings, it might be more problematic to cure without acquitting or sending back for retrial.

Cross-reference

Part IIA, s.1: General principles: fairness.
Part IIA, s.23: Right to silence.

[56] *Austria v Italy* (1966) (788/60) 6th Yearbook of the ECHR 740, where a breach is so gross as to distort the course of the proceedings, cure may not be possible.
[57] *Adolf v Austria*, March 26, 1982, Series A, No.49.
[58] *Arrigo and Vella v Malta*, (6569/04) (Dec.) May 10, 2005.

20. Public hearing and judgment

Key provision:

II–166 Article 6, para.1 (right to public hearing and public pronouncement of judgment).

Key case-law:

Albert and Le Compte v Belgium, February 10, 1983, Series A, No.58, 5 E.H.R.R. 533; *Pretto v Italy*, December 8, 1983, Series A, No.71, 6 E.H.R.R. 182; *Axen v Germany*, December 8, 1983, Series A, No.72, 6 E.H.R.R. 195; *Sutter v Switzerland*, February 22, 1984, Series A, No.74, 6 E.H.R.R. 272; *Campbell and Fell v UK*, June 28, 1984, Series A, No.80, 7 E.H.R.R. 165; *H v Belgium*, November 30, 1987, Series A, No.127–B, 10 E.H.R.R. 339; *Ekbatani v Sweden*, May 26, 1988, Series A, No.134, 13 E.H.R.R. 504; *Hakansson and Sturesson v Sweden*, February 21, 1990, Series A, No.171–A, 13 E.H.R.R. 1; *Helmers v Sweden*, October 29, 1991, Series A, No.212–A; *Jan-Ake Andersson v Sweden*, October 29, 1991, Series A, No.212–B, 15 E.H.R.R. 218; *Fejde v Sweden*, October 29, 1991, Series A, No.212–C, 17 E.H.R.R. 4; *Schuler-Zgraggen v Switzerland*, June 24, 1993, Series A, No.263, 16 E.H.R.R. 405; *Fredin v Sweden (No.2)*, February 23, 1994, Series A, No.283–A; *Diennet v France*, September 26, 1995, Series A, No.325–A, 21 E.H.R.R. 554; *Botten v Norway*, February 19, 1996, R.J.D. 1996–I; *Bulut v Austria*, February 22, 1996, R.J.D. 1996–II, No.5; *Stallinger* and *Kuso v Austria*, April 23, 1997, R.J.D. 1997–II, No.35; *Werner v Austria* and *Szucs v Austria*, November 24, 1997, R.J.D. 1997–VII, No.56; *Eisenstecken v Austria*, October 3, 2000, ECHR 2000–X; *Riepan v Austria*, November 14, 2000, ECHR 2000–XII; *B and P v UK*, April 24, 2001, ECHR 2002–III; *Goç v Turkey*, July 11, 2002, ECHR 2002–V; *Jussila v Finland*, November 23, 2006, ECHR 2006–XIII

1. General considerations

II–167 There are two hearing aspects: whether the proceedings are open to the public and whether there is an oral hearing at which the applicant may address the court. There are, in practice, many exceptions to this right, as with the requirement for public judgment.

2. Public hearing

II–168 The public character of proceedings before judicial bodies protects litigants against the administration of justice in secret without public scrutiny. It maintains public confidence in the courts and, in rendering the administration of justice visible, contributes to the achievement of a fair trial, a fundamental guarantee in a democratic society.[1] While practice varies in States as regards hearings and pronouncement of judgments, the Court will look at the realities of the procedure,

[1] *Axen v Germany*, December 8, 1983, Series A, No.72, 6 E.H.R.R. 195, para.25, *Werner v Austria* and *Szucs v Austria*, November 24, 1997, R.J.D. 1997–VII, No.56, para.45; *B and P v UK*, April 24, 2001, ECHR 2002–III, para.36.

the purpose underlying the guarantee rather than at the formalities which are of lesser importance.[2]

Generally a public hearing is required before the court of first and only instance.[3] Lack of public hearing will not be cured by a public hearing before an appeal or cassation instance where that body does not consider the merits of the case or is not competent to deal with all aspects of the matter.[4] Where a public hearing has not been provided at first instance, exceptional reasons will be required to justify refusal of one at second instance.[5]

In criminal cases, given the possible detrimental effects on fairness of a lack of public hearing at first instance, this could only be remedied by a complete re-hearing before the appeal court.[6]

In criminal cases, even where there has been a public hearing at first instance, the Court has held that before an appeal court, which had full jurisdiction on facts, law and sentencing, a public hearing was also required.[7]

Even in a relatively trivial civil case, a claimant cannot generally be denied a public hearing in court procedures aimed at simplifying or expediting cases.[8] While there may be an argument for holding no hearing at all (see further below) in very technical social security cases, the Court was not persuaded that, in proceedings concerning preventive confiscation of possessions, on grounds of alleged organised crime connections, the holding of no public hearing at either first instance or appeal was sustainable.[9] Nor, where disciplinary proceedings concerned a Supreme Court president, was the Court persuaded of the reasons given for excluding the public; as regarded the alleged need to protect the applicant's dignity, he himself had repeatedly asked for the proceedings to be public, while as regarded the alleged aim of protecting judicial dignity as a whole, the Court considered that this was not sufficient to outweigh the legitimate public interest in the proceedings.[10]

In the context of court martials, a hearing may still be sufficiently public where access to the hearing room on a military base is conditional on members of the public signing in, such measure justified by reasonable security and safety

[2] *Axen*, see fn.1 above, para.26.

[3] e.g. *Gautrin v France*, May 20, 1998, R.J.D. 1998–III, No.72, where no public hearing occurred in a medical disciplinary case.

[4] e.g. *Albert and Le Compte v Belgium*, February 10, 1983, Series A, No.58, 5 E.H.R.R. 533, para.37, where a public hearing in the Court of Cassation did not cure the lack of publicity before the professional tribunal; *H v Belgium*, November 30, 1987, Series A, No.127–B, 10 E.H.R.R. 339, where in reinstatement proceedings by a lawyer struck from the roll the proceedings were not heard in public nor was the decision pronounced in public—there were no circumstances such as to warrant the proceedings being held in camera, no indication of waiver and this was not cured by later hearings as there was no appeal; *Diennet v France*, September 26, 1995, Series A, No.325–A, 21 E.H.R.R. 554, no public hearing in a disciplinary body, not cured by medical appeal body being in public since it was not judicial with full jurisdiction; *Hummatov v Azerbaijan*, November 29, 2007, para.151.

[5] *Stallinger and Kuso v Austria*, April 23, 1997, R.J.D. 1997–II, No.35, para.51; *Goç v Turkey*, July 11, 2002, ECHR 2002–V, para.47; mutatis mutandis, *Malhous v Czech Republic*, July 12, 2001, where the applicant did not have a public hearing before a tribunal at first instance and the subsequent court reviews were conducted without any hearing.

[6] *Riepan*, para.41, where the appeal court had the power to review facts, law and sentence but did not re-hear witnesses and its review did not have the requisite scope.

[7] *Hummatov v Azerbaijan*, November 29, 2007, 142.

[8] *Scarth v UK*, July 22, 1999, the applicant, suing for £697, was refused a public hearing in arbitration procedure in the County Court.

[9] *Bocellari et Rizza v Italy*, November 13, 2007, paras 35–41.

[10] *Olujic v Croatia*, February 5, 2009, paras 69–76.

concerns.[11] The fact that a hearing may be open to the public in a formal sense may not, however, be enough where the proceedings are taking place outside normal court facilities. Thus in *Riepan v Austria*, where the criminal trial took place inside a prison, the Court found that practical obstacles to public attendance arose and that inadequate compensatory measures were taken to ensure that the public had notice that the hearing was taking place together with information about how to obtain access.

3. Absence of a hearing

II–169 It is not uncommon for no hearing to take place and for domestic courts to make decisions on the basis of written submissions. However, it generally flows from the notion of a fair trial that an accused person is entitled to attend a trial hearing in criminal matters.[12] The Court has nonetheless distinguished between the hard core of criminal law and matters such as fiscal surcharges, finding in *Jussila v Finland* that fairness may not, in technical matters and where the issues may be effectively dealt with in writing, require an oral hearing. In that case, the Court also took into account the very minor sum of money at stake and that the applicant had the opportunity to apply for a hearing, in respect of which the court gave reasons for its refusal.[13] It is fairness that is the overriding consideration.[14]

Where, in civil proceedings, there is no hearing before the first and only judicial instance, and the proceedings raise issues of fact and law, problems may arise.[15] Exceptional reasons will generally be required.[16] However, in *Schuler-Zgraggen v Switzerland*, there was no oral hearing before the Federal Insurance Court in respect of a claim for invalidity insurance. While the Court found that the rules made provision for the possibility of a hearing on application by a party or by the court's own motion and that there was unequivocal waiver from the applicant's failure to ask for a hearing, it also made reference to the nature of the proceedings, which were highly technical concerning private medical details and no issues of public importance, in which circumstances it considered domestic courts could have regard to reasons of expedition, efficiency and economy in avoiding holding hearings systematically. Similarly, no oral hearing was shown to be necessary in a testamentary case concerning pure points of law[17]; in a social security benefits

[11] *Hood v UK*, (Rep.) May 28, 1998, ECHR 1999–II, para.120. Security and identity checks acceptable also in *Allen v UK*, (35580/97) (Dec.) October 22, 1998.

[12] *Findlay v UK*, February 25, 1997, Reports 1997–I, para.79.

[13] See *Martinie v France*, April 12, 2006, ECHR 2006–. . . , where a decisive factor in finding a violation for lack of a hearing in the Court of Audit was the inability even to apply for a hearing.

[14] *Jussila v Finland*, November 23, 2006, ECHR 2006–XIII, para.42.

[15] *Fredin v Sweden (No.2)*, February 23, 1994, Series A, No.283–A, where the Supreme Administrative Court was the only instance but refused a hearing—it had jurisdiction over facts and law and the submissions were capable of raising issues of fact and law as shown by a dissenting minority who considered that it was necessary to obtain clarifications at an oral hearing; *Miller v Sweden*, February 8, 2005, where the Court considered the issues, factual and legal, were not clear-cut and that it could not be said that the applicant's doctor could not have added something useful.

[16] e.g. *Koottummel v Austria*, December 10, 2009, paras 18–21, no exceptional circumstances justified lack of oral hearing in the only instance concerning an employer's challenge of a refusal of a work permit for a foreign chef.

[17] *Varela Assalino v Portugal*, (64336/01) (Dec.) April 25, 2002; see also *Pursiheimo v Finland*, (57795/00) (Dec.) November 25, 2003, withdrawal of a gun licence (undisputed alcohol abuse): the evidence which the applicant wanted to present was not relevant and the issues of fact and law could adequately be dealt with on the basis of the written file.

dispute where the medical reports were in agreement and no witnesses had been requested[18]; in disputes of a technical nature[19]; or other situations in which the facts were not disputed.[20] Where a hearing concerned technical matters of the applicability of a treaty, without the hearing of any witnesses or the need to hear the applicant or to establish any facts, the Court found no violation as regards the lack of public hearing of proceedingson the forfeiture of assets in execution of a foreign judgment.[21]

The Government argument that the same approach should be taken to real property transaction disputes was, however, rejected by the Court in *Eisenstecken v Austria*, which noted that matters of contract did not appear highly technical and took into account the importance of what was at stake for the applicant (ownership of substantial parcels of land). Administration of justice and accountability of the State also outweighed considerations of speed and efficiency in a case for compensation for unlawful detention, where the issues could not be said to be technical in nature nor could be dealt with properly on the basis of the case file alone.[22] Nor was the Court persuaded by the argument that no hearing was required before an investment regulatory instance as financial professionals might be reticent to have their dealings reviewed under the public eye.[23]

A hearing is not automatic for appeal or later proceedings, the Court allowing for factors of dealing expeditiously with court caseloads. The question must be settled with regard to the nature of the proceedings, the scope of examination and powers of the domestic court and the manner in which the applicant's interests are presented and protected.[24]

In leave to appeal proceedings, appeal or cassation proceedings involving only questions of law, the lack of hearing may be justified by these special features.[25] Leave to appeal against conviction proceedings in a criminal case, where the applicants were not able to attend or submit oral arguments, did not raise issues of such a nature as to require their presence and since they had received free legal advice as to appeal (they had been advised no grounds arose) and were able to present written arguments on all relevant issues, the interests of justice and fairness were satisfied.[26]

[18] *Döry v Sweden*, November 12, 2002; in contrast, a violation arose in *Salomonsson v Sweden*, November 12, 2002, where the medical reports did differ and the applicant wished to give information on the points of difference.

[19] *Gasparini v Italy and Belgium*, (10750/03) (Dec.) May 12, 2009, the Court also appeared to take into account the need for a speedy decision and to ensure harmonious internal workings in such an organisation as NATO.

[20] *Speil v Austria*, (42057/98) (Dec.) September 5, 2002.

[21] *Saccoccia v Austria*, December 18, 2008, paras 78–80.

[22] *Goç*, see fn.5 above, even if the unlawfulness and length of detention were not in doubt, elements of suffering relevant to moral damage and the level of compensation required that the applicant be heard.

[23] *Vernes v France*, January 20, 2011, para.32.

[24] e.g. *Monnell and Morris v UK*, March 2, 1987, Series A, No.115, para.56.

[25] *Monnell and Morris*, see fn.24 above, *Axen v Germany*, see fn.1 above, and *Sutter v Switzerland*, February 22, 1984, Series A, No.74, 6 E.H.R.R. 272; see also *Bulut v Austria*, February 22, 1996, R.J.D. 1996–II, No.5, where no violation arose for lack of hearing when the Supreme Court rejected a plea of nullity in summary proceedings as manifestly lacking in merit, these being akin to leave to appeal proceedings and the nature of the grounds not such as to require a hearing.

[26] *Monnell and Morris*, see fn.24 above. Similarly, no problem arose in *Meftah v France*, July 26, 2002, ECHR 2002–VII, where the lay applicants were not allowed an oral hearing in the Court of Cassation; *Blücher v Czech Republic*, January 11, 2005, no violation for lack of hearing in Constitutional Court, or in appeal proceedings in *Rippe v Germany*, (5398/031) (Dec.) February 2, 2006, where there had been a hearing at the lower level.

The fact that an appeal instance has jurisdiction over facts as well as law is not decisive, the nature of the issues to be decided in the particular case being more relevant.[27] In *Ekbatani v Sweden*, the Court found that the Court of Appeal could not fairly or properly determine the issues without hearing the complainant or applicant in person as the crucial question appeared to be their credibility. Nor was the Court persuaded that no oral hearing was required in an appeal against a refusal of medical insurance for the applicant's gender re-assignment, considering that issues of fact concerning the necessity of the treatment arose on which the applicant should have been heard.[28] In *Helmers v Sweden* (a private prosecution in defamation by the applicant), the Court of Appeal had to examine questions of fact and law and make a full assessment of the defendant's guilt or innocence.[29] The Court also had regard to the seriousness of what was at stake for the applicant's professional reputation and career, though it is not apparent why this would require an oral hearing which otherwise was not warranted by the factual or legal issues to be decided.[30] The minor importance of what is at stake appeared to play a decisive role in two other cases, *Jan-Ake Andersson v Sweden* (a road traffic offence and small fine) and *Fejde v Sweden* (illegal possession of a firearm and small fine), where the Court, referring to the minor nature of the penalties and the inability of the courts to increase them, found no violation for lack of oral hearings on appeal, since, though the court had jurisdiction over facts and law, there were no issues which could not adequately be determined on the basis of the case file.[31]

4. Waiver

II–170 A public hearing may be waived by the applicant if by his own free will and unequivocal.[32] Waiver must, however, not run counter to any important public interest, which appears to suggest that in serious cases the appearances of justice will

[27] e.g. *Helmers v Sweden*, October 29, 1991, Series A, No.212–A.

[28] *Schlumpf v Switzerland*, January 8, 2009, paras 63–70, the appeal court had taken the view that only legal points were in issue. See also *Igual Coll v Spain*, March 10, 2009, where the appeal court reversed an acquittal, reaching differing conclusions as to the applicant's intentions vis-à-vis his maintenance obligations, the Court considered that the domestic court had had regard to more than interpretation of points of law and that a hearing should have been held.

[29] See similar reasoning in *Tierce v San Marino*, July 25, 2000, where the principal issue before the appeal judge concerned the guilt or innocence of the accused; also *Constantinescu v Romania*, June 27, 2000, paras 53–61; *Lundevall v Sweden*, November 12, 2002, para.39, concerning an assessment of the applicant's needs due to a speech handicap, the appeal court could have benefited from seeing him in person and a hearing could have provided relevant information for the determination of the issues; *Garcia Hernandez v Spain*, November 16, 2010, the appeal court overruled the lower instance, changing the assessment of the facts (medical negligence), without hearing the applicant; *Arnarsson v Iceland*, July 15, 2003, violation where the Supreme Court reversed an acquittal without a hearing on the basis of its re-assessment of predominantly factual issues.

[30] The lack of particularly convincing elements which might require a further hearing is indicated by the large dissenting minority. The importance of what was at stake for the applicants in *Monnell and Morris*, see fn.24 above, was apparently not relevant in leave to appeal proceedings. See also *Botten v Norway*, February 19, 1996, R.J.D. 1996–I, where the Supreme Court had full jurisdiction and overturned the acquittal on its assessment of "neglect" and dealing with sentencing (issues of personality and character) without hearing the applicant—reference to the effect on the applicant's professional career.

[31] The Commission found the cases indistinguishable from previous authorities, finding violations since the appeal court had jurisdiction over facts and law and had to reconsider guilt and innocence.

[32] e.g. *Albert and Le Compte*, para.35, the Court found that there was nothing in the letter or spirit of Art.6, para.1 to prevent waiver of this aspect in medical disciplinary proceedings.

require a public hearing regardless of the applicant's views.[33] Where in *Hakansson and Sturesson v Sweden*, the appeal court (the only judicial instance) had the power to hold an oral hearing but the applicants did not ask for one, this was found to constitute an unequivocal waiver of their right to a public hearing and there were no questions of public interest which would have rendered one necessary.[34] Where domestic law excludes the holding of hearings however, it is considered irrelevant whether or not the applicant asked for one. In *H v Belgium* there was no waiver although the applicant did not ask for a public hearing, since there was no provision for it or practice in the procedures adopted, and little prospect of securing one.[35] In *Botten v Norway*, where the applicant made no request to be present nor any objection, the Court found that the Supreme Court was under a duty to take positive measures to ensure his presence as necessary to a proper assessment.

5. Exclusion of public

There are specified exceptions to the requirement that criminal proceedings be open to the public, e.g. morals, public order, national security, interest of juveniles, protection of private life of the parties or where strictly necessary in special circumstances where publicity would prejudice the interests of justice.[36] II–171

The interests of protection of private life and the interests of justice were considered to justify the Belgian system of holding *la procedure d'instruction* in camera—full publicity becoming applicable after the investigation/preparatory stage when the trial of the issues began.[37]

Criminal trials with security problems must almost always be open to the public.[38] An applicant's escape history did not justify holding a trial in a prison, without proper access to the public, the Court noting that security concerns would only in very rare cases justify excluding the public.[39] Where a hearing was held in a closed area of a prison to which the public did not have free access and the prison was at some distance from the city, without obvious public transportation, the Court considered that the authorities had not done enough by way of ensuring free access to the public over the six months the trial lasted.[40] However, as regarded disciplinary hearing in prisons, the Court considered in *Campbell and Fell* that practical difficulties in admitting the public to prison precincts or problems of transportation if the Board of Visitors met outside would render the requirement of public hearings a disproportionate burden on the State.

[33] *Hakansson and Sturesson v Sweden*, February 21, 1990, Series A, No.171–A, 13 E.H.R.R. 1, para.66.

[34] See also unequivocal waiver findings in *Zumtobel v Austria*, September 21, 1993, Series A, No.268–A, 17 E.H.R.R. 116, where the applicant was represented but did not request a hearing, as was possible, and the nature of the proceedings did not require a hearing; *Hermi v Italy*, October 18, 2006, ECHR 2006–. . . , para.79, where a represented applicant opted for a summary procedure without a hearing and no questions of public interest arose preventing waiver; *Lundevall*, fn.29 above, where the applicant did not request a hearing at first instance.

[35] Also *Werner*, fn.1 above, para.48, an applicant cannot be blamed for not making an application with no prospect of success; *Eisenstecken v Austria*, October 3, 2000, ECHR 2000–X, para.33.

[36] e.g. *Guisset v France*, September 26, 2000, ECHR 2000–IX, para.73, no justification forthcoming for lack of public hearing in a disciplinary finances court. The converse, that a party or accused could claim a right to in camera proceedings, has not been examined substantively as yet.

[37] *Ernst v Belgium*, July 15, 2003, paras 68–69.

[38] *Campbell and Fell v UK*, June 28, 1984, Series A, No.80, 7 E.H.R.R. 165, para.87.

[39] *Riepan v Austria*, November 14, 2000, ECHR 2000–XII, para.34.

[40] *Hummatov*, see fn.4, paras 142–152.

As regards the hearing of civil claims in chambers, this may be acceptable, depending on the nature of the issues being determined. In *B and P v UK*, where applicant fathers complained that applications for residence orders in respect of their children were heard in chambers, the Court considered that such proceedings were prime examples of cases where the exclusion of press and public could be justified, namely, to protect the privacy of the child and parties and to avoid prejudicing the interests of justice. In the latter context, it was essential, in order that the judge gain as full and accurate a picture as possible of the child's situation, for parents and other witnesses to feel able to express themselves candidly on highly personal issues without fear of public curiosity or comment.[41] At an appeal, at which the applicants enjoyed all other guarantees, the Court accepted the Government's argument that the exclusion of the public was justified by the importance of speedily ruling on claims of discriminatory treatment.[42]

6. Public pronouncement of judgment

II–172 The Court, faced with the apparent absolute wording of this part of Art.6, noted in *Pretto v Italy, Axen v Germany* and *Sutter v Switzerland* that domestic courts had a variety of ways of rendering decisions public. Assuming that the drafters of the Convention could not have overlooked this, the Court refused a literal interpretation and held that the form of "publicity" to be given to the "judgment" in domestic law must be assessed in the light of the special features of the proceedings and with reference to the object and purpose of Art.6, para.1. It may be sufficient for higher instances with limited reviewing functions to dispense with pronouncement in open court where provision is made for some form of scrutiny by the public via publications or registries.[43]

At lower instances, the requirements are more stringent. Where there is no access to lower court judgments, there is likely to be a violation as in *Werner v Austria* and *Szucs v Austria*, in which the courts of first instance and courts of appeal did not give judgment in public nor were the full texts of their judgments openly available to the public in their registries; access was limited to those with a "legitimate interest". A violation was found in *Campbell and Fell*, since not only did the Board of Visitors not pronounce judgment publicly, but also took no other steps to make their decisions public. Where only a brief operative part of a judgment was read out at a hearing, without any provision for public access to the text of the reasoned judgment in a civil case, the Court considered that insufficient information had been made

[41] See also *AF v France*, (34596/97) (Dec.) October 21, 1998, hearing in private in a medical disciplinary case justified by the evidence being given about the applicant's mental and physical state due to chronic alcholism.

[42] *Udorovic v Italy*, May 18, 2010, paras 48–51, concerning a preliminary and provisional procedure where the applicant challenged a municipal order evacuating an unofficial encampment.

[43] No violations in *Pretto v Italy*, December 8, 1983, Séries A, No.71, 6 E.H.R.R. 182, *Axen*, see fn.1 above, and *Sutter*, see fn.25 above, which concerned high instances of appeal or cassation, which had limited review powers, for example, being unable to alter the verdict but only to confirm, quash or render final. Regard was also had to whether there were public hearings and judgment at earlier stages. It was enough, by way of publication in *Pretto*, that the judgment of the Court of Cassation was deposited in the registry and available on demand. In *Sutter*, it was acceptable that the full text of the judgment of the Military Court of Cassation was available from the court and this case was published in an official collection, although a dissenting minority noted the considerable delay in publication and that access was only to persons who established an interest.

available from which the public could understand why the applicant's claims had been rejected, hence a violation.[44]

However, in the special context of childcare proceedings, the Court has found that the publication of judgments at first instance risked frustrating the aim of Art.6, para.1, which was to secure a fair hearing, and that a literal interpretation should be avoided.[45] It was sufficient therefore in *B and P v UK* that anyone who could establish an interest could consult or obtain a copy and that the judgments of the first instance and appeal courts in cases of special interest were published allowing public scrutiny of their approach on such issues. It may also be sufficient for there to be partial and delayed publication as in *Lamanna v Austria*, where first instance judgment on a compensation claim was summarised in the appeal court judgment which was only made public after the final decision by the Supreme Court.[46]

Cross-reference

Part IIA, s.15: Legal representation in criminal proceedings.
Part IIA, s.18: Presence in court.

[44] *Ryakib Biryukov v Russia*, January 17, 2008, paras 38–46.

[45] Particularly as it had been found justifiable to hold hearings in camera to protect the privacy of the children and parties and avoid prejudicing the interests of justice—to allow the publication of the judgment would defeat those aims.

[46] *Lamanna v Austria*, July 10, 2001.

21. Reasons for decisions

Key provisions:

II–173 Article 6, paras 1 (fairness) and 3(b) (adequate time and facilities).

Key caselaw:

H v Belgium, November 30, 1987, Series A, No.127, 10 E.H.R.R. 339; *Van de Hurk v Netherlands*, April 19, 1994, Series A, No.288, 18 E.H.R.R. 481; *Ruiz Torija v Spain* and *Hiro Balani v Spain*, December 9, 1994, Series A, Nos 303–B and C; *De Moor v Belgium*, June 23, 1994, Series A, No.292; *Georgiadis v Greece*, May 29, 1997, R.J.D. 1997–III, No.38; *Higgins v France*, February 19, 1998, R.J.D. 1998–I, No.62; *Garcia Ruiz v Spain*, January 21, 1999, ECHR 1999–I; *Taxquet v Belgium*, November 16, 2010, ECHR 2010–. . .

1. General considerations

II–174 Article 6, para.1 has been interpreted as obliging courts to give reasons for their decisions. This has been described as justifying their activities as a State authority, demonstrating to the parties that they have been heard and affording the possibility of having the decision reviewed on appeal.[1] A detailed answer to every argument is not required.[2] The Convention organs' resistance to constituting a fourth instance leaves little scope in practice for attacking the adequacy of the reasons given in judgments.[3] There has been no development under Art.6 as in the context of Arts 8, 9 and 10, that decisions must necessarily be supported by relevant and sufficient reasons, which only comes into play where it is established that there has been an interference with a protected right. Article 6 confers primarily procedural protection based on the paramount consideration of fairness. It does not guarantee as such the "right" result and, on the current approach by the Court reasoning of a decision, is only likely to disclose a violation where there is clear arbitrariness or gross inconsistency on the part of the domestic courts concerned or where a court has exceeded the limits of reasonable interpretation in such a way as to undermine legal certainty.[4] Where criminal trials are concerned, whatever form the decision takes, the applicant must be able to understand the verdict that has been given.[5]

2. Lack of reasons

II–175 Lack of reasons in a decision was taken as an aspect of procedural safeguards in *H v Belgium*. In that case, the Bar Council's procedure was open to criticism in two respects: lack of public hearing and the lack of precision in rules or case-law as to the meaning of the "exceptional circumstances" condition required for reinstatement

[1] *Suominen v Finland*, July 1, 2003, paras 36–37.
[2] *Van de Hurk v Netherlands*, April 19, 1994, Series A, No.288, 18 E.H.R.R. 481.
[3] e.g. *Garcia Ruiz v Spain*, January 21, 1999, ECHR 1999–I, para.28; *Papon v France (No.2)*, (54210/00) (Dec.) November 15, 2001, ECHR 2001–XII.
[4] e.g. *Blücher v Czech Republic*, January 11, 2005, paras 56–57
[5] *Taxquet v Belgium*, November 16, 2010, ECHR 2010–. . . , para.90

to the Bar. The imprecise nature of the statutory concept rendered it all the more necessary for impugned decisions refusing reinstatement to give sufficient reasons. Since the decision in the case merely said that no such circumstances existed without explaining why those relied on by the applicant did not qualify, there was found to be a breach of Art.6, para.1, together with the aspect of lack of public hearing. Failure of a criminal court to set out the constituent elements of the offence together with the facts supporting the applicant's guilt or to explain its apparent rejection of the applicant's evidence was seen as disclosing a lack of a fair hearing.[6]

Juries in criminal cases rarely give reasoned verdicts. The relevance of this to fairness has been touched on in a few cases. Where in an Austrian case the jury in a criminal case gave no reasons for a verdict, the Commission found no unfairness since the jurors were given detailed questions to answer on which counsel could apply to make modifications and this specificity made up for lack of reasons. In addition, the applicant could and did file grounds of nullity on the basis that the judge wrongly explained the law.[7] The Court has stated that the requirement that reasons given must accommodate any unusual procedural features, such as the lack of obligation for jurors to give reasons. In *Papon v France (No.2)*, it was sufficient that a list of questions was put to the jurors and that the prosecution and accused could challenge any question or request additional questions be raised, the court giving a reasoned judgment in case of dispute.[8] However, in *Taxquet v Belgium*, where only a few succinct questions were put in regard of the applicant in identical terms to the other accused and which did not allow him to tell on what factual or legal basis he was convicted, his inability to understand why he was found guilty disclosed an unfair trial. The framework of safeguards surrounding a Scots jury's unreasoned verdict was found sufficient for the accused to understand his verdict, given the pre-verdict addresses by the prosecution, defence and presiding judge, the duty of the judge to direct the jury on law, to ensure a fair trial and to direct no case to answer if the prosecution evidence did not support a conviction, and the powers of the appeal court to remedy any improper verdict by the jury by quashing any miscarriage of justice or result that was logically inconsistent or irrational.[9]

Lack of any reasoning is likely to be more acceptable in the higher instances, in the same way that it may be compatible at upper appellate levels to dispense with oral or public hearings.[10] The Convention organs are unlikely to be demanding as regards the reasons given where the issues raised, from their nature or subject-matter, may legitimately receive short shrift. In a case dealing with the relatively trivial matter of a tax disc on a car,[11] the Commission found no violation where a fine was imposed by the *Cour de Cassation* without reasons when dismissing an appeal. It was enough for the Commission to note that the grounds of appeal appeared manifestly ill-founded and that the *Cour de Cassation* had rejected them

[6] e.g. *Boldea v Romania*, February 15, 2007.

[7] (25852/94) (Dec.) May 15, 1996. See also (15957/90) (Dec.) March 30, 1992, 72 D.R. 195, where the Commission noted that the extent to which reasons had to be given depended on the individual case, particularly its nature and complexity: although the applicant had been convicted of homicide on the simple "yes" response of the jury, the judge had put questions on the facts to the jury and the defence could contest the questions or request modifications, which compensated for the lack of reasoning and formed the framework of the decision; (20664/92) (Dec.) June 29, 1994, 78 D.R. 97.

[8] See fn.3 above.

[9] *Judge v UK*, (35863/10) (Dec.) February 8, 2011.

[10] See Pt IIA, s.20: Public hearing and judgment.

[11] (15384/89) (Dec.) May 9, 1994, 77–A D.R. 5.

after a thorough and amply-reasoned examination.[12] In *Garcia Ruiz v Spain*, it was enough that the *Audiencia Provincial* endorsed the statement of facts and legal reasoning of the first instance court, although the Court commented that a more substantial statement of reasons might have been desirable.[13] Indeed, as regards the preliminary procedure for the examination and admission of appeals on points of law at higher instances, the Court has commented that an appellate court is not required to give more detailed reasoning when it simply applies a specific legal provision to dismiss an appeal on points of law as having no prospects of success without further explanation.[14] The same applied in the case of a public prosecutor at the Court of Cassation answering the request of a civil party to lodge an appeal on points of law.[15]

A higher court cannot limit itself to endorsing a lower court judgment where the latter has itself failed to give reasons.[16] Where there had been a detailed judgment on appeal, no problem arose where the Court of Appeal refused leave for further appeal to the House of Lords without reasons.[17]

3. Omissions and reliance on inadequate reasons

II–176 While a court has to give reasons, the Court has held that it is not required to answer all the points raised and that it is not its role to examine whether arguments are adequately met.[18] That said, it appears that in appropriate circumstances a violation may arise where domestic courts fail to answer relevant submissions which are not obviously ill-founded, or where they make a manifest error of appreciation in the reasoning, which reflects on the fairness of the proceedings.

By way of guidance, the Court stated that the extent of the obligation to give reasons may vary according to the nature of the decision. It was necessary to take into account also the diversity of submissions that a litigant may bring into a court and the differences in Contracting States with regard to statutory provisions,

[12] e.g. (12275/86) (Dec.) July 2, 1991, 70 D.R. 47, where the *Conseil d'Etat* judgment dismissing an appeal and imposing a fine did not state exactly why it was vexatious, this was sufficiently shown by the fact that it rehearsed all the appeal grounds in detail finding them groundless.

[13] Also *Immeuble Group Kosser v France*, (38748/97) (Dec.) March 9, 1999 and *Bufferne v France*, (54367/00) February 26, 2002, ECHR 2002–III, where the *Conseil d'Etat* merely stated, without explanation, that no relevant points of law were made out; *Burg v France*, (34763/02) (Dec.) January 28, 2003, *Cour de Cassation* summary dismissal; *Kok v Netherlands*, (43149/98) (Dec.) July 4, 2000, ECHR 2000–VI, Supreme Court summary rejection of grounds of appeal.

[14] *Salé v France*, (39765/04) (Dec.) March 21, 2006.

[15] *Gourou v Greece (No.2)*, March 20, 2009, paras 38–42, where to require more than an indication that there were no well-founded grounds of appeal would have imposed too heavy a burden on the public prosecutor given the nature of the civil party claim.

[16] *Boldea*, fn.6 above, para.33.

[17] *Sawoniuk v UK*, (Dec.) May 29, 2001, ECHR 2001–VI; also *Nerva v UK*, (42295/98) (Dec.) July 11, 2000.

[18] *Van de Hurk*, see fn.2 above, where, on a general assessment of the judgment, the Court did not find it insufficiently reasoned. See also the Commission's approach, e.g. (10153/82) (Dec.) October 13, 1986, 49 D.R. 67, while the applicants had complained that the courts had distorted the presentation of their case, it was not the Commission's task to interfere with the legal assessment of claims made by national courts under domestic law, the application and interpretation of which was, in principle, reserved to them. A failure to discuss or refer explicitly to each submission was not unfair as long as the court heard the parties and their pleadings were considered. The fact that the court may have considered them as irrelevant or unfounded and implictly rejected them could not amount to a breach.

customary rules, legal opinion, and the presentation and drafting of judgments—in other words, all the circumstances of the case.[19]

In *Ruiz Torija v Spain* (concerning an action against the applicant for breach in terms of lease of gaming machines), there was a total failure of the *Audencia Provincial* to address the applicant's clear and timely submission that the action was time-barred. The Court noted that it was not its role to rule if the objection was well-founded. It was enough that it was "relevant" in the sense that if the court had ruled in his favour the action would have been terminated. Conversely, the Court was not convinced that the objection was so ill-founded that it was unnecessary for the appeal court to refer to it. The first instance had allowed evidence on the point and, in absence of mention in the judgment, it was not apparent whether it was impliedly rejected or whether the court had merely neglected to consider it. Since the point required an express reply not contained in a decision on the merits, there was a violation. A similar approach was adopted in *Hiro Balani v Spain*, a trademark dispute in which the applicant's claim that her trademark had priority would have been decisive if upheld. There was no answer in the Supreme Court's judgment to this "clearly relevant" submission, and the Court did not consider that it could be assumed that it was impliedly rejected. It was not so clearly ill-founded that no reply was necessary and there was a violation in the absence of that reply.[20] In *Pronina v Ukraine*, in finding a violation, the Court based itself on the domestic courts' failure at all instances to address a "specific, pertinent and important" ground of claim,[21] while in *Kuznetzov v Russia*, the domestic court failed to deal with "the crux of the applicants' grievances".[22]

Lack of detailed explanation of the finding of "gross negligence" in *Georgiadis v Greece* disclosed a violation since the lack of precision of the concept, which was decisive for the applicant's claim for compensation, required more detailed reasoning.

A clear mistake in reasoning or a failure to give reasons based on the applicable law may disclose a lack of fairness. In *Dulaurans v France*, the Court found a violation where the *Cour de Cassation* rejected the applicant's appeal on grounds that she failed to invoke a particular ground, which ignored, without explanation, the finding of the lower court and the applicant's written pleadings—the Court referred to the fact that the rejection of the appeal was based solely on a manifest error of appreciation.[23] In *De Moor v Belgium*, the refusal of the Bar Council to admit the applicant as a pupil advocate disclosed a violation since it did not base itself on one of the grounds in the applicable code, but held that it rejected the application in line with the practice not to admit persons who had fulfilled a full career outside the Bar (which did not automatically disclose any unfitness or incompatibility under the

[19] *Ruiz Torija v Spain* and *Hiro Balani v Spain*, December 9, 1994, Series A, Nos 303–B and C, para.29; *Higgins v France*, February 19, 1998, R.J.D. 1998–I, No.62, para.26.

[20] See also *Higgins*, fn.19 above, para.43, violation where the *Cour de Cassation* gave no reasons for not ordering a transfer of the third of three interconnected cases from an appeal court on grounds of lack of impartiality, it being impossible to tell if this was oversight or a refusal and, if so, on what grounds.

[21] *Pronina v Ukraine*, July 18, 2006, para.25.

[22] *Kuznetzov v Russia*, January 11, 2007, para.87, the court also remained silent on "crucial" evidential points. See also *Georghe v Romania*, March 15, 2007, lack of specific response to the applicant's claim for damages, rendering it impossible to tell whether it had been overlooked or whether the court had made a manifest error as to the object of the action, deprived him of a fair hearing.

[23] *Dulaurans v France*, March 21, 2000. See also *Udorovic v Italy*, May 18, 2010, paras 57–61, appeal court stated, in manifest oversight, that the applicant had not raised a particular ground, whereas he had.

Code). The Court phrased its finding to the effect that the Bar Council did not give the applicant a fair hearing since the reason which it gave was not legally valid.[24] "Manifestly-deficient reasoning" will disclose a violation, as where a domestic court's decision rested on inaccurate and unverified assumptions.[25]

Confused and contradictory reasoning which gave the applicant no clear idea of why the decision was reached disclosed a breach in *Hirvisaari v Finland*, where the Pension Board reduced the applicant's invalidity pension, while at the same time referring to his deteriorating state of health, and the appeal court merely upheld the decision without giving reasons of its own.[26] Contradictory decisions in a criminal case where the second court failed to address the doubts as to sufficiency of evidence identified by the first, and gave no reasons for coming to a different conclusion, founded a violation in *Salo v Ukraine*.[27]

4. Effective access to appeal procedures

II–177 Lack of reasons may raise problems under Art.6, para.3(b) or access to court where it prevents effective use of appeal procedures. For example, issues may arise from lack of access to the judgment itself[28] or from insufficient detail as to the grounds of the first instance decision.[29] In the latter context, courts must indicate with sufficient clarity the grounds on which they base their decisions, since this is essential for the effective exercise of available rights of appeal.

[24] In addition to not providing a public hearing.

[25] *Tatishvili v Russia*, February 22, 2007, paras 58–63.

[26] *Hirvisaari v Finland*, September 27, 2001. No contradictory elements were found in subsequent cases, e.g. *Pirinen v Finland*, May 16, 2006.

[27] *Salo v Ukraine*, September 6, 2005, paras 91–92. See also criticism of inconsistent reasoning in *Kuznetzov*, fn.22 above.

[28] e.g. where the appeal to the Supreme Court was dismissed although the applicant had been unable to obtain copies of the judgments he was appealing against, (15553/89) (Rep.) January 17, 1995, settled after admissibility.

[29] *Hadjianastassiou v Greece*, December 16, 1992, Series A, No.252, the judgment of the Court Martials Appeal Court gave only a summary version of the answers to the points in issue and by the time the applicant received the full text he was barred from expanding his grounds of appeal. This restricted the defence to such an extent as to deprive him of the benefit of a fair trial.

22. Retrospectivity

Key provision:

Article 7 (prohibition of retrospective criminal offences or imposition of heavier penalties). II–178

Key case-law:

Sunday Times v UK (No.1), April 26, 1979, Series A, No.30, 2 E.H.R.R. 245; *Welch v UK*, February 9, 1995, Series A, No.307–A, 20 E.H.R.R. 247; *Kokkinakis v Greece*, May 25, 1993, Series A, No.260–A, 17 E.H.R.R. 397; *G v France*, September 27, 1995, Series A, No.325–B, 21 E.H.R.R. 288; *CR v UK*, November 22, 1995, Series A, No.335–B, 21 E.H.R.R. 363; *SW v UK*, November 22, 1995, Series A, No.335–C; *Cantoni v France*, November 15, 1996, R.J.D. 1996–V, No.20; *Baskaya and Okçuoglu v Turkey*, July 8, 1999, ECHR 1999–IV, 31 E.H.R.R. 292; *Coeme v Belgium*, June 22, 2000, ECHR 2000–VII; *Streletz, Kessler and Krenz v Germany*, March 22, 2001, ECHR 2001–II; *Veeber v Estonia (No.2)*, January 21, 2003, ECHR 2003–II; *Achour v France*, March 29, 2006, ECHR 2006-. . .; *Scoppola v Italy (No.2)*, September 17, 2009, ECHR 2009–. . . ; *Kafkaris v Cyprus*, February 12, 2008, ECHR 2008–. . . ; *Korbely v Hungary*, September 19, 2008, ECHE 2008–. . . ; *Kononov v Latvia*, May 17, 2010, ECHR 2010–. . .

1. General considerations

Article 7, an essential element of the rule of law, aims at the provision of effective safeguards against arbitrary prosecution, conviction and punishment.[1] Its importance is indicated by the fact that no derogation is possible under Art.15. It embodies the general principle that offences must be based in law, and that an individual should be able to know from the wording of the relevant provision, and if need be, with the assistance of the courts' interpretation of it, what acts and omissions will make him criminally liable.[2] That generally entails that the law must be adequately accessible—an individual must have an indication of the legal rules applicable in a given case and he must be able to foresee the consequences of his actions, in particular, to be able to avoid incurring the sanction of the criminal law.[3] II–179

In terms of the standard of legal certainty or foreseeability, absolute certainty cannot be required, and indeed may be undesirable, entailing the risk of excessive rigidity, since the law has to be able to keep pace with changing circumstances.[4] A

[1] *SW v UK*, November 22, 1995, Series A, No.335–C, para.34.

[2] e.g. *Kokkinakis v Greece*, May 25, 1993, Series A, No.260–A, 17 E.H.R.R. 397, para.52; *SW*, see fn.1 above, para.35; *Baskaya and Okçuoglu v Turkey*, July 8, 1999, ECHR 1999–IV, 31 E.H.R.R. 292, paras 36–39, where "printed matter other than periodicals" covered books; *Schimanek v Austria*, (32307/96) (Dec.) February 1, 2000, where "activities inspired by National Socialist ideas" was sufficiently precise.

[3] e.g. *G v France*, September 27, 1995, Series A, No.325–B, 21 E.H.R.R. 288, para.25, where notwithstanding changes in legislation leading to reclassification of the sexual offences of which the applicant was accused, these fell within the scope of the Criminal Code provisions, which were accessible and foreseeable.

[4] e.g. *Streletz, Kessler and Krenz v Germany*, March 22, 2001, ECHR 2001–II, concerning the trial of East German leaders: the fact that domestic courts had different interpretations of the old regime's legal provisions reflected the legal complexity of the case and, as domestic law was largely for the interpretation of those courts, the Court did not find a problem under Art.7, particularly since in its view the conduct in question had been an offence at the relevant time; *Glassner v Germany*, (46363/99) (Dec.) June 28, 2001, ECHR 2001–VII, the conviction of a public prosecutor for deliberate perversion of justice in the trial of an opponent to the regime was acceptable.

standard of "reasonable foreseeability" is sufficient.[5] The Court in *CR v UK* and *SW v UK* noted that judicial interpretation of criminal law provisions was a widespread and even necessary feature. Article 7 could not be read as prohibiting the gradual clarification of the rules of criminal liability through judicial interpretation from case to case, but the resultant development must be within the bounds of reasonable foreseeability and not alter the "essence" of the offence.[6] Nor should the criminal law be extensively construed to an applicant's detriment, for example, by analogy.[7] Changes which are not to the accused's detriment escape the prohibition.[8]

Retrospective measures in other spheres are not expressly prohibited under the Convention and whether they offend will generally depend on the aims pursued and the proportionality of the effects.[9]

2. Retrospective criminal offences

II–180 The complaints brought tend to raise issues less of new statutes or laws being introduced or applied with retrospective effect, but of the uncertainty or lack of precision of those unarguably in existence.[10] In these cases, the issues depend on the analysis of whether or not in a particular jurisdiction, at a particular time a legal provision complied with the requirement of reasonable foreseeability. In assessing this, the Commission considered that knowledge of specialised or technical provisions may be assumed amongst those persons who work in a particular field.[11]

The Convention organs have also qualified the reasonable certainty test with reference to the hypothetical person seeking appropriate legal advice.[12] In *Cantoni v France*, where there was allegedly inconsistent case-law on the application of the term "medicinal product", the Court noted that a law may still satisfy the requirement of foreseeability, even if the individual has to take appropriate legal advice to assess the consequences of a given action. This was particularly so in

[5] *Sunday Times v UK (No.1)*, April 26, 1979, Series A, No.30, 2 E.H.R.R. 245, para.49.

[6] *SW v UK*, see fn.1 above, para.36; *CR v UK*, November 22, 1995, Series A, No.335–B, 21 E.H.R.R. 363, para.34; *Delbos v France*, (60819/00) (Dec.) September 16, 2004, ECHR 2004–IX, where the Court of Cassation ruled on a provision penalising alterations to health warnings on cigarette packets.

[7] *Baskaya and Okçuoglu v Turkey*, see fn.2 above, violation where domestic courts by analogy extended the power of sentencing to imprisonment from another provision. See also *Dragotoniu and Militaru-Pidhorni v Romania*, May 24, 2007, violation where the courts extended the offense of corruption by analogy from public officials to private employees.

[8] *Kokkinakis*, see fn.2 above, para.52; *G v France*, see fn.3 above, para.26, to the extent the law applied retrospectively, it mitigated the seriousness of the offence.

[9] See Pt IIA, s.16: Legislative interference in proceedings; Pt IIB, s.45: Tax.

[10] e.g. concerning overly broad and vague elements of the offence of abuse of position in *Liivik v Estonia*, June 25, 2009, paras 101–104.

[11] e.g. concerning a criminal prosecution of a butcher for failure to comply with food standards legislation, (8141/78) (Dec.) December 4, 1978, 16 D.R.141.

[12] (8710/79) (Dec.) May 7, 1982, 28 D.R. 77, the applicants, convicted for blasphemous libel, alleged that the law lacked clarity, e.g. that the lack of intention to blaspheme was not established until their own case. The Commission found that courts could clarify existing elements and adapt to new circumstances. The findings in the applicants' case were an acceptable clarification and reasonably foreseeable with appropriate legal advice; *Tolgyesi v Germany*, (554/03) (Dec.) July 8, 2008, a lorry driver, with appropriate advice, should have foreseen the German authorities would not accept an employment certificate as a formal work permit.

respect of persons engaged in professional or commercial activities entailing a certain degree of risk.[13]

The borderline between reasonable and unreasonable development is an uneasy one. Clarification of an element of an offence will presumably not infrequently extend the criminal law to conduct previously thought to be excluded. For example, where the German courts interpreted an offence of coercion as extending to the applicant's participation in a sit-in in a public road, the Commission commented that extensive interpretation with a view to adapting an offence to the developments in society was acceptable if it could be reasonably brought under the concept of the offence and was foreseeable by the citizen. It concluded that this example of judicial creativity was compatible with Art.7.[14]

In marital rape cases from the United Kingdom, which concerned the domestically controversial judicial abolition of an exemption from rape previously enjoyed by husbands, the Court had no difficulty accepting that the interpretation was reasonably foreseeable as part of a discernable trend of judicial interpretation.[15] In *Pessino v France*, the Court distinguished the character of the offending conduct which involved building without planning permission from that in the marital rape cases, finding that the change in case-law made by the Court of Cassation was made without the necessary minimum of prior judicial interpretation which could render the step reasonably foreseeable.[16]

In the marital rape cases, the Court also had regard to the nature of the conduct, namely, rape which was essentially degrading, as showing that the development could not be said to be contrary to the purpose of Art.7 and was in fact in conformity with the fundamental objectives of the Convention, the essence of which was respect for human dignity and freedom. This would seem to indicate that judicial developments which are otherwise in conformity with the spirit of the Convention or relate to inherently objectionable conduct will be more readily found to be reasonably foreseeable.

In a similar vein, the Court commented that the ex-leaders of the East German regime who had flagrantly disregarded the principles of legality could not plead the protection of Art.7 after German re-unification when they were tried concerning their responsibility for the deaths of persons shot while attempting to cross to the West.[17] Nor could a prosecutor for a former communist regime rely on the defence of "obeying orders" in conniving at show trials which had led to executions, where the impugned acts were done in knowledge of the lack of legal basis for the charges and the contravention of constitutional and international law provisions.[18]

[13] See also *Chauvy v France*, (64915/01) (Dec.) September 23, 2003, where an editor and publishing house were to be presumed as having access to specialised legal advice and to be aware of the risks involved in publishing; and *Eurofinacom v France*, (58753/00) (Dec.) September 7, 2004, ECHR 2004–VII, where a telecommunications company was expected to take requisite care that it did not facilitate the transmission of material that might be contrary to the law as interpreted by the domestic courts.

[14] (13079/87) (Dec.) March 6, 1989, 60 D.R. 256.

[15] There was a line of cases whittling away the application of the immunity. See, however, the substantial dissenting minority of the Commission who found that the abolition of a defence to husbands in circumstances in which it had previously been available went too far and should have been done by legislation, not retrospectively by the courts, a view shared by the Law Commission.

[16] *Pessino v France*, October 10, 2006.

[17] *Streletz, Kessler and Krenz*, see fn.4 above, para.88. Nor in *KH v Germany*, March 22, 2001, ECHR 2001–I, could an individual soldier who shot unarmed people crossing the border rely on blind obedience to orders and the attitude of the regime where the acts nonetheless flagrantly infringed legal principles and internationally protected human rights.

[18] *Polednova v Czech Republic*, (2615/10) (Dec.) June 21, 2011.

A certain amount of common sense may be relevant in assessing what applicants could or could not foresee. Where Greenpeace activists claimed that due to lack of clear maps and signposts it was not possible to tell the extent of the defence area in a remote corner of Greenland, the Court considered that they plainly knew, from their intentions and actions, that they were penetrating into a prohibited area; their conviction for trespassing was plainly foreseeable.[19]

Laws which are incoherent and obscure will be likely to offend the quality of law criterion. Where circumstances operated, inevitably, to render an applicant in breach of rules without any intention or knowledge, the Court noted that a moral connection between the offending behaviour and the person to be found guilty was generally a necessary element, supporting its conclusion that the punishment in question did not have the quality of law.[20]

Changes in procedural rules which affect applicants' prospects of conviction detrimentally do not per se infringe Art.7, the Court recognising the general principle that procedural rules apply immediately to proceedings already under way. Thus, extension of a limitation period through the immediate application of a procedural law was not in violation of Art.7 in *Coeme v Belgium* where the relevant offences had never become subject to limitation. It was left open whether there would be a breach if a law restored the possibility of prosecuting acts which had become time-barred under the previous provisions. For a Contracting State to rely on the argument that the applicant's conduct constituted a continuing offence committed after the entry into force of new or amended criminal provisions, the acts concerned must be clearly set out in the indictment and the decision of the courts must make it clear that the ingredients of a continuing offence were made out by the prosecution.[21] Where offences related exclusively or even partly to acts which predated the amendment in the law, this did not form part of a "continuing offence".[22]

Nor does Art.7 prevent the prosecution in a Contracting State of serious criminal offences such as torture committed elsewhere; in such a case the relevant consideration is whether the acts were prohibited in the Contracting State and under international law. The intervening issuing of an amnesty by the country where the offence was committed intended to prevent any prosecutions is not a factor which affects the Contracting State's competence, given the importance in international law of preventing impunity. It might be different, however, if the amnesty arose as part of a reconciliation procedure in which impunity was balanced with other important factors of public order.[23]

As regards the prosecution of crimes against humanity, an international crime which has been developing over the last century, the Court has on several occasions had to consider whether the acts for which an accused stood trial did in fact fall under the scope of this crime as it stood at the time at which the acts took place. Thus, in *Korbely v Hungary*, where the applicant was convicted in the 1990's for

[19] *Custers, Deveaux and Turk v Denmark*, (11849/03) (Dec.) May 3, 2007.

[20] *Sud Fondi Srl v Italy*, January 20, 2009, where the applicant company's property had been confiscated for abuse for planning irregularities.

[21] *Ecer and Zeyrek v Turkey*, February 27, 2001, ECHR 2001–III, para.33, in this case the terms of the indictment were inconsistent with the idea of a "continuing offence", not specifying any acts after the crucial date.

[22] *Veeber (No.2)*, January 21, 2003, ECHR 2003–II, paras 35–36; *Puhk v Estonia*, February 10, 2004, para.39.

[23] *Ould Dah v France*, (13113/03) (Dec.) March 17, 2009.

multiple murders of insurgents in 1956, the Court found that the relevant provisions of international law required the acts to be pursuing a State policy, which had not been examined, and that the victims, reasonably believed to be armed and participating in the insurrection, fell outside the provisions which extended at that time only to protection of non-combatants; the conviction therefore disclosed a violation. In contrast, in *Kononov v Latvia*, where the applicant was convicted for war crimes, namely the killing of villagers for alleged collaboration with the Nazis, the Court examined the status of international law in 1944 and found that it would have been reasonably foreseeable that such acts were punishable. It was not persuaded by the applicant's argument that as a young soldier he could not have been expected to understand the content of international law; even a "cursory reflection" would have led him to realise the atrocities would have risked being regarded as war crimes. Nor was it a defence that there was a prescription period in domestic law and that it was only later that international law specified that such crimes were inprescriptible, since at no time had it in fact been the case that the offences had become statute-barred under international law.

Where the relatively new crime of "genocide" in international law was open to differing interpretations at the relevant time, the Court considered that the question was whether the approach of the domestic courts could be reasonably foreseen: since the wide approach accorded with known authorities, the applicant could have foreseen the risk that it would apply to him at the time of the offences.[24]

Notwithstanding the long analyses in Grand Chamber judgments seeking to establish the meaning of various international law provisions, the Court rejected the argument of an applicant, convicted of a war crime for selling mustard gas to Saddam Hussein, that the legislation was too vague in relying on the standards of international law. The Court considered that during the relevant period a norm of customary international law existed prohibiting the use of such gas, which, taken with the repeated condemnations by the United Nations, made plain that the applicant could reasonably be expected to have realised that his actions might be of a criminal nature and to take appropriate advice.[25]

Conversely, there is nothing per se incompatible with the Convention if a State chooses to freeze presciption periods, which might otherwise have operated to render past actions immune to prosecution.[26]

3. Imposition of heavier penalties

Article 7, in its second sentence, prohibits the imposition of a heavier penalty than that applicable at the time of the offence. This may be contravened by a failure to apply the relevant sentencing rules[27] as well as by the retrospective application of new laws.[28] II–181

[24] *Jorgic v Germany*, (74613/01) (Dec.) July 12, 2007, the German courts held that genocide applied to acts of ethnic cleansing aimed at eradicating certain groups socially, and was not limited to attempts at physical or biological destruction.

[25] *Van Anraat v Netherlands*, (65389/09) (Dec.) July 6, 2010.

[26] *Polednova,* fn.18 above.

[27] *Gabarri Moreno v Spain*, July 22, 2003, paras 23–34.

[28] See *Ecer and Zeyrek*, fn.21 above, where the applicants were tried for assisting the PKK by conduct carried out in 1988–1989, but sentenced according to a 1991 statute that increased the applicable sentence by 50 per cent.

However, not all changes which have sentencing consequences to the detriment of persons awaiting trial or already convicted will fall foul of this provision. It does not apply where on appeal a sentence is increased within the statutory maximum which could have been imposed at first instance.[29] Where an offence is reclassified to allow it to be tried in a different court where the powers of sentencing are different, the applicant may be sentenced more heavily than he might have otherwise anticipated, but if the sentence is still within the statutory maximum applicable at the time of the offence the provision is not breached.[30] Nor was there any retroactivity where, due to delay in the trial, the applicant became 15 and thus eligible for a custodial sentence.[31]

It is also compatible with Art.7 where the penalties for recidivism are increased, since, even if a prior offence is taken into account, the punishment is imposed in respect of the repeat offending after the legislation has come into force.[32]

In some circumstances however, procedural changes can raise issues. Alteration in the regime of summary procedure, which had deprived the applicant of an essential advantage in sentencing guaranteed by law and which had prompted his decision to opt for summary trial, was found to breach Art.6 in *Scoppola v Italy (No.2)*.

A significant impact on punishment was felt by life prisoners when the practice in parole changed to exclude the possibility of release before a minimum of 20 years for certain categories of murderers and other serious offenders. However, since the harsh effect related rather to the execution of the penalty than to its imposition, the measure was compatible with Art.7.[33] In contrast, in *Kafkaris v Cyprus*, where the meaning in law and application of the sentence of "life imprisonment" was found to pose a problem of "quality of law," there was a violation. The applicant had been sentenced to life imprisonment at a time where the term served was effectively understood only to mean 20 years, the courts subsequently clarified that life imprisonment meant life. The situation should also be distinguished where differing views as to the effective length of a sentence emerge in a particular case: where the domestic court finally rules on the matter in line with established case-law, this does not involve any retrospective change in sentence.[34]

The notion of a "penalty" has also been considered in a number of cases.[35] For the Court, the starting point is whether the measure in question is imposed following conviction for a criminal offence.[36] Other relevant factors in identifying a "penalty" are the nature and purpose of the measure; its characterisation under domestic law; the procedures involved in its making and implementation; and its severity. It was

[29] e.g. (12002/86) (Dec.) March 8, 1988, 55 D.R. 218.

[30] (14099/88) (Dec.) April 14, 1989, where the sentencing powers of the Sheriff in Scotland in particular cases increased between the applicant's conviction and sentence—the Sheriff had always had powers to refer to a higher court if he considered his own powers inadequate.

[31] *Taylor v UK*, (48864/99) (Dec.) December 3, 2002.

[32] *Achour v France*, March 29, 2006, ECHR 2006, para.59.

[33] (11653/85) (Dec.) March 3, 1986, 46 D.R. 231; similar approach in *Kafkaris v Cyprus*, February 12, 2008, ECHR 2008–. . . , para.151, change of law removing possibility of remission did not impose a heavier sentence; *Grava v Italy*, July 10, 2003, para.51, a Presidential decree on a pardon concerned the execution of the sentence not the penalty itself.

[34] *Garagin v Italy*, (33290/07) (Dec.) April 29, 2009.

[35] See Pt IIA, s.1a: Criminal charge (penalties).

[36] See e.g. *Jamil v France*, June 8, 1995, Series A, No.317, 21 E.H.R.R. 65, para.31.

not found to cover the retrospective imposition on released sex offenders of an obligation to register with police.[37]

However, in *Welch v UK*, the retrospective imposition of a confiscation order on a suspect convicted of drugs offences concerned penalties having regard to its integral part of the conviction and sentencing process and the punitive nature of the measure.[38] Similarly, imposition of imprisonment ordered by a criminal court for non-payment of fines where intended to be a deterrent has also been found to involve a penalty and Art.7 was accordingly violated where a drug trafficker on conviction was subject to application of a retrospective law which increased the period of imprisonment in default of payment from a maximum of four months to two years.[39]

A distinction has also been drawn between preventive confiscation and punitive confiscatory measures, retrospectivity being prohibited only in respect of the latter. In *M v Italy*,[40] where a suspected participant in organised crime was subject to confiscation measures imposed retrospectively by an administrative tribunal separate from the criminal proceedings taken against him, the Commission distinguished between penal measures and measures with a preventive aim, such as the judicial investigation of the probable source of revenue of a person and its removal to prevent future use in a criminal organisation. However, retrospective imposition of an extension in preventive detention was regarded as concerning a "penalty"—as such detention nonetheless was regarded as having a punitive and deterrent element—and thus in violation of Art.7.[41]

While expulsion measures do not generally fall within the scope of Art.6 at all, where a regime of sentencing which replaced the discretionary substitution of a sentence of imprisonment for expulsion with a limit on return of 3 to 10 years by an obligatory replacement of the prison term by expulsion for 10 years, the Court considered that the applicant could claim to have had imposed a more severe penalty when the latter was imposed. This appears to be restricted to the particular circumstances of the case and legal system which treated the expulsion measure as a penal alternative to prison.[42]

4. Benefit to a more lenient penalty

Old Commission case-law did not consider that Art.7 could be interpreted to extend as far as guaranteeing the right to benefit from a more lenient penalty provided for in a law subsequent to the offence. However, in *Scoppola v Italy (No.2)* the Court, taking into account international law developments, considered that there was a II–182

[37] *Adamson v UK*, (42293/98) (Dec.) January 26, 1999, registration was seen as an administrative and preventive measure imposed separately from ordinary sentencing procedures; *Gardel v France*, (16428/05) (Dec.) December 17, 2009, sex offenders' register seen as administrative and preventive measure even if linked to criminal conviction.

[38] e.g. the sweeping statutory assumptions that all money in the possession of a convicted trafficker were proceeds of crime unless proved otherwise; that the judge could take into account culpability in allotting confiscation between various co-accused; and the possibility of imprisonment in default of payment.

[39] *Jamil v France*, see fn.36 above, where the Court rejected the Government's argument that the measure was analagous to the seizure of property to compensate the damage suffered through the illegal import of prohibited goods.

[40] (12386/86) (Dec.) April 15, 1991, 70 D.R. 59.

[41] *M v Germany*, December 17, 2009, paras 127–137.

[42] *Gurguchiani v Spain*, (16012/06) December 15, 2009, paras 32–34.

consensus in Europe and elsewhere that this was a fundamental principle of criminal law. It took the view that not giving the benefit of a more lenient penalty would be disregarding the legislative change favourable to the accused and thus in conflict with the rule of law. Therefore, there was a breach of Art.7 where an applicant had been sentenced to a strict regime of life imprisonment and deprived of the benefit of new legislative provisions enabling the sentence to be substituted in a summary procedure by a sentence of thirty years' imprisonment.[43]

5. The exception: general principles of law of civilised nations

II–183 This exception in the Art.7, para.2 has been applied in several French cases, where the applicants had been convicted of crimes for acts committed during the Second World War. The Commission noted that the purpose of para.2 was to ensure that the rule against retrospectivity did not affect laws which were passed in the wholly exceptional circumstances at the end of the Second World War in order to punish war crimes, treason and collaboration.[44] The Court has held that it applies equally to subsequent legislation on crimes against humanity.[45] Where the exception applies, it appears that the Court will not intervene to review the correctness of domestic courts' decisions or their interpretation of the applicable law.[46]

The role of para.2 has proved limited. In *Kononov v Latvia*, concerning a prosecution for war crimes committed in 1944, the Court commented that in any event "war crimes" had been held to have been declaratory of the international law position prior to Nuremberg and thus, impliedly, no separate issue would arise in the case which would turn on para.1.[47]

In *SW v UK*, the trial judge in the domestic proceedings had taken the view that the case fell within the exception in para.2 as concerning conduct (rape) which, at the time it was committed, was criminal according to the general principles of civilised nations. The Court and Commission's majority did not deal with the point. Mr Loucaides in his dissenting opinion in the Commission noted that the *travaux préparatoires* indicated that this provision was intended to cover prosecution of crimes against humanity in the context of the Nuremberg trials. While he did not exclude that other conduct might fall within the meaning of the phrase, a similar common law immunity for rape in the marital area existed or had existed until recently in a number of common law jurisdictions and he was not prepared to find sufficient international consensus as regarded marital rape. Rape as a systematic policy or inflicted by soldiers, however, is now expressly included within the definition of crimes against humanity and war crimes in the Statute of the International Criminal Court.

[43] See also the dissenting minority of six judges who took the view that this new approach to Art.7 went beyond the plain wording of the text and overstepped the bounds of judicial interpretation.
[44] (29420/95) (Dec.) January 13, 1997, 88–B D.R. 148.
[45] *Papon v France*, (54210/00) (Dec.) November 15, 2001, ECHR 2001–XII.
[46] *Papon*, fn.45 above. See also *Kolk and Kislyiy v Estonia*, (23052/04) and (24018/04) (Dec.) January 17, 2006, where the Court accepted the domestic court's finding that deportation of the civilian population constituted a crime against humanity under international law at the relevant time (1949).
[47] *Kononov v Latvia*, May 17, 2010, ECHR 2010–. . . , para.186.

23. Right to silence

Key provision:

Article 6, paras 1 (right to a fair trial) and 2 (presumption of innocence). **II–184**

Key case-law:

Funke v France, February 25, 1993, Series A, No.256–A, 16 E.H.R.R. 297; *John Murray v UK*, February 8, 1996, R.J.D. 1996–I, No.10, 22 E.H.R.R. 29; *Saunders v UK*, December 17, 1996, R.J.D. 1997–VII, No.53, 23 E.H.R.R. 313; *Condron v UK*, May 2, 2000, ECHR 2000–V, 31 E.H.R.R. 1; *Heaney and McGuinness v Ireland*, December 21, 2000, ECHR 2000–XII; *JB v Switzerland*, May 3, 2001, ECHR 2001–III; *Allan v UK*, November 5, 2002, ECHR 2002–IX; *Jalloh v Germany*, July 11, 2006, ECHR 2006–IX; *O'Halloran and Francis v UK*, June 29, 2007, ECHR 2007–. . .

1. General considerations

The right to silence has made a relatively recent appearance in the case-law dealing with procedural fairness in criminal trials. It appears to achieve more prominence in the Anglo-saxon systems, with the formalised system of cautions and the importance attached to oral evidence. There is, however, all over Europe an increase in the type of criminal/fiscal provisions which place defendants in the position whereby they are required to provide information on pain of a penalty. **II–185**

In *Funke v France*, the Court laid down the general principle that Art.6, para.1 contains the right to anyone charged with a criminal offence to remain silent and not to incriminate himself. The right to remain silent under police questioning and the privilege against self-incrimination were found in *John Murray v UK* to be generally recognised international standards lying at the heart of the notion of a fair procedure and, by providing an accused with protection against improper compulsion, contributed to avoiding miscarriages of justice.

Although the cases are difficult to reconcile at times, the Court has stated that, in assessing whether a procedure has extinguished the essence of the privilege against self-incrimination, it has regard in particular to the nature and degree of the compulsion, the existence of any relevant safeguards in the procedures and the use to which any material so obtained may be put.[1] It has also referred to taking into account, in determining whether there has been a violation, the weight of the public interest in the investigation and punishment of the offence at issue.[2]

2. Coercion to provide incriminating documents or oral testimony

There are two situations which appear: firstly, where an individual is punished in some way for failing to provide information or material and, secondly, where information obtained by use of compulsory powers is used in a criminal prosecution. **II–186**

[1] *Jalloh v Germany*, July 11, 2006, ECHR 2006–IX, para.101.
[2] *Jalloh*, see fn.1 above, para.117.

The approach taken by the Court in these cases is somewhat hard to reconcile analytically, and the leading case, *Funke*, has, as decided on its facts, attracted particular criticism.[3]

(a) Penalties imposed for failure to provide information or documents

II–187 In *Funke* itself, the Court found that the imposition of fines by the French Customs on the applicant for failing to disclose documents concerning his financial transactions violated Art.6, para.1 as offending the principle against self-incrimination. The Commission had reached a different opinion, considering that the protection of a State's vital economic interests legitimately and reasonably required individuals to produce documents relating to matters within customs and fiscal control. It was to be viewed, not as a means of facilitating prosecutions, but as essential for the implementation of the legislation in question and as a reasonable corollary of the trust reposed in citizens generally, allowing the State to forgo more restrictive measures of control and supervision. The Commission had in mind fiscal powers common everywhere in Europe which require disclosure of income which can be used as the basis of tax evasion proceedings. The Court found, without elucidating, that the special feature of customs law did not justify the coercion applied in this case.

Since then, it has been recognised that the requirement, per se, to provide information to the authorities under threat of penalty does not infringe the privilege against self-incrimination. However, penalising someone for refusing to provide information when they are charged, or likely to be charged with an offence, may raise problems, even if the information is not in fact later used in criminal proceedings.[4]

Thus, in *Saunders v UK*, where the applicant gave oral testimony under compulsory powers in a company inquiry conducted by DTI inspectors, the procedure in the inquiry itself was not regarded as falling under the scope of Art.6. The applicant had not been charged at that time. It was the use of the transcripts in the subsequent criminal prosecution that offended Art.6. The Court also distinguished, in that case, material obtained through coercion or oppression against the will of the accused (e.g. confessions, incriminating statements) from the use of material obtained through compulsory powers, such as blood or other physical samples, and documents obtained pursuant to a warrant, which have an existence independent of the will of the accused and do not fall under any privilege against self-incrimination.

Following the approach of the Court in *Saunders* rather than *Funke*, the Commission subsequently found no infringement of Art.6, para.1 in the context of blood samples obtained under threat of prosecution[5]; and the requirement to provide information to the tax authorities.[6]

Unacceptable compulsion was imposed on the applicants in *Heaney and McGuinness v Ireland*, when they were convicted for failing to account for their movements to the police, as required by s.52 of the Offences against the State Act 1939, and

[3] e.g. S.H. Naismith, "Self-incrimination: Fairness or freedom" [1997] 3 E.H.R.L.R.
[4] *Shannon v UK*, April 10, 2004.
[5] (30551/96) (Dec.) April 9, 1997.
[6] e.g. (27943/95) (Dec.) February 26, 1997, 88–A D.R. 120, where the information was used in tax fraud and evasion proceedings.

sentenced to six months' imprisonment. As they had been arrested on suspicion of involvement in a bombing and could be regarded as subject to a criminal charge at the time, the application of s.52 with a view to compelling them to provide information relating to charges against them destroyed the very essence of their privilege against self-incrimination and their right to remain silent. It would also appear that in *JB v Switzerland* it was the imposition of fines, which were not inconsiderable, upon the applicant's failure to provide documents about his income at the time criminal tax evasion proceedings were pending that infringed the privilege against self-incrimination. However, the finding of self-incrimination concerning failure to provide documents would seem difficult to reconcile with the *Saunders* classification of documents as having an existence independent of the person concerned and therefore outside the category of information obtained in defiance of the will of that person.

In a later case, *Allen v UK*,[7] the Court emphasised that the right not to incriminate oneself was primarily concerned with respecting the will of an accused person to remain silent in the context of criminal proceedings and the use of compulsorily obtained statements in criminal prosecutions: it did not per se prohibit the use of compulsory powers to require persons to provide information about their financial or company affairs. The Court noted that the obligation to disclose income and capital for the purpose of tax assessment was a common feature in Contracting States and it would be difficult to envisage taxation systems functioning effectively without it. It also pointed out that not every measure taken to encourage individuals to give information must be regarded as improper compulsion. The requirement, therefore, for an applicant to provide details of his assets under threat of a fine of up to £300 did not infringe Art.6. This appears to imply that measures imposing small fines will not be regarded as oppressively coercive. The fact that the applicant was then prosecuted for giving inaccurate information could also be distinguished from cases involving convictions based on the incriminating content of the statements provided. Privilege against self-incrimination could not, the Court said, be regarded as giving a general immunity to actions (e.g. perjury) motivated by the desire to evade investigation by the revenue authorities.[8] Similarly, a penalty imposed on a car owner for giving inaccurate information about the driver at the time of a speeding offence was found acceptable in *Weh v Austria*. Although the Commission had previously found it acceptable to fine owners when their cars were caught in speed traps, or illegally parked, and they did not name the driver at the time,[9] the Court noted that these decisions did not take into account the right to silence identified in *Funke*. However, as the owner in this case was penalised for giving inaccurate information about the driver of the car at the relevant time and no prosecution was pending against him in respect of the speeding charge, the majority considered there was insufficient connection with a "criminal charge" to cause a self-incrimination problem.

That not all direct compulsion to give incriminating evidence will offend is also shown by the Court's approach in *O'Halloran and Francis v UK*, in which weight was

[7] (76574/01) (Dec.) September 10, 2002, ECHR 2002–VIII.

[8] See also *Van Vondel v Netherlands*, (38258/03) (Dec.) March 23, 2006, where the applicant was convicted for perjury arising out of compulsory evidence to a Parliamentary inquiry (manifestly ill-founded).

[9] (23816/94) (Dec.) May 17, 1995, where a car owner was fined when his car was caught in a speed trap and he alleged coercion, either to be convicted himself or inform on another. The Commission saw no problem with the right to silence since the car used to commit the offence was registered in the applicant's name and he had the overall responsibility for the use to which the car was put.

given to special road traffic context where car owners may be regarded as knowingly taking on certain responsibilities and obligations (such as informing the authorities of the identity of the driver in the event of suspected offences) and the limited nature of the enquiry, which was restricted to the identity of the driver.[10]

Where a person is fined for failure to give evidence in proceedings in which he is a witness, the approach has been similarly unclear. In *K v Austria*,[11] the fine was treated as interference with freedom of expression, Art.6 not being applicable to proceedings in which the applicant was not subject to a criminal charge. In *Serves v France*, however, where the applicant refused to take the oath to appear as a witness before an investigating judge in a murder case, the Court found that the applicant could be considered subject to "criminal charge" for the purposes of Art.6. However, the fines imposed on him for his refusal did not constitute measures compelling himself to incriminate himself. Although the applicant had, on his account, refused since he did not wish to answer incriminating questions, the Court took the rather narrow view that the fines were imposed on him for refusing to take the oath, a requirement to ensure truthfulness which did not force witnesses to answer specific questions.[12]

(b) Use of material obtained by compulsion in criminal prosecutions

II–188 As stated above, the right not to incriminate oneself does not generally extend to the use in criminal proceedings of material which may be obtained from the accused under compulsory powers but which has an existence independent of the will of the suspect (e.g. documents or material produced by the normal functioning of the body such as breath, blood, hair, tissue or voice samples). Where obtaining the material goes beyond the mere passive endurance of a minor interference with bodily integrity, a problem may arise as in *Jalloh v Germany*, where an emetic was forcibly administered to induce the regurgitation of swallowed drugs. This was at risk to the applicant's health, and most importantly, a procedure which violated the prohibition of inhuman and degrading treatment under Art.3. The use as evidence of material obtained in this way infringed the right not to incriminate oneself and rendered the trial unfair.

In *Saunders v UK*, where transcripts of evidence given by the applicant under compulsory powers of DTI inspectors were used in the later criminal prosecution, the Court identified the essence of the privilege against self-incrimination as requiring the prosecution to prove their case without resort to evidence obtained through coercion or oppression against the will of the accused and accordingly found a violation of Art.6. While the Government argued that the statements to the inspectors were in fact exculpatory, the Court found that use of admissions of knowledge, which were relevant to credibility or contradicted other evidence, could be used by the prosecution to incriminatory effect.

[10] *O'Halloran and Francis v UK*, June 29, 2007, ECHR 2007–. . . , paras 57–58, distinguishing *Funke v France*, February 25, 1993, Series A, No.256–A, 16 E.H.R.R. 297, *Heaney and McGuinness v Ireland*, December 21, 2000, ECHR 2000–XII, *J.B. v Switzerland*, May 3, 2001, ECHR 2001–III and *Shannon*, fn.4 above, where the applicants were subject to wide-ranging requirements to produce documents or an account of themselves.

[11] (16002/91) (Rep.) October 13, 1992, Series A, No.255–B (settled before the Court).

[12] The Court minority and the Commission majority found that the fines were penalties attracting the guarantees of Art.6 and that a violation arose from the imposition of the fine without taking the privilege against self-discrimination properly into account.

As to whether there may be legitimate restrictions on the privilege against self-incrimination, the Court in *Saunders* also rejected the Government's argument that the complexity of corporate fraud and the vital public interest justified the measures applied, even with alleged procedural safeguards. The right applied in criminal proceedings without distinction. However, it may be noted that in assessing the nature of the compulsion imposed on the owners of cars requiring them, under pain of a fine, to disclose the driver at the time of a suspected offence, which information, if implicating the owner, was used against them in criminal proceedings, the Court had regard to the context of road traffic offences and the perception that car owners knowingly subject themselves to a special regulatory regime. It was also taken into account that the identity of the driver was only one element in the offence of speeding and that there was no question of a conviction arising solely due to that information.[13]

Requiring a suspect to take an oath during questioning was regarded as exerting a form of coercion. When incriminating statements so obtained were used as evidence, there was a breach of the right to silence.[14]

Indirect methods of coercion in obtaining incriminating statements may also fall foul of Art.6. In *Allan v UK*, the applicant's conviction rested to a significant degree on the evidence given by an informer who had been placed in his cell and coached by the police to "push him for what you can" while at the same time putting him under pressure in normal police interviews. The Court noted that freedom to remain silent was effectively undermined where a suspect, who has remained silent during police questioning, is subject to subterfuge to elicit answers to the same questions. In this case it found that the applicant had been subject to psychological pressures while he was in a susceptible position and thus the information could be regarded as having been obtained involuntarily and in defiance of his will. Thus the use of the information at trial impinged on his right to silence.

Where there are plausible allegations that a confession was obtained by coercion by the police, the lack of a proper investigation into whether the confession was gained by illicit means or other safeguards protecting the right against self-incrimination may render use of the confession in breach of Art.6.[15]

In a somewhat anomalous case, where the applicant stopped for a check by the police made a prejudicial statement about the source of petrol in his van without being warned of his privilege against self-incrimination, the Court found a violation of Art.6. This case should not be interpreted as requiring a "Miranda-type" warning to all potential suspects; the crucial element appears rather to be the way in which the domestic court placed exclusively decisive weight on the statement and did not allow the applicant an effective opportunity to put forward his defence. Thus, the case was less about use of coercion in the self-incrimination context but about the overall fairness of the taking of evidence.[16]

3. Drawing of inferences from silence

In *John Murray*, the Court held that the right to silence was not absolute and, while it might be incompatible to base a conviction solely or mainly on an accused's silence or on a refusal to answer questions, it was equally obvious that the privilege **II–189**

[13] *O'Halloran and Francis*, fn.10 above, paras 57–62.
[14] *Brusco v France*, October 14, 2010, paras 44–55.
[15] *Yaremenko v Ukraine*, June 12, 2008, paras 78–81.
[16] *Aleksandr Zaichenko v Russia*, February 18, 2010, paras 52–59.

did not prevent an accused's silence being taken into account in situations which clearly called for an explanation. It had been alleged that the inferences which could be drawn from the failure of a suspect in Northern Ireland either to give explanations to the police for his presence at the scene of a crime or to give evidence at trial amounted to violations of both the right to fair trial and presumption of innocence. However, in this case, the applicant had not been subject to direct coercion of the type in *Funke* and *Saunders*, being neither fined nor threatened with imprisonment. Having regard to the position in other Contracting States where the conduct of the accused can be freely taken into account in the assessment of the evidence, the Court found that the use of inferences was an expression of the common sense implication drawn where an accused fails to provide an innocent explanation for his actions or presence at the scene of a crime. In the particular case, where the applicant was found at a house where an IRA kidnap victim was being held and there was other evidence implicating him, there were sufficient safeguards to comply with fairness and the general burden of proof remained with the prosecution who had to establish a prima facie case before the inference could be brought into play by the judge, who sat without a jury.[17] The Court did, however, find a violation of Art.6, para.3(c) in that the applicant was denied access to legal advice as to his position at a stage of police questioning which might irretrievably prejudice the defence.

Where it is the jury, rather than the judge, which has the role of drawing any adverse inferences, the Court examines whether the judge's direction to the jury reflects the proper balance between the right to silence and the circumstances in which an adverse inference can be drawn from silence. Particular caution is required when weight is to be attached to silence to police questioning and where an accused has been advised by his lawyer to maintain silence, this must be given appropriate weight.[18] In *Condron v UK*, there was a breach of fairness where the judge mentioned the applicants' reasons for not answering police questions (namely the advice of their solicitor who had doubts about their fitness to cope) but did so in terms that left the jury at liberty to draw inferences even if satisfied as to the plausibility of the explanation. As it was not possible to tell what significance inferences played in the jury's decision to convict and as it was their role to draw properly directed inferences, the defective summing-up could not be cured on appeal.[19]

It is not, however, every shortcoming in a summing-up that will be incompatible with the exercise of an accused's right to silence, whether in a police station or in the witness box. Examining the essential gist of the judge's direction and whether the key elements regarding the exercise of the right to silence appear, the Court has in a number of cases found the alleged misdirections or omissions did not render the

[17] See also *Averill v UK*, June 6, 2000, paras 44–52, where the presence of incriminating fibres on the applicant called for an explanation and no violation arose from the judge's drawing of very strong adverse inferences from his silence to police questioning.

[18] *Condron v UK*, May 2, 2000, ECHR 2000–V, 31 E.H.R.R. 1, para.59.

[19] See fn.18 above, paras 63–66, distinguishing *Edwards v UK*, December 16, 1992, Series A, No.247–B, paras 34 and 39. See also *Beckles v UK*, October 8, 2002, paras 61–66, where the judge failed to direct the jury not to draw inferences if satisfied by the accused's explanation for silence and indeed his comments had undermined the explanation. Contrast *Adetoro v UK*, April 20, 2010, an omission in the judge's direction on drawing inferences did not mislead or confuse the jury in the circumstances where the reason given for his silence in police custody was linked to his substantive defence which the jury rejected, there being no indication therefore that the jury might have drawn inferences or convicted even if they had believed his reasons for silence were genuine.

proceedings unfair and that the direction was nonetheless confined in a manner compatible with the applicant's exercise of his right to silence.[20]

Cross-reference

Part IIA, s.1: General principles: fairness.
Part IIA, s.15: Legal representation in criminal proceedings.
Part IIA, s.19: Presumption of innocence.

[20] The Court has also had regard to whether counsel objected at the time to the judge's direction and to other procedural safeguards, e.g. that the judge has verified whether the accused is aware of the possible consequences of not giving evidence. See *Marlow v UK*, (42015/98) (Dec.) December 5, 2000; *Smith v UK*, (64714/01) (Dec.) December 12, 2002.

24. Sentencing

Key provisions:

II–190 Article 6 (fair trial); Article 3 (inhuman and degrading punishment).

Key case-law:

Weeks v UK, March 2, 1987, Series A, No.114, 10 E.H.R.R. 293; *Hussein v UK and Singh v UK*, February 21, 1996, R.J.D. 1996–I, No.4; *V v UK*, December 16, 1999, ECHR 1999–IX.

1. General considerations

II–191 Matters of sentencing generally fall outside the scope of the Convention.[1] It is irrelevant whether a burglar is sentenced to five years or ten years, or whether a court refuses to suspend a sentence for mitigating circumstances. There have been a few hints that a sentence may be so disproportionate that it could disclose a violation. For example, in *Hussein v UK* and *Prem Singh v UK*, the Convention organs agreed with the applicants that a true life sentence imposed on children, even for murder, would raise problems under Art.3, while in *V v UK*, the Court referred to the ban on life imprisonment of children without possibility of release in Art.37 of the UN Convention on the Rights of the Child.[2] Indeterminate sentences for adults have been found compatible with the Convention where there is sufficient link between the original conviction and continuing detention,[3] although there are also indications that an "irreducible" life sentence for an adult without possibility of release could raise issues under Art.3.[4] Issues of arbitrariness could also arise under Art.5 where sentencing provisions make no allowance for the individual circumstances of the offender or the offence.[5]

2. Discrimination

II–192 However, a measure, which might not in itself offend, may do so if applied in a discriminatory manner. As regards sentencing policies or practices, this has been

[1] e.g. *Weeks v UK*, March 2, 1987, Series A, No.114, 10 E.H.R.R. 293, para.72; *Sawoniuk v UK*, (Dec.) May 29, 2001, ECHR 2001–VI, concerning the imprisonment for life of a very elderly and infirm convict.

[2] While it accepted that children could be subject to punitive sentences and detained under an indeterminate sentence, allowing for continued detention where necessary for the protection of the public, it commented that an unjustifiable and persistent failure to fix the tariff (the minimum period representing punishment and deterrence), leaving the applicant in uncertainty for many years over his future could raise issues under Art.3.

[3] *Weeks v UK*, (Rep.) December 12, 1993, para.73.

[4] (7994/77) (Dec.) May 6, 1978, 14 D.R. 239; *Einhorn v France*, (71555/01) (Dec.) October 16, 2001, ECHR 2001–XI. Some prospect of release, even slight, seems to suffice, e.g. *Kafkaris v Cyprus*, February 12, 2008, paras 107–108; *Garagin v Italy*, (33290/07) (Dec.) April 29, 2008.

[5] e.g. *Partington v UK*, (58853/00) (Dec.) June 26, 2003, concerning s.2 of the Crime (Sentences) Act 1997 which required the imposition of a life sentence on the commission of a third serious offence: since, however, the Court of Appeal had interpreted the legislation to allow a lesser sentence to be imposed in "exceptional circumstances", no arbitrariness arose under Art.5, para.1.

touched on in a number of cases. In *P v UK*, complaints concerning different sentencing applicable to boys and girls was settled.[6] In *Nelson v UK*, a juvenile offender in Scotland claimed that he was not able to benefit from remission in sentence unlike adults or children in England and Wales. The Commission commented that, while complaints about length of sentence, passed after due process of law by a judge in possession of the facts of the case, would not fall within the scope of the Convention, a settled sentencing policy which affected individuals in a discriminatory fashion might raise issues of Art.14 in conjunction with Art.5. However, in the actual case, any difference with adults was justified since different considerations applied in relation to children and any difference between the regime in Scotland and that in England and Wales was based on geographical grounds and not on personal status.[7]

In *Grice v UK*, the Commission also commented that discriminatory release procedures would be problematic but did not find that the applicant AIDS sufferer had substantiated his complaint that prisoners suffering from other illnesses were better treated than he was as regarded compassionate release.[8] Where different procedures for release applied to persons sentenced to over 15 years' imprisonment than to those serving less or an indefinite term, the Court found a violation of Art.14 in conjunction with Art.5, considering that it was an unacceptable anomaly, unrelated to the risk posed by the prisoner, that those serving over 15 years required the approval of the executive for release.[9]

3. Fair trial

Procedural rights under Art.6 apply equally to criminal proceedings dealing with sentencing. Thus, failure to conform with fairness and guarantees of legal representation in sentencing decisions may lead to a violation.[10] II–193

The sentencing aspect of a trial cannot be usurped by the executive. The role of the Home Secretary in the fixing of the tariff (the part of sentence representing punishment and deterrence) in various types of life sentences imposed by courts disclosed a violation of Art.6, in particular as he could not be said to be a tribunal independent of the executive.[11]

[6] (15397/89) (Dec.) January 8, 1992.

[7] (11077/84) (Dec.) October 13, 1986, 49 D.R. 170.

[8] (22564/93) (Dec.) April 14, 1994, 77–A D.R. 90; see also (22761/93) (Dec.) April 4, 1994, 77–A D.R. 98, where an AIDS sufferer claimed that AIDS was not taken into account as a mitigating factor in sentencing unlike other illnesses, but was specifically excluded. However, no discrimination was made out on the facts of the case.

[9] *Clift v UK*, July 13, 2010, paras 55–63, distinguishing *Gerger v Turkey*, July 8, 1999, para.69, where the law was seen as making a distinction between different types of offences not categories of persons.

[10] e.g. lack of legal aid on sentencing appeal in *Murdoch v UK (No.2)*, (25523/94) (Rep.) October 16, 1996; independence and impartiality in *Findlay v UK*, February 25, 1997, R.J.D. 1997–I, No.30; *Csikos v Hungary*, December 3, 2006, violation where the appeal court increased the sentence in the absence of the applicant and his lawyer.

[11] *V v UK*, December 16, 1999, ECHR 1999–IX, para.120, concerning children detained during Her Majesty's pleasure; *Easterbrook v UK*, June 12, 2003, paras 26–29 and *Stafford v UK*, May 28, 2002, ECHR 2002–IV, para.87, concerning adult mandatory life prisoners.

Cross-reference

Part IIA, s.1: General principles: fairness.
Part IIA, s.15: Legal representation in criminal proceedings.
Part IIA, s.22 sub-s.3: Retrospectivity: imposition of heavier penalties.

25. Tribunal established by law

Key provision:

Article 6, para.1 (fair trial before a tribunal established by law). II–194

Key case-law:

Le Compte v Belgium, June 23, 1981, Series A, No.43, 4 E.H.R.R 1; *Campbell and Fell v UK*, June 28, 1984, Series A, No.80, 7 E.H.R.R 165; *Sramek v Austria*, October 22, 1984, Series A, No.84, 7 E.H.R.R. 351; *H v Belgium*, November 30, 1987, Series A, No.127, 10 E.H.R.R. 339; *Belilos v Switzerland*, April 29, 1988, Series A, No.132, 10 E.H.R.R. 466; *Demicoli v Malta*, August 27, 1991, Series A, No.210, 14 E.H.R.R. 47; *Pfieffer and Plankl v Austria*, February 25, 1992, Series A, No.227, 14 E.H.R.R. 692; *Van de Hurk v Netherlands*, April 19, 1994, Series A, No.288, 18 E.H.R.R. 481; *Beaumartin v France*, November 24, 1994, Series A, No.296–B, 19 E.H.R.R. 485; *Procola v Luxembourg*, September 28, 1995, Series A, No.326, 22 E.H.R.R. 193; *Bulut v Austria*, February 22, 1996, R.J.D. 1996–II, No.5, 24 E.H.R.R. 84; *Coeme v Belgium*, June 22, 2000, ECHR 2000–VII; *Posokhov v Russia*, March 4, 2003, ECHR 2003–IV.

1. General considerations

Civil rights and obligations or criminal charges must be determined by a "tribunal established by law". II–195

A tribunal does not have to be a court of the "classic" kind integrated with the standard judicial machinery,[1] but the fact that it carries out judicial functions is not enough.[2] Even a court which generally fulfills the ordinary conception of a judicial organ may in certain circumstances lose this classification. According to the case-law it must be a body which is impartial and independent of the parties, in particular of the executive, and, upon which national legislation confers a power of binding decision in a particular area.[3] This is sometimes expressed as involving substantive aspects, namely its judicial function in determining matters within its competence on the basis of rules of law and after proceedings conducted in a prescribed manner, and also procedural aspects, inter alia, independence, impartiality, and duration of members' terms of office.[4] There is an obvious overlap with the separate requirements of independence and impartiality contained in Art.6, para.1.

[1] *Campbell and Fell v UK*, June 28, 1984, Series A, No.80, 7 E.H.R.R 165, para.76.

[2] *Le Compte v Belgium*, June 23, 1981, Series A, No.43, 4 E.H.R.R 1, para.55.

[3] *Sramek v Austria*, October 22, 1984, Series A, No.84, 7 E.H.R.R. 351, para.36; *Le Compte*, see fn.2 above, para.55; Commission report, para.114, in *McMichael v UK*, February 24, 1995, Series A, No.307–B, the Children's Panel was not a tribunal as, inter alia, it was intended not to be a court but to deal with children's cases in a non-contentious manner; *Savino v Italy*, April 28, 2009, paras 91–99, the internal adjudicatory bodies of the Chamber of Deputies had qualified as "tribunals" with a basis in constitutional law.

[4] *Belilos v Switzerland*, April 29, 1988, Series A, No.132, 10 E.H.R.R. 466, para.64. See also *Stojakovic v Austria*, November 9, 2006, paras 46–50, concerning the status of a Ministry Appeals Commission.

2. Lack of legal basis

II–196 The criterion "established by law" is to avoid tribunals being composed and set up at the discretion of the executive. A practice is not sufficient to give legal basis to a tribunal; its composition, functioning and competence must be set down in law.[5] A court which acts in disregard of legal provisions governing its jurisdiction and composition may cease to be regarded as "established by law".[6]

In *Coeme v Belgium*, there was not, at the relevant time, any basis in domestic law for the Court of Cassation to try anyone but a minister and therefore the Court of Cassation could not be considered a "tribunal established by law" in conducting the trial of four other applicants at the same time as the minister. Failure to conform with the rules regarding the listing of names of lay members of the District Court and their length of service disclosed a violation in *Posokhov v Russia*, where there was no legal basis for the participation of two jurors in the applicant's trial.[7]

The mere fact a special court has been set up for a particular purpose is not a problem, where there is unequivocal legal basis for its functioning set out in legislation.[8]

Since it is primarily for domestic courts to interpret national law, including the rules governing their own constitution and procedures, the Court has stated that its supervisory role will only come into play in cases of flagrant disregard of applicable laws.[9] Where the applicant, a foreigner resident abroad, was tried in Germany for genocide in respect of incidents in former Yugoslavia, the Court found that the domestic courts' interpretation of applicable domestic laws and international law were not arbitrary and they had reasonably assumed jurisidiction.[10]

3. Plurality of roles

II–197 The mere fact that a body has a plurality of functions (administrative, regulatory, adjudicative, advisory or disciplinary) does not exclude it from being a tribunal. Thus, in *H v Belgium*, the Court considered that the *Conseil de l'ordre d'avocats* could be considered a tribunal as it was exercising a judicial function in deciding on the application for re-admission and its impartiality and independence were beyond dispute.[11] However, in *Procola v Luxembourg*, in the context of structural impartiality, the Court found that the fact that four out of five members of the *Conseil d'Etat*

[5] *Pandjikidze v Georgia*, October 27, 2009, paras 103–111, presence on the bench of lay judges who were not governed by any statutory framework in force at the time.

[6] *Buscarini v San Marino*, (31657/96) (Dec.) May 4, 2000.

[7] See also *Lavents v Latvia*, November 28, 2002, para.115, where the Regional Court which reheard an application sent back by the Senate of the Supreme Court was made up of the same composition as the original tribunal contrary to its ruling.

[8] *Fruni v Slovakia*, June 21, 2011, special courts for dealing with fraud and corruption provided for in legislation.

[9] *Coeme v Belgium*, June 22, 2000, ECHR 2000–VII, para.98; *Lavents*, fn.7 above, para.114; *Buscarini*, fn.6 above.

[10] *Jorgic v Germany*, (74613/01) (Dec.) July 12, 2007, paras 64–72.

[11] It did find the fairness of the procedures contrary to Art.6, para.1 in two respects—no reasons for the decision and no public hearing—whereas the Commission had stated robustly that it was not a tribunal due to the nature of its functions, constitution and lack of procedures.

acted in both advisory and judicial functions in the same case was capable of casting legitimate doubt on their impartiality.[12]

Where the President of a Court has an administrative as well as judicial role, the Court has held that the importance of judicial independence and legal certainty required rules concerning the re-assignment of cases to be of a particular clarity and attended by safeguards to ensure objectivity and transparency. Where a President re-assigned a case to himself and then rejected it, the Court noted that this had not been part of a general re-organisation of work and it had not been possible to establish if it had been re-assigned on objective grounds and that any administrative discretion had been exercised within transparent parameters. This had deprived the court of its character as a tribunal established by law.[13]

4. Disqualified judges

The Court has held that the right to be tried by a court whose composition is in accordance with law is a right of essential importance, whose exercise does not depend on the parties alone. There was a violation therefore in *Pfeifer and Plankl v Austria*, where two disqualified judges sat in circumstances where domestic law did not permit waiver. Where, however, in *Bulut v Austria*, there was a disqualified judge who sat but counsel waived objection during the proceedings, the Court found that domestic law permitted waiver and noted that the matter was examined by higher courts which found the composition of the lower court complied with the law.[14] II–198

5. Power to decide

The power to render a binding decision, which may not be altered by a non-judicial authority to the detriment of a party, is a basic attribute of a tribunal. In *Van de Hurk v Netherlands*, the tribunal deciding milk quota disputes was subject to a legislative provision which gave the Government the power to deprive judgments of their effect. There was a violation therefore, notwithstanding the Government's argument that the power was never used. II–199

Problems will arise where a court defers in its decision-making to an external body. Thus, in *Beaumartin v France*, the character of "tribunal" was not satisfied where the *Conseil d'Etat* referred the question of interpretation of the treaty to the Foreign Minister and thus had neither full jurisdiction nor independence from the executive.[15] Nor was it compatible with tribunal status for the Supreme Court of Cassation to defer, without any scrutiny, to the National Bank's assessment of the solvency of a company subject to a winding-up petition.[16] Allowing a medical expert

[12] It found it unnecessary to decide if it was an independent tribunal—*Procola v Luxembourg*, September 28, 1995, Series A, No.326, 22 E.H.R.R. 193, paras 43–45; see also *Savino v Italy*, April 28, 2009, paras 91–99, while qualifying as a "tribunal" the internal appellate body of the Chamber of Deputies included officials who had adopted the regulations in dispute, disclosing a lack of independence. See *Kleyn v Netherlands*, May 6, 2003, ECHR 2003–VI, it was not fatal where the body was not dealing with the "same case" in its dual roles (Pt IIA, s.10: Independence and impartiality, sub-s.3(c): Dual roles).

[13] *DMD Group a.s. v Slovakia*, October 5, 2010.

[14] *Bulut v Austria*, February 22, 1996, R.J.D. 1996–II, No.5, 24 E.H.R.R. 84, para.29.

[15] See also *Chevrol v France*, February 13, 2003, where the *Conseil d'Etat* deferred to the view of the Foreign Minister on the application of a bilateral agreement about recognition of medical qualifications.

[16] *Capital Bank AD v Bulgaria*, November 11, 2005.

to put questions to child victims did not deprive a judge of this status, however, where he continued to monitor the questioning through a two-way mirror.[17]

6. Procedural guarantees

II–200 Lack of independence and impartiality may operate to deprive a body of the necessary character of a "tribunal" or disclose a violation per se. In *Belilos v Switzerland*, where a police officer sat in a judicial function deciding cases on a Police Board, the Court referred to its case-law on the characteristics of a "tribunal", but its finding of a violation of Art.6 centred on the legitimate doubts as to the independence and organisational impartiality of a civil servant who would return to other departmental duties and would tend to be seen as a member of the police force subordinate to superiors and loyal to colleagues. Similarly, the Court in *Demicoli v Malta* found that the House of Representatives played a judicial function in determining the applicant journalist's guilt of breach of privilege, but it was not impartial since two members impugned in the publications participated throughout proceedings. The Commission had doubted whether part of the legislature could by its very nature be considered a court, having regard to its links with the executive. In Bulgaria, where public prosecutors enjoyed a range of decision-making powers, some seemingly judicial, the Court commented that the mere fact that they acted as guardians of the public interest could not be regarded as conferring on them a judicial status or the status of independent and impartial actors.[18]

Cross-reference

Part IIA, s.2: Access to court.
Part IIA, s.10: Independence and impartiality.

[17] *Accardi v Italy*, (30598/02) (Dec.) January 20, 2005, ECHR 2005–II.
[18] *Zlinzat, spds.r.o. v Bulgaria*, June 15, 2006.

26. Witnesses

Key provision:

Article 6, para.3(d) (right to examine and cross-examine witnesses). II–201

Key case-law:

Unterpertinger v Austria, November 24, 1986, Series A, No.110, 13 E.H.R.R. 175; *Bricmont v Belgium*, July 7, 1989, Series A, No.158; *Kostovski v Netherlands*, November 20, 1989, Series A, No.166, 12 E.H.R.R. 434; *Brandstetter v Austria*, November 28, 1991, Series A, No.211, 15 E.H.R.R. 378; *Windisch v Austria*, September 27, 1990, Series A, No.186, 13 E.H.R.R. 281; *Isgro v Italy*, February 19, 1991, Series A, No.194; *Delta v France*, December 19, 1990, Series A, No.191, 16 E.H.R.R. 574; *Asch v Austria*, April 26, 1991, Series A, No.203, 15 E.H.R.R. 597; *Vidal v Belgium*, April 22, 1992, Series A, No.235–B; *Saidi v France*, September 20, 1993, Series A, No.261–C, 17 E.H.R.R. 251; *Ludi v Switzerland*, June 13, 1992, Series A, No.238, 15 E.H.R.R. 173; *Edwards v UK*, December 16, 1992, Series A, No.247–B, 15 E.H.R.R. 173; *Baegen v Netherlands*, October 27, 1995, Series A, No.327–B; *Doorson v Netherlands*, March 26, 1996, R.J.D. 1996–II, No.6, 22 E.H.R.R. 330; *Ferrantelli and Santangelo v Italy*, August 7, 1996, R.J.D. 1996–III, No.12, 23 E.H.R.R. 288; *Van Mechelen v Netherlands*, April 23, 1997, R.J.D. 1997–III, No.36, 25 E.H.R.R. 647; *Sadak v Turkey (No.1)*, July 17, 2001, ECHR 2001–VIII; *SN v Sweden*, July 2, 2002, ECHR 2002–V.

1. General considerations

Courts are allowed a fair measure of discretion in governing their proceedings. Judges may assess to what extent a requested witness may provide admissible or relevant testimony and intervene to prevent, for example, time-wasting or irrelevant questioning.[1] While the exercise of this discretion is subject to the overriding fairness principle, fairness is judged in relation to the proceedings as a whole and it will be rare that isolated, limited interventions by a judge will exceed that margin, however annoying or frustrating to the defence. Since matters of the assessment of evidence are primarily for judges and courts, decisions that a proposed witness's testimony is irrelevant will not disclose a violation unless clearly arbitrary, unreasonable, or if it is substantiated that the witness was essential to the fair conduct of the proceedings or, in criminal proceedings, to secure the rights of the accused.[2] II–202

[1] *Vidal v Belgium*, April 22, 1992, Series A, No.235–B, para.33, referring to "appropriate"; *Bricmont v Belgium*, July 7, 1989, Series A, No.15, "necessary" or "advisable". See *Perna v Italy*, May 6, 2003, finding that the applicant had not shown the relevance to the issues of evidence of two witnesses and the complainant, whom the courts had refused to hear in defamation proceedings; *Kok v Netherlands*, (43149/98) (Dec.) July 4, 2000, ECHR 2000–VI, where the Court did not question the domestic courts' assessment of particular questions as irrelevant.

[2] See, e.g. *Bricmont*, fn.1 above, para.89, "exceptional circumstances" required to find domestic courts' decisions in this area incompatible with fairness. Also *Barbera, Messegué and Jabardo v Spain*, December 6, 1988, Series A, No.146, 11 E.H.R.R. 360, para.68, it was not for the Convention organs to assess whether or not evidence was correctly admitted and assessed, but to ascertain whether the proceedings as a whole, including the way in which evidence was taken, were fair; and *Wierzbicki v Poland*, June 18, 2002, where the courts gave detailed reasons for refusing to hear the applicant's witnesses, which were "not tainted by arbitrariness".

"Witness" as used in the Convention is an autonomous term, not governed by domestic law classifications, and will cover situations where statements by a person are used by a court or read out at trial.[3] Whatever the position in domestic law, it covers statements made by co-accused which may serve to a material degree as the basis for a conviction and thus constitute evidence for the prosecution.[4]

The most difficult problems arise where witnesses are not available for cross-examination even though their statements are admitted in evidence for the prosecution, whether by reason of vulnerability to threats (organised crime, terrorism), lack of compellability (wives, etc), security of undercover policemen, or where the witness has died or disappeared. The Court is alert to the inherent dangers of anonymous witnesses. While it claims not to underestimate the importance of fighting organised crime, it considers that the right to fair administration of justice holds so prominent a place in democratic society that it cannot be sacrificed to expediency. A series of sometimes contradictory Court judgments deals with the problems arising in different situations.

2. Use of anonymous witnesses or written evidence from unexamined witnesses

II–203 A number of principles have been established[5]:

- in principle all evidence must be produced in the presence of the accused at a public hearing with a view to adversarial argument;
- use of statements in absence of oral testimony is not per se incompatible with Art.6, paras 1 and 3(d), but must be compatible with the rights of the defence;
- this rule generally means that the accused must be given a proper and adequate opportunity to challenge and question a witness against him either when the witness makes the statement or later[6];
- it is generally not compatible, where there has been no opportunity to challenge the evidence given by witnesses, for a conviction to be based solely, or to a decisive extent, on their statements.[7]

[3] e.g. *Isgro v Italy*, February 19, 1991, Series A, No.194, para.33.

[4] *Luca v Italy*, February 27, 2001, ECHR 2001–III, para.41. See also *Kaste and Mathison v Norway*, November 9, 2006, where the applicants' counsel were effectively prevented from questioning a co-accused due to the courts' view that he was not a "witness" and did not have to answer their questions.

[5] e.g. *Kostovski v Netherlands*, November 20, 1989, Series A, No.166, 12 E.H.R.R. 434; *Unterpertinger v Austria*, November 24, 1986, Series A, No.110, 13 E.H.R.R. 175.

[6] e.g. *Isgro*, fn.3 above, where the opportunity at trial to confront and question a witness, unavailable before the investigating judge, was sufficient to respect the rights of the defence; *Padin Gestoso v Spain*, (39519/98) (Dec.) December 8, 1998, ECHR 1999–II, no problem arose from the inability of the accused's lawyer to question a co-accused during the investigation where there was an opportunity to do so during the public trial.

[7] e.g. *Unterpertinger*, fn.5 above, a violation was found where the conviction for assault was mainly based on the complainants' written statements; *Windisch v Austria*, September 27, 1990, Series A, No.186, 13 E.H.R.R. 281, the conviction was based largely on anonymous witness statements; *Ludi v Switzerland*, June 13, 1992, Series A, No.238, 15 E.H.R.R. 173, a violation was found where the conviction was not based solely on the written statements of the undercover agent but these played a role in establishing the facts leading to conviction; *Doorson v Netherlands*, March 26, 1996, R.J.D. 1996–II, No.6, 22 E.H.R.R. 330, where the Court seemed to suggest that even in the presence of counterbalancing features (e.g.

Any measure restricting the defence should be strictly necessary and if a less restrictive measure can suffice then that measure should be applied.[8] The Court does not consider that genuine fear of reprisals or of revelation of the identity of undercover police officers can be decisive or overrule the interests of fairness to the defence.[9] Domestic courts also must make proper assessment of any alleged threat to witnesses.[10] While in *Ludi v Swizerland* there was a legitimate interest in maintaining the anonymity of the undercover policeman, the Court was not persuaded that this rendered it impossible to arrange an opportunity for a confrontation or opportunity to question him in such a way as would preserve that anonymity. In *Van Mechelen v Netherlands*, where the undercover policemen gave evidence in a room separate from the defence but connected by a sound link, the Court was not convinced that these extreme limitations had been shown to be necessary in that case and they were not counterbalanced by the fact that the investigating judge who had ascertained the agents' identities had, in a detailed report for the court, stated his opinion as to their reliability and credibility.[11]

The Court has found it insufficient to respect the rights of the defence that an accused is only able to put written questions to an anonymous witness, since this deprives him of the opportunity to demonstrate the unreliability or prejudice of the witness.[12] Reference has been made to the importance that the trial court itself should hear the anonymous witness to be able to judge reliability.[13] However, the Court has acknowledged that it may prove necessary in certain circumstances for the judicial authorities to refer to depositions made during the investigative stage and, as long as the accused has been given an adequate and proper opportunity to challenge those depositions, when made or at a later stage, their admission in evidence may not in themselves contravene Art.6, paras 1 and 3(d).[14] However, the Court has

possibility of counsel questioning the witnesses) a conviction should not be based solely, or to decisive extent, on anonymous witness evidence; *Asch v Austria*, April 26, 1991, Series A, No.203, 15 E.H.R.R. 597, where the alleged victim refused to testify, the Commission found the case indistinguishable from *Unterpertinger*, but the Court found no violation, seeming to rely on the fact that the conviction was not solely based on her statement.

[8] *Van Mechelen v Netherlands*, April 23, 1997, R.J.D. 1997–III, No.36, 25 E.H.R.R. 647, para.58.

[9] *Kostovski*, fn.5 above; *Saidi v France*, September 20, 1993, Series A, No.261–C, 17 E.H.R.R. 251, where the Government argued that the witness drug addicts were fragile psychologically, but the Court found that notwithstanding their state and the difficulties in obtaining evidence, such a restriction on rights of the defence was not justified (i.e. conviction decisively based on their anonymous statements).

[10] *Van Mechelen*, see fn.8 above, para.61. See also *Visser v Netherlands*, February 14, 2002 and *Krasnicki v Czech Republic*, February 28, 2006, where the courts did not carry out an examination of the well-foundedness of anonymous witnesses' for fear of reprisals; contrast *Kok*, fn.1 above, where there were sufficient reasons to keep secret the identity of the informant.

[11] However, in *Kok*, fn.1 above, the hearing of an anonymous witness by the investigating judge apart from counsel was attended by sufficient safeguards—the case appears to be distinguishable on the basis that the defence was handicapped to a lesser degree as the anonymous testimony was not decisive for the conviction and there were adequate reasons supporting the anonymity of the witness.

[12] *Kostovski*, fn.5 above, para.42; *Van Mechelen*, fn.8 above, para.62.

[13] e.g. *Isgro*, fn.3 above, where the investigating judge saw the witness (no violation); *Delta v France*, December 19, 1990, Series A, No.191, 16 E.H.R.R. 574, where the court did not (violation).

[14] *Sadak v Turkey (No.1)*, July 17, 2001, ECHR 2001–VIII, para.65, the accused had had no opportunity at any stage to examine witnesses on whose testimony the courts had largely based their decisions and *AM v Italy*, December 14, 1999, ECHR 1999–IX, where the applicant's lawyer was expressly banned from attending the examination of the alleged abuse victim and other witnesses under letters rogatory. Contrast *Solakov v FYROM*, October 31, 2001, ECHR 2001–X, where the applicant and his lawyer failed to take up any opportunity to participate in the examination of witnesses in the US.

waivered from its strict stance on occasion. Where an informer did not appear to give evidence for fear of reprisals, the Court considered that the court could admit his written statements since, even though he was the main witness for the prosecutor, the conviction of the applicant was somehow not decisively based on his evidence.[15]

Some allowances may also be made with respect to victims of sexual offences, particularly children. Due to the special features of such cases, the Court has said that Art.6, para.3(d) cannot be interpreted so as to require that questions be put directly by the accused or his counsel through cross-examination or other means.[16] In *Baegen v Netherlands*, the Commission narrowly found no violation where an accused was able to confront the alleged victim of sexual abuse but did not have the opportunity to question her. The Commission had regard to special features of rape and sexual offences trials and accepted that, in criminal proceedings concerning sexual abuse, measures may be taken to protect the victim provided such are reconcilable with an adequate and effective exercise of the rights of the defence. Since the accused had not used his opportunity to put written questions or applied to the court to hear her and he had the opportunity to contradict her evidence by submitting to blood or other tests, it was not established that he was unable to challenge the victim's credibility. Similarly in *SN v Sweden*, where the initial police interview with the 10–year-old victim was videotaped and the applicant's counsel was able to arrange for questions to be put in a second taped interview, the Court noted that the applicant's counsel had consented to the form of the second interview, not insisting on postponement to allow him to be present and apparently satisfied that all his questions had been covered. As the courts had taken requisite care in assessing the child's statements and credibility, the Court found no violation arose from the failure to hear the child in court.[17] Where defence counsel had the opportunity to have questions put to child victims, and to observe the questioning from behind a mirror, the examination being recorded for viewing by the court, this was sufficient for the defence to be able to challenge the credibility and substance of their evidence.[18]

In several cases, the Court seemed to accept that the applicant may claim a right to "confront" the witnesses against him, namely, to be physically present and question the persons who have identified him as a suspect.[19] But there may be circumstances where it is sufficient for counsel to confront and question a witness in the absence of the accused, as in *Doorson v Netherlands*, where the Court found that there were relevant and sufficient reasons for the anonymity of the drug addict

[15] *Sapunarescu v Germany*, (22007/03) (Dec.) September 1, 2006, the court also relied on the applicant's and his co-accused's confessions. The Court acknowledged that it was impossible to assess the credibility of the informer and the extent to which he induced the drug deal, which would have been relevant to sentencing, yet still rejected the case.

[16] *SN v Sweden*, July 2, 2002, ECHR 2002–V, para.52. See also *Oyston v UK*, (42011/98) (Dec.) January 22, 2002, where the Court found no unfairness arising from limitations put on questioning victims of sexual offences about previous sexual experiences.

[17] See, however, *PS v Germany*, December 20, 2001, where a conviction for sexual offences was decisively based on the eight-year-old victim's statement to the police and the victim had not been heard in the court itself for very vague reasons. While the second instance court ordered a psychological expert report on the victim's credibility, this occurred some eighteen months after the event and did not enable the defence to challenge her evidence effectively.

[18] *Accardi v Italy*, (30598/02) (Dec.) January 20, 2005.

[19] e.g. *Saidi*, fn.9 above, where the conviction was based solely on the statements of witnesses identifying him to police as a drug dealer and he wished a "confrontation" with them.

witnesses and the domestic court knew the identities of the witnesses and was able to assess their credibility.[20]

Where a witness is no longer available due to death or disappearance, the Court appears to give weight to whether the authorities are at fault in failing to produce him. In *Isgro v Italy*, the Court noted that the authorities had attempted to find the missing witness.[21] In *Ferrantelli and Santangelo v Italy*, where the applicants complained that there was no confrontation with a witness who died, the Court noted that the Government was not responsible for the death and that the statement was found by the domestic courts to be corroborated by other evidence.[22] Where the authorities had not been guilty of neglect in failing to obtain the appearance of the three alleged rape victims, the Court commented that in that event there had been no obligation to discontinue the prosecution and that, as it could not be said that the conviction was solely or decisively based on their written statements, their use at trial was not contrary to defence rights.[23] Where the rape victim died days after the alleged attack, the inability of the accused to question her was not the fault of the authorities; the only question was the role played by her evidence. As the court heard other witnesses and had forensic reports, it was considered that her statement had been corroborated by other evidence and thus did not play a decisive role in the conviction.[24]

Failure to request explicitly the hearing of particular witnesses may not be fatal to an applicant's complaints. Any waiver of rights must be unequivocal and, where the testimony is a significant part of the court's decision and the accused has complained, albeit in indirect terms, of his inability to challenge it, it is expected that the authorities take positive steps themselves to ensure the accused's rights are enjoyed in an effective manner.[25]

3. Refusal to call witnesses or to allow questioning of witnesses by the defence

Although a trial and appeal procedure which results in no witness being questioned by the accused may show an imbalance that does not respect the rights of the defence,[26] Art.6, para.3(d) does not require the attendance and examination of every II–204

[20] *Doorson v Netherlands*, see fn.7 above, paras 70–73, however the conviction was not solely or decisively based on the statements; contrast *Saidi*, fnn.9 and 19 above.

[21] Also *Doorson*, fn.7 above, para.80, where despite the court's efforts it was impossible to secure the attendance of a witness, there was no unfairness in relying on his statement, especially since it was corroborated by other evidence; also *Kennedy v UK*, (36428/97) (Dec.) October 21, 1998, where a key witness had been unable to appear during a retrial due to mental illness, the Commission had regard to the fact that the defence had been able to examine him during the first trial and appeal and part of the retrial; *Calabro v Italy and Germany*, (59895/00) (Dec.) March 21, 2002, where the Italian authorities had done all that could be expected in tracing a witness in Germany; *Verdam v Netherlands*, (35253/97) (Dec.) August 31, 1999, where the victims could not be traced; *Wester v Sweden*, (31074/96) (Dec.) January 14, 1998, concerning the illness of a former co-accused.

[22] The Commission found a violation since it was the Government's fault that they had not acted more speedily and the statement had, as in *Ludi*, fn.7 above, played an important role in establishing the facts leading to conviction.

[23] *Sheper v Netherlands*, (39209/02) (Dec.) April 5, 2005, though it may be noted that both the domestic court and the Court gave weight to the similarity of the three alleged offences, committed over a short time, although none of the victims was subject to challenge by the defence.

[24] *Mika v Sweden*, (31243/06) (Dec.) January 27, 2009.

[25] *Sadak*, see fn.14 above, para.67; see also *Craxi v Italy (No.1)*, December 5, 2002, no waiver of rights where any challenge to the use of written statements, lawfully admitted, by witnesses whom the applicant had not had the chance to question would have had little chance of success.

[26] *Vaturi v France*, April 13, 2006.

witness requested by the defence.[27] Nor will the domestic authorities be held responsible where it is impossible to obtain the attendance of a particular witness required by the defence.[28]

The essential aim has been stated as ensuring equality of arms in examining witnesses, though considerations of equality do not exhaust the provision. A violation was found in *Vidal v Belgium* where the Court of Appeal heard no witnesses for the prosecution or defence, refusing to call the four witnesses requested by the defence. Since, however, it overturned the acquittal on the basis of the co-accused's statement and case file, and increased the sentence without giving reasons for rejecting the defence's request, the Court found that this was inconsistent with the notion of fair trial and that the rights of the defence were restricted in breach of Art.6. Similarly, in *Destrehem v France*, there was an unfair restriction of defence rights where the Court of Appeal had grounded the applicant's conviction on its own interpretation of the evidence given by witnesses it had not itself examined (despite the applicant's request) and which the court of first instance had found sufficiently unconvincing to justify an acquittal.[29]

Circumstances may also arise which require, for the sake of fairness, that a court agrees to the rehearing of witnesses, as in a case where a decisive witness had sent a letter to the court retracting his testimony.[30] However, where the trial court thoroughly examined the circumstances of a key witness' (V's) withdrawal of incriminating statements and came to the conclusion that the repudiation was not trustworthy, no violation arose from the failure to cross-examine V at trial; it was enough the applicant had had a prior opportunity to question V during a confrontation and it was not the authorities' fault that V did not appear, since it had taken search measures including use of Interpol.[31]

Where, as in *Brandstetter v Austria*, a court appoints an expert, the fact that he issues a report unfavourable to the defence will not require the court to appoint another on request of the defence. Where there was no reason to challenge the objectivity of the expert, there was no breach of equality of arms or otherwise and the procedure would continue *ad infinitum*. In *Doorson*, the Court found no problem where the domestic court refused to call a defence expert to give general evidence that drug addicts were not reliable witnesses, noting that it was a matter for the domestic court which could consider that the evidence did not, as such, elucidate the facts of the case and would not contribute much since similar evidence had already been given by other experts.

Nonetheless, the Court has found that the failure to call an expert witness may render proceedings unfair in breach of Art.6, para.1 where the questions of fact and law could not otherwise be adequately resolved. In *Elsholz v Germany*, a violation arose where the domestic courts in a child access proceedings failed to seek psychological expert evidence requested by the applicant father, and supported by the youth office, as to the five to six-year-old child's views. However, in a later case concerning alleged failure of domestic courts to seek psychological reports on the child's views on access, the Grand Chamber reiterated that as a general rule it was

[27] *Vidal*, see fn.1 above, para.33.

[28] *Ubach Mortes v Andorra*, (46253/99) (Dec.) May 4, 2000, ECHR 2000–V, where the witness was in Spain and also could not attend on health grounds.

[29] *Destrehem v France*, May 18, 2004.

[30] *Orhan Cacan v Turkey*, March 23, 2010, paras 39–43.

[31] *Bykov v Russia*, March 10, 2010, para.97.

for domestic courts to assess the evidence before them, including the means to ascertain relevant facts and having regard in particular to the age and maturity of the child who was heard in the proceedings, and found the courts well able to reach a reasoned decision on the issues without the expert evidence requested by the applicant.[32]

Where the court draws on expert evidence relevant to establishing the elements of the offence, failure to make the experts available for questioning by the defence at some point will be problematic.[33]

Cross-reference

Part IIA, s.8: Equality of arms.
Part IIA, s.9: Evidence.

[32] *Sommerfeld v Germany*, July 8, 2003, ECHR 2003–VIII, concerning failure to order expert opinion on the negative views to contact expressed by a 13–year-old, where the Court's reasoning was under the procedural aspect of Art.8, with no separate issue under Art.6. Similar reasoning regarding the failure of the court to hear a five-year-old concerning contact, where there was expert evidence as to the undesirability of direct questioning—*Sahin v Germany*, July 8, 2003, ECHR 2003–VII.

[33] *Balsyte-Lideikiene v Lithuania*, November 4, 2008, where four experts had submitted reports (historical, bibliographical, psychological, on political science) as to whether a nationalistic calendar posed a threat to Lithuanian society, there was a violation as, despite repeated requests, the defendant had not been able to question them.

B. OTHER

1. Abortion

Key provisions:

Articles 2 (right to life), 3 (prohibition on torture and inhuman treatment), 8 (respect for family and private life), 9 (freedom of conscience and religion), 10 (freedom of expression) and 11 (freedom of assembly). II–205

Key case-law:

Open Door Counselling and Dublin Well Woman v Ireland, October 29, 1992, Series A, No.246, 15 E.H.R.R. 244; *Vo v France*, July 8, 2004, ECHR 2004-. . .; *Tysiac v Poland*, March 20, 2007; *A, B and C v Ireland*, December 16, 2010, ECHR 2010–. . .

1. General considerations

Abortion continues to be a controversial subject in Council of Europe States generally and reveals widely differing approaches, ranging between liberal freedom of choice to women in Norway to almost total prohibition in Ireland. Sensitive to the difficult moral and ethical issues involved and to the lack of consensus, the Commission was reluctant to intervene and condemn any particular State policy that has been adopted, with the result that no cases on the practice of abortion ever reached the Court until relatively late. The Court has largely followed the Commission's approach and accorded a wide margin of appreciation to States.[1] However, with the entry to the system of another very restrictive country, Poland, difficult and sensitive cases are now arising. Nonetheless the Court has so far refrained from examining whether there is as such a right to abortion or whether a refusal of an abortion constitutes per se an interference with rights.[2] II–206

There have been peripheral issues arising around abortion, in particular, the steps taken, publicly, to support or criticise the practice, which have given rise to case-law in the context of Art.10.

2. Who can complain?

Only a person directly affected by the measure or legislation in question may bring a complaint. This includes any woman of child-bearing age (it is not required for a woman to be pregnant)[3]; the husband of a woman who intends to have an II–207

[1] *Vo v France*, July 8, 2004–. . ., ECHR 2004, para.82, concerning the moment at which life begins.
[2] *Tysiac v Poland*, March 20, 2007, paras 104 and 108.
[3] *Brüggeman and Scheuten v Germany*, (6959/75) (Dec.) May 19, 1976, 5 D.R. 103.

abortion[4]; and the putative father of a foetus carried by an unmarried mother.[5] It does not include a minister who considers that domestic legislation permitting abortion is wrong[6] or a man (husband and father of children) who objects to legislation on principle.[7]

3. Right to life of the unborn child

II–208 The Commission tended to the view, without deciding, that the foetus or unborn child was not protected by Art.2.[8] It referred to the terms of Art.2 as not appearing to apply to an unborn child. In *Boso v Italy*, the Court left the question open and stated that, even assuming the foetus could attract the protection of Art.2, in the circumstances of the case, where abortions were only permitted on grounds of risk to the mother, the State had not exceeded the margin of appreciation accorded to it in this delicate area.[9] It may be noted though, that in a controversial French case dealing with adoption it has found that measures taken by the State with a view to avoiding the number of abortions carried out, in particular illegal abortions, pursued the legitimate aim of respecting life.[10]

This does not necessarily exclude the application of the Convention in other circumstances, perhaps outside the medical context of abortion.[11] In *Vo v France*, where the mother lost the foetus due to a mistake by a doctor, the Court considered, in the absence of any European consensus, that it was neither appropriate or desirable to decide whether the unborn child was a person for the purposes of Art.2. However, on the assumption that Art.2 was applicable, it considered that it was sufficient by way of procedural protection that a prosecution lay for any injury to the mother and damages were payable for negligence. It was not necessary that under domestic law the option of charging the doctor with involuntary killing should have been available.

4. Inhuman treatment

II–209 In *H v Norway*,[12] the potential father raised the issue of the pain possibly caused to the 14-week-old foetus by the abortion procedure. The Commission found this allegation to be unsubstantiated by the material before it.

[4] (8416/79) (Dec.) May 13, 1980, 19 D.R. 244; *Boso v Italy*, (50490/99) (Dec.) September 5, 2002, ECHR 2002–VII.

[5] *H v Norway*, (17004/90) (Dec.) May 19, 1992, 73 D.R. 155.

[6] (11045/84) (Dec.) March 8, 1985, 42 D.R. 47.

[7] (7045/75) (Dec.) December 10, 1975, 7 D.R. 87.

[8] *Brüggeman and Scheuten v Germany*, (6959/75) (Rep.) July 12, 1977, 10 D.R. 100. In *Open Door Counselling and Dublin Well Woman v Ireland*, October 29, 1992, Series A, No.246, 15 E.H.R.R. 244, the Court left open whether the restriction on abortion could be considered as pursuing the aim of protecting the rights of others in the sense of the unborn child.

[9] See fn.4 above. See also *Evans v UK*, April 10, 2007, paras 54–56, where it was within the margin of appreciation for stored embryos to be excluded from the domestic right to life.

[10] *Odievre v France*, February 13, 2003, ECHR 2003–III, para.45.

[11] *Mentes v Turkey*, (23186/94) (Dec.) January 9, 1995, where the Commission declared admissible complaints alleging the security forces' expulsion of villagers from their homes, including a claim that in the resulting trauma a pregnant woman gave birth prematurely to twins who died. Her claims were rejected as unsubstantiated when she failed to give evidence before the Commission delegates: (Rep.) March 7, 1996, R.J.D 1998–IV.

[12] See fn.5 above.

5. Rights of a potential father

A potential father cannot derive a claim to be consulted in advance of any abortion. While his rights to potential family life may be interfered with by an abortion, they have to be weighed against the rights of the mother. Where the abortion is on grounds of the medical welfare of the mother, the rights of the mother have been found to outweigh those of the father.[13] Where the abortion was not on health grounds but social hardship, as in *H v Norway*, the Commission still found that the rights of the woman, as the person primarily concerned by the pregnancy and its termination, prevailed over the father, notwithstanding that the couple had planned to marry and had together planned the pregnancy. The Court reached the same conclusion in *Boso v Italy*, where the applicant complained that his wife had obtained an abortion without any possibility of intervention on his part.[14] II–210

6. Rights of the woman

(a) Availability of abortion

As indicated above, where domestic legislation allows abortion, whether on health or non-health-related grounds, the woman's rights prevail over the putative father's. II–211

The position is different where the legislation restricts abortion and it is the woman who claims a wider right under domestic law. There is no right, as such, to abortion, but the issues as relate to the health and well-being of the mother generally fall within the scope of Art.8 in its private life aspect.[15] In a German case,[16] a law was struck down by the Constitutional Court as unconstitutional, which permitted abortion within 12 weeks without particular ground of necessity. Abortion was subsequently limited to particular grounds. The Commission found that this legislation did not constitute an interference with the applicant women's rights to respect for private life. It had regard to the fact that abortion was permissible, that the health and distress of the mother were taken into account (albeit in restricted scope) and that the criminal provisions did not penalise women excessively (i.e. a pregnant woman was exempt from punishment if the abortion was performed by a doctor within 22 weeks and she had made use of counselling). In *H v Norway*, the Commission referred to the fact that laws on abortion differed considerably between the Contracting States and that "assuming that the Convention may be considered to have some bearing in this field" it found that in such "a delicate area" States must have a certain discretion. A wide margin of appreciation applies, largely due to widely-differing views held as to when life begins. Thus, it was acceptable, given the access to information to abortion abroad and freedom of travel for that purpose, that in Ireland no abortion was possible for mere health and well-being grounds (as opposed to a substanitial risk to life ground). The profound moral views of the Irish people as to the nature of life was given recognition in the context of the protection of morals justification to the restriction.[17]

[13] See fn.4 above.

[14] See fn.4 above.

[15] *A, B and C v Ireland*, December 16, 2010, ECHR 2010–. . . , para.214.

[16] *Brüggeman and Scheuten*, (Rep.), see fn.8 above.

[17] See the substantial partial dissent by Judge Rozakis and five other judges, which pointed out that this was the first time that national moral values had been allowed to trump a clear European consensus. It may also be noted that the moral views of the population in Northern Ireland were not given much weight in the context of the criminalisation of adult homosexual relation in *Dudgeon v UK*, October 22, 1981, paras 56–62.

So far, therefore, varying restrictions appear acceptable, though it may be noted that even if the Court continues to deny there is a right to abortion, in the aforementioned cases it took into account the ability of women to obtain an abortion in at least some circumstances or the availability of abortion elsewhere.

Where serious implications for the mother's health do appear to arise, even if short of life-threatening, the Court has taken a procedurally-based stance. Where it was confronted, in *Tysiac v Poland,* with a case in which a woman had been refused an abortion on therapeutic grounds, it examined the matter under Art.8 as regarded the positive obligation on the State to protect the physical integrity of the applicant mother, who had, allegedly, become effectively blind due to her pregnancy coming to term. It placed particular emphasis on procedural safeguards. Contracting States had to provide a form of procedure before an independent body competent to review the refusal to permit a therapeutic abortion. In this procedure the pregnant woman should have the possibility of being heard in person and have her views considered, as well as receiving written grounds for the eventual decision. The procedural failings in this case, therefore, disclosed a violation of Art.8.[18] Where in *A, B and C v Ireland*, the third applicant had serious concerns as to the impact on her own health of the pregnancy due to recent cancer treatment, the Court found a violation since the state of law was such that, although in theory abortion should have been available in life-threatening circumstances, the scope of the right in practice was uncertain and there was no framework or procedure in which the applicant could seek to assert that right effectively and in due time.[19] In other words, if abortion is made available within a State, there should be legal mechanisms, properly accessible and effective, to allow the right to be exercised.

Lack of availability of abortion within the Contracting State, rendering it necessary for women to travel abroad to obtain an abortion, although arduous physically and psychologically, did not meet the threshold of inhuman treatment under Art.3.[20]

Even if the Commission was tentative about the Convention organs' competence to strike down any particular substantive legal regime on abortion, the possibility is still there.[21]

(b) Information about abortion

II–212 Even where abortion is not lawful however, women may claim the right to access to information from others relating to abortions performed lawfully in another Contracting State, at least where another person or body is willing to give the

[18] *Tysiac*, see fn.2 above, there had been a difference of medical opinion as to the extent to which the pregnancy would affect the applicant's sight, and a lack of will on the part of medical staff to explain or accord to the applicant the available procedures.

[19] See fn.15 above, paras 250–267, the Court was not persuaded that a full-blown constitutional action was an effective and accessible procedure to a woman in a vulnerable situation; nor that the unregulated medical consultative procedures would be effective, given the overt resistance of the medical establishment to abortion.

[20] *A, B and C v Ireland*, see fn.15 above, paras 164–165, though it was left open whether the State was responsible under the Convention for any such "treatment".

[21] The case of *Att Gen v X* in Ireland in 1992 was an example of how a blanket prohibition could affect a teenage girl, pregnant from an alleged rape, who had been prevented by injunction from leaving Ireland to seek an abortion in the UK. The Irish Supreme Court, on March 5, 1992, did accept that termination of pregnancy could be permissible under the Irish Constitution where it was established as a matter of probability that there was a real and substantial risk to the life of the mother if the termination was not effected, with the result that the case did not come to Strasbourg. There would conversely be the other end of the spectrum where, for example, in the case of a mentally ill woman, steps were taken to carry out an abortion dispensing with her consent.

information. It is arguable whether the State or public authority could be obliged to make available such information themselves.

In *Open Door Counselling and Dublin Well Women v Ireland*, where two women's counselling organisations, two individual counsellors and two women of child-bearing age complained about an Irish Supreme Court injunction which restrained the two organisations from providing certain information to pregnant women concerning abortion facilities outside Ireland in the context of non-directive counselling, the Court found a breach of Art.10. The Court considered that the State did not have an unfettered or unreviewable discretion in the field of morals and held that the restriction was unnecessary, giving weight to the sweeping nature of the injunction regardless of the age, health or circumstances of the woman concerned, the fact that it was not against the law for a woman to travel abroad and that it prevented the provision of information about abortion facilities which were available lawfully in other Contracting States. It noted that in any case the information was available in other forms (via magazines and telephone directories) and that the ban appeared to penalise women who were less resourceful or educated and created a risk that women, in the absence of proper counselling, might seek abortion at later stages and fail to take advantage of medical supervision after an abortion.

7. Expression of views in respect of abortion

The Commission found it justifiable under Art.10 for individuals to be penalised II–213
where they expressed their views on abortion in certain circumstances to which others might object. It held that it was an acceptable restriction on freedom of expression where a doctor employed by a Catholic hospital was sacked following expression of views favourable to abortion in a letter to a newspaper.[22] It had regard to the contractual link freely undertaken by the doctor with an organisation whose convictions on abortion were well-known. On the other hand, the Commission also found it justified for the protection of the reputation of others under Art.10, para.2 where a doctor was fined for expressing the opinion that abortion advice centres were embryo-killer syndicates and the trade union organisation advocating them was "Nazi".[23] The Commission had regard to the light penalty. Such restrictions might perhaps be found disproportionate if they went beyond relatively small fines or sanctioned persons for the expression of more moderate or considered views outside the context of special contractual relationships.

Where an applicant in Poland was convicted of aiding and abetting abortion and sentenced to one and a half years' imprisonment and fined, the Court found that Art.10 did not even apply as it was not the expression of views held by the applicant in respect of the legal status of abortion which was in issue, nor had the applicant engaged in any kind of public debate.[24]

However, authorities cannot rely on purported grounds of public order to stop associations expressing their opposition to restrictive abortion policies without showing, convincingly, a necessity for such measures. Thus, the Court noted, in a case where several associations wished to pursue informational activities on board a

[22] (12242/86) (Dec.) September 6, 1989, 62 D.R. 151.
[23] (12230/86) (Dec.) December 12, 1987.
[24] *Tokarczyk v Poland*, (51792/99) (Dec.) January 31, 2002.

ship, there was no serious basis for allegedly suspecting that the associations would breach domestic law by selling prohibited abortion drugs and that, even if there were, there were other measures that could be carried out, such as seizing the drugs, instead of taking the intimidatory and draconian step of sending a warship to enforce an interdiction against entering territorial waters.[25]

8. Position of medical staff

II–214 There has only been one case indirectly raising issues as to the participation of medical staff in abortion procedures. In a Swedish case, three trainee midwives objected to being required in their training to insert contraceptive coils which they considered to have an abortive effect.[26] However, the case was struck off when the midwives were allowed to qualify with their certificate indicating that they had not conducted such procedures.

9. Freedom to demonstrate

II–215 Where an association against abortion carried out a public demonstration which was disrupted by others in favour of abortion, the Commission found that it had a right to be protected by the State in the exercise of its freedom of assembly although, in the circumstances of the case, the State had not failed in its obligations (i.e. it accepted the argument, inter alia, that more intrusive police intervention would in fact have escalated the violence that occurred).[27]

States may restrain the activities of protesters for or against abortion, in a proportionate manner, in the interests of preventing crime or disorder and protecting the rights of others. Thus it was a legitimate restriction to impose an injunction to prevent an applicant handing out leaflets at the door to an abortion clinic and seeking to dissuade women from entering. Under Art.9, the activities which primarily aimed at persuading women not to have an abortion did not constitute the expression of a belief.[28]

[25] *Women on Waves v Portugal*, February 3, 2009, the Court gave a high level of protection to the form of expression chosen by the associations who had, in any event, been able to take part in informational activities on land; it clearly considered the military armed response was overkill with an unacceptable chilling effect on the expression of views perceived as dissident.

[26] (12375/86) (Dec.) October 7, 1987.

[27] *Plattform Ärzte v Austria*, (10126/82) (Dec.) October 17, 1985, 44 D.R. 65.

[28] (22838/93) (Dec.) February 22, 1995, 80–A D.R. 187; (30936/96) (Dec.) September 10, 1997, the applicants' conviction for breach of the peace for entering an abortion clinic to conduct a communal praying session was considered justified for the protection of the rights and freedoms of others.

2. Aids

Key provisions:

Articles 3 (prohibition of inhuman treatment), 5 (liberty and security of person), 6 (fair trial within a reasonable time), 8 (respect for private life) and 14 (prohibition of discrimination). II–216

Key case-law:

X v France, March 31, 1992, Series A, No.234–C, 14 E.H.R.R. 483; *Vallée v France*, April 26, 1994, Series A, No.289, 18 E.H.R.R. 549; *Karakaya v France*, August 26, 1994, Series A, No.289–B; *A v Denmark*, February 8, 1996, R.J.D. 1996–I, 22 E.H.R.R. 458; *Z v Finland*, February 25, 1997, R.J.D. 1997–I, 25 E.H.R.R. 371; *D v UK*, May 2, 1997, R.J.D. 1997–III, 24 E.H.R.R. 423; *Enhorn v Sweden*, January 25, 2005, ECHR 2005–I; *N v UK*, May 27, 2008, ECHR 2008–. . . ; *Aleksanyan v Russia*, December 22, 2008, ECHR 2008–XII.

1. General considerations

The first cases dealt with by the Court rose in the context of proceedings for compensation for those contaminated through infected blood banks. More recently, claims have been made alleging that a State has failed to protect an individual's right to respect for life or security of person through inadequate regulation of public blood bank facilities, and concerning compatibility of keeping HIV/AIDS sufferers in detention and the adequacy of medical treatment in prison. For the moment it has not been shown that any prisoner has contracted, or been at serious risk of contracting, HIV/AIDS due to the lack of proper precautions by the authorities in the detention context.[1] II–217

Issues have also arisen concerning the disclosure of medical details of AIDS sufferers; the risk of inhuman treatment resulting from expulsion to a country where no drugs treatment or support care is available[2] and detention, sentencing and release procedures applicable to persons suffering from AIDS.[3]

The stigma and social difficulties facing AIDS sufferers have not been subject to much exposure in applications, presumably since these are matters of pervasive effect rather than express Governmental policy. However, in a case where an applicant who had settled in Russia with his family was refused a residence permit solely due to his HIV status, the Court underlined the unacceptability of imposing differential treatment on such sufferers without compelling justification.[4]

2. Protection of the right to life

A person infected with HIV by transfusions from a public blood bank may claim to be a victim of a violation of Art.2 given that his or her life has been put at risk.[5] Positive obligation arises under Art.2 for Contracting States to put in place a II–218

[1] *Korobov v Russia*, (67086/01) (Dec.) March 2, 2006.
[2] *D v UK*, May 2, 1997, R.J.D. 1997–III, 24 E.H.R.R. 423.
[3] *Grice v UK*, (22564/93) (Dec.) April 14, 1994, 77–A D.R. 90; *RM v UK*, (22761/93) (Dec.) April 14, 1994, 77–A D.R. 98.
[4] *Kiyutin v Russia*, March 10, 2011, paras 64–65.
[5] *Karchen v France*, (5722/04) (Dec.) March 4, 2008; *GN v Italy*, December 1, 2009, paras 67–69.

regulatory framework in hospitals, whether public or private, ensuring the adoption of measures protecting the lives of patients.[6]

This would require them to take reasonable steps to address a risk to life that was or should have been known to the authorities. Where Italian applicants complained of being contaminated from public hospital blood supplies, the Court accepted the findings of domestic courts as to the dates from which the Minister of Health could be regarded as knowing the risks of contamination from the blood bank supplies and thus found no failings in this regard before that time.[7]

A State is also under an obligation to provide a system of effective judicial protection, in particular the possibility of applying in civil proceedings for damages, but penal proceedings punishing those responsible will not always be required where there was no intentional harm.[8]

Discrimination contrary to Art.14 in conjunction with Art.2 was disclosed by the fact that compensation provisions benefited only a particular category of those infected from the bloodbanks, namely haemophiliacs, to the exclusion of those who had a different type of condition.[9]

3. Delay in compensation proceedings

II–219 Proceedings for compensation brought by those who developed HIV from contaminated blood supplies concern the determination of civil rights within the meaning of Art.6, para.1, as the outcome would be decisive for private rights to damages for injuries.[10] The Convention organs have emphasised the particular need for expedition in proceedings where the applicant is suffering from a disease such as HIV or full-blown AIDS where deterioration and death may ensue very rapidly. In *X v France*, the applicant, a haemophiliac who had received blood transfusions in a State hospital, discovered that he was HIV positive and filed for compensation to the relevant Government authority. When he died just over two years later, his appeal was still pending at the Administrative Court of Appeal. The Court found that the period of over two years was unreasonable. Though the matter of establishing the State's liability was complex, the Government should have been aware that proceedings were imminent and ought to have commissioned an objective report on liability immediately after the commencement of the cases against them. While two years might not have been dilatory for the average administrative court proceedings, the Court considered that, given the incurable nature of the infection and the applicant's reduced life expectancy, exceptional diligence was called for on the part of the domestic authorities, notwithstanding the number of similar pending cases.[11]

[6] *GN*, see fn.5 above, para.79.

[7] *GN*, see fn.5 above, paras 91–95.

[8] *Karchen*, see fn.5 above, the applicant, an infected haemophiliac, obtained compensation; the Court found nothing arbitrary in the domestic courts' rejection of criminal action for administering a harmful substance for lack of responsibility by the defendants, noting that blood bank officials had been convicted of other offences concerning the quality of the blood products; the French system had therefore provided sufficient protection.

[9] *GN*, see fn.5 above, paras 124–134, where the authorities only offered substantial settlements to haemophiliacs, apparently because they were the largest group affected.

[10] In *X v France*, March 31, 1992, Series A, No.234–C, 14 E.H.R.R. 483, the Court dismissed the Government's argument that the proceedings raised public law issues of the State's exercise of its regulatory authority rather than civil rights.

[11] See also *Vallée v France*, April 26, 1994, Series A, No.289, 18 E.H.R.R. 549, and *Karakaya v France*, August 26, 1994, Series A, No.289–B, where proceedings for compensation had lasted four or more years; *A v Denmark*, periods of over five and six years disclosed violations.

Even where the applicants had themselves contributed not inconsiderably to the delay, the Court found this did not dispense the courts from ensuring compliance with the requirement of reasonable time which in these cases involved the need for exceptional diligence. Furthermore, although in *Karakaya v France* and *Vallée v France* the applicants had received compensation from a State fund during an administrative procedure, the Court found that what was at stake in the civil proceedings continued to be of great importance, in both pecuniary and non-pecuniary terms. The requirement of exceptional diligence did not apply, however, to proceedings brought by relatives of a deceased AIDS victim.[12]

Complaints concerning the inadequate judicial response to claims of State responsibility for infection may also be examined under the procedural aspect of Art.2, though largely the same considerations as to the need for special diligence under Art.6 seem to apply.[13]

4. Detention issues

(a) Detention on remand or conviction

It is not inhuman or degrading per se to keep an HIV/AIDS sufferer in detention. II–220
The Court will, however, examine whether there is adequate medical treatment and whether the applicant's condition is compatible with detention. In *Gelfmann v France*, where the applicant had suffered HIV/AIDS for over 20 years and his chances of survival were compromised in the short to medium term, the Court noted that the applicant had made no complaint about the treatment available and that there was medical evidence that his condition did not exclude detention. It flagged as relevant the procedural possibility to challenge continued incarceration if his condition changed and to obtain expert evidence on the matter.[14] In *Khudobin v Russia*, the lack of qualified or timely medical assistance available in prison and the strong feeling of insecurity this engendered in the applicant, who suffered from several serious health problems including AIDS, did disclose degrading treatment contrary to Art.3.[15] Where there were strong indications that a prisoner's condition could not be treated adequately in the prison hospital, and the Government refused an interim measure requiring that the applicant's state of health be clarified by a bi-partisan medical commission, the Court drew adverse inferences and found that the failure to transfer him to a specialised facility amounted to inhuman and degrading treatment and that his prolonged pre-trial detention was not based on relevant and sufficient

[12] *A v Denmark*, February 8, 1996, R.J.D. 1996–I, 22 E.H.R.R. 458.

[13] See *GN v Italy*, fn.5 above, paras 96–102. See further Part IIB, s.43: Right to life.

[14] *Gelfmann v France*, December 14, 2004. See also *Ceku v Germany*, (41559/06) (Dec.) March 13, 2007, and *Colak v Germany*, (77144/01) and (35493/05) (Dec.) December 11, 2007, the Court was not prepared to substitute its own view for the domestic courts' which declined to order the release of the prisoner, suffering from HIV and a two year life expectancy, noting that such prisoners were provided with the appropriate medical care in prison and that they could re-apply to the courts if there was a change in circumstances.

[15] *Khudobin v Russia*, October 26, 2006. Contrast *ID v Romania*, (40155/02) November 24, 2005, where certain gaps in treatment caused distress but did not show any failure to protect health.

grounds. In those exceptional circumstances, the Court held that the applicant's detention should be discontinued.[16]

(b) Sentencing and release procedures

II–221 While in older cases the Commission noted that questions of length of sentence generally fell outside the scope of Art.5, and that there was no right as such to early release, it did find that where procedures relating to the release or sentencing of prisoners appeared to operate in a discriminatory manner, an issue could arise under Art.14 in conjunction with Art.5. It rejected the cases on their facts, however, for perhaps less than convincing reasons.

In *Grice v UK*, where the applicant, suffering from full-blown AIDS and sentenced to four years, was refused early release from prison on compassionate grounds, he argued that the Home Office was discriminating against HIV/AIDS sufferers, none of whom had ever been released early on compassionate grounds, whereas prisoners suffering from other non-life-threatening illnesses, such as senile dementia or treatable illnesses like cancer, were being released. The Commission noted that the applicant's life expectancy had been given by his doctor at trial as two years and then later as 6–12 months, but while in prison he had not suffered any sudden deterioration and he had not been incapacitated in any way or threatened by the development of the opportunistic infections to which AIDS sufferers are prone. The Commission concluded that there was no indication that the applicant had been treated differently by the Home Secretary in the exercise of his discretion as to early release on compassionate grounds.[17]

In *RM v UK*, in sentencing the applicant who had AIDS, the Court of Appeal expressly refused to take into account his medical condition. It took the approach that on appeals on sentence by AIDS sufferers it was not for the court to alter an otherwise proper sentence to achieve a desirable end, which was rather a matter for the royal prerogative of mercy. Before the Commission, the applicant argued that there was a general practice by the courts of accepting as a substantial mitigating factor in sentence, an illness which would definitely shorten the offender's life and that the Court of Appeal had singled out HIV/AIDS sufferers for less favourable treatment. The Commission noted the medical monitoring which, even a year into his sentence, still gave him a life expectancy of months, possibly up to two years, and found that he had not suffered any serious deterioration or failed to receive proper care in prison. In these circumstances the Commission found that it was not unreasonable or disproportionate for the Court of Appeal not to take his illness into account in mitigating the sentence to be imposed. There was also a reference to the margin of appreciation. The Commission did not address the applicant's arguments

[16] *Aleksanyan v Russia*, December 22, 2008, ECHR 2008–XII, there had been domestic medical recommendations for transfer and an investigator had applied for the applicant's release on bail, but then changed his mind for unknown reasons. See also *Yakovenko v Ukraine*, October 25, 2007, breach of Art.3 where the applicant, diagnosed with HIV and TB, did not receive prompt care and monitoring, was kept in an institution without a resident doctor and was only transferred as recommended by doctors when required to do so by the Court.

[17] It is to be noted that the Commission did not comment on the applicant's arguments disputing the Government's contention that death had to be imminent for a person to obtain early release (citing the sufferers of senile dementia or treatable cancer). It is difficult to assess, if it was correct that persons threatened with less urgent conditions were benefitting from early release, what objective or reasonable justification there could be for treating those with AIDS differently.

that, reasonable or not, other sufferers of illnesses which limited life expectancy in a less or equally drastic way were benefitting from mitigation of sentence.[18] The Commission's reasoning was not persuasive. While there may indeed have been nothing wrong or unreasonable in the way the applicant was treated in prison, where fortunately he did not become very ill, the Commission's approach ignored the point that Art.14 complaints are about the risk of particularly vulnerable groups being singled out for different treatment and that such differences are not compatible under Convention principles if not objectively and reasonably justified.

(c) Isolation measures

Detention under Art.5, para.1(e) "for the prevention of the spreading of infectious diseases" is justifiable in the case of a person suffering from HIV/AIDS where the spreading of the infectious disease is dangerous to public health or safety, and where detention of the person infected is the last resort in order to prevent the spreading of the disease. In the latter context, less severe measures must have been considered and found to be insufficient to safeguard the public interest. When these criteria are no longer fulfilled, the basis for the deprivation of liberty ceases to exist. Accordingly, in *Enhorn v Sweden*, the first limb was satisfied in respect of the applicant, who had already infected a partner, but not the second as the Government did not point to any other measures which had been considered or tried, such as psychiatric treatment. Given that the applicant showed no predilection for spreading the infection further, the compulsory detention orders over a period of seven years did not strike a proper balance. II–222

5. Disclosure of medical condition to others

Publication of information about a person's HIV/AIDS status is clearly an interference with private life. Disclosure of such medical details may be accepted as justified under Art.8 where there are legitimate interests in permitting disclosure and there are adequate safeguards. However, where general public disclosure is concerned, there is less likely to be a convincing justification: publication to satisfy prurient interest does not contribute to any debate of general interest to society.[19] The Court has emphasised that the interest of the individual in confidentiality of medical records will weigh very heavily in the balance and measures compelling disclosure attract the most careful scrutiny.[20] Respect for confidentiality of health data is identified as being a vital principle in the legal systems of all the contracting parties, crucial not only to respect the privacy of the patient but also to maintain confidence in the medical profession and health services.[21] Safeguards to prevent leaks from health clinics are thus necessary to discourage disclosures which might II–223

[18] There was the example of Ernest Saunders who had his sentence reduced by the Court of Appeal in the light of medical evidence of pre-senile dementia (May 16, 1991).

[19] *Armoniene v Lithuania*, November 25, 2008, para.43.

[20] *Z v Finland*, February 25, 1997, R.J.D. 1997–I, 25 E.H.R.R. 371, para.96.

[21] *Z v Finland*, see fn.20 above, the Court cited a recommendation of the Committee of Ministers (Council of Europe), which pointed out that lack of confidence might lead persons to avoid seeking assistance, endangering their own health and the general community—Rec. (89) 14 on the ethical issues of HIV infection in health care and social settings, adopted October 24, 1989, explanatory memorandum paras 166–168.

have a negative impact on the voluntary testing of others.[22] Hospitals must ensure that medical data is adequately secured against unauthorised access.[23] Severe monetary limits on compensation for unauthorised disclosures may also fail to deter recurrence of abuses and redress damage suffered, disclosing lack of respect for private life.[24]

In *TV v Finland*,[25] in respect of allegations concerning the disclosure of a prisoner's HIV condition to persons within the prison, the Commission found that access by prison and medical staff to information concerning his HIV status prima facie constituted an interference with his right to respect for his private life guaranteed under Art.8 of the Convention. However, this was not unlawful as it pursued the aim of protecting the rights of others with whom he came in contact and there was no evidence that the information was passed beyond the staff who dealt with him and who could justifiably expect to receive information relating to a disease carried by him which could be passed on through contact with blood. Impliedly, the case might have gone further if, in fact, it had appeared that the personal information relating to his condition had been circulated more widely than those immediately dealing with him, or that the information had been stored in such a way as to make it accessible to others unconnected with him.

In *Z v Finland*, disclosure of the applicant's HIV status was made during a criminal trial where her ex-husband was facing charges of attempted manslaughter on the basis that he had had forced sexual intercourse with women when he knew that he was HIV positive. Four principal points were at issue: the court orders requiring the applicant's doctors to give evidence at the trial; the seizure of her medical records; the decision to make the material in the file accessible to the public from 2002; and the disclosure of her name and medical condition in the Court of Appeal's judgment. All four were undisputed as constituting interferences with private and family life and the principal argument concerned the justification of the measures. The Court found that the first three pursued legitimate aims—the prevention of crime in relation to measures of investigation and protection of the rights of others in maintaining the transparency of court proceedings through public access to files. However, the Court doubted that the publication of the applicant's full name, as well as her medical condition, following their disclosure in the Court of Appeal's judgment could be justified for any aim, including the prevention of crime.

As to whether the four measures could be justified as necessary under Art.8, para.2, the questioning of the applicant's doctors was acceptable since it was carried out in camera and the proceedings were bound by confidentiality enforceable under civil and criminal law: this furnished adequate and effective safeguards against abuse. The seizure of her medical records and inclusion in the file was also proportionate. The Court was uninterested in allegations that not all the material was relevant to the investigation and was not prepared to question the domestic court assessment in that respect. However, the order which would make the material public by 2002 was disproportionate in its effects on the applicant, which outweighed any general interest in making files public. It also found that the

[22] *Armoniene*, fn.19 above, para.44.

[23] *I v Finland*, July 17, 2008, where a hospital failed to limit access to the applicant nurse's data to the health professionals directly involved in the applicant's treatment, or to keep a log of all persons who had accessed the file.

[24] *Armoniene*, fn.19 above, para.47.

[25] (21780/93) (Dec.) March 2, 1994.

publication of her identity and condition in the appeal judgment was disproportionate, in particular, since the lower court had felt able to issue an abridged version of its judgment excluding the name and part of the reasoning.[26]

6. Expulsion

Issues concerning access to medical treatment have arisen in connection with expulsion of persons from Contracting States to countries where the standard of care and treatment are deficient. The UK Government strenuously resisted the claims in *D v UK*, where an applicant suffering AIDS alleged that on expulsion to St Kitts his life-expectancy would be shortened and his final days subject to lack of medical care and support. The Government argued that finding a violation would open the floodgates to claims from persons with AIDS who were refused entry to European States where inevitably higher standards of medical and support care were available. The Commission dismissed this on the basis that United Kingdom responsibility was engaged in this particular case because, rather than expelling the applicant on arrival, they prosecuted him for drugs possession and held him in jail, where he became dependent on the drugs treatment provided. The argument that he would suffer the natural consequences of a disease contracted outside the United Kingdom did not divert responsibility either, since the Commission considered that the lack of treatment and adequate support would lead in all probability to painful and degrading circumstances prior to his death. The Court found that Government responsibility could arise from expelling an AIDS sufferer, but in finding a violation emphasised the exceptional facts, in particular the very severe deterioration in the applicant's health by the time of the hearing. Subsequent cases have distinguished the judgement on that basis. Where the applicant has not been in an advanced or terminal stage and there is some prospect of medical care and family support, expulsions have been found acceptable.[27] II–224

Following *D v UK*, there lingered some uncertainty as to what exactly were the circumstances in which a State would not be allowed to expel an HIV/AIDS sufferer. The Grand Chamber examined the matter again in *N v UK*, which concerned a Ugandan woman who had entered the country illegally in a very ill state and was suffering from AIDS, with a CD4 cell count of 10 (normally over 500). It was found in the domestic expulsion proceedings and that the cruel reality was that if she was returned to Uganda her position would be similar to having a life-support machine turned off. The Court clarified that aliens cannot, in principle, claim to remain in a Contracting State in order to continue to benefit from medical

[26] See also *CC v Spain*, October 6, 2009, where a civil court should have granted the applicant's request to have his name removed from the judgments relating to a medical insurance dispute which had disclosed his HIV status.

[27] See, e.g. *SCC v Sweden*, (46553/99) (Dec.) February 15, 2000, no problem arose out of the deportation of the applicant, who was suffering from HIV, to Zambia where some treatment and family support were available; *Henao v Netherlands*, (13669/03) (Dec.) June 24, 2003, expulsion of the applicant, who was HIV-positive, to Colombia was acceptable, as treatment was, in principle, available and he had family there; *Ndangoya v Sweden*, (17868/03) (Dec.) June 22, 2004, drugs were available in Tanzania, albeit expensive; *Amegnigan v Netherlands*, (25629/04) (Dec.) November 25, 2004, adequate treatment available, in principle, in Togo; conversely, *BB v France*, (30930/96) (Rep.) March 9, 1998, R.J.D. 1998–VI, pp.2613–2614, the Commission found that expulsion would breach Art.3 where the applicant's infection was at an advanced stage necessitating repeated hospital stays and the care facilities in the Congo were precarious.

assistance and the decision to remove would only breach Art.3 where the humanitarian grounds were compelling, such as in *D* where the applicant was critically ill and appeared close to death. A high threshold therefore applied to cases where the future harm flowed from a naturally occurring illness rather than the intentional acts or omissions of public authorities. The fact that, as in this case, treatment would only be available to the applicant in Uganda at substantial cost, and it was not apparent her family could assist her, did not reach this threshold. The effect on her life expectancy was regarded as speculative. The Court pragmatically acknowledged that to find otherwise would impose a great burden on Contracting States to provide long-term and expensive medical care to aliens.[28]

7. Discrimination

II–225 There have been hardly any cases to date alleging that information relating to a person's HIV status has been used to their detriment, for example, as a basis for dismissal from employment or as the basis for depriving them of some service or benefit. Whether that would raise a problem would depend very much on the facts of the case. There is no right to employment as such under the Convention and acts by private companies or bodies would not necessarily engage the responsibility of the State. The circumstances of the case would have to support the contention that the act or deprivation interfered with an aspect of private life and that the State owed an obligation to provide protection against such interference even by private bodies.

The sole finding of discrimination on HIV/AIDs grounds so far has been where an applicant of Uzbek origin living in Russia with his family was expressly refused a residence permit due to his HIV status. Referring to the vulnerability of this group of people, the Court accorded a narrow margin of appreciation to measures of differential treatment. It referred to international materials indicating that there was no objective justification for a travel ban on HIV/AIDS sufferers and that the mere presence of such a person in a country was not a public health risk. It noted that other measures were available for preventing irresponsible transmission of infection. Nor since free medical treatment was not available in Russia was the country likely to be overburdened financially by a drain on its medical resources by allowing such persons to settle. There was accordingly no compelling justification for the refusal in this applicant's case of a residence permit allowing him to remain with his family.[29]

Cross-Reference

Part IIA, s.17: Length of proceedings.
Part IIB, s.9: Deprivation of liberty.

[28] See the dissenting minority, who considered that there was no doubt that the applicant would face an early and painful death if removed and such a situation should have been regarded as falling within D's test of "exceptional circumstances". They did not consider States could rely on budgetary constraints where Art. 3 was concerned and considered the "floodgate" argument misconceived. While they quoted the number of HIV/AIDS expulsion cases before the Court in the previous years as being relatively low, they did not comment on whether a finding of violation by the Court in this case could have provoked more attempts by those who were ill to gain entry illegally to Convention countries.

[29] *Kiyutin*, fn.4 above, paras 67–74.

Part IIB, s.29: Immigration and expulsion.
Part IIB, s.42: Review of detention.
Part IIB, s.43: Right to life.

3. Armed forces

Key provisions:

II–226 Articles 5 (liberty), 6 (fair trial), 8 (private life) and 10 (freedom of expression).

Key case-law:

Engel v Netherlands, June 8, 1976, Series A, No.22, 1 E.H.R.R. 647; *Hadjianastassiou v Greece*, December 16, 1992, Series A, No.252–A, 16 E.H.R.R. 219; *Vereinigung demokratischer Soldaten Osterreichs v Austria,* December 19, 1994, Series A, No.302, 20 E.H.R.R. 55; *Mitap and Mûftüglü v Turkey*, (Rep.) December 8, 1994, annexed to the judgment of the Court, March 25, 1996, R.J.D. 1996–II, No.6; *Findlay v UK*, February 25, 1997, R.J.D. 1997–I, No.30, 24 E.H.R.R. 221; *Kalaç v Turkey*, July 1, 1997, R.J.D. 1997–IV, No.41, 27 E.H.R.R. 552; *Grigoriades v Greece*, November 25, 1997, R.J.D. 1997–VII, No.57, 27 E.H.R.R 464; *Larissis v Greece*, February 24, 1998, R.J.D. 1998–I, No.65, 27 E.H.R.R. 329; *Hood v UK*, February 18, 1999, ECHR 1999–I, 29 E.H.R.R. 365; *Smith and Grady v UK*, September 27, 1999, ECHR 1999–VI; *Cooper v UK*, December 16, 2003, 29 E.H.R.R. 493; *Grieves v UK*, December 16, 2003; *Bayatyan v Armenia*, July 7, 2011, ECHR 2011-. . .

1. General considerations

II–227 Armed forces personnel continue to enjoy the rights guaranteed under the Convention although the special disciplinary context may allow certain limitations on their exercise which could not be imposed on civilians.[1] Obvious and inevitable restrictions following on military service will not raise issues, e.g. rules on uniform and haircuts,[2] but joining up does not waive fundamental rights to liberty and fair trial.

2. Military discipline

II–228 Matters purely of internal discipline are unlikely to raise issues where the sanctions do not involve deprivation of liberty or other punishments serious enough to fall within the concept of a criminal penalty.[3] Any detention which involves a deprivation of liberty within the meaning of Art.5 will attract its procedural guarantees. Whether a restriction for a soldier, as opposed to a civilian, constitutes a deprivation of liberty depends on the extent to which it deviates from the normal conditions of life in the armed forces of Contracting States. The case-law indicates that light arrest, involving restriction to quarters in off-duty hours, was not sufficient, but that strict arrest, involving being locked in a cell day and night and exclusion from normal duties, was.[4] The procedural guarantees will include the right to be brought promptly before an officer exercising judicial functions who has the

[1] *Engel v Netherlands*, June 8, 1976, Series A, No.22, 1 E.H.R.R. 647, para.57; *Konstantin Markin v Russia*, October 7, 2010, para.52, pending Grand Chamber.
[2] (8209/78) (Dec.) March 1, 1979, 16 D.R. 166.
[3] See Pt IIA, s.1a: Criminal charge.
[4] *Engel*, see fn.1 above, paras 59–63. See also *Pulatli v Turkey*, April 26, 2011, para.32.

power to order release and the right to bring proceedings challenging the lawfulness of the detention.[5] In *Hood v UK*, the commanding officer of an arrested soldier was not regarded as sufficiently independent or impartial to fulfil the role of a judicial officer in deciding on pre-trial detention under Art.5, para.3, due in particular to his responsibilities for internal discipline and order in his command and his significant involvement in any subsequent prosecution. Nor where a soldier was placed under strict arrest for seven days by his superior officer was his detention regarded as ordered "by a competent court" by a procedure attended by the requisite guarantees for the purposes of Art.5, para.1(a).[6]

While dismissal from the armed forces previously fell outside the scope of Art.6, para.1 as not concerning the determination of civil rights and obligations due to the public service aspect,[7] Art.6 guarantees may now still apply if the domestic system itself has allowed access to court. Even where it does not, any exclusion must be justified by the nature of the applicant's post, involving a special bond of trust and loyalty or the exercise of public power, and the subject matter of the dispute must call the bond into question or be related to the exercise of public power.[8] Dismissal of higher ranking officers on grounds of conduct is likely still to fall into such category while mere disputes about salary or other entitlements may well not.[9]

3. Military justice

Where a criminal charge is involved, Art.6 rights play a full role. A prisoner is entitled, inter alia, to a fair hearing before an independent and impartial tribunal and within a reasonable time.[10] Potentially, this may mean legal representation and legal aid for such if he cannot afford it.[11] II–229

The Convention organs appear to dislike, in principle, situations where civilians are subject to the jurisdiction of military courts. In *Mitap and Müftülu v Turkey*, the Commission considered that this per se raised doubts as to independence and impartiality, and found that the presence on the court martial of an army officer and two military judges (who were linked with the military hierarchy for the purposes of their career, and subordinate to the commander of the state of martial law whose security forces were carrying out the arrests) was not cured by the presence of two civilian judges and was sufficient to give objective reason to doubt the independence and impartiality of the tribunal.[12] The Court has recently affirmed that it would only be in very exceptional circumstances that the trial of civilians by a military court would be compatible with Art.6 and that reasonable doubts about objective

[5] Art.5, para.3, e.g. *De Jong, Baljet and Van den Brink v Netherlands*, May 22, 1984, Series A, No.77; Art.5, para.4, e.g. *Engel*, fn.1 above.

[6] See also *Pulatli*, fn.4 above, para.32, nor did the detention fall under Art.5, para.1(b) as it was a punishment, not intended to obtain the performance of an obligation required by law for the future.

[7] e.g. *Batur v Turkey*, (38604/97) (Dec.) July 4, 2000.

[8] *Eskelinen v Finland*, April 19, 2007, ECHR 2007–. . . , para.62.

[9] e.g. *Kanayev v Russia*, July 27, 2006, (Art.6 inapplicable) concerning a naval officer's dispute about travel expenses—would perhaps be decided differently post-*Eskelinen*, fn.7 above; *Sukut v Turkey*, (59773/00) (Dec.) September 11, 2007, Art.6 not applicable where a sergeant was dismissed for conduct undermining discipline.

[10] e.g. *Jordan v UK (No.2)*, December 10, 2002, unreasonable length of court martial, over four years, seven months.

[11] *Morris v UK*, February 26, 2002, ECHR 2002–I, para.89, it was not contrary to Art.6, para.3(c) to require the applicant to pay £240 contribution to legal aid.

[12] See also *Incal v Turkey*, June 9, 1998, R.J.D. 1998–IV, paras 72 and 78.

impartiality would inevitably arise where such a court tried civilians for acts against the armed forces.[13] Overly harsh sentences imposed by military tribunals on civilian functionaries were frowned on by the Court, which found no reasons for a civilian secretary to be tried by a military body for what essentially boiled down to breaches of working hours and a propensity to argue back.[14]

There is, however, nothing in the provisions of Art.6 which, in principle, exclude the determination by service tribunals of criminal charges against service personnel.[15] Whether or not there are justifiable doubts as to the independence and impartiality of a particular court-martial will depend on the circumstances. Some weight has been given to the presence of irremovable civilian judges, the irremovability of military members during their mandate and as to whether the military members were not answerable to any authority.[16] Where military members remain subject to military discipline and assessment reports for promotion purposes, or remain part of the hierarchical chain of command, problems of independence and impartiality have arisen.[17] Strong administrative links between military judges and the Ministry of Defence can cause problems, as in a case where the judges were provided with housing by the executive and thus were subordinate to the Ministry hierarchy which directly financed the court on a daily basis.[18]

Serious structural problems were disclosed in *Findlay v UK*,[19] where there were hierarchical links between the officers on the District Court Martial and the convening officer, who acted as prosecutor. The fact that the decision of the court martial was not effective until confirmed by the convening officer was also contrary to the well-established principle that a "tribunal" had the power to give a binding decision, which may not be altered by a non-judicial authority. In *Grieves v UK*, concerning naval courts martial, there were insufficient guarantees where the judge advocate was a serving officer on whom reports were made to his hierarchical superiors and there was no permanent presiding officer who was irremovable and not subject to reports. The Court was not convinced by arguments that the unique nature of naval service required these roles to be filled by serving officers who had detailed knowledge of the naval way of life. In *Cooper v UK*, which concerned air force courts martial, the presence of a civilian judge advocate and a permanent president did, however, furnish sufficiently strong guarantees of independence taken in conjunction with detailed briefing notes to the two service members of the court martial, who were not assessed in conjunction with their judicial decision-making.[20] The reviewing authority's power to alter verdicts and sentences was not, however, found to be a problem as in any event the final decision was always taken by a judicial body, the Court Martial Appeal Court.

[13] *Ergin v Turkey (No.6)*, April 6, 2006, breach of Art.6 where the applicant, a civilian newspaper editor, was tried in a military court for incitement to evade military service.

[14] *Icen v Turkey*, May 31, 2011, paras 39–46.

[15] *Cooper v UK*, December 16, 2003, 29 E.H.R.R. 493, para.110.

[16] e.g. (12717/87) (Dec.) September 8, 1988, 57 D.R. 196; (8209/78) (Dec.) March 1, 1979, 16 D.R. 166.

[17] e.g. *Sahiner v Turkey*, September 25, 2001, concerning Martial Law Courts.

[18] *Miroshnik v Ukraine*, November 27, 2008, paras 62–64.

[19] See also *Coyne v UK*, September 24, 1997, R.J.D. 1997–V, No.48 and *Cable v UK*, February 18, 1999, reaching similar findings concerning RAF courts martial.

[20] See also *Yavuz v Turkey*, (29870/96) (Dec.) May 25, 2000, where military officers on the Supreme Military Administrative Court offered sufficient independence, e.g. irremovability during term of office and no supervisory assessment by military authorities.

4. Health and safety and conscription

The Court is increasingly imposing standards of treatment to which soldiers and conscripts may not be exposed. A person must perform military service in conditions compatible with respect for human dignity; the procedures and methods of military training should not impose distress or suffering of an intensity exceeding the unavoidable level of hardship inherent in military discipline; and, given the practical demands of such service, health and well-being must be adequately secured by medical assistance. Thus, where a conscript with a spinal condition suffered serious and lasting injury from a disciplinary punishment of some 350 kneebends, the Court found a breach of Art.3 of the Convention.[21] II–230

Requisite precautions should also be taken to ensure that conscripts or soldiers with mental disabilities are not placed in situations where they commit suicide due to undue stress. There should be adequate screening on entry to the army to spot any problems or difficulties; officers should be adequately trained so as to refrain in their conduct from driving their soldiers over the edge; and where problems are known, or ought to have been known, precautions should be taken to remove access to weaponry and exposure to stressful situations and to obtain medical treatment or monitoring.[22]

Adequate investigations should be taken concerning the deaths of soldiers and conscripts in order to put the families' suspicions to rest as to whether the cause was suicide, accident or foul play.[23]

Aptitude for military service also covers age. Where a 71-year-old man was conscripted and after a month was hospitalised, the Court found that requiring him to serve and subjecting him to duties and hardships unsuited for his age disclosed degrading treatment.[24]

Conversely, where there is a system of national military service and a requirement to pay an exemption tax where a person is found unfit to serve, the Court found, in the case of a person considered as under a disability due to the condition of diabetes, but who wished to fulfill his obligation to serve, that there was discrimination; it considered that it would be possible to provide a form of substitute service adapted to the level of disability.[25]

5. Restrictions on private and family life

Members of the armed forces do not waive their rights under Art.8. While an old Commission case considered that a prohibition on homosexual acts between soldiers could be considered as necessary for the protection of morals and the prevention of II–231

[21] See *Chember v Russia*, July 3, 2008, paras 50–57.

[22] See *Kilinc v Turkey*, June 7, 2005, paras 41–57, failure to send conscript to hospital, requiring him to perform duties with a rifle when known to be suicidal; *Salgin v Turkey*, February 20, 2007, paras 69–84, authorities were not at fault in not foreseeing the soldier's suicide, no previous history or incidents; *Abdullah Yilmaz v Turkey*, June 17, 2008, paras 55–76, failings in NCOs training, conduct and supervision, in particular use of abuse and physical violence on the conscript who committed suicide; *Servet Gunduz v Turkey*, January 11, 2011, paras 63–84, failings in regulations as regarded admitting as a conscript a person with a drugs addiction and subsequent failures in treatment.

[23] See e.g. *Caliskan v Turkey*, May 27, 2008, paras 49–61.

[24] *Tastan v Turkey*, March 4, 2008, paras 27–33.

[25] *Glor v Switzerland*, March 3, 2008, paras 71–98, conscientious objectors had been allowed to do a form of substitute service for example.

disorder given the special conditions of army life,[26] the Court has since held that it was an unjustified interference with private life to hold investigations into soldiers' private lives, including detailed interviews with the soldiers and third parties, and that their consequent administrative discharge on the sole ground of sexual orientation constituted a disproportionate interference with the right under Art.8.[27] It was unconvinced by the Government's arguments that the presence of homosexual personnel would have a negative effect on morale and risk diminishing operational effectiveness, noting that the applicants concerned had not been shown to pose disciplinary or other problems and that any untoward effects from inappropriate behaviour could be dealt with by a conduct code, rather than a blanket ban. The Court required particularly serious reasons for interference in this intimate part of an individual's life, even in the army context, and although there was a reference to the State's margin of appreciation in matters of national security, it found a lack of any concrete evidence to support the Government's fears. To the extent that these were based on negative attitudes held by some service personnel, it emphasised that this prejudice could not justify interferences with rights any more than negative attitudes to race, origin or colour.

Similarly, interferences with family life must be justified. It is not regarded as an area where, per se, military life requires special measures; restrictions based on operational efficiency require to be justified. Discrimination was found where men in the army were not able to enjoy the three years' parental leave open to women in the armed forces. The Court did not find that the authorities had substantiated the refusal, there being nothing to support the assertion that this would disrupt the fighting capacity.[28]

6. Restrictions on freedom of expression and freedom to receive information

II–232 Interferences with soldiers' access to outside sources of information have been treated with some robustness by the Commission and Court which have not been overly sympathetic to the protective attitude of State authorities, although acknowledging that the proper functioning of an army presupposes rules preventing the undermining of military discipline.[29]

Soldiers still enjoy freedom of expression and freedom to receive and impart information. An assertion by the Austrian authorities that a magazine was a threat to discipline and to service efficiency had to be substantiated by specific examples, of which none were given.[30] The magazine in question was not found by the Court to overstep what was permissible in the context of a mere discussion of ideas, including army reform, which must be tolerated in the army of a democratic State. There was thus a violation in respect of both the magazine producers, whose publication was not allowed to be distributed internally and in respect of the soldier who was fined

[26] (9237/81) UK, (Dec.) October 12, 1983, 34 D.R. 68.
[27] *Smith and Grady v UK*, September 27, 1999, ECHR 1999–VI; *Lustig-Prean and Beckett*, September 27, 1999.
[28] *Konstantin Markin v Russia*, fn.1 above, paras 53–59, pending GC.
[29] *Vereinigung demokratischer soldaten Osterreichs v Austria*, December 19, 1994, Series A, No.302, 20 E.H.R.R. 55, para.36; *Grigoriades v Greece*, November 25, 1997, R.J.D. 1997–VII, No.57, 27 E.H.R.R 464, para.45.
[30] *Vereinigung demokratischer soldaten*, see fn.29 above.

for distributing it. Where an applicant was prosecuted for distributing leaflets to British soldiers, there was a distinction to be drawn, the Commission found, between publications aimed at inciting disaffection and those expressing opinions as to the policy of using the army in Northern Ireland. Since the applicant was expressly encouraging soldiers to go absent without leave as a means of protest, and had not been dissuaded by other means from giving up her activities, the Commission found that her conviction and sentence of eight to nine months' imprisonment was not disproportionate to the aim pursued.[31] Where the applicant editor published an article concerning conscripts which was hostile to the military, his conviction disclosed a violation, the Court, considering that the article aimed at the general public, did not seek to precipitate desertion.[32]

Security considerations are given full weight where measures are applied in respect of the disclosure of information by army personnel. In *Hadjianasstiou v Greece*, where an officer was sentenced to five months for revealing military data in a study submitted to a private company, the Court referred to the special responsibilities incumbent on military life. Since the officer was involved in an experimental missile programme and bound by a duty of discretion, the Court agreed with the Government that the disclosure was capable of revealing the State's progress in weapons development and thus damage security interests.

Where a soldier expresses criticism of the armed forces, the domestic authorities' reaction must be proportionate. In relation to an admiral who made critical statements on television, the Commission accepted that suspension was a proportionate reaction given the nature of his comments which were found by the domestic courts to discredit Government information policy and, by condemning modern warfare and matters of defence policy, give rise to doubts that he would fulfil his obligations to the State.[33] Where, however, the criticism was conducted internally, by means of a letter to a senior officer, in terms which did not name any other officer critically but raised matters of public concern, the Commission found a disciplinary sanction of three months' imprisonment disproportionate.[34]

Weight was given to maintaining confidence in the army's reputation and loyalty to the Constitution, where a reserve officer's recall for training was revoked due to his membership of an extremist right party; the measure was not found to be disproportionate.[35]

7. Freedom of religion

It was previously held, in light of the exception for military service contained in Art.4, para.3(b), the Convention does not guarantee a right to refuse military service on conscientious grounds.[36] However, given a virtually general consensus in member II–233

[31] *Arrowsmith v UK*, (7050/75) (Rep.), October 12, 1978, 19 D.R. 5.

[32] *Ergin*, fn.13 above.

[33] (23576/94) (Dec.) November 29, 1995.

[34] *Grigoriades*, see fn.29 above, the Court found the prosecution not necessary in a democratic society as the letter had had insignificant impact on military discipline.

[35] *Erdel v Germany*, (30067/04) (Dec.) February 13, 2007.

[36] See earlier Commission case-law (7705/76) (Dec.) July 5, 1977, 9 D.R. 196, the Commission, unsympathetically noting the burden of military service to be shared equitably between citizens, found it legitimate for States to restrict exemptions (military or substituted) and acceptable, under Art.14 together with Art.9, for total exemption to be applied only to members of religions whose position was well known, e.g. Jehovah's Witnesses. Other persons, not so affiliated, had to suffer to avoid the possibility of shirkers! (10410/83) (Dec.) October 11, 1984, 40 D.R. 40.

States towards the recognition of conscientious objection as an aspect of the right to freedom of though, conscience and religion, the court has recently held that it falls within the scope of Art.9. Conviction of an application Jehovah's Witness for refusal to be drafted thus disclosed a breach where there was no provision for alternative service and the State had recognised itself the need for reform.[37] Impositions of persistent penalties on a pacifist for a failure to wear a uniform, without provision for other forms of service for conscientious objectors disclosed a breach of Art.3.[38]

Where members of the armed services have been penalised or subject to measures resulting from religious affiliations or activities, issues have arisen under Art.9. These cases primarily relate to steps taken in the Greek army against proselytisers and in the Turkish army against Islamic fundamentalists.[39] The importance of respecting the inner spiritual convictions of a person is such that it is arguable that espousal of a particular religion should, without more, justify sanctions of dismissal. However, in contrast to the approach taken to homosexuals in the army cases under Art.8, the Court has found that disciplinary measures may be imposed in respect of Islamic fundamentalism without reference to any requirement to show demonstrable prejudice to discipline or the functioning of the service.

In *Kalaç v Turkey*, where a military judge was forced into early retirement allegedly as a result of his religious convictions, the Court found that in choosing to pursue a military career he had accepted the restrictions implied by a system of military discipline, including regulations forbidding, inter alia, an attitude inimical to the established order reflecting the requirements of military service. Since the applicant was able to fulfil the normal forms through which a Muslim practised his religion and the reasoning for the order was based not on his religious opinions but his conduct and attitude,[40] it found that the compulsory retirement had not interfered with any right guaranteed under Art.9. Thus, since no interference was found, the Court had no need to examine the necessity or proportionality of any measures under para.2. Since then the Court has stated in terms that disciplinary regulations may include a duty for military personnel to refrain from participating in the Islamic fundamentalist movement, whose aim and programme is to ensure the pre-eminence of religious rules.[41]

A distinction was drawn by the Convention organs in a Greek case where air force officers who were members of the Pentecostal church were tried for proselytism.[42] The interference with their rights to manifest their beliefs was found to be justified where the proselytism related to servicemen in the applicants' unit having regard to

[37] *Bayatyan v Armenia*, July 7, 2011, ECHR 2011–. . .

[38] *Ulke v Turkey*, January 24, 2006, paras 61–62

[39] See, e.g. *Kalaç v Turkey*, July 1, 1997, R.J.D. 1997–IV, No.41, 27 E.H.R.R. 552; *Larissis v Greece*, February 24, 1998, R.J.D. 1998–I, No.65, 27 E.H.R.R. 329.

[40] A fine distinction—the conduct included the adoption of unlawful fundamentalist opinions. The Court has effectively accepted that disciplinary action based on military objection to particular alleged opinions does not interfere with rights under Art.9. This approach has been followed in numerous other dismissal cases, where grounds included the applicants' wives' wearing of headscarves—this was still viewed as concerning conduct and activities in breach of military discipline and the principle of secularism rather than based on the applicants' religious beliefs or opinions or the observance of their religious duties, e.g. *Tepeli v Turkey*, (31876/96) (Dec.) June 12, 2001 and *Sen v Turkey*, (Dec.) July 8, 2003.

[41] e.g. *Sen*, fn.40 above, citing *Yanasik v Turkey*, (14524/89) (Dec.) January 6, 1993, 74 D.R. 14, where a military cadet was dismissed from an academy in Turkey. No interference with religious belief was found as the Commission accepted that the dismissal was for disciplinary reasons, although these included grounds that he had participated in fundamentalist activities.

[42] *Larissis*, see fn.39 above.

the special character of the relationship between a superior and subordinate in the army which rendered the subordinate more susceptible to influence. Conversely, where the offences related to proselytism of civilians, outside this special relationship, the interferences were not found to be justified.

8. Restrictions on freedom of movement

Where ex-military personnel were automatically subject to travel bans abroad, as they had been allegedly privy to secrets of national importance, the Court found the measures disproportionate. It noted that Art.2 of Protocol No.4 did not distinguish between civilians and the military as regarded the enjoyment of freedom to leave one's country and considered that the ban did not, in any event, achieve its protective function, since in post-Soviet times a travel ban did not prevent persons from passing on secrets to other powers by other easily available means. Further, there had been no grounds in the individual cases for any apparent risk of a breach of national security.[43] II–234

Cross-reference

Part IIA, s.1a: Criminal charge.
Part IIB, s.22: Freedom of expression.
Part IIB, s.40: Religion, thought and conscience.
Part IIB, s.43: Right to life (concerning use of lethal force).

[43] *Bartik v Russia*, December 21, 2006, paras 47–52; *Soltysyak v Russia*, February 10, 2011, paras 49–54.

4. Arrest

Key provision:

II–235 Article 5 para.1(c) (right to liberty, exception of lawful arrest for the purpose of bringing before the competent legal authority on reasonable suspicion of committing an offence, or where reasonably necessary to prevent the commission of an offence or fleeing after the commission of an offence).

Key case-law:

Brogan v UK, November 29, 1988, Series A, No.145–B, 11 E.H.H.R 117; *Fox, Campbell and Hartley v UK*, August 30, 1990 Series A, No.182, 13 E.H.R.R. 157; *Murray v UK*, October 28, 1994, Series A, No.300–A, 19 E.H.R.R. 193; *Lukanov v Bulgaria*, March 20, 1997, R.J.D. 1997–II, No.34; *Erdagöz v Turkey*, October 22, 1997, R.J.D. 1997–VI, No.54, 32 E.H.R.R. 443; *K-F v Germany*, November 27, 1997, R.J.D. 1997–VII; *Wloch v Poland*, October 19, 2000, ECHR 2000–XI; *O'Hara v UK*, October 16, 2001, ECHR 2001–X.

1. General considerations

II–236 Arrest in this section refers to the use of power to detain to investigate or prevent crime. The key issues have arisen from the standard of suspicion justifying arrest and, only to a lesser extent, the conditions and procedural safeguards surrounding the arrest. Requirements of lawfulness lay emphasis on conformity with domestic procedural safeguards and generally the Convention organs have not been overly rigorous in their scrutiny, assuming the bona fides of the police and requiring only the minimum indications of grounds for the arrest, sufficient to exclude clear arbitrariness or oppressiveness.

2. Existence of arrest or detention

II–237 In the ordinary course of events, there is no doubt as to whether a person has been held or detained by means of the exercise of a power of arrest. Occasionally, there is a question mark as to the nature and degree of the loss of liberty.[1]

3. Grounds of arrest

II–238 Three heads of arrest are included in Art.5, para.1(c). Most cases have concerned arrest on reasonable suspicion of having committed an offence, while the heads of "reasonably necessary to prevent an offence"[2] or "to prevent a person fleeing after an offence" have been seldom invoked.[3] A general purpose of preventing a dangerous offender of committing future, unspecified criminal acts does not qualify.[4]

[1] See Pt IIB, s.9: Deprivation of liberty.

[2] Preventive detention outside the scope of criminal proceedings does not fall within Art.5, para.1(c): *Jecius v Lithuania*, July 31, 2000, paras 50–52.

[3] See, however, *Lukanov v Bulgaria*, March 20, 1997, R.J.D. 1997–II, No.34, the Commission found that where there is no reasonable suspicion of an offence having been committed the applicant's detention cannot be justified by an alleged danger of fleeing after having committed an offence; the Court found it unnecessary to decide. See also *Eriksen v Norway*, May 27, 1997, R.J.D. 1997–III, para.86, concerning detention pending a decision whether to impose a further period of security detention of a person convicted of an offence and subject to a special preventative sentence.

[4] *M v Germany*, December 17, 2009, para.89.

"Offence" in this context appears to enjoy a wide definition. In *Brogan v UK*, the applicants argued that arrest under prevention of terrorism legislation, on suspicion that a person is or has been involved in acts of terrorism, was not on suspicion of having committed a specific offence but of involvement in unspecified acts of terrorism which could not be regarded as an "offence" for the purposes of Art.5, para.1(c). The Court found that the definition of terrorism as the use of violence for political ends was well in keeping with the idea of an offence.[5]

4. Reasonable suspicion of having committed an offence

The standard is simply one of a reasonable suspicion. It is not required that the existence and nature of the offence be definitely proved since that is the purpose of the investigation.[6] II–239

The fact that domestic law does not set the same standard of suspicion will not necessarily disclose a violation on arrest, since the Convention organs will examine whether on the facts of the individual case there nonetheless existed a reasonable suspicion.[7]

The Court found that "reasonable suspicion" presupposed the existence of facts or information that would satisfy an objective observer that the person concerned may have committed the offence. However, what is to be regarded as reasonable will depend on the circumstances.[8] Terrorist crime, it held, fell into a special category due to considerations of urgency and reliance on information which might be reliable but could not be revealed without risk to the source. Therefore the same standards could not always apply, subject to the rider that the criterion is not stretched to the point that the essence of the safeguard is impaired.[9]

That said, there is a fine line between those cases where the suspicion grounding an arrest is sufficiently founded on fact and those where it is not.[10] In *Fox, Campbell and Hartley v UK*, where the applicants were arrested on suspicion of being terrorists, the Court considered that some factual elements capable of satisfying the Court that the applicants were reasonably suspected must be furnished by the Government, particularly since domestic law set a lower threshold of merely honest suspicion. The fact that the two suspects had had previous convictions for acts of terrorism connected with the IRA was not sufficient for an arrest some seven years later.[11]

[5] The Court cited its findings in *Ireland v UK*, January 18, 1978, Series A, No.25, paras 196–197. Breach of the peace has also been regarded as an offence: *Steel v UK*, September 23, 1998, R.J.D 1998–VII, No.91, para.49.

[6] e.g. (8083/77) (Dec.) March 13, 1980, 19 D.R. 223, where a solicitor who failed to appear before the court when a case was relisted was arrested for contempt of court, the fact that the court of appeal found that there had been no contempt did not mean that a reasonable suspicion had not existed at the time; (9627/81) (Dec.) March 14, 1984, 37 D.R. 15. For a recent Court statement, see *O'Hara v UK*, October 16, 2001, ECHR 2001–X, para.36.

[7] *Fox, Campbell and Hartley*, August 30, 1990 Series A, No.182, 13 E.H.R.R. 157, para.31.

[8] *Fox, Campbell and Hartley*, see fn.7, para.32; (27143/95) (Dec.) January 14, 1997, 88–A D.R. 94, where the Commission noted the risks attaching to basing reasonable suspicion on statements of Mafia *"pentitii"* and had regard to whether the domestic courts had assessed their credibility.

[9] *Fox, Campbell and Hartley*, see fn.7, paras 31–32; *O'Hara*, para.35; *Cisse v France*, (51346/99) (Dec.) January 16, 2001, ECHR 2001–I; also (8098/77) (Dec.) December 13, 1978, 16 D.R. 11, concerning an arrest on espionage (ordered by a judge) where suspicion was based on a small number of elements and qualified as reasonable, the decision giving weight to the judge's knowledge and experience in assessing the basis of suspicion.

[10] *O'Hara*, see fn.6, para.41.

[11] See also *Berktay v Turkey*, March 1, 2001, paras 199–201, finding a violation where the Government provided no basis justifying the arrest of the applicant during a house search.

Where, however, the Government is able to point to even indirect facts supporting their suspicion, as in *Murray v UK*, where the applicant was arrested under a similar provision as in *Fox, Campbell and Hartley*, there may be no violation.[12] In that case, where the applicant was arrested for involvement in IRA fundraising, the Court emphasised the special exigencies of investigating terrorism and recognised the need for use of confidential sources in fighting terrorism. It was also influenced by findings of domestic courts in the applicant's false imprisonment action where the judge had found the arresting officer transparently honest and believed that the applicant was genuinely suspected of having been involved in collecting funds for the purchase of arms for the IRA. Honesty and bona fides were, the Court said, indispensable elements of reasonableness. It added a new factor, the short period that the arrest lasted, four hours which strangely suggests the strength of the suspicion required for an arrest is influenced by the subsequent duration of the arrest.

Sufficient accountability in domestic proceedings, where the Convention test of reasonable suspicion is applicable, may meet the requisite standard and provide the necessary guarantee against arbitrary arrest, even where, as in the *O'Hara* case, there was, in the domestic court's view, "scanty evidence" of any connection between the applicant and the murder under investigation.[13]

There is a certain reluctance, perhaps, by the Court to find that authorities have acted in bad faith in carrying out arrests, at least where there is some putative connection with a suspected offence.[14] In *Erdagöz v Turkey*, the applicant alleged that his arrest for allegedly producing false evidence of an attack on his shop was motivated by police resentment against him for previous complaints which he had made. No fact was apparently adverted to by the Government as justifying the arrest and the Commission noted that in fact a suspect was prosecuted for the attack on the shop which he had reported. However, the Court considered that the suspicion was based on specific facts (e.g. the applicant's conduct) and saw no reason to disagree with the public prosecutor's finding that the 24-hour detention was for the purpose of confirming or dispelling the suspicion that he had falsely reported a criminal offence. The Court accordingly appears to require convincing evidence before it will find arbitrariness on the part of the police or other authorities, such as in *RL and MD v France*, where the police, apparently taking sides in a quarrel, forcibly arrested a restaurant owner apparently for fixing a sign on a door to which the neighbouring restaurant took exception,[15] or in *Stepuleac v Moldova*, where the applicant was arrested although his name had not been mentioned by any witness and the public prosecutor made no enquiry as to whether there was a factual basis to verify if the measure was well-founded.[16]

[12] The Commission had found a violation seeing no real distinction with *Fox, Campbell and Hartley*, see fn.7, the elements relied on by the Government being insufficient to found reasonable suspicion (e.g. her brother's conviction in the US on arms-buying charges).

[13] The applicant alleged that, as a prominent member of Sinn Fein, he was targeted by the police as an automatic suspect.

[14] See *Karakoz v Turkey*, November 8, 2005, where the police took the applicant from prison several times, either without any stated purpose or any connection with a new offence. The Court found this was an attempt to circumvent judicial control of detention and applicable procedural guarantees.

[15] *RL and MD v France*, May 19, 2004. See also *Smirnova v Russia*, July 24, 2003, ECHR 2003–IX, paras 65–71, where the repeated detaining of the applicants during an investigation on the basis of insufficiently reasoned decisions disclosed a violation of Art.5, para.1, as well as para.3.

[16] *Stepuleac v Moldova*, November 6, 2007.

However, where the allegations in proceedings against a suspect rely on matters which do not disclose an offence, the arrest and detention may fall outside the permitted exception, since the existence of reasonable suspicion requires that the facts relied on can be reasonably invoked as falling under prescribed criminal behaviour. Thus, in *Lukanov v Bulgaria*, where the applicant, a minister of the previous regime, was arrested and detained allegedly for misappropriation of funds, the Commission observed that the grounds of the accusations referred solely to his transfers of monies in aid to the Third World, which was not an offence. Thus the facts invoked against the applicant at the time of his arrest and during his continued detention could not, in the eyes of an objective observer, be construed as amounting to the criminal offence of misappropriation of funds and there was no reasonable suspicion of his having committed an offence to justify the detention. Conversely, the problem may be treated as lack of "lawfulness", which was the approach of the Court in *Lukanov*.[17] In *Wloch v Poland*, the uncertainties surrounding the interpretation of the domestic law imposing an offence in trading in children caused the Court to doubt the legality of the applicant's detention on suspicion of such activities; it felt able to rely nonetheless on the domestic investigation into the factual aspects of the suspicion and the suspicion that he had also committed the offence of inciting persons to give false evidence as showing that there was nothing arbitrary or unreasonable in his detention.[18]

This ground of detention does not include a policy of general prevention directed against an individual or a category of individuals who present a danger on account of their continuing propensity to crime. It does no more than afford the Contracting States a means of preventing a concrete and specific offence.[19] The mere fact that a person's name is on a "surveillance database" as a member of a human rights organisation did not form sufficient basis for an arrest, even of only 45 minutes.[20]

5. Purpose to bring before a competent legal authority

This is the purpose underlying Art.5, para.1(c) read in conjunction with Art.5, para.3. Applicants arrested under the three heads must all be brought before a judge or released.[21] II–240

It has sometimes been argued that the apparent purpose of an arrest was not to bring before a competent legal authority, but to gather information without necessarily intending to charge the person with anything. In *Brogan*, where the applicants argued that they were neither charged nor brought before a court, the Court agreed with the Commission that the existence of the purpose (to bring before a court if sufficient and usable evidence had been obtained during the police

[17] *Lukanov*, see fn.3 above, paras 42–45, the Court reasoned that as none of the criminal provisions that relied on specified or implied criminal liability could be incurred by participating in collective decisions of this kind, the deprivation of liberty was not "lawful".

[18] *Wloch v Poland*, October 19, 2000, ECHR 2000–XI, paras 108–117.

[19] *Haidn v Germany*, January 13, 2011, paras 76 and 90.

[20] *Shimovolos v Russia*, June 21, 2011, paras 53–57.

[21] *Lawless v Ireland*, July 1, 1961, Series A, No.3, pp.51–52, para.14, where the Government unsuccessfully argued a construction excluding the second and third heads, i.e. suspicion that a person would commit an offence or flee having committed one. The arrest of persons suspected of IRA membership for the purposes of internment, without the prospect of bringing them before a judicial authority was found by the Court to be contrary to Art.5, paras 1(c) and 3, though covered by Ireland's derogation under Art.15.

investigation) had to be considered independently of the achievement of that purpose. Arrest under Art.5, para.1(c) did not presuppose that charges have to be brought, but that the criminal investigation be furthered by way of confirming or dispelling the concrete suspicion. Evidence may prove unobtainable or impossible to produce in court. In that particular case, there was no indication that the police investigation was not in good faith and it could be assumed that, if they had been able, the police would have laid charges and brought the applicants before the competent legal authority. The fact that they were questioned about specific offences showed that their arrest was grounded in concrete suspicions.[22]

6. Lawfulness and procedural safeguards

II–241 It is not required that arrest be ordered by a judge,[23] but the individual must be brought promptly before a judge for the purposes of Art.5, para.3.[24] The arrest must be carried out in accordance with a procedure prescribed by law according to the second sentence of Art.5, para.1, and must also be "lawful" in terms of the various sub-paragraphs.[25] Reasons for the arrest must also be given promptly under Art.5, para.2.

Cross-reference

Part IIB, s.9: Deprivation of liberty.
Part IIB, s.35: Pre-trial detention.
Part IIB, s.39: Reasons for arrest and detention.
Part IIB, s.42: Review of detention.

[22] See also *K-F v Germany*, November 27, 1997, R.J.D. 1997–VII, paras 57–62; *Perry v UK*, (63737/00) (Dec.) September 26, 2002, where the applicant suspect was brought to the police station ostensibly for questioning and was filmed, without his knowledge, for identification purposes, the Court considered that this covert purpose did not render the detention either unlawful or arbitrary.

[23] (7755/77) (Dec.) May 18, 1977, 9 D.R. 210.

[24] See Pt IIB, s.35: Pre-trial detention.

[25] See, e.g. *Steel*, fn.5 above, the Court found that the conduct of three applicants handing out leaflets peacefully about arms sales did not justify any fear of a breach of the peace and their arrests were not lawful (paras 62–65); *Lucas v UK*, (39013/02) (Dec.) March 18, 2003, the arrest of the applicant for sitting in the road was regarded as lawful under Art.5, para.1; *Lukanov*, see fn.3 above, paras 42–45.

5. Childcare cases

Key provisions:

Articles 6 (fair hearing), 8 (respect for family life) and 14 (prohibition of discrmination). II–242

Key case-law:

W, B and R v UK, July 8, 1987, Series A, No.121, 10 E.H.R.R. 29; *O and H v UK*, July 8, 1987, Series A, No.120, 10 E.H.R.R. 82 and 95; *Olsson v Sweden*, March 24, 1988, Series A, No.130, 11 E.H.R.R. 259; *Eriksson v Sweden*, June 22, 1989, Series A, No.156, 12 E.H.R.R. 183; *Margareta and Roger Andersson v Sweden*, February 25, 1992, Series A, No.226–A, 14 E.H.R.R. 615; *Rieme v Sweden*, April 22, 1992, Series A, No.226–B, 16 E.H.R.R. 155; *Keegan v Ireland*, May 26, 1994, Series A, No.290, 18 E.H.R.R. 342; *Hokkanen v Finland*, September 23, 1994, Series A, No.299–A, 19 E.H.R.R. 139; *Kroon v Netherlands*, October 27, 1994, Series A, No.297–C, 19 E.H.R.R. 273; *McMichael v UK*, February 24, 1995, Series A, No.307–B, 20 E.H.R.R. 205; *Johansen v Norway*, August 7, 1996, R.J.D. 1996–III, No.13, 23 E.H.R.R. 33; *Bronda v Italy*, June 9, 1998, R.J.D. 1998–IV, No.77; *Soderback v Sweden*, October 28, 1998, R.J.D. 1998–VIII, No.94, 29 E.H.R.R. 95; *Ignaccolo-Zenide v Romania*, January 25, 2000, ECHR 2000–I; *Nuuttinen v Finland*, June 27, 2000, ECHR 2000–VIII; *Elsholz v Germany*, July 13, 2000, ECHR 2000–VIII; *Scozzari and Giunta v Italy*, July 13, 2000, ECHR 2000–VIII; *TP and KM v UK*, May 10, 2001, ECHR 2001–V; *K and T v Finland*, July 12, 2001, ECHR 2001–VII, 31 E.H.R.R. 212; *Kutzner v Germany*, February 26, 2002, ECHR 2002–I; *P, C and S v UK*, July 16, 2002, ECHR 2002–VI; *Sylvester v Austria*, April 24, 2003; *Covezzi and Morselli v Italy*, May 9, 2003; *Sahin v Germany*, July 8, 2003, ECHR 2003–VII; *Sommerfeld v Germany*, July 8, 2003, ECHR 2003–VIII; *Pini v Romania*, June, 22, 2004, ECHR 2004–V.

1. General considerations

This section concerns three situations where care, custody and contact with children may raise issues under the Convention. The first category involves the most common cause of complaint, namely, intervention by State authorities to remove children from their families and subsequent decisions taken as to contact, custody and adoption. The second category concerns regulation by the courts of custody and contact disputes following divorce or separation of the parents. Thirdly, there is a small group of cases dealing with issues of parental rights arising in non-conventional family groupings. II–243

Given the seriousness of the interferences in the first category, the Court gives complaints careful scrutiny. It has generally confined its role in line with its pronouncements on the nature of European supervision, in particular, that it is not its function to substitute its view on the merits for that of the domestic authorities. In this area, the domestic courts are particularly well placed to assess the requirements of the welfare of the children and, under the "margin of appreciation" doctrine, a significant measure of discretion is accorded to domestic authorities in the performance of their functions and in their evaluation of the factors which may appear to them to be critical for the protection of the health or morals of a child.[1] Consequently, if, after judicial proceedings in which the parent's interests are fairly protected, a judgment is issued removing custody or contact on the basis that the measure is necessary for the welfare of the child(ren), it is unlikely that an application would succeed on the basis of a complaint that the decision was wrong.[2]

The cases have concentrated on procedural aspects: access to court, delay, legal representation, etc. The merits of a decision may, however, be challenged indirectly through the requirement, outlined below, that decisions must be supported by relevant and sufficient reasons.

2. Interferences by domestic authorities

Parents

II–244 Steps taken regulating parents' contact with their children, removing custody or parental responsibility, prima facie constitute interferences with family life which require justification under Art.8, para.2. Conducting an investigation into allegations that the parent has abused the child is also an interference.[3]

Parents include natural fathers, where there has been cohabitation or other factors showing a relationship of sufficient constancy as to create de facto family ties.[4] Sporadic contact and disputed biological ties may not qualify.[5] Further, even a proven biological link does not confer an absolute right to obtain parental rights, the

[1] e.g. *Bronda v Italy*, June 9, 1998, R.J.D. 1998–IV, No.77, para.59; *TP and KM v UK*, May 10, 2001, ECHR 2001–V, para.70. The Court also takes into account the fact that perceptions as to the appropriateness of intervention by public authorities vary between Contracting States, depending, inter alia, on traditions relating to the role of the family, see *K and T v Finland*, July 12, 2001, ECHR 2001–VII, 31 E.H.R.R. 212, para.154, and *Kutzner v Germany*, February 26, 2002, ECHR 2002–I, para.66.

[2] The notion of "necessity" as applied by the courts requires more pressing justification than the placement of the child in a more beneficial environment, e.g. *K and T v Finland*, see fn.1 above, para.173, *Kutzner*, see fn.1 above, para.69. See also *Sabou and Pircalab v Romania*, September 28, 2004, violation where parental rights were automatically removed due to the imposition of a prison sentence for an offence unconnected with the parental role or welfare needs of the children; and *Wallova and Walla v Czech Republic*, October 26, 2006, where children were removed due to inadequate housing, without any indication of abuse or lack of parental ability to look after the children.

[3] *K and T v Norway*, September 25, 2008, the investigation was, however, justified by concerns to protect the child. Contrast *D v UK*, (38000(1)/05) (Dec.) February 12, 2008, the Court doubted that placing a sick child in hospital on the 'at risk' register, without any other measures, was sufficient to interfere with the mother's rights under Art.8.

[4] See *Keegan v Ireland*, May 26, 1994, Series A, No.290, 18 E.H.R.R. 342, para.44, a child born out of a relationship of two persons cohabiting outside marriage *ipso iure* is part of the "family unit" and a family bond exists even if at the time of birth the parents no longer cohabit or the relationship has ended; *Kroon v Netherlands*, October 27, 1994, Series A, No.297–C, 19 E.H.R.R. 273, para.56, the natural father did not cohabit but there was a longstanding relationship from which four children were born; *Lebbink v Netherlands*, June 1, 2004, ECHR 2004–IV, para.37, where the applicant, although not cohabiting, had been auxiliary guardian of the child—mere blood ties were not enough.

[5] In (22920/93) (Dec.) April 6, 1994, 77–A D.R. 108, the Commission were not prepared to find "family life" where the applicant claimed to be the father of a child of a married woman, nor a right to prove the link through a blood test—it distinguished *Keegan* on the basis the mother disputed his claims, there was no element of planning or cohabitation and thus insufficient links in fact or law to bring the case within Art.8. Similar conclusion in *Nylund v Finland*, (27110/95) (Dec.) June 29, 1999, ECHR 1999–VI. *Haas v Netherlands*, January 13, 2004, ECHR 2004–I, no family life where the putative father had only had sporadic contact with the applicant who, as an adult, only sought to have the paternity recognised for an inheritance claim.

interests of the child prevailing over the natural father's where any clash of Art.8 rights occur.[6] An adoption, carried out in accordance with the law and practice of the Contracting State, bestows family life, even where the adoptive parents have had minimal contact with the child.[7]

Blanket, automatic removal of parental responsibilities without judicial supervision as to the paramount interests of the child is likely to offend. Where the removal of rights flowed automatically from a criminal conviction, Art.8 was breached; even though the offence was serious, there had been no finding that the applicant father had in any way harmed the child or failed to provide proper care.[8]

Failure by a divorced father to pay child support cannot be relied on as somehow decisively forfeiting family life rights.[9]

Relations between adoptive parents and an adopted child receive equivalent protection under Art.8, the State being under an obligation to promote family unity in this context also.[10] It is doubtful that there is a right for an adopter to annul an adoption, whether on the basis of the misconduct of the adopted child or otherwise.[11]

Family life may be subject to interference where a parent is prevented from enjoying the company of both his children together on access visits by separate contact arrangements with each child.[12]

Other relatives

The extent to which interferences may occur in respect of other family members or concerned persons depends on the nature of the relationship with the child. In grandparent cases,[13] the Commission took the view that links between grandparents and grandchildren varied from family to family and each case had to be examined on its facts to determine whether there were sufficient links to constitute "family life" and thereby bring the relationship within the protection of Art.8. In determining whether the decisions taken by the social services interfered with the rights guaranteed under this provision, the Commission considered that different standards would normally apply than where a parent was involved. For example, a grandparent's access to a child was normally at the discretion of the child's parents in any case and regulation of access by a local authority would not, as such, constitute an interference. There might, however, be an interference where a local II–245

[6] e.g. *Youssef v Netherlands*, November 5, 2002, where the mother had died and the child was living with her uncle, the courts' refusal to give legal recognition of paternity, which the applicant intended to use to disrupt her current family situation, struck the right balance.

[7] *Pini v Romania*, June, 22, 2004, ECHR 2004–V, where it was not the applicant couple's fault that no closer links were forged (due to lack of enforcement of the adoption order) and their conduct showed that they viewed themselves as the childrens' parents.

[8] *Iordache v Romania*, October 14, 2008; see also *Sabou and Pircalab*, fn.2 above.

[9] *Eberhard and M v Slovenia*, December 1, 2009, para.131.

[10] *Kurochkin v Ukraine,* May 20, 2010, breach where the courts annulled the adoption, the alleged failure of the adoptive father to maintain discipline, the breakdown of the child's relations with the adoptive mother and the apparent intention to sanction the child's violent behaviour not justifying the measure.

[11] *Gotia v Romania*, (24315/06) (Dec.) October 5, 2010, paras 30–36, however, even if Art.8 did apply, there was no failure to comply with a positive obligation where domestic law did not provide for adoptive parents to annul the adoption where the adult child was "ungrateful".

[12] *Mustafa and Armagan Akin v Turkey*, April 6, 2010, para.21.

[13] (12399/85) (Dec.) March 9, 1988; (12402/86) (Dec.) July 14, 1988, 55 D.R. 224; (12763/87) July 14, 1988, 57 D.R. 216.

authority diminished the access necessary to preserve a normal grandparent-grandchild relationship. The Court has acknowledged that ties between near relatives such as grandparents and grandchildren fall within "family life" since such relatives may play a considerable part in family life.[14]

The Commission accepted that an uncle may have a relationship with a child of such a nature as to attract the protection of Art.8, where he had acted as a "father figure" and lived in close contact with the child, such that refusal of access by the social services when the child was taken into care disclosed an interference.[15] An old case indicated that a foster-parent may have sufficient links with a child to attract the protection of Art.8 of the Convention.[16] More recently, the Court found that where a foster family had established close bonds with a baby, who had been placed with them at one month old, and the foster parents acted in all respects as her parents, "family life" existed for the purposes of Art.8. The fact that the foster parents had applied to adopt the child was a relevant but not decisive element, demonstrating the strength of the bond.[17] However, a married couple who had lodged an orphan from another country over a period of eighteen months could not claim that "family life" had been established.[18]

Where sisters had been separated at birth by care measures, it was doubtful that they could claim "family life" with each other.[19]

Standing of children themselves

II–246 Children in care may themselves, through an appropriate representative, complain that their rights under the Convention have been infringed by measures taken by social services. Although in early cases the Commission had regard to whether the parent had any legal right to represent the child,[20] the Court has stated that the conditions concerning standing under the Convention are not necessarily the same as those in national law. In order to ensure that the child's interests are put forward and effectively protected, it has held that a natural parent may introduce an application on behalf of the child even if he or she no longer has parental rights

[14] See *Scozzari and Giunta v Italy*, July 13, 2000, ECHR 2000–VIII, para.221, no problem was found concerning the grandmother's complaints of denial of access due to her own inconsistent behaviour and lack of co-operation; *Bronda*, fn.1 above, paras 59–63, where the child's interest in remaining with her foster parents outweighed that of her grandparents; *Ticli and Mancuso v Italy*, March 23, 1999, contrast *Clemeno v Italy*, October 21, 2008, where complaints by uncles, aunts and a grandmother were rejected due to their lack of any previous interest in the child.

[15] *Boyle v UK*, (Rep.) February 9, 1993, Series A, No.282–B.

[16] (8257/78) (Dec.) July 10, 1978, 13 D.R. 248.

[17] *Moretti and Benedetti v Italy*, April 27, 2010, paras 50–52.

[18] *Giusto, Bornacin and V v Italy*, (38972/06) (Dec.) May 15, 2007, where it was part of an exchange and holiday programme, with no intention of giving the child a new family.

[19] *I and U v Norway*, (75531/01) (Dec.) October 21, 2004, the two elder sisters had applied for access rights to the youngest.

[20] In *Hokkanen*, since in the domestic proceedings the father no longer had legal custody and had no right in domestic terms to represent the child, the Commission found that he could not complain on behalf of the child in Strasbourg.

under domestic law.[21] In this context, the Court has distinguished situations where the applicant parent, without custodial or parental rights, is in dispute with a guardian appointed by the State from those in which the dispute, about matters of the child's welfare other than custody, is between the parent with custody and the parent without custody. To ensure that the minor's interests may be vindicated before the Court, the applicant in the former situation has standing; in the latter situation, it is for the parent holding the custodial rights to safeguard the child's interests and the other parent does not have standing before the Court in respect of the child.[22]

Children may complain where measures result in them being separated from their siblings and being unable to enjoy contact visits together.[23]

The case-law has established a number of key areas where violations may arise.

(a) Procedural protection of rights

The first UK cases before the Court established the important principle that the decision-making process in childcare matters must afford sufficient procedural protection of parents' interests.[24] Where in *W v UK*, for example, the local authority passed a parental rights resolution in respect of the applicant's child (S) and proceeded to take a series of decisions—placement in long-term foster care with a view to adoption, restriction and termination of access—without advance consultation or discussion with the applicant or his wife, the Court noted that it was crucial in an area where decisions may prove irreversible (i.e. a child may form new bonds with his alternative carers) that there is adequate protection for parents against arbitrary interferences. In the circumstances of this case, the Court found that the applicant had been insufficiently involved in critical stages of the decision-making which affected his relationship with S. Accordingly he had not been afforded the requisite consideration of his views or protection of his interests in violation of Art.8 of the Convention. II–247

Since these decisions, particular attention has been paid to the procedural fairness of the decision-making process regarding parents and other members of the family whose relationship with a child has been subject to interference.[25] Relevant factors,

[21] *Scozzari and Giunta*, see fn.14 above, paras 138–139; *P, C and S v UK* (Dec.) December 11, 2001, where the child had been adopted and the natural parents were not considered safe guardians by the authorities, it was still considered essential that potential claims be put forward on her behalf. See also *SP, DP and AT v UK*, (23715/94) (Dec.) May 20, 1996, where the Commission allowed a case to be introduced on behalf of three children by the solicitor who had represented them in care proceedings and who complained of the unjustifiable delay as prejudicing their welfare. Although he no longer represented them in domestic terms, the Commission noted the importance that children's rights be practically and effectively protected and that in the absence of any conflict of interest or the existence of more appropriate representation, found the solicitor had sufficient links with the children and the subject-matter of the claim to represent them in Strasbourg.

[22] *Eberhard and M v Slovenia*, fn.9 above, paras 87–88, citing *Sahin v Germany*, (30943/96) (Dec.) December 12, 2000.

[23] *Mustafa and Armagan Akin*, fn.12 above, para.21.

[24] This does not automatically require access to court, lack of which would instead raise issues under Art.6 where civil rights were concerned, but covers the intervention by the social services, which may be crucial for the development of events.

[25] No explicit procedural requirements are contained in Art.8: the emphasis is on fairness and due respect to the interests to be safeguarded, e.g. *McMichael v UK*, February 24, 1995, Series A, No.307–B, 20 E.H.R.R. 205, para.87; *Buscemi v Italy*, September 16, 1999, ECHR 1999–VI, para.58 (no violation concerning expert evidence procedure).

assessed on the particular facts of each case, include the opportunity to make submissions, in person or in writing, before decisions are reached[26]; access to the reports and documents relied on in the decision-making[27]; the provision of legal representation to parents[28]; expert reports taking into account examination of the parent[29]; the holding of public hearings; and the obtaining of necessary independent psychiatric opinions.[30] Procedural requirements do not go so far as to require domestic courts always to hear the child in court on the issue of access, this issue depending on the specific facts of the case with due regard to the age and maturity of the child.[31]

Although the responsibility lies on the authorities to ensure that a parent is placed in a position where he or she can obtain access to information upon which care measures were based, there is no absolute right of a parent to view materials. In *TP and KM v UK*, the applicant mother complained that she was prevented for a year from viewing a video of a disclosure interview crucial to the decision to remove her daughter into care as the doctor and social worker involved considered that this was not in the interests of the child. The Court emphasised, to the Government's argument that she had not applied to the court for disclosure, that it was not the sole responsibility of the parent, nor lay at her initiative, to obtain the evidence on which the removal was based and that the local authority should have submitted the issue of disclosure to the court for it to determine the issues.[32]

[26] e.g. *Boyle*, fn.15 above, where the uncle was a de facto father to the child in care, a violation flowed from the lack of meaningful consultation with him by the social services, which ended access without prior invitation of his views; (17071/90) (Dec.) February 13, 1990, where a mother complained of the inclusion of her child's name on a child abuse register, her position was adequately safeguarded by the opportunity to submit her views in writing beforehand; *Covezzi and Morselli v Italy*, May 9, 2003, paras 134–139, violation arose from the applicants' inability to put forward effectively their objections to the care measures over significant periods; *Hunt v Ukraine*, December 7, 2006, decision to remove parental rights taken without hearing the applicant or seeking his views through international legal assistance.

[27] e.g. *McMichael v UK*, fn.25 above, where the Children's Hearing only summarised orally the reports concerning the applicant parents and their baby; *Kosmopoulou v Greece*, February 5, 2004, delayed access to psychiatric report; *Tsourlakis v Greece*, October 15, 2009, father denied access to social welfare report (even if it had not been decisive in the proceedings, it might have assisted him in his future relations with the child).

[28] *P, C and S v UK*, July 16, 2002, ECHR 2002–VI, paras 92–100, and 134–137, violations of both Arts 6 and 8 where the court continued the hearing of a care order and freeing for adoption applications when the applicant parents were unrepresented. See also Pt IIA, s.14: Legal aid in civil cases.

[29] *Kosmopoulou*, see fn.27 above, para.49.

[30] *Elsholz v Germany*, July 13, 2000, ECHR 2000–VIII, paras 52–53, the courts did not obtain independent psychological evidence concerning the child's (aged five to six) position on access with her father, where the child, questioned by the judge, knew of the mother's objections and had shown hostility to the father: violations of both Arts 6 and 8. However, in *Sommerfeld v Germany*, July 8, 2003, ECHR 2003–VIII, paras 69–75, no violation arose from a failure to obtain a psychological report on the access possibilities between child and natural father: the distinction with *Elsholz* appears to be the age of the child—she was 13 and had been questioned several times by the judge who was recognised as being able, in the case of such a mature child, to evaluate her statements and assess whether she was capable of making up her own mind without expert evidence. See also *C v Finland*, May 9, 2006, where there was no oral hearing or expert evidence before the Supreme Court which overturned lower court decisions giving custody to the father.

[31] *Sahin v Germany*, July 8, 2003, ECHR 2003–VII, paras 73–74, no violation for failure to hear a child aged three to five years during the access proceedings.

[32] *TP and KM*, see fn.1 above, paras 80–83. See also *KA v Finland*, January 14, 2003, para.105, stating that as a general rule the authorities have an obligation to make available all case materials, even in the absence of a request by the parents.

The level of consultation or involvement in the decision-making process required may differ in respect of non-parental relatives.[33]

Where adoption procedures are concerned, the Court has accepted that it is acceptable for a short time-limit of two months to be imposed for the mother to reconsider her consent to the adoption of her baby[34]; it also accepted that such consent may be deemed irrevocable by domestic law.[35]

(b) Emergency measures

A wide margin of appreciation applies to the authorities' assessment of the necessity of taking a child into care.[36] Effective protection of children from harm even imposes a requirement for emergency measures.[37] The Court also accepts that when emergency care orders are made it may not be possible, due to the urgency of the situation, to involve the parents in the decision-making process, and that it may deprive the measure of effectiveness to give prior warning of the measure to those seen as the source of possible harm to the child. However, the Court will examine whether there exist circumstances justifying an abrupt removal without prior consultation or notification and whether the authorities have carried out a proper assessment of the impact of the measures and the existence of possible alternatives.[38] Extraordinarily compelling reasons must exist for a baby to be physically removed from the mother after birth.[39] In *K and T v Finland*, the Court found the removal of a baby from her mother at birth was not so justified, as the authorities were well aware of the mother's mental problems, both mother and child were in hospital care, and no consideration was given to other less drastic ways of protecting the child from harm.[40] In *P, C and S v UK*, the Court found that there were sufficiently compelling reasons to issue an emergency protection order for a new born baby whose mother had a conviction for previously harming a child and was suspected of II–248

[33] (12763/87), see fn.13 above, while the decision to end all contact with their grandchild constituted an interference with family life, the Commission did not expect that grandparents be involved in the procedures to the same extent as parents: it was sufficient that the local authority consulted the grandparents regularly, allowed them to make representations at case conferences and provided a procedure for review.

[34] *Kearns v France*, January 10, 2008, the Court considered that the mother was 36, accompanied by her mother, received advice from a lawyer and had had two lengthy interviews with the social services; two months was therefore sufficient for her to reflect. The French authorities had also adequately made clear the time-limit; no requirement to provide a qualified interpreter to the Irish applicant was found where medical staff with knowledge of English had acted as interpreters.

[35] *VS v Germany*, (4261/02) (Dec.) May 22, 2007, although it was possible for the mother to have examined whether her consent had been validly given at the time.

[36] e.g. *Johansen Norway*, August 7, 1996, R.J.D. 1996–III, No.13, 23 E.H.R.R. 33, para.64.

[37] *Clemeno*, fn.14 above, paras 51–52, children have a right to protection: emergency measure regarded as proportionate in case of suspected sexual abuse.

[38] *K and T v Finland*, fn.1 above, para.166.

[39] *K and T v Finland*, see fn.1 above, para.168.

[40] *K and T v Finland*, see fn.1 above, para.168, conversely, the emergency care order for the older child was justified as he was already in voluntary care and had shown signs of disturbance—para.169; *TP and KM*, see fn.1 above, para.74, where the emergency removal of a four-year-old, later found to be based on mistaken assumptions, was, at the time, justified by strong suspicions of abuse and the inability of the mother to protect her; *Covezzi and Morselli*, fn.26 above, para.104, where the removal of four children was justified by multi-generational sexual abuse and doubts about parental protection; *KA v Finland*, fn.32 above, paras 98–102, removal into care justified even though investigation into incest allegations was not completed.

suffering from Munchhausen's Syndrome by proxy. It did, however, find a violation concerning the implementation of the protection order, namely, the removal of the baby from the hospital into care rather than a less drastic form of supervision of mother and baby within the hospital.[41]

(c) *Access to court*

II–249 A parent's rights to contact with, and custody of, a child constitute "civil rights", the determination of which requires a fair hearing before an independent and impartial tribunal pursuant to Art.6. In less technical terms, where an important issue concerning a parent's relationship with a child is at stake, a parent should be able to challenge the decision in a court. A violation was found, for example, in *R v UK*, where the mother of a child in care under a parental rights' resolution, and to whom access had been refused by the local authority, was unable to go to a court to challenge that refusal. Where a natural father had no standing in care proceedings concerning a child taken into care and no prospect of applying for contact, the case was settled after being declared admissible.[42] Inability of a natural father to challenge the adoption of a child before a court disclosed a violation in *Keegan v Ireland*. Exclusion of the natural mother from adoption proceedings, as she had been deprived of legal capacity due to mental illness, was a breach; she should still have been given the opportunity to be heard and to express her views, and her relationship with her daughter should have been assessed.[43] There is an indication that domestic authorities may be under an obligation to assist parents in Hague Convention disputes to obtain access to court in the other jurisdictions.[44]

Access to court for other relatives would not appear to be regarded as an automatic requirement, having regard to the basic principle that Art.6, para.1 only applies to procedures concerning the recognition of a right which has a legal basis in domestic law. Thus, the Commission found that Art.6, para.1 could not be invoked by grandparents, since it did not consider that under English law grandparents enjoyed a right of custody of or access to their grandchildren.[45]

(d) *Delay in proceedings*

II–250 Childcare proceedings must be managed with particular expedition, having regard to the importance of what is at stake and since the nature of the issues is such that the lapse of time may influence their outcome.[46] In *H v UK*, where an application for access was not decided for almost two years, the judge had refused access, but criticised the delay as "quite deplorable" and commented that it had seriously

[41] See also *Venema v Netherlands*, December 17, 2002, where the mother was also suspected of Munchhausen Syndrome by proxy, the issuing of an emergency care order violated Art.8, essentially because, in contrast to *P, C and S v UK*, fn.28 above, the authorities had not allowed the parents any input before the order was made; and *Haase v Germany*, April 8, 2004, ECHR 2004–III, paras 102–103.
[42] (11468/85) (Dec.) October 15, 1986, 50 D.R. 199; (11240/84) (Rep.) May 13, 1988, 56 D.R. 108, where a natural father had no access to court to challenge a reduction in access.
[43] See *X v Croatia*, July 17, 2008, breach of Art.8.
[44] See *Mamousseau and Washington v France*, December 6, 2007, paras 103–104, where the French Central Authority had been found to have offered assistance and acted in accordance with its obligations.
[45] (12763/87), fn.13 above.
[46] e.g. *Johansen*, see fn.36 above, para.88; *Hoppe v Germany*, December 5, 2002, para.54; *Eberhard and M*, fn.9 above, para.142, referring to lack of promptness.

prejudiced the position of the applicant, who by that point had not seen the child for three and a half years, during which time she had been settled for 19 months with prospective adopters. The Court found a violation under Art.6 since the applicant had not received a fair hearing within a reasonable time having regard to the importance of what was at stake for her.[47] Under Art.8, the violation lay in that the delay had led to a de facto determination of the issue whereas an effective respect for the applicant's family life required that the question be determined solely in light of all the relevant considerations and not by the mere effluxion of time.

Whether the length of childcare proceedings will disclose a violation under Art.8 will depend largely on the prejudicial effect on the outcome of the proceedings. Protracted criminal proceedings which have the direct consequence of seriously curtailing enjoyment of family life may also raise issues.[48] Under Art.6, the general considerations applicable to length complaints are relevant, such as the complexity of the case and whether the applicant contributed to the delay.[49] A delay at one stage may be acceptable if the overall duration of the proceedings is not excessive.[50] (See Pt IIA, s.17: Length of proceedings.)

(e) Relevant and sufficient reasons

As stated above, the Court does not consider itself a court of appeal for domestic courts. Particularly in this area, it shies away from substituting its opinion on the merits. However, it does not, as a result, limit its review of a case solely to procedural matters. This was established in *Olsson v Sweden*, where the applicants' three children were taken into care, the social authorities considering that their development was in danger due, inter alia, to their parents' inability to satisfy their need for stimulation and supervision. In care the children were separated and placed in foster homes up to 600km from their parents' home. In assessing whether this interference with the parents' rights was justified under Art.8, para.2 as "necessary" in the children's interests, the Court repeated the principle that a margin of appreciation was left to the State in assessing the necessity of measures but held that it exercised a supervisory jurisdiction which was not confined to ascertaining whether the State had exercised its discretion reasonably, carefully and in good faith. It had also to consider whether the reasons adduced to justify an interference were "relevant and sufficient". On the facts of the case, it found that the decision to take the children into care initially was supported by such reasons (e.g. evidence that the children were retarded in their development, the fact that other measures had been **II–251**

[47] Also *Nuutinen v Finland*, June 27, 2000, ECHR 2000–VIII, paras 109–120, violation for proceedings lasting over five years; *Paulsen-Medalen and Svensson v Sweden*, February 19, 1998, R.J.D. 1998–I, No.63.
[48] *Schaal v Luxembourg*, February 18, 2003, violations of Arts 6 and 8 due to the five-year duration of the investigation into allegations of sexual assault of a child by the applicant father. Until his acquittal, his contact rights had been terminated to safeguard the child.
[49] e.g. (13288/87) (Dec.) February 13, 1990, where a judge found no sensible explanation for a 20-month delay in wardship proceedings, the Commission found that the time was not unreasonable under Art.6 nor had the case been determined solely by the effluxion of time contrary to Art.8: it had regard, in particular, to the complexity of the case, involving four children, and the failure of the applicant to take steps to expedite the matter (e.g. she agreed to the procedural steps which led to the longest periods of delay). Unlike *H v UK*, July 8, 1987, Series A, No.120, 10 E.H.R.R. 82 and 95, the applicant had had contact with the children during the proceedings and she had been partly successful, obtaining the return of two children.
[50] *MC v Finland*, (28460/95) (Dec.) January 25, 2001.

tried without success). Regarding the implementation of the care order however, the Court found that, particularly since the measure was seen as temporary, the placing of the children in separate homes at such long distances was not supported by relevant or sufficient reasons. In this respect, there was a violation of Art.8.[51]

The Court will therefore review the decisions of domestic courts to determine whether they are supported by reasons which are both relevant and sufficient.[52] Where a court did not go into detail in its judgment, for example, expressly refraining from repeating evidence out of sympathy for the mother, the Commission took into account the evidence (medical and other reports) before the court in assessing whether the decision was adequately supported.[53] It is questionable whether, if a domestic court failed to give any reasons at all for its decision,[54] although there was material before it which might have furnished "relevant and sufficient reasons", the Court could or should embark on a reconstruction of what the court might have been thinking. In a more recent judgment, the Court has stated that the decision-making authorities and courts must give such detailed reasons as would allow the parent or custodian to appeal effectively, and that vague descriptions or reference to "documentation on file" would be insufficient.[55] A court's findings must be based on adequate and objective evidentiary basis, with proper corroboration and expert analysis where appropriate.[56]

However, mistaken judgments or assessments by professionals do not themselves render protective measures incompatible with Art.8. The fact that a suspicion of abuse turns out to be ill-founded will not render the authorities liable as long as there were genuine and reasonably-held concerns about the safety of children which could require action. Thus, where a baby had an unexplained bone fracture, there

[51] See also *Mustafa and Armagan Akin*, fn.12 above, where, in rejecting the application by the applicant father to enjoy contact at the same time with both his children (who had been separated between the parents while exchanging simultaneous visits), the courts failed to respond to his detailed submissions and gave inadequate reasons. Contrast *Covezzi and Morselli*, fn.26 above, paras 128–130, the separate placement of four children was supported by psychological evidence.

[52] e.g. *Johansen*, fn.36 above, where there were relevant reasons to support the permanent placement in the mother's conduct and the need for stability but these were not sufficient, i.e. the mother's lifestyle was improving and access was going well; *Margareta and Roger Andersson v Sweden*, February 25, 1992, Series A, No.226–A, 14 E.H.R.R. 615, where there were relevant reasons in the child's difficulties and stress, but that these were not sufficient to justify the almost complete deprivation of contact, by even letter and telephone, for over one and a half years; *EP v Italy*, November 16, 1999, where there were relevant and sufficient grounds for taking the child into care based on the mother's psychiatric disorders but no convincing explanation of why all contact was broken off; *Kutzner*, fn.1 above, paras 77–82, where the removal into care, access restrictions and separate placements of the children, which could only lead to "alienation" from the parents, were not supported by sufficient reasons, e.g. although the applicants were lacking in intellectual capacity, expert reports indicated that the children's welfare was not in jeopardy and other measures of educational support were available; *Scozzari and Giunta*, fn.14 above, para.171, where the authorities acted "irresponsibly" in suspending contact visits on the basis of allegations of sexual assault in the absence of proper and prompt verification.

[53] e.g. (13288/87), fn.49 above.

[54] e.g. *Moretti and Benedetti*, fn.17 above, paras 69–71, violation where no reasons were given for rejecting the foster parents' application to adopt the baby in their care.

[55] *KA v Finland*, fn.32 above, para.105.

[56] *Saviny v Ukraine*, December 18, 2008, paras 56–58, lack of sufficient reasons where, in accepting the municipal authorities' assertions as to the conditions in the family home, the court failed to analyse in any depth the extent to which inadequacies were attributable to the applicant parents' irremediable incapacity to provide proper care as opposed to financial and objective difficulties which could have been overcome by financial and social aid and effective counselling. Contrast *Haase and Others v Germany*, (34499/04) (Dec.) February 12, 2008, where the courts' withdrawal of parental authority over seven children was based on two expert reports, foster home reports, reports of the *curator ad litem* and the declarations of the children.

was no violation due to her removal into care, even though it proved later that the cause was a rare bone condition; the measures were proportionate to the concerns and once a further fracture occurred outside the applicants' care, prompt action was taken to settle the diagnosis and return the child home.[57] This may be contrasted with a case where, although the authorities were not to blame for failing to diagnose the medical cause for the child's injury, they delayed unduly in conducting the risk assessment of the family and in returning the child to the parents' care when the assessment was in their favour.[58]

(f) Rehabilitation

The taking into care of a child should normally be regarded as a temporary measure to be discontinued as soon as circumstances permit and any measures of implementation should be consistent with the ultimate aim of reuniting natural parent and child.[59] In *Hokkanen v Finland*, it was said that Art.8 confers a right for parents to have measures taken with a view to being reunited and that there is an obligation on the authorities to take such measures.[60] However, while there is a presumption of rehabilitation in favour of the parent, particular importance is attached to the best interests of the child, which may override those of the parent. A parent cannot claim a right to measures which would harm the child's health and development.[61] II–252

Thus, measures taken with the aim of permanently depriving a parent of contact or custody, for example permanent placement with a view to adoption, must only be applied in exceptional circumstances and can only be justified if motivated by an overriding requirement pertaining to the child's best interests. While authorities enjoy a wide margin of appreciation in assessing the necessity of taking a child into care, a strict scrutiny will apply to any further restrictions which entail the danger of curtailing relations between parent and child.[62] Where, prior to termination of access, a mother's contact with her daughter in care was going well and there were

[57] *RK and AK v UK*, September 30, 2008, while the applicant parents were understandably aggrieved at being suspected mistakenly of abuse, the Court was not persuaded that the welfare authorities, under a duty to protect children, should have given them the benefit of any doubt or that they were wrong to have acted on the worst case scenario. See also *AD and OD v UK*, March 16, 2010, where the medical authorities could not be faulted for not having reached a brittle bone disease diagnosis at an earlier stage; *D v UK*, (38000(1)/05) February 12, 2008, where there were sufficient, if eventually mistaken, grounds to suspect the applicant mother of inducing illness in her child, and therefore the child was put on the at risk register, which measure was speedily revoked once the suspicion had dispelled.

[58] *AD and OD*, fn.57 above. See also *MAK and RK*, March 23, 2010, where there was undue delay in obtaining a dermatologist's opinion on symptoms which would have cut short the care measures by clearing the parents of suspicion.

[59] *Johansen*, fn.36 above, para.78; in *Rieme*, the Court found that the gradual re-introduction of access between the applicant and his daughter did not disclose any hindrance of their reunion, having regard to the length of time she had lived in the foster home.

[60] e.g. *Eriksson v Sweden*, June 22, 1989, Series A, No.156, 12 E.H.R.R. 183, where the care order had been lifted but the social authorities continued to prohibit removal from the foster home, the Court noted that while difficulties might arise on the termination of care where children have spent long periods away from their parents, the unsatisfactory situation ensued in this case from a failure to ensure any meaningful access between mother and child with a view to reuniting them. See *Olsson v Sweden*, March 24, 1988, Series A, No.130, 11 E.H.R.R. 259, para.81; *Margareta and Roger Andersson*, fn.52 above, para.91; in *Kutzner*, fn.1 above, para.76, the Court considered that the positive duty to take steps to facilitate reunification took on progressive force as the separation continued.

[61] *Johansen*, fn.36 above, para.78; *EP v Italy*, fn.52 above, para.62.

[62] e.g. *Johansen*, fn.36 above, para.64; *Gnahoré v France*, September 19, 2000, ECHR 2000–IX, para.54.

signs of improvement in her life, the difficulties experienced by the social authorities in respect of measures concerning her son and the risk of disrupting the daughter's placement if access was given, did not disclose such an overriding requirement.[63] In *K and T v Finland*, in finding a failure by the authorities to take sufficient steps towards reunification, the Court noted the exceptionally firm negative attitude shown by the authorities which only carried out enquiries once during seven years as to the possibility of reuniting parent and child. The minimum that could have been expected was for the situation to be examined anew from time to time to see if there had been improvements, while the restrictions and prohibitions on access contributed to hindering any progress. It referred to a failure to make the serious or sustained effort to facilitate family reunification expected for the purposes of Art.8.[64]

The obligation to take measures to reunite parent and child is not absolute however. The Court has acknowledged the need for preparatory steps and the requirement to balance the interests, rights and freedoms of all concerned. Nonetheless, there would appear to be an obligation that they take all necessary steps to facilitate reunion as can reasonably be demanded in the special circumstances of each case. Failure to give proper consideration to rehabilitation may, therefore, raise issues.[65] In *Gnahoré v France*, the Court considered that the failure of a parent to cooperate in preparatory measures could be a relevant, although not an "absolutely decisive" factor,[66] and in light of the genuine efforts towards rehabilitation made by the authorities in that case, and the fact that the applicant's behaviour caused the failure of the measures implemented, no lack of respect was shown by the omission of possible additional steps.[67] Where a child had been in long-term foster care and would benefit from the security of adoption by his foster parents, cutting legal links with his biological mother, the Court found that this step was justified by the child's best interests, noting that the mother had not built up a strong relationship with the child despite available access arrangements. It gave particular weight, however, to the findings of the domestic courts that the adoptive parents could be relied upon to allow continued access to birth relatives, thus ensuring that the child was not severed from his roots.[68]

[63] *Johansen*, fn.36 above, para.84; *EP v Italy*, fn.52 above, where the suspension of parental responsibility was not based on accurate information or informed medical opinion and no apparent consideration was given to supervision of contact.

[64] *K and T v Finland*, fn.1 above, paras 177–179; *KA v Finland*, fn.32 above, paras 142–147, a similar lack of "serious and sustained effort" and lack of genuine or regular reviews of the situation; *Scozzari and Giunta*, fn.14 above, paras 174–183, where the social authorities altered the practical effect of contact orders by providing only sporadic visits and accentuating the rift between children and parents: the courts did not conduct thorough reviews of the situation, and paras 210–216, concerning the negative influence of the placement in the "*Il Forteto*" community which was not sufficiently under the supervision of the relevant authorities; *Clemeno*, fn.14 above, paras 60–62, breach due to complete severance of contacts with the entire family and a lack of any steps taken to reunite the child with her family after the father was acquitted of suspected abuse. Contrast *Haase and Others v Germany*, fn.41 above, where the authorities re-assesed the situation at regular intervals and showed no "culpable disregard, discernable bad faith or lack of will."

[65] e.g. (18546/91) (Dec.) August 31, 1992, where social services took an immediate decision to have a baby adopted where the mother, after birth, was admitted to a psychiatric unit—the case was struck off after settlement.

[66] Obstruction and withdrawal from the proceedings by the parents were significant factors in finding no violation arising from prolonged interruption in contact in *Covezzi and Morselli*, fn.26 above, para.122.

[67] See fn.62 above, para.63. See also *Couillard-Maugery v France*, July 1,2004, paras 306–307.

[68] *Aune v Norway*, October 28, 2010, paras 65–80.

(g) *Other issues*

It is not inconceivable that admissible complaints could arise under Art.3 concerning the alleged inhuman or degrading treatment of children subject to the perhaps overzealous attentions of a local authority. The circumstances surrounding the removal of a child from its home by a local authority, as well as the subsequent medical examination and interviews, could inflict a level of distress and suffering on the child that brought the treatment within the scope of Art.3. However, the mere fact that a removal of a child was based on a mistaken suspicion, is not sufficient to render the measures inhuman or degrading, notwithstanding the distress or humiliation felt by the parents, since it would be contradictory to the responsibility of the authorities to protect children from serious abuse if their every error rendered them in breach of the Convention. Thus some additional factor is required.[69] II–253

In the context of compulsory medical treatment, the Court has found that as a general rule treatment which was a therapeutic necessity would not violate Art.3[70]; action by a local authority which had the bona fide intention of protecting that child might, however, still fall foul of Art.3 if it had departed from perceived ideas about desirable practices. On the other hand, it is now established that failure by the authorities to protect a child from abuse can disclose a violation of Art.3 where they did not take reasonable steps to prevent ill-treatment of which they knew or ought to have known.[71]

Unjustified removal of a child from its home could also raise problems concerning arbitrary detention under Art.5. A failure to respect the religious affiliations of a child in care could fall within the scope of Art.9 (freedom of religion) and a failure to ensure the proper education of a child in care could raise a problem under Art.2 of the First Protocol (right to education).

Although no right of access to court to obtain damages for the negligence of social services can be derived from Art.6, where domestic law does not provide a substantive right of action, issues may arise under Art.13 if the remedies available do not include the possibility of obtaining a determination of the allegations of breach of rights and an enforceable award of compensation.[72]

3. Regulation of disputes by the courts

Increasingly, the State is not directly involved in taking children into care but is called on to regulate the custody between different claimants, generally, in divorce and separation cases. Mostly these cases have been dismissed by the Convention organs since the decisions taken by the courts, having regard to the margin of appreciation, could be justified as being in the interests of the child, even where, for II–254

[69] *MAK and RK v UK*, fn.58 above, para.35.

[70] *Herczegfalvy v Austria*, September 24, 1992, Series A, No.244, 15 E.H.R.R. 437.

[71] *Z v UK*, May 10, 2001, ECHR 2001–V; *E v UK*, November 26, 2002.

[72] See *Z*, fn.71 above, where there was no possibility of obtaining determination of negligence claims or an enforceable award of damages for failure to protect the children from abuse and neglect by their parents; *TP and KM*, see fn.1 above, no possibility of negligence findings or an enforceable award for any damage caused to mother or child by the removal into care on the basis of mistaken assumptions.

example, an adoption order in favour of the mother's new husband severed the applicant father's links with the child.[73]

The case of *Hoffman v Austria* indicated that reliance by the courts on discriminatory factors, not related to the welfare of the children, would disclose a violation of Art.8 in conjunction with Art.14. But the narrow margin in the Court (five to four) indicated that disapproval of a domestic court approach to the facts of a case may resemble an overruling of its assessment of the welfare of the children.[74] Prejudicial reliance by the Portuguese court in awarding custody of a child to the mother on the homosexual orientation of the applicant father founded a similar violation in *Salguiero da Silva Mouta v Portugal*.[75] The decision by German courts refusing a natural father access to a child born out of wedlock on the basis that, where the mother was deeply opposed to contact, only special circumstances could justify an assumption that access was in the child's best interests, was found to be discriminatory in *Sahin v Germany*.[76]

Failure to enforce court orders as to custody and contact may also raise issues. The test appears to be whether the authorities have taken all necessary steps to enforce decisions as can reasonably be demanded in the special circumstances of each case. In *Hokkanen v Finland*, a violation of Art.8 arose from the authorities' inaction over several years in enforcing the court orders for access where the grandparents refused to return a child to the applicant father. While the Government argued that there were limited options open to the authorities in face of wilful intransigence of the persons with custody, the Court, without specifying what they could have done and noting that coercion was undesirable, found that the only steps taken by the social authorities had been to hold three meetings and that it could not be said that reasonable efforts to facilitate reunion had been made.[77] In *Amanalachioai v Romania*,

[73] *Soderback v Sweden*, October 28, 1998, R.J.D. 1998–VIII, No.94, 29 E.H.R.R. 95, paras 30–34, allowing the mother's partner to adopt was in the interests of the child, who had lived with the adoptive father since she was eight months old, and not disproportionate in its effects due to the relatively weak ties between the child and the biological father, who had never had custody or care of the child. Contrast the increasing emphasis on the severance of parental-child ties being only exceptionally justified, e.g. *Aune v Norway*, fn.68 above, in the context of children taken into care and fostered.

[74] The applicant mother, a Jehovah's witness, while awarded custody by the two lower courts, lost to the father in the Supreme Court which overruled the lower courts' assessment of the children's welfare based on expert evidence, which held that the children were at risk of being social outcasts, and from the mother's refusal of blood transfusions. The Court majority found that the Supreme Court was influenced, as shown by its tone and phrasing, by considerations regarding the applicant's religion. The minority considered that it was legitimate for the Supreme Court to look at the effect of the mother's religious affiliation on the children's welfare, that the decision could not be said to be based only on her religion and that it was not for the Convention organs to substitute their opinion concerning the children's welfare. Similar violation found in *Palau-Martinez v France*, December 16, 2003.

[75] *Salguiero da Silva Mouta v Portugal*, December 21, 1999, ECHR 1999–IX, paras 35–36, the applicant's sexual orientation was the decisive factor in the custody decision, a distinction not acceptable under the Convention.

[76] German law at the time gave married fathers a right of access whereas fathers of children born out of wedlock had to show it was in the child's best interests. Similar violation in *Sommerfeld*, see fn.30. Contrast *Elsholz*, fn.30 above, no discrimination as the courts had made specific findings of detriment to the child from access which would have had the same result in the case of a married father.

[77] See also *Hansen v Turkey*, September 23, 2003, the imposition of three small fines was not adequate and no steps were taken by the authorities to locate the children before scheduled access visits; *Eberhard and M*, fn.9 above, where fines were not enforced and no adequate or effective efforts made to enforce the access order. *Nuutinnen v Finland*, June 27, 2000, ECHR 2000–VIII, no violation arising from lack of enforcement of the father's contact rights against a mother whom he had assaulted, as drastic measures of enforcing escorted visits would not have been in the child's best interests and overall the courts had acted reasonably in a very difficult conflict.

where grandparents kept a child without any legal right of custody, there was a breach where the authorities, remaining totally passive, did nothing to maintain the links between father and child, providing the child with no psychological counselling. They had effectively allowed the matter to be resolved by passage of time in favour of the child's total integration with the grandparents and complete rupture with her biological parent.[78] The Court has acknowledged that the authorities may face significant difficulties from the intransigence of the party refusing to comply with contact or custody orders for which they cannot be held liable.[79] As long as courts act reasonably in face of a difficult conflict, the failure to enforce visits by taking draconian measures will not disclose a violation.[80]

Where the court provides for contact between the non-custodial parent and child, it must do so in such a manner as to render the contact practical and effective. An order which did not take into account the father's work schedule or a suitable location for the visits failed to protect his right to family life.[81]

A finding that the child currently enjoys a more comfortable or advantageous environment is not a sufficient basis for failing to ensure the return of a child from its maternal grandparents to its biological father, where the father can offer adequate care and his parental capabilities have not been put in doubt.[82]

Where one party is in breach of a court order, the applicant cannot claim, however, that the authorities bear an absolute duty to enforce it and he or she must bear a certain share of the responsibility in making the appropriate applications and actively and constructively participating in the proceedings and enforcement attempts.[83] The Court has also stated that authorities are under an obligation to take practical measures to encourage conflicting parties to co-operate and provide assistance to that end.[84]

Difficulties in enforcement may arise with particular complexity where one parent takes the children to another jurisdiction and seeks to thwart adverse custody decisions reached in the original country of residence. The Court has stated that the State's obligations under Art.8 to secure the reunification of the custodial parent and the children must be interpreted in light of the Hague Convention of October 25, 1980 on the Civil Aspects of International Child Abduction, in particular where the respondent State is a party.[85] Even if a country is not under an obligation as such to ratify the Hague Convention, it must provide an alternative and effective framework to deal with child abduction.[86]

[78] *Amanalachioai v Romania*, May 26, 2009, paras 91–103.

[79] See *Glaser v UK*, September 19, 2000, where the mother went into hiding.

[80] *Nuutinnen*, see fn.77 above. See also *Kallo v Hungary*, (70558/01) (Dec.) October 14, 2003, where it was enough that warnings had been issued and maximum fines imposed on the obstructive mother, the applicant not himself wishing for or requesting more coercive measures to be applied.

[81] *Gluhakovic v Croatia*, April 12, 2011, paras 60–80.

[82] *Amanalachioai*, fn.78 above, para.94.

[83] *Glaser*, fn.79, para.70; see also *Nuutinen*, fn.77, para.135, where reference was made to the applicant's inappropriate and aggressive behaviour to officials involved in the procedures; *Fusca v Romania*, June 22, 2010, where the applicant did not accompany the bailiff when he sought the child at the mother's home and appeared to give up efforts in pursuing contact; *Kaleta v Poland*, December 16, 2008, where the applicant father neglected to improve his relations with the daughter, who when older decided herself to end contact.

[84] *Zawadka v Poland*, June 23, 2005.

[85] *Ignaccolo-Zenide v Romania*, January 25, 2000, ECHR 2000–I, paras 95 and 113, it took into account that the authorities did not take the measures required in Art.7 of the Hague Convention; *Sylvester v Austria*, April 24, 2003, para.57; *Iglesias-Gil et AUI v Spain*, April 29, 2003, paras 56–57.

[86] *Bajrami v Albania*, December 12, 2006, paras 65–67.

The Court has emphasised that the adequacy of measures depends on the swiftness of their implementation, noting also the obligations under the Hague Convention to act expeditiously and account for any period of inaction of more than six weeks.[87] It has rejected arguments that decisons for ordering prompt return breached Art.8 in not allowing a complete assessment of the child's welfare and best interests.[88] While the Court has generally stated that coercive measures involving children are not desirable, in this context it has stated that the use of sanctions must not be ruled out in the event of unlawful behaviour by the parent with whom the children live.[89] Nor will the use of such measures by itself breach Art.8 either as regards the abducting parent where the situation had been brought about by the latter's obstructive conduct and was conducted under proper and due authority.[90] Violations of Art.8 have accordingly been found in a number of cases where State authorities failed to take measures with the requisite promptness or effectiveness in enforcing the return of children or to facilitate the preparatory contact with the children to prevent alienation from the custodial parent.[91] As the Government is under an obligation to equip itself with the effective means to comply with the Convention, it cannot rely on any gaps in domestic law allowing for measures or sanctions to be imposed,[92] nor can it rely on any purported procedural or other omissions by applicants to absolve it of its obligations.[93] The authority responsible for implementing the Hague Convention should also ensure that the ordinary courts are aware of the enforcement proceedings to prevent any judgment on the merits of a divorce and custody action pre-empting the Hague proceedings.[94]

Furthermore, while a change in relevant facts affecting the assessment of the child's best interests may exceptionally justify the non-enforcement of a return order, the Court requires to be satisfied that the change in situation was not brought

[87] The strict obligation of expedition is illustrated in *Sylvester*, fn.85 above, paras 67–68, where delays of two and three and a half months in the proceedings were regarded as important; see also lack of speed finding in *Iosub-Caras v Romania*, July 27, 2006, eighteen months for final decision; *Stochlak v Poland*, September 22, 2009, continuous delays by courts and authorities. Contrast *RR v Romania (No.1)*, November 10, 2009, where the authorities were sufficiently expeditious.

[88] See *Mamousseau and Washington v France*, fn.44, where the child's return to the US was enforced although French courts had found that it would inflict serious trauma due to separation from her mother. The Court noted that otherwise the primary purpose of the Hague Convention would be rendered void and abducting parents allowed to obtain legal recognition, through passage of time, of the de facto situation that they had created.

[89] *Ignaccolo-Zenide*, fn.85 above, para.107. See also *Paradis v Germany*, (4783/03) (Dec.) May 15, 2003, where the applicant mother had breached a Canadian order by taking the children to Germany, the Court found that the German court's decision to order their return to Canada, if necessary by force, did not violate Art.8.

[90] *Mamousseau and Washington*, fn.44 above, where the police officers acted under the supervision of the public prosecutor; they had to desist due to resistance by the mother and her supporters.

[91] *Ignaccolo-Zenide*, fn.85 above, paras 107–113; *Sylvester*, fn.85 above, paras 66–72. See also *Iglesias-Gil*, fn.85 above, paras 58–62, violation due to the lack of adequate steps taken by Spain, where the applicant mother resided, to enforce decisions against a father who had absconded to the USA with the child; *Maire v Portugal*, June 26, 2003, violation where the authorities took over four years to locate the abducted child and mother; *Stochlak v Poland*, fn.87 above, where the police lagged in locating and promptly securing the child, the father having to rely finally on a private detective agency.

[92] *Ignaccolo-Zenide*, fn.85 above, para.108; *Sylvester*, fn.85 above, para.68. See also *Iglesias-Gil*, fn.85 above, para.61, where the authorities could not rely on the legislative hole which prevented the issue of an international arrest warrant for the absconded father.

[93] *Ignaccolo-Zenide*, fn.85 above, para.111; *Sylvester*, fn.85 above, para.71. Contrast, however, the references to applicants' responsibilities in non-Hague Convention cases, fn.83 above.

[94] *Iosub-Caras*, fn.87 above, para.36.

about by the State's failure to take the measures reasonably expected to enforce the return order.[95] As in ordinary domestic childcare proceedings, effective respect of family life requires that the issues should not be decided by the mere effluxion of time.[96] Where the "abducting parent" complains to the Court about an order of enforcement of the child's return, the Court has generally found no violation.[97] A notable exception was *Neulinger and Shuruk v Switzerland*, where the mother had clandestinely removed the child from Israel and the Swiss court ordered the return of the child. The Court emphasised that developments since the order had to be taken into account to ensure the best interests of the child were duly considered; since the child was well settled in Switzerland and the mother refused to return to Israel due to fears of prosecution, it was not regarded as in the child's best interests to return alone to Israel where there were doubts as to the father's capability of caring for him. This case is not easy to reconcile with the approach in other cases where more emphasis was given to upholding the Hague Convention's aims; it also glances over the fact that the the primary reason for the child settling in Switzerland over a long period was the issuance of an interim measure by the Court preventing return of the child for almost three years during its proceedings. It remains to be seen whether this signals a change away from the previous presumption in favour of upholding Hague Convention decisions.[98]

The relevance of the child's own views varies according to age and the situation. The Court has stated that, particularly in the adoption context, the child's interests must prevail over those of the adoptive parents: adoption means "providing a child with a family, not a family with a child". There was thus no question of forcing a child, aged over ten years, into an adoption overseas.[99] Nor was it compatible with the father's rights for a court to effectively give a veto power to children over twelve, without carrying out an examination of where their best interests in fact lay, in an oral hearing with expert evidence.[100]

4. Parental rights in non-conventional families

Presumptions of paternity in favour of the married father have been found to pursue the legitimate aims of certainty and security in family relationships. However, there may be circumstances where the presumption clearly flies in the face of common sense and social and biological reality should prevail. In *Kroon v Netherlands*, an irrebuttable presumption of paternity in favour of the husband of the mother of the child was found to disclose a lack of respect, where the husband had long II–255

[95] *Sylvester*, fn.85 above, para.63. See also *Serghides v Poland*, November 2, 2010, paras 70–71, the applicant father had contributed to the deterioration of relations with his daughter, including an attempt to remove the child from the country while the courts were still examining his request under the Hague Convention.

[96] *Sylvester*, fn.85 above, para.69.

[97] e.g. *Eskinazi and Chelouche v Turkey*, (14600/05) (Dec.) December 6, 2005, where the Court found no flagrant risk of denial of justice or breach of Art.8 rights in returning a child to Israel where rabbinical courts had jurisdiction; *Mattenklott v Germany*, (41092/06) (Dec.) December 11, 2006, risk of US courts finding against the mother was not enough to justify undermining the basic premise of the Hague Convention; *Mamousseau and Washington*, fn.44 above.

[98] *Neulinger and Shuruk v Switzerland*, July 6, 2010, paras 141–151, the Swiss courts had discounted the mother's alleged fears of prosecution in Israel and considered that she could have returned with the child. Contrast with *Mamousseau and Washington*, fn.44 above.

[99] *Pini*, fn.7 above, paras 155–165.

[100] *C v Finland*, fn.30 above.

disappeared from the scene and the biological father was unable to have his paternity recognised.[101] Procedural obstacles which effectively prevented the applicant obtaining registration as the father of his biological child after its birth disclosed a lack of respect for his family life also, where he had lived with the mother for four years and established ties with the child.[102] However, a wide margin of appreciation as to the legislative approach to matters of filiation apparently still applies. Thus, an inability of the applicant, who claimed to be the biological father of the three children of the wife of a married couple, to challenge the husband's legal paternity, did not disclose a violation where since, in fact, the children were living with the applicant undisturbed by either the mother or presumed father, the inconveniences were minor and it was possible for the applicant to gain legal protection of his parental role by other means, such as adoption or an application for parental responsibility. The Court also noted that it was open to the children to contest paternity if they so wished on gaining their majority.[103]

Adoption procedures should not fly in the face of common sense either. In *Emonet v Switzerland*, where the first applicant, who was an adult, but was handicapped, sought to be adopted by her mother's partner, the Court found that it breached her right to respect for family life where the legal consequence of the adoption was that the first applicant's legal link to her mother was severed, contrary to the wishes of all concerned.[104] There was a failure to accord with social reality also where the Luxembourg courts refused to recognise the applicant's adoption of a child in Peru on the basis that the applicant was single and Luxembourg law only allowed married couples to adopt. The child having been abandoned in an orphanage in Peru and her adoption having been properly approved by the Peruvian courts, there had been a failure to recognise her paramount interest in full, legal integration in her adoptive family.[105]

Homosexual relationships for a long time were not acknowledged by the Convention organs as falling within the scope of "family life" for the purposes of Art.8. In a case where two women lived together sharing parental roles in respect of a child, born to one of them by artificial insemination by donor (AID), the partner of the mother could not rely on Art.8 to claim a right to obtain parental authority over the child.[106] The Commission considered only that homosexual relationships could raise issues under the concept of "private life", although the restriction

[101] Contrast *Youssef v Netherlands*, fn.6 above; (22920/93), fn.5 above, where the applicant claimed to be the father of a child born in wedlock living with the mother and her husband, the Commission found no issues under Arts 6, 8 and 14 arising from the courts' refusal to order a blood test on the child, in particular, since this risked disrupting the stability and security of the child's home. Issues could also arise where a married father separated from the mother of a child was unable to rebut the presumption of paternity. See also Part IIB, s.37: Private Life, sub-s.10: Other personal relationships.

[102] *Rozanski v Poland*, May 18, 2006, the mother's consent was needed and once her new partner recognised the child, the biological father's claims were barred.

[103] *Chavdarov v Bulgaria*, December 21, 2010, paras 39–56, the distinction with *Kroon*, see fn.4 above, is not made clearly; it appears that the mother had herself put the husband's name on the birth registrations even when she was living with the applicant; since the applicant was no longer cohabiting with her, there was also an ongoing, united family reality flying in the face of the legal presumption. However, as in *Rozanski*, fn.102 above, the mother also did not consent.

[104] *Emonet v Switzerland*, December 13, 2007, ECHR 2007–. . . , the Swiss law had been based on the aim of clarity and avoiding proliferating conflicts of interest, but its blind, mechanical operation in this situation failed to secure respect for the applicants' family life.

[105] *Wagner et JMWL v Luxembourg*, June 28, 2007.

[106] (15666/89) (Dec.) May 19, 1992.

complained of in the case was not found to reveal any curtailment of the enjoyment of private life. Some years later, in *Schalk and Kopf v Austria*, the Court finally held that a cohabiting same-sex couple living in a stable relationship enjoyed "family life" under the protection of Art.8.[107]

Where a domestic system did not provide for the recognition of the change of gender of a transsexual, the Court, referring to the controversial nature of the transsexual phenomenon and the use of AID, rejected the claim that Art.8 imposed a positive obligation to recognise in law the parental role of the transsexual father.[108] It did accept that the relationships of a transsexual, his partner and the partner's child fell within the scope of Art.8 as a de facto family life, but did not consider that they suffered any practical prejudice from the lack of formal legal recognition as would impose an obligation on the State to take any steps. The Commission, differing in its opinion, had given weight to the emotional or psychological needs of the family against which it found no overriding factor militating against recognition. Following the finding in *Christine Goodwin v UK* that the refusal of legal recognition to a post-operative transsexual violated her right to respect to private life and the right to marry, it would appear likely that the Court's view on the family life aspect of Art.8 will also be subject to modification.[109]

Cross-reference

Part IIA, s.2: Access to Court.
Part IIB, s.27: Homosexuality.
Part IIB, s.8: Defamation and right to reputation (sub-s.4: State's obligation to protect reputation).
Part IIB, s.47: Transsexuals.

[107] *Schalk and Kopf v Austria*, June 24, 2010, para.94, however, although the complaint came within the scope of Art.8, the Court by a narrow majority found no discrimination arising from the couple's inability to marry under Austrian law.

[108] *X, Y and Z v UK*, April 22, 1997, R.J.D. 1997–II, No.35, 24 E.H.R.R. 133.

[109] *Christine Goodwin v UK*, July 11, 2002, ECHR 2002–VI.

6. Compensation for detention

Key provision:

II–256 Article 5, para.5 (enforceable right to compensation for arrest or detention contrary to the provisions of Art.5).

Key case-law:

Wassink v Netherlands, September 27, 1990, Series A, No.185–A; *Brogan v UK*, November 29, 1988, Series A, No.145–B, 11 E.H.R.R. 117; *Fox, Campbell and Hartley v UK*, August 30, 1990, Series A, No.182, 13 E.H.R.R. 157; *Thynne, Gunnell and Wilson v UK*, October 25, 1990, 13 E.H.R.R. 666; *Sakik v Turkey*, November 26, 1997, R.J.D. 1997–VII, 26 E.H.R.R. 662; *NC v Italy*, December 18, 2002, ECHR 2002–X, 28 E.H.R.R. 82.

1. General considerations

II–257 The right to compensation for arrest or detention is conditioned on the existence of a breach of one of the other four paragraphs of Art.5. Such a breach must have been established directly or in substance. Where the Court has given a decision as to a breach in a previous application, or where a domestic court had found a breach of one of the paragraphs but rejected the claim for compensation, the Court can proceed directly to consider Art.5, para.5. If there is no finding by domestic courts, the Court must examine whether the applicant is a victim of arrest or detention in contravention of the provisions of Art.5 before proceeding to para.5.[1]

2. Availability of compensation

II–258 The right to compensation must be enforceable. An opportunity to apply for ex gratia payment would not be adequate. It presumably extends only to financial compensation. However, in *Bozano v France*,[2] the Commission stated that the right to compensation might be of broader scope than mere financial compensation, but could not confer a right to secure release since that was covered by Art.5, para.4.

The existence of the right in domestic law to obtain compensation for the breach must be established with a sufficient degree of certainty. In *Sakik v Turkey*, where the Government argued that the applicants could have made various applications for compensation, the Court noted that there was no example of any person obtaining compensation by these methods and that the constitutional provisions relied on appeared to cover only detention which was unlawful in domestic terms. It accordingly found a violation.[3]

The availability of compensation for the deprivation of liberty concerned may suffice for the purposes of Art.5, para.5, even if it is not given expressly for an

[1] e.g. (6821/74) (Dec.) July 5, 1976, 6 D.R. 65; (7950/77) (Dec.) March 4, 1980, 19 D.R. 213.
[2] (9990/82) (Dec.) May 15, 1984, 39 D.R.119.
[3] cf. *AC v France*, (37547/97) (Dec.) December 14, 1999, the possibility of using Art.L.781–1 of the Judicial Procedure Code to obtain damages had become sufficiently certain over time.

alleged breach of Art.5. In *NC v Italy*, the Court found no violation where the applicant could apply for compensation for pre-trial detention on the grounds of his acquittal without having to prove that his detention had been unlawful or too long. Such damages would have been "indissociable" from any compensation to which the applicant might have been entitled under Art.5, para.5 as a consequence of his deprivation of liberty, being contrary to Art.5, paras 1 or 3.

Compensation must be available in practice, as well as theory. Where the system of remedies in Chechnya was effectively not functioning, the Court found the applicants were not required to apply and a violation arose.[4] Where a tort action lay for damages for unlawful detention, but the court rejected a validly-introduced claim basing itself on arbitrary findings of fact, this denied the applicant an enforceable right to compensation.[5] However, the mere fact that a court has rejected a claim for damages for an arrest or detention, found by this Court to be unlawful or in breach of Art.5, appears to be sufficient to ground a violation. Nor will the fact that an application for damages was unsuccessful require the applicant to try another remedy which did not offer any better prospects of success.[6]

3. Existence of damage

The Commission and Court disagreed as to whether the existence of the right could, in domestic law, be made dependent on the existence of damage. In *Wassink v Netherlands*, there was a failure to comply with procedure prescribed by law[7] under Art.5, para.1, but the applicant could only apply for compensation under Dutch law if he could show damage. The Commission took the view, based on its earlier case-law,[8] that the Art.5, para.5 right to compensation was not conditional on damage. The Court held that there would be compliance with Art.5, para.5 where it was possible to apply for compensation in respect of a deprivation of liberty effected in conditions contrary to the other paras 1–4, but that States were not prohibited from making the award dependent on the ability of the person to show damage resulting from the breach. It distinguished this element from victim status which could exist even if there was no damage, but held that there could be no question of compensation if there was no pecuniary or non-pecuniary damage to compensate. This was stated to be without prejudice to just satisfaction (Art.41) considerations. 11–259

Where, however, domestic law operates in such a way as to render non-pecuniary damages effectively unavailable, the Court has considered that this derived the person detained of any possibility of obtaining compensation. This arose in a case in which there operated a domestic legal presumption that moral damage of unlawful imprisonment ceased on the moment of release and that any damage which persisted after that date would have manifest and external signs. It may be noted that the Court, in its own practice under Art.41, operates the contrary presumption, that even a short period of irregular detention must be regarded as causing the

[4] *Chitayev and Chitayev v Russia*, January 18, 2007, para.195.

[5] *Fedotov v Russia*, October 25, 2005.

[6] *RL and M-JD v France*, May 19, 2004, para.137.

[7] No registrar was present at the hearing.

[8] e.g. (10313/83) (Dec.) July 12, 1984, 39 D.R. 225, citing *Artico v Italy*, May 13, 1980, Series A, No.37, para.35, in which the Court stated that for Art.6, para.3(c) an applicant need not show that lack of legal representation caused actual prejudice and the existence of a violation was conceivable even in the absence of prejudice: prejudice was only relevant in the context of Art.50 (now Art.41).

victim moral suffering. Thus, requiring such a victim somehow to give objective proof of this internal state of affairs was not compatible with the right at stake.[9]

4. Domestic lawfulness

II–260 Where there is no possibility of applying for compensation for a breach of Art.5, paras 1–4, there will be a violation. The Convention organs have rejected arguments by the UK Government that the right should only accrue where the arrest or detention was unlawful in domestic terms or arbitrary. Until the Convention was incorporated in domestic law, it was only possible to challenge domestic unlawfulness in the courts in the United Kingdom and this led to automatic breaches of Art.5, para.5 where arrest or detention under the other provisions was lawful in domestic terms but failed to comply with Convention standards.[10]

Violations of Art.5, para.5 were accordingly found in *Brogan v UK* (breach of Art.5, para.3 for delay in being brought before a judicial officer); in *Fox, Campbell and Hartley v UK* (a lack of conformity with Art.5, para.1(c) standard of reasonable suspicion on arrest); and in *Thynne, Gunnell and Wilson v UK* (breach of Art.5, para.4 for lack of review of the lawfulness of the continued detention of discretionary lifers).

5. Adequacy of compensation under domestic law

II–261 Issues may arise if the amount of compensation is derisory. An applicant awarded £350 for four and a half hours unlawful detention by the police argued that it did not reflect the seriousness of the breach, would not discourage other infringements, was out of proportion to the costs of an action and would lead to the refusal of legal aid in future cases. The Commission agreed that since the Convention guaranteed rights that were practical and effective, a right of compensation which set levels too low might no longer be "enforceable" in practical terms. However, it considered that the amount awarded for the short detention period could not be said to be so low as to be negligible for the purposes of Art.5, para.5.[11]

[9] *Danev v Bulgaria*, September 2, 2010 paras 32–37.

[10] See, for other jurisdictions, e.g. *Harkmann v Estonia*, July 11, 2006.

[11] (28779/95) (Dec.) November 27, 1996. See *Attard v Malta*, (46750/99) (Dec.) September 28, 2000, where the Court rejected the applicant's arguments about the paucity of the compensation (MTL 100), plus legal costs, paid to him for an unlawful arrest of a few hours.

7. Corporal punishment

Key Provisions:

Articles 2 of the First Protocol (right to education and respect for the right of parents to ensure education of children in conformity with their religious and philosophical convictions), 3 (prohibition of inhuman and degrading treatment), and 8 (respect for family and private life). II–262

Key case-law:

Campbell and Cosans v UK, February 25, 1982, Series A, No.48, 4 E.H.R.R. 293; *Tyrer v UK*, April 25, 1978, Series A, No.26, 2 E.H.R.R. 1; *Costello-Roberts v UK*, March 25, 1993, Series A, No.247–C, 19 E.H.R.R. 112; *A v UK*, September 23, 1998, R.J.D. 1998–VI.

1. General considerations

The Convention organs have taken a generally critical view of corporal punishment. This reflects the position that, almost alone within Contracting States, the United Kingdom considered, and still does to a certain degree, that there may be legitimate physical punishment of children. II–263

2. Judicial corporal punishment

There is only one case. It concerned the use of the birch in the Isle of Man as a punishment of the 15-year-old applicant *Tyrer*, for assault on another pupil of his school, to which he had pleaded guilty in the juvenile court. The punishment, three strokes, was inflicted in circumstances where he was required to take down his clothing and bend over a table, held by two policemen while a third administered the strokes. The skin was raised, but not cut by the birch and the applicant was sore for a week and a half afterwards. II–264

In finding this treatment was degrading punishment contrary to Art.3, the Court gave particular significance to the institutionalised nature of the violence, referring to the deliberate treatment of an individual as an object in the power of the authorities and the infliction of punishment which constituted an assault on personal dignity and physical integrity. It also had regard to the psychological effect—mental anguish—resulting from the delay of three weeks from sentencing and the way the applicant was kept waiting in the police station before the punishment. The fact that the applicant was required to strip aggravated the degrading nature, but was not a determining factor.

It is clear that in finding the punishment degrading and rejecting the argument that local conditions justified the practice,[1] the Court was heavily influenced by the

[1] The Government argued under Art.63, para.3, that Art.3 had to be applied with due regard to the local requirements within the specific territory. However, the Court found that public opinion in favour of the punishment was not sufficient—there would have to be positive and conclusive proof of a requirement for the punishment imposed by the conditions on the island and there was no indication that criminal justice would falter without it.

fact that judicial corporal punishment was not found in the great majority of Contracting States. The risk of corporal punishment, such as flogging, on an applicant's threatened expulsion to another country, may disclose issues under Art.3 and provide grounds for interim measures under r.39.[2]

3. As a means of discipline in school

II–265 The United Kingdom has singlehandedly produced the leading cases in this area. The use of corporal punishment in its State schools was held to be incompatible with parental convictions and, where suspension resulted, could disclose a denial of education.[3] Whether or not it would constitute punishment contrary to Art.3 depends on the circumstances of each personal case.[4]

(a) *Interference with education and parental convictions*

II–266 Concerning State schools, the Court found that, where parents objected to the use of the belt ("tawse") in the schools attended by their children, there was a breach of the right of parents to ensure their children's education in accordance with their religious and philosophical convictions. The rejection of physical punishment was found of the necessary cogency and seriousness to constitute a "philosophical conviction" and a view worthy of respect in a democratic society. Where one child was suspended since the parents refused to accept his return to school subject to the condition of accepting physical punishment as a disciplinary sanction, there was an additional violation of the child's right to education.

(b) *Inhuman and degrading treatment*

II–267 In privately-run schools, the Court has found that the State is responsible for regulating the conduct of those schools and it can examine whether disciplinary measures infringe the provisions of the Convention. However, in *Costello-Robberts v UK*, it found that the punishment complained of—the boy was slippered three times on the buttocks through his shorts with a rubber-soled gym shoe—was not of the level of severity required to fall within the scope of "degrading punishment". There was, in particular, no evidence of any severe, long-lasting effects. It merely expressed reservations about the automatic imposition of this kind of punishment (after reaching a certain number of demerit marks) and the way in which the boy had to wait for three days for the punishment to be inflicted.

However, in *Y v UK*,[5] the Commission had found a violation of Art.3. The circumstances were more severe, since the boy was caned four times through his trousers by the headmaster who took several steps back and ran before striking. The boy had complained of severe pain afterwards and had four weals across his buttocks

[2] e.g. *Razaghi v Sweden*, (64599/01) (Dec.) March 11, 2003, where the applicant faced the alleged risk of 99 lashes for immoral behaviour on return to Iran.

[3] *Campbell and Cosans v UK*, February 25, 1982, Series A, No.48, 4 E.H.R.R. 293.

[4] *Y v UK*, October 8, 1991, Series A, No.247–1; *Warwick v UK*, (9471/81) (Rep.) July 18, 1986, 60 D.R. 5, the Commission observed that, as a general rule, moderate corporal punishment in schools would constitute institutionalised violence of the kind observed in *Tyrer*.

[5] See fn.4 above.

with heavy bruising and swelling. The Commission found this disclosed degrading treatment and punishment having regard to the significant physical injury and humiliation which he suffered. The case was settled before the Court.

The Commission found that the humiliation aspect of corporal punishment was of particular significance in *Warwick v UK*,[6] concluding that there was a violation of Art.3 by way of degrading punishment where a 16–year-old girl, a female of marriageable age, was caned on her hand by a male headmaster in the presence of another male teacher.

(c) Invasion of physical and moral integrity

The argument that the infliction of minor corporal punishment discloses a violation of Art.8, respect for private life, as an invasion of moral and physical integrity is unlikely to be successful in light of the Court's judgment in *Costello-Robberts*. The Commission, rejecting a violation of Art.3, nonetheless had considered that the scope of Art.8 was wider and that a separate issue arose which disclosed a violation. Corporal punishment was, in its view, an invasion of physical and moral integrity, respect for which had not been consented to by reason of enrolment in a private school, and there was no justification advanced for its necessity. The Court did not exclude the possibility that Art.8 might afford protection in the disciplinary field wider than Art.3. However, it considered that sending a child to school inevitably involved some degree of interference with private life and the treatment in this case did not entail such adverse effects on physical or moral integrity sufficient to bring it within the scope of the prohibition of Art.8. **II–268**

4. Parental chastisement

Conversely, there have been parents who have claimed the right to chastise their children. In cases introduced by Swedish parents objecting to the complete prohibition on physical punishment of children in the Code of Parenthood, the Commission held that the Swedish law, which imposed a normal measure for the control of violence extending to the chastisement of children by their parents, was intended to protect the potentially weak and vulnerable and did not interfere with the parents' right to respect for private and family life.[7] The claim that philosophical views of parents should enable them to birch their children met with no sympathy. **II–269**

Where the law permits physical chastisement, issues may arise where this level is set too high, or is too vague to apply effectively, and allows inhuman and degrading treatment to be inflicted on a child. A Contracting State is under a positive obligation to ensure the children are effectively protected from treatment contrary to Art.3 through its laws. Thus where a step-father was prosecuted for assault on a boy with a cane, but later acquitted, the Court found that the provision in English law for the defence of reasonable chastisement as applied in practice deprived children of adequate protection.[8]

[6] See fn.4 above.

[7] (8811/79) (Dec.) May 13, 1982, 29 D.R. 104 and (12154/86) (Dec.) October 23, 1987.

[8] *A v UK*, paras 21–24, the nine-year-old applicant had been beaten with a garden cane applied with considerable force on several occasions leaving weals and bruises. The burden of proof had been on the prosecution to prove that the assault went beyond the limits of lawful punishment. Although the applicant had been subjected to treatment of a severity prohibited by Art.3, the jury acquitted the step-father.

Cross-reference

Part IIB, s.13: Education.
Part IIB, s.46: Torture, inhuman and degrading treatment.

8. Defamation and the right to reputation

Key provisions:

Articles 6 (access to court), 8 (respect for private life) and 10 (freedom of expression). II–270

Key case-law:

Lingens v Austria, July 8, 1986, Series A No.103, 8 E.H.R.R. 103; *Oberschlick v Austria*, May 23, 1991, Series A No.204, 19 E.H.R.R. 389; *Castells v Spain*, April 23, 1992, Series A No.236, 14 E.H.R.R. 445; *Prager and Oberschlick v Austria*, April 26, 1995, Series A No.313, 21 E.H.R.R. 1; *Tolstoy v UK*, July 13, 1995, Series A No.316–B, 20 E.H.R.R. 442; *De Haes and Gijsels v Belgium*, February 24, 1997, R.J.D. 1997–I, 25 E.H.R.R. 1; *Oberschlick v Austria (No.2)*, July 1, 1997, R.J.D. 1997–IV, No.42; *Janowski v Poland*, January 21, 1999, ECHR 1999–I; *Bladet Tromso and Stensaas v Norway*, May 20, 1999, ECHR 1999–III; *Nilssen and Johnsen v Norway*, November 25, 1999, ECHR 1999–VIII; *Bergens Tidende v Norway*, May 2, 2000, ECHR 2000–IV; *Lopes Gomes da Silva v Portugal, September 28, 2000*, ECHR 2000–X; *Jerusalem v Austria*, February 27, 2001, ECHR 2001–II; *Feldek v Slovakia*, July 12, 2001, ECHR 2001–VIII; *Nikula v Finland*, March 21, 2002, ECHR 2002–II; *McVicar v UK*, May 7, 2002, ECHR 2002–III; *A v UK*, December 17, 2002, ECHR 2002–X; *Cordova v Italy (No.1)*, January 30, 2003, ECHR 2003–I; *Cordova v Italy (No.2)*, January 30, 2003, ECHR 2003–I; *Lesnik v Slovakia*, March 11, 2003; *Steel and Morris v UK*, February 25, 2005, ECHR 2005–II.

1. General considerations

The right to protection of reputation is now recognised as being part of the right to private life guaranteed by Art.8.[1] Most complaints arise in the context of proceedings for defamation, or procedural problems connected with obtaining redress through the courts for slights to reputation. There are two categories of claimant: those claiming protection of private life and those who have an interest in publishing information free of court sanction. In a Swedish case, the Commission noted the conflict of interest, commenting that where a question arose of interference with private life, by publication in the mass media, the State had to find a proper balance between the Convention rights involved, the right to respect for private life and freedom of expression.[2] The Court has stated that there is no hierarchical relationship between the rights guaranteed by both articles; journalists and those relying on freedom of expression apparently can claim no priority of interest.[3] II–271

[1] *Pfeifer v Austria*, November 15, 2007, para.35. Previously, the Commission had excluded this from the scope of Art.8.

[2] (11366/85) (Dec.) October 16, 1986, 50 D.R.173, the fact the applicant was not successful in his defamation action did not show a lack of protection, the courts giving adequate consideration to the applicant's interests in striking the balance.

[3] *Timciuc v Romania*, (28999/03) (Dec.) October 12, 2010.

2. Access to court

II–272 The right to enjoy a good reputation is a civil right for the purposes of Art.6, para.1, and applicants may generally claim the right of access to court to pursue defamation proceedings,[4] to the extent such is provided in domestic law.[5]

The general principle is that, while access to court is not absolute, it may only be restricted for legitimate aims pursued in a proportionate manner and a restriction must not impair the essence of the right.[6] The procedural and substantive limitations on defamation actions must be assessed in light of those considerations.

(a) Lack of legal aid

II–273 Since, in the United Kingdom, there is an exclusion of legal aid for defamation actions, a number of cases have arisen alleging that this deprives applicants of effective access to court. While a blanket ban, allowing no discretion or regard to prospects of success, might appear per se disproportionate, the Commission had exclusive regard to the individual circumstances in each case, the merits of the claims and to what extent each applicant has managed to take proceedings relating to the substance of his case without legal aid. It considered that legal aid could legitimately be restricted with regard to financial criteria and certain categories of cases, referring to the inherent riskiness of such claims, and found no arbitrariness arising from the lack of legal aid.[7] This approach has been essentially adopted by the Court in *McVicar v UK*, where it found that the applicant, defendant in defamation proceedings brought by a wealthy celebrity, was not prevented by lack of legal aid from presenting his defence effectively in the High Court. It did not consider that the law of defamation was sufficiently complex as to require a person in the applicant's position to have legal assistance. In the exceptional circumstances of *Steel and Morris v UK*, where two Greenpeace members were sued by McDonald's in complex proceedings, lasting over 313 court days and requiring them to prove the truth of numerous factual assertions, the Court found that the denial of legal aid prevented them presenting their case effectively and led to an unacceptable inequality of arms.

(b) Privilege and immunities from actions for defamation

II–274 Where certain categories of persons are protected from actions for defamation, issues arise as to whether this constitutes restriction on access to court.

Parliamentary privilege is generally recognised as compatible with the Convention, pursuing the legitimate aim of free Parliamentary debate in the public

[4] *Helmers v Sweden*, October 29, 1991, Series A No.212, 15 E.H.R.R. 285, citing *Golder v UK*, February 21, 1975, Series A, No.18, I E.H.R.R. 524.

[5] e.g. where domestic law excludes actions for group defamation, there is no civil right to attract the guarantees of Art.6; (11862/85) (Dec.) July 10, 1986, the applicant could not sue as a member of the class of gypsies in regard to disparaging posters.

[6] *Ashingdane v UK*, May 28, 1985, Series A, No.93, 7 E.H.R.R. 528.

[7] (10871/84) (Dec.) July 10, 1986, 48 D.R. 154, the applicant pursued proceedings himself and obtained a settlement; (10594/83) (Dec.) July 14, 1987, 52 D.R. 158, the applicant could bring the issues before the Industrial Tribunal in proceedings for unfair dismissal, where the reasonableness of the employer's belief in his dishonesty was considered.

interest.[8] Even where a MP named the applicant in a speech in Parliament about anti-social behaviour, making extremely serious allegations which were clearly unnecessary in a debate on municipal housing policy, the Court essentially found that it was justified in light of the importance of protecting free speech in Parliament, similar immunities being a feature of most Contracting States of the Council of Europe, and that the absolute privilege attached to speech inside Parliament was not disproportionate in the circumstances.[9] While the Court referred to the applicant's possibility of obtaining alternative redress through her own MP taking up the matter internally,[10] the importance of legislators' free speech was found to outweigh the lack of any remedy.[11]

Where, however, in *Cordova v Italy (No.1)* immunity was attached to an ex-President enjoying the status of a senator for life, the Court found that the rejection of the applicant's claims for defamation disclosed a disproportionate bar on his access to court. It noted that the derisory letters sent to the applicant were not linked to the exercise of legislative or parliamentary functions, but rather to a personal quarrel between individuals. The same conclusion was reached in *Cordova v Italy (No.2)* where immunity had applied to the statements of an MP outside the legislature during an electoral meeting and the Court again noted a lack of connection between the statements made and parliamentary function.

Privilege attached to Department of Trade Inspectors' reports was found to respect the proportionality principle in *Fayed v UK*, as it was in the public interest in regulating public companies that the inspectors report freely and they were bound by rules of rationality, legality and procedural propriety. The Court also found that the limits of acceptable criticism were wider where businessmen in large companies were concerned, particularly, where they have knowingly laid themselves open to close scrutiny of their acts through their conduct.

3. Interference with freedom of expression

Convictions or damage awards imposed in respect of defamatory statements constitute interferences with the freedom of expression and the cases generally turn on issues of necessity and proportionality. Where the media is involved, journalist applicants tend to win. Great emphasis is laid on freedom of expression as one of the essential foundations of a democratic society and on the importance of the freedom of the press to impart ideas and information and act as a public watchdog.[12] In that role, journalists are allowed a certain leeway to exaggerate, to use satirical humour,[13] II–275

[8] (3374/67) Collection of Decisions 29, p.29; *Golder v UK*, (4451/70) (Rep.) June 1, 1973, p.44, para.93; conversely a Parliamentarian cannot claim a right to privilege where the legislature waives it: (19890/92) (Dec.) May 3, 1993, 74 D.R. 234.

[9] *A v UK*, December 17, 2002, ECHR 2002–X.

[10] (25646/94) (Dec.) January 17, 1996, 84–A D.R. 122; (29099/95) (Dec.) January 17, 1996, the Commission in finding the privilege of Irish parliamentarians proportionate had regard to the fact that the complaints were reviewed by the Committee of Privileges.

[11] *Zollman v UK*, (62902/00) (Dec.) November 27, 2003, parliamentary privilege still prevailed where the foreign applicants, "named and shamed" in Parliament did not have that option.

[12] e.g. *Lingens v Austria*, July 8, 1986, Series A No.103, 8 E.H.R.R. 103, paras 41 and 44; *Bladet Tromso and Stensaas v Norway*, May 20, 1999, ECHR 1999–III, para.59; *Feldek v Slovakia*, July 12, 2001, ECHR 2001–VIII, para.78.

[13] e.g *Nikowitz and Verlagsgruppe News Gmbh v Austria*, February 22, 2007, paras 25–28.

and even to be provocative[14] or harsh,[15] as long as there is an issue of public interest[16] and an underlying basis of fact,[17] and they act in good faith in order to provide accurate and reliable information in accordance with the ethics of journalism.[18] Indeed a degree of exaggeration should be tolerated, according to the Court, in any public debate of general concern,[19] though both journalists and others must not overstep certain bounds.[20] Reporters are generally under a duty to verify facts when attacking the reputation of a named individual,[21] but it is not always expected that they need to distance themselves from the statements made by others.[22] Also, where they make a reasonable mistake of fact in good faith and rectify the mistake when it becomes apparent, a finding of defamation and liability in defamation may be disproportionate.[23] Where official documents are concerned, journalists are generally entitled to rely on the contents without carrying out their own

[14] *Prager and Oberschlick v Austria*, April 26, 1995, Series A No.313, 21 E.H.R.R. 1, para.38.

[15] *Feldek*, fn.12 above, para.84.

[16] This is given a wide interpretation, e.g. *Bergens Tidende v Norway*, May 2, 2000, ECHR 2000–IV, where the Court rejected the Government's argument that the allegations about a cosmetic surgeon's negligent treatments at a private clinic were private matters, considering that they concerned an important aspect of public health; *Maronek v Slovakia*, April 19, 2001, para.56, the applicant, involved in a housing dispute, addressed an open letter to the Prime Minister which did not exclusively concern his individual problems but also issues of public interest.

[17] e.g. *Prager and Oberschlick*, fn.14 above, para.38; see *Oberschlick v Austria (No.2)*, July 1, 1997, R.J.D. 1997–IV, No.42; *Lopes Gomes da Silva v Portugal, September 28, 2000*, ECHR 2000–X, paras 34–35.

[18] *Bergens Tidende*, fn.16 above, para.53; see also *Sellisto v Finland*, November 16, 2004, para.67, where the Court noted that the journalist had given the complainant the opportunity to comment on articles criticising his conduct; *Tonsberg Blad AS and Haukom v Norway*, March 1, 2007, para.101, apparently less checking is required where the defamatory element is minor. Contrast *Flux v Moldova (No.6)*, July 29, 2008, where the article accusing school officials of bribery had been based on an anonymous letter, the journalist had done no investigative checking and the newspaper refused a right of reply: the Court found no violation, noting the "unprofessional conduct" and the minor sum of damages imposed; *Brunet-Lecomte v France*, February 5, 2009, no violation where a newspaper director and editor were liable in damages to a bank for "virulent" allegations of money-laundering, specific allegations of fact, which, while based on an interview, were also combined with comments adopting the assertions, but without any verification with the bank or distancing from the interviewee, or adding context that there had been no criminal convictions.

[19] *Nilsen and Johnsen v Norway*, November 25, 1999, ECHR 1999–VIII, para.52, a heated public debate between the police, prosecution and researchers who had published findings on police brutality and where professional reputations on both sides were at stake.

[20] e.g. *Constantinescu v Romania*, June 27, 2000, ECHR 2000–VIII, where the applicant was convicted for calling three teachers "*delapidatori*", the Court found that he could have contributed to the debate on trade union affairs without using this word.

[21] *Pedersen and Baadsgard v Denmark*, December 17, 2004, ECHR 2004, para.78; *Rumyana Ivanova v Bulgaria*, February 14, 2008, para.65, where the applicant journalist, in her haste, failed to consult trustworthy sources but relied on ones which were not dependable; *Europapress Holding d.o.o. v Croatia*, October 22, 2009, when publishing an article alleging the deputy prime minister had pointed a gun at a journalist (E.V.) and threatened to kill her, the newspaper should have verified E.V's story, not being entitled to merely rely on the fact that she was a journalist herself.

[22] e.g. *Thoma v Luxemburg*, March 29, 2001, where the applicant had repeated controversial passages from another article, the Court commented that journalists could not generally be expected to distance themselves formally when quoting from other sources (para.64).

[23] e.g. *Aquilina v Malta*, June 14, 2011, in a chaotic court situation where the applicant journalist, as well as the prosecutor, were under the impression that a lawyer had been found in contempt, the liability in damages for defamation went too far: the newspaper had printed a retraction and apology when, from the court minutes, no contempt charge was recorded.

independent research.[24] A sarcastic and cynical slant to opinions based on facts should not be struck down, even if allegedly portraying the victim in a negative light.[25] Nor is it always expected of a journalist to specify the legal technical details in reporting to the wider public about criminal procedure, as long as he has essentially based himself on facts, even if this might not appear to give the full picture.[26]

The ordinary meaning of words, or the sense understood by the average reader, is the relevant one; more abstruse or subtle interpretations of otherwise offensive passages do not furnish a defence.[27]

Nor does the Court approve of domestic courts taking passages out of context and isolating particular phrases as defamatory. Thus where a political figure recounted in a book an incident during his trial in which he likened the public prosecutor to those magistrates who functioned for special courts during the Second World War, the Court found that his conviction for defamation was not justified, the domestic court's reasoning failing to take into account the author's description of how he came to make such an outburst, but treating it as if it was a statement of fact made in bad faith.[28]

Private individuals and associations lay themselves open to scrutiny when they enter the arena of public debate.[29] Although writers of historical works contribute to ongoing historical debate shaping opinion and interpretation about important events, they must adhere to proper historical methods and observe proper caution in their treatment of sources.[30] Accusations of plagiarism in the academic and university world are serious matters, but where not without foundation and expressed in the context of a faculty debate, the condemnation and fine of a university dean for defamation of two academic authors by court decisions that did not pay due regard to the evidence in support of his assertions, was not justified.[31]

Where critical comment by journalists is made on matters of public interest and relating to the conduct of politicians, the importance of the freedom of political debate, and the consideration that limits of critical comment are wider as politicians

[24] See *Bladet Tromso*, fn.12 above, concerning an impugned article which accused seal hunters of cruelty, the journalist had also been entitled to rely on the contents of an official inspector's report without carrying out his own research; *Sellisto v Finland*, fn.18 above, no general duty to verify the statements contained in documents such as pre-trial records can be imposed on reporters, who must be free to report on events based on information gathered from official sources (para.60); journalists may also rely on official documents such as the Strasbourg institutions' judgments and the transcripts of evidence therein: *Saygili v Turkey*, January 8, 2008. No such reliance can be made upon documents such as press releases of a political origin: *Standard Verlagsgesellschaft v Austria (No.2)*, February 22, 2007, para.42.

[25] *Gorelishvili v Georgia*, June 5, 2007, paras 39–43.

[26] *Ormanni v Italy*, July 17, 2007, para.69, where, in raising doubts about a prosecutor's independence in a case, the journalist did not clarify that it was not the prosecutor who had the final say in whether to pursue charges.

[27] *Vitrenko v Ukraine*, (23510/02) (Dec.) December 16, 2008, where a politician called another one "a thief", the domestic court was entitled to regard it as defamatory assertion of fact, despite the applicant's claim that she meant the word in the sense of a value judgement, such as "crook" or "sly, deceitful person".

[28] *Roland Dumas v France*, July 15, 2010, nor was the Court convinced of the need to protect the "parquet" since the statement had already been made in court without any reaction from the judges or magistrates present.

[29] *Jerusalem v Austria*, February 27, 2001, ECHR 2001–II, paras 38–39. See also *Artbeiter v Austria*, January 25, 2007, para.26, the expert who had been criticised had repeatedly given his own views to the press.

[30] *Chauvy v France*, June 29, 2004, ECHR 2004–VI, paras 69–77.

[31] *Boldea v Romania*, February 15, 2007, paras 56–62.

inevitably and knowingly open themselves to public scrutiny, are key factors. Very strong reasons are required to justify restrictions on political speech in particular[32] and those participating in public debate, such as activist groups may claim a high level of protection.[33] However, public figures may be given protection from the publication of rumours about their private life which have no relation to their public functions.[34]

The Court distinguishes between factual assertions and value judgments, and expects that domestic courts will correctly do the same.[35] The former being susceptible to proof, the defendant should have an effective opportunity for his evidence to be considered.[36] The Court has stated that it should be possible to make true declarations in public irrespective of their tone or negative consequences for those who are concerned by them.[37] In *Lingens v Austria*, where a journalist was convicted in a private prosecution for criticising the Chancellor of Austria for supporting an individual allegedly involved in war crimes and accusing him of immoral, undignified conduct, the Court found the articles relevant to current debate and that the position at domestic law, which required a journalist to prove not only facts but value judgments, imposed an impossible requirement.[38] In *Oberschlick v Austria*, where a journalist was fined for quoting a formal complaint lodged against a politician in criminal proceedings which accused him of making discriminatory statements concerning immigrant women's rights to family allowances, the Court found the article contributed to a debate of public importance on the treatment of foreigners and that it was undisputed that the publication was factually correct in reproducing the complaint. In these circumstances, the interference could not be justified as necessary, even if the applicant had been provocative and misleading in his form of presentation.[39] However, even though

[32] *Feldek*, para.83. See also *Lombardi v Malta*, April 24, 2007, paras 54–61.

[33] *Steel and Morris v UK*, February 25, 2005, ECHR 2005–II, paras 88–89.

[34] *Standard Verlags GMBH (No.2) v Austria*, June 4, 2009, concerning a fine and order to publish the court judgments in respect of articles alleging the President's marriage was in trouble and his wife was having an affair with another politician. In the protection of private life context, the newspapers cannot complain of not being allowed to prove the truth of the allegations.

[35] See e.g. *Gorelishvili v Georgia*, fn.25 above, paras 38–40, where the domestic courts wrongly treated certain passages as facts that required to be proved rather than value judgments or opinions.

[36] See violations where the courts, convicting the applicant, did not properly examine the evidence in support of his allegations: *Dalban v Romania*, September 28, 1999, ECHR 1999–VI, para.50; *Boldea v Romania*, February 15, 2007, para.60.

[37] *Csanics v Hungary*, January 20, 2009, para.43, where the domestic courts refused to allow the applicant to prove the factual basis of his assertions, holding them defamatory merely due to their offensiveness.

[38] The Commission had commented that where a politician's own statements had been provocative, others had a right to be provocative back. See also *Oberschlick (No.2)*, fn.17 above, where the journalist was fined for calling a politician a "*trottel*"—the Court found a violation noting that the article responded to deliberately provocative statements by the politician and had a factual basis; *Lopes Gomes da Silva*, fn.17 above, the Court noted that the applicant's comments had been "polemical" but supported by an objective explanation. Contrast the uncharacteristic majority ruling in *Lindon, Otchakovsky-Laurens and July v France*, October 22, 2007, which found the imposition of minimum standards of moderation acceptable in a case where a novelist had lambasted the National Front and its provocative leader, and was convicted, along with the publisher, for comparing him, inter alia, to a vampire.

[39] e.g. *Jerusalem*, see fn.29 above, where the Austrian courts had required the applicant to prove the truth of her value judgments about an alleged "sect" but refused to consider her evidence; *Ukrainian Media Group v Ukraine*, March 29, 2005, paras 66–69, violation where the newspaper was required to prove the truth of value judgments criticising two political party leaders.

value judgments must have a certain factual basis,[40] the Court gives considerable leeway, inter alia, noting that "political debate does not require unanimous agreement on the interpretation of particular words".[41] Where the applicant writer accused a Government minister of a fascist past in *Feldek v Slovakia*, the Court rejected the proposition that a value judgment could only be considered such if it was accompanied by the facts on which the judgment was based. It noted that in this case the value judgment was based on information already known to the wider public from earlier publications. It has also commented that the distinction between statements of fact and value judgments is of less significance where the impugned statement is made in the course of a lively political debate at local level and where elected officials and journalists should enjoy a wide freedom to criticise the actions of a local authority, even where the statements made may lack a clear basis in fact.[42]

The important role played by politicians themselves in contributing to public debate and a free democratic process has also been recognized. Elected representatives represent their constituents, defending their concerns, and interference in their role calls for the closest scrutiny. In *Castells v Spain*, a violation of Art.10 was found where a member of Parliament was convicted for an article attributing acts of violence to the Government, subsequently receiving a suspended sentence of one year and being barred from public functions for one year. It was accepted that the purpose of the conviction was to protect order, but the matter concerned issues of public interest and he was not allowed to rely on truth or good faith. The Court stated that the limits of permissible criticism was wider in relation to governments than to private individuals or even politicians, and that the dominant position of governments made it necessary for them to respond with restraint.[43]

On the other hand, where defamatory attacks are made on the judiciary, special regard is had to the need of the judiciary to enjoy public confidence and the limits of permissible criticism may be narrower. In *Prager and Oberschlick v Austria*, the Court, by a narrow margin, found the conviction of a journalist for alleging serious misconduct by certain judges justified for maintaining the authority of the judiciary and protecting judges' reputations. Referring to the "special role of the judiciary" as the guarantor of justice, it considered that the classification by the domestic courts of the impugned passages as unjustifiably defamatory fell within the margin of appreciation and that the applicant journalist could not invoke good faith or compliance with professional ethics since the research which he had undertaken did not appear adequate to substantiate such serious allegations and he had not given any judge an opportunity to comment on the accusations against him.[44] Particular

[40] *De Haes and Gijsels v Belgium*, February 24, 1997, R.J.D. 1997–I, 25 E.H.R.R. 1, para.47; *Cumpana and Mazare v Romania*, December 17, 2004, ECHR 2004–XII, para.101; *Grüner Klub im Rathaus v Austria*, (13521/04) (Dec.) February 2, 2007, where allegations of interference in the course of justice by the Minister of Justice, even if a value judgment, had no basis of fact: conviction for breach of reputation justified.

[41] *Lombardo v Malta*, April 24, 2007, para.59, where the domestic courts classified the comment, wrongly, as fact rather than a value statement.

[42] *Lombardo*, fn.41 above, para.60.

[43] See, concerning narrower limits applying to criticism of private individuals, *Tammer v Estonia*, February 6, 2001, ECHR 2001–I, paras 62–68; concerning the important role of municipal elected representatives, *Jerusalem*, fn.29 above, para.36.

[44] Narrow majorities in Commission and Court. The minority considered that judges also had to act under public scrutiny. Contrast *De Haes and Gijsels*, fn.40 above, where journalists were convicted for defaming judges in articles about a controversial custody case, the Court noted that, though they might have been polemical and aggressive, their comments had a factual basis and were proportionate to ongoing public debate.

weight was given by the Court to the importance of the judicial role where carrying out a balance of interests between a Ministry of Justice official who leaked critical comments and the senior judge who sued him for defamation; the Court noted that he required to enjoy public confidence in order to fulfill his functions.[45]

While civil servants acting in an official capacity are, like politicians, subject to wider limits of acceptable criticism, the Court seems to give weight to the need to protect them in the performance of their functions from offensive and abusive remarks, particularly those who should enjoy public confidence. In *Janowski v Poland*, it was not disproportionate to fine the applicant for heated words in a "lively exchange" in which he called two municipal guards "oafs" and "dumb".[46] Nor was it disproportionate to protect public prosecutors in *Lesnik v Slovakia*, where the applicant was convicted of insulting conduct for writing letters to a public prosecutor and his superior alleging misconduct, including the taking of a bribe, which allegations the Court majority held were serious and unsubstantiated.[47] However, where defence lawyers are concerned, in *Nikula v Finland*, the Court taking into account the possible chilling effect on the performance of their duties in ensuring a fair trial for accused under Art.6, found it unacceptable to convict defense counsel for making remarks during a trial about the prosecutor's conduct of the case.

Campaign groups, such as Greenpeace, which raise debate on matters of public interest may claim a certain protection, while multinational companies must expect to attract a certain amount of criticism and have their activities scrutinised. Thus, adequate procedural safeguards must be provided where such companies take action to defend their reputation to prevent a chilling effect on the free circulation of information.[48]

Journalists themselves are public figures who must accept a certain amount of criticism. However, where a journalist was found liable in defamation for remarks about other journalists, this was not disproportionate where it was not part of a public debate, but a reflection of personal animosity.[49]

The difficulty, and importance, of fighting child abuse within the family was given weight as against the interests of the parents who might be the subject of accusation. Where a grandmother was convicted of defamation when she repeated her suspicions to the child's doctor as to the origins of bruising on the child after a visit to his father, and the doctor then contacted the social services, the Court considered that this flew in the face of the more important need for persons to be able, in the interests of children, to pass on information or suspicions in good faith

[45] *Poyraz v Turkey*, December 7, 2010, paras 71 and 77–78, a heightened obligation of discretion was also considered to apply to officials who carried out official enquiries which could impinge on an individuals' reputation.

[46] The Court majority had regard to the fact that the applicant insulted them in front of bystanders and seemed to regard the dispute as akin to a personal quarrel rather than exercise of freedom of expression on a matter of public debate, though, as the minority noted, the applicant had been objecting to the guards moving on market stallholders when they had no legal authority to do so.

[47] The minority considered that private citizens should be free to make complaints to public officials and their superiors without risking prosecution for defamation or insult, particularly where the allegations were not made in the media. Judges Bratza and Maruste thought that civil servants should tolerate criticism, even where expressed in abusive, strong or intemperate terms and the allegations serious and unfounded. See also *Perna v Italy*, May 6, 2003, conviction and fine justified for attack on a public prosecutor's alleged abusive conduct.

[48] *Steel and Morris*, fn.33 above, paras 94–95.

[49] *Katamadze v Georgia*, (6987/01) (Dec.) February 14, 2006.

to the relevant authorities.[50] It also commented that there should be no chilling effect through the requirement to pay damages either. Similarly, employees in the public sector should be able to bring issues of misconduct to the appropriate authority; Art.10 thus protected a trade union official who brought not wholly baseless allegations of misappropriation of state property at a school to the attention of the school inspectorate and prosecutor.[51]

4. State's positive obligation to protect reputation

The Commission had been reluctant to accord much protection to notions of reputation and honour under the Convention outwith the general procedural protection under Art.6. In *Pfeifer v Austria*, the Court departed from this approach, stating categorically that the right to reputation fell within the scope of Art.8 of the Convention.[52] Other cases have expressly included the somewhat emotive notion of "honour".[53] This has sparked a line of cases in which the issue concerns a positive obligation on the State, through courts, to uphold reputation and honour, whatever that might mean, against defamation and excessive criticism. This has led the Court to look at freedom of expression cases from the other side of the mirror and supervise domestic courts to make sure that they do not err on the side of overly favouring the media or those publishing their views at the expense of their disgruntled subjects. Domestic courts cannot err on the side of protecting freedom of expression without risking breaching Art.8 as regards someone's right to reputation or vice versa.[54] II–276

The same principles come into play as in the freedom of expression cases. Thus, where, in defamation proceedings, the domestic courts wrongly treated a statement as a value judgment rather than a statement of fact which required to be proved, the Court found they failed to strike a fair balance between the competing interests.[55] Similarly, where Moldovan courts rejected defamation claims by a historian accused of having collaborated with the KGB as expression of subjective opinion, the Court found this was a statement of historical fact susceptible of proof and highly damaging in nature and that the approach of the courts had failed to give due protection to the historian's right to reputation.[56] Issues of political interest notwithstanding, journalists must have at least some basis of fact before making assertions as to an individual's collaboration with or membership in notorious state security services.[57] A fair balance was also not struck where courts refused redress to

[50] *Juppala v Finland*, December 2, 2008.

[51] *Marchenko v Ukraine*, February 19, 2009, paras 43–47.

[52] See fn.1 above.

[53] *Sanchez Cardenas*, October 4, 2007, para.38, concerning allegations of child abuse; *A v Norway*, April 9, 2009, para.74, concerning allegations against a past repeat offender of implication in two child murders.

[54] See *Karako v Hungary*, April 28, 2009, para.28, where the applicant invoked Art.8 due to a negative opinion published by a rival politician, the Court noted that he was himself a politician active in political life and that the statement was made during an electoral campaign; in these circumstances, if the courts had upheld his defamation action this would, in the Court's view, have been disproportionate interference with freedom of expression under Art.10.

[55] *Pfeifer*, see fn.1 above, where editor of a right-wing publication claimed the applicant, was a "member of a hunting society" that had hounded a professor to death by suicide because of his alleged national socialist views, the Court disagreed with the domestic courts' assessment that this was a value judgment, considering that this statement contained an alleged causal link which was a fact susceptible of proof and was tantamount to accusing him of criminal behaviour.

[56] *Petrenco v Moldova*, March 30, 2010.

[57] *Petrina v Romania*, October 14, 2008.

an individual, with a criminal record, who had been identified by the press as a suspect in shocking child murders with serious repercussions on his life, the public interest in reporting on the crimes not extending to defamatory allegations against the innocent individual.[58] Where, however, the journalist has acted with due diligence in checking his source concerning serious allegations and has invited the subject to comment, it is not a bar to publication that the person concerned denied the allegations.[59]

The positive obligation to protect reputation also extends towards making damages available for non-pecuniary damage. Where police officers, acquitted of torture and other abuses, brought proceedings for damages due to an unlawful ministerial decision dismissing them for the same alleged conduct, the Court found that the Supreme Court, in reversing a lower court award on the basis that moral damages were not available for unlawful administrative acts, had not given an adequate explanation for this reversal or a comprehensive assessment of the police officers' rights.[60]

Nor can domestic courts lightly make statements infringing unwarrantably on private life or reputation in their own pronouncements. In a child access case, where a court made an obiter statement of suspicion that the applicant father had abused his son, it was found that this had had a stigmatising and traumatic effect, for which no cogent reasons or justification had been given.[61] Authorities which publish inaccurate, damaging information on individuals may also fall foul of Art.8, as in a case where the police erroneously issued a report in court proceedings that the applicant had a previous criminal record and from which faulty information was picked up and reported by the press.[62] Procedural safeguards should be provided so that applicants can seek retraction or clarification of faulty public sources of information which might damage reputation.[63]

5. Injunctions and size of awards

II–277 Outside the sphere of journalistic and political debate, restraints on defamatory publications have been found more justifiable. An injunction imposed on Count Tolstoy, sued by Lord Aldington for passages in a book alleging involvement in sending prisoners of war and refugees to the Soviet Union where they were massacred, was found to be proportionate, not exceeding the purpose of preventing repetition of allegations found to be defamatory. There is, however, no duty of pre-notification imposed on the media to disclose intended publications to those who are concerned to allow them the opportunity to obtain an injunction. Such a duty could only be effectively enforced by imposing potentially high fines or damages which would have a chilling effect on publication generally.[64]

[58] *A v Norway*, fn.53 above.

[59] *Polanco Torees and Movilla Polanco v Spain*, September 21, 2010.

[60] *Taliadorou and Stylianou v Cyprus*, October 16, 2008, paras 49–59.

[61] *Sanchez Cardenas*, fn.53 above.

[62] *Celahattin Canli v Turkey*, November 18, 2008, the wrongful disclosure was an interference with private life that was not "in accordance with law" as it breached the relevant regulations.

[63] *Mikolajova v Slovakia*, January 18, 2011, even though the charges were dropped, police records stated an investigation disclosed the applicant had assaulted her husband; an insurance company accessed the record and requested reimbursement of the husband's medical costs: violation as she had no means of obtaining removal or rectification of the police record.

[64] *Mosley v UK*, May 11, 2011, paras 125–132

The size of the damages award imposed on Tolstoy by a jury, which exceeded one million pounds, was, however, disproportionate and in breach of Art.10. There was a lack of adequate safeguards in the procedure, since national law allowed the jury great latitude and awards could only be set aside on appeal on limited grounds.[65] Awards of £36,000 and £40,000 were disproportionate in *Steel and Morris*, given the lowly means of the two applicants and the fact that the defendant, a multinational company, had not had to prove any actual financial loss from the leaflets which they had distributed.[66] The unfettered and unpredictable power of juries to award damages in defamation was the subject of a complaint by *The Times*, which considered that this disclosed an unjustifiable restriction on their journalistic activities in general. The Commission found that a newspaper could claim to be a victim even if no defamation proceedings had been brought if the state of the law was too vague to allow the risk of proceedings to be predicted, but that they had not established such vagueness by reference to any award or any specific article in which it had in any way been inhibited from imparting information.[67]

6. Right of reply

While doubtful that a right of reply to defamatory comments would be implied **II–278**
under the Convention, the Commission found that where it existed in domestic law this did not impinge on the freedom of expression of the other party obliged to publish.[68] While it may also be compatible with Art.10 to require a newspaper to publish a notice indicating the institution of proceedings for defamation, it was not necessary to impose fines for failure to publish a notice concerning the decision of the first instance court in favour of the complainant, where the appeal proceedings were still pending and undecided.[69] More recently, the Court has held that there may be circumstances where the media are required to publish a reply, an apology or a judgment and that States must ensure that any denial of access to the media is not arbitrary or disproportionate interference with freedom of expression. Accordingly, the State was under a positive obligation to ensure that an individual had a reasonable opportunity to exercise his right of reply by submitting a response for publication to a newspaper which had published criticism of his poetry and, further, that he had an opportunity to contest the newspaper's refusal to publish his response before the domestic courts.[70]

[65] Contrast with *Independent News and Media and Independent Newspapers Ireland Ltd v Ireland*, June 16, 2005, where an award of IR£300,000 did not disclose a violation as apparently there were adequate procedural safeguards, namely the jury had been given some specific guidance and the appellate review examined the award in light of principles of fairness and proportionality.

[66] *Steel and Morris*, fn.33 above, para.97, it was irrelevant no steps had been taken to enforce the award, which remained enforceable. Contrast *Chauvy*, fn.30 above, para.78, where awards of 400,000 FRF plus fines were regarded as modest.

[67] (14631/89) (Dec.) March 5, 1990, 65 D.R. 307.

[68] (13010/87) (Dec.) July 12, 1989, 62 D.R. 247, it was not necessary for courts to verify the content of the reply as it had to be prompt to be effective; *Societe Prisma Presse v France*, (66910/01) (Dec.) July 1, 2003, containing comments as to the appropriateness of a requirement on a magazine to publish the court's finding of a breach of privacy. See also *Hachette Filipachi Associés v France*, June 14, 2007, where it was proportionate to require a periodical to publish a statement from the family of a murdered official indicating that they had not consented to publication of the photographs of his body and that, in their view, this breached their right to privacy.

[69] *Krone Verlag GmbH v Austria (No.2)*, November 6, 2003.

[70] *Melnychuk v Ukraine*, (28743/03) (Dec.) July 5, 2005.

Cross-reference

Part IIA, s.2: Access to court.
Part IIB, s.22: Freedom of expression.
Part IIB, s.37: Private life.

9. Deprivation of liberty

Key provision:

Article 5, para.1 (right to liberty and security of person), subject to exceptions: sub-paras (a)–(f). II–279

Key case-law:

Lawless v Ireland, July 1, 1961, Series A, No.3, 1 E.H.R.R. 15; *De Wilde, Ooms and Versyp v Belgium*, June 18, 1971, Series A, No.12, 1 E.H.R.R. 373; *Engel v Netherlands*, June 8, 1976, Series A, No.22, 1 E.H.R.R. 706; *Ireland v UK*, January 18, 1978, Series A, No.25, 2 E.H.R.R. 25; *Van Droogenbroeck v Belgium*, June 24, 1982, Series A, No.50, 4 E.H.R.R. 443; *Guzzardi v Italy*, November 6, 1980, Series A, No.39, 3 E.H.R.R. 333; *Bozano v France*, November 18, 1986, Series A, No.111, 10 E.H.R.R. 175; *Weeks v UK*, March 2, 1987, Series A, No.114, 10 E.H.R.R 293; *Nielsen v Denmark*, November 28, 1988, Series A. No.144, 11 E.H.R.R 175; *Ciulla v Italy*, February 22, 1989, Series A, No.148, 13 E.H.R.R 346; *Drozd and Janousek v France*, June 26, 1992, Series A, No.240, 14 E.H.R.R. 745; *Kemmache v France (No.3)*, November 24, 1994, Series A, No.296–C, 19 E.H.R.R. 349; *Benham v UK*, June 10, 1996, R.J.D. 1996–III, No.10, 22 E.H.R.R. 293; *Amuur v France*, June 25, 1996, R.J.D. 1996–III, No.11; *Bizzotto v Greece*, November 15, 1996, R.J.D. 1996–V, No.21; *Lukanov v Bulgaria*, March 20, 1997, R.J.D. 1997–II, No.34, 24 E.H.R.R. 121; *K-F v Germany*, November 27, 1997, R.J.D. 1997–VII, No.58; *Raninen v Finland*, December 16, 1997, R.J.D. 1997–VIII, No.60, 26 E.H.R.R. 563; *Riera Blume v Spain*, October 14, 1999, ECHR 1999–VII; *Witold Litwa v Poland*, April 4, 2000; *Jecius v Lithuania*, July 31, 2000, ECHR 2000–IX; *Mancini v Italy*, August 2, 2001, ECHR 2001–IX; *Conka v Belgium*, February 5, 2002, ECHR 2002–I; *Stafford v UK*, May 28, 2002, ECHR 2002–IV; *Vasileva v Denmark*, September 25, 2003; *Assanidze v Georgia*, April 8, 2004, ECHR 2004–II; *Ilaşcu v Moldova and Russia,* July 8, 2004, ECHR 2004–VII; *HL v UK*, October 5, 2004, ECHR 2004–IX; *Ocalan v Turkey*, May 12, 2005, ECHR 2005–IV; *Mooren v Germany*, July 9, 2009, ECHR 2009–. . . ; *A and Others v UK*, February 19, 2009, ECHR 2009–. . . ; *Medvedyev v France*, March 29, 2010, ECHR 2010–. . . ; *Al-Jedda v UK*, July 7, 2011, ECHR 2011–. . .

1. General considerations

The case-law indicates the importance of physical freedom and emphasises that exceptions are exhaustively limited to those set out in the sub-paras of Art.5, para.1 (see sections below) and are to be interpreted narrowly.[1] If the detention does not fall within any of these categories then it cannot be justified under Art.5, para.1, however "useful" the aim might be.[2] II–280

[1] *Winterwerp v Netherlands*, October 24, 1979, Series A, No.33, 2. E.H.R.R. 387, para.37.

[2] e.g. *Ciulla v Italy*, February 22, 1989, Series A, No.148, 13 E.H.R.R 346, para.41, arrest and detention of a mafia suspect as a preventive measure based on suspicion could not be regarded as following conviction within sub-para.1(a) or for the purpose of bringing him before a court within sub-para.1(c), despite the acknowledged importance of the fight against the mafia. See also *Engel v Netherlands*, June 8, 1976, Series A, No.22, 1 E.H.R.R. 706, para.57, the claim of special exclusion for military discipline was not accepted.

The principal aim is to prevent arbitrary deprivation of liberty. The emphasis is on procedural rights and safeguards, with perhaps limited scope for challenging the merits of decisions of deprivation of liberty. However, in the context of detention of alcoholics, the Court has held the detention of an individual is such a serious measure that it can only be justified where other, less severe measures have been considered and found insufficient to protect the individual or public interest.[3]

2. Existence of deprivation of liberty

II–281 Whether someone is deprived of their liberty depends on examination of the concrete situation, account being taken of a whole range of criteria, such as the type, duration, effects and manner of the implementation of the measure in question.[4] In ordinary circumstances, any element of compulsion restricting a person to custody or to attend a particular location falls within the scope of Art.5, para.1,[5] even if for a very short time.[6]

Detention by private individuals will attract State responsibility if connived at or permitted by the police.[7] Even where a person has submitted voluntarily to a particular regime of detention, this does not exclude the operation of Art.5 with regard to challenging the lawfulness or seeking discharge. For example, in *De Wilde, Ooms and Versyp v Belgium*, where the Government argued that the applicants had given themselves up to the police voluntarily, the Court considered that liberty was too important for a person to lose the benefit of protection under Art.5 merely because he might have surrendered himself. Scrupulous supervision was still required to ensure that measures were necessary for the purposes of Art.5, para.1.

The apparent ability of a person to leave the alleged place of detention may not be decisive, regard being had to the reality of the situation. In respect of asylum claimants restricted, on arrival in airports, to particular zones or holding areas, the

[3] *Witold Litwa v Poland*, April 4, 2000, para.78; *Ambruszkiewicz v Poland*, May 4, 2006, para.31.

[4] *Guzzardi v Italy*, November 6, 1980, Series A, No.39, 3 E.H.R.R. 333, para.92; (8334/78) (Dec.) May 7, 1981, 24 D.R. 103, though a threat to detain in accordance with the law could not infringe Art.5, para.1, it was implied that a threat of arbitrary or unjustified detention could infringe the right to security of person.

[5] Order to be taken by force to undergo a blood test fell under Art.5, para.1(b): (8278/78) (Dec.) December 13, 1979, 18 D.R. 154; (24722/94) (Dec.) April 10, 1995, 81–A D.R. 130, an applicant, suffering from a nervous disorder, was taken to the police station, the Commission found no deprivation of liberty, since he agreed to go, the police acted out of humanitarian reasons and in the station he was free to move around; conditional release or release on licence has not yet been found to affect liberty; nor the fact that an arrest warrant or order for detention was in force where the person was still at liberty, e.g. (12778/87) (Dec.) December 9, 1988, 59 D.R. 158. House arrest qualified as detention in *Mancini v Italy*, August 2, 2001, ECHR 2001–IX, as did forcible deprogramming of cult members in a hotel in *Riera Blume v Spain*, October 14, 1999, ECHR 1999–VII; confinement of crew to their cabins on board a ship arrested on the high sea also qualified in *Medvedyev v France*, March 29, 2010, ECHR 2010–. . . , paras 74–75, even if the cabin restrictions had been lifted, the fact that the ship's course was imposed by the French navy apparently meant the crew were still deprived of their liberty; where being transported by the police for forced expulsion, even if a matter of hours, Art.5 applied: *Iskandarov v Russia*, September 23, 2010, para.140.

[6] See e.g. *Shimovolos v Russia*, June 21, 2011, para.50, the applicant was taken to the police station for only 45 minutes, but was subject to coercion and not allowed to leave during that time: deprivation of liberty was found.

[7] e.g. *Riera Blume*, see fn.5 above. See also *Rantsev v Cyprus and Russia*, January 7, 2010, paras 314–321, the police were held responsible where they handed over a foreign girl to a cabaret owner who then locked her up in his flat.

Commission considered that, since they were able to leave the airport by taking a plane elsewhere, they were not in fact deprived of their liberty.[8] The Court in *Amuur v France*, however, found that the mere fact that an asylum seeker may leave the country does not exclude a deprivation of liberty, since this may be only a theoretical possibility if no other country is offering the protection which they seek or is prepared to take them in. Thus an asylum seeker held in restricted conditions for an extended period of time may claim to be deprived of liberty.[9] Short periods while practical matters were arranged, e.g. repatriation or granting of asylum, would only constitute a restriction on movement.[10] Where applicants' asylum claims were rejected within a few days, they retained their passports and were not under any supervision or surveillance, the Court found that they were not to be regarded as detained in the transit zone.[11] In the case of a mentally incapacitated person kept in hospital as a "voluntary patient", the Court did not consider it decisive that the applicant was compliant and never sought to leave, but found a deprivation of liberty as he was under continuous supervision and control and was not free to leave.[12]

In certain contexts, restrictions which might constitute deprivation of liberty if imposed on an adult civilian will not for other categories of person. In *Engel v Netherlands*, it was found that military life imposed a special disciplinary regime on persons stricter than in civilian life and it was necessary to examine whether a restriction clearly deviated from normal conditions of life in the armed forces in Contracting States, having regard to the nature, duration, effects and manner of execution of the penalty in question. Light arrest which meant confinement in off-duty hours to military premises, without being locked up, was not covered. Nor was aggravated arrest, where for 12 days an applicant was confined in off-duty hours to a specially designated place and barred from recreation. However, strict arrest, even for short periods where a person was locked in cell by day and night and no longer fulfilled duties, was a deprivation of liberty, as was committal to a disciplinary unit where persons were held in a particular establishment which they could not leave for periods of months and were locked in cells at night. The Court has underlined that deprivations of liberty within the army must be imposed by due judicial authority.[13]

Special considerations also apply to children, since they are inevitably subject to restrictions in the home and school. The taking of a girl from school for questioning by the police about pilfering was not a deprivation of liberty, apparently since it was not intended to be and there were no irregularities.[14] In *Nielsen v Denmark*, measures taken by a mother involving admittance of her son of 11 or 12 years to a hospital psychiatric ward against his will, were not found by the Court to disclose a deprivation of liberty. It emphasised parental rights and the inevitable restrictions imposed on children who, in school and elsewhere, have to abide by certain rules

[8] (19066/91) (Dec.) April 5, 1993, 74 D.R. 179.

[9] Twenty days qualified as deprivation of liberty in *Amuur v France*, June 25, 1996, R.J.D. 1996–III, No.11; 14 days in *Shamsa v Poland*, November 27, 2003; 11 and 15 days in *Riad and Idiab v Belgium*, January 24, 2008, para.68, where the Government purported to comply with court orders for release of the applicant asylum seekers by placing them in the transit zone.

[10] *Amuur*, see fn.9 above, para.43.

[11] *Mahdid and Haddar v Austria*, (74762/01) (Dec.) December 8, 2005.

[12] *H v UK* , October 5, 2004, ECHR 2004–IX, paras 82–89. See also *Storck v Germany*, June 16, 2005, where even if initially compliant, the applicant showed her lack of consent by attempts to abscond.

[13] *Pulatli v Turkey*, April 26, 2011, para.32.

[14] (8819/79) (Dec.) March 19, 1981, 24 D.R. 158.

and who may have to be hospitalised for medical treatment. Since the decision to place the child was taken by a parent, on the basis of medical advice, with the view to protect the child's health, and the conditions in the ward and the treatment which he received were not inappropriate (though the door was locked this was to protect the children and avoid disturbance to other patients), the nature of the restrictions was not such as to be similar to the cases of deprivation specified in Art.5, para.1. The Court gave little weight to the view of the child, since at age 12 it must still be possible for him to be admitted to hospital at the request of the holder of parental rights. The Commission had found a deprivation of liberty which was not justified, since he was not mentally ill in any real sense and, having regard to his understanding and views, it could not be regarded as a voluntary placement.[15]

It would therefore appear that as long as there is some medical or educational justification for the placement by parental rights holders, confinement of children to particular establishments will not constitute a deprivation of liberty.[16] Rather dubiously the Court relied on the *Nielsen* case in the context of the forcible removal of an 84-year-old from her home to a care establishment and found that Art.5, para.1 did not apply, apparently because she was not placed in a closed ward and retained freedom of movement and the placement was in her own interests.[17]

Not surprisingly perhaps, prisoners who are already under detention cannot claim a deprivation of liberty as occurring when they are transferred elsewhere[18] or subject to a more restrictive form of confinement.[19] This is regarded instead as a modification of the conditions of lawful detention or imprisonment.[20] Thus prisoners cannot invoke Art.5 in relation to the type of regime to which they are subjected, or in relation to the location of their prison.[21] Where there was a "deplorable delay" in transferring a prisoner from one regime to one far more suitable, he was still subject to the same lawful deprivation of liberty, although the difference in quality of life was of immense significance for him.[22] Issues could only arise if there was some failure to conform to lawful requirements with regard to the type of detention.[23]

Whether or not temporary measures restricting demonstrators to a limited area by police for security and safety reasons—a technique known as "kettling"—was a deprivation of liberty is under consideration in a case before the Grand Chamber.[24]

[15] There had been behavioural difficulties since, although the mother had won custody after divorce, the boy had repeatedly run away to live with his father.

[16] Where local authorities place children under their care in pure disciplinary or specialist facilities however, either under court orders or under statutory provisions providing for "secure" accommodation, there is likely to be a deprivation of liberty, e.g. *DG v Ireland*, May 16, 2002, ECHR 2002–III, *Koniarska v UK*, (33670/96) (Dec.) October 12, 2000.

[17] *HM v Switzerland*, (Dec.) January 29, 2002, ECHR 2002–IX, as Art.5 did not apply the Court did not have to deal with the applicant's argument that "neglect" was not a ground for deprivation of liberty. The Court in *HL v UK* distinguished this case, emphasising that she apparently agreed, at least at times, to the placement.

[18] e.g. *Perry v UK*, (63737/00) (Dec.) September 26, 2002, where the applicant, held on remand, was transferred to a police station where he was being covertly filmed for identification purposes. This raised issues under Arts 6 and 8, but not 5.

[19] e.g. *Bollan v UK*, (42117/98) (Dec.) May 4, 2000, ECHR 2000–V.

[20] (7754/77) (Dec.) May 9, 1977, 11 D.R. 216.

[21] (11703/85) (Dec.) December 9, 1987, 54 D.R. 116; (11208/84) (Dec.) March 4, 1986, 46 D.R. 182.

[22] *Ashingdane v UK*, May 28, 1985, Series A, No.93, 7 E.H.R.R. 528.

[23] See below, sub-s.5: "In accordance with a procedure prescribed by law" and lawfulness.

[24] *Austin v UK*, (39692/09) et al, communicated in October 2010, the House of Lords had found that the good faith, proportionate measures of crowd control did not qualify as deprivation of liberty. Judgment unlikely before early 2012.

3. Relationship with freedom of movement

The borderline between a deprivation of liberty and a restriction on freedom of movement, subject to separate protection under Art.2 of Protocol 4, is a difference of degree and intensity and not nature or substance.[25] In the UK context, exclusion orders which may restrict persons suspected of terrorism from entering mainland UK from Northern Ireland have not been found to impose restrictions of such a nature or degree as to constitute a deprivation of liberty (see Part IIB, s.23: Freedom of movement). II–282

4. Relationship with "security of person"

While Art.5, para.1 guarantees not only the right to liberty but "security of person", this latter aspect has proved to have no real independent existence. It cannot be used to cover ideas of physical integrity which have been found to fall, where appropriate, within the scope of Art.8 and, in more extreme cases, Art.3.[26] In *East African Asians v UK*,[27] the Commission found the use of the concept of "security of person" in juxtaposition to the right to liberty referred to by the aspect of arbitrary interference with liberty. The application of entry regulations did not constitute an interference with this right, notwithstanding the threat to the applicants' personal existence posed by the measures excluding them from the UK. II–283

The Court in *Bozano v France* also appeared to equate the notion to the arbitrary aspect of interference with liberty. Where an applicant was removed from France by the police by way of a "disguised extradition", it stated that what was at stake was not only the right to liberty but the right to security of person and concluded that the measures taken to circumvent a court decision against extradition were neither "lawful" or compatible with the right to security of person.[28] In *Ocalan v Turkey*, the Court also commented that an arrest made by the authorities of one State on the territory of another without the consent of the latter, would affect the person's individual rights to security under Art.5, para.1.[29]

In the case of disappearances in custody, where arbitrariness and lack of safeguards are acutely in issue, the Commission and Court found a violation of the aspect of "security of person" together with the right to liberty. They noted that compliance with procedures and the existence of safeguards were essential to prevent the risk of extra-judicial execution and torture.[30] Indeed disappearances disclose a particularly grave violation of Art.5.[31] Where disappearances are concerned, a continuing procedural obligation may arise under Art.5 which requires the

[25] *Guzzardi*, see fn.4 above, para.93.

[26] e.g. (5573/72) (Dec.) July 16, 1976, 7 D.R. 8; (7050/75) (Dec.) October 12, 1978, 19 D.R. 5; (11208/84), fn.21 above, where it did not apply to an integration policy of republican and unionist prisoners alleged to place them at physical risk; nor in *Akdivar v Turkey*, (Rep.) R.J.D. 1996–IV, No.15, para.229, concerning destruction of home, livelihood and personal security.

[27] (4403/70) et al (Rep.) December 14, 1973, 78–A D.R. 5.

[28] See also *Iskandarov*, fn.5 above, paras 148–151, concerning police action to remove the applicant unlawfully from the country.

[29] *Ocalan v Turkey*, May 12, 2005, ECHR 2005–IV, para.85.

[30] *Kurt v Turkey*, May 25, 1998, R.J.D. 1998–III, No.74, para.129; *Cakici v Turkey*, July 8, 1999, ECHR 1999–IV, para.105, concerning the importance of keeping accurate custody records.

[31] *Kurt*, fn.30 above; *Cakici*, fn.30 above, para.107; *Luluyev v Russia*, November 9, 2006, para.125; *Batayev v Russia*, June 17, 2010, para.225

authorities to carry out an effective investigation into the fate and whereabouts of persons who went missing while arguably under their control.[32]

5. "In accordance with a procedure prescribed by law" and lawfulness

II–284 Article 5, para.1 imposes two lawfulness criteria: firstly, in para.1, that a deprivation of liberty must be in accordance with a procedure prescribed by law; and, secondly, in each sub-paragraph listing the exceptions, a requirement that the detention, arrest or order be lawful.[33] These overlap, since the Court considers that "lawful" covers procedural as well as substantive rules, and are regarded as underlining the importance of the aim of Art.5, para.1 to prevent arbitrary detention.[34]

Most cases appear to consider both requirements of "lawfulness" together.[35] It is regarded as referring essentially to domestic lawfulness, both substantive and procedural, which is for national authorities to interpret.[36] The Court has also stated that it is not its role to assess the facts which led a national court to adopt one decision rather than another, otherwise it would be acting as a court of third or fourth instance.[37] Nonetheless, since compliance with domestic law is an integral part of the obligations of Contracting States, the Court is competent to satisfy itself of such compliance where relevant, subject to its inherent limits in the European system of protection.[38] The Convention organs have a certain jurisdiction to review whether domestic law has been complied with and the manner in which it is done, in particular that domestic law is not interpreted or applied in an arbitrary manner,

[32] *Varnava v Turkey*, September 18, 2009, paras 208–209.

[33] No legal basis for arrest and detention, e.g. *Denizci v Cyprus*, May 23, 2001, ECHR 2001–V, para.392; *Baranowski v Poland*, March 28, 2000, ECHR 2000–III, paras 53–58, pre-trial detention by executive order; *Shamsa*, fn.9 above, paras 55–60, detention in transit zone not based on a judicial decision or specific legal provision. Failure to comply with legal requirements, e.g. *Voskuil v Netherlands*, November 22, 2007, para.83, authorities omitted to inform the applicant in writing of the detention order within the 24 hours required by law.

[34] *Winterwerp v Netherlands*, see fn.1 above, para.4.

[35] e.g. *Raninen v Finland*, December 16, 1997, R.J.D. 1997–VIII, No.60, 26 E.H.R.R. 563, unlawful arrest of conscientious objector.

[36] It can include measures based on custom, as in *Drozd and Janousek v France*, June 26, 1992, Series A, No.240, 14 E.H.R.R. 745, where applicants, sentenced in Andorra but held in France, alleged there was no statutory or legal basis for their detention there, but the Court found that the practice was based on well-established custom.

[37] *Kemmache v France (No.3)*, November 24, 1994, Series A, No.296–C, 19 E.H.R.R. 349, para.44; (10689/83) (Dec.) July 1984, 37 D.R. 225, where Barbie claimed that his arrest was not lawful (i.e. disguised extradition), the Commission found that the decision of the Court of Cassation upholding the arrest as lawful was not arbitrary.

[38] *Lukanov v Bulgaria*, March 20, 1997, R.J.D. 1997–II, No.34, 24 E.H.R.R. 121, para.41, on examination of the Criminal Code the Court was not persuaded that the applicant's participation in a collective decision to send aid to the Third World constituted a criminal offence; conversely, see *Wloch v Poland*, October 19, 2000, ECHR 2000–XI, where the applicant's arrest and detention on child trafficking charges was found compatible with Art.5, as, notwithstanding difficulties of interpretation of the law, it was not shown that the domestic court's approach was arbitrary or unreasonable.

since no arbitrary detention can ever be regarded as "lawful".[39] For example, the measures applied by the domestic authorities in *Conka v Belgium* were incompatible with Art.5, para.1, where the applicant gypsies were lured under false pretences to the police station in order to facilitate their expulsion and in circumstances which removed any realistic possibility of challenging the measure. A flagrant example was furnished in *Assanidze v Georgia*, where the applicant continued to be detained for several years despite a court order for his release, the Court noting that detention must be based on a specific statutory provision or judicial decision or it will be incompatible with the principle of legal certainty and, therefore, arbitrary, running counter to the fundamental aspects of the rule of law.[40] A legal basis for detention must be in existence for each and every part of the period.[41] A special context, even such as the high seas, cannot remove the requirement for any detention to be properly based on legal provisions[42]; an ad hoc diplomatic note permitting the seizure of the ship was not an adequate legal basis for the measure of arresting and detaining its crew.[43]

It is irrelevant in this context that law enforcement officers acted in good faith and believed that there was a legal basis for the detention, if in fact there was no lawful basis.[44] Indeed, where the police purported to comply with legal requirements but re-detained an asylum seeker minutes after he had signed his release papers, the Court found that this offended the purpose of Art.5, para.1, effectively seeking to subvert the three-month maximum detention period under domestic law.[45]

As in references to lawfulness under other provisions of the Convention, it has been interpreted as referring in addition to the "quality of law", i.e. compatibility with the rule of law, that the rules be sufficiently accessible and precise,[46] sometimes

[39] *Winterwerp*, fn.1 above, paras 40 and 45; *Tsirlis and Kouloumpas v Greece*, May 29, 1997, R.J.D. 1997–III, No.38, 25 E.H.R.R. 198, where Jehovah's Witness ministers were detained for refusing national service, although under domestic law ministers of known religions were exempt, their detention had no basis in domestic law and was arbitrary; *PL v France*, (21503/93) (Rep.) April 11, 1996, R.J.D. 1997–II, No.34, where convicted prisoners had the right to deduction of pre-trial detention, the refusal to take into account the period on remand which the courts had annulled as unlawful (thus ceasing to have legal existence) was arbitrary; *Erkalo v Netherlands*, September 2, 1998, R.J.D. 1998–VIII, No. 88, where the applicant's detention was not based on any judicial decision, although in Dutch law the failure of the prosecutor to lodge the extension request until after the expiry of the time-limit did not effect the lawfulness of the continued detention.

[40] *Assanidze v Georgia*, April 8, 2004, ECHR 2004–II, para.175. See also *Gusinskiy v Russia*, May 19, 2004, ECHR 2004–IV, where the investigating officer ignored the amnesty applicable to the applicant; also *Lexa v Slovakia*, September 23, 2008, where the applicant was detained following an invalid attempt to revoke an amnesty; *Kolevi v Bulgaria*, November 5, 2009, prosecutor detained despite immunity under the law.

[41] See e.g. *Kucheruk v Ukraine*, September 6, 2007, where a court order for detention expired on July 22 and no other court order authorised detention, as opposed to dealing with other matters, until August 6.

[42] *Medvedyev*, fn.5 above, para.81, persons must always be covered by a legal system affording the requisite guarantees against arbitrary detention.

[43] *Medvedyev*, fn.5 above, paras 95–103, applying a "narrow" approach; contrast the minority opinion which considered that this approach was too narrow in the circumstances of action against drug smuggling at sea, where the crew caught *in flagrante delicto* were seeking to evade capture and the relevant Governments had reached a bilateral agreement.

[44] *Fedotov v Russia*, October 25, 2005, where the applicant's name, in error, figured on a wanted list and he was arrested.

[45] *John v Greece*, May 10, 2007, paras 30–37.

[46] *Amuur*, fn.9 above, where the rules applying to the holding of asylum seekers in international airport zones did not have the quality of law, since they contained no guarantees against arbitrary interferences, e.g. court review, access to legal or social assistance, time-limits, or procedures.

also emphasised as the general principle of legal certainty, which is of particular importance where the exercise of powers to detain is involved.[47] For example, while in general decisions by courts running counter to legal provisions will offend legal certainty, if the grounds the exceptions are based on are sufficiently foreseeable on the basis of case-law, legal certainty may be respected.[48]

In practice, this gives some leeway to domestic systems but might also be said to avoid breaches which are technical and lacking, essentially, in merit.[49] The fact that a conviction is quashed on appeal does not render it unlawful,[50] nor the fact that detention is found to be justified by the courts on an interpretation which is novel, although reasonably foreseeable.[51] Continued detention for two months pending examination of a prolongation request, regarded as lawful by the domestic courts, was not found arbitrary.[52] Lack of precision in the issuing by a court of a detention order was not regarded as fatal, where jurisdiction existed and the meaning was clear to all present.[53] Lack of reasons, or reasons referring to a legal provision, may, however, render the detention arbitrary.[54] The Court has sometimes referred to a finding stating that the domestic court did not act in bad faith.[55] On the other hand, it looks very poorly on failures to conform to basic formalities of recording arrest and detention, finding such in contravention of lawfulness and the purpose of Art.5.[56]

Where an order for detention is later quashed by a superior court, it does not automatically affect the validity of the detention retrospectively.[57] In *Benham v UK*, where the applicant was committed for failure to pay his poll tax by magistrates who failed to comply with the requirement to verify if his failure was due to culpable neglect; the Court had regard to the position at domestic law concerning the review by higher courts of magistrates' decisions. Since it found that the Divisional Court's decision could not be said to indicate with any certainty that the

[47] e.g. *Baranowski*, fn.33 above, para.52; *Shamsa*, fn.9 above, para.49; *Hafsteinsdottir v Iceland*, June 8, 2004, lack of precision as to duration of detention for alcoholism; *Kolevi v Bulgaria*, November 5, 2009, the Court commented that if after 10 years in the Convention system the domestic case-law had not been settled on the issue of immunity of prosecutors from detention, this was in itself an absence of clarity contrary to the requirements of Art.5. At para.178, the duties on the State under Art.5 were held to include "an obligation to secure, in legislation and case-law in matters concerning deprivation of liberty, a high level of legal certainty, clarity and foreseeability of the law".

[48] e.g. *Mooren v Germany*, July 9, 2009, ECHR 2009–. . . , paras 92–93.

[49] e.g. (9997/82) (Dec.) December 7, 1982, 31 D.R. 145, where the applicant complained that the appointment of an emergency duty judge was not valid, the Commission found that there was no reason to interfere with the Constitutional Court's appreciation of domestic lawfulness, no arbitrariness arising; (28574/95) (Dec.) November 25, 1996, 87–A D.R. 118, where the Court of Appeal did not find that procedural irregularities affected the lawfulness of detention, the Commission found the defect sufficiently remote from the procedural and substantive requirements for detention; *Douiyeb v Netherlands*, August 8, 1999, where the error in the order of detention was clerical.

[50] (7629/76) (Rep.) March 9, 1978, 13 D.R. 57.

[51] (9174/80) (Rep.) October 11, 1983, 40 D.R. 42.

[52] *Rutten v Netherlands*, July 24, 2001.

[53] *Jecius v Lithuania*, July 31, 2000, ECHR 2000–IX, paras 68–70.

[54] *Belevitskiy v Russia*, March 1, 2007, para.91, order was a pre-printed template without giving reasons; *Khudoyorov v Russia*, November 8, 2005, para.157, court order "laconic", not giving indication of ground of detention.

[55] *Jecius*, fn.53 above, para.69.

[56] *Menesheva v Russia*, March 9, 2006, where the police had apparently arrested the applicant on a fictitious charge to force disclosure of the whereabouts of her boyfriend; *Shchebet v Russia*, June 12, 2008, para.63, failure to record the applicant's arrest.

[57] *e.g. Bozano*, para.55; *Douiyeb*, fn.49 above, paras 44–45.

magistrates' decision was in excess of jurisdiction as opposed to an error made within its jurisdiction, it was not established that the order was invalid ab initio and the detention unlawful. Nor did it find any element of arbitrariness in the magistrates' decision to commit, referring to no apparent bad faith or failure to attempt to apply the legislation.[58] In subsequent cases, the Court has had to examine whether orders quashing magistrate's committals were based on failure to observe a statutory condition precedent for jurisdiction or on any gross or obvious irregularity which took the matter outside the magistrates' jurisdiction, sometimes a matter of fine distinctions.[59] In a recent case, the Court further explained that the distinction was between detention orders which were prima facie valid and effective unless and until they have been overturned by a higher court,[60] and those which were ex facie invalid, as where given by a court in excess of jurisdiction or where a party did not have proper notice or where the flaw in the order amounted to a "gross and obvious irregularity in the exceptional sense indicated by the Court's case-law.[61] It is not fatal if the reviewing court does not put right the defect itself but remits it to the lower court, as this may benefit the administration of justice, and as long as there is not undue prolongation of any situation of uncertainty.[62]

Where the place and condition in which a prisoner is detained appears to contravene a requirement of domestic law, or is manifestly not geared for the purpose, there may be scope for an issue to arise. There must be some relationship between the ground of permitted deprivation of liberty relied on and the place and conditions of detention.[63] In *Bizzotto v Greece*, where a judge convicted a drug addict and indicated that he should be detained in an appropriate clinic for treatment, the Commission found that his detention in an ordinary jail did not comply with the measures ordered against him in domestic law. The Court took the view that since the applicant had been convicted and sentenced for the purposes of punishment, the decision of the court at the same time to order his detention in a prison with medical facilities did not affect the main ground for his detention, which lay under Art.5, para.1(a). It considered that provisions merely laying down the arrangements for implementing sentences could not, in principle, have any bearing on the "lawfulness" of a deprivation of liberty.

If the location of the detention concerns something more fundamental than a manner of implementation of a sentence, for example, detention of a mental health

[58] The Commission had differed. See also the detailed separate opinion from Mr N. Bratza and the dissenting opinions in the Court. In the later cases, e.g. *Perks v UK*, October 12, 1999, no violation arose where the High Court quashed orders of detention which were regarded as falling within the jurisdiction of the magistrates.

[59] See *Lloyd v UK*, March 1, 2005, failure to hold a proper means inquiry or to have proper regard to the alternatives to imprisonment and committal, ordered in the applicant's absence without being satisfied that the applicant had been properly summoned, disclosed errors of jurisdiction, rendering the detention unlawful for the purposes of Art.5, para.1.

[60] *Mooren*, fn.48 above, paras 86–89, failure to set out in sufficient detail the facts and evidence was a formal defect only, not rendering the order void. That the distinction is still not easy to apply is illustrated by the narrow majority, eight dissenting judges considering that the defect was a serious irregularity rendering the detention unlawful. See also *Liu v Russia*, December 6, 2007, para.79, failure to set out necessity to keep the applicant in detention was not a fatal defect.

[61] *Mooren*, fn.48 above, para.75; for examples of gross and obvious irregularities see *Kolevi v Bulgaria*, fn.47 above, para.177, the detention order ignored prosecutors' absolute immunity from prosecution and detention.

[62] *Mooren*, fn.48 above, paras 95–96.

[63] *Ashingdane*, fn.22 above, para.44; *Saadi v UK*, January 29, 2008, para.69

patient in a prison, the result may be different. The Court has said that in principle the "detention" of a person as a mentally ill prisoner would only be "lawful" if effected in a hospital, clinic or other appropriate institution.[64] In *Mancini v Italy*, the three day delay in releasing the applicants from prison to house arrest violated Art.5, para.1, as, although house arrest involved a form of deprivation of liberty, it was of a different nature from prison detention and could not be regarded as a continuation of the latter. It is unlikely, though, that a person convicted of offences in respect of whom a judge had made comments or recommendations on the need for treatment could claim successfully under Art.5 if the authorities failed to respond.

6. The permitted exceptions

II–285 These are not exclusive of each other. Detention may fall within more than one category.[65] Different approaches apply to assessing the arbitrariness of detention under the various heads.[66]

(a) Article 5, para.1(a): conviction by a competent court

II–286 This sub-paragraph refers to lawful detention after conviction. It does not require the conviction itself to be lawful in the sense that it is maintained on appeal. The fact that the first instance court's ruling is overturned as disclosing an error does not take the detention pending the appeal outside the exception.[67] A violation was found, however, where an applicant ended up serving a longer sentence than that imposed by the relevant courts, taking into account the applicable reductions.[68]

"Court" for the purposes of this exception has been described as an organ which is judicial, in that it is independent of the executive and the parties to the case, and offers adequate procedural guarantees.[69]

Detention after conviction by a competent court requires not only that the detention follow the conviction in point of time but must result from, follow and depend upon or occur by virtue of the conviction.[70] The passage of time may break the causal link between a conviction and period of detention or continued detention, where the prolongation no longer has any connection with the objectives of the initial detention or was based on an assessment that was arbitrary or unreasonable in

[64] *Aerts v Belgium*, July 30, 1998, R.J.D. 1998–V, No.83, para.46; *Hutchison Reid v UK*, February 20, 2003, ECHR 2003–IV, para.54.

[65] e.g. *Silva Rocha v Portugal*, November 15, 1996, R.J.D. 1996–V, No.23, where a prisoner was detained by a court after committing acts constituting an offence but without criminal responsibility due to his mental state: Art.5, paras 1(a) and 1(e) applied; *Eriksen v Norway*, May 27, 1997, R.J.D. 1997–III, No.37, detention on special security grounds was based on Art.5, paras 1(a) and 1(c).

[66] See *Saadi v UK*, fn.63 above, paras 70–71.

[67] e.g. (7629/76) (Rep.) March 9, 1978, 13 D.R. 57; (9132/80) (Dec.) December 16, 1982, 31 D.R. 154, Art.5, para.1(a) applies even where by domestic law detention after the first instance is classed as detention on remand pending the appeal.

[68] *Grava v Italy*, July 10, 2003.

[69] e.g. (7341/76) (Rep.) March 4, 1978, 15 D.R. 35, the chief military prosecutor did not qualify; (17571/90) (Dec.) September 2, 1993, 75 D.R. 139, the Military Court of Appeal did; *Dacosta Silva v Spain*, (69966/01) November 2, 2006, a senior officer in the *Guardia Civil* did not qualify when imposing house arrest on a subordinate.

[70] *Weeks v UK*, March 2, 1987, Series A, No.114, 10 E.H.R.R 293, para.42.

terms of those objectives.[71] Sufficient causal connection between the conviction and detention has been found where a discretionary life prisoner is recalled to prison on revocation of his licence[72]; where the Court of Appeal has ordered that time spent in custody pending the appeal not be counted towards the sentence[73]; when orders for the preventive detention of convicted recidivists have been renewed[74]; where a convicted paedophile was retained in prison on preventive detention grounds[75]; and where two sentences for separate convictions were combined under domestic law to provide a life sentence.[76] However, where a prisoner sentenced to a mandatory term of life imprisonment for murder was released on licence and then subject to recall due to the risk of his committing further non-violent offences (i.e. fraud), the Court found that no sufficient causal connection between his detention after recall and the original sentence for murder.[77] Where due to a change in the law a prisoner was continued in preventive detention beyond the maximum authorised at the time of conviction, the Court considered the causal link between conviction and subsequent detention was broken.[78]

A sufficient causal connection exists where a convicted prisoner is transferred to serve his sentence in his own country, though the Court has flagged that problems might arise if an applicant is likely to serve a flagrantly longer de facto sentence.[79]

Where a sentence of life imprisonment is imposed, even on a juvenile, by a competent court in accordance with domestic law, problems are unlikely to arise, as the Court generally considers that matters of appropriate sentence fall outside the Convention.[80] However, in *Leger v France*, concerning the exceptionally long detention of a life prisoner (over 40 years), a Chamber did appear to examine the justification of the measure, finding the imposition of the sentence for a brutal murder of a child had not been arbitrary and that subsequent decisions refusing release had been appropriately motivated by his continuing dangerousness.[81] The case referred to the Grand Chamber was, however, struck off following the death of the applicant.

If a "conviction" results from proceedings which were a "flagrant denial of justice", i.e. were "manifestly contrary to the provisions of Article 6 or the principles embodied therein", the resulting deprivation of liberty would not be justified under Art.5 para.1(a).[82]

[71] *Van Droogenbroeck v Belgium*, June 24, 1982, Series A, No.50, 4 E.H.R.R. 443, para.40. See *Weeks*, fn.70 above, para.51, recall to prison of a discretionary lifer due to his aggressive, unstable behaviour was not arbitrary or unreasonable in terms of the objectives of the sentence imposed on him.

[72] *Weeks*, fn.70 above.

[73] *Monnell and Morris v UK*, March 2, 1987, Series A, No.115, 10 E.H.R.R. 205.

[74] e.g. (9167/80) (Dec.) October 15, 1981, 26 D.R. 248.

[75] *De Schepper v Belgium*, October 13, 2009, paras 38–50.

[76] *Garagin v Italy*, (33290/07) (Dec.) April 29, 2008.

[77] *Stafford v UK*, May 28, 2002, ECHR 2002–IV, paras 81–82, the Government could not claim any power to detain the applicant to prevent future indeterminate offending under the original sentence.

[78] *M v Germany*, December 17, 2009.

[79] *Veermäe v Finland*, (38704/03) (Dec.) March 15, 2005.

[80] *V v UK*, December 16, 1999, ECHR 1999–IX, para.104.

[81] *Leger v France*, April 11, 2006, paras 64–77.

[82] *Ilaşcu v Moldova and Russia*, July 8, 2004, ECHR 2004–VII, para.461, where the detention was imposed by a "court" set up by an illegal, unrecognised entity without a constitutional and legal basis reflecting a judicial tradition compatible with the Convention; see also *Stoichkov v Bulgaria*, March 24, 2005, violation where the applicant was detained after a refusal to re-open his conviction in absentia.

Enforcement by a Contracting State of a custodial sentence passed by the courts of another State falls within this exception, although the enforcing State should not provide assistance if the conviction is the result of a flagrant denial of justice.[83]

(b) Article 5, para.1(b): obligation imposed by law or non-compliance with order of the court

II–287 The two heads are not exclusive.

As concerns detention for non-compliance with the order of a court, it has covered: failure to pay a court fine[84]; failure to undergo medical examinations ordered by a court,[85] failure to comply with a decision to hand over children to a parent[86]; and failure to observe binding-over orders.[87] While non-payment of a fine has been included, the Court has expressed a view as to the growing archaicness of custodial penalties for failure to pay debts and left the matter open in *Gatt v Malta*. In that case, it held in any event that the length of detention imposed must not be disproportionate or fail to take into account the ability to pay; the imposition of over five years for failure to pay €23,000, where the applicant had been under strict bail conditions for the previous five years and unable to work, did not strike a fair balance.[88]

As concerns the head "in order to secure the fulfillment of an obligation imposed by law", this head of detention requires that a measure is taken to secure the execution of specific and concrete obligations. The obligation does not have to arise from a court order but may also derive from the law per se, although it must be sufficiently specific and concrete.[89] This has included: arrest for non-compliance with a compulsory residence order[90]; obligation to submit to a security check on entry to Great Britain[91]; committal by magistrates to secure fulfilment of the obligation to pay the community charge[92]; and detention in order to establish a person's identity.[93]

The aim of the detention must be to secure the fulfilment of the obligation, not to punish.[94] In *McVeigh v UK*,[95] the Commission noted that as soon as the obligation had been fulfilled, the basis for the detention under this leg ceased.[96] It was also of

[83] e.g. *Drozd and Janousek*, fn.36 above; (16462/90) (Dec.) January 19, 1994, 76 D.R. 18.
[84] *Airey v Ireland*, (6289/73) (Dec.) July 7, 1977, 8 D.R. 42.
[85] See *X v Austria*, (8278/78) (Dec.) December 13, 1979, 18 D.R. 154; and *X v FRG*, (6659/74) December 10, 1975.
[86] *Paradis v Germany*, (4065/04) (Dec.) September 4, 2007.
[87] e.g. *Steel v UK*, September 23, 1998, R.J.D. 1998–VII, paras 69–70.
[88] *Gatt v Malta*, July 27, 2010, paras 37–43.
[89] *Guzzardi*, fn.4 above, para.101, where the warning of a police chief to a *mafiosi* suspect was not sufficient; *Lawless v Ireland*, (Rep.) December 19, 1959, measures to secure public order and State security were not concerned with the execution of specific obligations.
[90] (8916/80) (Dec.) October 7, 1980, 21 D.R. 250; see, however, *Ciulla*, fn.2 above, where the arrest and detention predated the compulsory residence requirement and so fell outside Art.5, para.1(b).
[91] *McVeigh v UK*, (8022/77) etc. (Rep.) March 18, 1981, 25 D.R. 15.
[92] *Benham v UK*, June 10, 1996, R.J.D. 1996–III, No.10, 22 E.H.R.R. 293, para.39.
[93] (16810/90) (Dec.) September 9, 1992, 73 D.R. 136; *Vasileva v Denmark*, September 25, 2003, para.40.
[94] (7341/76) (Rep.) April 3, 1978, 15 D.R. 35, punishment for breach of military discipline; (10600/83) (Dec.) October 14, 1985, 45 D.R. 155, detention of conscientious objector to secure acceptance of military service.
[95] See fn.91 above.
[96] See also *Nowicka v Poland*, December 3, 2002, para.64, violation found where the applicant's detention continued after the psychiatric examination.

the view that, while there was no express requirement to that effect, the provision was primarily intended to cover the situation where a person has wilfully or negligently failed to perform an obligation. Therefore, while detention in the absence of a prior breach of duty was not excluded, it considered that in order to exclude arbitrary deprivation of liberty the circumstances had to warrant the use of detention to secure the obligation, and generally it would be required to show that the person was given an opportunity to fulfil the obligation and had failed to comply.[97] Imprisonment imposed in respect of non-payment of a fine has been held to be punitive, detention rarely facilitating a person's fulfilment of a financial burden, particularly where already indigent.[98]

Relying on *McVeigh*, the Court has stated that a balance must be drawn between the importance in a democratic society of securing the immediate fulfilment of the obligation and the importance of the right to liberty, in which balance duration is a significant factor. Thus, in *Nowicka v Poland*, the detention of the applicant for 83 days, for the purpose of obtaining two psychiatric examinations in the context of a private neighbour dispute, disclosed a violation, particularly as she was held for weeks before each examination and post-examination.[99] In *Vasileva v Denmark*, detention for more than 13 hours of a 67-year-old woman, who had refused to give the police information about her identity, was found to exceed the time proportionate to the cause of her detention.[100] Where an applicant had determinedly resisted and blocked an order to return children to the custodial parent, an order of detention which lasted for six months was not found disproportionate given the importance of enforcing the law in child abduction cases, the lack of an effective alternative and the ability for her to apply to end the detention.[101]

(c) *Article 5, para.1(c): suspicion of committing a criminal offence, etc.*

See Pt IIB, s.4: Arrest. II–288

(d) *Article 5, para.1(d): detention of minors*

The purpose of the deprivation of liberty of a minor must be either for "educational supervision" or the purpose of bringing the minor before the competent legal authority. Where, in *Bouamar v Belgium*, a 16-year-old juvenile was held in a remand prison without any purpose of bringing proceedings, the Court rejected the Government's claim that the measure was part of an educative programme in a II–289

97 Despite any prior failure by the applicants, their arrest and detention on entry to Great Britain was justified exceptionally by the exigencies of fighting terrorism and the short duration of the measures. The Commission talked of striking a balance between the need to ensure the fulfilment of the obligation and the right to liberty. See also (10719/84) (Dec.) May 13, 1987, 52 D.R. 111, where it was acceptable to hold a person for several hours at a police station for an identity check.

98 *Gatt*, fn.88 above, para.48. The Court also criticised the lack of proper guidelines governing enforcement of bail conditions and lack of ceilings on penalties, which had led to the somewhat bizarre result of the applicant being subject to detention for over five years for a curfew irregularity.

99 See fn.96 above.

100 The applicant had been in dispute with a bus ticket collector. The Court looked at the earlier Commission cases, noting the special context of terrorist checks in *McVeigh* and implying that more than six hours would not be acceptable in normal circumstances. No problem arose for one hour's detention while police checked the applicant's identity in *Novotka v Slovakia*, (47244/99) (Dec.) November 4, 2003.

101 *Paradis v Germany*, (4065/04) (Dec.) September 4, 2007.

general sense. The only reason for the placement was that no proper place was available and there were no staff or facilities available in the prison to carry out any educational aim.[102] However, more recently, the Court has commented that "educational supervision" is not to be equated rigidly with notions of classroom teaching and includes many aspects of the exercise by a local authority of parental rights for the benefit and protection of the person concerned. Thus, the detention of a teenager in a secure centre for seriously disturbed young people, which had a multi-disciplinary approach, was covered even though the applicant attended few, if any, classes.[103] A month in a juvenile holding centre for unspecified purposes, where the two minors did not participate in any form of programme or education, fell outside para.1(d).[104]

Detention of a minor held for observation in a specialist centre was found to be for the purpose of bringing him before the competent legal authority, since he was suspected of committing offences and was to be brought before the Juvenile Commission in due course. The length of time (eight months) was not so excessive or unjustifiable as to cast doubt on the genuine purpose of the detention, i.e. to obtain medical reports.[105] However, the detention of two minors, who had confessed to theft, for one month in a juvenile holding centre was not regarded as for the purpose of being brought before a legal authority as criminal proceedings had not in fact been commenced until after they had been released.[106]

(e) Article 5, para.1(e): mental health patients, vagrants, alcoholics, prevention of infectious diseases, etc.

II–290 The link between the categories under this sub-paragraph is that the persons concerned may be deprived of their liberty either to be given medical treatment or because of considerations dictated by social policy, or on both medical and social grounds. The Court takes the view that the predominant reason why the Convention allows their deprivation of liberty is not only that they are dangerous for public safety but also that their own interests may necessitate their detention.[107]

For mentally ill persons, see Pt IIB, s.32: Mental health.

In respect of vagrants, the Court in *De Wilde* accepted the Belgian definition of persons without fixed abode or means of subsistence and no regular trade or profession. The detention applied to the applicants in the case was found to fall within that definition and disclosed no arbitrariness in the decision or procedure whereby they were placed at the disposal of the Government.[108]

The term "alcoholics" has been held to cover not only those in a clinical state of alcoholism but also those whose conduct and behaviour under the influence of alcohol pose a threat to public order or to themselves.[109] In *Witold Litwa v Poland*,

[102] *Bouamar v Belgium*, February 29, 1988, Series A, No.129.

[103] *Koniarska*, fn.16 above. However, in *DG v Ireland*, fn.16 above, there was a breach where a teenager was held for a month in a penal institution, where any educational or recreational facilities were entirely voluntary and optional.

[104] *Ichin v Ukraine*, December 21, 2010, para.37.

[105] (8500/79) (Dec.) December 14, 1979, 18 D.R. 238.

[106] *Ichin v Ukraine*, fn.104 above, paras 38–39.

[107] *Witold Litwa*, fn.3 above, para.60.

[108] In *Guzzardi*, fn.4 above, the Government failed in their argument that mafia suspects were subject to restrictions as a type of vagrant.

[109] *Witold*, fn.3 above, paras 61–62; *Hafsteinsdottir*, fn.47 above, para.42, arrest was justified on this ground where the applicant was abusive, threatened to strike police officers and slammed a bin; *Kharin v Russia*, February 3, 2011, para.44, aggressive behaviour, attempt to start a fight and causing a disturbance qualified.

where the applicant, who was severely sight-impaired, was taken for over six hours to a sobering up centre, the Court found the detention arbitrary as it was based on a rather trivial factual basis and other less severe measures, provided for by law, such as being escorted home, had not apparently been considered.[110] A domestic ground of detaining a drunken person due to undignified or offensive appearance in public was not considered as sufficient to justify taking away their liberty.[111] It is not apparently necessary that the authorities prove the state of drunkenness by objective medical tests; the opinion of a medically qualified person suffices.[112]

Even fewer cases have arisen concerning detention for quarantine purposes. In the principal case to date, *Enhorn v Sweden*, the Court laid down the criteria that the spreading of the infectious disease must be dangerous to public health or safety and that the detention of the person infected is the last resort in order to prevent the spreading of the disease: less severe measures should have been considered and found to be insufficient to safeguard the public interest. In the particular case, it found a violation as, although the HIV virus was dangerous to public health and safety, the compulsory isolation order on the applicant over seven years was not justified by his conduct and other measures, such as psychiatric counselling, had not been tried.[113]

As in mental health cases, as soon as the criteria are no longer fulfilled, the basis for detention ceases to exist.[114]

(f) Article 5, para.1(f): pending expulsion or extradition

See Pt IIB, s.11: Detention pending extradition and expulsion. II–291

7. Types of detention not covered by the exceptions

Where a court has ordered release, some delay in carrying out the decision may be inevitable although the authorities should keep this to a minimum. Where an applicant remained in custody for a further seven hours, while certain formalities were being carried out, the Court found no violation.[115] The authorities are held strictly accountable for the lapse of time before release and a violation was found where the applicant was released a day late when the documents indicating that she had satisfied the conditions for release had been sent to the prison the previous afternoon.[116] Nor was the Court impressed by the Government's excuse where the court order for release on Friday afternoon was not implemented until after the weekend as the prison administrative staff had already left.[117] Where applicants have been deliberately retained in custody pending the authorities' intention to apply II–292

[110] Contrast *HD v Poland*, (33310/96) (Dec.) June 7, 2001, where the detention of the applicant was lawful—her conduct having been "rowdy", "aggressive", etc.

[111] *Kharin v Russia*, fn.109, para.43.

[112] *Kharin v Russia*, fn.109, paras 38–39.

[113] *Enhorn v Sweden*, January 25, 2005, ECHR 2005–1.

[114] *Enhorn*, fn.113 above, para.44.

[115] *Giulia Manzoni v Italy*, July 1, 1997, R.J.D. 1997–IV, No.41.

[116] *Bojinov v Bulgaria*, October 28, 2004. See also *Calmanovici v Romania*, July 1, 2008, paras 77–80, violation where there was a 16–hour delay between the court order for release becoming effective and the actual release.

[117] *Ogica v Romania*, May 27, 2010, para.64.

other measures, the detention has been found to fall outside the exceptions allowed by Art.5.[118] Detention on arrest which exceeded the statutory maximum of 12 hours by 45 minutes was also found to disclose a violation in *KF v Germany*.[119] It distinguished the cases in which some delay in release had been accepted, since in those cases the period of detention was not laid down in advance by statute, but ended as a result of a court order; in *KF v Germany* the maximum period was laid down in law as obligatory and the authorities were under a duty to comply with it. Yet a further refinement is illustrated by a case where a person was detained essentially for half an hour beyond the 72-hour statutory arrest period without a legal basis. Here the Court considered that as the prosecutor had lodged the application with the court to obtain further lawful detention within the proper time-limit and the hearing commenced only half an hour after the expiry of the time-limit, the delay was acceptable, and the situation distinguishable from the *KF* case, apparently as there was no imminent regularisation of the situation in that case.[120]

Internment or detention without trial is excluded. In *Lawless v Ireland*, the ministerial power to detain persons suspected of being engaged in activities prejudicial to public order or State security could not be considered as detention for failure to comply with an order of court or to secure the fulfilment of an obligation prescribed by law, nor for the purpose of bringing the person before a court under Art.5, para.1(c). In *Ireland v UK*, the internment power in Northern Ireland fell outside Art.5, para.1(c), since whether or not persons were in fact suspected on reasonable grounds of involvement in terrorist offences, their detention was not for the purpose of bringing them before a judicial authority which was the other essential element of para.1(c).[121] More recently, internment without trial or charge of alien terrorist suspects was struck down as outside the list of exceptions, the Court rejecting the Government argument that Art.5 permitted a balance to be struck between the individual's right to liberty and the State's interest in protecting its population from terrorist threat.[122]

It has been left open whether detention outside the permitted grounds could be justified where required by other international obligations imposed on the Contracting State. The United Kingdom Government sought to argue that detention without trial of terrorist suspects in Iraq was carried out as part of its functions in keeping order under a UN resolution. The Court found that, while the UN resolution authorised use in general terms of various security measures, it could not be said that it required the indefinite detention without charge of the applicant; there was no conflict between the United Kingdom's Convention and UN obligations and this ground of exception did not have to be decided.[123]

Other examples of detention not permitted by Art.5, para.1 include deprivation of liberty of a person confined and placed under guardianship for extravagance and

[118] *Quinn v France*, March 22, 1995, Series A, No.311, 21 E.H.R.R. 529; *Doran v Netherlands*, (15268/89) (Rep.) July 8, 1993. Also *Labita v Italy*, April 6, 2000, ECHR 2000–IV, paras 172–173, where 12 hours' detention after acquittal was not due to relevant administrative formalities but merely the absence of the registration officer.

[119] The Commission found that a delay of 45 minutes was not such as to deprive the applicant of his liberty in an arbitrary manner contrary to the spirit and purpose of Art.5, para.1: *KF v Germany*, (Rep.) September 10, 1996.

[120] *Ignatenco v Moldova*, February 8, 2011, para.68.

[121] However, in both *Lawless*, fn.89 above, and *Ireland v UK*, January 18, 1978, Series A, No.25, 2 E.H.R.R. 25, valid derogations under Art.15 had been lodged.

[122] *A and Others v UK*, February 19, 2009, ECHR 2009–. . . , paras 171–172.

[123] *Al Jedda v UK*, July 7, 2011, ECHR 2011–. . . , paras 98–110.

idleness[124]; possibly, collusion by State agents with private individuals to bring a person living abroad within State territory against his will[125]; preventive measures, including compulsory residence, based on a policy of general prevention against dangerous individuals such as *mafiosi* (without reference to the commission of any specific offence)[126]; detention of cult members for "deprogramming" purposes[127]; preventive detention in connection with unspecified banditism and criminal association where no criminal proceedings were pending[128]; and extra-territorial measures seizing the applicant outside the Contracting State, where that State has acted in a manner inconsistent with the sovereignty of the host State and contrary to international law.[129] Where an applicant was arrested and detained in order to put pressure on his fugitive brother, the Court found that this use of detention to exert moral pressure was not compatible with Art.5: even if the authorities did have grounds for suspicion against the applicant himself, as later alleged, the Court frowned on the misleading way in which this was never made properly apparent at the time.[130]

Cross-reference

Part IIB, s.4: Arrest.
Part IIB, s.11: Detention pending extradition and expulsion.
Part IIB, s.18: Extradition.
Part IIB, s.32: Mental health.
Part IIB, s.35: Pre-trial detention.
Part IIB, s.42: Review of detention

[124] (7397/76) (Dec.) December 13, 1977, 11 D.R. 58, settled (Rep.) March 8, 1979, 15 D.R. 105.
[125] *Stocké v Germany*, (Rep.) March 19, 1991, Series A, No.199, the Commission considered this, if proved, might render arrest and subsequent detention unlawful within the meaning of Art.5, para.1; see, however, *Reinette v France*, (14009/88) (Dec.) October 2, 1989, 63 D.R. 189, where a suspected terrorist on St Vincent was dragged onto a runway near a French military plane where officers executed letters rogatory, the Commission found no reason why co-operation between St Vincent and French authorities could raise problems under Art.5.
[126] *Guzzardi*, fn.4 above, para.102; see also *Ciulla*, fn.2 above, the arrest and detention predated the court order of compulsory residence and thus fell outside Art.5, para.1(b).
[127] *Riera Blume*, fn.5 above.
[128] *Jecius*, fn.53 above.
[129] *Ocalan*, fn.29 above, paras 93–99, in particular para.90, the arrest of Ocalan by Turkish officials in Nairobi was, however, conducted in co-operation with the Kenyan authorities.
[130] *Giorgi Nikolaishvili v Georgia*, January 13, 2009, paras 56–59.

10. Derogation: states of emergency

Key provision:

II–293 Article 15 (derogation from Convention obligations in time of war or public emergency).

Key case-law:

Lawless v Ireland, July 1, 1961, Series A, No.3, 1 E.H.R.R. 15; *Ireland v UK*, January 18, 1978, Series A, No.25, 2 E.H.R.R. 25; *Brannigan and McBride v UK*, May 26, 1993, Series A, No.258–B, 17 E.H.R.R. 539; *Aksoy v Turkey*, December 18, 1996, R.J.D. 1996–VI, No.26, 23 E.H.R.R. 553; *Sakik v Turkey*, November 26, 1997, R.J.D. 1997–VII, No.58; *A and Others v UK*, February 19, 2009, ECHR 2009–. . .

1. General considerations

II–294 Article 15 permits a Contracting State to derogate from its obligations under the Convention, excepting Arts 2 (save in respect of deaths resulting from lawful acts of war), 3, 4 and 7 in time of war or other public emergency threatening the life of the nation, and to the extent strictly required by the exigencies of the situation.

In derogation cases the Convention organs have adopted the approach of examining the substantive complaint first, and then, if there is a violation, proceeding to examine whether it is covered by the derogation in question.[1] This leaves no uncertainty as to what measures are in breach of the Convention. While there is a requirement of strict limitation of derogations to the exigencies of the crisis, in practice the Convention organs have given States considerable leeway.

The latest derogation lodged in respect of the United Kingdom (concerning the "war against terrorism" response to the September 11 attacks and extended powers of arrest and detention) has been withdrawn.[2]

2. Obligation to inform the Secretary General of the Council of Europe

II–295 The Secretary General should be informed without undue delay of the reasons for the derogation and the measures being taken. This appears to require identification of the laws concerned, and possibly also provision of the texts concerned.[3]

[1] Violations of Art.5 were found in respect of internment without trial in *Lawless v UK*, July 1, 1961, Series A, No.3, 1 E.H.R.R. 15, Arts 5, paras 1(c) and 3; *Ireland v UK*, January 18, 1978, Series A, No.25, 2 E.H.R.R. 25, extra judicial detention imposed on terrorist suspects was not in compliance with Arts 5, paras 1(c), 2, 3 or 4; *Brannigan and McBride v UK*, May 26, 1993, Series A, No.258–B, 17 E.H.R.R. 539, there the power to hold persons for up to seven days without being brought before a judge infringed the requirement of promptness in Art.5, para.3, as did the 14–day period in *Aksoy v Turkey*, December 18, 1996, R.J.D. 1996–VI, No.26, 23 E.H.R.R. 553. In all but *Aksoy*, the derogation conformed with the requirements of Art.15.

[2] Declaration, dated December 18, 2001, setting out the extended power of arrest and detention provided in the Anti-terrorism, Crime and Security Act 2001 and derogating from Art.5, para.1(f). Previously the UK had a derogation in place in respect of the Northern Ireland conflict, which was lifted in February 2001, following the peace process. Turkey, until recently, had derogations concerning primarily the security situation in the southeast.

[3] In *Lawless*, fn.1 above, the Irish Government had provided a copy of the relevant Proclamation and Act and the reasons were given as being "to prevent the commission of offences against the public peace and order and to prevent the maintaining of military or armed forces other than those authorised by the Constitution". No issue arose from notification of the UK derogations in *Ireland v UK* and *Brannigan and McBride*, see fn.1 above.

In *Aksoy*, where compliance was not adverted to before the Commission, the Court stated that it could raise the point of its own motion, though in view of its finding that the measure was not strictly required, it did not do so. There was a strong hint that the Turkish notification to the Secretary General was insufficient: no specific measures relating to Art.5 had been detailed beyond a reference to the power of the State of Emergency Governor, which was irrelevant to the case.[4]

Where a derogation is expressed as applying to a particular part of a country, the State cannot rely on the derogation applying to events taking part elsewhere, even if it was part of a response to the general problem underlying the derogation.[5]

There is no requirement for the Contracting State to promulgate the notice of derogation in its territory.[6]

3. Time of war

No derogation concerning a state of war has yet been in issue. II–296

4. State of emergency threatening the life of the nation

This refers to an exceptional situation of crisis or emergency which affects the whole population and constitutes a threat to the organised life of the community.[7] The Court allows a wide margin of appreciation. It is primarily for the Contracting State with its responsibility for the life of the nation to determine whether that life is threatened by a public emergency and, if so, how far it is necessary to go to overcome it. By reason of their direct and continuous contact with the pressing needs of the moment, the national authorities are in a better position than international judges to decide both on the presence of such an emergency and the nature and extent of the derogations necessary to avert it. The margin of appreciation is not altogether unlimited, the Convention organs being empowered to rule on whether States have gone beyond the extent strictly required by the exigencies of the crisis.[8] II–297

In *Brannigan and McBride*, the Court rejected the submissions of the applicants and intervenors, arguing against a wide margin of appreciation, particularly where the crisis was of a quasi-permanent nature as in Northern Ireland, and the rights essential for the protection of detainees. It merely repeated its earlier view and stated that in exercising its supervision it would give appropriate weight to relevant factors such as the nature of the rights affected, the circumstances leading to and the duration of the emergency situation.[9] Arguments that an emergency had to be "temporary" were also rejected in *A and Others v UK*, the Court noting that crises can last for many years and that the anti-terrorism measure in response to the September 11 attacks on the US were reviewed every year.

[4] *Aksoy*, fn.1 above, paras 31–32.

[5] *Sakik v Turkey*, November 26, 1997, R.J.D. 1997–VII, No.58, paras 36–39, the derogation, aimed at fighting terrorism, was framed as applying to the state of emergency region and the arrest of the applicants took place elsewhere; see also *Abdulsamet Yaman v Turkey*, November 2, 2004, paras 68–69.

[6] *Lawless*, fn.1 above, para.47.

[7] *Lawless*, fn.1 above, para.28.

[8] *Ireland v UK*, fn.1 above, para.207; *Lawless*, fn.1 above, para.28; *A and Others v UK*, February 19, 2009, ECHR 2009–. . . , para.180.

[9] *Brannigan and McBride*, see fn.1 above, paras 41–43.

The existence of an emergency claimed by a Government has not yet been rejected. In *Lawless*, the Court found that the existence of such an emergency was reasonably deduced by Irish Government having regard, inter alia, to the existence on their territory of a secret army engaged in unconstitutional activities and using violence to attain its aims, the operation of this army outside its territory seriously jeopardising its relations with its neighbour and the steady, alarming increase in terrorist activities from 1956–1957. The existence of such an emergency at the relevant time (early 1970s) was not in issue in the *Ireland v UK* case. The issue was also not contested in the *Aksoy* case, in relation to the extent and impact of PKK activity in southeast Turkey.

The nature of the situation arising from the attacks on September 11, 2001, which was claimed by the UK Government to justify a derogation of Art.5 rights in respect of foreign nationals suspected of involvement in terrorism, was challenged in *A and Others v UK*. The applicants relied on the view of Lord Hoffman that an emergency had to do more than threaten serious physical damage and loss of life; it should threaten the institutions of a country or the existence of civil society. However, the Court stated that it took a broader view and contented itself in giving weight to the view of Parliament and adopting the conclusion of the majority of the House of Lords that an emergency existed. While remarking that the United Kingdom was the only Contracting State that had felt the need to derogate following 9/11, the Court noted that it was for each Government as guardians of their citizens to assess the threat on the basis of the facts known to them.[10]

5. "Strictly required by the exigencies of the situation"

II–298 The Court has accepted measures as justified by this high standard even where there was, arguably, considerable doubt as to their efficacy or necessity. It has paid considerable attention to the existence of safeguards mitigating against abuse and given weight to the willingness of the authorities to introduce additional safeguards as the situation evolves. Notably, in one of the few cases, *Aksoy*, where the derogation fell foul of this requirement, the Government failed to provide a convincing reason for the length of time of incommunicado detention and there was a manifest lack of safeguards against abuse.

In *Lawless* and *Ireland v UK*, the Court accepted the arguments that the ordinary law had proved unable to check terrorism and steps were necessary to counter the difficulties of obtaining evidence to convict persons involved with the IRA due to the secret and terrorist nature of the groups and the fear inspired by them. In *Ireland v UK*, the Court found that a power to detain someone unsuspected of a crime or offence for the purposes of obtaining information could only be justified in very exceptionable circumstances, but that these existed in Northern Ireland at this time (e.g. the alleged need to question persons who were too scared to give evidence freely). The Court did not accept the argument that the use of extra-judicial detention was ineffectual (the Irish Government stated it clearly did not brake terrorism while the United Kingdom had abandoned it gradually and then wholly). The Court stated that it was not its role to judge in the place of the UK Government what was the most prudent or most expedient policy to combat terrorism and it had to exercise its power of supervision, not in light of retrospective

[10] *A and Others v UK*, fn.8 above, para.180.

considerations, but only having regard to the conditions and circumstances reigning at the time.

In contrast, in *Aksoy*, which concerned the power to detain for up to 30 days,[11] the Court acknowledged the difficulties of investigating terrorist crimes but found the period unacceptable, as being exceptionally long and leaving the applicant vulnerable to arbitrary interference with the right to liberty and to torture. It noted a lack of detailed reasons as to why judicial intervention was not practicable. The Government had referred solely to difficulties of investigations in a vast geographical area.

The factor of abuse of power may be relevant. In *Lawless*, the Court included in its reasoning that it had found no indication that the powers were used against the applicant for any other purpose than that for which they were granted (e.g. suspected involvement with the IRA).

In *Brannigan and McBride v UK*, it was argued that the derogations were not a genuine response to an emergency situation but to avoid implementing the Court's decision in *Brogan v UK*, where the power of detention of terrorist suspects for up to seven days was found in breach of Art.5, para.3. The Court observed that the power had been considered necessary under emergency measures in effect since 1974 to deal with terrorism and found that the derogation was clearly linked to the persistence of the emergency situation. As regarded the apparent interim nature of the derogation, the Court found that, as this was expressed to be pending review of other possibilities of judicial control, this disclosed a process of continued reflection entirely in keeping with the spirit of Art.15. It found that absence of judicial control could be regarded as necessary having regard to the various reports on terrorism issued in relation to the difficulties of investigating and prosecuting terrorist crime. It noted, without rejecting, the Government's view that it was essential to prevent disclosure to the detainee and his legal advisers of the information on which the extension of detention was required and that the independence of the judiciary would be compromised if judges were involved in the granting of extensions, particularly as in Northern Ireland the judiciary was small and vulnerable to attack and the Government understandably attached importance to public confidence in their independence.

On the issue of safeguards, recourse to formal courts has not been required, but weight has been given to any participation by courts or the judiciary in a reviewing procedure of the measures as applied.[12] Reference has also been made to the constant supervision by Parliament or other independent bodies, though the practical effectiveness of this is not apparent.[13] In *Ireland v UK*, where the safeguards were less apparent or effective than in *Lawless*, the Court placed emphasis on the fact that the authorities responded to the situation by evolving towards protecting individual liberties in the measures as amended and commented that while the provision of satisfactory judicial, or at least administrative, remedies was desirable from the outset, it would be unrealistic not to distinguish the phases. It could not be

[11] The applicant was held for 14 days.

[12] In *Lawless*, fn.1 above, reference is made to a detention commission (two of the three members were judges); in *Ireland v UK*, fn.1 above, to a valuable, if limited, recourse to the courts and a certain measure of protection from an advisory committee, commissioners and appeal tribunal; and in *Brannigan and McBride*, fn.1 above, to regular independent review of the legislation.

[13] See *Marshall v UK*, (41571/98) (Dec.) July 10, 2001, the Court dismissed objections that the annual Parliamentary debate or executive review of the measures were meaningless exercises—it was enough that the authorities addressed the issues with sufficient frequency.

expected of a State struggling against a public emergency to render itself defenceless by being required to provide complete safeguards from the outset. On this view, Art.15 allows, pragmatically, for progressive adaptations in providing human rights protection, without the apparent need to establish that the initial draconian response was in fact necessary.

Similarly, leeway is given as regards the timing of the complete removal of restrictions. Where in 1998 an applicant was held for seven days without being brought before a judge, it was argued that the security situation in Northern Ireland had been transformed due to the peace process and the power was no longer justified. The Court found that it could still be said that the measures were required by a state of emergency, noting that outbreaks of terrorist violence were still occurring and emphasising that the national authorities were best placed to decide both the presence of an emergency and the nature and scope of the derogation necessary to avoid it.[14]

In *Aksoy*, the Court found insufficient safeguards available to protect detainees. There was a denial of access to lawyers, doctors, relatives and friends which left the applicant completely at the mercy of those holding him. The Government's reliance on supervision by public prosecutor and the prohibition of torture in Turkish law was not enough.[15]

Measures which, on their face, apply arbitrarily to a particular group of people may offend, irrespective of applicable safeguards and procedures. In *A and Others v UK*, emergency measures providing for the detention of alien terrorist suspects without trial post-9/11 was not found to be "strictly required" as they discriminated unjustifiably between national and non-nationals. The Court upheld the conclusions of the House of Lords and domestic courts who had found, inter alia, that the threat was not any greater from the latter category.

6. Consistency with other obligations under international law

II–299 The only case where other international obligations were identified was *Brannigan and McBride*, where the applicants referred to the UK's obligations under the International Covenant and Civil and Political Rights and claimed that it was essential for valid derogation from Art.4 of the Covenant that the derogation had been officially proclaimed. The Court noted that the Secretary of State had made a statement to the House of Commons detailing the reasons for the derogation, which was sufficiently formal and public in its view.

[14] *Marshall*, fn.14 above.

[15] In contrast to *Brannigan and McBride*, fn.1 above, where the Court found important measures of protection against arbitrary detention, e.g. habeas corpus, the right to see a solicitor after 48 hours and to inform a relative or friend.

11. Detention pending extradition and expulsion

Key provisions:

Article 5, paras 1 and 1(f) (lawful detention pending extradition or expulsion) and para.4 (review of lawfulness of detention). II–300

Key case-law:

Bozano v France, December 18, 1986, Series A, No.111, 9 E.H.R.R. 297; *Soering v UK*, July 7, 1989, Series A, No.161, 11 E.H.R.R 439; *Kolompar v Belgium*, September 24, 1992, Series A, No.235–C, 16 E.H.R.R. 197; *Quinn v France*, March 22, 1995, Series A, No.311, 21 E.H.R.R. 529; *Chahal v UK*, November 15, 1996, R.J.D. 1996–V, No.22, 23 E.H.R.R. 413; *Dougoz v Greece*, March 6, 2001, ECHR 2001–II; *Slivenko v Latvia*, October 9, 2003, ECHR 2003–XI; *Saadi v UK*, January 29, 2008, ECHR 2008–I; *A and Others v UK*, February 19, 2009, ECHR 2009–. . .

1. General considerations

II–301 Article 5 para.1(f) permits the lawful arrest or detention of a person in two circumstances. The first is arrest or detention to prevent the person effecting an unauthorised entry into the country. The second is the arrest or detention of a person against whom action is being taken with a view to deportation or extradition. It should be noted that a person allowed temporary admission to a country, pending decision on his status, may still be regarded as someone against whom measures can be taken to prevent "unauthorised" entry.[1]

Undue length of detention may render it incompatible with this provision. Conditions of the detention may also raise issues under Art.3 as disclosing inhuman and degrading treatment.[2]

2. Lawfulness

II–302 The detention must be "in accordance with a procedure prescribed by law" and also be "lawful".[3] The dominant theme is the prevention of arbitrariness. (See Pt IIB, Deprivation of liberty.)

In *Chinoy v UK*, where the applicant complained that in the extradition proceedings in the United Kingdom the magistrate had regard to tapes allegedly obtained in breach of French law, the Commission found no breach of the lawfulness

[1] *Saadi v UK*, January 29, 2008, ECHR 2008–I, paras 61–66.

[2] e.g. *Dougoz*, where the serious overcrowding and lack of sleeping facilities where the applicant was held for several months pending his expulsion breached Art.3. See Pt IIB, s.36: Prisoners' rights, sub-s.3: Conditions of confinement and Pt IIB, s.46: Torture, inhuman and degrading treatment.

[3] e.g. *Doran v Netherlands*, (15268/89) (Rep.) July 8, 1993, where notwithstanding the order to release of the applicant the public prosecutor told the prison to retain him pending an intended extradition, the detention was not in accordance with a procedure prescribed by law; *Dougoz*, where the detention of the applicant on the opinion of a public prosecutor as to the applicability by analogy of a ministerial decision on administrative expulsion was not based on a "law" of sufficient "quality" within the meaning of the Court's case-law; *S.D. v Greece*, June 11, 2009, where there was no provision under domestic law to detain an asylum-seeker before his asylum claim was heard since until then he could not be expelled.

criteria of the detention since the use was not in breach of English law and not arbitrary.[4] Where steps are taken by the authorities by way of "disguised extradition", issues may however arise as to the lawfulness. In *Bozano v France*, the French courts had refused an extradition request. The procedure whereby the police proceeded to enforce a deportation order, which had the effect of delivering the applicant to the requesting State, was found by the Court to disclose arbitrariness, in particular having regard to the way in which it was executed, suddenly and forcibly, preventing the applicant from making use of any remedies theoretically available to him and not giving him the choice of destination.[5] Elements of bad faith and deception may thus render detention arbitrary, as in *Conka v Belgium* where the applicants were lured to the police station under false pretences and expelled in such a manner as to subvert any of the safeguards required by Art.5.[6]

Notions of legal certainty may play a role in findings of lack of lawfulness and arbitrariness. Where the applicable regime and safeguards to detention pending extradition were subject to confusion and contradictory approaches, the Court considered that the provisions of law were not sufficiently precise or foreseeable in their application and thus failed to protect the detainees from arbitrariness.[7] On the same basis, even if there is a legal basis for the detention, failure to provide "procedure prescribed by law" governing the modalities of the detention, in particular setting out safeguards, will fall foul of the Convention requirements under Art.5.[8]

The place and conditions of detention may also render a measure "unlawful" or "arbitrary" for the purposes of Art.5, as where an extremely vulnerable five-year-old unaccompanied child was held in unsuitable adult detention facilities pending her return to Kinshasa. This disclosed a failure by the Belgian authorities to provide her with sufficient protection of her right to liberty.[9] Where an asylum-seeker was placed in a centre adapted for asylum seekers with facilities, inter alia, for recreation, medical care and legal assistance, the detention was free from arbitrariness in that regard.[10]

Flaws in a detention order will not necessarily render the period of detention unlawful within the meaning of Art.5, para.1, particularly where the putative error

[4] *Chinoy v UK*, (15199/89) (Dec.) September 4,1991.

[5] See also *Iskandarov v Russia*, September 23, 2010, paras 148–152, flagrant flouting of decision refusing of an extradition request through unlawful removal by the police, aggravated by unacknowledged nature of the detention, violation.

[6] February 5, 2002. Contrast *Al-Moayad v Germany*, (35865/03) (Dec.) February 20, 2007, where the applicant had been tricked onto German soil, the Court noted that it was not the respondent Government or anyone for whom they were responsible that had been involved in any deception; no arbitrariness or unlawfulness in the German authorities detaining the applicant for extradition purposes in the circumstances.

[7] *Nasrulloyev v Russia*, October 11, 2007, paras 72–78, in particular it was not sufficiently clear whether persons detained pending extradition fell under the provisions of the Criminal Code which imposed the safeguards of regular judicial review and time-limits on the maximum length of detention.

[8] *Soldatenko v Ukraine*, October 23, 2008, paras 112–114, the Minsk Convention, as part of the legal order, gave the legal basis to detain the applicant pending extradition, but neither it nor ordinary domestic law set out the procedure applicable to such detention.

[9] *Mubilanzila Mayeka and Kaniki Mitunga v Belgium*, October 12, 2006, paras 95–105. See also *Muskhadzhiyeva and Others v Belgium*, January 19, 2010, breach due to the detention of four minors (three months to seven years' old) in an adult holding centre for a month; it was irrelevant that they were with their mother during this period; *Rahimi v Greece*, April 5, 2011, paras 102–110, a 16-year-old held automatically for two days, in appalling conditions, without regard to the overriding principle of the best interests of the child.

[10] *Saadi v UK*, fn.1 above, para.78.

is immediately detected and redressed by the release of the persons concerned.[11] Failure to comply with domestic requirements or preconditions for detention will generally offend though as not following "a procedure prescribed by law" stipulated in Art.5, para.1.[12]

3. With a view to extradition or expulsion

Only the existence of extradition or expulsion proceedings justifies the detention. In *Quinn v France*, the failure to release for 11 hours pending the French authorities' instigation of extradition proceedings by the Swiss constituted detention outside the scope of the exceptions in Art.5, para.1. II–303

In *Chahal v UK*, in the context of expulsion, the Court has said that all that is required is that action is being taken with a view to deportation and that it is immaterial for the purposes of Art.5, para.1(f) whether the underlying decision to expel can be justified under national or Convention law.[13] In extradition cases, there is no requirement for a prima facie case to be established before suspects can be detained pending extradition.[14]

There is no proportionality test as is sometimes applied under other heads of Art.5, para.1, nor requirement to show that the detention is necessary for the purpose or that without detention the person would abscond.[15] Under sub-paragraph 1(f), the State's right to control aliens' entry and residence has led to a less rigorous interpretation. The emphasis is rather on the detention being in good faith and the detention being closely connected to the purpose of preventing unauthorised entry or with a view to deportation or extradition. Thus, taking an asylum-seeker into detention for seven days while his case was being fast-tracked was part of the policy to speed up asylum decisions and thus was closely connected to preventing unauthorised entry and residence.[16] Nor was it a problem to retain an asylum-seeker in the transit zone, even when removal was no longer possible due to the application of an interim measure under r.39, where the Court saw no reason to doubt the good faith of the Government's assertion that it was necessary first to verify his identity as part of the process of "lawful" entry.[17]

Where the detention is for some other purpose resulting from some misuse of power it may cease to be justifiable.[18] Further, where for a legal, practical or administrative reason, a person held for the purposes of extradition or expulsion cannot in fact be removed, issues may arise as to whether the detention can in those circumstances be considered as justified as being "with a view to extradition". In *Ali v Switzerland*, the Commission noted that the Swiss wanted to extradite the applicant to Somalia but could not as he had no travel document. Since the execution of the

[11] *Slivenko v Latvia*, October 9, 2003, ECHR 2003–XI, para.149, citing *Benham v UK*, June 10, 1996, R.J.D. 1996–III, No.10, paras 42–47. Contrast *Garabayev v Russia*, June 7, 2007, where the defect in the order was so fundamental as to render it arbitrary and invalid.

[12] *Jusic v Switzerland*, December 2, 2010, paras. 75–83.

[13] See also *Slivenko*, fn.11 above, para.146.

[14] *Babar Ahmad v UK*, (24027/07) et al, (Dec.) July 6, 2010, para.180.

[15] *Soldatenko v Ukraine*, fn.8 above, para.109. Contrast *Jusic*, fn.12 above, where as domestic law itself required concrete proof of an intention to avoid expulsion, the detention fell foul of the lawfulness criteria under Article 5, para.1 in the absence of such proof.

[16] *Saadi v UK*, fn.1 above, paras 70–74.

[17] *Gebremedhin v France*, April 26, 2007.

[18] (7317/75) (Dec.) October 6, 1976, 6 D.R. 141.

extradition was impossible, the detention could no longer be regarded as "with a view to extradition" within the exception of Art.5 para.1(f) and infringed Art.5 para.1.[19] A similar approach was adopted where the Estonian authorities could not practically expel the applicant without his co-operation, which was unforthcoming, such that his detention could not be regarded as with a view to his expulsion; nor could the detention be justified for a period over three years in the expectation of the introduction of the legal measures enabling the expulsion.[20]

Where alien suspected terrorists were detained for a matter of a few days or just under three months and were released when they voluntarily agreed to return to their own countries, it was considered that during this period action was being taken with a view to deportation as the the authorities were still at the state of establishing their identities and whether their removal elsewhere was possible. However, where alien suspects could not be removed without risk of ill-treatment contrary to Art.3 and were detained for periods from two to four years, they could not be regarded as persons against whom action was being taken with a view to deportation or expulsion; domestic legal proceedings which concerned the lawfulness of their detention rather than any form of expulsion procedure were not relevant in this connection.[21]

4. Effect of length

II–304 If insufficient diligence is shown in the extradition or expulsion proceedings, the detention may also cease to be justifiable for the purpose of Art.5, para.1(f).[22] Although in *Quinn v France*, a period of almost two years detention pending extradition was found to exceed a reasonable time, the Convention organs will accept considerable delays and the Court in *Chahal* has considered it relevant to have regard to lack of arbitrariness.[23]

Two years and eight months was found by the Court in *Kolompar v Belgium* to be not unreasonable since the extradition proceedings proper were completed less than one month after the decision to release in respect of other criminal charges and the detention was continued due to the applicant's successive applications for release, in which the courts gave their decisions within a normal time. He could not, the Court said, complain of a situation which he had largely created.[24] Nor could an applicant

[19] (24881/94) (Rep.) February 26, 1997, later struck off by the Court due to the applicant's disappearance.

[20] *Mikolenko v Estonia*, October 8, 2010, EU-Russian admissions agreement eventually provided for travel documents to be issued despite the person's refusal to co-operate.

[21] *A and Others v UK*, February 19, 2009, ECHR 2009–. . . , paras 167–172.

[22] e.g. (8081/77) (Dec.) December 12, 1977, 12 D.R. 207; (7317/75), fn.9 above.

[23] *Chahal v UK*, November 15, 1996, R.J.D. 1996–V, No.22, 23 E.H.R.R. 413, paras 117 and 123; (15933/89) (Dec.) October 14, 1991, the longest detained person without trial in the UK (almost six years at the time of his second application) facing extradition to Hong Kong; as regarded the length of proceedings, the Commission considered that an assessment of diligence depended on all the circumstances. It looked at the complexity of the case (several countries involved, voluminous documentation), the conduct of the applicant (his failure to ask for expedition and his repeated habeas corpus applications) and, since he appeared to be protracting the proceedings deliberately, found that he could not complain of delay.

[24] The Commission considered that there must be a responsibility on States to prevent the undue prolongation of extradition proceedings in finding the correct balance between the restrictions on the right to liberty and international obligations. Belgium could not just adopt a passive attitude and was required to take positive steps to expedite the proceedings.

complain of ten and a half months in detention where she refused, five times, to board a plane, the authorities showing no lack of diligence in seeking to enforce the expulsion.[25]

In *Chahal v UK*, a period of over three years five months was acceptable to the Court due to the seriousness and difficulties of the issues (allegations of risk on return to India and national security aspects) and the procedural safeguards in place against arbitrary detention. This overruled the Commission which noted delays between procedural steps in the domestic proceedings and gave weight to the need for utmost expedition where the person was unconvicted and without charge.[26]

In the more recent case, *Saadi v UK*, the test was phrased in terms that the detention should not exceed that reasonably required for the purpose. That case however concerned the specific taking into detention of an asylum-seeker for a week for the purposes of fast tracking the determination of his case and was not considered as exceeding what was reasonably required for that purpose. It is not apparent that this test replaces that previously applied to the more usual detention pending the expulsion or extradition itself.

A period of detention prior to extradition where the applicant is serving a prison sentence following conviction by the sending State is not taken into account as it falls under Art.5, para.1(a) and not (f).[27]

5. Remedies

Where there is a breach of Art.5, para.(1)f, the applicable provisions with regard to effective redress are Art.5, para.4 which requires access to a review of the lawfulness of the detention by an appropriate judicial body[28] and Art.5, para.5 which requires an enforceable right in domestic law to receive compensation. II–305

The Commission found that habeas corpus complied with Art.5, para.4 in providing the means to challenge the lawfulness of the detention for the purposes of extradition.[29] Neither habeas corpus or judicial review however was found by the Court to furnish an adequate review of the lawfulness of the expulsion of the applicant in *Chahal v UK*, where the courts could not scrutinise the national security grounds relied on by the authorities.

A delay of two-and-a-half months in habeas corpus proceedings challenging lawfulness in a deportation case was found to comply with the requirement of promptness in Art.5 para.4. This is longer than has been found compatible in review of other types of detention but was with regard to the complexity of the issues and the significance the case had for all asylum-seekers at that time, and may be regarded as an exceptional decision.[30] In *Kadem v Malta*, a cumbersome procedure

[25] *Ntumba Kabongo v Belgium*, (52467/99) (Dec.) June 2, 2005, the applicant could not blame the authorities for not using physical force. See also *Eid v Italy*, (53490/99) (Dec.) January 22, 2002, one and a half years' detention was acceptable.

[26] Contrast *Mikolenko*, fn.20 above, where three years and eleven months was not acceptable, where the applicant could not in fact be expelled due to lack of papers.

[27] *Raf v Spain*, June 17, 2003, para.64.

[28] e.g. violations in *Dougoz*, where appeals to the leniency of government ministers did not satisfy Art.5, para.4; and *Conka v Belgium*, February 2002, ECHR 2002–I, where the applicant gypsies were tricked into coming to a police station, arrested and expelled without any effective possibility of challenging the measure in a court.

[29] (19319/91) (Dec.) September 2, 1992.

[30] (28201/95) (Dec.) November 27, 1996.

which failed to obtain a hearing before the applicant's release 23 days after his arrest was not regarded as "speedy" for the purposes of Art.5 para.4.[31]

Cross-reference

Part IIB, s.9: Deprivation of liberty.
Part IIB, s.18: Extradition.
Part IIB, s.39: Reasons for arrest and detention.
Part IIB, s.42: Review of detention.

[31] *Kadem v Malta*, January 9, 2003.

12. Discrimination

Key provision:

Article 14 (prohibition against discrimination). II–306

Key case-law:

Belgian Linguistic case, July 23, 1968, Series A, No.6, 1 E.H.R.R. 252; *Kjeldsen, Busk Madsen and Pedersen v Denmark*, December 7, 1976, Series A, No.23, 1 E.H.R.R. 711; *Marckx v Belgium*, June 13, 1979, Series A, No.31, 2 E.H.R.R. 330; *Van der Mussele v Belgium*, November 23, 1983, Series A, No.70, 6 E.H.R.R. 471; *Abdulaziz, Cabales and Balkandali v UK*, May 28, 1985, Series A, No.94, 7 E.H.R.R. 163; *Lithgow v UK*, July 8, 1986, Series A, No.102, 8 E.H.R.R. 329; *Johnston v Ireland*, December 18, 1986, Series A, No.112, 9 E.H.R.R. 203; *Darby v Sweden*, October 23, 1990, Series A, No.187, 13 E.H.R.R. 774; *Pine Valley Developments Ltd v Ireland*, November 29, 1991, Series A, No.222; *Hoffman v Austria*, June 23, 1993, Series A, No.255–C, 17 E.H.R.R. 293; *Schuler-Zraggen v Switzerland*, June 24, 1993, Series A, No.263, 16 E.H.R.R. 405; *McMichael v UK*, February 24, 1995, Series A, No.307–B, 20 E.H.R.R. 205; *Gayguzuz v Austria*, September 16, 1996, R.J.D. 1996–IV; 23 E.H.R.R. 364; *Stubbings v UK*, October 22, 1996, R.J.D. 1996–IV, 23 E.H.R.R. 213; *Van Raalte v Netherlands*, February 21, 1997, R.J.D. 1997–I, 24 E.H.R.R. 503; *Petrovic v Austria*, March 27, 1998, R.J.D. 1998–II; *Smith and Grady v UK*, September 27, 1999, ECHR 1999–VI, 29 E.H.R.R. 493; *Thlimmenos v Greece*, April 6, 2000, ECHR 2000–IV; *Ch'are Shalom Ve Tsedek v France*, June 27, 2000, ECHR 2000–VII; *Elsholz v Germany*, July 13, 2000, ECHR 2000–VIII; *Cyprus v Turkey*, May 10, 2001, ECHR 2001–IV; *Wessels-Bergervoet v Netherlands*, June 4, 2002, ECHR 2002–IV; *Willis v UK*, June 11, 2002, ECHR 2002–IV; *Sahin v Germany*, July 8, 2003, ECHR 2003–VII; *Sommerfeld v Germany*, July 8, 2003, ECHR 2003–VIII; *Nachova v Bulgaria*, July 6, 2005, ECHR 2005–VII; *DH and Others v Czech Republic*, November 13, 2007, ECHR 2007–. . . ; *Burden v UK*, April 29, 2008, ECHR 2008–. . . ; *Orsus and Others v Croatia*, March 16, 2010, ECHR 2010–. . .; *Carson and Others v UK*, March 16, 2010, ECHR 2010–. . . ; *Serife Yigit v Turkey*, November 2, 2010, ECHR 2010. . . ; *Stummer v Austria*, July 7, 2011, ECHR 2011–. . .

1. General considerations

Article 14 encapsulates a crucial human right. Discrimination, in its many insidious forms, could be described as one of the fundamental evils afflicting society and is at the heart of many tangible atrocities. However its role in the Convention system has been limited both by its drafters and approach adopted by the Convention organs. There has nonetheless been a recent emphasis on the condemnation of racism and ethnic hatred with corresponding positive obligations on the State to maintain the confidence of minorities in the ability of the authorities to protect them from racist violence and to investigate properly incidents of racial hatred[1]; this also extends to II–307

[1] *Menson v UK*, (47916/99) ECHR 2003–V; *Nachova v Bulgaria*, July 6, 2005, ECHR 2005–VII, paras 145 and 160.

violence of a religious extremist character.[2] Positive obligations are developing elsewhere also, in the area of protection against domestic violence and discrimination on grounds of trade union membership.[3]

While difficulties may often arise in establishing unacceptable motivations for official actions and decisions, where holders of public office express discriminatory opinions, the Court takes into account that this may influence others whose employment and careers depend on their approval and thus vitiate the decision-making procedure.[4] In court decisions, decisive reliance on a factor of personal status, such as homosexuality or race, will raise issues of discrimination, notwithstanding that there might be other justifying features present.[5]

According to the case-law, an applicant must establish that he is subject to a difference in treatment from others in a comparable position in the enjoyment of one of the rights guaranteed under the Convention, which difference cannot be objectively and reasonably justified, having regard to the applicable margin of appreciation. Once a difference in treatment is established, it is however for the respondent Government to show that it was justified.[6] Recent developments indicate that where indirect discrimination is concerned—where a general measure or policy couched in neutral terms has disproportionately prejudicial effects on a group, as demonstrated through, for example, reliable and significant statistical material—it is not necessarily required to show any discriminatory intent and once a prima facie case of indirect discrimination has been shown by the applicant, the burden then shifts to the Government to show that the difference in impact of the legislation or measure was the result of objective factors unrelated to ethnic origin.[7]

2. Protection only of enjoyment of guaranteed rights and freedoms

II–308 By its formulation, the provision has been tied inexorably to the other substantive rights in the Convention. An applicant complaining of discrimination must allege it in respect of, for example, freedom of religion or fair trial. It is useless to invoke it the area of employment rights, political office, pay, access to private leisure facilities, or the media. The new Protocol No.12, which was opened for signature on November 4, 2000, contains a wider guarantee against discrimination and has come into force for those countries which have ratified.[8]

[2] *Milanovic v Serbia*, December 14, 2010, paras 96–101.

[3] *Opuz v Turkey*, June 9, 2009; *Danilenkov v Russia*, July 30, 2009.

[4] *Baczkowski v Poland*, May 3, 2007, where in an interview the Mayor of Warsaw said that a march should be banned as being "propaganda for homosexuals" at the time the application for approval was pending; the application was rejected, purportedly, on technical grounds.

[5] *EB v France*, January 22, 2008, paras 85–98; *Salgueiro Da Silva Mouta v Portugal*, December 21, 1999, para.36. Cf. *PV v Spain*, November 30, 2010, para.36.

[6] *Serife Yigit v Turkey*, November 2, 2010, ECHR 2010. . . , para.71.

[7] *DH and Others v Czech Republic*, November 13, 2007, ECHR 2007–. . . , paras 179–195, statistical data showing that a large percentage of children in special schools were Roma, very few other pupils being allocated there. Contrast *Orsus and Others v Croatia*, March 16, 2010, ECHR 2010–. . . , para.152, statistics did not show indirect discrimination over the country as a whole, with special classes having mixed composition; however, in one district, the placement of children in special classes, due to insufficient command of Croation, was carried out on Roma children only and this, together with protests of non-Roma families against mixed classes, was prima facie evidence of a difference in treatment which required justification.

[8] April 1, 2005, e.g. Croatia, Finland, the Netherlands. The UK has neither signed nor ratified; Ireland has signed.

In *Belgian Linguistics*, the Court noted that the provision had "no independent existence" and it was as though it was an integral part of each of the substantive articles.[9] Further, extreme discrimination has been held by the Convention organs to constitute degrading treatment contrary to Art.3.[10]

Where the alleged discrimination relates to a matter which falls within the "ambit" of one of the substantive articles, the provision may become operable.[11] Thus special treatment of taxation under Art.1 of the First Protocol bestows on it an exclusion from the normal guarantee of protection for property but where taxation legislation appears to single out persons for unfavourable treatment, issues may arise under that provision in conjunction with Art.14.[12] The Court rejected a narrow interpretation advocated by the House of Lords, finding that measures requiring applicants to pay money will also come within the ambit for the purposes of Art.14.[13] In *Inze v Austria*, concerning a difference in land inheritance between children born in and out of wedlock, the Court emphasised that under Art.1 of the First Protocol it was not for the Court to say who should inherit. However Art.14 came into play where by operation of law a distinction operated based on birth in or out of wedlock as regarded the differences in inheritance rights. While there is no right for any social security scheme or benefits system to be provided, once legislation provides for the payment as of right of a welfare benefit—whether conditional or not on the prior payment of contributions—this generates a proprietary interest falling within the ambit of Art.1 of Protocol No. 1 for persons satisfying its requirements.[14] The test is whether but for the condition of entitlement about which the applicant complains (whether national origin, sex or other), he or she would have had an enforceable right to receive the benefit concerned.[15] Where a mother complained about a discriminatory denial of priority housing for herself and her son, this was regarded as affecting home and family life and thus within the ambit of Art.8, even though there is no right to social housing under Art.8 itself.[16]

[9] *Belgian Linguistic case*, July 23, 1968, Series A, No.6, 1 E.H.R.R. 252, p.34, para.9; for a more recent statement, *Petrovic v Austria*, March 27, 1998, R.J.D. 1998–II, para.22.

[10] In relation to race discrimination: *East African Asians v UK* (Rep.) December 14, 1973 78 D.R.5; *Cyprus v Turkey*, May 10, 2001, ECHR 2001–IV, para.303, concerning the severe discrimination against the Karpas Greek community in northern Cyprus. The same argument did not succeed in respect of sex discrimination in *Abdulaziz, Cabales and Balkandali v UK*, May 28, 1985, Series A, No.94, 7 E.H.R.R. 163, while the Commission found a degrading treatment finding inherent in a violation of Art.14, the Court found no separate issue under Art.3.

[11] This is in practice a wider concept than that of falling within the "scope" of substantive provisions: see Judge Bratza's analysis in his separate concurring opinion in *Zarb Adami v Malta*, June 20, 2006. See also e.g. *Petrovic*, fn.9 above, para.28, the issue of parental leave allowances, granted to mothers but not fathers, was thus considered to fall under Art.8 as a means by which the State demonstrated respect for family life; *Willis v UK*, June 11, 2002, ECHR 2002–IV, paras 35–36, right to receive widow's benefits was sufficiently pecuniary to fall under of Art.1 of Protocol No.1 without the Court needing to decide whether the benefit could constitute a "possession" under that provision; *Frette v France*, February 26, 2002, ECHR 2002–I, see the minority dissenting opinion at p.32–33, explaining at some length why, though there was no right to adopt under Art.8 and France had gone beyond what was required, it had a duty to implement the system so that there was no unwarranted discrimination on grounds listed in Art.14.

[12] (11089/84) (Dec.) November 11, 1986, 49 D.R. 181.

[13] *JM v UK*, September 28, 2010, paras 46–49.

[14] *Stummer v Austria*, July 7, 2011, ECHR 2011–. . . , para.82, Art.14 applicable to prisoner's claims that his years of work in prison should count towards entitlement for a pension as other forms of work did.

[15] *Stec v UK*, (65731/01) and (65900/01) (Dec.) July 6, 2005, para.55.

[16] *Bah v UK*, September 27, 2011, para.40.

Sentencing and release from prison are matters generally falling outside the scope of Art.5 but issues have been held as possibly arising if sentencing policy appears to effect individuals in a discriminatory manner.[17]

A somewhat attenuated approach to welfare benefits awarded to parents has been adopted. Initially, it was regarded as a problem of discrimination in enjoyment of property rights or a legitimate expectation to such. Latterly, the motive behind the legislation of promoting families was regarded as bringing discrimination in not awarding such benefits to non-national residents within the scope of Art.8.[18]

3. Difference in treatment

II–309 Not all differences in treatment are relevant for the purposes of Art.14. The examination for discrimination is only meaningful if the applicant is seeking to compare himself to others in comparable positions or analogous situations or, in another formulation, is in a "relevantly similar" situation to those others.[19]

For example, married couples are in many cases not in analogous situations with unmarried couples since they have chosen a particular legal regime to govern their relations, marriage having a special status which continues to be characterised by a distinct corpus of rights and obligations[20]; sisters who cohabit cannot claim to be comparable to those who live together in marriage or a civil partnership[21]; a live-in carer cannot claim to be in the same position as a spouse or partner, when it comes to claims to continue tenancies after a person's death[22]; IRA Category A prisoners could not seek to compare themselves with prisoners of no security risk[23]; advocates are not in analogous positions to other professions, even with those connected with the law like the judiciary or bailiffs, the professions in question being characterised by a corpus of rights and obligations of which it would be artificial to isolate one element[24]; companies subject to nationalisation are not in an analogous situation to property owners subject to compulsory purchase[25]; and insurance companies obliged

[17] (11077/84) (Dec.) October 13, 1986, 49 D.R. 170; (22761/93) (Dec.) April 14, 1994, 77–A D.R. 98; *Clift v UK*, July 13, 2010, para.42.

[18] See *Zeibek v Greece*, July 9, 2009, violation of Art.14 in conjunction with Art.1 of Protocol No. 1 where denial of large family benefit to applicants perceived as having forfeited their Greek nationality; *Weller v Hungary*, March 31, 2009, breach of Art.14 in conjunction with Art.8 where children of a foreign mother were not eligible for claims of maternity benefit on their behalf; Art.8 was in issue as the benefit was aimed at assisting families though in *Zeibek* the complaint under Art.14 with Art.8 was rejected as the refusal to pay a benefit had no preventive effect on existing family life; *Fawsie v Greece*, October 28, 2010, where a resident refugee was denied a large family benefit, the *Weller* approach was followed.

[19] *Marckx v Belgium*, June 13, 1979, Series A, No.31, 2 E.H.R.R. 330, para.32; *Van der Mussele v Belgium*, November 23, 1983, Series A, No.70, 6 E.H.R.R. 471, para.46; *Larkos v Cyprus*, February 18, 1999, ECHR 1999–I, 30 E.H.R.R. 597, para.30, where the applicant as a tenant renting State-owned property was in a relevantly similar situation to tenants renting from private landlords; *Stummer*, fn.14 above, paras 91–95, a working prisoner was in a relevantly similar position to an ordinary employee insofar as whether or not the purpose and conditions of the work were markedly different, both had the need to provide for their old age through pension affiliation arrangements..

[20] (11089/84), fn.12 above.

[21] *Burden v UK*, April 29, 2008, ECHR 2008–. . . , para.66.

[22] *Korelc v Slovakia*, May 12, 2009, para.90.

[23] (19085/91) (Dec.) December 9, 1992. See also *Halis v Turkey*, (30007/96) (Dec.) May 23, 2002, concerning differences in legal regime applicable to those arrested of terrorist offences and other offences, distinctions not based on characteristics of a particular group but the gravity of particular crimes.

[24] *Van der Mussele*, fn.19 above.

[25] *Lithgow v UK*, July 8, 1986, Series A, No.102, 8 E.H.R.R. 329.

to pay a percentage of car insurance premiums to public road safety funds were not comparable to other businesses who did not benefit from the universal obligation on car users to subscribe to road insurance.[26] Nor can pensioners living abroad, subject to different social, economic and fiscal conditions, claim to be in the same position as pensioners at home where eligibility to uprating is concerned.[27]

This may appear at times to overlap with the objective and reasonable justification concept (see s.5, below) since a finding that two situations are not comparable will generally rely on reasons, akin to objective and reasonable justification, disclosing material difference.[28]

While violations of Art.14 have generally concerned situations where the State has treated differently persons in analogous situations without providing a reasonable or objective explanation, the Court has extended the provision to situations where a State without an objective and reasonable justification fails to treat differently persons whose situations are significantly different. Thus, in *Thlimmenos v Greece*, the Court found a violation of Art.14 in conjunction with Art.9 where the applicant, a Jehovah's Witness had been convicted for refusal to wear a military uniform on religious grounds. He was then excluded from exercising the profession of chartered accountant on the basis that he had a serious criminal conviction. Taking the view that the applicant's conviction on conscientious grounds differed from other criminal offences which might render a person unsuitable to enter the profession, it found there was no objective and reasonable justification for not treating the applicant differently from other persons convicted of a felony. The discrimination therefore lay in failing to introduce appropriate exceptions to the bar on entry. This approach has yet to produce a violation in any other case however.[29]

4. On grounds of personal status

The Court has stated that Art.14 is only concerned with discriminatory treatment having as its basis a personal characteristic or "status" by which persons or groups of persons are distinguishable from each other.[30] It thus aims to strike down the offensive singling out of an individual or members of a particular group on their personal attributes.[31] Art.14 lists the obvious ones: sex, race, colour, language, **II–310**

[26] *Allianz-Slovenska poistovna, a.s. v Slovakia*, (19276/05) (Dec.) November 9, 2011.

[27] *Carson and Others v UK*, March 16, 2010, ECHR 2010–. . .

[28] See, e.g. *Stubbings v UK*, October 22, 1996, R.J.D. 1996–IV, 23 E.H.R.R. 213, where the Court effectively held that victims of deliberate and negligently inflicted injury were not in analogous positions since the prescription rules applicable to the two categories had developed separately with different characteristics and even if they were in analogous positions, there was reasonable and objective justification since they had different characteristics. See also *Gouveia Gomes Fernandes and Freitas E Costa v Portugal*, (1529/08) (Dec.) May 26, 2009, concerning complaints that judges were exempted from legal fees when sued, where the Court doubted that the applicant plaintiffs could claim to be relevantly similar to judges but in any event there was objective and reasonable justification in granting legal fee exemption to judges who in the exercise of their functions might be frequently sued by discontented litigants.

[29] See, e.g. *Chapman v UK*, January 18, 2001, ECHR 2001–I, para.129, where the applicant failed to persuade the Court that as a gypsy it was discriminatory to apply the same planning rules to her as to the sedentary majority.

[30] *Kjeldsen, Busk Madsen and Pedersen v Denmark*, December 7, 1976, Series A, No.23, 1 E.H.R.R. 711, para.56.

[31] See *Jones v UK*, (42639/04) (Dec.) September 5, 2005, there was no difference of treatment of the applicant merely because one parish council banned photographs on graves and municipal cemeteries did not.

religion, political or other opinion, national or social origin, etc. The list is not exhaustive, Art.14 referring to "any ground" and concluding with "or other status". It has applied also where the ground of difference was genetic disease[32]; where compensation for forced labour was interpreted as being available to conscripts to some units but not others[33] and where different procedures for release applied to persons sentenced to over 15 years' imprisonment than to those serving less or an indefinite term.[34]

The definition or limits of the concept of personal status have not been much discussed, although it has recently been stated that "personal characteristic" is not limited to the sense of innate or inherent personal traits.[35] Legal status, such as immigration or residence, counts.[36] Doubt was expressed that ineligibility for an Estonian pension while in receipt of a foreign one came within this concept.[37] While the element of choice in the "status" in issue does not remove it from the definition, it may be taken into account when considering the margin of appreciation and weighing whether there was sufficient justification for the difference in treatment.[38]

"Status" has been held not to be concerned in differences in treatment deriving from differing rules applicable between regional jurisdictions within a State, where, in other words, the difference results from the geographical location where the person finds himself and not any personal characteristic. Thus it is not a difference in treatment on grounds of personal status for people in Scotland to be subject to the poll tax before people living in England[39] or where a juvenile offender in Scotland did not enjoy an entitlement to remission accorded to such offenders sentenced in England and Wales[40] or where different practices allegedly applied between Northern Ireland and England and Wales concerning access of terrorist suspects to solicitors on arrest.[41] This reflects the fact that many Contracting States have regional jurisdictions, with differing rules and procedures and avoids interpreting Art.14 to require universally identical laws throughout each country. Geographical difference presumably could base a claim for discrimination where perhaps it was apparent that a particular area was subject to a law because its citizens were individuals sharing a common personal element, beyond their residence in the location.

However, it must also be borne in mind that place of residence can constitute an element of personal status for the purposes of Art.14, where it is the same legislation applying to persons, who are treated differently because of where they live, as in *Carson and Others v UK*, where the pension legislation affected United Kingdom pensioners differently depending on which country they were living in. It was nonetheless considered in that case that the applicants could not be considered

[32] *GN v Italy*, December 1, 2009, paras 126–127.

[33] *Beian v Romania*, December 6, 2007, paras 51–65.

[34] *Clift v UK*, July 13, 2010, paras 55–63, distinguishing *Gerger v Turkey*, July 8, 1999, para.69, where the law was seen as making a distinction between different types of offences not categories of persons.

[35] *Clift v UK*, fn.34 above, paras 58–59 no justification was then found for making release of long-term prisoners subject to political approval of a minister, where such was not required for indeterminate sentences and shorter-term sentences (paras 73–79).

[36] *Bah*, fn.16 above, para.46.

[37] *Tarkoev v Estonia*, November 4, 2011, para.59, in any event, the ex-Russian army pensioners could not claim to be in a comparable situation to other pensioners.

[38] *Bah*, fn.16 above, para.47.

[39] (13473/87) (Dec.) July 11, 1988.

[40] (11077/84), fn.15 above.

[41] *Magee v UK*, June 6, 2000, ECHR 2000–VI, para.50.

in a relevantly similar position to others, in effect because they were non-residents, living away from the United Kingdom, with weaker links and subject to different economic and sociable variables where they lived.

Indirect discrimination aside, there is generally an element of deliberate targeting implicit in a discriminatory difference in treatment. Where there is a particular pattern of application of a measure, it may simply flow from the fact that various state organs are more efficient than others, as the Court commented in a Polish case where one region was more rigorous in revoking mistakenly granted pensions.[42]

5. Justification for difference in treatment

While Art.14 is not expressly subject to exceptions, it has been interpreted as incorporating the practical recognition that not every difference in treatment in the enjoyment of the protected rights and freedoms can be prohibited. The Court in the *Belgian Linguistics case* noted that a literal application of the French version "*sans aucune distinction*" would lead to "absurd results" and referred to the inherent differences existing in legal situations and problems which call for differing legal solutions. The test applied to assess which differences in treatment are objectionable or not is whether they are based on objective and reasonable justification. The existence of the justification has to be assessed in relation to the aims and effects of the measure under consideration, regard being had to the principles which normally prevail in democratic societies. It must not only pursue a legitimate aim but there must be reasonable relationship of proportionality between the means employed and the aim sought to realised. Therefore the concepts of legitimate aim, proportionality, are brought in and, inevitably, the margin of appreciation.[43] It may also be relevant whether there are procedural safeguards provided domestically to avoid discriminatory effects of a measure and. for guaranteeing adequate and appropriate judicial supervision of restrictions.[44] II–311

Whether there is objective and reasonable justification will depend on the circumstances of each situation.

Administrative difficulties generally should not suffice a justification, as in *Darby v Sweden* where this was the sole basis for barring non-residents who worked in Sweden from an exemption to church tax available to residents in Sweden. The Court has also stated that society can be expected to put up with a certain inconvenience to enable individuals to live in dignity and worth.[45] Nor can objective and reasonable justification for the interferences with rights be derived purely from negative attitudes, varying from hostility or unease that a particular minority might arouse. In *Smith and Grady v UK*, the Court held that, insofar as the ban on homosexuals in the army represented a predisposed bias on the part of a heterosexual majority against a homosexual minority, this could not justify discriminatory treatment any more than similar negative attitudes towards those of a different race, origin or colour.

A certain allowance is, however, given to States as regards the timing of changes which reflect a shift in society's attitudes, as in *Petrovic v Austria*, where it noted that the grant of parental leave to fathers was a recent development and the Austrian

[42] *Moskal v Poland*, September 15, 2009, ECHR 2000–VI, para.100.
[43] *Belgian Linguistics case*, fn.9 above, p.35, para.10.
[44] *Sidabras and Dziautas v Lithuania*, July 27, 2004, ECHR 2004–VIII, para.59.
[45] *Unal Tekeli v Turkey*, November 16, 2004, ECHR 2004–X, para.67.

legislature could not be criticised for extending measures to fathers as well as mothers in a gradual manner. This was where there was no common standard amongst Contracting States on the issue at the relevant time and Austria, whose legislation could be regarded in fact as progressive, could not be held to have exceeded its margin of appreciation. The timing of the change to a single pension age and the introduction of the change over a long transitional period was found also to fall within the State's margin of appreciation, given the economic and social implications and lack of common standard.[46] Furthermore, where a domestic court makes a finding of discrimination which requires legislative change, the Court found that the continued application of the discriminatory provisions for a short period of time pending legislative amendment may be regarded as proportionate.[47]

Regard is often had to the existence or not of a common European consensus. Where most European countries extended parental leave to both mothers and fathers, the Court took this into account in finding no convincing reasons for the Russian army to extend leave to the former but not the latter.[48] Absence of a European consensus on age-limits for parents seeking to adopt children gave the Swiss authorities a wide margin of appreciation on the subject.[49] Where the European approach to recognition of same-sex relationships was assessed as one of "evolving rights with no established consensus", this gave rise to a certain margin of appreciation in the Government's favour.[50]

While it is primarily for domestic courts to interpret national law, they are required to do so, having regard to realities and changes in society and also in the manner which most closely corresponds to Convention principles; thus it was discriminatory to interpret a will in such a manner as to exclude adopted children.[51]

Where welfare benefits and pensions are concerned, the Court has underlined that in this context that it will look at the compatibility of the system overall, without giving undue weight to the particular circumstances of the individual, since welfare systems to be workable have to deal in broad categorisations which will inevitably impact some more prejudicially than others.[52] This seems to reflect the Court's general approach, in the area of complex social and economic policy, of accepting the legislature's approach save where "manifestly without reasonable foundation."[53] Where a prisoner complained of lack of affiliation to an old age pension scheme in respect of work done in prison, the Court considered the matter could not be looked

[46] *Stec v UK*, fn.15 above; see also *Schalk and Kopf v Austria*, June 24, 2010, para.105, margin of appreciation applicable to timing of introduction of changes permitting recognition of same-sex relationships; *Stummer*, fn.14 above, paras 106–110, gradual extension of social cover to prisoners was proportionate, but to be kept under review.

[47] *Walden v Liechtenstein*, (33916/96) (Dec.) March 16, 2000, 7–month period. See also *Runkee and White v UK*, May 10, 2007, para.41, where it was acceptable for the widows' pension paid to women only to be phased out gradually, the Court noting the impossibility of pinpointing the exact date at which elderly women ceased to need this extra help; *Andrle v Czech Republic*, February 17, 2011, paras 56–60, gradual phasing out of differential pension treatment between men and women based on presumed child caring roles was justified.

[48] *Konstantin Markin v Russia*, October 7, 2010, para.49, pending before the Grand Chamber.

[49] *Schwizgebel v Switzerland*, June 10, 2010, paras 91–92.

[50] See *Schalk and Kopf*, fn.46, para.105.

[51] *Pla and Puncernau v Andorra*, July 13, 2004.

[52] *Carson and Others*, fn.27 above, para.62. See also *Andrle*, fn.47 above, distinguishing between pension entitlements which are part of economic and social planning with serious financial ramifications and more short term measures without systemic significance such as parental leave; a wide margin of appreciation applied to the former.

[53] e.g. *James v UK*, February 21, 1985, Series A, No.98, para.46.

at in isolation but was one feature in an overall system linked to issues of general penal policy and social strategy where a wide margin of appreciation applied.[54] A wide margin of appreciation has also been said to apply in the context of sensitive moral and ethical issues such as artificial procreation treatment.[55]

Matters of fiscal and economic policy falling within the prerogative of the State, nonetheless arguments of financial necessity cannot be used to justify differences of treatment which are arbitrary, as where the Italian authorities had provided compensation to the numerous haemophiliacs contaminated by tainted blood supplies but not to the numerically smaller group of persons suffering from a more rare genetic illness. Thus, even purported monetary imperatives must hold up to scrutiny.[56] An unsupported claim that military efficiency would suffer if paternity leave was extended to men in the army as well as women was rejected.[57]

6. Relationship with substantive complaints

In many cases, an applicant subject to a particular measure will argue that the measure infringes a substantive right, without necessary justification and that he is, by the implementation of that measure, subject also to unjustifiable discrimination. Where a violation is found of the substantive article, it is often the case that the Court will find no separate issue arising under Art.14. It is a practice which may not be based on unavoidable logic but may rather give proof of a certain judicial economy. For example, in *Moustaquim v Belgium*, the Court found the proposed measure of expelling the applicant, a second generation immigrant, to a country in which he had no family, disclosed a violation of Art.8, but found it unnecessary to examine the complaint under Art.14. However, his claim that this measure constituted discrimination since the measure was imposed on him due to his nationality was arguably a separate legal issue, the fact that the complaint concerned the same measure not logically precluding the existence of two separate grounds of violation.[58] II–312

Conversely, a finding of no violation of a substantive article does not preclude the examination of the discrimination complaint, as in *Abdulaziz v UK* where the claims under Art.8 were rejected.[59] This is the type of case where the essence of the complaint is the discriminatory application of the measures, which otherwise disclose no fundamental incompatibility with the provisions of the Convention.

There are some cases where it is more difficult to analyse whether the case is primarily about the substantive provision or discrimination. There have accordingly

[54] *Stummer*, fn.14 above, paras 101–102. See also wide margin applicable to housing policies in *Bah*, fn.16 above, where it was legitimate to prioritise allocation of scarce housing resources to those with a permanent, unconditional right of abode in the UK.

[55] *SH and Others v Austria*, November 3, 2011, paras 97, 100 and 120.

[56] *GN v Italy*, fn.32 above, para.129.

[57] *Konstantin Markin*, fn.48 above, pending before the Grand Chamber.

[58] *Moustaquim v Belgium*, February 18, 1991, Series A, No.193. Similarly, no separate issue arose under Art.14 in the gays in the army cases once a breach of Art.8 was found (e.g. *Smith and Grady v UK*, September 27, 1999, ECHR 1999–VI, 29 E.H.R.R. 493, paras 115–116) or in the transsexual cases (*Christine Goodwin v UK*, July 11, 2002, ECHR 2002–VI, para.108).

[59] *Abdulaziz, Cabales and Balkandali v UK*, May 28, 1985, Series A, No.94, 7 E.H.R.R. 163, there was no interference with family life since the applicants and their spouses had no expectation of a grant of residence and could live together elsewhere; whereas discrimination arose as the rules applied differently to male and female spouses.

been decisions, where the Convention organs have chosen to examine the complaints under Art.14 alone. In *Hoffman v Austria*, the applicant, who lost custody of her children to her divorced spouse in a decision which gave considerable weight to her beliefs as a Jehovah's Witness, invoked Arts 8 and 14. Since the deprivation of her family rights was based on apparent discrimination on religious grounds, the Court found a violation of Art.14 and considered that it was not necessary in its view to look at Art.8 alone since it would involve the same arguments.[60]

To succeed in establishing violations of a substantive provision and a discrimination violation would require showing that separate arguments and considerations of some significance arose.

7. Particular discrimination areas

(a) Sex

II–313 The Court has emphasised that, advancement of equality of the sexes being a major goal in Contracting States, it would require very weighty reasons for a difference in treatment on grounds of sex to be compatible with the Convention. Such reasons have been lacking in a number of cases, which, interestingly, tend more to concern discrimination against men than against women.

No convincing justification was found for: a court decision refusing a woman a disability pension which had as its only basis the assumption that women give up work on having children, a difference of treatment based on sex for which there was no objective and reasonable justification[61]; the inability of a man to add his surname before that of his wife's, while the law allowed a woman to add hers to her husband's name[62]; an obligation on a man to pay a fire service levy in lieu of actual service based on a local tradition of male participation in fire brigade where women, who did not serve, did not have to pay either[63]; rules allowing the entry of foreign wives of citizens but not foreign husbands, which might pursue the legitimate aim of protecting the labour market but that aim could not be justified by differentiating between men and women for impact on employment[64]; exemption of childless women over 45 from paying social security contributions towards child benefit, as whether or not it was a legitimate aim to spare the feelings of childless women, there were equally men who could not procreate[65]; the ineligibility of widowers to apply for benefits on the deaths of their spouses in circumstances where a woman

[60] See also the Commission's approach in *Stubbings*, fn.28 above, the complaint was analysed by the Commission as alleging that the hindrance on access to court from prescription rules was unreasonable and disproportionate since it did not apply to other categories of litigant suffering from injuries—essentially discrimination and to be treated under Art.14.

[61] *Schuler-Zgraggen*.

[62] *Burghartz v Switzerland*, February 22, 1994, Series A, No.280–B, 18 E.H.R.R. 101; see also *Losonci Rose and Rose v Switzerland*, November 9; 2010, discriminatory rules applying to names depending on whether the woman was Swiss or not.

[63] *Karlheinz Schmidt v Germany*, July 18, 1994, Series A, No.291–B, 18 E.H.R.R. 513, while it might have been once justified in imposing the service on men alone, there was no justification for a difference in financial obligations.

[64] *Abdulaziz, Cabales and Balkandali v UK*, fn.60 above.

[65] *Van Raalte v Netherlands*, February 21, 1997, R.J.D. 1997–I, 24 E.H.R.R. 503, paras 42–43.

could obtain a Widow's Payment or Widowed Mother's Allowance[66]; for a 38 per cent difference in the old age pension which the applicant woman received compared with a man[67]; a requirement that a woman bear her husband's name on marriage, with no possibility of her retaining her maiden name[68]; the practice whereby it was mainly men who bore the burden of jury service as women were effectively exempted[69]; and the denial of the parental leave to men but not women in the army.[70]

The Commission to some extent accepted positive discrimination in favour of women as objective and reasonable justification for difference in treatment in the context of tax.[71] This was where rules had developed with the aim of encouraging women to work and advance the equality of the sexes, which resulted in a situation that where the wife was the major breadwinner of a married couple the tax allowance proved more favourable than where the major breadwinner was the man. The Commission accepted the aim as legitimate, noting that the difference only applied in three per cent of cases. It considered the margin of appreciation must be wider in the realm of taxes and pragmatically accepted that systems of taxation inevitably differentiated between groups of taxpayers and marginal situations might arise. As the discrepancy in treatment was not particularly large or widespread, it is possible that the case would have proceeded differently if there had been a significant financial disparity. The Court has since found objective and reasonable justification in providing a widow's pension, for which men did not obtain an equivalent, as this was aimed at eradicating hardship suffered in the past by a category of elderly women.[72] Similarly, it was justified for a lower pensionable age to be accorded to women who had raised children where this had pursued the legitimate aim of compensating factual inequalities and hardship arising of historical circumstances where women had been responsible for the upbringing of children and for the household while also being under pressure to work.[73]

In the context of domestic violence, there are now positive obligations on the State to protect women. Domestic violence indeed being regarded as a form of discrimination against women in international law, the Court found in a Turkish case that as domestic violence affected mainly women and that the general and discriminatory judicial passivity in Turkey created a climate that was conducive to domestic violence, the failures of the authorities to respond actively to a series of attacks on the applicant and her mother by her violent husband, in particular by pursing criminal law and injunctive measures of their own initiative, disclosed a breach of Art.14 in conjunction with Arts 2 and 3.[74]

[66] *Willis*, fn.11 above; see also *Matthews v UK* (friendly settlement), July 15, 2002, where the male applicant complained that unlike women who became eligible at age 60, he had to wait until 65 for a free London bus pass.

[67] *Wessels-Bergervoet v Netherlands*, June 4, 2002, ECHR 2002–IV.

[68] *Unal Tekeli*, fn.45 above, para.66, it was not sufficient that they could add their maiden name before their husband's.

[69] *Zarb Adami*, fn11 above.

[70] *Konstantin Markin v Russia*, fn.48 above.

[71] (11089/84) fn.12 above.

[72] *Runkee and White*, fn.43 above, however, there was no such justification in difference of treatment in widow's payment which aimed at offsetting immediate expenses at the time of the death of a spouse, which difficulties were suffered by both sexes (paras 44–47).

[73] *Andrle*, fn.47, paras 52–60, this case was distinguished from *Konstantin Markin*, fn.48 above, as the pension age was part of important social and economic structural policy rather than a short term benefit (i.e. parental leave) without wider significance.

[74] *Opuz v Turkey*, fn.3 above, paras 184–202.

(b) Marital status

II–314 Marriages consisting of a special legal regime, differences of treatment between non-married couples and married couples have, in some cases, been found not to disclose discrimination; the entry into marriage, a choice with personal, social and legal consequences, still confers a particular status.[75] Thus, it was legitimate for legislation to provide for survivors' benefits in marriage which does not extend to cohabiting couples[76] or to couples in a civil partnership.[77] Similarly, there was objective and reasonable justification for a regime which did not recognise religious marriages for the purposes of extending benefits to the survivor, where the insistence on civil marriages pursued the aim of improving the situation of women in society and where the situation had always been known to the applicant and her partner.[78]

Differences in the parental rights or responsibility over children accruing to natural fathers and married fathers were accepted in particular due to the differences in the nature of relationships of fathers with children born out of wedlock.[79] Where concrete decisions however are taken in respect of contact rights however, the Court has examined the circumstances of the case. In *Elsholz v Germany*, notwithstanding apparent differing tests applying between natural and married fathers (a presumption of contact being beneficial for the child operating in favour of the latter), the Court examined the court decisions and found that on the facts of the case it had not been shown that a divorced father would have been treated more favourably. However, in two later cases, *Sahin v Germany* and *Sommerfeld v Germany*, the Court found that the procedures showed that the applicants as natural fathers were treated less favourably in that the mother's refusal of access to a child could only be overridden by a court where access had been shown to be in the interest of the child. This heavy burden of proof was apparently found to have played a role in the negative decisions reached.[80] A natural father also did not enjoy a right of appeal which was available to a divorced father, which was not found to be justified.[81] The impossibility of an unmarried father to be awarded joint custody of a child where the mother refused, irrespective of the interests of the child or the circumstances of the case, was a violation.[82] Denial of child benefits to a natural father was not acceptable, where such benefits were given to other carers of children, mothers, adoptive parents and guardians.[83]

[75] See *Burden and Burden v UK*, paras 63–65, no discrimination disclosed by favourable inheritance tax exemption enjoyed by married couples but not sisters.

[76] *Shackell v UK*, (45851/99) (Dec) April 27, 2000, no discrimination for differential treatment in social security benefits between a widow and a bereaved non-married partner. Contrast *Zubczewski v Sweden*, (16149/08) (Dec.) January 12, 2010, no issue where the applicant's pension dropped some 50€ when he married on the strange legislative assumption that having a wife would diminish his expenses: this was regarded as within the margin of appreciation.

[77] *Manenc v France*, (66686/09) (Dec) September 21, 2010.

[78] *Serife Yigit v Turkey*, fn.6 above, paras 83–88. This case is to be distinguished from *Munoz Diaz v Spain*, December 8, 2009, where there was discrimination in denying survivors' benefits to a woman married by the unrecognised Roma marriage rite, since in practice the Spanish authorities had recognised the family unit previously and accorded them status and benefits.

[79] *McMichael v UK*, February 24, 1995, Series A, No.307–B, 20 E.H.R.R. 205, para.98; see also (29779/96) (Dec.) October 21, 1998, where the Commission found objective and reasonable justification for legislative provisions which permitted parental responsibility to be removed by a court from unmarried fathers, whereas no such possibility existed for married, divorced or separated fathers.

[80] *Sahin v Germany*, July 8, 2003, ECHR 2003–VII, paras 89–95; *Sommerfeld v Germany*, July 8, 2003, ECHR 2003–VIII, paras 88–94.

[81] *Sommerfeld*, fn.81 above, paras 95–98.

[82] *Zaunegger v Germany*, December 3, 2009.

[83] *Weller v Hungary*, see fn.18 above, paras 33–35.

However, where national authorities limit adoption to married couples, this does not justify a failure to give legal recognition to an overseas adoption by a single parent, decisive weight being attached to the interests of the child, otherwise left in a legal vacuum.[84]

Differences in rules applying to married and unmarried status were not justified by any objective and reasonable factors where in prison only married prisoners could talk on the phone to their partners, such possibility being refused to the applicant who had a long-term but unmarried relationship with the mother of his child.[85]

(c) Race

The Court has issued strong recent statements emphasising the importance of condemning racism and requiring positive steps to be taken to enforce criminal law against those who carry out racial violence.[86] **II–315**

Discrimination based on race had already been recognised by the Commission in the *East African Asians* case as forming a special form of affront to human dignity which, in aggravating circumstances, can amount to degrading treatment in breach of Art.3. The passing of legislation targeting a particular racial group for exclusion from entry to the United Kingdom was found to reach this level, having regard to the serious difficulties in which this placed Asians who were being expelled from their East African homes and were at risk of being "shuttlecocked" from one place to another. The extreme restrictions imposed on the Karpas Greek community in Northern Cyprus based on their ethnic origin, race and religion, which controlled and isolated them to an extent found to be debasing and contrary to the very notion of respect for human dignity, also disclosed a violation of Art.3 in *Cyprus v Turkey*.[87]

Where racist violence may be in issue, the authorities are under an obligation under Art.2 to pursue an official investigation with vigour and impartiality, inter alia, to maintain confidence of minorities in their ability to protect them. This applies where the alleged perpetrator is an official or a private person.[88] Failure thoroughly to investigate possible racist motives for the shooting of two unarmed Roma conscripts by military police, where the use of force was grossly excessive and a witness allegedly heard an officer shout racial abuse immediately after the event, was found in *Nachova v Bulgaria* to disclose a procedural breach of Art.14. It had regard in that finding to other international bodies' concerns about racist violence in Bulgaria and two previous cases against Bulgaria in which Roma had died in State custody in breach of Art.2. However, the Grand Chamber disagreed with the approach of the Chamber which had found that, in the absence of a proper investigation into the shooting of two unarmed Roma conscripts by military police, the burden of proof shifted onto the Government to disprove that the killing itself was in substantive breach of Art.14. While it did not exclude that in certain

[84] *Wagner and JMWL v Luxembourg*, June 28, 2007.

[85] *Petrov v Bulgaria*, May 22, 2008, paras 53–56.

[86] *Menson*, fn.1 above; *Nachova v Bulgaria*, July 6, 2005, ECHR 2005–VII, paras 145 and 160.

[87] See also *Moldovan v Romania (No.2)*, July 12, 2005, where the living conditions and the authorities' treatment of the grievances of the applicant Roma, burnt out of their homes, disclosed degrading treatment, in addition to breaches of Arts 8 and 6, alone and in conjunction with Art.14: there was overtly racist remarks throughout the proceedings, the length and outcome of which, could, as a result, be said to be based on their ethnicity.

[88] *Secic v Croatia*, May 31, 2007, para.67, attack on a Roma by extremist skinheads.

situations it might be for the Government to provide a convincing explanation that the events were not shaped by discrimination, it considered that where it was alleged that an act of violence was racially motivated such an approach would amount to requiring the respondent Government to prove the absence of a particular subjective attitude on the part of the person concerned.[89] In *Stoica v Romania*, where there was evidence of police officers using stereotypical abuse of a Roma before beating him, it was found that the assault was carried out in a racial context; substantive violation of Art.14 in conjunction with Art.3 was thus found.[90]

From subsequent cases, it would appear that there must be some overt sign of racist motivations before the procedural obligation is engaged,[91] and that where the indications are weak, the obligation will be discharged if the authorities show that they have given racist motivation consideration and reasons for discounting it.[92] Treating crimes of violence inspired by racial hatred in the same way as others fails to account for the distinction between the two; there is accordingly a requirement that criminal proceedings specify, and sanction expressly, offenses of this nature.[93] Pejorative or slighting remarks made by prosecutors themselves during investigations may, as an aggravating factor, disclose a situation in which there has been a failure properly to investigate racial motivation for attacks.[94]

Statements by authorities singling out ethnic minorities for adverse comment may pose serious problems under Art.14 in other contexts. Where in refusing to suspend a sentence on a Roma suspect, the court referred to the impunity reigning amongst minorities as the reason, the Court considered this gave rise to an appearance that heavier sentences were imposed on Roma defendants; no justification for such difference in treatment had been provided by the Government.[95] Similarly, exclusion from the benefits of particular legislation, even in the delicate area of power sharing in the aftermath of a civil conflict, will require convincing justification. Thus, inability of Roma or Jewish individuals to stand for office in Bosnia-Herzegovina, the legislation taking great pains in balancing the three major ethnic groups, was in breach, the Court not persuaded that smaller ethnic minorities could not be catered for.[96] Undue formalism in applying laws to the exclusion of minorities was struck down in a case where a Roma family, the parents married only by Roma rite, had been acknowledged by the authorities for the purposes of various social benefits, yet when the father died, the mother was denied widow's benefits due to the lack of recognition of the marriage in civil law. It was not sufficient argument that the couple could have married under civil law if they had wished.[97]

Where the racism alleged is less overt, it is likely to be harder to substantiate or bring under Art.14. In *Abdulaziz*, where rules rendered it more difficult for spouses in arranged marriages from India and Pakistan to enter,[98] the Court found that these rules applied without differentiation between persons on grounds of race or

[89] *Nachova v Bulgaria*, July 6, 2005, ECHR 2005–VII, para.157.

[90] *Stoica v Romania*, March 4, 2008, paras 128–133.

[91] See *Bekos and Koutropoulos v Greece*, December 13, 2005, para.66, the seriousness of misconduct of police officers was not sufficient to prove the ill-treatment was based on discrimination.

[92] *Green v UK*, (28079/04) (Dec.) May 19, 2005.

[93] *Anguelova and Iliev v Bulgaria*, July 26, 2007, paras 116–117.

[94] *Cobzaru v Romania*, July 26, 2007, para.99; *Moldovan (No.2)*, fn.87 above.

[95] *Paraskeva Todorova v Bulgaria*, March 25, 2010.

[96] *Sejdic and Finci v Bosnia-Herzegovina*, December 22, 2009.

[97] *Munoz Diaz v Spain*, see fn.78 above.

[98] Concerning ancestry links with the UK and that the parties to a marriage must have met.

ethnic origin and that it was legitimate for immigration purposes to favour persons having close links with the United Kingdom. Similarly, different treatment as to entry and residence applying to non-citizen aliens from in and outside the European Union has been found to be objectively and reasonably justified by the special legal regime concerned.[99] However, where treatment of persons within the State's jurisdiction is concerned, there should be less scope for such distinctions. Where an applicant was barred from entering a town on the basis of an order concerning only Chechens, the Court in finding a violation of Art.14 in conjunction with Art.2 of Protocol No.4 noted that the Government had not given any explanation for this treatment and commented that in any event no difference in treatment which was based exclusively or to a decisive extent on a person's ethnic origin was capable of being objectively justified in a contemporary democratic society built on the principles of pluralism and respect for different cultures.[100]

More recently, indirect indiscrimination has been found to arise in several cases concerning Roma children, a disproportionate number of whom were allocated to special schools or special classes. Even though these schools or classes may have been provided with the best intentions of providing educational support, the Court criticised the way in practice these became ways of excluding the Roma children from mainstream schooling, without effective procedural safeguards, either through tests which were in themselves biased [101] or through a lack of tests, without any real prospect of transfer to normal classes or any indication of a curriculum geared to the purported deficiencies.[102] The fact that the parents may themselves have consented to the placements was not a defence, the Court finding that they had not been in a position to give informed consent through proper information or availability of choice. In any event, it was stated that no waiver of the right not to be subjected to racial discrimination could be accepted.[103] Further, as regarded the high drop-out rate of Roma children from school, the Court stated that the authorities should take structured and active measures to encourage school attendance.[104] A particularly nasty violation was found where Roma children were excluded from a primary school following agitation by local people, in the culmination of which their separate teaching annex was burned down, resulting in total lack of access to primary education.[105]

As regards verbal discrimination, the Court found that the reproduction of pejorative phrases about gypsies in a dictionary did not disclose a breach of Article 14 in conjunction with Article 8, since they were not the author's own comments but examples of the perception of Roma people in Turkey and they were preceded by the qualification of the expressions as being of a "metaphorical" nature. Weight was also apparently given to the lack of apparent bad faith or intention to insult.[106]

[99] *Moustaquim*, fn.58 above, para.49.
[100] *Timishev v Russia*, December 13, 2005, ECHR 2005–XII, para.58.
[101] *DH and Others*, fn.7 above, paras 199–202.
[102] *Orsus and Others*, fn.7 above, paras 158–175.
[103] *DH and Others*, fn.7 above, paras 203–204, *Orsus and Others*, fn.7 above, paras 178–179. See also *Sampanis v Greece*, June 5, 2008, paras 93–94, parental consent was not a defence for the authorities where the choice was between insisting on integration with risks of provoking local fury and a place in a "ghetto" class.
[104] *Orsus and Others*, fn.7 above, paras 176–177.
[105] *Sampanis v Greece*, fn.104 above.
[106] *Aksu v Turkey*, July 20, 2010, pending before the Grand Chamber.

(d) Religion

II–316 Reliance on a parent's membership of a religious community (Jehovah's Witnesses) in a court decision on the custody of the children constituted a difference in treatment in *Hoffman v Austria*. While it pursued a legitimate aim (protection of health and rights of the children) it was not reasonably proportionate to base the decision essentially on a difference in religion. This was a majority of five to four, the minority agreeing with the Austrian Supreme Court that account could be taken of blood transfusions and risk of social isolation concerning the children's welfare. The majority essentially relied on the tenor of the Supreme Court's judgment, finding that its tone and attitude were negative on the religious aspect without taking into account the evidence accepted in the lower courts of the emotional need of the children for their mother. Also the Supreme Court gave undue weight to its view that the mother had infringed domestic law in bringing the children up as Jehovah's Witnesses since this was not the religion of the parties at the time of their marriage, an objection based purely on disapproval of the mother unrelated to the children's welfare.[107]

The Court found no objective and reasonable justification in *Canea Catholic Church v Greece* for the situation whereby the applicant church could not take legal proceedings to protect its property rights due to a denial of its legal personality, whereas the Orthodox Church and Jewish Community could do so, without any formality or required procedure.[108]

The mere fact however that one religious body or group enjoys more favourable treatment than others will not always disclose discrimination contrary to Art.14.

With a narrow majority, the Court found in *Cha'are Shalom Ve Tsedek v France* that no discrimination arose from the authorities' decision to give exclusive rights for ritual slaughter to one mainstream Jewish body and to refuse permission to the applicant association whose Jewish members wished to observe stricter rules. The majority considered that it had not been shown that the applicants' members were seriously affected (as they could obtain *glatt* meat from other sources, e.g. Belgium) and allowed leeway to the authorities in the "delicate relations" between the State and religions.[109] In a Spanish case, the Court also rejected complaints from Protestant bodies about the favourable position enjoyed by the Catholic Church due to provisions allowing taxpayers to allocate part of their income tax either to the Catholic Church or for other charitable purposes. It again referred to the margin of appreciation that had to apply to the "fragile relations that exist between the State and religions" and referred to the different financing arrangements of churches existing between Contracting States based on their individual history and traditions. Since Protestants could make other kinds of donations on fiscally advantageous terms to their own churches and the Catholic Church had entered into a specific agreement with the Government which imposed reciprocal obligations (the Catholic Church undertook to place at the service of Spanish society its historic, artistic and documentary heritage) any difference in treatment was not disproportionate.[110]

[107] Similar violation found in *Palau-Martinez v France*, December 16, 2003.
[108] *Canea Catholic Church v Greece*, December 16, 1997, R.J.D. 1997–VIII, 27 E.H.R.R. 521.
[109] The minority was not happy about substituting their own opinion as to the seriousness of an interference with a group's religious beliefs for that of the persons concerned, noting that the essential object of Art.9 was to protect individuals' most private convictions. They did not consider the monopoly had been shown to pursue a legitimate aim or to be proportionate, given the importance of ensuring religious pluralism.
[110] *Alujer Fernandez and Cabellero Garcia v Spain*, (53072/99) (Dec.) June 14, 2001, ECHR 2001–VI.

Nonetheless, differences in applicable rules may not be sufficiently justified. Where different legal regimes applied to religions not perceived to be old or established, in particular a longer waiting period for registration, the Court considered that this was not supported by reasonable justification in the case of the Jehovah's Witnesses who were well-known and present in the country for many years.[111] Restrictions on access to court, requiring a greco-catholic church to apply first to a non-judicial commission concerning disputes, which was not applied to other religious bodies was not justified either.[112] Inconsistent application of rules concerning which religious bodies could provide religious education in schools and conduct recognised marriages offended, where the authorities' decision refusing to enter such an agreement with certain reform churches disclosed that the qualifying criteria were not being applied to religious bodies in an equal manner.[113]

Failure to protect a religious group from violence, and lack of effective follow-up by the authorities to such incidents may disclose discriminatory practices in conjunction with Arts 3 and 9, as in a case where a meeting of Jehovah's Witnesses was attacked by supporters of an unfrocked, rabble-rousing orthodox priest, the official inaction being regarded as a "corollary" of the applicants' convictions.[114] Where a Hare Krishna applicant was victim of recurring attacks, the Court found under Art.3 not only that the official investigation was ineffective and half-hearted but that the authorities had failed to protect him from a real and predictable threat. There was a further procedural breach under Art.14 in conjunction with Art.3 as there was a duty to investigate properly violent crimes motivated by religious extremism; the authorities had unjustifiably refused to take the applicant seriously carrying out a pro forma investigation only.[115]

Situations which result in unwarranted stigmatisation of individuals through disclosure of their religious affiliations may raise issues. Where school certificates indicated an absence of a mark for religious/ethics studies, but schooling in the latter option was practically non-existent, it was considered that this could label a child who had chosen not to follow the course as not adhering to the majority religion of the country and impose pressure to join such classes.[116]

(e) *Birth*

While it may be legitimate to protect and nurture traditional family relationships, the Court considers, having regard to the importance of social integration, that there is no justification for subjecting children out of wedlock to different rules in relation to the possibility of inheriting property from parents. In *Marckx v Belgium*,[117] the Court found no objective or reasonable justification under Art.14 in conjunction with Art.8 in that a child born out of wedlock was subject to rules whereby the II–317

[111] *Religionsgemeinschafe der zeugen Jehovas and others v Austria*, July 28, 2008, paras 96–99.

[112] *Paroisse Greco Catholique Sâmbata Bihor v Roumania*, January 12, 2010, paras 79–82.

[113] *Savez crkava "Riječ Života" v Croatia*, December 9, 2010, paras 89–93.

[114] 97 *Members of the Gldani Congregation of Jehovah's Witnesses and 4 others v Georgia*, May 3, 2007, there was ample evidence of official indifference and inaction allowing "Father Basil" and his supporters to act with impunity.

[115] *Milanovic v Serbia*, fn.2 above, paras 87–90 and 96–101.

[116] *Grzelak v Poland*, June 15, 2010, effectively overruling an inadmissibility decision on a similar complaint in *Saniewski v Poland*, (40319/98) (Dec.). June 26, 2001.

[117] See also *Johnston*, a similar situation in Ireland, but with a finding of a violation of Art.8, no separate issue arose under Art.14.

mother had to take special steps for the family link to obtain legal recognition and which limited the unmarried mother's ability to leave property to a child born out of wedlock. It was not enough, as the Government argued that the mother could take other steps to protect the child's interests.[118] The Court also rejected the notion that unmarried mothers were less likely to wish to take the responsibility for caring for a child as unproved by the figures or that the risk of upsetting "legitimate" families by allowing "illegitimate" members to share family property was an acceptable motive for deriving a child of fundamental rights.

A variant in *Inze v Austria* concerned the precedence taken by a legitimate child over one born out of wedlock as regarded designation as the principal heir of a farm in case of intestacy. Examining the case under Art.14 in conjunction with Art.1 of the First Protocol, the Court found the justifications general and abstract. It rejected the Government's reference to the "convictions" of the local rural population as part of the "traditional outlook." Nor was it persuaded by the arguments of the Government in *Mazurek v France* that it was justified, for inheritance purposes, to penalise the applicant as an adulterine child, noting that such children could not be blamed for circumstances for which they were not responsible. Arguments as to legal certainty were not sufficient to justify legislation that only gave inheritance rights to children born out of wedlock after 1949 and where the father was resident in the former GDR; this was seen as unduly penalising the applicant who in the particular case had been recognised after the birth by her father and no doubt arose as to paternity.[119] Given the common European acceptance of the importance of equality between children born in and out of wedlock, very weighty reasons would now have to be advanced before a difference of treatment on that ground could be regarded as compatible with the Convention.[120]

Discrimination also arose where domestic courts interpreted a will in such a manner as to exclude an adopted child, as opposed to a natural child.[121]

(f) National origin and national minorities

II–318 Very weighty reasons are required for difference of treatment based solely on national origin.[122]

National origin is not a permissible ground for excluding an applicant from employment or welfare benefits where he otherwise satisfies all the eligibility criteria[123] or where a national in exactly the same circumstances would have

[118] Referring to the recognition by the Committee of Ministers that the single mothers and children were a form of family no less than others (resolution of social protection); see *Marckx*, fn.19, p.14).

[119] *Brauer v Germany*, (3545/04) (Dec.) May 28, 2009.

[120] *Mazurek v France*, February 1, 2000, ECHR 2000–II, paras 48–55; see also a finding of a violation of Art.14 in conjunction with Art.8 where the applicant, born out of wedlock, was treated differently from those children similarly born out of wedlock but recognised by their father, *Camp and Bourimi v Netherlands*, October 3, 2000, ECHR 2000–X; and in *Merger and Clos v France*, December 22, 2004, concerning inability of a child born out of wedlock to receive a gift from its father, inter vivos or testamentary of more than a certain amount.

[121] *Pla and Puncernau*, fn.51 above.

[122] *Luczak v Poland*, November 27, 2007, para.52; *Andrejeva v Latvia*, February 18, 2009, para.87.

[123] *Gaygusuz v Austria*, September 16, 1996, R.J.D. 1996–IV; 23 E.H.R.R. 364, the applicant had worked and paid contributions, the sole reason for exclusion being his alien status; *Koua Poirrez v France*, September 30, 2003, it was not relevant that the applicant's country of origin had not signed a reciprocity agreement with France on invalidity or other benefits.

obtained the benefit.[124] Nor were convincing reasons put forward for excluding a farmer of foreign origin from a social security scheme restricted to purely Polish farmers, the economic reasons being rather vague and the impact on the individual of exclusion from important social protection correspondingly crucial[125] or where a mother was refused large family benefits due to her perceived status as a foreigner.[126] Refusal of legal aid to a Congolese woman seeking to regularise the paternity of her daughter by a Belgian father on the basis that she did not have a residence permit was found to concern a matter crucial to the family and private lives of several persons, in respect of which the distinction between persons with and without right of abode was not justified by any weighty reasons.[127]

Restriction of an amnesty for war crimes to Italian citizens was considered justified by the purpose of post-war reconciliation between Italian citizens; no issue arose from the exclusion from the amnesty of a German accused of participation in a massacre of Italian villagers.[128]

It is not an answer to a difference in treatment on grounds of nationality that the applicant could avoid the problem by "naturalisation"; in other words placing the burden on the applicant to connive at the discrimination by removing the element of personal status which was stigmatizing; this would render Art.14 devoid of purpose.[129]

Arguments have been attempted that discrimination is revealed where members of a particular national minority appear to be more at risk of death or ill-treatment. However, as regards allegations in applications from the south-east Turkey that forcible evacuation of villages, torture and death in custody disclosed discrimination against people of Kurdish origin, the Court, relying on the Commission's findings, found them unsubstantiated.[130] Where it was argued in cases from Northern Ireland that the vast majority of victims of security force killings were Catholics, the Court commented that statistics by themselves could not disclose discrimination.[131] In other contexts, however, statistics revealing a particular group are impacted disproportionately by a measure have disclosed a prima facie case which the Government have to rebut (see General considerations and (c) Race above).

[124] *Andrejeva,* fn.122 above, paras 87–92, where the periods of work in Russia before independence were not taken into account for pension entitlement purposes for a permanent non-national resident, whereas they would have for a national; the applicant was stateless so no arguments that she had protection from another system were valid.

[125] *Luczak v Poland*, fn.118 above, paras 53–60.

[126] *Zeibek v Greece*, fn.18 above, violation of Art.14 in conjunction with Art.1 of Protocol No. 1; the Court commented adversely on the approach of the authorities in justifying the payment of such benefits as encouraging native Greeks to have large families for demographic reasons, irrespective of whether the persons excluded in fact had or could claim Greek nationality. See also *Weller v Hungary*, fn.18 above, breach of Art.14 in conjunction with Art.8 where children of a foreign mother were not eligible for claims of maternity benefit on their behalf; *Fawsie v Greece*, fn.16 above, violation where a resident refugee was denied a large family benefit.

[127] *Anakomba Yula v Belgium*, March 10, 2009, breach of Art.14 in conjunction with Art.6 concerning access to court.

[128] *Sommer v Italy*, (36586/08) (Dec.) March 23, 2010.

[129] *Andrejeva*, fn.118 above, para.91.

[130] *Akdivar*, para.99.

[131] e.g. *Hugh Jordan v UK*, May 4, 2001, para.154. See, however, *DH and Others v Czech Republic*, fn.7 above, which indicates that a presumption of indirect discrimination can arise effectively requiring rebuttal by the Government (violation of Art.14 in conjunction with Art.2 of Protocol No.1, where a disproportionately high number of Roma children were being segregated in special schools).

(g) *Sexual orientation*

II–319 It was not discriminatory to deny a survivor's pension to a gay partner, where French law restricted such benefits to those in marriage: there was no comparable situation.[132] On the other hand, calculation of child maintenance obligations of an applicant mother living with another woman which did not take into account reductions applicable where the absent parent entered into a new relationship were discriminatory, the Court seeing no reason for treating the applicant differently than if she had entered a new relationship with a man.[133] See further sections Homosexuality and Transsexuals.

(h) *Place of residence*

II–320 Rules concerning eligibility for benefits can, it seems, legitimately be geared to conditions of residence. In *Carson and Others v UK*, where United Kingdom pensioners living abroad in Australia and Canada did not benefit from uprating of their pensions. Those living abroad had weaker links with the home country, not paying tax or subject to the same social and economic conditions and so could not compare themselves with those remaining at home. Similarly, no problem arose where a person living in Algeria who had contributed to a pension scheme before Algeria's independence from France was excluded from claiming under the scheme in France many years later due to his non-residence status.[134]

(i) *Other*

II–321 Discrimination arose where dockers, claiming that they were being treated adversely due to their trade union membership, were unable to bring their complaints before a court. The Government was found to have failed to fulfil its positive obligation to adopt measures of effective and clear judicial protection against discrimination on the ground of trade union membership.[135]

In a rare case concerning the treatment of the handicapped, the Court took the opportunity to refer to the existence of a European and global consensus on the importance of protecting the handicapped from discrimination. It found the Swiss authorities had discriminated against the applicant, ruled as unfit for military service due to his diabetes but required instead to pay an annual tax instead. They had failed to strike a fair balance, in particular due to the failure to provide the applicant who had been willing to do his service with an alternative form of duty, the non-negligible amount of the sum and duration of the obligation imposed on the applicant and the insignificance of the tax as regarded the system of military conscription as a whole.[136]

As concerns other health conditions, the Court found it unjustified to refuse a residence permit to the Uzbek husband and father of Russian citizens on the ground that he had HIV. International materials indicated public health concerns about

[132] *Manenc v France*, (66686/09) (Dec.) September 21, 2009.
[133] *JM v UK*, September 29, 2010.
[134] *Si Amer v France*, October 29, 2009.
[135] *Danilenkov v Russia*, fn.3 above.
[136] *Glor v Switzerland*, April 30, 2009.

HIV did not require travel restrictions; indeed imposing penalties on HIV sufferers might drive the illness underground, preventing proper treatment and prevention. The Court also disliked the blanket nature of the refusal, which did not allow the applicant's family circumstances to be taken into account.[137]

There are barely any cases so far invoking "ageism". The principal case so far accepted that the authorities were entitled to impose a maximum age for those seeking to adopt children. The applicant was refused as there was a 47 to 48 year age difference between her and the child concerned; this was perceived as not being in the best interests of the child, such interests trumping those of the would-be parent.[138]

Cross-reference

Part IIB, s.27: Homosexuality.
Part IIB, s.47: Transsexuals.

[137] *Kiyutin v Russia*, March 10, 2011, paras 64–74.
[138] *Schwizgebel*, fn.49, paras 93–99.

13. Education

Key provisions:

II–322 Article 2 of Protocol No.1 (right to education) and Art.14 (prohibition of discrimination).

Key case-law:

Belgian Linguistics case, July 23, 1968, Series A No.6, 1 E.H.R.R. 252; *Kjeldsen, Busk Madsen and Pedersen v Denmark*, December 7, 1976, Series A No.23, 1 E.H.R.R. 711; *Campbell and Cosans v UK*, February 25, 1982, Series A No.48, 4 E.H.R.R 293; *Costello-Roberts v UK*, March 25, 1993, Series A No.247–C, 19 E.H.R.R. 112; *Valsamis v Greece*, December 18, 1996, R.J.D. 1996–VI, 24 E.H.R.R. 294; *Cyprus v Turkey*, May 10, 2001, ECHR 2001–V, 23 E.H.R.R 244; *Leyla Sahin v Turkey*, November 10, 2005, ECHR 2005–XI; *Folgero v Norway*, June 29, 2007, ECHR 2007–. . . ; *Lautsi v Italy*, March 18, 2011, ECHR 2011–. . .

1. General considerations

II–323 Until recently there have been relatively few cases exploring the substance of this provision, "no person shall be denied the right to education". This possibly reflects the fact that in general the Contracting States cater adequately for perceived educational needs. The issues which have tended to arise concern alleged prejudicial treatment of ethnic minority children in schools and perceived indoctrination in schools of some religious flavour.

The Court in an early case held that the provision enshrines the right of everyone to education.[1] But education is a wide concept. It is not just children who require education; there is a whole range of technical, vocational and professional training as well as undergraduate and postgraduate studies which may be pursued until the grave. And it would be an expensive exercise for a State to guarantee such further studies and training on an unlimited scale.[2] The Court has recognised that the development of the right to education, the content of which will vary in time and place according to social and economic circumstances, will depend largely on the needs and resources of the community.[3] The rights under this provision must also be interpreted in light of each other but also the other provisions of the Convention, in particular, Arts 8, 9 and 10.[4]

There is Commission case-law to the effect that the right to education is concerned primarily with elementary education and not necessarily advanced studies such as technology.[5] The Court has changed emphasis. Elementary education has

[1] *Kjeldsen,Busk Madsen and Pedersen v Denmark*, December 7, 1976, Series A No.23, 1 E.H.R.R. 711, para.50.

[2] The only reservation made by the United Kingdom under the Convention relates to Art.2 of Protocol No.1, stating that the principle in the second sentence of Art.2 is accepted only so far as it is compatible with the provision of efficient instruction and training, and the avoidance of unreasonable public expenditure. The validity of the reservation is untested.

[3] *Leyla Sahin v Turkey*, November 10, 2005, ECHR 2005–. . . , para.136.

[4] *Folgero v Norway*, June 29, 2007, ECHR 2007–. . . , para.84(a).

[5] (5962/72) (Dec.) March 13, 1975, 2 DR 50, where the Commission rejected in very brief terms the complaint of the 27–year-old applicant that he was unable to continue specialised technological studies in prison; (7671/76) (Dec.) May 19, 1977, 9 D.R.185, where the Commission found that foreign students, who were claiming to follow various studies but were being expelled from the UK under applicable immigration measures, could not rely on Art.2 as granting them a right to stay in the country.

been underlined as being of primordial importance to a child's development[6] and it has gone on to hold that Art.2 also applies to existing institutions of higher education in Contracting States. It found a violation in respect of a failure of the Turkish Cypriot authorities in northern Cyprus to make available appropriate secondary school facilities to the Greek Cypriots[7] and held that university education falls within the scope of the education right.[8] The manner in which the right applies though will be influenced by the context.[9]

Art.2 of Protocol No.1 is silent as to the standard of education provided. However, differing types of education made available to children on the basis of ethnic or other origin clearly raises issues in conjunction with Art.14 (see below, 8. Discrimination). There is also some support for the proposition that vulnerable groups of children may require positive measures in order to ensure that they are able to benefit from the education on offer, including active steps to combat absenteeism.[10]

Art.2 of Protocol No.1 is the *lex specialis* in the area of education and schooling, so that complaints about alleged religious indoctrination in schools fall to be examined under this provision rather than Art.9.[11]

2. Access to education

Access to education cannot, practically, be without limitations, notwithstanding the absence of any express restrictions in Art.2 of the First Protocol. The Contracting States enjoy a certain margin of appreciation in this sphere therefore but any restrictions should not impair the essence of the right and deprive it of effectiveness.[12] While there must be a legitimate aim, there is no exhaustive list as in other provisions of the Convention.[13] A lawful basis for measures is required.[14] II–324

Access may be restricted to those who apply for entrance in accordance with applicable formalities and pass any necessary examinations.[15] While the Court may consider itself competent to examine whether an applicant was being denied access on unlawful, unreasonable or arbitrary grounds,[16] it is likely to resist being dragged into debates as to academic ability, concerned rather with fairness of procedures, and any element of discrimination on racial or other grounds to the extent that such could be proved (see below, 8. Discrimination).

Disciplinary measures, which ensure compliance with internal rules and are part of the process by which an institution seeks to achieve its objects, should in principle acceptable. The Commission found a complaint inadmissible where a 16–year-old

[6] *Timishev v Russia*, December 13, 2005, ECHR 2005–XII, para.64.

[7] *Cyprus v Turkey*, May 10, 2001, ECHR 2001–V, 23 E.H.R.R 244, paras 278–280.

[8] *Eren v Turkey*, February 7, 2006, where the applicant was denied entry to university despite obtaining one of the highest results due to an apparently arbitrary decision that he must have obtained the results by cheating; *Leyla Sahin*, fn.3 above, where Art.2 was applicable to medical studies at university.

[9] *Leyla Sahin*, fn.3 above, para.142.

[10] *Orsus and Others v Croatia,* March 16, 2010, paras 148, 176–177.

[11] *Lautsi v Italy*, March 18, 2011, ECHR 2011–. . . , para.59.

[12] *Leyla Sahin*, fn.3 above, para.154 ; see, however, *Ciftci v Turkey*, (71860/01) (Dec.) June 17, 2004, which refers to a "considerable discretion".

[13] *Leyla Sahin*, fn.3 above, para.154.

[14] *Timishev*, fn.6 above, where the exclusion of Chechen children from primary school was unlawful; see also lack of legal basis in *Eren*, fn.8 above.

[15] *Lukach v Russia*, (40841/99) (Dec.) November 16, 1999.

[16] e.g. *Eren*, fn.8 above.

was suspended for bad behaviour: it was not found to be a denial of education for his return to school to be made conditional on his undertaking to be of good behaviour.[17] Similarly, expulsion or exclusion for cheating, where lawful and with a rational basis, does not generally injure the substance of the right.[18] A suspension of university students for one or two terms for making petition for Kurdish-language classes was found to be disproportionate, given that the students had not disrupted discipline or order in any way.[19]

Restrictions should not conflict with other provisions of the Convention and Protocols, being read together where appropriate (for example with Arts 8, 9 or 10).[20] Where, in *Campbell and Cosans*, a boy was suspended as a result of a refusal by himself and his parents to accept the disciplinary use of the "tawse" in a Scottish school, which conflicted with the parents' right to ensure the teaching of their children in line with their philosophical convictions, there was also a finding by the Court of a denial of education to the boy. However, the exclusion of a female student from university for wearing a headscarf did not disclose a denial of her right to education, where that restriction had already been found to be compatible with the right to manifest religion as pursuing the legitimate aim of preserving the secular character of educational institutions in a proportionate manner, with due safeguards protecting student interests.[21]

Interruptions in education caused by lawful detention[22] or restrictions incidental to immigration measures[23] found compatible with Art.8 of the Convention have not raised issues. Where local authorities issue enforcement notices to remove gypsy caravans stationed on land without planning permission, the Court has so far held that the applicant gypsies have failed to substantiate complaints that the children were effectively denied the right to education as a result of the legitimate planning measures.[24] Restriction on access to one particular aspect of the curriculum has also not been found to constitute a denial of education, where a girl in a wheelchair had no access to the science labs.[25]

Prisoners cannot rely on Art.2 of Protocol No.1 to impose an obligation on the State to organise any particular type of education or training in the prison.[26] Where educational courses are provided, it is undecided to what extent any issues could arise from any discriminatory or arbitrary denial of access to the facilities.

However while there may be a right to education for a child—so much is clear—there is no right of access to a particular State school of choice. Parents who

[17] (13477/87) (Dec.) October 4, 1989.

[18] *Sulak v Turkey*, (24515/94) (Dec.) January 17, 1996, 84–A D.R. 98; cf. *Mürsel Eren*, para.50, where the exclusion for presumed cheating in a university entrance examination was arbitary.

[19] *Irfan Temel v Turkey*, March 3, 2009; *Ali v UK*, January 11, 2011, finding no breach arising from the temporary suspension of a secondary school student under investigation for setting fire to a classroom.

[20] *Leyla Sahin*, fn.3 above, para.155.

[21] *Leyla Sahin*, fn.3 above; see also *Köse and 93 others v Turkey*, (26625/02) (Dec.) January 24, 2006, where rules excluding girls wearing headscarves in a state secondary school were compatible with Art.2.

[22] *Slivenko v Latvia*, (48321/99) (Dec.) January 23, 2002, ECHR 2002–II, brief periods of detention pursuant to deportation measures did not to pose a significant obstacle to an applicant's secondary education; *Durmaz v Turkey*, (46506/99) etc (Dec.) September 4, 2001, interruption in full-time education during lawful detention after conviction was not construed as deprivation of the right to education; *Arslan v Turkey*, (31320/02) (Dec.) June 1, 2006, lawful detention interrupting university education was not a deprivation of education.

[23] e.g. (23938/94) (Dec.) October 23, 1995; (26922/95) (Dec.) November 29, 1995; *Vikulov v Latvia*, (16870/03) (Dec.) March 25, 2004.

[24] e.g. *Lee v UK*, January 18, 2001.

[25] *Molly McIntyre v UK*, (29046/95) (Dec.) October 21, 1998.

[26] *Valasinas v Lithuania*, July 24, 2001.

complained of the closure of a local school had their application to the Commission rejected on the basis that the children were able to attend another school a mile further away.[27]

Nor is there any obligation on the State to provide any specific educational system. The provision does however guarantee that persons subject to the jurisdiction of a State should have the right to avail themselves of the educational institutions existing at a given time.[28]

While there is a right to start and run a private school, this must be subject to conditions, namely, regulation by the State to ensure fulfilment of its responsibility to provide a proper educational system, even in the private sector. The Commission found in *Ingrid Jordebo v Sweden*[29] that the State's refusal to allow a private school to run senior classes (above 16 years) was not incompatible, having particular regard to the reasons given, i.e. an absence of teachers with the requisite qualifications.

3. State schools and public schools

The Commission and Court both found that the State is responsible for both State schools and privately run or public schools.[30] The State cannot absolve itself from its responsibility of securing the right of education to everyone by delegating its obligations to private bodies or individuals. II–325

On the other hand, States are not obliged to grant subsidies to private education, for the establishment or running of private education.[31] A right cannot be derived to obtain from the authorities the creation of a particular kind of establishment.[32] Problems may however arise where they hand out money to some educational institutions but not others or permit discrimination in the entrance requirements (see below).

4. Education in accordance with philosophical convictions

There is in effect no absolute right for parents to have their children educated in accordance with their philosophical convictions, only a right to have such right respected,[33] although this has been said to mean more than acknowledgment or that they are taken into account, implying a positive obligation.[34] Furthermore respect is only due to convictions which do not conflict with the right of the child to education.[35] Setting and planning of school curricula fall in principle within the competence of the State, along with questions of expediency which may legitimately vary from country to country. It is not forbidden to impart through education information or knowledge of a directly or indirectly religious or philosophical kind. II–326

[27] (11644/85) (Dec.) December 1, 1986.

[28] *Belgian Linguistics case*, July 23, 1968, Series A, No.6, 1 E.H.R.R. 252, pp.31–32.

[29] (11533/85) (Dec.) March 6, 1987, 51 D.R. 125.

[30] e.g. *Kjeldsen, Busk Madsen and Pedersen v Denmark*, December 7, 1976, Series A, No.23, 1 E.H.R.R. 711; *Costello-Roberts v UK*, March 25, 1993, Series A, No.247–C, 19 E.H.R.R. 112.

[31] (6853/74) (Dec.) March 9, 1977, 9 D.R. 27; (23419/94) (Dec.) September 6, 1995, 21 D.R. 41.

[32] i.e. in the context of language teaching in the *Belgian Linguistics case*, fn.28 above, para.9.

[33] (10233/83) (Dec.) March 6, 1984, 37 D.R. 105.

[34] *Folgero v Norway*, June 29, 2007, ECHR 2007–. . . , para.84(c).

[35] *Konrad v Germany*, (35504/03) (Dec.) September 11, 2006, where parents wished to withdraw their children from primary school due to their religious convictions.

Nor can parents object to the integration of such teaching into the school curriculum or otherwise all institutionalised teaching would risk becoming impracticable. Many subjects cannot avoid having some philosophical complexion or even religious elements, bearing in mind that some religions have a very broad dogmatic base and offer answers to every kind of philosophical, cosmological or moral question.[36] Thus, the mere inclusion of ideas which were contrary to a particular faith is not problematic, there being no right not to be exposed to contrary opinions in religious and ethical matters.[37] State responsibility in this context also covers, not only the content of the curricula, but may also be engaged by the organisation of the school environment, such as the presence of crucifixes in State-run classrooms.[38]

The concept of "convictions" has been defined by the Court as denoting views that attain a certain level of cogency, seriousness, cohesion and importance.[39] It has had more difficulty with the notion of "philosophical" which has varying meanings and connotations from the serious to the trivial but it has held that it denoted in this context such convictions as are "worthy of respect in a democratic society". In *Campbell and Cosans*, the Court found that the applicants' views as to the use of the "tawse" in the Scottish school attended by their sons related to a weighty and substantial aspect of human life and behaviour, namely, the integrity of the person and the propriety or otherwise of the infliction of corporal punishment. It found that the provision of education subject to this disciplinary condition failed to respect the applicants' philosophical convictions. Supporters of secularism may also claim their views attain the level of "conviction".[40]

Where a disciplinary measure is mild, the Court has given less weight to parental convictions. In *Valsamis v Greece*, a child Jehovah's Witness was suspended for one day for failing to participate in Greek National Day celebrations, to which her parents had objected as a nationalistic event commemorating a war. The Court noted that the child was exempted from religious studies and found nothing in the purpose of the parade or its arrangements which could offend the applicants' pacifist convictions to an extent prohibited by Art.2 or deprive them of their right to guide their children in line with their convictions.[41]

On the issue of the substance of what is taught, the Court has held that the State in fulfilling its duties must take care that information is conveyed in an objective, critical and pluralistic manner and must not pursue the aims of indoctrination that might be considered as not respecting parents' philosophical convictions. What that might mean will vary according to one's own views. In *Kjeldsen v Denmark*, the parents objected to sex education. The Court, having examined the material in question, found that Denmark had not overstepped the limit in the conveying of necessary factual information to enable the children "to take care of themselves and show consideration for others in that respect" without in any way attempting to

[36] *Valsamis v Greece*, (Comm. Rep.), December 18, 1996, R.J.D. 1996–VI, 24 E.H.R.R. 294, para.38; *Kjeldsen*, fn.30 above, para.53.

[37] *Appel-Irgang v Germany*, (45216/07) (Dec.) October 6, 2009.

[38] *Lautsi*, fn.11 above, paras 63–65.

[39] e.g. *Folgero*, fn.34 above, para.84(c).

[40] *Lautsi*, fn.11 above, para.58.

[41] A minority of the Commission and Court however thought compelling children to participate on a school holiday day could be seen as an indirect attempt to indoctrinate them with a patriotic value system which was difficult to reconcile with the parents' right freely to choose the manner in which their children are educated. There was no plausible reason why it was necessary for her education to attend, particularly where she was already excused religious education classes.

exalt sex or incite them in such practices. The Court also gave weight to the fact that those parents who nonetheless objected were free to send their children to private schools or even to educate them at home.[42] Similarly, no problem arose where there was a rule barring children under 12 from attending Koranic classes at school, where this restriction, aimed at preventing indoctrination of the young, did not prevent the parents from guiding their children in a path in line with their own convictions.[43] Conversely, in *Folgero v Norway*, the authorities were found to have gone too far in the compulsory school subject of Christianity, Religion and Philosophy, which despite intentions to provide an open and inclusive school environment regardless of children's backgrounds, went beyond imparting knowledge about Christianity. It was based on the object of giving children a "Christian and moral upbringing" and laid preponderant stress on promoting Christianity and its values, together with learning texts by heart and engaging in activities such as prayer, psalms and plays.[44]

The mere fact that a preponderant part of religious education focuses on the dominant religion of the State is not necessarily a problem, as long as it meets the criteria of objectivity and pluralism and respects the convictions of the parents.[45] Failure to give coverage coverage to the range of religions within the State may however cause problems. Where the compulsory religious curriculum in Turkish schools failed to cover the applicants' faith, Alevism, to which many Turkish citizens adhered, the crucial safeguard of pluralism in particular was not met. The Court noted that it was only pluralism in education which could enable pupils to develop a critical mind with regard to religious matters in the context of freedom of thought, conscience and religion.[46] Complete evenhandedness is presumably the most likely to conform with the Convention standard. Where a State opted for a compulsory ethical course which was neutral and gave no precedence to any belief, the applicants' complaints that the subject gave insufficient weight to the majority education of Protestantism were unsuccessful.[47]

As to the availability of exemption from courses with objectionable content, an imbalance on the side of indoctrination was not redressed in *Folgero* by the possibility of partial exemption since this imposed an onerous and intrusive burden on parents, and accordingly full exemption should have been possible. Where, on the other hand, an ethics course hit the right note of objective pluralism, no problem arose from the fact the subject was compulsory, without possibility of exemption.[48] A system of dispensation which required the parents to disclose their convictions or faith to the authorities would be regarded as objectionable.[49]

[42] See a similar approach in *Jiminez and Jiminez Merino v Spain*, (51188/99) (Dec.) May 25, 2000, ECHR 2000–VI. However, where religious indoctrination was concerned, the availability of private schools for objecting parents was not relevant: *Folgero*, fn.34 above, para.101, as the State was under an obligation to ensure pluralism in State schools generally.

[43] *Cifti v Turkey*, (71860/01) (Dec.) June 17, 2004, ECHR 2004–VI.

[44] See, however, the large dissenting minority who, given Norway's history and its state religion, saw nothing objectionable in the fact that Christianity took up about half of the subject, noting that the curriculum aims covered humanist as well as Christian values with no indication that it would not be taught in an objective, critical or pluralistic manner. They also saw nothing onerous in expecting parents who wished partial exemption to take steps to inform themselves of the procedure.

[45] *Folgero*, fn.34 above, para.89; *Hasan and Zeylem Zengin v Turkey*, October 9, 2007, para.63. See also *Lautsi*, fn.11 above, paras 68–78, the presence in school of purely passive symbols of the predominant religion of the country was an allowable reflection of tradition and history.

[46] *Hasan and Zeylem Zengin*, fn.45 above, paras 56–69.

[47] *Appel-Irgang*, fn.37 above.

[48] *Appel-Irgang*, fn.37 above.

[49] *Hasan and Zeylem Zengin v Turkey*, fn.45, paras 71–76.

Where the teaching erred on the side of indoctrination, it was no answer that the parents could put their children in private schools where religion was concerned there was a State obligation to safeguard pluralism for everyone in State schools.[50]

Nor does Art.2 of Protocol No.1 as such guarantee education in a particular language in accordance with the parents' preferences.[51] A failure to provide education in a particular language may however disclose a violation where it in effect denies the substance of the right, as in *Cyprus v Turkey*, where the Turkish authorities in Northern Cyprus abolished secondary schools in Greek while continuing to assume responsibility for the provision of Greek-language primary schools and where the possibility of sending the children away from home to secondary schools in the south could not be regarded as practical or reasonable option given the impact on family life (see below, Discrimination).[52]

The presence of crucifixes in the classroom in State schools in Italy did not denote a process of indoctrination on the respondent State. It was a traditional and historical symbol of importance to the country, which even if of a Christian persuasion, was essentially of a passive nature, unaccompanied by any practices of intolerance to other convictions or proselytising tendencies. It was noted that the parents retained full rights to enlighten their children in line with their own philosophical convictions.[53]

5. State education and home education

II–327 The State may provide for a compulsory system of education. This is not without controversy, since, not infrequently, parents objecting to the State system prefer to educate their children at home. The Commission considered that State regulation of home education was part of its responsibilities to enforce educational standards and where refusal of permission for home education was based on its inadequacy, it effectively found that the State's assessment of the children's right to education prevailed over the parents' particular convictions.[54] The Court has accepted that the exclusion of home schooling at primary school level in Germany, which measures were aimed at ensuring children were integrated into society and preventing the emergence of parallel societies based on separate philosophical convictions.[55]

[50] *Folgero*, fn.34 above, para.101.

[51] *Belgian Linguistics case*, fn.28 above, para.3; *Skender v FRYOM*, (62509/00) (Dec.) November 22, 2001.

[52] See also *Catan and Others v Moldova and Russia*, (43370/04) et al (Dec.) June 15, 2010, admissible complaints under Arts 8 and 2 of Protocol No.1 and Art.14 in conjunction with Arts 3 and the previous provisions, arising out the Transdneistran authorities' measures against schools refusing to use the Cyrillic script. Pending before the Grand Chamber.

[53] *Lautsi*, fn.11 above, paras 68–78.

[54] In (10233/83), fn.33 above, the applicants, who were educating their dyslexic children at home, had been convicted for failing to comply with orders requiring their attendance at a State school. The Commission found that it was not its task to decide whether the parents' or the State's views on education were better for the children and that State had a responsibility to verify and enforce educational standards. Thus obliging parents to co-operate in the assessment of their children's educational standards to ensure a certain level of literacy and numeracy while nevertheless allowing children to be educated at home could not be said to disclose a lack of respect. In a Swedish case, (17678/91) (Dec.) June 30, 1993, the parents obtained permission to educate their children until a certain age, when permission was withdrawn on ground that their education required social contact and a specialisation which the parents were not qualified to give—the Commission found the State had acted within its margin of appreciation in assessing the parents' ability to provide a viable alternative to state schooling.

[55] *Konrad*, fn.35 above.

6. Special educational needs cases

A series of UK cases raised the issue of conflict between parents and education authorities as to the educational needs of children with problems. The Commission gave leeway to the educational authorities in assessing what a child might require, and as to the efficient use of educational resources, with only the weak rider that parental views be taken into account as far as might be consistent with the needs of the child. In *Graeme v UK*,[56] where the child was epileptic with other associated problems, the parents felt he should be catered for within the normal system. The education authority made the child a ward of court and placed him in a special school. The Commission found the child's right to effective education prevailed over the parents' view, to the extent that such could be regarded as a philosophical conviction. While it examined the complaints as to the standard of the education, including complaints of abuse and lack of access to Christian teaching, it found them ill-founded. Impliedly therefore, the Convention organs still retain a supervisory role and in a grossly unreasonable or arbitrary case might find the education authority were not in fact pursuing the effective education of the child. II–328

7. Access to court

Whether proceedings relating to educational matters attracted the guarantees of Art.6 had been left open for some time. Finally, a dispute as to enrolment in a university was found by the Court to involve civil rights and thus fall under the protection of Art.6. The Government's argument that the matter was one of public law failed, the Court considering that the applicant student was not making claims vis-a-vis the public authorities' discretionary powers but in her personal capacity as a beneficiary of a public service. Further, the matter was of considerable importance to the applicant, falling within the ambit of her personal rights and was civil in character within the meaning of Art.6, para.1.[57] II–329

8. Discrimination

Where unequal treatment is apparent as regards access to education, violation may arise under Art.14. In the *Belgian Linguistics case*, a violation was found where French-speaking children resident in a particular Flemish area were denied access to French-speaking schools outside that area but compelled to attend local Dutch-speaking schools.[58] Segregation of Roma children in so-called special classes or schools has also been found to be discriminatory when shown not to be objectively justified by their educational situation.[59] II–330

[56] (13387/88) (Dec.) February 5, 1990; (25212/94) (Dec.) July 4, 1995, 82 D.R. 129.

[57] *Emine Arac v Turkey*, September 23, 2008, the applicant had been refused enrolment due to her identity photograph not conforming to the rules (she was wearing a headscarf)—Art.6 was breached due to lack of adversariality in the Supreme Administrative Court.

[58] Though other complaints of unequal treatment were dismissed as not having been made out, the Court accepted the aim of promoting linguistic unity within regions and knowledge of the normal language of a region as being in the public interest and not disclosing any discrimination. See *Skender v FRYOM*, fn.51 above, where the applicants' complaints about refusal of access to a Turkish-speaking school on the basis of her father's residence in a different district have been declared admissible.

[59] See *DH and Others v Czech Republic* (GC), November 13, 2007, *Sampanis v Greece*, June 5, 2008 and *Orsus and Others v Croatia* (GC), March 16, 2010. See further, Pt IIB, s.12: Discrimination and Pt IIB, s.24: Gypsies and minorities.

While a State is not obliged to fund particular educational schemes, Art.14 requires that authorities do not discriminate in the provision of available financial subsidies. However there is no discrimination where the State makes lesser grants available to private educational institutions than to public ones[60] or gives preference to organisations providing a particular need.[61] Leeway is also given to education authorities as regards the measures taken to accommodate handicapped children in school buildings.[62]

Cross-reference

Part IIB, s.7: Corporal punishment.
Part IIB, s.12: Discrimination.
Part IIB, s.24: Gypsies and minorities.

[60] (7782/77) (Dec.) May 1, 1978, 14 D.R. 179, where it was legitimate and not unreasonable for the State to require the private body to foot 15 per cent of capital costs.

[61] (23419/94), fn.31 above, state subsidies were provided to church schools which were a widespread feature of the educational system.

[62] *Molly McIntyre*, fn.25 above, where the applicant, suffering from muscular dystrophy, could not negotiate the stairs to the science labs and complained that she did not have the same access to the curriculum as her able-bodied peers, the Commission found that the authorities had taken other steps to facilitate her use of the school and the decision, in a small school, not to build an expensive lift, was not disproportionate and struck a fair balance between the demands of the area's school and her needs.

14. Electoral rights

Key provisions:

Art.10 (freedom of expression and to receive and impart information) and Art.3 of Protocol No.1 (free elections ensuring the free expression of the people in the choice of the legislature). II–331

Key case-law:

Mathieu-Mohin and Clerfayt v Belgium, March 2, 1987, Series A, No.113, 10 E.H.H.R 1; *Gitonas v Greece*, July 1, 1997, R.J.D. 1997–IV, No.42; *Pierre-Bloch v France*, October 21, 1997, R.J.D. 1997–VI, No.53, 26 E.H.H.R 202; *Bowman v UK*, February 19, 1998, Reports 1998–I, No.63; *Ahmed v UK*, September 2, 1998, Reports 1998–VI, No.87, 29 E.H.R.R. 1; *Matthews v UK*, February 18, 1999, ECHR 1999–I, 28 E.H.R.R. 361; *Rekvenyi v Hungary*, May 20, 1999, ECHR 1999–III, 30 E.H.R.R. 519; *Labita v Italy*, April 6, 2000, ECHR 2000–IV; *Podkolzina v Latvia*, April 9, 2002, ECHR 2002–II; *Melnychenko v Ukraine*, October 19, 2004, ECHR 2004–X; *Hirst v UK (No.2) v UK*, October 6, 2005, ECHR 2005–IX; *Zdanoka v Latvia*, March 16, 2006, ECHR 2006–. . . ; *Yumak and Sadak v Turkey*, July 8, 2008, ECHR 2008–. . . ; *Sejdic and Finci v Bosnia-Herzegovina*, December 22, 2009, ECHR 2009–. . . ; *Tanase v Moldova*, April 27, 2010, ECHR 2010–. . . ; *Paksas v Lithuania*, January 6, 2011, ECHR 2011–. . .

1. General considerations

The Convention ascribes much importance to the values of a democratic society. The human rights guaranteed in it are seen as being best guaranteed by "an effective political democracy" (preamble). The proper and fair functioning of the mechanisms of electing proper democratic and representative law-making bodies could therefore be expected to assume key importance. II–332

The sparse early case-law may previously have been an indication of healthy democratic systems. There have been a growing number of cases from more recently-established democracies in many of which serious electoral irregularities have been in issue. However, also significant is the fact that Art.3 of the First Protocol is the only provision which is phrased in collective and general terms, rather than as a specific individual right. The case-law has however interpreted the provision as conferring rights. In *Mathieu-Mothin and Clerfayt v Belgium*, the Court explained that the impersonal phrasing is in fact intended to give greater solemnity to the commitment and reflect the fact that it was not concerned with abstention or non-interference but with a positive obligation to hold democratic elections. There are, however, implied limitations and a wide margin of appreciation, while considerable weight is given to a measure which has received serious parliamentary scrutiny.[1] Such limitations must not impair the essence of the rights such as to deprive them of their effectiveness and should pursue a legitimate aim in a

[1] *Hirst (No.2) v UK*, October 6, 2005, ECHR 2005–IX, para.79; *Sukhovetsky v Ukraine*, March 28, 2006, para.65.

proportionate manner.[2] Nonetheless, even if the individual may have some difficulty in establishing that personal restrictions or particular electoral practices in fact thwart the "free expression of the people" as a whole, there is a growing emphasis in recent cases on lack of arbitrariness and safeguards in procedures and decisions related to electoral matters, as well as on the requirement of clear, well-defined, not overly-broad legislative provisions to prevent arbitrary restrictions on rights.

2. Legislature

(a) *National legislature*

II–333 The legislature is not necessarily restricted to the national parliament or assembly. Having regard to the federal or cantonal structure of some Contracting States, regard must also be had to the particular constitutional system. For example, the diets of the German *Länder* are legislature for the purpose of Art.3,[3] as are Regional Councils a constituent part of the legislature in Italy.[4] In the highly particular situation in Bosnia-Herzegovina, where the present, electoral system was founded on a backdrop of brutal violence and ethnic conflict, the Grand Chamber majority considered that the House of Peoples, as the second house in the Parliament, was part of the legislature as it enjoyed wide powers to control the passage of legislature, decide upon State revenues and to consent to the ratification of treaties, even though, as a dissenter pointed out, it was a non-elective organ with the specific function of giving the three major ethnic groupings a veto power to protect the interests of their peoples.[5]

Local authorities with purely delegated powers will not qualify. While the regional councils of Belgium could submit bills, this was not enough, as they did not become law until passed by the national Parliament in which legislative powers were exclusively concentrated.[6] The abolition of the GLC in London did not raise a problem since it was a creature of statute, its powers purely derivative, subordinate and subsidiary to Parliament which held absolute constitutional authority. While the GLC had considerable power, it was of an administrative nature, often subject to approval from executive authority. In particular, it did not exercise any inherent rule-making power and those powers delegated to it by Parliament were exercised subject to its ultimate control.[7]

Referenda, however significant in national politics, do not generally form part of an election for the legislature.[8] Nor do presidential elections generally fall within the

[2] *Mathieu-Mohin and Clerfayt v Belgium*, March 2, 1987, Series A, No.113, 10 E.H.H.R 1, para.52; *Gitonas v Greece*, July 1, 1997, R.J.D. 1997–IV, No.42, para.39; *Matthews v UK*, February 18, 1999, ECHR 1999–I, 28 E.H.R.R. 361, para.63.

[3] (27311/95) (Dec.) September 11, 1995, 82–A D.R. 158.

[4] *Santoro v Italy*, July 1, 2004, para.52; see also *Py v France*, January 11, 2005, ECHR 2005–I, where Congress in New Caledonia was sufficiently involved in the legislative process through making local territorial laws with the rank of statute.

[5] *Sejdic and Finci v Bosnia-Herzegovina*, December 22, 2009, ECHR 2009–. . . , paras 40–41, the members of the upper house were chosen by the delegates from the Entities' separate legislatures. See Judge Myjer's dissenting opinion finding the complaint outside the scope of Art.3.

[6] (6745) and (6746/74) (Dec.) May 30, 1975, 2 D.R. 110.

[7] (11391/85) (Dec.) July 5, 1985, 43 D.R.236; also not qualifying were local authorities in Northern Ireland: (5155/71) (Dec.) July 12, 1976, 6 D.R. 13; municipal authorities in Vladivostok: *Cherepkov v Russia*, (51501/99) (Dec.) January 25, 2000; and Provincial Councils: *Santoro v Italy*, (36681/97) (Dec.) January 16, 2003.

[8] e.g. (7096/75) (Dec.) October 3, 1975, 3 D.R. 165; *Hilbe v Liechtenstein*, (31981/96) (Dec.) September 7, 1999, ECHR 1999–VI.

scope of Art.3,[9] although it may be that where the Head of State had powers to initiate or adopt legislation to such control the passage of legislation or to censure the legislative bodies the office might be capable of being regarded as part of the legislature.[10]

(b) European Parliament

Initially doubtful that the drafters intended to cover anything but national legislatures, the Commission considered in 1979 that the European Parliament was an advisory body with certain supervisory and budgetary powers but noted that developments in the structure of the EEC might make it necessary for the Contracting States to guarantee Art.3 rights if new representative bodies assumed at least in part the powers and functions of the national legislative bodies.[11] Eight years later, when a "Green" challenged the voting system in France for the European Parliament,[12] the Commission noted that the European Parliament's role had increased following the Single European Act but that it still did not constitute a legislature within the ordinary meaning of the term. By the time of *Matthews v UK*, which came after the Maastricht Treaty, the European Parliament's powers were no longer only "advisory and supervisory". The Court found that it was sufficiently involved in specific legislative processes leading to the passage of legislation and in the general democratic activities of the European Community to constitute part of the legislature for Gibraltar.[13] II–334

3. Right to vote

Art.3 does not expressly guarantee the individual right to vote but refers generally to "conditions" to ensure free expression of the "people". There is a wide margin of appreciation, the Court noting that rules reflecting the need to ensure both citizen participation and knowledge of the particular situation of the region in question will vary according to the historical and political factors peculiar to each State.[14] II–335

There is however recent emphasis on individual electoral rights as central to democracy and the rule of law; the right to vote, it was emphasised, was not a privilege and that universal suffrage was the basic principle.[15] However, the case-law also establishes that the right to vote is not absolute or without limitation.[16] Exclusions must however pursue a legitimate aim, be proportionate and any conditions imposed must not thwart the free expression of the people in the choice of the legislature- any exclusions being reconciliable with the underlying purpose of Art.3.[17]

[9] (15344/89) (Dec.) December 14, 1989, 64 D.R. 211; (41090/98) (Dec.) October 21, 1998; *Paksas v Lithuania*, January 6, 2011, ECHR 2011–. . . , para.72.
[10] *Boskoski v FYROM*, (11676/04) (Dec.) September 2, 2004, ECHR 2004–I. Under Protocol No.12, where there was no need for Art.3 to be applicable, there was discrimination where persons of Roma and Jewish origin could not stand for the Presidency: *Sejdic and Finci*, fn.5 above, paras 52–56.
[11] (8612/79) (Dec.) May 10, 1979, 15 D.R. 259.
[12] (11123/84) (Dec.) December 9, 1987, 54 D.R. 52.
[13] *Matthews v UK*, February 18, 1999, ECHR 1999–I, 28 E.H.R.R. 361, paras 48–54.
[14] e.g. *Py*, fn.4 above, para.46.
[15] *Hirst (No.2)*, fn.1 above, paras 58–59.
[16] e.g. *Matthews*, fn.2 above, para.63.
[17] (27614/95) (Dec.) May 21, 1997, 89–B D.R.76; *Hirst (No.2)*, fn.1 above, para.62.

While a wide margin of appreciation applies in this area, this could not be relied on by the Government in *Hirst v UK (No.2)* to justify a blanket ban on prisoners' voting where this was derived from historic tradition and not from considered legislative debate. The Court held that the severe measure of disenfranchisement could not be lightly imposed and that the principle of proportionality required a discernible and sufficient link between the sanction and the conduct and circumstances of the individual concerned, which was not apparent where the ban automatically restricted the rights of those sentenced to prison for one day or life, for minor offences to serious ones. It hinted that the withdrawal of political rights should preferably be carried out by express judicial decision, a court procedure providing a strong safeguard against arbitrariness.[18] A system which disenfranchised convicted prisoners sentenced to more than a year was also found to offend the principle of proportionality, where the Court emphasised even more strongly that disenfranchisement should be an exception with prisoners.[19]

In the context of persons deprived of the vote because they were under guardianship for mental disability, the Court accepted that it was a legitimate aim to seek to ensure that only citizens capable of assessing the consequences of their actions and of making conscious and judicious decision should participate in public affairs. However, it noted that the bar applied to anyone under guardianship, irrespective of the nature or degree of their disability, and that it was not apparent that the legislature had ever sought to assess the proportionality of the restriction. The blanket ban was accordingly indiscriminate and not compatible with Art.3 of Protocol No.1.[20]

That said, the Convention organs have accepted limitations:

- on persons convicted of collaboration during the war[21];
- based on residence requirements[22] and citizenship[23] which are geared to

[18] The Court distinguished (24927/94) (Dec.) April 14, 1998, 93 D.R. 15, where the Commission found acceptable the inability of an Irish prisoner to vote during an 18–month sentence, noting that the Commission had not referred to the elements of legitimate aim and proportionality identified in *Mathieu-Mohin*, fn.2 above.

[19] *Frodl v Austria*, April 8, 2010, where the Chamber somewhat creatively interpreted *Hirst (No.2)*, fn.1 above, as requiring that decisions had to be taken by a judge and that there should be a link between the offence committed and issues relating to elections and democratic institutions; also *Scoppolo v Italy (No.3)*, January 18, 2011, Where a Chamber went similarly far finding a violation for automatic removal of vote of life prisoner, without a properly reasoned decision on the point by a judge (paras 43–51)—referral has been accepted to the Grand Chamber which will in due course rule on whether *Hirst (No.2)* stands or is to be further developed.

[20] *Alajos Kiss v Hungary*, May 20, 2010.

[21] (6573/74) (Dec.) 1974, 1 D.R. 87, concerning discrimination, the Commission found objective and reasonable justification in preventing persons who had, in wartime, grossly misused their right to participate in public life from misusing their political rights in the future; (8701/79) (Dec.) December 3, 1979, 18 D.R. 250, where permanent deprivation of the vote for a person convicted of collaboration offences was not found arbitrary or calculated to prejudice the free expression of the opinion of the people.

[22] (7566/76) (Dec.) December 11, 1976, 9 D.R. 124, where a British citizen living abroad could not vote in Parliamentary elections; nor was it discrimination that diplomats and servicemen overseas could vote since they were abroad on duty and remained closely linked with their country and under Government control—impliedly accepting as a valid consideration an alleged risk of electoral fraud in the use of postal votes by other persons; *Hilbe*, fn.7 above, where a Liechtenstein citizen, resident in Switzerland for four years, had lost the right to vote in Liechtenstein; *Doyle v UK*, (30158/06) (Dec.) February 6, 2007, not disproportionate that a UK citizen lost the vote after living abroad for 15 years.

[23] (27614/95), fn.17 above.

ensuring that the ballot reflects the will of the "concerned" population or those with strong ties to the territory[24];
- imposition by a court, at the same time as a three-year prison sentence, of a two-year disqualification from exercising public functions, including voting, on a member of Parliament for fiscal fraud[25];
- imposition of a minimum age.[26]

The striking off the electoral roll of suspect Mafia members subject to special police supervision was found to pursue a legitimate aim, but it was disproportionate to continue the measure after a suspect's acquittal.[27] The Court did not accept a disenfranchisement imposed for five years on bankrupts, finding the aims of the measure, intended to shame and stigmatise, were not legitimate.[28]

Exclusion of geographical areas from voting for a particular part of the legislature may be justified by historical or constitutional considerations, as in the case where a citizen of Jersey could not claim the right to vote for the UK Parliament although it had legislative power over the Channel Islands. The Commission noted that Channel Islanders were not resident in the UK and that they had their own elected legislature, making reference to the exceptional and particular historical relationship between the two areas.[29] However, in *Matthews v UK*, the exclusion of the applicant as a resident in Gibraltar in voting in the European Parliament elections was found to disclose a violation as the legislation which emanated from the European Community formed part of the legislation in Gibraltar and the applicant was directly affected by it.[30] Similarly, as regards exclusion of particular minority groups, the inability of a Turkish Cypriot from any form of participation in legislative elections in Cyprus for more than thirty years was not justified by the division of the island.[31]

In special circumstances, measures which might otherwise be regarded as disproportionate can be justified under Art.56 by compelling considerations arising out of local conditions. Thus a ten-year residence condition for the right to vote in New Caledonia was found warranted by the particular status and history of the territory, where a transitional system was in place following a period of turbulent conflict.[32]

A wide margin of appreciation applies to the formalities or conditions which an individual must fulfil to claim the right to vote.[33]

[24] e.g. *Melnychenko v Ukraine*, October 19, 2004, ECHR 2004–X, para.56; *Py*, fn.4 above, para.50; see also *Erel and Damdelen v Cyprus*, (39973/07) (Dec.) December 14, 2010, exclusion of persons voting in the occupied part of the country was not disproportionate as due to the exceptional circumstances they were not directly affected by legislative measures and the link with the Cypriot jurisdiction had been effectively severed.

[25] *MDU v Italy*, (58540/00) (Dec.) January 28, 2003, the punishment pursued the legitimate aim of ensuring effective functioning of the democratic regime and, given the short duration, was not arbitrary or disproportionate.

[26] *Hirst (No.2)*, fn.1 above, para.62.

[27] *Labita v Italy*, April 6, 2000, ECHR 2000–IV, para.203; see also irregularities in imposition of the restriction in *Santoro*, fn.4 above, rendering the measure neither necessary or lawful.

[28] *Albanese v Italy*, March 23, 2006, paras 48–49.

[29] (8873/80) (Dec.) May 13, 1982, 28 D.R. 99.

[30] *Matthews*, fn.2 above, para.64.

[31] *Aziz v Cyprus*, June 22, 2004, ECHR 2004–V, para.29.

[32] *Py*, fn.4 above, paras 58–64.

[33] e.g. *Benkaddour v France*, (5/685/99) (Dec.) November 18, 2003.

Nor can the right to vote be construed as containing any guarantee that any particular candidate or party will be on the ballot. Thus, although there was a violation as regarded a party which was disqualified in an election, the individual applicant, who had wished to vote for it, could not claim that he had been prevented thereby from voting freely in the election.[34]

Modalities of voting have not received much attention so far, save in *Sitaropoulos v Greece*, where expatriate Greeks complained that they had to return to Greek soil to exercise the right to vote. A Chamber considered that since the applicants retained the right to vote even though resident overseas and the domestic Constitution provided for postal voting, the failure of the Greek authorities over decades to set up a mechanism for voting overseas in some fashion breached the applicants' right to vote.[35]

4. Right to stand for election

II–336 While an individual right to stand for election has also been implied as contained in principle by Art.3, it is not absolute or without limitation either. States are allowed considerable latitude in their constitutional regulation of parliamentarians' eligibility.[36] Stricter requirements may be imposed on eligibility to stand than on voting.[37] However, once elected by the free and democratically expressed wishes of the people, no subsequent amendment to the organisation of the electoral system may call that choice into question, except in the presence of compelling grounds for the democratic order.[38]

Examination of complaints seem to focus on two criteria: whether there has been arbitrariness or lack of proportionality and whether the restriction interferes with the expression of the opinion of the people. The Court has also held, more recently, that, in order to avoid arbitrary exclusion of candidates, the rules concerning eligibility must be expressed with sufficient precision and decisions concerning a particular candidate taken by a body presenting minimum guarantees of impartiality and not enjoying an unfettered discretion.[39] Furthermore, failure to abide by final decisions in electoral appeals will offend in that it renders the system ineffective.[40]

Age-limits on candidates in Belgium (25 for House of Representatives and 40 for the Senate) were not arbitrary or unreasonable.[41] In *Podkolzina v Latvia*, the Court did not object to a requirement as such that a candidate show a certain mastery of

[34] *Russian Conservative Party of Entrepreneurs v Russia*, January 11, 2007, paras 79–80.

[35] *Sitaropoulos v Greece*, July 8, 2010, paras 40–41, pending before the Grand Chamber, judgment not likely before 2012.

[36] *Gitonas*, fn.2 above, para.39; *Zdanoka v Latvia*, March 16, 2006, ECHR 2006–. . . , para.83.

[37] *Melnychenko*, fn.24 above, para.57, citing the Venice Commission's election guidelines (candidates may hold public office and a greater public interest may require exclusion).

[38] *Lykourezos v Greece*, June 15, 2006, where a member of Parliament was disqualified on the basis of rules coming into force after the election, without any ground of pressing significance to the democratic order.

[39] *Podkolzina v Latvia*, April 9, 2002, ECHR 2002–II, para.35. See also *Grosaru v Romania*, March 2, 2010, where rules concerning attribution of seats to minority candidates were unclear and the electoral commission's largely constituted from rival parties without judicial supervision of decisions.

[40] *Petkov v Bulgaria*, June 11, 2009, paras 63–67, where the Supreme Administrative Court had set aside the electoral commission decisions removing the applicants as candidates but the commissions refused to comply. See also *Grosaru v Romania*, March 2, 2010, where rules concerning attribution of seats to minority candidates were unclear and the electoral commission's largely constituted from rival parties without judicial supervision of decisions.

[41] (6745) and (6746/74), fn.6 above.

the national language, but found fault in the procedure, lacking objectivity and legal certainty, whereby the applicant, already holding a certificate, was required for unspecified reasons to undergo a special test.

Eligibility criteria may require candidates to show loyalty to the State, not to the Government; such loyalty encompassing respect for the country's Constitution, laws, institutions, independence and territorial integrity, to the extent that any desire for change should be pursued in accordance with the laws of the State.[42] The Court strongly doubted that a law banning candidates with dual nationality from being elected was aimed at securing loyalty, rather than strengthening the present Government's position against opposition parties. The restriction was struck down as disproportionate. In particular it had not been imposed in the aftermath of independence when there might arguably particular need for stability but more than seventeen years later that it gave the impression of a blanket ban, unsupported by any credible threat to State interests having been made out. It also offended as tending to exclude some persons or groups of persons from participating in political life.[43]

Exclusions of particular groups for whatever goal will need justification. The Court also found no objective and reasonable justification to prevent persons of Roma and Jewish origin standing for election. Even if the requirement for a candidate to declare affiliations with one of majority constitutent ethnic groups was understandable against the background of a brutal conflict, the Court noted that there mechanisms of power-sharing which did not automatically lead to the exclusion of representatives of other communities.[44]

It also may be legitimate for States to defend the democratic order by preventing certain persons from standing, e.g. due to racist or treasonous history.[45] The Court found that it was proportionate in *Zdanoka v Latvia* to bar a candidate due to her past membership of a communist party, which had been actively subversive in the early days of Latvia's new democratic regime. It was acceptable to exclude a certain category of individuals as long as the statutory distinction itself was not disproportionate or discriminatory; was sufficiently clear and precise; and there was access to courts which could examine whether the person belonged to the category. The Court did warn that the restriction should be kept under a review, and lifted once democratic security allowed.[46] Where a party had been dissolved due to its anti-secular stance contrary to the Constitution, the Court found it nonetheless disproportionate to single out the applicant and a few others for the penalty of restriction on their future political activities, when it appeared that the leaders of the party had not been so disqualified.[47] While it was a legitimate aim to bar erstwhile officers of the KGB from standing, the ambit of the bar was found to be too broad and undefined: its application to a former border-guard who had not been implicated in any undemocratic activities and had since shown his commitment to

[42] *Tanase v Moldova*, April 27, 2010, ECHR 2010–. . . , paras 166–167.

[43] *Tanase*, fn.42 above, paras 170–179. The applicant had been required to renounce his Romanian citizenship to stand.

[44] *Sejdic and Finci*, fn.5 above, paras 42–50.

[45] (16692/90) (Dec.) April 12, 1991; (8348/78) and (8406/78) (Dec.) October 11, 1979, 18 D.R. 187.

[46] The Court rejected the applicant's arguments that her own personal conduct had to be shown to necessitate the exclusion.

[47] *Kavakci v Turkey*, April 3, 2007, where the Court noted with approval new measures restricting the grounds for dissolving parties and less drastic ways of sanctioning their conduct. See also *Sobaci v Turkey*, November 29, 2007.

the new State through fulfilling important posts without any doubt as to his loyalty, was thus disproportionate.[48] In contrast, it was proportionate for Spanish law to dissolve parties found, after due judicial examination of each case, to have supported violence and the activities of the terrorist organisation ETA.[49]

Where disqualification for standing for office is concerned, the Court frowns upon blanket, open-ended bars. Thus, it considered barring an impeached President from ever standing for office, including Parliament, ever again, was disproportionate. This was where there was no provision for review of the measure in the future and the bar was virtually unchallengeable due to the constitutional framework. This immutability, and paternalistic, measure was seen as contrary to the spirit of Art.3 and as eroding the "free expression of the will of the people", seemingly implying that it was for the people to decide whether they wanted to vote for a candidate who as President had breached his oath, the law and the Constitution.[50]

The requirement to submit information on a candidate's property, earnings and sources of income enables voters to make an informed choice and promotes the overall fairness of elections and thus the disqualification of individual candidates for irregularities would pursue a legitimate aim. Disqualifying an entire party because of failings by one of their top three candidates was however disproportionate to that aim.[51]

It is legitimate to require candidates to submit truthful information about their employment and party affiliations. Thus there was no violation where a candidate was disqualified for stating that he was head of a district council which had ceased to exist, such untrue information have been deliberately submitted and capable of misleading voters. However, where the reasons for disqualification given were inconsistent, and referred to matters such as failing to indicate the location of the employment or its permanent or temporary nature, which could not seriously be regarded as misleading the voters, the Court found the measure dubiously justified and disproportionate.[52]

The ineligibility of clergymen from standing for election may in principle be acceptable, but the legislative provision must be sufficiently clear and precise, to prevent arbitrary decisions as to whose rights are restricted. Thus, where it was not clear from the law or practice who qualified as a "clergyman", or what constituted "professional religious activity", and where the domestic court decisions did not give any explanation either, the Court found an impairment in the enjoyment of Art.3 rights.[53]

As concerns residence requirements on candidates, while the Court did not exclude a five-year continuous residency requirement, which could be appropriate to

[48] *Adamsons v Lithuania*, June 24, 2008. The Court also frowned on the way in which the charges of ineligibility were brought relatively late and the extenstion of the ground of ineligibility from 2004 for another ten years without explanation and despite the stability of the State.

[49] *Etxeberria v Spain*, June 30, 2009. The Court was satisfied that the measure was not arbitrary, since some parties had not been found to have links with impugned groups, and the existence of other parties with an independantist stance showed that the measures were not part of a policy of trying to sanction the expression of separatist ideas.

[50] *Paksas*, fn.9 above, paras 103–110. See also para.107 where the Court, somewhat unfortunately, gives scant regard to the serious, undermining effect on a democracy that corruption may have.

[51] *Russian Conservative Party of Entrepreneurs*, fn.34 above, paras 62–66.

[52] *Krasnov and Skuratov v Russia*, July 19, 2007.

[53] *Seyidzade v Azerbaijan*, December 3, 2009, where the applicant, a muslim clergyman, had resigned from his offices and posts but continued to work for a journal which published religious articles; the electoral bodies and courts had not referred to the latter function but merely noted that his resignations did not rule out his engaging in professional religious activity.

enable candidates to have sufficient knowledge of issues before the national parliament, it found that the manner in which the Ukrainian authorities applied the criterion disclosed a violation. It appeared that the candidate had had a valid registered place of residence in the country, that it was not an absolute requirement but individual circumstances were to be taken into account and that his absence from the country had been due to a justifiable fear of persecution.[54]

Systems of subsidies to political parties according to the number of votes gained (which may penalise smaller parties) was not found by the Commission to be a condition which blocked the free expression of the people.[55] Nor was objection taken to the conditions imposed on any group putting itself forward in an election to obtain 100 or 500 signatures of support. This was considered to be justified as preventing the electorate from being confused by groups which could not assume political responsibility.[56] A requirement of 200 signatures or three members of the regional parliament on a list was compatible in an Austrian case, given the Constitutional Court's reasoning that the conditions were easily satisfied by a party with a reasonable chance of success and pursued a legitimate aim of preventing undue splitting of the vote in a proportional representation system.[57]

Obligations to pay deposits have been found acceptable where the amount was not excessive or impose an impenetrable barrier to serious but economically disadvantaged candidates. The practice is seen as pursuing a legitimate aim of guaranteeing effective streamlined representation by enhancing responsibility and confining elections to serious candidates, while avoiding unreasonable outlay of public funds.[58]

Authorities are apparently not under an obligation to assist candidates, even where such assistance may be indispensable. Where a German prisoner complained that the authorities refused to circulate in prisons his publications and official forms to collect the 500 signatures necessary for a candidate to stand for election, the Commission recalled that the right to stand was not absolute, noted that prisoners were not prohibited from standing or voting, that the circulation of materials might have an effect on internal order and security and that other parties were also not afforded the possibility of circulating material in prison or collecting signatures.[59]

Disqualifications may legitimately be imposed where an elected member is already a member of another legislature. This was challenged by a member elected for the Northern Ireland Assembly in 1982, who was disqualified since he was a member of legislature of the Republic of Ireland. The Commission found the restriction not irreconcilable with Art.3 without much discussion. Under Art.14, where complaint was made that this condition was not applied to Commonwealth countries, the Commission considered it sufficient to rely on the special historical tradition and special ties existing with Commonwealth countries as reasonable and objective justification.[60]

Whether persons should be disqualified because of service for local authorities was challenged in Greece and the United Kingdom. In *Gitonas v Greece*, the rule

[54] *Melnychenko*, fn.24, paras 60–67. See also *Erel and Damdelen*, fn.24 above, exclusion of candidates resident outside the Government-controlled area was proportionate.

[55] (6850/74) (Dec.) May 18, 1976, 5 D.R. 90.

[56] (6850/74), fn.55 above.

[57] (7008/75) (Dec.) July 12, 1976, 6 D.R. 120.

[58] *Sukhovetsky*, fn.1 above, paras 50–74, inter alia citing older Commission decisions.

[59] (11728/85) (Dec.) March 2, 1987.

[60] (10316/83) (Dec.) March 7, 1984, 37 D.R. 129.

disqualifying persons who had held particular public offices in the constituency over the previous three years was found to pursue the legitimate aim of preventing undue influence on the electorate or unfair advantage vis-à-vis other candidates and not to be arbitrary or disproportionate. Nor was it found disproportionate in *Ahmed v UK* that local authority officers were required to resign if standing in elections, the rules reflecting a legitimate concern to maintain the political impartiality of local government officers.[61] The aim of maintaining the independence and impartiality of judges justified the requirement in Latvia that judges resign before they stand as candidates in elections.[62] In a case concerning an absolute disqualification from professional activities while holding a seat, the Court ruled on a narrower technical ground but commented that this blanket prohibition was rare in Europe.[63]

Disqualification from founding or joining a political party based on a conviction for hate speech and incitement to violence was not found to disclose an issue.[64]

A candidate may claim an interference with his right to stand where there have been irregularities or abuse in the gathering of votes, even without showing that it realistically affected his chances of being elected. Thus, Government arguments that the difference in votes was such that the alleged irregularities could not have effected the ultimate result have failed, the Court holding that candidates are entitled to stand in fair and democratic conditions regardless of their chances of success.[65] It will not be quick to assume a factfinding function as to the extent of misconduct itself, but where the allegations are supported by some evidence and potentially capable of thwarting the will of the people, it will verify that the State has provided for an effective system for the examination of complaints and that the respective bodies decide without arbitrariness and necessary impartiality. Thus, where the domestic courts rejected complaints with excessive formalism and failed to respond to serious allegations, the Court found a violation. Not only should the courts not have applied rigid procedural rules as regarded evidence, but given the seriousness of the matter, should have taken the initiative in verifying the accuracy of the allegations casting doubt on the free and fair character of the elections in the applicant's constituency.[66]

5. Conditions ensuring the free expression of the opinion of the people

II–337 Elections should not be under any form of pressure as to the choice of one or more candidates and an elector must not be induced unduly to vote for any party.[67] No constraint must be exercised in respect of parties or candidates, particularly where there are minorities involved, in which context particular aspects may take on significance. Thus there was careful scrutiny of allegations concerning the way language groupings were "juggled" in various Belgian regional and legislative bodies.[68]

[61] *Ahmed v UK*, September 2, 1998, Reports 1998–VI, No.87, 29 E.H.R.R. 1, para.75.
[62] *Brike v Latvia*, (47135/99) (Dec.) June 29, 2000.
[63] *Lykourezos*, fn.38 above, para.53, the applicant was a lawyer; it appeared few countries barred a continuance of legal practice, although conditions to safeguard independence and prevent conflicts of interest were applied.
[64] *Güzel v Turkey*, (54479/00) (Dec.) September 20, 2005, the ban appeared to be short-term, until the criminal conviction.
[65] *Namat Aliyev v Azerbaijan*, April 8, 2010, para.75.
[66] *Namat Aliyev*, fn.65 above, paras 80–93.
[67] (9267/81) (Dec.) July 12, 1983, 33 D.R. 97, at p.131.
[68] *Mathieu-Mohin*, fn.2 above.

Art.3 does not as such require any type of electoral system, e.g. proportional, or majority vote with one or two ballots (all of which are part of the common heritage of political traditions in Contracting States).[69] Nor did the Court see that it had to decide on the particular way of counting votes as regarded blank ballots[70] or that it was objectionable that the onus was put on voters to take the steps to ensure accuracy of entries in a so-called "active system of voter registration."[71]

There is reference to a "wide margin of appreciation" and the necessity to assess any electoral system in light of the historical and political evolution of the country concerned.[72] This margin also applies to the formalities attaching to the valid lodging of a vote with the aim of preventing electoral fraud.[73]

However, whatever the chosen system, a general principle of equality of treatment of all citizens has been identified.[74] This does not mean however that all votes must have the same weight as regards the outcome of the election or that all candidates have equal chances of success. There is an acceptance that wasted votes are inevitable in all systems. There is reference also by the Court to the conflicting objectives sought by electoral systems which aim both to reflect fairly faithfully the opinion of the people and yet to channel currents of thought to promote the emergence of a sufficiently clear and coherent political will.[75] Systems which aim to restrict the number of candidates or parties have been acceptable in light of the latter factor.[76]

A considerable latitude has thus been given as regards electoral thresholds. The Court noted that the 10 per cent national threshold in Turkey was the highest in Europe and resulted, in 2002, in over 45 per cent of voters not being represented. However, considering that the Constitutional Court had been vigilant in preventing any excessive effects of the electoral threshold, it referred to the diversity of systems in existence in Europe and found that this solution was acceptable in the specific political context in Turkey.[77] It did comment adversely on the way in which the system encouraged parties to make use of strategems contrary to transparency of the electoral process.[78]

[69] e.g. *Yumak and Sadak v Turkey*, July 8, 2008, ECHR 2008–. . . , para.110. Nor is there any requirement that a candidate represent a region, rather than the country as a whole, para.124.

[70] *Paschalidis, Koutmerdis and Zaharakis v Greece*, April 10, 2008, para.29.

[71] *The Georgian Labour Party v Georgia*, July 8, 2008, paras 90–91.

[72] *Mathieu-Mohin*, fn.2 above, para.54, features existing in one perhaps might be unacceptable in another but could be justified by the context; see also strong statement on margin of appreciation in *Podkolzina*, fn.39 above, para.34; *Yumak and Sadak*, fn.69 above, para.111.

[73] *Tsimas v Greece*, (74287/01) (Dec.) September 26, 2002, where the applicant lost his seat when votes were assessed as null and void due to lack of appropriate signatures.

[74] *Mathieu-Mothin*, fn.2 above, para.54.

[75] *Mathieu-Mothin*, fn.2 above, para.54; *Yumak and Sadak*, fn.69 above, para.62.

[76] (1123/84), fn.12 above, the discounting of parties/lists with less than 5 per cent of the vote in a proportional representation system was legitimate to foster the emergence of sufficiently representative currents of thought and the forfeiture of deposits, and no repayment of publicity expenses incurred by such lists was compatible in pursuit of this aim; *Federacion Nacionalista Canaria v Spain*, (56618/00) (Dec.) June 7, 2001, the setting of thresholds of vote percentages for parliamentary representation pursued the aim of preventing the excessive and dsyfunctional fragmentation of Parliament; *Gorizda v Moldova*, (53180/99) (Dec.) July 2, 2002.

[77] *Yumak and Sadak*, fn.69 above, where there had been twenty changes of Government in nineteen years before the introduction of the threshold; fewer since.

[78] e.g. candidates joined larger parties for the election and once elected switched back. See the minority dissenting opinion, which considered that the contribution of the threshold to political stability, or the need for its continuance, had not been shown and found that the system failed to accommodate the interests of a large part of the electorate.

A proportional representation system which was favourable to minority groups was accepted as enabling the people to express their opinion freely and as such clearly in line with the requirements of Art.3 of the First Protocol. To the extent that this disclosed discrimination it was justified in pursuing the aim of protecting the minority.[79] In respect of the Liberal Party's complaints about the majority vote system in the United Kingdom, the mere fact that not all votes would have the same weight was not sufficient to disclose a problem. It was left open whether there would be a problem if the system used resulted in a pattern whereby particular religious or ethnic groups or communities could never be represented.[80]

Rules in Belgium concerning the eligibility of candidates who took the parliamentary oath in either French or Flemish to sit in particular groupings in the legislature and with different powers was not incompatible with Art.3 given the intention to achieve an equilibrium between the country's various regions and communities and to defuse language disputes in the country. Regard was also had to the wide margin of appreciation, a margin which was even greater given the system was incomplete and provisional pending installation of a permanent system.[81] Restrictions placed on candidates who refuse to take a prescribed oath on taking up their seat have been found not to interfere with rights under Art.3, the Court finding the requirement of affirming loyalty to the constitutional principles underlying a representative democracy was a reasonable condition attaching to parliamentary office.[82]

Access of candidates to media coverage is an important aspect of campaigning. In a French case, the Commission appeared to accept that issues could arise from the way air time was distributed on radio and television between different groupings but given the wide margin of appreciation the regulations in question were not unjustified or disproportionate as regarded the disadvantage suffered by smaller parties.[83] On the same basis it was not in breach of Art.3 where the national television channel only invited parties with representatives in Parliament already or who had at least 4 per cent electoral support to participate in televised debates.[84]

Matters of party financing have not yet come under detailed scrutiny in this context though in one case the less favourable financial State support given to small parties was not found to disclose any problems.[85]

Where procedural irregularities occur during an election, these will not necessarily impinge on the expression of the will of the people. The Court has expressed doubt

[79] (8364/78) (Dec.) March 8, 1978, 15 D.R. 247, unionists alleged that the proportional representation system with the single transferable vote in operation in Northern Ireland (a simple majority vote applied elsewhere in the UK) unduly favoured the republican community.

[80] (8765/79) (Dec.) December 18, 1980, 21 D.R. 211.

[81] *Mathieu-Mothin*, fn.2 above.

[82] *Martin McGuinness v UK*, (39511/98) (Dec.) June 9, 1998; see mutatis mutandis where there was a violation of freedom of religion under Art.9 where three candidates elected to the General Grand Council were required to take the oath "on the Holy Gospels": *Buscarini v San Marino*, February 18, 1999, ECHR 1999–I, 30 E.H.R.R. 208.

[83] (11123/84), fn.12 above, 30 minutes to big parties, 5 minutes to small parties; also (24744/94) (Dec.) June 28, 1995, an independent candidate at EP elections complained of not being allotted air time, which was confined to main political parties (at least 12.5 per cent vote): no problem with this under Art.10 since air time was inevitably limited; *Antonopoulos v Greece*, (58333/00) (Dec.) March 29, 2001. Nor was it not contrary to Art.3 not to annul an election where parties had obtained an advantage in publicity over rivals through overspending the allowable budget: *Partija "Jaunie Demokrati" and Partija "Musu Zeme" v Latvia*, (10547/07) and (34049/07) (Dec.) November 29, 2007.

[84] *Partija "Jaunie Demokrati" and Partija "Musu Zeme"*, fn.83 above.

[85] *Antonopoulos*, fn.83 above.

as to a practice of discounting all votes at a polling station due to apparent irregularities regardless of the extent of the misconduct and its impact on the outcome of the result of the constitutency.[86] It will supervise whether the decisions of domestic authorities declining to annul elections for breach of electoral rules are not arbitrary or unreasonable, agreeing that such measures should only be taken in exceptional and serious cases where the expression of the popular will had been shown to be compromised by the misconduct.[87] Where, however, an electoral commission annulled votes from particular stations with the result that another candidate won, the Court found that their decision was based on a provision lacking clarity as to the circumstances in which annulment should apply and failed in particular to explain why the perceived breaches obscured the outcome of the vote to the extent that it was no longer possible to establish the wishes of the voters.[88] Similarly, where an electoral commission, hastily and arguably acting beyond its powers, excluded the results from two electoral districts in de facto disenfranchisement of a significant section of the electorate, without investigating the alleged evidence or considering other measures for gathering the votes, the Court found a failure to comply with the rule of law and provide relevant and sufficients reasons, in breach of Art.3 of Protocol No.1.[89] Annulling the election of an applicant candidate without showing that the irregularities had obscured the outcome of the voting was not compatible with the spirit of free elections, particularly where the two officials at fault had been tampering with a view to favouring the applicant's opponents who had still lost.[90]

Sudden changes in electoral systems, particularly on the eve of elections, may undermine respect and confidence in the electoral process, but may be justified in very specific circumstances. The Court will require the Government to provide relevant evidence to support their claim as to the aim of the changes, particularly where the measure has been detrimental to opposition parties' ability to compete against the one in power.[91] Thus, where one entire election failed largely due to the absence of an accurate electoral roll, the Court accepted that the solution adopted for the repeat election was not without defects but more could not realistically have been expected in the circumstances.[92] Changes post-election require even stronger justification. Thus where the Supreme Court struck down an electoral provision after the election with the result that the three applicants lost their seats, the Court found that this ran counter to the expressed will of the people in a lawfully-held election and infringed principles of legitimate expectation and legal certainty for both the candidates and the electorate.[93]

[86] *Kovach v Ukraine*, February 7, 2008, para.52.

[87] *Partija "Jaunie Demokrati" and Partija "Musu Zeme"*, fn.83 above, where two parties amongst seventeen had spent over double the allowed amount on publicity; the Court obviously considered the domestic courts gave the matter proper and thorough consideration, giving weight to the fact that the applicants participated in the proceedings and were able to put forward their arguments on the matter.

[88] *Kovach*, fn.86, paras 57–62, the provision referred to unspecified "other circumstances" which contrasted with another provision which set a threshold of 10 per cent spoiled ballots for annulling results.

[89] *Georgian Labour Party v Georgia*, fn.71 above, paras 126–141.

[90] *Kerimova v Azerbaijan*, September 30, 2010.

[91] *Tanase*, fn.42 above, para.169.

[92] *Georgian Labour Party*, cited fn.71 above, paras 86–89.

[93] *Paschalidis, Koutmeridis and Zaharkis*, cited fn.70 above, paras 30–35. It also noted a lack of equality of treatment since the change in law was not applied to all candidates, only those in Central Macedonia.

As concerns electoral commissions, the Court has afforded a margin of appreciation to the authorities, there being no uniform European system and a diversity flowing from historical and political factors specific to each State. It has approved of the existence of some form of guarantees against the appointment of those who could reasonably considered to have a conflict of interest and which would avoid the commission becoming another forum of political competition. However although seven out of fifteen members on an electoral commission was a high proportion to be appointed by the President and the system lacked sufficient checks and balances, the Court perceived no indication on the facts of the case that the applicant party had suffered any detriment from the commission's acts and found no violation.[94]

6. Free elections at reasonable intervals

II–338 The Commission found that an increase from four to five year intervals for elections to the diet of a German *Länder* was not incompatible. It commented that the purpose of Art.3 was to ensure that fundamental changes in public opinion were reflected in the opinions of the representatives of the people, which aim however had to be balanced by the consideration that a Parliament must be able to develop and execute legislative programmes and that too short an interval would act as an impediment to planning and lead to petrification of the political groupings in Parliament which might then cease to bear any resemblance to the will of the electorate.[95]

7. Article 10: freedom of expression

II–339 This provision cannot be interpreted as bestowing the right to vote on an individual.[96] However freedom of expression and to receive and impart information may be relevant in the electoral process where restrictions are placed on candidates' or others' ability to communicate their ideas and policies.

A concern to prevent groups which espouse terrorist causes and violence from achieving public exposure in the political arena generated controversial cases in Ireland and the United Kingdom.[97] However restrictions imposed on the broadcasting of interviews with members of Sinn Fein were accepted, even though it was a lawful political party and presented candidates who could take office locally and in the legislature. It was argued in support of these measures that terrorists drew sustenance and support from the media coverage. The Commission gave particular weight to the aims pursued by both Governments in respect of fighting terrorism and assessed the measures as proportionate, since the information itself could be broadcast in the United Kingdom (using actor voice-overs) and other means existed in the media in Ireland.

Restriction on the activities of an applicant publicising a single issue during campaigns was however found to be disproportionate. In *Bowman v UK*, where the applicant had been prosecuted for distributing leaflets publicising the views and

[94] *The Georgian Labour* Party, cited fn.71 above, paras 105–111.
[95] (27311/95), fn.3 above.
[96] (27614/95), fn.17 above.
[97] (15404/89) (Dec.) April 16, 1991, 70 D.R. 262; (18714/91) (Dec.) May 9, 1994, 77 D.R. 42.

voting record of candidates on abortion, the Court found that the expenditure limit of £5 operated as a total barrier to her publishing the information and it was not satisfied that this very low limit was necessary for achieving the stated aim of securing equality between the candidates. More leeway was accorded to the restrictions imposed on political canvassing by local government officials in *Ahmed v UK*, which were found to be justified by the importance of maintaining their impartiality and political neutrality towards both council members and the electorate who cast their votes to enable the political complexion of the council to reflect their views.[98] In *Rekvenyi v Hungary*, the Court also found that limitations on the political activities of police officers, in particular barring membership of a political party, did not disclose a disproportionate restriction on their freedom expression, having regard to the historical background in Hungary and the fact that not all political activities were barred.

8. Article 6: access to court

In general, electoral and political rights of a candidate, voter or elected representative fall outside the scope of Art.6 as not concerning "civil rights". Its guarantees have been held not to apply to proceedings reviewing the legality of an election,[99] the eligibility of a candidate for election,[100] the dissolution of a political party,[101] where an electoral observer brought proceeedings for failure of a body to provide documents[102]; and whereby an elected candidate was removed from office for expenses irregularities.[103] The latter case, *Pierre-Bloch v France*, relating to proceedings involving the disqualification of the applicant, elected to the National Assembly, for one year and the imposition of a payment order, confirmed that civil rights and obligations did not cover political ones, such as the right to stand for election or the obligation to limit campaign expenditure. The fact that there was an economic aspect to the disqualification proceedings did not render them civil.[104] Nor so far have the penalties imposed, such as disqualification and payment orders, been found to be of a nature or severity as to render Art.6 applicable in its criminal aspect.[105] **II–340**

[98] *Ahmed*, fn.61 above, para.63, the Court did give weight to their perception that the restrictions were carefully aimed at visibly objectionable partisanship and did not prevent officers from all political activity or speech.

[99] (11068/84) (Dec.) May 6, 1985, 43 D.R. 195.

[100] *Brike*, fn.52 above; also *Zdanoka v Latvia*, (58278/00) (Dec.) March 6, 2003.

[101] *Refah Partisi v Turkey*, (41340/98) and (41342–44/98) (Dec.) October 3, 2000.

[102] *Geraguyn Khorhurd Patgamavorakan Akumb v Armenia*, (11721/04) (Dec.) April 14, 2009, paras 28–29.

[103] *Pierre-Bloch v France*, October 21, 1997, R.J.D. 1997–VI, No.53, 26 E.H.H.R 202.

[104] See also *Shirley Porter v UK*, (Dec.) April 8, 2003, where the Court noted that the surcharge imposed on the applicant for losses caused to Westminster Council arose from regulations governing the conduct of public officials and could be considered as pertaining to public law, but as the domestic courts had treated the case as involving the applicant's civil rights and obligations had assumed Art.6 applied.

[105] (24359/94) (Dec.) June 30, 1995, 82–B D.R. 56; in *Pierre-Bloch*, fn.103 above, while the applicant was liable to prosecution with heavy fines and the possibility of imprisonment, this, if it occurred, would be separate from the disqualification proceedings. See also *Shirley Porter*, fn.104 above, where the imposition of a surcharge on the leader of Westminster Council for wilful misconduct in selling council housing was not criminal as it was repayment of losses to the local authority and applicable only to public officials; the considerable size of the surcharge (millions of pounds) was not sufficient to render it criminal.

Cross-reference

Part IIA, s.2: Access to Court.
Part IIB, s.22: Freedom of expression.

15. Environment

Key provisions:

Articles 8 (private life and home) and 13 (right to an effective remedy), and Art.1 of the Protocol No.1 (peaceful enjoyment of possessions). II–341

Key case-law:

Powell and Rayner v UK, February 21, 1990, Series A, No.172, 12 E.H.R.R. 355; *Lopez Ostra v Spain*, December 9, 1994, Series A, No.303–C, 20 E.H.R.R. 277; *Balmer-Schafroth v Switzerland*, August 26, 1997, R.J.D. 1997–IV; *Guerra v Italy*, February 19, 1998, R.J.D 1998–I; *Athanassoglou v Switzerland*, April 6, 2000, ECHR 2000–IV; *Hatton v UK*, July 8, 2003, ECHR 2003–VIII; *Taskin and Others v Turkey*, November 10, 2004, ECHR 2004–X; *Fadeyeva v Russia*, June 9, 2005, ECHR 2005–IV.

1. General considerations

There is no provision specifically geared for protection of any "environmental" rights. It is perhaps difficult to fit the traditional notion of individual human rights with the collective interest of protection of ecosystems, the atmosphere or other environmental concerns. An early unpromising case by the Commission stated unreservedly: "no right to nature preservation is as such included among the rights and freedoms guaranteed by the Convention" with the result that an organisation set up to protest military use of marshland was accordingly unable to claim infringement of any protected right.[1] The Court has most recently stated that there is no explicit right in the Convention to a clean and quiet environment[2] and that there is no right to housing, or conditions for housing, that meet particular environmental standards.[3] Applicants who take actions for "the collective good", without showing an impact on their individual rights, will not standing as victim: such an "*actio popularis*" is outside the Court's competence.[4] II–342

But it is a reflection of the growing recognition of the crucial importance of the environment that matters concerning the quality of the environment and assertions of the need for protection against, or information concerning, environmental threats are increasingly being taken up. Public interest attaching to environmental and public health issues has been given weight in relation to freedom of expression and the role of NGOs in pursuing environmental causes obtained recognition.[5]

[1] (7407/76) (Dec.) May 13, 1976, 5 D.R. 161.

[2] *Hatton v UK*, July 8, 2003, ECHR 2003–VIII, para.96; also *Fagerskiold v Sweden*, (37664/04) (Dec.) February 26, 2008.

[3] *Ward v UK*, (31888/03) (Dec.) November 9, 2004.

[4] *Caron v France*, (48629/08) (Dec.) June 29, 2010, where environmental activists were convicted of damaging GM crops, the Court noted no geographical proximity or other links, direct or indirect between the targeted fields and their own private or family life interests.

[5] *Mamere v France*, July 11, 2006, para.20; *Collectif Stop Melox and Mox v France*, June 12, 2007, para.116, concerning possible chilling effect of adverse costs effects in proceedings brought by an NGO. See also *L'Erabliere A.S.B.L. v Belgium*, February 24, 2009, an association to protect the environment of the March-Nassogne region could claim a "civil right" was at stake in court proceedings brought to annul a permit to extend a tip.

Nonetheless, despite findings of State responsibility for risks to health from industrial operations, a wide margin of appreciation is still said to apply in this context.[6]

2. Indirect environmental interests

II–343 In numerous cases concerning complaints by persons of restriction on use of their own land, the Convention organs have held that measures of town planning, building restrictions, and sometimes even confiscation, have been justified, protection of the environment being necessary in the "general interest" or for the protection of the rights of others. Preservation of rural areas thus obtains recognition under the Convention where it comes to State action in controlling their citizens' use of property. For example, when an applicant was prosecuted for infringing regulations prohibiting her living in an old bunker on land in Jersey, the Commission recognised that planning controls are necessary and desirable to preserve areas of natural beauty.[7] Stringent fishing restrictions affecting water-owners' rights in Finland have been accepted as pursuing the important general interest in conserving fish stocks.[8] Positive obligations placed on landowners, for example, to plant particular types of tree in their forest land have also been found in the general interest as part of protection of environmental interests.[9] Restrictions on landowners' use of land have, however, been found on occasion to fall foul of Art.1 of Protocol No.1, even though the aim was to preserve the environment, where there was insufficient procedural protection to the individual property owner's interests.[10]

3. State responsibility for environmental problems

II–344 Where an individual complains that the State is responsible for harming the environment, the Convention organs have been less ready to find infringement of Convention rights. However, Government responsibility may flow from the fact that a official decision or regulation directly provides for the contested environmental nuisance or from a failure to regulate private industry in a manner securing proper respect for individual rights.[11]

Since there is no general environmental right guaranteed, an application will generally only be feasible where there is a direct individual interest at stake which

[6] *Taskin and Others v Turkey*, November 10, 2004, ECHR 2004–X, para.116.

[7] (11185/84) (Dec.) March 11,1985, 42 D.R. 275.

[8] e.g. *Alatulkkila v Finland*, July 28, 2005, para.67. See also *Pindstrup Mosebrug A.S. v Denmark*, (34943/06) (Dec.) June 3, 2008, prohibition on the applicant company extracting peat from bogs which came under protective measures was a justified interference, despite a prior Government permit and lack of compensation due to a finding by the domestic court that the financial impact was minor.

[9] (12570/86) (Dec.) January 18, 1989, 59 D.R. 127; it is also legitimate, for example, to regulate car exhausts to prevent pollution: *Svidranova v Slovak Republic*, (35268/97) (Dec.) July 1, 1998.

[10] e.g. *Papastavrou v Greece*, April 10, 2003, where the decision to re-afforest an area, thereby seriously restricting the use of the applicants' land, was confirmed without proper consideration of individual rights or the possibility of compensation.

[11] *Hatton*, fn.2 above, para.119, the same considerations broadly apply in either case; see also the Commission finding in *Powell and Rayner v UK*, (Rep.) February 21, 1990, Series A, No.172, 12 E.H.R.R. 355, that the State was responsible for noise nuisance at airports since it regulated air traffic and built airports.

can be brought under expressly guaranteed rights, for example, the right to respect for home and private life, or peaceful enjoyment of property. The individual has to point to direct and strongly prejudicial effect[12], substantiating his claims in that regard[13], and even then for a violation to be found, there must be no key public interest to outweigh his.[14] Proportionality is a key consideration.

In a Norwegian case, while accepting that the building of a dam, which would flood large areas of land traditionally used for reindeer herding, could constitute an interference with the private life or lifestyle of two Lapps, the Commission found the measure justified in view of the relatively small area concerned in the vast northern region and that the actual impact on the individual was outweighed by the general and economic interest.[15]

However, increasingly, the Court has been prepared to find violations of Art.8, where there is a combination of a clear and significant risk to health or serious impingement on private life and home and a lack of timely and effective steps to deal with the situation. In that context it is now established that States bear responsibility for the activities of private companies, where such are subject to regulation from local authorities and there are elements of unlawfulness or breach of internal domestic standards[16] or otherwise a sufficient nexus between the pollutant emissions and the State to raise an issue of the State's positive obligation under Art.8.[17]

In *Lopez Ostra*, the applicant complained of pollution from a plant treating waste which began to operate without a licence and was situated 12 metres from her home. The Court noted that she had had to live with the plant for a number of

[12] e.g. (12816/87) (Dec.) January 18, 1989, 59 D.R. 186, a complaint about a military shooting range was rejected where it was not used in such a way as to cause important noise nuisance and the applicants had not been exposed to an intolerable or exceptional level or frequency of noise as to amount to an interference with private life or their right to enjoyment of their property (while on some days the noise was alleged to be unbearable, no firing was carried out on weekends or public holidays and a limit was in place during during other days); (28204/95) December 4, 1995, 83–B D.R. 112, where the applicants in the Pacific areas under French jurisdiction complained unsuccessfully that the overground tests at Muratoa placed their lives and health at risk from the radiation and contamination of the water and sealife: however, since they lived at considerable distances, the Commission found that the potential consequences were too remote to be considered as directly affecting their personal situation (no sufficiently established degree of probability that damage would occur to their health where they were or that tests would, for example, fracture the atoll); *Asselbourg v Luxembourg*, (29121/95) (Dec.) June 29, 1999, ECHR 1999–VI, mere suspicions and conjectures arising from pollution risks inherent in steel production were not sufficient.

[13] e.g. *Furlepa v Poland*, (62101/00) (Dec.) March 18, 2008, where the applicant did not substantiate her claims that an adjacent illegal car repair shop produced significant levels of noise or pollution or impinged on her health; *Borysiewicz v Poland*, July 1, 2008, where the applicant did not produce any reports or evidence concerning sound levels from a neighbouring tailoring workshop.

[14] e.g. *Khatun v UK*, (38387/97) (Dec.) July 1, 1998, where the Commission weighed the importance of regeneration of the Docklands against the dust nuisance suffered by the applicants and found the former prevailed.

[15] (9278/81) and (9415/81) (Dec.) October 3, 1983 35 D.R. 30.

[16] *Lopez Ostra v Spain*, December 9, 1994, Series A, No.303–C, 20 E.H.R.R. 277, the State was responsible for the private plant as it had given a subsidy and planning permission; nor had the local authority done much to resolve the unlawfulness of the plant's activities and had even appealed against the closure.

[17] See also *Fadeyeva v Russia*, June 9, 2005, ECHR 2005–IV, paras 90–92, concerning State responsibility for monitoring pollution from a privately-run steelworks which operated in breach of local environmental standards. Contrast *Ward*, fn.3 above, where the gypsy applicants complained about pollution and noise from a motorway which were not the result of any activity carried out by, or in any sense authorised by, a local authority or linked to any unlawfulness in domestic terms.

years and considered the domestic findings of significant health effects were convincing.[18] It seemed to accept that actual damage to health was not required for Art.8, since "unnaturally severe environmental pollution may affect individuals' well-being and prevent them from enjoying their homes in such a way as to affect their private and family health adversely without however seriously endangering their health".[19] There was a violation of Art.8, but the conditions were not severe enough for Art.3 to bite.

In a later case, the Court stated that successful claims concerning pollution would have to show, arguably and in a detailed manner, a sufficient degree of probability of damage to health or quality of life due to inadequate precautions by the authorities and that the consequences of the acts complained of must not be too remote.[20] Where an applicant could show that severe pollution from a steel works had tangible effects on her health, the Court refrained from finding any obligation on the State to provide her free housing elsewhere as claimed but considered that it had failed to protect individual interests as it had neither provided an effective solution to help moving away from the dangerous zone nor taken measures to reduce the pollution to acceptable levels.[21] Very recent cases no longer seem to require evidence of impact on health as such. There was no actual proof of damage to health in a case where a motorway had been routed through the applicant's street; however the cumulative effect of noise, vibration and air and soil pollution was regarded as preventing her from enjoying her rights guaranteed by Article 8, which was thus applicable.[22]

Where an individual is therefore directly or seriously affected by noise or other pollution, an issue may arise under Art.8.[23] The adverse effects of the environmental pollution must however reach as certain minimum level of severity.[24] The threshold set has been described as high.[25] The same applies where people are likely to be exposed to an activity which has been assessed having potentially dangerous effects.[26] Sensibility to noise of night flying of certain applicants living in close proximity to Heathrow runways was not, however, considered by the majority of the Court in *Hatton v UK* to intrude into an aspect of private life in such a manner as to attract the narrow margin of appreciation applicable to intimate interests under Art.8. A wide margin was applied instead as the night flying regulations at an airport with key economic importance concerned general policy decisions on which the role of the domestic policy maker had to be given special weight. It also

18 e.g. the applicant's child suffered from acute bronchopulmonary infections.

19 *Lopez Ostra*, fn.16 above, para.51.

20 *Asselbourg*, fn.12 above, the conditions of operation imposed by the authorities on the steel plant were not shown to be so inadequate as to disclose a serious infringement of "the principle of precaution"; *Greenpeace EV v Germany*, (18125/06) (Dec.) May 12, 2009, where the State had taken measures in respect of vehicle particle emissions, the Court was not persuaded by the applicants' claims that they should go further in regulating car manufacturing or that the authorities had failed to strike the right balance.

21 *Fadeyeva*, fn.17 above, paras 132–134.

22 *Grimkovskaya v Ukraine*, July 21, 2011, para.61.

23 *Hatton*, fn.2 above, para.96.

24 e.g. *Fagerskiold*, fn.2 above, wind turbines some 300–400 metres from the applicants' holiday home which emitted 40db noise level was not found to affect the applicants seriously or prevent them enjoying their home and private and family life (the WHO recommended maximum level was 50db).

25 e.g. *Borysiewicz*, fn.13 above, concerning alleged noise nuisance from a tailoring workshop.

26 *Taskin and Others*, fn.6 above, para.113, where local people complained of cynidation processes in a nearby gold mine.

appeared significant that, unlike *Lopez Ostra*, the airport in question was not acting unlawfully or in breach of regulations. The Court found that the applicants' interests were sufficiently protected by the consultation and monitoring processes and the possibility of taking judicial review proceedings for procedural irregularities and was not prepared to find that the authorities' decisions could only be justified if comprehensive data and research had been carried out on every aspect of the situation. Given the perceived minimal effect on health and private life therefore and the consideration that their property could still be sold without difficulty allowing the applicants to move away,[27] the Court considered that the balance had been fairly struck.

Once a risk to health is apparent, the balance may well tip away from economic interest, as in *Bacila v Romania*, where the Court acknowledged the importance of the metallurgical plant as the principal employer in the area, but found that the high levels of heavy metal and sulphur dioxide pollution had been shown to be a risk to health, the applicant herself having excessive traces of lead in her blood and being hospitalised for various pollution-linked conditions. In that situation, it considered the Government was under an obligation to take positive steps to ensure that the plant implemented the measures required to bring pollution down to acceptable levels.[28]

In contrast, in a case of little economic impact, where an applicant was in an area acoustically-saturated by over one hundred night clubs, the Court found, without much discussion, that the authorities' toleration of the repeated flouting of its own regulations breached Art.8.[29] Similarly, the long duration of a smell nuisance from a tip which had been running without the necessary autorisation, and which reports confirmed imposed considerable discomfort on those living close-by was sufficient to disclose a lack of respect for private life, even without showing a concrete effect on health.[30]

Normal levels of noise or other side-products of ordinary modern urban life will not generally engage Art.8 as people are presumably meant to be able to tolerate such annoyances. Thus, two families' complaints about flat renovation and the noise

[27] Contrast two old Heathrow cases before the Commission, involving very serious noise nuisance, settled after admissibility: (7889/77) (Dec.) July 15, 1980, 19 D.R. 186, (Rep.) May 13, 1982, 26 D.R. 5 and (9310/81) (Dec.) October 16, 1985, 44 D.R. 13, (Rep.) July 8, 1987, 52 D.R. 29, where there were difficulties in selling property and moving away.

[28] *Bacila v Romania*, March 30, 2010, this would presumably involve ordering closure of the plant if it continued in its recalcitrance.

[29] *Moreno Gomez v Spain*, November 16, 2004, ECHR 2004–XI. Contrast *Furlepa*, fn.13 above, where the illegality of the workshop and inaction of the authorities was irrelevant as the applicant had not shown substantiated evidence that the noise nuisance impinged on her private life or health; *Galev v Bulgaria*, (18324/04) (Dec.) September 29, 2009, as the applicants had not shown that there was any nuisance from the dental office in their building, there was no interference with their rights and the lack of lawfulness did not come into play.

[30] *Branduse v Romania*, April 7, 2009, the tip operated under the supervision of the authorities, which delayed in taking action in respect of the tip which was running without authorisation or conformity with regulations, in particular with regard to proximity to habitations and which had failed to give information about the situation to the public or give access to the studies evaluating the risk posed by the tip. See also *Tatar v Romania*, January 27, 2009, where the applicants, living near to a metallurgical processing plant, could not point to concrete effects to health or studies assessing the potential risks, but could rely on numerous reports indicating that the pollution level was above international and national norms to bring the case within the ambit of Art.8; and *Greenpeace EV v Germany*, fn.20 above, where Art.8 applied to complaints about motor vehicle emissions in heavy traffic areas as reports clearly supported the contention that particle pollution was a serious risk to health.

during office hours of a business operating in their apartment block did not disclose Art.8 interferences. However, a computer club operating round the clock went beyond the normal level and triggered Art.8 protection; as it was operating unlawfully, the failure of the authorities to enforce the prohibition of its activities infringed the right to respect for the families' home, as well as family and private lives.[31]

More recently, it has been stated that such cases can be examined from a substantive and procedural perspective, namely whether the domestic measures taken respect individual rights under Art.8 and whether the decision-making procedure affords individuals protection of their interests. The latter appears to require that adequate studies and reports are made on any activities that are environmentally harmful and that interested individuals have adequate access to those materials in order to assess any danger, as well as the possibility of appealing against any decision, act or omission which they consider fails to take their interests into account.[32] A similar procedural violation arose in respect of a hazardous waste treatment plant where the authorities failed in their domestic law obligation to conduct an environmental-impact assessment prior to any project with potentially harmful environmental consequences, deprived concerned citizens of the opportunity to participate in the licensing procedure and failed to enforce domestic decisions which had found certain activities unlawful.[33] Where the authorities did not undertake a prior environmental feasibility study before routing a motorway down a residential street, failed to take steps to mitigate effects on nearby residents and to provide them with effective means of participating in the decision-making or challenging the decision, a fair balance had not been struck in terms of Article 8.[34] Authorities may also be required to re-assure the public as to the measures of prevention in place against industrial accidents and to provide information as to emergency procedures in case of such accidents.[35]

4. Effect on property rights

II–345 There is no property right as such under Art.1 of Protocol No.1 to sound environmental conditions. However, it has been said that where pollution seriously damages the value of land or renders it unsellable there might be a de facto expropriation capable of raising issues under that provision.[36] Where it was claimed

[31] *Mileva v Bulgaria*, November 25, 2010, paras 90–102. See also *Dees v Hungary*, November 9, 2011, significant increase in heavy lorry traffic throught the applicant's town, which caused noise above the statutory level, was a nuisance within the scope of Art.8; however, the brevity of reasoning for finding the Government in breach despite measures to alleviate the problem skims over the margin of appreciation and balancing of public and private interests: it is not a strong precedent in this context.
[32] *Taskin and Others*, fn.6 above, paras 115–125, where the failure of the authorities to enforce a judicial decision suspending mining activities was in breach of the procedural aspect of Art.8. See also *Lemke v Turkey*, June 5, 2007, similarly ineffective procedural guarantees concerning exploitation of gold mine.
[33] *Giacomelli v Italy*, November 2, 2006. See also *Tatar v Romania*, fn.29 above, where the authorities failed to provide any information, or render public various impact reports, to the local people concerned about the risks to their health of a nearby metallurgical plant which had already caused an environmental accident in leaking large amounts of water contaminated with sodium cyanide into the river system and in respect of which there were various reports indicating high levels of heavy metal and cyanade pollution around the plant.
[34] *Grimkovskaya*, fn.22 above, paras 58–73.
[35] e.g. *Tatar v Romania*, fn.30 above, para.122.
[36] *Taskin and Others v Turkey*, (46117/99) (Dec.) January 29, 2004.

genetically-modified crops were a risk to agriculture, the environmental activists concerned had not shown their own lands had been at risk from the crops targeted.[37]

5. Access to information about environmental risks

Where there are risks to health from severe environmental pollution, it now appears that persons who are affected may derive a right to obtain information about those risks from the relevant authorities under Art.8 of the Convention. While Art.10 contains a freedom to obtain information, this relates basically to information which others wish to impart. In *Guerra v Italy*, the applicants, who lived near a chemical factory, which had experienced a serious explosion in the past and had been found to fall short of standards, claimed that they had not been given information about the risks presented by the factory or the measures to be adopted in case of an accident. The Court, although holding that Art.10 could not in the circumstances of the case impose an obligation on the State to collect and disseminate information, nonetheless found a violation of Art.8, considering that the State had not fulfilled its obligation to secure the applicants' right to respect for private and family life through its failure to provide the applicants with essential information about the risks posed to them by severe environmental pollution. In subsequent cases, the lack of access to information has been examined in terms of the procedural obligation under Art.8 (see above). II–346

6. Access to court and remedies

The protection of environmental interests at domestic level may also be problematic. Where access to court under Art.6 is concerned, an applicant must be able to claim a dispute concerning a civil right.[38] II–347

In *Balmer-Schafroth v Switzerland*, the Court found Art.6, para.1 was not applicable to the procedure before the Federal Council which granted the extension of an operating licence to a nuclear plant near the applicants' villages, overruling the objections raised by the applicants on grounds of health. The Court's reasoning, perhaps less than convincing, appeared to focus on the lack of any proof from the applicants that the grant of the licence would have any decisive effect on their physical well-being, and thus on their rights. The new Court maintained this view however, though by a narrowing majority of 12 to 5, in *Athanossoglou v Switzerland*, finding that the report relied on by the applicants did not show that the power plant exposed the applicants personally to a danger that was serious, specific and, above all, imminent. This approach would seem to impose a high threshold, in effect requiring the applicants to prove their case on the merits in Strasbourg in order to vindicate a right to access to court on a domestic level.[39] The Court was not

[37] *Caron v France*, fn.4 above.

[38] e.g. *Lam v UK*, (41671/98) (Dec.) July 5, 2001, where the domestic courts found no cause of action arose from the applicants' negligence claims against the local authority for licensing industrial activity not covered by planning regulations and failing to take steps to end the health risks from toxic fumes, no right arose engaging Art.6.

[39] The minority commented that this reversed the subsidiarity principle, the Court reaching its own judicial assessment of risk to the applicants whereas in their view it was for the domestic courts to assess whether there was a sufficiently close link between the operation of the power plant and the applicants' rights to life and physical integrity.

impressed by the argument of the applicants that judicial examination of the risks of nuclear energy was the appropriate way to examine deficiencies, considering that the question of how best to regulate the use of nuclear power was a policy decision for each Contracting State to take according to its democratic processes. A less restrictive approach was taken in *Okyay v Turkey*, concerning the allegedly hazardous operation of thermal power plants, where the Court found that there was an acknowledged domestic law right to a healthy and balanced environment, linked to a right to compensation where the authorities failed to comply with court orders, such that the proceedings taken as a whole could be considered to relate to the applicants' civil rights.[40]

Thus, if domestic law does not acknowledge an applicant's standing to bring a particular claim against an alleged polluter, no issues of lack of access to court may arise.[41]

Failure by Governments to take steps to enforce judgments successfully obtained by applicants against polluters may more clearly raise issues under Art.6.[42]

In two UK cases, houseowners complained of the serious interference with their lives caused by noise of aircraft. Two of them, which were settled after admissibility, involved very serious noise interference from extensions and increased flights to Heathrow airport and a lack of any redress, including an inability to sell the property with change of use to obtain a reasonable price.[43] Though the issues were never settled on the merits, the cases implied that where developments occur which seriously impinge on occupation of private homes, without counterbalancing compensation to enable sale and removal elsewhere, there will be potential problems of access to court or lack of remedies under Arts 6 and 13.[44] Subsequently, in *Hatton v UK*, the Court found that judicial review did not provide sufficient scope of review of complaints about the impact of an increase in night flying on on the applicants' private and family lives and homes and the applicants accordingly did not have an effective remedy as required by Art.13.

Associations and non-governmental organisations formed to protect the environment have been found to come under the protection of Art.6 with regard to access to court where they could either claim to be linked to the region concerned [45] or where there was a domestic public right to information involved.[46] Thus, there was violation in respect of access to court, where the courts applied technical and

[40] *Okyay v Turkey*, July 12, 2005, paras 64–69.

[41] *Asselbourg*, fn.12 above.

[42] e.g. *Okyay*, fn.40 above, violation where Council of Ministers decided to continue the activities of three power plants which the courts had ordered to be suspended due serious pollution from nitrogen and sulphur dioxide.

[43] (7889/77), fn.27 above, admissible under Arts 6, 8, 13 and 14 of the Convention and Art.1 of the Protocol No.1: settled on payment of £7,500 by the Government; (9310/81), fn.27 above, where the house, a quarter of a mile from a runway, was overflown day and night, resulting in "intolerable conditions": admissible under Arts 8 and 13 of the Convention and Art.1 of the Protocol No.1 and settled on payment of £24,000. The report referred to recent legislation enabling the airport authority to buy noise blighted property in future.

[44] The Commission found a violation in *Powell and Rayner*, fn.11 above, under Art.13 since there was no possibility of action for increase in noise since entry to the property, no possibility of compensation and official noise control measures were ineffective. The Court, finding no arguable claim on the substantive provisions, did not consider the matter further (see Pt IIB, s.41: Remedies).

[45] See *L'Erabliere A.S.B.L*, fn.5 above, there was no hint of "*actio popularis*" as the association had specific geographic interests and the members lived in the region concerned.

[46] *Collectif Stop Melox and Mox*, fn.5 above.

formalistic rules to reject an association's application to annul a permit to extend a tip.[47]

[47] *L'Erabliere A.S.B.L.*, fn.5 above.

16. Euthanasia

Key provisions:

II–348 Articles 2 (right to life) and 8 (respect for private life).

Key case-law:

Pretty v UK, April 29, 2002, ECHR 2002–III.

1. General considerations

II–349 The subject of euthanasia or assisted suicide has rarely been considered. It may be observed that the term "euthanasia" itself has no common or established meaning within Contracting States.[1] While it would be inaccurate to state that there was any common approach to the controversial question of when people, terminally ill or otherwise, should be allowed, either by their own hand or with active or passive assistance, to take their own lives, it would appear that the countries which permit, as opposed to condone where appropriate, assisted euthanasia are few.[2] The principal case is *Pretty v UK*. While no violation was found in that case where the applicant, suffering from motor neurone disease, wished her husband to assist her to commit suicide, the Court's decision was limited to the facts of that case, in which the authorities had refused, before her death, to issue a declaration that her husband would not be prosecuted for any assistance given to her. It may nonetheless be deduced from the reasoning that prohibition of euthanasia, where one person actively brings about the death of another, may be regarded as compatible with the Convention.

2. Victim status

II–350 No victim issue arose in the *Pretty* case, where the application was lodged by the individual suffering from a terminal illness. Attempts have been made by various Dutch applicants to claim that the state of law in the Netherlands infringed their right to life. In the absence of any real or immediate likelihood that these individuals, in good health, were at risk of being killed by enthusiastic medical euthanasia-supporters, these cases have been disposed of as inadmissible.

Difficulties of victim status are likely to arise even where relatives of terminally-ill or profoundly-handicapped persons claim violations of the Convention. The fact that a domestic court had permitted artificial nutrition and hydration to be withdrawn in a case of irreversible vegetative state was not sufficient to give standing to relatives of other seriously-incapacitated patients to complain that this had caused prejudice to the position of their own loved ones.[3] In a Spanish case,[4] the applicant was sister-

[1] e.g. Council of Europe Report, Replies to questionnaires for Member States relating to euthanasia, CDB1 (220) II.

[2] The Netherlands is the famous example, followed in 2002 by Belgium.

[3] *Ada Rossi v Italy*, (55185/08) et al (Dec.) December 16, 2008, nor could the applicant associations dedicated to protection of the rights of the vulnerable claim to be affected by the decision.

[4] *Sanles Sanles v Spain*, (48335/99) (Dec.) October 26, 2000.

in-law, and heir, of a young man, tetraplegic, who had challenged in the courts the prohibition on assisted suicide. He had died with assistance before the conclusion of proceedings and the Spanish courts had refused to allow the applicant to continue the proceedings after his death. The Court considered that his claims in the domestic proceedings under Arts 2, 3, 8, 9, 13 and 14, were personal, non-transferable rights and that the applicant could not claim to be a victim, even if she was affected personally by the distressing circumstances in which her brother-in-law found himself.[5] A close relative of a person who died due to a deliberate intervention would be more likely to be found to have standing to bring on the deceased's behalf a claim that the death had been in some way unlawful or contrary to the Convention.

3. Right to life

The Court rejected the arguments in the *Pretty* case that Art.2 included not only the right to life but the right to die.[6] It left open the question of whether the practice of euthanasia would infringe the right to life, noting that issues of personal autonomy and public policy arose and that conflicting considerations might arise that could only be resolved on examination of the particular facts of the case.[7] **II–351**

Conversely, where it was argued that doctors could withhold life-saving treatment in breach of Art.2, the Court found that there was no indication that the applicant faced a real or imminent risk of death, noting that the presumption of domestic law was strongly in favour of prolonging life. It refused to hold that doctors should be under a wide-ranging duty to seek the authority of the court in all cases when withdrawing artificial nutrition and hydration.[8] It did find that a hospital should have sought a court order when the doctors' view as to treatment clashed with the relatives.[9]

4. Inhuman treatment

The suffering caused by illness or injury that leads a person to wish to end their life may clearly reach the threshold of severity covered by Art.3 of the Convention. Where however the Government cannot be held responsible for the injury or illness and is providing the necessary medical care and support, no "treatment" arises for which the State can be held responsible and no positive obligation arises requiring the State to permit or facilitate assisted suicide.[10] **II–352**

[5] See *Koch v Germany*, (497/09) (Dec.) May 31, 2011, the complaints of an applicant that his wife was denied drugs to end her life peacefully in Germany and was forced to travel to Switzerland have been declared admissible: the issue of the applicant's standing to complain on behalf of his deceased wife and his own victim status as her spouse and close relative were joined to the merits. Pending at the date of publication.

[6] *Pretty v UK*, April 29, 2002, ECHR 2002–III, para.39.

[7] *Pretty*, fn.6 above, para.41.

[8] *Burke v UK*, (19807/06) (Dec.) July 11, 2006. See also *Glass v UK*, ECHR 2004–II, March 9, 2004, para.75.

[9] *Glass*, fn.8 above, the relatives viewed the administration of morphine as likely to "help" the patient to die.

[10] *Pretty*, fn.6 above, paras 53–55.

5. Self-determination

II–353 While the Court's judgment in the *Pretty* case largely mirrored the conclusions of the House of Lords in the domestic proceedings, the Court differed in finding that the right to respect for private life provided for in Art.8, para.1 arguably covered the right to self-determination in the sense of deciding how or when to end one's life. It laid emphasis on the notions of "human dignity" and "human freedom". The reference to the concerns about increasing medical sophistication keeping people alive in states of advanced physical or mental decrepitude would appear to hint at freedom of choice extending at least so far as bestowing on applicants a choice to refuse medical treatment that kept them alive.[11] The Court did not however find the refusal of the DPP to give Mr Pretty an advance guarantee against prosecution an unjustified interference with the right under Art.8. It appeared particularly influenced by the risk to the vulnerable and sick by allowing exceptions to the general ban but noted that there was flexibility in the system of prosecution and criminal justice to deal sympathetically with so-called mercy killings.[12]

This approach has been largely confirmed in a recent Swiss case where the applicant, suffering from a chronic bipolar disorder, had been refused access to the drugs, which he wished to use to end his life, due to lack of a medical prescription. The Court stated that the choice of a person as to how and when to end his life fell within Art.8. It found that restrictions on access to lethal drugs was justified by the risk of abuses and found that, even if there was an obligation of the State to facilitate a dignified death, it had not been shown that this had been breached, since in Switzerland there existed the possibility to obtain assistance for suicide and a prescription could have been provided by a doctor who had examined him and attested to his mental capacity to make an informed and rational decision.[13]

6. Freedom of conscience and discrimination

II–354 The arguments raised in the *Pretty* case under Arts 9 and 14 received short treatment, the Court obviously not considering that a wish to commit euthanasia was the type of belief falling within the scope of Art.9 or that the law prohibiting assisted suicide could be considered as discriminatory of the physically disabled unable to act for themselves.

7. Criminal proceedings

II–355 No cases have yet been brought by persons prosecuted or otherwise sanctioned, either as medical personnel or a relative, for assisting someone to die. It is unlikely that a doctor could rely on any of the rights under Arts 2, 3 or 8 of the Convention. Even assuming that a doctor succeeded in claiming that a belief in the moral necessity of euthanasia fell within the scope of Art.9, or that a relative's actions came under Art.8 in its family life aspect, a measure applied in "accordance with the law" would be likely to be found justified in pursuit of the legitimate aim of

[11] *Pretty*, fn.6 above, para.65; see *B v NHS Hospital*, Court of Appeal judgment of March 22, 2002, cited at para.18.
[12] *Pretty*, fn.6 above, paras 74–77.
[13] *Haas v Switzerland*, January 11, 2011, paras 50–61.

protecting public order or health. Possibly if the punishment was grossly disproportionate a problem might arise—however, if the fact finding domestic bodies found the act was not in good faith or abusive, the Court would hesitate to overrule them. Nor would it be possible to rely on Art.6 concerning the proceedings other than on generally applicable aspects of fairness since that provision does not concern itself with the content of the criminal law being applied.

Cross-reference

Part IIB, s.37: Private life.

17. Expropriation, confiscation and control of use

Key provisions:

II–356 Article 1 of Protocol No.1 (peaceful enjoyment of possessions) and Art.6 (access to court/fair hearing).

Key case-law:

Sporrong and Lonnroth v Sweden, September 23, 1982, Series A, No.52, 5 E.H.R.R. 35; *James v UK*, February 21, 1985, Series A, No.98, 8 E.H.R.R. 123; *Lithgow v UK*, July 8, 1986, Series A, No.102, 8 E.H.R.R. 329; *Agosi v UK*, October 24, 1986, Series A, No.108; *Erkner and Hofauer v Austria*, April 23, 1987, Series A, No.117, 9 E.H.R.R. 464; *Hakansson and Sturesson v Sweden*, February 21, 1990, Series A, No.171, 13 E.H.R.R. 1; *Papamichalopoulos v Greece*, June 24, 1993 Series A, No.260–B, 16 E.H.R.R. 440; *Hentrich v France*, September 22, 1994, Series A, No.296–A, 18 E.H.R.R. 440; *Holy Monasteries v Greece*, December 9, 1994, Series A, No.301–A, 20 E.H.R.R 1; *Air Canada v UK*, May 5, 1995, Series A, No.316, 20 E.H.R.R. 150; *Matos e Silva v Portugal*, September 16, 1996, R.J.D. 1996–IV, No.14; *Akkus v Turkey*, July 9, 1997, R.J.D. 1997–IV, No.43; *Beyeler v Italy*, January 5, 2000, ECHR 2000–I; *Former King of Greece v Greece*, November 23, 2000, ECHR 2000–XII; *Bosphorus Airways v Ireland*, June 30, 2005, ECHR 2005–VI; *Jahn v Germany*, June 30, 2006, ECHR 2006–. . . ; *J.A. Pye (Oxford) Ltd and J.A. Pye (Oxford) Land Ltd v UK*, August 30, 2007, ECHR 2007–. . .

1. General considerations

II–357 Considerable room for manoeuvre is accorded in respect of expropriations and confiscations. A wide margin of appreciation applies to planning, nationalisation or other legislative interventions due to the complex or policy nature of the issues.[1] Examination of these cases tends to focus on whether a fair balance has been struck between the public and private interest and whether the applicant has been left with a disproportionate burden.[2] Deprivations of property must also conform with requirements of lawfulness, both as regards the existence of a basis for the measure in domestic law and the requisite quality of the law.[3]

Since property rights fall within the scope of Art.6, para.1 as civil rights, procedural safeguards generally apply regarding access to court for determination of

[1] *Sporrong and Lonnroth v Sweden*, September 23, 1982, Series A, No.52, 5 E.H.R.R. 35, para.26; *James v UK*, February 21, 1985, Series A, No.98, 8 E.H.R.R. 123, para.46, the margin is applied both to the assessment of the existence of a problem of public concern and the remedial action necessary. Where the legislature has made a choice by enacting a law in the general interest, the possible existence of alternative solutions does not in itself render the contested legislation unjustified, e.g. *Mellacher v Austria*, December 19, 1989, Series A, No.169, para.53; (33091/96) (Dec.) March 23, 1999, concerning restitution of property measures after the fall of communism; *Jahn v Germany*, June 30, 2006, ECHR 2006–. . . , paras 91 and 113, radical changes in political and economic regime on reunification of Germany.

[2] *Lithgow v UK*, July 8, 1986, Series A, No.102, 8 E.H.R.R. 329, para.120.

[3] *Iatridis v Greece*, March 25, 1999, ECHR 1999–II, expropriation measure unlawful; *Carbonara and Ventura v Italy*, May 30, 2000, ECHR 2000–VI, arbitrary and unforeseeable application of a constructive-expropriation rule.

claims and regarding requirements, inter alia, of fairness, reasonable length of proceedings, independent and impartial tribunals (See Pt IIA: Fair Trial).

2. Expropriation

(a) De facto deprivation

Generally, where ownership of the property remains or some form of exploitation, by way of sale or receipt of rents for example, the measure is not regarded as a de facto expropriation or deprivation of property within the meaning of the second sentence of the first paragraph of Art.1 of Protocol No.1 but an interference with peaceful enjoyment of possessions within the meaning of the first sentence.[4] However in *Papamichalopoulos v Greece*, where the navy constructed a naval base and officers' resort on the applicants' land, the Court found that, although there had been no formal expropriation, their land was occupied and being unable to sell, bequeath mortgage or even gain entry, they had lost all ability to dispose or make use of it. This, combined with the failure of attempts to remedy the situation, entailed sufficiently serious consequences for the situation to disclose a de facto expropriation incompatible with the general guarantee set out in the first sentence of Art.1. II–358

Revocation of duly registered title to land, or a title acquired in good faith, is likely to be regarded as a deprivation of a possession, notwithstanding claims by the authorities that the land in question had been in the public domain and thus not capable of private ownership. Where there is a strong public interest such as preservation of forest or coastline, the main issue is likely to be whether the individual interest has been sufficiently taken into account through compensation.[5]

Whatever the classification of the measure under Art.1 of Protocol No.1, the balancing exercise underlies the Court's examination.[6]

Where the "expropriation" is carried out by private persons, positive obligations may fall on the authorities to take steps to enforce the owner's rights, including the use of force where there are no strong public interests against such.[7]

(b) Public interest

The Court has stated that it will respect the legislature's judgment as to what is in the public interest unless it is "manifestly without reasonable foundation"[8] and that the notion of "public interest" is necessarily extensive.[9] II–359

Public interest has been accepted as being involved in almost all cases so far. It has included de facto expropriation for national defence policy in building a base and officers' resort[10]; transfer of monastery land for the purpose of ending illegal sales

[4] e.g. *Sporrong*, fn.1 above, para.65; *Matos e Silva v Portugal*, September 16, 1996, R.J.D. 1996–IV, No.14, para.85.

[5] See *Turgut v Turkey*, July 8, 2008; *Koktepe v Turkey*, July 22, 2008, violations in both due to total absence of, or lack of effective means of obtaining, compensation.

[6] *Sporrong*, fn.1 above, para.69.

[7] *Matheus v France*, March 31, 2005, referring to the rule of law and preventing "private justice".

[8] *James*, fn.1 above, para.46; *Lithgow*, fn.2 above, para.122.

[9] *Hentrich v France*, September 22, 1994, Series A, No.296–A, 18 E.H.R.R. 440, para.39.

[10] *Papamichalopoulos v Greece*, June 24, 1993 Series A, No.260–B, 16 E.H.R.R. 440.

and encroachments and controlling development[11]; expropriation of estates of the former ruling royal house[12]; price control systems for land purchase and rights of pre-emption for the prevention of tax evasion[13]; expropriation of a site of historic and cultural significance[14]; preservation of sites of cultural heritage[15]; expropriation of land for use of the Port of Riga[16]; and social justice in land reform.[17]

While expropriation of property may initially be justified for a public purpose, a failure to use the land may, after a certain passage of time may remove that earlier justification and impose an obligation of restoration.[18]

Where an applicant was unable to recover possession of property as the State had allowed it to be occupied by a foreign body purportedly enjoying State immunity, the Court expressed doubt that this pursued a "public interest".[19]

(c) Proportionality—striking a fair balance

II–360 In assessment of whether a fair balance has been struck, or the applicant required to bear an excessive and disproportionate burden, the Court looks at the circumstances as a whole, considering issues of lawfulness, the length of time involved, procedural safeguards and the effect on the applicant, in particular, whether compensation is available.[20]

Arbitrariness and lack of procedural safeguards were found to render the pre-emption measure in *Hentrich v France* disproportionate. The use of the power was selective, unforeseeable and punitive, no reasons were given and the applicants were not afforded an adversarial procedure in which to counter the allegations of tax evasion.[21] In *Hakansson and Sturesson v Sweden*, however, there was no lack of proportionality where the applicants were aware of the risk of not obtaining a

[11] *Holy Monasteries v Greece*, December 9, 1994, Series A, No.301–A, 20 E.H.R.R 1, while the Court acknowledged doubts as to the reasons why the property was not given to needy farmers but to co-operatives and public bodies, this nonetheless did not deprive the measure of its overall objectives as being in the public interest.

[12] *Former King of Greece v Greece*, November 23, 2000, ECHR 2000–XII, paras 87–88, interests of clarifying the status of the republic.

[13] *Hakansson and Sturesson v Sweden*, February 21, 1990, Series A, No.171, 13 E.H.R.R. 1; *Hentrich*, fn.9 above; also (12736/87) (Dec.) May 5, 1988, 56 D.R. 254, compulsory purchase for motorway construction; (13135/87) (Dec.) July 4, 1988, 56 D.R. 268, compulsory purchase to enforce habitable standards of housing.

[14] *Kozacioglu v Turkey*, February 19, 2009.

[15] *Potomska and Potomski v Poland*, March 29, 2011, para.64, a Jewish cemetery.

[16] *Vistins and Perepjolkins v Latvia*, March 8, 2011, paras 79–80. Pending before the Grand Chamber.

[17] *Jahn*, fn.1 above.

[18] *Beneficio Cappella Paolini v San Marino*, July 13, 2004, ECHR 2004–VII.

[19] *Hirschhorn v Romania*, July 26, 2007, ECHR 2007–. . . , paras 98–100, particularly since the lease concerned had expired, previous rents had not been paid to the applicant and the State immunity status of the US Peace Corps was in doubt. Contrast *Manoilescu and Dobrescu v Romania*, (60861/00) March 3, 2005, ECHR 2005–. . . , paras 93–98, ongoing occupation of the Russian Embassy; respect for State immunity was, without any debate, in the public interest.

[20] e.g. (12736/87), fn.13 above, compulsory purchase by a local authority of premises below habitable standards was proportionate since warnings and time for repairs were given and the property was in substantial disrepair; (13135/87), fn.13 above, expropriation of parts of a Highland estate for road widening was reasonably proportionate, having regard to the compensation fixed by a Land Tribunal after a hearing with representation for the applicants.

[21] Also *Zvolsky and Zvolska v Czech Republic*, November 12, 2002, ECHR 2002–IX, where, in revoking a transfer of property, the courts took no account of evidence as to the voluntariness of the transaction or the compensation paid at the time.

permit to retain the estate bought at auction and although they had paid more, they received a sum reasonably related to the market price plus the auction costs.[22]

The manner and effects of the de facto expropriation were incompatible in *Papamichalopoulos*, namely, the seizure of the land, the length of deprivation and lack of any remedial action by the State.

The length of the proceedings concerning the expropriation measures may disclose of a violation under Art.6, para.1 where there is an unreasonable delay in the determination of civil rights and obligations. It may also form a decisive or significant part in the finding of violation under Art.1 of Protocol No.1. Thus in *Erkner and Hofauer v Austria*, where land consolidation proceedings took more than 16 years, the Court said that the complaints about the unreasonable length of proceedings under Art.6 could be distinguished from the question as to whether the disputed transfer was compatible with right of property, in which context delay was one element. On the latter, the Court found a violation referring to the disproportionate burden imposed on the applicants resulting from the uncertainty and also the lack of flexibility of the system (e.g. no compensation for loss on the forced exchange where worse land was allotted and no means of altering the position of owners during that time).[23] In other cases, where the essence of the complaint has been the delay in the proceedings, with no separate effect on property rights, the Court has found it unnecessary to decide whether the delay in the proceedings also disclosed a violation of Art.1 of Protocol No.1. Any effect on value of property or pecuniary damage is in that context to be taken into account in assessing just satisfaction for the breach of Art.6.[24]

The right to compensation is not express. The reference to deprivation being subject to the conditions provided by principles of international law was found to be relevant only to the position as regards non-nationals and it does not therefore incorporate international law principles for nationals as regards compensation.[25] However, the existence and extent of compensation is a material factor in the balance of the general interest and private rights, otherwise the protection of Art.1 of Protocol No.1 against confiscations would be illusory and ineffective.[26]

On the issue of the standard of compensation, deprivation without compensation in an amount reasonably related to the value of the property would normally be disproportionate, exceptional circumstances being required to justify a lack of

[22] In *Hentrich*, fn.9 above, however, the risk of preemption was also known and the applicants received the purchase price plus 10 per cent and costs. The Court found that this was not sufficient to compensate for the loss of a property acquired without fraudulent intent. The arbitrary, punitive nature of the measure seems to be the main distinguishing feature.

[23] Also *Matos e Silva*, fn.4 above, violations of Art.6 and Art.1 of Protocol No.1 for 13–year expropriation proceedings since the prolonged uncertainty aggravated the detrimental effects of the measures; *Almeida Garrett v Portugal*, January 11, 2000, 24 years' delay in finalising the amount of compensation for the expropriation; *Skibinscy v Poland*, November 14, 2006, inability to effectively exploit land subject to a future, indefinite expropriation order and without any compensation.

[24] e.g. *Brigandi v Italy*, February 19, 1991, Series A, No.194–B.

[25] *Lithgow*, fn.2 above, paras 111–119.

[26] e.g. (7987/77) (Dec.) December 13, 1979, 18 D.R. 31, expropriation of property for road construction: complaint about level of compensation; the Commission took the view that there was no right to any particular amount of compensation but there would be a problem if there was a substantial reduction in compensation such as could be regarded as affecting the very substance of the right to compensation.

compensation.[27] However, full compensation is not necessarily required since measures of economic or social reform may call for less than full market value.[28] In *Lithgow v UK*, concerning nationalisation, to which other considerations might apply than to ordinary expropriation, the Court stated that it would respect the legislature's judgment unless manifestly without reasonable foundation, the test generally applied since.[29] Extreme disproportion between market value and compensation did not disclose a violation, in a situation of land regularisation where the State had returned land illegally expropriated by the former communist regime and then, following proper procedures, expropriated the land by law for use in vital economic port activities. The applicants were not regarded as bearing an excessive burden, as they had received the land by donation and not invested in the land during the brief period it was in their hands; they had also received compensation for loss of previous use.[30] Where there was a distinct expropriation outside the context of any reform process, the Court did not find any legitimate objective in the public interest justifying less than market value.[31] However, where an applicant enters into an agreement with the authorities and there is no element of oppression or coercion, the Court is unlikely to find a violation of Art.1 of Protocol No.1 in respect of allegations that the settlement did not properly reflect the value of the property.[32]

Lack of any compensation is therefore a significant feature. In *Erkner and Hofauer v Austria*, the lack of compensation for forced transfer of good land for worse, combined with delay and the inflexibility of the procedure, rendered the measures in violation of Art.1 of Protocol No.1. In the *Holy Monasteries*, where there was no compensation for the transfer of ownership of large areas of monastery land, the Court found a violation, rejecting the Government's arguments as to the exceptional, historical circumstances in which the property was acquired and used. However, in the unique context of German re-unification where the legislature intervened after a short interval on grounds of social justice to put right a loophole which gave the applicants a "windfall", the Court found that the lack of compensation did not upset the "fair balance".[33]

Methods of calculation have generally been unsuccessfully attacked and indeed, having regard to the standard of "manifestly without reasonable foundation" an assessment procedure would have to be grossly unfair or arbitrary to offend. In *Lithgow v UK*, where the applicant companies made numerous criticisms of the unfairness of the calculation process, the Court, inter alia, found the fact that there

[27] e.g. *Holy Monasteries*, fn.11 above, para.71. See also *Former King of Greece*, fn.12 above, para.98, no convincing explanation for absence of compensation for expropriation of royal estates; *Yagtzilar v Greece*, December 6, 2001, ECHR 2001–XII, no compensation paid for over 70 years; *Zvolsky and Zvolska*, fn.21 above, where there was no possibility of indemnity on revocation of a donation of property; *Jahn*, fn.1 above, para.94.

[28] *Lithgow*, fn.2 above, para.121; *Holy Monasteries*, fn.11 above, paras 70–71; *Papelachas v Greece*, March 25, 1999, ECHR 1999–II, para.48.

[29] e.g. *Hakansson and Sturesson*, fn.13 above, para.54; *Papachelas*, fn.23 above, para.48.

[30] *Vistins and Perepjolkins v Latvia*, fn.16, paras 89–97.

[31] *Sciordino v Italy (No.1)*, March 29, 2006, less than 50 per cent was allotted, subject to tax.

[32] *Guerrera and Fusco v Italy*, April 3, 2000.

[33] *Jahn*, fn.1 above, paras 109–117, the applicants had apparently obtained entitlement to inherit land by operation of reforms passed shortly before reunification although they had never farmed the land as had previously been required. See also *Weber v Germany*, (5578/00) (Dec.) October 23, 2006, no compensation was also acceptable where the applicant had only had the formal title to the land taken in 1944, which had had no economic value nor had she paid tax on the land.

was an international practice in some areas of calculation did not indicate that this was the only way, referring to the thorough Parliamentary process during which valuation issues had been thrashed out.

In other cases, failure to make payments inflation-proofed or to discount certain heads of damage has not been enough to render the compensation unreasonable.[34] An assessment method therefore that is geared at least ostensibly to compensating for the property will pass muster even if the method used or figure reached differs greatly from that preferred by the aggrieved owner. The approach that the valuation is "reasonably related" to the property in question is sometimes used.[35] A gross disparity between market value and compensation, without public interest justification, may however disclose a violation.[36] A system which penalised owners of expropriated property of historic value for depreciation in the state of the property but prohibited taking into account the special value of the site from its cultural features was unfair and disproportionate; the property's specific features should be taken into account to a reasonable degree.[37]

Where the court fees payable by the applicants for the proceedings by which they challenged the amount of compensation for their expropriated land exceeded that amount, the Court considered that this imposed an excessive burden. The Government argument that the State obligation to pay compensation for expropriation and the applicants' obligation to pay court fees were two separate matters was rejected, the Court considering the reality of the situation in which the second would not have arisen but for the first which was the responsibility of the State. Nor was it persuaded that the applicants were at fault for bringing the proceedings and claiming higher sums.[38]

Delay by the State in paying compensation due on expropriation which, due to 70 per cent inflation, caused the applicant substantial loss, was found by the Court to render the compensation inadequate.[39] An inflexible presumption that adjoining owners of expropriated land used for roads benefitted from the development and could not claim compensation for damage was "manifestly without reasonable foundation", leaving the applicants to bear an individual and excessive burden.[40]

[34] e.g. (13135/87), fn.13 above, where the Land Tribunal granted about one sixth of the claimed losses and future costs of upkeep, the Commission found the method of assessment reasonable and that the lack of inflation proofing did not bring it outside the margin of appreciation; (7987/77) (Dec.) December 13, 1979, 18 D.R. 31, where assessment of agricultural value without account being given to future mineral potential was not unreasonable; (14265/88) (Dec.) January 19, 1989, 59 D.R. 281, where the applicant who had never lived in the property only received site value on expropriation.

[35] e.g. *Liakopoulou v Greece*, (20627/04) May 24, 2006, para.31.

[36] e.g. *Platakou v Greece*, January 11, 2001, ECHR 2001–I, property expropriated for a museum with compensation one quarter/one fifth of the market value and the reason given by the authorities (its ruinuous state) was contradicted by the experts' valuations; *Jokela v Finland*, May 21, 2002, ECHR 2002–IV, where the amount paid for compensation for expropriation was based on a purported value of the property grossly inconsistent with the tax valuation; *Pincova and Pinc v Czech Republic*, November 5, 2002, ECHR 2002–VIII, where compensation was set at the price thirty years earlier and bore no reasonable relation to the current value, with no regard to costs of the upkeep of the property.

[37] *Kozacioglu*, fn.14 above, para.72, for just satisfaction the Court did not give the full value of the expert assessment but, due to the legitimate public aim pursued, awarded a lesser sum.

[38] *Perdigao v Portugal*, November 16, 2010.

[39] *Akkus v Turkey*, July 9, 1997, R.J.D. 1997–IV, No.43; also *Malama v Greece*, March 1, 2001, ECHR 2002–II, where the courts did not take the delay (70 years) in paying compensation for expropriated land into account, nor award interest for delay; *Yetis v Turkey*, July 6, 2010, paras 47–60, court awards did not take into account steep depreciation in value of compensation during the proceedings.

[40] *Katikarides v Greece*, November 15, 1996, R.J.D. 1996–V, No.20, paras 49–50, the applicants had strong arguments that the fly-over deprived their remaining land of value.

Indeed a failure to take into account the relevant factor that the expropriation would have the effect of devaluing the applicant's remaining land disclosed a breach.[41] Nor should the authorities require applicants to have recourse to multiple proceedings to recover different elements of loss from an expropriation, as this delays payment and puts too much of a burden on the individual.[42] It may also provide insufficient protection to put the burden on the applicant to apply for compensation as well as to operate, retrospectively, a time-limit for claims which allowed the authorities to benefit from the already existing situation.[43] Similarly, a lack of legal certainty which places an excessive burden on property owners arises where public authorities are permitted to occupy private land by way of effecting an informal expropriation without utilising legislative procedures, leaving it to the aggrieved landowner to seek to regularise the situation and obtain compensation in the courts. Allowing the public authorities to benefit from a lower interest rate on damages also encouraged them not to use formal expropriation procedures, again to the detriment of the landowners.[44]

A wide margin of appreciation applies where a Contracting State takes measures to remedy expropriations carried out by previous non-democratic regimes.[45] No issue arose where applicants received compensation, rather than restitution of the property and at less than market value.[46] Similarly, steps taken to restore justice and the rule of law by reinstating property arbitrarily taken without compensation did not disclose a violation, although measures went too far and no fair balance was struck where individuals had property removed without adequate compensation merely due to technical errors in title for which the authorities were responsible.[47]

3. Adverse possession

II–361 The operation of rules of adverse possession by which, after a limitation period, the beneficial owner lost title or the ability to recover the land was regarded as not a deprivation but a regulation of questions of title which amounted to a "control of use" within the meaning of the second paragraph of Article 1 of Protocol No. 1 and which could be regarded as within the legislature's wide margin of appreciation where it came to social and economic policies A fair balance was struck, given the relatively long limitation period of 12 years, the fact that the rules had been in force for many years and that the applicants could have stopped time running at any time by the requisite action for re-possession. The fact that no compensation was available for loss of land worth substantial sums was an inevitable feature of the operation of limitation periods which govern legal certainty; the value of the land and the windfall nature of the gain were not arguments relevant to the regime.[48]

[41] *Bistrovic v Croatia*, May 31, 2007.

[42] *Efstathiou and Michaelidis v Greece*, July 10, 2003, paras 30–33.

[43] *Börekciogullari (Cökmez) v Turkey*, October 19, 2006.

[44] *Sarica and Dilaver v Turkey*, May 25, 2010, paras 38–52.

[45] *Maltzan and Others v Germany*, (71916/01), (71917/01) and (10260/02), (Dec.) March 2, 2005, ECHR 2005–XI, para.111.

[46] *Põder v Estonia*, (67723/01) (Dec.) April 26, 2005.

[47] *Velikovi v Bulgaria*, March 15, 2007, it may be noted that some compensation had been available even in those cases where there had been abuse or material housing irregularities by the applicants.

[48] *JA Pye (Oxford) Ltd and JA Pye (Oxford) Land Ltd*, August 30, 2007, ECHR 2007–. . . , paras 66, 71, and 77–85. See the minority view that the general interest pursued in the case was not evident since the land was not abandoned or its usage in need of State intervention, while on the other hand there were insufficient procedural safeguards to prevent the owner losing his land through inadvertence and no convincing reason why the adverse possessor should benefit by gaining the full title.

4. Fines

Fines imposed by the authorities generally fall within the second paragraph of Art.1 which inter alia safeguards the State's ability to impose taxes and penalties, and they thus attract a wide margin of appreciation. However, a fine may nonetheless offend the basic principle of proportionality where its size is such as to amount to a de facto deprivation of the applicant's entire property.[49] II–362

5. Forfeiture and confiscation measures

Draconian powers for the seizure of goods in the customs or criminal context which pursue lawful and legitimate purposes have proved acceptable,[50] subject to minimum requirements of procedural safeguards and domestic lawfulness.[51] II–363

The approach of the Court has been to regard confiscations as a control of use of property rather than deprivation. This approach places an emphasis on the general purpose of the measure rather than the effect on the applicant's property rights. In *Agosi v UK*, smuggled kruggerrands obtained from the applicants by fraud had been seized by Customs which refused to exercise its discretion to return them to the applicant. The Court considered that, while in one sense the seizure disclosed a deprivation, it formed a constituent part of the procedure for the control of use of gold in the United Kingdom. Similarly, in *Air Canada v UK*, where an airliner was seized on discovery of a large cannabis resin shipment on board but released on payment of £50,000, the Court did not accept, as argued by the applicant, that they had been deprived of both airplane and money but found that the measures were part of the system for the control of use of an aircraft used to carry drugs.[52]

It is accepted that smuggled goods will generally be the object of confiscation, a practice existing in many Contracting States. While the Commission in *Agosi v UK* considered that there had to be a link between the behaviour of the owner of smuggled goods and the breach of the law, such that the innocent owner should be entitled to recovery, the Court observed that this was not a common practice in Member States, where the fault of owner might be only one element in the balancing exercise.

However the Court did hold in *Agosi v UK* that there were procedural requirements implicit in the protection of property rights, namely that there should be procedures which enabled reasonable account to be taken of the link between the conduct of owner and breach of law and to afford the owner to put his case to the

[49] *Mamidakis v Greece*, January 11, 2007, violation: extraordinarily high fines of millions of euros.

[50] e.g. *Handyside v UK*, December 7, 1976, Series A, No.24, para.62, where there was seizure and destruction of copies of *The Little Red Schoolbook*, the Court commented that the second paragraph on control of use set up the State as sole judges of the necessity of an interference. Later cases mitigated this extreme approach.

[51] e.g. *Baklanov v Russia*, June 9, 2005, no legal basis for the confiscation of some $250,000 in respect of which the applicant had committed no offence; *Zlinsat, SPOL, S.R.O. v Bulgaria*, June 15, 2006, vague, unreviewable powers applied to suspend a privatisation contract and evict the applicant from its hotel development. See also *Smirnov v Russia*, June 7, 2007, where the prosecution kept the applicant's lawyer's seized computer, not itself an instrument or object of a criminal offence, long after their use for it had finished: this failed to strike the balance between the general and individual interest.

[52] See also *Bosphorus Airways v Ireland*, June 30, 2005, ECHR 2005–VI, para.144, detention of aircraft pursuant to sanctions regime was a control of use; and *Islamic Republic of Iran Shipping Lines v Turkey*, December 13, 2007, para.87, seizure of ship due to suspected arms smuggling was a control of use.

responsible authorities. In both *Agosi* and *Air Canada*, the possibility of judicial review of the Customs Commissioners' decisions were found to furnish sufficient procedural protection although the decisions were essentially unreasoned, limiting the ability to challenge them.[53] There is a presumption of compliance with Art.1 of Protocol 1 and adequate legal safeguards where confiscations or seizures are made pursuant to European Union laws.[54]

Forfeiture of £240,000 found by customs officers in the applicant's car was a control of use and the Court did not find the proceedings to be unfair since the applicant had the opportunity to show the money was not connected with drug trafficking. Nor did the domestic court rely automatically on any statutory presumptions.[55] However, confiscation of money assessed by a court to be drug trafficking proceeds following conviction was not a control of use but a measure to secure the payment of a penalty within the meaning of the second paragraph of Art.1 of Protocol No.1 and not disproportionate where the procedure was fair.[56] The confiscation of buildings which had been unlawfully used for lodging foreigners and which had been in a state unfit for human habitation was justified where the applicant had been convicted of criminal offences with regard to the property in a procedure which had fully and fairly taken into account the applicant's fault.[57]

Rules on declaring the entry of currency into a country are justifiable in pursuit of various aims of fighting crime, but the Court has struck down various regimes which overly penalised people who were not themselves proved to be involved in nefarious activities. Where foreign currency was confiscated on entry into Russia due the failure to declare the amount, the Court found that the measure was disproportionate as the importation of the currency had not in fact been unlawful, nor had the State been deprived of any duties or taxes on the sum concerned. The Court noted that the money had been lawfully obtained, not being a product of organised crime or drug trafficking; the applicant had merely been at fault for not declaring the correct sum and had received the requisite punishment of a suspended prison sentence, which it had not been argued was of insufficient deterrent or punitive effect.[58] Also disproportionate was a fine of half the amount of undeclared currency and confiscation of the whole sum (some €200,000), again where there was no indication that there was any element of money laundering or fiscal fraud involved and only a failure to declare the sum.[59]

[53] In *Air Canada v UK*, May 5, 1995, Series A, No.316, 20 E.H.R.R. 150, although no reasons were given at the time of the confiscation beyond the presence of drugs, the Court considered that, against the history of previous warnings about security laxness by Customs, the company could not realistically claim to be unaware of the reasons. Taken with the important aim of combatting drug trafficking, the measures of seizure and return of the aircraft on payment of money were not disproportionate.

[54] *Bosphorus Airways*, fn.52 above.

[55] *Butler v UK*, (41661/98) (Dec.) June 27, 2002. The forfeiture of cars, used to carry drugs, has also been found a legitimate control of use of property, even if belonging to innocent third parties, where there was a procedure whereby they could apply for the return of their property: *CM v France*, (28708/95) (Dec.) June 26, 2001, ECHR 2001–VII; similar approach to forfeiture of a coach used in smuggling of illegal immigrants: *Yildirim v Italy*, (38602/02) (Dec.) April 10, 2003. Concerning confiscation of money unlawfully obtained or from organised crime: *Riela v Italy*, (52439/99) (Dec.) September 4, 2001; and *Honecker v Germany*, (53991/00) (Dec.) November 11, 2001, ECHR 2001–XII. For forfeiture of pensions, see Pt IIB, s.33: Pensions, sub-s.3: Property rights.

[56] *Phillips v UK*, July 5, 2001.

[57] *Tas v Belgium*, (44614/06) (Dec.) May 12, 2005.

[58] *Ismayilov v Russia*, November 6, 2008, paras 31–39.

[59] *Grifhorst v France*, February 26, 2009, paras 87–106.

Draconian regimes operating to confiscate property outside implication in criminal activity seem to attract more rigorous scrutiny. Where land and buildings were confiscated almost in their entirety due to breach of plannning regulations, the Court found this was unacceptable due to the arbitrariness and lack of compliance with the rule against retrospective criminal penalties, but was also not proportionate, in particular since the applicants had been in good faith (acting under assurances of various officials) and the confiscation exceeded the purported aim of the measure, to ensure enforcement of the regulations, which could have been achieved by requiring dismantling of the offending structures.[60] Confiscation of innocent goods which had been carried in a lorry in which drugs had been found but where the owner was of good faith and not implicated in any wrongdoing was found not to be justified by the need to prevent drug trafficking, the inability of the owner to make application for return of those goods disclosing a *lacuna*.[61] As regards the power of pre-emption of sales of works of art by the authorities to prevent masterpieces leaving the country, in *Beyeler v Italy*, the legitimacy of this aim was not put in doubt but the Court emphasised that, when using powers in the general interest, it was incumbent on the authorities to act in good time, in an appropriate manner and with utmost consistency. The delay and vacillation of the authorities, together with the lack of clarity in the law and unjust enrichment from their acquisition of the painting at well below market value, thus disclosed a violation.

Where property is confiscated pending criminal proceedings, the applicant in principle should be able to get them back or their value, once acquitted. A procedure which placed the burden on the acquitted suspect to prove that his property had been lost or deteriorated, rather than holding the authorities properly to account for what they had done with the property, was regarded as imposing an excessive burden on the individual.[62] Where, after acquittal for smuggling, proceedings to obtain compensation for forfeited furs took over seven years, this was also regarded as imposing an excessive burden due to the length of time.[63] However, where the applicant was merely claiming for depreciation of his car, held in a pound for 14 months, the Court considered the availability of court action for any wrongdoing on the part of the public prosecutor for false prosecution or for tortious action damaging the car struck a fair balance.[64]

As in other contexts, decisions which are flagrantly arbitrary will raise issues. Thus where a Cypriot ship carrying arms was seized by Turkish authorities on suspicion of arm smuggling and the seizure prolonged despite the fact that the suspicion was shown to be founded on the pretext, contradicted by the relevant State institutions, that Turkey was at war with Cyprus, the Court found that the seizure had been a disproportionate interference.[65]

[60] *Sud Fondi Srl v Italy*, January 20, 2009, paras 130–142.
[61] *Bowler International Unit v France*, July 23, 2009, paras 34–47.
[62] *Tendam v Spain*, July 13, 2010.
[63] *Jucys v Lithuania*, January 8, 2008; *Borzhonov v Russia*, January 22, 2009, paras 57–63, bus seized and held for excessive period during proceedings. See also *Smirnov v Russia*, June 7, 2007, para.54, where the authorities retained the applicant's computer, not the object or instrument of a crime, even though the information required by way of evidence had been extracted: failure to strike a fair balance.
[64] *Adamczyk v Poland*, (28551/04) (Dec.) November 7, 2006.
[65] *Islamic Republic of Iran Shipping Lines*, fn.52 above, paras 94–103.

6. Bankruptcy and insolvency measures

II–364 Imposition of bankrupcy on a person, with removal of the power of disposal of his possessions, is regarded as a control of use of property that pursues in general terms a legitimate aim and falls within the margin of appreciation. However, the interference with property rights can become disproportionate if it lasts too long due to judicial inactivity, as in *Luordo v Italy*.[66] Imposition of receivership on a business will also constitute a control on possessions. While the Court may refrain from verifying whether the authorities were correct to take the measure, it has stated that the business must be able to obtain an effective judicial review of the imposition of receivership, including access to the documents necessary to raise its grounds of appeal, as a guarantee against arbitrariness.[67]

Creditors' claims may constitute possessions protected under Art.1 of Protocol No.1. However, where court-ordered debt adjustments in bankruptcy effectively wiped out the applicant creditor's claims, the measure, implementing legislation to cope with a recession, was not considered disproportionate, the Court noting that the creditor had knowingly undertaken a financial risk, any prospects of any repayment had become highly precarious and there had been the opportunity to put forward his interests in the court procedures.[68]

The actions of liquidators in distributing assets may attract the responsibilty of the State, even if it is not responsible as such for the insolvency of private business enterprises nor is there any expectation necessarily that a creditor recoup all his losses. Where an applicant had a judgment debt in his favour against an insolvent bank and was a priority creditor, there was a violation where, in breach of the law, the liquidator distributed assets to others, failing to give the applicant priority.[69]

Where forced sales are made in order to pay debts, this is a deprivation of property. The Court will examine the procedures to verify whether the applicant has borne a disproportionate burden. In a case where a co-owner was able to exercise a power of pre-emption at a low price before such a sale, the Court considered that this denied the applicant the possibility of obtaining a price at the sale closer to market value.[70]

Cross-reference

Part IIA, s.1b: Civil rights and obligations.
Part IIA, s.2: Access to court.
Part IIB, s.34: Planning and use of property.
Part IIB, s.38: Property.

[66] *Luordo v Italy*, July 17, 2003, bankruptcy lasted over 14 years.
[67] *Druzstevni Zalozna Pria v Czech Republic*, July 31, 2008, breaches of Art.1 of Protocol No.1 and Art.6, as courts could not examine the factual basis justifying the measure or lawfulness in a wider sense.
[68] *Back v Finland*, July 20, 2004.
[69] *Kotov v Russia*, January 14, 2010, the liquidator was regarded as fulfilling public duties. Currently pending before the Grand Chamber.
[70] *Kanala v Slovakia*, July 10, 2007.

18. Extradition

Key provisions:

Articles 2 (right to life), 3 (prohibition on torture, inhuman and degrading treatment), 13 (right to effective remedy), and 34 (obligation on States not to hinder the effective exercise of the right of individual petition). **II–365**

Key case-law:

Soering v UK, July 7, 1989, Series A, No.161, 11 E.H.R.R. 439; *Chahal v UK*, November 15, 1996, R.J.D. 1996–V, No.22, 23 E.H.R.R. 413; *Mamatkulov and Askarov v Turkey*, February 4, 2005, ECHR 2005–I; *Shamayev v Georgia and Russia*, April 12, 2005, ECHR 2005–III; *Ocalan v Turkey*, May 5, 2005, ECHR 2005–IV; *Bader and Kanbor v Sweden*, November 8, 2005, ECHR 2005–XI.

1. General considerations

Extradition is accepted by the Convention organs as a legitimate and desirable means of enforcing criminal justice between States.[1] There is no right not to be extradited.[2] Principally issues arise under the Convention regarding the detention pending extradition and regarding allegations of breaches of human rights which will occur in the receiving State if the extradition is carried out. **II–366**

2. Risk of violations in receiving country

(a) Ill-treatment

Where on proposed extradition an applicant faces a real risk of treatment contrary to Art.3 in the receiving State, the responsibility of the expelling State is engaged and a violation arises. This principle was established in *Soering v UK*, where conditions on death row in Virginia were found to expose the applicant, facing two charges of capital murder, to the real risk of inhuman and degrading treatment. **II–367**

The risk must relate to a treatment which reaches a certain minimum level of severity, taking into account all the circumstances, including the physical and mental effects and where relevant the age, sex and health of the victim.[3] General

[1] *Soering v UK*, July 7, 1989, Series A, No.161, 11 E.H.R.R. 439, paras 86 and 89, noting the legitimate interests of the international community in facilitating the bringing to justice of offenders who move easily about the globe and the dangers facing States which were obliged to become safe havens for alleged criminals.

[2] *Soering*, fn.1 above, para.85. See *Babar Ahmad v UK*, (24027/07) et al (Dec.) July 6, 2010, paras 175–177, where there is no risk of ill-treatment on return to the receiving State it is not relevant that it might be more proportionate for the sending State to carry out the trial itself or send to a third State.

[3] In *Soering*, fn.1 above, death row disclosed inhuman treatment having regard to the average length of detention pending execution (six to eight years) with the ever present and mounting anguish of awaiting an execution, the stringency of the custodial regime in the Mecklenburg Correctional Centre over that time, the applicant's personal circumstances, in particular his youth and some indications that he had suffered from an impairment of mental responsibility for his acts; cf. (10479/83) (Dec.) March 12, 1984, 37 D.R. 58, the Commission had not found that death row would involve Art.3 treatment having regard to the fact that the element of delay derived from procedural safeguards used by prisoners.

reliance on a poor humans right record generally is not enough to establish risk.[4] Where there are substantial grounds for believing that the person would be subject for example to torture by the authorities, extradition has been held to contravene Art.3, whether the risk flowed from the applicant's particular circumstances[5] or from an exceptional situation in which all criminal suspects ran the risk of torture and abuse, applied indiscriminately without aim or purpose.[6] It has been left open whether the extradition to face the imposition of life sentence without possibility of early release would infringe Art.3.[7]

The way in which the extradition is enforced, even if involving the use of tranquillizers, has not generally been found to go beyond the inevitable trauma involved in the legitimate enforcement of an extradition decision.[8] However, in *Shamayev v Georgia and Russia*, in finding a breach of Art.3, the Court heavily criticised the way in which the detained applicants were kept in uncertainty as to the reasons for their detention and their fate and took into account the panic and anguish caused by the announcement of imminent expulsion to Russia where they had legitimate grounds to fear how they might be treated, together with the severity of injuries caused when they resisted the execution of the extradition.

The Court has emphasised that the prohibition contained in Art.3 is absolute.[9] Therefore, if there is a real risk of such prohibited treatment in the receiving State, no principle of international enforcement of justice would justify implementing the extradition.

Before extraditing the authorities should make a proper assessment of risk, with reference to the facts which were known or ought to have been known at the time of the extradition. This may require them to seek assurances of the applicant's safety from the State seeking extradition or other safeguards such as medical reports or visits by independent observers.[10] The assessment should not be limited merely to asylum considerations but address other alleged grounds of risk of ill-treatment.[11]

[4] See e.g *Puzan v Ukraine*, February 18, 2010, para.34, the applicant had not shown that he belonged to a vulnerable group such as political prisoners or distinguished any personal circumstances substantiating his fears of ill-treatment in Belarus.

[5] See e.g. *Klein v Russia*, April 1, 2010, where the poor human rights record in Colombia was combined with the applicant's circumstances as a person convicted of aiding paramilitary activities in respect of whom the Vice-President of the country had made threatening statements; *Iskandarov v Russia*, September 23, 2010, paras 130–131, international reports of widespread torture where the applicant had been a political opponent of the current President in Tajikistan and there was a history of persecution of persons in such a situation.

[6] See e.g. *Kaboulov v Ukraine*, November 19, 2009, para.112, concerning Kazakhstan.

[7] e.g. *Gonzalez v Spain*, (43544/98) (Dec.) June 29, 1999, the Court, assuming that the life imprisonment without release was contrary to Art.3, took into account the fact that the Spanish courts had imposed the condition that he should not be imprisoned for his whole life; *Nivette v France*, (44190/98) (Dec.) July 3, 2001, ECHR 2001–VII, the Court had regard to the undertaking on oath by the District Attorney that he would not apply for the death penalty or a whole life sentence; *Einhorn v France*, (71555/01) (Dec.) October 16, ECHR 2001–XI, where the Court did not exclude the possibility, referring to various Council of Europe texts on the treatment of long-term prisoners. Later cases, e.g. *Salem v Portugal*, (26844/04) (Dec.) May 9, 2006 and *Saoudi v Spain*, (22871/06) (Dec.) September 18, 2006, appear to assume that Art.3 applies to irreducible life sentences.

[8] (25342/94) (Dec.) September 4, 1995, 82–A D.R. 134, where the applicant, who had attempted to commit suicide under strain of the imminent extradition, had to be given sedatives in view of her resistance to departure.

[9] *Chahal v UK*, November 15, 1996, R.J.D. 1996–V, No.22, 23 E.H.R.R. 413, paras 80–81.

[10] *Garabayev v Russia*, June 7, 2007, where the applicant was sent back to Turkmenistan.

[11] *Ryabikin v Russia*, June 19, 2008, paras 118 and 120, the authorities only considered whether the applicant had been persecuted, not whether he faced other forms of ill-treatment such as inhuman prison conditions.

Failure to provide any judicial recourse against removal for extradition purposes, thus removing a basic safeguard, will offend.[12]

The fact that the requesting State has recognised the right of individual petition may be relevant. Where IRA prisoners were to be extradited from the Netherlands to the United Kingdom and were alleging that they would be ill-treated in the Maze prison, the Commission, in dismissing the complaints as manifestly ill-founded, had regard to assurances given to the Dutch authorities by the Deputy Director of the Maze prison and the fact that the United Kingdom had ratified the right of individual petition.[13] Diplomatic Notes from the USA were considered a satisfactory form of guarantee concerning an undertaking that terrorist suspects would not be classified as enemy combatants taking them outside the civil justice system or that they would be subject to extraordinary rendition to Egypt.[14] Not all assurances are sufficient. In *Soering* the undertaking by the US authorities to inform the trial court of the wish of the United Kingdom that the death penalty should not be applied was not enough to diminish the risk in view of the prosecution's intention to seek the death penalty as merited. Nor are diplomatic assurances from a State in which reputable international sources assert that torture is endemic likely to suffice.[15] The source of the promises is also crucial, the Court having found no indication on a number of occasions that the official concerned had the power to make the assurances on behalf of the State.[16]

Risk of extradition should be of some immediacy. Where a person under extradition order to India swallowed a razor blade rendering travel impossible, the Court rejected complaints under Art.3 noting that the applicant currently could not be removed and that when his medical status changed he could obtain a judicial review of the situation as at that time.[17]

Failure to comply with a request by the Court to suspend an extradition pending its proceedings may lead to a finding of a violation of the State's obligation under Art.34 of the Convention not to hinder the effective exercise of the right of individual petition. In *Mamatkulov and Askarov v Turkey*, the applicants were sent, despite such a request, to Uzbekistan where they allegedly risked serious ill-treatment as terrorist suspects. The applicants had not been in contact with their representatives after the extradition, which hampered their ability to prove their substantive complaints. The Court found that, although no breach of Art.3 had been established, the Government had failed to abstain from measures that prejudiced the integrity and effectiveness of the Court's final judgment and were thus in breach of Art.34.

[12] *Iskandarov*, fn.5, para.133, where in fact the authorities unlawfully removed the applicant without obtaining an extradition order against which he could appeal.

[13] (12543/86) (Dec.) December 2, 1986, 51 D.R. 272. See also Pt IIB, s.29: Immigration and expulsion, on the Convention organs's increased readiness to find problems within Contracting States which are not cured by their acceptance of the right of individual petition.

[14] *Babar Ahmad*, fn.2 above, paras 104–116.

[15] *Ismoilov v Russia*, April 24, 2008, para.127, assurances of humane treatment by the Uzbekistan Government were not considered a reliable guarantee; *Ryabikin*, fn.11 above, para.119, same view taken of assurances from Turkmenistan—due to prohibition of access of international observers to places of detention, the lack of any means of monitoring compliance deprived such assurances of value.

[16] *Soldatenko v Ukraine*, October 23, 2008, para.73, concerning assurances given by the First Deputy Prosecutor General of Turkmenistan.

[17] *Ghosh v Germany*, (24017/03) (Dec.) June 5, 2007. Contrast *Ryabikin*, fn.11 above, para.115, where though no decision to extradite had yet been taken, the parties did not dispute that he was under threat of extradition, the applicant keeping his whereabouts secret due to fear of removal at any moment.

(b) Death penalty

II–368 Extradition to face the death penalty, if imposed judicially after a fair trial, did not previously raise an issue by itself under Art.3. In *Soering*, the Court rejected the argument of Amnesty International that while Art.2 allowed judicial execution it was nonetheless contrary to Art.3 to impose it. The two provisions had to be read in harmony with each other and Art.3 could not have been intended to include a general prohibition of the death penalty. The Court did not exclude however that in certain circumstances an issue might arise under Art.3 concerning, for example, the disproportionality of the sentence to the crime committed and personal circumstances of the accused, as well as the conditions of detention awaiting executions such as the death row phenomenon.

Now, where a country has ratified Protocol No.6 (abolition of the death penalty save in time of war) or Protocol No.13 (abolition of the death penalty in all circumstances), it would appear to be in potential violation of those provisions and Art.3 to extradite or expel someone to face a real risk of imposition of the death penalty.[18] In *Ocalan v Turkey*, the Court, noting that almost all Contracting States has ratified Protocol 6, gave a strong indication that this almost universal abandonment of the death penalty in peace time constituted a de facto abrogation or modification of Art.2 and a rejection of capital punishment as an unacceptable, if not inhuman, form of punishment.[19] Since in that case the imposition of the death penalty on an applicant after an unfair trial before a tribunal lacking independence and impartiality was found to disclose a breach of Art.3, extradition to face trial in such circumstances would appear to be incompatible with the Convention on that basis also.[20]

Assurances from the requesting State will be relevant to the existence of any potential violation from the extradition. In *Einhorn v France*, where the applicant was to return to Pennsylvania to face a murder charge, the Court considered the Government had obtained sufficient assurances such as to remove the danger of the applicant being sentenced to death in the United States of America, namely, affidavits sworn by the District Attorney that she would not seek the death penalty and that the court would have no power to impose it of its own motion.[21]

In addition, where the laws in the receiving country have changed and the death penalty is no longer applicable, that bar to extradition may be lifted.[22] A moratorium on imposition of the death penalty which is effective and likely to last may also remove this element of risk.[23]

[18] (22742/93) (Dec.) January 20, 1994, 76–A D.R. 164; *Ismaili v Germany*, (58218/00) (Dec.) March 15, 2001, where Germany had ratified Protocol No.6 but it was not substantiated that the offences facing the applicant in Morocco attracted the death penalty; mutatis mutandis, *Bader and Kanbor v Sweden*, November 8, 2005, ECHR 2005–XI, where the applicant had been sentenced to death in absentia, a breach of Arts 2 and 3 was found in respect of his proposed expulsion to Syria.

[19] *Ocalan v Turkey*, May 5, 2005, ECHR 2005–IV, paras 163–165.

[20] *Bader and Kanbor*, fn.18 above, para.42.

[21] See fn.7 above; also (22742/93) fn.18 above; *Salem* and *Saoudi*, fn.7 above, where the specific assurances and information obtained from the Indian and Algerian authorities respectively removed the risk of the death sentence or an irreducible life sentence; *Babar Ahmad*, fn.2 above, Diplomatic note and assurances supported by fact indictment on non-capital charges was already drawn up.

[22] See *Ismoilov*, fn.15, para.119, the risk of imposition of the death penalty in Uzbekistan had been eliminated.

[23] See *Kaboulov v Ukraine*, fn.6 above, para.102.

(c) Other violations in receiving State

There is no general principle that a State cannot surrender an individual unless satisfied that the conditions awaiting him in the receiving country are in full accord with each of the safeguards of the Convention.[24] II–369

Where in *Soering* the applicant invoked Art.6, claiming that if he was extradited he would face a breach of Art.6, para.3(c) because of lack of legal aid for certain appeal applications, the Court did not exclude that an issue might be raised under Art.6 where the fugitive to be extradited had suffered, or risked suffering, a "flagrant denial" of a fair trial in a requesting country,[25] particularly where there is a risk of execution.[26] That was however not the case in *Soering* where flattering remarks had been made as to the democratic character of the legal system which respected the rule of law and afforded considerable procedural safeguards.[27] The Court has rejected a submission that an applicant should only have to show a "real risk" of unfairness as opposed to a risk of a "flagrant denial" of his rights or that he was entitled to have his Art.6 right protected on the first relevant occasion.[28]

The meaning in practice of a "flagrant denial" of a fair trial is not yet established, but the standard would appear to be set very high. Where an applicant complained of extradition to Hong Kong, the Commission did not find his allegations that at his trial he would face contested evidence taken in his absence in Malaysia or that a co-accused might be offered immunity to testify against him disclosed such a risk.[29] Nor was the trial facing a Russian facing extradition from Finland to Russia found to disclose the exceptional circumstances adverted to by the Court.[30] Evidence of extremely hostile media coverage in Pennsylvania where the applicant faced jury trial for murder did not furnish substantial grounds for believing that his trial would not take place in conditions complying with Art.6.[31] In *Mamatkulov and Askarov v Turkey*, a majority of the Grand Chamber considered that, although there was a doubt that the applicants would receive a fair trial in the Uzbekistan, there was insufficient evidence to show that possible irregularities would constitute a flagrant denial of justice. Three dissenting judges however differed, considering that the materials from, *inter alia*, Amnesty International gave credible grounds for believing confessions obtained by torture were routinely used and that access to lawyers was frequently denied, which fears proved justified when the applicants were held incommunicado on their return, their trial held in camera and their convictions

[24] *Soering*, fn.1 above, para.112.

[25] *Soering*, fn.1 above, para.113. See also (10383/83) (Dec.) May 3, 1983, 36 D.R. 209, where the Commission stated that a violation could not be ruled out if there was a risk of prosecution for political reasons which could lead to an unjustified or disproportionate sentence.

[26] *Ocalan*, fn.19 above, paras 166–175.

[27] See, mutadis mutandis, *Tomic v UK*, (17837/03) (Dec.) October 14, 2003, where the concerns about trials of war criminals in Croatia was not sufficient for the applicant's expulsion to raise issues under Art.6, particularly since Croatia was a Contracting State.

[28] *Stapleton v Ireland*, (56588/07) (Dec.) May 4, 2010.

[29] (15933/89) (Dec.) October 14, 1991; (19319/91) (Dec.) September 2, 1992, his complaints that although Hong Kong had given procedural assurances, this would not protect him when China took over, were rejected on the basis that the complaints were largely hypothetical and the lack of responsibility of the UK for the future acts of China.

[30] (16832/90) (Dec.) May 28, 1991, 69 D.R. 321, the applicant alleged that KGB cases were decided by the Supreme Court as the only instance, with minimal publicity; (22742/93), fn.18 above, risk to fairness of trial from alleged media publicity too hypothetical.

[31] *Einhorn*, fn.7 above.

principally based on self-incriminating statements made while in custody without access to their lawyers.[32]

There has been some recent guidance however. Where a terrorist suspect was being sent to the United States, the Court found no issue arising due to assurances that he would not stand trial in any controversial military tribunal, but commented that a flagrant denial of justice would be threatened if there were substantial grounds for believing that he would be held incommunicado without access to a lawyer and without access to or trial in the ordinary US criminal courts.[33] It was not established that terrorist suspects extradited to the US were at risk of being coerced into guilty pleas or would not be able to communicate effectively with their lawyers, or that evidence obtained by torture would be admitted in evidence against them.[34] It was not sufficient to show flagrant denial of justice that there might have been delay in prosecuting the crime.[35]

Summary trial, where no oral evidence was taken at the hearing, all evidence submitted by the prosecutor and both the accused and his lawyer absent, has also been regarded as disclosing a flagrant denial of justice.[36]

3. Extradition proceedings: fairness

II–370 Extradition proceedings in the sending State do not fall within the scope of Art.6, para.1 since they do not involve the determination of the criminal charge.[37] Even where a limited examination of the merits is undertaken in committal proceedings by the magistrates this is not considered part of the determination of the charges on which the extradition is sought.[38]

4. Remedies

II–371 Where it is alleged that there is a risk of Art.3 treatment on return, the Court held in *Soering*, disagreeing with the Commission, that judicial review furnished an effective remedy against extradition. The Court found that the approach of the courts, giving the "most anxious scrutiny" to claims of risk of ill-treatment, was sufficient notwithstanding the formally limited scope of the examination in judicial review. While in *Chahal v UK*, concerning expulsion, judicial review was inadequate, this was due at least in part to the inability of the courts to undertake any independent scrutiny of the national security considerations which were at the basis of the decision to expel. Despite criticism of the inability of the courts to decide the question solely on the question of risk without reference to security considerations, the Court did not appear to overrule its previous case-law and it remains to be seen

[32] See also *Olaechea Cahuas v Spain*, August 10, 2006, para.61, doubts about fairness of trial of person suspected of financing local terrorists not sufficient.

[33] *Al-Moayad v Germany*, (35865/03) (Dec.) February 20, 2007.

[34] *Babar Ahmad*, fn.2 above, paras 133 and 159, the applicants had claimed that the authorities would monitor their conversations with their lawyers; however, there had only been one example, in wholly exceptional circumstances and the material had not been passed to the prosecution; there were also means of contesting admissibility of evidence obtained by illicit means in US courts.

[35] *Stapleton v Ireland*, fn.28 above.

[36] *Bader and Kanbor*, fn.18 above, para.47, where the applicant was tried in absentia in Syria: however, this did not found a separate breach of Art.6 in addition to Arts 2 and 3.

[37] *Mamatkulov and Askarov v Turkey*, February 4, 2005, ECHR 2005–I, para.80.

[38] (10479/83), fn.3 above; also (24015/94) (Dec.) May 20, 1994, 77–A D.R.144.

whether it would maintain its general view of the effectiveness of judicial review in an extradition case, where risk was not the sole question but other elements irrelevant to Art.3 played a decisive role in the decision to uphold the extradition.

Cross reference

Part IIB, s.11: Detention pending extradition or expulsion.
Part IIB, s.25: Hindrance in the exercise of the right of individual petition.
Part IIB, s.29: Immigration and expulsion.
Part IIB, s.46: Torture, inhuman and degrading treatment.

19. Forced labour

Key provision:

II–372 Article 4 (prohibition of slavery, forced or compulsory labour)

Key case-law:

Van der Mussele v Belgium, November 23, 1983, Series A No.70, 6 E.H.R.R. 163; *Karl Heinz Schmidt v Germany*, judgment of July 18, 1994, Series A, No.291–B, 18 E.H.R.R. 513; *Siliadin v France*, February 1, 2005, ECHR 2005–VII; *Zarb-Adami v Malta*, June 20, 2006; *Rantsev v Cyprus and Russia*, January 7, 2010, ECHR 2010–. . . ; *Stummer v Austria*, July 7, 2011, ECHR 2011. . .

1. General considerations

II–373 There have been few substantive cases, and only one concerning the first paragraph prohibition against slavery and servitude.[1] The trafficking of women is the area where cases are appear likely to arise at the present time.

Article 4 enshrines a fundamental value in democratic society and cannot be subject to derogation. Where forced prostitution is concerned, this would be likely to raise issues also under Art.3.[2]

In interpreting this provision, the Court takes into account, in particular, the ILO Conventions.

2. Protection by the State

II–374 The State must not only refrain from inflicting treatment of this kind itself but is also under a positive obligation to provide for the penalisation and effective prosecution of any act by another maintaining a person in a situation falling under Art.4. In *Siliadin v France*, the Government were in breach where the "employers" of a girl working in effective servitude in their home could only be prosecuted, unsuccessfully, for exploitation of labour in conditions incompatible with human dignity, under vague provisions open to differing interpretations. French law did not classify slavery or servitude as offences nor provide for effective sanctions against such.

In *Rantsev v Cyprus and Russia*, the Court also indicated that in addition to criminal law measures to punish traffickers, States must take adequate measures to prevent businesses being used as a cover for trafficking as well as ensuring that immigration rules cannot be suborned in such a way as to encourage or facilitate trafficking. Thus, in a situation where a large number of young women were entering Cyprus from abroad to work as "cabaret artistes", the Court noted the way in which the artiste visa regime operated encouraged trafficking, in particular where

[1] *Siliadin v France*, February 1, 2005, ECHR 2005–VII.

[2] *Tremblay v France*, (37194/02) (Dec.) September 11, 2007, para.25, on the facts, the Court did not find that the imposition of social security charges on a woman trying to leave prostitution placed her under any constraint to remain in that activity.

the young woman was rendered dependent on the employer or agent and apt to be exploited under cruel living and working conditions. In the particular case, the police aliens service had handed the Russian girl back to the cabaret manager after she had given up working as if he was somehow her owner; she had later been found dead, apparently having fallen from the manager's apartment balcony. This regime of artiste visas was found not to afford the victim a practical and effective protection against trafficking and exploitation, nor had the police authorities reacted appropriately to the girl's situation, failing to take steps to protect her. The Court also examined possible failings on the side of the Russian authorities but noted that they were unaware of any particular risk to the victim prior to her departure for Cyprus; as regarded their awareness of the general problem of young Russian women being lured abroad to work in the sex industry, the authorities had issued warnings in that regard.

An obligation to investigate situations of potential trafficking has been also read into Art.4. As with Arts 2 and 3, the obligation is triggered as soon as the matter has come to the attention of the authorities; the investigation must fulfill the requirements of independence and impartiality, promptness and reasonable expedition, urgency where there is a possibility of removing the individual from a harmful situation; it must be capable of leading to the identification and punishment of the individuals of those responsible and involve the victim or their next-of-kin to the extent necessary to safeguard their legitimate interests.[3] In *Rantsev*, the Russian Government were in breach of this procedural obligation in that they failed to investigate the recruitment in Russia of the young woman who had gone to work as a cabaret artiste and died in suspicious circumstances in Cyprus, while the Cypriot authorities failed properly and thoroughly to investigate how her death had occurred.

In addition, given the international context of trafficking, states must co-operate effectively with the relevant authorities of other states in investigation of cross-border situations.[4]

3. Slavery and servitude

Slavery involves a condition in which powers of ownership are exerted over a person or status as an object[5]; servitude involves a particularly serious form of denial of freedom and may include, in addition to the obligation to provide services, an obligation to live on the other's property and the impossibility of changing status.[6] Servitude was found in *Siliadin* where a girl, brought to France from Togo at age fifteen, was required to work in a house fifteen hours a day, sleeping in the children's room, with no free time or freedom of movement. II–375

4. Forced or compulsory labour

Labour covers not only manual but other types of work.[7] The notion of "forced" or "compulsory" is interpreted as involving two considerations: whether the work is exacted under menace of a penalty, or unpleasant consequences such as arrest for II–376

[3] *Rantsev v Cyprus and Russia*, January 7, 2010, ECHR 2010–. . . , para.288.
[4] *Rantsev*, fn.3 above, para.289.
[5] *Siliadin*, fn.1 above, para.122.
[6] *Siliadin*, fn.1 above, para.123.
[7] *Van der Mussele v Belgium*, November 23, 1983, Series A No.70, 6 E.H.R.R. 163, para.33.

immigration irregularities[8] and whether the person had "offered himself voluntarily" for the work in question.[9] In the latter context, it is relevant whether the service required was excessive or disproportionate. Thus in *Van der Mussele* the fact that advocate had chosen to enter his profession with prior knowledge of the requirement to provide certain services to the indigent was not in itself decisive but no violation arose as the Court found that such services did not fall outside the ambit of normal activities of an advocate; in addition there were compensatory factors to be found in the advantages attaching to the profession, the service was founded on a conception of social solidarity and could not be regarded as unreasonable; nor was it disproportionately costly or time-consuming, leaving ample time for paid work.[10] Remuneration does not prevent work being "forced" but is relevant to the proportionality assessment.[11] The Court was not prepared to read any element of objectionable physical or psychological constraint into a situation where a teenager in care was involved in giving assistance to an instructress in a riding centre programme for handicapped children.[12]

Forced labour does not cover deduction of salary in prison to take into account food and lodging[13]; withholding by an employer of tax on wages and other contributions[14]; transfer of employment to less lucrative conditions[15]; the requirement of an advocate to take unpaid work for indigent accused[16]; the requirement of a notary to receive reduced fees when acting for non-profit making organisations[17]; the requirement for a doctor to participate in an emergency medical cover scheme[18]; or the condition imposed on social benefit seekers to make demonstrable efforts in order to obtain and take up generally accepted employment.[19]

Where an employee is not paid for work done, there is no issue under Art.4 when the work was performed voluntarily and entitlement to payment for work done is not in dispute—the dispute falls instead within the scope of Art.6 as concerning civil rights.[20]

As regards prisoners, the Court rejected a prisoner's argument that obligatory work done in prisons without being affiliated to the pension system could not be regarded as "work required to be done in the ordinary course of detention". It found no basis in current State practice for finding effectively that in current times all work normally had to recognised under the social security system. Prison work

[8] *Siliadin*, fn.1 above, para.118.
[9] *Van der Mussele*, fn.7 above, paras 35–36.
[10] See also (22956/93) (Dec.) May 15, 1996, 85 D.R. 58, where it was not oppressive to require a lawyer to be on 24-hour call once every 200 days for assisting persons in police custody; (20781/92) (Dec.) June 19, 1984, 78 D.R. 116, where judges had to perform work of absent colleagues without remuneration; *Steindel v Germany*, (29878/07) (Dec.) September 14, 2010, where requiring a doctor in the private sector to be available six days a month for a remunerated participation in an public emergency medical scheme was not outside the ambit of his normal medical activities and was not disproportionate, as it did not impinge on his ability to manage his private practice; it also was based on professional and civil solidarity.
[11] *Van der Mussele*, fn.7 above, para.40.
[12] *Roda and Bonfatti v Italy*, November 21, 2006, paras 90–91.
[13] *Puzinas v Lithuania*, (63767/00) (Dec.) December 12, 2005.
[14] (8500/79) (Dec.) September 27, 1976, 7 D.R. 148.
[15] *Antonov v Russia*, (38020/03) (Dec.) November 3, 2005, no elements of coercion.
[16] *Van der Mussele*, fn.7 above.
[17] (8410/78) (Dec.) December 13, 1979, 18 D.R 216.
[18] *Steindel*, fn.10 above.
[19] *Schuitemaker v Netherlands*, (15906/08) (Dec.) May 4, 2010, the applicant, a philosopher by profession, objected to a possibility of being required to take other types of employment.
[20] *Sokur v Ukraine*, (29439/02) (Dec.) November 26, 2002.

therefore continued to be excluded from "forced labour" even if not earning entitlement towards a pension as ordinary work did.[21]

5. Trafficking in human beings

While noting in *Rantsev v Cyprus and Russia* that trafficking was often described as a form of modern slavery, the Court took the view that it was in itself an affront to human dignity incompatible with democratic and Convention values and thus within the prohibition of Art.4, without needing to classify it as "slavery", "servitude" or "forced labour". The elements of trafficking identified—namely, the treating of human beings as commodities, close surveillance and circumscribing of movement, use of violence and threats, poor living and working conditions, little or no payment—cut across these three categories and presumably would have led to artifical and fine distinctions being drawn from case to case.[22] II–377

6. Situations outside the scope of the prohibition

The situations set out in the third paragraph do not limit the right but define its content by setting out what is not included.[23] These cover work done in the ordinary course of detention under Art.5 or on conditional release, military service or its substitute,[24] service required during an emergency of calamity threatening the community or any work or service forming part of normal civic obligations. II–378

It has been left open whether normal civic obligations include obligations incumbent on a specific category of citizens by reason of their position or function.[25] Compulsory service in the fire brigade, or payment of a levy in substitution of service,[26] and service on the jury[27] have been regarded as "normal civic obligations". While imposition of such duties may not disclose in themselves a substantive breach of Art.4, they fall within the ambit of the provision and discriminatory treatment in that respect may breach Art.14 of the Convention.[28] They have also been held to include the requirement of a holder of hunting rights to participate in the gassing of foxholes as counter-measure to an epidemic; this also fell within the exception of service required in an emergency under Art.4, para.3(c).[29]

[21] *Stummer v Austria*, July 7, 2011, ECHR 2011. . . , paras 124–134.

[22] *Rantsev*, fn.3 above, paras 279–282.

[23] *Van der Mussele*, fn.7 above, para.38.

[24] Substitution of civilian service for objectors, where such is provided, is compatible with this exception: (10600/83) (Dec.) October 14, 1985, 44 D.R. 155.

[25] *Van der Mussele*, fn.7 above, para.41.

[26] *Karl Heinz Schmidt v Germany*, judgment of July 18, 1994, Series A, No.291–B, 18 E.H.R.R. 513, para.23.

[27] *Zarb-Adami v Malta*, June 20, 2006.

[28] See *Karl Heinz Schmidt*, fn.26 above, and *Zarb-Adami*, fn.27 above, where women were exempted, in law or in practice, from service.

[29] (9686/82) (Dec.) October 4, 1984, 39 D.R. 90.

20. Freedom of assembly

Key provision:

II–379 Article 11 (freedom of peaceful assembly).

Key case-law:

Platform "ärzte für das leben" v Austria, June 21, 1988, Series A, No.139, 13 E.H.R.R. 204; *Ezelin v France*, April 26, 1991, Series A, No.202, 14 E.H.R.R. 362; *Stankov and the United Macedonian Organisation Linden v Bulgaria*, October 2, 2001, ECHR 2001–IX; *Cissé v France*, April 9, 2002, ECHR 2002–III; *Djavit An v Turkey*, February 20, 2003, ECHR 2003–III.

1. General considerations

II–380 Exercise of this freedom is often closely connected with other rights, such as freedom of expression and thought, conscience and religion. Article 11 is the *lex specialis* where an assembly is concerned but the other two rights, Arts 9 and 10, may be taken into account in examining the effect and proportionality of the interference.[1] As with freedom of expression, freedom of peaceful assembly is one of the foundations of a democratic society[2] and protects demonstrations that may annoy or give offence to persons opposed to the ideas or claims that are being promoted.[3] It covers not only public but private meetings,[4] static gatherings as well as public processions, and in *Cissé v France*, it covered the occupation of a church by protesting aliens without valid residence permits. The right is capable of being exercised by not only individuals but by those organising the assembly, such as associations.

The right does not extend to demonstrations where organisers and participants have violent intentions which result in public disorder.[5] Where a Government argued that an assembly was unlikely to be peaceful due to reactions of other groups, the Commission considered that it was the intention to hold a peaceful assembly which was significant and the possibility of violent counter demonstrations could not as such remove the right from the scope of the first paragraph. The Commission expressed the opinion that it did not guarantee a right to pass and re-pass in public places, such as shopping centres, or to assemble for purely social purposes.[6]

[1] (25522/94) (Dec.) April 6, 1995, 81–A D.R. 146; *Ezelin v France*, April 26, 1991, Series A, No.202, 14 E.H.R.R. 362, para.35.

[2] e.g. (8191/78) (Dec.) October 10, 1979, 17 D.R. 93.

[3] *Platform "ärzte für das Leben" v Austria*, June 21, 1988, Series A, No.139, 13 E.H.R.R. 204, para.32; *Stankov and the United Macedonian Organisation Linden v Bulgaria*, October 2, 2001, ECHR 2001–IX, paras 86 and 107, emphasising that national authorities must be alert to ensure public opinion is not protected at the expense of the assertion of minority views however unpopular. See *Alekseyev v Russia*, October 21, 2010, paras 78–86 where the Court rejected the Government's arguments that the ban on Gay Pride marches was justified to prevent offence to the religious and harm to morals and to protect children and vulnerable adults.

[4] (8191/78), fn.2 above.

[5] (8440/78) (Dec.) July 16, 1980, 21 D.R. 138.

[6] (33689/96) (Dec.) October 27, 1997, where West Indian youths were banned from a shopping centre; see, however, *Appleby v UK*, May 6, 2003, where Art.10, and impliedly Art.11, applied to the applicants' campaigning in a shopping centre against a development of public playing fields.

Article 11 is not to be interpreted restrictively; reasons for interfering with exercise of its freedoms must be convincing and compelling.[7] The fact that an assembly is illegal will not necessarily remove it from the scope of the right, at least where it is peaceful in nature. Thus where an applicant was convicted for participation in an organised sit-in in a road, the Commission found that, though it was illegal, it was not actively violent and that the interference had to be justified in terms of the second paragraph.[8] Nor will the fact that proceedings brought against a person for participation in a demonstration end in an acquittal remove victim status, if there has nonetheless been a chilling effect on the exercise of the right or other aspect of the interference which has not been redressed.[9]

2. Regulation of assemblies

The requirement to obtain prior authorisation or give notification of an intended assembly will not constitute an interference or necessarily act as a deterrent,[10] although formalities and regulations should not form a hidden obstacle to exercising assembly rights.[11] For example, onerous administrative formalities purportedly to deal with road traffic aspects, and brought out by the authorities as a ground for refusing authorisation, were not compatible with the freedom of assembly.[12] In contrast, where the organiser of a public protest meeting was convicted for failing to give the statutory three-day notice to the authorities, the Court found that the time-delay was not unreasonable, being geared to allowing time for the authorities to make due arrangements for public and traffic safety; it also took into account that the applicant's meeting had not been interfered with and that the fine imposed was for the failure to notify, not for participation in the meeting, which was neither spontaneous or arising in circumstances in which prior notification was not practicable.[13] **II–381**

Where disbanding a demonstration on grounds of lack of prior notice is concerned, it would undermine the enforceability of such rules if the authorities never had this option. Thus, the Court stated in *Bukta v Hungary* that it was only where an immediate response to a political event was called for by way of demonstration that the actions of the authorities to disband it would be disproportionate. In that case, where the demonstrators wished to respond to an announcement by the Prime Minister of his intention to attend a controversial reception the next day and were unable to give the requisite three-day notice, the disbanding of

[7] See e.g. *Makhmudov v Russia*, July 26, 2007, para.64.

[8] (13079/87) (Dec.) March 6, 1989, 60 D.R. 256.

[9] *Balcik v Turkey*, November 29, 2007.

[10] *Rai and Evans v UK*, (26258/08) (Dec.) November 17, 2009, where the Court rejected the argument that the requirement of pre-authorisation of meetings in designated areas in London, such as near Whitehall, was objectionable as deterring exercise of the freedom of assembly.

[11] *Oya Ataman v Turkey*, December 5, 2006, para.38.

[12] *Baczkowski v Poland*, May 9, 2007, even though the domestic courts later ruled the refusal of permission for the procession on these grounds was unlawful, the applicant organiser could still claim victim status; even though the procession had gone ahead after the refusal of permission, in the circumstances the uncertainty about legality could have had a chilling effect on potential participants, .

[13] *Skiba v Poland*, (10659/03) (Dec.) July 7, 2009. See also *Rai and Evans*, fn.10 above, where fines and unconditional charges for failure to obtain prior authorisation for an anti- Iraq war protest in a "designated area" was not disproportionate: there was nothing spontaneous about the protest preventing such notice and the police intervention was calm and reasonable, ending the meeting only after the applicants had declined their invitation to do so.

the peaceful protest went too far.[14] In contrast, in *Eva Molnar v Hungary* the Court did not consider that the only adequate response by the protesters was an immediate demonstration, since it concerned election results known months before and it was satisfied the requirement to give notification did not impose an unreasonable restriction, judicial review being speedily available if the police decided to ban the protest.[15] However, the Court considered, slightly departing from its earlier words in *Bukta*, that even where a non-notified demonstration in support of Palestine could not be said to be a spontaneous reaction, the police went too far in acting immediately to break up the peaceful, small-scale protest. Tolerance and some nod in the direction of allowing people the opportunity of exercising the freedom of assembly even in those circumstances appears to be the theme.[16] In general, cases do emphasise that freedom of assembly, however crucial, does not justify ignoring formalities save in special circumstances; those exercising the freedom must equally play by the rules of the democratic game as well as the authorities.

Grounds for refusal of permission for peaceful assemblies are scrutinised quite rigorously by the Court. Where permission was repeatedly refused for a peaceful and silent protest of some 20 persons intending to stand in a line outside the Prime Minister's house on the pavement on grounds that this would disrupt the traffic, the Court was not persuaded that a protest of such a size or nature would indeed have had a significant effect and took the view that it should have been tolerated even if causing some inconvenience to passers-by and road users.[17] Similarly, consistent refusals to allow a congregation to hold a religious open air service on the ground that it was a minority faith were not found to be justified, since there were no concrete indications that this would in fact spark any adverse reactions for those of other religions.[18] On the other hand, official tolerance is allowed its limits. Where an organisation was banned from distributing food in public to the homeless, the Court found that the interference was justified since the organisation made a highly publicised and contentious point of using pork products that would be offensive to individuals of a certain religious persuasion, which could be regarded as discriminatory, provocative and a potential risk of public order.[19]

Whether a complete ban on processions is justified will depend on whether other less restrictive measures, including the imposition of conditions on the assembly as to time or place, are practicable. Where there was a one-month ban on processions in London imposed by the police, the Commission considered that a general ban could only be justified if there was a real danger of disorder which could not be avoided by less stringent measures. In that case, it accepted that there was a tense atmosphere; that the police presence at other processions had not stopped damage to persons and property; and that 2,400 officers were necessary to police a National Front march. It also noted as regarded proportionality that the meetings could still be held in London, as well as processions outside London.[20]

[14] *Bukta v Hungary*, July 17, 2007.

[15] *Eva Molnar v Hungary*, October 7, 2008, the Court also noted that the police did not act immediately to disband the protest but allowed the demonstrators leeway to exercise their freedom of assembly half the day despite considerable disruption to traffic.

[16] *Samut Karabulut v Turkey*, January 27, 2009, the Court may also have been influenced in deviating from the *Bukta* line by the fact that disproportionate force was used in arresting the applicant, disclosing a breach of Art.3, showing the police had overall not reacted in a moderate manner.

[17] *Patyi v Hungary*, October 7, 2008.

[18] *Barankevich v Russia*, July 26, 2007.

[19] *Association Solidarité v France*, (267877/07) (Dec.) June 16, 2009.

[20] (8440/78), fn.5 above.

Once there was some connection with public order, the Commission tended to afford a broad margin of appreciation to authorities' measures.[21] Where a ban on rallies in Trafalgar Square concerning Northern Ireland was applied to "Peace Now", a non-partisan group advocating negotiations, the Commission accepted the necessity to prohibit the meeting even though there was no real expectation of violence. The policy, based on politically sensitive considerations, was perceived as following the aim of prevention of disorder in a general sense. Nor was it disproportionate since it appeared that in the past a meeting by an Ulster group had turned into a political rally and it was reasonable for the authorities to seek to avoid a recurrence. It again was noted that it was open to hold the rally in other locations.[22] However, the Court seems to require some concrete evidential basis for public order or security reasons for revoking permission for a meeting. Where the authorities cancelled permission for a protest meeting critical of the mayor, on alleged grounds of a terrorist threat to mass meetings, the Court noted that other city-wide festivities continued undisturbed and no other special security measures seemed to be taken; it concluded that the refusal was arbitrary.[23] The Court nonetheless refers to applying in this context a wide margin of appreciation once some public interest justification arises.[24] Considerable leeway was given in *Cissé v France*, where, although the Court regretted the manner of police eviction of illegal aliens from the church in which they had taken refuge, it considered that the authorities had shown a sufficient amount of toleration in permitting the occupation for two months and that it was not unreasonable to end the occupation. The grounds of justification were somewhat vague, since the protest had been peaceful and there had been no breach of public order. Reference was made instead to the deterioration in the health of hunger strikers inside the church and the inadequate sanitary conditions. Applying the wide margin of appreciation to these circumstances, the Court concluded that the restriction was not disproportionate.

In contrast, in *Stankov and the United Macedonian Organisation Ilinden v Bulgaria*, which concerned prohibitions over many years on commemorative meetings by a Macedonian association perceived by the authorities to be a threat to the territorial integrity of Bulgaria, the Court emphasised the right of the inhabitants of a region to assert a minority consciousness and that the key issue was whether there had been any incitement to violence. In the absence of any espousal of violent aims or likelihood of violence arising at the meetings, the risk of separatist declarations being made was not sufficient to justify a systematic and sweeping ban; the authorities had therefore overstepped the margin of appreciation.[25] The Court has

[21] e.g. (8191/78), fn.2 above, where there was a ban on all political meetings following a controversy over cantonal reorganisation with local feeling running high; (9905/82) (Dec.) March 15, 1984, 36 D.R.187, where there was a ban on a meeting of a pro-German unification group justified by Austria's constitutional and international obligations to safeguard its statehood; (31416/96) (Dec.) October 19, 1998, concerning restrictions on assemblies near Stonehenge.

[22] (25522/94), fn.1 above; also *Gypsy Council v UK*, (66336/01) (Dec.) May 14, 2002, where restrictions on the traditional gypsy fair at Horsmonden were not disproportionate having regard to the possibility to hold a larger event at another location and the perceived disruption to public order relied on by the police.

[23] *Makhmudov v Russia*, fn.7 above, nor, in domestic proceedings was any supporting evidence adduced either as to the existence of the alleged threat, the courts basing themselves on assumptions..

[24] *Cissé v France*, April 9, 2002, ECHR 2002–III, para.53.

[25] *Stankov and the United Macedonian Organisation Ilinden v Bulgaria*, October 2, 2001, ECHR 2001–IX, paras 90 and 107, while States enjoyed a wider margin of appreciation where there has been incitement to violence, the Court rejected the Government argument that this also applied to issues touching on national symbols or national identity.

also stressed that the authorities should have a certain tolerance for gatherings on subjects of public concern and rejected traffic regulation justification for police intervention in breaking up, with some force, an unauthorised but peaceful demonstration during the rush hour.[26]

States must also refrain from applying unreasonable indirect restrictions upon the right to assemble peacefully. Thus in *Djavit An v Turkey* the refusal to grant permits to the applicant to cross into southern Cyprus which prevented him from attending bi-communal meetings for six years constituted an interference with the applicant's freedom of assembly and disclosed a violation of Art.11 in the absence of any adequate law in existence regulating such restrictions. The requirement that members of associations had to obtain permission to attend meetings abroad was not found to pursue a legitimate aim.[27]

3. Penalties for participation in public demonstrations

II–382 Previously minor criminal sanctions following protests which breached public order or obstructed the highway had not been found disproportionate.[28] In *Steel v UK*,[29] where the five applicants had participated in various protest activities and been arrested and detained, the Court examined the circumstances of each incident. Where two applicants had acted in a way likely to cause a breach of the peace, by walking in front of a grouse shooter about to take aim or climbing into trees about to be felled, the measures were not considered disproportionate. Where however three applicants were involved in a peaceful protest, giving out leaflets against the sale of fighter helicopters at a conference centre, the Court was not satisfied that the police had reasonable grounds for apprehending that breach of the peace might arise and the interference with their rights was disproportionate. The issues were dealt with by the Court under Art.10 and it did not consider it necessary to give separate consideration to the complaints raised under Art.11. It may be noted however that the Court has recently been more inclined to tolerance of those demonstrating on topics of public interest with no more than a risk of minor traffic disruption.[30] It now refers to the need for convincing and compelling reasons for interfering with peaceful assemblies, specifying that the authorities must exercise their discretion

[26] *Oya Ataman*, fn.11 above. Contrast *Ciloglu v Turkey*, March 6, 2007, no violation, where the police only intervened in an irregular sit-in after tolerating the demonstration for over three years.

[27] *Izmir Savas Karsitlari Dernegi v Turkey*, March 2, 2006.

[28] (9728 and 9415/81) (Dec.) October 3, 1983, 35 D.R. 30, where Lapps were arrested for a public protest outside Parliament after four days in a tent in an area open to public traffic; (13079/87), fn.7 above, conviction for road sit-in as a non-violent obstruction of traffic; *Caroline Lucas v UK*, (39013/02) (Dec.) March 18, 2003, where it was not disproportionate under Arts 10 and 11 to arrest the applicant for sitting in the road during a protest, conduct reasonably regarded as falling within the concept of breach of the peace.

[29] *Steel v UK*, September 23, 1998, R.J.D. 1998–VII, No.91.

[30] *Oya Ataman*, fn.11 above, although the applicants were not prosecuted, there was a violation for the forcible police intervention in the unlawful demonstration; contrast *Ciloglu*, fn.26 above, the Court noted that the applicants had been able to air their protest for over three years, dispersion of the sit-in by the police at that stage was not disproportionate; *Barraco v France*, March 5, 2009, a suspended sentence and fine on the applicant for a "snail" protest on the roads which brought an entire motorway to a halt for several hours was not disproportionate to the authorities' aims of regulating traffic, since they acted in a restrained manner allowing the applicant his moment of public protest.

reasonably, carefully and in good faith, in accordance with an acceptable assessment of the relevant facts and in light of the relevant principles of Arts 10 and 11.[31]

Where a penalty is imposed on a person for participation in a lawful assembly in which there is no indication that they behaved in an unlawful or unruly manner, serious issues of proportionality are likely to arise. In *Ezelin v France*, the applicant lawyer participated in demonstration during which some participants shouted insults and painted graffiti. Disciplinary proceedings were brought against him and he was reprimanded for breach of professional discretion. The argument that the applicant had been free to participate but sanctioned only afterwards was not successful. There was an interference resulting from the sanction imposed on him for failing to disassociate himself from the demonstrators' insulting acts by leaving the procession. While the Court accepted that it pursued the prevention of disorder and that the penalty was light, the importance of the right was such that no sanction was compatible with Art.11 where a participant was not guilty of any reprehensible act in taking part in a demonstration that had been lawful.[32] However, even if an assembly is unlawful but peaceful, Art.11 extends protection. Where an applicant was punished with a prison sentence for mere presence at a press conference that turned into a demonstration, considered unlawful by the authorities, and without reference to any reprehensible conduct on his part, there was a breach.[33]

Interferences with assembly and demonstrations must also, of course, be prescribed by law. This requires the prescriptive rules applied to marches and demonstrations to be have a clear basis in domestic law, be accessible and foreseeable in their effects. In *Mkrtchyan v Armenia*, where it was not at all clear the extent to which ex-Soviet rules on unauthorised gatherings remained valid in the new democratic regime, the Court was not convinced by arguments of necessity to prevent a legal vacuum and considered that in an area so important as freedom of assembly the new Government should not have waited some eleven years before adopting a new law.[34]

4. Protection of "peaceful assemblies"

Freedom of peaceful assembly, if it is to be effective, cannot be limited merely to an obligation on the State not to interfere. The Court has found that positive measures may be required to regulate conduct between individuals. Participants must be able to hold a demonstration without fear of physical violence from those who oppose their ideas otherwise they will be deterred from openly expressing their opinions.[35] II–383

[31] e.g. *Sergey Kuznetsov v Russia*, October 23, 2008, para.39, punishing the applicant for a picket protesting at a local court was on that basis not justified on any of the three grounds put forward, namely the technical reason that he had only given eight instead of ten days' notice did not correlate to any lack of official readiness for the incident; the finding that he had blocked access to the building was not supported by the evidence, nor a convincing reason since he had complied immediately with a direction to clear the stairway; insofar as it was asserted that the picket had not been for the stated purpose of protesting lack of access to justice, the fact that he had instead made critical comments calling for the court's president to resign had not been shown to be defamatory or outside legitimate political speech which was in any event equally protected.

[32] See also *Galstyan v Armenia*, November 15, 2009, where the applicant's conviction and sentence to three days administrative detention for participation in a peaceful demonstration, purportedly for blocking traffic and making a noise, was disproportionate.

[33] *Cetinkaya v Turkey*, June 27, 2006, paras 28–32.

[34] *Mkrtchyan v Armenia*, January 11, 2007, paras 39–45.

[35] e.g. *Alekseyev*, fn.3 above, para.73, the Court dismissed the Government claim that it was necessary to ban Gay Pride marches in Moscow due to alleged fears of violent reactions from sections of the public.

In a democracy the right to counter-demonstrate cannot extend to inhibiting the exercise of the right to demonstrate.[36] At the same time the unconditional banning of a counter-demonstration itself requires particular justification, particularly if intended to express an opinion on an issue of public interest.[37]

Positive measures appear to include a duty to take reasonable and appropriate steps to enable lawful demonstrations to proceed peacefully. It does not involve an absolute guarantee and there is a wide discretion accorded to the authorities as to the means to be used. No violation was found in *Platform Arzte v Austria*, where counter-demonstrators disrupted the applicant association's open air service, interrupting with loudspeakers and throwing eggs. Although the applicant association claimed the authorities had failed to protect its freedom of peaceful assembly, the Commission found, and the Court agreed, that the authorities had not failed in their duty since the police had been present in large numbers and had interposed themselves between the opposing groups and no damage or serious clash had occurred. Where a counter-demonstration, intending to attend a cemetery hosting a SS commemoration ceremony, was banned, the Court considered that, given the avowedly peaceful intentions of the group and the fact that previous occasions had given rise, at most to heated discussions, that preventive measures, such as police presence, would have been a viable alternative and found a breach.[38] Mere risk of violent reaction cannot justify banning a procession: where the authorities used this ground to ban Gay Pride marches, the Court stated that it was necessary for there to be a concrete assessment of the potential risks from counter-demonstrators and to consider what precautions would counter any risks.[39]

Banning public meetings on the ground of the need to protect the participants from violent reaction will not necessarily be a compelling reason, bearing in mind the authorities are under an obligation to give protection to individuals to allow them to exercise their freedom of assembly.[40]

There is however no positive obligation to require privately-owned shopping centres to allow access to individuals for the purpose of campaigning on issues of public interest.[41]

Cross-reference

Part IIB, s.21: Freedom of association.
Part IIB, s.22: Freedom of expression.
Part IIB, s.40: Religion, thought and conscience.

[36] *Ollinger v Austria*, June 29, 2006, para.44.

[37] *Platform ärzte*, fn.3 above, para.32.

[38] *Ollinger*, fn.36 above.

[39] *Alekseyev*, fn.3 above, paras 73–77.

[40] *Barankevich v Russia*, fn.18 above, paras 32–33, where the authorities repeatedly refused a religious congregation permisssion to hold an open-air service allegedly due to fears for their safety from other faiths.

[41] *Appleby*, fn.6 above. The case was examined principally under Art.10, but the Court found that largely identical considerations arose under Art.11 (para.52).

21. Freedom of association

Key provision:

Article 11 (freedom of association) II–384

Key case-law:

National Union of Belgian Police v Belgium, October 27, 1975, Series A, No.19, 1 E.H.R.R. 518; *Swedish Engine Drivers' Union v Sweden*, February 6, 1976, Series A, No.20, 1 E.H.R.R. 617; *Schmidt and Dahlstrom v Sweden*, February 6, 1976, Series A, No.21, 1 E.H.R.R. 632; *Le Compte, Van Leuven and de Meyere v Belgium*, June 23, 1981, Series A, No.43, 4 E.H.R.R. 1; *Young, James and Webster v UK*, August 13, 1981, Series A, No.44; 4. E.H.R.R. 38, *Sibson v UK*, April 20, 1993, Series A, No.258–A, 17 E.H.R.R. 193; *Sigurjonsson v Iceland*, June 30, 1993, Series A, No.264, 16 E.H.R.R. 462; *Gustafsson v Sweden*, April 25, 1996, R.J.D. 1996–II, No.9, 22 E.H.R.R. 409; *United Communist Party v Turkey*, January 30, 1998, R.J.D. 1998–I, No.62, 26 E.H.R.R. 121; *Sidiropoulos v Greece*, July 10, 1998, R.J.D. 1998–IV, 27 E.H.R.R. 633; *Chassagnou v France*, April 29, 1999, ECHR 1999–III; *Rekvenyi v Hungary*, May 20, 1999, ECHR 1999–III, 30 E.H.R.R. 519; *Grande Oriente d'Italia di Palazzo Guistiniani v Italy*, August 2, 2001, ECHR 2001–VIII; *Wilson, National Union of Journalists v UK*, July 2, 2002, ECHR 2002–IV; *Refah Partisi (the Welfare Party) v Turkey*, February 13, 2003, ECHR 2003–II; *Gorzelik v Poland*, February 17, 2004, ECHR 2004–I; *Partidul Comunistilor (Nepeceresti) et Ungureanu v Romania*, February 3, 2005, ECHR 2005–I; *Sorensen and Rasmussen v Denmark*, January 11, 2006, ECHR 2006–. . . ; *Demir and Baykara v Turkey*, November 12, 2008, ECHR 2008–. . .

1. General considerations

The freedom of association is a general capacity for all persons to join with others without interference by the State to attain a particular end.[1] It does not imply a right to attain the end sought.[2] It implies a negative right, not to be compelled to join an association, an aspect which has had relevance in the area of trade unions. Freedom of assembly is an associated right which is dealt with separately. The ability of citizens to join together collectively is recognised as part of the proper and healthy functioning of a democracy which respects pluralism and diversity.[3] II–385

Laws governing associations must not err on the side of vagueness or bestow untrammelled discretion on the authorities to interfere in their activities; detailed rules governing the scope and extent of power to intervene in the internal management and activities of associations and minimum safeguards providing sufficient guarantees against the risk of abuse and arbitrariness are required.[4]

[1] It does not guarantee a general ability to mix socially with others, e.g. a prisoner cannot derive right to associate with other prisoners—where applicants were in isolation punishment the Commission took the view that the complaints were incompatible *ratione materiae* as Art.11 concerned freedom to form or be affiliated to group or organisation pursuing particular aims. Despite the Government's argument in *United Communist Party v Turkey*, January 30, 1998, R.J.D. 1998–I, No.62, 26 E.H.R.R. 121, it applies to political parties.

[2] (6094/73) (Dec.) July 6, 1977, 9 D.R. 5.

[3] *Gorzelik v Poland*, February 17, 2004, ECHR 2004–I para.92.

[4] See e.g. *Tebieti Mühafize Cemiyyeti and Israfilov v Azerbaijan*, October 8, 2009, paras 59–65.

2. Formation and dissolution of associations

II–386 The dissolution of, or refusal to give legal status to an association through registration,[5] constitute interferences within the scope of Art.11, para.1, as may delays, and prevarications, in registration[6] and restrictions on means of financing.[7]

Where decisions by the authorities relating to the formation and dissolution of associations are found to interfere with the rights under Art.11, assuming such measures are prescribed by law, a considerable margin of appreciation was previously left to the authorities as to the necessity of the regulation. Refusal of registration on grounds of objection to the proposed name was acceptable where there was no indication that the association could not be registered under another name.[8] In a French case, concerning refusal of registration of the applicant's association promoting surrogate motherhood as contrary to the criminal code (incitement of child abandonment), the Commission found the interference justified having regard in particular to the margin of appreciation applying to the controversial subject of surrogacy and considering that the applicant could still carry out activities.[9] Similar leeway was given where a Portuguese association supporting the old royal house of Braganza was dissolved, the Commission finding that such a decision could be considered as necessary to promote public order.[10]

More recently the Court stresses the need for convincing and compelling reasons to justify restrictions. Where an association aiming to restore the Bulgarian monarchy was refused registration as being contrary to the current constitution, the Court, in finding a violation, pointed out that it was possible to campaign for constitutional change in a legal and peaceful manner conforming with fundamental democratic principles.[11]

Mere suspicions of an association's intention to pursue illicit goals is generally not enough, as in a case where the courts refused registration of a so-called anti-mafia guard as the intention of mobilising citizens against organised crime was seen as seeking to trespass on the functions of the public prosecutor despite riders in the articles of association as to acting in conformity with the law and not usurping the prerogatives of the authorities.[12] The Court scrutinises decisions purporting to justifying dissolution of associations; it requires the authorities to rely on, and courts to verify the existence of, hard evidence of alleged illegal activities, not general and vague assertions.[13]

Justification was found for the ban, on grounds of protecting the public order and litigants, of an association which intended to set up rival bars to the national

[5] *Sidiropoulos v Greece*, July 10, 1998, R.J.D. 1998–IV, 27 E.H.R.R. 633, para.31; *Gorzelik*, see fn.3 above, para.52.
[6] *Ramazanova v Azerbaijan*, February 1, 2007, para.60.
[7] *Basque Nationalist Party and Ipparalde-Regional Organisation v France*, June 7, 2007, although the ban on receiving funds from overseas parties was found justified to safeguard national sovereignty.
[8] *APEH v Hungary*, (32367/96) (Dec.) August 31, 1999, the name, using the title of the tax authority, was allegedly defamatory and a potential source of confusion.
[9] (14223/88) (Dec.) June 5, 1991, 70 D.R. 218.
[10] (23892/94) (Dec.) October 16, 1995, 83–A D.R. 57, though the activities of the association hardly seemed a real threat to undermine the State; also (8652/79) (Dec.) October 15, 1981, 26 D.R. 89, banning Moon sect associations; (6741/74) (Dec.) May 21, 1976, 5 D.R. 83.
[11] *Zhechev v Bulgaria*, June 21, 2007, para.47.
[12] *Bozgan v Romania*, October 11, 2007.
[13] *Tebieti Mühafize Cemiyyeti and Israfilov*, fn.4 above, paras 85–89.

advocates' union.[14] It was also acceptable to refuse to register an association defaming a public institution; and it was an abuse within the meaning of Art.17 where the association's aims sought to revive anti-semitism.[15] A refusal to register an association which through its memorandum of association sought to achieve the status of a national minority and thereby electoral privileges not accorded by domestic law was found justified to protect the existing democratic order and not disproportionate as it was not aimed preventing its cultural activities or manifestations of Silesian identity.[16]

States cannot assume a paternalistic role of protecting citizens and institutions from the activities of associations, which approach seems based on a deep mistrust of non-official initiatives and "meddling" in public affairs. Thus, where a rather innocuous association for the preservation of natural habitat in one region was refused registration due to a myriad of apparent failures to comply with the law, the Court was not impressed by the need for such restrictions imposed on associations, for example, prohibiting lobbying on issues or publishing, involvement in economic activities or activities outside the particular region and engaging volunteers, noting merely that the association intended to pursue purely peaceful and democratic aims and functions.[17]

Where political parties are concerned, the Court has emphasised that only conduct which might endanger political pluralism or fundamental democratic principles could justify a ban on their activities.[18] In view of the essential role played by political parties in the proper functioning of democracy, the exceptions set out in Art.11 are, where political parties are concerned, to be construed strictly; only convincing and compelling reasons can justify restrictions on such parties' freedom of association. Thus in *United Communist Party v Turkey*, the Court found that the reference in the Party's constitution to the Kurdish problem, perceived by the Government as a threat to the State's territorial integrity, did not justify the dissolution of the party. The UCP's constitution was geared to the democratic process and it had not engaged in activities at variance with that.[19] In subsequent cases about dissolution of political parties in Turkey, the Court emphasised that the essential factor was whether the programme of the party in question contained anything which could be regarded as a call for violence, an uprising or any other form of rejection of democratic principles.[20] Though the Court noted the Government's arguments in these cases as to the real underlying intentions of the banned parties and accepted that it might be necessary to compare official documents with acts and declarations in practice, none of the parties concerned had acted in a way

[14] *Bota v Romania*, (24057/03) (Dec.) October 12, 2004.

[15] *WP v Poland*, (42264/98) (Dec.) September 2, 2004, ECHR 2004–VII.

[16] *Gorzelik*, fn.3 above. Contrast *Zhechev*, fn.11 above, para.56, where the ban on an association merely for having "political aims" offended, as this did not bypass electoral checks and balances. See also *Artyomov v Russia*, (17582/05) (Dec.) December 7, 2006, where it was proportionate to refuse registration as a political party of an association, which promoted one ethnic group, since this did not prevent the association continuing its activities, only from nominating candidates in elections: mention was made of the principle of respect for national specificity in electoral policy.

[17] *Koretskyy v Ukraine*, April 3, 2008.

[18] *Christian Democratic People's Party v Moldova*, February 14, 2006, para.76.

[19] *United Communist Party*, fn.1 above, para.46; *Freedom and Democracy Party (Ozdep) v Turkey*, December 8, 1999, ECHR 1999–VIII, para.44.

[20] *Socialist Party v Turkey*, May 25, 1998, R.J.D. 1998–III, paras 46–47; *Freedom and Democracy Party (Ozdep) v Turkey*, fn.19 above, para.40.

justifying their dissolution.[21] Similarly, where a new communist party's constitution and political programme contained nothing contrary to democratic principles, the refusal to register it was not justified by its implied criticism of the post-1989 regime, since democracy allowed differing strands of political opinion, even if irksome and disturbing; in the absence of any overt violent or non-constitutional actions, it was not enough to argue that the country could not allow the emergence of a new communist party. Indeed, a political party must be allowed to campaign for a change in the law or the legal and constitutional structures of the State on two conditions: firstly, the means used to that end must in every respect be legal and democratic, and secondly, the change proposed must itself be compatible with fundamental democratic principles.[22]

A temporary ban on a political party's activities due to its organisation of allegedly unlawful meetings outside the parliament building was found disproportionate, the Court commenting that even if the meetings, non-violent, had been unlawful, it would not have justified such a serious measure.

However, in *Refah Partisi v Turkey*, where the Constitutional Court dissolved a popular political party perceived as advocating Islamic fundamentalism, the Court found that the Party could be regarded as posing a risk to the democratic constitution of the State in that it intended to set up a plurality of legal systems based on religious differences which would infringe the principle of non-discrimination and to introduce sharia which was incompatible with the democratic ideals of pluralism or human rights. It also took into account, somewhat rigorously, that the Party did not expressly exclude recourse to force to implement its policy. The dissolution therefore met a "pressing social need" and was proportionate.[23] Where political parties, through the conduct of their leaders and members taken as a whole, could be construed as giving implicit support to a terrorist organisation and pursuing policies in contradiction with democratic values, the Court considered their dissolution was justified.[24]

There has also been an increased recognition of the role associations play in expressing and promoting the identity and culture of national and ethnic minorities.[25] Where therefore measures are taken against associations alleged to pursue

[21] *United Communist Party*, fn.1 above, para.48; *Yazar (HEP Party) v Turkey*, April 9, 2002, ECHR 2002–II, para.60; *DEP Party v Turkey*, December 10, 2002, para.47, though the speech of an ex-leader of the party given in Iraq was identified as approving the use of force, this one incident did not justify the dissolution of the party. Nor did the Court take into account the conviction, subsequent to the dissolution, of several DEP MPs of terrorist offences, noting that the trial had violated Art.6 (*Sadak v Turkey*, July 17, 2001, ECHR 2001–VIII) and that in any event these matters had not played a role in the Constitutional Court's decision to dissolve the party.

[22] *Partidul Comunistilor (Nepeceresti) et Ungureanu v Romania*, February 3, 2005, ECHR 2005–I. See also lack of convincing reasons to refuse registration of a political party in *Linkov v Czech Republic*, December 7, 2006.

[23] The Grand Chamber was unanimous. The earlier Chamber judgment of July 31, 2001 had found no violation by a narrow margin. The minority found no convincing evidence that the party used or encouraged the use of violence or undemocratic means to destroy the secular system or establish the supremacy of an Islamic regime, in particular since when it was in power it took no such steps. It considered the Constitutional Court's reasoning, concerned with the anti-secularism of the party, did not justify the extreme measure of dissolution. See also *Kalifatstaat v Germany*, (13828/04) (Dec.) December 11, 2006, concerning acceptable ban on a party advocating an islamic regime based on *sharia*.

[24] *Herri Batasuna and Batasuna v Spain*, June 30, 2009, taken into account were not just failure to condemn ETA or to exclude violence but also speeches and slogans which could be construed as expressing support to ETA, symbols on websites, recognition and honours bestowed on ETA members etc

[25] *Gorzelik*, fn.3 above, paras 89–93.

objectives contrary to the State, the Commission and Court have emphasised that democratic societies have to tolerate a wide range of opinions, including those opposed to officially-sanctioned positions and that interferences have to be convincingly justified. The refusal of Greek authorities to register a Macedonian cultural association was an undisputed interference with its members' freedom of association which was not justified by relevant and sufficient reasons or proportionate. It was not established that the association harboured separatist intentions or violent intentions, and the fact that it promoted the idea of a "Macedonian" minority did not justify the measure.[26] Similarly the mere fact that an association's name may have evoked unpopular connotations and its purposes offensive to the majority do not justify refusal to register. Thus, where an association pursued an interpretation of history with a view to denying the existence of an ethnic "Macedonian" identity and asserting "Macedonians" were Bulgarian, the Court underlined that democracy thrived on freedom of expression and solving disagreements through discourse, however irksome. It found no basis for the court's finding that a denial of Macedonian identity was equivalent to a violent destruction of the constitutional order as there was nothing to indicate the association intended to use any other than democratic means.[27]

As concerns religious associations, the believers' right to freedom of religion encompasses the expectation that the community will be allowed to function peacefully, free from arbitrary State intervention. Nor is it acceptable for the State, in regulating such associations, to assess whether religious beliefs or the means used to express such beliefs are legitimate. Thus, where the authorities refused to re-register a branch of the Salvation Army, on spurious grounds showing a lack of good faith and neutrality, there was a breach of Art.11 in conjunction with Art.9 (freedom of religion).[28] Nor did the Court find that the domestic courts had adduced relevant and sufficient reasons for refusing to re-register the Jehovah's Witnesses community as a legal entity, holding that the purported grounds had not been substantiated or grounded on a reasonable assessment of the relevant facts. For example, insofar as it was alleged that members refused blood transfusions, there was a right to decline medical treatment; insofar as it was alleged that the community dominated the way their members lived their lives, it was a common feature of many religions to set down doctrinal standards of behaviour.[29]

While it is permissible for the authorities to set down formalities of structure and functioning for associations and to verify due compliance, the Court frowns heavily on authorities policing associations and holding them to account for every minor infringement of their internal rules. Thus, quibbling about minutiae of membership records has been regarded as a heavy-handed and unjustified interference in internal workings. Sanctions for administrative failings on the part of associations should be proportionate, with due notice and effective opportunity to put matters right being afforded: dissolution as the only penalty was not acceptable.[30]

[26] *Sidiropoulos*, fn.5 above, paras 40–47; similar violation found when the authorities refused to register an association which implied the existence of a Turkish minority within Greece, *Bekir-Ousta v Greece*, October 11, 2007, the Court noted that the State had means to take appropriate measures if the association, which had given no concrete indication of intention to carry out unlawful activities, did in fact do so: mere suspicions beforehand were not enough.

[27] *Association of Citizens Radko and Paunkovski v former Yugoslav Republic of Macedonia*, January 15, 2009.

[28] *Moscow Branch of the Salvation Army v Russia*, October 5, 2006. Similar violation in *Church of Scientology v Russia*, April 5, 2007.

[29] *Jehovah's Witnesses of Moscow v Russia*, June 10, 2010, nor had it been shown that the community had lured minors into joining or incited members not to fulfil their civic duties.

[30] *Tebieti Mühafize Cemiyyeti and Israfilov*, fn.4 above.

Actions short of dissolution may interfere with freedom of association, such as rules on an association's funding. However, such milder measures may be easier for States to justify. Where a Basque political party in southern France was banned from receiving funding from foreign sources, namely Spanish Basque parties, the Court considered it pursued the legitimate aim of preserving national sovereignty and given the lack of consensus in Contracting States on the issue, found it an "eminently political" matter which fell with the French State's margin of appreciation, it remaining possible for the applicant party to seek and receive funding from within French borders.[31]

3. Positive and procedural obligation

II–387 The authorities may be required to take steps to protect associations. Where the affixing of a sign in Macedonian at the headquarters of a party aiming to protect the interests of the Macedonian minority in Greece sparked protests by local townspeople, the authorities' own actions in exacerbating the situation, and the lack of police response when a mob smashed the building, breached Art.11. Noting the prosecutor's dilatory response to the incident, the Court also stated that the authorities were under an obligation to carry out an effective investigation into interferences by individuals with the freedom of association.[32]

4. Public law institutions and compulsory membership

II–388 Article 11 does not cover public law institutions. An obligation on a person to join a professional or occupational institution which is of a public law nature, pursuing aims of public regulation, will not offend, although it is relevant whether the applicant is able to join other professional associations to protect his interests.[33]

The fact that an association fulfills some statutory functions will not be decisive as to "public" status where the principal object is to protect the professional interests of its members. In *Sigurjonsson v Iceland*, the Government argued that FRAMI (a taxi association) was a professional organisation of public law character, carrying out a role in price-fixing of services under approval of the administration. The Court found, notwithstanding these aspects, that it was primarily a private law association which protected the professional interests of its members and promoted solidarity, for example, by negotiation and presenting demands relating to working hours. The domestic characterisation of the institution has only relative value as the term "association" has an autonomous meaning under the Convention. The key question is whether the body is an association for the purposes of Art.11.[34]

[31] *Parti Nationaliste Basque-Organisation Regionale d'Iparalde v France*, June 7, 2007.

[32] *Ouranio Toxo v Greece*, October 20, 2005.

[33] *Le Compte, Van Leuven and de Meyere v Belgium*, June 23, 1981, Series A, No.43, 4 E.H.R.R. 1, obligation to join the *ordre des architectes*; (13750/88) (Dec.) July 2, 1990, 66 D.R. 188, bar association in Spain; (14596/89) (Dec.) July 10, 1991, 71 D.R. 158, Austrian chambers of trade; (44319/98) (Dec.) April 3, 2001, compulsory membership of notary chambers.

[34] *Chassagnou v France*, April 29, 1999, ECHR 1999–III, paras 100–102, where hunting associations were not public law institutions, consisting of private individuals and not exercising any processes of a public authority. Contrast *Herrmann v Germany*, January 20, 2011, paras 78–79, where hunting associations qualified as public law associations under the control of the hunting authority: pending before the Grand Chamber.

Outside public law and professional institutions, the Court has looked less leniently on compulsory membership of associations. In *Chassagnou v France*, the Court found the imposition of membership of hunting associations on the applicant landowners violated their freedom of association, giving particular weight in that case to the fact that they were being forced to join an association fundamentally contrary to their ethical convictions.[35]

5. Trade union aspects

Trade union freedom is a special aspect of the freedom of association. But it does not guarantee any particular treatment of trade unions or their members by the State. The phrase "for the protection of his interests" indicates that the provision is intended to protect the occupational interests of members by trade union action. This includes the right to form and join a trade union, the prohibition of closed-shop agreements and the right for a trade uinon to seek to persuade the employer of what it has to say on behalf of its members.[36] Under national law, trade unions should be enabled in conditions not at variance with Art.11 to strive for the protection of their members' interests.[37] II–389

(a) *State responsibility*

Even if a Government is not directly responsible for the actions of or agreements reached by unions and employers, where the domestic law renders lawful such measures, State responsibility under Art.1 is engaged. Contracting States must therefore maintain supervisory control over trade unions and the way they wield their powers[38] and ensure that domestic law secures the rights contained in Art.11.[39] II–390

(b) *Right of consultation*

The right to be consulted by the executive before measures are adopted is not implied. In *National Union of Belgian Police v Belgium*, where only a restricted number of trade unions were officially consulted, the National Union was able to present claims and make representations nonetheless, and while its lack of formal consultative status may have made it less attractive to prospective members, this did not disclose an interference under Art.11. II–391

(c) *Collective action and collective bargaining*

Article 11 does not secure any particular treatment of unions or their members by the State such as the right that the State enter into any collective agreement with II–392

[35] *Chassagnou*, fn.34 above, paras 103–117.

[36] *Demir and Baykara v Turkey*, November 12, 2008, ECHR 2008–. . . , para.145.

[37] *National Union of Belgian Police v Belgium*, October 27, 1975, Series A, No.19, 1 E.H.R.R. 518, para.39.

[38] *Young, James and Webster v UK*, August 13, 1981, Series A, No.44; 4. E.H.R.R. 38.

[39] *Wilson, National Union of Journalists and Others v UK*, July 2, 2002, ECHR 2002–IV, para.41. See also responsibility under Art.1 of Protocol No.1 where the authorities permitted trade union deduction from salaries of employees without allowing them to check how the money was spent: *Evaldsson v Sweden*, February 13, 2007.

them. Nor is there any guarantee that a collective agreement on a particular matter be maintained for an indefinite period.[40]

While in an early judgment, it had been considered that collective bargaining was not indispensable for the effective enjoyment of trade union freedom, even where this could damage the union through reducing its membership[41] this position has evolved. Taking into account that the right to bargain collectively is recognised by the ILO, the European Social Charter, the European Union and the majority of Contracting States, the Court has now held that it has become one of the essential elements of the right to form and join a trade union for the protection of one's interests.Thus, the retrospective annulment by the authorities of a collective agreement of public servants based merely on a legislative gap was an interference which lacked the requisite convincing justification and disclosed a breach of Art.11.[42]

A requirement on a trade union to provide an employer with the list of members before voting on industrial action was not regarded as a significant or disproportionate restriction on the right to take collective action.[43] Nor does the freedom of a trade union to make its voice heard extend to imposing on an employer an obligation to recognise a trade union.[44]

(d) *Preferential treatment/discrimination*

II–393 As implied above, the practice by State authorities in conferring special recognition or status on particular unions has been found to be compatible with the Convention. The Belgian system of conferring consultation status on three unions of State officials and not on the applicant police union was found to pursue a legitimate aim of ensuring a coherent and balanced staff policy, avoiding "trade union anarchy". Nor were the means used disproportionate as the disadvantage to the applicant was not deemed to be excessive.[45] A similar policy in Sweden did not offend proportionality, where the State preferred to sign collective agreements only with widely representative unions, to avoid excessive numbers of negotiating parties. The Court found no ill-intentioned designs in that policy.[46]

[40] *Swedish Transport Workers' Union v Sweden*, (53507/99) (Dec.) November 30, 2004, ECHR 2004–XII, where the agreement was struck down after some years for being anti-competitive.

[41] *Schmidt and Dahlstrom v Sweden*, February 6, 1976, Series A, No.21, 1 E.H.R.R. 632, para.34; see also *Swedish Engine Drivers' Union v Sweden*, February 6, 1976, Series A, No.20, 1 E.H.R.R. 617, where the State had entered into a collective agreement with three large federations but refused to accept the smaller union, the Court noted that it was not mentioned specifically as a right, nor accepted in all Contracting States. Since individuals were free to join any trade union and the applicant union was able to engage in various kinds of activity, the refusal of the executive to enter into a collective agreement did not disclose a breach even if the union membership was suffering as a result; *Wilson, NUJ and Others*, paras 44; (18881/91) (Dec.) January 13, 1992, 72 D.R. 278.

[42] *Demir and Baykara*, fn.36 above, paras 147–170.

[43] (28910/95) (Dec.) April 16, 1998, where the Commission found nothing sinister or intimidatory in the requirement.

[44] *Wilson, NUJ and Others*, fn.39, above, para.44.

[45] *National Union of Belgian Police*, fn.37 above.

[46] Also (6094/73), fn.2 above, where one student association was chosen as the official body with compulsory membership and another association complained of discrimination, the Commission found nothing unreasonable in the authorities choosing one union for the purpose of concentrating students together to facilitate the proper administration of the university.

(e) Right NOT to join a trade union

In the leading case of *Young, James and Webster v UK*, the Court found that the notion of a "freedom" implied some choice in its exercise. Thus a negative right could not be excluded from the ambit of Art.11.[47] The test applied was to examine whether in the particular case the form of compulsion struck at the very substance of the right guaranteed. Since the three applicants had received notices terminating their employment for failure to join a union, this was found to be the case. The Court noted that, even had the applicants joined another union, they would still have been dismissed and it considered that their freedom of action had been rendered non-existent or of no practical value. This individual right outweighed the alleged general desirability of closed shops in the public interest. The Court was not persuaded that unions could not pursue their interests without compulsory memberships.[48] It was of no relevance in *Sorensen and Rasmussen v Denmark* that both applicants had taken up their jobs in the knowledge of the closed shop agreement; there was still an element of compulsion. Even if one of the applicants was in fact only looking for a temporary job and could have looked for work with an employer without a closed shop, the fact that he was dismissed for failing to join the trade union disclosed hardship and struck at the substance of the right. Nor was it sufficient that the applicants could have subscribed to a "non-political membership" of the union, since they still had to pay the full fee and potentially provide indirect support for the political agenda of the union. The Court was even less convinced in this more recent case that closed-shop agreements were indispensable to trade union freedoms, taking into account that few countries still allowed them, the manner in which the 1961 Social Charter had been applied and the EU instruments on the subject. II–394

While in *Young, James and Webster*, the Court emphasised the element of exertion of pressure to compel someone to join an association contrary to his conviction, which had to be considered also in light of Arts 9 and 10, it is not necessary for an applicant to object to trade union membership on any particular point of principle.[49] In *Sigurjonsson v Iceland*, the Government argued that the taxi association was non-political and that membership was not a question of the applicant's beliefs since he had previously joined the association. The Court considered that Arts 9 and 10 could still be affected since the applicant held a belief in freedom of occupation. Since he now wished to leave and was subject to compulsion striking at the heart of the right, there was a violation. The nature and strength of the objection may however be of relevance in the balancing exercise in assessing the proportionality of any interference.[50]

The Court's approach is to consider whether a proper balance is struck between the interests of the individual and any general interest in maintaining the compulsory membership, but has stated its objections to what may be construed as abuse of a dominant position.[51]

[47] Also *Sigurjonsson v Iceland*, June 30, 1993, Series A, No.264, 16 E.H.R.R. 462, where the Court's views on the negative right were stronger, noting that few Contracting States imposed compulsory membership and referring to international materials, i.e. ILO, EU, Council of Europe.

[48] Also *Sigurjonsson*, fn.47 above, para.41.

[49] Two applicants had objected to trade union policies and one to its political affiliations.

[50] e.g. *Sibson v UK*, April 20, 1993, Series A, No.258–A, 17 E.H.R.R. 193, para.29.

[51] *Young, James and Webster*, fn.39, above, para.63.

A compulsory requirement on an individual to pay a charge to an industrial federation of which he was not a member and to the policies of which he objected was regarded as an infringement of his freedom of association, regardless of the minor nature of the fee involved. There were relevant reasons for this—the Government's aim to promote the industry concerned—but these were not sufficient, as there was no transparency or accountability to non-members as to the use of the funds or safeguards against non-members being placed at a disadvantage by the federation.[52]

Compulsion which falls short of dismissal or removal of livelihood[53] may not strike at the heart of the right. In *Sibson v UK*, where an employee was faced with being sacked or moved to another depot, on roughly equivalent terms and pursuant to the terms of his contract, there was no violation.

(f) Trade union relationships with members

II–395 The right to join a trade union does not include the right to join a union of one's choice regardless of the rules. Protection is primarily against interference by the State, although the State has to protect the individual against abuse of a dominant position. Expulsion from a union which was in breach of union rules, pursuant to arbitrary rules or entailing exceptional hardship, could constitute such abuse. However, where a union was prevented from expelling a member who was member of a right-wing nationalist party, the Court found that the wrong balance had been struck, giving weight to the right of the union to limit membership to those espousing the same values and finding that the individual suffered no particular detriment from being excluded.[54]

Other objections of members to internal union rules have not disclosed abuse, e.g. where a union subscribed to compulsory collective home insurance on behalf of members.[55]

(g) Trade union pressure on employers

II–396 The position of the employer who may be the subject of intense union pressure is perhaps less protected by the Convention. While Art.11 applies to an employer forced to sign a collective agreement by a trade union, it does not extend to granting a right not to join a collective agreement.[56] The Court has referred to a wide margin of appreciation, noting the sensitive character of the social and political issues involved and the wide divergence of practice in Contracting States. It also gives weight to the interests of trade unions in undertaking industrial action, observing that the individual right to join trade unions for the "protection of his interests" implies action can be taken to protect occupational interests of trade unions.[57]

Thus, in *Gustafsson v Sweden*, where a restaurant owner was placed under considerable pressure by lawful industrial action aimed at securing his participation

[52] *Vördur Olafsson v Iceland*, April 27, 2010.
[53] *Sigurjonsson*, fn.47, above, removal of taxi licence.
[54] *ASLEF v UK*, February 27, 2007.
[55] (13537/88) (Dec.) May 7, 1990, 65 D.R. 202.
[56] *Gustafsson v Sweden*, April 25, 1996, R.J.D. 1996–II, No.9, 22 E.H.R.R. 409, para.52.
[57] *Gustafsson*, fn.56 above, para.45.

in a collective bargaining agreement, the Court found no violation having regard in particular to the margin of appreciation, the special character of collective bargaining in Sweden[58] and the consideration that the applicant could have avoided membership of an employer's association by an alternative, substitute agreement.[59] The view of the Court majority seemed to discount the relevance of the applicant's political objection to joining a collective agreement and to imply that the infliction of economic damage was not enough to strike at the heart of the right where an employer is concerned.

(b) *Prohibition on trade union membership*

A special exception is contained in the second paragraph of Art.11, namely, the lawful imposition of restrictions on the exercise of rights by police, armed forces and administration of the State, which is not expressly qualified by reference to the necessity of the measure. When GCHQ staff were not permitted to join any existing trade union, the Commission found that their functions were similar to that of the police and vital to national security and therefore to be considered as part of the administration of the State. While the applicants had argued that "restrictions" could not mean extinction of the right, the Commission found that, having regard to the wide margin of appreciation accorded in the protection of national security and the previous disruption by industrial action, the measure was not arbitrary.[60] II–397

However, more recently, the Court has applied this limitation very restrictively. It considered that the nature of the duties of municipal civil servants had not been such as to require them to be regarded as "members of the administration of the State".[61] Further, it has held, in light of numerous international instruments upholding the rights of public servants to join trade unions, that members of the administration could not be excluded from the scope of Art.11[62] nor, even, their right to strike.[63] Any restriction imposed on the ability of public employees to join or act in trade unions will therefore be scrutinised to verify whether it is necessary to safeguard the essential interests or functioning of the State. Thus, where there was an absolute ban on any civil servants forming trade unions, the Court found that, in the absence of any concrete evidence to show that the founding or the activities of *Tüm Haber Sen* represented a threat to Turkish society or the Turkish State, the restriction disclosed a breach.[64] Where the Court of Cassation held that a trade union of municipal workers could not be formed due to lack of legal provision for

[58] The Government emphasised that the applicant was challenging an important element in the "Swedish model" of industrial relations which was important to their welfare state, i.e. control by collective agreements rather than legislation.

[59] See also the Commission's opinion that the harsh measures (resulting in the sale of the applicant's restaurant) were not counterbalanced by strong legitimate interests in forcing him to sign a collective agreement; and two dissenting judges who considered that compulsion to enter a collective bargaining system was equally an infringement on negative freedom of association incompatible with an element inherent in that freedom, e.g. freedom for the applicant to negotiate his own labour agreements.

[60] (11603/85) (Dec.) January 20, 1987, 50 D.R. 228.

[61] *Demir and Baykara*, fn.36 above, para.107.

[62] *Demir and Baykara*, fn.36 above, paras 98–108.

[63] *Enerji-Yapi-Yol Sen*, April 21, 2009, paras 32–33, only a restriction on public servants exercising the power of the State seems to remain.

[64] *Tum Haber Sen and Cinar v Turkey*, February 21, 2006, concerning telecommunications workers. The Court noted that Turkey had ratified ILO instruments protecting public sector employees' rights to form trade unions.

such a union, the Court found that this was an insufficient ground on which to deny the workers' rights.[65]

(i) Disincentives on trade union membership

II–398 Where domestic law permitted employers to offer financial incentives to employees to enter into new contracts by which they relinquished the right to trade union representation and the right to certain forms of industrial action, the Court found in *Wilson, National Union of Journalists and Others v UK* that this effectively undermined or frustrated the trade union's ability to strive for the protection of its interests. By thus permitting employers to induce employees to surrender important union rights, the State had failed in its positive obligation to secure the enjoyment of Art.11 rights.

(j) Right to strike

II–399 The right to strike is not expressly guaranteed.[66] Where a German teacher, a civil servant, was fined for voting to go on strike, the Commission noted that Germany generally accepted the right to strike but that civil servants were excluded due to the special character of their functions. Since there were no other elements restricting rights under Art.11, para.1, the Commission considered the ban acceptable.[67] It was also proportionate to issue an order prohibiting the strike of oil rig workers and to impose mediation and collective bargaining, where the union had already exercised its right to strike for 36 hours to some effect and there was the prospect of serious consequences to State revenue and damage to the installations if matters dragged on. The Court did emphasise that this did not mean a system of compulsory arbitration for bringing lawful strikes to an end would be considered proportionate in all cases and referred to specific and exceptional circumstances existing in that case.[68] Nor was it disproportionate for a court to prohibit a strike intended to force a public employer into protecting hypothetical future employees by effecting agreements with private companies to which it might transfer its functions, the Court finding that this did not effectively prevent the trade union's current members from safeguarding their own interests.[69] However, where the authorities issued a circular prohibiting all civil servants from joining a national strike action and sanctioned those that took part, the Court considered that this was a disproportionate measure, there being nothing to show that the national action had been banned or was indiscriminate in its extent; it considered that the bar on striking was only extendable to those public servants exercising the power of the State.[70]

6. Prohibitions on, or penalties flowing from, membership of an association

II–400 Where a person is penalised due to membership or activities as member of an association or party or barred from such, the Court has often examined the issues under Art.10 of the Convention and dealt with Art.11 complaints as subsidiary. For

[65] *Demir and Baykara*, fn.36 above, paras 119–127.
[66] *Schmidt and Dahlstrom*, fn.41 above, para.36.
[67] (10365/83) (Dec.) July 5, 1984, 39 D.R. 237.
[68] *Federation of Offshore Workers' Trade Unions v Norway*, (38190/97) June 27, 2002, ECHR 2002–VI.
[69] *UNISON v UK*, January 10, 2002, ECHR 2002–I.
[70] *Enerji Yap-Yol Sen v Turkey*, fn.63, paras 31–33, this authority would appear to overrule the Commission precedent at fn.60 above.

example in *Vogt v Germany*, where the applicant school teacher had been dismissed due to her membership of the Communist Party, the Court carried out its assessment of legitimate aim, necessity and proportionality under Art.10 and after finding a violation of Art.10 on the basis of a lack of convincing justification for the measure, even in light of historical considerations attaching to the independence of the civil service, concluded that there was a violation of Art.11 on the essentially the same grounds.[71] However, in *Rekvenyi v Hungary*, where the applicant police officer was barred from political activities, including membership of any party, the Court found no violation under Art.10, acknowledging the importance in newly post-Communist Hungary of de-politicising the police, and for the same reasons, no violation of Art.11.

In *Grande Oriente d'Italia di Palazzo Guistiniani v Italy*, a freemason association complained of a new law barring freemasons from regional public office. While accepting that the law had the legitimate aim of maintaining public order and national security in an atmosphere of suspicion by the public of the role played by freemasons, the Court found that the chilling effect on the freedom of association in circumstances where membership was not in itself a reprehensible act could not be regarded as necessary in a democratic society.[72] However, it was acceptable to impose an obligation on public servants to declare their membership of particular organisations, in the interests of transparency and to dismiss them for failure to comply, where there were adequate procedural safeguards.[73]

Given the international network of organisations, the requirement that members of associations had to obtain permission from the authorities to attend meetings abroad was not found to pursue a legitimate aim.[74] Nor was it compatible with Art.11 to transfer a civil servant to another district, purely because of his trade union activities.[75]

Cross-reference

Part IIB, s.20: Freedom of assembly.

[71] *Vogt v Germany*, September 26, 1995, Series A, No.323; also *Ahmed v UK*, September 2, 1998, R.J.D. 1998–VI, where the restrictions on local authority officers' political activities was found proportionate under Art.10, no violation followed under Art.11.

[72] See also *Grande Oriente d'Italia di Palazza Guistiniani v Italy (No.2)*, May 31, 2007, breach of Art.14 in conjunction with Art.11 where only members of freemasonry associations had to declare their membership when applying for regional offices.

[73] See *Siveri and Chiellini v Italy*, (13148/04) (Dec.) June 3, 2008, there was evidence that the applicants would not have been dismissed if revealing their masonry affiliations, others having made their declarations in due form and being maintained in their positions.

[74] *Izmir Savas Karsitlari Dernegi v Turkey*, March 2, 2006.

[75] *Metin Turan v Turkey*, November 14, 2006.

22. Freedom of expression

Key provisions:

II–401 Articles 10 (freedom of expression and to impart and receive information) and 17 (bar on interpreting Convention to confer rights to engage in any activity aimed at the destruction or limitation on its rights and freedoms).

Key case-law:

Handyside v UK, December 7, 1976, Series A, No.24; *Sunday Times (No.1) v UK*, April 26, 1979, Series A, No.30, 2 E.H.R.R. 245; *Barfod v Denmark*, February 22, 1989, Series A, No.149, 13 E.H.R.R. 493; *Oberschlick v Austria (No.1)*, May 23, 1991, Series A, No.204; *The Observer and The Guardian v UK*, November 26, 1991, Series A, No.216, 14 E.H.R.R. 153; *Sunday Times v UK (No.2)*, November 26, 1991, Series A, No.217, 14 E.H.R.R. 229; *Thorgeir Thorgeirson v Iceland*, June 25, 1992, Series A, No.239, 14 E.H.R.R. 843; *Chorherr v Austria*, August 25, 1993, Series A, No.266–B, 17 E.H.R.R. 358; *Verenigung Weekblad Bluf! v Netherlands*, February 9, 1995, Series A, No.306–A, 20 E.H.R.R. 189; *Piermont v France*, April 27, 1995, Series A, No.314; *Prager and Oberschlick v Austria*, April 26, 1995, Series A, No.313, 21 E.H.R.R. 1; *Goodwin v UK*, March 27, 1996, R.J.D. 1996–II, No.7, 22 E.H.R.R. 123; *De Haes and Gijsels v Belgium*, February 24, 1997, R.J.D. 1997–I, No.30, 25 E.H.R.R. 1; *Oberschlick v Austria (No.2)*, July 1, 1997, R.J.D. 1997–IV, No.42, 25 E.H.R.R. 357; *Worm v Austria*, August 29, 1997, R.J.D. 1997–V, No.45; *Lehideux and Isorni v France*, September 23, 1998, R.J.D. 1998–VII, No.92, 30 E.H.R.R. 665; *Fressoz and Roire v France*, January 21, 1999, ECHR 1999–I, 31 E.H.R.R. 28; *Bladet Tromso and Stensaas v Norway*, May 20, 1999, ECHR 1999–III; 29 E.H.R.R. 125; *Bergens Tidende v Norway*, May 2, 2000, ECHR 2000–IV; *Lopes Gomes da Silva v Portugal*, September 28, 2000, ECHR 2000–X; *Roy and Malaurie v France*, October 3, 2000, ECHR 2000–X; *Tammer v Estonia*, February 6, 2001, ECHR 2001–I; *Jerusalem v Austria*, February 27, 2001, ECHR 2001–II; *Feldek v Slovakia*, July 12, 2001, ECHR 2001–VIII; *Perna v Italy*, May 6, 2003, ECHR 2003–V; *Roemen and Schmit v Luxembourg*, February 25, 2003, ECHR 2003–IV; *Cumpana and Mazare v Romania*, December 17, 2004, ECH 2004–XII: *Pedersen and Baadsgaard v Denmark*, December 17, 2004, ECHR 2004–XII.

1. General principles

II–402 Freedom of expression has provoked some of the most concentrated and emphatic case-law from the Convention organs. It often involves the cleaner cases (fewer terrorists, criminals or other undesirables) and raises nice defined issues of principle for practitioner, politician, academic and civil right activist alike.

Freedom of expression is, the Court has underlined, one of the key pillars on which an effectively functioning democracy rests. This fundamental importance underlies the cases. Since the media are the most public and identifiable manifestation of the passage of ideas, information and opinions and therefore the most likely to feel the effect of any official interference or restriction, a large percentage of the cases involve journalists. The Court has recognised the role of the media in the free flow of information and ideas in a democratic society. They are the "watchdog" of democracy and there is a very strong presumption in practice towards the necessity of the media being able to operate unhindered. As the case-law has developed, there is little scope for restrictions on political speech or on debate of questions of public interest, with elected officials, journalists and activist groups able to claim strong levels of protection in contributing to public debate.[1]

The restrictions allowed under the Art.10, para.2 must be narrowly interpreted and the necessity for restrictions convincingly established, in addition to being lawful and pursuing legitimate aims. While the exercise of freedom of expression may be made subject to compliance with certain formalities, where a failure to comply with a formal procedure in exercising a form of freedom of expression constitutes a criminal offence, the law must clearly define the circumstances in which it will apply.[2]

However the above must be read subject to the Court's view of the role of the Convention organs. The adjective "necessary" implies a "pressing social need" in respect of interferences. Contracting States have a certain margin of appreciation in assessing whether such a need exists though this is subject to a "European supervision" of both the law and decisions applying it. This involves examining whether in light of the case as a whole the measure was proportionate to the legitimate aim pursued and whether the reasons adduced by the national authorities were relevant and sufficient.[3] Factors of significance in balancing the interest in freedom of expression against other claimed interests include the nature and severity of the restriction, its duration,[4] the public interest for and against exercise of the right,[5] whether the reasons for the restriction continue to be valid in light of changing circumstances and the nature of the publication/expression in issue, in particular its tone and balance, its factual accuracy and the relevance to public debate of any comment or opinion. The Court will also take into account whether the national authorities applied standards in conformity with the principles of Art.10 and based themselves on an acceptable assessment of the relevant facts.[6] It has stated that, where a domestic court thoroughly examines the relevant issues under

[1] e.g. *Castells v Spain*, April 23, 1992, Series A, No.236, 14 E.H.R.R. 445, para.43, *Thorgeir Thorgeirson v Iceland*, June 25, 1992, Series A, No.239, 14 E.H.R.R. 843, para.63; *Murphy v Ireland*, July 10, 2003, para.67; *Sürek v Turkey (No.1)*, July 8, 1999, ECHR 1999–IV, para.61, very strong reasons required to justify restrictions on political speech; *Steel and Morris v UK*, February 15, 2005, ECHR 2005–II, paras 88–89, concerning Greenpeace.

[2] *Karademirci v Turkey*, January 25, 2005, ECHR 2005–I, para.40, where trade unionists were convicted for making a statement to the press without prior filing of the document with the public prosecutor, it was not foreseeable from the legal provisions that this formality would extend to such statements.

[3] e.g. *Sunday Times v UK (No.2)*, November 26, 1991, Series A, No.217, 14 E.H.R.R. 229, para.47.

[4] *Sunday Times (No.1) v UK*, April 26, 1979, Series A, No.30, 2 E.H.R.R. 245, it was relevant that the Thalidomide case had been dormant pending settlement for many years, in a "legal cocoon" from public enquiry.

[5] Where measures are taken to protect public order against disturbance, as in *Chorherr v Austria*, August 25, 1993, Series A, No.266–B, 17 E.H.R.R. 358, a protester arrested at a military parade, or in (28979/95) and (30343/96) (Decs.) January 13, 1997, 88–A D.R. 137, (terrorist aspect—see below sub-s.10: Threats to national security and public safety) the balance is more readily found to have been respected. See, however, *Piermont v France*, April 27, 1995, Series A, No.314, where measures against a MEP were not regarded justified by public order. On topics of public health and the environment there should be less restriction on freedom of expression: *Mamere v France*, November 7, 2006, para.20, concerning levels of radiation.

[6] e.g. *Pedersen and Baadsgaard v Denmark*, December 17, 2004, ECHR 2004–XII, para.70; *Perna v Italy*, May 6, 2003, ECHR 2003–V, para.39(c); *Karman v Russia*, December 14, 2006, paras 42–43, where the courts wrongly treated the term "neo-fascist" as a fact to be proved, not a value judgment and held the journalist to too high a standard of proof.

the Convention and gives detailed reasons for its decision, it would require strong reasons for the Court to substitute its view.[7]

Measures covered by Art.10 primarily concern interference by public authorities, either directly or through pressure.[8] There are a few cases showing that in some circumstances a positive obligation may arise requiring the State to take action to protect freedom of expression from interference from others (see sub-s.15: Positive obligations to protect expression).

2. Scope of the right

II–403 The freedom covers not only information and ideas of a popular, uncontroversial nature but also those which might offend, shock or disturb. It protects the substance of the ideas and information expressed and the form or mode in which they are conveyed.[9] It covers artistic expression and commercial speech (see sub-ss.6 and 11 below).

There has not been much discussion over what means of expression is included. In *Groppera* the Government argued that music and advertising on radio did not constitute information or ideas for the purposes of Art.10. The Court did not consider it necessary to decide since broadcasting was separately mentioned in Art.10 as a form of expression without specifying its content. In an early case, the Commission said that Art.10 did not protect the commercial interests of newspapers, save possibly where the State failed in its duty to protect against excessive press concentrations.

The right cannot be invoked where, as set out in Art.17, it would imply the right to engage in any activity or perform any act aimed at the destruction of any of the rights and freedoms in the Convention, or limit them to an extent greater than provided for therein. Article 17 is very rarely applied however. It was unsuccessfully invoked by the French Government in *Lehideux and Isorni v France*, where the applicants complained of their convictions for statements allegedly implying support of collaboration with the Nazis during the war. The Court did not consider that issues about Petain's role, which were part of an ongoing debate amongst historians, belonged to the category of clearly established historical facts, such as the Holocaust, whose negation or revision would be removed from the protection of Art.10 by Art.17.[10] The Court also rejected the Government argument that the wearing of a

[7] e.g. *MGN Ltd v UK*, January 18, 2011, paras 144–150.

[8] e.g. *Saliyev v Russia*, October 21, 2010, paras 52–61, the applicant's article, which was critical of the municipality, had been printed in a municipally-owned newspaper; when the edition was abruptly withdrawn by the editor, without justification, this was seen as a measure carried out on behalf of a "public authority"; Art.10 was breached.

[9] e.g. *Oberschlick v Austria (No.1)*, May 23, 1991, Series A, No.204, para.57; *Jersild v Denmark*, September 24, 1994, Series A, No.298, para.31. See also *Women on Waves v Portugal*, February 3, 2009, para.30, where the abortion activists were barred from entering national waters in their campaign boat, this was an interference with their chosen form of conveying information, even though they could have entered Portugal by another mode of transport. By way of exception, in *Hachette Filipacchi Presse Automobile et Dupuy v France*, March 6, 2009, paras 48–50, in the context of indirect advertising through photographs of racing drivers bearing tobacco logos, the Court envisaged that the magazine could have been required to blur or otherwise fiddle with the image to render the logos illegible: this was not considered as distorting any factual representation of a particular sporting moment.

[10] *Lehideux and Isorni v France*, September 23, 1998, R.J.D., 1998–VII, No.92, 30 E.H.R.R. 665, para.47. See similar finding as regarded writings by a former general about the Algerian war in *Orban, De Bartillat*

red star by a left-wing politician at a lawful demonstration propagated or conveyed a justification of totalitarian practices contrary to the Convention's underlying values.[11] However, in *Garaudy v France*, where the applicant disputed the reality, breadth and severity of the persecution of the Jews during the Holocaust, the statements were found to conflict with fundamental values of the Convention and pursuant to Art.17 the applicant could not rely on Art.10 concerning his conviction for disputing crimes against humanity.[12] A general and vehement attack on one ethnic or religious group is also considered as being in contradiction with the Convention's underlying values, notably tolerance, social peace and non-discrimination. Art.17 applied where an applicant complained of his conviction for publications inciting hatred of the Jewish people[13] and where an applicant was convicted for displaying a poster implying that Muslims as a whole were responsible for a grave act of terrorism.[14]

3. Who can invoke the right?

Legal persons which are editors and publishers of magazines may claim to be victims as well as individuals such a journalists.[15] Trade unions, such as the NUJ, cannot claim to be victim of restrictions affecting their members[16] but journalists and producers of programmes could claim to be affected by measures aimed at broadcasting companies where as employees they were bound to comply with them.[17] Actors in a theatre troupe refused permission to perform a particular play may claim interference with their freedom of expression.[18] **II–404**

There is no right as such for a journalist or other person to obtain publication of his views by the media; newspapers will have their own editorial policies and cannot be required to accept all offerings in effect. Access to the media is a limited right so far. However, where an article has been accepted and printed, measures taken to withdraw the newspaper from circulation due to the contents of the article will constitute an interference.[19]

and Editions Plon v France, January 15, 2009, paras 35–37, even if some passages could be regarded as seeking to justify war crimes, it was primarily intended as contributing to a serious and ongoing public debate; *Leroy v France*, October 2, 2008, para.27, a cartoon was condemned for supporting terrorism through apparent approving terms of the 9/11 attacks, but was intended as a comment on American imperialism in a broader context, Art.17 did not apply.

11 *Vajnai v Hungary*, July 8, 2008, paras 23–26.

12 (65831/01) (Dec.) June 24, 2003, ECHR 2003–IX, the Court doubted whether other passages of the book, found by the courts to incite racial hatred, could fall within the scope of Art.10, but in any event found the conviction justified under para.2. In (8348/78) and (8406/78) (Dec.) October 11, 1979, 18 D.R. 187, the Commission found that Art.10, pursuant to Art.17, did not apply to a racially discriminatory publication.

13 *Ivanov v Russia*, (35222/04) (Dec.) February 20, 2007.

14 *Norwood v UK*, November 16, 2004, ECHR 2004–XI.

15 (9615/81) (Dec.) May 5, 1983, 32 D.R. 231. See more recently *Urper v Turkey*, October 20, 2009, para.19, editors, directors, journalists and owners of the newspapers could claim to be victims of measures suspending publication of the newspapers.

16 e.g. (11553/85) and (11658/85) (Dec.) March 9, 1987, 51 D.R. 136.

17 *Purcell v Ireland*, (15404/89) (Dec.) April 16, 1991, 70 D.R. 262.

18 *Ulusoy v Turkey*, May 3, 2007.

19 e.g. *Saliyev*, fn.8 above, paras 52–61, the applicant's article criticising the municipality which owned the newspaper had been printed but the edition was withdrawn by the editor, seemingly under pressure from the local authority.

4. Media

II–405 The Court scrutinises closely measures penalising publication by the press. While it may accept that measures pursue legitimate aims, it has required convincing justification. Where matters of public interest are concerned, the presumption is heavily in favour of freedom; public interest has a wide interpretation but a private sphere exists where care should be taken.[20]

Journalistic freedom is accepted as covering possible recourse to a degree of exaggeration, even provocation,[21] with allowances to be made for satirical humour.[22] The defences of justification and fair comment should also be available.[23] Value judgments should not be treated as matters of fact requiring proof but in such cases the proportionality of an interference may depend on whether there is a sufficient factual basis as even a value judgment without any factual basis may be excessive.[24]

There is not unlimited freedom even for press coverage of matters of serious public concern, with reference being made to the duties and responsibilities inherent in the exercise of the freedom of expression, particularly where the rights of others are involved, requiring journalists to act in good faith in order to provide accurate and reliable information in accordance with the ethics of journalism.[25] This involves taking sufficient steps to verify the truth of allegations,[26] but journalists may rely on official reports and documents[27] and are not required to distance themselves formally

[20] e.g. *Hachette Filipacchi Associé ("Ici Paris") v France*, July 23, 2009, para.44, articles concerning Johnny Halliday's lifestyle and alleged monetary problems were not part of a public debate of interest to society.

[21] e.g. *Prager and Oberschlick v Austria*, April 26, 1995, Series A No.313, 21 E.H.R.R. 1, para.38, *De Haes and Gijsels v Belgium*, February 24, 1997, R.J.D. 1997–I, No.30, 25 E.H.R.R. 1, para.46.

[22] e.g. *Nikowitz and Verlagsgruppe News GmbH v Austria*, February 22, 2007, paras 25–28.

[23] e.g. *Lingens*; *Oberschlick (No.1)*, fn.9 above; *Colombani v France*, June 25, 2002, ECHR 2002–V, where the defence of justification had not applied to *Le Monde*'s article making allegations damaging to the reputation of a head of State.

[24] e.g. *De Haes and Gijsels*, fn.21 above, para.47; *Oberschlick v Austria (No.2)*, July 1, 1997, R.J.D. 1997–IV, No.42, 25 E.H.R.R. 357, para.33.

[25] e.g. *Fressoz and Roire v France*, January 21, 1999, ECHR 1999–I, 31 E.H.R.R. 28, para.48; *Bergens Tidende v Norway*, May 2, 2000, ECHR 2000–IV, para.53; *Harlanova v Latvia*, (57313/00) (Dec.) April 3, 2000, where the journalist did nothing to verify the basis of serious allegations or to identify sources of information; *Pedersen and Baadsgaard*, fn.6 above, lack of sufficient factual basis for allegations of a criminal offence concerning a senior police officer; *Stangu and Scutelnicu v Romania*, January 31, 2006, lack of good faith and any substantiation in allegations made about a police officer and judge.

[26] e.g. *Verdens gang and Aase v Norway*, (45710/99) (Dec.) October 16, 2001, where the newspaper did not verify the truth of the allegations published about a cosmetic surgeon; *Tonsberg Blad AS and Haukom v Norway*, March 1, 2007, para.101, less rigorous level of checking of facts sufficient where defamatory element was limited; *Cuc Pascu v Romania*, September 16, 2008, no violation where the journalist accused an academic-turned-politician of plagiarism on the basis of unsubstantiated assertions and was fined for criminal insult; *Mihaiu v Romania*, November 4, 2008, no violation where journalist accused a public figure, on the basis of unchecked assertions, of accepting a bribe, and had acted in bad faith; *Europapress Holding d.o.o. v Croatia*, October 22, 2009, where reporting that the deputy prime minister had pointed a gun at a journalist (EV), the newspaper should have verified EV's story, not being entitled to rely on her status as a journalist.

[27] e.g. *Bladet Tromso and Stensaas v Norway*, May 20, 1999, ECHR 1999–III, 29 E.H.R.R. 125, where the majority found that the newspaper could reasonably rely on an official report without carrying out its own research into its accuracy; *Selisto v Finland*, November 16, 2004, para.60, no obligation on journalists to check the veracity of official documents such as pre-trial records; or of facts and evidence contained in decisions of the Strasbourg institutions, in *Saygili v Turkey*, January 8, 2008. Contrast *Standard Verlagsgesellschaft v Austria (No.2)*, February 22, 2007, para.42, where the newspaper should have checked the accuracy of a source quoted in a political press release, which could not be relied on as an official record.

from the contents of quotations.[28] Reasonable mistakes made in good faith which are rectified promptly should not be disproportionately sanctioned.[29]

Where the subject in issue contributes to a debate on a matter of public interest, the scope of freedom of expression is wider; where the subject is not, it is narrower.[30]

(a) *Injunctions and preventive measures*

Where the matter to be reported is of public interest or importance, it is hard for a State to find justification for the restriction in the absence of established damage to an interest of at least equal importance. Prior restraints are not inherently incompatible with Art.10 but call for careful scrutiny.[31] The Court has noted that delay in publication in the press leads to staleness quickly depriving news of interest and value.[32] Refusals of registrations which are tantamount to the prohibition of publication must be scrutinised under the terms of the second paragraph.[33] II–406

An injunction was not found to be "necessary" in *Sunday Times (No.1) v UK*, where articles on the Thalidomide drug scandal raised matters of undisputed public concern and were moderate and balanced in nature. Notwithstanding the domestic courts' concern to prevent "trial by newspaper" in pending civil proceedings, the Court commented that courts could not operate in a vacuum; the media had a role in reporting matters that came before the courts and the public a right to receive such information. An injunction against one newspaper preventing repetition of certain accusations was found proportionate where the domestic courts found that the statements had a competitive aim, including untrue and disparaging statements of fact, beyond participation in a matter of public debate.[34]

Measures to prevent publication or distribution on the basis of the confidential nature of the subject matter generally cease to be justifiable or proportionate once the material has been made public. Seizure of a weekly periodical publishing security classified material from the Dutch security service was found to be disproportionate since 2,500 copies had already been sold at night and the continued ban on the distribution of the copy no longer served any purpose, notwithstanding the Court's acknowledgment that the security services could claim a high level of protection.[35]

[28] e.g. *Thoma v Luxembourg*, March 29, 2001, ECHR 2001–III, where the imposition of a penalty on a journalist for repeating quotations from another source was disproportionate, the Court noting that there could be no general requirement on journalists to systematically and formally distance themselves from the contents of a quotation.

[29] See *Aquilina v Malta*, June 14, 2011, paras 45–52, where in a chaotic court scene, the journalist, as well as others, received the mistaken impression that the judge had found a lawyer guilty of contempt, the finding of a liability for damages was disproportionate, particularly as a retraction had been published.

[30] e.g. *Hachette Filipacchi Associé*, fn.20 above, para.44, articles concerning Johnny Halliday's private life did not attract the wider scope of Art.10.

[31] *The Observer and The Guardian v UK*, November 26, 1991, Series A, No.216, 14 E.H.R.R. 153, para.60; *Gaweda v Poland*, March 14, 2002, ECHR 2002–II, para.35; *Association Ekin v France*, July 17, 2001, para.56, where a blanket executive power to ban foreign books was unjustified.

[32] *Sunday Times (No.2)*, fn.3 above, para.51.

[33] *Gaweda*, fn.31 above.

[34] *Krone Verlag GmbH & CoKG and Mediaprint v Austria*, (42429/98) (Dec.) March 20, 2003. See also *Andreas Wabl v Austria*, March 21, 2000, paras 40–45, where an injunction preventing a politician repeating the epithet "Nazi-journalism" about a newspaper was justified; it was no excuse that the newspaper had defamed him first.

[35] *Verenigung Weekblad Bluf! v Netherlands*, February 9, 1995, Series A, No.306–A, 20 E.H.R.R. 189, see also (10038/82) (Dec.) May 11, 1984, 38 D.R. 53 (settled after admissibility), where a solicitor, who allowed a journalist to read documents produced by the Government and which were read out in open court, was found in contempt of court.

Similarly, although initially an interlocutory injunction on the *Observer* and *Guardian* preventing publication of material from the *Spycatcher* book by an ex-MI5 official could be justified as necessary to maintain the authority of the judiciary and also protect national security, once the book was published in the United States with no ban on importation into the United Kingdom, the Court found that the interest of the plaintiff litigant in maintaining confidentiality had ceased to exist for the purposes of the Convention.[36] The interest identified at that later stage of maintaining confidence in MI5 and preventing their agents publishing in an unauthorised fashion did not justify the injunctions against the newspapers (as opposed to steps against the author himself and accounts for profits for use of confidential material).

Although exception is often taken to the use of photographs in the press, the Court has stated that there is little scope for an absolute prohibition to publish a public person's picture in an article contributing to a public debate.[37] There are however contexts where a photograph may unduly stigmatise without any countervailing public interest in which context conditional prohibitions on publication may be acceptable.[38]

Where injunctions are issued even for the limited purpose of preventing the repetition of an allegedly insulting criticism, the Court will require it to be supported by relevant and sufficient reasons. It does not hesitate to disagree with domestic court's interpretations of phrases. In *Ferihumer v Austria*, where the courts applied the approach of taking the most negative interpretation of the impugned phrases, namely that the applicant parent had accused teachers of unlawful conduct, the Court considered that this failed to take into account the overall context in which the applicant was expressing an opinion and value-judgment. It also gave weight to the fact that the applicant parent acted for a parents' association, which presumably fortified the legitimacy of his role in commenting on school activities.[39]

No obligation arises on the press to pre-notify subjects of articles of the contents in order to allow them an effective opportunity to apply for an interim injunction. The Court considered that imposition of such a requirement would have a chilling effect on freedom of expression; it could only be effectively enforced by imposing punitively high damages or fines, which would impact on publication on matters of public interest as well as less savoury media disclosures about celebrity private lives.[40]

A particularly narrow margin of appreciation applies where it comes to such measures as ordering the suspension of the publication or distribution of newspapers

[36] The measure was initially proportionate and supported by relevant and sufficient reasons since the book was only in manuscript form at that time, it was unclear what damaging disclosures might be made and the substantive action would be prejudiced by the publication. See also *Plon Société v France*, June 18, 2004, ECHR 2004–IV, where a temporary ban on publication of a book disclosing confidential medical information about President Mitterrand was justified in the aftermath of his death, but a continued ban ceased to be necessary due to the passage of time and the fact the information was available on the internet and elsewhere.

[37] *Verlagsgruppe News GmbH v Austria (No.2)*, December 14, 2006, para.40. See also *Österreicherischer Rundfunk v Austria*, December 7, 2006, paras 68–71, concerning the photograph published on release from prison of a notorious person, where the accuracy of the article was not in question and linked to the photo and other newspapers had been able to publish the photograph.

[38] *Österreichischer Rundfunk v Austria*, (57597/00) (Dec.) May 25, 2004, a photo of a released convict was to be published without mentioning that he had been acquitted of the bomb attacks in question and that he had served his sentence and been released.

[39] *Ferihumer v Austria*, February 1, 2007.

[40] *Mosley v UK*, May 11, 2011, paras 125–132.

by the authorities due to their disapproval of particular articles or features. Suspension is seen as a punitive measure seeking to interfere with the way in which newspapers conduct their role and even if for relatively short periods will be regarded as an unnecessary restraint. Instead of banning an entire periodical, the authorities should consider less draconian measures, such as confiscations of particular issues or prohibition of particular articles.[41]

Ban on a ship operated by abortion campaigners entering territorial waters through despatch of a warship was found to be a disproportionate interference, where there was no evidence of a threat to public order or any serious risk that the applicants would breach the criminal law by giving prohibited medicaments to women; even if there had been such risk, the Court considered that less draconian and more targeted measures could have been taken to counter such a problem such as seizing the drugs.[42]

A requirement, subject to criminal law enforcement, that before publication an interview had to be authorised by the interviewee, was regarded as incompatible with press freedom, giving a veto to the interviewee to prevent publication. The Court took the view that interveiwees enjoyed other more proportionate methods of redress if a journalist failed truthfully to reproduce what was said.[43]

(b) *Penal sanctions for publication*

Where an article has been published and the journalist, editor or publisher pursued under the criminal law, the sanction constitutes an interference that requires convincing justification under the second paragraph. Where an article is based on fact and addresses matters of public interest, the balance is in favour of freedom of expression, notwithstanding polemical, aggressive or even provocative aspects.[44] Using mockery and jokes is also part of the journalistic battery, which has to be tolerated.[45] II–407

(i) Slights on the judiciary

In this area, a certain weight is given to the need to protect judges from disparaging attacks. Although the Court has stated that courts as with other public institutions cannot be immune from criticism and scrutiny, a clear distinction had to be drawn II–408

[41] *Urper*, fn.15 above, paras 43–45, where various "pro-Kurdish" newspapers were subject to closure orders for 15 days up to one month due to alleged propaganda in favour of illegal armed groups.

[42] *Women on Waves*, fn.9 above, paras 36–44.

[43] *Wizerkaniuk v Poland*, July 5, 2011, paras 64–87, where an editor was convicted for reproducing parts of an interview with an MP who had not given authorisation for publication.

[44] e.g. *Oberschlick (No.2)*, fn.24 above, where the journalist, in calling a prominent politician an idiot ("*trottel*"), was commenting on public statements of the politician which were themselves provocative; *Lehideux and Isorni*, fn.10 above, paras 52–55, polemical advertisement on the sensitive topic of Petain's collaboration, where Court considered that the authorities should allow open debate on their history and that it was inappropriate to react with the same severity as decades ago; *Fressoz and Roire*, fn.25 above, paras 51–52, public right to receive information about finances of public figures; *Bladet Tromso*, fn.27 above, para.73, the important public interest in seal hunting outweighed the seal hunters' interest in protecting their reputation; *Scharsach and News Verlagsgesellschaft v Austria*, November 13, 2003, para.44, labelling a politician as a "closet Nazi" did not exceed what was acceptable.

[45] *Bodrozic and Vujic v Serbia*, June 23, 2009, where a male lawyer was ridiculed as a "blonde" with a photograph of a blonde woman in a state of undress, the Court rejected as derisory reasoning that comparing a man to a blonde woman was an attack on his dignity and integrity justifying a criminal conviction.

between criticism and insult. In the latter case, it has gone so far as to comment that an appropriate punishment would not violate Art.10.[46] Thus, the "special role of the judiciary" which as the guarantor of justice must enjoy public confidence to function successfully outweighed other considerations in *Barfod v Denmark*, where a journalist was convicted for defamation in respect of an article criticising lay judges[47] and in *Prager and Oberschlick v Austria*, where the applicants published a strongly worded critique of the Vienna criminal judges, stepping over the limit of permissible exaggeration.[48] Where however in civil proceedings journalists were found to have defamed judges in *De Haes and Gijsels v Belgium*, there was a violation since despite certain provocative elements the articles had an undisputed factual basis.[49] Comments disclosing a certain lack of regard for the Constitutional Court, but which were not grave or insulting, should not have been subject to sanction[50] nor was a criminal penalty justified in respect of a journalist's somewhat exaggerated criticism of a judgment with allegedly homophobic overtones but which did not constitute an attack on the judge or the judiciary as such.[51] Where an article could reasonably be assessed as prejudicing the outcome of a trial by stating an opinion of guilt, the interests in maintaining the authority and impartiality of the judiciary rendered the imposition of a relatively light penalty by way of fine a not disproportionate interference.[52] On the other hand, an overly broad injunction geared to preventing any publication of "the opposite view" of a car accident involving the applicant journalist and a judge was contrary to the essence of pluralism and went beyond any legitimate aim in protecting the authority of the judiciary or the integrity of pending proceedings.[53]

(II) Politicians

II–409 Criticism of politicians has been subject to a more robust approach and a keen concern to avoid the stifling of open debate.[54] In *Lopes Gomes da Silva v Portugal*, in finding disproportionate the conviction of the applicant journalist for an article

[46] *Skalka v Poland*, May 27, 2003, para.34.

[47] The journalist criticising the composition of the court implied that they voted in favour of their local government employer in Greenland in relation to a controversial tax measure.

[48] Narrow majorities: Court 5–4, Commission 15–12. The majority were influenced by the serious nature of the allegations (including breach of law and professional obligations), finding that the applicant journalist could not invoke good faith or compliance with professional ethics since his research did not appear adequate to substantiate such allegations and he had not given any judge a chance to comment. The minority put less weight on the need to protect judges. In the Commission, the minority considered that judges had to act under public scrutiny and tolerate even exaggerated forms of criticism if based on irrefutable fact.

[49] The articles referred to a controversial child custody case, including allegations of abuse imputations of cowardice and bias towards the father. See also *Skalka*, fn.46 above, where a journalist was convicted for derogatory remarks about regional judges, the eight-month prison sentence was disproportionately severe to the aim of maintaining the authority of the judiciary.

[50] *Amihalachioaie v Moldova*, April 20, 2004. See also *Hrico v Slovakia*, July 20, 2004, criticism of a Supreme Court judge, who had entered the political arena, not found to offend or humiliate, but was based on fact and concerning a matter of public interest.

[51] *Kobenter and Standard Verlags GmbH v Austria*, November 2, 2006.

[52] *Worm v Austria*, August 29, 1997, R.J.D. 1997–V, No.45, paras 52–58.

[53] *Obukhova v Russia*, January 8, 2009.

[54] See, e.g. *Worm*, fn.52 above, para.50; *Ukrainian Media Group v Ukraine*, March 29, 2005, para.67, politicians must accept the burden of robust scrutiny and criticism; Also Part IIB, s.8: Defamation and the right to reputation.

describing a political candidate as 'buffoonish" and "grotesque", the Court commented that political invective often spilled over into the personal sphere, such being the hazards of politics and the free debate of ideas. The article was not however a gratuitous personal attack but was based on facts, supported by an objective explanation on a matter of political debate. However, there may even be a certain protection for the untrue statements, a violation being found when an applicant was convicted for disseminating false information, alleging inter alia that a rival presidential candidate was dead; the Court put more weight on the importance of the public debate and the failure of the courts to take it into account that the applicant had expressed his own doubt about the veracity of the information and passed on copies to only eight persons.[55] Further, where councillors and a journalist criticised the local council for not consulting the public or taking account of public opinion on a topic of public interest, the Court found it largely irrelevant whether this was a statement of fact or a value judgment since in lively debate on a topic of public importance elected officials and journalists should enjoy a wide freedom to criticise the actions of the local authority even if a statement lacked a clear basis in fact.[56]

On the other hand, no violation was found in respect of the journalist's conviction in *Tammer v Estonia* for offensive remarks on a public figure about her role as a mother and in breaking up another politician's marriage, which could have been expressed without resort to insult and could not be regarded as pursuing issues in the public interest. There were also relevant and sufficient reasons for convicting journalists who made serious allegations, which could lead to criminal proceedings against a public official, without proper substantiation.[57]

(III) Civil servants

The Court has drawn a distinction between civil servants and politicians. The limits of acceptable criticism may be wider of civil servants than of private individuals, but it could not be said that they knowingly lay themselves open to close scrutiny of their words and deeds to the same extent as politicians.[58] Indeed, as they had to enjoy public confidence in conditions free of perturbation to fulfill their duties, it may be necessary for the State to protect them from unfounded accusations, particular reference being made to public prosecutors and superior police officers.[59] This consideration may, as in other areas, be outweighed by the public interest in the matter raised for debate and proper opportunity must be given for good faith II–410

[55] See *Salov v Ukraine*, September 6, 2005, paras 113–117.

[56] *Lombardo v Malta*, April 24, 2007, para.60. Also *Lepojic v Serbia*, December 10, 2007, disproportionate to convict a journalist for describing a politician as "near-insane" in his handling of public money and attributing criminal conduct to him. Contrast the restrictive approach inconsistent with this emphasis on tolerance for attacks on politicians, even offensive or in strong terms, in *Lindon, Otcharovsky-Laurens and July v France*, October 22, 2007, where there was an uncharacteristic finding of a need for a minimum standard of moderation when the National Front and its leader were excoriated in a fictional novel, the novelist being convicted, inter alia, for likening the right-wing figure to a "vampire".

[57] *Pedersen and Baadsgaard*, fn.6 above, para.80.

[58] *Cumpana and Mazare v Romania*, December 17, 2004, ECH 2004–XII, paras 104–109.

[59] *Lesnik v Slovakia*, March 11, 2003, para.53, no violation disclosed by conviction of a non-journalist for impugning a public prosecutor who, as an official in the administration of justice, attracted protection from unfounded accusations. See also *Perna*, fn.6 above, where emphasis was laid on the highly offensive and gratuitous nature of the criticisms of the chief public prosecutor, which the journalist had not sought to verify.

and the factual basis of allegations to be shown.[60] Criticism of the speed and inefficiency of an investigation by investigating judicial officers, with use of the pejorative term'"rocambolesque" did not support a finding of lack of good faith, nor justify a criminal conviction of the journalist.[61]

(IV) Heads of State

II–411 Presidents, or Heads of State, cannot claim any special protection against insult or criticism, there being no pressing reason for such a restriction or why they cannot make use of standard procedures for defamation.[62] Where a political party spokesman accused the King of Spain of being responsible for torture and violence as head of the army, the Court drew a distinction between provocative, even hostile criticism of a monarch head of state in his role as institutional leader and an attack on personal honour. The former, where concerning an issue of public interest did not justify a conviction for insult to the King and a sentence of one year in prison. The Court was not persuaded that the neutral and apolitical stance of the monarch in the Spanish system gave him any particular immunity from criticism.[63]

(V) Anti-semitism, racism and attacks on religion

II–412 Criminal sanction of individuals who make racist or anti-Semitic statements was generally found justifiable by the Commission.[64] Incitement to racial hatred may justifiably lead to convictions, even of parliamentarians, the Court noting that in the electoral context a xenophobic message can have particularly wide deleterious impact.[65] Seizure of a calendar containing anti-Jewish, anti-Russian and anti-Polish sentiments was found not disproportionate, given the obligation on the Government to protect against ethnic hatred.[66] However, the official approach adopted to protecting "Turkishness", which included any criticism or allegations relating to the Armenian genocide, could not be regarded as preventing incitement to racial hatred—in that context, the search for historic truth and participation in a debate of public interest was the decisive element attracting Convention protection.[67]

[60] *Mamere v France*, November 7, 2005; see also *Thorgeirson v Iceland*, fn.1 above, the conviction of a journalist for defamation of the police ("beasts in uniform") was not found to be justified to protect the rights of police officers. The Court noted that the article was based on objective fact—a known case of ill-treatment—and though expressed in strong terms it concerned a matter of public interest, urging the setting up of an impartial enquiry.

[61] *July and Liberation SARL v France*, February 14, 2008.

[62] *Columbani v France*, June 25, 2002, ECHR 2002–V, para.69, where journalists could not rely on the defence of justification concerning foreign heads of state; *Pakdemirli v Turkey*, February 2, 2005, where elevated damages were awarded due to the president's status; *Artun and Guvener v Turkey*, June 26, 2007, paras 30–32, where prison sentences were imposed for insulting the President.

[63] *Otegi Mondragon v Spain*, March 3, 2011, paras 55–62.

[64] e.g. (9777/82) July 14, 1977, 34 D.R. 158, conviction for denying the extermination of the Jews. See also *Ivanov v Russia*, fn.13 above, complaints by an editor for his conviction for accusing Jews of causing all the evils in Russia did not fall under the protection of Art.10 (see above, sub-s.2: Scope of the right, concerning Art.17).

[65] *Feret v Belgium*, July 16, 2007. See also *Willem v France*, July 16, 2007, no violation where a mayor was convicted for calling for a boycott on Israeli goods, found by domestic courts to be discriminatory against Israeli producers, even if not expressly anti-Semitic. The fact that the mayor's intention was to protest against the Israeli policy, not to incite racial hatred or discriminate was irrelevant as the means used went beyond this.

[66] *Balsyte-Lideikiene v Lithuania*, November 4, 2008.

[67] *Dink v Turkey*, September 14, 2010.

However there is a fine line between legitimate reporting of nasty social phenomena and the unacceptable repetition of racist propaganda. In *Jersild v Denmark*, a television programmer was convicted in relation to a documentary on "greenjackets" during which they expressed racist views. The case turned on the weight given to the freedom of the press to report versus the weight given to the offensive nature of the views reported on and the possible risk of encouraging those views by exposure. For the majority of the Court finding a violation,[68] the key factors were that the applicant did not express the racist views himself but was participating in the current public discussion on racism in the country, intending to portray the mentality and background of those racist individuals. It was relevant that the film was part of a serious news programme aimed at an informed audience and that its presentation made it clear that its aim was not the propagation of racism. "Interviewing" was also noted to be an important means of TV journalism and punishment of a journalist for views of the person interviewed would seriously hamper the contribution of the press to discussion of matters of public interest and should not be envisaged without particularly strong reasons.[69]

Measures may be taken in respect of publications to protect against offensive attacks on religion.[70] However, even ideas which shock or offend may be permissable if not gratuitously abusive or insulting and where contributing to a debate on a point of indisputable public interest.[71] Nor can members of a religion claim to have been disparaged or discredited, requiring protection from interference with their freedom of religion, where a journalist makes provocative criticism of a high functionary in that church.[72]

(vi) Severity of penalties

The Court has generally not been impressed by Government arguments that the penalty resulting from a prosecution was minor, considering that what matters is that the journalist was convicted at all.[73] Regard is sometimes had to the existence of alternative means of intervention and rebuttal, particularly through civil remedies[74] or in *Du Roy and Malaurie*, to the existing protection provided to rights of the accused where the applicant journalists were convicted for disclosing details about II–413

[68] *Jersild v Denmark*, fn.9 above, 12–7, the minority emphasised the importance of fighting racism which endangered the rights of others and outweighed the "good intentions" of journalists who were expected actively to criticise racial discrimination (the applicant had not expressly condemned the racist views).

[69] See, mutatis mutandis, *Muslum Gunduz v Turkey*, December 4, 2003, the prosecution of an applicant for extreme religious views expressed during a television programme was disproportionate, where it was part of an ongoing public debate.

[70] See *IA v Turkey*, September 13, 2005, where a book attacked the Prophet in an offensive manner: in finding the conviction of the publisher proportionate, the Court noted that the book itself had not been banned and that the fine was small. See also sub-s.6: Artistic, cinematic, theatrical and literary.

[71] *Giniewski v France*, January 31, 2006, violation for convictions for publication of article on the influence of certain Catholic doctrines on the origins of the Holocaust.

[72] *Klein v Slovakia*, October 31, 2006, paras 51–55.

[73] *Jersild*, fn.9 above, para.35; *Lopes Gomes da Silva v Portugal*, September 28, 2000, ECHR 2000–X, para.36; *Bodrozic and Vujic*, fn.45, unjustified conviction and fining of journalists for making fun of a male lawyer through comparisons to a blonde woman. Yet in *Tammer v Estonia*, February 6, 2001, ECHR 2001–I, para.69, the limited fine was taken into account in finding the conviction proportionate and in *Perna*, fn.6 above, para.39(d), the Grand Chamber referred to the nature and severity of the sentence as relevant factors.

[74] *Lehideux and Isorni*, fn.10 above, para.57.

criminal proceedings. Prison sentences for journalists can only exceptionally be justified due to the chilling effect, as with penalties removing their civil rights or suspending them from practising journalism; hate speech or incitement to violence has been given as a possible exception.[75] A conditional discontinuation of proceedings is still regarded as having an objectionable discouraging censorship effect[76] as well as convictions followed only by fines.[77] Imposition of prison sentences on private individuals for defamation are also likely to be regarded as excessive, as in the case of a woman facing a suspended 15-month sentence for giving a published interview in which she accused a plastic surgeon of butchering her through a series of botched interventions. [78]

Where disclosures are made in the public interest by public employees, even where it may be justified to convict for defamation insofar as the allegations prove baseless or ill-founded as regards the complainant, the imposition of a prison sentence, even if suspended, will render the measure disproportionate.[79]

(vii) Other factors

II–414 It seems that more leeway towards freedom of expression is given where a spokesperson makes provocative and hostile remarks in a press conference, the Court noting that in such a context there is no possibility, as in written or otherwise recorded form, to reformulate them or withdraw them before publication.[80]

Different, less liberal considerations apply where the purpose of the expression is commercial without contributing to any public debate.[81]

(c) Other restrictions on reporting

(i) Awards of damages and legal costs

II–415 Awards of damages in civil defamation proceedings may disclose unjustified or disproportionate interference with freedom of expression, raising similar considerations as considered above in the context of penal sanctions (see further Pt IIB, s.8: Defamation and the right to reputation). Journalists themselves are public figures who must expect to attract criticism, but there was no violation where a journalist was found liable in defamation for statements about other journalists where this was not part of a public debate but the targetting of people she disliked.[82]

The imposition of exorbitant success fees for claimants in actions against newspapers may also breach Art.10. Where a fashion model was awarded £3,500 for

[75] *Cumpana and Mazare*, fn.6 above, paras 115–119; *Fatullayev v Azerbaijan*, April 22, 2010, para.103, unjustified prison sentence (over two years) given to journalist for articles claiming Government soldiers involved in an infamous massacre attributed to Armenians; nor could his statements criticising the treatment of minorities be regarded as incitement of ethnic violence (para.126). Contrast *Palusinski v Poland*, (62414/00) (Dec.) October 3, 2006, where, as the applicant stood to gain financially from the sale of a book found to incite drugs use, it was not disproportionate to impose a suspended sentence of 13 months.

[76] e.g. *Dabrowski v Poland*, December 19, 2006, para.36.

[77] e.g. *Dupuis v France*, June 7, 2007, para.48.

[78] *Kannelopoulou v Greece*, October 11, 2007, para.38.

[79] *Marchenko v Ukraine*, February 19, 2009, para.52.

[80] *Otegi Mondragon*, fn.63, para.54.

[81] *Perrin v UK*, (5446/03) (Dec.) October 18, 2005, ECHR 2005–XI, concerning an internet porn site.

[82] *Katamadze v Georgia*, (69857/01) (Dec.) February 14, 2006.

damages for breach of confidence against a newspaper which also had to pay some £500,000 to her lawyers due to a "success fee" agreement, the Court noted that this system had been criticised in public consultations, in particular since there were no qualifying conditions, the lack of any incentive for claimants to minimise their costs, the chilling effect which drove opposing parties to settle early despite a good case and the opportunity for lawyers to cherry-pick cases likely to succeed while avoiding claims with smaller chances of success, thus defeating the alleged purpose of such agreements in opening access to court to a wider range of people. The imposition of such a large sum for fees in this case was found disproportionate and outside the authorities' margin of appreciation.[83]

The Commission found that the administration of justice could require the exclusion of the press from court[84] or that secrecy of jury deliberations be maintained.[85] It is also compatible to impose conditions of accreditation on journalists who attend courts in a privileged capacity.[86] Prohibitions on publishing certain details may raise issues, if not shown to be necessary. In one case, settled before admissibility, the name of a witness was subject to prohibition even though she was named in open court to avoid prejudicing the defence.[87]

(II) Court reporting and administration of justice

Regarding restrictions imposed on publications about pending court proceedings, comment on criminal trials may not extend to statements likely to prejudice, whether intentionally or not, the fair trial of an accused.[88] The Commission found it legitimate to impose a postponement on a TV programme about the Birmingham Six, scheduled for the close of the appeal hearing with portrayal of judges, counsel and witnesses by actors. It considered the restriction proportionate, agreeing that this method differed from press reports on the proceedings which were unaffected and having regard to its duration of eight weeks until the judgment was given. Although objectively judges would not be influenced, the appellants had a right to be assured that they would not be affected by external matters.[89] Similarly, the banning of a Channel Four "Court Report" intending to report a controversial official secrets trial, by way of dramatic reconstruction with actors reading edited highlights of the proceedings, was justified having regard to the real risk of prejudice if watched by the jury and as the programme could be issued with the same information read by newsreaders.[90] Contracting States also have a wide margin of II–416

[83] *MGN Ltd v UK*, January 18, 2011, paras 198–220.

[84] (13366/87) (Dec.) December 3, 1990, 67 D.R. 244, exclusion of press during sentencing. The Commission assumed that there was an interference, given the important role played by media in the administration of justice, but Art.6 was of particular weight in a trial context (it allowed for in camera proceedings) and the exclusion was at the request of the defendant whose interests outweighed the journalists.

[85] (24770/94) (Dec.) November 30, 1994, heavy fines for newspaper and editors for contempt of court for publication of jurors' opinions on a controversial trial were justifiable, e.g. protection for jurors to speak freely in the jury room. The question whether the interests of justice at a particular trial could justify disclosure was left open.

[86] (23869/94) December 24, 1995, 80–B D.R. 162.

[87] (11552/85) (Dec.) July 15, 1988, 56 D.R. 148.

[88] e.g. *Worm*, fn.52 above, para.50; *Roy and Malaurie v France*, October 3, 2000, ECHR 2000–X, para.34; *News Verlags GmbH & CoKG v Austria*, January 11, 2000, ECHR 2000–I, para.56.

[89] (14132/88) (Dec.) April 13, 1989, 61 D.R. 285.

[90] (11553/85) and (11658/85), fn.16 above.

appreciation in regulating the freedom of the press to transmit court hearings live. Thus it was compatible with Art.10 to refuse a radio station permission to transmit a murder trial live on radio, where the restriction applied to the media as a whole and steps had been taken to give access to the press on a non-discriminatory basis.[91]

As indicated by the Birmingham Six and Channel Four examples above, television journalism has an impact and immediacy which sometimes attracts interference from State authorities anxious to protect from nefarious influences. The Commission accepted the necessity felt by both the Irish and UK Governments to prevent any television exposure of members of the Sinn Fein (and other groups) which might serve the ends of the violent terrorists with whom they were purportedly linked. In *Purcell v Ireland*,[92] the measure prevented coverage of, inter alia, Sinn Fein members by way of interviews or recordings on any subject. In finding the restriction proportionate, the Commission stated that the defeat of terrorism was a public interest of the utmost importance and referred to the difficulty of striking a fair balance where advocates of this violence seek access to the media for publicity purposes. It was noted that TV and radio were media of considerable power and influence and that their opportunity to correct, qualify or comment was more limited compared to the press. It was also relevant that the ban, although inconvenient, did not in fact prevent them from producing news items on any subject. Regarding a similar ban in the United Kingdom which allowed coverage of live interviews on TV but with use of actors' voice-overs, the Commission observed that there was no restriction as to the words or images transmitted and while the logic of the voice-over might be open to dispute, it could be regarded as one aspect of a very important area of domestic policy, namely, combating terrorism.[93]

As regards photographs published of accused, the prohibition on the publication by an Austrian newspaper of the photograph of a suspect in pending proceedings had not been shown to be necessary either to protect him against defamation or against violation of the presumption of innocence.[94] Nor were there sufficient reasons to render a journalist liable in damages for breach of privacy where the name and photograph of an accused was published while criminal proceedings were pending. The Court noted that there was an issue of public interest at stake, namely, abuse of public funds, and considered that the domestic courts had not given weight to the fact that the photograph published had been first made available in another publication with the complainant's consent and the information was largely based on the bill of indictment, clearly indicating that the person concerned had merely been charged.[95] These last cases are perhaps hard to reconcile with the approach in *Egeland and Hanseid v Norway*, where there was no violation where newspaper editors were fined for publishing photographs of a criminal suspect shortly after conviction and in a state of distress. Norwegian law gave particular protection to persons not in "a state of control" and the courts also invoked the aim of safeguarding the judicial process. It may have been judicial restraint on the Court's part not to interfere with the domestic courts' weighing of the interests in respect of an invasive, not very newsworthy, photograph.[96]

[91] *P4 Radio Hele Norge ASA v Norway*, (76682/01) (Dec.) May 6, 2003.
[92] *Purcell*, fn.17 above.
[93] (18714/91) (Dec.) May 9, 1994, 77 D.R. 42.
[94] *News Verlags GmbH*, fn.88 above.
[95] *Eerikainan v Finland*, April 16, 2009.
[96] *Egeland and Hanseid v Norway*, April 16, 2009.

The public interest in receiving information about criminal proceedings requires that newspapers have an effective opportunity to challenge court orders prohibiting the reporting of proceedings. Informal procedures, even if flexible, do not offer sufficient safeguards, where there is no right as such to be heard or for hearings to be publicly notified.[97]

(III) Journalistic sources

Journalists may claim some protection in their role as public watchdogs, in particular as regard protection of their sources.[98] This does not extend to an immunity from providing information or film when ordered to do so by a court which considers the material relevant in criminal proceedings.[99] However in *Goodwin v UK*, where a journalist was fined for contempt of court for refusing to identify the source of his information about a private company's confidential financial report, the Court found that the £5,000 fine for contempt of court was a restriction on his freedom of expression and that the coercion exerted on a journalist risked having a chilling effect on future reporting and the willingness of sources to give information. Safeguards to the press were seen as of particular importance in maintaining freedom of expression in the interests of a democratic society. Thus, limitations on the confidentiality of journalistic sources called for the most careful scrutiny. Since an injunction had effectively stopped the leak through the press, the alleged need to uncover the source to obtain the missing plan and prevent other possible leaks was not sufficient in the balance against the vital public interest in the protection of journalistic sources. The malicious conduct or bad faith of a source in intending damage through leaking information can never be decisive; even where there is an allegation that the information was deliberately distorted or falsified, courts should be slow to assume the truth of one-side assertions by the aggrieved party. The Court found no distinction between an obligation to reveal the identity of a source or the documents that might lead to the identification of the source, since either will have a chilling effect. [100] II–417

Detaining for over two weeks a journalist who refused to name his source of information allegedly disclosing wrongdoing by the police was regarded as going far too far. The Court was not impressed that the source was needed to prevent a miscarriage of justice, noting that the courts found other witnesses who could give evidence; nor did it find that the authorities had an interest to know which police officer might have been the source.[101] An order by a public prosecutor requiring disclosure of a CD-ROM containing photographs of an illegal road race in respect of which the newspaper had promised the participants confidentiality was regarded as a violation on the procedural ground that domestic law failed to provide the requisite independent examination of whether the interests of the criminal investigation outweighed journalistic protection of sources.[102]

[97] *Mackay and BBC Scotland v UK*, December 7, 2010.

[98] e.g. *Roemen and Schmit v Luxembourg*, February 25, 2003, ECHR 2003–IV, para.46.

[99] Where the BBC were summonsed to produce a film of a riot, the Commission found that it was a normal civic duty to give evidence and it was not satisfied that this would result in greater risk to camera crews beyond that already incurred in filming such episodes: (25978/94) (Dec.) January 18, 1996, 84–A D.R. 129.

[100] *Financial Times Ltd v UK*, December 15, 2009, violation for a disclosure order of a leaked document concerning a potential takeover bid even though it had affected the stock market prices of the companies concerned.

[101] *Voskuil v Netherlands*, November 22, 2007.

[102] *Sanoma Uitgevers BV v Netherlands*, September 14, 2010, ECHR 2010–. . .

There is a distinction between ordering disclosure of journalistic sources who have voluntarily given information and research material, such as footage taken of people unaware. The "chilling effect" consideration did not apply to the latter and disclosure could more easily be justified for the purposes of prevention of crime.[103]

(iv) Searches and seizures

II–418 Searches targeting journalists are regarded as even more serious. In *Roemen and Schmidt v Luxembourg*, Art.10 was breached where the authorities conducted a search of a journalist's home and office seeking to discover sources of leaked information concerning a government minister.[104] It would seem therefore that only an overriding requirement in the public interest, perhaps to prevent a serious crime or unmask the perpetrator of a serious crime, would justify coercive measures taken to identify journalistic sources. However, the right of protection of journalistic sources has been emphasised as attaching to even illicit sources and even where there was an accusation that a journalist had committed an offence of corruption in using bribes to obtain the leaked information from a public official, the Court condemned not only the fact that the search led to an indiscriminate seizure of large amounts of the journalist's materials but also that it was geared to identify the source rather than pursue a purported criminal investigation.[105]

(v) Travel and movement

II–419 Public order measures preventing journalists attending particular places or events may raise issues. The Court found that police action stopping a bus on its way to Davos for the World Economic Forum interfered with the freedom of expression of the journalist on board intending to report on aspects of the forum. Whether the measure could have been justified by needs of security and prevention of disorder was not resolved as there was a violation due to the lack of lawfulness of the police action.[106]

While there is no right for foreigners to be granted entry to a country, immigration controls must be exercised in conformity with Convention rights, including Art.10. Where therefore an American lecturer was banned from re-entering Turkey to continue teaching in university due to her expression of views on the Armenian genocide and treatment of Kurds, the Court found this was an unjustified interference with her freedom of expression.[107]

(vi) Confidential or unlawfully obtained material

II–420 Where journalists deliberately breach confidentiality, sanctions may be found justified. Where a parliamentary journalist was convicted and fined for publishing a confidential parliamentary document, the Commission found the measure could be

[103] *Nordisk Film & TV A/S v Denmark*, (40485/02) (Dec.) December 8, 2005, concerning film and notes taken by a journalist investigating paedophile networks.

[104] The Court noted that there were other methods by which the authorities could have pursued the leaks, i.e. questioning the civil servants concerned. Similar violation also found in *Ernst v Belgium*, July 15, 2003, where sweeping search warrants were issued to uncover sources of leaks from judicial investigation files.

[105] *Tillack v Belgium*, November 27, 2007.

[106] *Gsell v Switzerland*, October 8, 2009, the authorities claimed to be acting on a very general and indistinct provision of law and did not distinguish between those likely to offer violence and those not.

[107] *Cox v Turkey*, May 20, 2010, there was nothing to support allegations of security grounds for her exclusion.

justified for preventing disclosure of material received in confidence and was not disproportionate since the applicant was an accredited journalist who had known the document was confidential and use of penalties was aimed at maintaining the credibility of the system.[108] However, convictions of journalists in *Fressoz and Roire* for breach of professional confidence in respect of their use of confidential tax documents but whose contents were in the public domain was not considered proportionate. Nor was conviction for incitement to reveal official secrets of a journalist who obtained information about prior convictions of suspects in a high profile case from a willing official, such information also being available in judicial decisions and old newspapers.[109]

Accounting for profits on publication of confidential material was held justifiable in the *Spycatcher* case.[110] While *The Times* alleged a vital public interest in the information about Government misdeeds, the Commission found no problem as the interference with newspaper's freedom of expression was minor, there was no prior restraint and few profits to account for and the information was obtained from an employee bound by confidentiality, which *The Times* had deliberately and knowingly published.

The fact that material may have been obtained unlawfully by third parties does not deprive the media of its Art.10 protection, where there is no indication of unlawfulness or bad faith on the part of the journalists and the matter is one of public interest.[111]

(VII) Financial privileges and obligations to make amends

Withdrawal from a magazine of preferential fiscal and postal rates was an interference but not disproportionate, given that it encouraged use of unproven therapies for serious illnesses and was not prevented from continuing to publish.[112] II–421

Nor was it a chilling effect on a periodical for it to be required to publish a press release from the relatives of a murdered official indicating that the photographs of his dead body in the street had been published without their consent and that it had breached their right to privacy.[113]

[108] (10343/83) (Dec.) October 6, 1983, 35 D.R. 224. See also *Leempoel & S.A. Ed. Ciné Revue v Belgium*, November 9, 2006, measures to prevent publication of confidential material from a parliamentary inquiry, also relevant to an investigating judge's defence, were justified, the public interest being protected by the public nature of the inquiry. *Stoll v Switzerland*, December 10, 2007, fine of journalist for disclosing a confidential diplomatic document was proportionate, given the truncated and misleading way it was used.

[109] *Dammann v Switzerland*, April 25, 2006, the journalist had decided not to publish the information and there was no identifiable damage to third parties. See also *Dupuis v France*, fn.77 above, conviction of journalists for using confidential material from a pending criminal investigation in a book was disproportionate: it was a matter of political controversy of high public interest, a lot of the information was likely to be in the public domain already, and the journalists were fulfilling their role of public watchdog.

[110] (14644/89) (Rep.) October 8, 1991, 73 D.R. 41. See also *Blake v UK*, (68890/01) (Dec.) October 25, 2005, where it was not disproportionate to hold the ex-spy accountable for profits linked to a breach of confidentiality and his own serious criminal misconduct.

[111] *Radio Twist A.S. v Slovakia*, December 19, 2006, violation where a radio programme broadcasted a taped telephone conversation between two ministers and was required to air an apology and pay compensation.

[112] *Vérités Santé Pratique SARL v France*, (74766/01) (Dec.) December 1, 2005.

[113] *Hachette Filipachi Associés v France*, June 14, 2007, the courts imposed this requirement rather than ordering the seizure of the magazines.

5. Broadcast licensing and programming

Key case-law:

II–422 *Groppera Radio v Switzerland*, March 28, 1990, Series A, No.173, 12 E.H.R.R. 321; *Autronic AG v Switzerland*, May 22, 1990, Series A, No.178, 12 E.H.R.R. 485; *Informatsverein Lentia v Austria*, November 24, 1993, Series A, No.276, 17 E.H.R.R. 93; *VgT Verein Gegen Tierfabriken v Switzerland*, June 28, 2001, ECHR 2001–VI; *Murphy v Ireland*, July 10, 2003.

Article 10 contains specific reference in the third sentence of the first paragraph to the provision not preventing States from requiring the licensing of broadcasting, television or cinema enterprises. Briefly, national licensing systems are accepted as necessary for the orderly regulation of broadcasting enterprises and to give effect to international rules. Licensing is for the purpose of organising the technical aspects primarily. However, even where the licensing fulfills that function, it must still satisfy the requirements of para.2.[114] According to the Commission, the third sentence only applied to broadcasting, not to receipt of broadcasts whereas the Court found no need to decide since, even if it was applicable, there still had to be compliance with the requirements of the second paragraph.[115]

There is a recognition that restrictions should be minimal, with a presumption in favour of free access to transmissions.[116] Where a monopoly is imposed, even if it can be said to contribute to the quality and balance of programmes and be consistent with third sentence, it may not prove to be justified in terms of the second paragraph, particularly since it requires a pressing need to justify such a severe restriction. A refusal of a licence to broadcast will constitute an interference that must be justified in terms of the third sentence of the first paragraph and the second paragraph, even if the refusal is in the context of a tender system.[117] A system which gives only vague indications of reasons for refusal without procedural safeguards of accountability and judicial review preventing arbitrariness will offend the lawfulness criterion.[118]

Pluralism is a key consideration in this area, with the State acting as an ultimate guarantor that television and radio media are not dominated by one voice. Where the State itself sets up a public broadcasting service, particularly where it is the dominant player, the State must still ensure that it provides the public with impartial and accurate information and a range of opinion and comment, reflecting the diversity of political outlook within the country and that journalists and other

[114] e.g. *Tele 1 Privatsfernsehgesellschaft MBH v Austria*, September 21, 2000.

[115] In *Groppera Radio v Switzerland*, March 28, 1990, Series A, No.173, 12 E.H.R.R. 321, a ban on cable re-transmission of radio programmes in Switzerland from an unlicensed Italian station fell within the third sentence and pursued the legitimate aim of protecting the international telecommunications order and the rights of others (those stations with licences).

[116] See *Autronic AG v Switzerland*, May 22, 1990, Series A, No.178, 12 E.H.R.R. 485, para.61, where the Court stated that rejections should not be manifestly arbitrary or discriminatory and the necessity for any restriction convincingly established. It found no necessity to refuse authorisation to receive uncoded Russian television programmes which concerned no confidential information and were aimed at the general public.

[117] See *Meltex Ltd and Movsesyan v Armenia*, June 7, 2008, para.74.

[118] See *Glas Nadezhda Eood v Bulgaria*, October 11, 2007, paras 45–51. See also the violation in *Meltex Ltd and Movsesyan*, fn.117 above, no reasons given for refusal, lack of transparency in the tender system.

professionals working in the audiovisual media are not prevented from imparting this information and comment. In a case where senior television journalists and editors had complained that on election the Communist Government had inserted their own staff to control programming, the Court found a violation of Art.10 in that the applicable law did not ensure sufficient independence of the public service or provide safeguards against intervention in editorial policy by the ruling party.[119]

In *Informatsverein Lentia v Austria*, a violation arose in circumstances where it was impossible to set up a private radio or TV station. The argument that this was necessary to prevent private monopolies was not, in the Court's view, borne out by other European countries of comparable size. Quality and variety could be maintained by other means (licensing conditions, etc.); there was no technical need for restrictions as frequencies were available; and the raison d'etre of rigid monopoly no longer held since transmissions entered from other countries. However, where a terrestrial television broadcasting monopoly was mitigated by the ability of private broadcasters to create and transmit programmes via the cable net, the refusal of a territorial licence was no longer disproportionate.[120] A ban on applications for national radio broadcasting licence by religious bodies was justified to prevent any one group predominating and proportionate in the circumstances as they could apply for local licences.[121] Ban on a particular station broadcasting for up to a year was justified by its airing of programmes which incited violence and hatred.[122]

Some preferential treatment may be acceptable. The Dutch system of offering regional frequencies on a priority basis to public TV broadcasting organisations was compatible with the third sentence, and pursued the legitimate aim of maintaining pluralism, diversity and non-commercialism for audiences in the area.[123]

Regarding restrictions on the broadcasting of particular programmes, the Court found objectionable a ban on political advertising that prevented the airing of the applicant association's commercial denouncing the industrial farming of pigs. Although it found that the ban pursued the legitimate aim of preventing financially powerful groups from obtaining a competitive advantage, it placed emphasis on the need for convincing reasons to restrict participation in an ongoing public debate. As the association in question was not a powerful body which could endanger independent broadcasting or unduly influence public opinion, no "relevant and sufficient" grounds had been shown to arise in the particular case.[124] Where some years later, despite the Court's judgment, the applicant's commercial had still not been aired, the Court found a new violation, rejecting the argument that it might offend or upset the meat-eating public or meat producers, freedom of expression covering even shocking material. Insofar as the domestic courts had considered that the applicant had not shown that with the passage of time it still had an interest in airing the commercial, the Court considered that this rather fell within the applicant's purview; anyway the courts had not indicated how time could have effected the relevance of the subject matter.[125] It also struck down a blanket ban on political advertising which had led to a TV station being fined for airing commercials

[119] *Manole v Moldova*, September 17, 2009.

[120] *Tele 1 Privatfernsehgesellschaft MBH*, fn.114 above, paras 36–41.

[121] *United Christian Broadcasters v UK*, (44802/98) (Dec.) November 7, 2000.

[122] *Medya FM Reha Radyo Ve Iletism Hizmetleri A.S. v Turkey*, (32842/02) (Dec.) November 14, 2006.

[123] (25987/94) (Dec.) November 29, 1995, 84–A D.R. 149.

[124] *VgT Verein Gegen Tierfabriken v Switzerland*, June 28, 2001, ECHR 2001–VI.

[125] *VgT Verein Gegen Tierfabriken v Switzerland (No.2)* (GC), June 30, 2009.

for a small party that otherwise did not get much coverage. The Court was not impressed by arguments as to the general aims of the ban in preventing abuse by the richer parties, since this did not in fact apply to the case in hand; it was not persuaded either that a case-by-case approach rather than a blanket ban was not viable.[126]

However in *Murphy v Ireland*, concerning a ban on religious advertising, the Court found no violation arising from the refusal to air on radio an advertisement about a presentation on the Resurrection. It found a wider margin of appreciation was to be accorded to the authorities in the sphere of morals and religion than in political speech and had regard to the divisiveness of religion in the history of Ireland, the limitation of the ban to broadcast media and the distinctly partial objectives of advertising, in finding that the Irish State could pursue the policy of a "level playing field" for all religions in the medium with the most powerful impact.

6. Artistic, cinematic, theatrical and literary

Key case-law:

II–423 *Muller v Switzerland*, May 24, 1988, Series A, No.133, 13 E.H.R.R. 212; *Otto Preminger Institute v Austria*, September 20, 1994, Series A, No.295, 19 E.H.R.R. 34; *Wingrove v UK*, November 25, 1996, R.J.D. 1996–V, No.23, 24 E.H.R.R. 1.

There have been few cases, authorities perhaps feeling their interests less challenged by works of art. The nature of the form of artistic expression may mean that it has a very limited audience, without the impact of mass media and that may affect the seriousness of any alleged risk to public disorder flowing from it.[127]

Controversy tends to arise where the "work" provokes religious or moral outrage. Freedom to receive and impart information and ideas includes the opportunity to take part in the public exchange of cultural, political and social information and ideas of all kinds, including artistic expression.[128] Artists cannot claim an unlimited freedom however but are subject to duties and responsibilities under the second paragraph of Art.10. In *Otto Preminger v Austria*, the Court stated that these included an obligation to avoid gratuitously offending others and infringing their rights, since this could not contribute to any public debate capable of furthering progress in human affairs. This approach would appear to place a strict burden on artists to avoid offending, since what is or is not gratuitous may be rather subjective, as shown in the *Otto Preminger* case, where the Court appeared to agree with the authorities that the provocativeness of the film outweighed the artistic merits, while the Commission took the view that the satirical elements predominated.

A wide margin of appreciation is generally afforded by the Court to Contracting States when regulating freedom of expression in relation to matters liable to offend intimate personal convictions within the sphere of morals, or especially, religion.[129] The Court considers that there is no uniform concept of morals, or of the requirements of the protection of religious beliefs, which differ from place to place

[126] *TV Vest AS Rogaland and Pensjonistparti v Norway*, December 11, 2008.
[127] *Karatas v Turkey*, July 8, 1999, ECHR 1999–IV, para.52, where a poet was given allowance for his colourful imagery that would have limited impact; *Arslan v Turkey*, July 8, 1999, para.48, similar approach to impact of a literary work.
[128] *Muller v Switzerland*, May 24, 1988, Series A, No.133, 13 E.H.R.R. 212, para.27.
[129] e.g. *Wingrove v UK*, November 25, 1996, R.J.D. 1996–V, No.23, 24 E.H.R.R. 1, para.58.

and time to time. Local State authorities which are in direct and continuous contact with the vital forces of their country are thus, in principle, in a better position to give an opinion on the exact contents of these requirements as well as the necessity of the measures designed to meet them.[130] It found in *Muller v Switzerland*, where a painter and exhibitors were convicted for displaying paintings depicting sexual acts, that the domestic court's view that the emphasis on sexuality in some of its cruder forms was "liable grossly to offend the sense of sexual propriety of persons of ordinary sensitivity" was not unreasonable. It was not persuaded by the applicant's arguments that there had been no public outcry[131] and that he had been able to exhibit abroad and other areas of Switzerland without trouble. The Court was also influenced by the factor that the paintings were open to the public at large without restriction.

There was arguably more public outrage in *Otto Preminger*, where the Salzburg authorities, at the prompting of the Catholic diocese, ordered the seizure and forfeiture of a film about to be shown portraying God, Christ and the Virgin in a satirical manner. The Court emphasised the protection of religious beliefs and the responsibility of the State to ensure the peaceful enjoyment of those rights under Art.9. It accordingly found that the measure pursued the legitimate aim in protecting others from being insulted in their religious feelings. The seizure was necessary since there was a high proportion of Catholics in Tyrol (87 per cent), and although the film was only open to adults, there had been sufficient publicity about the film for the public to have an idea about its subject-matter and to render the proposed screening "public" enough to cause offence. The Court considered that the authorities had weighed up the artistic elements against offensiveness and it could not disagree with their view of the provocativeness of film. Consequently, the measures taken to ensure religious peace in the region and protect persons who might feel under attack, were within the margin of appreciation of the authorities.[132]

The element of risk to public outrage and religious peace was nevertheless absent from *Wingrove v UK*, where a short video did not pass the British Board of Film Classification on grounds that it was blasphemous in its portrayal of Christ in a sexual context. The Court however found that the decision pursued the legitimate aim of protecting the rights of others not to be offended in their religious beliefs. Having regard to the wide margin of appreciation and the particular contents of the film, the decision was not found arbitrary or unreasonable. It did not accept that argument that such a video could be restricted in its distribution by its classification, since once videos were marketed they were commonly lent, copied and otherwise escaped any regulation.[133]

As concerns novels and literary works, the Court has given recognition to the notion of a European literary heritage to which access should not be barred. Where

[130] *Muller*, fn.128 above, para.35; *Wingrove*, fn.129 above, para.58; (17634/91) (Dec.) September 2, 1991, conviction of artist and gallery owner for outraging public decency by the display of freeze-dried foetus earrings as a sculpture was justified—given the wide margin of appreciation in the area of morals and the public element of the display: no issue arose from the lack of a defence of artistic merit.

[131] There had been some complaints—one man had thrown a painting on the floor and stamped on it.

[132] The Court found no violation by six to three, while the Commission majority voted for violation, noting that the film was based on a play freely available in shops and was only open to an interested, fee-paying adult audience.

[133] See also the *Gay News case*, (8710/79) (Dec.) May 7, 1982, 28 D.R. 77, where there was a conviction for blasphemy for a poem detailing homosexual acts by Christ, the Commission found it compatible for a State to prohibit attacks of a particular severity on others' beliefs, noting that the material was available to the general public and that the judicial authorities found it blasphemous after a thorough investigation.

a translation into Turkish of a work by Apollinaire, an acknowledged classic work included in the prestigious French *Pléiade* collection and available widely in Europe, led to criminal proceedings against the publisher for obscenity, the Court gave greater weight to the cultural elements than to any perceived shock or offensiveness within Turkey due to the graphic sexual content. The fine and seizure of the books thus were not found justified.[134] It has also been said that a novel is a "creation of the imagination" contributing to the exchange of ideas and opinions, on which the State should not encroach unduly. Since this form of expression appeals to a narrower audience than the media, the limited extent of any potential damage should be taken into account. Thus it was not per se objectionable to use a real political figure, Jean-Marie Le Pen in a fictional setting in order to attack what he stood for. However, perhaps surprisingly, the Court accepted the domestic court's approach in requiring some basic verification of the alleged underlying facts and a sufficiently dispassionate approach. Thus, it found the conviction of a writer and a publisher for passages asserting the politician was head of a gang of killers and a vampire thriving on the bitterness of the electorate was not disproportionate, considering it permissible in political debate to ensure a minimum of moderation.[135]

No special protection however attaches to autobiographies as such. The refusal of the prison authorities to pass on to a convicted murderer his manuscript about his various murders and mutilations was found amply justified by considerations of protecting the victims' families and preventing public outrage at such publication which, the Court agreed, could be seen as an affront to human dignity. It distinguished the murderer's self-justifying writings from a serious academic or criminological study of his crimes.[136] This case may be contrasted with a French one, in which author and publishers of military memoirs of a senior officer involved in the Algerian wars were found guilty by domestic courts of justifying war crimes. The Court considered that the memoirs offered direct testimony of a participant in controversial events and thus contributed to an important public debate, even if at times it sought to argue that torture and atrocities had been inevitable. It did not consider that the publishers should have distanced themselves from the contents; on the other hand, its finding that the presentation of the book had not sought to glorify the author as a hero, perhaps hints that a more subjective and polemical presentation might have offended. The passage of some 40 years from events was also considered as rendering the subject less sensitive.[137]

It is relatively rare that theatrical performances are banned by the authorities for their alleged political agenda. Where a theatre troupe were intending to perform a play in Kurdish, the authorities took the view, given some actors had criminal records for separatist or other offences, that it would be used as an occasion to encourage support of the PKK. The Court required some evidential indication that public order issues would arise; it noted that the play had already been performed by the applicants without any incident and there was nothing to support the allegation that the play would be used as a pretext for another agenda.[138]

[134] *Akdas v Turkey*, February 16, 2010.

[135] *Lindon, Otchakovsky-Laurens and July v France*, October 22, 2007, paras 47–59. Contrast the persuasive dissent of Presidents Rozakis, Tulkens and Bratza and Judge Sikuta which homed in on the domestic courts' essential failure to treat the novel as an artistic creation, imposing on it a set of rigid rules not appropriate to this mode of expression. In their view, politicians known for the virulence of their own discourse had to accept a high degree of tolerance vis-à-vis the reactions that they provoke.

[136] *Nilsson v UK*, (36882/05) (Dec.) March 9, 2010.

[137] *Orban, Le Bartillat and Editions Plon v France*, fn.10 above.

[138] *Ulusoy*, fn.18 above, paras 47–53.

7. Pornography

Key case-law:

Scherer v Switzerland, March 25, 1994, Series A, No.287, 18 E.H.R.R. 276. II–424

Criminal measures taken in respect of sale, distribution or trade in pornographic materials were generally found by the Commission to conform with the requirements of Art.10 as being necessary for the prevention of crime or the protection of morals.[139]

A key factor is whether the pornographic material is on display to the general public or suitably restricted to those adults interested. In *Scherer v Switzerland*, the Commission found a violation arose from the conviction of a porn shop owner for showing obscene homosexual films in part of his premises that was not open to the public where there was no question of the protection of morals of adults generally as none were confronted unintentionally with the material.[140] There were no particularly compelling reasons for the prosecution given. This case distinguished an early application rejected as inadmissible where the measures related to a chain of video shops open to the general public.[141] Protective measures aimed at children will be easier for the authorities to justify. No violation was disclosed by the criminal prosecution and seizures in respect of *The Little Red Schoolbook* in *Handyside,* which contained factual and useful information on sex education but also passages capable of being interpreted as encouragement to indulge in activities harmful for children or even to commit criminal offences. Similarly, it was not disproportionate to convict an applicant for obscene material viewable on his internet preview site, the Court dismissing arguments that other similar material was easily available on the internet or that there were other methods of restricting access of young people to such sites.[142]

8. Internet

Cases touching on freedom of expression as affected by the internet are a recent phenomenon. That the internet has an important role to play in enhancing the public's access to news and the dissemination of information generally has been acknowledged by the Court.[143] II–425

When *The Times* was held liable for each time an article was accessed on its website, the Court rejected its argument that a single publication rule was required to prevent a chilling effect on the maintenance of internet archive material, in other words that the provider could only be held liable when the article was placed on the website. Notwithstanding the importance for education and research of the

[139] (9615/81) (Dec.) March 5, 1983, 32 D.R. 231, seizure of magazines destined for overseas markets was justified for protection of morals, not as safeguarding those outside the jurisdiction, but as a legitimate concern to stop the UK becoming the centre of the flourishing export trade.

[140] Case was struck off before the Court when the applicant died.

[141] (16564/90) (Dec.) April 8, 1991.

[142] *Perrin*, fn.81 above, a prison sentence was proportionate given the commercial nature of the site and the lack of any contribution to public debate.

[143] *Times Newspaper (Nos 1 and 2) v UK*, March 10, 2009, para.27.

accessible and free archives now online, the Court considered that a wider margin of appreciation applied to historical materials than to the reporting of current affairs. It also noted that it was open to the newspapers operating such sites to attach a notice warning as to the truth of the archive copies, a not very onerous condition, and that the newspaper in this case had failed to do, even when the first action had been brought. Nor had there been, in the Court's view, any real chilling effect or any real problem of continuous liability. Thus, the interference was not disproportionate. The Court did, however, warn that proceedings brought by an aggrieved person against a newspaper after a significant lapse of time might no longer be justified, thus hinting that in practice repeated libel actions based on archive materials would not be acceptable under Art.10.[144]

Use of internet material by journalists should also be regulated by domestic law in order for them to enjoy the usual protections for freedom of expression. Thus where a newspaper was held liable for defamation for reproducing a letter from a website, as the civil law exemption for journalistic accurate reproduction of material did not apply to the internet, the Court found a lack of adequate legal safeguards.[145]

9. Parliamentary and electoral context

Key case-law:

II–426 *Castells v Spain*, April 23, 1992, Series A, No.236, 14 E.H.R.R. 445; *Piermont v France*, April 27, 1995, Series A, No.314, 20 E.H.R.R. 301; *Ahmet Sadik v Greece*, November 15, 1996, R.J.D. 1996–V, No.15, 24 E.H.R.R. 323; *Bowman v UK*, February 19, 1998, R.J.D. 1998–I, No.63, 26 E.H.R.R. 1; *Jerusalem v Austria*, February 27, 2001–II.

The importance of freedom of expression for those participating in the democratic process has been affirmed. The requirement for elected representatives to be able to participate freely in political debate received recognition in *Castells v Spain*, where a conviction of a senator for an article on the Basque situation which "insulted" the Government disclosed a violation. The Court found that freedom of expression was "especially important" for an elected representative who represents his electorate and defends their interests. This applied to political debate inside and outside the legislature, any interferences calling for the closest scrutiny. The Court further considered that it was permissible to criticise governments more widely than in relation to private citizens and that governments should show restraint in resorting to criminal proceedings. While it might be compatible to take action against defamatory accusations devoid of factual basis or formulated in bad faith, in the case itself, the senator had not been afforded the chance to prove the factual basis of the article was true.

Special privileges for Parliamentarians by way of immunity from suit have been found compatible with the Convention.[146] In *A and Others v UK*, the absolute immunity from suit enjoyed by members of Parliament for statements made within Parliament was found to be justified under Arts 6 and 8 by the crucial importance of

[144] *Times Newspaper (Nos 1 and 2)*, fn.143 above, paras 44–50.
[145] *Editorial Board of Pravoye Delo and Shtekel v Ukraine*, May 5, 2011, paras 60–68.
[146] See Pt IIB, s.8: Defamation and the right to reputation.

freedom of political debate by the elected representatives of the people. The Court stated that very weighty reasons were required to justify interference with freedom of expression within the legislative forum. In *Jerusalem v Austria*, where an elected politician was sued for an alleged defamatory speech in a council meeting not covered by parliamentary immunity, the Court considered that the statements which were issued during a debate on a matter of public concern attracted the protection of Art.10. On the other hand, blanket immunity to statements made outside the parliamentary context or outside the scope of parliamentary activity went too far.[147] Indeed, liability in civil suit of a MP for untrue factual statements made outside parliament was not disproportionate.[148] Nor can Parliamentarians claim any special protection for their own private life. Increased penalties for the invasion of an MP's privacy were not considered proportionate, where the impugned articles had no bearing on the MP's performance of her parliamentary duties and were minimally invasive.[149]

Article 10 also extends to visiting European Union Parliamentarians. Measures to expel and prohibit the entry to French Polynesia of a German MEP invited by a political party to be present at elections were not justifiable, notwithstanding the tense political atmosphere at the time, since the meeting had been peaceful, no disorder had arisen from the visit and her views had been a contribution to the existing local democratic debate in Polynesia.[150]

Where it is considered that an elected MP is expressing views that are dangerously provocative, States must still react in a suitable and adequate manner, using the means usually available in a democratic State. While the Commission noted in *Sadik v Greece*[151] that moderation in political debate may be desirable, to avoid, for example, exacerbating ethnic tensions, the imposition of a prison sentence on a MP for words used in an election campaign could not be regarded as proportionate in the absence of clear elements of incitement to violence.[152]

In the context of election campaigns, the rules may legitimately limit expenditure to ensure equality between candidates. However, in *Bowman v UK*, where an anti-abortion campaigner was prosecuted for distributing leaflets about particular electoral candidates' views on abortion and related issues, the Court found it disproportionate to impose, through a £5 limit, what was effectively a total barrier on her participation in the electoral debate, particularly where there was no limit on the press to support or oppose any particular candidate or on parties or their supporters to advertise on a national level.

9. Threats to national security and public safety

Key case-law:

Zana v Turkey, November 25, 1997, R.J.D. 1997–VII, No.57, 27 E.H.R.R. 667; *Incal v Turkey*, June 9, 1998, R.J.D. 1998–IV, No.78, 29 E.H.R.R. 449; *Sürek v Turkey (No.1)*, July 8, 1999, ECHR 1999–IV; *Karatas v Turkey*, July 8, 1999, ECHR II–427

[147] *Cordova v Italy (No.1)* and *Cordova v Italy (No.2)*, January 30, 2003.

[148] *Keller v Hungary*, (33352/02) (Dec.) April 4, 2006.

[149] *Karhuvaara and Italehti v Finland*, November 16, 2004, ECHR 2004–X.

[150] Cf. (28979/95) and (30343/96), fn.4 above, the exclusion order preventing the Sinn Fein leader from attending a political meeting in London was justified in the context of the fight against terrorism and sensitivity of the peace process.

[151] The Court upheld the Government's preliminary objection on exhaustion.

[152] The words "Turks" or "Turkish" to identify Moslems of Western Thrace did not qualify.

1999–IV; *Ceylan v Turkey*, July 8, 1999, ECHR 1999–IV, 30 E.H.R.R. 73; *Baskaya and Okçuoglu v Turkey*, July 8, 1999, ECHR 1999–IV, 31 E.H.R.R. 10; *Özgür Gündem v Turkey*, March 16, 2000, ECHR 2000–III, 31 E.H.R.R. 49; *Erdogdu v Turkey*, June 15, 2000, ECHR 2000–VI.

Where measures are taken in response to perceived terrorist threats by way of suppressing publications, a certain leeway is accorded to Contracting States in acknowledgment of the seriousness and complexity of the situations that are often involved.[153] In imposing penalties for forms of expression allegedly endangering national security, the domestic courts should, nonetheless, give relevant and sufficient reasons and apply standards in conformity with Art.10 principles.[154]

Thus, the Court has accepted, in the context of southeast Turkey, that steps taken to prosecute and convict a person for statements in support of the PKK (an illegal terrorist organisation) could be said to pursue the legitimate aims of maintaining national security and public safety. Whether the measures could be justified as necessary and proportionate under Art.10, para.2 appear to turn on a consideration of the perceived impact of the statements concerned. In finding a conviction justified in *Zana v Turkey*, the Court noted that there had been serious disturbances in the region at the time and gave weight to the fact that the applicant was a former mayor of Diyarbakir (the principal city of the region) and that his statement gave express support to the PKK as a "national liberation movement" and referred in ambiguous, contradictory terms to PKK massacres as "mistakes". While the applicant did not express approval of violence as such, his words were, in the Court's view, open to several interpretations, and in light of the tensions existing at the time, they could be viewed as likely to exacerbate an already explosive situation.

In following cases, the Court has continued to examine whether the statements subject to criminal proceedings can be regarded as capable of inciting or advocating violence, giving a wide margin of appreciation to the authorities even where the courts have been examining different issues, such as whether the statements had a separatist content.[155] However, as long as the impugned statements could not be construed, by tone, content or context, as inciting violence,[156] the mere fact that interviews or statements contained strongly disparaging views of Government policy or the expression of support for the idea of a separate Kurdish entity, would not justify a conviction.[157] The public had a right to be informed of different perspectives

[153] e.g. *Öztürk v Turkey*, September 29, 1999, para.59, where the Court gave the authorities the benefit of the doubt that a prosecution for publishing a book pursued the legitimate aim of preventing crime and disorder.

[154] e.g. *Kommersant Moldovy v Moldova*, January 9, 2007, where the courts gave no sufficient reasons justifying the closure of the newspaper.

[155] e.g. *Sürek v Turkey (No.1)*, July 8, 1999, ECHR 1999–IV, paras 61–63.

[156] e.g. *Erdogdu v Turkey*, June 15, 2000, ECHR 2000–VI, para.71, "Where a publication cannot be categorised as inciting to violence, Contracting States cannot with reference to the prevention of disorder or crime restrict the right of the public to be informed by bringing the weight of the criminal law to bear on the media."

[157] *Özgür Gündem v Turkey*, March 16, 2000, ECHR 2000–III, 31 E.H.R.R. 49, paras 63 and 70; *Incal v Turkey*, June 9, 1998, R.J.D. 1998–IV, No.78, 29 E.H.R.R. 449, para.50, the appeal to Kurdish citizens to oppose the government through "neighbourhood committees" was not an incitement of violence or hatred; *Ceylan v Turkey*, July 8, 1999, ECHR 1999–IV, 30 E.H.R.R. 73, paras 33–35, the trade union leader's article was virulent in tone but did not encourage the use of armed resistance; *Karatas v Turkey*,

of security problems, however unpalatable that might be to the authorities,[158] just as media professionals had to exercise particular caution in publishing the views of representatives of organisations which resorted to violence to prevent the media becoming a vehicle for hate speech and the promotion of violence.[159] Nor can newspapers disclaim responsibility for the contents of statements by terrorist groups which they publish; they will be accountable if they incite violence.[160] Automatic convictions for reproducing written material of banned organisations, without reasoning or justification in terms of prevention of violence or other legitimate aims, will offend.[161]

The Court has been less than impressed with criminal measures taken against publications on the ground that they have named State officials engaged in fighting terrorism and rendered them targets of retaliation. Where the news articles concerned events of public interest and the information was already, at least in part, in the public domain, it has found insufficient justification.[162] Nor was it justified to convict an applicant for expressing views hostile to the army and conscription where he did not seek to precipitate desertion or incite violence or hatred.[163] Participation in demonstrations allegedly in support of Ocalan and the PKK was not sufficient justification for criminal convictions where there was no element of violence and the applicants themselves were not accused of chanting particular slogans capable of inciting to violence.[164] Chanting slogans, even of a violent tone, did not justify convictions and prison sentences, where carried out in a lawful, non-violent demonstration and without any real element of riot or incitation to violence and insurrection.[165]

Prohibition of a newspaper without reasons given for the decision or any adequate judicial control of the administrative measure was not good enough, even with a certain weight being given to problems of terrorism in the region.[166]

July 8, 1999, ECHR 1999–IV, paras 49–50, the poems were aggressive with "colourful imagery" about self-sacrifice for "Kurdistan" but since poetry is an artistic form of expression with a small audience, they were more an expression of distress than a call to uprising; *Baskaya and Okçuoglu v Turkey*, July 8, 1999, ECHR 1999–IV, 31 E.H.R.R. 10, paras 64–65, the authorities had not had sufficient regard to freedom of academic expression in penalising a socio-economic essay on the Kurdish problem which contained strong criticism of Government policy but did not incite to violence. Contrast *Osmani v FRYOM*, (50841/99) (Dec.) October 11, 2001, where the impugned statements had identifiable effects of incitement, justifying a significant prison sentence; *Sürek (No.1)*, fn.155 above, where the statements were regarded as "hate speech" and the "glorification of violence"; *Sürek v Turkey (No.3)*, July 8, 1999, para.40, where the article expressed a call to armed force, the applicant newspaper owner had provided the writer with an outlet for the stirring up of violence, even if he had not associated himself personally with the views.

[158] e.g. *Baskaya and Okçuoglu*, fn.157 above, para.65; *Sürek and Özdemir v Turkey*, July 8, 1999, para.61, concerning a conviction for publishing interviews with a leader in a proscribed organisation which had newsworthy content.

[159] e.g. *Erdogdu and Ince v Turkey*, July 8, 1999, para.54.

[160] e.g. *Falakaoglu and Saygili v Turkey*, January 23, 2007, para.34.

[161] e.g. *Gözel and Özer v Turkey*, July 6, 2010, penalties included fines and closure of the periodicals for periods of one to two weeks.

[162] *Sürek v Turkey (No.2)*, July 8, 1999, para.40; *Özgür Gündem*, fn.157 above, paras 67–68.

[163] *Ergin v Turkey*, May 5, 2006, para.34.

[164] *Yilmaz and Kilic v Turkey*, July 17, 2008, paras 60–69.

[165] e.g. *Gül v Turkey*, June 8, 2010, the Court considered the chants to be stereotypical left-wing slogans, without any impact on national security or public order.

[166] *Çetin v Turkey*, February 13, 2003, ECHR 2003–III, concerning the banning of a newspaper critical of the Government policy in the region.

However, less drastic measures imposed with a view to stopping the IRA or other groups using the media to express their views were not found, with due regard to a wide margin of appreciation, to fall foul of Art.10. In *Purcell v Ireland*, the Commission found that the exigencies of the situation justified the banning of the airing on television or radio of interviews with or statements by Sinn Fein members; the more bizarre measure of using actors' voice-overs for such interviews was accepted for the United Kingdom.[167]

Where apologies for terrorism are concerned, the Court has noted the principal difficulty in punishing such acts without trespassing on freedom of expression, particularly since the media are entitled to publish views and opinions that offend, shock and provoke. Issues and questions concerning acts of global terrorism are clearly part of a crucial public debate. However, the press must keep to certain limits and the domestic authorities are entitled to have regard to the apparent meaning of the words without reference to the author's intentions. The publication of a cartoon which appeared to support and approve of the 9/11 attacks as culmination of a shared dream was therefore justifiably prosecuted, and a moderate fine was not disproportionate. The Court appeared to give more weight than usual to public sensibilities in the immediate aftermath of the horrific and world-shaking tragedy, on which sensibilities the cartoon would have had considerable impact.[168]

A restrained approach appears to be taken where persons are prosecuted for espionage, the Court not rushing to impose its own interpretation on events. It was not prepared to find incompatible with Art.10 a domestic legal approach to espionage which included non-classified information and information publicly available, not excluding that provision of this information could also be legitimately regarded as potentially damaging to national security. However, in the case concerned, information relative to defence issues had been involved; a ten year sentence was not found disproportionate against a background of wilful involvement with, and collection of information for, the intelligence service of another power.[169]

The Court has also not been unduly sympathetic to protesters who wilfully flout the law and ignore available means of airing grievances. Where the applicant went beyond protest against a ban on supporting the activities of the PKK and a plea that the ban be lifted, signing a declaration that she did not acknowledge the ban and deliberately ignoring it, the Court noted that she was only convicted of contravening the ban, not protesting against it and that instead of applying her protests to the Ministry with power to lift the ban, she had incited thousands of persons to flood the public prosecution with such declarations in a deliberate attempt to overburden that public service. The thorough examination of the issues by the courts and the minor fine imposed were also relevant to the finding of no violation.[170]

The imposition of criminal sanctions for the wearing of controversial symbols is likely to raise issues, however potent the associations. Where a left-wing politician, wearing a red star as emblem of the international workers' movement, was convicted for wearing a symbol of totalitarian oppression, the Court noted that this was not the only connotation of the red star and that even if one of its meanings was obnoxious, this was not enough to equate it with dangerous propaganda

[167] *Purcell*, fn.17 above; see also (18714/91), fn.93 above.
[168] *Leroy v France*, fn.10 above, paras 38–48.
[169] *Bojoylan v Armenia*, (23693/03) (Dec.) November 3, 2009.
[170] *Aydin v Germany*, January 27, 2011, paras 57–63.

requiring criminal measures. There was nothing in fact to indicate any risk, even remote, of public disorder being triggered by the display of the symbol. Sentiments of uneasiness or public feeling, real or imaginary, could not be allowed to set the limits on freedom of expression.[171] The ban on a prisoner wearing an Easter lily (a Republican symbol) outside his cell was found justified to prevent disorder in the prison and to protect prison staff; the setting in a prison where there was an acute risk of disorder was a key element.[172]

10. Advertising and unfair competition

Key case-law:

Barthold v Germany, March 25, 1985, Series A, No.90, 7 E.H.R.R. 383; *Markt Intern Verlag GmbH v Germany*, November 20, 1989, Series A, No.165, 12 E.H.R.R. 161; *Casada Coca v Spain*, February 24, 1994, Series A, No.285–A, 18 E.H.R.R. 1; *Jacubowski v Germany*, June 23, 1994, Series A, No.291, 19 E.H.R.R. 64; *Hertel v Switzerland*, August 25, 1998, R.J.D. 1998–VI, No.87, 28 E.H.R.R. 534. II–428

Commercial speech is covered. Matters relating to professional practice are not removed from the sphere of Art.10 because of the financial element.[173] In *Markt Intern Verlag GmbH v Germany*, the Commission considered that democratic society was based on the articulation of a wide spectrum of views, including those relating to economic interests.[174] It rejected the Government view that Art.10 only covered artistic, religious, political and scientific matters and excluded purely competition-related promotional statements.[175]

Regarding professional rules against press exposure, these appear justifiable, where the penalties are slight and pure advertising is involved. Noting the wide variety of rules throughout Contracting States, the Court has commented that the domestic authorities are in the best place to assess where to strike the balance, special considerations attaching to the role of lawyers in the administration of justice and to doctors with general obligations to health of the community.[176]

In *Barthold v Germany*, the injunction on a vet for making statements in the press was based on a a disproportionately wide prohibition since it covered his expression of views about the problems of emergency night service and might discourage vets from giving their views in public debate and hamper the press in its role as public watchdog.[177] A ban on pure commercial advertising by a lawyer who sent circulars

[171] *Vajnai*, fn.11 above, paras 48–58.

[172] *Donaldson v UK*, (56975/09) (Dec.) January 25, 2011.

[173] *Barthold v Germany*, (Rep.) March 25, 1985, Series A, No.90, 7 E.H.R.R. 383, para.61, the Court did not find it necessary to decide since the article included information and opinions on matters of public concern. The issue was undisputed by the parties in *Stambuk v Germany*, October 17, 2002.

[174] *Markt Intern Verlag GmbH v Germany*, (Rep.) November 20, 1989, Series A, No.165, 12 E.H.R.R. 161, paras 202–203.

[175] See also *Casada Coca*, February 24, 1994, Series A, No.285–A, 18 E.H.R.R. 1, para.35: no distinction between profit-making forms.

[176] *Casada Coca v Spain*, fn.175 above, paras 54–55; *Stambuk*, fn.173 above, paras 40–41, which seems to imply stricter restrictions can apply to lawyers than to doctors however.

[177] See also *Stambuk*, fn.173 above, where the applicant doctor was fined for an interview in the press about new techniques (accompanied by a photograph), the Court considered that that the publicity aspect was secondary and that it impinged on the ability of the press to report on the subject.

to collection agencies was found justified in the interests of clients and the profession and not disproportionate given the lightness of the penalty.[178] A stratagem by which a cosmetic surgeon benefited from the publicity of an intermediary business which directed clients his way led to a disciplinary suspension; this interference was justifiable as part of the duties and obligations attached to the practice of medicine, which was not a commercial enterprise but an integral part of public health protection: the Court rejected the surgeon's argument that such a consideration only applied to reparative, not cosmetic, medicine, noting that cosmetic grafts also involved risks to health.[179] A disciplinary warning given to a lawyer for breaching an advertising ban was not disproportionate in *Casada Coca v Spain*.[180]

Restrictions on publications found by domestic courts to damage commercial interests of others have not been found objectionable. Indeed the Court has stated that a margin of appreciation for the authorities is essential in an area as complex and fluctuating as that of unfair competition,[181] although it will be reduced where what is at stake is not purely "commercial" statements but participation in a debate concerning the public interest, such as public health.[182] In *Markt Intern*, where an injunction was issued against a magazine to prevent publication of critical information about the trading practices of particular enterprises, the Court found that, while large undertakings opened themselves to public scrutiny and specialised press served a legitimate purpose, there were limits on criticism. It gave weight to the fact that the domestic courts had assessed the issues, and the fact that different views were possible did not permit substituting its opinion for that of the domestic courts.[183] An injunction placing detailed restrictions on a newspaper's price-comparison adverts was found not to strike the correct balance, impairing the essence of that type of advertising,[184] while a satirical, mocking response by a magazine mimicking the deliberately shocking publicity campaign of a food company should not have led to an award of damages, since it was a contribution to a public debate provoked by the business itself and not an attack on the commercial interests and reputation of the business as had been found by the courts.[185]

Convictions and fines for indirect publicity or advertising of cigarettes was not found to breach Art.10 where a magazine published a photograph of famous racing drivers who bore logos on their clothing. The important public health interest in not encouraging young persons to smoke was given considerable weight, and in this

[178] (14622/89) (Dec.) March 7, 1991, 69 D.R. 272; in *Stambuk*, fn.173 above, paras 29–30, the ban on advertising by doctors pursued the legitimate aim of protecting the interests of other medical practitioners and the proper regulation of community health.

[179] *Villnow v Belgium*, January 29, 2008.

[180] See also *Colman v UK*, settled before the Court, (16632/90) (Rep.) October 19, 1992, Series A, No.258–D, no violation where a doctor was prevented from newspaper advertising for patients.

[181] *Krone Verlag GmbH & CoKG v Austria*, December 11, 2003, para.30.

[182] e.g. *Hertel v Switzerland*, August 25, 1998, R.J.D. 1998–VI, No.87, 28 E.H.R.R. 534, the conviction of an academic for publication of research setting out alleged risks of microwaves to health was not justified, nor the injunction preventing repetition of these claims. Where in the subsequent case more limited restrictions, i.e. a requirement to add a qualifying statement, were imposed on future publications, the Court found this could be justified under the second paragraph in pursuing the legitimate interests of maintaining fair competition: *Hertel v Switzerland*, (53440/99) (Dec.) January 17, 2002.

[183] See also *Jacubowski v Germany*, June 23, 1994, Series A, No.291, 19 E.H.R.R. 64, where prohibition of a circular on grounds of unfair competition was proportionate.

[184] *Krone Verlag GmbH*, fn.181 above, paras 34–35.

[185] *Kulis and Rozycki v Poland*, October 6, 2010.

context, where the photos were themselves a pre-arranged publicity exercise, not the record of a particular event or sporting moment, it would not have usurped the choice of means of expression if the magazine had blurred or altered the photographs to render the logos illegible.[186] It was irrelevant in another case that the intention of the magazine guilty of the indirect advertising of tobacco logos through photographs was to criticize the sporting stars bearing such logos and the whole sponsorship ethos.[187]

As far as advertising and publicity seeking by non-commercial organisations is concerned, the Court gave a certain leeway to the authorities when they refused an application by the Raelien Movement, an organisation which, inter alia, had the goal of establishing first contact with visiting extra-terrestrials, for authorisation to put up a poster campaign in the public space. Even if the poster seemed harmless enough, the Court accepted that the authorities could take exception to the included reference to a website which arguably sponsored illegal cloning activities and to the organisation's stance on paedophilia and geniocracy. A wide margin of appreciation was held to apply in this context.[188]

11. Research and the academic sphere

The Court has underlined the importance of academic freedom, which comprises the academics' freedom to freely express their opinion and the freedom to distribute knowledge and truth without restriction.[189] This includes the freedom to criticise the institution or system in which they work. Thus where an academic was found liable for defamation for critical comments on academic appointments while giving a paper at a scientific conference, the Court found that the domestic courts had not allowed the academic to seek to prove the factual basis of his allegations or that they were comments made in good faith and had insufficiently justified why the personal rights of the plaintiff, who had not shown any damage to his career or private life, had automatically prevailed over the academic's freedom of expression.[190] II–429

Perhaps not surprisingly, issues arose from the refusal to renew a university professor's post as philosophy lecturer at a catholic university due to the allegation that his "positions" were contrary to catholic doctrine. In the proceedings which he brought challenging the refusal, the courts did not examine the purported basis for the refusal, or enquire into the details of the alleged incompatibility of his positions. The Court found a violation since, due to lack of procedural safeguards, the professor had been unable to counter the allegations against him or vindicate his rights. The procedural emphasis allowed the Court to refrain from confronting the knotty question of whether Art.10 requires that academic institutions, even when run and funded by religious bodies, should refrain from penalising their employees due to the expression of opinions of which their sponsors did not approve.[191]

[186] *Hachette Filipacchi Presse Automobile et Dupuy v France*, March 6, 2009.

[187] *Societé de Conception de Presse et d'Edition et Ponson v France*, March 6, 2009.

[188] *Mouvement Raelien suisse v Switzerland*, January 13, 2011, paras 51–60, pending before the Grand Chamber.

[189] *Sorguc v Turkey*, June 23, 2009, para.35; *Sapan v Turkey*, June 8, 2010, para.34, where, in finding a violation, weight was given to the fact that a seized book referring to a pop idol was based on a doctoral thesis concerning the phenomenon of stardom rather than part of the sensationalist press.

[190] *Sorguc*, fn.189 above, paras 35–40.

[191] *Lombardi Vallauri v Italy*, October 20, 2009. Compare *Schuth v Germany*, and *Obst v Germany*, September 23, 2010, where under Art.8 courts were required to give due protection against dismissal by religious employers due to private life conduct allegedly contrary to their moral teachings: see Pt IIB, s.37: Private Life, sub-s.4: Privacy and protection of private life.

Access to original documentary sources for legitimate historical research was protected by Art.10 as regarded a historian researching the Communist era. The prolonged failure of the Ministry of the Interior to comply with a court order requiring access was seen as a "misuse of power" and thus a measure not "prescribed by law".[192] Conversely, a university researcher cannot, it seems, claim any right to maintain the confidentiality of his own research material where the domestic courts, in line with data access legislation, order that it be made available to other researchers with a legitimate interest and subject to appropriate conditions. The Court rejected the claim of the applicant professor that researchers should enjoy privilege vis-à-vis their subjects as did lawyers with their clients.[193]

The ability of academics and researchers to publish criticism of each other's works was recognised by the Court as an essential part of scientific, intellectual and cultural debate. Thus, where a passage in one book on a cultural and historic monument gave scathing criticism of an earlier work on the same subject, the Court considered that the earlier writer had laid herself open to criticism by publishing her own views. The conviction of the later author for defamation did not sufficiently distinguish between facts and the expression of comment; the imposition of even a token fine of a few euros was not minor given that prison was the sanction for failure to pay.[194]

As in other contexts, where an academic publishes a contribution as part of a debate of the utmost public interest, a high level of protection attaches; a requirement to retract or issue a rectification will affect his credibility and thus have a chilling effect on the academic's role.[195]

Nor can the expression of opinion be a legitimate ground for banning an academic from re-entering a country, without the Government providing relevant and sufficient reasons. Thus, Art.10 was breached where an academic was banned from re-entering Turkey due to her views on controversial subjects.[196]

12. Obligations and restrictions in employment or the professional sphere

Key case-law:

II–430 *Glasenapp v Germany*, August 28, 1986, Series A, No.104, 9 E.H.R.R. 25; *Kosiek v Germany*, August 28, 1986, Series A, No.105, 9 E.H.R.R. 328; *Vogt v Germany*, September 26, 1995, Series A, No.323, 21 E.H.R.R. 205; *Rekvenyi v Hungary*, May 20, 1999, ECHR 1999–III, 30 E.H.R.R. 519; *Guja v Moldova*, February 12, 2008; *Palomo Sanchez v Spain*, September 12, 2011, ECHR 2011. . .

Where a person is bound contractually by reasonable terms of confidentiality or loyalty, measures to suspend or dismiss for breach have generally been compatible,

[192] *Kenedi v Hungary*, May 26, 2009, paras 43–45.

[193] *Gillberg v Sweden*, November 2, 2010, no breaches of Arts 10 or 8 where the applicant university professor was convicted of abuse of office for refusing to make the research materials available (he claimed that he had promised the participants in the paediatric studies anonymity). Pending before the Grand Chamber.

[194] *Azevedo v Portugal*, March 27, 2008.

[195] *Karzai v Hungary*, December 1, 2009, where an historian was ordered to rectify an article analysing the way in which right-wing sources had been rehabilitating a former prime minister and "Jew bashing".

[196] *Cox v Turkey*, fn.107 above.

for example, where a doctor expressed views on abortion objectionable to his Catholic hospital employer,[197] or where civil servants have been penalised for revealing official secrets. General restrictions on participation in political debate and activity may also be acceptable in certain sectors as was found in respect of members of the police in *Rekvenyi v Hungary*, where particular importance was attached to the political neutrality of the police after forty years of communist rule. Nor was it a disproportionate or unjustified interference where the call up of a reserve officer was cancelled due to his membership of a right-wing populist party considered as under suspicion of being disloyal to the Constitution: it was relevant that the applicant had been a full-time lawyer and had not lost his livelihood by the measure and that the measure had been taken against a background where persons of similar leanings had brought the army into damaging disrepute.[198]

In *Vogt v Germany*, however, where the applicant was an appointed civil servant, and a teacher, the Court narrowly found a violation where she was suspended from a post for communist party activities.[199] While it was open to a State to impose a duty of discretion on civil servants, freedom of expression still applied to them. Since she was member of a lawful party, there was no criticism of her work (as regarded the alleged risk of indoctrinating children), the majority found the interference disproportionate.[200] On the other hand, dismissal of a municipal employee for breach of discretion and calling into doubt the integrity of the public service by issuing a statement outside the workplace using terms of approval in reference to the 9/11 attacks was not disproportionate.[201]

Dismissal on the basis of lack of appropriate professional qualification or proper professional conduct does not, without more, infringe Art.10.[202] Failure to promote a police officer to a senior position was an interference with his freedom of expression as it was based on his membership of a party regarded as pursuing anti-constitutional goal, but it was not disproportionate, being less severe than the measure in the *Vogt* case and coming late in his career. The Court seemed also to accept that his political views could legitimately be taken into account in a post with special responsibility towards the public.[203]

Nor can employees claim impunity as to the form and content of their expressed views as concerns reaction by employers where they are unduly offensive and insulting. Dismissal of four applicant trade union activists due to misconduct in

[197] (12242/86) (Dec.) September 6, 1989, 62 D.R. 151.

[198] *Erdel v Germany*, (300677/94) (Dec.) February 13, 2007, reference was also made to the specific historical context in Germany. Similar reasoning where a conscript was subject to early termination of national service due to membership of an extremist party: *Lahr v Germany*, (16912/05) (Dec.) July 1, 2008.

[199] In *Glasenapp v Germany*, August 28, 1986, Series A, No.104, 9 E.H.R.R. 25 and *Kosiek v Germany*, August 28, 1986, Series A, No.105, 9 E.H.R.R. 328, where the applicants, probationary civil servants, were dismissed for expression of particular political views, the Court found no violation on the special consideration that there was no right of entry to the civil service.

[200] Ten votes to nine: the minority gave greater weight to German history, the State's commitment to democratic order and considered that, since the civil service was vital to the proper functioning of the State, it was within its margin of appreciation to insist on conformity to strict rules.

[201] *Kern v Germany*, (26870/04) (Dec.) May 29, 2007.

[202] *Petersen v Germany*, (39793/98) (Dec.) November 22, 2001, ECHR 2001–XII, where, on reunification of Germany, the applicant civil servant was dismissed after scrutiny of his qualifications, which included political, rather than research-based, theses; also *Volkmer v Germany*, (39799/98) (Dec.) November 22, 2001, where a teacher was dismissed not purely for his past political opinions but for abuse of position by using a pupil as a spy.

[203] *Otto v Germany*, (27574/02) (Dec.) November 24, 2005.

publishing offensive cartoons and texts about a manager and fellow employees was found not to be punishing them for their trade union views but for breach of contract as employees; the domestic courts were found to have properly assessed the conflicting interests.[204]

The duty of loyalty and discretion does not apply with as much force to journalists as regards their relationship to their employer due to their role in promoting public debate. Thus, where a television journalist was reprimanded by her employer for criticising programming policy, the Court found the interference unjustified, noting that she had commented on a matter of public interest, that there was a factual basis to her remarks, there was no element of personal or offensive attack and that an overly broad approach had been taken to the contractual requirement to refrain from damaging her employer's good name.[205]

In the context of disciplinary rules of professional etiquette applied to doctors, the Court rejected the argument that matters of professional practice fell outside Art.10. The imposition of a reprimand on a doctor for unethical conduct in issuing a report to a patient which contained criticism of another doctor was an interference with his freedom of expression. While there might be a legitimate requirement for solidarity between doctors, there was also the important interest that patients receive an objective evaluation of their health and treatment previously received; the domestic courts had not assessed the relevant factors, indeed had regarded them as irrelevant, in particular ignoring whether the doctor had been pursuing a socially-justified interest rather indulging in a gratuitous attack.[206]

As regards "whistleblowing", protection of the disclosure of information of public concern has been found to extend to private-law employment relationships as well as the public sector.[207]

In *Guja v Moldova* the Court considered that dismissal for disclosing information was an interference with the freedom to impart information; it rejected the Government argument that the applicant had neither written the leaked letters or the article in the press that disclosed them, or that the dismissal was formally for breach of the internal regulations of the Prosecutor's Office where the applicant worked as a press officer. While the duty of discretion on civil servants must generally be strong, the disclosure by a civil servant of conduct that was illegal or wrongful should be protected in certain circumstances. The relevant factors are whether the civil servant had alternative means of bringing the illegal conduct to book, for example by raising it within the hierarchy, the strength of the public interest, the damage to the public authority, the motive of the whistleblower (vengeance or spite does not attract protection), the authenticity of the information and the penalty imposed on the whistleblower. In the particular case, the Court gave weight to the fact that the applicant's superiors appeared to be complicit in the wrongdoing; further, the issue of administration of justice was of public importance and the applicant had acted in good faith and on principle. The penalty, dismissal, was also regarded as overly severe and likely to have a chilling effect on other civil servants making public any misconduct.

In *Heinisch v Germany*, where a geriatric nurse was dismissed for bringing a criminal complaint against her employer, a nursing home, by way of making public

[204] *Palomo Sanchez v Spain*, September 12, 2011, ECHR 2011. . . , paras 63–77.

[205] *Wojtas-Kaleta v Poland*, July 16, 2009.

[206] *Frankowicz v Poland*, December 16, 2008.

[207] *Heinisch v Germany*, July 21, 2011, para.64, a private-law nursing organisation, albeit with a public authority as majority shareholder.

allegedly appalling care conditions for the elderly, the Court emphasised that "whistleblowing" must be the last resort for the employee. As the nurse had brought her allegations of inadequate care several times to the attention of her employer who had not reacted, the Court did not consider that she was to blame for not specifying that the alleged conduct amounted to "aggravated fraud" or seeking further clarifications. Nor was her good faith in doubt through use of a criminal complaint, even if this was eventually rejected as unfounded. Her dismissal for disclosing a matter of public concern about care of the elderly was thus found to be disproportionately severe.[208]

13. Judges, lawyers and defendants

Key case-law:

Schopfer v Switzerland, May 20, 1998, R.J.D. 1998–III, No.72; *Wille v Liechtenstein*, October 28, 1999, R.J.D. 1999–VII, 30 E.H.R.R. 558; *Nikula v Finland*, March 21, 2002, ECHR 2002–II; *Kyprianou v Cyprus*, December 15, 2005, ECHR 2005–XII. II–431

As regards judges' freedom of expression, senior members of the judiciary may be expected to show restraint, moderation and propriety in situations where the authority and impartiality of the judiciary could be called into question, but any interference with the freedom of expression of a judge of this position calls for close scrutiny.

In *Wille v Liechtenstein*, where the President of the Administrative Court was informed by the ruling Prince that he would not be re-appointed due to a statement made at a lecture on a controversial constitutional issue, the Court, finding a violation of Art.10, noted that the judge had not commented on a pending case and that there was no suggestion that his view had any bearing on his conduct as a judge or the performance of his office. Similarly, where a judge was demoted for conduct undermining the honour and dignity of the judiciary, the Court noted the vague nature of the allegations and, insofar as the sanction related to the judge's reading of Kurdish newspapers and watching of Kurdish television, this interference was hardly "necessary".[209] The authorities went too far in removing a judge for comments in media interviews which were highly critical of the Moscow City Courts but which had a foundation of fact in her own irregular removal from sitting in a case due to intervention from the court president; the comments had also been on a subject of public interest, rather than motivated by mere personal grievance. The Court also had regard to the lack of procedural safeguards disclosed by the failure to transfer the matter out of the impugned courts' jurisdiction and the fact that a severe measure such as removal could have a chilling effect on judges.[210]

However, in *Harabin v Slovakia*, the Court did not find that the removal of the President of the Supreme Court breached Art.10, as it was essentially related to the applicant's ability to properly exercise the judicial duties; although there was some reference to his expression of views, the proposal to remove the applicant from office was not exclusively or preponderantly prompted by that aspect.[211]

[208] *Heinisch v Germany*, fn.207 above, paras 71–95.
[209] *Albayrak v Turkey*, January 31, 2008.
[210] *Kondrashina v Russia*, February 26, 2009.
[211] (62584/00) (Dec.) June 29, 2004, ECHR 2004–VI. See also *Pitkevich v Russia*, (47936/99), where a judge was dismissed not for expression of religious opinion but because of specific activities incompatible with judicial office, e.g. promising a favourable outcome if parties joined her church.

Public prosecutors, as civil servants, are also bound by duties of loyalty and discretion. However, it is important that the public have confidence in their freedom to fearlessly pursue their duties in upholding the law. Thus while it was justifiable to impose a disciplinary warning on a public prosecutor who had used his position to publicise his own views as to the need to pursue the military officers who had carried out the 1980 coup, it went too far to hold him liable additionally for insulting the army due to steps taken in the exercise of his functions and to remove him altogether from his post.[212]

Disciplinary sanctions imposed on lawyers by professional bodies may be acceptable where pursuing legitimate aims in a suitably proportionate manner. In *Schopfer v Switzerland*, the Court found no violation arising from a 500 CHF fine imposed on a lawyer for serious criticisms of the courts issued at a press conference, reference being made to the key role of lawyers in contributing to the proper administration of justice and maintaining public confidence therein. Nor was there a problem where a lawyer was convicted and fined for defamation of the police, when, during a controversial trial, she issued a press statement, accusing the police of serious misconduct and brutality. There was no factual basis to the allegations, which were more a "personal diatribe" than any vindication of the rights of her client.[213] Using the media as a shortcut to resolving issues in a trial is likely not to attract protection. Thus, fining a lawyer for improper conduct during a trial was acceptable where he had leaked to the press evidence which had been excluded from the case file and the lay jurors; it could have prejudiced the courts' conduct of the trial. Insofar as the lawyer alleged he was acting in the interests of his client, the Court noted that the available method of redress within the proceedings had been available to him and had, indeed, been successful.[214] Conversely, where a lawyer was sanctioned with a disciplinary fine for interviews with the media in which he criticised the conduct of a criminal investigation in which his clients were civil parties, the Court considered that it was in the context of an affair of public interest and that he had not gone beyond criticism of officials in their carrying out of public functions. In that case it was not impressed by any need to penalise lawyers who make use of the media, finding no indication of any concerted press campaign.[215]

Any measures interfering with counsel's freedom of expression during a trial, however, threatens to conflict with Art.6 guarantees and the Court has stated it could only be in exceptional cases that a criminal sanction of even a lenient kind could be imposed on defence counsel's freedom of expression.[216] Even a simple admonition by a disciplinary council on defence counsel for alleging that his client had been put under pressure by an investigating officer was found to have an unjustified "chilling" effect.[217] Conviction for criminal contempt offended where comments of the applicant counsel, although disrespectful of the court, concerned

[212] *Kayasu v Turkey*, November 13, 2008. See also *Poyraz v Turkey*, December 2010, duty of restraint on a Ministry of Justice inspector who had commented publicly on a report without distancing himself from potentially defamatory elements concerning a senior judge.

[213] *Coutant v France*, (17155/03) (Dec.) January 24, 2008, the Court noted that even if the "mass trial" had been controversial, the lawyer had not shown that she had not had other methods of raising legitimate issues.

[214] *Furuholmen v Sweden*, (53349/06) (Dec.) March 18, 2010.

[215] *Foglia v Switzerland*, December 13, 2007.

[216] *Nikula v Finland*, March 21, 2002, ECHR 2002–11, breach of Art.10 where a defence lawyer was privately prosecuted by a public prosecutor for alleged defamation in court.

[217] *Steur v Netherlands*, October 28, 2003.

the conduct of the case.[218] However, a mere written reprimand imposed on a lawyer for comments in pleadings accusing the prosecuting authority of "playing a trick" on his client, without any factual element being put forward to justify the allegation, did not go beyond the margin of appreciation in disciplining lawyers who contribute to the proper administration of justice.[219]

Where a defendant himself was punished for contempt due to remarks made while addressing the court, the Court acknowledged that he could have criticised the functioning of the court without personally attacking the judges and that it was arguably necessary to take steps to protect the authority of the judiciary. However, the six-month prison sentence, two in solitary confinement, was found to be disproportionately heavy.[220]

14. Freedom to receive information

Key case-law:

Open Door and Dublin Well Woman v Ireland, October 29, 1992, Series A, No.246, 15 E.H.R.R. 244; *Guerra v Italy*, February 19, 1998, R.J.D. 1998–I, No.64; *Cyprus v Turkey*, May 10, 2001, ECHR 2001–IV. II–432

Article 10 cannot be used to derive a general right of access to information. In *Guerra v Italy*, the Court stated unequivocally that the freedom to receive information essentially prohibited a government from restricting a person from receiving information that others wished to impart. It did not impose on the authorities in that case the obligation to collect and distribute information about the health risks to the local community from the nearby factory.

In *Open Door and Dublin Well Woman v Ireland*, there was a violation where a court injunction prevented the provision of information services concerning abortion by the applicant counsellors. The Court found the ban disproportionate in the circumstances, since it was absolute, the counselling given was neutral and the information lawfully available elsewhere in Ireland or by contact outside in a less supervised manner, which imposed a risk to those women who sought abortion at a later stage and who did not receive counselling or proper after-care. The vetting by the TRNC authorities in northern Cyprus in respect of school-books destined for primary school Greek-Cypriot children, which resulted in the unilateral censorship or rejection of large numbers of schoolbooks, no matter how innocuous their content, was a denial of freedom of information in *Cyprus v Turkey*.

More recently, the Court has paid more attention to issues of access to information by the press and by bodies, such as non-governmental organisations, who play the role of social watchdog. It has stated in that context that the authorities are under an obligation not to impede the flow of information or erect obstacles in that regard. Thus, where a NGO requested access to a constitutional application lodged with the courts by a member of Parliament on drugs issues, the

[218] *Kyprianou v Cyprus*, January 27, 2004, ECHR 2005–XIII, para.179.

[219] *Schmidt v Austria*, July 17, 2008. This case differs from *Steur*, fn.217 above, in which case the lawyer claimed to have factual support for his allegation, but the courts did not examine any issues of relevance or good faith.

[220] *Saday v Turkey*, March 30, 2006.

Court considered the refusal interfered with its freedom of expression. It considered that the information, at most conveying the MP's opinion on the issues, did not attract the protection of personal data and did not require any effort of collection by the authorities; hence there was no justification for barring access.[221] The Court has also held that access to original documentary material for legitimate historical research was to be regarded as an essential element of a historian's freedom of expression, though it may be noted that in the case in question the academic had a court order for access to the Communist-era documents and the breach flowed from the authorities failure to comply with that order.[222]

Receiving television channels through a satellite dish has been found to be covered by the freedom to receive information. The order to evict the family for refusing to take down the dish was disproportionate, disclosing a violation.[223]

15. Positive obligations to protect the exercise of freedom of expression

Key case-law:

II–433 *Özgür Gündem v Turkey*, March 16, 2000, ECHR 2000–III, 31 E.H.R.R. 49; *Fuentes Bobo v Spain*, February 29, 2000; *Appleby v UK*, May 6, 2003, ECHR 2003–VI.

Genuine and effective exercise of this key freedom does not depend merely on the authorities' duty not to interfere, but may require positive measures of protection, even between individuals. Thus, the Court found the authorities were under a positive obligation in *Özgür Gündem v Turkey* to take investigative and protective measures where an allegedly pro-PKK newspaper had been victim of a campaign of violence. A general obligation on the State to protect freedom of expression has also been found to arise in the employment context,[224] while positive steps must be taken to ensure freedom of expression where the Court has already found a particular interference has infringed Art.10.[225] Where it is known that a journalist faces a real risk to his life arising out of exercise of his freedom of expression, a positive obligation to take steps to protect him may arise. In a case where the journalist, killed by extremists known to the authorities, had also been subject to an unjustified conviction for alleged denigration of Turkishness, exacerbating his situation as a target, the failure of the security forces to take any steps to protect him from assassination breached that obligation.[226]

As with positive obligations in other contexts, issues of striking a fair balance arise, with a margin of appreciation to the State as regards appropriate policies, priorities and use of resources. Nor will the Court interpret the provision in such a manner as to impose an impossible or disproportionate burden on the authorities. Thus, in *Appleby v UK* where the applicant campaigners had other means available to them to circulate their views, the Court did not consider that a positive obligation

[221] *Tarsasag Szabadsagjokokert v Hungary*, April 14, 2009.
[222] *Kenedi*, fn.192 above, para.43.
[223] *Khurshid Mustafa and Tarzibachi v Sweden*, December 16, 2008, paras 44–50
[224] *Fuentes Bobo v Spain*, February 29, 2000, para.38. Contrast *Palomo Sanchez v Spain*, September 12, 2011, where the courts properly balanced rights and interests at stake where trade union employees were dismissed for offensive cartoons and texts in a newsletter.
[225] *VgT Verein Gegen Tierfabriken v Switzerland (No.2)* (GC), fn.125 above, para.91.
[226] *Dink*, fn.67 above, paras 137–138.

arose requiring that the State should ensure access to privately-owned shopping centres for the exercise of their freedom of expression. Article 10 did not bestow freedom of forum, though the Court did not exclude that where the bar on access to private property effectively destroyed the essence of the right, such as in a company-owned town, a positive obligation might arise for the State to regulate property rights in favour of exercise of freedom of expression. The finding of a lack of any obligation on the State to provide access to private property or public buildings for information events was not applied to a case where applicant abortion activists were banned from entering territorial waters in the boat that they used for their information events. The Court distinguished it on the basis that the sea was in principle an open public space and that the ban was an interference; the case, thus interpreted, did not impose a burdensome positive obligation.[227]

While there is no right of access as such to the media for private individuals who wish to express their views and newspapers must enjoy editorial freedom, there may be circumstances where a newspaper is required to publish a retraction, apology or a judgment and States should prevent any denial of access to media which is an arbitrary or disproportionate interference with freedom of expression. Thus, where the applicant's poetry had been criticised robustly by a critic writing for a newspaper, the State was under an obligation to ensure he had a reasonable opportunity to exercise his right of reply by submitting a response to the newspaper for publication and, secondly, that he had an opportunity to contest the newspaper's refusal before the domestic courts. The first was apparently satisfied by the fact he could write a letter to the newspaper, which refused to publish it due to his use of abuse; as to the second, the courts' decisions showed no arbitrariness. This approach would appear to require States to provide the possibility of suing for a right of reply in the courts.[228]

Where tenants were evicted from their flat for refusing to dismantle the satellite dish with which they received programmes in their national language, the Court considered that this interfered with their freedom to receive information. The State had failed in their positive obligation to protect that freedom, since the courts had ordered their eviction. The Court did not find the reasons given for the need to forbid a satellite dish, safety or aesthetics, had been made out.[229]

Cross-reference

Part IIB, s.3: Armed forces, sub-s.6: Restrictions on freedom of expression and freedom to receive information.
Part IIB, s.8: Defamation and right to reputation.
Part IIB, s.15: Environment, sub-s.4: Access to information about environmental risks.
Part IIB, s.20: Freedom of assembly, sub-s.3: Penalties for participation in public protests.
Part IIB, s.36: Prisoners' rights, sub-s.10: Education, leisure facilities and expression.
Part IIB, s.37: Private life, sub-s.5(b): Access to personal information.

[227] *Women on Waves*, fn.9 above, paras 43–44.
[228] *Melnychuk v Ukraine*, (28743/03) (Dec.) July 5, 2005.
[229] *Khurshid Mustafa and Tarzibachi*, fn.223 above, paras 44–50.

23. Freedom of movement

Key provision:

II–434 Article 2 of Protocol No.4 (liberty of movement within a State and freedom to leave).

Key case-law:

Guzzardi v Italy, November 6, 1980, Series A, No.39, 3 E.H.R.R. 333; *Raimondo v Italy*, February 22, 1994, Series A, No.281–A, 18 E.H.R.R. 237; *Piermont v France*, April 27, 1995 Series A, No.314, 20 E.H.R.R. 301; *Labita v Italy*, April 6, 2000, ECHR 2000–IV; *Baumann v France*, May 22, 2001, ECHR 2001–V; *Denizci v Cyprus*, May 23, 2001, ECHR 2001–V; *Olivieira v Netherlands*, June 4, 2002, ECHR 2002–IV, 28 E.H.R.R. 289; *Luordo v Italy*, July 17, 2003; *Timishev v Russia*, December 13, 2005, ECHR 2005–XII.

1. General considerations

II–435 Where restrictions on movement are concerned, Art.2 of Protocol No.4 is regarded as the *lex specialis*. Article 5, which concerns deprivation of liberty, has not been extended by the Convention organs beyond the conventional context of physical detention.

2. Restriction on movement

II–436 Whether there has been a deprivation of liberty rather than a restriction on movement depends on examination of the concrete situation, but is a distinction of degree and intensity, not of nature or substance. Account is taken of a whole range of criteria: the type, duration, effects and manner of implementation of the measures restricting the individual's liberty. In *Guzzardi v Italy*, the confinement of an applicant to the island of Asinara was found to be cumulatively a deprivation of liberty within the meaning of Art.5. While the area of confinement was much larger than a cell, it covered a tiny fraction of an island, nine-tenths of which consisted of a prison. He had to remain in his dwelling between 22.00 and 07.00 hours, report twice per day to the authorities and could only leave the island under strict supervision—a state of affairs which lasted 16 months. Conversely, in *Raimondo v Italy*, special police supervision, where the applicant could not leave home without informing the police and was under an obligation to report on certain days and to remain at home between 21.00 and 07.00 hours, was considered only a restriction on movement. Also, exclusion orders restricting persons in Northern Ireland from entering mainland UK have not been considered to be of such a degree as to constitute a deprivation of liberty.[1]

Refusal of a passport which did not prevent the applicant in Sweden from moving to other Nordic countries was still an interference with freedom of movement since freedom to leave a country implies freedom to leave for any country to which he

[1] e.g. (13709/88) and (13944/88) (Dec.) October 11, 1989.

may be admitted.[2] Seizure of a passport or other similar identity document also constitutes an interference,[3] as does stamping the passport with a mention which prevents its use in leaving the country.[4] A ruling under the Hague Convention as to the lawfulness of a removal of a child overseas by its mother did not constitute an interference with their freedom of movement as it did not constitute a ban on quitting the country or an order to return.[5]

Minor impediments or conditions imposed on the freedom of movement will not be seen as interfering, e.g. the obligation to carry an identity card and present it on request of the police.[6] However, in *Denizci v Cyprus*, the requirement to report to the police every time the applicants wished to move their place of residence or visit friends or family in the north was found to disclose an interference with freedom of movement.[7] Refusal to allow a Chechen to pass a checkpoint to reach the town where he lived was also an interference.[8]

3. "Lawfully" within the territory

Freedom of movement applies only to persons lawfully within the territory. This refers to domestic law, which may lay down the conditions to be fulfilled. Thus aliens provisionally allowed to stay in a certain district can only be regarded as lawfully in the territory as long as they comply with the conditions of their admission.[9] Also, the provision applicable to an alien who has had his residence permit revoked.[10] Where an applicant has been resident in the country for some time, it appears that it is for the authorities to establish the "unlawfulness" and that the Court will scrutinise the factual and legal basis of that assertion.[11] II–437

An alien who has entered immigration control cannot claim necessarily to be "lawfully" in the territory, a claim made by the applicant MEP in *Piermont v France* who was only stopped after her passport had been checked at New Caledonia airport. The Court considered that at such an airport passengers remained liable to checks as long as they were in its perimeter. Since the applicant was served with the order preventing her entry while still in the airport she could not be considered as having been lawfully within the territory.

[2] (19583/92) (Dec.) February 20, 1995, 80 D.R. 38.

[3] *Baumann v France*, May 22, 2001, ECHR 2001–V, paras 60–62, where the Court dismissed the Government's argument that no restriction had taken place in fact as the applicant had been arrested shortly after requesting the return of his passport; *Napijalo v Croatia*, November 13, 2003, para.69.

[4] *Sissanis v Romania*, January 25, 2007, para.64.

[5] *SDJ and AK-R v Romania*, (34175/05) (Dec.) October 20, 2010, para.74.

[6] (16810/90) (Dec.) September 9, 1992, 73 D.R. 136.

[7] In *Luordo v Italy*, July 17, 2003, the obligation on the applicant not to leave his district without permission was, without discussion, within the scope of the provision, even though it was not apparent that he had ever wished to or that permission had ever been refused.

[8] *Timishev v Russia*, December 13, 2005, ECHR 2005–XII.

[9] (14102/88) (Dec.) October 9, 1989, 63 D.R. 195; (12068/86) (Dec.) December 1, 1986, 51 D.R. 237; *Omwenyeke v Germany*, (44294/04) (Dec.) November 20, 2007, an asylum seeker subject to a requirement to remain in a particular district could not rely on Art.2 of Protocol No.4 when he was convicted for travelling outside that area as he was not "lawfully" on the territory when he did so.

[10] (21069/92) (Dec.) July 9, 1993, 75 D.R. 245.

[11] *Tatishvili v Russia*, February 22, 2007, paras 38–43, where the applicant, born in Georgia, claimed the status of a citizen of the former USSR, the Government had not shown that she had Georgian citizenship or was a stateless person to whom special formalities applied.

4. Legitimate restrictions

II–438 Considerations of lawfulness,[12] necessity, legitimate aim and proportionality apply.

Refusal by Finland to issue a passport to a Finnish citizen resident in Sweden was an interference with freedom of movement but justified as necessary in the interests of national security and the maintenance of the *ordre public* since the applicant had failed to report for his military service. The Commission noted that the applicant had not invoked any ground warranting a departure from the usual rule, e.g. special need for travel, and that he was able to re-apply at any time. It considered also that Contracting States were entitled to a wide margin of appreciation in the organisation of their national defence.[13] An injunction prohibiting an anti-abortionist campaigner from entering within 250 metres of an abortion clinic for six months was justified for the protection of the rights of others having regard to the limited area and duration of the measure.[14] A court order prohibiting a Spanish mother from leaving Italy with her children was regarded as necessary to protect the rights of the Italian father and to maintain the *ordre public* in the sense of the administration of justice,[15] while an order excluding a habitual drugs user from the centre of Amsterdam for 14 days was found a proportionate measure for the prevention of crime and the maintaining of public order.[16]

Where the authorities exceed the justification in domestic terms, issues may arise. In *Raimondo v Italy*, special supervision measures imposed against the applicant, suspected of mafia crimes, were considered as necessary and proportionate in view of the threat to democracy posed by the Mafia. The measures ceased to be necessary or lawful from the filing of the revocation decision by the court in the registry or, at the latest, when the applicant was informed a week later. Continued retention of a passport of an applicant initially suspected of crime, but who was not prosecuted or needed as a witness, ceased to be justified in *Baumann v France*.[17]

In *Labita v Italy*, continuation of severely restrictive measures against an applicant on grounds of alleged mafia links were found unnecessary after his acquittal.[18] The Court considered that it was legitimate for special supervision measures, including restriction on movement, to be taken against persons suspected of mafia membership prior to conviction where they were intended to prevent crimes being committed. It did not rule out that special measures could continue after an acquittal, but only where there was concrete evidence which, even if insufficient to

[12] *Olivieira v Netherlands*, June 4, 2002, ECHR 2002–IV, 28 E.H.R.R. 289, paras 47–59, the Court examined whether the 14–day order excluding the applicant from the centre of Amsterdam on grounds of drugs use had a basis in domestic law and the quality of law (e.g. foreseeable and accessible); also *Denizci v Cyprus*, May 23, 2001, ECHR 2001–V, paras 404–406, where the Government had advanced no legal basis for the restriction on the movements of Turkish Cypriots; *Santoro v Italy*, July 1, 2004, where the order had expired; *Timishev*, fn.8 above, where an informal, unrecorded oral instruction did not provide a legal basis for barring Chechens at a road block.

[13] (19583/92), fn.2 above.

[14] (22838/93) (Dec.) February 22, 1995, 80–A D.R. 147; *Sissanis*, fn.4 above, lack of precision and clarity or basis in domestic law.

[15] *Roldan Texiero v Italy*, (40655/98) (Dec.) October 26, 2000.

[16] *Olivieira*, fn.12 above, paras 64–65.

[17] See also *Napijalo v Croatia*, November 13, 2003, lack of justification for continued retention of a passport by customs where they did not pursue any proceedings against him.

[18] The applicant's wife was from a mafia family. The restrictive measures included weekly reporting to the police, a curfew between 20.00 and 06.00 hours, a prohibition on attending bars or public gatherings or on leaving home without informing the supervision authorities.

secure a conviction, justified reasonable fears that the person might commit criminal offences in the future.

There must also be a sufficient link between a travel ban and the protective purpose. Where an applicant was prohibited from travelling abroad due to his knowledge of "State secrets", the Court found that in the absence of any control of correspondence or contacts with foreigners there was no indication that the ban served its purported purpose.[19] Overseas travel restrictions on retired army personnel due to alleged knowledge of such secrets was noted to apply in Russia and was not considered to have the requisite compelling justification.[20]

Duration of a measure may render it disproportionate, particularly where the necessity for the restriction weakens with the passage of time. Thus, in *Luordo v Italy*, although the Court accepted that the requirement on the applicant not to leave his place of residence without permission during bankruptcy proceedings was not in itself objectionable, the duration of those proceedings over fourteen years was disproportionate to any legitimate aim, even if it was not apparent that the applicant had ever wished to leave the area or that permission had ever been refused. Six and a half years' duration during criminal proceedings was also too long.[21] Conversely, where a measure restricting movement during a criminal prosecution lasted over four years and the applicants had twice been granted permission to leave the area, there was no lack of proportionality.[22]

In order to prevent arbitrariness, procedural safeguards are required by which the authorities assess the continued justification of a ban. Thus, the nine-year seizure of the applicant's passport under a travel ban imposed due to her considerable fiscal debts disclosed a violation where it was of an automatic nature, giving no account of her family links abroad, whether any other measures had been taken to recover the money and whether her travelling abroad would undermine debt recovery.[23] Lack of reasons for decisions extending a prohibition on leaving an area may also offend, particularly as with lapse of time the necessity for the measure will diminish.[24] There must therefore be an effective judicial scrutiny of the imposition and continuation of such prohibitions which allow all the relevant factors to be taken into account, including the proportionality of the measure.[25] It has been left open whether the size of the debt or its importance to the claimant (e.g. maintenance) would be a factor justifying an otherwise excessive duration of a ban on movement.[26] The mere fact that a person has been criminally convicted and not yet rehabilitated does not justify in itself the imposition of an automatic removal of a passport.[27]

[19] *Bartik v Russia*, December 21, 2006, the Court also referred to the length of the ban and the fact that the applicant had handed in all confidential materials after he left the sensitive post.

[20] *Soltysyak v Russia*, February 10, 2011, paras 50–54.

[21] *Rosengren v Romania*, April 24, 2008.

[22] *Fedorov and Fedorova v Russia*, October 13, 2005.

[23] *Riener v Bulgaria*, May 23, 2006; see also *Földes and Földesne Hajlik v Hungary*, October 31, 2006, automatic ban of long duration disclosing a violation; and *Gochev v Bulgaria*, January 26, 2009, ban on debtor leaving the country during enforcement proceedings offended due to its automatic and indefinite nature.

[24] *Rosengren v Romania*, fn.21, para.39.

[25] *Gochev*, fn.23, paras 54–55, the Supreme Administrative Court had no jurisdiction to examine the appropriateness of the ban or its continuation against the applicant who was subject to proceedings as a debtor, nor did any other judicial body.

[26] *Gochev*, fn.23, para.57.

[27] *Nalbantski v Bulgaria*, February 10, 2011, para.66.

5. Overlap with other provisions

II–439 While in *Piermont v France* the applicant MEP, as an alien subject to lawful expulsion measures, did not succeed in claims based on freedom of movement in respect of measures taken by the authorities to prevent her attending meetings in French Polynesia and New Caledonia, breaches of Art.10 were found since the measures interfered with her freedom of expression.[28] There was no point taken that Art.2 of Protocol No.4 was the *lex specialis* or that no separate issues could arise where an alien was lawfully restricted in her movements. When Gerry Adams, Sinn Fein President, was stopped from attending a meeting in the House of Commons by an exclusion order allegedly for that purpose, the Commission noted that Art.2 of Protocol No.4 had not been ratified by the United Kingdom. While it examined the case on the basis that there had been an interference with freedom of expression, it found the measure justified as necessary to protect national security and prevent disorder and crime.[29]

Cross-reference

Part IIB, s.9: Deprivation of liberty.
Part IIB, s.21: Freedom of association.

[28] See Pt IIB, s.22: Freedom of expression.
[29] (28979/95) and (30343/96) (Dec.) January 13, 1997, 88–A D.R. 137.

24. Gypsies and minorities

Key provisions:

Articles 8 (private life, family life and home) and 14 (discrimination), Art.1 of the Protocol No.1 (peaceful enjoyment of property), Art.2 of the Protocol No.1 (right to education), and Art. 3 of the Protocol No.1 (right to stand for election and to vote). II–440

Key case-law:

Bryan v UK, November 22, 1995, Series A, No.335–A, 21 E.H.R.R. 342; *Buckley v UK*, September 25, 1996, R.J.D. 1996–IV, 23 E.H.R.R. 101; *Chapman v UK*, January 18, 2002, ECHR 2001–I; *Conka v Belgium*, February 5, 2002, ECHR 2002–I; *Nachova v Bulgaria*, July 6, 2005, ECHR 2005–VII; *Connors v UK*, May 28, 2004; *Moldovan v Romania (No. 2)*, July 12, 2005, ECHR 2005–. . . ; *DH and Others v Czech Republic*, November 13, 2007, ECHR 2007–. . . ; *Orsus and Others v Croatia*, March 16, 2010.

1. General considerations

The Convention guarantees rights in respect, primarily, of the individual. The Convention case-law emphasises this in an insistence that an applicant must be able to claim to be a victim, with direct effect on enjoyment of a protected right. It sits uneasily therefore for a person to complain because he is a member of a group which is prejudiced in a general, less direct or less immediate way. II–441

Complaints tended until recently to slip between the provisions.[1] Until the entry of Central and Eastern European States into the Convention system, which have large Roma and other minority populations, the cases derived principally from the United Kingdom relating to the siting of gypsy caravans. These highlighted the difficulties facing gypsies, whose ability to lead nomadic lives has been seriously hindered, inter alia, by legislative provisions rendering unauthorised stationing of caravans on the highway or other land a criminal offence; the shortfall of official sites throughout the country; and difficulties of obtaining local authority planning permission for their own sites. This is a global situation that could be described as undermining the viability of the gypsy way of life, but which is difficult for the Court to examine as a whole, confined as it is to the individual circumstances of each case and being reluctant to embark on abstract investigations. The recent cases indicate, more promisingly, that disproportionately prejudicial effects of a policy or

[1] e.g. (11862/85) (Dec.) July 18, 1986, where posters in shops opposed gypsy sites implying that gypsies were dirty and attracted vermin, the applicant gypsy could not take action for group defamation under English law and consent was not given for prosecution for incitement to racial hatred—the Commission held that Art.6 could not grant substantive rights of defamation and no issues arose under Art.8; (18401/91) (Dec.) May 6, 1993, where a gypsy on an official site was threatened with summary eviction, it was argued with some force that she was in an impossible situation, due to the general shortfall of sites and the designation system in the area making it a criminal offence for gypsies to station their caravans on public or private land without consent. However, when during the proceedings the applicant was granted permission by the local council to remain where she was, the Commission avoided looking at the effect of the general situation, since it found no real indication that she wanted to travel elsewhere; she was no longer a victim.

measure on a particular individual or group may be sufficient to ground a breach of discrimination without examining individual cases.[2] A change in emphasis might also be noted with statements by the Court specifying that while cases concern the individual situation of Roma applicants, their identity as members of a minority cannot be ignored and the position of the Roma population can be taken into account.[3]

There is little case-law on what constitutes an ethnic minority. Where the members of the Countryside Alliance, united in their love of hunting, argued, somewhat inventively, that the hunting ban was an attack on their minority way of life, the Court gave them short shrift, stating that "mere participation in a common social activity, without more, cannot create membership of a national or ethnic minority". Interpersonal ties, however strong, of a social nature did not therefore create a discrete minority.[4]

2. Right to respect for private life, family life and home

II–442 Planning controls on the use of land, a common feature in Contracting States, have generally been found by the Commission and Court to be justified in the public interest, for example prohibiting development in green belt or areas of rural amenity,[5] or as justified to protect the rights of others, for example, the contractual rights of a site owner.[6] An individual who has been refused permission to occupy land is not in a strong position under the approach adopted in Convention case-law, which holds that Art.8 does not contain an express right to living accommodation. The Court has stated that individual preferences cannot outweigh the public interest.[7] The fact that planning and site provision is an area of policy and discretion has also resulted in a wide margin of appreciation being accorded to the authorities and a reluctance to impose positive obligations on the State to provide accommodation in a particular place.[8]

Where, however, a gypsy family was established on a particular site and faced with expulsion, the Commission found that issues could arise. The lack of reasonable alternatives for the Buckley family, who had been refused planning permission for the caravan on their own land and were faced with enforcement measures, was the basis for the Commission's finding of a violation. Both the Court and Commission accepted that the family's settlement on their land, even though never authorised, nonetheless fell within the scope of "home" under Art.8. The Commission also

[2] *DH and Others v Czech Republic*, November 13, 2007, ECHR 2007–. . ., paras 184 and 209.

[3] e.g. *Orsus and Others v Croatia*, March 16, 2010, para.147.

[4] *Friend v UK*, (16072/06) and (27809/08) (Dec.) November 24, 2009, nor was the Court persuaded that hunting was a particular lifestyle so inextricably linked to the identity of those who practised it that to impose a ban on hunting would be to jeopardise the very essence of their identity. So no hope for smokers claiming to be an endangered minority either.

[5] e.g. (11723/85) (Dec.) May 7, 1987, 52 D.R. 250; (11185/84) (Dec.) March 11, 1985, (Dec.) 42 D.R. 275.

[6] (14751/89) (Dec.) December 12, 1990, 67 D.R. 264.

[7] *Buckley v UK*, September 25, 1996, R.J.D. 1996–IV, 23 E.H.R.R. 101, para.81.

[8] *Buckley*, fn.7 above, para.75; (14455/88) (Dec.) September 4, 1991, where the applicant gypsies had sought unsuccessfully in the courts to enforce the statutory obligation on local authorities to provide sufficient sites to prevent being continually moved on from place to place, the Commission, though noting the lack of adequate provision, was not prepared to find that the respect for family and private life extended to obliging the authorities to build sites. Article 8 was about respect for lawfully established homes already in existence.

relied on a Norwegian case concerning Lapps which held a minority could claim the right to respect for its particular lifestyle as being "private life", "family life" and home".[9] In its view a gypsy could therefore claim that her way of life, which involved living in a caravan, attracted protection under Art.8.

Regarding the compliance with the requirements of Art.8, the Court took a stricter line than the Commission. The Commission approached the balancing exercise from the point of view that gypsies, from their lifestyle, had more limited options open to them and that they had special requirements. It found that the applicant's interest in security for herself and her children and the continuation of their lifestyle outweighed the slender public interest in planning controls in that case. The Court emphasised, however, that in the area of planning controls the authorities enjoyed a wide margin of appreciation under Art.8. Although it noted the importance of respect for home, in effect this was given little weight. It was unimpressed by allegations of the unsuitability of the alternative site available nearby, commenting only that it was not as satisfactory as her own land and discounting matters of individual preference. The Court considered that it was not its role to enter into the merits of planning decisions, and it was sufficient to verify, as in this case before the planning inspectors, that the competing claims were given due consideration in a fair procedure. This approach was confirmed in *Chapman v UK*, where, though reference was made to some special consideration being given to the needs of gypsies, the Court found that Art.8 could not be interpreted as imposing a far-reaching positive obligation on the State to make an adequate number of suitably equipped sites available to the gypsy community. It also stated that it would be slow to grant protection to those who, in conscious defiance of the prohibition of the law, established their home on an environmentally protected site.[10]

In light of the Court's judgments above, a finding of violation is unlikely where a gypsy is refused planning permission for their land. Issues might still arise perhaps where eviction measures are imposed arbitrarily or in circumstances of extreme hardship. It will generally be difficult for any gypsy to establish that there is no viable alternative at all to remaining on their own land.[11]

As regards a homeless gypsy, it has not been excluded that Art.8 could impose a positive obligation on the authorities to provide accommodation which facilitates their "gypsy way of life". This obligation is very restricted, potentially arising only where the authorities had such accommodation at their disposal and were making a choice between offering such accommodation or offering accommodation which was not "suitable" for the cultural needs of a gypsy.[12]

[9] (9278/81) and (9415/81) (Dec.) October 3, 1983, 35 D.R. 30.

[10] *Chapman v UK*, January 18, 2002, ECHR 2001–I, paras 90–116; also similar findings of no violations in respect of enforcement measures against gypsy occupation of land in *Beard*, *Coster*, *Jane Smith*, and *Lee*, judgments of January 18, 2001; it may be noted that the Government settled a sixth case, *Varey v UK*, December 12, 2000, in which the planning inspector's decision to grant the gypsy family's appeal was overridden twice by the Secretary of State.

[11] This will be particularly hard where a gypsy has given up a nomadic way of life, through force of circumstance, and adopted conventional housing, as in (31600/96) (Dec.) September 10, 1996, where the applicant had lived in housing for 17 years and when dying of cancer tried to end her days in a caravan: the Commission found that the local authority had made not unnegligible attempts to find a place for her caravan, but in the circumstances they could not be held in breach of Art.8 in failing to provide such a site.

[12] *Codona v UK*, (485/05) (Dec.) February 2, 2006, where there was no such site, there was no positive obligation to create one.

However, where a gypsy family had long been lawfully resident on a local authority site, the Court found in *Connors v UK* that their summary eviction had not been attended by adequate procedural safeguards, in particular the requirement that the local authority establish proper justification for the serious interference with their home, private and family life. The Court was not convinced by Government arguments that the nature of such sites or the purported reluctance of the occupants to participate in official proceedings justified the lack of effective court scrutiny of evictions.

Not surprisingly, where the authorities had been implicated in the violent destruction by a mob of the Roma villagers' homes, the Court found that the failure to provide replacement homes and proper compensation, leaving the applicants in long term uncertainty as to their fate and in unsanitary and overcrowded conditions, disclosed a serious violation of Art.8.[13]

As concerns defamation or breach of personal integrity through racist publications, a Chamber of the Court accepted that a Roma could claim to be affected by alleged insulting references to gypsies in a historical textbook and dictionary since, even though he was not targeted personally, he had had standing to bring proceedings for compensation in the domestic courts. These claims had been unsuccessful but the Chamber considered that there had been no failure to respect his private life in the circumstances, as the impugned passages were part of an academic study setting out, in a historical and socio-economic analysis, perceptions of the Roma people which were not adopted by the applicant who had made clear that Roma should be respected. The dictionary definitions had also been clearly labelled "metaphorical".[14]

3. Discrimination

II–443 Justifications for differences in treatment based on ethnicity are to be approached strictly; indeed the Court has said that no difference in treatment based solely or to a decisive extent on a person's ethnic origin is capable of justification in a democratic society which adheres to the principles of pluralism and respect for different cultures.[15]

Where evidence of direct discrimination arises, the Court has shown itself rigorous in its approach, insisting that racial motivation must be investigated seriously in cases of assault, ill-treatment and killings (see further below).

However, even where there is no direct evidence of discrimination, the Court now applies the principle that a discriminatory difference in treatment may be disclosed by the disproportionately prejudicial effects of a general policy or measure on a particular minority, even if it is couched in neutral terms, or on its face intended to benefit the group concerned.[16] Statistical evidence may be relied on, therefore, to show such potential imbalance in a policy's effect, though it is not the only evidence

[13] *Moldovan v Romania (No.2)*, July 12, 2005, paras 107–109.
[14] *Aksu v Turkey*, July 27, 2010, pending before the Grand Chamber.
[15] *DH and Others*, fn.2 above, paras 176 and 196.
[16] *DH and Others*, fn.2 above, para.184.

that can be used.[17] A rebuttable presumption can arise in those circumstances, the burden shifting to the Government to show that the difference in impact is the result of objective factors unrelated to ethnic origin.[18]

There can be no waiver of the right not to be subjected to racial discrmination, the Court considering that such would be against an important public interest. Thus, where the Government argued in a school segregation case that the parents of the Roma children had all signed consent forms, the Court doubted that the parents could be considered as waiving their rights, being poorly educated and disadvantaged,[19] but in any event held that no waiver could be permitted.[20]

4. Ill-treatment, persecution and expulsion

Allegations of serious physical ill-treatment and unlawful killing of Roma victims led early on to findings of breaches of Arts 2 and 3 in a series of cases from Bulgaria.[21] Lack of effective investigation or remedy, with procedural breaches of Arts 2 and 13, was an accompanying feature of these incidents. Initially, the judgments laid no emphasis on the ethnic identity of the victims and the Court found that there was no material enabling it to conclude beyond reasonable doubt that the killings, ill-treatment and ineffective investigations were motivated by racial prejudice.[22] However, in *Nachova v Bulgaria*, where the two unarmed, absconding Roma conscripts were shot dead in a blatantly excessive use of force and the military policeman involved was reported as using racial insults, the Court emphasised the importance of the fight against racism and stated that the authorities were under an obligation to investigate with rigour and impartiality to unmask any racist motives. The absence of such an investigation disclosed a procedural breach of both Arts 2 and 14. The alleged shouting of racist slurs by the officer responsible had not been II–444

[17] See also *Sampanis v Greece*, June 5, 2008, where not only were the only children in the segregated preparatory classes of Roma origin, but there were striking and nasty incidents where non-Roma parents shouted insults and blocked access of Roma families to the school, making plain their desire that Roma children should not attend classes with non-Roma children. Contrast *Orsus and Others*, fn.3 above, para.152, where the statistical evidence of Roma children attending ordinary and special classes within primary schools did not provide prima facie evidence of a discriminatory practice as Roma children were attending both; however, it was evident that in some schools the measure of putting children in separate classes on the basis of insufficient command of the Croatian language only applied to Roma children; there was also evidence of non-Roma parents agitating against "mixed" classes.

[18] *DH and Others*, fn.2 above, paras 185–195.

[19] See Judge Borrego's dissenting criticism of this condescending attitude to the ability of Roma parents to make informed decisions, which reminded of historic examples of so-called well-intentioned people deciding what was best for ethnic children in place of their parents.

[20] *DH and Others*, fn.2 above, paras 203–204; see also identical reasoning in *Sampanis*, fn.17, paras 93–95, *Orsus and Others*, paras 178–179.

[21] *Assenov v Bulgaria*, October 28, 1998, R.J.D. 1998–VIII, violation of Art.3 for failure to investigate allegations of beatings by the police of the 14–year-old applicant, as well as violations of Art.5, paras 3 and 4, 13 and former Art.25 of the Convention; *Velikova*, May 18, 2000, ECHR 2000–VI, violations of Art.2 for the beating to death of a Roma in police custody and Arts 2 and 13 for the lack of effective investigation or remedy; *Anguelova*, June 12, 2002, ECHR 2002–IV, violations of Art.2 for death from injuries in custody of a 17–year-old Roma boy and for the failure to provide timely medical care, as well as violations of Art.5, para.1 and Arts 2 and 13 for lack of effective investigation or remedy; *Nachova v Bulgaria*, July 6, 2005, ECHR 2005–VII, breaches of Arts 2 and 14 for the killing of two conscripts of Roma origin.

[22] *Velikova*, fn.21, para.94; *Anguelova*, fn.21, para.168, see Judge Bonello's partly dissenting opinion where he criticises the Court's insistence on using such unrealistic and high burden of proof as inappropriate for its functions.

enough to lead to a conclusion that the State was liable for a racist killing in a substantive violation. In *Stoica v Romania*, the racist context of an assault on a Roma by police officers was established by a range of evidence, including eye witness reports and the manner in which the investigation itself was conducted with racial bias.[23]

It appears that, as regards a substantive violation, a mere assertion that racist assaults by the police are common is not enough by itself to give an incident of ill-treatment racist and discriminatory overtones.[24] Nor will reprehensible conduct towards a Roma by itself be evidence of racist motivation.[25] Against a background of such abuses, the authorities should nonetheless be sensitive to the issue and properly investigate whether there was any such racist element, lack of which investigation may lead to a violation of Art. 14. In *Bekos and Koutropoulos v Greece*, even where there was no direct or independent evidence that the police had been overtly racist in beating two Roma youths, the Court found the applicants' own accounts of being racially abused during the incident, and an attested background of racist attitudes to Roma by the police, enough to engage Art.14 in its procedural aspect; a breach followed from a lack of proper investigation into any possible racist overtones.[26] However, even where there are alarming reports of police brutality towards Roma people, this may not always be enough to trigger the obligation to investigate a racial motivation; objective evidence relative to the particular incident still seems to be required. Thus, where there were no overt racist elements in an incident, and the victim's relatives made no allegation of such during the domestic procedures, there was no procedural failure under Art.14.[27]

A failure to conduct a proper investigation into an allegedly racist motivation for an attack does not shift the burden onto the Government as regards as the substantive aspect.[28]

The same obligations of promptness, diligence and effectiveness in investigating applies to racist attacks by third parties.[29] It is not necessary, as such, for a State to provide for specific offenses of serious racist violence as long as there is a means of

[23] *Stoica v Romania*, March 3, 2008, paras 119–128, where the Court found the prosecutors too quick to discard racial motivation despite disquieting evidence surrounding an incident of police intervention at a bar; it also was not impressed by the Government's attempt to claim the way in which the word "gypsy" appeared in official reports was racially neutral.

[24] *Cobzaru v Romania*, July 26, 2007, the applicant did not, for example, allege that the police officers made any racial remarks or insults during the assault, thus the Court did not find a basis for establishing that the ill-treatment had been racially motivated, but did find the investigation had fallen short in not pursuing this element further.

[25] *Mizigarova v Slovakia*, December 14, 2010, para.117.

[26] *Bekos and Koutropoulos v Greece*, December 13, 2005, there was a breach of Art.3 concerning the ill-treatment.

[27] *Mizigarova v Slovakia*, fn.25 above, para.122; *Beganovic v Croatia*, June 25, 2009, paras 93–97, the applicant had made no mention during the domestic procedures of any racial insults during the assault.

[28] *Nachova*, fn.21 above, para.157; *Mizigarova v Slovakia*, fn.25, para.117.

[29] *Anguelova and Iliev v Bulgaria*, July 26, 2007, where a Roma was killed by a seven adolescents with racist motivations the Court found a procedural breach of Art.2 as, despite the fact the perpetrators were identified rapidly, the criminal proceeding dragged on inconclusively for over eleven years, and a breach of Art.14 since, despite the avowed racist motivations of the attackers, the suspects were not brought to trial and no charges were brought against them which reflected the dimension of racial hatred. See breaches of Arts 3 and 14 also in *Secic v Croatia*, May 31, 2007, where the police showed insufficient diligence in failing to question members of a skinhead group implicated in an attack on a Roma or to ask the courts to compel a journalist to reveal information about a skinhead source who had information on the incident.

including the racist motivation in some way as an element of the offences charged so that it can be seen that the State refuses to tolerate such acts which are regarded as particularly destructive of fundamental rights.[30]

Prisoners at risk of violence due to their ethnic origin require special protection.[31]

Where a group is openly singled out for differential treatment on the basis of ethnic origin, race and religion, proof is less of a problem, as in *Cyprus v Turkey*, where the hardship and restrictions suffered by an enclave of Greek Cypriots in the northern part of the island had been so severe and long lasting as to violate the very notion of respect for their human dignity.[32] The Court found aggravated breaches of Art.8 and a breach of Art.3, with no separate issue under Art.14. In *Moldovan (No.2)*, there was also degrading treatment in breach of Art.3 where the authorities left the applicants living in appalling conditions after they had been burnt out of their homes and publicly subjected them to remarks about their ethnic origin when dealing with their grievances.

Public remarks by the authorities concerning ethnicity may also disclose discrimination contrary to Art.14 in conjunction with other rights.[33]

Allegations are not uncommonly made that gypsies are treated more unfavourably than others who make applications for planning permission. However, difficulties in establishing that a refusal to a gypsy was based on grounds of his ethnic origin to the exclusion of normal planning considerations or that permission was granted to a non-gypsy in comparable circumstances rendered, and continue to render, success before the Court problematic. It would be required to show blatant reliance on irrelevant planning factors, or a planning policy based on a clearly discriminatory element for serious issues to arise.[34] In *Chapman v UK*, where the applicant complained that the legal system failed to accommodate the gypsies' traditional way of life by treating them in the same way as the majority population and in that way discriminated against them, the Court avoided looking at the general situation, finding no lack of objective or reasonable justification for the measures taken against this individual applicant.[35]

Steps taken to expel Roma from one country to another must also comply with certain procedural standards. Where, in *Conka v Belgium*, the authorities used a ruse to bring the families to the police station to be detained pending their expulsion, the Court had regard to the limited information made available in their own language

[30] *Anguelova and Iliev*, fn.29 above, Bulgarian law allowed racist motivation to be put forward as an aggravating factor in sentencing for violent crimes (para.104); however, the authorities failed in the event to put forward any racist charges (para.117).

[31] *Rodic v Bosnia-Herzegovina*, May 27, 2008, where Serbs convicted of war crimes, prisoners were kept in the general population and assaulted by other prisoners, the Government excuse of shortage of space not allowing for separate confinement was not accepted; no other measures of protection had been taken either. Breach of Art.3.

[32] *Cyprus v Turkey*, May 10, 2001, ECHR 2001–IV, the absence of normal means of communication, unavailability of Greek-Cypriot press, lack of secondary education in Greek, effect on residence rights on children sent to school in the south, limitations and conditions imposed on freedom of movement, with effects on access to medical treatment and participation in communal or religious events, and inability to preserve property rights on departure or death.

[33] *Moldovan (No.2)*, fn.13 above, in conjunction with Arts 6 and 8, where both the courts and the authorities made adverse remarks.

[34] In (31006/96) (Dec.) July 2, 1997, where the applicant gypsies claimed that special allowance was required in the application of planning laws to them, the Commission found no such disregard of their position as to disclose discrimination.

[35] *Chapman*, fn.10 above, para.129.

and the speed of the removal, which rendered futile any possibility of applying to the courts, and found that the strategem contravened the principles implicit in the Convention. The measure also contravened the prohibition on collective expulsions set out in Art.4 of Protocol No.4, namely the decision to enforce the expulsion was taken without a procedure affording sufficient guarantees that the personal circumstances of each individual had been genuinely taken into account.

5. Education and culture

II–445 Where planning measures concerning occupation of land by gypsies have been found to be in conformity with Arts 8 and 14, the Court has given short shrift to complaints that the restrictions disclosed any breach of Art.2 of Protocol No.1. Ignoring any difficulties resulting in attendance at school or continuity of school education, the Court found that the applicants had not substantiated that there had been in the circumstances any denial of education to the children of the families concerned.[36]

However, where the number of Roma children segregated in special schools was disproportionately high, the Court found a strong presumption of indirect discrimination. The Government could not, however, show the imbalance was due to objective factors unrelated to ethnic factors, in particular since the tests used to assess the children's abilities doubtfully reached a proper evaluation of their true abilities[37]; placement of the Roma children in the special classes had been quasi-automatic with no adequate psychological or pedagogical assessment; and that while the intention of the authorities had in fact been to achieve social and educational integration, they had failed to instal sufficient safeguards in the system to counter discriminatory tendencies.[38] Even where the aim of putting Roma children in a separate class temporarily to cater for language difficulties was not noted to be automatically contrary to Art.14, the Court noted that in practice the tests applied to the children were not designed to identify such difficulties, the placement never extended to non-Roma children, there were no regular tests to check progress and no extra lessons in Croatian appear in fact to have been given with very few Roma children ever transferring into mixed classes; this situation, despite the well-meaning efforts of the authorities, showed a lack of the safeguards necessary to prevent a discriminatory situation arising.[39] Positive measures to address the poor attendance rates of Roma children and their high drop out rate were also required in order to raise awareness of the importance of education amongst the Roma population and to assist the children with any difficulties.[40]

Gypsies and other minorities cannot claim claim any overriding right to continue traditional cultural activities, or even reside, in a particular location. Cases so far

[36] *Coster*, para.137; *Jane Smith*, para.129; *Lee*, para.125: judgments cited in fn.10 above.

[37] The tests were designed for the majority population and did not take Romany specifics into account; this factor put the Romany children at a disadvantage from the very beginning.

[38] *DH and Others*, fn.2 above; see also *Sampanis*, fn.17 above, where local people showed violent and threatening resistance to Roma children attending the local school and the Roma children were placed in "preparatory" classes separate from the other children, the Court found discrimination as the Government failed to show any justification for this effective segregation, unable to show that it was based on objective testing or that any of the children had ever been transferred into the ordinary school at a later stage.

[39] *Orsus and Others*, fn.3 above, paras 158–175.

[40] *Orsus and Others*, fn.3 above, paras 176–177, reference to involving the social services.

have found measures to be proportionate where alternative solutions have been provided.[41] Nor can Roma claim that their rites of marriage should receive equal recognition in law as certain religious forms of marriage, it being sufficient that the civil marriage ceremony was equally open to all.[42]

6. Access to court

Regarding the adequacy of court review of planning decisions, the Court's judgment in *Bryan v UK* indicates that special considerations apply in the planning sphere. The applicant, facing enforcement measures in respect of his barn conversion, had argued that the inspector in planning enquiries was not sufficiently independent of the Executive and the High Court's scope of review on points of law insufficient to address his complaints on the merits. The Court found that while the inspector did not provide guarantees of independence, the procedures were basically fair and the possibility of appeal on points of law to the High Court was sufficient review in a special area of administrative discretion. As a result, it would appear that gypsies who generally have problems on the merits of cases (for example, whether the planning considerations outweigh the compassionate circumstances) will effectively be deprived of any independent scrutiny of their cases and the planning authorities given an almost exclusive decision-making power if they keep within domestic law.[43] II–446

7. Property rights

Where land of ethnic groups has been expropriated in the past, it is likely that the act itself will fall outside the temporal jurisdiction of the Court. Nonetheless, where there are subsequent procedures which can be examined, the Court, in determining whether a fair balance has been struck between the general interest and the individuals concerned, is also likely to give leeway to the domestic courts which carry out the factual assessment and calculation of losses.[44] II–447

Measures also have to be shown to have a concrete effect on the value or exercise of current proprietary rights. The Court found no interference with traditional Sámi fishing rights where these were maintained but also extended to all the local residents in particular areas.[45]

Where a Roma widow found that she was not entitled to a pension on the death of her husband (the Roma marriage not being legally recognised), the Court considered that her claim to a social benefit fell within the scope of Art.1 of Protocol No.1 and that the refusal of the pension, despite the fact that the authorities had recognised the family unit for other official purposes and in light of applicant's good

[41] *Gypsy Council v UK*, (66336/01) (Dec.) May 14, 2002, where a prohibition order was issued severely restricting the traditional horse fair at Horsemonden (a limited procession was allowed in the village and an alternative venue provided some 20 miles away): *Noack v Germany*, (46346/99) (Dec.) May 25, 2000, ECHR 2000–VI, where a community of Sorbs were required to transfer to another village to make room for lignite mining with accompanying measures aimed to protect their language and culture.

[42] *Munoz Diaz v Spain*, December 8, 2009.

[43] See e.g. *Chapman*, fn.10 above, paras 123–126, applying the *Bryan* approach to a gypsy case.

[44] *Hingitaq and 53 others v Denmark*, (18584/04) (Dec.) January 12, 2006, where Inuit complained of the expropriation of land for the US airbase in Thule in 1951.

[45] *Johtti Sapmelaccatry v Finland*, (42969/98) (Dec.) January 18, 2005, even where there was a restriction in the use of certain equipment, this was justified by conservation concerns.

faith and belief that her marriage was thus officially-accepted, showed inconsistency and a disproportionate inflexibility to her situation which was discriminatory.[46]

8. Electoral rights

II–448 Where the power-sharing mechanisms set up in Bosnia-Herzegovina to cater for the three major "consituent" peoples did not provide the possibility for Roma (and Jewish) candidates to stand for the House of Peoples, the Court found no justification for the exclusion, even in the delicate and difficult post-conflict situation.[47]

Cross-reference

Part IIA, s.2: Access to court.
Part IIB, s.12: Discrimination.

[46] *Munoz Diaz*, fn.42 above, paras 54–71.
[47] *Sejdic and Finci v Bosnia-Herzegovina,* December 22, 2009, paras 47–50.

25. Hindrance in the exercise of the right of individual petition

Key provision:

Article 34, *in fine* (undertaking not to hinder the effective exercise of the right of individual petition) formerly Art.25, para.1, *in fine*. II–449

Key case-law:

Cruz Varas v Sweden, March 20, 1991, Series A, No.201, 14 E.H.R.R. 1; *Akdivar v Turkey*, September 16, 1996, R.J.D. 1996–IV, No.15, 23 E.H.R.R. 143; *Aksoy v Turkey*, December 18, 1996, R.J.D. 1996–VI, No.26, 23 E.H.R.R. 553; *Aydin v Turkey*, September 25, 1997, R.J.D. 1997–VI, No.50, 25 E.H.R.R. 251; *Petra v Romania*, September 23, 1998, R.J.D. 1997–VII, No.92; *Kurt v Turkey*, May 25, 1998, R.J.D. 1998–III, No.74, 27 E.H.R.R. 373; *Tanrikulu v Turkey*, July 9, 1999, ECHR 1999–IV; *McShane v UK*, May 28, 2002, *Mahmatkulov and Askarov v Turkey*, February 4, 2005, ECHR 2005–I; *Shameyev v Georgia and Russia*, April 12, 2005, ECHR 2005–III; *Ocalan v Turkey*, May 5, 2005, ECHR 2005–IV; *Paladi v Moldova*, March 10, 2009, ECHR 2009–. . .

1. General considerations

The right of individual petition is the keystone of the supervision process, since it is individuals and private organisations who provide the vast bulk of the cases under Art.34. The final sentence intends to safeguard the open and unimpeded access of the individual to Strasbourg by imposing the obligation on Contracting States not to hinder the exercise of the right of individual petition. In examining issues arising under Art.34 (former Art.25), the Commission and Court had regard to the fundamental principle of interpretation of the Convention, that it must guarantee rights which are practical and effective as opposed to theoretical and illusory.[1] As an indication of its importance, the Commission used to raise any apparent problems of hindrance *ex officio*, such being a matter pertinent to its own functioning[2]; the Court continues to do so.[3] II–450

Express obligations are imposed on States which sign the European Agreement relating to persons participating in proceedings of the European Court of Human Rights. This covers for example interference with prisoners' correspondence with the Convention organs (Art.3) and co-operation in allowing applicants to enter or leave territory for the purpose of attending hearings (Art.4).

It is a healthy sign that relatively few complaints are made that a Contracting State has either failed to co-operate with the Convention organs in the examination process or that it has interfered with the applicant in some way. Where allegations do arise of deliberate interference by a Government with an applicant during

[1] e.g. *Cruz Varas v Sweden*, March 20, 1991, Series A, No.201, 14 E.H.R.R. 1, para.99; *Aydin*, (Rep.) March 7, 1996, para.212.

[2] (13590/88) (Rep.) July 12, 1990, Series A, No.233–A, p.33. The Court would be likely to adopt the same view, now that it has taken over sole responsibility for applications.

[3] *DB v Turkey*, July 13, 2010, para.61; *Lopata v Russia*, July 13, 2010, para.147.

pending proceedings, which the Government denies, the Court is in a difficult position and may be faced by factual problems which it is ill-equipped to resolve.[4]

In brief, the obligation has been defined as requiring Contracting States not only to refrain from pressurising applicants but also covers any act or omission which, by destroying or removing the subject-matter of an application, would make it pointless or otherwise prevent the Court from considering it under normal procedure. Thus, the purpose of the rule being to render effective the right of individual petition, the Court has stated that the intentions of the authorities or their reasons are of little relevance; the question is whether the situation created as a result of the authorities' act or omission conforms to Art.34.[5]

2. Substantive or procedural right

II–451 Former Art.25 was described in *Cruz Varas v Sweden* as a procedural right which could be invoked by individuals. The Commission followed a practice of making findings as to whether a Government had failed to comply with its obligations. Then, in *Akdivar v Turkey* the Court made a finding of a violation of Art.25, although specifying that it was of a procedural nature distinguishable from the substantive rights. The terminology used by the new Court tends to use the previous Commission formulation, though references to violation or non-violation of Art.34 also appear. No matters of relevance appear to flow from the varying usage.

Having regard to the procedural character of the right, the admissibility criteria appear to have no role.[6] Although the Court might not consider it appropriate to apply the six-month time-limit, it might well be that a failure to raise an allegation for a considerable period without any convincing reason would be a factor against the matter being taken up.

3. Hindrance

II–452 Hindrance in its normal meaning is not synonymous with complete obstruction, but would appear to cover any step which renders the application process more difficult. Indeed, though it was initially questioned whether there could be hindrance where an applicant pursued his petition, it would have meant that no successful allegations of interference could be made since the applicants who were most effectively

[4] e.g. *Kurt v Turkey*, May 25, 1998, R.J.D. 1998–III, No.74, 27 E.H.R.R. 373, para.161, where the applicant produced contradictory statements, her lawyers claimed Government pressure while the Government alleged PKK coercion to produce anti-State propaganda. Some allegations may prove impossible to clarify, as in *Aksoy v Turkey*, December 18, 1996, R.J.D. 1996–VI, No.26, 23 E.H.R.R. 553, where the applicant was tortured in custody and then shot dead shortly after his case was communicated to the Government. His lawyer stated that the applicant had claimed that he was being followed and that his life was in danger. The Commission was "deeply concerned" by the death of the applicant but unable to resolve the matter. It therefore did not find any failure to comply with former Art.25, nor did the Court. See more recently *Akhmadova and Saduleyeva v Russia*, May 10, 2007, para 55–62 and 130–134, where the applicants complained of harassment by police, including physical assaults, the Court had insufficient evidence on which to make any findings; *Bitiyeva and X v Russia*, June 26, 2007, where the first applicant was killed after introducing her application, the Court found that she and other family members had been executed by security forces in breach of Art.2 but that there was nothing to show a link to the application before the Court.

[5] *Paladi v Moldova*, March 10, 2009, ECHR 2009–. . . , para.87.

[6] *Ergi v Turkey*, July 28, 1998, R.J.D. 1998–IV, No.81, para.105; *Al-Moayad v Germany*, (35865/03) (Dec.) February 20, 2007, para.117, rejecting applicability of the six-month rule.

intimidated would have ceased to pursue their cases at all.[7] The Court made this position clear in *Akdivar*, where indeed one applicant had withdrawn his application entirely before the Commission Delegates and the remaining applicants had continued notwithstanding the alleged intimidation.[8]

4. Types of hindrance

(a) *Prisoners' correspondence, solitary confinement and access to lawyers and documents*

The occasional stopping of a letter to the Commission was not considered sufficient to raise an issue,[9] and in *Campbell v UK* the opening of letters to the Commission, without tampering or delaying, was insufficient to disclose any prejudice in the presentation of his application to the Commission.[10] No violation of Art.34 arose from delays of some weeks in transmitting the applicant's letters to the Court as they were not regarded as significant or hindering the exercise of his right of petition.[11] The stopping of two letters to the Court which delayed the submission of an application for eight months did interfere with the right of individual petition[12] as did a refusal to forward an application for failing to comply with rules on exhausting local remedies first.[13] However, where the main complaint concerns the opening or censorship of letters and the Court finds a breach of Art.8, no separate issue under Art.34 is likely to arise.[14] II–453

Where the same applicant in *Campbell* alleged that he was being punished in solitary confinement for his applications to Strasbourg, the Commission took the complaint seriously enough to pursue the matter with the Government. It transpired, however, that he was held in segregation because he wanted to spend time on his various litigations and had refused to go on normal routine which would have involved working instead of spending time in his cell with his books and papers. Thus, there was no clear punitive intent and no indication that it hampered his right of petition.[15] In *Petra v Romania* however, the Court found a violation of former Art.25 where the applicant had been threatened twice by the prison authorities when he had asked to write to the Commission.[16] Refusal to provide writing materials for pursuing an application may also disclose a hindrance.[17]

[7] In *Kapan v Turkey*, (Dec.) January 14, 1997, 88–A D.R. 17, the applicant failed to appear at a hearing in Strasbourg and in Turkey, his lawyers claiming that he feared for his life. However, following his continued silence, including a failure to provide written confirmation of his intention to continue the application, the Commission struck the case off. To give up these cases is perhaps unsatisfactory. But it underlines the reality that the system relies on applicants with the courage to complain and to maintain their complaints actively.

[8] See also *Shamayev v Georgia and Russia*, April 12, 2005, ECHR 2005–III, para.478.

[9] (18264/91) (Dec.) September 8, 1993.

[10] The Commission did find a violation of the Art.8 correspondence right, as did the Court. Former Art.25 was not pursued before the Court.

[11] *Valasinas v Lithuania*, July 24, 2001, ECHR 2001–VIII, para.136, the Court had, however, found a breach of Art.8 in respect of censorship of the correspondence.

[12] *Poleshchuk v Russia*, October 7, 2004, para.27.

[13] *Nurmagomedov v Russia*, June 7, 2007, paras 57–62.

[14] e.g. *Klamecki v Poland (No.2)*, April 3, 2003, para.158.

[15] *Campbell v UK*, (12323/86) (Dec.) July 13, 1988, 57 D.R. 148.

[16] *Petra v Romania*, September 23, 1998, R.J.D. 1997–VII, No.92, para.44; mere questioning for clarification did not disclose improper pressure in *Manoussos v Czech Republic and Germany*, (46468/99) (Dec.) July 9, 2002.

[17] *Cotlet v Romania*, June 3, 2000, where there were also delays in the mail which was sent and systematic opening of Strasbourg correspondence.

As regards prisoners' access to lawyers for the Convention purposes, in *Ocalan v Turkey* the refusal to grant the applicant's lawyers' permission to enter the territory and alleged difficulties for the applicant in communicating with his lawyers did not in fact prevent them from submitting an application to the Court on his behalf and thus there was no indication that his exercise of his right of individual petition had been impeded to any significant extent.[18] Where an applicant complained under Art.3 of alleged ill-treatment and lack of proper medical treatment in prison, the failure of the authorities to allow his lawyers and doctors access to him and his prison medical file disclosed a failure to comply with Art.34 and an aggravated breach of Art.3.[19] The inability of an applicant and lawyer to consult about a Strasbourg application without an intervening glass partition that prevented the passage of documents, and was also suspected, on reasonable grounds, of being bugged, disclosed an unacceptable hindrance.[20] While lawyers and representatives may be required to fulfill certain formalities, for reasons of security and to prevent obstruction of justice, in order to visit applicants in prison, these should not be of such a nature or degree as to effectively bar access.[21] This was the case where the applicant's representative before the Court could not obtain access to him in prison as she was not his counsel in criminal proceedings.[22]

(b) Applicants' access to documents

II–454 Art.34 may extend to requiring access by applicants to documents necessary for submitting their application. Where there was a four month delay by the prison authorities in providing the applicant with copies from his prison and medical file, the Court noted that these documents had been required by the Rules of Court to support his application form and this, together with dissuasive remarks by prison officials, infringed Art.34.[23] No problem arose, however, where tapes of court hearings were, as a rule, destroyed after two months, the Court finding no indication that the applicant's inability to obtain the tape-recording had hindered him in his application.[24] Where there was no provision for providing prisoners with copies of documents from domestic court files and an applicant was refused copies of the petitions which he had lodged, the Court was not precluded from finding a breach of Art.34 by the fact that the Government provided these documents some time later during the Strasbourg proceedings.[25]

[18] *Ocalan v Turkey*, May 5, 2005, ECHR 2005–IV, para.200.
[19] *Boicenco v Moldova*, July 11, 2006, paras 158–159. See also the six-month ban on contact with lawyer while the applicant was in a mental hospital: *Shtukaturov v Russia*, March 27, 2008, paras 139–140.
[20] *Ofert Plus Srl v Moldova*, December 19, 2006, para.156.
[21] *Melnikov v Russia*, January 14, 2010, keeping the lawyer waiting while verifying the applicant's authorisation of representation was not excessive; *Lebedev v Russia*, October 25, 2007, where the additional court authorisation had been easily obtained and only restricted access over a few weeks.
[22] *Zakharkin v Russia*, June 3, 2010, as the Court permitted non-legally qualified representatives, domestic law should not have restricted access to counsel only.
[23] *Gagiu v Romania*, February 24, 2009, the applicant had claimed the prison authorities required him to pay for the photocopies and as he had had no funds he was forced to sell his food to other prisoners to obtain the money. See also *Zdravko Petrov v Bulgaria*, June 11, 2011, paras 60–64, violation due to obstructiveness of authorities to supplying the applicant with court documents relevant to his application to Strasbourg.
[24] *Holland v Sweden*, (27700/08) (Dec.) February 9, 2010.
[25] *Naydyon v Ukraine*, October 14, 2010, paras 62–69.

(c) *Applicants' access to lawyers and court facilities*

Where a disabled applicant complained of being unable to access public buildings, including court premises and lawyers' offices, the Court seemed to envisage that Art.34 might come into play if an applicant was unable to exhaust domestic remedies which is a precondition to coming to Strasbourg. However, on the facts of the case, the Court considered that the applicant had been able to use the post to lodge claims with the Court and to enlist the aid of lawyers and thus difficulties of access to the buildings had not been a hindrance.[26] II–455

(d) *Intimidation of applicants*

Contact by State authorities with applicants concerning their applications to Strasbourg is likely, save in exceptional and convincingly innocuous circumstances, to raise serious issues. The Court's approach in *Aydin v Turkey*, however, indicates that applicants must provide some concrete and independent proof of any harassment alleged.[27] II–456

Unacceptable pressure includes direct coercion and flagrant acts of intimidation of applicants or potential applicants or their families or legal representatives and also other improper indirect acts or contacts designed to dissuade or discourage them from pursuing a Convention remedy. The vulnerability of the complainant is taken into account in assessing the propriety of any such contacts.[28] Intimidation of the chief executive officer has been regarded as interfering with the right of individual petition of an applicant company.[29] Intimidatory contacts with witnesses who have provided statements supporting an applicant's case are also prohibited.[30]

[26] *Farcas v Romania*, (32596/04) (Dec.) September 14, 2010, paras 49–54.

[27] *Aydin v Turkey*, September 25, 1997, R.J.D. 1997–VI, No.50, 25 E.H.R.R. 251, paras 116–117, it disagreed with the Commission's more liberal approach requiring the Government to make a proper response to allegations. Also, *Demiray v Turkey*, November 21, 2000, ECHR 2000–XII, where the Court found insufficient facts to conclude that the applicant's family had been questioned about the application or otherwise harassed by the authorities; *Denizci v Cyprus*, May 23, 2001, ECHR 2001–V, paras 419–421, insufficient evidence to show that improper pressure had been placed on the applicants to retract their allegations; *Berktay v Turkey*, March 1, 2001, para.208.

[28] e.g. *Kurt*, fn.4 above, para.60; *Assenov v Bulgaria*, October 28, 1998, R.J.D. 1998–VIII, No.96, para.170, where the applicants were questioned and led to make a sworn declaration denying that they had made an application; *Bilgin v Turkey*, November 16, 2000, para.135, where the applicant was questioned about his application by the gendarme authorities against whom he had made serious complaint; *Akkoç v Turkey*, October 10, 2000, ECHR 2000–X, para.126, where the applicant was questioned about her application during an interrogation involving torture; *Ilaşcu v Moldova and Russia*, July 8, 2004, ECHR 2004–VII, paras 481–482, where the applicants' conditions of detention deteriorated after they had lodged their application, the President of Moldova accused the first applicant of being the cause of the continued detention of the other applicants through his refusal to withdraw his application and the Russian Government had interceded with the Moldovan Government to influence the course of the proceedings.

[29] *Oferta Plus Srl*, fn.20 above, para.136, sufficiently strong grounds supported the inference that unfounded criminal proceedings against the CEO were intended to discourage the company from pursuing its case in Strasbourg.

[30] *Novinskiy v Russia*, February 10, 2009, paras 119–123, in prison condition cases, where most information was in the hands of the authorities, applicants relied on fellow-prisoners to substantiate their complaints and interferences with such witnesses hampered their right of petition. In this case, the witness had been questioned by police about his statement to the Court under threat of fines and conviction but in the absence of any suspicion of any criminal offence.

Questioning of applicants about their applications will generally amount to an illicit and unacceptable form of pressure on applicants to withdraw their applications.[31] Even if contact by the authorities with a view to investigate their complaints on a domestic level was compatible, the Commission considered that applicants' lawyers should be present and that it was never legitimate to question applicants about the circumstances in which they made their application, their motivation or what they intended to say in the application with a view to testing the accuracy of submissions made on their behalf.[32] The Court regards statements of applicants retracting their complaints following visits by State officials with the utmost suspicion and appears to require convincing explanation of the contents of such conversations to rebut allegations of intimidatory or illicit purposes.[33] In *Tanrikulu v Turkey*, the questioning of the applicant by the Chief Public Prosecutor as to the authenticity of the letter of authority provided by her lawyers to the Commission was, with other actions, interpreted as a deliberate attempt to cast doubt on the validity of the application and the applicant's credibility and a bid to frustrate the applicant's successful pursuit of her application. The Court agreed with the Commission that if a Government were concerned about forged documents they should bring their misgivings before the Convention organs.[34] In exceptional circumstances, no pressure, intimidation or harassment may be disclosed by questions put by the authorities to applicants, as in *Sisojeva v Latvia*, where although a police officer had exceeded his remit in asking about the applicant's case in Strasbourg, the Court accepted that the interview principally concerned allegations of corruption which the applicant had made on television shortly before and was not aimed at interfering with the Strasbourg proceedings.[35]

(e) Intimidation of lawyers

II–457 Attempts to institute criminal and even disciplinary proceedings against lawyers in connection with their participation in applications to Strasbourg will disclose a failure by the State to comply with obligations under Art.34, since this may have

[31] *Akdivar v Turkey*, September 16, 1996, R.J.D. 1996–IV, No.15, 23 E.H.R.R. 143, violations of former Art.25 found where the Government produced a videotape of an applicant, and a villager mistaken for an applicant, denying the introduction of any application and stereotyped denials signed by other applicants; *Popov v Russia*, July 11, 2006, repeated questioning of the applicant in prison in a vulnerable situation.

[32] Also *Kurt*, (Rep.) December 6, 1996, para.247, where the Commission found that contacts with an applicant to verify whether the application was genuine were unacceptable, since where such doubts existed it was for the Commission to verify the existence of a valid application; *Ergi*, fn.6 above, the Convention organs found no plausible reason for the authorities, particularly the anti-terror police, to question the applicant about his application, even to verify his legal aid claim; *Akdeniz v Turkey*, May 31, 2000, paras 119–120, where applicants were questioned about their applications and in two cases detained overnight.

[33] See *Lopata*, fn.3 above, paras 154–159.

[34] Also *Salman v Turkey*, June 27, 2000, ECHR 2000–VII, paras 131–132, where the applicant was questioned about her legal aid declaration of means from the Commission and blindfolded while at the Anti-Terror Department.

[35] *Sisojeva v Latvia*, January 8, 2007, para.124. See also *Manoussos*, fn.16 above, where the questioning of the prisoner did not disclose any improper pressure on the facts; *Matyar v Turkey*, February 21, 2002, where the majority found insufficient evidence to support allegations of intimidation when an applicant was summoned for questioning by gendarmes, the minority considered that the presumption that this amounted to illicit pressure had not been rebutted in the absence of a convincing explanation about why it was necessary; *Imkayeva v Russia*, November 9, 2006, para.206, no indication of any threats or intimidation in circumstances when the applicant was questioned incidentally by a criminal investigator and army officer about her application; similar approach adopted in *Bitiyeva and X*, fn.4, para.166.

the effect of dissuading an applicant or his or her lawyer from pursuing a case, place obstacles in the path of pursuing an application and deter future applications. A hindrance was found in *Kurt v Turkey* where a Government representative took the initiative in contacting the prosecution authorities after a Commission hearing with a view to taking action against the applicant's lawyer for making allegations which the applicant had not maintained in her oral evidence.[36] An investigation by the police, rather than the appropriate tax authority, into the regularities of the applicant's disbursements to her lawyer concerning her application in Strasbourg was also potentially intimidatory contrary to Art.34.[37] Even where the lawyer is later acquitted or the proceedings dropped, the institution of the proceedings is regarded as having a potential chilling effect.[38] There was, on that basis, a sufficient connection with an application to the Court for an adverse finding under Art.34 in *McShane v UK*, where the police lodged a disciplinary complaint, later dropped, against the applicant's lawyer in inquest proceedings for allegedly infringing an undertaking in passing on documents to the applicant for use in her Convention application. Generalised threats which could be construed as having an objectionable chilling effect on petition to the Court may also suffice, as in *Colibaba v Moldova*, where a letter by the Prosecutor General to an applicant's lawyer, threatening prosecution for making false allegations of human rights breaches to an international organisation, fell foul of Art.34 regardless of whether it was intended to cover the Court or whether the authorities were aware of the particular application to the Court.[39]

Where Governments suspect lawyers of improper conduct in the lodging of an application to the Court, they should restrict themselves to informing the Court.[40]

5. Failure of the Government to comply with procedural requests

(a) *Failure to comply with interim measures*

The refusal of a Government to comply with a Commission request for suspensive measures under its rules of procedure was not per se a failure to comply with its former Art.25 obligations. In *Cruz Varas v Sweden*, where the authorities expelled the applicant to Chile despite the Commission's request to suspend the measure pending examination of allegations that he risked torture and ill-treatment on return, the Court found that no power to impose binding interim measures could be derived from former Art.25 or the Commission's Rules.[41] II–458

36 See also *Sarli v Turkey*, May 22, 2001, paras 85–86, where criminal proceedings were commenced against a Turkish lawyer for submitting an application for the purpose, inter alia, of anti-State propaganda. It was irrelevant that the lawyer was not one of the applicant's named representatives in Strasbourg as he had nonetheless been assisting them and was instrumental in introducing the application.

37 *Fedotova*, April 13, 2006, paras 47–52. See also *Ryabov v Russia*, January 31, 2008, paras 59–65, where the authorities inappropriately targeted the applicant's representative, sending the police to question him about their relationship and the purportedly fraudulent nature of the legal assistance agreement which he had entered into.

38 *Sarli*, fn.36 above, para.85.

39 *Colibaba v Moldova*, October 23, 2007, para.68.

40 *Ryabov*,fn.37, para.59.

41 Now r.39 of the Rules of Court. See Procedure Before the Court, Interim Relief. An approach which it confirmed regarding its own rules of procedure until as recently as *Conka v Belgium*, (51564/99) (Dec.) March 13, 2001, where the Belgian authorities failed to suspend the expulsion measures against the gypsy applicants without explanation, the Court rejected the Art.34 complaint.

Nonetheless, when the new Court came years later to consider the status of its own interim measures in *Mamatkulov and Askarov v Turkey*, it emphasised the need to make the system effective and the status of the Convention as a living instrument, concluding that Contracting States were under an obligation to comply with requests for interim measures and to refrain from any act or omission which might impinge on the integrity and effectiveness of a future binding judgment under Art.46. In the particular case, it found that the failure of the Government to suspend the extradition of two applicants to Uzbekistan disclosed a violation of Art.34, essentially as, since the applicants' extradition, their lawyers had been unable to communicate with them and it was for lack of substantiation that their complaints under Art.3 were rejected. Thus, there had been irreparable damage to the level of protection the Convention system could provide.[42] Where a suspected Islamic terrorist had been expelled by Italy to Tunisia despite an interim measure, the Court noted that this prevented him from submitting further information in his application and that his lawyer could no longer contact him. Further, the fact that the applicant was now outside Italian jurisdiction would pose obstacles for the Italian Government under Arts 1 and 46 to efface the consequences of any violations found.[43] However, even where on expulsion to Peru, in defiance of an interim measure, the applicant had apparently come to no harm and had been released, with no difficulties in continuing his application in Strasbourg, the Court found that the failure to comply with the indication, in itself, was a serious infringement of Art.34.[44]

It appears that deliberate expulsion of an applicant, in knowledge that a request for interim relief has been made to the Court by an applicant, but before the Court reached its decision, might breach the obligation to co-operate in good faith imposed on Governments by Art.34.[45] There is furthermore an obligation on the authorities to organise themselves in such a way as to be able to respond promptly to an interim measure, a breach being found where the Court Registry had been unable to contact the Government Agent concerning implementation of the measure and also due to the subsequent delays in the measure being carried out.[46]

It is not decisive that, notwithstanding failure to comply with a measure, the applicant was able to continue his application to the Court. Thus, where the authorities failed to comply with a direction to allow the applicant, while in mental hospital, to consult with his lawyer, it was no defence that he had pursued his application once he had been released and renewed contact with his lawyer, as making it more difficult for an applicant to petition Strasbourg amounted to a hindrance for the purposes of Art.34.[47] Where the Government had failed, as required under r.39, for two months to transfer the applicant, seriously ill with

[42] See also *Shamayev*, fn.8 above, where the extradition, executed despite a r.39 indication, frustrated the gathering of evidence; *Aoulmi v France*, January 17, 2006, paras 101–112.

[43] *Ben Khemais v Italy*, February 24, 2009.

[44] *Olaechea Cahuas v Spain*, August 10, 2006, para.81.

[45] *Al-Moayad*, fn.6 above, there was, however, no evidence that the German authorities were aware that the applicant had made a request to the Court before they extradited him.

[46] *Paladi*, fn.5 above, where the Court had indicated that the applicant prisoner should not be transferred from hospital to prison until it had examined his complaints about inadequate medical care in prison.

[47] *Shtukaturov*, fn.19, para.147. See also *DB v Turkey*, fn.3 above, paras 65–67, delay in allowing detained asylum seeker access to his lawyers as directed by an interim measure seriously hampered his case before the Court and even placed him in jeopardy since he could not substantiate his claims of risk on return to Iran.

AIDS and opportunistic infections, to a specialised hospital and to co-operate in setting up a medical commission including the applicant's own doctor to establish his state of health, the Court again rejected arguments that the prisoner had nonetheless been able to pursue his application and noted that the delay had put the applicant's life in danger and had also hampered the gathering of objective information about his medical condition, in hindrance of the right of individual petition.[48] Frequently, interim measures have to be issued as a matter of urgency and without full information before the Court; even if the situation later is found not to be so serious, this does not remove the obligation of compliance on the State. It is not for the State to substitute its own judgment as to whether there is risk of irreparable damage to an applicant; if it has information to the contrary, it should merely inform the Court with a view to obtaining a lifting of the measure.[49] Its obligation is to act urgently.[50] While objective impediments to complying with a measure may provide justification for failure to do so, the Court has scrutinised such explanations rigorously.[51] Even where the United Kingdom Government were under a treaty obligation to hand over detainees to the Iraqi authorities, the Court found that this did not relieve them of making the necessary efforts to ensure that they nonetheless acted in compliance with their Convention obligations, in particular by obtaining satisfactory assurances before transfer that the detainees would not be subject to the death penalty.[52]

Not all failures to comply with interim measures may breach Art.34 however. The Court reserved its position in *Ocalan v Turkey*,[53] stating that in the exceptional circumstances of that case the failure of the Government under a r.39 request to make available certain information did not prevent the applicant setting out his case in Strasbourg.

(b) *Documents and other facilities*

A failure by a Government to provide documents or information, or to facilitate the taking of evidence before Delegates from the Court might also potentially raise issues under Art.34 where this substantially hindered the Strasbourg examination of the case. In cases of this kind, however, the Court tends instead to make a finding that the State has failed to comply with Art.38 (former Art.28 para.1(a)), which provides that States "shall furnish all necessary facilities" in the investigation of a case,[54] emphasising the importance of the Government's co-operation in Convention II–459

[48] *Aleksanyan v Russia*, December 22, 2008, paras 228–232.
[49] *Paladi*, fn.5 above, paras 89–90 and 104.
[50] See e.g. *Grori v Albania*, July 7, 2009, paras 190–191, where there was a seventeen day delay in transferring the applicant from prison to hospital, the Court rejected excuses of the need for time to deal with security matters.
[51] *Paladi*, fn.5 above, paras 95–102, where there had been a delay over the weekend in obtaining the applicant's return to hospital, the Court rejected the Government's claims that it had not been possible to organise compliance more promptly; *Kamiliyevy v Russia*, June 3, 2010, where the notification had gone to the Government, on a working day, twenty-six hours before the applicant had been expelled, with no reported difficulties in communication, the Court did not accept that the time difference had rendered it impossible for the Government to contact the authorities in one of its more remote regions.
[52] *Al-Saadoon and Mufhdi v UK*, March 2, 2010, paras 162–166.
[53] *Ocalan v Turkey*, fn.18 above, para.201.
[54] e.g. *Cakici v Turkey*, July 8, 1999, ECHR 1999–IV, para.76, where the Government gave no satisfactory explanations for failure to provide custody records or the non-attendance of witnesses at a

proceedings.[55] This has included providing access to the country, applicants and the premises where applicants were held, the Court dismissing various excuses including the alleged refusals of the domestic courts to grant access to prisoners or difficulties of timing.[56] In cases raising issues of the effectiveness of investigations into unlawful killings and forced disappearances, the material in the investigation file is regarded as crucial to the establishment of the facts; thus, the provision of formal procedural decisions, without providing copies of witness interviews and forensic reports was found to fall short of Art.38 obligations.[57]

No issues under Arts 34 or 38 arose where, impliedly, a Government witness had lied on oath before Commission delegates.[58]

Governments must provide concrete, reasoned grounds for refusing to provide documents to the Court. It was not sufficient for the Russian Government to rely without explanation on Art.161 of the Code of Criminal Procedure which stated that the contents of preliminary investigation files could not be disclosed without permission of the public prosecutor and where, inter alia, such disclosure would not prejudice the investigation or infringe the rights of participants in the proceedings.[59] Nor could the Government rely on the status of a report on an alien as a State secret and the lack of domestic legal provision for making available such documents to international organisations; it was under a Convention obligation to make provision for such a procedure, in which it would be possible to address any legitimate security concerns by, for example, editing sensitive passages.[60]

Alternatively, the Court may draw inferences from the failure of a Government to respond to questions or requests and proceed to find substantive violations.[61] The Commission referred, in a number of cases involving the taking of evidence, to the Court's statement in *Ireland v UK* that the conduct of the parties when evidence is being taken may be taken into account in the assessment of evidence.[62]

It appears that in cases in which the admissibility and merits are considered together and there has been no failure by the Government to respond to a specific request for documents, the Court may content itself with drawing inferences from a

fact-finding hearing; *Aktas v Turkey*, April 24, 2003, where the Government refused on short notice to make 11 witnesses available to the Commission without special security conditions barring the applicant's lawyers from participation; *Tas v Turkey*, November 14, 2000, where the Government delayed in providing information; *Tanis v Turkey*, August 2, 2005, ECHR 2005–VIII, paras 163–164, failure to provide unexpurgated file or provide a key witness.

[55] e.g. *Tepe v Turkey*, May 9, 2003, para.135; *Baysayeva v Russia*, April 4, 2007, para.168, Art.34, the *lex generalis* in relation to Art.38's specific obligation: breach of the latter for failing to provide almost no documents from the case file; contrast *Musayeva and Others v Russia*, July 26, 2007, inferences drawn from failure to provide some requested documents, but no breach of Art.38.

[56] *Shameyev v Georgia and Russia*, April 12, 2005, ECHR 2005–III, paras 498–504.

[57] *Kukayev v Russia*, November 15, 2007, para 121–123.

[58] *Timurtas v Turkey*, June 13, 2000, paras 72 and 123.

[59] *Imakayeva, v Russia*, fn.35 above, paras 123 and 201; *Kukayev*, fn.57.

[60] *Nolan and K v Russia*, February 12, 2009, a failure to comply with Art.38 for refusing to communicate a classified report to Court about reasons for denial of entry to a foreign national; the Court noted that the applicant's counsel had seen a copy though was bound not to disclose its contents, which showed there was no objection to showing the report outside the security services and high levels of government (paras 56–57).

[61] e.g. *Ergi*, fn.6 above, failure to provide requested gendarme witnesses was taken into account in assessing the evidence.

[62] *Ireland v UK*, January 18, 1978, Series A, No.25, para.161; *Ergi*, fn.6 above; *Betayev and Betayeva v Russia*, May 29, 2008, para.70.

lack of documentary evidence.[63] However, it is not precluded from finding a breach of Art.38 in such a joint procedure, where the Government has signally failed to provide relevant materials without plausible explanation.[64]

6. Immunity in Strasbourg proceedings

The European Agreement relating to Persons Participating in Proceedings of the European Court of Human Rights provides immunity to those participating in proceedings in Strasbourg. The Court has emphasised that this is to ensure free and open communication in its proceedings and to protect those who plead before it from being sued or prosecuted for their statements. In view of the importance of this objective for the proper conduct of its proceedings, it has stated that it will waive such immunity only in exceptional circumstances, for example where the impugned statements are manifestly excessive or plainly irrelevant. Thus, it refused to lift immunity where a witness for an applicant wished to sue the Government Agent for statements in written pleadings which were pertinent to credibility and not excessive.[65] II–460

[63] *Betayev and Betayeva*, fn.58, paras 4 and 131–133, the text rejects complaints raised by the applicants under Arts 34 and 38 in departure from the traditional approach of the Convention organs in treating these provisions as not falling under the admissibility criteria.

[64] *Enikidze and Girvliani v Georgia*, April 26, 2011, paras 295–302, the Government did not provide a full copy of the surveillance recordings or other evidence relevant to the investigation into a death.

[65] *Andersson v Sweden*, (41102/07) (Dec.) July 6, 2010.

26. Home

Key provision:

II–461 Article 8 (respect for home).

Key case-law:

Gillow v UK, November 24, 1986, Series A No.109, 11 E.H.R.R. 335; *Chappell v UK*, March 30, 1989, Series A, No.152–A, 12 E.H.R.R. 1; *Niemietz v Germany*, December 16, 1992, Series A, No.251–B, 16 E.H.R.R. 97; *Funke v France*, February 25, 1993, Series A, No.256–A, 16 E.H.R.R. 287; *Murray v UK*, October 28, 1994, Series A, No.300–A, 19 E.H.R.R. 193; *Buckley v UK*, September 25, 1996, R.J.D. 1996–IV, 23 E.H.R.R. 101; *Mentes v Turkey*, November 28, 1997, R.J.D. 1997–VIII, 26 E.H.R.R. 1; *Camenzind v Switzerland*, December 16, 1997, R.J.D. 1997–VIII, 28 E.H.R.R. 458; *McLeod v UK*, September 23, 1998, R.J.D. 1998–VII, 27 E.H.R.R. 493; *Chapman v UK*, January 18, 2001, ECHR 2001–I; *Cyprus v Turkey*, May 10, 2001, ECHR 2001–IV; Stés *Colas Est v France*, April 16, 2002, ECHR 2002–III; *Roemen and Schmit v Luxembourg*, February 25, 2003, ECHR 2003–V; *Ernst v Belgium*, July 15, 2003; *Prokopovich v Russia*, November 18, 2004, ECHR 2004–XI; *Keegan v UK*, July 18, 2006.

1. General considerations

II–462 Home has been given a wide definition by the Convention organs. It is not necessary that a home be lawfully established, significance attaching rather to the nature of the occupation.[1] Nor is ownership decisive,[2] though where there are no legal ties and no realistic expectation, after a passage of time, of resuming occupation, lack of ownership may be relevant.[3] Secondary homes used for recreational purposes may be covered, having regard to the nature of the use and strength of links.[4] Where an extended family had left their home due to fear of

[1] *Buckley v UK*, September 25, 1996, R.J.D. 1996–IV, 23 E.H.R.R. 101, paras 52–54, where the applicant gypsy established her home on land without planning permission—also *Buckley*, (Rep.) para.63, where the Commission found that "home" is an autonomous concept which does not depend on classification under domestic law, but on the factual circumstances, namely, the existence of sufficient and continuous links, citing (7456/76) (Dec.) February 8, 1978, 13 D.R. 40; *Gillow v UK*, November 24, 1986, Series A, No.109, 11 E.H.R.R. 335, para.46, where, though the applicants were absent from their house for almost 19 years for professional reasons, they intended it to be their home, keeping furniture there and having no home established elsewhere; recent statement in *Prokopovich v Russia*, November 18, 2004, ECHR 2004–XI, para.18; *McCann v UK*, May 13, 2008, para.43, "home" still applied even if the applicant had lost right of occupation.

[2] *Khamidov v Russia*, November 15, 2007, para.129, where two brothers and their kin lived close together in adjoining premises as one family, it was not relevant that the applicant brother did not own both houses in claiming interference with the whole.

[3] *Demopoulos v Turkey*, (46113/99) et al (Dec.) March 1, 2010, para.136. See also *Vrahimi v Turkey*, September 22, 2009, paras 50 and 60, where the applicant had been living at the time of the invasion, in 1974, on land owned by a company and in which she held no current legal interest.

[4] *Demades v Turkey*, July 31, 2003, paras 31–32; *Fagerskiold v Sweden*, (37664/04) (Dec.) February 26, 2008.

violence, maintaining the intention to return and not establishing a home elsewhere, Art.8 still applied.[5] However, with the lapse of time, links with a family "home" may weaken and cease to attract protection. Thus, where a member of a family was very young at the time that the family were forced to leave and had no ongoing connection with the property, some thirty years later she was not be able to claim concrete and persisting links to the claimed "home".[6]

Further, since "home" and "private life" may overlap with business and professional activities, the scope of Art.8 has been found to extend to offices. This is seen as consonant with the essential purpose of Art.8 to protect the individual against arbitrary interferences by public authorities.[7] Since companies may claim rights as applicants under the Convention, it has also been interpreted as covering company premises.[8] It has, however, been found contrary to common sense to extend the notion to pig breeding buildings.[9] Nor did it extend to the temporary and short use by a conductor of a dressing room in a concert hall,[10] to the buildings on an estate used as mill, bakery and storage facility,[11] or to the occasional use of a communal laundry room.[12]

As in other aspects of Art.8, while it is primarily interferences by public authorities which are concerned, there may in certain circumstances be positive obligations imposed on a State to protect the right to respect for home from others[13] or from environmental threats for which they can be held responsible.[14] However, there is no right as such to be provided with a home.[15]

[5] *Khamidov v Russia*, fn.2 above, para.41, in the families' absence, security forces had moved in, preventing their return. Violations arose due to the prolonged unlawful occupation and the damage caused to their adjoined houses.

[6] *Demopoulos v Turkey*, fn.3 above, paras 136–137.

[7] *Niemietz v Germany*, December 16, 1992, Series No.251–B, 16 E.H.R.R. 97, paras 30–31, where a search of a lawyer's office and seizure of documents by the police interfered with private life, home and correspondence; *Chappell v UK*, March 30, 1989, Series A, No.152–A, 12 E.H.R.R. 1, search of premises used for residential and business purposes; *Roemen and Schmidt v Luxembourg*, February 23, 2003, ECHR 2003–V, search of a lawyer's office; *Keslassy v France*, (51578/99) (Dec.) January 8, 2002, ECHR 2002–I, where the person's domicile was also head office of a company. Not all business activities will qualify: (23953/94) (Dec.) September 6, 1995, 82 D.R. 51, where a bar open to the public, which showed pornographic videos, was searched and videos seized, the Commission found that nature of the premises and the business activities had to be taken into account—no interference with home or private life was found; (44568/98) (Dec.) September 18, 2003, police entry of a restaurant impliedly not covered.

[8] *Sté Colas Est v France*, April 16, 2002, ECHR 2002–III, para.41, referring to the role of the Convention as a living instrument reflecting current conditions.

[9] *Leveau et Fillon v France*, (63512/00) and (63515/00) (Dec.) September 6, 2005, even where the barns were near to one farmer's house.

[10] *Hartung v France*, (10231/07) (Dec.) November 3, 2009.

[11] *Khamidov*, fn.2 above, para.131.

[12] *Chelu v Romania,* (40274/04) (Dec.) January 12, 2010.

[13] (20357/92) (Dec.) March 7, 1994, 76 D.R. 80. Positive obligations are only likely to arise from serious infringements in the personal sphere such as deliberate, health-threatening persecution. Unsolicited mail is insufficient: (24967/94) (Dec.) February 20, 1995, 80 D.R. 175.

[14] See IIB, s.15: Environment, sub-s.3: State responsibility for environmental problems.

[15] *Chapman UK*, January 18, 2001, ECHR 2001–I, para.99. See however, *Fadeyeva v Russia*, June 9, 2005, ECHR 2005–IV, para.133, although the authorities were under no obligation as such to resettle the applicant outside a polluted area, they had not taken steps either to bring pollution levels down to acceptable levels and thus had not provided her with any effective solution.

2. Regulation of occupation

II–463 Any interferences with "home" must comply with the requirements of Art.8, para.2. The Court has stated that the importance of the right to respect for home, which is pertinent to personal security and well-being, must be taken into account in determining the scope of the margin of appreciation allowed to Governments.[16] However, in the balancing exercise of private against the general interest, certain features such as the perceived nature of planning controls have taken on significance. A wide margin of appreciation has been held to apply to the implementation of town and country planning schemes.[17]

In *Gillow v UK*, where the applicants were refused permission to reside in their house in Guernsey, the Court's emphasis was on the lack of any pressing social need for the restriction, with a failure on the part of the authorities to give sufficient weight to the applicants' personal circumstances notwithstanding the legitimate interest in controlling population on the island. In contrast, in *Buckley v UK*, the applicant gypsy's right to respect for the home established on her land was not of manifest weight against the Court's consideration that in the area of planning controls national authorities are in principle better placed to evaluate local needs and conditions and in the exercise of discretion involving a multitude of factors the authorities enjoy a wide margin of appreciation. In *Buckley*, the emphasis was accordingly on whether there was a procedure whereby the local authorities assessed the competing interests. Since the planning inspectors reached their decisions on the basis of relevant and sufficient reasons, the refusal of planning permission was not found to exceed the margin of appreciation. Although the applicant had argued that no practical alternative was open to her and that her personal circumstances were pressing, the Court, with less sympathy than in *Gillow*, stated that Art.8 did not allow individual's preferences as to their place of residence to override the general interest. In a later gypsy case, *Chapman v UK*, the Court has stated, as regards measures taken against occupation of land without proper planning permission, that it would be slow to grant protection to those who, in conscious defiance of the law, established a home on an environmentally protected site.[18]

Where social housing is concerned, the importance of home is such that tenants, who have lost the right to occupation under domestic law, should still be able to challenge the proportionality of the measure. Thus, in *McCann* where the applicant and his wife had been joint tenants of a three-bedroom house and the applicant lost the right under domestic law to occupy the house when his wife left giving notice to quit, the summary eviction procedure by the housing authority, which did not allow him to argue that he should be able to stay due to his new family situation, did not provide sufficient procedural safeguards.[19] Eviction from home by private landlords must also be protected. Procedure of summary judicial sale of a debtor's home was regarded as overly draconian, in particular given the small amount of money in

[16] *Gillow*, fn.1 above, para.56.

[17] *Buckley*, fn.1 above, para.75; also *Noack v Germany*, (46346/99) (Dec.) May 25, 2000, ECHR 2000–VI, where the Sorbian minority in a village was resettled elsewhere to permit extension to mining activities.

[18] *Chapman*, fn.15 above, para.102, while a Grand Chamber majority found no violation of Art.8, considering that the authorities had struck a proper balance, the dissenters gave greater weight to the interests of the individual gypsy in maintaining her caravan on her land.

[19] See fn.1 above. See also *Cosic v Croatia*, January 15, 2009, where the applicant was evicted after 18 years' tenancy in court proceedings which did not take her personal circumstances into account.

issue; there was also a lack of proper safeguards where the applicant, mentally incapacitated, had no means of challenging the sale after the event due to an inflexible time-bar.[20]

More drastic interferences by state authorities with dubious legal basis are more easily condemned. Exclusion of displaced persons from returning to their homes in northern Cyprus was found in *Cyprus v Turkey* to infringe Art.8 as having no basis in law. Nor was the Court sympathetic to claims by Turkey that the policy should be regarded as justified pending the outcome of intercommunal talks on a whole range of sensitive issues. It further found aggravated breaches of Art.8 in its aspects of private and family life and home arising out of the surveillance, monitoring of movements and other restrictions imposed on the enclaved Greek Cypriot community remaining in the northern part of the island.[21]

3. Entry and search of property

Where the authorities enter property to search, the interference may well cross the boundaries of most, or all, the separate protected interests under Art.8.[22] Requirements of customs control, investigation of terrorism or other crime, protection of the rights of others in the area of copyright and investigations into anti-competition agreements between companies have been accepted as legitimate aims for searches.[23] II–464

The case-law has concentrated on the requirements that searches be "lawful" and attended by adequate procedural safeguards against arbitrariness and abuse.[24] There is no requirement as such that searches be ordered by a court,[25] although where orders are issued by courts, with an element of judicial supervision built in, there is likely to be sufficient safeguard, as in *Chappell v UK* where the applicant

[20] *Zehentner v Austria*, July 16, 2009. See, mutatis mutandis, eviction from a flat of tenants due to refusal to remove a satellite dish, *Khurshid Mustafa and Tarzibachi v Sweden*, (23883/06) (Dec.) December 16, 2008, breach of Art.10; no separate issue under Art.8.

[21] *Cyprus v Turkey*, May 10, 2001, ECHR 2001–IV, see paras 281–301, these highly intrusive and invasive measures included the physical presence of State agents in Greek Cypriot homes during social events or visits by third parties.

[22] e.g. *Niemietz*, fn.7 above, search of lawyer's office; *Mentes v Turkey* November 28, 1997, R.J.D. 1997–VIII, 26 E.H.R.R. 1, where soldiers searched and burned houses, there was grave interference with private and family life and home.

[23] *Funke v France*, February 25, 1993 Series A, No.256–A, 16 E.H.R.R. 287; *Murray v UK*, October 28, 1994, Series A, No.300–A, 19 E.H.R.R. 193; *Chappell*, fn.7 above; *Sté Colas Est*, fn.8 above. Also *Camenzind v Switzerland*, December 16, 1997, R.J.D. 1997–VIII, 28 E.H.R.R. 458, aim of maintaining telecom regulations.

[24] *Funke*, fn.23 above, paras 54–57, where Customs had exclusive competence to assess the expediency, number, length, and scale of investigation and the procedural safeguards were too lax and full of loopholes, the Court was not impressed by the supervision of a senior customs official or the presence of a police officer; *Camenzind*, fn.23 above, search of house by a PTT official verifying conformity of telephones with regulations had adequate safeguards (including attendance of local public official on request), given the limited nature of the search; *Stés Colas Est*, fn.8 above,where there was no pre-judicial approval of the "visits" of investigators and insufficient safeguards governing the very wide powers of the administrative authority; *Van Rostem v Belgium*, December 9, 2004, where the terms of the search warrant were too wide and no inventory of items taken was drawn up.

[25] *Smirnov v Russia*, June 7, 2007, para.54, where domestic law permitted such orders to be made by a deputy prosecutor and there was an *ex post factum* judicial review; however, in the particular case, the courts failed to rigorously scrutinise the grounds for the search and how it was carried out.

unsuccessfully attacked the draconian nature of Anton Pillar orders.[26] The Court was not prepared to accept a general power to search under terrorist provisions as justifying a search in the absence of individual authorisation of the measure, delimiting its object and scope, and drawn up in accordance with the relevant legal provisions.[27] However, even where a court makes the order, it is necessary for its scope to be contained within identifiable limits. In *Niemietz v Germany*, the Court found the order for search and seizure of documents without any limitation to be disproportionate, particularly in the context of the confidentiality attaching to correspondence and documents of a lawyer.[28] The minor nature of the offence which led to the search was also of relevance in that case.[29] In *Roemen and Schmidt v Luxembourg*, where a lawyer's office was searched with a view to discovering a confidential source of her client journalist, a judicial officer was present but the Court considered that the terms of the search were framed too widely and indiscriminately.[30] In finding the search disproportionate, it also took into account the speed with which the search was carried out (the same day as the court order issued) and its link with a breach of the Art.10 rights of the journalist. Rules must not only be provided to prevent breach of lawyer-client privilege but must be effective in practice, a violation arising where a lawyer's client notes were read, notwithstanding the presence of an officer of the Bar Association and the lack of any suspicion that the lawyer was implicated in any offence with his client.[31]

There must also be relevant and sufficient reasons for carrying out a search at the particular location.[32] Further, the authorities must take reasonable steps to ensure that they are acting on accurate information, a violation arising where police broke into the applicants' home under the mistaken, but honest, belief that it was occupied by a putative armed robber. The Court rejected the Government's argument that the limitation of liability to instances of malicious conduct was necessary to protect the police in their vital functions of investigating crime.[33]

The manner in which the entry or search is conducted must also be compatible with the requirements of Art.8, in particular the means employed should be proportionate to the legitimate aim pursued. In *McLeod*, while a power for the police

[26] It was sufficient that the plaintiff's solicitor rather than a court official carried out the order, since he would be subject to heavy sanctions for breach of undertakings to the court; also the order was only granted ex parte if certain conditions fulfilled and was subject to limitation. Also *Tamosius v UK*, (62002/00) (Dec.) September 19, 2002, where sufficient supervision was provided by counsel independent of the search team; *Funke*, fn.23 above, where the Court commented on lack of judicial supervision of wide Customs powers.

[27] *Imakeyeva v Russia*, November 9, 2006, paras 187–188, the search showed a complete lack of accountability.

[28] The possibility of an independent observer was referred to as a special procedural safeguard that might be required in that context. See (15882/89) March 29, 1993, 74 D.R. 48, where search of a lawyer's office was accepted as attended by necessary safeguards, including a representative from a lawyers' association.

[29] Also *Funke*, fn.23 above, para.58, where the lack of any criminal complaint against the applicant whose home was searched was relevant.

[30] *Roeman and Schmidt*, fn.7 above, para.70, the search warrant covered any item useful, or harmful, to the investigation. See similar breach in *Ernst v Belgium*, July 15, 2003, where the applicant journalists were not charged with any offence and the warrant was without any limitation; and *Smirnov v Russia*, June 7, 2007, warrant in too broad terms giving police "unrestricted discretion" in removing items.

[31] *Andre v France*, July 24, 2008, paras 41–49.

[32] *Smirnov*, fn.25 above, where the authorities gave no, or no satisfactory, reasons as to why a search should be carried out at the applicant lawyer's premises.

[33] *Keegan v UK*, July 18, 2006, paras 32–36.

to enter a house to prevent a breach of the peace was generally acceptable, the entry was not in fact justified in the circumstances of the case, in particular as the applicant was not present in the house at the relevant time and it should have been clear to the officers that there was little or no risk of disorder or crime arising. In *Kucera v Slovakia*, the Court found it disproportionate to use special forces to descend upon and enter the applicant's home at dawn to serve an investigating officer's decision and summons to answer questioning on an extortion charge, without either obtaining a signed record that the applicant consented to their entry or entering in the presence of an independent observer.[34] However, the circumstances existing in Northern Ireland were found to necessitate the precautions used by the army on entering houses.[35]

While the Court did not rule out that a search could be carried out on a third parties' premises to uncover evidence of another's crime, it considered that in light of the seriousness of such an interference, a search to uncover the identity of a road traffic offender was disproportionate.[36]

Concerned with preventing any abuse of power, the Court has recently stated that it is incumbent on the authorities to take meaningful steps to investigate claims that a search has been carried out without apparent legal authority with a view to identifying those involved. This appears to import a procedural obligation into Art.8 akin to those in Arts 2 and 3.[37]

4. Nuisance and enjoyment of home

Problems of noise, pollution and neighbouring industrial hazards are considered under Part IIB, s.15: Environment. II–465

5. Discrimination

While there is still no right as such to be provided with a home, discriminatory treatment as regards allocation of housing to those in need could raise a issue under Art.14.[38]

Cross-reference

Part IIB, s.15: Environment.
Part IIB, s.24: Gypsies and minorities.
Part IIB, s.28: Housing and tenancy.
Part IIB, s.37: Private life.
Part IIB, s.46: Torture, inhuman and degrading treatment (particularly sub-s.4(g): Village destruction).

[34] *Kucera v Slovakia*, July 17, 2007, paras 117–124.
[35] *Murray*, fn.23 above, where the occupants were briefly confined in one room.
[36] *Buck v Germany*, April 28, 2005.
[37] *HM v Turkey*, August 8, 2006, case closed after five days without taking evidence from the family members which was consistent and convincing.
[38] See *Bah v UK*, September 27, 2011, para.40.

27. Homosexuality

Key provisions:

II–466 Articles 8 (private and family life) and 14 (discrimination).

Key case-law:

Dudgeon v UK, October 22, 1981, Series A, No.45, 4 E.H.R.R. 149; *Norris v Ireland*, October 26, 1988, Series A, No.142, 13 E.H.R.R. 186; *Modinos v Cyprus*, April 22, 1993, Series A, No.259, 16 E.H.R.R. 485; *Laskey, Jaggard and Brown v UK*, February 19, 1997, R.J.D. 1997–I, 24 E.H.R.R. 39; *Smith and Grady v UK*, September 27, 1999, ECHR 1999–VI, 29 E.H.R.R. 493; *Lustig-Prean and Beckett v UK*, September 27, 1999, 29 E.H.R.R. 548; *Salguiero da Silva Mouta v Portugal*, December 21, 1999, ECHR 1999, 31 E.H.R.R. 1055; *ADT v UK*, July 31, 2000; *Sutherland v UK (striking out)*, March 27, 2001; *L and V Austria*, January 9, 2003, ECHR 2003–I; *Karner v Austria*, July 24, 2003. *EB v France*, January 22, 2008, ECHR 2008–I.

1. General considerations

II–467 The Convention organs have made a limited contribution to tackling the problems of stigmatisation and discrimination facing persons who are homosexual. While they made an early and important step in rejecting the criminalisation of adult homosexual acts, there have been somewhat slow and conservative responses to claims in the realm of family life, differing ages of consent and discrimination. There has been more readiness in the last few years to scrutinise the justifications for treating individuals in a less favourable manner merely on account of their sexual orientation, most notably in army cases.

2. Right to private life

II–468 *Dudgeon v UK* established the important principle that private sexual conduct, which is a vital element of an individual's personal sphere, cannot be prohibited merely because it may shock or offend others. In such an intimate aspect of private life, there must exist particularly serious reasons before interferences can be justified. The Court underlined in this context two of the hallmarks of a democratic society, tolerance and broadmindedness. In *Norris v Ireland*, it rejected the claim that States should enjoy extensive leeway as to what morals should require. Therefore, the prohibition by criminal law of consensual sexual activities between adult homosexuals in private constitutes an unjustified interference with the right to respect for private life. A homosexual applicant can claim to be a victim of such a violation through the mere existence of the criminal offence since this has a direct and continuous effect on his life. The Convention organs have not been persuaded by arguments that an individual applicant had not been prosecuted or threatened with prosecution, that there was no real incidence of prosecutions[1] or that there was a claimed policy of no prosecutions.[2]

[1] *Dudgeon v UK*, October 22, 1981, Series A, No.45, 4 E.H.R.R. 149 and *Norris v Ireland*, October 26, 1988, Series A, No.142, 13 E.H.R.R. 186. It was noted in *Dudgeon* that private prosecutions were possible.

[2] *Modinos v Cyprus*, April 22, 1993, Series A, No.259, 16 E.H.R.R. 485, where the Attorney-General could not bind his successors.

As to what activities fall within the scope of "private life", the Court doubted that it covered group sado-masochistic activities.[3] In any event, it found that the prosecution of such acts as assault and wounding, notwithstanding the consent of the adult victims, was justified for the aim of the protection of health, having regard to the extreme nature of the acts concerned. In a later case, *ADT v UK*, the post-1998 Court noted the obiter nature of the expressed doubts and found without reservation that the arrest and conviction of the applicant for engaging in acts, mainly of oral sex, with up to four other adult men in his own home disclosed an interference with his private life. It was not convinced that the mere videotaping of the activities, in the absence of any actual likelihood of the tapes being rendered public, was sufficient to take the acts outside the scope of "private life". In the absence of public health considerations in this case and given the purely private nature of the behaviour, the Court found the prosecution and conviction were not justified.

The way in which gays in the army were investigated in respect of their sexual orientation and sexual relationships and then discharged was found in the cases of *Lustig-Prean and Beckett v UK* and *Smith and Grady v UK* to disclose a violation of the right to respect private life.[4] The Court scrutinised in some detail the reasons put forward for the policy pursued by the Ministry of Defence and found them unconvincing, in particular as there was no concrete evidence to substantiate alleged damage to morale or fighting power from the presence of homosexuals in the armed forces. It observed that negative attitudes expressed in an internal army survey, to the extent that these reflected a predisposed bias of a heterosexual majority against a homosexual minority, could not by themselves amount to sufficient justification for the interferences with the applicants' rights any more than similar negative attitudes towards those of a different race, origin or colour. Accordingly, it had not been shown that conduct codes or disciplinary rules could not adequately deal with any behavioural issues arising on the part of either homosexuals or heterosexuals. Regard was also had to the small number of Contracting States that maintained a blanket legal ban on gays in the armed forces and the widespread, if relatively recent, developments in the domestic law of Contracting States on this issue.

Insofar as a homosexual asylum seeker claimed that his right to private life would not be respected on return to his home country, where such relationships were criminalised, the Court was not prepared to find Contracting States were barred from expelling such persons, finding in the particular circumstances that it had not been established that the applicant's moral integrity would be substantially affected to a degree falling within the scope of Art.8 of the Convention.[5]

3. Age of consent

Measures prohibiting acts with minors under 21 were found justified in *Dudgeon v UK*, the Court finding that a margin of appreciation was left to Contracting States as to appropriate safeguards, including the age of consent, required for the II–469

[3] *Laskey, Jaggard and Brown v UK*, February 19, 1997, R.J.D. 1997–I, 24 E.H.R.R. 39, where the group was large, organised and circulated videos.

[4] This departs robustly from the early Commission decision which accepted the alleged need, in the context of the armed forces, to prevent blackmail and coercion and maintain trust and confidence: (9237/81) (Dec.) October 12, 1983, 34 D.R. 68.

[5] *F v UK*, (17341/03) June 22, 2004, this was where there was apparently a certain toleration in practice and no substantial evidence of prosecutions for adult homosexuality alone, an argument which had been rejected in cases as regarded the Contracting States themselves: the Court is reluctant effectively to impose Convention standards of rights where expulsion to non-Contracting States is concerned.

protection of the young. The Commission noted that 21 might seem high but considered that the Government could rely on the report of the Wolfenden Committee, which had recommended the age of 21 as necessary to protect young men from influences of an undesirable kind.[6]

By the 1990s when the UK age limit had been reduced to 18,[7] the Commission found a violation of Art.14 in conjunction with Art.8 concluding that there was no objective and reasonable justification for the difference in age of consent of 18 for male homosexuals and 16 for heterosexuals.[8] It dismissed the argument that society was entitled to indicate disapproval of homosexual conduct and its preference for a heterosexual lifestyle, finding that this could not furnish objective and reasonable justification for inequality under the criminal law. The Court struck the case out after the Sexual Offences (Amendment) Act 2000 equalising the age of consent at 16 as of January 8, 2001.

Differing ages of consent were also rejected in *L and V v Austria*, where the applicants were convicted for homosexual acts with consenting adolescent males between 14 and 18 years old, which criminal prohibition did not apply to girls of the same age for either heterosexual or lesbian relations. The Court effectively followed the Commission's approach in *Sutherland* and found a violation of Art.14 in conjunction with Art.8, noting the growing European consensus to apply equal ages of consent for heterosexual, lesbian and homosexual relations.

4. Right to family life

II–470 For a long time, the relationship of gays and lesbians did not, according to the Convention organs, fall within the scope of the right to family life. Consequently, where the United Kingdom refused the homosexual partner of a British citizen leave to enter to live with his partner, the Commission found the refusal could not interfere with any family right. While it could raise issues as regarded private life, the Commission found that it had not been shown that the applicants were not able to live somewhere else or that their link to the United Kingdom was an essential element of their relationship.[9] Similarly, where the lesbian partner of the applicant died, her eviction from the partner's home (the partner was a secure tenant in public housing) did not concern any family life rights.[10] The Court left open the question in *Karner v Austria*, as in that case the threatened eviction of a homosexual after his partner's death fell within the "home" aspect of Art.8.[11]

This approach was continued, for a time, by the new Court which maintained an emphasis on the traditional married heterosexual couple as the core of the notion of

[6] (7215/75) (Rep.) October 12, 1978, 19 D.R. 66, referring to a German case citing studies indicating a specific social danger in masculine homosexuality (e.g. male homosexuals often constituted a distinct socio-cultural group with a clear proselytising tendency towards adolescents and a resulting social isolation); (5935/72) (Dec.) September 30, 1975, 3 D.R. 45.

[7] The Criminal Justice and Public Order Act 1994 which pre-empted a pending case introduced by two applicants, aged 20, in *Wilde, Greenhalgh and Parry v UK*, (22382/93) (Dec.) January 19, 1995, 80–A D.R. 132, struck off as the matter was resolved.

[8] *Sutherland v UK (striking out)*, March 27, 2001, the Commission noted that reports now gave a very different picture as to the desirability of introducing an equal age of consent, in particular, that the sexual pattern in young males was fixed by 16 and that the existing law might inhibit efforts to improve the health of young homosexual and bisexual men.

[9] (9369/81) (Dec.) May 3, 1983, 32 D.R. 220.

[10] (11716/85) (Dec.) May 14, 1986, 47 D.R. 274; also (28318/95) (Dec.) May 15, 1996.

[11] *Karner v Austria*, July 24, 2003, para.33.

family.[12] However, the slow extension of "family life", as understood by Art.8, to situations where there was de facto family life between heterosexuals outside marriage has finally been applied to a cohabiting same-sex couple living in a stable de facto partnership.[13] The Court noted the rapid evolution in social attitudes in many member States, in particular that a considerable number had afforded legal recognition to same-sex couples.[14]

Where there have been children in the household, a restrictive approach has also been longstanding. In *Kerkhoven v Netherlands*,[15] where two lesbians lived in a long-term relationship and shared parenting roles in respect of the child born by artificial insemination by donor, the courts refused an application by the mother's partner for parental authority. The Commission considered that, while homosexual relationships could fall within the scope of private life, the refusal of parental authority did not infringe on the private lives of the applicants. This approach seemed to overlook or discount the problems which might arise on the death of the child's mother, where in the absence of any legal recognition of a parenting role of the partner, the partner might be at a disadvantage in upholding claims for continued custody of the child. Even where an effect on private or family life was assumed by the Court in the case of *Helen Craig v UK*, it found that the court orders in a child custody case, which forbade any contact between the lesbian partner of a divorced mother and her children, did not disclose any unjustified interference.[16] Given the development above as regards family life existing between gay partners, it would not seem unlikely that if a similar case arose today the Court might now accept that family life existed between the couple and the biological child of one partner.

Where the homosexual applicant is the parent of a child, an interference with family life would probably arise from any decisions on custody or contact requiring justification under Art.8, para.2. In *Salguiero da Silva Mouta v Portugal*, where the Court of Appeal had reversed an order giving custody to the applicant father on the grounds that his homosexuality gave rise to an "abnormal situation", the Court avoided ruling on the Art.8 complaint and instead found a violation of Art.14 in conjunction with Art.8, on the basis that the court's decision was based decisively on considerations of the applicant's sexual orientation, a discriminatory distinction which it stated was not acceptable under the Convention.

A homosexual, as is the case for everyone, is unable to claim a right to adopt a child as such. Nor, initially, did any discriminatory issue arise where permission to adopt was refused on grounds related to sexual orientation. In *Frette v France*, the applicant, a homosexual, complained that, unlike single heterosexuals, he was unable to adopt a child.[17] The Court found that, although there was no guaranteed right, as such, to adopt a child under Art.8, as domestic law authorised single persons to

[12] *Mata Estevez v Spain*, (56501/00) (Dec.) May 10, 2001, ECHR 2001–VI, where the rules allowing a surviving spouse to claim social security allowances did not apply to a homosexual partner, the Court found the difference in treatment pursued the legitimate aim of the protection of the family based on marriage bonds.

[13] *Schalk and Kopf v Austria*, June 24, 2010, para.94, although the difference in treatment was found within the State's margin of appreciation as regarded inability to marry.

[14] *Schalk and Kopf*, fn.13 above, para.93.

[15] (15666/89) (Dec.) May 19, 1992.

[16] (45396/99) (Dec.) March 21, 2000, the Court put weight on the fact that the mother of the children had in fact agreed to the limitations on contact. The children were in the custody of the father, who strenuously opposed any contact with his former wife's lesbian partner, and there is no indication that the partner had ever enjoyed any meaningful contact with them.

[17] *Fretté v France*, February 26, 2002, ECHR 2002–I.

apply for adoption and the decisive reason for refusing the applicant permission was his "choice of lifestyle", issues arose under Art.14 in conjunction with Art.8. However, it concluded, albeit by a fine majority, that the difference in treatment pursued the legitimate aim of protecting the health and rights of children. Given the lack of common ground in Contracting States and the divided opinion in the scientific community as to the possible consequences of a child being adopted by one or more homosexual parents, there was a broad margin of appreciation which the Government had not exceeded. The majority, as with the claim of a transsexual to recognition of family rights in *X, Y and Z v UK*, appeared to take the cautious approach of finding that exclusion of rights could be justified where it had not been proved that having an "unconventional" parent was not harmful to a child. In contrast, the minority pointed out that the decision of the French authorities was based solely on the fact that he was a homosexual, without any reference to any specific conduct or traits that might be detrimental to a child's upbringing. This position has now been overruled effectively by the Grand Chamber in *EB v France*, in which a lesbian applicant was similarly refused authorisation to adopt. It found that, notwithstanding the way in which the courts purported to avoid discrimination, the fact that they placed emphasis throughout on the lack of a "paternal referent", along with other references to her lifestyle and circumstances, showed that her sexual orientation was, unacceptably, at the centre of the deliberations; it was thus irrelevant that one valid ground of refusal had been put forward with reference to the lack of commitment to the adoption of the applicant's partner. As it considered that there had to be convincing and weighty reasons for treating persons differently on grounds of sexual orientation and none were forthcoming, there was a violation. The alleged ground of protection of children was not even considered worthy of discussion.[18]

5. Right to marry

II–471 In view of the express wording of Art.12—"Men and women. . . have the right to marry"—and the reference to applicable national laws, the Court is perhaps unlikely to find that a right to marry could exist for homosexuals where the Contracting State forbids it. It has stated that while a number of Contracting States have extended marriage to same-sex partners, this reflected their own vision of the role of marriage in their societies and did not flow from an interpretation of the fundamental right as laid down by the Contracting States in the Convention in 1950. Where, therefore, national law excluded a transsexual from remaining married to her female partner once her change of gender had been recognised, there was no problem under Art.12.[19]

While in the context of transsexuals the Grand Chamber had emphasised the evolution of the institution in marriage since the Convention was adopted, a Chamber of the First Section was not persuaded to extend a dynamic interpretation to a complaint of inability to marry introduced by a same-sex couple. It also relied on the phrasing of Art.12 and the sense of marriage in the 1950's as indicating that it was intended to cover heterosexual marriage; it distinguished the case from the

[18] *EB v France*, January 22, 2008, ECHR 2008–I, paras 91–98. See the dissenting opinions of Judges Costa and Mularoni, who were not convinced that the refusal was decisively based on consideration of sexual orientation or "contaminated" by such consideration.

[19] See *Parry v UK*, (42971/05) November 11, 2006; *R and F v UK*, (35748/05) November 28, 2006.

situation in *Christine Goodwin v UK*[20] of a transsexual applicant whose inability to marry had been in breach of Art.12; that case had not concerned the claim to marry a person of the same gender as that acquired by the applicant after gender re-assignment.[21] It appears that the fact that some six out of forty-seven Contracting States allowed marriage of same-sex couples was decisively not indicative of a European consensus on the subject; the matter is left for the moment to the regulation of the national law of the Contracting State.[22] However, it may be that the failure to provide any legal protection to a same-sex relationship, such as a form of registered partnership as found in a growing number of States, could disclose a breach of Art.14 in conjunction with Art.8, although such partnership would not have to offer all the rights and obligations of marriage.[23]

6. Discrimination

Where differences of treatment are concerned, it has depended very much on the area of rights concerned and whether the Convention organs accepted that a homosexual could claim to be in an analogous position for the purpose of comparison. Even if he or she could do so, there still remains the obstacle of establishing that the difference concerned a substantive right under the Convention and that there is no objective or reasonable justification for the difference. II–472

In the context of family life, for example, the Commission found in *Kerkhoven* that a lesbian couple could not claim to be in a relevantly similar position as a heterosexual one as regarded parental authority, while the Court in *Mata Estevez v Spain* considered that it was within the State's margin to pursue the aim of protecting traditional married couples in providing them with social security allowances in the event of the death of one partner.[24]

Regarding justifications for differences of treatment, the alleged need to protect young men has at last been found not to be sustainable in *Sutherland v UK* and *L and V v Austria*, which refer to studies indicating that sexual proclivities are fixed by early adolescence and young males are not in any special need of protection from being "perverted" away from heterosexuality.

Apart from the somewhat unfortunate case of *Frette*, where the majority held that a broad margin of appreciation applied in the context of adoption by homosexuals due to the lack of "common ground" or "uniform principles" in Contracting States, an approach which the minority considered as liable to take the protection of fundamental rights backwards,[25] the clear trend from the gays in the army cases onwards is towards the inacceptability of making distinctions based on considerations of sexual orientation.[26] The Court has stated that just like differences in sex,

[20] *Christine Goodwin v UK*, July 11, 2002, ECHR 2002–VI, paras 84–85.

[21] *Schalk and Kopf v Austria*, fn.13 above, paras 54–63.

[22] *Schalk and Kopf*, fn.13 above, paras 58 and 61–63.

[23] *Schalk and Kopf*, fn.13 above, paras 101–110, during the proceedings Austria introduced legislative provision for registration of same-sex couple partnerships; the majority found no violation due to the failure to introduce such a measure earlier; see the dissenting minority's view that there was no justification for prior non-recognition of relationships and thus no scope for a margin of appreciation as to the timing of introduction of reforms.

[24] See fn.12 above; also *Manenc v France*, (66686/09) (Dec.) September 21, 2010, within the margin of appreciation that a survivor of a marriage, but not a same-sex civil partnership, should benefit from a reversionary pension.

[25] *Fretté*, fn.17 above, paras 41–42, and opinion of Judges Bratza, Fuhrmann and Tulkens.

[26] *Smith and Grady v UK*, September 27, 1999, ECHR 1999–VI, 29 E.H.R.R. 493, para.97; see also *Salguiero da Silva Mouta*, December 21, 1999, ECHR 1999–. . . , 31 E.H.R.R. 1055, para.36.

differences based on sexual orientation require particularly serious reasons by way of justification. Thus in the absence of any convincing or weighty reasons for excluding persons in a homosexual relationship from protection under Rent Acts, the Court found a violation of Art.14 in conjunction with Art.8.[27] Where in an interview the Mayor of Warsaw made prejudicial statements about homosexuals, in stating that a march should be banned, the Court found that this vitiated the decision-making procedure and disclosed discrimination.[28] Further, where Art.14 is applicable, in light of *EB v France*, it appears that once the authorities appear explicitly, or even implicitly, to be motivated by reliance on sexual orientation, they will be required to produce the requisite justification.[29]

Cross-reference

Part IIB, s.3: Armed forces.
Part IIB, s.12: Discrimination.
Part IIB, s.37: Private life.

[27] *Karner*, fn.11 above, para.37, citing *Smith and Grady*, fn.26 above, para.90. See also on tenancy succession: *Kozak v Poland*, March 2, 2010.
[28] *Baczkowski v Poland*, May 3, 2007. See, as concerns unjustified ban on Gay Pride marches in Moscow examined under Art.11: *Alekseyev v Russia*, October 21, 2010.
[29] *EB v France*, fn.18 above, paras 80–90.

28. Housing and tenancy

Key provisions:

Article 1 of Protocol No.1 (peaceful enjoyment of possessions) and Art.6 (access to court/fair hearing). II–473

Key case-law

Sporrong and Llonroth v Sweden, September 9, 1982, Series A, No.52; *James v UK*, February 21, 1986, Series A, No.98, 8 E.H.R.R. 123; *Gillow v UK*, November 24, 1986, Series A, No.109, 11 E.H.R.R. 335; *Mellacher v Austria*, December 19, 1989, Series A, No.169, 12 E.H.R.R. 391; *Spadea and Scalabrino v Italy*, September 28, 1995, Series A, No.315–B, 21 E.H.R.R. 482; *Scollo v Italy*, September 28, 1995, Series A, No.315–C, 22 E.H.R.R. 524; *Velosa Barreto v Portugal*, November 21, 1995, Series A, No.334; *Larkos v Cyprus*, February 18, 1999, ECHR 1999–I, 30 E.H.R.R. 597; *Immobiliare Saffi v Italy*, July 28, 1999, ECHR 1999–V, 30 E.H.R.R. 756; *Hutten-Czapska v Poland*, June 19, 2006, ECHR 2006–. . .

1. General considerations

There is no right to housing or accommodation as such in the Convention.[1] Generally, for issues to arise, an applicant must have an already existing property right or occupy the property, although a right attracting protection of Art.1 of Protocol No.1 may even arise where a house is built illegally on State land.[2] The cases have related principally to Government regulation of leases and rents. Such measures generally constitute a control of use and, if severe enough, de facto expropriation or outright deprivation as in *James v UK* where a statute conferred a right to long leaseholders to acquire the freehold of the Duke of Westminster's property in London. Where a person enjoys a property right to the housing, an interference will raise issues under Art.1 of Protocol No.1,[3] while Art.8 may become applicable, if the circumstances are such that his occupation of the property render it his home (see Pt IIB, s.26: Home). Once property or contractual rights are in issue, an applicant may generally also claim access to court and procedural safeguards of Art.6. II–474

[1] e.g. *Marzari v Italy*, (36448/97) (Dec.) May 4, 1999, where the applicant, suffering from a serious illness, was evicted from local authority housing—the Court stated that although Art.8 did not guarantee the right to have one's housing problems solved by the authorities, a refusal to provide assistance to someone seriously ill might raise an issue because of the impact on his/her private life. In this case, however, the authorities had provided an alternative flat and the Court refused to enter into dispute about its adequacy. See also *Fadeyeva v Russia*, June 9, 2005, ECHR 2005–IV, where the authorities bore responsibility for the serious pollution in the area, they had to provide an effective solution for the applicant's problems, whether by resettlement elsewhere or remedial actions.

[2] *Oneryildiz v Turkey*, November 30, 2004, ECHR 2004–XI, violation where authorities' shortcomings led to a methane explosion destroying the applicant's home, which was illegally established, but officially tolerated for some five years.

[3] See, however, (19217/91) (Dec.) January 12, 1994, 76–A D.R. 76, where the Commission held that the right to live in a property of which one was not the owner was not a possession right (dispute about inheritance rights over a chateau); *JLS v Spain*, (41917/98) (Dec.) April 27, 1999, ECHR 1999–V, where a serviceman could not claim a property right when ordered to leave his military quarters.

In these cases, the Convention organs carry out a balancing exercise in which effect on the applicant's rights is weighed against the wider interests.[4] Measures pursuing social or economic policies tend to attract a wide margin of appreciation.[5]

2. Regulation of ownership

II–475 The compulsory transfer of property from one private person to another is not per se contrary to the Convention.[6] Transfers may pursue legitimate social and economic policies and implement social justice, as in *James*, where the transfer of long leases could reasonably be considered to remedy a social injustice. The margin of appreciation, where expropriation is concerned, is wide due to the nature of the political, economic and social issues involved. The Court in this area has stated that it will respect the legislature's judgment as to what is in the public interest unless it is "manifestly without reasonable foundation".[7] Measures involving loss of the property altogether will generally require an element of compensation to satisfy the requirement of proportionality.[8] While less than market value compensation may be justified where measures pursue economic reform or social justice, in other cases substantially undervalued compensation may impose an excessive burden on the landowner, as in a case where land was transferred to allotment gardeners without compensation of comparable value and the Court was not persuaded that the declared public interest was sufficiently broad and compelling to justify the substantial difference; allotment gardening did not qualify, it seems, as a significant means of agricultural production or of assisting the impoverished.[9]

3. Rent and tenancy control

II–476 A wide margin of appreciation applies also to rent control measures. Measures intervening in existing contracts may be acceptable where there are legitimate social and economic aims to make accommodation more accessible to the less affluent. Thus in *Mellacher v Austria*, the striking reductions, up to 79 per cent in some cases, did not disclose a violation. The Court did not consider that it violated the principle of freedom of contract in that parties had entered into the agreement as to rents on freely determined market principles. The burden on the landlords was not found to be disproportionate and it was not for the Court to decide whether this was the best solution.[10] On the other hand, where the tax payable on compulsorily-let property

[4] *Sporrong and Llonroth v Sweden*, September 9, 1982, Series A, No.52, para.69.

[5] *James v UK*, February 21, 1986, Series A, No.98, 8 E.H.R.R. 123, para.46; *Hutten-Czapska v Poland*, June 19, 2006, ECHR 2006–. . . , para.166.

[6] *James*, fn.5 above, para.46.

[7] *James*, fn.5 above, para.46; *Immobiliare Saffi v Italy*, July 28, 1999, ECHR 1999–V, 30 E.H.R.R. 756, para.49, the Court is not keen to enter into assessments of policy and the margin is applied both to the assessment of the existence of a problem of public concern and the remedial action necessary; *Hutten-Czapska*, fn.5 above, para.166.

[8] See Pt IIB, s.17: Expropriation, confiscation and control of use.

[9] *Urbarska Obec Trenciasnske Bikupice v Slovakia*, November 27, 2007, paras 113 and 126–133; See also *Dokic v Bosnia-Herzegovina*, May 27, 2010, inability of applicant, classed as "disloyal", to obtain restitution of his pre-war flat not shown convincingly enough to pursue social justice and compensation was not reasonably related to market value.

[10] Also, e.g. (15434/89) (Dec.) February 15, 1990, 64 D.R. 232, where the applicant who let property by licence to avoid application of Rent Acts was affected by a House of Lords judgment requiring courts to look at the true legal nature of transactions and not to give effect to sham devices. The Commission referred to the wide margin of appreciation enjoyed by States in determining and remedying social problems and found that it was not a disproportionate effect to reduce rent.

by their owners was less than the rate of minimal rent imposed by legislation, a fair balance had not been struck.[11]

Restrictions on landlords' ability to recover their property and evict tend to satisfy the requirements of the Convention where they pursue social policies without disproportionate hardship to the individual property owners. Where an applicant complained that legislation was discriminatory in that it protected tenants to the detriment of landlords, the Court considered that, due to the fundamental differences between landlords and tenants, the two situations could not be considered as analogous and thus did not raise any issue of discrimination.[12] It was acceptable for agricultural land to be assigned to tenants' heirs preventing recovery of possession by the landowners, where it was the policy to facilitate medium-size agricultural holdings and family farming and the owner continued to receive a rent which was not alleged to be inadequate; also the owner did have the possibility of recuperating the land in certain specific circumstances, such as using the land personally.[13] It was also acceptable for an automatic rule to protect the occupation of tenants of more than 20 years longstanding, where the landlord had freely entered into the agreement at a market rent and was aware of this rule.[14]

In Italy, where there was a shortage of rented accommodation, owners of rented flats were obtaining eviction orders but were unable to have them enforced, due to emergency laws suspending the enforcement of evictions. Since the owners in *Spadea and Scalabrino v Italy* and *Scollo v Italy* could still sell the property and receive rents this was a control of use not a deprivation of property. The Court found that the suspension was a legitimate measure aimed at managing the effects of expiry of many leases, and the resulting hardship and social tensions. As regarded proportionality, while the applicants attacked the government policy which led to the situation of many leases expiring together without taking steps to make sure other accommodation was available, the Court noted that shortage of housing was a universal problem in modern society and that the law provided exceptions for landlords who urgently required their property. Where in *Spadea*, the tenants were very old and infirm and the period involved was not overly excessive, the measure was not disproportionate. However in *Scollo*, where the applicant claimed priority, since he was disabled and the tenant had stopped paying rent, there was a violation since the authorities failed to implement their own provisions to give him priority. Some years later however, when restrictions on landlords obtaining possession continued, the Court commented in *Immobiliare Saffi v Italy* that, while the staggering of enforcement of court orders to reinstate landlords was not itself incompatible with the Convention, the risk of imposing an excessive burden on landlords required the provision of procedural safeguards. As the system showed inflexibility and, in practice, non-priority cases remained outstanding, without any deadline for recovery of possession, and the applicant in the particular case had waited some eleven years without the possibility of compensation, the Court found that a fair balance had not been achieved and that there was accordingly a violation of Art.1 of Protocol No.1. Where restrictions on termination of tenancies were combined with stringent rent controls unmitigated by any means for landlords to recoup maintenance costs or to derive any profit from their property, the Court

[11] *Urbarska Obec Trenciasnske Bikupice*, fn.9, paras 140–146.
[12] *Palumbo v Italy*, November 30, 2000, para.52.
[13] *Gauchin v France*, (7801/03) June 19, 2008.
[14] *Almeida Ferreira and Melo Ferreira v Portugal*, December 21, 2009, paras 33–35.

found that the proper balance had not been struck, notwithstanding the dire housing shortage and difficult socio-economic situation.[15]

A fair balance was struck in *Velosa Barreto v Portugal*, where the applicant was prevented from taking possession of an inherited house to live in himself. The measure aimed at the social protection of tenants and the domestic courts had found that he had no urgent need for the property as he lived with other members of his family.

Conversely, the removal of protection to tenancies may not disclose any interference with respect for home, where there is no immediate danger of eviction.[16] However, there was discrimination contrary to Art.14 together with Art.8 in *Larkos v Cyprus* where the tenants of State properties enjoyed less protection from eviction than private tenants. The Court considered that the Government when acting as landlord was in an analogous situation to other landlords and found no public interest grounds for treating their tenants differently.

A stricter scrutiny applies where the Government requisitions, and subjects to permanent tenancy, private property for the purpose of housing government offices rather than helping the homeless or deprived. The imposition of a minimal rent which did not meet the applicants' entitlement to obtain a profit from their property disclosed a violation.[17]

4. Housing restrictions

II–477 The Channel Island's strict residential housing control was found in *Gillow v UK* to pursue the legitimate aim of regulating population to prevent overdevelopment and maintaining the economy. However, refusal of both temporary and permanent licences to the applicants, who returned to live in their house on Guernsey, which they had built 20 years before, was found disproportionate. In the balancing exercise, the Court emphasised the importance of "home" as pertinent to personal security and well-being and that special circumstances weighed in favour of the applicants, namely, that they had been in lawful occupation, had rented out the house as part of the available housing stock on the island, the house now needed repairs and no one else could have lived there in the meantime. In contrast, an applicant, who lost resident status on divorce and was refused a licence and was not subject to disproportionate interference since he was offered the possibility of part-occupation if he carried out certain alterations.[18]

5. Enjoyment and protection of occupation

II–478 In separation and divorce, the occupation rights of a spouse may be trumped by the spouse with custody of the children, the interests of the latter justifying the exclusion of the non-custodial parent from his or her property.[19]

Loss of home being an extreme form of interference, the Court has held that a tenant of public housing faced with eviction should have the opportunity of

[15] *Hutten-Czapska*, fn.5 above, para.225.

[16] *Strunjak v Croatia*, (46934/00) (Dec.) October 5, 2000, ECHR 2000–X.

[17] *Fleri Soler and Camilleri v Malta*, (35349/05) September 26, 2006, paras 74–78. See also *Ghigo v Malta*, September 26, 2006.

[18] (7456/76) (Dec.) February 8, 1978, 13 D.R. 40.

[19] *Mancini v Italy*, (41812/04) (Dec.) October 13, 2005.

challenging the proportionality of the measure as the requisite procedural safeguard under Art.8. It was not accepted that the aim of regulating social housing required the blanket availability of summary proceedings, in which the only ground of challenge was unlawfulness.[20] Nor did the Court approve of the application of a summary judicial sale procedure of a debtor's home, which the applicant, mentally incapacitated, was unable to challenge due to an inflexible time-bar.[21] Once proportionality enters into the examination of these cases, breach of conditions of tenancy per se may no longer be sufficient to justify an eviction from a home.[22]

Evictions, even of persons in illegal occupation, must be "in accordance with the law".[23] Formalistic and inconsistent rulings by domestic courts denying occupation rights may disclose arbitrariness and denial of justice in breach of the requirement to protect rights under Art.1 of Protocol No.1.[24]

Cross-reference

Part IIB, s.15: Environment.
Part IIB, s.17: Expropriation, confiscation and control of use.
Part IIB, s.26: Home.
Part IIB, s.34: Planning and use of property.
Part IIB, s.38: Property.

[20] *McCann v UK*, May 13, 2008, paras 46–55, the Court was not persuaded that the grant of the right to the occupier to litigate his rights under Art.8 would have had a negative effect on the functioning of social housing system or landlord and tenant law. See similar violations due to lack of ability to challenge proportionality of home evictions, e.g *Cosic v Croatia*, January 15, 2009, and *Paulic v Croatia*, October 22, 2009.

[21] *Zehentner v Austria*, July 16, 2009.

[22] Mutatis mutandis, eviction for refusal to remove a satellite dish as required by conditions of tenancy was disproportionate under Art.10, no separate issue under Art.8: *Khurshid Mustafa and Tarzibachi v Sweden*, (23883/06) (Dec.) December 16, 2008.

[23] *Prokopovich v Russia*, November 18, 2004, ECHR 2004–XI, paras 44–45.

[24] *Saghinadze v Georgia*, May 25, 2010, where the manifestly unlawful eviction of internally displaced persons from authorised housing was not properly reviewed by the domestic courts, and therefore did not apply the protection applicable to such persons' occupation.

29. Immigration and expulsion

Key provisions:

II–479 Articles 3 (inhuman and degrading treatment), 8 (respect for private and family life), 13 (effective remedy before national authority), 14 (prohibition against discrimination) and Art.2 of the First Protocol (right to education). Article 3 of Protocol No.4 (specific prohibition on expulsion of nationals) has not been ratified by the United Kingdom.

Introduction

1. General considerations

II–480 Immigration, and the arrival of people seeking asylum, if once tolerated or encouraged by Western European States for economic reasons or by virtue of political and philosophical conviction, are now subject to increasing restrictions. This has an effect not only on those outsiders seeking entry but also on people belonging to long-established communities in Contracting States, who do not enjoy full citizenship status and find the host authorities depressingly keen to resort to deportation as a measure of control. A not insignificant number of countries have changed their laws of nationality and citizenship placing the possibility of obtaining security of residence for non-nationals and their families even further out of reach.

The Convention organs have not been immune to the general atmosphere of "Fortress Europe". They have recognised the legitimate concerns of immigration control, without questioning too deeply the motivation behind it.[1] It is an area where, given the current political sensitivity of the issues, the Convention organs are unlikely to give vent to much creative interpretation. Their record may, to some, be disappointing. Immigrant communities and refugees are particularly vulnerable and, it might be thought, in special need of protection. The Commission was responsive to the hardship disclosed in some cases and there was a number of settlements, which left the issues on the merits unresolved. Both Commission and Court have found violations where the exercise of the power to expel exceeded what they found acceptable. However overall, the case-law is negative and has been criticised as unhelpful and, on occasion, inconsistent. There is some recent development however, focussing on the treatment of asylum-seekers pending determination of their claims and on the procedures and remedies available to them.[2]

There are two important groups of cases. The first concerns situations where applicants claim that the expulsion will expose them to torture or ill-treatment—this will often be a refugee case, where the applicant has applied unsuccessfully for asylum under the Geneva Convention[3] or where refugee status has been revoked.

[1] e.g. *Moustaquim v Belgium*, February 18, 1991, Series A, No.193, 13 E.H.R.R. 802, para.43, "The Court does not in anyway underestimate the Contracting States' concern to maintain law and order, in particular in exercising their right, as a matter of well-established international law and subject to their treaty obligations, to control the entry, residence and expulsion of aliens." Also *Abdulaziz, Cabales and Balkandali v UK*, May 28, 1985, Series A, No.94, 7 E.H.R.R. 471, para.67 "the Court cannot ignore that this present case is concerned not only with family life, but also with immigration. . ."
[2] e.g. *M.S.S. v Belgium and Greece*, January 21, 2011, ECHR 2011–. . . See para.II–503: Access to court and remedies.
[3] United Nations 1951 Convention on the Status of Refugees.

The second concerns decisions by immigration authorities to expel, or refuse entry to, persons seeking to remain with or join other family members. There are also associated issues, of private life; denial of education where children are obliged to accompany a parent who is being expelled; discrimination, where the immigration rules appear to treat some groups less favourably than others; and the problem of effective remedies before national authorities for applicants claiming to be at risk of torture and ill-treatment or interference with their family lives.

Before dealing with the substantive issues, the problem of exhaustion of domestic remedies deserves individual mention.

2. Exhaustion of domestic remedies

Key case-law:

Bahaddar v Netherlands, February 19, 1998, R.J.D. 1998–I, No.64, 26 E.H.R.R. 278; *Jabari v Turkey*, July 11, 2000, ECHR 2000–VIII.

The requirement for exhaustion of domestic remedies applies in the normal way. II–481
Special considerations arise as to the "effectiveness" of remedies as regards the scope of the review of immigration decisions and having regard to the potential irreversibility of expulsions where individuals may face death or torture on their return.

The Commission's case-law established that a remedy without suspensive effect was not effective for expulsion complaints for the purposes of Art.35 (former Art.26) where there was a risk of persecution.[4] Where a person, if successful in the application, could later return from the country to which they had been sent and where there were no allegations of ill-treatment, lack of suspensive effect did not render an available remedy ineffective.[5] The Court has so far followed this approach.[6] It has further specified that the remedy must have automatic suspensive effect without the requirement that the applicant apply for suspension separately.[7] An application for a stay which is dealt with as a subsidiary, albeit urgent, matter and may be refused after a limited review of the merits, is not sufficient as it may still result in an applicant being expelled without there having been a rigorous scrutiny of his claims of risk.[8]

Where a person alleges risk of death or ill-treatment if expelled, the Court, differing from the Commission (see below: Access to Court and Remedies) has found in the context of Art.13 that judicial review furnishes an effective remedy for refusal of asylum. Consequently, judicial review or its equivalent must be considered in light of current case-law as potentially an effective remedy which must be exhausted if the case is to be declared admissible.

An application can be rejected as premature, as in a French case concerning Tamils, where the request for asylum had been refused but no expulsion order had

[4] e.g. (7465/76) (Dec.) September 29, 1976 7 D.R. 153; (14312/88) (Dec.) March 8, 1989, 60 D.R. 284.

[5] e.g. (12097/86) (Dec.) July 13, 1987, 53 D.R. 210, where a Swiss, Austrian and Algerian, complaining under, inter alia, Arts 8 and 9 were to be returned from Denmark to their countries of origin.

[6] e.g. *Sultani v France*, September 20, 2007, paras 49–50.

[7] e.g. *Gebremedhin v France*, April 26, 2007, para.66; *Abdolkhani and Karimnia v Turkey*, September 9, 2009, para.58; *Diallo v Czech Republic*, June 23, 2011, para.74.

[8] *M.S.S*, fn.2 above, paras 388–390.

been made and it was still possible once the order issued to appeal to the administrative courts which would have suspensive effect. This avenue of appeal was rigorous since it required a written application to be made within 24 hours of service of the expulsion order (though an applicant had the right to ask for an interpreter and legal counsel). The applicants' arguments that this rendered the appeal nugatory as a safeguard in practice were unsuccessful before the Commission, and ultimately the Court, indicating a somewhat strict approach.[9]

However, in special circumstances, a failure to pursue remedies through non-compliance with procedural formalities may not disclose a basis for rejecting an application for non-exhaustion. In *Bahaddar v Netherlands*, where the asylum appeal of an Bangladeshi applicant was rejected as his lawyer failed to submit grounds within the time-limit, the Commission considered that, where there was a serious allegation that an applicant would be ill-treated if expelled, the domestic authorities should examine the case on the merits.[10] The Court upheld the Government's non-exhaustion objection though, as it was still possible for the applicant to lodge a fresh application in the courts. However, in *Jabari v Turkey*, where the applicant had failed to apply for asylum within the five-day time-limit after her arrival, the Court found a breach of Arts 3 and 13, considering that the authorities had not provided a proper scrutiny of the factual basis of her claims. The Government's argument that the applicant had failed to comply with procedural requirements of a domestic remedy was rejected. Though the Court emphasised that applicants in Art.3 expulsion cases were not dispensed from exhausting available and effective domestic remedies, the rigid application of the five-day rule to the applicant took no account of her language difficulties and lack of a lawyer or other support and denied her any effective possibility of submitting an asylum request for consideration on the merits.[11]

It appears that where an applicant has made numerous unsuccessful applications, he will not be penalised for failing to renew his application one more time despite the theoretical availability of further recourse, since the Court will have regard to the practical realities of the situation in assessing whether there would be any reasonable prospects of success.[12]

There must also be practical access to any avenue of redress. The Greek system was found deficient from a number of cumulative factors; a very high rate of rejection of asylum claims, lack of information and misinformation to asylum seekers about the procedure to be followed; lack of any system of communication between the authorities and asylum seekers concerning their applications; a dearth of available lawyers and no provision of information about other bodies capable of furnishing assistance in claims; and undue delay in processing, as well as indications that asylum seekers were at risk of being expelled before the claims were examined.[13]

[9] *Vijayanathan and Pusparajah v France*, August 27, 1992, Series A, No.241–B, the Court upheld the Government's preliminary objection that the applicants could not yet claim to be victims.

[10] (25894/94) (Dec.) May 22, 1995, (Rep.) September 13, 1996.

[11] *Jabari v Turkey*, (Dec.) October 28, 1999. See, mutatis mutandis, *Conka v Belgium*, February 5, 2002, ECHR 2001–I, where the manner of expulsion of the Roma applicants made it practically impossible for them to apply to the courts (breach of Art.5, para.4).

[12] *NA v UK*, July 17, 2008, para.91. See also *M.S.S.*, fn.2 above, para.394, no certainty of success is required for an effective appeal, but lack of any prospect of success due to constant rejections of similar cases may be relevant.

[13] *M.S.S.*, fn.2 above, paras 301–320. See also *Rahimi v Greece*, April 5, 2011, para.79, minor asylum seeker speaking only Farsi had not practical access to alleged remedies for bad conditions, the brochure handed out being in Arabic.

Expulsion: risk of ill-treatment

Key case-law:

Soering v UK, July 7, 1989, Series A, No.161, 11 E.H.R.R. 439; *Vilvarajah v UK*, October 30, 1991, Series A, No.215, 14 E.H.R.R. 248; *Nasri v France*, July 13, 1995, Series A, No.320, 21 E.H.R.R 458; *Chahal v UK*, November 15, 1996, R.J.D. 1996–V, 23 E.H.R.R. 413; *Nsona v Netherlands*, November 28, 1996, R.J.D. 1996–VI, No.23, 32 E.H.R.R. 170; *Ahmed v Austria*, December 17, 1996, R.J.D. 1996–VI, No.26, 24 E.H.R.R. 423; *HLR v France*, April 29, 1997, R.J.D. 1997–III, No.36, 26 E.H.R.R 29; *D v UK*, May 2, 1997, R.J.D. 1997–III, No.37, 24 E.H.R.R. 423; *Jabari v Turkey*, July 11, 2000, ECHR 2000–VIII; *Bensaid v UK*, February 6, 2001, ECHR 2001–I; *Hilal v UK*, March 6, 2001, ECHR 2001–II; *Saadi v Italy*, February 28, 2008, ECHR 2008–. . . ; *N v UK*, May 26, 2008, ECHR 2008–. . . ; *M.S.S. v Belgium and Greece*, January 21, 2011, ECHR 2011–. . . II–482

1. Responsibility of the expelling Government

While there is no right to asylum as such guaranteed under the Convention, where an applicant faces a real risk of torture or ill-treatment, including extra-judicial or arbitrary execution[14] on expulsion to a particular country, issues arise under Art.3 of the Convention. This is also where the Court may apply its discretion under r.39 to request interim measures pending the determination of the case in Strasbourg (see Pt IA, s.3: Interim relief). Under Art.3, the obligation of the State extends in respect of everyone within their jurisdiction to a duty not to expose them to an irremediable situation of objective danger even outside their jurisdiction.[15] The argument of the UK Government in *Soering v UK* that a State should not be held accountable for acts committed outside its jurisdiction was rejected by the Court which found that Art.3 enshrined one of the fundamental values of the democratic societies making up the Council of Europe and considered that the provision should be interpreted so as to make its safeguards practical and effective. A State cannot therefore deport any persons with callous and convenient disregard for their likely fate once they have left its soil. In *TI v UK*, the Court considered that State responsibility could potentially arise in sending an asylum applicant to his European port of entry if, in the circumstances, there was a real risk that the applicant would then be sent on to a country where he faced treatment contrary to Art.3.[16] The same applied where there was good reason to believe that Iranian asylum seekers deported to Iraq from Turkey would be promptly, and without judicial safeguards, be moved onto Iran where they would be at risk.[17] This approach has been II–483

[14] See further Pt IIB, s.18: Extradition, sub-s.2(b): Death penalty.

[15] (10479/83) (Dec.) March 12, 1984, 37 D.R. 158, where the applicant alleged the risk of the death penalty on extradition to the US.

[16] (43844/98) (Dec.) March 7, 2000, where, without examing his asylum claims, the UK were expelling the applicant Tamil to Germany, which had already rejected his claims, under the Dublin Convention. On the facts, the Court was satisfied that he was not at risk of being expelled directly to Sri Lanka but could make a fresh application to the German authorities, which could take into account his complaints under Art.3. It was not concerned as such with whether or not Germany was unduly restrictive in its approach to non-State sources of risk but rather with the existence of any effective procedural safeguards protecting the applicant from removal.

[17] *Abdolkhani and Karimnia*, fn.7 above, paras 88–90.

confirmed in *M.S.S. v Greece and Belgium*, where the Grand Chamber held that a State had a duty to verify that an asylum seeker would be properly treated in the intermediate country, both as regarded the examination of his claims before being expelled to his country of origin and the way he was treated in in interim.[18]

Responsibility arises whether the source of the risk is the Government or authorities in the receiving State or other groups, such as rival warring or political factions[19] or organised crime groups,[20] where there is no indication of the authorities being able to provide protection.[21] The Commission seemed also prepared to accept risk to a Lebanese woman from her husband's family of being confined to a rigorous form of "house arrest" for refusal to comply with her husband's wishes.[22]

Threat to life may also arise from impact of an expulsion on a person's health apart from deliberately inflicted injury by others, although a high threshold has been held to apply particularly where a case does not concern the direct responsibility of the Contracting State for the infliction of harm.[23] For example, former r.36 was applied by the Commission where the removal of a pregnant woman with a history of premature labour posed a significant risk to the life of the unborn child, though the application was later rejected once after the birth there was no apparent risk to health to mother or child from an expulsion.[24] The psychological impact of the threatened expulsion to Algeria of the applicant *Nasri*, born deaf and dumb, was found by the Commission to constitute treatment of such severity as to breach Art.3. It had regard to his upbringing since the age of four in France where all his family lived and to his extremely limited communication and perception skills. The expulsion threatened him with prolonged sensory deprivation in an unfamiliar environment and to inflict on him such fear and anguish as might humiliate him and crush his personality.[25]

Lack of medical care and support in the receiving State may, in exceptional circumstances attracting compelling humanitarian considerations, disclose a breach, as in *D v UK* where the applicant, extremely ill in the advanced stages of AIDS, was threatened with expulsion to St. Kitts where no treatment or family care would be available. In cases where some medical and/or family assistance have been available

[18] *M.S.S.*, fn.2 above, paras 359 and 365–368.

[19] (23985–87–88/94) (Dec.) November 28, 1994, concerning deportation of Lebanese applicants who alleged that the Hezbollah would target them as collaborators, the Commission cited an Amnesty report describing the Hezbollah as an important political force with semi-governmental services and the largest faction in the Parliament.

[20] *HLR v France*, April 29, 1997, R.J.D. 1997–III, No.36, 26 E.H.R.R 29, where the applicant alleged that on return to Colombia he would be at risk from the drug trafficking circles on whom he had given information to the police. The Court, unlike the Commission, found that the risk was not substantiated.

[21] e.g. *Ahmed v Austria*, December 17, 1996, R.J.D. 1996–VI, No.26, 24 E.H.R.R. 423, where a violation arose from the proposed expulsion of the applicant to Somalia in a state of civil war where he risked treatment contrary to Art.3 with no indication of any public authority able to protect him. Contrast *AM v Sweden*, (38813/08) (Dec.) June 16, 2009, no indication that Russian authorities would not protect the applicants from a rogue officer.

[22] (25849/94) (Dec.) November 16, 1994. Former r.36 was applied, though the case was later rejected for lack of substantiation.

[23] *Bensaid v UK*, February 6, 2001, ECHR 2001–I, para.40.

[24] (26985/95) (Dec.) May 15, 1996; also (27949/95) May 13, 1996, where a woman had a history of psychiatric illness, with medical evidence indicating that the stress of removal to an environment where little treatment was available would lead to a risk of suicide, the case was communicated but declared inadmissible when she moved to Ireland and the risk of expulsion disappeared.

[25] *Nasri v France*, July 13, 1995, Series A, No.320, 21 E.H.R.R 458, the Court, finding a breach of Art.8, strangely found it unnecessary to look at the Art.3 allegations.

for applicants suffering from mental or physical illness, the Court has not found a sufficiently real risk that removal would be contrary to Art.3.[26] In some cases it appears to put the burden of proof on the applicant to show that no medical care is available.[27] In any event, it appears that the Court applies a higher threshold where the harm flows from a naturally-occurring illness rather than intentional ill-treatment by public authorities, based on the pragmatic consideration that otherwise it would impose too heavy a burden on Contracting States to provide a haven of medical care to people from overseas.[28]

Nor is the considerable stress that might accompany a fear of removal enough to engage State responsibility.[29]

As regards the risk that an applicant faces other types of human right violations if sent back to his home country, the Court has said, pragmatically, that it cannot be required that an expelling Contracting State only return an alien to a country which is in full and effective enforcement of all the rights and freedoms set out in the Convention.[30] However, there is some authority that an applicant might succeed if he could show a real risk of "flagrant denial" of Arts 5 and 6 rights,[31] and possibly Art.9, although the Court considered that it was unlikely that any such risk as regarded the latter would not amount to a breach of Art.3.[32] For example, no issues have so far arisen in respect of bans on homosexual conduct[33] or difficulties in practising religion.[34] Where an applicant has been, or risk being, sentenced to death after an unfair trial, there may be a violation of Arts 2 or 3.[35]

2. Type of ill-treatment alleged

The type of ill-treatment to be established is, in line with Art.3 case-law,[36] severe. Generally, a significant risk to health, physical or psychological, from deliberate ill-treatment or conditions has to be alleged. However even alleged risk to life is generally still considered in the context of Art.3. The Commission stated that Art.2 would only be in issue where the loss of life was a "near certainty" as a consequence of the expulsion.[37] II–484

[26] See *Salkic v Sweden*, (7702/04) (Dec.) June 29, 2004, post-traumatic stress disorder; *Dragan v Germany*, (33743/03) (Dec.) October 7, 2004, hepatitis and suicidal tendencies; *Hukic v Sweden*, (17416/05) (Dec.) September 27, 2005, Downs Syndrome. See also concerning HIV-associated problems: Pt IIB, s.2: AIDS.

[27] See *Aoulmi v France*, January 17, 2006, para.57, concerning treatment for hepatitis in Algeria.

[28] *N v UK*, May 26, 2008, ECHR 2008–. . ., paras 42–45.

[29] e.g. *Nasimi v Sweden*, (38865/02) (Dec.) March 16, 2004.

[30] See *F v UK*, (17341/03) (Dec.) June 22, 2004.

[31] See *Soering v UK*, July 7, 1989, Series A, No.161, 11 E.H.R.R. 439, para.113; *Drozd and Janousek v France and Spain*, June 26, 1992, Series A, No.240, para.110; *Tomic v UK*, (17837/03) (Dec.) October 14, 2003, no risk of flagrant breach of Arts 5 or 6 where a former Serb paramilitary was returning to Croatia. See also PtIIB, s.18: Extradition, sub-s.2(c): Other violations in receiving State.

[32] See *Z and T v UK*, (27034/05) (Dec.) February 28, 2006.

[33] *F v UK*, fn.30 above.

[34] *Z and T*, fn.32 above, concerning an expulsion to Iran.

[35] *Bader and Kanbor v Sweden*, November 8, 2005, ECHR 2005–XI, para.42, citing *Ocalan v Turkey*, May 12, 2005, ECHR 2005–IV, paras 165–169.

[36] See Pt IIB, s.46: Torture, inhuman and degrading treatment.

[37] *Bahaddar*, fn.10 above.

The following are generally not covered: risk of criminal trial and imprisonment following a criminal conviction or for desertion[38]; economic hardship[39]; risk of difficulties in travelling through military checkpoints from lack of identity cards[40]; refusal of a passport on return[41]; and threat of prosecution and heavy sentence (e.g.10 years) for conscientious objection to service in the army.[42]

However, threat of prosecution for political offences may constitute Art.3 treatment, though the Commission considered that there must be a definite and serious risk of being prosecuted on such a basis and of receiving a long and severe sentence if convicted.[43]

The way in which a person is expelled may raise issues of inhuman and degrading treatment, particularly if they are ill. However, if suitable medical precautions are taken, no violation will be found in respect of expulsion of persons with medical problems.[44] In highly exceptional circumstances, as in *D v UK*, threat of expulsion of person, severely ill and thus unfit to travel, may found a violation, particularly where there is no prospect of any assistance, medical or otherwise on his return.[45]

Conditions of detention and living conditions imposed on asylum-seekers while their claims are pending may raise issues under Art.3 also (see para.II–505: Treatment of asylum seekers and irregular immigrants pending domestic procedures).

3. Absolute right

II–485 The right under Art.3 is absolute. Once a risk of Art.3 treatment is established, the threat posed by the applicant cannot reduce the level of protection afforded by the Convention. Thus in *Chahal v UK*, the Court rejected the Government argument that the risk to the Sikh applicant, an alleged terrorist, on return to India had to be weighed against the threat to UK security if he remained. The Convention guarantee is thus wider than the Geneva Convention pursuant to which a refugee can forfeit his status. A Contracting State has to make do (not unreasonably perhaps) with using its criminal law to deal with any threat posed by a person on its territory.[46] A further attempt by the United Kingdom Government to modify this absolute approach was made in *Saadi v Italy*, in which they argued that, where the individual posed a threat to national security and the community due to international terrorism, this should weigh more heavily in the balance; in such cases stronger evidence would have to be shown that the individual to be expelled would be likely to be subjected to ill-treatment contrary to Art.3. The Court however re-

[38] (28152–3/95) (Dec.) September 11, 1995, existence of criminal proceedings in Romania did not raise issues on expulsion from France; (7334/76) (Dec.) March 8, 1976, 5 D.R. 154, deserter from Jordanian army; also cases of persons evading military service in the Serbian army, e.g. (22508/93) (Dec.) October 21, 1993; (25129/94) (Dec.) January 11, 1995, concerning a Muslim Albanian being returned to Serbia.

[39] *Tomic*, fn.31 above.

[40] *Vilvarajah v UK*, October 30, 1991, Series A, No.215, 14 E.H.R.R. 248.

[41] *Beldjoudi v France*, (Rep.) March 26, 1992, Series A, No.235–A, para.74.

[42] e.g. (11017/84) (Dec.) March 13, 1986, 46 D.R. 176.

[43] (11933/86) (Dec.) April 14, 1986, 46 D.R. 257.

[44] eg *Y v Russia*, December 4, 2008, paras 93–95, the applicant, who had suffered from a stroke, had been examined by a neurologist and announced fit to travel; he was accompanied by a doctor on the flights.

[45] *D v UK*, May 2, 1997, violation for return of advanced AIDS sufferer to St Kitts; contrast *N v UK*, May 27, 2008, no violation for return of stablised AIDS sufferer to Uganda. See Part IIB, s.2: AIDS.

[46] *Chahal*, (Rep.) November 15, 1996, R.J.D. 1996–V, 23 E.H.R.R. 413, paras 79–81, para.104.

affirmed the *Chahal* approach and the absolute nature of Art.3, rejecting the appropriateness of any kind of balancing test where a person faces a substantial risk of ill-treatment which can hardly be lessened merely because he is perceived to be a threat to the host State.[47]

Where refugee status has been granted, a State will be required to have proper reasons, when revoking that status, for expelling the individual. In *Ahmed v Austria*, a conviction of an applicant for robbery did not justify the threatened expulsion, in the absence of any circumstances rebutting the risk of persecution.

4. Existence and assessment of risk

An applicant has to substantiate that he faces a real risk of torture or ill-treatment.[48] It is in principle for the applicant to adduce evidence capable of proving that there are substantial grounds for believing that, if the measure complained of were to be implemented, he would be exposed to a real risk of being subjected to treatment contrary to Art.3. Where such evidence is adduced, it is for the Government to dispel any doubts about the risk that the applicant might face.[49] While the Court has said that the assessment of the existence of a real risk must necessarily be a rigorous one, the Strasbourg approach has evolved over the last decade and if anything there is a more scrupulous regard to avoid underestimating the risk that applicants may face if returned to particular countries.[50] Indeed, it has been stated that due to the special situation in which asylum seekers often find themselves, it is frequently necessary to give them the benefit of the doubt when it comes to assessing the credibility of their statements and the documents submitted in support thereof, although when information is presented which gives strong reasons to question the veracity of an asylum seeker's submissions, the individual must nonetheless provide a satisfactory explanation for the alleged inaccuracies in those submissions.[51] II–486

(a) Imminence and safeguards

Expulsion must be imminent.[52] II–487

[47] *Saadi v Italy*, February 28, 2008, ECHR 2008–. . . , paras 137–142.

[48] e.g. *Vilvarajah*, fn.40 above, paras 103 and 111.

[49] e.g. *NA v UK*, fn.12 above, para.111. See also *N v Sweden*, July 20, 2010, para.61, where it was for the Government to bring forward evidence negativing the applicant's claims that she had no male support available in Afghanistan (which would render her existence as a woman perilous) rather than for her to substantiate them.

[50] e.g. *Chahal*, fn.46 above, para.96; *Saadi v Italy*, fn.47 above, paras 128–129.

[51] e.g. *Elezaj v Sweden*, (17654/05) (Dec.) September 20, 2009, citing *Collins and Akasiebie v Sweden*, (23944/05) (Dec.) March 8, 2007 and *Matsiukhina and Matsiukhin v Sweden*, (31260/04) (Dec.) June 21, 2005.

[52] e.g. *Vijayanathan*, (Rep.) September 5, 1991, paras 118–121; *Kalantari v Germany*, October 11, 2001, ECHR 2001–X, the case was struck off as, with the annulment of the decision to expel the applicant to Iran, there was no risk of a breach of Art.3, distinguishing *Ahmed*, fn.21 above, where the measure had been suspended and the decision to expel remained in force. See also *Salah Sheekh v Netherlands*, January 11, 2007, where temporary arrangements for Somali asylum seekers to remain did not resolve the matter as expulsion might still be ordered after further review.

Nor will there be a problem if the expelling authorities have provided safeguards sufficiently diminishing the risk.[53]

Where the applicant to be expelled suffers from problems of health or disability, assurances by the expelling State that steps will be taken to ensure appropriate treatment have proved relevant.[54] Adverse comment was made by the Commission in finding violations in *Nasri v France* and *D v UK* of the absence of any steps taken by the expelling Government as regards verifying the available facilities or treatment.[55]

Available safeguards have also been of crucial relevance where the expulsion is of children, with the ill-treatment alleged deriving from the circumstances of their removal. Safeguards such as ensuring reception by welfare authorities and the existence of a care structure in the receiving State can be identified as reducing any alleged risk of psychological or physical harm. The failure of the Netherlands Government to investigate the personal situation of a nine-year-old girl who was being returned to Zaire or to take adequate steps themselves to ensure that she was properly met on her return received critical comment in *Nsona v Netherlands*, but since Swissair had taken their own initiatives the Government escaped a finding of violation.

Assurances, or the lack of assurances, made by the Governments of receiving States can be relevant.[56] When assurances are given they are scrutinised carefully. In *Chahal*,[57] an assurance of the Indian Government given to the UK authorities that the applicant, a Sikh militant, would receive the same legal protection as any other Indian citizen on his return did not satisfy the Convention organs as providing an effective guarantee.[58] Nor was a reference to adherence to "international treaties" by the Tunisian authorities sufficient in *Saadi v Italy*.[59] Where, in respect of a terrorist suspect transferred to Tunisia, the Italian Government sought to rely on more detailed assurances given by an advocate-general, the Court noted that there was no indication that this official had competence to give binding assurances on the part of the State and found that, although his local lawyer and family had been able to visit, neither his lawyer before the Court nor the Italian consular officials had been able to gain access. Thus, even if it was not apparent that he had been ill-treated to date,

[53] e.g. (27249/95) (Dec.) September 15, 1995, 83–A D.R. 91, where two teenage Ugandan brothers were held in Sweden in psychiatric care inter alia for suicidal tendencies, their complaints under Art.3 regarding an expulsion order were rejected since no enforcement would be possible while compulsory medical care was necessary and the order would only be enforced if the applicants were met in Uganda by a child welfare official and a Swedish consulate officer.

[54] (29244/95) (Dec.) April 18, 1996, the applicant's complaints of expulsion to Senegal on the basis of mental illness were rejected since inter alia the French Government had ensured that appropriate care would be available on his return; (31362/96) (Dec.) January 23, 1997, the French Government's statement that the expulsion to Morocco would only occur if the applicant's treatment in an appropriate establishment for his mental condition was guaranteed was sufficient even if the level of care differed from that available in France; (37384/97) (Dec.) October 30, 1998, where the Swiss Government undertook to pay for the applicant's diabetic treatment on return to Angola.

[55] *Nasri v France*, (Rep.) February 28, 2008, ECHR 2008–. . . , para.61; *D v UK*, (Rep.) para.59.

[56] *Bader and Kanbor*, fn.35 above, para.45, where the Court noted that the Swedish Government had not obtained any guarantees that the applicant's conviction and death sentence *in absentia* would be re-opened and that the prosecutor would not ask for the death penalty.

[57] *Chahal*, fn.46 above, para.105; also (Rep.), para.113.

[58] i.e. there was insufficient judicial control of police activities targeting Sikhs.

[59] *Saadi*, fn.47 above, para.147. See also *Daoudi v France*, December 3, 2009, para.70, where an amnesty did not apply to the applicant, reference to benefiting from the "spirit" of the amnesty was not a sufficient safeguard.

there were insufficient guarantees for the future.[60] It is conceivable that in a particular case a Government could provide sufficient guarantees to offset a prima facie risk of ill-treatment but their quality and strength would presumably have to increase where the evidence of risk was strong or the nature of the risk particularly grave.[61]

Where a person claims ill-treatment likely if expelled to a Contracting State, some weight has been given to the possibility of an applicant exercising the right of individual petition, presumably on the basis that a State's adherence to the Convention renders risk of ill-treatment less likely to materialise, taking into account the mechanisms which should be in place to safeguard the guaranteed fundamental rights.[62] That problems may however arise in Contracting States is illustrated by reports by the CPT (the European Committee for the Prevention of Torture) on conditions in places of detention which have revealed serious problems in a number of countries. Interim measures have been applied on occasion, e.g. to an expulsion from France to Spain of an ETA member, possibly motivated by severe criticisms of the methods of the *guardia civil* by the CPT,[63] and to expulsion of Kurds to Turkey.[64] Until recently however, no violation based on a proposed expulsion from one Contracting State was found. That changed with *M.S.S v Belgium and Greece*, where Belgium was found in breach of Art.3 for sending an asylum seeker to Greece under the Dublin Regulations when it was well-known that asylum procedures were not properly functioning nor adequate assistance made available as regarded conditions of detention or living conditions. A Contracting State can no longer automatically rely on being able to expel people to another but will have to give due attention to warnings by the UNHCR and other bodies as to deficiencies in standards of treatment.[65] Not even the fact that the Court itself has declined to apply r.39 to suspend an expulsion will absolve the State from its responsibilities in that regard.[66]

Internal flight has been rejected as offering a reliable guarantee against the risk of ill-treatment where human rights problems have not been confined to one part of the country and there are institutional links between the police authorities in the different regions.[67] Nor was the intention to send the applicant to a "relatively safe" area in Somalia sufficient since there was no guarantee that the authorities there would accept or protect an outsider.[68]

[60] *Ben Khemais v Italy*, February 24, 2009, paras 55–56.

[61] See, e.g. *Salem v Portugual*, (26844/04) (Dec.) May 9, 2006, where the specific and detailed guarantees given by the Indian authorities concerning the trial and sentencing of a terrorist suspect were found to remove any risk of the death sentence; *Saoudi v Spain*, (22871/06) (Dec.) September 18, 2006, where the specific assurances and information obtained from the Algerian authorities removed the risk of an irreducible life sentence

[62] e.g. (12543/86) (Dec.) December 2, 1986, 51 D.R. 272; (28152–3/95), fn.38 above; *Tomic*, fn.31 above; *AM v Sweden*, (38813/08) (Dec.) June 6, 2009, where the Court was not persuaded that the Russian authorities would not protect the applicants from purported threats from a criminally-minded military officer.

[63] (31113/96) (Dec.) December 5, 1996.

[64] e.g. *Incedursun v Netherlands*, June 22, 1999.

[65] *M.S.S.*, fn.2 above, paras 344–359 and 362–368.

[66] *M.S.S.*, fn.2 above, para.355, decisions of interim measures are taken by a President of a Section urgently, on the basis of limited materials, and do not prejudge the merits of the case.

[67] See *Chahal*, fn.46 above, para.104; *Hilal v UK*, March 6, 2001, ECHR 2001–II, paras 67–68, where there was also the possibility of extradition from mainland Tanzania to Zanzibar where the situation was particularly precarious.

[68] *Salah Sheekh*, fn.52 above, paras 143–144.

(b) *Substantiating the level of risk*

II–488 The Court holds that, given the absolute character of the provision and the fact it enshrines one of the fundamental values of the democratic societies making up the Council of Europe, its examination of the existence of a risk of ill-treatment in breach of Art.3 must be rigorous. It will, if necessary, assess the risk in light of material obtained *proprio motu.*[69]

That said, the mere possibility of ill-treatment is not enough.[70] Thus it may not be sufficient for an applicant to point to the general unsettled situation in a country or his membership in a group which occasionally faces problems.[71] It seems that the applicant has to establish that he faces a specific, personal risk of treatment contrary to Art.3. In *Vilvarajah v UK* concerning the expulsion of five Tamil applicants to Sri Lanka, the Court did not consider that it was enough that the situation was unsettled or that some Tamils might possibly be detained or ill-treated. This threat was apparently not specific enough to these five applicants, even in light of the fact that during the Convention proceedings three of the applicants were subjected to ill-treatment in Sri Lanka. The Court found that there was no special distinguishing feature which would have enabled the Secretary of State to foresee that they would be treated in this way. This case can now be contrasted with the recent *NA v UK*, in which it was considered that where an applicant was a young male, with scarring which was regarded by Sri Lankhan authorities as indicative of Tamil Tiger involvement, with a history of past arrests, there was a real risk on his return that he would be picked up by the authorities as a suspected rebel and thus be subject to ill-treatment.[72] Similarly, as regards the current climate of the "War against Terror" in which arbitrary arrest and detention and torture of suspected terrorists is widely reported, the Court found a substantial risk of ill-treatment where terrorist suspects were to be expelled to countries which had a record of using torture with impunity on such persons.[73]

Where there are indications of a high level of risk attaching to a particular group due to its systematic persecution, it should be possible to establish the requisite substantiation of risk to the individual applicant merely through his membership,[74] particularly where the person is known to be implicated or wanted in connection with that group or its activities.

[69] *Vilvarajah*, fn.40 above, paras 107–108.

[70] *Vilvarajah*, fn.40 above, para.111; *Salah Sheekh*, fn.52 above, para.148.

[71] e.g. *Katani v Germany*, (67679/01) (Dec.) May 31, 2001, where the Court appeared to reject the applicants' complaints on the basis that they had not shown that they were treated particularly worse than any other members of the Yezidi minority or other Georgian citizens and that the police lack of response to attacks by third parties was rather a sign of a general structural weakness in the country; *Aoulmi*, fn.27 above, para.66, unstable situation in Algeria not enough; *Sultani*, fn.6 above, para. 67, generalised violence in Afghanistan not show sufficient risk; *NA v UK*, fn.12 above, para.114.

[72] *NA v UK*, fn.12 above, paras 138–147.

[73] *Saadi v Italy*, fn.47 above, paras 143–146, risk of return to Tunisia. See also *Daoudi*, fn.59 above, risk concerning expulsion of a convicted Islamist terrorist to Algeria where reports consistently highlighted abuses and torture of suspected terrorists.

[74] e.g. *Saadi v Italy*, fn.47 above, para.131; see *Y v Russia*, December 4, 2008, para.80, on the facts of this case, while the Falun Gong sect was under threat of persecution in China, there was no indication that the applicant, who claimed to be a member, had suffered ill-treatment before leaving the country or that he was known to the Chinese authorities as an active member, which together with some doubts as to his credibility, did not disclose a real risk of ill-treatment if he was returned. Contrast *Abdolkhani and Karimnia*, fn.7 above, paras 77–92, where, in light of known episodes of persecution and lack of access by UNHCR to recent returnees, the applicants as members of the People's Mojahedin Organisation were at risk if returned to Iran.

The difficulties of reaching an assessment of risk to a particular person may be demonstrated in *Paez v Sweden*[75] where the Commission by 15 votes to 14 found no violation if applicant was returned to Peru. He was a supporter of the Sendero Luminoso, a terrorist group, and other family members had been arrested and one had disappeared. However, the majority noted that he was not a leading figure, had not participated in any terrorist atrocities and in particular he could not point to any warrant of arrest or similar evidence which would show that he would be of particular interest to the authorities. The minority noted, inter alia, that his mother and sisters had been granted asylum; that the refusal to the applicant seemed to rely on his terrorist affiliations, a ground not relevant under Art.3; and that the interest shown by the Peruvian press in the asylum seekers in Sweden was a significant factor increasing the risk. More recently, where a Somali was member of a vulnerable minority and he and his family had already suffered ill-treatment from a warring clan, the Court considered that it was not necessary for him to show any further special distinguishing features in his particular case.[76]

Risk must exist at the time when the person is expelled, or if the person has not been expelled, it is assessed at the time the Court considers the case.[77] Previous conditions only remain relevant to the extent that they cast light on the present situation. There was evidence supporting the allegations of the applicant *Cruz Varas* that he had suffered torture in the past but his complaints concerning his expulsion to Chile failed since at the time when he was returned democratic developments and voluntary return of refugees had begun. Conversely in *Chahal*,[78] the Convention organs found that, despite apparent improvements in treatment of Sikhs by members of the Indian security forces and a change in Government attitude, including the creation of a National Human Rights Commission, they were still not satisfied that the police in the Punjab in particular and security forces elsewhere in the country were under effective democratic control. Thus, there was a real risk that the applicant, a high profile and leading Sikh militant, would be a target of special interest on his return and there were substantial grounds for believing that he would be exposed to a real risk of ill-treatment

On occasion the Court appears to expect a certain level of robustness from applicants in themselves preventing the ill-treatment. While it acknowledged that female genital mutilation was a practice in breach of Art.3, it took the view that in light of the official prohibition of the practice and its apparently diminishing prevalence, the applicant, who had been able to overcome practical and financial obstacles in reaching Sweden, had not shown that she would not be able to protect herself and her daughter from any risk.[79]

[75] (28942/95) (Rep.) December 6, 1996; settled before the Court, October 30, 1997, R.J.D. 1997–VIII, No.56.

[76] *Salah Sheekh*, fn.37 above, para.148. See also *Hilal*, fn.67 above, the applicant's claims of previous torture in Tanzania were medically supported, his brother had died in custody and ordinary members of the opposition group, such as he, were also at risk of police brutality; *Said v Netherlands*, July 5, 2005, para.54, where country materials indicated that deserters were at risk of torture and ill-treatment and the applicant's name would be on a list and known to the Eritrean authorities.

[77] At the time the Court considers the case if the person has not been expelled, e.g. *Chahal*, fn.46 above, para.97; *Saadi v Italy*, fn.47 above, para. 133.

[78] *Chahal*, fn.46 above, paras 99–107, (Rep.) paras 108–114.

[79] *Collins and Akaziebie v Sweden*, (23944/05) (Dec.) March 8, 2007.

(c) Factors and materials taken into account

II–489 Existence of a real risk may be supported by previous incidences of ill-treatment on arrest and detention, in respect of which medical and psychiatric reports are very useful, if not essential. Also relevant are considerations whether an applicant's involvement in opposition has been publicised and likely to be known to the authorities or other groups in the receiving State. The Court will also refer to Amnesty Reports and the UNHCR as well as reports by the UN Committee against Torture and country reports of the US State Department, and these sources may be regarded as highly relevant and persuasive, particularly where they are consistent with each other.[80] Where there was some dispute as to the weight to be placed on UNHCR reports, the Court noted that those which were couched in terms of Art.3 risk assessment were more relevant than those dealing with broader social and economic issues[81]. It has acknowledged that Contracting States' embassies may be the source of recent information about the situation in particular places.[82] The reports of the CPT are treated as particularly relevant when concerned with Contracting States (see, for example, its Public Statements on Turkey).[83] In *Jabari v Turkey*, where the applicant claimed to be at risk of stoning for adultery if expelled to Iran, the Court gave weight to the UNHCR's assessment of her credibility and its finding that she had a well-founded fear of persecution.

Factors which cast doubt on an applicant's case include inconsistencies in accounts to national authorities and serious doubts as to the authenticity of the documents.[84] Weight, often decisive, is given to domestic authorities' experience in dealing with applications.[85] Applicants must therefore be able to point to flaws or shortcomings in any assessment by the domestic authorities of the merits of their case.[86] However, the Court will review the domestic authorities' reasoning to satisfy itself that their assessment is adequate and sufficiently supported, taking into account not only the material before the domestic bodies but other reliable objective information about

[80] e.g. *Vilvarajah*, fn.40 above, UNHCR reports on Sri Lanka and Amnesty International's position on return; *Ahmed v Austria* (Rep.), fn.21 above, information requested from the UNHCR on the situation in Somalia; *Paez v Sweden* (Rep.), the UN Committee against Torture, Peru's report to ECOSOC, US State Department Report, the HRC report on Peru, Human Rights Watch and Amnesty International; *TI v UK*, fn.10 above, UNHCR intervention concerning the effect of the return, under the Dublin Convention, of an asylum seeker to Germany; *Saadi v Italy*, fn.40 above, para.143, Amnesty International, Human Rights Watch, US State Department.

[81] *NA v UK*, fn.12 above, para.122. See *M.S.S. v Belgium and Greece*, fn.2 above, para.349, where "critical" weight was given to a letter by the UNHCR to the Belgian authorities warning of risk of ill-treatment if an asylum seeker was sent to Greece.

[82] e.g. *NA v UK*, fn.12 above, para.121.

[83] e.g. its First Public Statement on Turkey was cited in *Aydin v Turkey*, (23178/94), (Rep.) March 7, 1996, para.159.

[84] e.g. *Nsangu v Austria*, (25661/94) (Rep.) May 22, 1995, the Commission noted inconsistencies in the story, delay in mentioning relevant grounds and doubts about the documents; (31026/96) (Dec.) October 24, 1996 where the alleged arrest warrant was undated and contained outdated wording. See also the strong weight given by the Court in *Nsona* to the fact that the aunt lied trying to bring her niece in, presenting a forged document: the authorities could not be blamed for refusing, once this was discovered, to accept claims unsupported by evidence.

[85] e.g. *Cruz Varas v Sweden*, March 20, 1991, Series A, No.291, para.81.

[86] *Jabari*, fn.11 above, para.40, where the domestic authorities had not carried out any meaningful examination of the applicant's claims of being at risk of stoning; *Hilal*, fn.67 above, para.62, where new evidence was not scrutinised by the Special Adjudicator and in reaching their decisions, the Secretary of State and courts relied not on any assessment of its credibility but on an "internal flight" argument.

the situation[87]; and may differ with their conclusions, on occasion in a case turning on credibility appointing delegates to hear the applicant and other witnesses themselves.[88]

Other factors taken into account include known practices by receiving countries in scrutinising returning asylum seekers with a view to taking action against them or otherwise rendering it likely that they come to the attention of the authorities in a negative way.[89] Also, intervening events or even the fact of residence in the expelling country may be a source of risk of ill-treatment, such as where the applicant has changed religion, been involved in political opposition or, in the case of women returning to Islamic areas, they have separated or become estranged from their husbands, or liable to accusations of adultery.[90]

(d) Shuttlecocking

State immigration policies sometimes give rise to the risk of asylum seekers or stateless persons being shunted from country to country. "Shuttlecocking" was an element in the Commission's finding of a violation of Art.3 in the East African Asians case,[91] where applicants holding British citizenship were refused entry to the United Kingdom and in some cases, forced to and fro unable to obtain entry to the United Kingdom or elsewhere. **II–490**

The Commission also stated that the repeated expulsion of an individual to a country where his admission is not guaranteed, may raise an issue, particularly where it occurs over a long period of time without any country taking measures to regularise his position.[92] Deliberate steps to render oneself stateless are however likely to prejudice a case.[93]

(e) Expulsion of children

Issues have arisen as to whether the manner of implementation of expulsion or its effects are so traumatic for children as to constitute treatment contrary to Art.3. **II–491**

Where unaccompanied minor children are held pending further measures, the receiving State is under an obligation to provide them with adequate care and protection. There was a lack of humanity, amounting to inhuman treatment, where the Belgian authorities placed a five-year-old Congolese child in a closed adult centre, without facilities, counselling or educational assistance.[94] Two days for a 16-

[87] *Salah Sheekh*, fn.52 above, para.136.

[88] e.g. *N v Finland*, July 26, 2005.

[89] e.g. *RC v Sweden*, March 9, 2010, para.56.

[90] e.g. *N v Sweden*, fn.49 above, paras 56–62.

[91] (4403/70) and others, (Rep.) December 14, 1973, 78–A D.R. 5.

[92] (7612/76) (Rep.) July 17, 1980, 21 D.R. 73, the applicant was of African origin with no identity papers, subject to a series of arrests and moving to and from one country to another—settled when he left for Senegal with a travel document from the Belgian Government; cf. (10798/84) (Dec.) March 5, 1986, 46 D.R. 112, the applicant of Algerian origin claiming to be stateless was repeatedly expelled from the Netherlands (over 20 times) but was found primarily responsible for his plight, e.g. he had not taken steps to seek Algerian citizenship nor substantiated that he was ever expelled back to the Netherlands rather than going back of his own free will.

[93] (28152–3/95), fn.38 above, where the applicants renounced their Romanian citizenship in an apparent effort to render themselves stateless and avoid expulsion from France.

[94] *Mulilanzila Mayeka and Kaniki Mitunga v Belgium*, October 12, 2006, the lack of information and attitude of the authorities also disclosed breaches of Art.3 in respect of the mother who was seeking to have her daughter join her in Canada.

year-old held in "abominable conditions" was sufficient for a breach of Art.3, as was the authorities' release of the minor to fend for himself for some 10 days without ensuring proper supervision and care.[95] States also must take adequate precautions and make necessary arrangements to ensure that when expelling a child there are appropriate family members or structures to care for them on arrival. In *Nsona*, where a nine-year-old girl was sent back to Zaire, the Court made critical comment of the failure of the Dutch authorities properly to investigate her personal situation and to take adequate measures in respect of her arrival. However, the circumstances did not reach the minimum level of severity prohibited by Art.3, in particular since the girl was not left unattended at the airport due to the initiative of the airline and she was brought back to the people previously taking care of her. Where however the Belgians sent back the five-year-old child, the Court found a lack of adequate preparation and supervision, as they did not arrange for her to be accompanied on the flight or make sure that a family member would come to meet her at the airport.[96]

In exceptional circumstances, the conditions facing children on expulsion to another country may disclose treatment of such a severe nature as to inflict on them inhuman and degrading treatment contrary to Art.3. A high threshold is set for treatment from mere change of environment and living standards to fall within the scope of Art.3 and allegations require specific and concrete substantiation.

In *Fadele v UK*, children with British citizenship living in the United Kingdom lost their mother in an accident and the Nigerian father was refused leave to join the children in the United Kingdom, with the consequence that the children were forced to join him in Nigeria. The case was declared admissible, reflecting the extreme hardship which the children faced, but not resolved on the merits since the case settled when the Government granted the father a residence permit and the family returned.[97] However, where the level of hardship is low, hypothetical or unsubstantiated, complaints have been rejected, for example, from a three-year-old British child, threatened with removal to Kenya with her mother who claimed that the child would have difficulties in obtaining treatment for problems with her hands and risk isolation from the Asian and African communities[98]; from children, where obliged to accompany their mother to Jamaica, about the alleged risk to their psychological health and physical well-being from the change in environment[99]; and from a four-year-old child allegedly at risk if sent to Colombia where his father was involved in drug trafficking circles.[100]

The situation where a child has the right to stay in a Contracting State but the custodial parent is being expelled also did not in the Commission's view constitute Art.3 treatment, even though it places the parent in the dilemma of taking the

[95] *Rahimi*, fn.13 above, paras 81–85, 87–94, the minor had to shift for himself on release, travelling from Lesbos to Athens, relying on ad hoc assistance from various unofficial sources.

[96] *Mulilanzila Mayeka*, fn.94 above, the Court did not, this time, give any credit for the fact that the air crew arranged for the child to be supervised and that the Congolese authorities provided an alternative solution when, after six hours, no relative had appeared to meet her at the airport.

[97] The family lived in a compound which was filthy, with open sewers. The children attended no school and spoke no Nigerian language. The youngest suffered bouts of malaria including convulsions requiring blood transfusions and hospitalisation and all three suffered from typhoid, respiratory infections and gastro-entiritis—(13078/87) (Rep.) July 4, 1991, 70 D.R.159.

[98] (23938/93) (Dec.) October 23, 1995.

[99] (25297/94) (Dec.) January 16, 1996.

[100] (24865/94) (Dec.) October 23, 1995.

child, who will then lose educational and other advantages, or of leaving it in the United Kingdom in care. The Commission appeared to find it compatible with the requirements of Art.3 that the parent has the opportunity to bring the child and they are not forced to be separated.[101] The mere loss of benefits to which the children are entitled by their citizenship are not enough.[102]

Effect on family life

Key case-law:

Abdulaziz, Cabales and Balkandali v UK, May 28, 1985, Series A, No.94, 7 E.H.R.R. 471; *Moustaquim v Belgium*, February 18, 1991, Series A, No.193, 13 E.H.R.R. 802; *Berrehab v Netherlands*, June 21, 1988, Series A, No.138, 11 E.H.R.R. 322; *Beldjoudi v France*, March 26, 1992, Series A, No.234–A, 14 E.H.R.R. 801; *Gül v Switzerland*, February 19, 1996, R.J.D. 1996–I, No.3, 22 E.H.R.R. 93; *Boughanemi v France*, April 24, 1996, R.J.D. 1996–II, No.8; *C v Belgium*, August 7, 1996, R.J.D. 1996–III, 32 E.H.R.R 19; *Nsona v Netherlands*, November 28, 1996, R.J.D. 1996–VI, No.23; *Ahmut v Netherlands*, November 28, 1996, R.J.D. 1996–VI, No.24; *Bouchelkia v France*, January 29, 1997, R.J.D. 1997–I, No.28, 25 E.H.R.R. 686; *Mehemi v France*, September 26, 1997, R.J.D. 1997–VI, No.51; *El Boujlifa v France*, September 26, 1997, R.J.D. 1997–VI, No.51, 30 E.H.R.R. 223; *Boujlifa v France*, October 21, 1997, R.J.D. 1997–VI, No.54, 30 E.H.R.R. 419; *Baghli v France*, November 30, 1999, ECHR 1999–VIII; *Ciliz v Netherlands*, July 11, 2000, ECHR 2000–VIII; *Ezzouhdi v France*, February 13, 2001; *Boultif v Switzerland*, August 2, 2001, ECHR 2001–IX; *Sen v Netherlands*, December 21, 2001, 24 E.H.R.R. 93; *Amrollahi v Denmark*, July 11, 2002; *Jakupovic v Austria*, February 6, 2003; *Slivenko v Latvia*, October 9, 2003, ECHR 2003–X; *Maslov v Austria*, June 23, 2008, ECHR 2008–. . . II–492

Apart from Art.3 ill-treatment issues, the principal ground on which expulsion measures have been contested has been Art.8 in respect of their disruption of "family life".

Approach to the cases is a balancing exercise whether viewed as an interference where a decision is taken to expel a person previously lawfully resident or an allegation of failure to comply with a positive obligation to respect family life by granting entry. In weighing the individual's interest against the general policy concerns, a restrictive approach is taken to almost every factor: from the weight given to the nature of family life concerned; the importance of immigration concerns and public order; the high threshold of acceptable hardships to individuals; and the wide margin of appreciation accorded to the State.

It should go without saying that measures should comply with requirements of lawfulness under the second paragraph of Art.8.[103]

[101] e.g. (22471/93) (Dec.) September 6, 1994, the mother was expelled while the children remained in the UK as wards of court. However there was evidence that the mother consented to wardship, i.e. there was no forcible separation.

[102] Cases cited at fnn.98–100 above.

[103] e.g. *Estrikh v Latvia*, January 18, 2007, violation where the applicant was expelled, contrary to domestic law, before his appeal was terminated. Lack of procedural safeguards may also disclose lawfulness problems, see further, para.503: Access to court and remedies.

Where unequivocal and not counter to any important public interest, an applicant may waive his right to remain in a particular country, as where a former Russian officer, who lived many years in Estonia, voluntarily signed up to a resettlement scheme outside Estonia.[104]

1. Existence of "family" links

(a) "Family life"

II–493 For the Court, where a child is born of a marriage, there is *ipso iure* family life between the parent and child, which only exceptional circumstances can break. This has been extended to parent-child relationships where there has been no cohabitation or marriage.[105] The fact in *C v Belgium* that the father was imprisoned, then deported or that the son went to live with an aunt did not constitute exceptional circumstances. The Court did not comment on the aunt-niece relationship in *Nsona*.

The Commission in older cases excluded the mere existence of blood ties as being sufficient save between married parents and their minor children. It held that adult children and other relatives must show elements of dependency going beyond normal emotional ties, e.g. monetary and practical links, evidence of regular contact.[106] This does not make allowance for the extended families found in some cultures,[107] or where families are poor, unable to contribute to each others support financially and are separated over time, with no opportunity to make contact and develop demonstrable relationships. In *Slivenko v Latvia*, the Court stated that "family life" is normally limited to the core family, without however specifying what that meant, beyond excluding one of the applicant's elderly parents who had been shown to have no links of dependency.[108]

(b) Verification procedures

II–494 Applicants seeking leave to enter often find themselves required to prove the claimed relationships with persons resident in the country. This has not been found to raise problems as long as a fair opportunity has been given to present family claims.

Where an applicant complained about the procedures whereby his purported wife and son were refused entry, the Commission found that a country was entitled to set up domestic verification procedures for family claims and that it could not intervene as a supervisory body to decide if a decision was wrong but only whether the authorities had acted outside what might reasonably be required of them in ensuring the right to respect for family life.[109] Refusal of entry to a child when the

[104] *Nagula v Estonia*, (39203/02) (Dec.) October 25, 2005, it was irrelevant that Estonia was not a party to the Russo-American resettlement agreements.

[105] *Gül v Switzerland*, February 19, 1996, R.J.D. 1996–I, No.3, 22 E.H.R.R. 93, para.32; *Boughanemi v France*, April 24, 1996, R.J.D. 1996–II, No.8, para.35; *Boultif v Switzerland*, August 2, 2001, ECHR 2001–IX, para.28; *Al Nashif v Bulgaria*, June 20, 2002, paras 112–113.

[106] e.g. (9492/81) (Dec.) July 14, 1982, 30 D.R. 232.

[107] (26373/95) (Dec.) October 16, 1995, whether the applicant's mother, two sisters, seven brothers, etc. qualified as "family" in a refugee family re-unification case where the applicant had become head of the family in Somali terms was left open.

[108] *Slivenko v Latvia*, October 9, 2003, ECHR 2003–X, para.94.

[109] (8378/78) (Dec.) May 14, 1980, 20 D.R. 168.

immigration authorities were not satisfied that he was the son of the putative father in the United Kingdom was not a problem, even though a DNA test later revealed a biological link and entry was refused since the son was no longer a minor. The Commission found no bad faith on the part of the immigration authorities at the time of the initial refusal and there had been a fair opportunity to present the claims.[110]

2. Spouses

The principles governing the extent of the State's obligation to admit spouses is laid down by the Court in *Abdulaziz, Cabales and Balkandali v UK*: II–495

- there is no general obligation on a Contracting State to respect the choice of married couples as to the country of matrimonial residence;
- States enjoy a wide margin of appreciation;
- it is relevant whether there are obstacles to establishing the marital home elsewhere, in the country of the spouse or the applicant's own origin or whether there are any special reasons why they should not be expected to do so;
- it is relevant whether, when marrying, they were aware of the problems of entry or limited leave situation.

Since in *Abdulaziz* there were no obstacles or special reasons and the couples were aware of their problematic immigration status at the time of marriage, no violation of Art.8 was found. It remains to be seen what relevance would or should be given to a situation where an applicant married in circumstances where neither spouse knew the problems of immigration status. Arguably, they would have to give a convincing explanation for ignorance of a potential problem. It is not obvious, however, that expectations at the time of marriage could ever play a significant role in finding a violation.

Many cases are rejected using the above criteria, with reference to the lack of obstacles to the spouses living elsewhere and in particular their knowledge of the precarious immigration status beforehand.[111] Occasionally, reasons have been put forward that an applicant cannot be expected to join a spouse elsewhere, for example, health, or the fact that the spouse would leave a business or employment[112] but the Convention organs have rarely accepted any as constituting a sufficient obstacle or special circumstances. The fact that an applicant suffered illness on a previous visit to Pakistan was not enough;[113] where a wife submitted that she was unable to live in Bangladesh as she was constantly ill there, the Commission found "no serious obstacles" existed and noted that she had lived there herself for 12 years

[110] (19546/92) (Dec.) March 13, 1992; also (36287/97) (Dec.) July 10, 1998, where the Commission held that the procedural guarantee in Art.8 did not require decision-making authorities to afford the opportunity to lodge further submissions if the evidence of family relationship was not considered sufficient.

[111] e.g. *Darren Omoregie v Norway*, July 31, 2008, paras 61–64, where the spouses had never had reasonable expectation that the husband, who had never had a lawful right of residence, could claim an entitlement to stay. (25073/94) (Dec.) February 28, 1996.

[112] e.g. (25073/94) (Dec.) February 28, 1996.

[113] (17229/90) (Dec.) February 12, 1992.

previously.[114] A successful claim would require strong substantiation and a high level of danger to health. However, even where it was argued that no appropriate treatment was available in Sierra Leone for a particular intestinal disorder and epilepsy, supported by the only qualified neurologist in Sierra Leone, this argument was outweighed by the fact the illness was of long standing, known before the spouses married and that the deportation order on the husband was issued before the marriage.[115]

It may be noted that in most of these unsuccessful cases the spouse with residence rights or citizenship is nonetheless of a similar background to the spouse to be expelled, for example, having originated from the same part of the world, which will render, for the Convention organs' purposes, the possibility of the couple being able to set up the family unit elsewhere as a practical option. Where the spouse has no such prior or family connections elsewhere, the hardship involved in setting up married life in an African or Asian country is conceivably more significant. In *Beldjoudi v France*, part of the reasoning for finding a violation in expelling the applicant to Algeria, was that his wife was French, with French parents, had always lived in France and to be uprooted to go to Algeria, where she did not speak the language, would cause her real practical or even legal obstacles: the interference might therefore imperil the unity or even existence of the marriage.[116] In *Amrollahi v Denmark*, the Court, in finding it would breach Art.8 to expel the Iranian applicant, considered that it would cause the applicant's Danish wife and Danish children 'obvious and serious difficulties' to live in Iran. This appears to put an unfortunate emphasis on the ethnic or racial origins of the spouse but would still appear to be only one factor in the balancing exercise against legitimate immigration interests. More recently, the Court appears to be moving away from this relatively strict approach. Where the applicant's wife, also of Nigerian origin, could have have joined him in Nigeria, the Court nonetheless gave more weight to the strength of the wife's and children's connections to the UK and held that the expulsion of the applicant was not proportionate.[117] In the cases where refusal to allow the foreign spouse to remain was in breach, it may be noted generally that the family had been established for some time in the Contracting State concerned.

The Commission accepted that a country may limit the number of wives as a matter of policy entering to live with a man settled in the United Kingdom. Excluding surplus wives pursued the legitimate aim of preserving the Christian-based monogamous culture dominant in that society (thereby protecting morals and the rights and freedoms of others) and a Contracting State could not be required to give full recognition to polygamous marriages in conflict with their own legal order or bigamy laws.[118]

[114] (18713/91) (Dec.) April 1, 1992.
[115] (24831/94) (Dec.) August 31, 1994.
[116] *Beldjoudi v France*, March 26, 1992, Series A, No.234–A, 14 E.H.R.R. 801, para.78.
[117] *Omojudi v UK*, November 11, 2009, paras 46–48. Also *Ciftci v Austria*, (24375/94) (Rep.) April 15, 1998, where the Commission found a violation of Art.8 where the applicant, to be expelled to Turkey, was married to an Austrian wife, with three children who were Austrian citizens; *Boultif v Switzerland*, August 2, 2001, ECHR 2001–IX, where the applicant's Swiss wife could not be expected to follow him to Algeria.
[118] (19628/92) (Dec.) June 29, 1992.

3. Children

(a) *Entry to join family*

Where a child previously living apart from a parent outside a Contracting State is refused entry to join the family, violations may conceivably arise where the child has no practical alternative. However, there must be shown to be substantial existing family ties, which may be difficult where the individual has lived at a distance for some time. For example in *Ahmut v Netherlands*, the 15–year-old son left Morocco, where he had been brought up by relatives, to join his father in the Netherlands. The Court noted that the boy had lived most of his life in Morocco with which he had strong linguistic and cultural links, there were other family members in Morocco, the separation was the result of the conscious decision of the father to move to the Netherlands and there was nothing to stop them continuing the degree of family life they had before. That the father might prefer to intensify his family links with his son in the Netherlands, the Court said, did not guarantee a right to choose the most suitable place to develop family life. II–496

The fact that the family is able to return to join the child may also be a decisive consideration. In *Gül v Switzerland* where the Turkish father lived in Switzerland and had applied unsuccessfully for his 12-year-old son to join him, the Court observed that the parents had caused the separation by moving to Switzerland and while it was admittedly difficult from a humanitarian point of view, there were no obstacles preventing them from living in Turkey, in particular since they could continue to receive their invalidity pension and benefits and it was not proved that the mother could not receive appropriate medical treatment in Turkey.[119]

The situation could conceivably change if the parent had succeeded in obtaining refugee status, in which case the argument that the family could return would be weaker. It may also be decisive if the parents can show a greater degree of integration into the society of the country. It was on this basis, in the case of *Sen v Netherlands*, that the Court distinguished the *Ahmut* case in finding that that the refusal to allow entry to the eldest daughter breached Art.8. The parents had both obtained long-standing and lawful resident status and two children had been born in the country. The Court gave weight to the consideration that these two children had no links with Turkey and commented, in contradiction of the approach in *Ahmut*, that the free choice of the parents to leave their eldest child in Turkey could not be regarded as an irrevocable decision that she should remain outside the family group. The *Gül* case was distinguished on the basis that the parents in that case did not have a permanent right of abode in the host country. Consequently, by placing the parents in the situation of having to choose between their established life in the Netherlands or giving up the company of their daughter, the State was found, in this case, not to have struck a proper balance.

(b) *Expulsion of custodial parent(s)*

Whether removal or exclusion of a parent from a Contracting State is incompatible with the requirements of Art.8 as regards a child with residence will depend on a number of factors: the extent to which family life is effectively ruptured, whether II–497

[119] Also *PR v Netherlands*, (39391/98) (Dec.) November 7, 2000, where the applicant had been refused entry for children left behind in the Cape Verde islands six years earlier, the Court noted that the separation had been her choice, there was no obstacle to the family living together in the islands and that Art.8 did not guarantee a right to choose the most suitable place to develop family life.

there are insurmountable obstacles in the way of the family living in the country of origin of one or more of them, whether there are factors of immigration control (e.g. history of breaches of immigration law) or considerations of public order (e.g. serious or persistent offences) weighing in favour of exclusion.[120] The "age" and "adaptability" of the children are regarded as particularly significant.[121]

While applicants argued that weight should be given to the British citizenship of children, the Commission found the factor to be of no material weight, whether obtained *ius sanguine* through a parent rather than the accident of *ius soli*.[122] The Commission was also unpersuaded by arguments as to "constructive expulsion" where a child British citizen, forced by circumstances to accompany a non-national parent, would be deprived of the benefits of the country of nationality and face long years of "exile" until able to return as an adult and face the difficulties adapting to life there again. Although this might constitute hardship, it would nonetheless not appear to disclose any effective bars to enjoying family life elsewhere.

Save for the case of *Fadele v UK*,[123] no case concerning the expulsion of custodial parent has been declared admissible, indicating that where young children are concerned, there are generally no Convention obstacles to them accompanying the parent abroad.

However, where the applicant custodial parent was expelled from Russia without being given the opportunity to organising that his baby son could accompany him to avoid their separation, the Court found a violation emphasising the State's positive obligation to protect young children, the authorities' knowledge of the applicant's status as the sole parent and the lack of any attempt by them to take this matter into account in their decisions and measures applied.[124]

(c) Expulsion of divorced or separated parent

II–498 Where a non-national parent is being expelled and the children are in the custody of the other parent (with citizenship or residence rights), after separation or divorce, family links may arguably be ruptured between parent and child since there is no possibility of the child accompanying the parent.[125]

Whether the expulsion will in this situation disclose a violation will depend on a number of factors, in particular, the nature and strength of the parent's links with the child.[126] In *Berrehab v Netherlands*, the application was brought by father, ex-wife and child in respect of the proposed expulsion of the father from the Netherlands,

[120] e.g. (9285/81) (Dec.) July 6, 1982, 29 D.R. 205; (11970/86) (Dec.) July 13, 1987.

[121] See cases cited fnn.71–73 above.

[122] e.g. (11970/86) (Dec.) July 13, 1987, where the Commission found it compatible with Art.8 to expect children of unlawful overstayers to follow their parents even if they had acquired theoretical rights of abode; cases cited at fnn.71–73.

[123] See fn.70 above.

[124] *Nolan and K v Russia*, February 12, 2009, paras 86–89.

[125] Paradoxically, an applicant who has been divorced may therefore derive a right to stay to enjoy access to a child whereas those who enjoy an ongoing married relationship may be expected to uproot every family member and leave.

[126] Mere allegations of interest or links are not enough: there must be strong indications of an ongoing relationship, e.g. (26985/95), fn.24 above, where the links of a boy with his father in the UK would be affected by removal to Ghana, the Commission noted the irregular nature of the contacts and that it had diminished to telephone contact such that the effect on "family life" would be minimal; (28627/95) (Dec.) January 17, 1997, where the child's father had not shown any commitment beyond a statement that he would like to see her.

after divorce, which threatened to break the ties between father and child. The fact the parents no longer cohabited was not decisive for the existence or otherwise of family life where the relationships arose out of a lawful and genuine marriage and the father saw the child four times a week, regular and frequent contact proving the strength of his ties.[127] The Court also had regard to the fact the father had been lawfully resident in the Netherlands for many years, had a home and job and that the Government had no real cause for complaint against him: therefore a balance had not been achieved between the interest of immigration control and the applicants' mutual interests in continuing their family ties.

The illegal nature of the parent's presence in the country has been a decisive factor in rejecting other cases.[128] However, where domestic courts had ruled that it was in the best interests for a child to remain in the Netherlands with her Dutch father, the Court held that it was excessively formalistic to hold against the Brazilian mother with whom she had close ties her failure to regularise her status in the Netherlands. Her relationship of three years with the father would have entitled her to obtain legal residence and this allowed the case to be distinguished from those where a parent or parents never had any reasonable expectation to remain.[129] In *Ciliz v Netherlands*, the decision-making procedure concerning the father's expulsion disclosed a violation of Art.8, where the authorities prejudged the outcome of contact proceedings by expelling him during a period of trial contact sessions and he had not been convicted of any criminal offences warranting his removal. The Court has underlined that decisions concerning the expulsion of a non-national parent must give proper regard to the best interests of the children.Thus, where the mother, who had been the custodial parent of two girls, was put under order of expulsion and ban of re-entry for two years, the Court found that her aggravated breaches of immigration law did not justify the traumatic impact of separation from the two children who had been placed, by court order, under the care of the father due to the expulsion order.[130]

(d) *Expulsion measures concerning unaccompanied minors*

In *Jakupovic v Austria*, the Court stated that very weighty reasons had to be put forward to justify the expulsion of a young person (16 years old in that case), particularly given the history of conflict in the country of origin and no evidence of close relatives remaining there. It gave close scrutiny to the boy's criminal record and giving weight to the absence of any elements of violence, found the expulsion II–499

[127] Also *Ciliz v Netherlands*, July 11, 2000, ECHR 2000–VIII, where the father, who was to be expelled to Turkey, had kept up contact, on a frequent, if not, regular basis. Contrast *Aoulmi*, fn.19 above, para.89, where the applicant did not specify the nature of ties or his role vis-à-vis his 16–year-old daughter.

[128] (26285/95) (Dec.) April 9, 1997, expulsion of a mother, entailing separation of a child from the father with whom she enjoyed frequent contact, was not disproportionate since the mother had been unlawfully in the country and started the relationship, bearing the child when her immigration status was irregular. Whereas in *Berrehab v Netherlands*, June 21, 1988, Series A, No.138, 11 E.H.R.R. 322, the relationship had developed while the father was lawfully resident and the residence was not revoked for any misconduct or breach of condition but only due to end of a marriage to a Dutch citizen.

[129] *Rodriguez da Silva and Hoogkamer v Netherlands*, January 31, 2006, paras 43–44.

[130] *Nunez v Norway*, June 28, 2006, paras 65–85, the Court also took into account the four-year delay in taking the decision to expel. The case may be anomalous in that if the custody of the children had remained with the mother, there would have been nothing to prevent their accompanying her on expulsion as they were of a relatively young age still.

would be a disproportionate interference with his right to respect for family and private life.

In a transit situation, where a five-year-old Congolese girl was found not to have the necessary travel papers in Belgium and was eventually expelled back to the Congo, the Court considered that the authorities had been under an obligation to facilitate her reunion with her mother in Canada, whereas the measures they had taken had in fact hindered this process and had not pursued the higher interest of the child, in particular by detaining her in an unsuitable adult centre rather than finding a more adapted structure. The Court emphasised that the child could not be blamed for the perhaps questionable conduct of her adult relatives.[131]

4. "Second-generation" immigrant expulsions

II–500 Where a State seeks to expel persons who have been legally settled in their territory but who have committed offences, the Convention organs look particularly at the extent of the links of the individual with the host State and receiving State: the length of residence; knowledge/ignorance of the language or culture; existence and strength of family links or friends in the respective countries; dependency on the family which remains behind in the Contracting State; and personal circumstances such as health or psychological state which might render removal of potentially drastic effect. These have to be balanced against the reasons for the removal and the assessment made whether the interests of the prevention of crime or disorder outweigh the effect of the removal on the applicant. This case-by-case approach has been criticised as a "lottery" for national authorities, lacking legal certainty and the opposing view has been put forward that there should be at least a very strong presumption that aliens who have lived most, or all their lives in a country should no more be expelled than nationals.[132] The Court's approach has crystallised in recent years more towards the latter. It now states straightforwardly that for a settled migrant who has lawfully spent all or the major part of his or her childhood and youth in the host country very serious reasons are required to justify expulsion, particularly where the person concerned committed the offences underlying the expulsion measure as a juvenile.[133]

Disproportionate effects were found in a number of cases, where in effect an applicant had lived most of his life in the expelling State, his family lived there and he had no real links with, or knowledge of, the receiving State.[134] Legal ties of

[131] *Mulilanzila Mayeka*, fn.94 above, breaches of Art.8 for child and mother.

[132] e.g. Judge Morenilla dissenting in *Nasri*, fn.55 above, considering that the expulsion of non-nationals for misconduct was discriminatory, cruel and inhuman; Judge Martens, dissenting in *Boughanemi v France*, April 24, 1996, R.J.D. 1996–II, No.8, considering that expulsion might be exceptionally justified where very serious crime (terrorism or lead drug trafficker) was involved and Judges Costa and Tulkens, dissenting in *Baghli v France*, November 30, 1999, ECHR 1999–VIII, with comments as to the unnecessarily punitive nature of such orders on persons who had lived practically their entire lives in the expelling country.

[133] See *Maslov v Austria*, June 23, 2008, ECHR 2008–. . . , para. 75.

[134] *Moustaquim*, fn.1 above, had arrived in Belgium aged two, all his close relatives were there and had acquired Belgian nationality, he had received all his schooling in French and visited Morocco only twice on holiday. *Beldjoudi* had been born and educated in France, knew no Arabic, had no links with Algeria apart from nationality and was married to a French woman who has always lived in France. In *Mehemi*, September 26, 1997, R.J.D. 1997–VI, No.51, the applicant had been born and schooled in France, most of his family lived there, including his wife and three children who had French nationality and who could not reasonably be expected to live elsewhere. See also *Lamguindaz v UK*, (16152/90) (Rep.) October 13, 1992, Series A, No.258–C, settled before the Court, where the Commission found a violation of Art.8 for expelling the applicant who had lived in the UK from age 7–8, was educated there, his close relatives lived there and no real links with Morocco.

nationality are not in themselves decisive.[135] However where applicants have retained some links with the country of origin, they have been less successful. In *Boughanemi*, the Court found it probable that the applicant retained links with Tunisia, noting that he did not claim that he could not speak Arabic, or that he had cut off all ties. It gave particular weight to his offences and none to the fact that he lived as man and wife with a Frenchwoman and had a child, since this had occurred after the deportation order.[136] In *C v Belgium*, the applicant also had only moved to Belgium at the later age of 11 and still had links with Morocco.[137]

While in earlier cases, the Court found that the personal interests of the applicant outweighed quite significant criminal records,[138] there was, for a while, an apparent hardening in attitude and greater sympathy given to the public order policies of Contracting States, with particular reference to understanding the firmness with which the authorities treat offenders who contribute to the 'scourge' of drug trafficking.[139] In *Boughanemi* (four convictions, theft and aggravated proxenetism attracting prison sentences) the Commission found a violation but the Court did not. While it found the applicant's actual links to France weak, it "above all" attached importance to the fact the deportation was decided after he had been sentenced to almost four years' imprisonment, for, inter alia, living on the earnings of prostitution in aggravating circumstances.[140] Although the applicant in *Bouchelkia* had lived in France since the age of two, the factor of his conviction of rape tipped the balance towards the interests of the State in expelling him.[141] A long history of criminal conduct, culminating in narcotics importation outweighed an applicant's strong links with Sweden and his close relationship with his children who lived with his ex-wife.[142] The Court has also sometimes referred negatively to applicants' lack of desire to acquire nationality of the expelling country.[143]

Where, however, there are effectively no links with the receiving country and the applicant's record is not regarded as serious or shows mitigating factors, the balance is more likely to tip against expulsion. In *Ezzouhdi v France*, where the applicant had lived in France since the age of five and had no apparent links but nationality with

[135] e.g. *Ezzoudhi v France*, February 13, 2001, para.34.

[136] Also *Bouchelkia v France*, January 29, 1997, R.J.D. 1997–I, No.28, 25 E.H.R.R. 686, where the marriage to a French national and birth of a child after the deportation order were discounted.

[137] e.g. he had married a woman there (later divorced).

[138] e.g. *Moustaquim*, fn.1 above, an alleged 147 offences, mainly petty theft, carried out as an adolescent, *Beldjoudi*, fn.116 above, seven custodial sentences, the last eight years for aggravated theft, *Nasri*, fn.55 above, over 10 convictions, one for gang rape.

[139] *Baghli*, fn.132 above, para.48.

[140] Also *C v Belgium*, August 7, 1996, R.J.D. 1996–III, 32 E.H.R.R 19, where the Court attached great importance to a drugs offence attracting five years; *Boujlifa v France*, October 21, 1997, R.J.D. 1997–VI, No.54, 30 E.H.R.R. 419, armed robbery, etc.

[141] Also *Benrachid v France*, (39518/98) (Dec.) December 8, 1998, ECHR 1999–II, where the applicant arrived from Algeria aged 7 and all his family were in France, the Court rejected his complaint on the basis of a serious conviction (armed robbery) and an assumption that he had not cut all links with Algeria; *Djaid v France*, (38687/97) (Dec.) March 9, 1999, where the applicant had arrived in France aged five months and had two French children born out of wedlock (his links with the children were apparently strong)—the Court gave weight to his drug convictions and his knowledge at the time of the conception of the first child that he was liable to expulsion: *Baghli*, fn.132 above, where the applicant arrived in France aged two, his family and social ties were in France, this was outweighed by the drug conviction (three-year sentence).

[142] *Najafi v Sweden*, (28570/03) (Dec.) July 6, 2004.

[143] *Boulifa*, fn.140 above, para.44; *El Boujaïdi v France*, September 26, 1997, R.J.D. 1997–VI, No.51, 30 E.H.R.R. 223, para.41; *Djaid*, fn.110 above, *Baghli*, fn.132 above, para.48, though it is not apparent whether these applicants would have had any prospect of obtaining citizenship.

Morocco, his conviction for minor drugs possession charges was not sufficient for him to be regarded a threat to public order necessitating his expulsion. While in *Boultif v Switzerland*, where the applicant had committed a serious offence of robbery, albeit one attracting the relatively light sentence of two years, the expulsion order was found to be disproportionate, when balanced against the fact that the applicant's wife, a Swiss national with no connections with Algeria or knowledge of Arabic, could not be expected to follow him. Since it was practically impossible for him to live his family life outside Switzerland, and, with recent good behaviour, he presented only a comparatively limited danger to the public order,[144] there was a violation of Art.8. A sexual offence which did not disclose an underlying problem or pattern of offending did not justify expulsion of a Nigerian long settled in the UK, the Court contrasting his situation with a previous applicant who had been a repeat drugs offender.[145]

The understanding of strict public policies against drugs offences has its limits, the Court being less impressed by the heinousness of offences of drug consumption, in particularly by the young. Indeed where minors are concerned, it has expressed the view that even where they have committed criminal offences, the principal object should be pursuit of their "best interests" and "re-integration". Expelling a minor then from the country where they have lived most of their lives and where their close family lives would rarely fit in with such an object, thus, Art.8 was been found to be violated where such a measure had been applied. Although in that particular case, the Court emphasised that the minor concerned had mostly committed non-violent and only drug consumption offences and contrasted cases where minors had committed rape and seriously violent offences, it would seem from the thrust of the reasoning that it would be in exceptional cases that the factors of protection of children would not be likely to prevail.[146]

In a handful of cases, even where the expulsion of second generation applicants was largely justified by the nature of the offences, the Court took exception to the imposition of an indefinite measure of prohibition of return to the expelling country where most of their family connections still existed.[147]

Where a "second generation" applicant has spent most of his or her formative life in a Contracting State and is refused renewal of a residence permit on technical grounds, the Court is likely to find issues arising. When a 15-year-old daughter of Somali parents settled in Denmark was sent back to Kenya to care for her grandmother and meanwhile her Danish residence permit expired due to failure to re-apply within the statutory time-limit, the Court found that a fair balance between her interests and immigration control had not been struck under Art.8.[148]

[144] See also *Maslov*, fn.133 above, paras 89–95, where the Court identified as a relevant factor the applicant's conduct between the latest offence and the date of the expulsion, viz. showing the level of danger posed by him to public order and security. Contrast *Mutlag v Germany*, March 25, 2010, para.57, where the lack of offending was seen as due to his incarceration or clandestine hiding, not good conduct.

[145] *Omojudi v UK*, fn.117 above, paras 42–44, distinguishing *Joseph Grant v UK*, January 8, 2009, no violation for deporting an applicant, long settled in the UK but with a considerable criminal record, to Jamaica.

[146] *Maslov*, fn.133 above, paras 77–101. Contrast *Mutlag*, fn.143 above, para.55, distinguishing *Maslov*, fn.133 above, inter alia, where the applicant had committed a series of violent offences.

[147] See *Yilmaz v Germany*, April 17, 2003, para.48; *Keles v Germany*, October 27, 2005, para.66.

[148] *Osman v Denmark*, June 14, 2011, paras 53–77.

Effect on private life

Expulsion of a person settled in a country may disclose an interference with private life, as well as family life.[149] Though most cases have turned on the aspects of family life, the Court has found expulsion measures to have violated both family and private life aspects in a few cases.[150] It considers that it must now be accepted that the totality of social ties between settled migrants and the community in which they are living constitutes part of the concept of "private life" within the meaning of Art.8.[151] II–501

Where in *Slivenko v Latvia*, the whole family was to be deported together, the Court examined the case primarily as regarded the disruption to their private life and home. Although the Court found nothing incompatible per se with the arrangements for the withdrawal of Russian troops and their families, it found that in the particular case it was disproportionate to apply the measure to the descendants of a long retired officer who had been integrated into Latvia and had no equivalent ties in Russia. Applicants present in a country on a short-term or provisional basis may not be able to claim an interference with any established private life.[152]

Expulsions which threaten to have significant adverse effects on an applicant's mental health and sanity may raise issues under Art.8 in its aspect of physical and moral integrity.[153]

Arguments by child applicants that their forced departure to accompany their foreign mothers would deprive them of growing and developing in their country of birth and nationality have been rejected.[154] Presumably, if there are no effective obstacles to a small child living family life with its mother elsewhere there is no interference with private life either. "Private life" doubtfully applies to future benefits of living in a particular environment: there must be at least something specific to existing private life or elements relating to past private life.[155] Whereas "family" life has been held to extend to the development of potential relationships by the Commission in the case of natural fathers and their children,[156] it remains to be seen whether such an approach could be accommodated under the Art.8 private life aspect.

[149] e.g. *C v Belgium*, fn.140 above, para.25; *Boujlifa*, fn.140 above, para.36; *El Boujaïdi*, fn.143 above, para.33; *Baghli*, fn.132 above, para.37, where the applicants had lived most of their lives in the expelling State.

[150] e.g. *Ezzoudhi*, fn.135 above, paras 26 and 33; *Mehemi*, fn.134 above, paras 35–37; *Jakupovic v Austria*, February 6, 2003, paras 22–26. Cf. *Beldjoudi*, fn.116 above, Judge Marten's concurring opinion finding a violation of the aspect of private life instead of family life, considering that this covered external relations with others and the right to establish and develop relationships with others.

[151] e.g. *Maslov v Austria* (GC), ECHR 2008–. . . , para.63; *Omujudi v UK*, November 24, 2009, para.37, concerning persons of Nigerian origin long settled in the UK.

[152] e.g. (9478/81) (Dec.) December 8, 1981, 27 D.R. 243, where the applicant was to be deported from Germany to Indonesia, the Commission said that to the extent that the circle of acquaintances established during her stay in Germany disclosed relationships recognised as 'private life' there could be no interference since the applicant knew at all times that her presence, and hence her ability to establish relationships, was temporary and subject to revocation.

[153] *Bensaid*, see fn.23 above, paras 46–48.

[154] See fnn.98 and 100 above.

[155] See *Gaskin v UK*, July 7, 1989, Series A, No.160, where information about past childhood was in issue.

[156] *Keegan v Ireland*, (Rep.) February 17, 1993, Series A, No.290, para.48.

Effect on education

II–502 Expulsion of a child of school age will inevitably entail disruption of education and claims have been made, so far unsuccessfully, under Art.2 of the First Protocol.[157] Education will, arguably, be available at least at elementary level if not higher in most countries. It may be difficult to argue that deportation will deny "education" as such, though it may diminish the choice or quality of the education. Also if a deportation measure is justifiable for the aim of legitimate immigration control where there is interference with family life it would be strange if Art.2 of the First Protocol granted residence rights for the purpose of education. The Commission had on that basis dismissed in very brief terms Art.2 of the First Protocol complaints where the expulsion has been found compatible with Art.8.[158] In *Ebibomi v UK*,[159] the two sons (aged 21 and 20) in full-time education claimed that they were supported by their mother financially and emotionally and if she was expelled their education would be prevented. The Commission had found that the practical difficulties which might arise from the removal of their mother, which was compatible with Art.8 as a legitimate measure of immigration control, could not be construed as a deprivation of their right to education.

Access to court and remedies

Key case-law:

II–503 *Soering v UK*, July 7, 1989, Series A, No.161, 11 E.H.R.R. 439; *Vilvarajah v UK*, October 30, 1991, Series A, No.215, 14 E.H.R.R. 248; *Chahal v UK*, November 15, 1996, R.J.D. 1996–V, 23 E.H.R.R. 413; *Jabari v Turkey*, July 11, 2000, ECHR 2000–VIII; *Maaouia v France*, October 5, 2000, ECHR 2000–X; *Bensaid v UK*, February 6, 2001, ECHR 2001–I; *Hilal v UK*, March 6, 2001, ECHR 2001–II; *Al-Nashif v Bulgaria*, June 20, 2002; *M.S.S. v Belgium and Greece*, January 21, 2011, ECHR 2011–. . .

The Commission considered that there was no "civil right" to nationality or to a right of residence and that Art.6 had no application to asylum, expulsion, deportation proceedings or the like.[160] In *Maaouia v France*, the Court confirmed this approach, holding that decisions regarding the entry, stay and deportation of aliens did not concern either the determination of an applicant's civil rights or obligations or of a criminal charge against him within the meaning of Art.6, para.1.[161]

This is a restrictive approach, based at least partly on the view that questions of entry or residence of aliens involve discretionary acts of public authorities or are governed by public law.[162] An alien may therefore reside lawfully in a country with

[157] Nor does disruption to schooling interfere with family life under Art.8: (9492/81) (Dec.) July 14, 1982, 30 D.R. 232.

[158] See fnn.98 and 100 above.

[159] (26922/95) (Dec.) November 29, 1995.

[160] (8118/77) (Dec.) March 19, 1981, 25 D.R. 105; (9990/82) (Dec.) May 15, 1984, 39 D.R. 119.

[161] *Maaouia v France*, October 5, 2000, ECHR 2000–X, paras 38–41.

[162] See, e.g. the Commission's approach in (7729/76) (Dec.) December 17, 1976, 7 D.R. 164, the expulsion of a US citizen from the UK on security grounds was considered an act of state falling within the public sphere. In *Maaouia*, fn.161 above, the majority interpreted an exclusion of aliens' rights in Art.6 from the specific provision for procedural guarantees in Art.1 of Protocol No.7.

his family for decades and be expelled, with drastic effects on family life, private life, employment, livelihood and health, without recourse to a court, with the full procedural guarantees, to challenge the decision. In other areas (see, e.g. social security, pensions, tax) the Commission and Court have seen less clear distinctions between public and private law areas and have had regard to effect on private life with analogies to matters such as contract.[163]

Though an applicant expelled or refused entry cannot claim a right as such under Art.6 to a court procedure to challenge the merits or lawfulness of the decision, there has been scope under Art.8 to lay claim at least to some procedural protections.[164] In *Al Nashif v Bulgaria*, the Court found a violation of Art.8 where the applicant's expulsion was ordered pursuant to a legal regime that did not provide the necessary safeguards against arbitrariness. In that case, where the applicant was to be expelled as an alleged threat to public order due to his religious activities, the Court held that, even where national security was at stake, the concepts of lawfulness and the rule of law required that the executive's discretion should not be unlimited and such measures be subject to some form of adversarial procedure before an independent body competent to review them.[165] The judicial scrutiny must be a meaningful one, examining the factual basis of the alleged grounds for expulsion and not merely taking the executive's assertions at face value.[166] Similarly, where a Chinese national who had established family life with his Russian spouse and child was expelled on national security grounds in a procedure at the discretion of the executive which fell outside the otherwise applicable judicial guarantees and judicial scrutiny, the Court considered the deportation was not based on provisions with the requisite "quality of law".[167]

Lack of access to court aside, applicants may invoke Art.13 of the Convention, a right to an effective remedy. This is subject to the precondition of Art.13—that there is an "arguable claim" of a violation of another provision of the Convention (see section "Remedies") and in practice will generally only become operative once a substantive complaint has been declared admissible.

Article 13 does not automatically require a court remedy. However bodies which fail to provide sufficient procedural safeguards or which function by way of discretionary powers will be unlikely to qualify. In *Chahal*, the Court found that the hearing before an advisory panel gave a restricted review to the case and also provided insufficient procedural safeguards, namely, no entitlement to legal representation, provision of few details to the applicant and only a power of recommendation, not decision. The Court made positive note of the system in Canada adverted to by intervenors. Failure to provide an appeal against the proposed expulsion of the applicant in *Al-Nashif v Bulgaria* breached Art.13. There the Court stated that, even

[163] Pt IIA, s.1b: Civil rights and obligations.

[164] See *Ciliz*, fn.127 above, and (sub-ss.3(c): Expulsion of divorced or separated parents and 1(b): Verification procedures.

[165] See also lack of protection against arbitrariness founding a lack of lawfulness violation in *Lupsa v Romania*, June 8, 2006, paras 39–44, e.g. order not served on applicant till after his deportation, no details given, no review of merits by courts.

[166] See *CG v Bulgaria*, April 24, 2008, paras 37–50, the domestic courts made a purely formal examination of the applicant's challenge to his expulsion on national security grounds, the Court noting with disapproval that the only element put forward to justify this measure being his alleged involvement in drug trafficking which could hardly be regarded as a national security threat, however widely that term could legitimately be interpreted.

[167] *Liu and Liu v Russia*, December 6, 2007, paras 59–69.

in national security cases, as a minimum there should be an independent appeals authority, which is informed of the reasons grounding the decision (even if such reasons are not publicly available), competent to reject the executive's assertions of the existence of a threat to national security, with some form of adversarial proceedings and capable of examining whether a fair balance has been struck between the public interest and the individual's rights.

Whatever the body however, it must also give an independent and 'rigorous scrutiny' of claims of a risk of ill-treatment contrary to Art.3 and be able to suspend the implementation of the measure.[168] Emphasis has been placed on this requirement of an automatic stay to prevent expulsion before a claim has been thoroughly examined. A procedure whereby a stay would only be granted after a limited review of the merits of the claim was found insufficient as it might still allow expulsion before a rigorous scrutiny was carried out.[169]

There must be practical and effective access to this body. Thus, the Belgian system was found lacking where an appeal was dismissed for the applicant's lawyer failure to appear although the hearing had been scheduled only a few hours after the appeal had been lodged and the lawyer's office was in a different city. It may also be relevant for the purposes of Art.13 what is the record of success for similar claims before the domestic courts; however this will not always be decisive since there is no requirement under Art.13 of the certainty of obtaining redress; it is apparently the lack of any prospect of success that will be fatal.[170] Deficiencies in information to asylum seekers about the remedies available and the legal assistance available , and lack of communication between the authorities and asylum seekers about progress of claims undermined the effectiveness of the Greek asylum procedure.[171]

In the United Kingdom, the limited scope of judicial review was previously insufficient in cases concerning family and private life issues. It remains to be seen whether the Human Rights Act 1998 provides effective court scrutiny. Where however an applicant was alleging risk to life or ill-treatment falling within the scope of Art.3, the Court accepted that the "reasonableness" test of judicial review would furnish the domestic courts with the possibility of reviewing the extradition in light of allegations of serious risk of inhuman and degrading treatment and that where a decision put a life at risk the courts, according to Lord Bridge, would give the case the "most anxious scrutiny". Judicial review therefore furnished an effective remedy in respect of an extradition in *Soering v UK*, in respect of refusal of asylum to Tamils in *Vilvarajah* and an application to prevent expulsion after release from prison for an AIDS sufferer in *D v UK*.[172] In *Chahal v UK*, however, concerning a Sikh militant who was threatened with deportation to India for reasons of national security, domestic courts could not examine the evidence as to the threat to national security on which the Secretary of State claimed to rely. The Court found that the domestic courts were unable to review the decision of the Home Secretary with reference solely to the question of risk but could only satisfy themselves that the Home Secretary had balanced the risk against the danger to national security. This was ineffective in the circumstances.

[168] *Jabari*, see fn.11 above, paras 49–50; *Diallo*, fn.7 above, paras 74, 83–85.
[169] *M.S.S. v Belgium and Greece*, January 21, 2011, paras 386–390.
[170] *M.S.S*, see fn.169 above, para. 394.
[171] *M.S.S*, see fn.169 above, paras 301–320, for a full analysis of the system's flaws.
[172] The scope of judicial review also satisfied Art.13 in *TI v UK*, fn.16 above, *Bensaid*, fn.23 above, paras 56–58 and *Hilal*, fn.67 above, paras 77–78.

The Secretary of State's ability to exercise his discretion in favour of an applicant on compassionate grounds or otherwise is unlikely to be regarded as an effective remedy. In *Youssef v UK*, where the applicant was applying for entry to enjoy access to his son in the United Kingdom, such leave could only be granted on an exceptional basis as being outside immigration provisions, and it was within the discretion of the Adjudicator whether to make a recommendation for leave and then within the discretion of the Secretary of State as to whether he followed the recommendation. For the Commission, this provided insufficient guarantees of efficacy for the purposes of Art.13 of the Convention.[173]

Discrimination

Discrimination has been found in immigration practices which differentiate between persons on ground of sex. In *Abdulaziz*, the Court found no objective or reasonable justification in applying different and restrictive rules to the entry of male spouses. It rejected the Government's argument that it could be assumed that women would live in the country of their husband or that entry of male spouses as opposed to female spouses had a distorting and adverse effect on the employment market. II–504

On the other hand, arguments relating to less conventional marriage practices have failed. It is not discrimination to refuse entry to more than one wife of a man settled in the United Kingdom,[174] any difference in treatment flowing essentially from the practice of polygamy for which the respondent Government was not responsible under the Convention.[175]

Immigration policies frequently are accused as being of racist in application. It is however difficult for an applicant of Asian or African ancestry to prove that he was refused entry whereas a white immigrant from a European or North American origin did or would have obtained entry in the same circumstances. Discrimination was established in the East African Asians case where statutory rules were introduced which could be shown to target persons of a particular origin. It may also be noted that a case in which it was claimed that the rules applying to the entry of adopted children treated those from India differently on grounds of their origin, without any objective and reasonable justification, was settled.[176]

The favourable treatment applying to EEC citizens as regards entry and residence has been found to be based on objective and reasonable justification, namely, the distinct Community legal regime involved.[177]

Treatment of asylum seekers and irregular immigrants pending domestic procedures

Restrictions on aliens pending procedures have rarely been looked at. Where an asylum seeker is subject to conditions of residence in a particular place, Protocol No. 4 will not apply as regards criminal prosecutions for breach of those conditions since protection is only given insofar as a person is "lawfully" on the territory.[178] II–505

[173] (14830/89) (Rep.) June 30, 1992, Resolution DH (95) 246.
[174] (19628/92), fn.90 above.
[175] (23860/94) (Dec.) November 29, 1995.
[176] *Singh v UK*, June 8, 2007, entry of the adopted child was granted.
[177] *Moustaquim*, fn.1 above, para.49.
[178] *Omwenyeke v Germany*, (44294/04) (Dec.) November 20, 2007, para.49.

Splitting up families as regards residence conditions however may cause problems under Art.8, as in a Swiss case where a husband and wife were assigned to reside in different cantons. It was stated, somewhat robustly, that the administrative costs and inconvenience of arranging relatives to be together had to yield to the family interests.[179] It appears that the families may be able to claim discrimination if, once they have been granted asylum, they are refused benefits available to others in the country.[180]

Where asylum seekers are kept in detention, it is apparent that very often these are makeshift places not geared for the purpose, or due to the numbers involved, seriously over-burdened, with serious problems of infrastructure and general neglect of the well-being of the inmates. Conditions have been found to be degrading contrary to Art.3 where the asylum-seeker had been kept locked up for several months in a prefabricated barracks, without provision for exercise and without hygiene facilities and bedding.[181] Even shorter periods of four days and a week will offend where there is serious overcrowding, appalling hygiene and minimal provision of sanitation, fresh air or bedding;[182]; two days in "abominable " conditions for a minor sufficed for a violation.[183] In cases of people already traumatised by persecution or ill-treatment in their countries of origin, there is scope for argument that as vulnerable individuals they should attract particular protection.

Until recently there has been no scrutiny of the conditions in which asylum seekers have to fend for themselves pending determination of their claims. However, in *MSS v Belgium and Greece*, the Grand Chamber further held Contracting States liable for how asylum seekers who were not held in detention fared. It emphasised the vulnerability of asylum seekers, often ignorant of the language and without means, often having already suffered traumatic experiences. Thus, where an asylum seeker lived on the streets in extreme poverty and insecurity for over a year, there was a violation. The Greek authorities were expected to take proactive measures to inform asylum seekers of the infrastructure or sources of assistance available to them and to keep in contact with them to faciliate such assistance and the speedy processing of their claims.[184]

Cross-reference

Part IIB, s.9: Deprivation of liberty.
Part IIB, s.11: Detention pending expulsion or extradition.
Part IIB, s.12: Discrimination.
Part IIB, s.18: Extradition.
Part IIB, s.41: Remedies.
Part IIB, s.46: Torture, inhuman and degrading treatment.

[179] *Mengesha Kimfe v Switzerland*, July 29, 2010, paras 67–72.
[180] *Fawsie v Greece*, October 28, 2010, paras 29–40, where a Syrian family was refused a "large family" allowance.
[181] *SD v Greece*, (Dec.) June 11, 2009, paras 49–54.
[182] *M.S.S.*, fn.169 above, paras 223–234, short periods of detention of four days and one week in asylum holding areas which were horrendously overcrowded, unhygienic and with minimal access to sanitation or fresh air disclosed violation.
[183] *Rahimi*, fn.13 above, paras 81–85.
[184] *M.S.S.*, fn.169 above, paras 249–263.

30. Interception of communications

Key provision:

Article 8 (respect for private life, home and correspondence). II–506

Key case-law:

Klass v Germany, September 6, 1978, Series A, No.28, 2 E.H.R.R. 214; *Malone v UK*, August 2, 1984, Series A, No.82, 7 E.H.R.R. 14; *Schenk v Switzerland*, July 12, 1988, Series A, No.140, 13 E.H.R.R. 242; *Huvig v France*, April 24, 1990 Series A, No.176–A, 12 E.H.R.R. 528; *Kruslin v France*, April 24, 1990, Series A, No.176–B, 12 E.H.R.R. 547; *A v France*, November 23, 1993, Series A, No.277–B, 17 E.H.R.R. 462; *Halford v UK*, June 25, 1997, R.J.D. 1997–III, No.39, 24 E.H.R.R. 523; *Kopp v Switzerland*, March 25, 1998, R.J.D. 1998–II; *Amann v Switzerland*, February 16, 2000, ECHR 2000–II, 27 E.H.R.R. 91; *Khan v UK*, May 12, 2000, ECHR 2000–V, 31 E.H.R.R. 1016; *MM v Netherlands*, April 8, 2003; *Craxi v Italy (No.1)*, July 17, 2003.

1. General considerations

Interception of communications, telephone tapping in its most well-known form, has generally been found, where it exists, to constitute an interference with one or more of the interests protected under Art.8, para.1. In *Klass v Germany*, the Court found that interception of communications (telephone and post) was an interference with private and family life, correspondence and, potentially, home.[1] Correspondence covers not just materials which cross by post but also telephone communications,[2] facsimiles,[3] and telexes.[4] Emails, and information derived from monitoring of personal internet usage, are also covered by the notions of "private life" and "correspondence".[5] II–507

The bulk of the Convention organs' examination of interceptions has concentrated on the lawfulness of the measures in the broad sense of conformity with the rule of law—that the powers are grounded in accessible and foreseeable legal rules—and verifying the existence of safeguards against abuse. There have been not inconsiderable findings of violations on this ground. It might therefore be claimed that the Convention has been a useful tool in subjecting the use of covert technological techniques by the State to proper regulation. The Court's approach is increasingly rigorous. Where statistics showed that practically all applications for measures had been granted, the Court felt it necessary to underline that telephone tapping was a very serious interference and that only very serious reasons based on a reasonable suspicion that the person is involved in serious criminal activity should be taken as a basis for authorising it: the figures therefore gave in themselves a strong indication that judges were not looking for compelling justification and that the system did not provide effective safeguards against abuse.[6]

[1] *Klass v Germany*, September 6, 1978, Series A, No.28, 2 E.H.R.R. 214, para.41.
[2] *A v France*, November 23, 1993, Series A, No.277–B, 17 E.H.R.R. 462, para.37.
[3] *Weber and Saravia v Germany*, (54934/00) (Dec.) June 29, 2006, para.77.
[4] (21482/93) (Dec.) June 27, 1994, 78–A D.R. 119.
[5] *Copland v UK*, April 3, 2007, para.41.
[6] *Iordachi v Moldova*, February 10, 2009, paras 51–54.

2. Telephone tapping

(a) Content of communication

II–508 Art.8 applies regardless of the content of the telephone conversation. In *A v France*, the Government argued that conversations taped relating to the commission of murder did not relate to private life. The Commission held that the mere fact that a conversation concerned the public interest did not deprive it of its private character, while the Court did not specify why it did not accept this argument. In *Halford v UK*, conversations by telephone were covered, whether business or private, as was use of office telephones.

However, where an applicant utilised an open air channel, the interception did not constitute interference with "private life" since the conversation, on a wave length accessible to other users, could hardly be classified as "private" communications.[7]

(b) Establishing a State interference/proof of victim status

II–509 As intended, many of the subjects of telephone tapping are oblivious to the interference. Others may suspect without any concrete proof. It may be only when the interception leads to a trial that the telephone tapping is disclosed in the interests of the prosecution. An interference however is disclosed by the process of interception, even where no use is made of the recorded material.[8]

In *Klass v Germany*, however, the applicants attacked the legislation known as G10 on the basis, inter alia, that while the State had the right to have recourse to interception measures, there should be provision for informing the subject after the measures had been lifted and for court control of the imposition and execution of such measures. They had no proof or indication that they were in fact subject to any measures. The Court stated in very broad terms that, "under certain conditions", an applicant may claim to be the victim of a violation occasioned by the mere existence of secret measures or of legislation permitting secret measures.[9]

This was repeated as a basis for finding interferences in *Malone v UK* "apart from any measures actually taken against him".[10] However the existence of victim status and interference was admitted by the UK Government who, without furnishing any details, accepted that as a suspected receiver of stolen goods he was member of a class of persons against whom such measures were liable to be employed. Regarding metering, although the Government stated that it had not been employed in his case, the Court still found that he was in a class of persons potentially liable to be directly affected by the practice and could, on the basis of the *Klass* case, claim to be a victim quite apart from any concrete measure taken against him.

However, the Commission which dealt at the admissibility level with many unsubstantiated, often delusional complaints, developed a more restrictive filter approach, unwilling to embark on a detailed examination of the state of domestic law and practice every time a complainant alleged that the CIA or the freemasons

[7] (21353/93) (Dec.) February 27, 1995, 80–A D.R. 101.
[8] *Kopp v Switzerland*, March 25, 1998, R.J.D. 1998–II, para.53.
[9] See fn.1, para.34.
[10] *Malone v UK*, August 2, 1984, Series A, No.82, 7 E.H.R.R. 14, para.64.

were tapping his telephone. A test, namely whether there was a reasonable likelihood that the applicant had been subject to such measures or was in a category of persons likely to be targetted, was taken from *Hilton v UK*,[11] which dealt with secret files.

The reasonable likelihood test was then used when an applicant trade union leader discovered from a television documentary that the telexes addressed to him from overseas were being routinely intercepted[12] and led to rejection of complaints about telephone tapping by nuclear test veterans who had not adduced sufficient evidence to demonstrate a reasonable likelihood that they would be subject to interception measures as a result of their campaigning.[13] A fine distinction was drawn in *Halford* where the Government accepted that there was a reasonable likelihood that calls on the applicant's office phone were intercepted, which was not unlawful in domestic law. In respect of allegations of bugging her home phone on the public lines however, the Court, adopting the Commission's approach, found no reasonable likelihood on the evidence presented, namely, the applicant had no specific information that her home phones were bugged and it would have been unlawful for the police to have taken this step.

More recently, there has been an apparent return to a broad approach to "victim status" citing *Klass* and distinguishing complaints against the conformity of the system as a whole from those in which individuals claim themselves to be subject to measures.[14] On this basis, it would seem that the Court will examine a complaint about the legislative framework of interception, without requiring more to prove "victim status" as long as the applicant does not assert that his own telephone is tapped. In a recent case, the Court referred to the mere existence of interception legislation entailing for those who fell within its reach a menace of surveillance. Thus, as it could not be excluded that secret surveillance measures were applied to the applicant lawyers, an organisation representing applicants before the Court which had already received threats from the authorities, or that they were potentially at risk of such measures, there was an interference with their rights.[15] This would appear to require an applicant to show that he could, under the law, be at risk of such measures. However, the importance of ensuring that secret measures are effectively challengeable seems to have induced the Court to lower the threshold still lower. Where an applicant, originally subject to such measures as a murder suspect, claimed that the police were continuing to intercept his business communications in order to harass him, the Court noted that he had not shown any reasonable likelihood that this was the case, nor did it appear that he fell within the ambit of interception measures due to his campaigning against injustice activities; however, since it could not be excluded that he might have been subject to harassment as he alleged, the objection to lack of victim status was rejected.[16]

[11] (12015/86) (Dec.) July 6, 1988, 57 D.R. 108.

[12] (21482/93), fn.4 above, the Government accepted that there was a reasonable likelihood of interception.

[13] (23413/94) (Dec.) November 28, 1995, 83–A D.R. 31; (21825/93) (Dec.) November 11, 1995.

[14] *Association for European Integration and Human Rights and Ekimdliev v Bulgaria*, June 28, 2007, para.59. See also *Weber and Saravia v Germany*, fn.3 above, paras 78–79, where interferences were disclosed by the existence of a system of interception, the extension of categories of official bodies to which data could be transmitted and provision for the destruction of material and for the refusal to notify the subjects of measures.

[15] *Iordachi v Moldova*, fn.6 above, paras 33–35.

[16] *Kennedy v UK*, May 18, 2010, paras 124–129.

Where police assist private individuals in taping telephone conversations to obtain evidence of criminal activities, State responsibility has been found to be engaged. In *MM v Netherlands*, the Court rejected the Government's argument that it was ultimately a Mrs S who was in control of events, in circumstances where it was the police who had suggested that she tape the applicant's conversations and who had connected the recorder to her telephone.[17] Similarly, even where the idea allegedly came from a private individual, the fact that the police provided the recorder and made at least one suggestion as to the kind of conversation to engage in with the suspect was a crucial contribution in executing the scheme; State responsibility followed.[18]

3. "In accordance with the law"[19]

II–510 The notion refers, first, to the interference having some basis in domestic law and, secondly, to the quality of law, i.e. those aspects which render it compatible with the notion of the rule of law, including accessibility, foreseeability as to the circumstances in which and conditions under which authorities are empowered to interfere, which should be such as to provide protection against arbitrary interferences.

Insufficient basis in domestic law was the basis for violations in *Malone*, where the powers relating to the interception of post and telephone communications, including metering, were not clearly incorporated in legal rules. An absence of a prohibition against measures was not sufficient. Similarly, the Court found in *Halford* that there was no basis in domestic law for interception of "private" telecommunications systems, since the Interception of Communications Act 1985 did not apply to it nor was there any general law of privacy.

When applicants alleged that the authorities failed to comply with the domestic law provisions, the Commission accorded domestic authorities a wide margin of appreciation in their assessment. Where, in an Italian case, the Court of Cassation found that the regulations were followed and conditions fulfilled as regarded the existence of adequate suspicion existed, the Commission did not find that the lawfulness criterion was breached.[20] The Court has also emphasised that it is primarily for the national authorities to interpret and apply domestic law and expressed reluctance to contradict the views of such authorities as to the legal basis of measures.[21]

As to the quality of law, interceptions are regarded as serious interferences which render it essential to have clear detailed rules on the subject particularly since

[17] Also *A v France*, fn.2 above, para.36.

[18] *Van Vondel v Netherlands*, October 25, 2007, para.49, even if the main reason for the recording was for the private individual to prove to the authorities that he had been telling the truth, the interception should have been governed by proper regulatory framework.

[19] See Pt IC: Convention principles.

[20] ". . . [I]ts power to review national authorities' compliance with domestic law is limited": (13274/87) (Dec.) September 6, 1990, 66 D.R. 164.

[21] e.g. *Kruslin v France*, April 24, 1990, Series A, No.176–B, 12 E.H.R.R. 547, para.29; *Huvig v France*, April 24, 1990 Series A, No.176–A, 12 E.H.R.R. 528, para.28; *Kopp*, fn.8 above, paras 59–60.

technology continually becomes more sophisticated.[22] Relevant factors are the existence of a definition of the categories of person or offences which may attract measures,[23] limits on duration, regulation of the circumstances in which records are destroyed, whether the originals are available for inspection by the judiciary.[24] The Commission recognised that flexibility was required by the subject-matter and that the concept of foreseeability did not require definition of terms like "national security"[25] or "economic well-being" when used as pre-conditions for the application of measures. It rejected the argument that the discretion afforded by these terms was too wide and undefined or that it should be subject to judicial input through adversarial argument in courts to establish full meaning of the terms. It considered that it was acceptable for the terms to be elaborated by administrative and executive statements and instructions.[26]

Where a virtually unlimited discretion on monitoring external communications was enjoyed by the Secretary of State, the Court held that insufficient details about the "arrangements" by which this discretion was exercised disclosed a problem, as there were no guidelines or code of practice accessible to the public giving an indication of the procedure followed in examining, sharing, storing and destroying intercepted material: the bare legislation requiring such arrangements be made had not been enough.[27]

An emphasis may be noted as to the provision of independent authorisation for interceptions and review of measures, legislation which has failed to provide checks and balances against arbitrary executive actions falling foul of the standard.[28] Importance has also been attached to provision for independent review of the accuracy of recorded material[29] as well as proper provision of clear rules where lawyer-client communications were concerned.[30]

Whereas previously case-law did not appear to require notification of measures to the victim in acknowledgment of security considerations, the Court seemes to have changed emphasis, commenting that some provision for notification should be made

[22] *Kruslin*, fn.21 above, para.33; *Huvig*, fn.21 above, para.32; also *Kopp*, fn.8 above, where a lawyer's phone was tapped, the law did not clearly state how legally privileged material was to be distinguished from other matters and the Court remarked on the "astonishing" practice of entrusting the task to an official of the executive, without supervision by a judge; *Amann*, where the law did not regulate in detail the case of persons, such as the applicant, who were fortuitously monitored during interception measures taken against other targets; *Doerga v Netherlands*, April 27, 2004, lack of clarity in rules surrounding taping of prisoners' telephone calls in prison; contrast *Weber and Saravia*, fn.12 above, paras 92–102, minimum safeguards satisfied.

[23] See *Iordachi*, fn.6 above, para.44, measures were applicable to to suspect, defendant and "other person involved in a criminal offence" which last category was insufficiently defined; as were the grounds of intervention "protection of morals", "protection of health", and "maintenance of legal order".

[24] e.g. *Kruslin*, fn.21 above, para.35; *Huvig*, fn.21 above, para.34; *Valenzuala Contreras v Spain*, July 30, 1998, R.J.D. 1998–V, No.83, para.59; *Prado Bugallo v Spain*, February 18, 2003, para.30.

[25] *Kennedy*, fn.16 above, para.159, the Court agreed, noting that "national security" was a term set out in Art.8, para.2.

[26] (21482/93), see fn.4 above.

[27] *Liberty v UK*, July 1, 2008, paras 64–69. Contrast *Kennedy*, see fn.16 above, concerning regulation of internal communications in respect of which the domestic law was set out with sufficient clarity and safeguards against abuse.

[28] *Dumitru Popescu v Romania*, April 26, 2007, the ordering and reviewing of measures by the public prosecutor only; *Association for European Integration*, fn.12 above, paras 85–89, overall control wielded by a minister without independent review or scrutiny; *Iordachi*, fn.6 above, para.41, no judicial control over the grant of interception; supervision on prosecutors.

[29] *Dumitru Popescu*, fn.28 above, paras 80–81.

[30] *Iordachi*, fn.6 above, para.50.

once this would not jeopardise the purpose of the restriction after the termination of the measure.[31]

4. Necessity

II–511 Interception is acknowledged as potentially pursuing the aim of preventing crime and disorder in the police investigation context[32] and in the sphere of national security, in which latter context the Court has acknowledged a wide margin of appreciation.[33] There has been no real scrutiny of the purposes of the systems as such in the absence of obvious abuses. The key point has been whether there exist adequate and effective guarantees against abuse.[34] This provides some overlap with "in accordance in law" but where the latter looks at whether the way the law as formulated provides sufficient safeguards by way of accessibility and foreseeability, this looks rather at the concrete procedural protections.

Relevant features include the existence of any independent scrutiny in the implementation process, significance attaching to judicial input or parliamentary supervision of the executive.[35] Though judicial control is regarded as ensuring the most effective supervision offering the best guarantees of independence, impartiality and procedure, the lack of it is not necessarily fatal where other independent bodies exist with sufficient powers and competence to exercise continuous and effective control.[36] Where an applicant argued that there was no court and parliamentary control in the United Kingdom, the Commission found that an independent tribunal with limited review powers and an independent commissioner of high judicial rank, whose thorough and critical approach to his functions was disclosed in his reports, were acceptable.[37]

Limitations as to duration of warrants and requirement for prior authorisation have also been considered as safeguards,[38] as have limitations and controls over the transmission of data for use by other public authorities.[39]

While no requirement that a person subject to measures be informed afterwards had been previously identified, the Convention organs allowing that the secrecy and efficacy of the system would be undermined by such notifications,[40] the Court has recently relied on the provision for notification as showing conformity with necessary safeguards.[41] It is not necessary, however, that a tribunal ruling on a complaint by

[31] *Association for European Integration*, fn.14 above, paras 90–91, this was seen as preventing victims taking action against unlawful measures. This aspect has also been taken into account under "necessity": see further below.

[32] *Malone*, fn.10 above; also (29839/96) (Dec.) May 18, 1998.

[33] *Klass*, fn.1 above, para.49; *Leander*, para.59.

[34] *Klass*, fn.1 above, para.50; (29839/96), fn.32 above, where the Dutch courts provided adequate and sufficient, if indirect, control as regarded alleged negligence in taping privileged conversations.

[35] e.g. *Klass*, fn.1 above, where an officer qualified for judicial office carried out scrutiny and there was supervision by a parliamentary body of the executive minister. Also (10439/83) (Dec.) May 10, 1985, 43 D.R. 34, where a senior judge was involved in review; (11811/85) (Dec.) March 8, 1988, 55 D.R. 182, where safeguards included judicial supervision within 24 hours.

[36] *Klass*, fn.1 above, paras 55–56. See the recent emphasis in *Kennedy*, fn.16 above, para.167, on judicial supervision being desirable.

[37] (21482/93), fn.4 above. See more recently *Kennedy*, fn.16 above, paras 167–170.

[38] (10439/83), fn.26 above; (13564/88) (Dec.) June 8, 1999.

[39] *Weber and Saravia*, fn.3 above, paras 121–122 and 126–129.

[40] *Klass*, fn.1 above; (21482/93), fn.4 above; (10439/83), fn.35 above; (11811/85), fn.35 above.

[41] *Weber and Saravia*, fn.3 above, paras 135–136.

an applicant give reasons for a negative decision, instead of confirming only whether or not there has been a contravention of the statutory provisions.[42]

The Commission and Court have shown a pragmatic attitude in assessing the efficacy of procedural safeguards. No system, it is said, can rule out abuse by over-zealous officials but where a procedure is in place designed to reduce measures to the necessary minimum and ensure their conformity with the necessary provisions, unless there is evidence to the contrary the Court will assume that the authorities are properly applying the legislation.[43] In the area of security checks, the Commission took a stance of setting a minimum necessary standard, rejecting arguments based on the existence of better protection systems elsewhere. Since the aim is to balance the needs of the State against the protection of individual rights a system of effective, not fool-proof, checks against abuses is required. For an issue to arise where there is a system of checks in place, it would generally require a fundamental inadequacy, evidence of abuse or failure to control or a clear gap in the protection, as in *Halford*, where the legislation omitted private telecommunication systems. The significant volume of measures taken in Bulgaria was taken into account as a factor showing the overall operation of the system was lacking in procedural safeguards.[44]

5. Postal interferences

The above considerations apply equally to interception of mail, though there are fewer cases dealing expressly with such allegations. While numerous complaints are made by persons suspicious of receiving envelopes or parcels which are torn and taped back together by the postal authorities, the Commission tended to apply a robust approach, requiring some form of substantiation of "interference" and applied the "reasonable likelihood" test to reject them.[45] As regards mishandling by the Post, an old Commission case states that Art.8 does not guarantee the perfect functioning of the postal service.[46] II–512

There are some contexts where interference with mail is in fact routine or not unexpected, e.g. prisons, bankruptcy. There are also criminal law provisions regulating what may be sent by post, in particular, pornography.[47] Interferences based on enforcement of criminal law provisions are likely to be found justifiable, when in compliance with domestic law.

[42] (21482/93), fn.4 above.

[43] *Klass*, fn.1 above, para.59; (21482/93), fn.4 above, the Commission found this evidence was not furnished by the fact that the Interception of Communications Tribunal had never made a determination in favour of an applicant nor was it impressed by unsubstantiated rumours in the media that there was routine interception of businessmen's communications.

[44] *Association for European Integration*, fn.14 above, para.92.

[45] (20591/92) (Dec.) December 2, 1992, where the applicant (involved with groups which attempt to visit Stonehenge at the solstice) alleged opening of his parcels, the Commission found that there was insufficient evidence that he was a person or in a category of persons in respect of whom the police would consider clandestine surveillance measures were necessary. No reasonable likelihood that his mail was interfered with by the police rather than merely damaged in transit (as claimed by the parcel service).

[46] (8383/75) (Dec.) October 3, 1979, 17 D.R. 227, reference to the volume of mail, statistical likelihood of some miscarriage which is generally known and special means provided to ensure safe delivery of particular letters on demand.

[47] e.g. (7308/75) (Dec.) October 12, 1978, 16 D.R. 32, stoppage of packages containing obscene materials.

6. Use of material in court proceedings

II–513 The use in evidence at trial of material obtained by the police using interceptions has been examined under Art.6 "fairness" considerations. It seems to be an accepted source of evidence in domestic courts where lawfully obtained subject to a warrant and procedural safeguards.

However, the lawfulness is not decisive to fairness under Art.6 as shown in *Schenk v Switzerland*, where the taping of a phone call by a hired assassin with the applicant handed over to the police was unlawful as not ordered by the investigating judge. The Court considered this did not render a trial automatically unfair or a disclose a ground of violation per se. It had regard to the circumstances, namely, the applicant had knowledge of the tape and how it was recorded and was able to challenge its use and contents by calling the assassin or police inspector as witnesses. The Court found that the rights of defence were not disregarded. Though it attached weight to the fact that it was not the only evidence on which the conviction was based, the case of *Khan v UK*, where the only evidence against the applicant had been obtained by covert surveillance conducted without proper legal basis, has since established that there will be no breach of Art.6 in basing a conviction solely on such evidence as long as there are adequate procedural safeguards by which the applicant can challenge the authenticity of, or unfairness of using, the material. Subsequent cases have underlined that use of material at trial obtained without a proper legal basis will not generally offend the standard of fairness imposed by Art.6, para.1 where proper procedural safeguards are in place and the nature and source of the material is not tainted, for example, by any oppression, coercion or entrapment which would render reliance on it unfair.[48] The way in which the material was obtained raises issues rather under Art.8 regarding the State's responsibility to secure the right to respect for private life in due form.[49]

Issues will arise under Art.8 if interception material of a private nature disclosed at trial is obtained or used without regard to domestic lawfulness or is made public in circumstances which infringe private life without any corresponding relevance to the interests of preventing crime.[50] In *Craxi v Italy (No.1)*, the Court objected to the lack of safeguards surrounding the transcripts of the accused's private telephone conversations, not used in court by the prosecution but which found their way out of the court registry file into the hands of the press and were duly published.[51] The use of other parts of the transcript at the trial was not in accordance with law either as the prosecution failed to comply with domestic procedural safeguards requiring the material to be lodged with the registry prior to being read in court which would have allowed the defence to present their comments.

[48] e.g. *Bykov v Russia*, March 10, 2009, paras 94–105.

[49] e.g. *Chalkley v UK*, (63831/00) (Dec.) September 26, 2002; *Perry v UK*, (63737/00) (Dec.) September 26, 2002. See also *Heglas v Czech Republic*, March 1, 2007, recording conversations from a covert body microphone was not "in accordance with the law" in breach of Art.8 but there was no procedural unfairness in use of the material at trial; similar findings in *Bykov*, fn.48 above.

[50] Mutatis mutandis, *Z v Finland*, February 25, 1997, R.J.D. 1997–I, where medical material concerning a witness was made public.

[51] Even if the leak had come from one of the parties rather than a public official, the Government's responsibility was engaged as there was an obligation of safe custody and it had not taken effective steps to investigate the incident and sanction any breach of confidentiality.

7. Procedures concerning complaints of interception measures

The Court has left open whether proceedings before tribunals which examine complaints about interceptions fall within the ambit of Art.6.[52] On the assumption that it did, it was nonetheless found that the security context justified the lack of public hearing, the restriction on access of the applicant to secret documents and the limited reasoning given in the decision. These limitations were assessed as necessary and proportionate in the context of a system of judicial challenge which was open to all and did not put an evidential burden on the applicant.[53] II–514

Cross-reference

Part IIA, s.9: Evidence.
Part IIB, s.36: Prisoners' rights, sub-s.7: Correspondence.
Part IIB, s.44: Surveillance and secret files.

[52] *Kennedy*, fn.16 above, paras 178–179, even though the tribunal itself had held that it was bound by Art.6.
[53] *Kennedy*, fn.16 above, paras 184–190.

31. Marriage and founding a family

Key provisions:

II–515 Articles 12 (right to marry and found a family) and 14 (prohibition against discrmination). Also Article 8 (right to respect for family life).

Key case-law:

Airey v Ireland, October 9, 1979, Series A, No.32, 2 E.H.H.H. 305; *Rees v UK*, October 17, 1986, Series A, No.106, 9 E.H.R.R. 56; *Johnston v Ireland*, December 18, 1986, Series A, No.112, 9 E.H.R.R. 56; *F v Switzerland*, December 18, 1987, Series A, No.128, 10 E.H.R.R. 411; *Cossey v UK*, September 27, 1990, Series A, No.184, 13 E.H.R.R. 622; *Christine Goodwin v UK*, July 11, 2002, ECHR 2002–VI; *B and L v UK*, September 13, 2005; *S.H. and Others v Austria*, November 3, 2011, ECHR–. . . ; *Serife Yigit v Turkey*, November 2, 2010, ECHR 2010–. . .

1. General considerations

II–516 The traditional marriage enjoys a favoured position in the Convention, with Art.12 singled out for separate treatment and resulting in special status, for example, where married relationships are considered in the context of family life and discrimination.[1] The Commission organs have interfered little in practice in how States choose to regulate this area. For the Court, the right to marry guaranteed by Art.12 refers to the traditional marriage between persons of opposite biological sex, which interpretation is supported by the reference to the founding of a family.[2]

2. The right to marry

II–517 Article 12 is dominated by the reference to "according to the national laws governing the exercise of this right" and the Court has stated that it will not rush to substitute its own judgment for that of the national authorities.[3] Persons are expected, for example, to comply with the procedural formalities imposed by the State. A German could not therefore claim a violation when the registrar refused to register his marriage which had not involved the completion of the necessary administrative forms but only a religious ceremony.[4] Nor was there any issue under

[1] (11089/84) (Dec.) November 11, 1986, 49 D.R. 181, married and unmarried couples are not in analogous positions for tax purposes since marriage relates to a special regime of rights and obligations; *McMichael v UK*, February 24, 1995, Series A, No.307–B, 20 E.H.R.R. 205, automatic parental rights for married fathers as opposed to unmarried fathers were objectively and reasonably justified.

[2] *Rees v UK*, October 17, 1986, Series A, No.106, 9 E.H.R.R. 56; see, however, the Commission's opinions in (7114/75) (Rep.) December 13, 1979, 24 D.R. 5 and (8186/78) (Rep.) July 10, 1980, 24 D.R. 72. See also analysis in *Schalk and Kopf v Austria*, June 24, 2010, para.55, where the Court found that although in isolation the wording might not exclude marriage between two men or two women, the choice of wording in avoiding, as in other provisions, "everyone" or "no-one", must be regarded as deliberate and seen in the context of the 1950's when marriage was understood in the traditional sense.

[3] *B and L v UK*, September 13, 2005, para.36.

[4] (6167/73) (Dec.) December 18, 1974, 1 D.R. 64. Nor does Art.8 require the State to recognise a religious marriage—*Serife Yigit v Turkey*, November 2, 2010, ECHR 2010–. . . , para.102.

Article 12 where a marriage under Roma tradition was not recognised under civil law.[5]

The principle is that the national laws may govern the exercise of the right but not injure its substance.[6] Generally-recognised limitations such as capacity, consent, consanguinity or prevention of bigamy are likely to be compatible. For example, the Commission rejected a complaint from a Muslim who complained that he could not marry a girl of 14 who had no legal capacity despite his assertion that his religion permitted marriage to a girl over 12. The Commission commented that it would not be compatible to deprive a person or a category of persons of the full, legal capacity to marry.[7] A case is pending which raises the issue as to a prohibition on marriage by legally-incapacitated persons, in the particular case, an applicant suffering from schizophrenia.[8]

Other legal bars which prevent marriage of consenting and legally capable adults may be expected therefore to raise issues[9] and it may be that traditional or historical limitations that have become anomalous could be challenged successfully. For example, in *B and L v UK*, the Court found a violation in the traditional domestic bar on marriage of parents-in-law with children-in-law, since, notwithstanding the significance to be attached to the national law and legislature's choice, there was a basic inconsistency between the purported aims of the bar (to protect children and the integrity of the family) and the fact such marriages were allowable, if the individuals concerned obtained, by a cumbersome, costly and ill-defined procedure, a private act of parliament.

Where domestic law permits, and the authorities even facilitate, gender re-assignment, the inability of a transsexual to marry someone of opposite gender to their re-assigned gender has been found to violate Art.12. Referring to findings in earlier UK cases, *Rees*, *Cossey* and *Sheffield and Horsham*, that this did not impair the essence of the right as the transsexual continued to enjoy the right to marry a person of the opposite birth gender, the Court in *Christine Goodwin v UK* rejected this argument as artificial and found that the United Kingdom could no longer restrict marriage to a union between a man and woman both of biological origin as defined at birth without reference to intervening phenomena. It noted that the corresponding and more recently drafted provision in the European Charter of Human Rights, Art.9, referred to the right to marry without framing it in terms of "men and women" and found no justification for preventing transsexuals from marrying. It is probably too early for changing attitudes and evolving practices in Contracting States with regard to homosexual marriages to lead the Court to find that Art.12 extends beyond marriage for opposite sexes (however defined). Indeed the Court found that the ban on same sex marriages which prevented a transsexual from remaining married to her partner after recognition of her gender was within

[5] *Munoz Diaz v Spain*, December 8, 2009, paras 78–81, civil marriage was open to all, no discrimination arose from lack of recognition of Roma marriages or the fact that there were specific arrangements between certain religious confessions and the authorities which permitted recognition of rites. There was, however, discrimination as regarded enjoyment of property rights, due to failure to pay a Roma "widow" benefits on the death of her "husband".

[6] (7114/75) and (8186/78), fn.2 above.

[7] (11579/85) (Dec.) July 7, 1986 48 D.R. 253.

[8] *Lashin v Russia*, (33117/02) (Dec.) January 6, 2011.

[9] *Selim v Cyprus*, July 16, 2002, the applicant's complaints under Art.12 that he was unable marry in Cyprus as there was no provision in domestic law for a Turkish Cypriot of the Muslim faith to contract a civil marriage, were settled after admissibility.

the margin of appreciation accorded to States in applying their concept of marriage.[10] Most recently, the Court, taking into account Art.9 and the diversity of national regulations, concluded that although the right to marry under Art.12 cannot be interpreted as in all circumstances limited to two persons of opposite sex, the question of same-sex marriage is left, "as matters stand", to the regulation by the national law of the Contracting State. It declined to "rush to substitute" its own judgment for that of the national authorities who were best placed to assess and respond to the needs of society.[11]

Practical prohibitions have disclosed problems in other contexts. The Commission held early on that prison authorities could not legitimately refuse a prisoner permission to get married while serving his sentence. It was irrelevant to the Commission that the respective couples would not have been able to consummate the marriage or cohabit. Marriage, to the Commission, was the formation of a legally binding association between a man and a woman. The delay imposed on them before they could exercise their right to marry on their release was found to injure the substance of their right to marry.[12] This approach has been confirmed by the Court, which stated unequivocally that personal liberty is not a precondition for the exercise of the right to marry.[13] Where a trial court refused an accused permission to marry due to its view that this was an attempt to prevent his girlfriend from testifying against him and not a genuine relationship, and also commented that a remand centre was not an appropriate place to hold such an important event, the Court held that it was not for the the authorities to assess whether the quality of a relationship was of a nature as to justify a decision to get married or to analyse which time or venue would be suitable for the ceremony. Only important considerations related to order in prison or prevention of crime would justify a refusal of permission to a prisoner.[14]

Conversely, it has been recognised that States can properly impose reasonable conditions on the right of a third-country national to marry in order to ascertain whether the proposed marriage is one of convenience and, if necessary, to prevent it. The aim of preventing immigrants making use of sham marriages to obtain entry is accepted as legitimate. However a general ban on people under immigration control or without sufficient "leave to remain" undertaking marriages, irrespective of their genuineness, was not acceptable.[15]

The imposition of time-limits has also been found incompatible in *F v Switzerland* where the Swiss attempted to regulate the frequency of divorces. A three-year prohibition on re-marriage was imposed on an applicant after having been granted his third divorce. The Government argued that such temporary prohibitions were not arbitrary or disproportionate, pursuing the aim of preserving the stability of

[10] See *Parry v UK*, (42971/05) November 11, 2006; *R and F v UK*, (35748/05) November 28, 2006.

[11] See *Schalk and Kopf*, fn.2 above, para. 60, thus two male homosexuals' complaints about inability to marry disclosed no violation. While the matter fell within the scope of Art.8 private life and family life for the purposes of Art.14, there could be derived no right to marry under this discrimination provision either. Nor did Art.14 require that legal partnerships provided in place of marriage had to have all the same legal effects as marriage.

[12] (7114/75) and (8186/75), fn.2 above, the prisoners were serving five years and life sentences respectively.

[13] See *Frasik v Poland*, January 5, 2010, para.91.

[14] *Frasik*, fn.13 above, para.95. See also *Jaremowicz v Poland*, January 5, 2010, where the refusal of marriage based on the prison authorities' negative views of a relationship claimed between the applicant prisoner and another detainee was found to breach Art.12.

[15] *O'Donoghue v UK*, December 14, 2010, paras 87–90.

marriage, the protection of the rights of the future spouse and compelling proper reflection (impliedly no bad thing in this applicant's case). The Court disagreed, finding the restriction unreasonable, disproportionate and affecting the very essence of the right. A paternalistic attitude to regulate the entering into marriage of legally capable adults was therefore rejected as constituting an acceptable public policy interest. The argument that a refusal of permission for prisoners to marry was of limited duration since the prisoners either obtained permission after some months or could have married once they were released were not successful was similarly not found to be a justification for a restriction on the right to marry.[16]

Imposition of fees in order to marry may offend Art.12, if the sum charged is prohibitive. The requirement for persons under immigration control to pay £295 for a certificate of approval allowing them to marry was sufficiently heavy for those in needy circumstances as to impair the right to marry.[17]

The right to marry does not, however, in principle include the right to choose the geographical location of the marriage, or obtain an entry visa for that purpose. A refusal to allow entry into a State of a foreign fiancé did therefore not contravene Art.12, where the couple were able to marry in the fiancé's country of residence.[18] An unjustified delay in registering the applicant's marriage to a foreigner was examined under Art.8 and found to be an unjustified interference.[19]

3. Divorce

The ordinary meaning of the provision is the formation of marital relationships and not their dissolution. The Court held that a restriction on divorce in a country adhering to the principle of monogamy cannot be regarded as injuring the substance of the right guaranteed by Art.12. Developments in society with regard to the availability of divorce were irrelevant having regard to the clear meaning of the text and to intent of the drafters, as shown from the *travaux préparatoires*, who deliberately omitted reference to dissolution of marriage. In *Johnston v Ireland* therefore, the applicant's inability to obtain the dissolution of the marriage with his first wife to allow him to marry the woman with whom he had lived for over eight years and with whom he had founded a family, did not disclose a violation of Art.12. II–518

Conversely, where divorce was permitted in domestic law, this has not been considered as infringing the right to marry.[20]

4. Founding a family

This limb does not as such create a right to procreate.[21] Nor is there any right to adoption to be derived from Art.12 or any of the other provisions of the II–519

[16] *Frasik*, fn.13 above, para.97; *Jaremowicz*, fn.14 above, para.61.

[17] *O'Donoghue v UK*, fn.15 above, paras 90–91, even if the fee could be refunded, the disincentive remained powerful to people who could either not work or were of low income.

[18] *Walter v Italy*, (18059/06) July 11, 2006.

[19] *Dadouch v Malta*, July 20, 2010, paras 47–61.

[20] See *F v Switzerland*, December 18, 1987, Series A, No.128, 10 E.H.R.R. 411, para.38; *SH v Austria*, (57813/00) (Dec.) November 15, 2007.

[21] Nor to have grandchildren: *Sijakova v Macedonia*, (67914/01) March 6, 2003, where the applicants complained about the church rules imposing celibacy on their children in orders.

Convention.[22] Where procedures for applying for adoption exist, any rights are subject under Art.12 to the requirements of "national laws". In a Dutch case the applicant and her husband who wished to adopt a Polish boy were refused permission as the proposed adoption did not fulfil the conditions set down in domestic law with regard, inter alia, to the difference in ages between themselves and the child. Their complaints were rejected as the measure was in accordance with national laws.[23] Nor was it unjustified or disproportionate for a State to refuse permission for an adoption placement due to the applicant's age—where she would have been 46–48 years older than the child in question.[24] In the absence of blatant arbitrariness, it would be unlikely that matters of eligibility or procedural requirements for adoption under domestic law would raise issues. Instead it has proved to be discrimination concerning Art.8 in its aspect of family life has been the area most relevant to adoption issues under the Convention.

In *Fretté v France*, where there was a right to adopt under domestic law, the Court considered that complaints about discriminatory application of the law could fall within the scope of Art.14 in conjunction with Art.8, though in the circumstances of that case, a narrow majority found that no violation arose from refusal to allow the applicant to adopt due to his homosexuality.[25] However, in a subsequent case *EB v France*, the Grand Chamber effectively overruled *Frette*, finding that where domestic law granted single persons the right to apply for autorisation to adopt and established a procedure to that end, the refusal of autorisation to the applicant based decisively on her "lifestyle" (her sexual orientation as a lesbian and lack of a so-called "paternal referent"), disclosed a difference in treatment without justification.[26]

A discrimination issue under Art.14 arose in an admissible case, settled without judgment on the merits, where more restrictive adoption rules applied to children being brought into the United Kingdom from India.[27]

Regarding practical obstacles to founding a family in the biological fashion, prisoners have unsuccessfully claimed the right to conjugal visits, the Commission finding that no such right could be derived from Art.12.[28] With increasing concessions being made in prison regimes particularly in the Nordic countries, the Commission hinted that the situation might be reviewable in the future. The issue

[22] (31924/96) (Dec.) July 10, 1997, 90 D.R. 134; *Fretté v France*, February 26, 2002, ECHR 2002–I, para.32 and (Dec.) June 12, 2001, rejecting as incompatible *ratione materiae* the complaints under Art.12 about a refusal of permission to adopt based on the applicant's homosexuality; *EB v France*, January 22, 2008, ECHR 2008–. . . , no right to adopt or found a family under Art.8, (para.41).

[23] (8896/80) (Dec.) March 10, 1981, 24 D.R. 177; also (7229/75) (Dec.) December 15, 1977, 12 D.R. 32.

[24] *Schwizgebel v Switzerland*, June 10, 2010, paras 86–99, the refusal had been based on considerations of the child's welfare.

[25] Three dissenting judges thought that the bar was not based on any individual consideration of the applicant's suitability or identified grounds of detriment to any adopted child; one of the majority judges found that Art.14 was not applicable, while the remaining three judges held that the refusal was based on the welfare of the children to be adopted and within the broad margin of appreciation, where the scientific community were divided on the possible consequences of such adoptions and bearing in mind the limited number of studies on the subject.

[26] *EB v France*, fn.22 above.

[27] *Singh v UK*, June 8, 2006.

[28] (8166/78) (Dec.) December 3, 1978, 13 D.R. 241, where husband and wife were detained in the same prison, lack of conjugal visits was justifiable in the interests of security and good order under Art.8, with no separate issue under Art.12. Also (6564/74) (Dec.) May 21, 1975, 2 D.R. 105, where there was no infringement in locking someone up as there was no right to be given the actual possibility at all times to procreate!

was subject to two communications to the United Kingdom in combination with a complaint about a refusal to allow artificial insemination treatment of prisoners' wives, who due to factors of the age or health could not await their husbands' release. Where it was a matter of allowing a brief procedure for a prisoner to provide the necessary sample for his wife's doctor, there appeared to be little justification to put in the balance against the enjoyment of the right under Art.12. However, the cases were struck off when permission was granted.[29] The Grand Chamber recently found a breach of Art.8, in its family and private life aspects, where the applicants, a prisoner and his wife, were refused artificial insemination facilities. This was where the applicable policy put a heavy burden on the applicants to show their case was exceptional and did not allow a balancing of competing of individual and public interests or an assessment of proportionality.[30]

Where an inability to procreate derives from infertility problems, the fact that there are medical alternatives to aid conception may give rise to issues of where persons are legally barred from using these methods. Thus in *S.H. and Others v Austria*, where two couples were refused in vitro fertilisation treatment as they required, respectively, use of donated ova and sperm banned under domestic law, a Chamber found the arguments put forward by the Government justifying the ban to be unconvincing. However, on referral, the Grand Chamber considered that there was a wide margin of appreciation applying to the sensitive domain of artificial procreation. The solution applied by the Austrian legislature did not exceed this margin, given that law in member States was still in a stage of development. The Court nonetheless warned a reassessment of the rules might be necessary in the future in light of the dynamic developments in science and society.[31]

Where a couple is infertile the extent to which they could derive a practical right of access to new medical technologies is unexplored. There are aspects of resource allocation and costs which would make it unlikely that a couple could require a State to furnish treatment free of charge. Where treatment is available, the decision-making procedure might perhaps be amenable to challenge on grounds of arbitrariness or discriminatory treatment.[32]

Abortion measures which are compatible with Art.8 cannot raise any separate issues under Art.12.[33]

Cross-reference

Part IIB, s.1: Abortion.
Part IIB, s.12: Discrimination.
Part IIB, s.27: Homosexuality.
Part IIB, s.47: Transsexuals.

[29] (10822/84) (Dec.) May 7, 1987 and (17142/90) (Dec.) July 10, 1991.

[30] *Dickson v UK*, December 4, 2007.

[31] *S.H. and Others v Austria*, November 3, 2011, paras 91–118.

[32] See, mutatis mutandis, *Tysiac v Poland*, March 20, 2007, concerning access to abortion and procedures for challenging refusals.

[33] *Boso v Italy*, (50490/99) (Dec.) September 5, 2002, ECHR 2002–VII.

32. Mental health

Key provisions:

II–520 Article 5, para.1(e) (lawful detention of persons of unsound mind); Article 5, para.4 (review of detention); and Articles 8 (private life) and 3 (prohibition of ill-treatment).

Key case-law:

Winterwerp v Netherlands, October 24, 1979, Series A, No.33, 2 E.H.R.R. 387; *X v UK*, November 5, 1981 Series A, No.46, 4 E.H.R.R. 188; *Luberti v Italy*, February 23, 1984, Series A, No.75, 6 E.H.R.R. 440; *Van der Leer v Netherlands*, February 21, 1990, Series A, No.170, 12 E.H.R.R. 567; *Wassink v Netherlands*, September 27, 1990, Series A, No.185–A; *Koendjbiharie v Netherlands*, October 25, 1990, Series A, No.185–B, 13 E.H.R.R. 820; *Keus v Netherlands*, October 25, 1990, Series A, No.185–C, 13 E.H.R.R. 700; *Megyeri v Germany*, May 12, 1992, Series A, No.237, 15 E.H.R.R. 584; *Herczegfalvy v Austria*, September 24, 1992, Series A, No.244, 15 E.H.R.R. 437; *Johnson v UK*, October 24, 1997, R.J.D. 1997–VII, No.55, 27 E.H.R.R. 296; *Aerts v Belgium*, July 30, 1998, R.J.D. 1998–V, No.83, 29 E.H.R.R. 58; *Musial v Poland*, March 25, 1999, ECHR 1999–II, 31 E.H.R.R. 720; *Matter v Slovakia*, 5 July 1999, 31 E.H.R.R. 783; *Varbanov v Bulgaria*, October 5, 2000, ECHR 2000–X; *Hutchison Reid v UK*, February 20, 2003, ECHR 2003–IV; *Rakevich v Russia*, October 28, 2003; *HL v UK*, October 5, 2004, ECHR 2004–IX.

1. General considerations

II–521 The principal cases concern the procedures and safeguards relating to detention of persons on grounds of mental illness. Surprisingly few cases relate to the other disabilities imposed on mentally ill persons in the enjoyment of basic rights and freedoms, or to any allegations of ill-treatment within institutions. This presumably is a sad reflection that this vulnerable group of people face grave problems in putting forward or establishing claims.[1] It may be noted though that mental patients have standing to introduce complaints before the Court even if their guardian at the domestic level has not approved; standing in Strasbourg does not mirror domestic rules and the rationale of protecting mentally ill persons applicable on the domestic level does not necessitate that they can only act through a guardian before the Court.[2]

2. Admissibility points

II–522 The admissibility criteria apply in the ordinary way. A mental health patient is required to exhaust effective domestic remedies and to comply with the six-month period. (See Pt IB: Admissibility Checklist).

[1] In *Aerts v Belgium*, July 30, 1998, R.J.D. 1998–V, No.83, 29 E.H.R.R. 58, where the applicant complained that the deficiencies on the psychiatric wing violated Art.3, the Court commented that it would be unreasonable to expect a severely mentally disturbed person to give a detailed or coherent description of what he had suffered but, even allowing for that difficulty, found it had not been established that the applicant had suffered inhuman or degrading treatment (para.66).
[2] See *Zehentner v Austria*, July 16, 2009, paras 37–41.

3. Grounds for detention

Article 5, para.1(e) refers to persons of "unsound mind". The Court in *Winterwerp v Netherlands* noted that this was not a term which leant itself to precise definition since psychiatry was a progressing field, both medically and in social attitudes. It is not sufficient that a person's views or behaviour deviates from the established norms. The concept is to be narrowly interpreted given the importance of the right to liberty. II–523

The Convention organs will examine whether domestic law is compatible with the Convention.[3]

There are three basic requirements to establish that detention of a person of "unsound mind" falls within sub-para.1(e)[4]:

- "a true mental disorder" has to be established by objective medical expertise before the competent domestic authority except where it is an emergency procedure;
- it has to be a kind or degree to warrant compulsory confinement; and
- the validity of the continued detention depends on the persistence of the disorder.

In the assessment of whether the person should be detained as of "unsound mind", the authorities have a certain discretion or margin of appreciation with regard to the evaluation of the evidence, subject to Convention supervision.[5] This will usually involve an examination of whether there was psychiatric evidence to support the assessment. No deprivation of liberty will be compatible with Art.5, para.1(e) if it has been ordered without seeking the opinion of a medical expert (save in emergency cases).[6] Nor is it acceptable that a person is placed in a psychiatric institution on the request of their guardian without a requisite medical opinion showing the necessity of the measure.[7] There has as yet been no case where the official medical view of the existence of mental illness has been negatived by the Court. The requirement that the applicant be suffering from a mental disorder warranting compulsory confinement does not import any condition that the condition is amenable to medical treatment, the so-called treatability criteria found in some domestic laws.[8] Confinement may be necessary not only where a person requires treatment or therapy but also where the person needs control and supervision to prevent harm to himself or others.[9] The medical opinion relied on

[3] e.g. *Winterwerp v Netherlands*, October 24, 1979, Series A, No.33, 2 E.H.R.R. 387, the law which covered persons with a mental disorder rendering them a danger to themselves or others was compatible.
[4] *Winterwerp*, fn.3 above, para.39.
[5] e.g. *Rakevich v Russia*, October 28, 2003, para.30, where the authorities received the benefit of the doubt as to the necessity of detaining the applicant after "a night-long emotional study of the Bible".
[6] e.g. *Varbanov v Bulgaria*, October 5, 2000, ECHR 2000–X, paras 47–48, the applicant was detained for psychiatric examination by a prosecutor without consulting a medical expert and no emergency was claimed—by not requiring a medical opinion prior to detention, domestic law failed to protect against arbitrariness; *CB v Romania*, April 4, 2010, paras 48–59, violation when the applicant was taken forcibly into custody following vexatioius complaints lodged by him against a police officer, handcuffed and transferred to a psychiatric hospital for 14 days on order of a public prosecutor without any medical examination by an appropriately qualified doctor.
[7] *Shtukaturov v Russia*, March 27, 2008, paras 115–116.
[8] *Koniarska v UK*, (33670/96) (Dec.) October 12, 2000.
[9] *Hutchison Reid v UK*, February 20, 2003, ECHR 2003–IV, para.51, where the applicant's psychopathic disorder was not appropriate for hospital treatment, the Court found that it was not contrary to Art.5, para.1(e) to detain him in hospital as it was not disputed that his mental disorder made him a risk to the public.

should however reflect the applicant's condition at the time of the decision, a delay between the medical examination and the presentation of the opinion in court being capable of disclosing arbitrariness contrary to the principle underlying Art.5.[10]

As to the moment when detention ceases to be justified, the Court had found that the authorities may legitimately proceed with caution and a certain time may lapse while the applicant's condition is considered.[11] The authorities also enjoy a certain discretion as to the timing and conditions under which a person is released. Thus, in *Johnson v UK*, the Court did not consider that it automatically followed from a diagnosis that an applicant's mental disorder no longer persisted that he should be immediately or unconditionally released. However, any deferral of release had to be compatible with the purpose of Art.5, para.1 and not be unduly delayed. Over three years elapsing from a tribunal finding that the applicant was not mentally ill until his release did not fall with the authorities' discretion in managing his release into society in that case.[12] It was also compatible with Art.5, para.1(e) for an applicant to continue to be detained if the order for discharge had been made conditional on provision of treatment which did not turn out to be available. In those circumstances though, the applicant had to have access to a procedure able to review the continuing detention in conformity with Art.5, para.4.[13] Once it has been established that an applicant's mental state does not require admittance to hospital, he cannot be kept in detention, even for a matter of hours, purely for administrative reasons.[14]

Concerning emergency procedures, the Court will examine the facts leading to the emergency detention and the available medical reports or evidence at the time.[15] In *Winterwerp*, it considered the applicant's bizarre behaviour justified the steps taken (he was stealing, stripped off his clothes, etc.).[16] The Commission in *O'Reilly v Ireland* found admissible issues arising as to the justification of the extreme step of emergency detention, based on the complaint of the applicant's spouse and a visual examination by a general practitioner from the end of a garden.[17] In *Kay v UK*, where the Secretary of State ordered the recall to hospital of a prisoner whose prison sentence expired without first obtaining an up-to-date medical report of his state of mental health, the Commission found a violation since there was no emergency to

[10] *Musial v Poland*, March 25, 1999, ECHR 1999–II, 31 E.H.R.R. 720, para.50, where the court decision ordering continued detention was based on an examination which took place some 11 months earlier; see also *Varbanov*, fn.6 above, para.47; *Magalhaes Pereira v Portugal*, February 26, 2002, ECHR 2002–I, para.49.

[11] *Luberti v Italy*, February 23, 1984, Series A, No.75, 6 E.H.R.R. 440, para.29, where the applicant's detention reasonably continued pending court examination of the file and reports.

[12] The Court commented critically that the Mental Health Review Tribunal and the authorities did not have the necessary powers to ensure that the conditions attached to his release (namely placement in a supervised hostel) could be implemented within a reasonable time.

[13] *Kolanis v UK*, June 21, 2005.

[14] *RL and M-JD v France*, May 19, 2004, paras 123–129; see also *Kucheruk v Ukraine*, September 6, 2007, paras 191–194.

[15] e.g. in *Wassink v Netherlands*, September 27, 1990, Series A, No.185–A, the judge had four medical reports (two doctors had appeared and two had spoken on the telephone), statements from the applicant's wife and a police report about an assault: there were thus no grounds for questioning the weight of the evidence on which the judge extended the emergency confinement by three weeks.

[16] Also *X v UK*, November 5, 1981 Series A, No.46, 4 E.H.R.R. 188, on recall of a person under conditional release, complaints by his wife of threats and fears for safety supported by her doctor were sufficient.

[17] (24196/94) (Dec.) January 22, 1996, 84–A D.R. 72; settled (Rep.) December 3, 1996.

justify this omission.[18] The time which should elapse before a full evaluation of the applicant's state occurs should be brief on any view of matters. The Court in *Winterwerp* found that a six-week delay was rather long but not so excessive as to render the detention unlawful.[19]

Since there must be some relationship between the ground of permitted deprivation of liberty and the place and conditions of detention, the detention of a person as a mental health patient will only be lawful for the purposes of Art.5, para.1(e) if effected in a hospital, clinic or other appropriate institution.[20] Thus in *Aerts v Belgium*, where the applicant, who suffered from a severe mental disturbance, was held, while awaiting trial, in the psychiatric wing of Lantin prison, the Court found a violation of Art.5, para.1 as the lack of appropriate medical supervision and treatment showed that the wing was not an institution appropriate for the detention of persons of unsound mind. While some lapse of time for assessing the appropriate custodial clinic to which an offender should be transferred was acceptable, 15 months in prison did not strike a reasonable balance.[21] Eight months' delay in transferring the applicant, who had been found to lack criminal responsibility due to a delusional disorder, from an ordinary detention centre to a specialised hospital was too long and disclosed a violation.[22] Conversely, where the prisoner is clearly a dangerous risk with detention falling within Art.5, para.1(a) and the expert medical opinion is that he is not yet ready or able to benefit from specialised treatment, the failure to transfer him from detention in prison to a hospital will not offend.[23]

States must also exercise appropriate supervision over private clinics to ensure that there are no interferences with the right to liberty of patients by private persons.[24]

4. Procedure prescribed by law

The authorities must conform to requirements imposed by domestic law in the proceedings concerning detention.[25] Violations of Art.5, para.1 may result even from technical breaches, as in *Wassink v Netherlands*, where the registrar of the court was not present at the hearing as required by law. In *Van der Leer v Netherlands*, the applicant was confined without being heard though pursuant to the relevant law the judge should have heard her where the psychiatrist had no objection to such a procedure. The Court commented that at the very least the judge should have given reasons for departing from the pyschiatrist's opinion and there was a violation since an essential procedural requirement was not satisfied. The latter seemed to hint that a non-essential infringement of domestic procedure might not fall foul of the Convention. II–524

[18] (17821/91) (Rep.) March 1, 1994. Contrast *Herz v Germany*, June 12, 2003, where the existing medical reports were over a year old but the applicant's violent conduct the day before provided sufficient basis for an emergency order.

[19] *Winterwerp*, fn.3 above, para.42.

[20] *Aerts*, fn.1 above, para.46; *Hutchison Reid*, fn.9 above, para.54.

[21] *Morsink v Netherlands*, May 11, 2004, paras 66–70. See also *Nelissen v Netherlands*, April 5, 2011, para.60, one year and one month delay not acceptable either.

[22] *CB v Romania*, April 4, 2010, paras 49–59.

[23] *De Schepper v Belgium*, October 13, 2009, paras 47–50, distinguishing *Morsink*, fn.21 above.

[24] *Storck v Germany*, June 16, 2005, paras 103–108, where the applicant was placed in a clinic by her family, without her consent or a court order.

[25] e.g. *Rakevich*, fn.5 above, para.35, failure to grant or refuse the hospital order within five days of application (39 days).

The key objective of preventing arbitrary detention also requires the existence in domestic law of adequate legal protections and fair and proper procedures. Thus, where an applicant was admitted as an "informal patient" which procedure lacked any fixed rules concerning the conditions and purposes of the admission or its duration, with no requirement of any representative being appointed for the patient or ongoing assessment of the continued need of admission, the Court found that the system failed to protect against arbitrary deprivation of liberty.[26] Similarly, where an applicant, under criminal investigation, was taken from lawful house arrest and held in a psychiatric institution for his criminal responsibility to be determined, the Court noted that this changed the nature and degree of the restrictions involved which required specific legal justification; as the removal was not based on a valid court order, the detention in hospital was not "lawful".[27]

5. Review of the lawfulness of the continued detention

II–525 A person of unsound mind who is compulsorily confined is entitled under Art.5, para.4 to take proceedings to challenge the lawfulness of their detention at reasonable intervals and to obtain a speedy judicial decision.[28] The applicant should enjoy a direct right of appeal or application and not have to rely on the intermediary of the detaining authority.[29] The provision of a system of periodic review independent of the applicant's initiative, is not sufficient on its own.[30]

Since the validity of detention under Art.5, para.1(e) depends on the persistence of the disorder, the review required by Art.5, para.4 includes verification of the applicant's mental state as necessitating detention.

Habeas corpus was not adequate in *X v UK*, where the applicant was recalled after his conditional release from a restriction order, since the court did not examine whether in fact the applicant's disorder persisted or whether the continuation of the compulsory confinement was necessary in the interests of public safety. Nor did judicial review provide an examination of the clinical views as to the necessity of the continuing detention of a patient.[31]

The Court previously held in *Ashingdane v UK* that there was no right to obtain a review of the location or conditions of detention, where the applicant disputed the justification of his continued detention at Broadmoor. Judicial control was not guaranteed of the legality of all aspects or details of the detention and it was not considered that the question of entitlement to a more appropriate regime concerned "lawfulness" for the purpose of Art.5, para.4.[32] Since *Aerts v Belgium*, however, where the Court held that issues of lawfulness would arise from placement of a mental patient outside a suitable therapeutic institution, it would appear issues could arise from lack of effective review of the suitability of the placement.[33]

[26] *HL v UK*, October 5, 2004, ECHR 2004–IX, paras 120–124.
[27] *Gulub Atanasov v Bulgaria,* November 6, 2008, paras 73–78. See also *Shopov v Bulgaria*, September 2, 2010, lack of lawfulness where a prosecutor had detained the applicant in hospital going beyond the court order for treatment as outpatient.
[28] *Musial*, fn.10 above, para.43.
[29] *Rakevich*, fn.5 above, paras 43–46.
[30] *Gorshkov v Ukraine*, November 8, 2005, paras 37–46.
[31] *HL v UK*, fn.26 above, paras 137–142.
[32] *Ashingdane v UK*, May 28, 1985, Series A, No.93, para.52–the applicant had been recommended as fit for transfer to an ordinary hospital.
[33] *Aerts*, fn.1 above, paras 54–56, the opportunity for the applicant to apply for an injunction satisfied Art.5, para.4 in that case.

(a) "Court"

The review must be conducted by "court", which must have a power to decide. In *X v UK*, the Mental Health Review Tribunal only had advisory powers and no binding power to release. A specialised body of this kind may be a "court" provided that it enjoys the necessary independence and offers sufficient procedural safeguards. A public prosecutor did not qualify in *Winterwerp v Netherlands*. II–526

(b) Procedural requirements

The review must provide the requisite procedural safeguards. In the context of mental illness, special safeguards may also be required to protect persons who are not fully capable of acting for themselves.[34] While mental illness may justify restricting or modifying the exercise of their right of review, it cannot however justify impairing the very essence of that right.[35] II–527

There was a violation in *Winterwerp*, where neither the applicant nor his representative were present before the courts which issued the orders of detention. The Court considered that the applicant must be heard either in person or through a representative. Further, answering the Government's point that the applicant had failed to instruct a lawyer, it was not for the person with unsound mind to take the initiative to obtain legal representation before applying to a court. The necessity for legal assistance was underlined in *Megyeri v Germany*, where the applicant challenged his detention in psychiatric hospital but was not represented before the court conducting the review. The Court found that where a person was confined in psychiatric institution on the basis of acts which would have been criminal offences for those criminally responsible, he should, unless there are special circumstances, receive legal assistance in subsequent proceeedings concerning that detention. It was doubtful that the applicant could address the medical and legal points arising and the Court emphasised the importance of what was at stake for him.[36]

What is required by way of procedure at the hearing may be minimal where emergency considerations apply. In *Wassink*, the Court found it compatible with Art.5, para.4 that the President of the court consulted experts and witnesses by phone, although failing to read his notes to the applicant or his counsellor and in the absence of the registrar who was required by law. The Court was influenced by the fact that the power exercised was an emergency one limited in duration to three weeks and considered that the President nonetheless had established the medical basis for continued detention.

Having regard to Art.5, para.4 cases dealing with other forms of detention, it is likely that access to documents and reports may be required, tempered however by the consideration whether an applicant should on health grounds be allowed to see particular documents.[37]

[34] *Megyeri v Germany*, May 12, 1992, Series A, No.237, 15 E.H.R.R. 584, para.22; *Magalhaes Pereira*, fn.10 above, para.56.

[35] *Wassink*, fn.15 above, para.60.

[36] Also *Magalhaes Pereira*, fn.10 above, paras 58–62, a breach of Art.5, para.4, for lack of effective legal assistance to the mentally disturbed applicant at the hearings concerning his detention. The Court rejected the Government's argument that an officially assigned lawyer was not required due to an alleged lack of legal issues—it was self-evident that such issues could arise.

[37] See Pt IIB, s.42: Review of detention.

It is for the authorities to prove that he satisfies the conditions for compulsory detention, not for the applicant to prove the converse. A violation of Art.5, para.4 arose in *Hutchison Reid v UK* where the applicant had to show that his mental disorder was not of a nature or degree making it appropriate for him to receive treatment in hospital and thus the burden of proof was on him to establish that his detention was not lawful.

6. Timing of reviews

II–528 A person detained as being of unsound mind is entitled both to a speedy decision and to take proceedings at reasonable intervals.[38] The latter applies where there is no automatic periodic judicial review, the Court commenting in *X v UK* that it was not its task to specify which system of judicial review was appropriate.

However, no initial review is required where detention is ordered by a court at the end of judical proceedings. In these circumstances, the review of lawfulness is regarded as incorporated. An initial review by a court is only required for the purposes of Art.5, para.4 where the decision to detain is taken by an administrative authority.[39]

A distinction may be made between the speed at which an applicant taken into detention or recalled should obtain a review and the time which should be taken in reaching decisions on release or continuance at later stages.

The first review should take place very rapidly. In *Wassink*, the Commission found that the applicant's discharge after three weeks of emergency confinement did not follow so speedily that it made a review of detention superfluous. Detention of 16 days without any judicial decision on an application for release disclosed a lack of promptness.[40] A five-month delay on a hearing after recall was, not surprisingly, excessive in *Kay v UK*.

Concerning later reviews, four months for a court to issue a decision on an application for release was not speedy in *Koendjbiharie v Netherlands*. Where in another case it took almost three months to decide an application for release, the Commission, rejecting the case as inadmissible, commented that while on first sight this seemed excessive and required factors to justify it, it was not excessive in light of the applicant's conduct in challenging the impartiality of the expert and the conducting of thorough medical examinations.[41]

Where an applicant's conduct contributes to the length of proceedings, rendering it impossible to obtain an examination, this will be a relevant factor in assessing whether the court has acted reasonably.[42] However, the fact that an applicant applies for adjournments or shows disinterest does not absolve the court from acting speedily. In *Kay v UK*,[43] the Commission found the system of review on recall inherently slow, since it frequently took six months for cases to come before the

[38] A court must decide speedily and at reasonable intervals—*Herczegfalvy v Austria*, September 24, 1992, Series A, No.244, 15 E.H.R.R. 437, para.75.

[39] *Luberti*, fn.11 above, para.31.

[40] *Van Glabeke v France*, March 7, 2006, paras 29–34.

[41] *Boucheras v France*, (14438/88) (Dec.) April 11, 1991, 69 D.R. 236.

[42] e.g. *Keus v Netherlands*, October 25, 1990, Series A, No.185–C, 13 E.H.R.R. 700; *Luberti*, fn.11 above. However, in *Van der Leer v Netherlands*, February 21, 1990, Series A, No.170, 12 E.H.R.R. 567, para.35, the fact that the applicant absconded while the application was pending did not absolve the court from reaching a speedy decision since she could have been brought back against her will at any moment.

[43] See fn.18 above.

Mental Health Review Tribunal. In this case there was a two-year delay, the applicant's own requests for adjournments and later disinterest not being relevant, since anyway the first hearing had been set for five months after recall. Similarly, in *Musial v Poland*, the fact that the applicant requested that examination by particular doctors did not discharge the domestic court from its obligation to rule speedily on his request for release. In that case, the Court also did not find the medical complexity of the file sufficient to constitute exceptional grounds justifying a delay of over one year and eight months. Where the system provides appeals, these must also be taken in to account in assessing the speed and cannot provide an excuse for lack of proper expedition.[44]

Regarding reviews at reasonable intervals, an automatic review once per year was considered reasonable in *Megyeri*. In *Herczegfalvy v Austria*, the Court found intervals of 15 months and 2 years were not speedy but in not remarking on the period of nine months seemed to find that was compatible. It referred to the fact that the Austrian system recommended a yearly interval.

7. Access to court

The factor of mental illness may justify restrictions on access to court. In *Ashingdane* where leave was required to bring actions in relation to acts done in pursuance of the Mental Health Act 1959 the Court found that this pursued the legitimate aim of preventing those responsible for the care of mental patients being unfairly harassed by litigation and that the essence of the right was not impaired, since it was only a partial exclusion.[45] II–529

However, the proceedings to detain a person per se do not involve the determination of a person's civil rights and obligations under Art.6, para.1. A different kind of court control is applicable to these cases under the special provisions of Art.5.[46]

8. Ill-treatment

In the context of force feeding, constraints and compulsory administration of drugs, the Court's view appears to be that such will not breach Art.3 if required for therapeutic reasons. In *Herczegfalvy*, the Commission doubted that it was necessary to apply massive force to administer medication and found that the fettering to bed for several weeks when the applicant was in a very bad physical state, combined with isolation, was excessive and disclosed inhuman and degrading treatment. The Court restricted itself to the medical necessity, holding that a measure which was a therapeutic necessity could not be inhuman or degrading. While the duration of the period of handcuffing and restriction in a security bed was "worrying", there was nothing to disprove the Government's argument that, according to the psychiatric principles accepted at the time, medical necessity required it.[47] Since then, in the II–530

[44] *Hutchison Reid*, fn.9 above, paras 77–80, where the applicant's proceedings for release were heard by four instances, lasting three years and nine months, and there were no exceptional grounds justifying the delay.

[45] See above, i.e. if there was bad faith or negligence the case could proceed with leave of the court.

[46] *Neumeister v Austria*, June 27, 1968, Series A, No.8, para.23.

[47] Also *Frommelt v Liechtenstein*, (49158/99) (Dec.) May 15, 2003, necessity for neuroleptic drug treatment: constant surveillance and threat to force feed the applicant did not offend Art.3.

context of prisoners on hunger strikes, the Court has reviewed more strictly the circumstances in which, and procedures by which, force-feeding is applied. It appears to require objective medical evidence as to the life-saving necessity and that the methods should not cause undue physical or mental suffering.[48] A rigorous approach has also been taken to the use of restraints, which require appropriate medical justification. Where a mentally-ill prisoner was kept handcuffed constantly while in a disciplinary cell, there was a violation of Art.3 since the use of the handcuffs had not been a measure approved by the appropriate psychiatric expert and patently had not been justified by the purported need to prevent the prisoner harming himself, since they caused him deep abrasions on his wrists and did not stop him banging his head on the wall in frustration.[49]

For an Art.3 case to have any chance of success, it would appear necessary to show that the authorities applied treatment clearly injustifiable by any established medical norm.[50]

Failure by the authorities to pursue an effective investigation into credible allegations of ill-treatment of a patient may disclose a procedural breach of Art. 3.[51]

9. Right to treatment

II–531 The Court has stated in old cases that no right to a specific treatment appropriate to the applicant's condition can be derived from Art.5, para.1(e).[52] However, the more recent case of *Aerts* discloses the possibility of challenging under Art.5 the holding of mentally ill prisoners in a regime where no adequate treatment or supervision is available. Lack of care and treatment appropriate to a prisoner with psychiatric problems in a prison context has also been found to disclose treatment contrary to Art.3.[53] As in other contexts, financial difficulties are no excuse for failure in this respect.[54] Lack of proper supervision of mentally-ill prisoners may raise issues, as in a case where a prisoner was able to hoard his medication and commit suicide.[55] Imposition of disciplinary punishments on mentally-ill prisoners who are particularly vulnerable has also been found to disclose breaches of Article 3.[56]

[48] *Nevmerzhitsky v Ukraine*, April 5, 2005, ECHR 2005–II, violation of Art.3.

[49] *Kucheruk v Ukraine*, September 6, 2007, paras 140–146.

[50] *Buckley v UK*, (28323/95) (Dec.) February 26, 1997, where the administration of drugs in circumstances which led to the death of a patient did not disclose ground for negligence in domestic law, there was no basis for the Commission to find a violation.

[51] e.g. *Filip v Romania*, December 14, 2006, paras 47–52, where the applicant alleged that he had been strapped to his bed and had not received necessary medical treatment.

[52] See *Ashingdane*, fn.32 above; *Winterwerp*, fn.3 above, where the applicant unsuccessfully claimed the right to have treatment to enable detention to be as short as possible and claimed that his meetings with psychiatrists were too short, too many tranquillisers, etc.

[53] e.g. *Riviere v France*, July 11, 2006, regarding a breach where the mentally-ill prisoner was kept in prison, rather than a hospital, without proper psychiatric care; *Kucheruk v Ukraine*, fn. 14 above, paras 147–152, breach for failure to execute the recommended transfer to a specialisted hospital and lack of adequate psychiatric supervision and care while in prison; *Slavomir Musial v Poland*, January 20, 2009, paras 89–96, lack of constant and specialised psychiatric supervision while in ordinary prison rather than in a hospital or specialised prison hospital ward.

[54] e.g. *Dybeku v Albania*, December 18, 2007, para.50, the applicant with chronic mental problems was treated essentially the same as other prisoners, with no provision being made for his particularly vulnerable condition, in particular as no specialised hospital had yet been built for such cases.

[55] *Renolde v France*, October 16, 2008, paras 85–110, breach of Art. 2. See Part IIB, s.42: Right to Life, sub-s.4(): Protection from self-harm.

[56] e.g. *Renolde*, fn.55 above, paras 119–130.

10. Respect for private life and home

Forcible examination for psychiatric purposes is an interference with private life within the scope of Art.8. Although it may generally be found to pursue the aim of protecting the applicant's own health, it must also be necessary and proportionate within the meaning of the second paragraph of Art.8. In *Matter v Slovakia*, it was not found to be disproportionate to impose compulsory examination in a hospital when the applicant had refused a voluntary procedure and it was a necessary part of their supervision that the authorities verify whether the applicant continued to lack legal capacity. II–532

Where other measures of control are applied to persons under mental health supervision, issues will arise where they do not comply with lawfulness criteria[57] or pursue legitimate aims or are disproportionate.[58] For example, the repeated summonsing of the applicant for psychiatric examination over a short period was not justified in *Worwa v Poland*.[59] Where an applicant was subject to compulsory outpatient treatment for five years, the Court found a breach of Art.8, since this indefinite measure had not been subject to the regular judicial review of its necessity as required by domestic law.[60]

Where treatment was imposed forcibly on an applicant in a private clinic, the Court found that it was not sufficient that the criminal law imposed liability for assault and the civil law gave the possibility of damages: the State was under a positive obligation to provide mechanisms to protect such vulnerable persons from breaches of their physical integrity.[61] Complaints that young, mentally ill women were sterilised without being informed or their consent being required have been communicated to the Government for observations, serious issues arising under Art.8, as well as Arts 3, 6, 12 and 14.[62]

Patients may be able to claim some say in which person is named as their "next relative", for purposes of being given information about admission and reviews. Two cases were settled with the United Kingdom undertaking to change the legislation.[63]

Where an applicant, who had lacked legal capacity, was subject to an order for sale and eviction from her apartment in summary proceedings in which she had not participated, the Court found a violation in that there had been no effective way in which, once her incapacity had been established, the procedure could have been re-opened due to the operation of strict time-limits. Given the severity of the interference, in taking away the applicant's home, the Court found insufficient procedural safeguards in the system, which was not justified by any requirements of legal certainty.[64]

57 e.g. (18969/91) (Rep.) June 30, 1993, complaints by person under guardianship of mail censorship; violation of Art.8 due to a total absence in law as to the permissibility of an interference with a ward's correspondence, the purpose and duration of such an interference, etc.

58 e.g. (26494/95) (Dec.) February 27, 1997, admissible under Art.8 concerning complaints from an involuntary patient that medical and other reports automatically went to a relative to whom she objected. Settled before the Court on March 30, 2000, on amending legislation permitting a patient to apply to court to change the designated "nearest relative".

59 *Worwa v Poland*, November 27, 2003, caused effectively by lack of proper co-ordination, the interference was not necessary under Art.8, para.2.

60 *Shopov*, fn.27 above, paras 45–49.

61 *Storck*, fn.24 above, paras 145–153.

62 *Gauer v France*, (61521/08) March 2011, decision or judgment not likely before 2012 at the earliest.

63 e.g. *M v UK*, (30357/03) (Dec.) February 13, 2007, where the person appointed, her adoptive father, had allegedly sexually abused the applicant as a child.

64 *Zehentner*, fn.2 above, paras 52–64.

A person suffering from mental illness cannot claim a right to have medication made available to him for the purpose of suicide.[65]

11. Limitation of capacity to act

II–533 The loss of capacity to administer property concerns "civil rights and obligation" under Art.6, para.1. In this context, lack of proper access to a court with requisite guarantees may constitute a breach.[66] There must be good reason for a court to rule on legal incapacity without the applicant being present or at least his representative, not only due to what was at stake personally but also as the judge should generally see the person under discussion for him or herself.[67] Indeed the Court has considered that deprivation of legal capacity was a very serious interference with Art.8 rights by itself and that the authorities were under an obligation to verify whether the measure continued to be justified.[68] A "tailor-made" response is also required when considering issues of legal capacity, the Court disapproving of the automatic imposition of full incapacity on a person with a mental illness without giving justification for the measure or considering intermediate or alternative solutions.[69] Procedural protection should also be available where persons deprived of capacity wish to acknowledge the paternity of a child. There was a violation where there was a legal void as regarded such a person's ability to prove a claim for paternity: only the social authorities could bring such an action on his behalf, but they could not be required to do so and there was no time-limit within which they had to respond to a request.[70]

A case concerning the incapacity of a schizophrenic, under legal disability, to marry was under examination at the time of publication.[71]

Cross-reference

Part IIA, s.2: Access to court.
Part IIB, s.6: Compensation for detention.
Part IIB, s.9: Deprivation of liberty.
Part IIB, s.42: Review of detention.
Part IIB, s.43: Right to life, sub-ss.4(ix): Protection from suicide, 4(x): Medical services, and 4(xi): Protection of the vulnerable.
Part IIB, s.46: Torture, inhuman and degrading treatment.

[65] *Haas v Switzerland*, January 20, 2011, the applicant suffered from chronic bipolar disorder.
[66] See *Winterwerp*, fn.3 above, where the applicant automatically lost capacity by law when committed to hospital in a process not affording the requisite guarantees; also *Matter*, paras 51–61: breach of Art.6 for unreasonable length of proceedings concerning the applicant's capacity.
[67] *Shtukaturov v Russia*, March 27, 2008, paras 71–75.
[68] *Matter v Slovakia*, 5 July 1999, 31 E.H.R.R. 783, para.68.
[69] *Shtukaturov*, fn.67 above, paras 90–96.
[70] *Kruskovic v Croatia*, June 21, 2011, paras 36–44, both the applicant and mother agreed he was the biological father of the child. Even though the social authorities eventually made an application to establish recognition of paternity on his behalf, they ignored his claims for some two and a half years meanwhile.
[71] *Lashin v Russia*, (33117/02) (Dec.) January 6, 2011, judgment not likely before 2012. See *Kruskovic*, fn.70 above, paras 90–96.

33. Pensions

Key provisions:

Article 6, para.1 (fair hearing guarantees); Article 1 of Protocol 1 (right to property), and Article 14 (prohibition of discrimination). II–534

Key case-law:

Schuler-Zgraggen v Switzerland, June 24, 1993, Series A, No.263, 16 E.H.R.R. 405; *Massa v Italy*, August 24, 1993, Series A, No.265–B, 18 E.H.R.R. 266; *Gaygusuz v Austria*, September 16, 1996, R.J.D. 1996–IV, No.14, 23 E.H.R.R. 364; *Süssman v Germany*, September 16, 1996, R.J.D. 1996–IV, No.58, 25 E.H.R.R. 64; *Stamoulakatos v Greece (No.2)*, November 26, 1997, R.J.D. 1997–VII; *Wessels-Bergervoet v Netherlands*, June 4, 2002, ECHR 2002–IV; *Stummer v Austria*, July 7, 2011, ECHR 2011–. . .

1. General considerations

Where a pension is based on private contract with private institutions, it will be considered as both a "civil right" for the purposes of attracting the procedural guarantees to determine disputes in proceedings and the right to a court under Art.6 and as a pecuniary right classifying as property within the meaning of Art.1 of Protocol No.1. Where the pension concerned is derived from a public or State context, the issues overlap to some extent with those arising in the area of social security or welfare benefits. Although once it was less automatic that these two provisions apply in this context, the distinction appears to be disappearing. II–535

The Convention organs have stated that there is no right as such to receive a pension guaranteed in the Convention.[1] Where no basis for entitlement exists, or has ever existed, it is unlikely that the Convention provisions can offer any ground of complaint.

2. Civil rights: applicability of Article 6, paragraph 1

Where a pension is linked to contract or akin to a private contractual relationship, Art.6, para.1 in its civil context is likely to be applicable and the normal guarantees apply.[2] II–536

Following the approach of the Court in *Schuler-Zgraggen v Switzerland*, where Art.6 applied to a benefits claim since it concerned an interference with the applicant's means of subsistence and related to an individual economic right, it appears that pension claims of a similar character attract the same treatment. Where civil servant pensions disputes have arisen, Art.6 has been held to apply notwithstanding the

[1] (9776/82) (Dec.) October 3, 1983, 34 D.R. 153; *Hadzic v Croatia*, (48788/99) (Dec.) September 13, 2001.

[2] e.g. (9630/81) (Dec.) October 13, 1986, 49 D.R. 59, where a pension was awarded after an industrial accident on the basis of contributions paid by the employer on behalf of his employees, such insurance was considered as grafted onto the employment contract, governed by private law and similar to insurance in private law; (10659/83) (Rep.) July 3, 1989, 69 D.R. 7.

public law context, on the basis of similarity with private law employment contract or the pecuniary nature of the pension entitlement.[3] In recent cases, the Court has stated, without qualification, that it found no reason to depart from its case-law that the right to a pension is a civil right.[4] Special diligence may attach to proceedings where the applicant's means of support is at stake, although due account has to be taken of the proper administration of justice in complex cases with importance for the system as a whole.[5]

3. Property rights

II–537 Where a person has contributed to a pension fund, this could, according to the Commission, in certain circumstances create a property right in a portion of such a fund and a modification of the pension rights under such a system could in principle raise an issue under Art.1 of Protocol No.1.

Where the payments are to a social security system, even assuming that this gives rise to a right to derive a benefit from the system, it cannot be interpreted as entitling that person to a pension of a particular amount.[6] A right to a pension based on employment can in certain circumstances be assimilated to a property right, where special contributions were paid or the employer has given a more general undertaking to pay a pension on conditions which can be considered part of the employment contract.[7] In *Walden v Liechtenstein*, where the Government argued that the payments made to the general pension system were on the basis of social solidarity and did not create a specific entitlement to a share in the fund, the Court nonetheless considered that the applicant had a pecuniary right to a common married couple's pension which fell within the scope of Art.1 of Protocol No.1.[8]

An applicant must however satisfy domestic legal requirements governing the right before Art.1 of the First Protocol can apply.[9] Thus where by moving to Australia, the applicants ceased to qualify for future pension increases, this did not

[3] *Massa v Italy*, August 24, 1993, Series A, No.265–B, 18 E.H.R.R. 266, para.26; *Süssman v Germany*, September 16, 1996, R.J.D. 1996–IV, No.58, 25 E.H.R.R. 64, para.42.

[4] e.g. *Stamoulakatos*, para.31. More recently, *Domalewski v Poland*, (34610/97) (Dec.) June 15, 1999, ECHR 1999–V, decision revoking an entitlement to a veterans' pension was decisive for pecuniary rights; *Trickovic v Slovenia*, June 12, 2001, para.40.

[5] e.g. *Sussman*, fn.3 above, paras 55–57; *Trickovic*, fn.4 above, paras 64–67 and 69, where proceedings of over two years, seven months was not excessive in the transition period to a democratic legal order.

[6] e.g. (5849/72) (Rep.) October 1, 1975, 3 D.R. 25, para.30; (10671/83) (Dec.) March 4, 1985, 42 D.R. 229; (25044/94) (Dec.) May 15, 1996, where the Commission held that the applicant was entitled to benefit from the social insurance system to which he had contributed, but not to any particular amount; *Domalewski*, fn.4 above; *Jankovic v Croatia*, (43440/98) (Dec.) October 12, 2000, ECHR 2000–X.

[7] (10671/83) fn.6 above; (12264/86) (Dec.) July 13, 1988, 57 D.R. 131.

[8] (33916/96) (Dec.) March 16, 2000. Also *Wessels-Bergervoet v Netherlands*, June 4, 2002, ECHR 2002–IV, paras 39–43; *Szrabjer and Clarke v UK*, (27004/95) and (27011/95) (Decs.) October 23, 1997, where the pension fund (SERPS) contained a social solidarity element but the right to a pension was still dependent on some contribution and therefore was a pecuniary right for the purposes of Art.1 of Protocol No.1.

[9] *Bellet v France*, (40832/98) (Dec.) April 27, 1999; *Hadzic*, fn.1 above, where the applicant did not fulfil the condition of having made himself available for service in the army prior to December 31, 1999. See however, *Klein v Austria*, March 3, 2011, where the disbarred applicant did not qualify for a pension as he was not practising law at the moment of claim as specified in the law, the Court nonetheless considered compulsory affiliation to an old-age pension scheme, based on compulsory membership of a professional organisation, could give rise to the legitimate expectation to receive pension benefits at the point of retirement and thus constitute a "possession". This reasoning is difficult to reconcile with the general principle.

amount to a deprivation of possessions.[10] The requirement to pay contributions for a minimum period to accrue a right must also be satisfied, where applicable.[11] Rules providing for the co-ordination of a pension with other State benefits or pensions have also been found compatible with Art.1 of Protocol No.1.[12]

Since the operation of a social security system is essentially different from the management of a private life insurance company, having to take account of political considerations particularly those of financial policy, it is conceivable that, due to a deflationary trend, a State may be obliged to reduce the amount of pension payable, as in the case of German re-unification. This kind of fluctuation was not seen by the Commission as having anything to do with the guarantee of ownership as a human right.[13] Thus the fact that an applicant's pension was less than he could have received under former East German system was not a problem. But the Commission did add that his level of pension was sufficient and did not deprive him of basic means of existence.[14] Proportionality issues (i.e. effect and hardship) could conceivably arise where a substantial reduction, affecting the substance of the right, is concerned.[15] Where an ex-public security officer lost his veteran status and the special pension that went with it, the Court found that the essence of his pension rights was not impaired as he retained all the rights attaching to his ordinary pension under the general system.[16]

Forfeiture or termination of pension could conceivably disclose a deprivation of property where disproportionate or failing to strike the right balance between public and private interests.[17] In *Azinas v Cyprus*, although the Grand Chamber later upheld the Government's preliminary objection, the Chamber found that the automatic forfeiture of a civil servant's pension on his dismissal interfered with his property right under the first sentence of Art.1 of Protocol No.1. Although the dismissal might pursue the aim of protecting the public and safeguarding the integrity of the administration, the retrospective forfeiture of pension rights did not serve any commensurate purpose. Given the drastic impact on him and his family of removal of their means of subsistence, a fair balance had not been struck.[18] The drastic nature of total forfeiture of an old age pension to a disbarred lawyer also led to the conclusion that the measure was disproportionate.[19] On the other hand, where a police officer had his pension reduced by the amount of State contributions (65 per cent) due to serious misconduct jeopardising public confidence in the police, the

[10] (9776/82), see fn.1 above.

[11] (7459/76) October 5, 1977, 11 D.R. 114, where the applicant, dismissed from his job after conviction, also lost his pension as he had not secured the necessary seniority.

[12] (10671/83) March 4, 1985, 42 D.R. 229; also *Bellet*, fn.9 above, where the ex-civil servants were not allowed by law to collect pensions from both France and Monaco.

[13] (5849/72), see fn.6 above.

[14] (24077/94) (Dec.) May 15, 1996.

[15] (25044/94), fn.6 above, where the Commission found that the calculation had not been carried out in an arbitrary manner.

[16] *Domalewski*, see fn.4 above; also *Jankovic*, see fn.6 above.

[17] See, mutatis mutandis, *Asmundsson v Iceland*, October 12, 2004, violation where, under legislation that only affected a tiny minority, the applicant lost a disability pension (received for the previous 20 years) which was a major part of his means of subsistence.

[18] June 20, 2002. See also *Apostolakis v Greece*, October 22, 2009, violation for removal of the applicant's civil service retirement pension due to fraud offences: it was his only means of subsistence and he was too old to resume working life; the Court saw no link between removal of the pension and the offences for which he served a prison term, referring to a double punishment.

[19] *Klein v Austria*, March 3, 2011, paras 48–58.

Court emphasised the procedural safeguards in the decision-making procedure in finding that the right balance had been struck.[20] Suspension of payments while an applicant was in prison justifiably prevented him from deriving financial enrichment from his detention when he was being supported at the State's expense.[21]

Where pensions or allowances are granted subject to continuous fulfilment of certain criteria, revocation when circumstances change and fall outside statutory entitlement will not generally disclose a problem. The Court has eschewed any claim that a pension can never be reduced or be regarded as irrevocable.[22] Pension fund arrangements in the private sector may be modified in line with legislative provisions to the beneficiaries' disadvantage also.[23] However, where the conduct or mistakes of the authorities has a prejudicial impact on the amount of, or the entitlement to, a pension, issues may arise of a disproportionate burden on the applicant, or of a failure to strike a fair balance between the individual and public interest. Thus, where legal provisions concerning backdating of pension entitlements ran, not from an objectively fixed date such as the lodging of the claim in question but from a date which depended on the actions of the authorities and thus subject to the vagaries of their delays, the Court considered that this imposed an excessive burden on the applicant, who had already been unlawfully paid a lower pension than his entitlement and was then in addition penalised when the benefit of the decision in his favour was backdated from the date of the court decision, which only occurred after years of proceedings.[24] The Court has on occasion referred to a principle of "good governance" in this context, considering that while accepting the authorities must be able revoke pensions granted in error, they must act in good time and in an appropriate manner and without imposing an excessive burden on the applicant. There was a violation where an applicant, acting in good faith, gave up her job to look after a sick child and obtained an early retirement pension, which however was subsequently revoked due to the lack of the requisite medical ground, leaving the applicant without her means of subsistence.[25]

4. Discrimination

II–538 Article 14 can only be invoked in respect of complaints falling within the ambit of another substantive provision. In light of *Schuler-Zgraggen v Switzerland, Gaygusuz v Austria*[26] and *Van Raalte v Netherlands*[27] it is apparent that issues could arise from differences on entitlements or contribution obligations based, inter alia, on sex or

[20] *Banfield v UK*, (6223/04) (Dec.) October 18, 2004.
[21] *Szrabjer and Clarke*, see fn.8 above.
[22] *Wieczorek v Poland*, December 8, 2009, paras 61–74, where after receiving an invalidity pension for 15 years, the applicant was found able to work and the pension stopped.
[23] *Aizpurua Ortiz v Spain*, February 2, 2010.
[24] *Reveliotis v Greece*, December 4, 2008.
[25] *Moskal v Poland*, September 15, 2009, a narrow decision by four votes to three, the minority did not consider that the authorities should be prevented from putting right an error and removing an entitlement that had erroneously been granted; nor did they consider the revocation disproportionate, as the authorities had acted without undue delay and had not required the applicant to repay the pension already received. It is likely that this case will receive further interpretation in the future.
[26] Where in the context of emergency subsistence, there were sufficient links with payments made from salary to bring the applicant's claim within the scope of Art.1 of Protocol No.1.
[27] *Van Raalte v Netherlands*, February 21, 1997, R.J.D. 1997–I, No.39, where differences in social security contributions paid by men and women fell within the scope of Art.1 of Protocol No.1 and disclosed discrimination contrary to Art.14.

race where a pension was sufficiently linked to employment or established pecuniary rights to fall within the scope of Art.1 of Protocol No.1 (see Pt IIB: Welfare Benefits).[28] There is now a general principle that legislation providing for payment of an old age pension, whether conditional or not on contributions, generates a proprietary interest falling within the ambit for those satisfying its requirements. The test is whether the applicant would have had an enforceable right to receive a pension, had it not been for the condition of entitlement alleged to be discriminatory.[29]

To disclose discrimination, differences in eligibility or quantification also have to be in respect of persons in relevantly similar situations and without reasonable and objective justification for difference in treatment.[30] Very strong reasons have to be put forward to justify differences based solely on ground of sex and marital status, as appears from *Wessels-Bergervoet*, where the Government argued that excluding the female applicant from a full pension was to prevent the undesirable accumulation of pension rights (she also received a pension from abroad); the Court noted that a man in her position could have benefitted from two pensions and found a violation. A wide margin applies however to States in regulating their social policy. Thus, it found that the payment of widow's pension to women was objectively and reasonably justified as correcting the hardship faced in the past by a certain category of women.[31]

Differences based on national origin will also be struck down, if, without reasonable and objective justification, the mere fact of being a foreigner not disclosing such a ground, if, apart from status of origin, the individual would otherwise qualify. Refusal, somewhat arbitarily, to pay a large-family retirement pension to a mother, of Turkish origin, living in Greece disclosed discrimination for example.[32]

Measures reducing pensions in pursuit of social justice or re-integration into the general system of previously privileged groups may also be acceptable. In *Domalewski v Poland*, for example, the Court found that there was objective and reasonable justification in removing special veterans' pensions from ex-security officers who had assisted in preserving the previous totalitarian regime.[33]

Some leeway in time is also given to Contracting States in redressing discriminatory differences in pensions, a gap of some seven months in changing the law being

[28] *Schwengel v Germany*, (552122/99) (Dec.) March 2, 2000, rights flowing from payments to a social insurance fund were considered property rights; *Wessels-Bergervoet*, fn.8 above, para.43, rights to a pension from general insurance scheme.

[29] *Stummer v Austria*, July 7, 2011, ECHR 2011–. . . , paras 81–86.

[30] *Buchen v Czech Republic*, November 26, 2002, where there was no apparent objective or reasonable justification for removing pension rights from some categories of ex-military judges but not others. See conversely (9776/82) fn.1 above, when, by moving to Australia, the applicants ceased to be eligible for future pension increases, there was reasonable and objective justification since they had left the United Kingdom and there was a relevant social security scheme in Australia; (24077/94) fn.14 above, even assuming that Art.14 applied, an applicant in East Germany was not in a comparable position to persons living in the West or to those in East Germany who paid supplementary contributions and anyway it was objective and reasonable to make pension rights conditional on the payment of contributions.

[31] *Runkee and White v UK*, May 10, 2007.

[32] *Zeibek v Greece*, July 9, 2009.

[33] See fn.4 above. See also *Schwengel*, fn.28 above, where the reduction in certain East German officials' special pensions to the average in East Germany was justified for reasons of social justice and not disproportionate; *Jankovic*, fn.6 above, where reduction in former Yugoslav army officers' pensions was part of the policy of integration of pensions into the general system.

compatible with Art.14 in *Walden v Liechtenstein*[34] as not imposing a disproportionate burden on the applicant. The phased implementation of legislation harmonising the ages in entitlement to State pensions for men (age 65) and women (60) in the United Kingdom over some decades has been found to fall within the State's margin of appreciation, given the significant financial and social implications.[35] Gradual extension of social benefits and cover to prisoners did not disclose any problem in a context of changing standards, where prisoners, although their years of prison work did not count towards the state pension, were provided with other forms of assistance. Standards were evolving in this area and to be kept under review for the future however.[36]

Cross-reference

Part IIA, s.1b: Civil rights and obligations.
Part IIB, s.12: Discrimination.
Part IIB, s.48: Welfare benefits.

[34] See fn.8 above, reference to the complexity of social security law and legal certainty.
[35] *Pearson v UK*, August 22, 2006, equalisation at age 65 not complete until 2020. See also *Runkee and White*, fn.31 above, acceptable to take time to "level down" widow's pensions after the justification for them had disappeared.
[36] *Stummer*, fn.29 above, paras 105–110. See, in contrast, the dissenters who considered that the right to an old age pension formed part of the social pact between citizens and the State.

34. Planning and use of property

Key provisions:

Article 1 of Protocol No.1 (peaceful enjoyment of possessions) and Article 6 (access to court/fair hearing). II–539

Key case-law:

Sporrong and Lonnroth v Sweden, September 23, 1982, Series A, No.52, 5 E.H.R.R. 35; *Allan Jacobsson v Sweden*, October 25, 1989, Series A, No.163, 12 E.H.R.R 56; *Tre Traktorer v Sweden*, July 7, 1989, Series A, No.159, 13 E.H.R.R. 309; *Fredin v Sweden*, February 18, 1990, Series A, No.192, 14 E.H.R.R 319; *Pine Valley Developments v Ireland*, November 29, 1991, Series A, No.222, 14 E.H.R.R 319; *Raimondo v Italy*, February 22, 1994, Series A, No.281–A, 18 E.H.R.R. 237; *Bryan v UK*, November 22, 1995, Series A, No.335–A, 21 E.H.R.R 342; *Phocas v France*, April 2, 1996, R.J.D. 1996–II, No.7, 32 E.H.R.R. 221; *Buckley v UK*, September 25, 1996, R.J.D. 1996–V, No.16, 23 E.H.R.R. 101; *Chassagnou v France*, April 29, 1999, ECHR 1999–III, 29 E.H.R.R. 615; *Chapman v UK*, January 18, 2001, ECHR 2000–I; *Depalle v France* and *Brosset-Triboulet v France*, March 29, 2010, ECHR 2010–. . .

1. General considerations

Control of use of property, the "third rule" of Art.1 of Protocol No.1, is compatible where necessary in accordance with general interest. A wide margin of appreciation is accorded to the authorities. Where planning considerations are involved, the Court has emphasised the complex issues[1] and that this is an area where the authorities exercise discretionary powers.[2] As with use of expropriation powers, weight is given to the exercise by the legislature of its role to implement measures in the general interest.[3] II–540

In older cases, the approach was taken that States were the sole judges of the necessity of a control of use and that the Convention organs were restricted to supervising the lawfulness and purpose (if legitimate) of the restriction.[4] More recently however, in line with the general development of case-law, there is some examination of the proportionality of the measures applied. Whether a planning restriction is regarded as an interference with peaceful enjoyment of possessions or a control of use appears to depend on the intended primary purpose of the measure but the same considerations appear to apply in this area whichever classification is used.[5] Even where property is seized and ownership is lost in the area of

[1] e.g. *Allan Jacobsson v Sweden*, October 25, 1989, Series A, No.163, 12 E.H.R.R 56.

[2] e.g. *Chapman v UK*, January 18, 2001, ECHR 2000–I, para.92.

[3] e.g. (11763/85) (Dec.) March 9, 1989, 60 D.R. 128, legislation ending exclusive fishing rights for landowners: weight given to decision of democratic institutions that measure was necessary in the general interest.

[4] e.g. *Handyside v UK*, December 7, 1976, Series A, No.24, para.62; (10378/83) (Dec.) December 7, 1983, 35 D.R. 235.

[5] *Sporrong and Lonnroth v Sweden*, September 23, 1982, Series A, No.52, 5 E.H.R.R. 35, para.69, striking a balance between the general and individual interest underlies the whole of Art.1 of Protocol No.1.

confiscation, this is regarded not as a deprivation of property but as a control of use due to the purpose of the measure in, for example, controlling the importation of gold or fighting drug-trafficking (See Pt IIB: Expropriation and confiscation). This section deals with planning type restrictions and preventive measures.

2. Planning restrictions

(a) General interest

II–541 The Convention organs accept without particular scrutiny planning restrictions which affect development of property or occupation rights. Environmental concerns provide grounds of justification in the most general terms.[6] Reference has been made to the community's general interest in environmental conservation policies being pre-eminent.[7] The aim of protecting cultural, architectural and archeological sites is a strong ground of justification in practice.[8]

(b) Proportionality

II–542 Consideration is given to whether the applicant knew or was subject to the restriction when he took over the property,[9] the existence of legitimate expectations or acceptance of the risk on purchase,[10] the extent to which the restriction prevents use of the land,[11] the availability of procedures importing flexibility and fairness[12] and the possibility of challenging the restriction.[13] Where measures are enforced against use of property for a home for planning reasons related to protection of the

[6] e.g. *Pine Valley*, development refused in green belt; *Fredin*, refusal of exploitation of a gravel pit; (20490/92) (Dec.) March 8, 1994 76–A D.R. 90, enforcement procedures against intensified use of house as Buddhist pilgrimage centre, where planning controls were found necessary to preserve and improve landscapes; *Depalle v France* and *Brosset-Triboulet and Others v France*, March 29, 2010, ECHR 2010–. . . , para.81.

[7] *Depalle*, fn.6 above, para.84, the applicant's argument that conservation interests did not, after his long years of occupation, require demolition of his house was rejected, the Court noting that even if the authorities had been less strict in the past, regional planning policies were evolutive and within State policy sphere, firmer management of coastal lands therefore not raising any problems. See also *Hamer v Belgium*, November 27, 2007, enforcement of a non-building zone in forests.

[8] See *Longobardi v Italy* (7670) (Dec.) June 26, 2007, absolute prohibition on building justifiable to protect views of an important archeological site.

[9] *Allan Jacobsson*, fn.1 above; (11723/85) (Dec.) May 7, 1987, 52 D.R. 250, concerning enforcement proceedings against applicants for use of property for vehicle repair and haulage which had always been unlawful; *Depalle*, fn.6 above, para.86, where the applicant was always aware that his continued occupation of public coastal land was subject to renewable prefectoral decisions.

[10] e.g. *Fredin v Sweden*, February 18, 1990, Series A, No.192, 14 E.H.R.R 319, the Court found no legitimate expectation to continue the exploitation of the gravel pit; *Pine Valley*, where the applicants were involved in commercial development which entailed risk.

[11] e.g. *Allan Jacobsson*, fn.1 above, where the applicant had one house on the property in which he could live but could not build a second; *Longobardi*, fn.8 above, concerning the imposition of an absolute building ban due to the vicinity of a heritage site, it was noted that this did not prevent the applicants continuing their prior usage of the land, and that during the period when building had been possible, they had shown no indication of wanting to build, as they made no application.

[12] e.g. *Allan Jacobsson*, fn.1 above, where prohibitions were reviewed every few years and applications for exceptions were possible.

[13] *Papastavrou v Greece*, April 10, 2003, para.37, inability to challenge merits of decision to zone land for reafforestation.

environment, the lawfulness of the initial occupation is highly relevant, if not decisive. In *Chapman v UK*, where a gypsy family had taken up unauthorised residence on their land in a Green Belt area, the Court stated that it would be slow to grant protection to those in conscious defiance of the law. Nor did it consider that humanitarian considerations could be relied on to exempt even applicants in difficult personal circumstances from planning laws. However, even where applicants had been in long-term and lawful occupation of homes on public coastal lands, the fact that their occupation had always been subject to renewed grants of permission and the importance of environmental policies in the general interest weighed more heavily than the impact on the applicants who were required to demolish their homes without any compensation.[14] Similarly, an order of demolition of a house built in a strictly-prohibited non-construction forestry zone was justifiable notwithstanding some 37 years of occupation.[15]

Indeed, relatively few situations have arisen where control of use in the planning sphere has been found disproportionate to the general interest being pursued.[16]

For example, where in *Tre Traktrorer v Sweden*, a restaurant lost its licence to sell alcohol, there was a control of use of the business and premises but no violation. There had been a progression of measures having regard to the company's discrepancies in its book keeping on alcoholic beverages and although there was a heavy burden on the company to justify itself (it alleged the shortfall was from thefts) there was a wide margin of appreciation and the measure not disproportionate.[17] In *Phocas v France*, where the restriction imposed on the applicant's ability to develop his property by an urban development plan was treated as an interference with enjoyment of possessions, the measure was found not disproportionate since there were procedures by which the applicant could require the State to buy his property. Refusal of the authorities to expropriate, and thus pay compensation for, land zoned as roads for a large area of building plots was found to inflict an excessive burden on the applicant company which could not use the land for anything else and had to build and maintain the roads which were essentially in public use.[18]

Severe restrictions on use of land, without compensation, due to proximity to listed historic buildings were found acceptable as there was nonetheless some

[14] *Depalle*, fn.6 above, *Brosset-Triboulet v France*, fn.6 above, although the Court did note some flexibility on the part of the authorities who had offered the applicants a chance to continue occupying the land for a further period subject to conditions, which had been refused. Contrast the dissenting minority who considered that requiring demolition after a century of occupation had led the owners to have hopes of permanency was too drastic, particularly since there were no concrete indications that the occupation harmed the coastal environment or that restrictions on use could not have adequately secured the general interest.

[15] *Hamer v Belgium*, fn.7, paras 82–89, demolition was regarded as the appropriate measure in the circumstances, no lesser alternative measure in conformity with the public interest.

[16] Interference with enjoyment of possessions under the first sentence of the first paragraph has been found more frequently where measures have been severe in their effects, e.g. *Sporrong*, fn.5 above, long term restrictions imposed by expropriation permits.

[17] Also (33298/96) (Dec.) October 21, 1998, where the measures prohibiting companies from deboning cattleheads were not regarded as disproportionate, notwithstanding the impact on their business, including closure (some compensation was paid and their capital assets remained); *Andrews v UK*, (37657/97) (Dec.) September 26, 2000, where legislation prohibiting gun shop owners from selling handguns did not impose an excessive individual burden, even though compensation was paid only for guns in stock not the reduction in value of the business; *Gallego Zafra v Spain*, (58229/00) (Dec.) January 14, 2003 (removal of authorisation for pharmacy).

[18] *Bugajny v Poland*, November 6, 2007.

possibility of development in the vicinity and procedures for obtaining permission.[19] Where, however, there was a moratorium preventing return of expropriated property protected since it had become an important museum and no prospect of damages or compensation, a fair balance had not been struck.[20] An excessive burden had been imposed where the applicants' land was declared a site of cultural heritage due to presence of an old Jewish cemetery, preventing any development. There had been no mechanism by which the applicants could either obtain compensation by requiring the State to expropriate the site nor a procedure with adequate safeguards for settling the allocation of appropriate property in exchange.[21] Imposition of strict planning controls in the environmental interest failed to strike a fair balance also, where the State had promised on purchase of an island from the family owners to allow them rights to build on the land which remained to them but had not long after the purchase ignored the contractual agreement, without exploring the possibility of limited development compatible with the area or offering compensation for the loss of building rights.[22]

A disproportionate control of use under the second paragraph of Art.1 was exceptionally found in *Chassagnou v France*, where a law imposed the compulsory transfer of hunting rights over the applicants' land to hunting associations. While it was in the general interest to avoid unregulated hunting and foster the rational management of game, the Court noted the unequal way in which the law affected landowners throughout France and found that the balance was struck unfairly in compelling the applicants, opposed themselves to hunting, to allow others to make use of their land contrary to their personal convictions.[23] Where, in a German case, the hunting regulations applied over the entire country in a coherent manner, thus clearly pursuing the stated goals of public interest, the Court found a fair balance had been struck.[24]

Fines imposed on companies for breaching planning conditions have not been found to breach Art.1 of Protocol No.1, even when high,[25] nor the requirement to remove the offending construction.[26]

Failure by the authorities to enforce decisions striking down illicit constructions impinging on the enjoyment by others of their neighbouring properties have been

[19] *SCEA Ferme de Fresnoy v France*, (61093/00) December 1, 2005.

[20] *Debelianovi v Bulgaria*, March 29, 2007.

[21] *Potomska and Potomski v Poland*, March 29, 2011, paras 65–80, the Court apparently did not accept the Government's arguments that the applicants must have known an old Jewish cemetery was on their land and had in fact obtained the land at knock down value, taking the risk that the land would not be exploitable.

[22] *Richet and Le Ber v France*, November 18, 2010, paras 115–125, the Government argument that the sale terms could not bind future planning regulations and that the applicants' legal advisers could have told them that was not accepted; the Court tends to take the view that Governments should act in good faith.

[23] See conversely *Aschan v Finland*, (37858/97) (Dec.) February 15, 2001, where the granting of fishing rights to the public, without payment of the loss of value to the landowners, was not disproportionate: there were only economic, not moral, objections to the measures; *Posti and Rahko v Finland*, September 24, 2002, where the restriction on fishing in coastal waters under the applicants' leases was a legitimate control of use, for which some compensation was paid.

[24] *Herrmann v Germany*, January 20, 2011, the applicant could claim compensation if the hunt damaged his property. Interestingly, less weight was given in this case to the landowner's personal convictions than in *Chassagnou v France*, April 29, 1999, ECHR 1999–III, 29 E.H.R.R. 615, the case has been referred to the Grand Chamber.

[25] *Valico v Italy*, (70074/01) (Dec.) March 21, 2006.

[26] *Saliba v Malta*, November 8, 2005, reference to wide margin of appreciation.

found in breach, particularly where the failure is flagrant, without excuse and has lasted a long time.[27]

3. Article 6 rights and planning cases

Proceedings relating to property rights, including disputes as to permitted use of the land, concern civil rights and obligations. However, following *Bryan v UK* it appears that limited court review of points of law in planning cases may suffice insofar as access to court is concerned. In *Bryan*, where the applicant alleged that the procedures before planning inspectors from which limited appeal lay to the High Court were insufficient to comply with the requirements of Art.6, para.1, the Court commented that limited review was a frequent feature of systems of judicial control of administrative decisions throughout Member States and this case illustrated the typical exercise of discretionary judgment in the regulation of citizens' conduct in the sphere of town and country planning. It found that the limited review by the High Court of factual questions was reasonably to be expected in specialised areas of law where the facts were already established in a quasi-judicial procedure conforming with many of the safeguards of Art.6, para.1. Thus, the Court found that the planning inspector was bound to decide fairly and impartially and gave a fair hearing, notwithstanding a lack of independence or decision-making power, and that the High Court's review powers were sufficient. II–543

4. Preventive measures

Measures aimed at preventing persons suspected of involvement in organised crime from using their property constitute a control of use and have generally been found to pursue the general interest and to be proportionate, in which context adequate procedural safeguards against arbitrariness are required.[28] In *Raimondo v Italy*, where the seizure was a temporary measure, the Court found that it aimed at preventing the use of property in organised crime, which purpose appeared to be decisive in light of the Court's emphasis on the importance of fighting mafia crime, in which context confiscation of this kind was a real and effective weapon. While the initial measures were not disproportionate however, the Court did find a violation when, after the domestic court ordered the property restored, there was a delay in removing the measures from the public register.[29] Since the court had ordered rectification, the continuation of the measure was neither provided for by law or necessary in public interest. II–544

5. Administrative measures

The imposition of levies or charges on milk producers is regarded as a control of use but a wide margin of appreciation applies, the general interest is strong and the Community framework presumed to give due protection to individual interests.[30] II–545

[27] *Paudicio v Italy*, May 24, 2007.

[28] (12386/86) (Dec.) April 15, 1991, 70 D.R. 59, where there was confiscation of property from a person suspected of mafia membership, the Commission found it was clearly in the general interest as designed to prevent the illicit use of possessions the lawful origin of which was not established, the State enjoying wide scope in preventive measures in face of a disturbing level of organised crime. It gave attention to whether there were effective judicial guarantees allowing the applicant a reasonable opportunity to put his case. Since a court established the facts in adversarial proceedings and there was no indication of arbitrary assessment of evidence, the measures were not disproportionate.

[29] A blot had remained on the title and caused practical difficulties in use.

[30] *Coopérative des agriculteurs de Mayenne and Coopérative laitière Maine-Anjou v France*, (16931/04) (Dec.) October 10, 2006.

Annulment of concession agreements for electricity transmission between the State and private companies was regarded as a control of use of possessions in the public interest; the lack of compensation for the annulment, based on fault-based reasons upheld during domestic court proceedings, did not offend against the public interest background.[31]

Cross-reference

Part IIB, s.17: Expropriation and confiscation.
Part IIB, s.24: Gypsies and minorities.
Part IIB, s.26: Home.
Part IIB, s.28: Housing and tenancy.
Part IIB, s.38: Property.

[31] *Uzan v Turkey*, (18240/03) (Dec.) March 29, 2010, the applicants had also been duly warned and given the opportunity to improve performance before the annulment.

35. Pre-trial detention

Key provision:

Article 5, para.3. II–546

Key case-law:

Neumeister v Austria, June 27, 1968, Series A, No.8, 1 E.H.R.R. 91; *Matznetter v Austria*, November 10, 1979, Series A, No.10, 1 E.H.R.R. 198; *De Jong, Baljet and Van Den Brink v Netherlands*, May 22, 1984, Series A, No.77, 13 E.H.R.R. 433; *Brogan v UK*, November 29, 1988, Series A, No.145–B, 11 E.H.R.R. 117; *B v Austria*, March 28, 1990, Series A, No.175, 13 E.H.R.R. 20; *Huber v Switzerland*, October 23, 1990, Series A, No.188; *Letellier v France*, June 26, 1991, Series A, No.207, 14 E.H.R.R. 83; *Kemmache v France (No.1)*, November 27, 1991, Series A, No.218, 14 E.H.R.R. 520; *Toth v Austria*, December 12, 1991, Series A, No.224, 14 E.H.R.R. 551; *Clooth v Au*stria, December 12, 1991, Series A, No.225, 14 E.H.R.R. 717; *Tomasi v France*, August 27, 1992, Series A, No.241–A, 15 E.H.R.R. 1; *Brincat v Italy*, November 26, 1992, Series A, No.249–A, 17 E.H.R.R. 60; *W v Switzerland*, January 26, 1993, Series A, No.254–A, 16 E.H.R.R. 591; *Yagci and Sargin v Turkey*, June 8, 1995, Series A, No.319, 20 E.H.R.R. 505; *Mansur v Turkey*, June 8, 1995, Series A, No.319–B, 20 E.H.R.R. 535; *Van der Tang v Spain*, July 13, 1995, Series A, No.321; *Aksoy v Turkey*, December 18, 1996, R.J.D. 1996–VI, No.26, 23 E.H.R.R. 553; *Scott v Spain*, December 18, 1996, R.J.D. 1996–VI, No.27, 24 E.H.R.R. 391; *Muller v France*, March 17, 1997, R.J.D. 1997–II, No.32; *Sakik v Turkey*, November 26, 1997, R.J.D. 1997–VII, No.58; 26 E.H.R.R. 662; *Assenov v Bulgaria*, October 28, 1998, R.J.D. 1998–VIII, No.96, 31 E.H.R.R. 372; *Hood v UK*, February 18, 1999, ECHR 1999–I, 29 E.H.R.R. 365; *Aquilina v Malta*, April 29, 1999, ECHR 1999–III; *Caballero v UK*, February 8, 2000, ECHR 2000–II, 30 E.H.R.R. 643; *Labita v Italy*, April 6, 2000, ECHR 2000–IV; *Jecius v Lithuania*, July 31, 2000, ECHR 2000–IX; *Kudla v Poland*, October 26, 2000, ECHR 2000–XI; *Kalashnikov v Russia*, July 15, 2002, ECHR 2002–VI; *McKay v UK*, October 3, 2006, ECHR 2006–. . . ; *Mangouras v Spain*, September 28, 2010, ECHR 2010–. . .

1. General considerations

There are two principal aspects under Art.5, para.3—first, concerning the time permissible for a person arrested on reasonable suspicion of committing an offence (or the other two grounds under Art.5, para.1(c)) to be held before being brought before a judicial officer; secondly, limiting the time on which a person should be held pending trial. II–547

While there is no right to bail as such, Art.5, para.3 does not give the judicial authorities the choice between bringing the accused to trial within a reasonable time or granting him provisional release, as the purpose of the provision is essentially to require release once continuing detention ceases to be reasonable.[1] The presumption is always in favour of freedom.

[1] *Neumeister v Austria*, June 27, 1968, Series A, No.8, 1 E.H.R.R. 91, para.4; *Jablonski v Poland*, December 21, 2000, para.83.

2. Initial arrest period

II–548 It is a fundamental safeguard against abuse of power by the police or any equivalent officer with the power of arrest or detention that the person is brought "promptly" before a judicial authority. It prevents oppression, coercion, arbitrary arrest and ill-treatment, giving less opportunity for marks to fade or for a person's will to be broken by pressure and isolation.[2] The Convention organs have emphasised the importance of judicial control against arbitrary deprivation of liberty as fundamental ingredient of the rule of law.[3]

Two principal issues have arisen in the case-law: exactly what qualifies as "promptly" and as a judicial officer.

(a) Promptly

II–549 The Court has held that the degree of flexibility attaching to the notion is very limited. While individual circumstances must be taken into account in assessing promptness, their significance can never be taken to the point of impairing the very essence of the right.[4]

Brogan v UK indicates that four days may in exceptional circumstances, such as the difficulties attaching to terrorist investigations, be acceptable but beyond four days was unacceptable, exceeding the plain meaning of the word "promptly" and allowing a serious weakening of the guarantee to the extent of impairing its essence.[5] In later cases, where the Government have relied on the exigencies of terrorist crime, the Court has refused to allow this to be used as a *carte blanche* by investigating authorities and has generally not accepted any period in excess of four days.[6] More than four days is regarded as prima facie too long.[7] Where juveniles are concerned, standards are stricter; three days and nine hours was not sufficiently prompt due to their status as minors, the lack of adequate safeguards available such as access to a lawyer and no indication as to any compelling reason for not bringing them before a judge sooner.[8]

For ordinary crimes, it would seem that the Court would set a shorter maximum but the point is as yet not expressly decided, save in one case where 3 days and 23 hours for a suspect arrested for a minor non-violent offence was found insufficiently prompt.[9] Excuses for more than four days are unlikely to be successful. A delay of

[2] *Aksoy v Turkey*, December 18, 1996, R.J.D. 1996–VI, No.26, 23 E.H.R.R. 553, para.76; the importance of this safeguard re-iterated in *Dikme v Turkey*, July 11, 2000, ECHR 2000–VIII, para.66.

[3] *Brogan v UK*, November 29, 1988, Series A, No.145–B, 11 E.H.R.R. 117, para.58; re-emphasised, inter alia, in *Sakik v Turkey*, November 26, 1997, R.J.D. 1997–VII, No.58; 26 E.H.R.R. 662, para.44.

[4] *Brogan*, fn.3 above, para.59.

[5] Violations found for periods of 4 days and 6 hours; 4 days and 11 hours; 5 days and 11 hours; and 6 days and 16 and a half hours. See also breach found in *O'Hara v UK*, October 16, 2001, ECHR 2001–X, 6 days and 13 hours.

[6] *Sakik*, fn.3 above, para.44 (12–14 days); also, *Gunay v Turkey*, September 27, 2001 (5–11 days); *Dikme*, fn.2 above, para.66, the Court rejected the Goverment's argument that the investigation required a longer period as the evidence had to be gathered from the suspects themselves.

[7] *Oral and Atabay v Turkey*, June 23, 2007, paras 43–44, violations for 4 days and 4 hours, and 4 days and 2 hours.

[8] *Ipek v Turkey*, February 3, 2009, paras 36–37, the police were not using the time for any essential investigative measures for example.

[9] *Kandzhov v Bulgaria*, November 6, 2008, para.66, no exceptional circumstances or special difficulties preventing the suspect being brought before a judge sooner.

five days for an applicant to be brought before a military court was not found to be justified on the basis of an intervening weekend and the involvement of personnel in manoeuvres, since this eventuality was foreseeable and steps could have been taken, such as sitting over the weekend.[10] Since the onus is on the authorities to provide judicial supervision, the arrested person cannot himself be blamed for taking any wrong procedural steps.[11] Nor was the excuse of bad weather accepted for seven days' delay.[12] However, in highly unusual circumstances, where applicant crew members were arrested by a naval vessel thousands of nautical miles from port, the Court found that the 13 days which it took to bring them before a judge did not breach the requirement of promptness as it was not apparent that this took longer than was practicable in the circumstances; the Court also noted with approval that on landfall the suspects only remained some eight—nine hours in police custody before being brought before a judicial authority.[13]

Extension of the period to seven days for terrorist suspects was found to be compatible with the power to derogate under Art.15, where this was limited by the exigencies of a state of emergency and attended by safeguards against abuse.[14] Extension of the period to 14 days in Turkey was considered prima facie to be too long, impliedly with or without attendant safeguards.[15] (See Pt IIB—Derogation).

The review of the merits of police or administrative detention should be automatic. It is insufficient that an applicant can apply for review.[16] Article 5, para.3 however does not include a right to be brought repeatedly before a judge.[17]

(b) Judge or other officer authorised by law to exercise judicial power

The judicial officer does not have to hold the status of a judge but he must have some of a judge's attributes or guarantees. This includes independence of the executive and of the parties; the procedural requirement of hearing the individual himself; the substantive requirement of reviewing the continuation of the detention by reference to legal criteria; and the power to order release.[18] **II–550**

Appearance before a court is not by itself a sufficient guarantee, where the question of justification for the continued detention is not to be dealt with until later.[19] Where the officer or tribunal has no power to release, they lack the requisite

[10] *Koster v Netherlands*, November 28, 1991, Series A, No.221

[11] *Samoila and Cionca v Romania*, March 4, 2008, para.48, no supervision of legality for nine days.

[12] *Ocalan v Turkey*, May 12, 2005, para.104.

[13] *Medvedyev v France*, March 29, 2010, ECHR 2010–. . . , paras 127–134. See similarly for arrest on high seas, *Rigopoulos v Spain*, (37388/97) (Dec.) January 12, 1999, ECHR 1999–II, 16 day delay acceptable in the exceptional circumstances.

[14] *Brannigan and McBride v UK*, May 26, 1993, Series A, No.258–B, a breach was found for 6 days and 14 hours, and 6 days and 6 hours respectively, but covered by the UK derogation in respect of the threats to the nation from terrorism.

[15] *Aksoy*, fn.2 above, paras 82–84.

[16] e.g. *De Jong, Baljet and Van Den Brink v Netherlands*, May 22, 1984, Series A, No.77, 13 E.H.R.R. 433, para.51; *Aquilina v Malta*, April 29, 1999, ECHR 1999–III, para.49; *Sabeur Ben Ali v Malta*, June 29, 2000, para.31.

[17] *Grauzinas v Lithuania*, October 10, 2000, para.25. Although Art.5, para.4 may in certain cases require a person be brought before a judge for the purpose of contesting the lawfulness of his detention when it lasts a long time: *Jecius v Lithuania*, July 31, 2000, ECHR 2000–IX, para.84.

[18] *Scheisser v Switzerland*, December 4, 1979, Series A, No.34, para.31.

[19] *Van der Sluijs, Suiderveld and Klappe v Netherlands*, May 22, 1984, Series A No.78, para.46.

judicial power.[20] A breach will therefore arise where the judicial officer has no power to release by operation of law, as for example, where a statutory provision removes the judge's discretion to release in certain categories of cases.[21] A magistrate's power of review must also be sufficiently wide to encompass the lawfulness of the arrest and detention and the existence of reasonable suspicion in the terms of Art.5, para.1(c): it does not have to encompass issues of release with or without conditions, which falls under the second limb, as concerning the reasonableness of continuing detention pending trial.[22]

An officer who combines functions of investigation and prosecution is likely to be lacking in independence and impartiality. There was a breach where the *auditeur militaire*, though independent from the military authorities, could be called upon to perform prosecution functions once a case was referred to the military court and was therefore not independent of the parties to the potential criminal proceedings.[23] Similarly, in *Huber v Switzerland*, where a district attorney took decisions relating to detention and also conducted the investigation and drew up the indictment, there was a violation.[24] Although the district attorney did not in fact act as prosecutor in the final proceedings, as was possible under the applicable procedure, he could not be regarded as independent of the parties and his impartiality was capable of appearing open to doubt. Though the Court has not ruled out that a judicial officer may carry out other functions, he must do so without calling his impartiality and independence into doubt. It is the objective appearances at the time of decision of detention on remand which are material.[25]

(c) Other procedural safeguards

II–551 Representation by a lawyer has not been found to be required for the purposes of Art.5, para.3[26] though issues may arise under Art.6 para.3(c) (see Pt IIA—Legal representation in criminal proceedings). The Court has also referred to Art.5, para.3 requiring the judicial officer to set out in the decision on detention the facts upon which that decision is based[27]; it has stressed the importance of "formal visible

[20] e.g. *De Jong*, fn.16 above, where the *auditeur militaire* made non-binding recommendations albeit accepted in practice; *Assenov v Bulgaria*, October 28, 1998, R.J.D. 1998–VIII, No.96, 31 E.H.R.R. 372, para.148, where the applicant was brought before an investigator whose decisions as to release, not legally binding, could be overturned by a prosecutor.

[21] e.g. mutatis mutandis, *Caballero v UK*, February 8, 2000, ECHR 2000–II, 30 E.H.R.R. 643; *SBC v UK*, June 19, 2001, breach of Art.5, para.3 where legislation removed the possibility of bail in serious cases.

[22] *McKay v UK*, October 3, 2006, ECHR 2006–. . . , paras 39–40. See, e.g. *Aquilina*, fn.16 above, violation where the magistrate could only examine one ground of lawfulness of his own motion.

[23] *De Jong*, fn.16 above, para.49.

[24] *Huber v Switzerland*, October 23, 1990, Series A, No.188, paras 42–43, which reversed *Scheisser*, fn.18 above, para.34, which appeared to indicate that it was the effective concurrent exercise of dual functions which was problematic.

[25] Also *Brincat v Italy*, November 26, 1992, Series A, No.249–A, 17 E.H.R.R. 60, para.41; *Hood v UK*, February 18, 1999, ECHR 1999–I, 29 E.H.R.R. 365, paras 57–58, where the applicant's commanding officer took decisions on pre-trial detention and was also liable to intervene in subsequent proceedings on behalf of the prosecuting authority; cases concerning decisions on pre-trial detention taken by Polish prosecutors, e.g. *Niedbala v Poland*, July 4, 2000, para.53, where the Court dismissed the Government argument that the prosecutors had a judicial status as guardians of the public interest.

[26] *Scheisser*, fn.18 above, para.36.

[27] *Scheisser*, fn.18 above, para.31; *Letellier v France*, June 26, 1991, Series A, No.207, 14 E.H.R.R. 83, para.35.

requirements stated in the 'law'" as opposed to standard practices.[28] In *Hood v UK*, it commented on the lack of any written record or opportunity for the applicant to make submissions but made no ruling on this aspect.[29]

(d) Relationship with Article 5, paragraph 4: review of lawfulness of detention

Article 5, para.4 is a guarantee of a different order to, and additional to, that provided by Art.5 para.3. They can be applied concurrently, though obviously the procedure for bringing a person before a judge may have a certain incidence on compliance with para.4.[30] Conversely, compliance with Art.5, para.3 cannot be ensured by making an Art.5, para.4 remedy available as the review must be automatic.[31] II–552

3. Length of detention on remand

It is not necessary that the magistrate who first verifies the lawfulness and grounds of arrest and attention deal also with bail and no requirement of promptness as such. However, the question of release should be examined with due expedition, in order to keep any unjustified deprivation of liberty to an acceptable minimum.[32] A blanket removal of the judicial control of pre-trial detention of certain categories of offences is not acceptable.[33] II–553

As concerns the continuation of detention on remand, the role of the domestic authorities is seen as ensuring that the pre-trial detention of an accused person does not exceed a reasonable period. They must examine all the circumstances arguing for or against the existence of a genuine public interest justifying, with due regard to the presumption of innocence, a departure from the rule of respect for individual liberty and set them out in decisions on the applications for release. It is essentially on the basis of the reasons given in these domestic decisions and of the established facts mentioned by the applicant in his appeals that the Court considers it is called upon to decide whether or not there has been a violation of Art.5, para.3.[34]

Continuation of a reasonable suspicion that the applicant has committed an offence (the principal ground under Art.5, para.1(c)) is a sine qua non for the validity of the detention but with the lapse of time this no longer suffices and the Court must then establish whether the other grounds given by the judicial authorities continued to justify the deprivation of liberty. Such grounds must be relevant and sufficient and the competent national authorities must display "special diligence" in the conduct of the proceedings.[35] A period of detention may not be

[28] *Duinhof and Duijf v Netherlands*, May 22, 1984, Series A, No.79, para.34.

[29] *Hood*, fn.25 above, para.60.

[30] e.g. *De Jong*, fn.16 above, where there was both a breach of Art.5, para.3 for delays of 7, 11 and 6 days before the applicants were brought before a court and a breach of Art.5, para.4 for an inability to obtain review of the lawfulness of their detention over the same period.

[31] *Aquilina*, fn.16 above, para.53.

[32] e.g. *McKay*, fn.22 above, para.46, three days was acceptable. The Court did not specify any upper limit but commented that it would not be less than the four days set out in *Brogan*.

[33] *Caballero*, fn.21 above, the Government conceded that s.25 of the Criminal Justice Act 1994, in removing the power to grant bail for serious offences, breached Art.5, para.3; *SBC v UK*, fn.21 above, the Court made an express finding of breach as regards the automatic denial of bail.

[34] e.g. *McKay*, fn.22 above, para.43.

[35] See, e.g. *Yagci and Sargin v Turkey*, June 8, 1995, Series A, No.319, 20 E.H.R.R. 505, para.50; *Letellier*, fn.27 above, para.35.

justified on the basis of the alleged shortness of time alone.[36] In the absence of reasons, or where an uninformative stereotyped form of decision is given by the courts, it would be unnecessary to consider whether they acted with particular diligence since there would be no sufficient grounds for the continued detention.[37] Thus, where the courts do not properly examine the issues or set sufficient grounds in their decisions, even relatively short periods of some months will offend due to lack of any apparent justification for the detention.[38] The Government cannot rely on grounds or evidence which were not referred to by the courts.[39]

The period of detention is calculated from the date of arrest/commencement of detention on Art.5, para.1(c) grounds until the judgment/conviction at first instance.[40] In systems where cases are remitted to first instance and there are consecutive periods of pretrial detention, the Court takes a cumulative approach in calculating the overall periods spent in detention.[41]

Assessment of reasonableness can take into account a period of detention which is itself outside the Convention' organs competence *ratione temporis*, since whether continued detention in the later period is justified may depend on how much time has already been spent in custody.[42]

A period of many years will appear prima facie unreasonable and will require exceptional circumstances to justify it.[43]

Article 5, para.3 does not place an obligation on authorities to release a detainee due to ill-health. Whether his condition is compatible with detention is largely a matter for the national courts and though issues could potentially arise under Art.3 that provision has not been interpreted as requiring release on health grounds or placement in a civil hospital to receive particular treatment.[44] However, where a detainee's state of health is so grave that trial proceedings have been suspended and treatment is precarious in prison, further detention may cease to have any meaningful purpose and may render that measure of restraint incompatible with Article 5.[45]

[36] *Yagci and Sargin*, fn.35 above, para.54.

[37] e.g. in *Mansur v Turkey*, June 8, 1995, Series A, No.319–B, 20 E.H.R.R. 535, where the court gave sterotyped identical orders renewing detention and on three occasions no reasons were given; *Yagci and Sargin*, fn.36 above, where the courts looked at the case four times in a three-month period, but gave stereotyped refusals, with no explanation of why there was a danger of absconding.

[38] *Stoican v Romania*, October 6, 2009, paras 40–44, periods of five, six and eight months.

[39] e.g. *Sarban v Moldova*, October 4, 2005, para.102; *LeLievre v Belgium*, November 8, 2007, para.104; *Aleksanyan v Russia*, December 22, 2008, para.183.

[40] *B v Austria*, March 28, 1990, Series A, No.175, 13 E.H.R.R. 20, para.39, even where domestic law classifies detention pending appeal as detention on remand; *Kudla v Poland*, October 26, 2000, ECHR 2000–XI, para.104.

[41] See e.g. *Solmaz v Turkey*, January 16, 2007, para.36, this may appear common sense but raised particular issues as to application of the six-month rule in which conflicting approaches had to be resolved.

[42] e.g. *Mansur*, fn.37 above, 1 year and 28 days after recognition of the Court's compulsory jurisdiction but five years and three months before; *Kalashnikov v Russia*, July 15, 2002, ECHR 2002–VI, 1 year, 2 months and 29 days after the Convention entered into force for Russia, but two years, ten months and six days before; *Prencipe v Monaco*, July 16, 2009, two years before, two years after approximately.

[43] *Lelievre v Belgium*, fn.39 above, para.91, a period of seven years and ten months.

[44] *Jablonski*, fn.1 above, para.82, citing *Kudla*, fn.40 above, para.93.

[45] See *Aleksanyan v Russia*, fn.39 above, paras 191–197, there had also been a breach of Art.3 due to lack of adequate medical care for the applicant's conditions, which included HIV and related illnesses.

(a) Relevant and sufficient grounds

(i) Seriousness of the alleged offences and strength of suspicion

Existence and persistence of serious indications of guilt are relevant but cannot alone justify a long period of pre-trial detention and cannot be used to anticipate a custodial sentence.[46] After a certain period of time, persistence of reasonable suspicion no longer suffices and the Court examines whether the other grounds relied on by the judicial authorities justify the deprivation of liberty.[47] It is not apparent up to what moment, or lapse of time that suspicion alone will continue to justify detention but it is likely to be a matter of months at most. The Commission found a violation in the period of 14 months in *Can v Austria*[48], while in *Jecius v Lithuania* the Court considered that suspicion against the applicant of having committed murder may initially have justified his detention but it could not constitute a "relevant and sufficient" ground for his being held in custody for almost fifteen months.[49] Shorter periods may well offend in particular circumstances. For example, where a minor was concerned who was being held in an adult prison, a period of 48 days exceeded what was justifiable merely due to the "state of the evidence". The Court has indeed expressed repeated concern about the practice of keeping children in pre-trial detention at all.[50] II–554

For reasonable suspicion to persist there must be facts or information satisfying an objective observer that the person concerned may have committed an offence. In *Labita v Italy*, the Court considered that while a suspect might be validly detained at the beginning of proceedings on the basis of *pentiti* statements (informant evidence raising issues of reliability) they necessarily became less relevant with the passage of time, particularly when no further evidence was uncovered. Where in this case the statements were uncorroborated and in fact contradicted, very compelling reasons were required to justify the applicant's detention for two years and seven months. The longer the pre-trial period of detention the stronger the reasons would have to be.[51]

It is not compatible with Art.5, para.3 for the burden to be placed on the applicant to establish grounds for his release, as this would be tantamount to overturning the purpose of the provision which makes detention an exceptional departure from the right to liberty. Thus, where the law provides for a presumption in respect of factors relevant to continued detention, the concrete facts outweighing the rule of respect for individual liberty must still be convincingly demonstrated.[52]

[46] e.g. a period of five years and seven months in *Tomasi v France*, August 27, 1992, Series A, No.241–A, 15 E.H.R.R. 1, para.89.

[47] *Letellier*, fn.27 above, para.35.

[48] (9300/81) (Rep.) July 12, 1984, Series A, No.96 (settled before the Court).

[49] *Jecius*, fn.16 above, para.94, particularly as the suspicion was proved unsubstantiated by the trial court which acquitted him.

[50] *Nart v Turkey*, May 6, 2008, paras 31–35. See also *Selcuk v Turkey*, January 10, 2006, para.35, where a 16–year-old was held for four months pre-trial in an adult prison: violation; *Guvec v Turkey*, January 20, 2009, paras 108–109, where a minor spent four-and-a-half-years on remand from age 15: violation.

[51] *PB v France*, August 1, 2000, para.30, particularly strong reasons required to justify a period of four years and eight months.

[52] *Ilijkov v Bulgaria*, July 26, 2001, para.85, violation where the courts relied on the presumption that the person should be detained unless he showed exceptional circumstances and made no mention of any concrete facts that might justify continued detention. See also *Rokhlina v Russia*, April 7, 2005, para.67, not for accused to show no risk of collusion or absconding.

(II) PROTECTION OF PUBLIC ORDER

II–555 Some offences by their gravity and the public reaction to them may give rise to public disquiet capable of justifying pre-trial detention at least for a time. However, the Court has rejected Government claims on this ground in a number of cases, considering that this can only provide justification in exceptional circumstances and must be based on sufficient evidence of facts indicating that the accused's release would actually disturb public order. There was insufficient evidence in *Letellier v France* where the Government referred to the "profound and lasting" disturbance to public order resulting from a premeditated murder.[53] While in *Tomasi v France*, where an officer was involved in an armed terrorist attack which resulted in death and serious injuries, some risk of disorder might have existed at the beginning but it must have disappeared after a certain time.[54]

(III) RISK OF PRESSURE ON WITNESSES OR COLLUSION WITH CO-ACCUSED

II–556 This is a relevant and unexceptional ground but as soon as the risk diminishes the ground will no longer be valid. With the passage of time, risk to the gathering of evidence has often been found to disappear, as in *Kemmache v France (No.1)* when the witnesses were questioned, the file was closed and sent to court. Where, as in *W v Switzerland*, findings of risk of collusion and interference are maintained on the basis of scrupulous examination of the evolving circumstances, the Court is unlikely to disagree but if, as in *Clooth v Austria*, decisions continuing detention are stereotyped and refer to the needs of investigation in a general and abstract fashion, it may be found that the detention ceases to be justified on this basis.[55]

(IV) RISK OF REPETITION OF OFFENCES

II–557 The Court and Commission have accepted the view of domestic courts that the existence of previous convictions for similar offences gives grounds for reasonable fears that the applicant might commit new offences.[56] But where domestic authorities relied on an alleged precarious psychological state of the suspect shown by previous offences of a different kind, this was found only to furnish a ground for extending confinement if accompanied by therapeutic measures.[57] A reference to the person's antecedents is not sufficient to justify refusing release.[58]

(V) DANGER OF ABSCONDING

II–558 The risk of absconding has to be assessed in light of the factors relating to the person's character, his morals, home, occupation, assets, family ties and all kinds of links with the country in which he is prosecuted. The expectation of heavy sentence

[53] *Kemmache (No.1)*, November 27, 1991, Series A, No.218, 14 E.H.R.R. 520, para.52, counterfeiting did not qualify.

[54] e.g. *Olstowski v Poland*, November 15, 2001, para.78, where the courts' reliance on the "heavy load of social harmfulness" of the offence could not by itself justify lengthy detention (almost three years and three months); *Prencipe v Monaco*, fn.42 above, paras 78–81, alleged risks not specified or sufficient to justify the detention.

[55] Also *Debboub alias Husseini Ali v France*, November 9, 1999, para.44, where the courts did not explain the basis of the alleged risk; *Szeloch v Poland*, February 22, 2001, para.91, where the decisions were succinct, absent concrete facts and repetitive; *Prencipe*, fn.42 above, para.86, risk not specified or explained.

[56] *Toth v Austria*, December 12, 1991, Series A, No.224, 14 E.H.R.R. 551, para.70.

[57] *Clooth v Austria*, December 12, 1991, Series A, No.225, 14 E.H.R.R. 717, para.40.

[58] *Muller v France*, March 17, 1997, R.J.D. 1997–II, No.32, para.44.

and the weight of evidence may be relevant but not as such decisive and the possibility of obtaining guarantees (e.g. payment of security, other forms of judicial supervision) may have to be used to offset any risk.[59] If the risk of absconding can be offset by bail or other guarantees, the Court has gone so far as to state the accused must then be released.[60] Furthermore the domestic courts must consider alternatives of their own motion; nor can the applicant be blamed for failing to raise the matter or specify the types of alternative measures which he would accept.[61] On the other hand, where other grounds are also relied upon to justify continued detention, inability to consider alternative guarantees does not pose a problem as such.[62]

The Convention organs have criticised domestic courts which rely on this ground without indicating any factual basis, repeat stereotyped decisions or fail to consider the possibility of obtaining guarantees from applicants to ensure their appearance, e.g. financial conditions. In *Tomasi v France*, the Court considered that the domestic courts gave no proper consideration to this aspect, their decisions unreasoned as to why the risk of absconding was decisive despite the applicant's clean record and status as shopkeeper.[63] The fact that he faced a serious prison sentence if convicted could not be the sole basis for finding such a risk.[64] On the other hand, where the likely sentence can be anticipated and the period in detention deductible, the lessening incentive to abscond should be taken into account.[65]

There must be continued grounds for believing the risk to subsist. In *Kemmache v France (No.1)*, there was some basis for suspicions since the applicant had previously failed to appear before the court on spurious grounds of car "mechanical" failure. Since however the courts did not rely on this reason after a particular date and added no fresh grounds, it could not be used to justify further detention.[66] However, findings of links with foreign countries, including funds or family, have provided sufficient grounds.[67] Although, even where there are sufficient grounds for fear of flight, as in *Erdem v Germany* where the alleged PKK terrorist suspect had no links with Germany, this could not justified prolonged detention up to 5 years and 11 months.[68] However, in contrast in *Chraidi v Germany*, the danger of absconding of a Lebanese terrorist suspect with no local ties was exceptionally found to justify a period of over five years and six months, where no other alternative guarantees were applicable and the courts had showed special diligence throughout.[69]

[59] e.g. *Letellier, Matzenetter, Hauschildt v Denmark* (10486/83) (Dec.) October 9, 1986, 49 D.R. 86.

[60] *Mangouras v Spain*, September 28, 2010, ECHR 2010 . . . , para.79.

[61] *Lelievre*, fn.39, paras 991–102.

[62] *Krejcir v Czech Republic*, March 26, 2009, paras 100–104.

[63] See also *Sarban*, fn.39 above, abstract, stereotyped decisions which did not explain how the grounds related to the facts of the applicant's case; *Moiseyev v Russia*, October 9, 2008, paras 152–155, no specific facts mentioned to support ground of risk of absconding.

[64] See also. *Letellier*, fn.27 above, para.43, concerning a mother of two children who ran a business.

[65] *Can*, fn.48 above.

[66] See also *Kudla v Poland*, fn.40 above, paras 111–115, where the applicant's initial failure to give an address for service and a medical certificate could not justify detention for two years and four months, no other element being adduced to support the alleged risk of absconding.

[67] e.g. *W v Switzerland*, January 26, 1993, Series A, No.254–A, 16 E.H.R.R. 591; *Van der Tang v Spain*, July 13, 1995, Series A, No.321. See also *Czesky v Czech Republic*, June 6, 2000, para.79, where the applicant had left the country and obtained a false passport; *Tinner v Switzerland*, April 26, 2011, para.56, suspects had no strong links with the country, one had his family in Thailand.

[68] *Erdem v Germany*, July 5, 2001, ECHR 2001–VII, para.44. See also *Adamiak v Poland*, December 19, 2006, over five years not justified by fear of flight in organised crime case.

[69] *Chraidi v Germany*, October 26, 2006.

Regarding the type or level of guarantees that may be legitimately required by domestic authorities, these are not limited to money but can include residence and movement restrictions.[70] The level of bail set should not be set too high and should not be aimed at reparation of loss but to ensure the presence of the accused.[71] The Court requires care to be taken by the authorities in assessing the appropriate amount of bail. Where the applicant is implicated in large scale, fraudulent financial dealings, higher sums may not be unreasonable.[72] Similarly, while the personal circumstances of the accused and his assets must be the principal criterion, it is not unreasonable in certain situations to take into account the amount of loss imputed to him. Thus, where a ship's captain was arrested in relation to a disastrous oil spill causing huge environmental and economic damage and bail was set in the sum of 3 million euros, the Court found that it was legitimate to take into account the implications for criminal and civil liability to ensure that the persons responsible had no incentive to evade justice. Even though the captain himself had no assets to cover such a sum, the courts could have regard to his employee relationship with the shipowner and shipowner's insurer who in fact provided the security.[73] Conversely, imposition of a relatively high sum on a mother of a small child and without a steady job failed sufficiently to have regard to her circumstances, resulting in her being retained in detention unjustifiably for over a year.[74]

Where there is a purported risk of flight abroad, the measure of requiring surrender of a passport should be considered, even where a foreign national is concerned.[75]

Continued detention of an applicant while the authorities sorted out the size and modalities of the bail payment led to a breach, where the court had already found that his release would not jeopardise the proceedings.[76]

(vi) Risk of harm to the accused

II–559 Where the accused was implicated in a series of child kidnappings and murders arousing a storm of public outrage and retained in pre-trial custody for over seven years, the Government argument that this was required for his own safety was smartly rejected by the Court as irreconcilable with the rule of law, since Contracting States were required to ensure the safety of all on their territory without recourse to locking them up.[77]

[70] e.g. *Schmid v Austria* (10670/83) (Dec.) July 9, 1985, 44 D.R. 195.

[71] e.g. *Can*, fn.48 above, where the Commission criticised the sum set at the value of property subject to the arson attack rather than assessed vis-à-vis the applicant, his assets and his relation to the persons to provide the security; *Neumeister*, fn.1 above, paras 13–14; *Mangouras*, fn.60 above, para.78; *Skrobol v Poland*, September 13, 2005, para.59.

[72] e.g. *W v Switzerland*, fn.67 above, the rejection of the applicant's offer of a CHF 30,000 guarantee was not unreasonable since the provenance of money unknown and the sum derisory in light of the size of the case (large scale fraud).

[73] *Mangouras*, fn.60 above, paras 82–92. See, however, the minority view which put strict emphasis on the accused's own assets rather than the losses caused by the alleged criminal acts and noted that in fraud cases there had been a strong suspicion of undisclosed assets held by the suspects which justified high levels of bail; in their view, other guarantees of appearance could also have been effectively imposed such as surrender of passport etc.

[74] *Hristova v Bulgaria*, December 7, 2006, paras 110–113; see also *Toshev v Bulgaria*, August 10, 2006, paras 69–72, where the domestic courts failed to carry out a review of the applicant's current financial situation when imposing a bail amount.

[75] *Lind v Russia*, December 6, 2007, para.81; *Aleksanyan*, fn.39 above, para.193.

[76] *Iwanczuk v Poland*, November 15, 2001, paras 68–70: 4 months and 14 day delay.

[77] *Lelievre*, fn.39 above, para.104.

(b) *Conduct of the proceedings: special diligence*

Courts must show "special diligence" in bringing cases of detained persons to trial, notwithstanding the existence of strong suspicion or other relevant grounds for the detention.[78] However, the requirement of special diligence had been held not to stand in the way of the proper administration of justice and there is an obligation on judges to clarify the facts and collect evidence prior to trial.[79] Even where a case was not particularly complex but was delayed when it was joined to another, the joinder was made in the interests of the proper administration of justice and the inevitable slowing down of the case was not incompatible with the speed requirement.[80] A finding of a domestic court of lack of due expedition or an extension of detention beyond the period normally acceptable in domestic law will not necessarily disclose a breach, since domestic and Convention standards may differ and the Court will examine the circumstances as a whole.[81] **II–560**

Consideration is given to the complexity of the investigation, the number of defendants, the nature of the legal issues and the international elements by way of letters rogatory.[82] A substantial gap in proceedings may be fatal as in *Vallon v Italy* where, although the Commission refused to question the merits of the decision to issue letters rogatory, an eight-month delay between the reply and the setting down for trial founded a violation.[83] Also relevant are: errors made by the authorities[84]; unnecessarily cumbersome procedures[85]; frequent adjournments and delays in issuing decisions[86]; the complexity of the case[87]; and the conduct of the applicant.[88] In respect of the latter, applicants are not required to co-operate actively with the

[78] e.g. *Letellier*, fn.27 above, para.35.

[79] e.g. *Matznetter v Austria*, November 10, 1979, Series A, No.10, 1 E.H.R.R. 198, para.12; *B v Austria*, fn.40 above, para.45.

[80] *Van der Tang*, fn.67 above; *Can*, fn.48 above. See also *Ferrari-Bravo v Italy* (9627/81) (Dec.) March 14, 1984, 37 D.R. 15, 4 years and 11 months was justified by the complexity of the affair and the exceptional difficulties due to the terrorist aspects; joining other accused to the case was reasonable for the administration of justice, so it was not required for the cases to be severed.

[81] *Wardle v UK*, (72219/01) (Dec.) March 27, 2003, although the judge criticised the extension obtained by the prosecution by lodging new charges on the expiry of the initial period, the Court noted relevant and sufficient reasons for the detention (previous absconding and offending on release), the complexity of the case and ongoing investigative measures: no lack of necessary despatch overall.

[82] e.g. *Matzenetter*, fn.79 above, para.12; *B v Austria*, fn.40 above, para.45; *Tinner*, fn.67 above, para.62.

[83] *Vallon v Italy*, (Rep.), Series A, No.95. Also *Woukam Moudefo v France*, (Rep.) October 11, 1988, Series A, No.141–B, where there was four-and-a-half months delay before the applicant was interrogated and a delay of a year in acting on the failure of certain witnesses to appear.

[84] In *Tomasi*, fn.46 above, there were numerous errors and omissions by the judicial authorities, e.g. proceedings instituted in courts without jurisdiction.

[85] e.g. *Toth*, fn.56 above, where on each new application for release or for extension in detention, the file was transferred (rather than copies) causing suspension of investigation.

[86] *Punzelt v Czech Republic*, April 25, 2000, paras 78–80; also *Vaccaro v Italy*, November 16, 2000, where no explanation was given, inter alia, for the ten months to transfer from one court jurisdiction to another.

[87] *W v Switzerland*, fn.67, exceptional complexity of large economic crime was a significant factor in finding no violation (by a narrow majority) for over 4 years; complexity of international terrorist crime in *Chraidi*, fn.69 above, over five years acceptable.Conversely, in *Scott v Spain*, December 18, 1996, R.J.D. 1996–VI, No.27, 24 E.H.R.R. 391, after 4 years and 16 days of investigation the alleged difficulties in serving letters rogatory abroad did not justify the delay and the duty of "special diligence" was not observed; *Erdem*, fn.68 above, para.46, the difficulties attaching to trial of PKK suspects did not justify detention of five years and 11 months; nor over five years for organised crime in *Adamiak*, fn.68 above.

[88] e.g. *Kalashnikov*, fn.42 above, where the protracted proceedings were not attributable either to the complexity of the case or the applicant's conduct.

judicial authorities and cannot be blamed for taking full advantage of the resources afforded by national law in their defence. Where conduct of an applicant goes beyond this, revealing an obstructive attitude, or contributing substantially to delaying proceedings, is perhaps a fine line.[89] Delay caused by the applicant will not rule out a breach where the dilatoriness of the authorities is still responsible for a significant lapse of time.[90]

4. Access to family

II–561 The authorities are under an obligation properly to regulate contact between persons detained in police custody and their families. Failure to provide a means enabling rapid communication disclosed a violation of Art.8 where the applicant father had been unable to contact his son who was for nine days in police custody.[91]

Table of lengths of detention

II–562

Previous Convention organs

Quinn v France—1 year: no violation
Can v Austria—14 months and 26 days: Commission violation (settled before the Court)
Di Stefano v UK[92]—19 months: manifestly ill-founded
Deschamps v Belgium[93]—23 months: manifestly ill-founded
Toth v France— 2 years, 1 month and 2 days: violation
Matznetter v Austria— 2 years and almost 2 months: no violation
B v Austria—2 years, 4 months and 15 days: no violation
Letellier v France— 2 years and 9 months: violation
Hauschildt v Denmark[94]—2 years and 9 months: manifestly ill-founded
Kemmache v France (No.1)—2 years and 10 months: violation
Van der Tang v Spain—3 years, 1 month and 27 days: no violation
Clooth v Austria—3 years, 2 months and 4 days: violation
Woukam Moudefo v France—3 years, 2 months and 25 days: Commission violation (settled before the Court)
Muller v France—almost 4 years: violation
W v Switzerland— 4 years and 3 days: no violation (narrow decision—5:4)

[89] *Yagci and Sargin*, fn.35 above, where the Government attacked the applicants' tactics (e.g. filing of evidence and leaving the court in protest at security arrangements) but there was no indication that they were obstructive.
[90] *Trzaska v Poland*, July 11, 2000, where the applicant refused to attend three hearings but the case came to a standstill for over eight months (e.g. change in compostion of court), the period of over four years disclosed a breach overall; *Jablonski*, fn.1 above, where the applicant's hunger strikes and self-mutilation did not prevent a breach for pre-trial detention of three years and nearly ten months.
[91] e.g. *Ucar v Turkey*, April 11, 2006, paras 139–141.
[92] (12391/86) (Dec.) April 13, 1989, 60 D.R. 182. Complex fraud with 100 witnesses and 3,000 pages of documents and though the applicant had strong ties with the United Kingdom for 20 years he was still an Italian citizen and also had alleged links with organised crime abroad.
[93] Dangerous personality, death threats to witness, not unduly prolonged.
[94] See fn.59 above, not excessive due, inter alia, to the substantial activity of the courts (136 court sessions in 18 months).

Scott v Spain—4 years and 16 days: violation
Ferrari-Bravo v Italy[95]—4 years and 11 months: manifestly ill-founded
Tomasi v France—5 years and 7 months: violation

New Court

Nart v Turkey—48 days for a minor: violation.
Stoican v Romania—two periods: 5—6 months and 8 months: violation
Jecius v Lithuania—14 months and16 days: violation
Kalashnikov v Russia—1 year, 2 months and 29 days (after pre-Convention period of 2 years,10 months and 6 days): violation
Jasinski v Poland[96]—1 year, 3 months and 6 days: manifestly ill-founded
Rokhlina v Russia—1 years and almost 6 months: violation.
Iliowiecki v Poland—1 year, 9 months and 19 days: violation
Svipsta v Latvia[97]—over two years and three months: violation.
Kudla v Poland—2 years, 4 months and 3 days: violation
Nevmerzhitsky v Ukraine[98]—over two years and five months: violation.
Moiseyev v Russia—2 years and 6 months: violation
Punzelt v Czech Republic—2 years, 6 months and 18 days: violation.
Labita v Italy—2 years and 7 months: violation
Pantano v Italy[99]—2 years, 8 months and 14 days: no violation
Ilijkov v Bulgaria—3 years, 3 months and 27 days: violation
Jablonski v Poland—3 years and almost 10 months: violation
Prencipe v Monaco—almost 4 years (including 2 years before ratification): violation.
Vaccaro v Italy—more than 4 years and 8 months: violation
Erdem v Germany—5 years and 11 months: violation
Chraidi v Germany[100]—over five years and six months: no violation

[95] (9627/81) (Dec.) March 14, 1984, 37 D.R. 15.
[96] (39865/96) (Dec.) January 21, 2003, no failure of diligence on part of authorities who were gathering evidence and laying new charges.
[97] *Svipsta v Latvia*, March 9, 2006.
[98] *Nevmerzhitsky v Ukraine*, April 5, 2005, ECHR 2005–II.
[99] *Pantano v Italy*, June 3, 2003.
[100] See fn.69 above.

36. Prisoners' rights

Key provisions:

II–563 Articles 3 (prohibition of inhuman and degrading treatment), 5, para.4 (review of lawfulness of detention), 8 (respect for family life, private life and correspondence), 13 (effective remedy for Convention breaches), and 14 (discrimination).

Key case-law:

Golder v UK, February 21, 1975, Series A, No.18, 1 E.H.R.R. 524; *Silver v UK*, March 25, 1983, Series A, No.61, 5 E.H.R.R. 347; *Campbell and Fell v UK*, June 28, 1984, Series A, No.80, 7 E.H.R.R. 165; *Schonenberger and Durmaz v Switzerland*, June 20, 1988, Series A, No.137, 11 E.H.R.R. 202; *McCallum v UK*, August 30, 1990, Series A, No.183, 13 E.H.R.R. 597; *Campbell v UK*, March 25, 1992, Series A, No.233, 15 E.H.R.R. 137; *Hercezegfalvy v Austria*, September 24, 1992, Series A, No.244, 15 E.H.R.R. 437; *Keenan v UK*, April 3, 2001, ECHR 2001–III; *Valasinas v Lithuania*, July 24, 2001, ECHR 2001–VIII; *Kalashnikov v Russia*, July 15, 2002, ECHR 2002–VI; *Van der Ven v Netherlands*, February 4, 2003, ECHR 2003–II; *McGlinchey v UK*, April 29, 2003, ECHR 2003–V; *Poltoratskiy v Ukraine*, April 29, 2003, ECHR 2003–V; *Ezeh and Connors v UK*, October 9, 2003, ECHR 2003–X; *Nevmerzhitsky v Ukraine*, April 5, 2005, ECHR 2005–II; *Hirst v UK (No.2)*, October 6, 2005, ECHR 2005–IX; *Stummer v Austria*, July 7, 2011, ECHR 2011. . .

1. General considerations

II–564 A convicted prisoner's deprivation of liberty does not mean that he loses protection of the other fundamental rights in the Convention. The enjoyment of these must, however, inevitably be tempered by the exigencies of his situation and the requirements of security will weigh in any balancing exercise of justification.[1] Where ill-treatment is concerned, Contracting States are under an obligation not only to refrain from inflicting treatment contrary to Art.3 but to take the steps necessary to protect the safety and health of prisoners under their responsibility.[2]

A large proportion of the cases before the Commission and Court have been introduced by prisoners, who are perhaps in a particularly vulnerable position, almost, if not all, aspects of their lives being subject to regulation by authority. The potential for interference and restriction in fundamental rights and freedoms is considerable and reflected by the wide number of issues raised in prisoner cases. These are examined below, following brief comment on non-exhaustion of domestic remedies.

2. Exhaustion and remedies issues

II–565 A prisoner, notwithstanding the difficulties of his position, financial and practical, is generally required to exhaust domestic remedies available in the United Kingdom. If a remedy is available, he is expected to find a lawyer, apply for legal aid and pursue proceedings in courts, including available appeals.

[1] *Hirst v UK (No.2)*, October 6, 2005, ECHR 2005–IX, paras 69–70.

[2] e.g. positive obligation to protect prisoners from the violence of other prisoners as in *Pantea v Romania*, June 3, 2003, paras 192–196, *Rodic v Bosnia-Herzegovina*, May 27, 2008, paras 71–73; and to provide adequate medical treatment as in *Nevmerzhitsky v Ukraine*, April 5, 2005, ECHR 2005–II.

The principle that only effective remedies need to be exhausted applies. The Board of Visitors, which could not enforce its conclusions, was not effective, nor was the Parliamentary Commissioner who has no power of rendering a binding judgment. The Secretary of State has been found to constitute an effective remedy where a prisoner is complaining about the misapplication of one of the prison rules in his case but not where the prisoner challenges the rule itself.[3] The Commission hinted a doubt at the former assumption in a case where the prisoner's complaint about interference with correspondence was summarily discounted as groundless by the Home Office though his allegations were later proved correct.[4] Notwithstanding suspicion that the prison authorities did not always give detailed consideration to prisoners' grievances, the basic approach was that they must be given an opportunity to remedy mistakes before the Strasbourg organs embark on examining State responsibility for alleged violations. Accordingly, the Commission, in the context of Art.13, gave the authorities the benefit of the doubt "in the absence of any indication or evidence that as a matter of practice petitions to the Secretary of State are not properly or adequately examined".

Whether the courts may furnish an effective remedy will depend on the subject-matter of the complaint. Mere doubts about prospects of success do not exempt from exhaustion.[5] Civil claims for assault, negligence, and/or trespass to goods would be required by Art.35, para.1, in appropriate cases.[6]

Where an applicant challenged the content of a prison rule, e.g. concerning censorship of correspondence, the position in *Silver* was that judicial review, limited to examining whether the measure was arbitrary, in bad faith, for an improper motive or ultra vires was not sufficient. However, where the prison rule is arguably ultra vires or there has been a misuse of power or failure to apply the rules, judicial review may furnish the possibility of an effective remedy: for example, where a prison rule allowed the reading and stopping of confidential letters with a solicitor on wider grounds than merely to ascertain if they were in truth bona fides communications[7]; where orthodox Jewish prisoners complained of the Secretary of State's rejection of the proposal of a Jewish welfare association to provide kosher food where it could be argued that the special dietary requirements had to be taken into account in providing sufficient food of the necessary quality[8]; and where complaints were made that conditions of confinement in a special detention unit (the Inverness cages) were contrary to Art.3.[9]

The scope for effective judicial examination of prisoners' complaints may be presumed to have been extended by the Human Rights Act 1998 which allows the provisions of the Convention to be invoked expressly. The remedy of obtaining a certificate of incompatibility where the violation arises from the content of a statutory provision has not yet been held to furnish an effective remedy for the purposes of Art.35, para.1 of the Convention.[10]

[3] *Silver v UK*, March 25, 1983, Series A, No.61, 5 E.H.R.R. 347, para.116.
[4] (16244/90) (Rep.) May 4, 1993.
[5] See Pt I, s.B: Admissibility Checklist, sub-s.2: Exhaustion of domestic remedies.
[6] e.g. (14462/88) (Dec.) April 12, 1991.
[7] (20075/92) (Dec.) August 31, 1994; (20946/92) (Dec.) August 31, 1994; (37471/97) (Dec.) September 2001.
[8] (13669/88) (Dec.) March 7, 1990, 65 D.R. 245.
[9] (9511/81) (Rep.) May 4, 1989, the applicant acceded to the Government's argument under Art.13 that where conditions were so severe as to be inhuman or degrading, justiciable issues could arise concerning the proper exercise of power.
[10] *Hobbs v UK*, (63684/00) (Dec.) June 18, 2002. See Pt I, s.B(2)(c): Particular remedies in the UK.

In countries where there is a systemic or structural problem of prison conditions, in particular overcrowding based on economic or financial difficulties, the Court has found that the remedies available did not address this situation and thus were not required to be exhausted.[11] However, where complaints even within such an overloaded system concerned specific acts or omissions for which the standard remedies could provide redress, prisoners should exhaust in respect of those aspects.[12]

3. Conditions of confinement

II–566 Minor unpleasantnesses, however unnecessary, petty or deliberately provoking, will not raise any issues under Art.3. More extreme treatment may receive examination by the Court, but the case-law indicates that the threshold is high and in fact, until recently, no prisoners held in prison after conviction had secured a finding of a violation before the Court. In *Selmouni v France* in 1999, some 21 years after the leading judgment in *Ireland v UK* set the standard for Art.3 cases, the Court found that an increasingly high standard was required in the area of protection of fundamental rights.[13] Since then, there have been a number of violations based on conditions of imprisonment, showing more stringent standards are perhaps being applied, though the Court continues to emphasise that the distress or hardship complained of must be shown to go beyond the unavoidable level of suffering inherent in detention and to take into account the practical demands of imprisonment.[14]

The Court has stated that it applies in these cases a cumulative approach, as well as examining specific allegations.[15] Where it does find a violation, it has tended to categorise the treatment as "degrading" rather than "inhuman treatment".

While the applicable burden of proof placed on the applicant prisoner to establish ill-treatment is sometimes stated as being "beyond reasonable doubt," this has been mitigated by the Court taking into account the practical difficulties that a prisoner might face in substantiating allegations. Thus in this context there may not be a rigorous application of the principle "*affirmanti incumbit probatio*" (he who alleges something must prove that allegation), in particular where the Government may be regarded as being the sole party with access to the information capable of proving the facts one way or another. Thus, inferences may well be drawn where the Government fails without satisfactory explanation to submit such information.[16]
It is also worth noting that the Court places considerable probative weight on reports issued by the CPT as to the conditions pertaining in places of detention.[17]

[11] *Kalashnikov v Russia*, (47095/99) (Dec.) September 18, 2001; *Petrea v Romania*, April 29, 2008, para.37.

[12] *Solovyev v Russia*, (76114/01) (Dec.) September 27, 2007.

[13] *Selmouni v France*, July 28, 1999, ECHR 1999–V, para.101, a case of assault in police custody.

[14] e.g. *Kalashnikov v Russia*, July 15, 2002, ECHR 2002–VI, para.95.

[15] e.g. *Dougoz v Greece*, March 6, 2001, ECHR 2001–II, para.46, *Kalashnikov*, fn.14 above, paras 95 and 102.

[16] e.g. *Khudoyorov v Russia*, February 22, 2005, para.113, Government failed to provide specifications/occupancy details of prison transport vans; *Ogica v Romania*, May 27, 2010, para.45, Government failure to provide documents on occupancy, hygiene and conditions in the cells.

[17] e.g. *Dimakos v Romania*, July 6, 2010, paras 46–47; *Gavrilita v Romania*, June 22, 2010, para.37.

(a) Solitary confinement

Segregation per se, or detention in a special high security regime, is not inhuman or degrading.[18] However, the Court has acknowledged that prolonged removal from association is undesirable and that complete sensory deprivation coupled with complete social isolation can ultimately undermine the personality and could, in certain circumstances, amount to inhuman treatment which could not be justified by the requirements of security. Pursuant to the general Art.3 approach, the Court will examine the particular circumstances, for example, the duration, stringency, objective of the measures and the effects on the person.[19] II–567

The Commission accepted quite rigorous regimes. Even where there were reports of marked physical and mental deterioration in prisoners in segregation, it found no sensory deprivation, having regard, inter alia, to the provision of radio, TV and exercise and no complete social isolation, since they had contacts with their lawyers and each other save for limited periods. It was also satisfied that there was no deliberate attempt to punish or break resistance.[20]

As to the duration of solitary confinement, 15 months in a cell of six square metres was not contrary to Art.3, even though the length was "undesirable".[21] 23 months cellular confinement (23 and half hours in the cell per day) for refusal to wear a prison uniform was "severe" isolation but mitigated by daily visits from various persons and not sufficiently serious.[22] Where an IRA prisoner complained of 760 days of solitary confinement, the Commission found that he did not suffer from either sensory or social deprivation, with no physical symptoms besides loss of weight, and that, though this length of time was "undesirable", it fell short of treatment contrary to Art.3.[23] Over eight years in solitary confinement for "Carlos the Jackal" was not a problem either, the isolation being partial and relative; the prisoner had frequent contact with his lawyers and his wife, as well as medical personnel. While the Court expressed some concern over the duration of the restrictive regime, there had been no signs of mental deterioration. It nonetheless emphasised that solitary confinement should not be imposed indefinitely but kept under review; it also laid weight on the existence of procedures by which an independent judicial authority could review the merits of prolongation.[24] Significantly, where a period of over two years in solitary confinement was found to inflict degrading treatment, the prisoner although difficult did not present security concerns: he also suffered from a spinal condition that meant he could not gain

[18] e.g. *Van der Ven v Netherlands*, February 4, 2003, ECHR 2003–II, para.50.
[19] See *Van der Ven*, fn.18 above, para.51 and citations therein.
[20] (7572/76), (7586/76) and (7587/76) (Dec.) July 8, 1978, 14 D.R. 64. See also (18942/91) (Dec.) April 6, 1991, fourteen month lockdown with some effects on applicant's health but no complete sensory deprivation as would undermine his personality; the applicant also had alleged that prisoners had gone for several days without food. In this kind of case, the ability of the Government to provide convincing records of conditions is significant.
[21] (10263/83) (Dec.) March 11, 1985, 41 D.R. 149, where the applicant had two half-hour periods of exercise and contact with prison staff, visits, and medical examinations. The reason for the confinement—the complexity and seriousness of the ongoing investigation—was taken into account.
[22] (8231/78) (Dec.) March 6, 1982, 28 D.R.5.
[23] (8158/78) (Dec.) July 10, 1980, 21 D.R. 95, the applicant received visits and exercise, and regard was had to his security classification, attempts to escape and influence on other prisoners.
[24] *Ramirez Sanchez v France*, July 4, 2006, ECHR 2006–. . . , paras 136–150. See also *Rohde v Denmark*, July 21, 2005, over 11 months in solitary confinement but the prisoner had regular contact with family, friends and others and was under medical monitoring.

access to outdoor exercise and fresh air without unnecessary and avoidable physical suffering.[25] Two years in a special security regime of solitary isolation was also found inhuman and degrading, where there were only very restricted opportunities for exercise outdoors and visitors, and constant handcuffing whenever the prisoner left his cell. In this case, the Court also appeared influenced by its view that the application of the regime to the applicant smacked of arbitrariness, no substantive reasons having been given and no history of incitement of disorder apparent.[26]

The prisoner's own conduct may be relevant to some extent. Where Republican prisoners on a "dirty protest" complained of severe disciplinary sanctions and oppressive conditions,[27] the Commission, noting the elements of self-imposition, found that the circumstances were not severe enough to disclose prohibited treatment, notwithstanding its criticism of the inflexible attitude of the authorities, who were more concerned to punish the offenders than to resolve the deadlock. Dealing separately with the complaint about the restricted diet imposed in combination with cellular confinement, for which there was no security or other justification, the Commission considered that this was a stringent and wholly undesirable form of punishment but though harsh, it was still not severe enough to infringe Art.3.[28] However, even where a prisoner may have brought punishment or harsh restrictions on himself by revolt or fundamental non-co-operation, the Government is not excused from its obligations and must constantly monitor conditions with a view to ensuring the health and well-being of all prisoners.[29]

The new Court has not questioned the necessity for special security regimes for particular prisoners[30] and, in *Messina v Italy*, was prepared to accept quite rigorous restrictions on Mafia prisoners as compatible with Art.3, in light of the security justifications for coping with their alleged dangerousness.[31] Where the authorities showed flexibility in lifting restrictions and taking account of illness, the Court found even extended periods of restriction did not offend.[32] The special security regime "EBI" in the Netherlands, however, was found to inflict degrading treatment on two applicants, Van der Ven and Lorse. Though in some respects the regime was less restrictive on contact with others than in the Italian case, the Court appears to have placed particular significance on the aspect of automatic strip searches, weekly and whenever the prisoner made visits, for example, to the clinic or dentist, which searches were not convincingly justified on security grounds. The

25 *Mathew v Netherlands*, September 29, 2005, he was also seven months in a cell open to the weather.

26 *Csullog v Hungary*, June, 7, 2011, paras 32–38, visitors only a few times a month: contrast cases at fn.24 above.

27 e.g. loss of remission, cellular confinement, loss of privileges, i.e. visits, letters, exercise, no clothing, cold temperatures, alleged 24–hour denial of toilet access, hosing down of cells and occupants with cold water, slopping out, strip searches, restricted and cold food. But there was no sensory or social deprivation in the Commission's terms.

28 (8317/78) (Dec.) May 15, 1980, 20 D.R. 44.

29 (8231/78), fn.22 above; (9511/81) (Dec.) July 9, 1984, where confinement in cages was under constant review; (7572/76) etc, fn.20 above; (18942/91), fn.20 above, the entire prison was locked down in extreme conditions—the Commission found a progressive relaxation and return to a normal routine; (8317/78), fn.28 above.

30 *Van der Ven*, fn18 above, para.55.

31 (25498/94) (Dec.) June 8, 1999, ECHR 1999–V, where there was no access to telephone, or participation in communal sports, recreation or handicrafts (tools were forbidden), limits on family visits (one per month) and limited exercise, the Court found that this only imposed relative social isolation, noting that he did have some contact with other prisoners and some exercise and recreation.

32 *Enea v Italy*, September 17, 2009, paras 60–67. Contrast *Khider v France*, July 9, 2009, paras 119–122, where measures were prolonged despite medical certificates as to the negative effects of isolation.

length of time over which this, and other stringent security measures, were imposed was also given weight, and there is some reference to both applicants showing signs of psychological damage.[33]

Where a prisoner was already seriously ill, placing him in an isolation cell for 25 days and depriving him of his prescribed nutritional diet, was in breach of Art.3.[34]

(b) Prison uniform, work and hair shaving

There is nothing inherently degrading about the requirement to wear a prison uniform or to work.[35] Where, however, a prisoner had his head shaved for punishment reasons, unrelated to considerations of hygiene, the Court found the measure to be degrading contrary to Art.3,[36] as was the somewhat bizarre, if dehumanising, requirement for a prisoner to continuously wear a balaclava outside his cell, even when meeting family visitors.[37] II–568

Prisoners can be prohibited from wearing symbols which pose an acute risk of provoking crime and disorder, as where a paramilitary prisoner was prevented from wearing the Republican lily out of his cell in a Northern Irish prison; the bar was also seen as necessary for safeguarding prison staff.[38]

Prisoners cannot yet claim a right for work done in prison to count towards the old age pension entitlement. It was neither forced labour nor discriminatory treatment for an ex-prisoner, provided with other forms of assistance on reaching pension age, not to have been affiliated to the pension system when working in prison, although the Court noted that standards were evolving and States had to keep the matter under review.[39]

(c) Cell conditions

Applying a cumulative approach, the Court has found conditions degrading in a number of cases, with various factors such as serious overcrowding, excessive temperatures, lack of natural light, open toilets, and lack of adequately hygienic or any sanitary facilities.[40] The length of time over which the conditions have been suffered has generally received a reference and in one case lack of private toilet facilities did not disclose a problem due to its temporary nature.[41] II–569

[33] *Van der Ven*, fn.18 above, three and a half years, signs of depression; *Lorse v Netherlands*, February 4, 2003, six years, depressive and panic disorders.

[34] *Gorodnitchev v Russia*, May 24, 2007, paras 93–97.

[35] e.g. (8317/78), fn.28 above; (8231/78), fn.22 above; *Nazarenko v Ukraine*, April 29, 2003, para.139 (on uniforms).

[36] *Yankov v Bulgaria*, December 11, 2003, paras 112–121.

[37] *Petyo Petko v Bulgaria*, January 7, 2010, paras 39–47, the purported reason, to avoid contamination of witnesses who might have crossed his path, was not sufficient to justify the extent of the practice.

[38] *Donaldson v UK*, (5666975/09) (Dec.) January 25, 2011.

[39] *Stummer v Austria*, July 7, 2011, ECHR 2011. . .

[40] See *Yakovenko v Ukraine*, October 25, 2007, paras 81–89, severe overcrowding, sleep deprivation due to lack of beds, lack of natural light; and cases cited in Pt IIB, s.46: Torture and inhuman degrading treatment, sub-s.4(d): Conditions of detention.

[41] *Valasinas v Lithuania*, July 24, 2001, ECHR 2001–VIII, para.108.

In regard to allegations of overcrowding, the Court, as elsewhere, has had regard to CPT recommendations, which are $4m^2$ for multiple occupancy cells.[42] Continuous conditions of less have disclosed breaches of Art.3.[43]

In the Ukrainian death row cases, where the applicants were locked up 24 hours per day in very restricted space without natural light, with little or no provision for exercise or activities and no water tap or sink in the cell, the Court found breaches of Art.3, commenting that though it bore in mind the difficult socio-economic conditions in Ukraine, lack of resources could not, in principle, justify prison conditions which were so poor as to reach the threshold of treatment contrary to Art.3.[44]

Where a prisoner's health condition so requires, it appears that the authorities are under an obligation to take measures to protect him from passive smoking, presumably ensuring non-smoking only cells.[45]

Transfer conditions may cross the threshold of severity, as in a case where an applicant was taken to and from court over 200 times in a van carrying over double its proper capacity, not receiving food or outside exercise on those days.[46]

Less severe conditions in a cell may still interfere with Art.8 rights, however. Private life rights attach in some degree to occupation of a cell as a personal living space; thus, longstanding and severe problems of smells from a nearby illegal tip disclosed a violation.[47]

(d) Nature of place of detention

II–570 It has occasionally been argued that a prisoner, by the nature of his health or sentence, requires a particular regime of detention. However, both in *Ashingdane* (mental health) and *Bizzotto* (drug addiction), the Court dismissed the contention that location of detention impinged on the lawfulness of the detention for the purposes of Art.5, para.1.[48] However, the Court in *Aerts v Belgium* held that in principle the detention of a person as a mental health patient would only be lawful for the purposes of Art.5, para.1(c) where effected in a hospital, clinic or other appropriate institution. As the Lantin psychiatric wing, due to lack of regular

[42] *Alexov v Bulgaria*, May 22, 2008, para.64. In some cases, in error, the figure of $7m^2$ is misquoted instead as $4m^2$ of living space for a single inmate in multi-occupancy cells (see *Rodić v Bosnia-Herzegovina*, May 27, 2008, para.77), $7m^2$ per detainee in single occupancy police cells (see *Malechkov v Bulgaria*, June 28, 2007, para.137), and $9m^2$ of living space in single prison cells (*Davydov v Ukraine*, July 1, 2010, para.299).

[43] Less than $2m^2$ per person: *Kadikis v Lithuania*, May 4, 2006; less than $2.5m^2$: *Melnik v Ukraine*, March 28, 2006; less than $3m^2$: *Sulejmanovic v Italy*, para.43. Where a regime is stringent, a relatively short period of overcrowding is enough to breach Art. 3, *Alexov*, fn.42 above, paras 112–115, combined with lack of sunlight, no outside exercise.

[44] *Poltoratskiy v Ukraine*, April 29, 2003, ECHR 2003–V; also Ukrainian judgments of the same date: *Aliev*, *Kuznetzov*, *Dankevich*, *Nazarenko* and *Khokhlich*.

[45] *Florea v Romania*, September 14, 2010, paras 57–65. See also *Elefteriadis v Romania*, January 25, 2011, paras 48–55, where the prisoner suffering from chronic pulmonary condition had to share a cell with two smokers, as well as being held in court waiting rooms in which prisoners smoked.

[46] *Khudoyorov v Russia*, November 8, 2005; see also *Tarariyeva v Russia*, December 14, 2006, Art.3 breach for transport of a post-operative patient in an ordinary van for over two hours.

[47] *Branduse v Romania*, April 7, 2009, paras 64–76.

[48] *Ashingdane v UK*, May 28, 1985, Series A, No.93; *Bizzotto v Greece*, November 15, 1996, R.J.D. 1996–V. See Pt IIB, s.9: Deprivation of Liberty, sub-s.5: In accordance with law and lawfulness, and s.32: Mental Health, sub-s.8: Right to Treatment.

medical attention or a therapeutic environment, was not an institution appropriate for the detention of persons of unsound mind, the proper relationship between the aim of the detention and the conditions in which it took place was deficient and there was a breach of Art.5, para.1.[49] An inappropriate regime may perhaps not always impose treatment amounting to Art.3, as in *Aerts* where, despite unsatisfactory conditions, there was no evidence of serious effects on the applicant.[50] Where, however, a psychotic prisoner with suicidal tendencies was kept in prison, the Court held that this imposed on him suffering beyond that normally associated with imprisonment and although the authorities had hospitalised him from time to time and provided monitoring, his state of serious mental illness required a permanent and specialised hospital setting.[51]

Long-term detention in a place geared only for short stays may reach the threshold of Art.3, as in *Kaja v Greece*, where there was no provision in the detention centre for, inter alia, outside exercise and no TV or radio for contact with the outside world.[52]

Frequent transfers of a prisoner from one prison to another may offend Art.3, particularly where the prisoner has mental problems which are exacerbated by the resulting disruptions to treatment and family visits and therefore prevent integration and adaptation to new environments.[53] Security concerns posed by a high risk prisoner with a history of escape attempts may justify frequent transfers.[54]

4. Medical treatment

States are under an obligation to secure the health and well-being of prisoners, inter alia, by providing the requisite medical assistance.[55] Where a prisoner enters detention in good health, and is later found to have developed a serious illness, the Court has said an issue under Art.3 may arise in the absence of a plausible explanation for this development.[56] **II–571**

Complaints about the adequacy of medical treatment offered and received are not uncommon from prisoners, however, and a significant defect or failing is generally required to reach the threshold of Art.3.[57] While the CPT has upheld that the standard of medical care in prison should be equivalent to that in the community, the Court states that it applies a more flexible standard, accepting that prison facilities may not match those outside, but requiring that treatment is compatible

[49] Also *Hutchison Reid v UK*, February 20, 2003, ECHR 2003–IV, para.54, sufficient link between the applicant's detention under a hospital order and the conditions of his detention in the State Hospital; *Brand v Netherlands*, May 11, 2004, paras 61–66, six months' delay in transfer from prison to custodial clinic was not acceptable, violation; *Hadzic and Suljic v Bosnia-Herzegovina*, June 7, 2011, paras 41–42, psychiatric annex not suitable therapeutic setting for mentally ill prisoners due to poor conditions and custodial nature.

[50] *Aerts v Belgium*, paras 65–66, no breach of Art.3 despite unsatisfactory conditions, largely as no evidence of serious effects on the applicant.

[51] *Rivière v France*, July 11, 2006.

[52] *Kaja v Greece*, July 27, 2006, the applicant was there for three months.

[53] *Khider v France*, fn.32, paras 111–112, also prolonged solitary confinement, repeated strip searches.

[54] *Payet v France*, January 20, 2011, paras 57–64.

[55] *Kudla v Poland*, October 26, 2000, ECHR 2000–IX, para.94.

[56] *Dobri v Romania*, December 14, 2010, para.45, the applicant had developed TB in prison, for which the State was held liable under Art.3.

[57] *Kudla*, fn.55 above, paras 95–100, no discernible shortcoming in the treatment of the applicant who suffered from psychiatric problems, e.g. suicidal tendencies.

with the human dignity of the inmate while taking into account the practical exigencies of imprisonment.[58] Where the lack of prompt or adequate medical treatment has endangered the life of a prisoner or contributed to his death, Art.2 may be breached.[59]

Failure to provide adequate or timely medical care has been disclosed where an applicant contracted tuberculosis in prison and there was a delay in diagnosis and treatment being given[60]; where there was a lack of proper monitoring and treatment of a prisoner, who was HIV-positive and epileptic with other chronic diseases, which led to further infections and deterioration[61]; and where a prisoner contracted a skin disease in prison and received no attention from a doctor for over a year.[62] Short delay in providing treatment may be acceptable.[63] In serious cases of ill-health, delays in addressing health problems and failure to follow up on diagnoses and to provide medical treatment, if necessary in exterior hospitals, may disclose inhuman and degrading treatment.[64] Where highly infectious diseases are concerned, the Court has highlighted the importance of screening to prevent sick prisoners from spreading infection to the healthy and found a violation where a prisoner was found to have developed T.B. while in prison.[65]

Prisoners with mental problems may be regarded as particularly vulnerable and the authorities are required to show particular vigilance to ensure that they are not subjected to treatment crossing the threshold of Art.3. Thus, treating a mentally-ill prisoner in the same manner as other prisoners is not a strong justifying argument from a Government.[66]

Nonetheless, failure to give proper medical supervision of prisoners with psychiatric or other health problems may disclose problems without always showing that the shortcoming had long-term effects on health or was causative of any deterioration.[67] Thus, prison authorities failed to comply with the standards imposed by Art.3 in *Keenan v UK*, where the applicant, mentally ill with suicidal tendencies, was not properly monitored and was subjected, without informed psychiatric input, to a disciplinary punishment of segregation during which he hung himself, even though it was not established that the authorities could have foreseen that he was likely to kill himself at that time.[68] Similarly, in *McGlinchey v UK*, where a prisoner

[58] See *Aleksanyan v Russia*, December 22, 2008, paras 139–140.

[59] See *Dzeiciak v Poland*, December 9, 2008, paras 93–101, where the applicant was suffering from severe heart problems and requiring surgery, but during four years of pre-trial detention these urgent health problems were largely ignored and he died before the re-scheduled surgery took place.

[60] *Melnik*, fn.43 above, paras 104–106, together with poor hygiene, sanitation, overcrowding, etc; see also *Yakovenko v Ukraine*, fn.40, lack of timely and adequate treatment for TB.

[61] *Khudobin v Russia*, October 26, 2006.

[62] *Nevmerzhitsky*, fn.2 above.

[63] *Gavrilita v Romania*, June 22, 2010, para.33, 14–day lapse before treatment for diagnosis of TB was not a problem.

[64] *Ghavtadze v Georgia*, March 3, 2009. See also *Kucheruk v Ukraine*, September 6, 2007, paras 147–152, concerning delay in a recommended transfer of a schizophrenic to the hospital; *Aleksanyan*, fn.58 above, para.158, breach of Art.3 where, despite specialist advice, a prisoner suffering HIV/AIDS was not transferred to an external hospital.

[65] *Dobri v Romania*, December 14, 2010, paras 46–56.

[66] *Dybeku v Albania*, December 18, 2007, paras 47–52.

[67] See *Rivière v France*, fn.51 above. Contrast *Aerts*, fn.50 above, para.66, where the applicant, who was mentally ill, was unable to show that the unsatisfactory conditions in the psychiatric wing had such serious effects on his mental health as would bring them within the scope of Art.3.

[68] See also *Renolde v France*, October 25, 2008, imposition on a mentally-ill prisoner of a 45–day stint in a punishment cell breached Art.3; it also breached Art.2 as the punishment and lack of proper medical supervision of the acutely ill prisoner was seen as playing a part in his suicide, the risk of which the authorities should have been aware and reacted appropriately to.

had died following complications from drug withdrawal symptoms, her family had dropped allegations under Art.2 as there was insufficient medical evidence to establish the lack of treatment caused the death. The Court still found a violation of Art.3 due to the lack of proper medical supervision of her deteriorating state and the delay in admitting her to hospital where more adequate treatment would have been available. Considerable anxiety suffered by a prisoner, who had been operated upon for cancer of the bladder and did not receive specialised examinations or tests for over a year to enable diagnosis and treatment of a feared recurrence, disclosed a breach of Art.3 together with poor conditions of detention.[69]

As regards complaints that ill-health or advanced age render an applicant unfit for detention, the Court has held that these elements do not per se render detention incompatible with Art.3, adopting a case-by-case approach. The Commission previously adopted a robust attitude and appeared to require convincing medical evidence that the prisoner was unfit for detention or that the facilities were inadequate.[70] Even where prisoners were suffering from potentially fatal illnesses such as HIV, with limited life expectancy, it was sufficient that they were receiving proper monitoring and care and that serious complications had not yet developed.[71] While the Court has yet to find that the factor of old age alone has subjected a prisoner to distress or hardship of an intensity exceeding the unavoidable level of suffering inherent in detention,[72] it reached findings of treatment contrary to Art.3 in *Farbtuhs v Latvia* where the prison itself had acknowledged its inability to cope with the needs of a prisoner who was over 80 years' old, paraplegic, and suffered from many chronic and incurable health problems.[73] Violations also arose in *Price v UK*,[74] where the prison did not have the facilities to look after the severely disabled applicant and in *Mouisel v France*,[75] where the applicant was suffering from cancer. There were significant degrading elements in both cases, in *Price*, where the female applicant had to be manhandled on and off the toilet by male prison officers, and in *Mouisel*, where the authorities insisted on handcuffing the applicant throughout his external hospital visits and treatment.[76] Where a partly-paralysed prisoner suffering from renal problems, requiring daily use of a catheter, was held in an overcrowded

[69] *Popov v Ukraine*, July 13, 2006.

[70] (13407/87) (Dec.) March 10, 1988, 55 D.R. 271, where a concentration camp survivor's claims of unfitness for detention were not substantiated by his own doctors, thus, despite the special hardship that detention might cause him, the claims were manifestly ill-founded; (8244/78) (Rep.) December 5, 1979, 18 D.R. 148, where the applicant (74) suffered diabetes and other disorders but the prison was found to have a medical service with considerable expertise.

[71] (22564/93) (Dec.) April 14, 1994, 77–1 D.R. 90; (22761/93) (Dec.) April 14, 1994, 77–A D.R. 98. See also *Ceku v Germany*, (41559/06) (Dec.) March 13, 2007, where it was relevant that the authorities were under an obligation to review any change in his situation.

[72] *Papon v France (No.1)*, (64666/01) (Dec.) June 6, 2001, ECHR 2001–VI, applicant over 90; *Sawoniuk v UK*, (63716/00) (Dec.) May 29, 2001, applicant almost 80–no evidence in either case that the applicants were not receiving any necessary treatment or supervision.

[73] *Farbtuhs v Latvia*, December 12, 2004.

[74] *Price v UK*, July 10, 2001, ECHR 2001–VII, Judge Bratza gave a separate opinion that the court should not have committed such a person (four-limb deficient thalidomide victim with defective kidneys) without verifying that the prison could cope with her needs.

[75] *Mouisel v France*, November 14, 2002, ECHR 2002–IX.

[76] The manner of providing treatment caused suffering beyond what was inevitably entailed by detention or cancer therapy. Also *Henaf v France*, November 27, 2003, handcuffing of 75–year-old prisoner in hospital bed disclosed inhuman treatment; *Huseyin Yildirim v Turkey*, May 3, 2007, violation where the applicant was so severely incapacitated that domestic courts found him unfit for prison.

cell with bad hygiene and hardly any access to sanitation facilities, the Court found the appalling conditions by themselves were incompatible with his handicap.[77]

Conversely, where there are complaints about treatment imposed on a prisoner against his will, complaints under Art.3 are unlikely to succeed where the measures are based on "therapeutic necessity". In *Herczegfalvy v Austria*, which concerned a person detained as mentally ill, the Commission found that the compulsory sedation, being fettered to a bed for several weeks and forced artificial feeding reached levels of inhuman and degrading as did the disproportionate and "brutal" manner in which these measures were applied. The Court, less emotive, considered that established medical principles were decisive and a measure which was therapeutic could not at the same time be inhuman and degrading. However, when considering the issue more recently, the Court emphasised that the medical necessity for forcible intervention in order to save life had to be convincingly shown and that, at the same time, the manner of intervention should not infringe Art.3. The force feeding of a prisoner without any apparent medical justification therefore disclosed a violation, while the forcible insertion of the tube into the resisting prisoner amounted in itself to torture.[78] Consideration should also be given to alternative, less invasive solutions.[79] Even where a measure is claimed to be medically necessary, the Court will verify that it was the appropriate medical expert that approved the measure, as in a case where a schizophrenic was handcuffed continuously in an isolation cell for a week without the approval of a psychiatrist and without follow-up monitoring as to the continuance of the restraint.[80]

The mere fact of a hunger strike does not give rise to a right to be released where there is no indication of a lack of appropriate medical care being provided by prison authorities.[81]

As regards preventive health measures, the Court has been more hesitant. In *Ghavadze v Georgia*, it commented that it would have been appropriate to screen the applicant for TB, endemic in Georgian prisons, on entry to prison.[82] However, where in Romania the problem of TB was apparently less serious, it was not initially prepared to criticise the authorities for not screening for the disease.[83] That changed where it was found that an applicant had developed TB while in prison. The Court heavily criticised the authorities for not screening prisoners to enable the infected to be kept apart from the healthy and found a violation based on the applicant's development of TB as well as appalling cell conditions.[84] Where the applicant prisoner was not able to point to any direct and immediate risk or effect on his own health, the Court declined to find that Arts 2, 3 or 8 required prison authorities to provide needle exchanges to prevent the transmission of HIV and hepatitis amongst the prison population. In the area of preventive policy, it was stated that there was little precedent for imposing obligations of intervention, and a margin of apprecia-

[77] *Flaminzeanu v Romania*, April 12, 2011, paras 82–100.
[78] *Nevmerzhitsky*, fn.2 above, the Court stressed procedural safeguards, e.g. prior medical examinations and opinions showing medical necessity.
[79] *Ciorap v Moldova*, June 19, 2007, para.87, intravenous drip.
[80] *Kucheruk*, fn.64, paras 141–145.
[81] *Horoz v Turkey*, March 31, 2009, paras 28–31.
[82] *Ghavadze v Georgia*, March 3, 2009, para.86.
[83] *Gavrilita v Romania*, June 22, 2010, para.33.
[84] *Dobri v Romania*, December 14, 2010, paras 49–56.

tion was applied, taking into account considerations of resources, medical health policy, priorities and a legitimate policy of seeking to reduce drugs use.[85]

Failure to provide dental treatment in serious cases may inflict on a prisoner treatment incompatible with Art.3,[86] while deprivation of glasses permitting prisoners to see properly may do so also. It may be that in these cases it is less a case of inflicting suffering, but rather a form of humiliation or attack on essential human dignity where a prisoner is deprived of the wherewithal to eat properly and adequately see his surroundings.[87]

5. Stripping and searches

Strip searches, including rectal examinations, have not been found a problem under Arts 3 or 8 where carried out for plausible security or crime prevention reasons[88] and in a manner avoiding unnecessary humiliation. Where a prisoner was required to urinate before a prison officer to provide a sample for testing for use of illegal drugs, the Commission accepted that it was desirable to control the use of drugs in prisons.[89] The circumstances were not severe enough for Art.3 and, while there was an interference with private life, regard was had to the reasonable and ordinary requirements of imprisonment in which wider measures of interference might be justified than for persons at liberty. The measure was accordingly necessary for the prevention of crime and disorder. Frequent strip searches were found to be necessitated by the exceptional security requirements of the Maze Prison, where smuggling of dangerous items had occurred. The Commission found that while the circumstances were humiliating they were not deliberately degrading, referring to the lack of physical contact and the presence of a senior officer to prevent abuse.[90] II–572

However, in *Valasinas v Lithuania*, the performance of a strip seach of a male prisoner in the presence of a female prison officer and without the use of gloves, disclosed degrading treatment contrary to Art.3.[91] Systematic, intrusive measures may also be objectionable, as in the weekly, automatic strip searching over long periods of prisoners in a high security facility in the cases of *Van der Ven v Netherlands* and *Lorse v Netherlands*, where the Court was not persuaded of the security justification and in *Frerot v France*, where systematic body searches involving visual anal inspection were imposed in an arbitrary manner.[92] Even as regards a prisoner attracting special security concerns, the Court was not convinced that strip

[85] *Shelley v UK*, (23800/06) (Dec.) January 4, 2008, however, as regarded differential treatment in that prisoners in Scotland benefited from needle exchanges and those in England did not, the Court noted the evidence that exchange programmes were beneficial but that tests were still being run in various jurisdictions; it found the margin of appreciation still applied under Art.14 also.

[86] *Slyusarev v Russia*, April 20, 2010.

[87] *VD v Romania*, February 16, 2010.

[88] *Valasinas*, fn.41 above, para.117; *Van der Ven*, fn.18 above, para.60.

[89] (21132/93) (Dec.) April 6, 1994, 77–A D.R. 75.

[90] See fn.22 above.

[91] Also *Iwanczuk v Poland*, November 15, 2001, para.59, where the strip search was accompanied by verbal abuse and derision.

[92] *Van der Ven*, fn.18 above, paras 60–62; *Lorse*, fn.33, paras 70–74, the Court disapproved of the automatic nature of searches which deterred one prisoner from using facilities such as the hairdressers and the lack of any concrete need for weekly searches; *Frerot v France*, June 12, 2007 and *Khider v France*, fn.32 above, concerning systematic, frequent strip searches without justification; *Iwanczuk*, fn.91 above, para.89, where no compelling justification was forthcoming for requiring the prisoner to strip before voting in the prison voting facilities.

searches were required at an intensity of 4 to 6 times a day, whenever the service supervising him changed; the presence of officers wearing balaclavas and the unregulated filming of searches was also condemned.[93]

While it might have been compatible with Art.3 to place the applicant, who had violently resisted prison guards, in a special security cell for a week, the Court considered that keeping him naked during that period humiliated and debased him and disclosed inhuman and degrading treatment: it was noted that if the concern was self-harm from use of his clothes, tearproof clothing, as recommended by the CPT, could have been used.[94]

As concerns strip searching of visitors, while there might be a legitimate aim in preventing the smuggling of drugs, the Court emphasised that, as regarded outsiders to the prison who might very well be innocent of any wrongdoing, the prison authorities were required to take rigorous precautions to protect the dignity of those being searched as far as possible. There was thus a violation of Art.8 when in searching a prisoner's mother and handicapped half-brother the prison officers failed to comply with their own regulations as to the manner in which the searches were to be conducted.[95]

Handcuffing of a female prisoner and the presence during a gynaecological examination of gendarme officers, even with use of a folding screen, were disproportionate measures capable of imposing degrading treatment in breach of Art.3; there was a breach even though the examination in the end did not take place due to the prisoner's refusal.[96]

6. Visiting rights and access to family

II–573 The Commission considered that continued contact by a prisoner with his family and friends took on added importance in the context of Art.8 since normal means of continuing relationships had been removed. It had noted the European Prison Rules which emphasise the need to encourage links. Consequently, the Commission found that Art.8 requires the State to assist prisoners as far as possible to create and sustain ties with people outside prison in order to facilitate their social rehabilitation.[97] The Court has since endorsed this approach.[98]

There is no right to unlimited visiting.[99] In theory there should be good reasons for obstacles placed in the way of contacts and an absolute ban could only be justified in exceptional circumstances.[100] Obstructiveness deriving from a policy of moving a prisoner around at short notice for "cooling off", with the result that

93 *El Shennawy v France*, January 20, 2011, paras 39–46.

94 *Hellig v Germany*, July 7, 2011, paras 52–58.

95 *Wainwright v UK*, September 26, 2006, the applicants were not given information and consent forms to sign beforehand, the blinds not drawn and the rule that they should not be more than half-undressed at any time ignored.

96 *Filiz Uyan v Turkey*, January 8, 2009, paras 32–35. For handcuffing, see Part IIB, s.46: Torture, inhuman and degrading treatment, sub-s.4(b): Handcuffing, police control and security measures.

97 e.g. (9054/80) (Dec) October 8, 1982, 30 D.R. 113, refusal of a visit of a campaign group to a prisoner did not disclose an interference under Art.8 however; (13756/88) (Dec.) March 12, 1990, 65 D.R. 265.

98 *Messina v Italy (No.2)*, September 28, 2000, ECHR 2000–X, para.61.

99 (9054/80), fn.97 above, reference to the burden placed on prisons by visits precluding unlimited visiting facilities.

100 *Lavents v Latvia*, November 28, 2002, para.141, long periods when the applicant was barred from family visits (up to one year and seven months) were unnecessary to prevent collusion or interference in the ongoing investigation.

relatives arrived at prison to find him gone, was the basis of an admissible complaint which settled.[101] Arbitrarily limiting numbers of visits from family members may not pursue, or be proportionate to, any legitimate aim, as in *Nowicka v Poland*, where the applicant, detained for psychiatric examination, was restricted to one visit per month for no particular reason.[102] Even where the applicant's wife was also a co-accused, the Court did not find that the ban on the applicant receiving visits from her for thirteen months was justified, in particular due to the length of time and the possibility of special security arrangements if it was suspected that such a meeting could have jeopardised the ongoing investigation due to collusion.[103] However, in *Messina v Italy (No.2)*, restrictions for long periods of only one visit or phone call per month were found justified due to the special security considerations attaching to the applicant as a mafia prisoner convicted of very serious offences.[104] Visiting arrangements whereby a prisoner could not have physical contact with his partner and children, but was separated from them by a partition, were found in breach of Art.8 where the restriction was arbitrarily applied. It seems the Court found acceptable such restriction where justified by plausible security concerns but that the continuing existence of any security risk had to be shown and a coherent policy applied, taking into account other methods of preventing any breach of security.[105]

Prisoners held in special security categories are unable to derive from Art.8 the right to unsupervised visits or to visits unencumbered by partitions or screens, in particular where IRA prisoners and their families were concerned. The Commission found that though such restrictions were prima facie an interference, they were justified in the interests of public safety and the prevention of crime and disorder.[106]

Visits by families are often rendered difficult and practically discouraged where a prisoner is held in a prison far from the district where his close relatives live. The Commission always started from the premise that a prisoner could not derive from Art.8 a right to choose the place of confinement and that separation from family and the hardship that caused inevitably flowed from imprisonment. It would only be in exceptional circumstances that the location of a prison a long way from a prisoner's home or family might infringe the requirements of Art.8.[107]

No exceptional circumstances arose from the separation of IRA prisoners, held in mainland UK, from their families, based entirely in Northern Ireland or the

[101] (9466/81) (Rep.) May 15, 1986, 36 D.R. 41.

[102] *Nowicka v Poland*, December 3, 2002, paras 75–77; also *Poltoratskiy*, fn.44 above, where limits of one visit per month (and a limit of one outgoing letter per month); *Khokhlich*, fn.44 above, strict limit on parcels from relatives was not based in law as required by Art.8, para.2.

[103] *Kucera v Slovakia*, July 17, 2007, paras 130–134. See also *Ferla v Poland*, May 25, 2008, where even if the fact that the applicant's wife was a witness may have initially justified restrictions on visits, the continuation over a year did not strike a fair balance, as she refused to give evidence and no other methods of preventing collusion were considered.

[104] See fn.98 above, paras 72–74, where the Court appeared to give weight to the periodic mitigation of the restrictions as showing the authorities taking the pains to assist the applicant in maintaining contacts with family; see, similarly, *Enea*, fn.32, paras 128–131 and *Kalashnikov v Russia*, (47905/99) (Dec.) September 18, 2001, where the restrictions on and supervision of family visits to a prisoner on remand was justified by the gravity of the charges against him and the risk of collusion or obstruction in the investigation.

[105] *Boguslaw Krawdzak v Poland*, May 31, 2011, paras 115–121.

[106] (8065/77) (Dec.) May 3, 1978, 14 D.R. 246.

[107] (5229/71) (Dec.) October 5, 1972, Coll. 42, p.14; (5712/72) (Dec.) July 15, 1974, Coll. 46, reference to thousands of miles overseas; (15817/89) October 1, 1990, 66 D.R. 251, the interference from a refusal to transfer a Scot from an English to a Scottish prison so he could see his fiancée was a proportionate interference, provision being made for temporary visits under strict security conditions.

Republic of Ireland.[108] In some cases, parents were elderly, in ill-health and unable to make the long journey, or other relatives, not in receipt of State assistance, could not afford the trip with the result that some prisoners received very few visits at all over long periods. The Commission commented on the fact that their place of imprisonment resulted from the prisoners' arrest and trial for serious offences committed in England and Wales and noted the serious security considerations attached to this category of prisoner. Where it was argued that there was no real security risk on transfer, or the prisoner was not a security threat due to health or classification, this was still insufficient to raise issues. Even if other prisoners of high security classification had been transferred, any difference in treatment was justified by the special and sensitive considerations arising out of the disposal of IRA prisoners within the prison system against the background of the political situation which remained subject to complex pressures.[109]

It would therefore appear that where transfers are concerned, there is a reluctance to impose positive obligations on Contracting States and an applicant would have to establish circumstances of extreme hardship and arbitrariness by the authorities.

As regards external visits, Art.8 does not guarantee a detained person an unconditional right for leave to attend the funeral of a relative. However, in *Ploski v Poland* where the applicant had lost both parents in the space of a month the Court considered that taking into account the seriousness of what was at stake for the applicant the authorities should only have refused him leave if there had been compelling reasons and in the absence of practicable solutions. As it did not appear that he had been held on charges concerning violent crime and there was the possibility, unconsidered, of escorted leave, the refusal was found disproportionate to the legitimate aims of public safety or the prevention of crime or disorder.[110] Where a prisoner's father was due to die in the Netherlands by euthanasia, the Court considered, in these exceptional circumstances, the Russian authorities should have sought the assistance of the Dutch authorities to enable a visit under suitable security conditions.[111] Where the family relationship has not been close, or where there have been strong security considerations or the degree of illness not substantiated as rendering a home visit necessary, refusals have been accepted.[112]

The mere fact that an applicant is a prisoner is not a justification for refusal of permission by the authorities for him or her to marry or to participate in a spouse or partner's fertility treatment.[113]

7. Correspondence

II–574 Article 8 expressly guarantees the right to respect for correspondence and the Commission emphasised that this applied to prisoners, subject to the ordinary and reasonable requirements of imprisonment. There should in principle be a free flow of

108 (18632/91), (19085/91) and (21596/93) (Decs.) December 9, 1992.

109 (23956/94) (Dec.) November 28, 1994; (23958/94) (Dec.) November 28, 1994.

110 *Ploski v Poland*, November 12, 2002, paras 37–39.

111 *Lind v Russia*, December 6, 2007, paras 95–97.

112 See *Marincola and Sestito v Italy*, (42662/98) (Dec.) November 25, 1999, no problem where a Mafia prisoner was refused permission to attend his brother's funeral, or in *Sannino v Italy*, (Dec.) May 3, 2005, where the applicant was dangerous and unstable and the request did not concern a close relative, only a grandparent; *Schemkamper v France*, (75833/01) (Dec.) October 18, 2005, where it was not established that the prisoner's father's health prevented him from visiting the prison. Contrast an earlier case, *Georgiou v Greece*, (45138/98) (Dec.) January 13, 2000, where the Court more brusquely dismissed complaints about refusal to attend a grandfather's funeral and visit a sick mother.

113 See Part IIB, s.31: Marriage and founding a family.

correspondence and any stopping of a letter to a prisoner requires justification in rules which are accessible and public. In *Silver v UK*, the stopping of letters to outside bodies or letters complaining about prisoners' convictions or treatment in prison was not "in accordance with law" as the measures were unforeseeable, the relevant orders not having been published.[114] Numerous similar findings have followed in other jurisdictions, where prison authorities have placed restrictions on correspondence which have not had sufficient basis in law or the requisite quality of law.[115]

Regarding justifiable restrictions, the Commission referred in *Silver* to the perhaps understandable desire to support prison staff by preventing floods of outside criticism, but it gave much greater weight to the need of prisoners to make outside contacts and express feelings to those outside contacts. Systematic censorship of an applicant's entire correspondence has not been found to correspond to a pressing social need or to be proportionate.[116] In *Silver*, many restrictions were found unnecessary, e.g. the restrictions on letters to family and friends, complaints about public authorities and the requirement of prior ventilation of complaints before letters could be sent to legal advisers or members of Parliament. Later cases found that it was unnecessary to stop letters to the press[117]; letters of complaint to lawyers which have not been put to prison authorities; letters from lawyers to a prisoner instructed by his wife on his behalf[118]; matters intended for publication; letters to persons unknown to prisoners before their imprisonment[119]; letters seeking pen friends[120]; complaints to the police about ill-treatment to others[121]; letters concerning the institution of private criminal prosecutions; and letters to unofficial organisations.[122] Nor is it legitimate to stop letters that insult the prison service or criticise the authorities,[123] or to exclude from "correspondence" letters which do not concern the prisoner addressee specifically or exclusively.[124] Where a prisoner had serious health problems, there was no justification for opening letters from a named external medical specialist who had agreed to mark her correspondence in an identifiable manner.[125]

The following measures may be necessary: restrictions on correspondence of a business nature (which may involve the proceeds of crime)[126]; the naming of other prisoners in the prison, which may raise security considerations[127]; the naming of

[114] Also (16244/90) (Rep.) May 4, 1993, where an unofficial agreement with police, whereby letters of complaint were held back while the governor investigated, was not "in accordance with the law".

[115] *Calegoro Diana v Italy*, November 15, 1996, R.J.D. 1996–V, No.21, where the power to censor mail was undefined; *Labita v Italy*, April 6, 2000, ECHR 2000–IV, paras 182–183, where the Minister of Justice had acted *ultra vires* in imposing restrictions and the restrictions continued though the court order had been rescinded; *Lavents*, fn.100 above, para.136, too wide discretion left to the authorities; *Niedbala v Poland*, July 4, 2000, paras 81–82.

[116] *Petrov v Bulgaria*, June 12, 2007, para.44.

[117] e.g. (9511/81), fn.9 above.

[118] *Schonenburger and Durmaz v Switzerland*, June 20, 1988, Series A, No.137, 11 E.H.R.R. 202.

[119] (8575/79) (Rep.) July 2, 1979.

[120] (11523/85) (Rep.) December 15, 1985.

[121] (9511/81), fn.9 above.

[122] (7291/75) (Rep.) October 18, 1985, 50 D.R. 5.

[123] *Ekinci and Akalin v Turkey*, January 30, 2007, para.47.

[124] *Frerot v France*, fn.92 above.

[125] *Szuluk v UK*, (36936/05) (Dec.) June 2, 2009.

[126] *Silver*, fn.3 above.

[127] *Silver*, fn.3 above.

prison officers in a context which raises a threat[128]; threats of violence[129]; letter naming a prison officer with imputations made against him intended for publication.[130]

Opening without stopping or delay may also be acceptable, as mere screening outside special categories of correspondence with courts or legal advisers is not by itself incompatible with Art.8.[131] Delay in sending a letter may disclose a violation, though this is subject to the practical acceptance that where instructions are required as to whether a letter should be stopped, some time will elapse. Three weeks for a letter, not urgent in nature, was found to be acceptable.[132]

Regarding other restrictions on correspondence, the imposition of letter quotas may be justifiable, having regard to the vast quantity of mail the authorities have to deal with, at least where the level set is not unduly restrictive and the effect is minimal.[133] There is no interference from the obligation to use prison notepaper assuming it is readily available[134] or from the insistence that the prisoner uses an official form.[135] A denial of notepaper altogether may disclose a violation.[136] As for the cost of correspondence, the State is not obliged as a general principle to pay postage for prisoners but depending on particular circumstances a failure to do so might severely restrict their ability to communicate by post. The provision of one paid letter a week was found sufficient by the Commission.[137] Where a prisoner does not have means to pay for his own correspondence to the Court in particular, a failure to provide the wherewithal, including stamps, founded a violation.[138] The prohibition on writing in a language not known to the prison censors was not disproportionate where translation facilities had been made available.[139] However, a practice of requiring prisoners writing in Kurdish to provide translations at their expense to obtain expedition of their letters was found incompatible with Art.8.[140] A disciplinary sanction imposed on a remand prisoner for contacting a journalist without prior judicial permission was acceptable where there was not a general ban on contacting third persons as such and the supervisory measure was geared to preventing a suspected terrorist contacting other members of her group or otherwise interfering with the ongoing investigation.[141] Nor was there a breach where a prisoner received a minor punishment for sending out a complaint about prison conditions outside available official prison channels.[142]

Errors and mistakes are no justification for a failure to send a letter, nor for not notifying that the Post Office has returned a letter as the address was incomplete,[143]

[128] (16244/90) (Dec.) December 12, 1991.

[129] *Silver*, (Rep.), fn.3 above, paras 413–415;(11523/85), fn.120 above.

[130] (16244/90), fn.128 above.

[131] *William Faulkner v UK*, (37471/97) (Dec.) September 18, 2001; *Puzinas v Lithuania (No.2)*, January 9, 2007, para.33.

[132] *Silver*, fn.3 above; (9511/81), fn.9 above, a delay of up to a month was acceptable while the authorities contacted the addressee.

[133] (12395/86) (Rep.) May 17, 1990, applicant had sent 600 letters, eight to thirty per week, during the course of his application, some weeks 30, and it was not unreasonable to limit him to 24 Christmas cards.

[134] (7291/75), fn.122 above.

[135] *William Faulkner*, fn.131 above.

[136] (8231/78) (Rep.) October 12, 1983, 49 D.R. 5.

[137] (9659/82) (Dec.) May 5, 1983.

[138] *Gagiu v Romania*, February 24, 2009, paras 89–92.

[139] *Chishti v Portugal*, (57248/00) (Dec.) October 2, 2003.

[140] *Mehmet Nuri Ozen v Turkey*, January 11, 2011, para.60.

[141] *Sotiropoulou v Greece*, (40225/02) (Dec.) January 18, 2007.

[142] *Puzinas (No.2)*, fn.129 above.

[143] (11523/85), fn.120 above.

or for mistaken opening of letters on a regular basis.[144] On the other hand, accidental opening due to an administrative oversight (e.g. novice censor, failure to notice a marking) when accompanied by an apology, may not disclose a problem where there is no indication of a deliberate flouting or disregard of the applicable rules.[145] A Government is expected to maintain proper records relating to the handling of mail and where a dispute arises as to whether letters have been received by prisoners, it cannot discharge its obligations by merely supplying a record of incoming mail.[146]

Although prison regimes are showing increasing flexibility as regards access to telephone facilities, the Convention organs' approach has been to hold that there is no right to communications by telephone where adequate provision by way of mail is made.[147] Where telephone use is allowed, restrictions on the number of calls or authorised recipients is unlikely to raise problems in the current climate.[148] Discrimination may arise where rules unjustifiabily exclude some from benefiting. It was discriminatory to bar an applicant from telephoning his long-standing partner and the mother of his children, where other prisoners were allowed to telephone their wives.[149]

8. Access to lawyer and to a court

A prisoner cannot be barred from taking action in the courts or be required to obtain prior consent by the Home Secretary to contact a lawyer for the purpose of taking possible action. Such a restriction is a breach of the principle of access to court, access for everyone being a crucial guarantee of the respect of the rule of law on a domestic level.[150] II–575

Further, even a Category A prisoner is entitled, under Art.6, to out-of-hearing visits with his legal adviser, as he can claim a legitimate and vital interest in keeping the subject-matter of such consultations confidential.[151] Other conditions imposed on

[144] *Demirtepe v France*, December 21, 1999, ECHR 1999–IX, paras 9 and 27,where mistakes were made due to volume of mail and use of a machine, the Court found this was not "in accordance with the law" contrary to Art.8.

[145] (14176/88) (Dec.) January 19, 1989; (18264/91) (Dec.) September 8, 1993, struck off when the Government admitted two letters had have been wrongly stopped and no further hindrance followed; *William Faulkner*, fn.131 above, the applicant ceased to be a victim under Art.34 in respect of a legal letter which the authorities accepted should not have been opened and gave an apology and assurance for the future; *Touroude v France*, (35502/97) (Dec.) October 3, 2000, and *Sayoud v France*, (70456/01) (Dec.) December 7, 2006, no interference where only one letter out of many was opened in error and no indication of deliberate intention or system breakdown; *Armstrong v UK*, (48521/99) (Dec.) September 25, 2001, "incidental errors" where apologies and an assurance given during ombudsman procedures concerning opening of letters with the Court and solicitors.

[146] *Messina v Italy*, February 26, 1993, Series A, No.257–H, the list contained the letters received at the prison and sent to the investigating judge to be censored, without trace of what happened afterwards. Similarly in *Gagiu*, fn.135, it was for the Government to provide due records showing that they had provided the applicant with postage stamps for his letters to the Court.

[147] (9658–9/82), fn.137 above; *AB v Netherlands*, January 29, 2002, para.92.

[148] (32783/96) (Dec.) September 11, 1997; (33742/96) (Dec.) September 11, 1997; *AB v Netherlands*, fn.147 above, para.93.

[149] *Petrov v Bulgaria*, fn.116, paras 53–56.

[150] *Golder v UK*, February 21, 1975, Series A, No.18, 1 E.H.R.R. 524, paras 35–36.

[151] *Campbell and Fell v UK*, June 28, 1984, Series A, No.80, 7 E.H.R.R. 165; also *Ocalan v Turkey*, May 12, 2005, ECHR 2005–V, para.133, where it was considered essential, despite security considerations, for the defence that the PKK leader have conferences with his lawyers out of hearing of security officers. The restriction on the number and length of the visits disclosed additional grounds for violation of Art.6, paras 1, 3(b) and 3(c).

access of a solicitor, including search and continual close presence of prison officers may be justified by security considerations.[152] Refusal of consultation with a doctor for an independent medical examination concerning alleged injuries may raise an issue under Art.6, para.1 where it concerns possible litigation for assault by prison officers, though there is as such no automatic right to such facilities.[153]

Regarding letters, imposing a delay on consultation by letter with a solicitor regarding possible claims pending internal enquiries—"prior ventilation rule"—was found to disclose violations of both Arts 6 (access to court) and 8 (respect for correspondence).[154] *Campbell v UK* settled that it was unjustified to open any correspondence with a lawyer outside the presence of the applicant and in the absence of a good reason. A blanket opening rule was incompatible and where there were reasons to suspect abuse or illicit enclosures, opening might be justified if guarantees against abuse were offered by allowing the prisoner to be present.[155] The opening of the applicant's letters with his defence lawyer was found to be a justified interference where special considerations attached to the suspected terrorist status of the applicant and the implementation was supervised by a magistrate unconnected with the criminal trial.[156]

In *Campbell*, the same strong presumption against opening was found to apply to correspondence with the Commission, which were likely to contain complaints about the prison and lead to risk of reprisals by staff, and in later cases to correspondence with the Court.[157] Restrictive measures concerning correspondence with the Convention organs may also disclose interference with the right of individual petition contrary to Art.34,[158] including the failure to provide the necessary writing materials.[159]

A prisoner without funds is in a difficult position as regards pursuing his civil rights in a court. The Commission found that refusal of legal aid on the basis that there were no prospects of success was not incompatible with requirements of access to court, given that there was no specific right to legal aid in respect of civil matters in the Convention. There was the rider that the refusal had not been shown to be arbitrary. However, the Commission accepted the refusal of legal aid even where counsel had stated there was a prima facie case supported by medical evidence.[160]

Where a prisoner's civil rights are in issue in internal disciplinary proceedings, access to court to review the imposition of restrictions is required (see below, sub-s.11: Internal prison discipline).

[152] (12323/86) (Dec.) July 13, 1988, 57 D.R. 48; *Ocalan*, fn.151 above, para.149.

[153] *Campbell and Fell*, (Rep.), fn.151 above, paras 153–156.

[154] *Campbell and Fell*, fn.151 above, paras 105–111; *McComb v UK*, (10621/83) (Dec.) March 11, 1985, screening of legal correspondence concerning pending court proceedings disclosed an admissible issue of interference with access to court: settled.

[155] A complete ban on correspondence with the applicant's representative in Strasbourg proceedings was also found unjustifiable in *AB v Netherlands*, fn.104 above, paras 86–88, although the representative, not a lawyer, was a former inmate of the same prison.

[156] *Erdem v Germany*, July 21, 2001, ECHR 2001–VII.

[157] Also *Rehbock v Slovenia*, November 28, 2000, ECHR 2000–XII, paras 96–101, no compelling reasons justifying the opening of letters from the Commission or Court; *Peers v Greece*, April 19, 2001, para.84, discounting the risk of Commission envelopes being forged to smuggle prohibited material into the prison as negligible; *Valasinas*, fn.41 above, para.129.

[158] e.g *Petra v Romania*, September 23, 1998, R.J.D. 1998–VII, No. 90, para.44. See Pt IIB, s.25: Hindrance in the exercise of the right of individual petition.

[159] *Cotlet v Romania*, June 3, 2003, para.71.

[160] (8158/78) (Dec.) July 10, 1980, 21 D.R. 95, the Commission commented that it was open to the prisoner to initiate proceedings by other means and noted that he had been able to find a lawyer to bring the case to Strasbourg.

Refusal of temporary leave from prison was found in one case to impact on a prisoner's rehabilitation in civil society and thus to require access to court to challenge the refusal. The somewhat surprising finding that this sufficed to disclose civil rights were at stake in the case is under review in the Grand Chamber.[161]

9. Practice of religion and beliefs

Occasional complaints have been made concerning interference with religious beliefs or matters of conscience by prison regimes. Few serious issues have yet been found to arise. II–576

Claims by Orthodox prisoners that prison food failed to respect dietary requirements was contested strongly by the UK Government and failed for non-exhaustion.[162] A proven failure to provide a dietary regime in conformity with religious requirements is likely to cause a problem. Where a Buddhist prisoner was not able to enjoy a meat-free diet, the Court found a violation, considering that he had not asked for any special items or for any particular method of cooking, and thus that the Government's claim that it would be administratively or financially onerous was not found convincing.[163]

What constitutes a religious commitment is perhaps a sensitive area. There has been no success as yet in claiming that working is against a religious belief.[164] Where a prisoner claimed that it infringed his vegan beliefs to work in a prison workshop which entailed contact with dyes, the Commission, which considered that vegan convictions in relation to animal products could fall within the scope of Art.9, appeared sceptical noting the Government's point that the applicant first refused the work on the basis that he preferred work outdoors and rejected the case, referring to the dubious substantiation of any link between the dyes and animals and the minor nature of the penalties which he suffered for refusing to work.[165] Where a life prisoner, converted after conviction to Islam, complained that while he had changed his name by deed poll the prison refused to use this name for some internal prison purposes, the question of whether this interfered with any religious belief was left undecided when the case settled.[166]

A personal belief that one is a political prisoner is not sufficient to constitute a right to wear personal clothing.[167]

The provision of facilities or the opportunity to worship or have contact with religious ministers is probably required by Art.9. In *Chester v UK*,[168] a prisoner complained that he had been deprived of the possibility of attending religious services in the chapel which the Government stated had been closed down as being insecure. The case was communicated but later struck off, after it appeared that the applicant had received visits from the chaplain in his cell, services were conducted in the segregation unit and the applicant lost interest in pursuing the complaint. In

[161] *Boulois v Luxembourg*, December 14, 2010.
[162] (13669/88), fn.8 above.
[163] *Jakobski v Poland*, December 7, 2010, paras 42–55.
[164] (8231/78) (Dec.) March 6, 1982, 28 D.R.5.
[165] (18187/91) (Dec.) February 10, 1993.
[166] (26651/95) (Dec.) May 13, 1996; (11046/84) December 10, 1985, 45 D.R. 236, where a murderer wished to lose his infamous name, it was compatible with Art.8 in the interests of prison administration to retain the name for internal use.
[167] (8231/78), fn.164 above.
[168] (14747/89) (Dec.) October 1, 1990.

Kuznetzov v Ukraine,[169] where a prisoner on death row was unable to attend the weekly religious services with other prisoners and was not visited by a priest for a number of years, the Court found a breach of Art.9 as the interference had no basis in law (not "in accordance with law") and thus did not need to consider the necessity of the restrictions.

10. Education, leisure facilities, expression and voting

II–577 Limitation on educational and leisure activities may be justified by security or associated considerations as in *Boyle v UK*, where a complaint concerning prohibition of pursuit of sculpting activities in his cell was found justified from the risk posed by the sculpting tools.[170] The refusal to Boyle, a prolific writer, of a typewriter was not a problem as there was no indication that the lack of one hindered his freedom to communicate or impart ideas in manuscript.[171] Where there were drastic restrictions on access to library, TV and radio facilities, the Commission had regard to the prisoners' own responsibility for the protest campaign being waged.[172] Similarly, restriction on access to the library to a prisoner who refused clothes was acceptable in light of his own difficult behaviour and the fact that he received books via the education officer.[173] However, severe, long-term restrictions on exercise and other activities played a role in the finding of Art.3 violations in the Ukrainian death row cases.[174]

Violation of freedom of expression was found where there was a restriction on access to newpapers and periodicals to a difficult prisoner, which reduced his contact with the outside world and was not, unlike other restrictions, justified by considerations of security or order.[175] In the same case a general prohibition on sending out academic or scientific writings fell foul of Art.10. Access to outside publications may be legitimately restricted to prevent crime and disorder or the protection of the rights of others, as in a case of a prisoner who complained that the authorities confiscated the anti-semitic "Gothic Ripples" literature.[176]

There were also relevant and sufficient reasons for prison authorities refusing to pass on to a prisoner copy of a manuscript of a draft book from his solicitor in which he described his crimes, namely the offense to public opinion and distress to the families of his victims. The Court distinguished a work by a murderer himself from an objective account by a third person; it found that his writings could not be considered a serious contribution to issues of criminal justice or other matters of public interest but was instead a platform for him to seek to justify himself, written in lurid and pornographic terms.[177]

Imposition of seven days' solitary confinement as punishment for a prisoner writing allegedly defamatory statements against police and prison officers in his private diary disclosed a violation, the Court commenting that the authorities should

[169] See fn.44 above, paras 148–151.

[170] Also *Messina*, fn.98 above, where the applicant was barred from craft activities requiring the use of dangerous tools and there was no indication that he was excluded from work altogether.

[171] (9659/82), fn.137 above.

[172] (8317/80), fn.28 above.

[173] (8231/86), fn.164 above.

[174] *Poltoratskiy*, et al in fn.44 above.

[175] (8231/78), fn.164, above.

[176] (13214/87) (Dec.) December 9, 1988, 59 D.R. 244.

[177] *Denis Nilsen v UK*, (36882/05) (Dec.) March 9, 2010.

have shown more restraint and provided particularly solid justification where the statements were written in the context of criticism of conditions of detention.[178]

A general and automatic ban on voting by all convicted prisoners was found disproportionate and in breach of Art.3 of Protocol No.1 as not showing a discernible and sufficient link between the sanction and the conduct and circumstances of the individual concerned. Impliedly, removal of the vote would have to be justified by the nature of the crime or its seriousness, with a strong hint that it should be imposed judicially.[179]

11. Internal prison discipline

Whether internal prison disciplinary proceedings attract the procedural guarantees of Art.6, para.1 depends on whether they fall within the *Engel* criteria (see Pt IIA, s.1a: Criminal charge). Loss of remission was found to constitute a penalty akin to a deprivation of liberty in *Campbell and Fell*, as was the addition of extra days to a sentence in *Ezeh and Connors v UK*, where the Court stated that there would be a presumption that Art.6 applied to the imposition of extra days unless the deprivations of liberty involved were not "appreciably detrimental" given their nature, duration or manner of execution.[180] **II–578**

Where Art.6 applies to prison disciplinary proceedings, the tribunal concerned must be impartial and independent of the executive and, even where there are good reasons to exclude the public from the proceedings, some steps must be taken to give public scrutiny to the proceedings.[181]

Lack of legal assistance, of a prisoner's own choosing, for consultation before or at the hearing also disclosed a violation of Art.6, paras 3(b) and (c) in *Campbell and Fell*.[182] It was, however, compatible with Art.6, para.3(b) that the prisoner was only informed of charges five days before the hearing and that he received notices relevant to the proceedings only the day before, it being noted that he did not make a request for an adjournment. It is perhaps unlikely in the context of prison detention that liberal facilities will be considered necessary for the purposes of Art.6. The requirement for free legal representation under Art.6, para.3(c) is, however, conditional on the interests of justice. Whether a person could claim such legal aid is likely to depend on the nature and complexity of the issues and the importance of what is at stake for the applicant.

Where disciplinary procedures and punishments impinge on the enjoyment of other rights, Art.6 may come into play in its civil head. For example, where visiting rights have a basis in domestic law, they will found a claim for access to court to

[178] *Yankov*, fn.36 above, paras 134–145.

[179] *Hirst (No.2)*, fn.1 above, paras 71, 77 and 82. See also *Frodl v Austria*, April 8, 2010, concerning a ban on voting for all prisoners sentenced to more than one year imprisonment: this was also found to lack a sufficient and discernible link between the crime and the disenfranchisement, and the lack of individualised judicial decision-making expressly criticised. See also Part IIB, s.14: Electoral Rights. The issue is again pending before the Grand Chamber in *Scoppola v Italy (No.3)*.

[180] *Ezeh and Connors v UK*, October 9, 2003, ECHR 2003–X, paras 120–129, 40 and 7 day penalties qualified. See *Engel*, where two days did not.

[181] *Campbell and Fell*, fn.151 above, where there were no steps to make the decision public. See also, mutatis mutandis, a violation in *Riepan v Austria*, November 14, 2000, ECHR 2000–XII, where a criminal trial took place in a prison without sufficient public access.

[182] Breach of Art.6, para.3(c) for lack of legal representation in *Ezeh and Connors*, fn.180 above, paras 131–134.

challenge restrictions, as they are regarded as personal rights in nature, and thus civil.[183] Failure to allow prisoners effectively to present their disciplinary appeals before the relevant tribunals may disclose violations.[184] On the same basis, prisoners should enjoy proper access to court to contest the imposition of detention of a restrictive regime which affects visiting and pecuniary rights.[185]

Cross-reference

Part IIA, s.1a: Criminal charge.
Part IIB, s.13: Education.
Part IIB, s.29: Immigration and expulsion, para.II–504: Treatment of asylum seekers and irregular immigrants pending domestic procedures.
Part IIB, s.31: Marriage and founding a family.
Part IIB, s.37: Private life.
Part IIB, s.42: Review of detention.
Part IIB, s.46: Torture, inhuman and degrading treatment.

[183] See e.g. *Gulmez v Turkey*, May 20, 2008, paras 28–30.
[184] See e.g. *Gulmez*, fn.183 above.
[185] *Enea*, fn.32, paras 103–107. See also *Stegarescu and Bahrin v Portugal*, April 6, 2010, paras 35–40, Art.6 applied where the applicants were contesting being placed in isolation which restricted visits, studying and sitting exams, and exercise: violation as there was no access to judicial review.

37. Private life

Key provision:

Article 8 (respect for private life). II–579

Key case-law:

Klass v Germany, September 6, 1978, Series A, No.28, 2 E.H.R.R. 214; *Dudgeon v UK*, October 22, 1981, Series A, No.45, 4 E.H.R.R. 149; *Rasmussen v Denmark*, November 28, 1984, Series A, No.87, 7 E.H.R.R. 371; *X and Y v Netherlands*, March 26, 1985, Series A, No.91, 8 E.H.R.R. 235; *Gaskin v UK*, July 7, 1989, Series A, No.160, 12 E.H.R.R. 36; *Niemietz v Germany*, December 16, 1992, Series A, No.251–B, 16 E.H.R.R. 97; *Funke v France*, February 25, 1993, Series A, No.256–A, 16 E.H.R.R. 297; *Costello-Roberts v UK*, March 25, 1993, Series A, No.247–C, 19 E.H.R.R. 112; *Burghartz v Switzerland*, February 22, 1994, Series A, No.280–B, 18 E.H.R.R.36; *Murray v UK*, October 28, 1994, Series A, No.300–A, 19 E.H.R.R. 193; *Stjerna v Finland*, November 25, 1994, Series A, No.299–B, 24 E.H.R.R. 195; *Laskey, Jaggard and Brown v UK*, February 19, 1997, R.J.D. 1997–I, No.29, 24 E.H.R.R. 392; *Z v Finland*, February 25, 1997, R.J.D. 1997–IV, No.44, 25 E.H.R.R. 371; *Amann v Switzerland*, February 16, 2000, ECHR 2000–II, 30 E.H.R.R. 843; *Rotaru v Romania*, May 4, 2000, ECHR 2000–V; *PG and JH v UK*, September 25, 2001, ECHR 2001–IX; *Mikulic v Croatia*, February 7, 2002, ECHR 2002–I; *Pretty v UK*, April 29, 2002, ECHR 2002–III; *Christine Goodwin v UK*, July 11, 2002, ECHR 2002–VI; *Peck v UK*, January 28, 2003, ECHR 2003–I; *Odievre v France*, February 13, 2003, ECHR 2003–III; *Hatton v UK*, July 8, 2003, ECHR 2003–VIII; *Perry v UK*, July 17, 2003; ECHR 2003–IX; *Smirnova v Russia*, July 24, 2003, ECHR 2003–IX; *MC v Bulgaria*, December 4, 2003, ECHR 2003–XII; *Glass v UK*, 9 March 2004, ECHR 2004–II; *Von Hannover v Germany*, June 24, 2004; *S. and Marper v UK*, December 4, 2008, ECHR 2008–. . .

1. General considerations

Private life is not a concept which has received any exhaustive definition by the Convention organs, which have generally preferred, as in most areas, to restrict themselves to the particular problem in hand. The scope of the term is potentially very wide. It is a notion which also tends to overlap with the other interests protected under Art.8—family life, home and correspondence, as in *Klass v Germany*[1] where interception of communications (mail and phone) was potentially an interference with family and private life, correspondence and home while, in *Mentes v Turkey*,[2] the Commission found that the deliberate destruction of the applicants' homes and possessions by the State security forces cut across the entire personal sphere protected by Art.8, family life, private life and home and it was not necessary to distinguish them. II–580

The concept stands for the sphere of immediate personal autonomy. This covers aspects of physical and moral integrity.[3] It is wider than the right to privacy.

[1] *Klass v Germany*, September 6, 1978, Series A, No.28, 2 E.H.R.R. 214, para.41.

[2] *Mentes v Turkey*, November 28, 1997, R.J.D. 1997–VIII, No.59, para.73, the Court adopted the Commission's reasoning.

[3] *X and Y v Netherlands*, March 26, 1985, Series A, No.91, 8 E.H.R.R. 235, para.22. See also *Bensaid v UK*, February 6, 2001, ECHR 2001–I, para.47, where mental health was regarded as a crucial part of moral integrity and the preservation of mental health a vital precondition to the effective enjoyment of private life.

According to the Commission, it ensures a sphere within which everyone can freely pursue the development and fulfillment of his personality.[4] This necessarily comprises the right to an identity[5] and includes the right to develop relationships with other persons, in particular in the emotional field and including sexual ones with other persons.[6] Thus for the Commission the notion of private life was not limited to "an inner circle" in which the individual might live his own personal life as he chose and exclude therefrom the outside world but extended further, comprising to a certain degree the right to establish and develop relationships with other human beings and the outside world.[7] The Court has been more hesitant in making broad statements[8] but was clear in its approach to intimate aspects of sexual life in the adult homosexual cases.[9]

An emphasis on human dignity has recently emerged,[10] with reference to the notion of "self-determination" and "quality of life" in *Pretty v UK*, where the Court found that the complaints of the applicant, suffering from a painful degenerative disease, about the inability to end her life with the assistance of her husband fell within the scope of Art.8 although the prohibition on assisted suicide was found justified as necessary to protect the vulnerable.[11] There is a strong hint that the Court would consider seriously complaints from a person who was prevented from exercising a choice to decline medical treatment that prolonged suffering or would continue life in a state of advanced mental or physical decrepitude.[12]

2. Extent of the "private" sphere

II–581 There are limits on the personal sphere or inner circle. While many measures by the State will affect an individual's possibility of developing his personality by doing what he wants, not all can be considered an interference with private life under Art.8. The Convention organs have tended, at least in the past, to find that the claim to respect for private life automatically reduces to the extent that an individual brought his private life into contact with public life or other protected interests.[13] In *Friedl v Austria*, the Commission considered it highly relevant, as regarded the

[4] (6825/75) (Dec.) May 18, 1976, 5 D.R. 86.

[5] *Burghartz v Switzerland*, (Rep.) February 22, 1994, Series A, No.280–B, 18 E.H.R.R.36, para.47; *Mikulic v Croatia*, February 7, 2002, ECHR 2002–I,, para.54, finding an entitlement to establish details of identity as a human being and to obtain information with important formative implications (i.e. in paternity proceedings); *Odievre v France*, February 13, 2003, ECHR 2003–III, para.29, the adopted applicant's claims to discover the identity of her natural parents/family/circumstances of her birth concerned her private life.

[6] (6959/75) (Rep.) July 12, 1977, 10 D.R. 100.

[7] *Friedl v Austria*, (Rep.) May 19, 1994, Series A, No.305–B, para.45.

[8] See *Stjerna v Finland*, November 25, 1994, Series A, No.299–B, 24 E.H.R.R. 195, para.37; *Burghartz*, fn.5 above, para.24.

[9] *Dudgeon v UK*, October 22, 1981, Series A, No.45, 4 E.H.R.R. 149, para.41. See Pt IIB, s.27: Homosexuality.

[10] *Pretty v UK*, April 29, 2002, ECHR 2002–III, para.65, *Christine Goodwin v UK*, July 11, 2002, ECHR 2002–VI, para.90.

[11] *Pretty*, fn.10 above, paras 61–78. See also *Haas v Switzerland*, January 20, 2011, paras 50–61, right of individual to decide when and how to end his life fell within Art.8 but the State was not obliged to make lethal drugs available to a chronic bipolar sufferer.

[12] *Pretty*, fn.10 above, para.64.

[13] Also *Ludi v Switzerland*, June 15, 1992, Series A, No.238, para.40, where the Court excluded criminal activities from "private life"; Mr Geus, dissenting in *Burghartz* (Rep.), fn.5 above, considered that the applicant's surname was a manifestly public feature.

extent to which the taking of photographs by the police and their retention in files amounted to an intrusion in the individual's privacy, whether it related to private matters or public incidents.[14] Thus no interference with private life arose where photographs were taken of a person participating in a public incident[15] nor in respect of communication of statements made during public proceedings.[16] Similarly while hunting might be a traditional and important part of the lives of some persons, it was primarily a public activity removed from the sphere of personal autonomy and the aspects of inter-personal relationships involved too broad to render regulation of hunting an interference with rights under Art.8. Nor was participation in a common social activity enough to constitute a minority or ethnic lifestyle protected by Art.8 either.[17]

In the Icelandic dog case,[18] the Commission stated that protection of Art.8 did not extend to relationships of the individual with his entire immediate surroundings insofar as they did not involve human relationships (see below: Pets) In the context of abortion, the Commission took the view that pregnancy could not be said to pertain uniquely to the sphere of private life.[19] The life of the pregnant woman was seen as closely connected with the developing foetus and not every regulation of the termination of unwanted pregnancies would constitute an interference with the right to respect for private life.

However, the mere fact that the individual is in a public area or the personal information about an individual is accessible to others or in the public domain will not always exclude the application of Art.8. The Court has stated that a number of elements are relevant to the consideration of whether a person's private life is concerned in measures effected outside a person's home or private premises. A person's reasonable expectations as to privacy may be a significant, though not necessarily decisive, factor[20] as well as whether the individual voluntarily supplied the information or there was reasonable anticipation of the later use made of the material.[21] For example, publication of photographs taken of Caroline of Hannover's daily life, showing her, inter alia, shopping, riding, in a restaurant and at a beach club, were considered as clearly falling within the scope of her private life,[22] as was a picture of an applicant taken by the police on arrest for investigative purposes which they handed over to the press. In the latter case, the applicant's status as an "ordinary person" enlarged the zone of interaction with others which may fall within

[14] *Friedl*, fn.7 above.

[15] (5877/72) 45 Coll. 90; *Steel and Morris v UK*, (68416/01) (Dec.) October 22, 2002, where McDonalds' use of inquiry agents to attend Greenpeace events did not fall within "private life", which was inapplicable to places freely accessible to the public.

[16] (3868/68) 34 Coll. 10.

[17] *Friend v UK*, (16072/06) and (277809/08) (Dec.) November 24, 2009.

[18] See fn.4 above.

[19] (6959/75), fn.6 above. See Pt IIB, s.1: Abortion.

[20] *PG and JH v UK*, September 25, 2001, ECHR 2001–IX, para.57; *Peck v UK*, January 28, 2003, ECHR 2003–I, paras 58–63, the applicant could not have foreseen that the CCTV recording of his suicide attempt would be broadcast on television; *Wypych v Poland*, (2428/05) (Dec.) October 25, 2005, political figures should have less expectation of privacy.

[21] e.g. *Lupker v Netherlands*, (18385/91) (Dec.) December 7, 1992, the photographs in the police album had not been obtained through any invasion of privacy but submitted in passport applications or taken on earlier arrests. Conversely, in *Perry v UK*, July 17, 2003, ECHR 2003–IX, para.41, the applicant, who had refused an identification parade, had no expectation that footage from a visible CCTV camera was being taken for identification: this was beyond normal or expected use of the camera.

[22] *Von Hannover v Germany*, June 24, 2004, para.53.

the scope of private life, and the fact that the applicant was the subject of criminal proceedings did not curtail the scope of such protection.[23] There was an interference with personality rights where insurance investigators monitored the applicant's movements, taking photographs and video footage in public places.[24]

However, where a person has entered the arena as a public figure, such as a politician, it appears that there are no restrictions applicable to the publishing of photographs by the media, as long as no other details of private life are disclosed thereby.[25] It appears that e-mails and internet usage at work may fall within private life, where the employee has not been warned that such would be liable to monitoring.[26] There is also a reasonable expectation of privacy in an office as regards personal belongings and documents in desks and filing cabinets.[27]

Disclosure of personal details and medical information concerns private life.[28] Also a systematic or permanent recording of material taken in the public domain, or any processing of such data will generally bring the measure within the scope of Art.8.[29] The collecting and storing of information about an applicant employee's use of the telephone, even legitimately obtained for payment purposes, constituted an interference.[30] The seriousness of the intrusion and the degree of public exposure resulting from the measure may also be relevant, as in *Peck v UK*, where the CCTV footage of the applicant's attempted suicide in a public place was shown on national television without adequate masking of his identity. The degree of targeted surveillance disclosed by permanent camera monitoring of a remand prisoner in his cell constituted an interference with private life, notwithstanding the setting or lack of processing of data.[31]

The right to protection of one's image extends not only to the unauthorised publication of photographs or footage but also to the taking of images without consent, otherwise a third party would effectively gain control over images and their subsequent use . Thus, even though the photographs taken of the applicants' baby

[23] *Sciacca v Italy*, January 11, 2005, para.29. See also *Khuzhin v Russia*, October 23, 2008; no legitimate aim, such as the need to locate suspects, pursued in releasing to the press the police photos of the applicants who had been arrested; and *Toma v Romania*, February 24, 2009, paras 90–91, violation where the police permitted the press to take footage of him on police premises which was shown on TV.

[24] *Verliere v Switzerland*, (41953/98) (Dec.) June 28, 2001, ECHR 2001–VIII, the domestic courts had struck the right balance, however, when finding that the interference had not gone beyond the insurers' legitimate and lawful interest in verifying her claims.

[25] *Krone Verlag GMBH Co KG v Austria*, February 26, 2002, para.37; no issues arose under Art.8 concerning publication of photographs of celebrities already known to the public which did not disclose details of private life: *Pipi v Turkey*, (4020/03) (Dec.) May 12, 2005.

[26] *Copland v UK*, April 3, 2007, para.42.

[27] *Peev v Bulgaria*, July 26, 2007, paras 37–39, a search of the applicant's office in a government building by prosecutors and removal of a draft resignation letter interfered with private life.

[28] e.g. *CC v Spain*, October 6, 2009, where a judge revealed the applicant's HIV status in the judgment.

[29] e.g. *Amann v Switzerland*, February 16, 2000, ECHR 2000–II; 30 E.H.R.R. 843, paras 65–66, concerning creation and storage of a card containing professional and business details; *Rotaru v Romania*, May 4, 2000, ECHR 2000–V, paras 43–44, where public information was systematically collected; *PG and JH*, fn.20 above, para.59, concerning covert taping of the applicants' voices in the police station for voice analysis; *Perry*, fn.21 above, paras 41–42, concerning covert videotaping of the applicant in the custody area for an identification video; *Verliere*, fn.24 above. Conversely, viewing a person in the street or over CCTV cameras, without recording, is not covered: *PG and JH*, fn.20 above, para.57.

[30] *Copland*, fn.26 above, although the Court hinted it could be justified if duly authorised in accordance with law (para.48).

[31] *Van der Graaf v Netherlands*, (8704/03) (Dec.) June 1, 2004, measure justified in highly sensitive criminal case to prevent any risk to the applicant from himself or others.

at the clinic were never published, there was an interference with private life as they had been taken without the parents' consent.[32]

Difficulties imposed on the way on which a person can interract with the outside world and live their daily lives as a whole may, if sufficiently serious, fall within the scope of Art.8, as in *Smirnova v Russia*, where the applicant's internal passport, which was crucial to everyday life, from buying train tickets to obtaining medical treatment, had been withheld for over four years.[33] Withdrawal of a passport for 15 years was found to impinge seriously on private life in an age where international travel was part of personal development and many individuals' lives were based in several countries.[34] Stop and search powers on the streets of London fell within the scope of Art.8, since people had to submit to a coercive and detailed search of their person, clothing and belongings; the fact that it was in a public place did not detract from this, since, unlike in the airport context, where there was forewarning, the individual had no choice to walk away rather than go through the search.[35]

The placing of a television under seal in the applicant's home for failure to pay his licence fee concerned his ability to receive information and his private life in a broad sense, even if the interference was justified.[36]

The employment and professional world are not excluded since it is in the workplace people forge relations with the world; thus a ban on entering into particular jobs may raise issues.[37] Where a Russian student who had pursued her legal studies in Greece was prevented, due to a nationality restriction, from sitting the final exam leading to inscription on the roll of barristers, the Court found that this had an impact on her chosen career path and professional life which interfaced with private concerns and relationships with others, thus falling within Art.8.[38]

Constraints on a person's choice of mode of dress may also constitute an interference with private life, although the requirements to wear prison uniform or to adhere to a workplace dress code have been found proportionate and justifiable restrictions.[39]

The Court found no direct link between the State's failure to ensure proper access for handicapped persons to a beach and the applicant's private life[40]; nor any lack of respect where a disabled person could not obtain access to a polling station, though it is not excluded that a lack of facilities could engage Art.8 if significantly

[32] *Reklos and Davourlis v Greece*, January 15, 2009, paras 38–41, the courts failed to protect the applicants' son's private life in refusing their claims for damages against the clinic which had retained the negatives.

[33] Also *B v France*, where daily aggravation arose from the anomalous gender identification on a transsexual's identity documents; *M v Switzerland*, April 26, 2011, paras 57–58, refusal to renew a passport of a citizen living overseas was an interference as lack of papers could impact on daily life.

[34] *Iletmis v Turkey*, June 12, 2005. See further, sub-s.8: Nationality.

[35] *Gillan and Quinton v UK*, January 12, 2010, paras 61–65, the Court rejected the Government's attempt to establish a distinction between particularly intrusive searches involving for example the perusing of personal documents and superficial ones.

[36] *Faccio v Italy*, (33/04) (Dec.) March 31, 2009, it was regarded as a tax funding a public service which was of a reasonable amount and not disproportionate to its purpose.

[37] e.g. *Sidabras and Dziautas v Lithuania*, (55480/00) and (59330/00) July 27, 2004, para.47; *Albanese v Italy*, March 23, 2006, where automatic imposition of various legal and professional incapacities following bankruptcy was unjustified, imposing a punitive moral stigma.

[38] *Bigaeva v Greece*, May 28, 2009, paras 23–25.

[39] (8317/78) (Dec.) May 15, 1980, 20 D.R. 91; (36528/97) (Dec.) October 22, 1998. See also *Tig v Turkey*, (8165/03) (Dec.) May 24, 2005, prohibition on having a beard in university was not found to infringe private life.

[40] *Botta v Italy*, (Rep.) R.J.D. 1998–I, No.66, para.35, the Commission referred to a wide discretion in the area of recreational activities.

restricting a disabled person's ability to enter into relations with others.[41] Where a handicapped person, refused the possibility of performing military or substitute service, was subjected to an exemption tax, this imposition based on the applicant's physical state was regarded as falling within the ambit of private life.[42]

The notion of personal living space may attract the protection of Art.8, where it is for example invaded by significant pollution. Thus, a prisoner could complain of the effect on his quality of life and potential health risk which he suffered in his cell due to the proximity of an unlawful, and highly noisome tip.[43]

Once Art.8 is applicable, the second paragraph imposes requirements of lawfulness and proportionality, including sufficient safeguards against abuse or disclosure inconsistent with private life rights. Lack of statutory regulation or provision of adequate protection for the individual has thus in a number of cases disclosed violation of Art.8.[44] The Court has also increasingly imported a positive obligation aspect, considering that where a breach of privacy has been shown to have arisen, the authorities have an obligation to ensure respect for private life by putting the matter right, whether by carrying out inquiries to rectify the matter as much as possible, including sanctioning those responsible.[45]

Further, protection of the right to privacy requires the State to offer adequate redress and provide deterrence against breaches of confidentiality. Thus, where domestic law limited compensation for even outrageous breaches of private life, there was a breach of the positive obligation.[46] Similarly as concerns damage to physical integrity, the domestic legal system must provide an adequate and effective means of obtaining reparation, including civil damages.[47]

It had been left open as to whether a criminal conviction imposed on a university professor for failure to comply with court orders to make available his research data to other researchers constituted an interference with private life. The professor had contended that his action was motivated by his ethical obligation of confidentiality to his child research subjects. In any event, the Court found that the conviction was for failure of public duty as an official head of department and that the domestic courts had not acted disproportionately, given their findings that there was no absolute obligation of confidentiality for research subjects under domestic law and the issue of disclosure, subject to conditions, had been settled by the administrative courts.[48]

[41] *Molka v Poland*, (56550/00) (Dec.) April 11, 2006. Also *Zehnalova and Zehnal v Czech Republic*, (38621/97) (Dec.) May 14, 2002, concerning lack of disabled access to public buildings, there was insufficient concrete proof of serious detriment to personal development or ability to enter into relations with others.

[42] *Glor v Switzerland*, April 30, 2009, the Court found discriminatory treatment contrary to Art.14 in conjunction with Art.8.

[43] *Branduse v Romania*, April 7, 2009, paras 64–67. See also Part IIB, s.15: Environment.

[44] e.g. findings of lack of "lawfulness" or proper legal regulation in *Amann*, *Rotaru*, *PG and JH*, and *Sciacca*, fn.21 above; insufficient protection of the applicant's position in *Peck*, fn.21 above, paras 80–87, no effort to obtain his consent to the TV transmission and inadequate masking of his identity.

[45] e.g. *Craxi v Italy (No.2)*, July 17, 2003, paras 74–75 above; *Giorgi Nikloaishvili v Georgia*, January 13, 2009, para.130.

[46] *Armoniene v Lithuania*, November 25, 2008, the maximum was set at approximately £2,000 and applied to a case where the newspaper had published details of the applicant's husband's HIV status as well as untrue allegations of infidelity and children born out of wedlock.

[47] *Codarcea v Romania*, June 3, 2009.

[48] *Gillberg v Sweden*, November 2, 2010. Pending before the Grand Chamber.

3. State obligations: non-interference and positive protection

A Contracting State must not only restrict its own interferences to what is compatible with Art.8, which provides a primarily negative undertaking, but may also be required to take steps to secure respect for its rights, whether through the protection of domestic law or more specific measures.[49] The extent to which a State may be under such a positive obligation will vary with the differing situations obtaining in Contracting States which enjoy in this respect a wide margin of appreciation in determining the steps to be taken to ensure compliance with the Convention having regard to the needs and resources of the community and individuals.[50] II–582

Insofar as positive obligations are concerned, the Court has helpfully indicated that the notion of "respect" is not clear cut. It has stated that a fair balance must be struck between the interests of the individual and those of the community and in striking that balance, the aims referred to in the second paragraph may be relevant.[51]

The cases illustrate that the impact on the applicant's rights must be serious and significant as in *X and Y v Netherlands* (which concerned a serious infringement of physical and moral integrity, i.e. rape), *Gaskin* (where fundamental values and essential aspects of private life or identity were concerned), *B v France* (where the interference was daily and acute) and *Moldovan v Romania (No.2)* (10 years' inaction and hindrance where the Roma applicants had been burned out of their homes).[52] No positive obligation was found in *Costello-Roberts* (where the chastisement was minor).[53]

Whether an important State interest is involved may also be significant as in *Abdulaziz v UK* (where vital State interests in immigration were concerned), *Hatton v UK* (economic interests in maintaining Heathrow's competitiveness) and *Rees* and *Cossey* (claimed State interest in maintaining a historical birth record). In the latter cases, concerning claims of transsexuals to legal recognition of their change of gender, the Court was also swayed by the perceived controversial nature of the phenomenon and the lack of consensus within Contracting States on the approach to be adopted. The Court has since changed its view in *Christine Goodwin v UK*, its judgment indicating that the issues were perceived as less controversial, the consensus in Contracting States was clear and that there were no significant factors of public interest to weigh against the individual right to personal development. In *Odievre v France*, the interests of the natural mother and her family together with the potential impact on the general interest in avoiding illegal abortions rendered the matter of allowing an adopted applicant to obtain information about her birth origins both complex and sensitive and no failure to respect the applicant's private life was thereby disclosed by maintaining confidentiality.[54]

[49] *Costello-Roberts v UK*, March 25, 1993, Series A, No.247–C; 19 E.H.R.R. 112, para.26. See recent statement of case-law on positive obligations in *Moldovan v Romania (No.2)*, July 12, 2005, paras 93–98.

[50] e.g. *Abdulaziz v UK*, May 28, 1985, Series A, No.94, para.67.

[51] *Rees v UK*, October 17, 1986, Series A, No.106, para.37.

[52] See fn.33. Also, (20357/92) (Dec.) March 7, 1994, 76–A D.R. 80 ,where the harassment was extreme and frequent.

[53] Also, (24967/94) (Dec.) February 20, 1995, 80–A D.R. 175, no positive obligation to protect from unsolicited mail, having regard to freedom of expression, a link with funding costs of student facilities: also the commercial information could be easily ignored.

[54] See, however, the persuasive dissent of seven judges who found an emerging consensus for the "right to know" and no significant prejudice arising from a procedure by which the competing interests, including the natural mother's desire for anonymity, could be balanced.

4. Privacy and protection of private life

II–583 The extent to which an issue might arise under private life for press intrusion or the disclosure of intimate, non-defamatory details of private life will be influenced, inter alia, by the extent to which the person concerned courted attention, the nature and degree of the intrusion into the private sphere and the ability of diverse domestic remedies to provide effective and adequate redress.[55] The press cannot rely on any notion of celebrity as justifying intrusive photography or coverage, the Court drawing a decisive distinction between the reporting of matters capable of contributing towards debate in a democratic society and the reporting of details of private life unlinked to official functions or public debate.[56] Thus, in *Von Hannover v Germany*, a breach was disclosed by the publication of photographs of the daily life of the applicant, who though "a figure of contemporary society 'par excellence'" did not exercise any official State functions and had a legitimate expectation of protection of her private life. But where a magazine mainly reprints commercial photographs already published, without distortion, and relies largely on the celebrity's own public statements on his lifestyle, conviction for breach of privacy is not justified.[57] Where no issues of legitimate public interest are engaged, public figures may also have a legitimate expectation of protection against the propagation of rumours relating to intimate aspects of their private life. Newspapers cannot rely in that context of any defence of truth.[58]

Where an applicant complained not only of difficulties in suing for defamation but of the lack of redress for revelations in a book of his love affairs, the Commission noted the need for domestic law to balance the conflicting rights of freedom of expression and right to private life but on the facts of that case (the applicant was relatively successful in his defamation action and settled the case) it was not established that the balance was unfairly struck.[59] Other cases concerning the taking of photographs[60] and a campaign of harassment by an ex-boyfriend which stopped short of actionable torts or crimes[61] were rejected for non-exhaustion of domestic remedies, indicating that problems of exhaustion may arise where the domestic law situation leaves a doubt as to the existence of a remedy or appears to be subject to progressive interpretation. The criteria applied by domestic courts should however ensure effective protection of private life, not being too vague as to prevent the persons concerned determining in advance when they must expect interference.[62]

[55] (28851/95) and (28852/95) (Dec.) January 16, 1998, 92 D.R. 56, introduced by Earl and Countess Spencer concerning press coverage—rejected for non-exhaustion as, in their case, an action for breach of confidence was available; (36908/97) (Dec.) October 21, 1998, where an indistinct photograph was shot through a window, the Commission noted that there had been no intrusion, harassment or exploitation and it was attached to an article in the public interest.

[56] *Hachette Filipacchi Associé ("Ici Paris") v France*, July 23, 2009, para.44, articles concerning Johnny Halliday's lifestyle and alleged monetary problems were not part of a public debate of interest to society; thus, the scope of freedom of expression was narrower and the margin of appreciation was narrower.

[57] *Hachette Filipacchi Associé*, fn.56 above.

[58] *Standard Verlags GmbH (No.2) v Austria*, June 4, 2009, concerning articles alleging the President's marriage had broken down and his wife engaged in adultery with another politician.

[59] (10871/84) (Dec.) July 10, 1986, 48 D.R. 154.

[60] (18760/91) (Dec.) December 1, 1993, where an insurance company had taken photographs of the applicant through a window in order to verify her state of health, the Commission found that she had failed to take an action to test the extent of constitutional protection.

[61] (20357/91), fn.36 above, where it was claimed that the piecemeal protection by domestic law was inadequate: as there were case-law developments extending injunctive relief to "harassment" threatening health, the applicant was expected to test the matter in the courts.

[62] *Von Hannover*, fn.22 above, paras 73–75.

Measures taken against individuals based on elements of their private life attract proper procedural safeguards. Where a judge was dismissed due to allegations centring on her private relationships with a lawyer and others, the Court found a violation as the dismissal was not supported by evidence that the relationships had impinged on her performance of her official duties and there had been insufficient procedural protection of her interests.[63] Domestic courts must strike a fair balance in the employment sphere where factors relating to individuals' private lives are concerned. This was the focus of two German cases, where an employee of the Mormon church was dismissed due to an extramarital relationship and the organist and choirmaster of a Catholic parish was dismissed for living with a new partner after leaving his wife. The domestic courts had upheld the dismissals as lawful bearing in mind the interests of the religious bodies in maintaining their credibility and requiring their employees to respect certain principles. The Court in Strasbourg had noted the existence of court protection and the possibility for the applicants to have their claims examined in light of the Court's jurisprudence. However, it found that the domestic courts in applying the relevant criteria had struck a proper balance in the former case, where the employee had been a high-level official whose conduct reasonably could be regarded as incompatible with obligations of loyalty to his employer.[64] In the latter case, the Court however found that the domestic courts had failed to give adequate weight to the interests of the less prominent individual, who had worked 14 years in his post as organist and choir master, could not easily obtain work outside the church organisation and could not be reasonably be regarded as having undertaken lifelong commitments to celibacy outside marriage through his employment contract; the domestic courts, it was said, did not explain why the parish's interests outweighed those of the individual.[65] Domestic courts, it seems, will have to pay due regard to the Strasbourg case-law as to the way in which they should take the competing interests into account and and should not accept too easily the restrictions placed on individuals' private lives by their employer, particularly where the organisation concerned enjoys a dominant position.

Issues may also arise where a court itself makes statements which affect private life or reputation. Where in a child access case, a court made an obiter statement of suspicion that the applicant father had abused his son, it was found that this had had a stigmatising and traumatic effect, for which no cogent reasons or justification had been given.[66]

5. Personal information

Protection of personal data falls within the scope of private life. II–584

(a) *Content of "personal data"*

Public information can fall within the scope of private life where it is systematically collected and stored in files held by the authorities, particularly were such information concerns a person's distant past or where it is false and likely to injure II–585

[63] *Özpinar v Turkey*, October 19, 2010, paras 67–79, e.g. the applicant had not been provided with copies of the inspector's report or witness' evidence, and only given belated hearing before a body of doubtful independence and impartiality.

[64] *Obst v Germany*, September 23, 2010.

[65] *Schuth v Germany*, September 23, 2010, see in particular para.73, where the Court noted the dominant position of the two principal churches in Germany and appears to have been concerned to prevent abuse of that position.

[66] *Sanchez Cardenas v Norway*, October 4, 2007.

reputation.[67] The Court has also stated that Art.8 corresponds with the Council of Europe's Data Protection Convention whose purpose is to secure for every individual his right to privacy with regards to the automatic processing of personal data relating to him and such personal data being defined as "any information relating to an identified or identifiable individual."[68] Thus it is arguable that the fact of recording and using any personal data is an interference.

While in one old case the obligation to carry identity cards and show them to police was considered not to constitute an interference if the cards did not disclose information relating to private life (the card included name, address, sex, date and place of birth and could exclude mention of personal identification number on request),[69] in *Friedl* the personal data relating to establishing of identity by the police was enough to fall within Art.8.[70] Cellular samples and DNA profiles taken by police in criminal investigations has been held, by their nature and the amount of personal information contained them, to be covered by private life. Even if the information can be considered objective and factual, it impinges on unique aspects of identity as well as being relevant to health issues.[71] Fingerprints contain less information but also constitute personal data; they contain external identification features comparable to personal photographs or voice samples and are unique to the persons concerned.[72] Information about ethnic origin recorded in the civil register and on documents is considered a detail pertaining to a particularly sensitive aspect personal identity.[73] Detailed information about an applicant's finances, income and property is also covered.[74]

Where in *Zdanoka v Latvia* the courts reached a decision imposing restrictions on the applicant's political activities based on her past conduct, the Court found that there had been no interference with her private life as the information had been contained in public official archives or was common knowledge due to her notoriety in recent events and related essentially to her public life.[75] It may be that the gathering of publicly accessible information or information relating to matters or records in the public domain (e.g. press cutting files or criminal records) would fall outside the scope of Art.8, where not obtained by specific or intrusive measures targeting a specific individual or stored long term in a secret file.

(b) Access to personal data

II–586 Where information is stored by public bodies which relates to the private life of a person, issues may arise from a refusal to grant access. The principal case so far is *Gaskin v UK*, which falls short of conferring any general right of access to data. The

[67] *Rotaru*, fn.29 above, paras 43–44.

[68] Convention for the Protection of Individuals with regard to the Automatic Processing of Personal Data, January 28, 1981, in force on October 1, 1985: *Amann*, fn.29 above, para.65; *Rotaru*, fn.29 above, para.43.

[69] (16810/90) (Dec.) September 9, 1992 73 D.R. 136.

[70] *Friedl*, fn.7 above.

[71] *S. and Marper v UK*, December 4, 2008, ECHR 2008–. . . , paras 70–77, the Court rejected the Government's argument that DNA profiles fell outside the personal sphere on the basis that the data was neutral and only intelligible to a few through sophisticated technology.

[72] *S. and Marper*, fn.71 above, paras 80–86, since fingerprints were less data-sensitive than DNA samples and profiles, the justification of interference might be less onerous, however.

[73] *S. and Marper*, fn.71 above, para. 66; also *Ciuboratu v Moldavia*, April 27, 2010, para.49.

[74] *Wypych*, fn.20 above.

[75] (58278/00) (Dec.) March 6, 2003, there was apparently no official or secret file compiled on the applicant.

applicant, in local authority care for most of his childhood, was refused access to his files, which were described as forming the only coherent record of the applicant's early childhood and formative years. A person's entitlement to information of that kind was derived from its relation to his identity and formation of his personality. The Commission held that persons should not be obstructed by the authorities from obtaining such information without specific justification.[76] The Court commented that the finding of violation in the case was without prejudice as to whether general rights of access to personal data and information could be derived from Art.8. Notwithstanding that confidentiality of the records protected the children and rights of the contributors and was important for the receiving of objective and reliable information, it concluded that the applicant had a vital interest in receiving the information and that there was a failure to strike the appropriate balance as there was no independent procedure whereby access could be allowed when a contributor gave an improper reason for refusing, failed to reply, gave consent or could not be traced.[77] Where an applicant had participated in nerve and mustard gas tests, the Court found that the State had a positive obligation to provide an effective and accessible procedure enabling the applicant to have access to all relevant and appropriate information allowing him to assess any risk to which he had been exposed.[78]

Where an applicant's access to personal information held by social services was made subject to certain conditions, the Commission examined the reasonableness of the conditions. It was not arbitrary or unreasonable, in respect of a person with a history of mental illness and where the records related to a brief period, to provide for access to be given to the applicant's doctor who was to judge whether or not the applicant should receive them.[79] Where health data relevant to fertility and past gynaecological treatment was concerned, the Court held that there was a right for access to such personal data, and while it was for the dataholder to determine modalities or the payment required for taking copies, the patient could not be required to provide justification for access; it was rather for the authorities to provide compelling justification for refusing this facility.[80]

On the matter of security files, the Convention organs have not found a general requirement of access or disclosure. Interferences, assessed against a wider margin of appreciation, may be justified where there are sufficient safeguards against the arbitrary use of powers.[81] In lustration proceedings, however, where an applicant seeks to displace an adverse security rating and the information relates to past activities of communist intelligence, the Court has found that there is less active public interest in maintaining confidentiality and that procedural safeguards for the subjects must be afforded. It therefore seems that in this context an applicant may

[76] *Gaskin v UK*, (Rep.) July 7, 1989, Series A, No.160, 12 E.H.R.R. 36, para.89.

[77] See *MG v UK*, September 24, 2002, paras 27–32, no breach for period after entry of force of new appeal procedure which the applicant had not utilised.

[78] *Roche v UK*, October 19, 2005, ECHR 2005–X, paras 157–168.

[79] (27533/95) (Dec.) February 28, 1996, 84–A D.R. 169; also (30039/96) (Dec.) May 20, 1998, access to a deceased mother's medical file by the applicant's doctor was sufficient.

[80] *K.H and Others v Slovakia*, April 28, 2009, paras 47–48; it was not enough that the applicants could access and copy the files by hand; any risk of abusive use of the information could be met by adequate safeguards in the legislative framework.

[81] (25099/94) (Dec.) April 5, 1995, 81–A D.R. 136, where the applicant had partial access. Applicants in other surveillance cases have had no access possibilities, but the Convention organs have not pursued these issues. See Pt IIB, s.44: Surveillance and secret files.

claim effective access to his file and disclosure of former security service rules and practices.[82]

As concerns information held by private bodies, there was no lack of respect for private life where the courts refused to order disclosure to the applicant of handwritten records archived by his bank of meetings at which he attended, such information not relating to his identity or personal history, or obtained by any measure invasive of his privacy, or stored for current use or release to others.[83]

(c) Collection and retention

II–587 The recording of personal information for purposes of criminal investigation generally will concern private life but may be justified. This includes records of past offences, but also information obtained by the police in investigations where no criminal proceedings are brought and even where there is no reasonable suspicion in relation to a specific offence, where special considerations such as fighting terrorism can justify retention. In *McVeigh v UK*,[84] questioning, searching, fingerprinting and photographing of the applicants and subsequent retention of the relevant records constituted an interference but was justified in the interests of public safety and prevention of crime. This was where the applicants were arrested and detained under prevention of terrorism legislation when they arrived in England from Ireland. Even though no criminal charge was brought against them, the Commission accepted that the information was relevant for intelligence purposes and found that there was a pressing social need to fight terrorism which outweighed what it considered as minor infringements of the applicants' rights. Similarly in *Murray v UK*, on the arrest of the applicant, the recording of personal details and photographing were within the legitimate bounds of an investigation of terrorist crime. None of the details were found to be irrelevant to the arrest and interrogation procedures, which seems to imply that the Court would at least impose a check on the nature and extent of the information which the police and security forces recorded, albeit subject to a wide margin of appreciation.

As concerns DNA profiles, the interference involved in taking and retaining the data may be justified where the applicant has been convicted of a serious offence, such retention serving the purpose of preventing crime in the future.[85] A blanket power to retain the data of persons unconvicted, as well as the physical samples themselves, was found to be disproportionate, the Court being unimpressed by claims that building up a huge database of those not convicted was crucial to the prevention of crime. The retention of fingerprints of unconvicted persons was similarly found to be unjustified.[86]

The mere taking and storing of photographs by the police of a public demonstration was not found even to constitute an interference in *Friedl v Austria*.

[82] *Turek v Slovakia*, February 14, 2006, paras 115–116.
[83] *Smith v UK*, (39658/05) (Dec.) January 4, 2007.
[84] (8022/77) (Rep.) March 18, 1981, 25 D.R. 15.
[85] *Van der Velden v Netherlands*, (29514/05) (Dec.) December 7, 2006, provisions applicable to persons convicted of offences carrying a maximum of four years' imprisonment or more and authorising retention for 20–30 years.
[86] *S. and Marper*, fn.71 above, paras 105–126, the Government had not substantiated their claims that DNA profiles, which otherwise would have been destroyed, had played a decisive role in obtaining a significant number of convictions.

There was no identification of the persons on the photographs apparently and the photographs remained in a general administrative file and were not put in a data processing system. The Commission emphasised that the photographs were not taken in any operation invading the applicant's home. The taking of personal data establishing identity and recording that data was an interference but justified since taken for the purpose of pursuing a prosecution even though that did not ensue due to the trivial nature of the offences. Also the data was kept only for a general administrative file about the event and not entered into any data-processing system. This was only a "relatively slight interference" with the applicant's right to respect for his private life.[87] The retention of files destined purely for archivage for period of 50 years did not constitute an interference since there was no effect on private life.[88]

Another major area of personal records is the medical. The taking and storing of such records associated with treatment will generally be justified under the second paragraph, unless there is some failure or shortcoming as regards its use or disclosure to others.[89]

The compulsory requirement to provide information to a census (including sex, marital status, place of birth) was found to be an interference with private and family life but the Commission was satisfied that the interests of the individual were sufficiently safeguarded (replies were strictly confidential, names not used in the computer analysis and original forms not to be released in the Public Records Office for 100 years) and that the aim of economic well-being of the country was pursued.[90]

Compulsion by tax authorities to reveal details of personal expenditure was an interference but justified where the applicant had recently sold properties and the issue arose as to how he had disposed of large sums. It was accepted as necessary in the interests of the economic well-being of the country that he establish these matters though there was a hint that such powers wielded more indiscriminately would be disproportionate.[91]

(d) *Disclosure of personal information*

Disclosure to the public or third parties of personal information constitutes interference less easily justified having regard to the recognition that the protection of personal data is of fundamental importance to a person's enjoyment of his private and family life.[92] The public interest in disclosure must outweigh the individual's right to privacy, having regard to the aim pursued and the safeguards surrounding its use. II–588

The showing of a photograph of an applicant from police files to third persons constituted an interference but was justified for prevention of crime and proportio-

87 See fn.7 above.

88 See fn.54 above.

89 (14461/88) (Dec.) July 9, 1991, 71 D.R. 141, the retention of information in hospital records about psychiatric confinement after the applicant's release was an interference, but it was justified as strict confidentiality was observed and the records served legitimate aims in running the hospital and safeguarding patients' rights, even though the applicant's detention had been unlawful.

90 (9702/82) (Dec.) October 6, 1982, 30 D.R. 239; also (9804/82) (Dec.) December 7, 1982, 31 D.R. 231.

91 (9804/82) (Dec.) December 7, 1982, 31 D.R. 231.

92 *Z v Finland*, February 25, 1997, R.J.D., 1997–IV, No.44, 25 E.H.R.R. 371, para.95; *MS v Sweden*, para.41; *LL v France*, October 10, 2006, para.44.

nate since the photograph was used solely for investigation, was not generally available to public and had not been taken in way which intruded on his privacy, i.e. lawfully by police during earlier arrest.[93] Use by a court of an old police report in order to assess the criminal responsibility of the accused was found to be necessary for the prevention of crime.[94] Disclosure of details of arrest by the police to the press was, assuming this to be an interference, justified as being factual, summary and pursuing the legitimate aim of informing the public on matters of general interest.[95] A requirement on a local councillor to disclose in a public register detailed information about his finances and property was justified by the interests of transparency and preventing corruption.[96] While in *Z v Finland* it was found necessary to order the disclosure of a witness's medical records for the purposes of a trial, the publication of the witness's name and HIV status in the appeal judgment was not justified as necessary for any legitimate aim.[97] The vital principle of confidentiality of medical data was emphasised in *Z v Finland* and *MS v Sweden*. However in the latter, the Court found that it was legitimate for State medical institutions to pass on to social insurance authorities details of the medical history of a claimant for benefits. The measure was proportionate since the details disclosed were relevant to the claim, there was a duty of confidentiality and staff incurred civil and/or criminal liability for abuse.

Provisions for general disclosure of categories of records to the public in the future may disclose issues where containing highly personal information. In *Z v Finland*, a further breach was disclosed from the fact that criminal files including the applicant's medical records (HIV status) would be made public within 10 years, while she might be still alive.[98]

A system of personal identity numbers (e.g. in civic registration and tax, health, social services, etc.) may not interfere as such but use of the system will be covered if it affects private life. Thus the Commission found an interference where the applicant's name appeared in a register of defaulting tax debtors to which the public had access, including credit companies.[99] However, the interference, of a minor nature, was accepted as necessary in the interests of the economic well-being of the country. The applicant had not shown that he was in fact refused credit because of the register and regard was had to the fundamental Swedish principle of public access to official documents. The Commission appeared to lend weight to the general desirability of public access to official data registers.

Personal information in the hands of the authorities, in particular concerning medical and health details, must be effectively protected from unauthorised disclosure. Where the patient records of a hospital were not adequately secured

93 (20524/92) (Dec.) November 29, 1993, 75 D.R. 231.

94 (8334/78) (Dec.) May 7, 1981, 24 D.R. 103; (7940/77) (Dec.) May 9, 1978, 14 D.R. 224, which hinted that the public disclosure of a criminal record would constitute an interference in defamation proceedings, this applicant, however, could apply for *in camera* procedure.

95 (24744/94) (Dec.) April 6, 1995, where details appeared in the press, following the applicant's arrest on suspicion of indecent assault on a boy, referring to confiscation at his home of large quantities of child pornography.

96 *Wypych*, fn.18 above.

97 See also *LL v France*, fn.92 above, lack of justification, and procedural safeguards, where a court cited a medical report on the applicant's alcoholism in a divorce decision; *CC v Spain*, fn.28 above, where the court cited the applicant's HIV status which was relevant to the legal issue but failed to keep his name anonymous: there was no pressing social need to make that public.

98 cf. (25099/94) fn.54 above, concerning a 50–year period.

99 (10473/83) (Dec.) December 11, 1985, 45 D.R. 121.

against such disclosure, in particular since there was no restrictions on access to the health professionals involved in treatment nor a system of recording those who had been given access, the State had failed in its positive obligation to ensure respect for private life.[100]

6. Reputation and defamation

Reputation falls within the scope of private life under Art.8.[101] The right to enjoy a good reputation is also a civil right for the purposes of Art.6, which guarantees access to court and fair determination of the issues. See Pt IIB, s.8: Defamation and the right to reputation. II–589

7. Names and aspects of personal identity

Names are not only a form of personal identification but also constitute a link to family and involve to a certain degree the right to establish relationships with others.[102] Since there is little common ground in Contracting States, the Court tends to afford a wide margin of appreciation as to the restrictions on permissible changes. There are accepted public interest considerations such as the importance given to the stability of family names, accurate population registration, safeguards to the means of personal identification and of linking the bearers of a particular name to a given family. II–590

Restrictions have, mostly, been found compatible with respect for private life.[103] In *Stjerna v Finland*, where the applicant claimed his Swedish surname caused problems since it was liable to be mispronounced by Finnish speakers, caused delays in mail and gave rise to the pejorative nickname "churn", the Court was not persuaded that there was any particular inconvenience or singularity in his name, noting that many names gave rise to nicknames.[104] In France, where strict rules apply to first names, the Court found that it was also compatible with Art.8 to prohibit the registration of a baby as "Fleur de Marie". Noting that the child could use the name in daily life, if not for official documents, the Court found the "certain complications" which might arise were insufficient to raise issues of interference with family or private life. The Commission, noting that the naming of a child was undeniably an intimate part of the emotional life of its parents, had found no violation by a narrow margin.[105] A shift in the Court's approach may perhaps be seen in *Johansson v Finland*, where the onus was put on the authorities to give a good reason for rejecting registration of the applicants' son as "Axl Mick". The Court, in finding a violation, noted that the domestic courts had not found that the name

[100] *I v Finland*, July 17, 2008.

[101] *Pfeizer v Austria*, November 15, 2007, para.35.

[102] *Stjerna*, fn.8 above, para.37, citing *Burghartz*, fn.5 above, para.24.

[103] Although discriminatory differences applied to men and women on marriage there was a breach of Art.14 in conjunction with Art.8: *Burghartz*, fn.5 above.

[104] The Commission majority commented that there could, in principle, be no right to change one's surname under Art.8, but did not exclude exceptional cases might arise where a name caused suffering or serious difficulties.

[105] *Guillot v France*, October 24, 1996, R.J.D. 1996–V, No.19, the large Commission minority, and two judges, considered that first names were well inside the private sphere and that there should be rigorous control of interferences in their choice. While the name was unusual, it was not any more ridiculous than anachronistic saints' names (e.g *Scholastique*, *Polycarpe*).

would cause any prejudice to the child or to Finnish cultural identity, particularly since the name had already been accepted for other children.[106] Similarly, undue rigidity and failure to strike a fair balance was found where a woman's married name, borne for some 50 years, was corrected in the new electronic state registry and the authorities refused, without convincing reasons, to allow her to continue to use her accustomed surname.[107] Nor was there any public interest in refusing to allow an applicant to correct her name in the civil register to its regional Kurdish spelling, particularly where the domestic law did not support clearly the authorities' proposition that only names found in the Turkish dictionary were permitted.[108]

Restrictions found acceptable include the refusal of the prison authorities for administrative purposes to use the name obtained by deed poll after an applicant's sentence began[109]; inability of a woman to use her maiden name for election (candidate or voter)[110]; inability of woman to take a name used by her ancestors 200 years before[111]; the prohibition of a woman's continued use of her ex-husband's name as her legal name;[112] the regulation of spelling of foreign names to accord phonetically with the official language of the country[113]; and the refusal to register names with letters not contained in the official language, where phonetic equivalents were available.[114]

Where ethnic identity is recorded in civil registers and identity cards, the Court found a violation where the applicant, registered at birth as ethnic Moldovan, had been unable to obtain a change of status to Romanian as he could not show that either of his parents had been so recorded. While it accepted that the State was entitled to require proof of status, the applicant should have been able to provide such by other objectively verifiable evidence which was available.[115]

A person's status as married, divorced or widowed has been held to be part of their personal and social identity. Undue delay by the Maltese authorities in registering the applicant's marriage to a foreigner disclosed a breach of Art.8.[116]

8. Nationality

II–591 There is no right to a particular nationality, it has long been said.[117] However, with recent events, the Court has held that arbitrary removal or denial of nationality may

[106] *Johansson v Finland*, September 6, 2007, paras 31–39.

[107] *Daroczy v Hungary*, July 1, 2008, even if it had been originally registered in error of the proper usage, the authorities had not shown how allowing her to keep it disrupted the system.

[108] *Guzel Erdogen v Turkey*, October 21, 2008.

[109] (11046/84) (Dec.) December 10, 1985, since it only concerned internal prison documents and official prison contexts, it related to public administration outside the scope of Art.8.

[110] (8042/77) (Dec.) December 15, 1977, 12 D.R. 202, the applicant could add the name to her married one.

[111] (16878/90) (Dec.) June 29, 1962.

[112] *Taieb dit Halimi v France*, (50614/99) (Dec.) March 20, 2001, the applicant could keep the name for professional and media use; the Court doubted that any inconvenience arose from the bar on use for administrative purposes capable of interfering with private life.

[113] *Mentzen alias Mencena v Latvia*, (71074/01) (Dec.) December 7, 2004, the inconvenience was not considered serious; the original spelling was included in the passport.

[114] *Kemal Taskin v Turkey*, February 2, 2010.

[115] *Ciuboratu*, fn.73 above.

[116] *Dadouch v Malta*, July 20, 2010, paras 47–61.

[117] See authorities cited in *Karassev v Finland*, (31414/96) (Dec.) January 12, 1999, ECHR 1999–II.

raise issues due to the impact on private life.[118] Where the names of numerous people who had lived for many years in Slovenia were erased from a Register of Permanent Residents, which had repercussions on the possibility of obtaining citizenship and enjoyment of numerous rights and benefits, the Court found that this interfered with private and family life and that the authorities' prolonged failure to regularise their situation in line with a Constitutional Court judgment disclosed a violation.[119]

Nor is there a right as such to renounce nationality, the Court not finding the alleged emotional distress from being required to retain Bulgarian citizenship amounted to an interference with private life.[120]

Imposition arbitarily of nationality restrictions on professional activities may fall foul of Art.8. Where a Russian student had pursued legal studies for almost two years, the Court found that the refusal to let her sit the final exams due to her nationality had lacked coherence and respect for her private life.[121]

9. Sexual and gender matters

The Commission established very early that a person's sexual life was an important aspect of private life. Thus the choice of affirming and assuming one's sexual identity comes within protection of Art.8.[122] The Court has, in the context of consensual sado-masochistic acts, commented that it is not however every sexual activity carried on behind closed doors which will necessarily fall within the scope of Art.8. It doubted in that case, where the activities were organised, involving numerous people and the making and distribution of video-tapes, whether the conduct fell entirely within the notion of private life, although in the absence of dispute by the Government or Commission it assumed the criminal proceedings for wounding and assault disclosed an interference with private life.[123] Where an applicant was involved in performances of bondage acts in a private club, with exposure of photographs on the internet, the Court also expressed doubts that these activities would fall within "private life".[124] II–592

Matters relating to individual sexual life are of a particularly intimate nature within the scope of private life and require particularly sound reasons to justify interference. The hallmarks of a democratic society, tolerance and broad mindedness, have to be borne in mind and it is not enough that a particular activity might

[118] *Karassev*, fn.117 above, the consequence of refusing a child Finnish nationality were not sufficiently serious, as he was allowed to remain in the country with his parents who received support; see also *Kolosovskiy v Latvia*, (50183/99) (Dec.) January 29, 2004, no arbitrary refusal of Latvian citizenship, given the applicant's links with Russia.

[119] *Kuric v Slovenia*, July 13, 2010. Pending before the Grand Chamber.

[120] *Riener v Bulgaria*, May 23, 2006, no other adverse consequences were shown to arise.

[121] *Bigaeva*, fn.38 above, paras 33–36.

[122] e.g. (9369/81) (Dec.) May 3, 1983, 32 D.R. 220; (6959/75) (Dec.) May 19, 1976, 3 D.R. 103.

[123] *Laskey, Jaggard and Brown v UK*, February 19, 1997, R.J.D., 1997–I, No.29, 24 E.H.R.R. 392. Contrast *ADT v UK*, July 31, 2000, ECHR 2000–IX, the Court accepted that group sex in the privacy of the home fell within the scope of Art.8. and found no likelihood of the videotape of the activities being made public. See, however, *KA and AD v Belgium*, February 17, 2005, para.78, where the Court left open if conviction, for facts found to amount to incitement to "debauchery" and prostitution, fell within Art.8.

[124] *Pay v UK*, (32792/05), (Dec.) September 16, 2008.

shock, disturb or offend.[125] Criminal law prohibition of consensual adult homosexual activity in private has accordingly found to be unjustified (see Pt IIB, s.27: Homosexuality).

Some aspects may be subject to State interference if in accordance with para.2, particularly where the protection of children is concerned.[126] Article 8 does not protect sex for remuneration professionally or activities amounting to prostitution.[127] While the disciplinary sanction of a police officer for cohabiting with a homosexual engaged in prostitution was an interference, it did not go beyond what was necessary for the purpose of prevention of disorder (i.e. to protect the good reputation of the police force).[128] Dismissal of a probation officer who supervised sexual offenders due to his involvement in organised bondage activities was found to be justified bearing in mind the need for probation officers to keep the respect of their clients and maintain the confidence of the public.[129]

In *Laskey, Jaggard and Brown v UK*, the Court found criminal sanctions on sado-masochistic behaviour, even conducted between consenting adults in private for sexual gratification, to be justified for the protection of health, taking the view that the State was entitled to regulate conduct involving physical harm which was not of a trifling or transient nature. This infliction of injury was sufficient to distinguish the case from the homosexual cases. It also commented, rather censoriously, that its finding on the grounds of health should not be interpreted as negativing the right of the State to deter acts of this kind on moral grounds.[130] Convictions for sado-masochistic acts were later found justified in the interests of protecting others where the domestic courts found that the participants exceeded the consent of the victims, matters sometimes escalating out of control.[131]

The daily aggravation of a humiliating nature facing a transsexual who was unable to obtain a change of name and official papers to reflect gender re-assignment was sufficient to disclose a breach of Art.8.[132] Inability to obtain legal recognition, which placed the transsexual in an anomalous position at risk of humiliation, vulnerability and embarrassment was also found to disclose a lack of respect for private life in *Christine Goodwin v UK*, weight being placed on the right of the transsexual to personal development and physical and moral security in the full sense[133] (See Part IIB, s.47: Transsexuals).

[125] *Dudgeon*, fn.9 above, para.60.

[126] (5935/72) (Dec.) September 30, 1975, 3 D.R. 46, justified to convict homosexual of acts with children under 16.

[127] (11680/85) (Dec.) March 10, 1988, 55 D.R. 178, conviction for unnatural debauchery (paid homosexual relations).

[128] (12545/86) (Dec.) December 12, 1988, 58 D.R. 126.

[129] *Pay v UK*, fn.124 above, the Court noted that while measures less than dismissal could have been envisaged, the applicant's own attitude in maintaining the acceptability of his conduct and his failure to keep his activities discreet rendered the authorities' reaction proportionate in the circumstances.

[130] The argument that the law prohibited commonly practised types of masochism, heterosexual or otherwise, was rejected in (22170/93) (Dec.) January 18, 1995. The applicants were not victims, unable to show any direct effect on their private lives, i.e. no threat of prosecution; the conduct was milder than in *Laskey* and there was no indication that such types of sado-masochism were being pursued.

[131] *KA and AD*, fn.123 above, paras 84–88.

[132] *B v France*, fn.33 above.

[133] See also *Van Kuck v Germany*, June 12, 2003, paras 73–86, where the Court found the decision of the court, rejecting the transsexual applicant's claims for payment of her gender re-assignment surgery from her insurance company, failed to respect her private life.

10. Other personal relationships

The determination of an applicant's legal relations with a putative child concerns private life, even where what is at issue is a father's attempt to disprove paternity.[134] In that context a fair balance has to be struck between the general interest of the protection of legal certainty of family relationships and a father's right to have the legal presumption of his paternity reviewed in the light of the biological evidence. A system which imposed a one-year inflexible time-limit from the date of birth was not acceptable where the applicant only learned that he was not the father of his wife's child after the expiry of that time-limit and tests confirmed that fact[135]; as was a system that imposed a complete bar on any challenge to paternity.[136] Courts should also take into account scientific developments, such as DNA testing in deciding whether to re-open previous decisions on paternity.[137] The Court has generally not been convinced that bars on proceedings which fly in the face of reality serve the interests of protecting the child, who, it has said, also has an interest in knowing its true father.[138] However, where the authorities refused to allow a challenge to paternity several years after the birth registration where the applicant had always known that the child was not his and did not bring an action within the six-month time-limit, the Court found that they were justified in finding the interests of the child, of young age, to continued financial support outweighed the applicant's.[139] Similarly, where the applicant had not appealed an earlier decision holding recognising him as the father of a child, the refusal of the domestic courts to order a subsequent DNA test to verify paternity was found to have properly given priority to the child's interests in continuing to enjoy the stability of the existing situation.[140] Persons under legal incapacity should also have due procedural protection of their rights and be able to obtain effective means of challenging a bar on acknowledging paternity.[141] II–593

The interests of the child will weigh heavily in the converse situation, where an outsider to the family unit claims paternity. Where an applicant claimed that respect for private life in the sense of establishing relationships was infringed by the refusal of a court to order a blood test to prove whether he, rather than the husband, was the biological father of a child of a married woman, the Commission found that the decision was taken in the interests of the child, who was remaining with the mother and her husband and required the stability and security of that home.[142] No such relevant reasons were given by the courts for refusing to register the biological

[134] *Rasmussen v Denmark*, November 28, 1984, Series A, No.87, 7 E.H.R.R. 371,, para.33, though the procedural inequality, whereby only husbands faced a time-bar in paternity matters, had objective and reasonable justification.

[135] *Shofman v Russia*, November 24, 2005.

[136] *Mizzi v Malta*, January 12, 2006. See also *Paulik v Slovakia*, October 10, 2006, where a father could not challenge paternity in the case of a 40–year-old daughter who had consented to a DNA test.

[137] *Tavli v Turkey*, November 9, 2006, where DNA evidence was not a domestic ground for re-opening a past decision.

[138] e.g. *Tavli*, fn.137 above, para.84.

[139] *Knakal v Czech Republic*, (39277/06) (Dec.) January 8, 2007.

[140] *ILV v Romania*, (4901/04) (Dec.) August 24, 2010, the child had refused consent for the test; its right to continued support, even though modest, would also have been in jeopardy.

[141] *Kruskovic v Croatia*, June 21, 2011, paras 42–50.

[142] (22920/93) (Dec.) April 6, 1994, 77 D.R. 108; also *Nylund v Finland*, (27110/95) (Dec.) June 29, 1999, ECHR 1999–VI, where the Court similarly rejected the applicant's complaints about the courts' refusal to investigate paternity of a child born to a married couple.

father of a stillborn child instead of the deceased husband, thus disclosing a lack of respect for the father's private life.[143]

Children may also claim rights in this regard. The delayed and ineffective procedure adopted by the courts in the paternity proceedings brought by the applicant against her putative father failed to secure her right to respect for private life in *Mikulic v Croatia*, as did the failure of the Swiss courts to order a DNA test of a deceased person to verify paternity postumously.[144] Time-bars on affiliation proceedings must allow for distinguishing between cases where a child knew or had reasonable grounds to suspect who was their biological father but took no steps and those where the child had no knowledge; thus, a 21–year period for claims offended where the law made no provision for the case of the applicant who was only told by her mother the name of her biological father when she was over 50.[145] Less weight is given to claims for recognition of more distant relatives, in which case interests of the family concerned and legal certainty may prevail.[146]

Close relationships short of family life will generally fall within the scope of private life, for example the links between a foster mother and foster child[147]; the establishment of paternal descent of a stillborn child[148]; relationships between fiancés[149]; relationships between homosexuals and their partners[150]; as may the links formed by a person who has lived for many years in a particular country, i.e. "the network of personal, social and economic relations that make up the private life of every human being".[151] The desire to become a genetic parent through implantation of a stored embryo fell within the scope of "private life", but the Court found the requirement that the donor father's consent was necessary for implantation of the stored embryo did not disclose a lack of respect.[152]

A claim for damages from third parties based on claims in respect of loss of dependency do not concern the relationship between the claimant and the deceased, but the claimant and the alleged tortfeasor which is not a private life matter.[153]

The means by which a person pursues relationships may attract the protection of Art.8 also. Penalties for use of a citizen's radio was an interference although justified by the need to regulate such use.[154]

[143] *Znamenskaya v Russia*, June 2, 2005.

[144] *Jaggi v Switzerland*, July 13, 2007. See also *Pascaud v France*, June 16, 2011, paras 55–64, where the French courts barred proper consideration of the applicant's claims as to his true biological father, refusing consideration of a DNA test.

[145] *Phinikaridou v Cyprus*, December 20, 2007.

[146] *Menendez Garcia v Spain*, (21046/07) (Dec.) May 5, 2009, the applicant had claimed that DNA tests should be taken to prove that her father was in fact the son of someone else, who was thus her grandfather: both persons were already deceased.

[147] (8257/78) (Dec.) July 10, 1978, 13 D.R. 248.

[148] *Znamenskaya*, fn.143 above.

[149] (15817/89) (Dec.) October 1, 1990, 66 D.R. 251.

[150] e.g. (9369/81) (Dec.) May 3, 1983, 32 D.R. 220. See Pt IIB, s.27: Homosexuality.

[151] e.g. *Slivenko v Latvia*, October 9, 2003, ECHR 2003–X, para.96.

[152] *Evans v UK*, April 10, 2007. See also *SH v Austria*, April 1, 2010, para.60, where the Court held that the right of a couple to conceive a child and to make use of medically assisted procreation for that end comes within the ambit of Art.8 as an expression of private and family life

[153] *Hofmann v Germany*, (1289/09) (Dec.) February 23, 2010, contrasting matters of inheritance and succession, and rights of maintenance which may concern family life under Art.8.

[154] (8962/80) (Dec.) May 13, 1982, 28 D.R. 112.

11. Pets

Many would argue that the nature and strength of links between an owner and his pet should bring the relationship within the scope of "private life". However, in the *Icelandic dog* case[155] where the applicant was refused permission to have a dog in the city of Reykjavik, the Commission did not consider that private life extended to relationships with dogs. It considered that the keeping of dogs overlapped into the public sphere, necessarily involving interferences with the life of others. II–594

In *Artingstoll v UK*,[156] an elderly man argued that, as a pet was good for his health, the refusal to allow a dog in his council communal sheltered housing was an unjustified interference with his private life. The Commission avoided categorically rejecting the idea of private life as encompassing the companionship of pets. Instead it relied on the fact that when the applicant took up the lease it should have been known by him that dogs were not allowed. Later cases, more drastically, had owners of allegedly dangerous breed dogs complaining that the destruction of their pets was in violation of their right to private life. The Commission returned to its view in the *Icelandic dog* case.[157]

12. Health, safety and security measures

The Commission found that numerous measures which States take to protect the public against various dangers cannot be considered as infringing private life, referring inter alia to safety appliances in industry, obligation to use pedestrian crossings or subways, and compulsory seatbelts.[158] II–595

A compulsory medical intervention, even of a minor nature, interferes with private life, although, in practice, physical interventions on the grounds of health have been found justified under the second paragraph of Art.8.[159] Compulsory vaccination, TB tests or X rays for children have been found to pursue the aim of protecting health while the disadvantages adverted to were not comparable to the former ravages of disease.[160] Where severe damage and death occurred in some cases as the result of a State-provided vaccination scheme, the Commission found that there was no lack of proper consent, there being a general knowledge of potential risks and the State had taken reasonable precautions.[161]

If there is a dispute between a parent and the doctors about the appropriate treatment for a seriously ill child, the Court has held that, in a non-emergency context, the doctors cannot ignore the lack of parental consent and should seek a ruling of the court.[162] In a non-urgent matter, proceeding to take blood samples and

[155] (6825/75) fn.4 above.

[156] (25517/97) (Dec.) April 3, 1995.

[157] e.g. (26280/95), (28846/95) and (26279/95) (Decs.) January 16, 1996.

[158] (8707/79) (Dec.) December 13, 1979, 18 D.R. 255.

[159] e.g. *Matter v Slovakia*, July 5, 1999, paras 67–72, where the applicant was forced by court order to undergo psychiatric examination; *Storck v Germany*, June 16, 2005, forcible medication; *Bogumil v Portugal*, October 7, 2008, no violation where a simple surgical procedure was conducted on an arrested person to remove swallowed drugs that threatened his life: the drugs were not to be used as evidence against him.

[160] (10435/83) (Dec.) December 10, 1984, 40 D.R. 251.

[161] (7154/75) (Dec.) July 12, 1978, 14 D.R. 31.

[162] *Glass v UK*, March 9, 2004, ECHR 2004–II, paras 78–83.

photographs of child, suspected of being a victim of abuse, without first obtaining the consent of the parents was a violation.[163]

Compulsory testing has also been found justified in the context of prisons, where urine tests are imposed on prisoners to check for drugs. This is generally regarded as necessary to prevent crime and disorder in prisons.[164] The Court also found it justifiable, for the protection of public safety and the rights of others, that crew members on Danish shipping undergo random urine testing.[165] Security and public safety considerations also justified testing of nuclear power plant employees.[166] Compulsory blood testing of a drunken driver was justified as necessary for the protection of the rights and freedoms of others[167] while compulsory psychiatric examination of a person facing criminal charges was justified for the prevention of crime even though the enquiries into private life were not relevant to the crime but criminal responsibility.[168] Court-ordered blood tests to resolve paternity have also been found justified for the protection of the rights and freedoms of others.[169]

Where in *YF v Turkey*, the applicant's wife had been forced in police custody to undergo a gynaecological examination for which no medical or investigation necessity had been shown, the Court emphasised that such interference with physical integrity had to be prescribed by law and generally required the consent of the detainee.[170] In a case where a female suspect was subjected to a gynaecological examination after nine days in custody, the Court considered that it was evident that she did not wish to undergo the examination and the fact that she did not, in the end, resist but allowed a doctor to persuade her did not indicate that she had given free or fully informed consent in her vulnerable circumstances; thus the examination interfered with her private life and this serious and intrusive interference was disproportionate to the purported aim of protecting security forces from false allegation of rape on arrest, which allegation she had not made.[171]

Applicability of Art.8 to health and medical choices of the individual is little explored. In *Pretty*,[172] the Court implied that an individual should have the right to refuse life-extending medication. In *Ternovszky v Hungary*, the Court considered that as Art.8 requires respect of the decision to become a parent, the circumstances of giving birth fell within its scope also. Thus, an arbitrary and inconsistent legal framework which imposed criminal penalties on health professionals who assisted at home births was regarded as unduly interfering with the applicant's choice as a pregnant woman to give birth at home.[173]

Police stop and search powers—to look for objects that could be used in terrorism—were found to be insufficiently attended by safeguards against arbitrary

[163] *MAK and RK v UK*, March 23, 2010, paras 75–80, there had been no reason to anticipate that the mother, due to arrive shortly, would not have given consent; if she had refused, the hospital could have asked for a court order.

[164] (21132/93) (Dec.) April 6, 1994, 77–A D.R. 75, it was hinted that testing might not be acceptable if applied to persons not detained.

[165] *Madsen v Denmark*, (58341/00) (Dec.) November 7, 2002, one test per year was not disproportionate.

[166] *Wretlund v Sweden*, (46210/99) (Dec.) March 9, 2004.

[167] (8239/78) (Dec.) December 4, 1978, 16 D.R. 184.

[168] (8344/78) May 7, 1981, 24 D.R. 103.

[169] (8278/78) (Dec.) December 13, 1979, 18 D.R. 154.

[170] *YF v Turkey*, July 23, 2003.

[171] *Juhnke v Turkey*, May 13, 2008, paras 74–82.

[172] *Pretty*, fn.10 above,paras 61–78.

[173] *Ternovszky v Hungary*, December 14, 2010, paras 22–28, the criminal provisions clashed with the constitutional right of self-determination disclosing, in the Chamber's somewhat creative view, a problem of "lawfulness".

use, due inter alia to the width of the discretion based on expediency, the fact that they had been automatically extended in a rolling programme without any real check on their necessity and that in practice the power had been massively used without apparently leading to any arrest.[174] Where however a parent complained about being investigated by the child welfare authorities due to malicious accusations by his ex-spouse, the Court considered there was justifiably a wide discretion given the important duty to protect children and rejected the contention that authorities should be limited to acting on the basis of reports checked for validity and reliability—there had been some objective ground for concern and the measures taken reasonable, which rendered the interference not disproportionate.[175]

13. Measures of administrative control

Removal of legal capacity is an evident and serious interference with private life, removing the ability to lead an independent life in almost all key areas.[176] Such measures should be tailor-made to the degree of inability to function, the blanket imposition of full incapacitation in all cases being disproportionate.[177] Appointment of guardians for mentally-ill persons has been found justified for the prevention of crime and disorder where, for example, the guardian had the power to consent to treatment without which the applicant was a risk to his warders.[178] II–596

The requirement of sex offenders to register with the police and give details of name and address interfered with private life but was justified for the prevention of crime and protection of the rights of others.[179]

Refusal to renew a passport to a citizen living overseas in order to require him to return to face a criminal investigation for fraud was regarded as a proportionate measure; his health did not preclude his return and it was a less draconian measure than seeking to execute an international arrest warrant or applying for extradition.[180]

14. Physical and moral integrity

Even where the State does not infringe itself on the private sphere of a person, it may be under a positive obligation to protect persons from incursions on their physical and moral integrity. The case establishing the principle was *X and Y v Netherlands*, where Y, mentally handicapped, was raped but had no legal capacity to appeal against the decision of the prosecution not to pursue criminal charges and her father had no standing to do so on her behalf. The Court found that positive obligations could arise requiring a State to adopt measures even in the sphere of the relations of individuals between themselves.[181] It found civil law remedies offered II–597

[174] *Gillan and Quinton*, fn.35 above, paras 76–87, the interference was not "in accordance with the law".
[175] *K and T v Norway*, September 25, 2008.
[176] *Shtukaturov v Russia*, March 27, 2008, paras 83, 90.
[177] *Shtukaturov*, fn.176 above, paras 90–96.
[178] (8518/79) (Dec.) March 14, 1980, 20 D.R. 193.
[179] *Adamson v UK*, (Dec.) January 26, 1999, there was no evidence that this gave rise to a risk of public humiliation or attack. See also, *Gardel v France*, December 17, 2009, retention of data on a sex offenders' register for as long as 30 years might have caused a problem, but the possibility for the applicant to apply to the prosecutor, appeal lying to a judge, for the data to be destroyed due to change in circumstances was an adequate safeguard.
[180] *M v Switzerland*, April 16, 2011, paras 61–68.
[181] See also (20357/92), fn.52 above, the Commission implied that failure to provide adequate protection in criminal and civil law to persons suffering from harassment by another could give rise to a positive obligation.

insufficient protection in cases of wrongdoing of this kind and that the criminal law suffered from a deficiency regarding Y which disclosed a lack of respect for her private life. It has been since confirmed in *MC v Bulgaria* that there is a positive obligation in Art.8, as well as Art.3, to enact criminal laws effectively punishing rape and to apply them in practice through effective investigation and prosecution. The lack of proper investigation of the "date rape" in that case, which resulted from undue emphasis on direct proof of lack of consent through signs of resistance by the victim, failed to provide the requisite effective protection.

The positive obligation of protection has extended still further to require protection of individuals from criminal assaults in general, by maintaining and applying in practice an adequate legal framework affording protection against acts of violence by private individuals. Where the State failed to prosecute the identified perpetrators of an assault, a minor offence procedure had ended due to a time bar and the applicant had been unable to bring a private prosecution for the assault, the Court found that criminal law mechanisms had not provided adequate protection of the applicant's physical integrity.[182] Proper enforcement of measures of deterrence and a legal framework permitting a global assessment of a situation of domestic violence rather than an unco-ordinated ad hoc approach were singled out as requirements of protection in a case where the applicant was repeatedly attacked and threatened by her husband who suffered from severe mental disorder. Although orders had been made for detention, fines and compulsory treatment, they had not been enforced, depriving the measures of any restraining or deterring effect.[183] Where there was a well-known public health risk from stray dogs in the city and the 71–year-old applicant had been attacked, knocked down and seriously injured by a pack of dogs, the Court found a breach of Art.8 due to a lack of sufficient measures taken by the authorities in addressing the issue of stray dogs in the particular circumstances of the case, combined with a failure to provide appropriate redress to the applicant for her injuries.[184] This is the first case which puts a focus on an obligation to take operational measures under Art.8, in addition to providing a proper legal framework, borrowing inspiration from Art.2 cases.[185]

Where damage to health from medical negligence is concerned, the domestic legal system must be capable of providing a means of allocating liability and giving reparation. Thus, where a doctor was able to escape paying damages for a botched operation through transferring his property to family members, the Court criticised the length of the proceedings which had facilitated his evasiveness and the fact that in the Romanian system the hospital could not be pursued for the doctor's negligence and that no compulsory insurance covered such medical malpractice for the protection of the victims.[186]

Similarly, a positive obligation can arise to protect psychological and moral integrity in the context of proceedings seeking reparation. Failure to protect the applicants' private life rights, including reputation, arose where the Supreme Court

[182] *Jankovic v Croatia*, March 5, 2009, paras 50–58.

[183] *A v Croatia*, October 14, 2010, paras 50–58.

[184] *Georgel and Georgeta Stoicescu v Romania*, July 26, 2011, paras 53–62.

[185] *Georgel and Georgeta Stoicescu*, fn.184 above, para. 51. Contrast *Beru v Turkey*, January 11, 2007, where a child's death from a stray dog bite was considered under Art.2; however, the problem of stray dogs was not so flagrant (fewer and outside a village) and the death of the victim was not regarded as reasonably foreseeable, even against a background of past attacks: no breach due to failure of the gendarmes to take preventive action.

[186] *Codarcea*, fn.47 above, paras 106–109.

reversed an award of compensation damages where police officers, acquitted of torture, had nonetheless been unlawfully dismissed, holding without due explanation or assessment of their rights, that no moral damages lay for unlawful administrative acts.[187]

The State must also take steps to ensure competent and regular supervisory control of private mental health clinics, in particular to avoid the wrongful confinement or administration of medication. Given the need for protection of those in a vulnerable position, it was not sufficient that retrospective criminal sanctions and civil damages might lie in respect of any infringements of patient rights.[188]

Positive obligations also arise in respect of children and the protection which they should receive from assaults. The Commission in *Costello-Roberts v UK* considered that Art.8 might afford wider protection that Art.3. Thus even though there was no violation of Art.3 (the slippering did not constitute degrading treatment), the same punishment could infringe the right to respect for private life.[189] However, while agreeing the slippering three times on the buttocks through his shorts by a rubber-soled gym shoe was not sufficiently severe for Art.3, the Court was not persuaded that Art.8 would provide wider protection in the area of physical integrity. While it did not rule out that disciplinary measures at school might in certain circumstances affect the right to respect for private life, not every act or measure which might affect adversely physical or moral integrity necessarily gave rise to interference. It had regard to the fact that the sending of a child to school necessarily involved some degree of interference with private life. More relevantly perhaps, the Court reasoned that the treatment in this case did not have sufficiently adverse effects for his physical or moral integrity to bring it within the scope of the prohibition contained in Art.8. A shift in approach perhaps may be discernable in more recent cases. Where information potentially inviting sexual advances was placed about a minor on the internet, it was considered that this posed a threat to his psychological welfare and that the the authorities were under a positive obligation to take protective measures; the failure in the legislative framework which made it impossible to compel the internet operator to identify the person who posted the information and thus to pursue the person in criminal proceedings disclosed a breach of Art.8.[190] There is also a statement by a Chamber that incidents of school bullying could trigger the State's positive obligations under Art.8 and require the relevant authorities to take concrete steps.[191]

15. Funerals and remains

Respect for private life may also extend after death as concerns the relatives of the deceased. In *Pannullo and Forte v France*, the delay in releasing the body of applicants' child for funeral after an investigation infringed Art.8 in both its private and family life aspects,[192] as did the refusal of the prison authorities to allow a II–598

[187] *Taliadorou and Stylianou v Cyprus*, October 16, 2008, paras 49–59.

[188] *Storck*, fn.159 above, paras 149–150.

[189] It considered that the sending of a child to a school did not amount to consent by the parents to corporal punishment; there was no necessity for such punishment in a democratic society.

[190] *KU v Finland*, December 2, 2008.

[191] *Durdevic v Croatia*, July 26, 2011, para.118, the allegations were too vague in the actual case.

[192] *Pannullo and Forte v France*, October 30, 2002, ECHR 2001–X; the treatment of bodies during investigations or post mortems may also raise issues, e.g. *Dennis v UK*, (76573/01), concerning the removal of the victims' hands without informing the relatives.

detainee to attend his parents' funerals.[193] The burial of a still-born baby in a common grave without consultation or informing the mother, together with the transport of the body in an ordinary van, was an interference with the mother's respect for private and family life which had no domestic legal basis.[194] However, while a refusal to allow the removal of a burial urn to a new resting place was an interference with the widow's private life, the Court accepted the domestic authorities' approach which required special reasons for disturbing a resting place beyond the fact that she had moved her place of residence.[195] Neither the deceased or his estate can claim that exhumation interferes with any private life rights.[196]

In more extreme situations of mutilation of bodies, these do not raise issues as concerns the deceased themselves but may inflict anguish and suffering on the relatives as to fall within Art.3.[197]

16. Environment

II–599 Although there is no explicit right to a clean and quiet environment, considerable noise or other nuisance and pollution can undoubtedly affect physical well-being and interfere with private life and the amenities of home. This may also give rise to a pressing personal interest in having access to information relating to the extent of any risk involved. However, a wide margin of appreciation will be accorded to Government's where the case concerns matters of general policy.[198]
(See Pt IIB, s.15: Environment.)

Cross-reference

Part IIB, s.8: Defamation and the right to reputation.
Part IIB, s.12: Discrimination.
Part IIB, s.15: Environment.
Part IIB, s.16: Euthanasia.
Part IIB, s.27: Homosexuality.
Part IIB, s.47: Transsexuals.

[193] *Ploski v Poland*, November 12, 2002.
[194] *Hadri-Vionnet v Switzerland*, February 14, 2008.
[195] *Elli Poluhas Dodsbo v Sweden*, January 17, 2006.
[196] *Estate of Kresten Filtenberg Mortensen v Denmark*, (1338/03) (Dec.) May 15, 2006.
[197] *Akpinar and Altun v Turkey*, February 27, 2007. See also *Khadzialiyev v Russia*, November 6, 2008, concerning the effect on the family of dismembered and incomplete remains of a disappeared relative breaching Art.3.
[198] *Hatton v UK*, July 8, 2003, ECHR 2003–VIII, para.122. See also, the summary of previous case-law on environmental issues at paras 96–104.

38. Property

Key provisions:

Article 1 of Protocol No.1 (peaceful enjoyment of possessions) and Art.6 (access to court/fair hearing). II–600

Key case-law:

Marckx v Belgium, June 12, 1979, Series A, No.31, 2 E.H.R.R. 330; *Sporrong and Lonnroth v Sweden*, September 23, 1982, Series A, No.52, 5 E.H.R.R. 35; *James v UK*, February 21, 1985, Series A, No.98, 8 E.H.R.R. 123; *Van Marle v Netherlands*, June 26, 1986, Series A, No.101, 8 E.H.R.R. 483; *Erkner and Hofauer v Austria*, April 23, 1987, Series A, No.117, 9 E.H.R.R. 464; *Inze v Austria*, October 28, 1987, Series A, No.126, 10 E.H.R.R. 394; *Tre Traktorer v Sweden*, July 7, 1989, Series A, No.159, 13 E.H.R.R. 309; *Fredin v Sweden*, February 18, 1991, Series A, No.192, 13 E.H.R.R. 784; *The Holy Monasteries v Greece*, December 9, 1994, Series A, No.301–A, 25 E.H.R.R. 640; *Stran Greek Refineries v Greece*, December 9, 1994, Series A, No.301–B, 19 E.H.R.R. 293; *Gasus Dosier v Netherlands*, February 23, 1995, Series A, No.306–B, 20 E.H.R.R. 360; *Pressos Compania Naviera v Belgium*, November 20, 1995, Series A, No.332, 21 E.H.R.R. 301; *Agrotexim v Greece*, October 24, 1995, Series A, No.330–A, 21 E.H.R.R. 250; *Phocas v France*, April 23, 1996, R.J.D. 1996–II, No.7, *Matos e Silva v Portugal*, September 16, 1996, R.J.D. 1996–IV, No.14, 24 E.H.R.R. 573; *National & Provincial Building Society v UK*, October 23, 1997, R.J.D. 1997–VII, No.55; 25 E.H.R.R. 127; *Brumarescu v Romania*, October 28, 1999, ECHR 1999–VII; *Former King of Greece v Greece*, November 23, 2000, ECHR 2000–XII; *Prince Hans-Adam II of Liechtenstein*, July 12, 2001, ECHR 2001–VIII; *Elia Srl v Italy*, August 2, 2001, ECHR 2001–IX, *SA Dangeville v France*, April 16, 2002, ECHR 2002–III; *Nerva v UK*, September 24, 2002, ECHR 2002–VIII; *Allard v Sweden*, June 24, 2003, ECHR 2003–VII; *Kopecky v Slovakia*, September 28, 2004, ECHR 2004–IX; *Maurice v France*, June 10, 2005, ECHR 2005–IX; *Anheuser-Busch Inc v Portugal*, January 11, 2007, ECHR 2007–. . . ; *J.A. Pye (Oxford) Ltd and J.A. Pye (Oxford) Land Ltd*, August 30, 2007, ECHR 2007. . .

1. General principles

Three limbs or distinct rules for the protection of property rights are contained in Art.1 of Protocol No.1—in the first sentence of the first paragraph which generally sets out the principle of non-interference with property; in the second sentence relating to deprivation (expropriation) subject to conditions; and in the second paragraph relating to control of use, also subject to specific conditions.[1] Before determining whether the first general rule has been complied with, the Court examines whether the second two are applicable. The three rules are not however unconnected. The second and third are concerned with particular instances of interference with the general right and are to be construed in light of the general principle of the first rule.[2] II–601

[1] *Sporrong and Llonroth v Sweden*, September 23, 1982, Series A, No.52, 5 E.H.R.R. 35, para.61.
[2] *James v UK*, February 21, 1985, Series A, No.98, 8 E.H.R.R. 123, para.37.

Interference with property, whether expropriation or control of use, will generally be justified if it respects the requirement of lawfulness and can be regarded as pursuing the general or public interest. The Convention organs have imported a requirement of proportionality and the necessity to strike a fair balance between the demands of the community and the protection of the individual's interests.[3] The possibility of obtaining compensation is an important element in assessing whether an individual bears an excessive burden.[4] General and public interest is given a wide meaning and where the legislature intervenes in an area of economic or social policy, the Court will respect the State's assessment unless manifestly without reasonable foundation.[5] Adequate procedural protection of the applicant's interests in proceedings decisive for property rights is also a relevant factor in assessing whether a fair balance has been struck.[6] Increasingly the Court imposes a standard of conduct on the authorities when wielding their powers, frowning on arbitrariness and requiring them to act in good time, in an appropriate manner and with utmost consistency[7] as well as finding failings of legal certainty, when legislative provisions and the interpretation of law by the courts is lacking consistency and requisite foreseeability in effects.[8] Reference has also been made to the principle of good governance.[9]

Where ownership remains and some ability to exploit the property, a finding of de facto expropriation in the sense of deprivation of property is unlikely. Such cases falling short of expropriation are rather dealt with as an interference in the peaceful enjoyment of possessions.[10] Where the purpose of the measure is not intended as

[3] *Sporrong*, fn.1 above, para.69.

[4] e.g. in *Sporrong*, fn.1 above, a violation disclosed by long-term expropriation permits on property, which affected ability to sell and was not counterbalanced by the possibility of compensation or shortening the duration; *Former King of Greece v Greece*, November 23, 2000, ECHR 2000–XII, no compensation provided for expropriation of royal family's estates; *Elia Srl v Italy*, August 2, 2001, ECHR 2001–IX, long term uncertainty and no possibility of compensation. See Pt IIB, s.17: Expropriation, confiscation and control of use, sub-s.2(c): Proportionality.

[5] e.g. *Lithgow v UK*, July 8, 1986, Series A, No.102, nationalisation; *James*, see fn.2 above, sweeping leasehold reform; *Pressos Compania Naviera v Belgium*, November 20, 1995, Series A, No.332, 21 E.H.R.R. 301, legislative intervention in pending tort claims. For rare examples of the Court finding no general interest in a measure, see *SA Dangeville v France*, April 16, 2002, ECHR 2002–III, where it perceived no general interest in not enforcing a community directive to allow the repayment of overpaid VAT; *Zwierzynski v Poland*, July 2, 2002, where police headquarters were squatting effectively in the applicant's property and refusing to leave.

[6] e.g. *Allard v Sweden*, June 24, 2003, ECHR 2003–VII, where the applicant's house was demolished before the conclusion of proceedings concerning her claims; *Tsironis v Greece*, December 6, 2001, where insufficient procedural protection of the applicant's rights to property meant that it was seized and sold at auction by a creditor; *Papastavrou v Greece*, April 10, 2003, no adequate protection against executive decision to zone land for reafforestation; *Bruncrona v Finland*, November 16, 2004, irregular termination of long-standing historic lease of islands precluding any compensation.

[7] *Megadat Com Srl v Moldova*, April 8, 2006, where the authorities removed the applicant company's licences in an inconsistent, arbitrary discriminatory manner, without giving them an effective opportunity to protect their interests.

[8] See e.g. *Nacaryan and Deryan v Turkey*, January 8, 2008, lack of legal certainty arising from the manner in which the courts applied a reciprocity bar to the Greek applicants' inheritance of Turkish property, based on a purported inability of Turkish heirs to inherit in Greece.

[9] *Moskal v Poland*, September 15, 2009, para.51, where the Court did not like the manner in which the applicant, acting in good faith, was penalised by a mistake made by the authorities which led her to act to her detriment in reliance on the pension awarded; *Plechanow v Poland*, July 7, 2009, the applicant's claim for damages was rejected for failure to sue the correct state body, which was due largely to inconsistent case-law, intervening reforms and lack of legal coherence.

[10] e.g. *Sporrong*, fn.1 above, where the applicant still owned the land and could dispose of it; Fredin where though the licence to exploit the gravel pit was removed the applicant did not thereby lose all meaningful use of the land, which also included a farm.

such to control the use of the property but to achieve other goals it will also tend to fall under the first sentence. For example, provisional land transfer in *Erkner and Hofauer v Austria* was dealt with under the first sentence of the first paragraph as there was no actual deprivation of property until the consolidation plan was issued and there was no aim to control use but to restructure and improve farming.[11] Public interest declarations (pre-expropriation measures) in *Matos e Silva v Portugal* were also dealt with under the first sentence of the first paragraph. There was no de facto deprivation since ownership remained and the applicants could still use the land in a restricted manner and were able to sell. In *Phocas v France*, restriction on use of property, together with uncertainty as to future expropriation, resulting from an urban development plan was dealt with as an interference under the first sentence of the first paragraph.[12]

2. Property

Property or possessions for the purposes of attracting the protection of Art.1 of Protocol No.1 covers a wide range of interests. Possession has an autonomous meaning independent of formal classification in domestic law,[13] although recognition of a proprietary interest by domestic courts is in practice highly relevant.[14] It is not limited to ownership of physical goods: other rights and interests constituting assets can also be regarded as property rights.[15] An interest in property, even if revocable in certain circumstances, can constitute a possession for the purposes of Art.1 of Protocol No.1, as in *Beyeler v Italy*, where the applicant had bought a work of art subject to the State's right of pre-emption.[16] Contracts to purchase real property may be regarded as giving "possessions" through a right of occupation acknowledged under domestic law even though title has not passed.[17] Authorised and longstanding occupation of public property by internally displaced persons, where such occupation was regarded as conferring a pecuniary right under domestic law, was found to give rise to "possessions".[18] Nor where, by operation of law, land becomes unrecoverable due to adverse possession does the beneficial owner cease to enjoy protection of Art.1 of Protocol No. 1 since the ownership was effectively lost due to the operation of the applicable legislation.[19] II–602

[11] See, similarly, *Elia Srl*, fn.4 above, effect of building restrictions short of final expropriation.

[12] Despite a serious effect on his ownership rights, the applicant was procedurally protected since he could apply for State to purchase his property within three years of his application.

[13] e.g. *Former King of Greece*, fn.4 above, para.60, royal estates were regarded as owned by the applicants as private persons and could not be regarded as sui generis or as State property.

[14] e.g. *Broniowski v Poland*, June 22, 2004, ECHR 2004–V, paras 125–134, where the domestic courts at the highest level had recognised the right to credit (compensation for property abandoned beyond the Bug River during WW2) as a transferable and inheritable proprietary right; *cf. Melchior v Germany*, (66783/01) (Dec.) February 2, 2006, where the courts ruled, on interpretation of applicable law and Agreement, that the applicant's claim to his estate had been extinguished.

[15] *Gasus Dosier v Netherlands*, February 23, 1995, Series A, No.306–B, 20 E.H.R.R. 360, where it was immaterial if the applicant's claim to the concrete mixer was a right of ownership or a security right in rem (ownership had passed to purchaser under contract subject to retention of title until full price paid which had not occurred at the time of seizure by tax authorities). Also, right by way from a restrictive covenant and receipt of annual rent are possessions—(10741/84) (Dec.) December 13, 1984, 41 D.R. 226—as are intellectual property, including patents and applications to register trademarks: *Anheuser-Busch Inc v Portugal*, January 11, 2007, ECHR 2007–. . . , paras 66–78.

[16] He had also had possession of the painting for some years and the authorities had treated him as the owner.

[17] *Dokic v Bosnia-Herzegovina*, May 27, 2010, para.50.

[18] *Saghinadze v Georgia*, May 27, 2010, paras 105–108.

[19] *J.A. Pye (Oxford) Litd and J.A. Pye (Oxford) Land Ltd*, August 30, 2007, ECHR 2007. . . , paras 61–63.

Where in *Matos e Silva v Portugal*, the Government disputed that the applicants owned part of the old royal lands subject to the expropriation measures, the Court found that the applicants had occupied them undisputed for almost a century and the revenue which they derived from working it could qualify as possessions. In *Holy Monasteries v Greece*, where the Government also disputed that the applicants were owners, the Commission considered that, even if they held no registered title, they had "patrimony" rights in personam, which could be "possessions" without being property rights protected in Greek law. The Court held that the transfer of possession and control of the properties affected ownership and could not be regarded as a mere procedural exercise. Where applicants occupied inalienable public coastal lands subject to unilateral evocation of permission by the Prefect, it was noted that they did not have rights in rem over the property but it was found that the fact of the longterm occupation by itself vested the applicants with a proprietary interest in the peaceful enjoyment of their houses which was sufficiently weighty and established to amount to a "possession".[20]

Article 1 of Protocol No.1 only applies to existing possessions and does not confer a right to obtain property, whether on intestacy or through voluntary dispositions.[21] This situation should be distinguished from that where infringement of the rule of legal certainty prevents applicants obtaining recognition of title to property which they have effectively possessed[22] or where title is revoked after acquisition in good faith or due registration due to unforeseen intervention by the authorities.[23] An applicant must generally fulfil the conditions set by domestic law for ownership.[24] However, case-law recognises in certain cases that "existing possessions" include claims in respect of which an individual can claim to have at least a "legitimate expectation" of obtaining effective enjoyment of a property right[25]: see further below sub-s 2(d): Debts and claims. No legitimate expectation arises where there is a dispute as to the correct interpretation of and application of domestic law and the applicant's submissions are rejected by the domestic courts.[26]

Driving licences are not items of property for purposes of Art.1 of Protocol 1.[27]

Where property rights cease or are altered pursuant to pre-existing requirements or conditions fulfilled by law there is generally no interference with property.[28]

[20] *Depalle v France* and *Brosset-Triboulet v France*, March 29, 2010, ECHR 2010–. . . See also proprietary interest generated by 27 years' occupation of a house built without permission: *Hamer v Belgium*, November 27, 2007, para.76.

[21] *Marckx v Belgium*, June 12, 1979, Series A, No.31, 2 E.H.R.R. 330, para.50; *Merger and Cros v France*, December 22, 2004, where gifts were set aside on distribution of an estate.

[22] See *Fener Rum Erkek Lisesi Vakfi v Turkey*, January 9, 2007, violation where in ruling that the applicant institution could not hold donated property although it had done so for over 30 years, the authorities erred against the principle of legal certainty, their application of the law unforeseeable; also *Bozcaada Kimisis Teodoku Rum Ortodoks Kilisesi Vakfi v Turkey*, March 3, 2009, religious organisation possessed the donated land for some 20 years but were refused registration.

[23] See *Turgut v Turkey,* July 8, 2008; *Koktepe v Turkey,* July 22, 2008, where title to land was revoked or annulled on the basis that the land was forest and thus in the public domain, incapable of private ownership.

[24] e.g. *Hadzic v Croatia*, (48788/99) (Dec.) September 13, 2001, where the applicant did not fulfil the conditions for a pension; *Nemcova v Czech Republic*, (72058/01) (Dec.) November 9, 2004, condition for restitution of coins not fulfilled.

[25] e.g. *Prince Hans-Adam II of Liechtenstein*, July 12, 2001, ECHR 2001–VIII, para.83; *Jantner v Slovakia*, March 4, 2003, where the applicant was not an owner of land, but a claimant with no legitimate expectation that the matter would be determined in his favour.

[26] *Kopecky v Slovakia*, September 28, 2004, ECHR 2004–IX, para.50.

[27] (9177/80) (Dec.) October 6, 1981, 26 D.R. 255.

[28] (10443/83) (Dec.) July 15, 1988, 56 D.R. 20, disciplinary suspension of civil servant's pension did not constitute and interference with property rights where suspension fulfilled legal requirements; (10426/83) (Dec.) December 12, 1984, 40 D.R. 234.

There is some authority for the view that a trivial effect on property rights will not constitute an interference.[29] Inflation does not impose an obligation on the State under Art.1 of Protocol No.1 to maintain the purchasing power of sums deposited with financial institutions.[30] A right to pre-emption or a conditional option to purchase has not been regarded as a possession.[31]

There is no "possession", or legitimate expectation to such, where the property was expropriated before a Contracting State ratified the Convention nor any obligations as to any scheme of restitution or compensation later implemented. However, where a State enacts legislation providing for the full or partial restoration of property confiscated under a previous regime, such legislation may be regarded as generating a new property right protected by Art.1 of Protocol No.1 for persons satisfying the requirements for entitlement.[32] The same may apply in respect of arrangements established under pre-ratification legislation, where still in force after ratification of Protocol No.1[33] (see further below: sub-s (f): Restitution of property).

(a) *Business and professional interests*

Possessions were concerned in the revocation of a licence to serve alcoholic beverages in a restaurant, since it formed part of the economic interests of the restaurant and loss of it affected good will and value of the restaurant.[34] Where accountants were refused registration as chartered accountants when the profession was regulated by new legislation, the Court found that they had built up a clientele over years, which had in many respects the nature of a private right and constituted an asset and hence a possession.[35] **II–603**

While the vested interests of a doctor in his private practice were "possessions", which could be interfered with by removal of a social security affiliation decisive to the running of his practice,[36] the withdrawal of doctors' licence to dispense medicine was not an interference with property, where the conditions for its exercise no longer existed.[37] Goodwill of a professional practice was an element in its valuation but did not constitute a possession to the extent not necessarily linked to the profession in

[29] *Langborger v Austria*, June 22, 1989, Series A, No.155, the Commission said the requirement in lease to pay small 0.3 per cent of rent to tenants' association for rent negotiations was so small it was not interference.

[30] e.g. *Gayduck v Ukraine*, (45526/99) (Dec.) July 2, 2002, ECHR 2002–VI; *Ryabykh v Russia*, July 24, 2003, ECHR 2003–IX, para.63.

[31] e.g. *Gavella v Croatia*, July 11, 2006; *Mirailles v France*, (63156/00) (Dec.) ECHR 2003–XI.

[32] *Maltzan and Others v Germany*, (71916/01), (71917/01) and (10260/02) (Dec.) March 2, 2005, ECHR 2005–XI, no property rights existed for the applicants who were not covered by the legislative scheme, their prior hopes based on earlier declarations and statements not being sufficient.

[33] *Broniowski v Poland* (GC), (31443/96) ECHR 2004–V.

[34] *Tre Traktorer v Sweden*, July 7, 1989, Series A, No.159, 13 E.H.R.R. 309; see also *Capital Bank A.D. v Bulgaria*, November 24, 2005, withdrawal of banking licence was an interference with possessions; *Megadat Com Srl v Moldova*, April 8, 2006, para.63, withdrawal of licence of internet service providers disclosed an interference with possessions.

[35] *Van Marle v Netherlands*, June 26, 1986, Series A, No.101, 8 E.H.R.R. 483, the interference was not disproportionate since it was a legitimate aim to regulate a profession vital to the economic sector and provision for registration was made by way of proving competence by diploma or before a board.

[36] (11540/85) (Dec.) March 8, 1988, 55 D.R. 157, this was found a control of use in the general interest and not disproportionate, since the applicant did not meet the condition of being recommended by the appropriate authority, as part of comprehensive health care reform.

[37] (10438/83) (Dec.) October 3, 1984, the applicants' licence was dependent on there being no chemist in the area and was withdrawn when a chemist began operating.

question. The Commission found that dispensing was not automatically connected with their practice. There could be no reasonable expectation as to the lasting nature of benefits which could be withdrawn in accordance with pre-existing lawful conditions, so there was no property right affected in the licence.

Future income does not constitute a possession unless the money has been earned or an enforceable claim to it exists. Mere expectations of notaries that existing rates of fees would not be reduced by law did not constitute a property right.[38] Customs officers' income affected by change of custom levying on the Greek entry to the European Union did not fall within "possessions".[39] Their licences were not revoked and it was not accepted that they had any vested economic interests or legitimate expectations of deriving future advantages. Nor had the income been earned or an enforceable claim to it in existence. Where exclusive rights of audience were removed from certain German courts, the lawyers' claims for loss of future income fell outside the scope of Art.1 of Protocol No.1, although their law practices and clientele could be regarded as assets and possessions. Any interference however was not disproportionate given the transitional period to allow those affected to adjust to the changes.[40] A tax consultant's clientele were also assets and the revocation of his appointment was a control of use of that property which was however justified given the applicant's lack of qualifications.[41] It was, however, disproportionate, on re-organisation of the accountants' profession, to require the applicants to repay fees lawfully gathered and declared over the prior period.[42]

Fishing rights attached to land ownership, used by professional fishermen or otherwise given proprietary character attract the protection of Art.1 of Protocol No.1, although restrictive measures to protect fishing stocks have generally been found to pursue an important public or general interest.[43] Extending fishing rights to other local residents did not constitute an interference with the historic rights of the Sami people to fish.[44]

(b) Intellectual property

II–604 Article 1 of Protocol No.1 applies but will depend largely on conditions applicable under domestic law and no issues will arise where courts regulate disputes without arbitrariness or manifest unreasonableness.[45] A trademark will be a protected possession once registered. However, an application for registration of a trademark

[38] (8410/78) (Dec.) December 13, 1979, 18 D.R. 216, where notaries were obliged to reduce fees for certain public bodies, e.g. universities—the claim for fees would only to be considered as a possession when it came into existence on grounds of services rendered and on basis of existing regulations for the fees.

[39] (24581/94) (Dec.) April 6, 1995, 81–B D.R. 123.

[40] *Wendenburg v Germany*, (71360/01) (Dec.) February 6, 2003, ECHR 2003–II; see also *Buzescu v Romania*, May 24, 2005, annulment of lawyer's Bar registration deprived him of his practice and "goodwill", violation as procedures lacked certainty and the authorities failed to act timeously to resolve the situation; *Lederer v Germany*, (6213/03) (Dec.) May 22, 2006, not disproportionate to remove bar membership from a lawyer on becoming a university professor, as he had rights of audience in the new function and it had become a secondary activity. Decision May 22, 2006.

[41] *Olbertz v Germany*, (37592/97) (Dec.) May 25, 1999, ECHR 1999–V.

[42] *Kliafas v Greece*, July 8, 2004.

[43] e.g. *Alatukkila v Finland*, July 28, 2005.

[44] *Johtti Sapmelaccat Ry v Finland*, (42969/98) (Dec.) January 18, 2005, it was not shown that this would appreciably impact on the enjoyment of their own rights.

[45] *Melnychuk v Ukraine*, (28743/03) (Dec.) July 5, 2005, ECHR 2005–IX.

itself could give rise to interests of a proprietary nature, even if of a conditional nature. The applicant in such circumstances was entitled to expect that the application would be examined in accordance with relevant domestic law and without arbitrariness.[46]

(c) *Inheritance and succession rights*

Article 1 of Protocol No.1 does not guarantee the right to obtain possessions by way of intestacy or involuntary dispositions, although difference in treatment in matters of inheritance may fall foul of Art.14 in conjunction with Art.1 of Protocol No.1.[47] In *Inze v Austria* where the applicant, born out of wedlock, had acquired a right of inheritance with other heirs, but was precluded by his birth from being a principal heir, there was a property right in issue, as in *Mazurek v France*, where under domestic law, the applicant had automatically acquired hereditary rights over his mother's estate.[48] II–605

Annulment of an inheritance in Turkey of Greek applicants due to purported lack of reciprocity of inheritance rights for Turkish citizens in Greece disclosed a violation due to lack of a proper legal basis.[49] Where the Turkish courts refused to grant the Greek applicants the right to inherit real property, they could not claim to have "possessions" as such but as they fulfilled all the conditions to so inherit, they could claim a legitimate expectation to obtain recognition of their rights; thus, when the courts' approach to the application of the reciprocity bar lacked coherence and legal certainty, there was an unjustified interference with the applicants' rights.[50]

(d) *Debts and claims*

Debts or claims in respect of property have to be sufficiently established to be enforceable.[51] The applicant must be at least able to argue that he has a legitimate expectation of obtaining effective enjoyment of a property right.[52] Hope of recognition of an old property right that it has been impossible to exercise effectively is not sufficient,[53] nor hope of a change of law to remove a condition for restitution[54] II–606

[46] *Anheuser-Busch Inc*, fn.15 above, no interference where the courts interpreted domestic law on priority of conflicting claims to a trademark.

[47] *Marckx*, fn.21 above, limitation on an unmarried mother's ability to make gifts/legacies to her child disclosed discrimination contrary to Art.14 in conjunction with Art.1 of Protocol No.1 but no violation under Art.1 of Protocol No.1 in relation to the child's inability to inherit.

[48] *Mazurek v France*, February 1, 2000, ECHR 2000–II.

[49] *Apostolidi v Turkey*, March 29, 2007.

[50] *Nacaryan and Deryan v Turkey*, fn.8 above.

[51] *Stran Greek Refineries v Greece*, December 9, 1994, Series A, No.301–B, 19 E.H.R.R. 293; *Anheuser-Busch Inc*, fn.15 above, para.65.

[52] e.g. *Stretch v UK*, June 24, 2003, where the applicant had entered into a building lease with an option for renewal for 21 years, he had a legitimate expectation to exercise the option even though it was found later to be invalid due to a technicality (the local authority had acted ultra vires at the time in granting the option). See *Kopecky*, fn.26 above, paras 45–52, for recent analysis of "legitimate expectation"; also a court order for a social tenancy agreement, although not giving a right to occupy a particular property, gave a "legitimate expectation" to obtain a pecuniary asset: *Teteriny v Russia*, June 30, 2005.

[53] e.g. *Prince Hans-Adam II of Liechtenstein*, fn.25 above, concerning the Prince's claim in the German courts for restitution of a painting expropriated from his father in 1946 by the former Czech authorities.

[54] *Gratzinger and Gratzingerova v Czech Republic*, (39794/98) (Dec.) July 10, 2002, ECHR 2002–VII, where the applicants did not fulfil the condition of Czech nationality and had no legitimate expectation, only a hope, that this condition would be set aside as unconstitutional.

or a conditional claim which lapses as result of non-fulfilment of the condition.[55] A statement of intention to pay compensation did not confer a right sufficient for the purposes of Art.1 of Protocol No.1.[56] The Court has in some cases left open whether there were "possessions" where the amount of reimbursement to be paid by the State was not defined, but to be fixed by a future regulation.[57] Where the law providing for restitution of property of victims of political repression made no reference to the property covered or any modalities, indeed stating that it should be subject to separate legislation, no "legitimate expectation" or sufficiently-established claim arose. Conversely, where the same law set conditions of eligibility for such victims to claim non-pecuniary damage, there was a claim based on law amounting to "possessions" as the applicants fulfilled the conditions, the facts having been established in court, and the fact that further legislation was required to specify the level of compensation did not detract from that position. Indeed the total inactivity of the legislature, leaving the applicants in a state of uncertainty for over 11 years, imposed on them a disproportionate burden that disclosed a violation.[58]

Measures affecting claims pursued in court actions may disclose interference with possessions where the claims are sufficiently established or final. No possession or legitimate expectation of obtaining a pecuniary asset arises where based on a particular interpretation of law in court decisions which are not final;[59] it may do so where there is sufficient basis in national law, for example where there is settled case-law of the domestic courts confirming it.[60] A legitimate expectation may be in play even where it is based on an erroneous decision.[61]

In *Stran Greek Refineries v Greece*, an arbitration award in favour of a company pursuing damages against the State for breach of contract to build an oil refinery constituted a "possession", since it was immediately enforceable, final and with no right of appeal on the merits. There was an interference when, due to a legislative measure, the award ceased to be enforceable. Although it might have not been in the State interest to pursue the contract, the State had intervened to alter the machinery set up under the agreement, after the judiciary had ruled on its validity and no provision for compensation had been made by way of counterbalance.

In *Pressos Compania Naviera v Belgium*, the claims of applicants for negligence in pending proceedings against pilots alleged to have caused damage to their vessels were assets as claims for compensation coming into existence under the rules of tort

[55] e.g. *Malhous v Czech Republic*, (33071/96) (Dec.) July 12, 2000, ECHR 2000–XII, where the applicant brought proceedings to claim restitution of land which failed, under the statutory conditions, as it was no longer owned by the State.

[56] *Teytaud v France*, (Dec.) January 25, 2001, ECHR 2001–I, where the applicants had no legal right to the compensation paid to the French State by Algeria for expropriated property notwithstanding statements of intention by the authorities.

[57] *OGIS-Institut Stanislas, OGEC St Pie X and Blanche de Castille v France*, May 27, 2004, no violation arose in that the amount reimbursed was a far lower figure than hoped.

[58] *Klaus and Iouri Kiladze v Georgia*, February 2, 2010, paras 57–62.

[59] *Klaus and Iouri Kiladze*, fn.58 above, paras 63–78.

[60] *Maurice v France*, June 10, 2005, ECHR 2005–IX, para.63, where the applicants' claim, but for enactment of a new retrospective law, gave them a legitimate expectation, on the basis of precedent, of obtaining compensation. See also *Weissman v Romania*, May 24, 2006, where the applicants' claim for payment of loss of income from expropriated property was regarded as clearly based in law and the State had no defence.

[61] *Chroust v Czech Republic*, November 20, 2006, however, the refusal not to continue to pay the allowance was not disproportionate, given that the applicant had no entitlement according to the domestic courts and he did not have to repay those sums mistakenly given.

at the moment damage occurred. The Court noted that the applicants had a legitimate expectation that their claims would be dealt with in accordance with the law of torts and found that the 1988 Act which exempted the State and its pilots from liability for negligent acts, amounted to a deprivation of possessions. While the Court accepted the Government's arguments that the Act pursued the public interest, e.g. to protect the State's financial interests, harmonise laws with the Netherlands, it found the measure disproportionate since there was no measure of compensation. The Court also accepted the applicants' view that legal certainty did not require retrospective extinguishing of claims.[62] This may be contrasted with a situation where claims in tort were more speculative (due to time-bar problems) and, although extinguished by new legislation, were replaced by a scheme of compensation which benefitted all without the burden of taking proceedings. Even though the compensation paid was less than that claimed, it was not considered against this background that the measure failed to strike a fair balance.[63]

Conversely, in *National & Provincial Building Society v UK*,[64] where the applicants had pending claims for the recovery of tax paid under invalid regulations, the Court expressed doubts that these claims constituted possessions, since they had not obtained an enforceable final judgment and it was questionable that they had a legitimate expectation of such given the Government's clear intention to rectify the defects in the regulations. However, assuming that there was a control of use to secure payment of taxes, the Court found that the measure was remedial legislation to give effect to the original intention of the legislators and there was an obvious and compelling public interest in achieving that intention.[65] As to balance, it considered that the Government had always made it clear that the sums should be liable to tax noting that the invalidity worked by way of giving a windfall for building societies to exploit; it accepted the Government view that liability imposed for the gap period when assessment periods changed was fair.[66] A claim for overpaid VAT did however constitute an asset in *SA Dangeville v France*, where the claim was based on a Community norm that was perfectly clear, precise and directly applicable and created a substantive right.

Judicial application of procedural law in a particular case may interfere disproportionately with claims to possessions as in *SA Dangeville v France* where the *Conseil*

[62] See also *Maurice*, fn.60 above, where a violation arose from retrospective removal of claim for considerable damages for medical failure to identify disabilities of a child before birth, other possibilities of compensation being uncertain and inadequate.

[63] *Poznanski v Germany*, (25101/05) (Dec.) July 3, 2007, concerning claims by forced labourers under the Nazi regime against I.G. Farben's successor.

[64] *National & Provincial Building Society v UK*, (21319/93) etc. (Rep.) June 25, 1996, as regarded "possessions", the Commission pointed out a divergence between the Court judgments in *Stran Greek*, fn.51 above, and *Pressos*, fn.5 above—the Court having found that the domestic court judgment acknowledging Stran's claim was not sufficiently established to be enforceable though the arbitration award was, while in *Pressos*, tort claims qualified though no judgments had issued.

[65] See also *EEG-Slachthuis Verbist v Belgium*, (60559/00) (Dec.) November 10, 2005, concerning retrospective legislation to make good defects in collection of animal health subsidies; *Sud Parisienne de Construction v France*, February 11, 2010, retrospective amendment to default interest for public works contract did not affect the principal claim, but was intended to remedy an inflationary dysfunction in the system as a whole. Contrast *Aubert v France*, January 9, 2001, no convincing evidence that the functioning of the health and social services required retrospective legislation to protect them from pending actions such as the applicants; *Joubert v France*, July 23, 2009, retrospective legislation impinging on recovery of tax rebates was a disproportionate interference not justified by any pressing state interest, mere avoidance of financial liability not being enough apparently.

[66] On Art.6, see: Pt IIA, s.16: Legislative interference.

d'Etat refused to give effect to a directly applicable provision of Community law on a technical ground which estopped repayment of overpaid VAT. In *Brumarescu v Romania*, intervention by the Supreme Court in overturning a final and irrevocable judgment ordering the return of the applicant's property unlawfully expropriated during the communist regime was not found to be supported by any public interest and to impose an excessive burden on the individual owner.

Where there were undue delays in repaying tax advances (some five to ten years) which were uncontested, the Court found the claims were property rights and that the uncertainty caused by the delays failed to strike a fair balance.[67] A violation may also arise where interest is not paid on claims paid after undue delay[68] or where interest due on a claim is reduced to a far lower rate due to the public status of the debtor.[69] Failure by the authorities to execute in due time[70] claims that have been upheld in final court judgments will also raise issues of interference with property rights.[71] Lack of funds cannot justify such omission,[72] although refusal to enforce against another State due to state immunity was not disproportionate.[73] Excessively high stamp duties or court fees which bar pursuit of actions to vindicate property rights may disclose a violation,[74] as will transfer by the State of the property under dispute to a third party thereby preventing recovery.[75] Where by the time a claim is awarded its value has considerably depreciated due to inflation, the lack of power in the courts to revalue the amount of money does not disclose a violation of Article 1 of Protocol No.1 which cannot be interpreted as imposing an obligation on States to maintain the value of claims or apply an inflation-compatible default interest rate.[76]

Claims for legal fees were possessions, where the client was liable for the fees for acts already carried out. The law which prevented the lawyer from recuperating those fees directly from the State which was party in the proceedings imposed an excessive burden on the lawyer, whose choice not to seek payment from her impoverished clients was not arbitrary or unreasonable.[77]

[67] *Buffalo SRL in liquidation v Italy*, July 3, 2003.

[68] *Eko-Elda Avee v Greece*, March 9, 2006.

[69] *Meidanis v Greece*, May 22, 2009, no justification as to why a public hospital needed to benefit from the much lower rate in order to fulfil its functions. See also *Zouboulidis v Greece*, June 25, 2009, where application of prejudicial limitation period and starting point for default interest applied to the applicant's awarded claims against a State body acting as a private employer: fair balance not struck in the circumstances

[70] Delays more than 12 months in ordinary cases of non-enforcement were generally regarded as unreasonable in Russian cases e.g. *Burdov v Russia (No. 2)*, January 15, 2009, para.67; where the judgment debt was in respect of damage for excessive delay in proceedings, a shorter time of six months was the threshold: *Simaldone v Italy*, March 31, 2009, paras 57–64.

[71] e.g. *Antonakopoulos v Greece*, December 14, 1999; *Dimitrios Georgiadis v Greece*, March 28, 2000, failure to pay pensions to which courts had found that the applicants were entitled; *Metaxas v Greece*, May 27, 2004: violation where the State paid the judgment debt to the applicant only after prolonged enforcement proceedings; *Mykhaylenky v Ukraine*, November 30, 2004, ECHR 2004–XI, violation where three to seven years' ongoing failure by State to comply with judgments against company for whose debts it was liable.

[72] *Burdov v Russia*, May 7, 2002, para.41; see also *"Amat-G" Ltd and Mebaghishvili v Georgia*, September 27, 2005, lack of Government funds was no excuse; an attempt to stagger payments imposed by an ordinance was also found to lack legal certainty.

[73] *Treska v Albania and Italy*, (26937/04) (Dec.) June 29, 2006, the applicants' claim against the Albanian Government remained, even though no steps would be taken to enforce against the Italian embassy.

[74] *Weissman*, fn.49 above.

[75] *Strain v Romania*, July 21, 2005.

[76] *Todorov v Bulgaria*, (65850/01) (Dec.) May 13, 2008.

[77] *Ambruosi v Italy*, October 19, 2000.

(e) *Shareholders' interests*

A share in a company with an economic value is a possession, such that the loss of shares can constitute an interference with possessions or deprivation of property.[78] Issue of new shares which reduced an applicant's majority shareholding, depriving it of the ability to wield influence or control over the company was regarded as interference with "possessions".[79] II–607

Shareholders in a company cannot claim per se that their property rights are affected by the expropriation of property of that company.[80] Despite the Commission's finding in *Agrotexim v Greece* that the shareholders' rights were affected by the interference with the company's property and its capacity to enter into developments projects, the Court upheld a preliminary objection of no victim status since in fact it was not the property of the shareholders which was affected by the expropriation but that of the company which could have acted through its liquidator. Thus the shareholders were not entitled to act on behalf of the company. It was not enough to allege a fall in the value of their shares. The corporate veil was maintained.

Nonetheless, in exceptional circumstances, shareholders may claim on behalf of the company, e.g. where it is clearly established that it is impossible for the company to apply to the Court through the organs set up under its articles of incorporation or—in the event of liquidation or bankruptcy—through its liquidators or trustees in bankruptcy[81]; or where there is direct effect on the property rights in the shares, the applicant can show that he is the sole shareholder or that the company is the means by which he runs his own affairs.[82]

(f) *Bank accounts*

Depositing money on account gives an applicant the entitlement to withdraw that sum, together with accrued interest. Claims to these sums consitute possessions notwithstanding difficulties the bank may have to honour the debt. The freezing of accounts is regarded as a "control of use" under the third rule, set out in the second paragraph, of Art.1 of Protocol No.1.[83] II–608

Temporary suspension of accounts due to emergency situations may be justified, as in a case where the applicant was unable to access his savings in a Chechen bank but was entitled to interest on the amounts over the two-year-period.[84] A wide margin of appreciation applies where the State intervenes in the banking sector due

[78] (8588–9/79) (Dec.) December 12, 1982, 29 D.R. 64; *Olczak v Poland*, (30417/96) (Dec.) November 7, 2002, ECHR 2002–X, measures which devalued the applicant's shareholding in a bank were justified by its mal-administration and the need to prevent its bankruptcy.

[79] *Sovtransavto Holding v Ukraine*, July 25, 2002, ECHR 2002–VII.

[80] *Agrotexim v Greece*, October 24, 1995, Series A, No.330–A, 21 E.H.R.R. 250; also (11189/86) (Dec.) December 11, 1986, 50 D.R. 121, the minority shareholder in a company could not claim to be victim of levying of tax or charges on company but was a victim where a new shareholder was introduced free of charge which diminished relative value of his own rights as shareholder.

[81] *Agrotexim*, fn.80 above, para.66.

[82] *Ankarcrona v Sweden*, June 29, 2000, ECHR 2000–VI; *Nosov v Russia*, (30877/02) (Dec.) October 20, 2005; *Pokis v Latvia*, (528/02) (Dec.) October 5, 2006.

[83] *Suljagic v Bosnia-Herzegovina*, November 3, 2009, paras 34–36.

[84] *Merzhoyev v Russia*, October 8, 2009, hostilities had given rise to security, social and financial difficulties, as well as loss of many bank documents and seals.

to either motives of financial, economic or social reform, or in the aftermath of serious civil upheaval and war.[85] While it was acceptable, against a background of reconstruction of a devastated economy, for authorities to implement schemes of staggered reimbursement of foreign currency savings through government bonds and to set levels of interest below the norm, the Court considered that, where they had undertaken to make payments, principles of the rule of law and lawfulness required them to keep to their promises with relative fidelity; thus, a series of delays in making payments disclosed a violation.[86]

The Court has held that the State is not obliged to guarantee the purchasing power of sums deposited with financial institutions.[87]

(g) Restitution of property

II–609 Following the disintegration of the Soviet Bloc, several of the new democratic governments passed legislation concerning the restoration of property expropriated by the communist regimes. This in some cases has caused more problems than it has solved.

There is usually no doubt that the aim of such legislation is in the public interest, whether redress of previous wrongs or administering social justice. However, difficulties arise where the confiscated property has meanwhile been acquired by other private parties. The Court has stated that, in order to strike a fair balance, the way in which the current occupiers acquired the property must be taken into account. The availability and adequacy of compensation or other methods of offsetting the loss of the property is also key. Where an applicant has obtained the expropriated property in good faith, in general compensation reasonably related to the value of the property is required.[88]

Delays in the restitution of property to which the applicant has an established right or, in default, payment of adequate compensation may disclose unjustified interference with property rights. Where the delay is aggravated by uncertainty, due to frequent changes in the legal regime and inadequate precision or time-limits for payment of compensation, violations have been found, particularly in the Romanian context where the authorities have been called upon to restore coherence, simplicity and effectiveness to the overly-complex and confused situation.[89]

3. Domestic court regulation of disputes

II–610 Domestic court regulation of property disputes according to pre-existing law does not as such engage the responsibility of the State under Art.1 of Protocol No.1. Nor can the order of a domestic court, consequent upon civil proceedings, requiring one party to the proceedings to pay the other party be equated to a deprivation of property, even if the successful party was a public authority.[90] The fact that one

[85] *Suljagic*, fn.84 above, para.42.
[86] *Suljagic*, fn.84 above, paras 49–57.
[87] *Appolonov v Russia*, (67578/01) (Dec.) August 29, 2002, one of many cases introduced by savers hit by the disastrous depreciation of currency following economic reform.
[88] e.g. *Kalinova v Bulgaria* November 8, 2007, paras 75–79, violation. No provision for compensation made; giving the applicant alternative accommodation at reduced rent was not sufficient.
[89] *Viasu v Romani*, December 9, 2008.
[90] e.g. *Blake v UK*, (68890/01) (Dec.) October 25, 2005.

party is inevitably unsuccessful is generally not sufficient, without some supervening act of administration or legislation affecting the applicant's position.[91] Where in *Nerva v UK*, the domestic courts ruled that the tips paid to the applicant waiters were the property of their employers and could be regarded as paid to them as part of their "remuneration", the Court considered that this was essentially a matter of interpretation of domestic law insufficient to engage the responsibility of the State under Art.1 of Protocol No.1.

Leeway is given for courts to interpret law to remedy anomalies and deficiencies. Change in application of law affecting property rights which were reasoned, foreseeable and in pursuit of a legitimate aim was not regarded as arbitrary or unlawful.[92]

Whether or not an applicant's property rights were determined in the courts fairly would generally fall to be examined under the procedural guarentees of Art.6, para.1. Rights of property have long been classified as falling "without doubt" within the scope of "civil rights" under Art.6, para.1.[93]

However, as the State is under a positive obligation to provide a judicial mechanism for settling effectively property disputes between private individuals and organisations, serious defects in the handling of such may raise issues under Art.1 of Protocol No.1 as well as Art.6.[94]

4. Obligation to protect property

The right in the first sentence of Art.1 of Protocol No.1 may include an obligation II–611
to take positive measures to protect property. However, in contrast to the obligation to take measures to protect life from known risks, the obligation to protect property is more limited. In *Budayeva v Russia*, where a mudslide devastated a community, the failures of infrastructure and to give warning led to a breach of Art.2 as regarded loss of life; however as regarded property the obligation only arose where there was a direct link between the measures an applicant might legitimately expect from the authorities and his effective enjoyment of his possessions and could not

[91] e.g. (10082/82) (Dec.) July 4, 1983, 33 D.R. 247, order by House of Lords to pay £40 million to BP following frustration of contract for exploitation of Libyan oil concession; (11949/86) (Dec.) December 1, 1986, 51 D.R. 195, eviction of tenant following annulment of lease by landlord; (8588–9/79), fn.63 above, redistribution of company shares. Though where State does intervene in legal relations of private individuals as regards property, the Commission stated that it must ensure the law does not create such inequality that a person is arbitrarily and unjustly deprived of property in favour of another, i.e. (13021/87) (Dec.) September 8, 1988, 57 D.R. 268.

[92] *Hoare v UK*, (16261/08) (Dec.) April 12, 2011, costs had been imposed on the applicant, a convicted prisoner sued by one of his victims when he had won the Lottery; in doing so, the House of Lords had overruled a precedent, identified by the Law Commission as apt for reform, iin interpreting limitation rules in favour of victims of sexual abuse; costs orders also discouraged unnecessary litigation and the applicant, offered a settlement, had refused.

[93] *Sporrong and Lonroth*, fn.1 above, para.79, where the Court overruled the Commission's approach that there had been no determination since expropriation did not take place nor had there been any change in ownership.

[94] See *Sovtransavto Holding*, fn.64 above, where the repeated annulation of decisions by the courts and varying interventions by the executive authorities in the proceedings concerning the lawfulness of share re-valuations disclosed violations of both provisions. Also, violations of Art.1 of Protocol No.1 in *Paduraru v Romania*, December 1, 2005, general legal uncertainty concerning property sales in good faith to third parties, and *Russian Conservative Party of Entrepreneurs v Russia*, January 11, 2007, where in proceedings breaching legal certainty the courts refused to order the restitution of the applicant party's electoral deposit.

extend beyond what was reasonable. It was not apparent to what extent the authorities could have been expected to prevent damage resulting from the freak weather conditions. Noting that the authorities provided free housing and disaster relief, the Court was not prepared to find that they were also obliged to make good pecuniary losses or that any disproportionate burden was laid on the applicants.[95]

Where property rights are interfered with by third parties, positive obligations to protect those rights by providing for effective criminal investigations and redress through civil proceedings may arise. However, standards of effectiveness are apparently less rigorous than in other contexts and criminal investigations into minor crimes will only offend if plagued by flagrant and serious deficiencies. Thus, where the applicant's house was burgled twice while she was detained, the Court examined whether the response to her complaints was adequate.[96] It is not altogether apparent why it is necessary to import a procedural obligation of this nature into Art.1 of Protocol No.1. Property rights are generally protected under Art.6 in its civil head, as well as Art.13. The human rights interest in regulating criminal investigations for matters of property—by its nature compensatable by money—does not seem particularly fundamental or pressing.

A positive obligation to provide a effective judicial mechanism for dealing with property disputes has also been referred to by the Court. In this regard, failings of legal certainty and inconsistency of case-law in property cases may deprive applicant's rights of practical and effective protection. Thus, where an applicant's claim for compensation failed on the ground that the wrong official body had been sued, the Court found a violation arising as the mistake had largely arisen due to conflicting case-law and new reforms. It also commented that, where actions against the State were concerned, there was a positive obligation on the State to facilitate the identification of the appropriate State organ to be sued.[97]

Procedural protection must also be provided to persons who lack legal capacity, ensuring that their interests are adequately protected and that they can effectively participate in any proceedings. Thus, where the flat of a mentally incapacitated applicant was subject to a summary judicial sale and the guardian was unable to obtain a re-opening of the procedure, the Court considered that legal certainty and the interests of a good faith buyer were not sufficient justification for imposing an inflexible time-limit to the applicant's prejudice.[98]

Cross-reference

Part IIA, s.1b: Civil rights and obligations.
Part IIA, s.2: Access to Court.

[95] *Budayeva v Russia*, March 20, 2008. Contrast *Oneryildiz v Turkey*, November 30, 2004, paras 135–138, where there was a causal link between the gross negligence that led to the engulfment of the applicant's house as well as the loss of life when the methane explosion destroyed the housing built on a tip with the acquiescence of the authorities. Violation of Art.1 of Protocol No. 1 for not taking the practical steps which would have avoided the destruction, such as installation of a gas-extraction system.

[96] *Blumberga v Latvia*, October 14, 2008, the criminal investigation was regarded as slow but not flagrantly deficient, and the option of civil proceedings against identified suspects had been open to the aggrieved applicant. Under domestic law, the police had the obligation to ensure the protection of property of the applicant while she was detained but this was not in fact relied on by the Chamber as a ground of responsibility.

[97] *Plechanow*, fn.9 above.

[98] *Zehentner v Austria*, July 16, 2009, paras 76–79.

Part IIB, s.17: Expropriation, confiscation and control of use.
Part IIB, s.25: Housing and tenancy.
Part IIB, s.34: Planning and use of property.
Part IIB, s.34: Pensions.
Part IIB, s.48: Welfare benefits.

39. Reasons for arrest and detention

Key provision:

II–612 Article 5, para.2 (right to be informed promptly in language understood of the reasons for the arrest or detention).

Key case-law:

X v UK, November 5, 1981, Series A, No.46, 4 E.H.R.R. 188; *Fox, Campbell and Hartley v UK*, August 30, 1990, Series A, No.182; *Van der Leer v Netherlands*, September 27, 1990, Series A, No.170, 12 E.H.R.R. 567; *Murray v UK*, October 28, 1994, Series A, No.300–A, 19 E.H.R.R. 193; *Conka v Belgium*, February 5, 2002, ECHR 2002–I; *Saadi v UK*, January 29, 2008, ECHR 2008–I.

1. General considerations

II–613 This is a safeguard against arbitrary arrest, requiring the person to be informed of the grounds of arrest. This also provides an opportunity to challenge the reasonableness of the suspicion justifying arrest and to use the remedy provided by Art.5, para.4 to challenge the lawfulness of the detention.[1]

2. Scope of the guarantee

II–614 Article 5, para.2 applies not only to persons arrested under Art.5, para.1(c) despite the apparent criminal law connotation of the words used, although it may be subsumed, as in *X v UK*, by a finding of a violation of Art.5, para.4.[2] In *Van der Leer v Netherlands*, concerning the recall of of a mental health patient, the Court held that the provision was to be interpreted autonomously as regards "arrested" and that it went beyond criminal law measures.[3] It was closely linked to Art.5, para.4 which was not limited in scope to any particular form of taking into detention. Thus, a failure to inform the applicant of the measures against her disclosed a violation. It was not subsumed by a finding of a violation under Art.5, para.4 for in this case the applicant, in voluntary residence at the hospital, was not informed at all that she had been deprived of her liberty by a compulsory measure and she should have been informed of this important change in her status, not merely to enable her to challenge the lawfulness.

3. Nature and form of the information

II–615 The Court has not been rigorous as to what form the information should take, though it should, at least, be in a language which the applicant understands.[4] The necessary information does not have to be given in writing to the applicant or

[1] (8098/77) (Dec.) December 13, 1978, 16 D.R.1 11 and 34 D.R. 119. Art.5, para.2 is a weaker guarantee than Art.6, para.3(a) which applies to preparation of the criminal trial.

[2] The Court found that it followed necessarily from the breach of Art.5, para.4 that to make effective use of his right to challenge recall the applicant had to be promptly and adequately informed of the facts on which the authorities relied: the issue was thus absorbed.

[3] *Van der Leer v Netherlands*, September 27, 1990, Series A, No.170, 12 E.H.R.R. 567, paras 27–28.

[4] (11539/85) (Dec.) July 12, 1986, 48 D.R. 237, paras 242–243; (34573/97) (Dec.) May 21, 1998, where the English-speaking applicant should have been nonetheless aware from certain Italian phrases that extradition was being sought on charges of use of a false passport; *Parlanti v Germany*, (45097/04) (Dec.) May 26, 2005, where an Italian arrested in Germany was informed in English which he did not deny understanding.

consist of a complete list of all the charges or disclose to the suspect all the information which might be available to the investigating judge.[5] For example, it was sufficient that the applicant was made aware that he was being detained for possession of drugs with the intent to supply as a result of allegedly having sold drugs to certain individuals, without being told when, where or to whom.[6] It may be acceptable that the information be given, orally, to his representative.[7]

It is not necessary for a person to be expressly informed of the reasons since the Court has indicated that the surrounding circumstances of the arrest or its aftermath may be sufficient for the person to deduce them,[8] although it is not enough for the Government to refer to a general statement of intent in Parliament.[9] As to how indirect the notification can be, the Commission and Court differed.

In *Fox, Campbell and Hartley v UK*, the Commission found a violation, since the applicants were not directly informed at the time of arrest that they were suspected, inter alia, of information gathering and courier work for IRA although they were questioned about particular activities. It considered that the elementary nature of the safeguard was such that it placed an obligation on the arresting authorities to provide a detainee with adequate information as to the reasons for the arrest as soon as was practicable. The Court did comment that being told on arrest that they were held as terrorists was not enough but found no violation since there was no ground to suppose that the reasons for the applicants' arrest were not brought to their attention during their interrogation within a matter of a few hours.[10]

In *Murray v UK*, the Commission found a breach where the applicant on arrest was questioned about money and the USA which gave her only a vague indication, not sufficiently precise to enable her to understand why she had been arrested. The Court again differed, noting that from the reference to her brother it must have been apparent that she was being questioned about involvement in the purchase of arms for which her brother had been convicted and thus the reasons for arrest were sufficiently brought to her attention.[11]

General policy information, such as parliamentary announcements are not sufficient; reasons relevant to the individual himself are required.

The degree of information will also depend on the kind of arrest or detention. In mere arrest for security check purposes unrelated to the existence of particular suspicions (i.e. an obligation under under Art.5, para.1(b)) it was sufficient if information was provided promptly as to the legal basis of the arrest and the nature of the check, namely, that they were to be fingerprinted, photographed, questioned and otherwise checked up on. Suspicion was not required under the relevant domestic order nor under Art.5, para.1(b) so it was compatible with Art.5 that the applicants were not told what suspicions were being held against them during the 45-hour period of detention.[12]

[5] (8098/77) (Dec.) December 13, 1978, 16 D.R. 11.

[6] *Jordanov v Bulgaria*, August 10, 2006.

[7] *Saadi v UK*, January 29, 2008, ECHR 2008–I, paras 84–85, although the Court appears to leave this open by using an "even assuming" formula.

[8] e.g. *Kerr v UK*, (40451/98) (Dec.) December 7, 1999, a delay between arrest and charging did not raise any difficulty as it could be assumed that the applicant gained a reasonable idea of the suspicions against him during questioning a few hours after his arrest. See *Dikme v Turkey*, July 11, 2000, paras 54–57, where the applicant's obstructive conduct was apparently regarded as prolonging matters.

[9] *Saadi*, fn.7 above, para.53.

[10] See also *Korkmaz v Turkey*, March 21, 2006, para.29, where the applicants could deduce from questioning that they were wanted as members of an illegal armed group.

[11] *Saadi*, fn.7 above, paras 84–85.

[12] *McVeigh v UK*, (8022–25–27/77) (Rep.) March 18, 1981, 25 D.R.15.

A lesser standard also applies to arrest with a view to extradition where the information given need not be so complete as in the case of arrest for the purpose of bringing someone to trial.[13]

An applicant cannot claim any particular right to see the documents which initiated the investigation.[14] Nor does Art.5, para.2 require the disclosure of the complete file, only provision of sufficient information to facilitate the pursuit of the remedy envisaged under Art.5, para.4.[15]

4. Promptly

II–616 The person must be informed at or soon after the time of arrest or be able to deduce the reasons from the questioning or circumstances within a few hours of arrest. In *Murray*, where the applicant was arrested at 7.00 and questioned from 8.20—9.35, this was sufficiently prompt. The Commission stated that no more than a few hours should elapse save in exceptional circumstances such as the serious incapacity of the arrested person to comprehend the reasons that might have been given. Thus, where an applicant was merely told that he was arrested under a particular provision and not questioned until next day, the Commission found that the alleged practical problems in assembling an interview team so late at night were not sufficient where the fundamental importance of the right to liberty was at stake.[16] The Court has since found violations where 4 days,[17] and 76 hours[18] elapsed before applicants were informed.

5. Access to legal representation or to contact family

II–617 Art.5, para.2 does not guarantee the right to call a lawyer.[19] Access to a lawyer is generally dealt with under Art.6, para.3(c), but as yet there is no automatic right to a solicitor from the first moment of arrest (see Pt IIA: Fair trial guarantees, legal representation in criminal proceedings). Access to doctors and relatives were mentioned as elements in safeguards justifying derogation under Art.15 by the United Kingdom in respect of Art.5, para.3, concerning provisions allowing the

[13] (10819/84) (Dec.) July 5, 1984, 38 D.R. 230, where an applicant informed that he was suspected of fraud and arrested for purpose of extradition to the United States; (23916/94) (Dec.) April 6, 1995, where a person was held for extradition, this did not involve the determination of a criminal charge so information given did not need to meet the requirements of Art.6, para.3: information from the judge that extradition was sought by the United States on a charge of false billing was enough.

[14] e.g. *Lamy v Belgium*, March 30, 1989, Series A, No.151, para.32, i.e. the allegedly tendentious report which had sparked off the judicial investigation: he had seen the arrest warrant and had an interview with the investigation judge.

[15] (9614/81) (Dec.) October 12, 1983, 34 D.R. 19, where a judge had removed certain documents from the case file to safeguard the investigation and the defence lawyers did not see them until a year later, the absence of the information did not hamper the exercise of an Art.5, para.4 remedy. In *Conka v Belgium*, February 5, 2002, ECHR 2002–I, the Roma family were given sufficient information, with an interpreter, about the purpose of their arrest being to deport them to satisfy Art.5, para.2, though the circumstances, in particular the shortness of time before their expulsion, deprived them of a realistic possibility of applying to court for a Art.5, para.4 remedy (para.52); while in *Shamayev v Georgia and Russia*, April 12, 2005, ECHR 2005–III, there was a violation for refusal to give any access to the file.

[16] (12690/87) (Rep.) October 14, 1991, C.M. Resolution DH (95) 4, January 11, 1995.

[17] *Shamayev v Georgia and Russia*, April 12, 2005, ECHR 2005–III, para.416.

[18] *Saadi*, fn.7 above, paras 84–85.

[19] (8828/79) (Dec.) October 5, 1982, 30 D.R. 93.

detention of suspects for up to seven days without being brought before a judicial officer.[20] Inability of detained suspects to contact their wives in *McVeigh v UK* led to a finding of violation by the Commission of Art.8.[21]

Cross-reference

Part IIA, s.11: Information about the charge.
Part IIB, s.42: Review of detention.

[20] *Brannigan and McBride v UK*, May 26, 1993, Series A, No.258–B, para.64.
[21] (8022–25–27/77) (Rep.) March 18, 1981, 25 D.R. 15. See also *Ucar v Turkey*, April 11, 2006, breach of Art.8 for lack of provision for contact by a father with his detained son.

40. Religion, thought and conscience

Key provision:

II–618 Article 9 (freedom of thought, conscience and religion).

Key case-law:

Darby v Sweden, October 23, 1990, Series A, No.187, 13 E.H.R.R. 774; *Hoffman v Austria*, June 23, 1993, Series A, No.255–C, 17 E.H.R.R. 293; *Kokkinakis v Greece*, May 25, 1993, Series A, No.260–A, 17 E.H.R.R. 397; *Manoussakis v Greece*, September 26, 1996, R.J.D. 1996–IV, No.17, 23 E.H.R.R. 387; *Valsamis v Greece*, December 18, 1996, R.J.D. 1996–VI, No.4, 24 E.H.R.R. 294; *Kalaç v Turkey*, July 1, 1997, R.J.D. 1997–IV, No.41, 27 E.H.R.R. 552; *Larissis v Greece*, February 24, 1998, R.J.D. 1998–I, No.65, 27 E.H.R.R. 329; *Buscarini v San Marino*, February 18, 1999, ECHR 1999–I, 30 E.H.R.R. 208; *Serif v Greece*, December 14, 1999, ECHR 1999–IX, 31 E.H.R.R. 561; *Thlimmenos v Greece*, April 6, 2000, ECHR 2000–IV, 31 E.H.R.R. 411; *Cha'are Shalom Ve Tsedek v France*, June 27, 2000, ECHR 2000–VII; *Hasan and Chaush v Bulgaria*, October 26, 2000, ECHR 2000–XI; *Cyprus v Turkey*, May 10, 2001, ECHR 2001–IV; *Metropolitan Church of Bessarabia v Moldova*, December 13, 2001, ECHR 2001–XII; *Leyla Sahin v Turkey*, November 10, 2005, ECHR 2005–XI; *Bayatyan v Armenia*, July 7, 2011, ECHR 2011–. . .

1. General considerations

II–619 The relationship of churches and State has a troubled history in Europe. Where a State has a bias to a particular religion (for example, constitutional protection) there is potential for issues arising as regards the effect of this preference on other religious groups. It is questionable to what extent in multi-ethnic Europe one group can justifiably be given preferential treatment over another and what weight should be given to the history and traditions of the particular country. The arrival on the scene of other "religions" with differing cultural and social dimensions poses special problems where practices conflict with expected ways of doing things. The Court's case-law increasingly emphasises that the State's neutral role and the importance of pluralism, tolerance and broadmindedness and that the views of the majority cannot always prevail against minority groups.[1]

Issues arise as to what may genuinely claim protection as a "religion" or matter of conscience; what may be considered manifestations of those beliefs which require protection; and what justifications exist for interfering with beliefs and practices. There are also questions as to what extent the State is under a positive obligation to protect the manifestation of religious beliefs from others.

As in other provisions of the Convention, interferences with the right guaranteed under Art.9 must conform with notions of the rule of law, namely, be prescribed by law.[2] In an accessible and foreseeable manner, pursue a legitimate aim and be justified as necessary. Exceptions in the second paragraph must be strictly construed and cannot be subject to additions[3]

[1] See, e.g. *Bayatyan v Armenia*, July 7, 2011, ECHR 2011–. . ., para.126.

[2] See, e.g. *Kuznetsov v Russia*, January 11, 2007, where police disrupted a meeting of Jehovah's Witnesses on spurious grounds without legal basis.

[3] *Nolan and K v Russia*, February 12, 2009, para.73, it had not been open to Russia to plead national security, a ground listed in some provisions but not in Art.9, para.2, as the aim for expelling a sect leader. The Court commented that this omission, deliberate, reflected the primordial importance of religious pluralism.

Where there is an overlap between freedom of assembly and association and religious expression in a case concerning religious meetings or religious associations, the case may be dealt with under Art.11, as *lex specialis*, interpreted in light of Art.9.[4]

2. Religion, thought and conscience

There has been little detailed discussion about the nature of the beliefs or principles which fall within the scope of these concepts. It is a sensitive area, what one person holds as sacred appearing absurd or anathema to another. The Commission showed a tendency to rely on other methods of rejecting cases based on the more controversial beliefs, using the justified exceptions under Art.9, para.2 and the possibility of finding that a particular claimed interference or restriction did not in reality prevent the manifestation of a particular religion, thought or belief. In a case which found the refusal of the authorities to register the Salvation Army as a religious body was in bad faith, the Court stated that the right to freedom of religion excludes any discretion on the part of the State to determine whether religious beliefs or the means used to express such beliefs are legitimate.[5] **II–620**

For the Commission, Art.9 covered "the sphere of private, personal beliefs", religious creeds or the "*forum internum*".[6] The Court emphasises its importance as a foundation of "democratic society and as part of the identity of believers and that their conception of belief is a precious asset to atheists, agnostics and the unconcerned".[7] The freedom guaranteed entails, inter alia, the freedom to hold or not to hold religious beliefs and to practise or not to practise a religion.[8]

More concretely, the Commission was prepared to assume that Veganism was a belief falling within Art.9[9]; pacifism was accepted as a philosophy involving the commitment in theory and practice to the securing of political and other objectives without the resort to the threat or use of force[10] Scientology was accepted without discussion[11]; Druidism was left open[12]; the Krishna consciousness movement was accepted without argument.[13] In the cases before the Court, Jehovah's Witnesses qualified.[14] Where there has been controversy as to whether a particular set of beliefs qualified as a religion, the Court has more recently taken the cautious view that it is not its task to rule in the abstract on such matters; in the absence of a European consensus, it stated that it would look to the domestic system for the nature of classification.[15] It may not, in any event, be a crucial matter, since even if

[4] See, e.g. *Barankevich v Russia*, July 26, 2007, violation of Art.11 in conjunction with Art.9 where Jehovah's Witnesses were refused permission to hold an open-air service.

[5] *Moscow Branch of the Salvation Army v Russia*, October 5, 2006, para.92.

[6] e.g. (10358/83) (Dec.) December 15, 1983, 37 D.R. 142; "primarily" added in (11308/84) (Dec.) March 13, 1986, 46 D.R. 200.

[7] *Kokkinakis v Greece*, May 25, 1993, Series A, No.260–A, 17 E.H.R.R. 397, para.31.

[8] *Buscarini v San Marino*, February 18, 1999, ECHR 1999–I, 30 E.H.R.R. 208, para.34.

[9] (18187/91) (Dec.) February 10, 1993.

[10] (7050/75) (Rep.) October 12, 1978, 19 D.R. 5.

[11] (7805/77) (Dec.) May 5, 1979, 16 D.R. 68; see also *Church of Scientology v Russia*, April 5, 2007.

[12] (12587/86) (Dec.) July 14, 1987, 53 D.R. 241, assuming Druidism was a religion, the closing of Stonehenge was a justified interference.

[13] (20490/92) (Dec.) March 8, 1994, 76–A D.R. 90.

[14] e.g. *Kokkinakis*, fn.7 above.

[15] *Kimyla v Russia*, October 1, 2009, paras 79–81, concerning Scientology: it was found that domestic authorities had recognised its activities as religious in nature.

not a religion, a suitably conscientious system of beliefs or thoughts could still fall under Art.9.

Article 9 does not cover mere "idealistic activities", for example the activities of a German legal association which gave advice to prisoners.[16] It also did not cover the stance taken by IRA prisoners with regard to "special category status"[17] or a lawyer's personal convictions which led him to refuse to carry out legal aid duty at police stations.[18]

Early Commission case-law held, in light of the exception for military service contained in Art.4, para.3(b), that there was no right to to refuse military service on conscientious grounds contained in the Convention.[19] In *Bayatyan v Armenia*, a Jehovah's Witness was convicted of draft evasion and sentenced to two and a half years' imprisonment for refusing to serve in the army; he had informed the authorities that he would perform alternative civilian service but this was not available. The Grand Chamber held that the mere fact that Art.4, para.3(b) removed civilian service from the scope of "forced or compulsory labour" did not mean that conscientious objection fell outside the scope of the separate and different provision governing freedom of religion, thought and conscience. Having regard to the almost universal consensus in Europe recognising a right to conscientious objection, it found that an opposition to military service, where motivated by a serious and insurmountable conflict between the duty to serve in the army and the person's conscience or deeply and genuinely held beliefs constituted a conviction of sufficient importance to attract the guarantees of Art.9.[20]

Article 9 does cover State intervention in disputes within a religious congregation, where such impacts on the running and organisation of the community. Government objections that disputes as to leadership were matters of control of administration and property not concerning religious practice as such have been rejected. Otherwise, the Court noted, the individual's practise of his religion would be rendered vulnerable if the organisational life of the community were not covered.[21] It has been left open whether merely revoking permission to use state property for religious purposes constitutes an interference with Art.9 rights.[22]

[16] (10358/83), fn.6 above.

[17] Nor was the wearing of non-prison uniform the manifestation of a belief under Art.9: (8317/78) (Dec.) May 15, 1980, 20 D.R. 44.

[18] (37489/97) (Dec.) October 21, 1998.

[19] See (7705/76) (Dec.) July 5, 1977, 9 D.R. 196, the Commission, unsympathetically noting the burden of military service should be shared equitably between citizens, found it legitimate for States to restrict exemptions and acceptable under Art.14 together with Art.9 for total exemption to be applied only to members of religions whose position was well known, e.g. Jehovah's Witnesses. Other persons, not so affiliated, had to suffer to avoid the possibility of shirkers!: (10410/83) (Dec.) October 11, 1984, 40 D.R. 40. However, impositions of persistent penalties on a pacifist for a failure to wear a uniform, without provision for other forms of service for conscientious objectors disclosed a breach of Art.3 in *Ulke v Turkey*, January 24, 2006, paras 61–62.

[20] *Bayatyan v Armenia*, fn.1 above, para.110, the applicant's beliefs as a Jehovah's Witness thus qualified.

[21] e.g. *Holy Synod of the Bulgarian Orthodox Church (Metropolitan Inokentiy) v Bulgaria*, January 22, 2009, paras 102–104.

[22] *Griechische Kirchengemeinde München und Bayern E.V. v Germany*, (52336/99) (Dec.) September 18, 2007, the orthodox community had used the church for some 150 years. The revocation was however found to be justified in the circumstances, in particular since they had been offered other locations for their religious rituals instead.

3. Victim status

Individuals, churches and associations with religious and philosophical objects are capable of exercising Art.9 rights.[23] A church or ecclesiastical body may also exercise on behalf of its adherents the rights guaranteed by Art.9.[24] However there is old authority that a legal person cannot exercise freedom of conscience[25] and a corporate profit-making body cannot rely on Art.9 rights.[26] II–621

Measures which do not impinge directly on an individual or religious organisation's exercise of Art.9 rights cannot be challenged. Thus, where a constitutional amendment banned the building of minarets, the Court noted that the applicants, a Muslim and several Muslim organisations, had not themselves been subject to any measure or decision impacting on their right and their complaints were rejected as an "*actio popularis*".[27]

4. Manifestation and practice

For an act to be considered as the manifestation of personal beliefs it must at the very least constitute an expression of a coherent view on a fundamental problem.[28] However, religion and beliefs pertaining especially to the inner sphere, the Commission emphasised that the term "practice" as employed by Art.9, para.1 does not cover each act which is motivated or influenced by a religion or belief. There is a distinction between "manifestation" and motivation. II–622

There is also the idea that the act must directly express the belief. It protects acts intimately linked to beliefs or creeds such as acts of worship and devotion which are the aspects of the practice of a religion or belief in a generally recognised form.

For example, the distribution of leaflets to soldiers may have been motivated by an applicant's pacifist ideals but was not a manifestation of her beliefs in the sense recognised by the Commission: rather it was specifically urging soldiers not to go to Northern Ireland.[29] Marriage, though considered desirable for Muslims, cannot be regarded as a form of expression, thought or religion.[30] Non-payment of taxes by Quakers to prevent contribution to arms is not covered[31] nor the wish to have one's

[23] (7805/77) (Dec.) May 5, 1979, 16 D.R. 68; (8118/77) (Dec.) March 19, 1981, 25 D.R. 105; (12587/86) (Dec.) July 14, 1987, 53 D.R. 241; *Cha'are Shalom Ve Tsedek v France*, June 27, 2000, ECHR 2000–VII, para.72, an ecclesiastical or religious body, such as a Jewish association promoting kosher rules, could exercise on behalf of its adherents the rights guaranteed by Art.9; *Metropolitan Church of Bessarabia*, para.101.

[24] See *Cha'are Shalom Ve Tsedek*, fn.23 above, para.72; *Leela Förderkreis E.V. v Germany*, (58911/00) (Dec.) November 6, 2008.

[25] (11921/86) (Dec.) October 12, 1988, 57 D.R. 81.

[26] (7865/77) (Dec.) February 27, 1979, 16 D.R. 85.

[27] *Ouardiri v Switzerland*, (65840/09) and *Ligue de Musulmans de Suisse et autres v Switzerland*, (66274/09) (Decs.) June 8, 2011.

[28] *Blumberg v Germany*, (14618/03) (Dec.) March 18, 2008, a doctor's dismissal flowing from his refusal to examine an apprentice was not covered, although he claimed it was the result of a moral dilemma; the facts showed no clear ethical basis to the refusal.

[29] (7050/75), fn.10 above; also (11567–8/85) (Dec.) July 6, 1987, 53 D.R. 150.

[30] e.g. (11579/85) (Dec.) July 7, 1986, 48 D.R. 253, where a Muslim claimed an interference with his religion as English law prevented marriage to a 14–year-old girl. Marriage is governed by Art.12, which allows European notions of marriage, as provided in national laws, to prevail.

[31] (10358/83) (Dec.) December 15, 1983, 37 D.R. 132. See the confirmation of this approach in *Bayatyan v Armenia*, fn.1 above, para.111

ashes scattered on one's own land,[32] or to have one's religion noted on an official identity card.[33] The distinction has more recently become fuzzier and watered down where a Buddhist prisoner claimed a meat-free diet. The Government had argued that it was not required by Mahayana Buddhism to be vegetarian; the Court took the view that the applicant's preference was motivated and inspired by his Buddhism and not unreasonably linked to it.[34]

Freedom to manifest one's religion has been found to include the right to try and convince one's neighbour[35]; kosher diet[36] and kosher slaughtering[37]; a vegetarian diet for a Buddhist[38]; wearing a headscarf[39]; refusal to report for military service by a Jehovah's Witness[40]; and it has been accepted that a high caste Sikh would transgress if he undertook such work as cleaning floors.[41]

Protection for organisation of religious communities may also be derived from Art.9, interpreted in light of Art.11 which safeguards associative life against unjustified State interference. Thus, in *Hasan and Chaush v Bulgaria*, the Court rejected the Government's argument that the alleged forced replacement of the leadership of the Muslim community had no bearing on the rights of the applicants to manifest their religion personally.[42] Restriction on a pastor's ability to minister to his flock or preach is an interference with a manifestation of religion, such acts falling within the ambit of that concept and the role of such a figure being of key importance in religious communities.[43]

5. Interferences with Art.9 rights

II–623 The Convention organs have consistently held that general legislation which applies on a neutral basis without any link whatsoever with an applicant's personal beliefs cannot in principle be regarded as an interference with his or her rights under Art.9 of the Convention. Thus, where applicants claimed that their official tax number

[32] (8741/79) (Dec.) March 10, 1981, 24 D.R. 137.

[33] (1988/02), (1997/02) and (1977/02) (Dec.) December 12, 2002.

[34] See, however, *Jakobski v Poland*, December 7, 2010, para.45, the Government had argued that it was not required by Mahayana Buddhism to be vegetarian; the Court took the view that the applicant's preference was motivated and inspired by his Buddhism and not unreasonably linked to it. This renders somewhat fuzzy the distinction previously drawn between manifestation and motivation as regards protected practices.

[35] *Kokkinakis*, fn.7 above, where a Jehovah's Witness had been convicted for proselytism (e.g. gaining entry to an Orthodox Christian's house to persuade her to convert) the Court acknowledged that where several religions co-existed some restrictions on this freedom might be necessary to reconcile their interests.

[36] (13669/88) (Dec.) March 7, 1990, 65 D.R. 245.

[37] *Cha'are Shalom*, fn.23 above, para.74.

[38] *Jakobski v Poland*, December 7, 2010, para.45.

[39] *Leyla Sahin v Turkey*, November 10, 2005, ECHR 2005–XI, para.78.

[40] *Bayatyan*, fn.1 above, para.112.

[41] (8231/78) (Dec.) March 6, 1982, 28 D.R. 5.

[42] *Hasan and Chaush v Bulgaria*, October 26, 2000, ECHR 2000–XI, paras 60–65, the first applicant was the Chief Mufti displaced by his State-supported rival and the second applicant a practising Muslim. See also *Canea Catholic Church v Greece*, December 16, 1997, R.J.D. 1997–VIII, a breach of Art.14 in conjunction with Art.6 due to the inability of the church to take proceedings to defend its civil rights: no separate issue arose under Art.9.

[43] *Perry v Latvia*, November 28, 2007, the Court rejected the argument that there was no interference since the pastor could, although banned from a preaching and pastoral role, participate in the community as an ordinary member.

marked them with the number of "the Beast" from Revelations, the Court considered that they were not required to make use of the number in any way and that the method of organisation of the State tax system could not be said to interfere with their freedom of religion, the clash with their beliefs being only an incidental effect of the generally applicable legislation.[44]

Measures preventing a person from manifesting his belief in a manner recognised under Art.9 or penalising him for doing so will generally constitute a limitation requiring justification under the second paragraph, as for example, criminal sanctions imposed on the use of premises as a place of worship[45] or, as in *Kokkinakis*, where the Jehovah's Witness applicant was convicted for proselytising.[46] The refusal of the State to give official recognition to a church with the consequence that its priests could not officiate or members meet to practise their religion was found to constitute an interference in *Metropolitan Church of Bessarabia v Moldova*. Severe restrictions on movement, with the consequence of curtailing the ability of enclaved Greek Cypriots in Northern Cyprus from attending places of worship outside their villages was found to infringe Art.9.[47] To the extent that it was an interference to require an applicant to give some evidence that he was a Muslim in order to enjoy the right to an exemption from work on Muslim religious holidays, this was considered justified in the context of his putting forward a claim for a privilege not commonly available to all.[48] Conviction of a Jehovah's Witness for manifesting his beliefs by refusing military service was an interference under Art.9 which failed to strike a fair balance between the individual's interests and those of society, in particular as alternative service was an available means by which an applicant with genuine objections of conscience could share the societal burden through an alternative form of service.[49]

Conversely, obligations imposed by the State which effectively require an individual to reveal his religious beliefs may be an interference. The inclusion of an indication of religion on an identity card had been found to be an unjustified interference. The possibility under domestic law of applying to correct a mistaken attribution of religion placed the individual in the position of having to provide the authorities with information about his beliefs.While even if the person could apply for the entry to be erased, the fact that the box was empty in itself would distinguish that person from others and have a specific connotation.[50] The requirement to make a public profession of belonging or not belonging to a particular religion had not been found to be justified in the context of both being sworn in as a lawyer and the form of swearing in or affirmation of a witness in

[44] *Skugar and Others v Russia*, (40010/04) (Dec.) December 3, 2009.

[45] *Manoussakis v Greece*, September 26, 1996, R.J.D. 1996–IV, No.17, 23 E.H.R.R. 387.

[46] Also *Larissis v Greece*, February 24, 1998, R.J.D. 1998–I, No.65, 27 E.H.R.R. 329, para.38; *Serif v Greece*, December 14, 1999, ECHR 1999–IX, 31 E.H.R.R. 561, where the applicant was convicted for usurping the functions of a minister of religion (where he had assumed the position of mufti on election by the mosque congregation in opposition to the State-appointed mufti).

[47] *Cyprus v Turkey*, May 10, 2001, ECHR 2001–IV, paras 244–246.

[48] *Kosteski v FYROM*, April 13, 2006. See cited cases therein concerning the justification for authorities to require strong evidence of religious affiliation for exemption from the duty of military service.

[49] *Bayatyan*, fn.1 above, paras 124–127.

[50] *Sinan Isik v Turkey*, February 2, 2010, the applicant had been recorded as a Muslim while he regarded himself as an Alevi. The Court disapproved also of the authorities taking it upon themselves to decide what categories people fell into. See in the context of discrmination, *Grzelak v Poland*, June 15, 2010, where non-Catholic children who were not provided with ethical classes were "stigmatised" by the absence of a mark for "religion/ethics" on their school report.

court.[51] However, a limited disclosure of this kind of information about a person may not be disproportionate as in a German case where an applicant's tax imposition card only revealed that he was not member of one of the six religious bodies which could levy a tax and kept on file by his employer, was never used in a public context.[52]

However, where an applicant's beliefs conflict with contractual and employment conditions, the Convention organs have adopted an approach of finding that the resulting dismissal does not necessarily interfere with the manifestation of religion. The alleged lack of protection of an applicant's beliefs, required to work on Sundays by her employer, did not disclose an interference with her beliefs since she was not dismissed for her beliefs but for failing to work certain hours.[53] In *Kalaç v Turkey*, compulsory retirement of a military judge for his fundamentalist beliefs was not an interference with his freedom of religion but a disciplinary matter, the Court noting that he had joined the army knowing of the restrictions imposed on its members. Similarly, where religious beliefs clash with professional obligations, the applicant cannot expect to give precedence to the former, as where two Catholic pharmacists were convicted for their refusal to sell contraceptives, which were legal and could only be supplied on medical prescription from a pharmacy.[54] The prohibition on a primary school teacher to wear a headscarf was a justifiable restriction, since it was a powerful external symbol that could have a proselytising effect and was not easily reconciliable with the messages of tolerance, respect, equality and non-discrimination that teachers in a democratic society should convey to pupils.[55] A distinction can be drawn between people in public positions which can reasonably require a duty of neutrality and other persons. Where members of a sect were convicted for wearing distinctive dress in public spaces, the Court distinguished their situation as individuals from those such as teachers with a public role and authority over others.[56] Further where the wearing of a religious symbol took on the nature of an ostentatious act that would constitute a source of pressure and exclusion, the State could legitimately take measures, as in the case of an 11-year-old who refused to remove her headscarf for sports activities at school.[57] This approach may still remain compatible with Art.9 where, given the principle of secular education enshrined in the particular system, a rule is enforced in schools against any non-discreet religious symbol, such as a Sikh headcovering.[58]

[51] *Alexandridis v Greece*, February 21, 2008, where the applicant was placed in the situation on being sworn in as a lawyer to state that he was not orthodox and wished to make a solemn declaration instead of swearing on the Bible; *Dimitras v Greece*, June 2, 2010, where the applicant witnesses had to reveal their beliefs to be dispensed from a religous oath.

[52] *Wasmuth v Germany*, February 17, 2011, paras 59–64.

[53] Also (29107/95) (Dec.) April 9, 1997 89–A D.R. 104, citing (24949/94) (Dec.) December 3, 1996, where the applicant (member of the Seventh Day Adventists Church which forbade work after sunset on Friday) was dismissed from the Finnish State Railways for failing to respect working hour: this was not a dismissal for his beliefs either.

[54] *Pichon and Sajous v France*, (49853/99) (Dec.) October 2, 2001, ECHR 2001–X.

[55] *Dahlab v Switzerland*, (42393/98) February 15, 2001, ECHR 2001–V. See also *Kurtulmus v Turkey*, (65500/01) January 24, 2006, ban on university lecturer wearing a headscarf.

[56] *Ahmad Arslan v Turkey*, February 23, 2010.

[57] *Dogru v France*, (27058/05) (Dec.) December 4, 2008, the ostensible reason was health and safety requirements, but respect for the principle of secularity was also taken into account; *Leyla Sahin*, fn.39 above, para.109; *Aktas v France*, (43563/08) (Dec.) June 30, 2009, where a girl wearing a veil was excluded from the school premises altogether.

[58] *Ranjit Singh v France*, (27561/08) (Dec.) June 30, 2009.

The Court will verify whether a dismissal is based on justified grounds related to job requirements or due to disapproval of the post holder's religious beliefs, examining the background circumstances. Thus, where a school swimming pool manager was dismissed after being pressured by two officials to renounce her adherence to an Evangelical Protestant group at the time of an official policy of intolerance, the Court rejected the Government assertions that the dismissal was due to job re-organisation.[59]

Where a restriction is not shown in fact to prevent a particular manifestion of belief, no interference with Art.9 rights may arise, as in *Cha'are Shalom Ve Tsedek v France* where the refusal to licence the applicant Jewish association to carry out its form of ritual slaughter had not been shown to prevent its members from obtaining "glatt" meat (i.e. from other sources).[60]

Requirements to act in a particular way will also not necessarily constitute an interference with Art.9 rights notwithstanding the person's objection to them on grounds of principle. Where it involves the obligation to make a religious declaration or to participate in religious activities, there is likely to be a problem.[61] Where the act required is one required of the community generally on public interest grounds and is of a general nature, it is more problematic for an individual to claim that this unacceptably conflicts with his or her beliefs.

In *Valsamis v Greece*, where a child Jehovah's Witness was suspended from school for failure to participate with her school in a procession on a Greek national day, the Court noted that she had been exempted from religious education and the Orthodox mass, and considered that the obligation to take part in the school parade was not such as to either offend her parents' religious convictions under Art.2 of Protocol No.1 or amount to an interference with her right to freedom of religion. Although the applicants objected to participation on the grounds of their pacifist beliefs, the Court considered that there was nothing in the purpose or arrangements of the parade to offend them to an extent forbidden by the Convention provisions. Its own view was that the national day, which the Government stated commemorated Greece's attachment to democracy, liberty and human rights, served both pacifist objectives and the public interest and a military presence at some of the parades did not alter their nature.[62] This case seems to show that the offensiveness of particular measures to religious beliefs must meet a certain threshold of seriousness.

Whether the requirement imposed on a non-church adherent to pay a church tax constitutes an interference with rights under Art.9 will depend on the circumstances. It was compatible with freedom of religion if a person could avoid the tax by leaving the church.[63] In *Darby v Sweden*, where the applicant, a non-resident who worked in Sweden, had no possibility of exemption, the Commission considered that though the existence of a State Church system could not in itself be considered to breach Art.9, there had to be safeguards to prevent anyone being forced to enter or

[59] *Ivanova v Bulgaria*, April 12, 2007.

[60] See, however, the strong dissenting minority who saw no reasonable or objective justification for treating the applicant association differently from the mainstream Jewish body, which had been given by the State exclusive slaughtering rights, contrary to the notion of pluralism.

[61] e.g. *Buscarini*, fn.8 above, where elected representatives were required to swear allegiance to the Gospels in order to take up their seats.

[62] Dissenters in the Commission and Court considered that the applicants' perception of the significance of the parade to their own beliefs should be accepted unless obviously ill-founded or unreasonable, finding no need for the child's participation in a public event of this kind.

[63] (10358/83) (Dec.) December 15, 1983, 37 D.R. 142.

prohibited from leaving. The Court commented that Art.9 protected everyone from being compelled to be involved in religious activities without being a member of the religious community concerned and thus the payment of a tax to a church for its religious activities could in certain circumstances be seen as such involvement. It considered however that the particular case disclosed primarily a discrimination problem in payment of taxes between residents and non-residents which was not founded on objective or reasonable justification. In a later case, the requirement of a non-church member to pay a portion of the tax to the Church of Sweden did not interfere with his freedom of religion since it was a contribution to the non-religious activities of the Church and its fulfilment of its civil responsibilities, such as burials.[64]

As concerns the requirement to take oaths, the obligation for elected representatives to swear on the Gospels was not regarded as necessary in *Buscarini v San Marino*; making the exercise of a mandate intended to represent different views of society within Parliament subject to a prior declaration of commitment to a particular set of beliefs was essentially incompatible with the democratic and pluralistic ethos of Art.9 and the Convention as a whole. On the other hand, in *McGuinness v UK*, where the applicant, an elected MP, was unable to use parliamentary facilities due to his refusal to take the oath of allegiance to the Queen, the Court considered that he was not thereby required to affirm allegiance to any religion on pain of taking up his seat or obliged to abandon his republican convictions.[65]

It has been left open whether the State, by describing a particular group as a sect or cult, thereby interferes with their Art.9 rights. However, the Court considered that it was a legitimate use of protective power by the State to contribute to a public debate on religious phenomena and to warn against aspects which it considered dangerous to the public; the use of the terms concerned did not step over the bounds of its role.[66]

Prisons must seemingly take into account the reasonable dietary requirements of religious inspiraction, striking a balance between any cost or administrative burden and the individual's interest. Thus, where a Buddhist prisoner wanted a meat-free diet, the Court considered that this imposed no disruption on meal preparations and did not require any special products or preparation; failure to provide such therefore breached Art.9.[67] Refusing to give fiscal status to a religious body which would exempt donations from tax was regarded as interfering with its freedom to excercise its Art.9 rights due to the impact this had on its primary source of income and thus its ability to function. As the refusal was essentially arbitrary, there was a violation in this regard.[68] This case seems strangely to bring claims for tax exemption within the scope of the freedom of religion. There was no interference by the State in any respect with the organisation's religious practices; importing a guarantee of financial protection for continuing such practices would seem to be extending Art.9 in a new direction.

[64] *Bruno v Sweden*, (32196/96) (Dec.) August 28, 2001.

[65] (39511/98) (Dec.) June 8, 1999, ECHR 1999–V.

[66] *Leela Förderkreis*, fn.24 above, it may be noted that the domestic courts had already struck down the use of stronger terms such as "destructive" and "pseudo-religious".

[67] *Jakobski*, fn.38 above, paras 48–55, this approach overlooks the fact that a proper vegetarian diet requires special care to ensure that the absence of meat is made up for, inter alia, by other sources of protein and iron. It is not a question of merely removing the bits of meat. The effort required of the prison authorities nonetheless might be regarded as not too burdensome.

[68] *Association des Temoins de Jehovah v France*, June 30, 2011, paras 52–72.

6. Justified limitations

Restrictions on manifestations of belief or practice, where in conformity with the requirements of lawfulness,[69] may be justified inter alia on grounds of health and public safety (e.g. motorcyle helmets), security (access to certain publications where the applicant is in prison) or where there is a clearly perceived harm or threat to others.[70] However, the Court will carefully scrutinise decisions by courts dissolving religious groups on grounds of public harm, not accepting the mere rehearsal of popular prejudice. Thus, in banning the Jehovah's Witnesses the domestic courts should have adduced "relevant and sufficient" reasons, substantiated by specific evidence, to show, as claimed, that the applicant community had forced families to break up, coerced them in their professional and private lives, incited its followers to commit suicide or refuse medical care, impinged on the rights of non-Witness parents or their children, or encouraged members to refuse to fulfil any duties established by law.[71] The Court noted inter alia that no details were given of persons whose rights had allegedly been infringed or who had refused legal duties, that it was a right to refuse medical treatment and that no coercion had been shown in any particular case. It commented that it was in any event a feature of many mainstream religions to lay down detailed, even demanding, rules as to appropriate conduct. II–624

Religious practices which conflict with justifiable regulatory restrictions pursuing a public interest are not exempted due to Art.9.[72]

The aim of protecting public safety was found to justify requiring a Sikh to remove his turban at an airport, the Court commenting, in response to the argument that the applicant could have been checked by other means, that the means lay within the State's margin of appreciation.[73] However, convictions of applicants for wearing tunics and turbans of a particular sect in a public place were not justified, since there was no evidence that this placed public order at risk or that they were seeking to put undue pressure on others.[74]

Where an applicant Krishna society was subject to enforcement notices relating to the increased influx of pilgrims to the manor used as a religious centre, the Commission found the factor of their religious freedom was sufficiently taken into account by the planning authorities despite an unfortunate letter from the planning authorities referring to the religious factor not being "relevant" to the decision. However the Commission interpreted this in the positive sense that the decision was

[69] "Prescribed by law": e.g. *Hasan and Chaush*, fn.42 above, paras 85–89, where the chief mufti was removed, the law was insufficiently defined as to the circumstances in which disputed leadership could be resolved and without any procedural safeguards before an independent body concerning the exercise of the executive discretion in that regard. See Pt I, s.C: Convention Principles and Approach, sub-s.8: Rule of Law.

[70] *Manoussakis*, fn.45 above, para.40, States are entitled to take steps to verify whether a movement, ostensibly for religious aims, carries on activities which are harmful to the population. This did not apply to Jehovah's Witnesses, a "known religion".

[71] *Jehovah's Witnesses of Moscow v Russia*, June 10, 2010.

[72] e.g. *Mann Singh v France*, (24479/07) (Dec.) January 13, 2008, concerning a requirement for a Sikh to present a photograph for a driving licence with his head bare; justified by considerations of road safety and public order.

[73] *Phull v France*, (35753/03) (Dec.) January 11, 2005, ECHR 2005–2005–I. See *also El Morsli v France*, (155885/06) (Dec.) March 4, 2008, requirement for a Muslim woman to remove briefly her veil for identification purposes when applying for a visa at a consulate was also justified.

[74] *Ahmet Arslan v Turkey*, February 23, 2010, the Government had argued the ban on such religious attire was necessary to protect laicity and prevent propaganda and proselytising.

taken on proper planning grounds and not on the basis of objection to the religious activities.[75] Druids who are barred access to sites in or around Stonehenge have also found their complaints have been rejected as justified in the interests of protection of a historical site as well for public safety and the prevention of crime and disorder.[76] The refusal to dispense a child of Seventh Day Adventists from attending school on Saturday mornings was found to be justified in order to safeguard the coherence of the teaching programme as a whole and to ensure the education of the child concerned.[77]

Where a Jehovah's Witness was convicted for proselytism, the Court considered that a distinction had to be drawn between bearing witness and proselytism by improper means (force, offering of material or social advantages by inducement, improper pressure on persons in distress or need). Indeed, seeking to persuade one's neighbour was not per se objectionable, otherwise there would be effectively little freedom to change one's religion. Since the liability of the applicant was established without any reference to whether he used improper means, but on the basis of a general prohibition and there was no indication of improper means on the facts,[78] the conviction was not justified by a pressing social need. In *Larissis v Greece* the Court found that the convictions of air force officers, members of the Pentecostal Church, for proselytising three airmen were justified to protect the latter from the risk of undue pressure, but not justified as regarded their proselytisation of civilians outside the hierarchical military structure. The imposition of criminal sanctions on Jehovah's Witnesses for using premises as a place of worship without authorisation was disproportionate where the framework of law and practice placed prohibitive conditions on the practice of religious non-orthodox movements; the relative leniency of the penalty was immaterial.[79]

Some administrative formalities for the use of premises for religious purposes may be acceptable where, for example, they protect the rights of others in a proportionate manner.[80] However, even if it may be compatible with the Convention to require religious groups to conform with certain formalities, convicting an individual for performing Muslim rituals on private premises on the ground that domestic law required all manifestations of unrecognised religions to be registered with the State was, in the Court's view, going too far and tantamount to excluding minority beliefs and dictating to people what they should believe.[81] Imposing too rigid restrictions on the registration of religious groups may also offend, as where only groups that

[75] (20490/92), fn.9 above.

[76] Also *Johannische Kirche and Peters v Germany*, (41754/98) (Dec.) July 10, 2001, ECHR 2001–VIII, where the refusal of permission to the church to use its land for a cemetery on planning grounds was justified under Art.9, para.2.

[77] *Casimiro and Ferreira v Luxembourg*, (44888/98) (Dec.) April 27, 1999, where the Court noted that special dispensation for particular religious events was permitted and found the right to education had to prevail in the circumstances against religious preferences.

[78] *Kokkinakis*, fn.7 above, the Court appears to have accepted the applicant's arguments that the woman concerned was an experienced adult with intellectual abilities who was not unduly infuenced by the applicant's actions in calling at her door.

[79] e.g. the Minister was not subject to any requirement to give a decision in a particular time (the applicants' request was still pending without any explanation) and had wide discretion; the Orthodox church also played a role in consenting to authorisation being given.

[80] *Tanyar v Turkey*, (74242/01) (Dec.) June 7, 2005.

[81] *Masaev v Moldova*, May 12, 2009.

had already been in existence for 15 years could register[82] or where proceedings for such registration took an excessive period.[83]

Exclusion of a Jehovah's Witness from appointment as a chartered accountant due to his conviction for refusal to wear a military uniform was found in *Thlimmenos v Greece* to be a disproportionate punishment.[84]

While States have a legitimate interest in preventing tension in religious communities and in taking measures to protect those whose legal relationships can be affected by the acts of religious ministers (where such have legal and administrative powers to conduct marriages for example), the Court emphasised that their interventions should be guided by the principle of pluralism and aimed to ensure competing groups tolerated each other rather than to seek to eliminate one or the other. In its relations with diverse religions and faiths, the State should remain neutral and impartial.[85] Nor does the State have to take measures to ensure that religious communities are brought under unified leadership[86] or to impose rules on admission or exclusion of membership.[87] The State should not enter into assessments of the legitimacy of a congregation's beliefs, nor rely on that assessment to seek to disband or replace one group in favour of another.[88] It may be noted that where schisms and doctrinal differences arise, there is no protected right to dissent within a religious community as such, only a right to leave to manifest that dissent in a new formation; it is not for the authorities to weigh in on one side or another.[89] But in all circumstances, the State should maintain its neutrality and any intervention must be convincingly justified and exercised with sensitivity and restraint.[90] Thus, where the authorities limited themselves to the civil law repercussions of congregational changes, there was no breach of neutrality.[91]

[82] *Kimyla v Russia*, fn.15 above.

[83] *Religionsgemeinschaft der Zeugen Jehovas and Others v Austria*, July 31, 2008, the proceedings took 20 years; there was also a breach of Art.9 in conjunction with Art.14 in that a requirement of waiting a further ten-year period for obtaining a higher protected status as a religious society as opposed to religious community had been somewhat arbitrarily imposed on the applicant but not other religious groups.

[84] The Court found a breach of Art.14 in conjunction with Art.9.

[85] *Serif*, fn.46 above, the Court found that the conviction of the rival mufti was not justified since there had been no proof that the existence of two religious leaders was causing disturbances or that the non-officially appointed one had tried to exercise legal or administrative functions; *Metropolitan Church of Bessarabia v Moldova*, December 13, 2001, ECHR 2001–XII, paras 116 and 123, where the Government lacked neutrality and impartiality in refusing to give recognition to the applicant church without approval from the Moldovan Church which regarded it as schismatic; *Supreme Holy Council of the Muslim Community v Bulgaria*, December 16, 2004, the Government went beyond neutral mediation in seeking to impose a single leadership.

[86] *Hasan and Chaush*, fn.42 above, para.78, where the State intervened to appoint one of two rivals in the muslim religious community. The Court did not however rule on necessity or proportionality as the measure was not "prescibed by law"; *Holy Synod of the Bulgarian Orthodox Church*, fn.19 above, violation where the State intervened in a situation of deep and genuine division in the Church by forcing the community under one of the rival leaderships and forcibly suppressing the other: this was in breach of neutrality, disproportionate.

[87] *Svyato-Mykhaylivska Parafiya v Ukraine*, June 14, 2007, para.150.

[88] *Mirobulovs v Latvia*, September 15, 2009, para.80(f), except in very exceptional (but undefined) circumstances.

[89] *Holy Synod of the Orthodox Bulgarian Church*, fn.21, para.141; *Mirolubovs*, fn.88, para.80(d).

[90] *Svyato-Mykhaylivska Parfiya*, fn.87 above, para.123; *Mirolubovs*, fn.88, para.87.

[91] *Griechische Kirchengemeinde München und Bayern E.V. v Germany*, (52336/99) (Dec.) September 18, 2007, the authorities had revoked permission to use a church which was State property to re-allocate it to conform with original intentions, the lawfulness of which was thoroughly reviewed by domestic courts.

Nonetheless, States may take measures against extremist political movements, that seek to impose on society as a whole their religious symbols or precepts, in particular where this is necessary to protect the rights and freedoms of others. Thus, it was justified, in light of the aims of secularism and to protect individuals from external pressure from extremist movements, to ban the wearing of headscarves in universities in Turkey.[92]

There is no right derivable from Art.9 to obtain entry or residence within a country; however immigration controls must be applied in conformity with the provisions of the Convention. Thus, where a foreign evangelical pastor's residence permit was renewed with a condition that he could not preach or minister, the Court found that this was an interference that had to be compatible with the second paragraph.[93] In *Nolan and K v Russia*, revoking residence status of a leading member of the Unification Church on the basis of his religious activities disclosed a breach, since the Government had not put forward a plausible legal or factual justification as to the necessity for the measure. While they had invoked national security this was not an allowed exception under the second paragraph; nor had they shown that he had been involved in any activity impinging on public order or the rights of others.[94]

7. State obligation to protect religion from others

II–625 Positive obligations may arise requiring the State to take steps to protect the exercise of religious freedom from others. A violation of Art.9 arose where the authorities failed to take any steps against a fanatical group that had attacked a congregation of Jehovah's Witnesses, assaulting them and burning books. The Court stated that the State was under an obligation to ensure that the group of orthodox extremists tolerated the applicants and allowed them freely to manifest their religion.[95]

As regards differing levels of protection inbuilt into domestic law, the Commission found the law of blasphemy an acceptable means of protecting the religious feelings of offended Christians.[96] However it rejected complaints of a Muslim applicant that the inability to prosecute blasphemous attacks on the Islamic faith was contrary to Art.9 and disclosed discrimination contrary to Art.14 as such protection was only available to Christians.[97] The Commission considered that the Government could not be said to have interfered in the applicant's right to manifest his beliefs and that Art.9 did not guarantee a right to bring proceedings against publishers of works that offended the sensitivities of any individual or group. Thus the discrimination complaint was rejected as incompatible *ratione materiae*, avoiding the necessity for finding any objective and reasonable justification in favouring the religious feelings of one group, albeit the historically dominant one.

[92] *Leyla Sahin*, fn.39 above, paras 112–123. See also similar ban justified in a religious high school: *Köse and 93 others v Turkey*, (26625/02) January 24, 2006.

[93] *Perry v Latvia*, fn.43.

[94] *Nolan and K v Russia*, fn.3 above.

[95] *97 members of the Gldani Congregation of Jehovah's Witnesses and 4 others v Georgia*, May 3, 2007, paras 129–135.

[96] (8710/79) May 7, 1982, 28 D.R. 77, where the applicants were convicted in a private prosecution of the criminal blasphemy for publication of a poem ascribing to Christ promiscuous homosexual practices, the conviction was found to pursue the legitimate aim of protecting the rights of others, namely the private prosecutor, not to be offended in religious feeling.

[97] (17439/90) (Dec.) March 5, 1991, concerning Salman Rushdie's *Satanic Verses*.

Cross-reference

Part IIB, s.3: Armed forces.
Part IIB, s.12: Discrimination.
PartIIB, s.13: Education, sub-s.4: Education in accordance with philosophical convictions.
Part IIB, s.31: Marriage and founding a family.
Part IIB, s.36: Prisoner's rights.

41. Remedies

Key provision:

II–626 Article 13 (effective remedy before a national authority).

Key case-law:

Delcourt v Belgium, January 17, 1970, Series A, No.11, 1 E.H.R.R. 355; *Klass v Germany*, September 6, 1978, Series A, No.28, 2 E.H.R.R. 214; *Silver v UK*, March 25, 1983, Series A, No.61, 5 E.H.R.R 347; *Abdulaziz v UK*, May 28, 1985, Series A, No.94, 7 E.H.R.R. 471; *James v UK*, May 11, 1984, Series A, No.98, 8 E.H.R.R. 123; *Lithgow v UK*, July 8, 1986, Series A, No.102, 8 E.H.R.R 329; *Leander v Sweden*, March 26, 1987, Series A, No.116; 9 E.H.R.R. 433; *Boyle and Rice v UK*, March 27, 1988, Series A, No.131, 10 E.H.R.R 425; *Kamasinski v Austria*, December 19, 1989, Series A, No.168, 13 E.H.R.R. 36; *Powell and Rayner v UK*, February 21, 1990, Series A, No.172, 12 E.H.R.R. 355; *Vereinigung Demokratischer Soldaten Österreichs v Austria*, December 19, 1994, Series A, No.302, 20 E.H.R.R. 56; *Chahal v UK*, November 15, 1996, R.J.D. 1996–V, 23 E.H.R.R. 413; *Aksoy v Turkey*, December 18, 1996, R.J.D. 1996–VI, No.26, 23 E.H.R.R. 553; *Valsamis v Greece*, December 18, 1996, R.J.D. 1996–VI, No.26, 24 E.H.R.R. 294; *D v UK*, May 2, 1997, R.J.D. 1997–III, No.37; 24 E.H.R.R. 423; *Halford v UK*, June 25, 1997, R.J.D. 1997–III, No.39, 24 E.H.R.R. 523; *Aydin v Turkey*, September 25, 1997, R.J.D. 1997–VI, No.50, 25 E.H.R.R. 251; *Kaya v Turkey*, February 19, 1998, R.J.D. 1998–I, No.65, 28 E.H.R.R. 1; *Smith and Grady v UK*, September 27, 1999, ECHR 1999–V, 29 E.H.R.R. 493; *Z v UK*, May 10, 2001, ECHR 2000–V; *Kudla v Poland*, October 26, 2000, ECHR 2000–XI; *Hatton v UK*, July 8, 2003, ECHR 2003–VIII; *McFarlane v Ireland*, September 10, 2010, ECHR 2010–. . . ; *M.S.S. v Belgium and Greece*, January 21, 2011, ECHR 2011–. . .

1. General considerations

II–627 Taking the principal consideration that it is the obligation first and foremost of Contracting States to secure to every individual their rights and freedoms,[1] Art.13 is the countervailing requirement that an individual has the opportunity to obtain redress for violations in the domestic system.[2] If a Contracting State fulfills this requirement, the Court's role will diminish. It may be said that observance of this provision is the most crucial to the effective protection of rights in Contracting States. It is however a technical and procedural provision and its role has been whittled away by interpretations and arguably not given its proper prominence.[3] Applicants are also sometimes reticent in raising Art.13 complaints, perhaps preferring to concentrate on what they see as the core substantives issues.[4]

[1] Art.1.

[2] See, e.g. *Boyle and Rice*, (Rep.), para.73, citing *Handyside v UK*, December 7, 1976, Series A, No.24, 1 E.H.R.R. 737, para.48.

[3] There is perhaps a suspicion that the Convention organs were, and are, seduced by the more interesting questions arising under the substantive provisions (possibly trespassing on the role of the domestic authorities when involving themselves in rather detailed factual assessments) whereas they should have been encouraging domestic bodies to carry out this function.

[4] e.g. in *McCann v UK*, September 27, 1995, Series A, No.324, where there was an Art.2 violation but no complaint raised under Arts 6 or 13 by the relatives of the dead terrorists, who had been unable to pursue civil proceedings due to the nature of the case.

Article 13 is not a general compensation provision. As seen below, it is limited to where there have been arguable claims of violations, and Art.13 cannot be relied upon to correct gaps in general compensatory frameworks, however desirable that may be.[5]

2. Limitation to "arguable claims" of violations

Article 13 requires a remedy for everyone whose rights under the Convention have been violated. Thus the provision is linked to breaches of substantive rights. No breach of Art.13 is possible in isolation. **II–628**

The words of the provision appear to require that a person must establish an actual breach of a substantive provision. The Court thought that this was unduly restrictive. Until a court or other body has investigated a claim, it will not necessarily be apparent whether there has been an unjustifiable interference with a right. Accordingly, it held that a remedy must be guaranteed to anyone who "claims" that his rights have been violated.[6] This was translated by the Court in *Silver* into the notion that a person with an "arguable claim" of being a victim of a violation of the rights in the Convention should be able to seek a remedy.[7]

The Commission, which was setting a high standard for the manifestly ill-founded inadmissibility criterion, applied the approach that Art.13 could be breached even if the substantive complaint was inadmissible, as there could still in the appropriate circumstances be an arguable claim.[8] The Court in *Boyle and Rice v UK* noted the Commission delegate's explanation that to be arguable a claim "only needs raise a Convention issue that merits further examination" and that a conclusion that a claim was manifestly ill-founded could be reached after considerable oral and written argument. It preferred its own view in *Airey v Ireland* that a finding of manifestly ill-founded meant that there was not even a prima facie case against the respondent State.[9] It held, bluntly, that on the ordinary meaning of the words it was difficult to conceive that a claim that was manifestly ill-founded could nevertheless be arguable. It declined to give an abstract definition of arguability, each case to be determined in the light of the particular facts and issues. It later commented, in face of Commission intransigence in *Powell and Rayner v UK*, that different standards between the manifestly ill-founded inadmissibility criterion (now Art.35, para.1) and Art.13 would undermine the coherence of the system of enforcement since a State could not be required to make available a remedy at national level for a grievance which was so weak as not to warrant examination on its merits on the international. This approach had the practical effect of lowering of the threshold of admissibility on the manifestly ill-founded ground and of increasing the number of admissible cases.

Since then, it is also rare to find a violation of Art.13 without the presence of a violation of a substantive provision.[10] On the basis of the case-law above, there

[5] e.g. *Zavaloka v Latvia*, July 7, 2009, where non-pecuniary damages were not claimable in fatal accidents caused by private individuals.

[6] *Klass v Germany*, September 6, 1978, Series A, No.28, 2 E.H.R.R. 214, para.64.

[7] *Silver v UK*, March 25, 1983, Series A, No.61, 5 E.H.R.R 347, para.113.

[8] e.g. *Boyle and Rice v UK*, (Rep.) March 27, 1988, Series A, No.131, 10 E.H.R.R 425, where the Commission had rejected as manifestly ill-founded Art.8 complaints but declared admissible the complaints about the lack of effective remedies for these complaints.

[9] *Airey v Ireland*, October 9, 1979, Series A, No.32, para.18.

[10] e.g. *Hatton v UK v UK*, July 8, 2003, ECHR 2003–VIII, no violation on Art.8, but a lack of effective remedy for an arguable claim under Art.13.

should at least be an admissible complaint.[11] Conversely, the fact that a complaint was declared admissible by the Convention organs did not require a finding of an arguable claim for Art.13. This still occurs where a number of complaints under different provisions are declared admissible together, the Court's practice being not to split issues based on the same facts, even if some complaints are clearly more substantial than others.[12]

3. Remedies for non-conformity of statute or law

II–629 The Commission took the view that Art.13 could not be interpreted as requiring a means by which the conformity of statute with the Convention can be examined at domestic law.[13] The Court endorsed this approach in *James v UK*.[14] To hold otherwise would be tantamount to requiring incorporation of the Convention in domestic law and this could not, in the Court's view, be imposed de facto by the Convention organs. In any event, it considered that if the substantive laws were found, as in *James*, to conform with Art.1 of Protocol No.1, it would be sufficient for the purposes of Art.13 that the aggrieved property owner could go to the courts to secure compliance with the relevant laws.[15] The new Court continues to apply this approach, where the applicant's complaints are directed against statutory provisions[16] or the state of domestic law.[17]

In relation to secondary legislation, the Commission found that the immigration rules in issue in *Abdulaziz v UK* did not attract the immunity of legislation to scrutiny under Art.13; and in *Boyle and Rice* held that the immunity did not apply to the prison rules, standing orders and administrative circulars, basing itself on the application of Art.13 in the *Silver* case to prison norms.[18] The Court agreed in

[11] See, however, the anomalous example, *Soysal v Turkey*, February 15, 2007, where the Art.11 complaint was unsubstantiated, manifestly ill-founded, there was nonetheless an arguable claim, and a violation, under Art.13.

[12] e.g. *Valsamis v Greece*, December 18, 1996, R.J.D. 1996–VI, No.26, 24 E.H.R.R. 294, where a girl Jehovah's Witness was suspended from school, the application was principally concerned complaints under Arts 9 and 2 of Protocol No.1 but the Art.3 complaint was also declared admissible: on the merits, arguable claims arose under the first two provisions but none under Art.3; *Halford v UK*, June 25, 1997, R.J.D. 1997–III, No.39, 24 E.H.R.R. 523, where complaints under Art.8 were admissible for claims of tapping of office and home phone, arguable claims under Art.13 arose in respect of the former alone.

[13] See *Young, James and Webster v UK*, (Rep.) December 14, 1979, interpreting the wording of Art.13 "notwithstanding that the violation has been committed by persons acting in an official capacity" as indicating that it was not meant to cover legislation.

[14] Referring to a dictum in *Swedish Engine Drivers' Union case*, February 6, 1976, Series A, No.20, para.50 and *Ireland v UK*, January 18, 1978, Series A, No.25; also *Lithgow v UK*, July 8, 1986, Series A, No.102, 8 E.H.R.R 329, para.206; *Observer and Guardian v UK*, November 26, 1991, Series A, No.216, para.76.

[15] See also concurring opinions in *James v UK*, May 11, 1984, Series A, No.98, 8 E.H.R.R. 123, which added that this restrictive interpretation was supported by the existing legislation of Contracting States since it was improbable that the drafters intended to cover statute as few states had provision for constitutional challenge by individuals of legislation, and the dissenters, who saw see no reason to exempt acts of the legislature from Art.13 and considered that the approach of the Court in *Silver*, fn.7 above, and *Abdulaziz v UK*, May 28, 1985, Series A, No.94, 7 E.H.R.R. 471, should be maintained.

[16] *A v UK*, December 17, 2002, ECHR 2002–X, para.112; *Maurice v France*, October 6, 2005, ECHR 2005–. . . , para.107.

[17] *Christine Goodwin v UK*, July 11, 2002, ECHR 2002–VI, para.113; *Hatton*, fn.10 above, para.138, with a reference also to Art.13 not allowing a challenge to a general policy as such—the Court nonetheless found a violation of Art.13 due to the limited scope of judicial review proceedings concerning lawfulness of the scheme applicable to night flying at Heathrow. Sir Brian Kerr, dissenting as ad hoc judge, considered that no violation arose as the applicants' complaints concerned the state of domestic law.

[18] *Boyle and Rice*, (Rep.), fn.8 above, para.78; *Silver*, fn.7 above, paras 124–127.

Abdulaziz, finding that the applicants were victims of norms that were incompatible with the Convention and that there was no effective remedy as required by Art.13.

The approach was extended by the Commission in *Johnston v Ireland* where it held that Art.13 does not guarantee an effective remedy in respect of a constitutional provision.[19]

4. Relationship with procedural guarantees under Art.6 (fair trial) and Art.5 (liberty)

Where an alleged violation is alleged in respect of a court's decision, Art.13 does not require appeal to a higher court, having regard to the approach that Art.6 does not require courts of appeal to be set up.[20] Where the highest national court is alleged to have breached the Convention, the application of Art.13 is subject to a similar implied limitation.[21] Presumably, where the court proceedings are themselves in compliance with the requirements of Art.6, this is sufficient for the purposes of the Convention. **II–630**

Where the specific guarantees of Art.6 apply, Art.13 as the more general provision does not apply, its requirements being less strict and accordingly absorbed by Art.6 which is the *lex specialis*.[22] Thus where proceedings falling within the scope of Art.6 are involved, there is, in general, no possibility of issues arising under Art.13, whether or not there is a violation of Art.6.[23] The exceptions to this so far concern, principally, complaints about length of proceedings. In *Kudla v Poland*, the Court rejected the Government's argument that Art.13 was never applicable where the alleged violation had taken place in judicial proceedings. It considered that the application of Art.13 to complaints of excessive delay in court proceedings would fulfil the purpose of ensuring that individuals could obtain relief at a national level and therefore reinforce the safeguards of Art.6, para.1, rather than being absorbed by it. As the remedy was only required in respect of delay, this would not impose a right of appeal on the merits of the decision. It also rejected the argument that imposing the obligation to provide a remedy would add to the already existing delays since experience showed that it was not impossible to create such remedies and operate them effectively.[24] As regarded the type of remedy, there is the

[19] *Johnston v Ireland*, (Rep.), Series A, No.112, para.151, the complaint was dropped by the applicants before the Court.

[20] *Delcourt v Belgium*, January 17, 1970, Series A, No.11, 1 E.H.R.R. 355, para.25; also (13135/87) (Dec.) July 4, 1988, 56 D.R. 268, where applicants could not require appeal to a higher court from the Land Tribunal's allegedly derisory compensation assessment.

[21] e.g. *Leander v Sweden*, (Rep.), May 17, 1985, Art.13 not normally grant a further remedy against the decisions by the highest national court; (14739/89) (Dec.) May 9, 1989, 60 D.R. 296, no right to review by a higher court in criminal matters; *Pizzetti v Italy*, Series A, No.257–C, (Rep.) December 10, 1991, para.41, the Convention did not guarantee the right to a second level of jurisdiction and provisions of the Convention could not be held to oblige States to set up bodies to exercise supervision over judicial bodies.

[22] e.g. in *Kamasinki v Austria*, December 19, 1989, Series A, No.168, 13 E.H.R.R. 36, para.110; *W v UK*, July 8, 1987, Series A, No.121, para.86.

[23] e.g. only where there is a criminal charge or civil right is Art.13 superceded by Art.6 which is more stringent: (8588/79) etc. (Dec.) December 12, 1983, 38 D.R. 18.

[24] e.g. *Gonzalez Marin v Spain*, (39521/98) (Dec.) October 5, 1999, ECHR 1999–VII, which rejected a length complaint for non-exhaustion where the applicant had not sought statutory compensation for delay; *Tome Mota v Portugal*, (32082/96) (Dec.) December 2, 1999, where the New Code of Criminal Procedure had provided a legal remedy to end or expedite criminal proceedings; *Mifsud v France*, (61166/00) (Dec.) September 11, 2000, ECHR 2000–VIII, Art.L 781–I (Code of Judicial Organisation) provided compensation for delays; *Charzynski v Poland*, (15212/03) (Dec.) March 1, 2005, non-exhaustion of remedy capable of accelerating court proceedings and resulting in a compensation award.

alternative of preventing the alleged violation or its continuation by providing for expedition or of providing adequate redress for past delays, such as compensation.[25] Where the courts, in line with the Court's case-law, acknowledge the unreasonable delay and pay sufficient non-pecuniary damage, the remedy was regarded as effective.[26] The possibility of seeking disciplinary proceedings against tardy judges impacts only on the personal situation of the judge, without providing effective redress for the excessive duration of proceedings.[27]

It also appears that as regards non-enforcement of court judgments contrary to Art.6, the Court may examine whether the legal system affords an effective remedy to applicants, enabling them to put forward their arguable complaint of non-enforcement of a final judgment, and to obtain redress, finding a breach where they could not.[28]

Article 5, para.4 (review of the lawfulness of detention) is also *lex specialis* in the area covered by it.[29]

5. No separate issue: procedural rights contained in substantive provisions

II–631 Not infrequently, where the violation under a substantive provision involves findings of lack of procedural safeguards, the Convention organs have found that no separate issues arise under Art.13. For example, in *Hokkanen v Finland*,[30] no separate issue was found under Art.13 since the complaints amounted in substance to those already dealt with under Arts 6 and 8 in regard to length of custody and child access proceedings and the non-enforcement of custody rights. However, in *Kaya v Turkey*, the Court held that its findings under Art.2 as regarded the procedural deficiencies of the forensic examination and investigation into a death did not exclude a further finding of a breach of Art.13, the requirements of which were broader, including the availability of compensation where appropriate. In *Ergi v Turkey*, where the Commission had found a violation of the Art.2 procedural obligation to carry out an effective investigation and no separate issue left under Art.13, the Court found a violation of both, considering that a failure to carry out an effective investigation undermined the exercise of any remedies available under Turkish law.[31] Although there have been some indications that it may be more appropriate to consider this matter under Art.13 alone, where Art.3 is concerned[32] the recent approach of the Court shows a preference to rely on the procedural

[25] *Kudla v Poland*, October 26, 2000, ECHR 2000–XI, para.158. Remedies ineffective in, e.g. *Hartmann v Czech Republic*, July 10, 2003; *Doran v Ireland*, July 31, 2003, where the constitutional remedy had not been shown to be sufficiently swift and no precedents of compensation existed; *Konti-Arvanti v Greece*, April 10, 2003, the possibility of suing in tort a tardy expert did not offer redress for a length problem; *Kangasluoma v Finland*, January 20, 2004, where mere delay was not a ground for compensation.

[26] e.g. *Cataldo v Italy*, (45656/99) (Dec.) June 3, 2004, ECHR 2004–VI.

[27] e.g. *Abramiuc v Romania*, February 24, 2009, para.134.

[28] *Zazanis v Greece*, November 18, 2004, paras 45–49.

[29] e.g. *Chahal v UK*, November 15, 1996, R.J.D. 1996–V, 23 E.H.R.R. 413.

[30] *Hokkanen v Finland*, September 23, 1994, Series A, No.299–A.

[31] *Ergi v Turkey*, July 28, 1998, R.J.D. 1998–IV, No.81, para.98. See also *Labita v Italy*, April 6, 2000, ECHR 2000–IV, paras 130–136, procedural breach of Art.3; *Assenov v Bulgaria*, October 28, 1998, R.J.D. 1998–VIII, No.96, procedural breach of Arts 3 and 13 on same basis.

[32] *Ilhan v Turkey* (GC), June 27, 2000, ECHR 2000–VII, paras 89–93; dissenting opinion of Sir Nicolas Bratza in *Kuznetsov v Ukraine*, April 29, 2003. See Pt IIB, s.46: Torture, inhuman and degrading treatment, sub-s.6(a): The obligation to investigate.

obligation of both Arts 2 and 3 and only to find an additional breach of Art.13 where there is a systemic failing or general undermining of available remedies.[33]

6. Effectiveness

Where an individual has an arguable claim that he is the victim of a violation of the rights set forth in the Convention he should have a remedy before a national authority which has the power both to decide his claim and if appropriate to give redress.[34] An absence of any possibility to seek relief at national level will disclose a violation.[35] II–632

A remedy must also be effective in practice as well as in law.[36] However, the fact that an application to a court fails is not sufficient to indicate that the remedy was ineffective.[37] Nonetheless, the lack of any prospect of success will raise an issue of effectiveness, as in where all other previous applications have been refused.[38]

Where settled case-law indicates that a person has no standing to lodge a complaint, the possibility to seek a review by the courts will not constitute an effective remedy.[39] In some circumstances, where systemic functioning is in issue, an overwhelming pattern of refusal, with stereotypical, unreasoned decisions may disclose a lack of effectiveness of a remedy.[40]

Generally, an aggrieved person must have direct access to the remedy, without reliance on an intermediary with standing.[41] Remedies should be practically accessible: where appeals are rejected due to failure to appear in circumstances where the hearing date was listed without giving sufficient notice to the applicant's lawyer to appear, the remedy was flawed.[42]

An inability by a court to address the core elements of the alleged violation may also render the procedure ineffective, as in *Smith and Grady v UK*, where the courts' examination on judicial review of the Ministry of Defence policy on homosexuals in the army could only consider irrationality, to which a high threshold applied, and could not examine whether the interference with the applicants' rights was justified by a pressing social need and was proportionate, the principles at the heart of the

[33] *Luluyev v Russia*, November 9, 2006, para.139; *Chitayev and Chitayev v Russia*, January 18, 2007, para.202.

[34] *Silver*, fn.8 above, para.113; *Klass*, fn.6 above, para.64.

[35] e.g. *Halford*, fn.12 above, no remedy against telephone tapping of office phones; *Valsamis*, fn.12 above, no remedy to challenge the requirement of Jehovah's witness pupils to participate in parades; *Ramirez Sanchez v France*, July 4, 2006, ECHR 2006–. . ., absence of remedy to challenge extension of solitary confinement.

[36] e.g. not hindered by acts or omissions of the authorities, as in *Kaya v Turkey*, February 19, 1998, R.J.D. 1998–I, No.65, 28 E.H.R.R. 1, para.106; *Ilhan*, fn.30 above, para.97; *Iatridis v Greece*, March 25, 1999, ECHR 1999–II, the applicant obtained a court order but the Finance Minister did not comply.

[37] e.g. *Amann v Switzerland*, February 16, 2000, ECHR 2000–II, para.89; *Murray Family v UK*, October 28, 1994, Series A, No.300–A, para.100, where an action for trespass to property furnished an effective remedy for a search of a home by soldiers, despite the feeble prospects of success; *Salah Sheekh v Netherlands*, January 11, 2007; para.154, "effectiveness" did not depend on the certainty of a favourable outcome.

[38] *M.S.S. v Belgium and Greece*, January 21, 2011, ECHR 2011–. . . , para.394.

[39] e.g. *Camenzind v Switzerland*, December 16, 1997, R.J.D. 1997–VIII, No.61, 28 E.H.R.R. 458.

[40] *M.S.S.*, fn.38 above, para.302.

[41] e.g. *Petkov v Bulgaria*, June 11, 2009, para.82, where the applicants had been struck off the list of candidates, only specified office-holders, institutions and a quorum of M.Ps could lodge complaints before the Constitutional Court.

[42] *M.S.S.*, fn.38 above, para.392.

Court's analysis under Art.8. The scope of review was also found inadequate in *Hatton v UK* where the courts were unable, on judicial review application, to examine whether the night flying scheme at Heathrow was a justified limitation on the private and family life rights of those living in the vicinity. An approach by a judicial disciplinary board which failed to distinguish aspects of private life unlinked to the exercise of professional duty from those were so linked did not comply with the requirements of Article 13.[43]

It does not necessarily have to be a judicial remedy although the body's powers and procedural guarantees are relevant in determining whether the remedy is effective.[44] A non-judicial body may well have difficulties satisfying notions of independence which in some administrative spheres may undermine any real efficacy of a remedy.[45] In the electoral sphere, the Court noted the Venice Commission's recommendation of the availability of judicial redress and found a violation where the applicant had no recourse for refusal to accord him a Parliamentary seat beyond the Electoral Commission which counted a large number of the representatives of other parties who had a conflict of interest.[46]

Impartiality is a requirement of effectiveness. Where the appeal from disciplinary sanctions on a public prosecutor lay to a formation within the Judicial Services Commission which included members who had participated in the impugned decisions, there was a lack of impartiality.[47]

Effectiveness as a standard may vary depending on the subject matter, or nature of the Convention right relied on.[48]

In respect of measures alleged contrary to the Convention, and whose effects may be potentially irreversible, effectiveness requires that the remedy can suspend their execution, in particular in expulsion cases.[49] Where expulsion cases are concerned, the suspensiveness of the remedy should have automatic suspensive effect; it is not good enough that an asylum seeker can apply for suspension of expulsion pending an appeal if the refusal of suspension can be issued on a limited examination of the merits, permitting expulsion before a rigorous examination has taken place.[50] Where detainees were transferred by the British army to the Iraqi authorities while their appeal was pending, this nullified the effectiveness of that remedy.[51] Where life and limb are concerned, authorities must carry out an independent and rigorous scrutiny as to the existence of any real risk of treatment contrary to Art.3.[52] Since remedies must be accessible in a practical sense, asylum seekers must be given access to legal advice, and they must be properly notified of decisions of deportation so that they can make use of available remedies.[53] They should also be clearly informed of the

[43] *Ozpinar v Turkey*, October 19, 2010, para.85.

[44] e.g. *Klass*, fn.6 above, para.67; *Z v UK*, May 10, 2001, ECHR 2000–V, para.110. Also the Commission in *Powell and Rayner v UK*, (Rep.) February 21, 1990, Series A, No.172, 12 E.H.R.R. 355, para.54, rejecting a submission that there was a general right to a court; (12573/86) (Dec.) March 6, 1987, 51 D.R. 283, effective remedy may be provided by non-judicial authority where it does not merely endorse decisions from below.

[45] *Chahal*, fn.29 above, paras 153–154.

[46] *Grosaru v Romania*, March 2, 2010, paras 54–62.

[47] *Kayasu v Turkey (No.1)* November 13, 2008, para.121.

[48] *Hasan and Chaush v Bulgaria*, October 26, 2000, ECHR 2000–XI, para.99.

[49] *Salah Sheekh*, fn.37 above, para.153; *Gebremedhin v France*, April 26, 2007, para.66.

[50] *M.S.S.*, fn.38 above, paras 293, 389–390.

[51] *Al-Saadoon and Mufdhi v UK*, March 2, 1010, where the transfer by the UK of detainees to the Iraqi authorities nullified a pending appeal to the House of Lords.

[52] *Abdolkhani and Karimnia v Turkey*, September 22, 2009, paras 108, 116.

[53] *Abdolkhani and Karimnia*, fn.52, paras 114–117.

procedures available to them and of legal or other assistance that might be available.[54] The authorities must also take the initiative in establishing viable channels of communication with asylum seekers who may not have a stable address.[55]

Timing of remedies can be crucial. Delays in decisions may impinge on effectiveness, as in post-hoc remedies for the banning of demonstrations on public issues of the moment which do not enable the demonstrators to protest at the opportune moment.[56] A remedy which will not bear fruit in sufficient time will not be adequate or effective.[57] Where a prisoner lodged an appeal against 45 days in a disciplinary cell and he was no longer in the cell by the time the case came before a judge, the Court found a breach of Art.13, noting that such disciplinary punishment had serious repercussions for the prisoner.[58]

Where secret surveillance was in issue, the Court took the approach in *Klass v Germany* that remedies only had to be as effective as they could be given the restricted scope for recourse inherent in such a system and referred to the possibility of an aggregate of remedies as satisfying the requirements of Art.13 (see below).[59] In the context of Art.9, the Court considered that a State's obligation could be discharged by making remedies in respect of registration of a religious community's leadership accessible only to certain representatives rather than to each individual believer.[60]

A more detailed and active scrutiny is required in cases concerning Arts 2 and 3. Generally, the Court has accepted that judicial review in the United Kingdom has sufficient scope as applied in expulsion cases to afford an effective remedy, since the courts have shown that they will apply a thorough scrutiny.[61] However, in *Chahal v UK*, where the applicant, a suspected terrorist, was found to risk torture or death on expulsion to India, the Court found that due to the irreversible damage which would be caused, the scope of the review was deficient since in the context of national security the courts did not carry out a scrutiny of the grounds and the possibility of review by the advisers who only had a power to recommend was insufficient.[62]

Where Arts 2 and 3 are concerned, a certain responsibility also lies on the authorities to take the initiative in respect of possible infringements. Thus, in *Aksoy v Turkey*, a violation was found in respect of the complete lack of reaction of the public prosecutor to the physical condition of the applicant who appeared before him after a long period in custody. In the series of cases arising out of the situation in south-east Turkey, where the public prosecutor played a central role in the system of criminal and civil remedies, the Court went so far as to state that Art.13 required the authorities to conduct a thorough and effective investigation capable of leading to the identification and punishment of those responsible, including effective access

[54] *M.S.S.*, fn.38 above, paras 304–308, such information as had been provided was misleading; *Rahimi v Greece*, April 5, 2011, para.79, information leaflet was not in a language which the applicant could understand.

[55] *M.S.S.*, fn.38 above, paras 308–319.

[56] *Baczkowski v Poland*, May 3, 2005, paras 82–83.

[57] *Pine Valley Developments Ltd v Ireland*, November 29, 1991, para.47.

[58] *Payet v France*, January 20, 2011, paras 127–134.

[59] *Klass*, fn.6 above, para.70.

[60] *Hasan and Chaush*, fn.48 above, paras 98–104.

[61] e.g. *Bensaid v UK*, February 6, 2001, ECHR 2001-I, paras 55–56, and authorities cited therein.

[62] *Chahal*, fn.29 above, paras 151–155, the procedures before the advisers were also lacking, i.e. no legal representation or information as to the grounds for expulsion.

for the complainant to the investigation procedure.[63] In *Aydin v Turkey*, the lack of prompt reaction by the public prosecutor to an allegation of rape of a girl in gendarme custody, failing to obtain the necessary expert medical examination or to seek any factual corroboration, together with the deferential attitude disclosed towards the gendarmes, disclosed a violation.[64] In respect of cases of killings by the security forces in the different context of Northern Ireland, the Court noted that generally an applicant who claimed the use of unlawful force had to exhaust domestic remedies by taking civil proceedings where the courts could establish facts, determine liability and award compensation. This process was not dependent on the proper conduct of criminal investigations as had been the situation in the Turkish cases. Thus, the Court found no violation of Art.13 as there was nothing to indicate that civil proceedings would not be capable of furnishing an effective remedy for alleged excessive use of force.[65] Insofar as the applicants' complaints disclosed defects in the inquest and criminal investigations these gave rise to breaches of the procedural obligation in Art.2 and no separate issue arose under Art.13.

Where complaints under Arts 2 and 3 of the Convention concern the failure of the authorities to protect the applicants from the acts of others, less stringent requirements are imposed as regards the investigative aspect of remedies. It may not always require the authorities to undertake the responsibility of launching an inquiry. There should be available a mechanism which the victim or victims' relatives can establish any liability.[66]

There are, in effect, two separate aspects of effective redress under Art.13. Firstly, there should be a procedure whereby the substance of the applicant's complaints under the substantive articles may be determined, including the finding of liability by the responsible Government body or authority and, secondly, the provision of adequate redress, which includes compensation where appropriate for non-pecuniary, as well as pecuniary, damage.[67] The inability of children to sue the local authority for alleged negligence in failing to protect them from their parents breached Art.13 as it prevented them obtaining a determination of their allegations and denied them the possibility of obtaining an enforceable award of damages.[68] However, the mere fact that a court awards a low amount of compensation is not enough to show a lack of effectiveness.[69] Where the alleged remedy for a breach of presumption of innocence only addressed breach of rights of privacy and did not address the liability for a procedural deficiency in defence rights, the Court found the availability of compensation was only a partial remedy.[70]

[63] *Kaya*, fn.356 above, para.107.

[64] See also *Bati v Turkey*, June 3, 2004, ECHR 2004–IV, where the dilatory investigation led to the prosecution being time-barred, allowing the perpetrators to enjoy virtual impunity despite overwhelming evidence.

[65] *McKerr v UK*, ECHR 2001–III, para.173; *Hugh Jordan v UK*, May 4, 2000, para.162. Contrast *Khashiyev and Akayeva v Russia*, February 24, 2005, para.185, where the civil remedies were undermined.

[66] *Z v UK*, fn.44 above, para.109.

[67] e.g. *TP and KM v UK*, May 10, 2001, ECHR 2001–V, para.107, concerning damages for allegedly negligent removal of child from home by social services.

[68] *Z v UK*, fn.44 above, paras 110–111. Breaches of Art.13 also found for lack of a practically available and enforceable right to compensation for the treatment of a mentally ill prisoner in *Keenan v UK*, April 3, 2001, and the inability of parents to obtain compensation for the death in custody of their son in *Paul and Aubrey Edwards v UK*, March 14, 2002, ECHR 2002–II.

[69] *Delle Cave and Corrado v Italy*, June 5, 2007, para.45.

[70] *Konstas v Greece*, May 24, 2011, paras 29 and 56. Constrast *Elsner v Austria*, May 24, 2011, para.151, where the remedy under the Media Act was expressly designed to protect presumption of innocence and could lead to a finding in that regard, thus was effective.

While preventive measures are stated as preferable, in some areas, compensatory remedies may be sufficient, as in length of proceedings or delayed enforcement of judgments. However, damages must be shown to be available in practice, at levels not unreasonable when compared to Court awards, the claim must be determined within a reasonable time[71] and the award paid within six months of the judgment, while legal costs for the applicant in pursuing the claim must not be prohibitive.[72]

In appropriate cases, non-pecuniary damage, as well as pecuniary damage for losses suffered must be available.[73] The Court rejected the view that unreasonable length of proceedings by itself did not give rise to non-pecuniary damage, noting that there might be some cases in which such damage was perhaps minimal or non-existent and stating that in such cases the judge in awarding no damages should give sufficient reasoning to that end.[74]

In other areas, compensation may not be enough. Where candidates unlawfully struck from the list before the election could apply for compensation, the Court considered this was an important part of redress but not by itself effective, since they should also have been able to apply to be reinstated: without such obligations of redress, rights to stand for election or to vote would have been ineffective in practice, Governments not correcting defects in the electoral system.[75]

As in the area of non-exhaustion of domestic remedies, there is a certain burden on the Government to show that the available remedies are effective. In *Vereinigung Demokratischer Soldaten Österreichs v Austria*, the Government alleged a number of remedies were available in the courts whereby the association could have had its journal distributed but the Court found that the Government had not put forward any example showing the application of the alleged remedies in a case similar to the present one; it had therefore failed to show that the remedies would have been effective.[76] Thus, Governments must give convincing proof of the effectiveness of a claimed remedy: one or a few isolated examples of a favourable decision does not suffice to show established case-law demonstrating the effectiveness of the avenue of redress.[77] The effectiveness must also be established in respect of the relevant period, a subsequent development in the case-law not being sufficient.[78] Thus, the Goverment argument that in assessing an untested remedy in a common law constitutional system the Court would infringe the principle of subsidiarity failed, the Court holding that less than full supervision of the existence and operation of domestic remedies would undermine and render illusory these guarantees of

[71] See, e.g. *Vidas v Croatia*, July 3, 2008, the effectiveness of the Constitutional Court remedy was undermined by its excessive length of three years.

[72] *Scordino v Italy (No.1)* (GC), (36813/97), para.182, ECHR 2006–V, paras 1995–213, concerning remedies for length of proceedings; see also *Wasserman v Russia (No.2)*, April 10, 2008, paras 54–58, where a claim for compensation for delayed enforcement of judgment was not heard speedily and the amount awarded manifestly unreasonable.

[73] *Burdov v Russia (No.2)*, January 15, 2009, paras 105–116.

[74] *Martins Castro and Alves Correia de Castro v Portugal*, June 10, 2008, para.54.

[75] *Petkov*, fn.41, para.79.

[76] The Government also failed to show purported remedies were effective in *Rotaru v Romania*, February 4, 2000, ECHR 2000–V, paras 70–72 and *Wille v Liechtenstein*, October 28, 1999, ECHR 1999–VII, para.77, absence of any precedent that court would entertain a claim.

[77] *Abramiuc*, fn.27above, para.128; *Wasserman*, fn.72 above, insufficiently established case-law showing a remedy gave damages for delay in enforcement of judgments against the State; *Burdov v Russia (No.2)*, fn.73 above, para.114, four examples were not sufficient.

[78] *Khider v France*, July 9, 2009, paras 138–145, where it was not apparent before 2007 that prison transfers were measures challengeable as administrative decisions.

Art.13.[79] However, in contrast, it is apparent that where Contracting States have furnished a new remedy specifically to address a Convention problem, the Court accords a certain time over which the remedy can be tested in practice.[80] Even then it will take more than a few examples of shortcomings before the Court will conclude a structural defect in the remedy provided.[81]

7. Aggregate theory

II–633 The Court applied for a while a theory that where no single remedy may itself entirely satisfy the requirements of Art.13, the aggregate of remedies provided for under domestic law may do so. Thus, in *Leander v Sweden*, in respect of allegations of invasion of privacy through secret files, the Court found overall that the safeguards of the Chancellor of Justice, ombudsman and the presence of parliamentarians on the national police board sufficed.[82] This may be logical where in the context of secret surveillance the thrust of the Convention organs' concern has been to ensure an adequate framework to guard against abuse of power. It is not a satisfactory approach where an applicant is in a situation where he seeks a remedy which should have a more tangible result. After a silence of some years the Court has made some recent reference to the principle; it has not yet been relied upon in a finding of non-violation.[83]

Cross-reference

Part IB: Admissibility, sub-s.2: Exhaustion of domestic remedies.
Part IIB, s.6: Compensation for detention.
Part IIB, s.29: Immigration and expulsion.
Part IIB, s.36: Prisoners' rights.
Part IIB, s.42: Review of detention.

[79] *McFarlane v Ireland*, para.112, where an alleged consitutional remedy for delay was found not to be effective, inter alia, due to lack of confirmed case-law, the doubt as to its existence and the complexity of the legal opinions on the point; also noted were the practical obstacles that proceedings between the Supreme Court were not particularly expeditious and likely to be costly given the procedural and legal complexity that would be involved.

[80] *McFarlane v Ireland*, citing, inter alia, *Grzinčič v Slovenia*, (26867/02), ECHR 2007–V, para.108.

[81] See *Simaldone v Italy*, March 3, 2009, paras 81–83, where some fifty or so examples of excessive delay in payment did not yet disclose a structural defect in the remedy when set against the apparent 16,000 decisions which had been rendered under the new law. The Court flagged its concern nonetheless.

[82] Cf. the dissent of President Ryssdal noting no binding power of decision or specific responsibility to enquire into particular complaints.

[83] e.g. *Al-Nashif v Bulgaria*, June 20, 2002, para.132, violation for lack of appeal against an expulsion on national security grounds; *M.S.S.*, fn.38 above, para.289.

42. Review of detention

Key provision:

Article 5, para.4 (right to speedy review of lawfulness of detention by a court). II–634

Key case-law:

De Wilde, Ooms and Versyp v Belgium, March 10, 1972, Series A, No.14, 1 E.H.R.R. 435; *Van Droogenbroeck v Belgium*, June 24, 1982, Series A, No.50, 4 E.H.R.R. 443; *Sanchez-Reisse v Switzerland*, October 21, 1986, Series A, No.107, 9 E.H.R.R. 71; *Weeks v UK*, March 2, 1987 Series A, No.114, 10 E.H.R.R. 293; *Bouamar v Belgium*, February 29, 1988, Series A, No.129, 11 E.H.R.R. 529; *Lamy v Belgium*, March 30, 1989, Series A, No.151, 11 E.H.R.R. 529; *E v Norway*, August 29, 1990, Series A, No.181–A, 17 E.H.R.R. 30; *Thynne, Wilson and Gunnell v UK*, October 25, 1990, Series A, No.190, 13 E.H.R.R. 666; *Toth v Austria*, December 12, 1991, Series A, No.224, 14 E.H.R.R. 551; *Megyeri v Germany*, May 12, 1992, Series A, No.237–A, 15 E.H.R.R. 584; *Herczegfalvy v Austria*, September 24, 1992, Series A, No.244, 15 E.H.R.R. 437; *Kampanis v Greece*, July 13, 1995, Series A, No.318–B, 21 E.H.R.R. 43; *Hussain v UK*, February 21, 1996, R.J.D. 1996–I, No.4, 22 E.H.R.R. 1; *Prem Singh v UK*, February 21, 1996, R.J.D. 1996–I, No.4; *RMD v Switzerland*, September 26, 1997, R.J.D. 1997–VI, No.51, 28 E.H.R.R. 224; *Chahal v UK*, November 15, 1996, R.J.D 1996–V; *Sakik v Turkey*, November 26, 1997, R.J.D. 1997–VII, No.58, 26 E.H.R.R. 662; *Assenov v Bulgaria*, October 28, 1998, R.J.D., 1998–VIII; *DN v Switzerland*, March 29, 2001, ECHR 2001–III; *Stafford v UK*, May 28, 2002, ECHR 2002–IV; *Hutchison Reid v UK*, February 20, 2003, ECHR 2003–IV; *Svipsta v Latvia*, March 9, 2006, ECHR 2006–. . . ; *A and Others v UK*, February 19, 2009, ECHR 2009–. . .

1. General considerations

There is a right of review of the lawfulness of all the categories of detention provided for in Art.5, para.1, regarded by the Court as a crucial guarantee against the arbitrariness of detention.[1] However the scope of the obligation under Art.5, para.4 is not identical and its requirements will vary according to the kind of deprivation of liberty in question. It no longer applies once a person is released.[2] II–635

Article 5, para.4 contains specific procedural guarantees for matters of deprivation of liberty that are distinct from the procedural guarantees of Art.6. Article 5 para.4 is the *lex specialis* in relation to Art.5.[3]

2. Review of detention imposed by a court

Where sentences of detention are imposed by competent courts, the supervision is incorporated in the decision made by the court at the close of the judicial proceedings. Thus in respect of sentences imposed by competent courts within the II–636

[1] e.g. *Varbanov v Bulgaria*, October 5, 2000, ECHR 2000–X, para.58; *Benjamin and Wilson v UK*, September 26, 2002, para.33.

[2] e.g. (12778/87) (Dec.) December 9, 1988, 59 D.R. 158, concerning conditional release; persons in hiding or on the run: (25527/94) (Dec.) November 29, 1995; *A and Others v UK*, February 19, 2009, ECHR 2009–. . . , para.200.

[3] *Reinprecht v Austria*, November 15, 2005, para.55, as concerns differences between the two, for example a public hearing is not specified in Art.5 (para.54).

meaning of Art.5, para.1(a), the review of lawfulness is inbuilt in the conviction and appeal procedures.[4] Only where the decision of detention is taken by other authorities, administrative or executive, is there a right of recourse to a court pursuant to Art.5, para.4. No right to parole or release on licence can therefore be derived from Art.5, para.4.

This principle was initially applied to mandatory life sentences for murder which were seen as being imposed by a court as fixed sentences reflecting the gravity of the offence.[5] In *Stafford v UK*, the Court considered that the mandatory life sentence could no longer be considered as imposing lifelong imprisonment as a punishment and that after the expiry of the tariff period representing punishment and deterrence, the sentence fell to be regarded as justified by considerations of risk and dangerousness as in indeterminate, or discretionary life sentences and thus requiring review (see further below).

3. Special types of sentences

II–637 Where sentences are passed with the aim of social protection and rehabilitation of offenders, since the grounds relied upon by the courts in sentencing (risk and dangerousness) are by their very nature susceptible of change with the passage of time, new issues may arise which affect the lawfulness of the detention. These types of sentence attract the right to review under Art.5, para.4. The principle was first applied in respect of sentences of detention imposed on recidivists in *Van Droogenbroeck v Belgium*[6] and then extended to the imposition of discretionary life sentences in the United Kingdom, which were found also to be based not only on the gravity of the offences but also on considerations of risk and dangerousness which could change with the passage of time.

In *Weeks v UK*, the applicant's recall after release on licence was compatible with Art.5, para.1(a) as derived from his original conviction when he was sentenced to a term of discretionary life imprisonment for robbery.[7] Nonetheless, Art.5, para.4 came into play as the Court found new issues of lawfulness in the Convention sense might arise if the decision not to release or to redetain was not based on grounds consistent with the objectives of the sentencing court. The right to review had to be wide enough to bear on those conditions which were essential for the lawful detention of a person subject to the special kind of deprivation of liberty both on recall to prison and at reasonable intervals during the course of his imprisonment. Thus the applicant whose sentence was imposed by the judge on the grounds of risk which his unstable personality presented, had the right to review on recall to prison after release to test that the legal basis for the detention still existed. Similarly in *Thynne, Wilson and Gunnell v UK*, three discretionary lifers, whose tariff had expired, could claim a review of their continuing detention.

Where minors convicted of murder were sentenced to detention at Her Majesty's Pleasure, the Commission and Court rejected the Government's argument that this

[4] *De Wilde, Ooms and Versyp v Belgium*, March 10, 1972, Series A, No.14, 1 E.H.R.R. 435, para.76.

[5] *Wynne v UK*, July 18, 1994, Series A, No.294–A.

[6] See also (11082/84) March 4, 1988, 69 D.R. 27, where in respect of an offender placed at the disposal of the Government as a recidivist, an additional penalty of 19 years was left to the discretion of the executive after the expiry of a four-year sentence, the judicial review required was not incorporated in the initial decision whereby the executive was empowered to order or not order a deprivation of liberty.

[7] At age 17, he had stolen 35 pence using a starter pistol with blank cartridges.

was a fixed sentence imposed due to the gravity of the offence, finding that it had to be regarded as an indeterminate sentence based on a special factor subject to change over time. Indeed both adopted the argument of the applicant's counsel that if the sentence did intend that the child forfeited its liberty for the rest of its days there might be problems under Art.3. The Court had regard to the nature and purpose of the sentence, noting that the sentence was imposed because of the youth of the offender and held that an indeterminate sentence on a young person could only be justified by the need to protect the public which must take into account any developments in the personality or attitude as he grew older. There was accordingly a violation of Art.5, para.4 in the lack of any judicial review of continued detention for two applicants, *Prem Singh v UK* and *Hussain v UK*, who had both served their tariffs.[8]

As concerns mandatory life sentences imposed on adults for murder, the Court held in *Stafford v UK* that the tariff fixed by the Secretary of State comprised the punishment element of the sentence and once it expired continued detention depended on elements of dangerousness and risk associated with the objectives of the original sentence. As these elements could change over time, it could no longer be maintained that the original trial and appeal proceedings satisfied, once and for all, issue of compatibility of detention with Art.5, para.1. Such prisoners could therefore claim, after expiry of tariff, a right to review of the lawfulness of their continued detention by a body satisfying the guarantees of Art.5, para.4.

4. Access to court and scope of review

Failure to make provision for a detained person to have the possibility of applying to a court for review of lawfulness of detention will disclose a straightforward breach[9] as will the refusal of a court to entertain an application.[10] **II–638**

More difficult questions arise where there is access to a court but limitations in the scope of its review. The "court" must be able to decide on the procedural and substantive conditions essential for "lawfulness". It is not required to cover every question and it does not guarantee a right to judicial control of such scope as to empower the "court" on all aspects of the case to substitute its own discretion for that of the decision-making authority.[11] However it is not enough for a court to confine itself to the existence of formal grounds for detention without examining the underlying lawfulness, such as the reasonableness of the suspicion underlying the arrest in remand cases and the legitimacy of the purpose of the varying types of detention.[12] Problems may also arise where the court treats as irrelevant, or

[8] See also *V v UK*, December 16, 1999, ECHR 1999–IX, paras 119–120, violation of Art.5, para.4, where after his conviction for murder, the 11–year-old applicant's tariff was set by the Home Secretary but quashed by the House of Lords, leaving inchoate his entitlement to access to a tribunal for review of the lawfulness of his detention.

[9] See, e.g. *Nasrulloyev v Russia*, October 11, 2007, paras 87–90, no access to a court for three years while in detention pending extradition.

[10] See, e.g. *Samoila and Cionca v Romania*, March 4, 2008, paras 58–61, where the Supreme Court claimed it had no jurisdiction, whereas it had already ruled on identical applications.

[11] *Weeks v UK*, March 2, 1987 Series A, No.114, 10 E.H.R.R. 293, para.59; *Van Droogenbroeck v Belgium*, June 24, 1982, Series A, No.50, 4 E.H.R.R. 443, para.49; *Toth v Austria*, December 12, 1991, Series A, No.224, 14 E.H.R.R. 551, para.87.

[12] e.g. *Jecius v Lithuania*, July 31, 2000, ECHR 2000–IX, paras 100–101; *Grauslys v Lithuania*, October 10, 2000, para.54, even in ordering release the court refused to examine the applicant's allegations of breaches of domestic law and specified no reasons for the release; *SD v Greece*, June 11, 2009, para.75, failure of administrative court to rule on "lawfulness".

disregards, concrete facts invoked by the detainee capable of putting in doubt the existence of conditions essential for the "lawfulness" in the Convention sense of the deprivation of liberty.[13] Security considerations, even relating to terrorism, do not provide a justification for a lack of judicial procedure to challenge detention as techniques are available to accommodate, for example, concerns about confidential intelligence material.[14]

Judicial review in the United Kingdom was previously not wide enough for review of the continued detention of the discretionary lifer, as this was unable to verify whether detention was consistent with and justified by the objectives of the indeterminate sentence imposed on him.[15] The same applied to judicial review, including habeas corpus, as concerned applications for release by mental patients since the procedure did not review the merits of the clinical decisions.[16]

5. Procedural requirements of review

II–639 The review must be of a judicial character and give the individual the guarantees appropriate to the kind of deprivation of liberty in question.[17] The fact that the review is conducted by a court or judge is not decisive. For example, in *De Wilde, Ooms and Versyp v Belgium*, magistrates ordered the detention on vagrancy but in a summary procedure without the requisite guarantees necessary to the seriousness of what was at stake, which gave it the character of an administrative decision. To constitute a "court" for the purposes of Art.5, para.4, the authority must be independent from the executive and from the parties, as well as providing the fundamental guarantees of judicial procedure.[18]

Direct access to court is not always required. In *Sanchez-Reisse v Switzerland*, where the applicant argued that he could not apply directly to court without his request going via the police office, the Court found it was legitimate and necessary for the executive to have the power to comment, access not thereby being impeded or the power of the court hindered.[19] An applicant must however be entitled to apply to a court for review of detention himself, without relying on the permission or good will of the authorities.[20] Article 5, para.4 also presupposes the existence of a procedure in

[13] e.g. *Nikolova v Bulgaria*, March 25, 1999, ECHR 1999–II, para.61, where the domestic court ignored the applicant's arguments concerning pre-trial detention, inter alia, that she had a permanent address and family and was in poor health; *Ilijkov v Bulgaria*, July 26, 2001, paras 97–98, rejecting the Government argument that the domestic court, by ruling on the persistence of reasonable suspicion relevant to pre-trial detention, would prejudge the merits and forfeit their impartiality.

[14] e.g. *Chahal v UK*, November 15, 1996, R.J.D 1996–V, para.131; *Al-Nashif v Bulgaria*, June 20, 2002, paras 94–98.

[15] *Weeks*, fn.11 above, para.69. See, after the Human Rights Act 1998, *Stewart v UK*, (25185/02) (Dec.) December 16, 2002, where the prisoner's complaints were rejected for non-exhaustion for failure to invoke the Convention in judicial review proceedings.

[16] *HL v UK*, October 5, 2004, paras 137–142.

[17] *De Wilde*, fn.4 above, para.76; also, in *Weeks*, fn.11 above, there was no full disclosure of adverse material on recall to prison.

[18] *Varbanov*, fn.1 above, paras 58–61, where the prosecutor who ordered detention was a party to the proceedings; *Dougoz v Greece*, March 6, 2001, para.62, where the applicant's appeal was to the leniency of Government ministers; *DN v Switzerland*, paras 50–57, concerning the lack of impartiality of a psychiatric panel member who had already expressed an opinion on key issues.

[19] *Sanchez-Reisse v Switzerland*, October 21, 1986, Series A, No.107, 9 E.H.R.R. 71, para.45.

[20] *Rakevich v Russia*, October 28, 2003, paras 43–47, mental health case where the initiative lay with the medical staff.

comformity with its requirements without the necessity of instituting separate legal proceedings in order to bring it about. Thus the Court rejected the argument of the Government in *Prem Singh v UK* that applicant could apply for judicial review of the Parole Board decision in order to obtain an oral hearing.

(a) Power to release

A power to release is necessary. In *Weeks*, the ability of the Parole Board to recommend release, which did not bind the Secretary of State, was not sufficient.[21] In *E v Norway*, the general power of the courts to review and rule invalid administrative decisions was found sufficient, notwithstanding no precedent of a court overriding such a decision. However, lack of precedents in successfully invoking an alleged remedy may indicate that the existence of the remedy is insufficiently certain, and that it is accordingly lacking the accessibility and effectiveness required for Art.5.[22] II–640

(b) Adversarial procedure and fairness

The procedure should be adversarial, providing the applicant with the opportunity to present his case effectively. While Art.5, para.4 is not to be interpreted as identical with Art.6, para.1,[23] the Court has stated that it should allow to the largest extent possible the basic requirements of a fair trial, such as the right to an adversarial procedure.[24] Where applicants had been subject for a long period to what appeared to be indefinite detention without charge, the Court in those circumstances did consider that substantially the same fair trial guarantees should apply under Art.5, para.4 as under Art.6, para.1.[25] II–641

While the Court has tended to acknowledge the need for a hearing before a judicial authority, the procedure required in each case is not identical.[26] Where in *Sanchez-Reisse* the applicant was challenging his detention with a view to extradition the Court found that he should have been provided in some way or other with an adversarial procedure. This could have included the possibility of submitting written comments on the objections of the Federal Police Office which went before the Federal Court with his request for release.

Failure to provide access to relevant documents and reports which deprives the applicant of the ability to participate properly in the proceedings and to challenge

[21] See also *Prem Singh v UK*, February 21, 1996, R.J.D. 1996–I, No.4, and *Hussain v UK*, February 21, 1996, R.J.D. 1996–I, No.4, 22 E.H.R.R. 1; *Benjamin and Wilson*, fn.1 above, where the practice of the Secretary of State in following the recommendation of the Mental Health Tribunal concerning the category of "technical lifers" did not alter the crucial fact that the decision to release was taken by the executive.

[22] e.g. *Sakik v Turkey*, November 26, 1997, R.J.D. 1997–VII, No.58, 26 E.H.R.R. 662, where there was no example of any person in police custody having successfully invoked the Constitution or human rights provisions when applying to a judge for a release; *Sabeur Ben Ali v Malta*, June 29, 2000, paras 38–42; *Vachev v Bulgaria*, July 8, 2004, para.73, no example of any successful challenge of a house arrest relying on Art.5, para.4.

[23] *Megyeri v Germany*, May 12, 1992, Series A, No.237–A, 15 E.H.R.R. 584, para.22, *Assenov v Bulgaria*, October 28, 1998, R.J.D., 1998–VIII, para.162. Although there is a certain overlap: *Svipsta v Latvia*, March 9, 2006, ECHR 2006–. . . , para.129(e).

[24] *Schops v Germany*, February 13, 2001, ECHR 2001–I, para.44; *Lietzow v Germany*, February 13, 2001, para.44; *Svipsta*, fn.23 above, para.129(e).

[25] *A and Others v UK*, fn.2 above, para.127.

[26] *De Wilde*, fn.4 above, para.78.

effectively the lawfulness of the detention has been found to render the review defective.[27] While some parts of a file may be kept secret, information which is essential for the assessment of the lawfulness of a person's detention should nonetheless be made available in an appropriate manner to the suspect's lawyer.[28] Where counsel was unable to inspect documents in the file before the court ruled on whether to hold the applicant on remand, whereas Crown counsel was familiar with the file, there was a failure to ensure equality of arms and the proceedings were not truly adversarial as required by Art.5, para.4.[29] Where prosecution counsel was present before the Court of Appeal whereas the applicant and his lawyer were not, the procedure did not ensure equal treatment and was not truly adversarial.[30] Procedures where submissions to the court by the prosecutor are not heard by or provided to the applicant or his lawyer, with an opportunity to make comments, have also been found to infringe the principle of equality of arms.[31]

Even though important public interests may be at stake where persons are detained as potential terrorist suspects, it was still found to be essential that as much information about allegations and evidence against applicants as possible be made available and any lack of full disclosure counterbalanced so that they can effectively challenge the case against them. Thus, where most of the evidence against a suspect was disclosed by the special tribunal and that material played the predominant role in the determination, the challenge had been practically effective; however where most of the evidence was not disclosed and the decision to detain based solely or to a decisive degree on that evidence, there was a breach due to the applicants'inability to challenge the allegations against them. The role played by a special advocate was not regarded as a counterbalance since although he or she could test the evidence before the tribunal, this was only of limited usefulness since the suspect, who was not given any information or contact with the advocate on the material, could not give effective instructions to the advocate.[32]

Not all evidence has to be disclosed for compliance with Art.5, para.4. Where there was ample evidence, including the fact the applicants had been caught red-handed, the failure to disclose to the defence a videotape of the scene was not in breach, as there were adequate grounds for finding reasonable suspicion that they had committed an offence and the court did not require to view the tape to rule on lawfulness of the detention in the circumstances.[33]

Overall appearances of fairness can come into play, as well as the other specific elements of Art.6, para.1, given that the Court increasingly considers that the importance of the right to liberty requires those guarantees to extend as far. Thus,

[27] *Weeks*, fn.11 above, paras 60–69; *Hussain*, fn.22 above, para.58; *Shameyev v Georgia and Russia*, April 12, 2005, ECHR 2005, para.432; *Svipsta*, fn.23 above, paras 137–139.

[28] *Lietzow*, fn.24 above, para.47; *Svipsta*, fn.23 above, para.137.

[29] *Lamy v Belgium*, March 30, 1989, Series A, No.151, 11 E.H.R.R. 529, para.29; also *Schops*, fn.24 above, paras 46–55, the Court rejected as over-formalistic the Government view that the applicant's lawyer should make requests to inspect the file at each stage of the proceedings, implying that the authorities should take some initiative in making files available; *Lietzow*, fn.24 above, para.47, where the Court did not accept refusal of access to the file was justified to avoid compromising the on-going investigations as this imposed a substantial restriction on the rights of the defence; *Mooren v Germany*, September 7, 2009, violation where applicant's lawyer had no access to that part of the case file submitted by the prosecutor and relied on by the courts as regarded suspicion against him.

[30] e.g. *Toth*, fn.11 above. See sub-s.(c): Oral hearing and cases cited below.

[31] e.g. *Trzaska v Poland*, July 11, 2000, para.78; *Wloch v Poland*, October 19, 2000, para.129.

[32] *A and Others v UK*, fn.2 above, paras 212–224.

[33] *Ramishvili and Kokhreidze v Georgia*, January 27, 2009, paras 124–127.

where the applicants were held in a metal cage, unable properly to communicate with their lawyers, while the judge made no attempt to maintain order in a courtroom filled with journalists and special security forces, the Court considered that the proceedings failed to reflect necessary considerations of presumption of innocence, independence and impartiality as well as hampering of the applicants and their lawyers from participating effectively in an adversarial procedure. In the circumstances, the hearing gave all the appearance of a sham.[34]

(c) *Oral hearing*

Equality of arms may require that the applicant be able to appear at a hearing, in addition to submitting written submissions, in particular where the prosecution is present.[35] II–642

In *Hussein v UK* and *Prem Singh v UK*, having regard to what was at stake (a substantial term of imprisonment) and as questions of the applicants' personality and level of maturity were important to deciding on their dangerousness, Art.5, para.4 required an oral hearing in the context of an adversarial procedure involving legal representation and the possibility of calling and questioning witnesses.[36] Similarly hearings, attended by the applicant and/or counsel have been found necessary in cases dealing with review of detention on grounds of mental health.[37] Emphasis was put on the "right to be heard" where the applicant, detained pending extradition, claimed release on health grounds.[38]

It is unclear the extent to which hearings, oral or public, are required for the review of persons detained pending trial (Art.5, para.1(c)). In *Assenov*, where the applicant was only entitled to one review during a two-year period, the lack of oral hearing was found to disclose a violation.[39] However, in *Reinprecht v Austria*, while the general principle was laid down that a hearing is required for a person whose detention falls within the ambit of Art.5, para.1(c), the Court accepted argument that the requirement to hold hearings speedily at short intervals might be hindered by an obligation to hold such hearings in public and stated that as a general rule such was not necessary. It considered that Art.5, para.4 had a different purpose than Art.6, and was more flexible and less strict in that regard.[40] In *Mamedova v Russia*,

[34] *Ramishvili and Kokhreidze*, fn.33 above, paras 128–133.

[35] e.g. *Kampanis v Greece*, July 13, 1995, Series A, No.318–B, 21 E.H.R.R. 43, the applicant was unable to attend the hearing although the prosecutor was present; *Niedbala v Poland*, July 4, 2000, para.67, where the applicant and his lawyer had no right to attend even when the prosecutor attended; *Grauzinas v Lithuania*, October 10, 2000, para.34, where the applicant was not present at remand hearings to give instructions to his counsel or factual information; *Giorgi Nikolaishvili v Georgia*, January 13, 2009, para.93, violation where the applicant was excluded from the hearing before the court at which the prosecutor was present and which dealt with the reasonableness of suspicion as well as continued detention.

[36] The Commission in *Prem Singh*, fn.21 above, had particular regard to the reasons for recall which were based on disputed facts relating to his conduct on which witnesses could have been heard. Also *Waite v UK*, December 10, 2002, where the applicant was recalled for alleged misuse of drugs, attempted suicide and relationship with a minor.

[37] See Pt IIB, s.32: Mental Health, sub-s.5(b): Procedural requirements.

[38] *Sanchez-Reisse*, fn.19 above, para.51.

[39] *Assenov v Bulgaria*, October 28, 1998, R.J.D., 1998–VIII, para.162, it is unclear whether the oral hearing also had to be public, although the law had changed to provide for such meanwhile.

[40] *Reinprecht v Austria*, November 15, 2005, paras 31–42, the applicant had no complaint about the three review hearings which he attended within short intervals, save that they were not in public.

the Court found a violation in that the applicant was not allowed to attend her appeal against pre-trial detention, giving emphasis to the "importance" of the first appeal hearing and noting that issues about her character and factual nature of the issues which she wished to raise rendered her presence necessary.[41] In *Allen v UK*, where the applicant had been denied the opportunity to attend the prosecutor's appeal against the decision to release her on bail, the Court noted that but for the appeal she would otherwise have been entitled to immediate release; it distinguished this situation from one where the applicant had been appealing against an order to detain.[42] It found a violation, not being convinced by the reasons for refusing to allow the applicant, in the building, to attend the hearing at which the prosecution was present.[43]

(d) Legal representation

II–643 Early cases talked about legal representation being required depending on the nature of the proceedings and the capabilities of the applicant. It was found to be essential in *Bouamar v Belgium*, concerning a juvenile, that a lawyer be present at the hearings where he was remanded in custody in prison, otherwise an essential safeguard would be denied; and in *Megyeri v Germany*, concerning a person detained on ground of mental illness. Where the detainees are foreigners and unfamiliar with the legal system, legal representation affords an important guarantee.[44] In *Woukam Moudefo v France*,[45] where the appeal concerned questions of law, the Commission found that the applicant was unable, without a lawyer, to present his case properly and satisfactorily. It was not enough that the court addressed questions of public order of its own motion and it was the fundamental role of defence counsel to stress the crucial problems which may be raised by an appeal and which may otherwise not be examined by the court, as well as clarifying the applicant's submissions.

More recently, with increasing reference to the desirability of guarantees of Art.6 being applied to the extent possible, it has been stated that adversarial proceedings for the purposes of Art.5, para.4 render a form of representation for the detainee implicit.[46] However it is possible for a court to overrule the detainee's choice of counsel for relevant and sufficient reasons; the replacement of counsel living over 100km away was justifiable in interests of saving costs and expediting the proceedings. There are riders: the replacement counsel must be appropriately qualified and where the applicant has installed a relationship of trust with a particular counsel, that counsel should be retained.[47]

The representation provided should be adequate.[48]

Detainees held on remand should be able to consult confidentially with their lawyers and consult documents brought by them. In *Castravet v Moldova*, the Court

[41] *Mamedova v Russia*, June 6, 2006, paras 91–92.

[42] *Jankauskas v Lithuania*, (59304/00) (Dec.) December 16, 2003, where the applicant's presence had not been required at the appeal hearing, which largely covered the same issues: he had been heard by a judge three weeks earlier and no new factual arguments necessitated his attendance.

[43] *Allen v UK*, March 10, 2010, paras 40–48.

[44] *Sanchez-Reisse*, fn.19 above, para.47.

[45] (10868/84) (Rep.) July 8, 1987 (settled before the Court) October 7, 1988, Series A, No.141–B.

[46] *Lagerblom v Sweden*, January 14, 2003, para.49, concerning Art.6 para.3(c).

[47] *Prehn v Germany*, (40451/06) (Dec.) August 24, 2010.

[48] See *Magalhaes Pereira v Portugal*, February 26, 2002, where the applicant mental patient received ineffective legal assistance from a trainee lawyer and a hospital official. The Court stated that only in special circumstances would it be compatible not to provide legal assistance to such a detainee (para.56).

found a breach of Art.5, para.4 as the applicant had reasonable grounds to suspect that the special consulting room in the detention centre was under surveillance, due to the Bar Association's own concerns, and as the glass screen dividing prisoner and lawyer did not permit the transfer of documents.[49]

(e) Effective access

Where a time-limit or procedural requirements render an apparent review procedure theoretical, the Commission found that it did not comply with Art.5, para.4. In *Farmakopoulos v Belgium*,[50] where the applicant was held in detention pending extradition, he had 24 hours from the service of the enforcement order to appeal though no mention of this possibility of appeal was included in the order. The Commission held that the shortness of time and lack of information made available did not afford the applicant a real opportunity to have the lawfulness of his detention reviewed, in particular noting the ignorance of aliens of language or procedures in this context. Lack of provision of information in the requisite language to a 16–year-old Afghan asylum-seeker together with lack of access to a lawyer was an element in rendering a review of detention inaccessible.[51] II–644

Circumstances in which the applicant is detained which render practical use of a remedy ineffective or unrealistic may disclose problems, as in *RMD v Switzerland* where the applicant was transferred from canton to canton depriving him of any real or effective access to the review procedures available in each jurisdiction and in *Conka v Belgium*, where the applicant gypsies were arrested and expelled before their lawyer could lodge an application in the court.[52] Lack of clarity in domestic law and practice as to review of procedures may also raises issues where it impairs the exercise of the right under Art.5, para.4.[53] Where inordinate delay in the review of the detention measure led to a court declining to rule on the challenge to lawfulness as meanwhile the applicant had been released, the Court considered that deprived the review process of pratical effectiveness—it did not find any reason why the court could not have ruled on the applicant's complaint earlier.[54]

Failure to provide information to an applicant as to why he has been arrested or detained may deprive a right of appeal of all substance in breach of Art.5, para.4 (as well as Art.5, para.2, concerning the obligation to give reasons for arrest and detention).[55]

(f) Reasoning of decisions

The failure to give any adequate reasons, or to give repeated stereotyped decisions which give no answer to the arguments of the applicant may disclose a violation, by depriving the guarantee of its substance.[56] II–645

[49] *Castravet v Moldova*, March 13, 2007, paras 52–61, distinguishing an old case, which found a glass screen compatible, on the basis that the prisoners had a violent history.

[50] *Farmakopoulos v Belgium*, (Rep.) December 4, 1990, struck off before the Court, March 27, 1992, Series A, No.235.

[51] *Rahimi v Greece*, April 5, 2011, para.120.

[52] *Conka v Belgium*, February 5, 2002, ECHR 2002–I, paras 45 and 55.

[53] *Shishkov v Bulgaria*, January 9, 2003, paras 89–90.

[54] *STS v Netherlands*, June 7, 2011, paras 58–62.

[55] *Shameyev*, fn.27 above, para.432.

[56] *Svipsta*, fn.23 above, paras 131–134. See also *Giorgi Nikolaishvili v Georgia*, fn.35 above, para.95, where the Court commented that the template form of the decision cast doubts as to whether the courts properly reviewed the matter.

(g) Burden of proof

II–646 The Court held that it is implicit in Art.5 case-law that it is for the authorities to prove that an individual satisfies the conditions for compulsory detention, not the converse. Thus it was contrary to Art.5, para.4 to require the applicant in *Hutchison Reid* to discharge the onus of proof that he was not suffering from a mental disorder rendering it appropriate for him to to detained in a hospital for medical treatment.[57]

(h) Appeals

II–647 Article 5, para.4 does not require appeals from decisions ordering or extending detention.[58] However, if domestic law allows for an appeal then in principle it must allow to detainees the same guarantees on appeal as at first instance.[59] Therefore in *Toth v Austria*, where the applicant appealed to the Court of Appeal against a court ruling continuing his detention on remand, there was a violation where the procedure was not adversarial as the representative of the prosecution was present and would have been able to respond to questions, whereas neither the applicant or his lawyer were present. In *Hutchison Reid*, the time taken by the appellate levels was taken into account in assessing the speediness of the procedure, while lack of speediness at the appeal level itself may found a violation (see further below).

6. Speedily

II–648 A person taken into detention is entitled to a decision as to the lawfulness of that detention being taken with some expedition. In appropriate cases, Art.5, para.4 also requires the opportunity for review of continued detention at reasonable intervals, where such is not provided automatically.[60]

Different considerations will apply depending on the nature and circumstances of the detention. Release within 16 days was not sufficient to render a review unnecessary in relation to a person taken into detention on mental health grounds.[61] Regarding detention under Art.5, para.1(c), gaps of 7, 11 and 6 days before applicants were brought before the military court were not speedy[62]; while a period of 21 days was too long for a habeas corpus application to be heard concerning release pre-trial.[63] The Court has stated that there is special need for a swift decision

[57] *Hutchison Reid v UK*, February 20, 2003, ECHR 2003–IV, paras 69–73. Also *Nikolova*, fn.13 above, para.59, and *Ilijkov*, fn.13 above, para.99, concerning incompatibility of a strong presumption that applicants held in pre-trial detention were likely to abscond or obstruct justice.

[58] e.g. *Jecius*, fn.12 above, para.100; *Ilijkov*, fn.13 above, para.103.

[59] e.g. *Samoila and Coinca*, fn.10 above, para.58, where the superior court wrongly declined jurisdiction, it was irrelevant that the lower court had given a full review with reasoning, as access to the appeal instance had been denied.

[60] *X v UK*, November 5, 1981, Series A, No.46, para.52.

[61] *Van Glabeke v France*, March 9, 2006, para.33. See also *Wassink v Netherlands*, September 27, 1990, Series A, No.185–A, 21 days too long; and *Rutten v Netherlands*, July 24, 2001, para.54, over five months at two instances for prolongation at a secure institution was too long.

[62] *De Jong, Baljet and Van den Brink v Netherlands*, May 22, 1984, Series A, No.77, paras 57–59, this was the first review after arrest.

[63] *Sarban v Moldova*, October 4, 2005, para.120; see also *Kadem v Malta*, January 9, 2003, para.53, over 23 days, not speedy; *Toma v Romania*, February 24, 2009, paras 75–77, 22 days too long, taking into account the short time-limits in the criminal code and lack of explanation for the various delays in the application being registered, transferred and acted upon.

where a trial is pending.[64] Thus, even though there is no requirement to provide an appeal instance, where there is such provision, lack of requisite speediness will also offend, more than 27 days for decision on appeal against decisions extending pretrial detention disclosing a violation.[65]

Thirty-one days and forty-one days was not sufficient for review of lawfulness of detention for extradition in *Sanchez-Reisse v Switzerland* where the case was not complicated, did not require detailed investigation, and the case file and information about the applicant's health were to hand. Almost eight weeks was too long in *E v Norway*, concerning challenge to a renewed order of preventive detention, where the Court rejected the excuse of a court vacation period, since it was for the State to organise necessary administrative arrangements to deal with urgent matters. Sixty-three days for appellate review of a custodial treatment measure for a minor was not per se a problem due to the range of evidence to gather, but 249 days for the Supreme Court to rule at the third instance was inordinate delay.[66] In *AT v UK*,[67] a gap of almost 14 months between the expiry of the applicant's tariff and the first review by the new system of Parole Board hearings was not justified by the difficulties in introducing a new procedure and the need to establish priorities amongst the prisoners. In such cases, there was indeed a particular need for expedition in holding the first review.

Regarding the intervals at which reviews of continued detention should be made available, a gap of two years between the reviews for a discretionary lifer was not justified, particularly where he had completed the set rehabilitative work within eight months.[68] A period of nine months has been impliedly accepted by the Court in mental health cases,[69] while over a year in one case was excessive.[70] Where detention on remand is concerned, the assumption is that the detention is to be of strictly limited duration and so periodic review at short intervals is called for.[71]

The dilatoriness of the applicant in pursuing proceedings may be a relevant factor, as in *Kolompar v Belgium*, where the Court noted the unusually long period but considered that the State could not be held responsible for the delays to which the applicant's conduct gave rise and that he could not complain validly of a

[64] *Jablonski v Poland*, December 21, 2000, para.93, 43 days was too long; *GB v Switzerland*, November 30, 2000, 32 days for two instances was too long; *Rehbock v Slovenia*, November 28, 2000, 23 days was too long.

[65] *Nazarov v Russia*, November 26, 2009, paras 127–128. See also *Mooren*, fn.29 above, paras 103–107, two months and 22 days too long for pretrial detention challenge, caused by appeal court decision to remit rather than rule itself.

[66] *STS v Netherlands*, fn.54 above, paras 45–50.

[67] (20488/92) (Rep.) November 29, 1995.

[68] *Oldham v UK*, September 26, 2000, ECHR 2000–X, paras 34–37, the Court commented that discretionary lifers appeared to be in a comparable position to mental health detainees; also *Hirst v UK*, July 24, 2001, periods of 21 months and two years between reviews. Exceptionally, a gap of two years was accepted in *Dancy v UK*, (55768/00) (Dec.) March 21, 2002, where the review system showed appropriate flexibility and due regard to the applicant's individual circumstances: a programme of offence-related work had been planned and a transfer to a Category C prison to facilitate further progress to release.

[69] *Herczegfalvy v Austria*, September 24, 1992, Series A, No.244, 15 E.H.R.R. 437, *Megyeri*, fn.23 above (see Part IIB, s.32: Mental Health).

[70] *Kolanis v UK*, June 21, 2005.

[71] *Bezicheri v Italy*, October 25, 1989, Series A, No.164, paras 20–21; *Assenov*, fn.39 above, paras 162–165, where the applicant was only entitled to one review of his detention on remand over a period of two years.

situation which he had created.[72] However, the complexity of medical issues and the obtaining of expert opinions in accordance with wishes of the applicant did not provide a justification for delay of over one year and eight months in reviewing his detention on mental health grounds in *Musial v Poland* as the primary responsibility for obtaining such evidence rested with the State.[73] The Court commented that only exceptional grounds could justify such a delay. Where appellate instances are provided, the State has the obligation to organise its judicial system in such a way as to comply with the requirements of Art.5, para.4 concerning speediness.[74]

7. Relationship with Art.13

II–649 Together with Art.5, para.5 which provides for compensation, Art.5, para.4 is the *lex specialis* for remedies in respect of detention. Art.5, para.4 requirements are stated as being stricter than those of Art.13.[75]

Cross-reference

Part IIB, s.6: Compensation for detention.
Part IIB, s.18: Extradition.
Part IIB, s.29: Immigration and expulsion.
Part IIB, s.32: Mental health.
Part IIB, s.35: Pre-trial detention.

[72] *Kolompar v Belgium*, September 24, 1992, Series A, No.235–C, applicant held for extradition for two years and eight months but had applied for postponements, successive applications for a stay of execution or for release. The Commission had found a lack of speed since despite the applicant's own conduct there was still an obligation on the State to take positive steps to expedite the proceedings. See *Magalhaes Pereira*, fn.48 above, paras 47–51, the fact that the applicant absconded for seven months was not taken into account as he was at his family home.

[73] *Musial v Poland*, March 25, 1999, ECHR 1999–II; also *Baranowski v Poland*, March 28, 2000, para.72, where the complexity of the medical issues could be taken into account but could not absolve the authorities from their essential obligations.

[74] *Hutchison Reid*, fn.57 above, paras 74–80, (mental health case) violation for more than three years and four months for four instances; *Grauzinis*, fn.35 above, para.32; *GB v Switzerland*, fn.64 above, para.38, 32 days for two instances concerning pre-trial detention. See, however, *Letellier v France*, November 23, 1991, Series A, No.207, para.56 and *Touroude v France*, (35502/97) (Dec.) October 3, 2000, where, although expressing doubts as to the speediness of pre-trial detention decisions before the Court of Cassation, the Court found no breach of Art.5, para.4, as, in the French system, the applicant was able to make fresh applications at any time and had made use of this possibility.

[75] *De Jong*, fn.62 above, para.60; *De Wilde*, fn.4 above, para.95.

43. Right to life

Key provision:

Article 2 (right to life). II–650

Key case-law:

McCann and Others v UK, September 27, 1995, Series A, No.324, 21 E.H.R.R. 97; *Andronicou and Constantinou v Cyprus*, October 9, 1997, R.J.D. 1997–VII, No.52, 25 E.H.R.R. 491; *Kaya v Turkey*, February 19, 1998, R.J.D. 1998–I, No.65, 28 E.H.R.R. 1; *Güleç v Turkey*, July 27, 1998, R.J.D., 1998–IV, No.80, 28 E.H.R.R. 121; *Ergi v Turkey*, July 28, 1998, R.J.D., 1998–IV, No.81, 32 E.H.R.R. 388; *Yasa v Turkey*, September 2, 1998, R.J.D. 1998–VI, No.88, 28 E.H.R.R. 408; *Osman v UK*, October 28, 1998, R.J.D., 1998–VIII, No.95, 29 E.H.R.R. 245; *Ogur v Turkey*, May 20, 1999, ECHR 1999–III, 31 E.H.R.R. 912; *Cakici v Turkey*, July 8, 1999, ECHR 1999–IV, 31 E.H.R.R. 5; *Kiliç v Turkey*, March 28, 2000, ECHR 2000–III; *Ilhan v Turkey*, June 27, 2000, ECHR 2000–VII; *Salman v Turkey*, June 27, 2000, ECHR 2000–VII; *Keenan v UK*, April 3, 2001, ECHR 2001–III; *Tanli v Turkey*, April 10, 2000, ECHR 2000–III; *Avsar v Turkey*, July 10, 2001, ECHR 2001–VII; *Calvelli and Ciglio v Italy*, January 17, 2002, ECHR 2002–I; *McKerr v UK*, May 4, 2001, ECHR 2001–III; *Paul and Aubrey Edwards v UK*, March 14, 2002, ECHR 2002–II; *Mastromatteo v Italy*, October 24, 2002, ECHR 2002–VIII; *Öneryildiz v Turkey*, November 30, 2004, ECHR 2004–XI; *Makaratzis v Greece*, December 20, 2004, ECHR 2004–XII; *Nachova v Bulgaria*, July 6, 2005, ECHR 2005–VII; *Ramsahai v Netherlands*, May 15, 2007, ECHR 2007–. . . ; *Varnava v Turkey*, September 18, 2009; *Giuliani and Gaggio v Italy*, March 24, 2011, ECHR 2011–. . .

1. General considerations

The right to life guaranteed under Art.2 is one of the most important rights from which no derogation is possible. The situations where deprivation of life may be justified are exhaustive and must be narrowly interpreted.[1] II–651

Interpretation of the scope and application of this provision has, after a very slow start (the first finding of a violation of Art.2 was by the Court in 1993)[2] been subject to recent, rapid and radical development. Article 2 concerns, most obviously, the use of lethal force by State agents. It was in this context that the early case-law principally evolved. But even from the first major case before the Court, *McCann and Others v UK*, the Court analysed Art.2 as comporting several strands, deriving from the phrasing of the first sentence which provides that the "right to life shall be protected by law". Thus, firstly, there is a dimension of positive obligation: a Contracting State must provide a proper legal framework protecting the right to life, which involves not only a body of laws and regulations as to when force may be properly used but a mechanism of courts and police which functions so as to effectively enforce these laws. There is a growing body of cases which extend this

[1] (10044/82) (Dec.) July 10, 1984, 39 D.R. 162.
[2] *McCann and Others v UK*, September 27, 1995, Series A, No.324.

obligation to a wide range of "life-threatening" circumstances, including, in particular situations, the taking of concrete steps of an operational nature to protect life from threats, both man-made and natural—this imposes positive obligations on the State. Secondly, a State must refrain from the unlawful, unnecessary and disproportionate use of force through its officers and agents—the "negative obligation". Thirdly, where some-one has been victim of violence or, arguably, an unlawful death, the State must provide an effective investigation into the circumstances of the death, the so-called "procedural obligation". While first applied to the situation of killings by security forces, this procedural obligation also increasingly applies to deaths falling under the first head, requiring investigations into fatal accidents. These three "obligations" have interrelated in a somewhat convoluted, overlapping, and occasionally inconsistent, fashion, probably due to the speed with which the case-law has been developing. It has also had perhaps unexpected effects on the application of the admissibility criteria, which deserves some mention. The extent of the application of Art.2 cannot therefore be simply, or easily, mapped out.

There is, however, no right to die to be implied from Art.2.[3] For the moment at least.

After discussion of the peculiarities of admissibility case-law on Art.2, the "negative obligation", dealing with situations where people are killed by forces of the State, is dealt with first. It has a positive obligation aspect as regards the domestic legal framework and standards applied to law enforcement, as well as an extensively developed corpus of principles on the procedural obligation to carry out effective investigations into the killings at the hands of the State. In a second part, the extent of the positive obligation applicable to where life has been put at risk from other quarters is tackled, along with the scope of the procedural obligation to investigate in these widely-differing situations.

2. Admissibility factors

II–652 Recent case-law has shown several marked trends as regards the application of admissibility criteria to Art.2 cases. This has stemmed partly from the way in which the provision has been split into two branches of violation—substantive responsibility of the State for the death and procedural failure to investigate the death properly—and also due to the fundamental importance of the right to life, leading arguably to a tendency for the Court to find domestic remedies ineffective in problematic contexts and to place quite a high bar on applicants losing their victim status.

(a) Ratione temporis

II–653 **Key case-law**: *Silih v Slovenia*, April 4, 2009, *Varnava and Others v Turkey*, September 18, 2009, ECHR 2009–. .

(I) Deaths

II–654 Where a death occurs before the date of ratification of the right of individual petition by the respondent State, complaints about this fact will fall outside the Court's temporal jurisdiction.[4] So much is clear.

[3] *Pretty v UK*, April 29, 2002, ECHR 2002–III, para.41.
[4] *Varnava and Others v Turkey*, September 18, 2009, para.134.

In the early cases, as the obligation to investigate concerned the factual circumstances of a death predating temporal jurisdiction, the Court took the view that the procedural obligation also failed *ratione temporis*.[5] This was overruled in *Silih v Slovenia*. The majority of the Grand Chamber held that the procedural obligation operated separately and autonomously from the substantive aspect of the death itself and that Court may examine, for conformity with Art.2, those procedural acts and/or omissions relative to investigation into the death which occurred or ought to have occurred after the date of ratification. In an apparent effort to exclude jurisdiction nonetheless for historic massacres far in the past, it added, not too helpfully, that there must exist a genuine connection between the death and the entry into force of the Convention in respect of the respondent State for the procedural obligations imposed by Art.2 to come into effect and that a significant proportion of the procedural steps, including proceedings into the cause of death and holding those responsible to account, will have been or ought to have been carried out after the critical date. If it was intended by those riders to limit temporal jurisdiction to those cases where the death occurred only shortly before the critical date and the proceedings evolved over the intervening period and mostly occurred afterwards,[6] this is not spelled out with any clarity. And it is not how the passage has been applied in subsequent cases, where it has proved sufficient that the investigation was pending for a certain period after the date of ratification, even where the death itself and abortive investigations dated back more than ten years. The "genuine connection" test appears to boil down in practice to whether there were any investigative steps pending or ongoing after the date of ratification.

Nor is understanding aided by the further statement that the Court would not exclude that in certain circumstances the "connection" between the death and date of ratification could also be based on the need to ensure that the guarantees and the underlying values of the Convention are protected in a real and effective manner, a formulation described as "Delphic".[7] Since Art.2 is the most important of the Convention rights, it is difficult to assess whether this is meant to ensure jurisdiction where a new investigation is launched into a particularly heinous or large scale incident occurring long before the crucial ratification date; however, it is difficult to see how a test could, without being arbitrary, hope to distinguish sensibly between numbers of victims and the kind of outrages involved in past incidents.[8] Given the contemporary predilection for holding public inquiries into past controversial events, particularly when the purported crimes occurred under the aegis of a previous regime, would temporal jurisdiction attach to the Katyn Forest massacre during World War Two[9] or even further back to the hotly-disputed "Armenian genocide" in the early twentieth century? Bearing in mind that a State would not be under an

[5] e.g. *Moldovan and Others v Romania*, (41138/98) and (64320/01) (Dec.) March 13, 2001; *Voroshilov v Russia*, (21501/02) (Dec.) December 8, 2005.

[6] See Judge Lorenzen's separate opinion which focuses on the temporal nature of the relevant "connection".

[7] See the Supreme Court's analysis of *Silih v Slovenia*, April 4, 2009 in *In the matter of an application by Brigid McCaughey and another for Judicial Review (Northern Ireland)*, May 18, 2011.

[8] See the dissenting opinions of Judges Bratza and Turmen disagreeing as to the "detachability" of the procedural obligation and pointing to the difficulties of understanding the test of a "genuine connection" between the death and the date of ratification and of a "significant proportion" of procedural steps.

[9] Complaints arising out of the murder of large numbers of Polish officers in 1940 have indeed recently been declared admissible: see *Janowiec v Russia*, (55508/07) and (29520/09) (Dec.) July 5, 2011, where the Government's objection on temporal jurisdiction has been joined to the merits. Judgment on the merits not likely to issue before 2012.

obligation to start an inquiry into a past alleged crime against humanity, if it chose, freely, to do so, it is not perhaps helpful for the State to attract as a result, the full weight of Art.2 supervision. Such a consequence might have a "chilling effect" on such exercises which may at that stage be not so much a conscientious exercise in imposing criminal justice but about political messages, transparency, achieving closure and setting history straight.

As to how the test has applied in concrete cases, in *Silih* itself, the death had occurred in May 1993 while Slovenia had ratified in June 1994; both the criminal and civil proceedings concerning the death had commenced shortly before that date and then dragged on for years afterwards. The Court found a close connection between the death and ratification (barely a year in time) and most of the procedures took place afterwards.[10] Temporal jurisdiction attached. In a case about violent suppression of a demonstration in 1989, the State had only ratified in June 1994, more than five years later. However, the Court merely noted, briefly, that most of the proceedings, which had been subject to various re-openings, had occurred after that date and thus were within its jurisdiction.[11]

(ii) Disappearances

II–655 Where a victim disappeared before the date of ratification of the right of individual petition, the event itself falls outside the Court's temporal jurisdiction. However, as held in *Varnava and Others v Turkey*, given the sui generis nature of disappearance, in particular the hallmark uncertainty attached to the fate of the missing person, the procedural obligation is of a continuing nature and may, potentially, persist as long as the fate of the person is unaccounted for. This is regardless of whether death may, eventually, be presumed. The *Silih* test does not apply. Thus, where men had gone missing in 1974 in life-threatening circumstances under the responsibility of the Turkish authorities and not been seen since, the Court had temporal jurisdiction some 13 years later at the date of ratification by Turkey to examine complaints whether the State had properly accounted for their fate and whereabouts through an effective Art.2 investigation.

(b) Exhaustion of domestic remedies

II–656 Before the extensive development of the procedural obligation, it was considered that exhaustion of domestic remedies applied to Art.2 in the same manner as other provisions of the Convention. It would be necessary for applicants to apply to the civil courts for findings of unlawful conduct and for an award of damages. There was the rider only that, to avoid States buying their way out of gross human rights violations, this did not apply to an administrative practice.[12]

[10] See also *Velcea and Mazare v Romania*, December 1, 2009, paras 85 and 88, death occurred in January 1993, some seventeen months before ratification, most of the procedures afterwards; temporal jurisdiction applied.

[11] See *Sandru v Romania*, December 8, 2009; also *Agache v Romania*, October 20, 2009. See also *Teren Aksakal v Turkey*, September 11, 2007, where the victim died in 1980 and over six years elapsed until the date of ratification; *Efimenko v Ukraine*, November 25, 2010, lapse of four years and three months between death and ratification.

[12] See *Caraher v UK*, (24520/94) (Dec.) January 11, 200, citing *Donnelly v UK*, (5577–5583/72) (Dec.) December 15, 1975, DR 4, p.4 at para.66.

Thus, in cases concerning killing by the security forces of alleged terrorist suspects in Northern Ireland, the Court did not consider any need to examine a complaint further where the family of a victim had accepted civil damages.[13] In cases from Northern Ireland, where civil proceedings were pending brought by families of victims shot by soldiers, the Court stated that it was not its role to seek, in place of the civil courts, to establish the facts and liability for any allegedly unlawful acts and declined to examine these complaints of substantive Convention responsibility for the deaths. It did, however, examine separately the procedural head, namely whether there had been an effective criminal investigation.[14]

When Strasbourg's attention was turned to problems of excessive use of force and killings by security forces in conflicts in south-east Turkey and the Chechnya region, the Court held that it was not required for families of victims killed allegedly by security forces to go to the civil courts to exhaust domestic remedies. However, this was in two very specific contexts. In Turkey, the Court considered that vulnerable victims were entitled to rely on public prosecutors finding facts, identifying perpetrators and bringing prosecutions which they could join as civil parties.[15] In the Chechen cases, where the civil court system did not effectively function during the period of conflict, it was found that civil actions were incapable, without the benefit of the conclusions of a criminal investigation of making meaningful findings as to the perpetrators of fatal assaults or to establish their responsibility; the civil system was regarded as undermined by the malfunctioning of the criminal justice system.[16] Against the background of these two lines of case-law and the circumstance that in many continental jurisdictions, families of victims may, and frequently do, choose the path of joining criminal prosecutions as civil parties of some kind, the Court's case-law from continental systems tends to find the availability of civil remedies beside the point and concentrate its examination on whether there was an effective investigation in both the context of domestic remedies and the procedural obligation in itself.[17] Both points are often decided together.[18]

Nonetheless, occasionally the Court continues to examine whether there any concrete factors which could deprive the civil courts of their ability to establish the facts and determine any liability for a death and has made findings that a civil remedy should have been exhausted for the purposes of Art.35, para.1 as regarded the complaint of a substantive obligation under Art.2; it has then examined the procedural obligation separately.[19] For the United Kingdom and Ireland, a victim's family would still be expected to bring civil proceedings if they claimed the State was responsible for the death; the existence of an effective criminal investigation would still be likely only to be relevant under the procedural head. The conflicting approaches may have to be brought before the Grand Chamber for resolution as

[13] *Caraher*, fn.12 above. See more recently *Obiora v Norway*, (55508/07) and (29520/09) (Dec.) June 21, 2011, where the applicant had settled his civil case concerning the death of a relative subjected to considerable force by police on arrest, in full and final settlement, he had renounced use of local remedies and could not claim to be a victim.

[14] See, e.g. *McKerr v UK*, May 2001, paras 116–121.

[15] See the Court's reasoning in *McKerr v UK*, fn.14 above, paras 116–121.

[16] See, e.g. *Khashiyev and Akiyeva v Russia*, February 24, 2005, paras 119–122, para.185, thus, the award of damages without a proper factual and liability assessment was not enough in that case.

[17] See, e.g. *Eugenia Lazar v Romania*, February 16, 2010, para.90, where civil remedies had no hope of success where there was no criminal conviction as notions of fault were allied to the penal sense.

[18] See, e.g. *Betayev and Betayeva v Russia*, May 29, 2008, paras 63 and 89–90.

[19] See, e.g. *Dvoracek and Dvorackova v Slovakia*, July 28, 2009, para.49.

under both Arts 2 and 3 there are now categorical statements in leading cases that seem to make an effective criminal investigation crucial both for remedies and victim status and to dispense families from troubling with civil proceedings (see further below on victim status). Where there is a fully-effective civil law system capable of attributing responsibility for deaths and awarding damages, this seems to run counter to the principle of subsidiarity and risks making the Court a compensation tribunal for relatives of victims of unlawful deaths.

(c) Victim status[20]

II–657 Where the domestic system does make some response to a death, the question will arise whether this is sufficient to redress any violations and render the deceased's relatives no longer victims for the purposes of the Convention. The test for whether victim status is lost is whether the domestic authorities have acknowledged the breach, expressly or in substance and then afforded redress to the victim.[21]

The Court has stated that an unlawful killing, however, cannot be remedied exclusively by an award of compensation—this would allow the State to buy its way out of serious human rights violations and afford impunity to the perpetrators. It has taken that approach which had previously only applied in relation to systemic practices and to remedies which did not allow any allocation of responsibility, whether criminal or civil, and extended it in such a way as to make the provision of an effective criminal investigation an indispensable part of redress offered to any person complaining of unjustified killing. Thus in *Nikolova and Velichkova v Bulgaria*,[22] where two police officers assaulted, without any justification whatsoever, a man who later died of his injuries, it was not sufficient to remove victim status that the victim's family had received an award of civil damages; the Court examined whether there had also been an effective criminal justice response.[23] Similarly, in *Leonidis v Greece*, where the victim's family had received €80,000 in compensation proceedings for the shooting by a policeman, the Court rejected the Government's objection of lack of victim status, considering the issue of effectiveness of the criminal investigation had to be determined first.[24] This can lead to confusion. The procedural aspect is separate from the substantive one; it is not logically, or otherwise, necessary to make victim status for a substantive breach dependent on whether or not there has been a procedural or investigative breach. In *Leonids*, as the victim issue had been joined to the merits, the Court overlooked in examining the justification for the killing, that the procedural point was outstanding and found a substantive breach of Art.2 due to the shooting by the police officer. Then, proceeding to examine the adequacy of the criminal investigation and trial, it found the procedures fully compliant with the Art.2 requirements. Thus, due to circular reasoning, the deceased's family retained victim status although they had received compensation and there had been a proper and thorough criminal investigation and trial. A purely formal finding of a substantive breach was reached, echoing the

[20] See general principles in Part IB: Admissibility Checklist, sub-s.3: Manifestly ill-founded, para.I–047, concerning loss of victim status.

[21] e.g. De *Scordino (No.1) v Italy*, March 29, 2006, para.193.

[22] *Nikolova and Velichkova v Bulgaria*, December 20, 2007.

[23] *Nikolova and Velichkova v Bulgaria*, see fn.22 above.

[24] *Leonidis v Greece*, January 9, 2009.

findings of the domestic bodies, and the Court made no award of just satisfaction as, after all, the family had already received damages on the domestic level.

Further, the Court's case-law has been extended in relation to what constitutes a satisfactory outcome to an investigation and trial to also cover adequate sentencing of the perpetrator. Where trials for unlawful deaths are concerned, "national courts should not under any circumstances be prepared to allow life-endangering offences to go unpunished" due to the need to maintain public confidence and the rule of law. So, in *Nikolova and Velichkova*, where the criminal courts convicted officers of negligently causing death by wilfully inflicting grievous bodily harm and only imposed the minimum prison sentence, a three-year sentence suspended for five years, the Court considered that this was an inadequate response and in manifest disproportion to the seriousness of the offence. Thus, the applicants could still claim to be victims of both the substantive killing and the procedural lack of effective investigation and trial. This approach, conflicting somewhat with the Court's oft-stated dictum that there is no right to obtain the prosecution and conviction of any particular person, seems to curtail the domestic court's discretion to mitigate a sentence. In *Nikolova and Velichkova*, the domestic courts had taken into account the young age and previous good record of the officers and considered that an immediate custodial sentence was not appropriate; this had apparently not been permissible.

In cases where the death is not caused intentionally, but from negligence, oversight or error, it has been acknowledged that criminal proceedings are not always relevant and that findings of responsibility by a civil or administrative court, as well an award of compensation, will generally remove victim status.[25] However just as with sentencing in the criminal cases, in assessing victim status being removed by civil court decision, the Court will examine the sufficiency of the award made. In *Oyal v Turkey*,[26] it was not enough that the civil courts awarded a large sum to the applicant, infected with HIV at birth from contaminated blood, since in fact this only covered one year of treatment; the Court considered that as the applicant required medical care for the rest of his life this redress was not satisfactory and he remained a victim. On a finding of a violation of Art.2, it then ordered that the Turkish Government provide him with free and full medical coverage for life.

(d) *Six months*

As concerns allegedly unlawful or unjustified deaths, the six month time-limit runs from the final decision in the process of exhaustion of domestic remedies under Art.35, para.1. Where criminal remedies are concerned, the relatives of the deceased II–658

[25] e.g. *Oyal v Turkey*, March 23, 2010, para.68, no requirement for criminal proceedings for allegedly negligent supervision of the blood banks; *Florea Pop v Romania*, April 6, 2010, paras 37–47, where the applicant's son died shortly after release from detention, from TB and other health complications, which it was found was not diagnosed promptly by the detention centre for minors due to a series of shortcomings in care and treatment from various persons and bodies involved in his care. It was sufficient to remove the victim status that the applicant's father obtained due to a finding from the civil courts of the responsibility of minister and department in charge of prisons, and award damages, which if on the small side, reflected in fact what the applicant had asked for.

[26] *Oyal v Turkey*, fn.25 above, paras 71–72 and 101.

are expected to take steps to keep track of the investigation's progress, or lack thereof, and to lodge their applications with due expedition once they are, or should have become, aware of the lack of any effective criminal investigation.[27] This is to prevent families waiting for years during an inactive investigation before bringing their complaints to Strasbourg. This approach also applies to the substantive aspect of disappearances; the families of the missing are required a certain diligence in bringing a complaint alleging State responsibility for the disappearance as soon as they become aware that the investigation is ineffective.[28] In practice this should mean complaints are lodged within months, or at most a few years of the death itself without waiting for long periods. In *Abuyeva and Others v Russia*, the Court found exceptionally no lack of diligence where complaints were lodged in 2005 about many deaths and injuries during a major military operation in a Chechen town in 2000: given the number of applicants, the complexity of the investigation and the failure of the authorities to keep the families informed of the investigative steps, it had not been unreasonable for the applicants to wait some time in expectation of being notified of the results.[29]

However, as the procedural obligation to investigate disappearances is based on a continuing situation, the ongoing failure of the authorities to account for the fate of the missing person, the six-month time-limit applies with more flexibility to reflect the uncertain circumstances. There remains however a duty of diligence on the families who should bring their complaints of lack of effective investigation to Strasbourg as soon as they have become aware that that no investigation has been instigated or that the investigation has lapsed into inaction or become ineffective and, in any of those eventualities, there is no immediate, realistic prospect of an effective investigation being provided in the future. Thus, in *Varnava*, where there was a complex international conflict scenario, the applicants were not penalised for awaiting developments in the UN-brokered Committee of Missing Persons; it was only as late as end of 1990 that they should have been aware that this avenue was so marred by problems and offered such limited redress as to remove its effectiveness as a remedy.[30] Nor where the applicant's husband went missing in 1995 in war-torn ex-Yugoslavia did she show undue diligence in introducing her complaint in Strasbourg some nine years later, since in the interval there had been considerable and meaningful international and domestic developments setting up a framework for investigating disappearances giving reasonable prospects for the launch of an effective investigation.[31]

Where an investigation into a death has long ended, it is possible that new developments occur such that a fresh obligation to investigate arises, for example, fresh evidence casting doubt on the results of an earlier investigation or trial. In these circumstances, the complaints will not be rejected for being more than six months since the end of the earlier investigation.[32] A fresh obligation arose where a

[27] See *Bulut and Yavuz v Turkey*, (73065/01) (Dec.) 28 May 2002; *Bayram and Yıldırım v Turkey*, (38587/97) January 29, 2001.

[28] *Eren v Turkey*, (42428/98) (Dec.) July 4, 2002; *Üçak and Kargili v Turkey*, (75527/01) and (11837/02) (Dec.) March 28, 2006.

[29] *Abuyeva and Others v Russia*, December 2, 2010, paras 172–182. See also *Kerimova v Russia*, May 3, 2011, paras 198–203, obstructiveness by the authorities in providing the applicants with decisions and informing them of the status of the case justified delays in coming to Strasbourg in 2004–2005 concerning deaths occurring in 1999.

[30] *Varnava and Others*, fn.4 above, paras 165–172.

[31] *Palic v Bosnia-Herzegovina*, February 15, 2011, paras 48–52.

[32] See *Brecknell v UK* November 27, 2007, paras 65–72.

witness came forward making plausible allegations about security force collusion in a sectarian killing,[33] and where the person convicted of a murder made revelations years after his trial alleging his confession had been false, seeking to protect the real killer.[34] The scope of the fresh obligation to investigate may be restricted to verifying the reliability of the new evidence and the authorities can legitimately take into account the prospects of launching a new prosecution at such a late stage.[35] Where long after an investigation is ended an applicant applies to the authorities who take some steps in response, this is insufficient in itself to generate a fresh obligation to investigate; in other words, an applicant cannot avoid the application of the due diligence criterion by prodding the authorities into some semblance of an investigation after a long lull in investigative activity, unless, that is, there is some new evidence or development casting fresh light on the death.[36]

(e) Applicability of Art.2

Article 2 applies mainly to situations where a person is killed, but may also, in exceptional circumstances, extend to life-threatening attacks or incidents where a person survives.[37] In *Ilhan v Turkey*, the Court found that Art.3, rather than Art.2, was violated by the excessive use of force on arrest which caused the victim serious brain damage. It commented that the degree and type of force, as well as the intention or aim of the perpetrators, would be relevant in assessing whether a particular use of force inflicting injury short of death infringed the object and purpose of Art.2. In *Makaratzis*, where an applicant was wounded during an uncontrolled and reckless high speed car chase by armed police officers, Art.2 applied as he was the victim of conduct which, by its very nature, put his life at risk. The impugned conduct of the police officers was also such as called for examination under Art.2.[38] II–659

The cases have been somewhat conflicting as to whether the injury suffered should in fact be serious or life-threatening or whether it is enough that the use of force was potentially life-threatening. In *Vasil Sachev Petrov v Bulgaria*, the Court found Art.2 applicable where the applicant was shot while running away and at close distance by police officers, one of whom deliberately aimed at him rather than in the air and inflicted injuries that were temporarily life-threatening, not least because the officers failed to inform the doctor treating the applicant that he had been shot and he later had to undergo an operation to remove a kidney and part of his liver: these circumstances rendered the applicant "the victim of conduct which,

[33] *Brecknell* fn.32 above, paras 73–75.

[34] *Hackett v UK*, (34698/04) (Dec.) May 10, 2005. See also *Gasyak v Turkey*, October 13, 2009, paras 61–63, new evidence of perpetrators of a killing.

[35] See *Brecknell*, fn.32 above, paras 79–81; *Hackett*, fn.34 above.

[36] See e.g. *Finozhenok v Russia*, (3025/06) (Dec.) May 31, 2011; *Hackett*, fn.34 above.

[37] See *Ilhan v Turkey*, June 27, 2000, ECHR 2000–VII, paras 76–77. Also cases, concerning positive obligations to protect life, in which Art.2 applied although the applicant was still alive: *Osman v UK*, October 28, 1998, R.J.D., 1998–VIII, No.95, 29 E.H.R.R. 245, paras 115–122, where the applicant had been injured and his father killed by a teacher against whom they had sought protection from the police; *Yasa v Turkey*, September 2, 1998, R.J.D. 1998–VI, No.88, 28 E.H.R.R. 408, paras 92–108, where the applicant had been shot eight times by an unknown gunman; *LCB v UK*, June 9, 1998, R.J.D. 1998–III, paras 36–41, concerning complaints by the daughter of a serviceman, who was exposed to radiation on Christmas Island, about lack of information from the authorities about the risks to her health.

[38] See also *Evrim Oktem v Turkey*, November 4, 2008, Art.2 applicable where a young demonstrator's knee was shattered when a police officer opened fire in circumstances putting life at risk.

by its very nature, put his life at risk, even though, in the event, he survived".[39] In a case concerning mass casualties during an operation to put down a prison riot, Art.2 applied to the prisoners who were seriously injured, and Art.3 to those whose injuries had been less severe.[40] Where the applicant was struck once in the back by a special riot control bullet and did not suffer life-threatening injury, Art.2 did not apply, even if such bullets could be lethal at short range.[41] In contrast where a TV journalist filming a police operation was shot by police officers, the Court downplayed the fact that the injury to his legs was not life-threatening, noting that he had been the target of a flurry of shots which had been potentially lethal: Art.2 applied.[42]

In some situations of mass casualties, where life has been lost and some victims survived, or only suffered injuries, by chance, Art.2 may be applied to all those who came under threat of danger. In *Budayeva v Russia*, where a village was engulfed by a mudslide, the provision covered those who lost relatives, those who were injured and those who escaped by the skin of their teeth.[43]

In disappearance scenarios, it may not be known whether the person has in fact died. However, where the person has disappeared in a life-threatening context[44] or in one case, where a vulnerable old person had been missing for a period of time which qualified for a presumption of death under domestic law,[45] Art.2 applied.

3. Use of lethal force

II–660 The situations listed in the second paragraph are the only justifications allowed for killing people: namely, defence of others, lawful arrest or prevention of the escape of a person lawfully detained or action lawfully taken for the purpose of quelling a riot or insurrection. The use of lethal force for these purposes must be no more than "absolutely necessary". This necessity test indicates that a stricter and more compelling test must be applied than under other provisions of the Convention which refer to necessity alone. The use of force must be "strictly proportionate".[46] There should therefore be no, or at least less, scope for the use of the "margin of appreciation". The Commission and Court have not made reference to the term expressly in this context.

However, as always, the Convention organs will have regard to the circumstances of the use of force, in particular, the nature of the aim pursued, dangers to life and limb inherent in the situation and the degree of risk that the force employed might result in loss of life.[47]

Allegations that State agents were involved in the lethal use of force in circumstances infringing Art.2 must be established by proof beyond reasonable

[39] *Vasil Sachev Petrov v Bulgaria*, June 10, 2010, paras 39–41. See also *Peker v Turkey (No.2)*, April 12, 2011, where the applicant was shot by gendarmes during a prison operation, his life had been put at risk and his survival "fortuitous": it was not specified whether his injury had been life-threatening though.

[40] *Perisan v Turkey*, May 20, 2010, paras 75–93.

[41] *Tsekov v Bulgaria*, February 23, 2006, paras 40–44, it might also be relevant that the conduct of the police officers was not grossly reckless or inappropriate having regard to their duties and the situation.

[42] *Trevalec v Belgium*, June 14, 2011, paras 53–60.

[43] *Budayeva v Russia*, March 20, 2008, ECHR 2008–. . .

[44] e.g. the violent conflict in southeast Turkey and in Chechnya— see further sub-s.3(c)(ii): Disappearance.

[45] *Dodov v Bulgaria*, January 17, 2008, para.68.

[46] (10044/82) (Dec.) July 10, 1984, 38 D.R. 162.

[47] (10044/82), fn.46 above.

doubt,[48] though this may include sufficiently strong, clear and concordant inferences.[49] Special presumptions operate in the contexts of disappearances and deaths in custody; and where a person is found dead or injured in an area under the exclusive control of the authorities, the burden lies on them to provide a satisfactory and convincing explanation of how the events in question occurred.[50] Where the authorities manifestly fail to elucidate the circumstances of a killing by State officers, the Court has taken this into account in assessing whether there was any Convention-compatible justification for the shooting, noting that to accept explanations not properly supported by an objective investigation would be to allow a Government to benefit from its own shortcomings. Thus, where it was never established whether the victim of a police shooting had in fact been armed with a knife as alleged by the officer, the Court rejected the Government's assertion that the killing had been in legitimate self-defence.[51]

(a) *Deliberate versus non-intentional infliction of loss of life*

Notwithstanding the use of the word "intentionally" in the first paragraph, Art.2 has been interpreted to cover the accidental deprivation of life by the use of lethal force. This question arose in the context of the death of a 13–year-old boy who was struck by a rubber bullet, fired by a soldier who was facing a barrage of missiles thrown by rioters. The domestic courts had found that the soldier had not intended to injure the boy; he had aimed at a rioter standing next to him and his aim was deflected when a missile struck his shoulder. The Commission considered that Art.2, taken as a whole, must be interpreted as defining the situations where it is permissible to use force which may, whether intended or not, result in the deprivation of life. Any other interpretation would not, in the Commission's view, have been consistent with the object and purpose of the Convention or with a strict interpretation of the obligation to protect life.[52] II–661

(b) *Standard of domestic law and regulatory frameworks*

In *McCann and Others v UK*, the applicants argued that the applicable domestic law should protect the right to life. The Commission agreed to the extent that this required national law to regulate in a manner compatible with the rule of law the II–662

[48] *Kaya*, fn.2 above, para.76. Insufficient factual and evidentiary basis for complaints led to no violation where the applicant alleged that his brother, a farmer, was riddled with bullets in his fields while the security forces alleged that he was killed during a clash with armed terrorists.

[49] e.g. *Aktas v Turkey*, April 24, 2003, inferences were drawn from the Government's unsatisfactory response to Commission requests for information and witnesses and this together with evidence of injuries in the autopsy report, consistent with death by mechanical asphyxia, furnished proof beyond reasonable doubt that the victim was subjected in custody to violence that caused his death.

[50] e.g. *Akkum v Turkey*, March 24, 2005, ECHR 2005–II, paras 210–211, the Government failed to account for the deaths of villagers during a military operation; *Mansurolu v Turkey*, February 26, 2008, paras 80–81, burden on the Government to show that the use of deadly force during an operation was absolutely necessary and strictly proportionate to an authorised aim.

[51] *Soare v Romania*, February 22, 2011, paras 141–150.

[52] (10044/82) (Dec.) July 10, 1984, 39 D.R. See, more recently, *Makaratzis v Greece*, December 20, 2004, ECHR 2004–XII, para.55, Art.2 applied irrespective of whether or not the police intended to kill the applicant; *Saoud v France*, October 9, 2007, Art.2 applicable to accidental death flowing from immobilisation techniques on arrest.

permissible use of force by its agents. Both Commission and Court did not accept that the fact that domestic law imposed a test of reasonableness as opposed to absolute necessity, indicated a failure to comply with the Convention standard.[53] A State was not bound to use the same formulation, which would be tantamount to requiring incorporation into domestic law of the Convention. The Court noted that the Convention test appeared stricter but did not consider that the difference between the two standards was sufficiently great to found a violation alone.[54]

A case, however, where the criminal and/or civil courts rejected an applicant's claims on the basis of reasonable necessity in light of facts which the Convention organs found disclosed no justification under the Convention would cast doubt on the adequacy of the domestic law standard. Thus, in *Nachova v Bulgaria*, where the authorities decided not to bring charges against an officer who shot dead two absconding conscripts on the ground that the regulations on the use of force had been complied with, the Court found that the legal framework was fundamentally deficient, failing to provide protection "by law" of the right to life: it had been lawful to shoot any fugitive who did not surrender immediately in response to an oral warning and a warning shot in the air, no relevance attaching to the crucial fact that the two men, who had committed non-violent offences, did not pose any threat to the arresting officers.[55]

To prevent arbitrariness and abuse, and even avoidable accident, the use of force by police or other security forces must not only be authorised under national law, but their operations must be sufficiently regulated by it, within a framework of adequate and effective safeguards.[56] While it was argued in *McCann and Others* that domestic law was too general and that specific, clear and detailed rules were required, reference being made, inter alia, to the UN Basic Principles on the use of Firearms by Law Enforcement Officials, the Court found that the rules of engagement for military and police personnel provided regulation of the use of force which reflected the domestic and Convention standard. In *Makaratzis*, the framework in place was "slender", consisting of a general prohibition without any detailed provisions regulating the use of weapons by the police or guidelines on the planning and control of police operations. The lack of proper structure, channels of communication and guidelines was responsible in that case for a largely uncontrolled car chase, where officers fired volleys of shots with pistols and machine guns. This failure to put in place an adequate legislative and administrative framework with safeguards to avoid risk to life breached the standard required by Art.2.[57]

[53] The Government had argued that in practice the reasonable necessity test took into account all requisite factors. The Commission found that whether or not the application of the reasonable necessity standard permitted the use of force in contravention of Art.2 could only be determined by an examination of the case before it: see also (17579/90) (Dec.) February 13, 1993, 74 D.R. 139.

[54] See also *Perk v Turkey*, March 28, 2006, para.60, no significant difference between domestic standard and Art.2; *Giuliani and Gaggio v Italy*, March 24, 2011, ECHR 2011–. . . , paras 211–215, insufficient difference in standards.

[55] *Nachova v Bulgaria*, July 6, 2005, ECHR 2005–VII, paras 99–102.

[56] *Makaratzis*, fn.52 above, para.58. See also *Nachova*, fn.55 above, para.96, concerning proper domestic approach to using force on arrest.

[57] See also *Hamiyet Kaplan v Turkey*, September 13, 2005, para.55, lack of clear and detailed guidelines on use of force in police operation; *Soare*, fn.51 above, paras 135–137, lack of clear guidelines and training on use of force in arrest situations.

(c) *Justifiable exceptions*

(i) Defence of others (Art.2, para.2(a))

In *McCann and Others*, SAS soldiers shot dead three IRA terrorists believing, they said, that the suspects were about to detonate a bomb in the centre of Gibraltar. In fact, there was no bomb in Gibraltar, nor were the terrorists carrying any arms or any object connected with any possible detonation of a bomb. Objectively therefore, three people were shot dead in circumstances where they posed no immediate risk and could have been taken into custody without difficulty. The case was surrounded by controversy. It was alleged that the security forces had deliberately executed the terrorists rather than bring them to trial. II–663

The Commission commented in strong terms on the alleged shoot-to-kill policy, which would be in flagrant violation of the Convention. A terrorist's right to life is also protected under Art.2 as is his or her right to fair trial on any allegations of criminal actions. Both the Commission and Court however, looking at the soldiers' actions, found that the soldiers were under an honest belief, due to the information given to them, that it was necessary to shoot the IRA suspects to prevent them detonating a bomb. Such an honest belief which is perceived for good reasons to be valid at the time could still be justified under Art.2 even if it turned out to be mistaken. To hold otherwise would put an unrealistic burden on law enforcement officers. The Court has since stated that it would require convincing evidence to find a premeditated plan by police to kill during an operation.[58]

A standard of honest belief, based on good reasons, also applied in *Andronicou and Constantinou v Cyprus*, where a security team shot both the hostage and the hostage-taker. The Court regretted the level of firepower used but giving allowance for "the heat of the moment" considered that the officers honestly and reasonably believed that they and the hostage were at risk from the armed hostage-taker and that they were entitled to open fire to eliminate that risk.[59] Where terrorist suspects opened fire on police first, the Court considered that in the circumstances the police were entitled to react by firing back, under the reasonable belief that this was necessary to protect their own and others' lives, without first attempting to neutralise the suspects through tear gas or stun grenades.[60] An honest belief by a police officer that his life was in danger from rioters attacking a jeep, one of whom appeared about to throw a fire extinguisher at him, rendered the use of force compatible with Art.2.[61]

The shooting of 50–55 bullets through a door, causing multiple and fatal injuries, on an unseen target in a residential block occupied by innocent civilians, women and children was found to be a grossly disproportionate response by special team officers in *Gül v Turkey*,[62] where the Court found that they had no reasonable belief that their lives were at risk.

[58] *Perk*, fn.54 above, para.59.

[59] Also *Brady v UK*, (55151/00) (Dec.) April 3, 2001, where a policeman killed a robber in the mistaken belief that the man had a gun, the Court found that this honest belief was explicable by "visual perception distortion" caused by stress and poor lighting; and *Bubbins v UK*, March 17, 2005, paras 139–140, where the officer was faced with a man with gun which he could not know was a replica.

[60] *Perk*, fn.54 above, para.72, although there was a procedural breach for failing in the investigation to examine the planning of the operation, particularly whether other means should have been used (para.81).

[61] *Guiliani and Gaggio*, fn.54 above, paras 189–196.

[62] *Gül v Turkey*, December 14, 2007.

(II) TO EFFECT A LAWFUL ARREST OR PREVENT THE ESCAPE OF SOMEONE LAWFULLY DETAINED (ART.2, PARA.2(B))

II–664 There is no justification for using lethal force under this head where the person to be arrested poses no threat to life or limb and is not suspected of having committed a violent offence, even if there is a risk of the suspect escaping.[63] Even pursuing non-violent suspects with gun in hand was found excessive, where the officer slipped and the weapon accidentally fired with lethal result.[64] As in the context of self-defence, the Court examines not only the proportionality of the use of force by the officer concerned, but also the manner in which the arrest operation was planned and controlled[65] and whether the national law regulating policing operations provides a system of adequate and effective safeguards against arbitrariness and abuse of force and avoidable accident[66] and in particular that law-enforcement agents have been trained to assess whether or not there is an absolute necessity to use firearms, not only on the basis of the letter of the relevant regulations, but also with due regard to the pre-eminence of respect for human life.[67]

There has been no case concerning the second limb.

As regards the first limb—the effecting of a lawful arrest—this was found to justify the use of lethal force by soldiers to stop a car of joy riders which drove through a Belfast checkpoint. The Commission accepted that given a reasonable belief that the occupants of the case were terrorists (their manner of driving put the soldiers at risk) the shooting at the car could be justified as absolutely necessary to effect a lawful arrest. This conclusion flew in the face of the domestic court's findings in the civil proceedings that the soldiers could not rely on the defence of arrest since the occupants of the car had not committed any serious offence when the incident arose. The Commission's decision does not explain this apparent contradiction. The level of force used to stop the car was also not found to be excessive or disproportionate, although the applicant had pointed out there was no attempt to fire at the tyres or take other steps to apprehend the vehicle and that no consideration was given to the known fact that cars going through checkpoints were as likely to be joy riders, drunken motorists or inadvertent drivers. The Commission gave special regard to the difficult situation in Belfast and to the extreme circumstances of the *Kelly* case, where the soldiers had only seconds to react to an apparently determined effort to evade the checkpoint which had caused one soldier minor injury.[68]

Conversely, in a Turkish case, where a soldier shot dead the driver of a car which passed through a checkpoint without stopping, the Commission distinguished it from *Kelly*, since the manner in which the driver, an ordinary civilian working for the State authorities, behaved was not shown to be suspicious.[69] A recent case, not

[63] *Kakoulli v Turkey*, October 22, 2005, paras 108 and 119, mere suspicious conduct is not enough even in a zone of tension; *Wasilewska and Kalucka v Poland*, February 23, 2010, paras 52–53, even if the suspects had posed a risk to the officers' safety initially, at the moment the officers opened fire that risk was no longer present and they were firing merely to stop the suspects escaping.

[64] *Alikaj v Italy*, March 29, 2011, para.73.

[65] e.g. *Bubbins*, fn.59 above, para.136.

[66] *Makaratzis*, fn.52 above, para.58

[67] *Wasilewska and Kalucka*, fn.63 above, para.45.

[68] *Kelly v UK*, May 4, 2001, ECHR 2001–III, para.114. Also see fn.53 above.

[69] *Aytekin v Turkey*, September 23, 1998, R.J.D 1998–VII, the Court did not consider the merits of the case, however, as material arose leading it to uphold the Government's preliminary objection on non-exhaustion.

too dissimilar from *Kelly*, would seem to indicate that a more rigorous approach is now being taken even where the car is being driven in a suspicious and dangerous manner. In *Wasilewska and Kalucka v Poland*, the Court seems to have accepted that the police officers were justified in using their weapons when the car full of suspects drove at them but it found the manner in which they did so was unjustified, in particular since most of the bullets were fired once the car had passed and the officers were no longer in danger. Further, although the officers claimed to have been shooting at the tyres, the bullets hit the body of the car, and the occupants instead. The Court also considered that the planning and conduct of the arrest operation was deficient, inter alia, since some police officers were in plain clothes, leading to some confusion as to their identity (the survivors claimed that they thought that they were being attacked by robbers), noting that for a pre-organised operation the plan seemed somewhat vague, that there was a confusion in the orders given and that no provision for an ambulance being present had been made although a gang-type conflict was predicted.[70] The case might possibly be distinguishable from *Kelly* on the ground that in the Northern Irish case, the incident arose without warning or the opportunity for prior planning, the soldiers having to react to an apparent threat in a matter of seconds. However, in *Juozaitienė and Bikulčius v Lithuania*,[71] where the police officers also responded to an unforeseen incident, the Court considered that firing many bullets at a car unjustifiably put the lives of the occupants at risk and could only be acceptable to counter a clear and imminent danger; there was accordingly a violation since there was no convincing case that the car, however recklessly it was being driven, was putting the police officers', or anyone else's, lives at risk or anyone else's at the time they riddled it with bullets.[72]

The use of lethal force in an attempt to arrest two absconding conscripts, who were unarmed and had no record of violence, disclosed grossly excessive force, in particular with regard to use of a rifle on automatic setting and the other options available to effect the arrest.[73]

Where a drug addict in a precarious state of health died after being forcibly arrested, there was no liability where the police officers had no reason to suspect any risk from conventional arrest techniques.[74] However, given the subsequent wealth of material attesting to the lethal danger of positional asphyxia flowing from the immobilisation technique of pinning a person chest down on the floor for any prolonged period, the Court found a violation where a suspect died after being so immobilised for 35 minutes, despite the fact that he was secured by wrists and ankles and was injured; it gave decisive weight to the complete lack of instruction on the matter given to the officers involved.[75]

[70] *Wasilewska and Kalucka v Poland*, see fn.63 above.

[71] *Juozaitien·e and Bikulčius v Lithuania*, April 24, 2008.

[72] It was midnight and the streets hardly thronged with innocent passers-by. On that basis, there should also, arguably, have been a violation in the *Kelly* case, where the danger to be prevented had been stated domestically to have been that of potential future terrorist crime, a danger neither clear nor imminent.

[73] *Nachova*, fn.55 above, paras 106–108.

[74] *Scavuzzo-Hager v Switzerland*, February 7, 2006, para.61.

[75] See *Saoud v France*, fn.52 above, paras 98–104. Contrast the earlier case *Douglas-Williams v UK*, (56423/00) (Dec.) January 8, 2002, where the applicant's brother died after arrest from positional asphyxia caused by the method of restraint used, but it was found that the use of force had not been excessive to restrain a man armed with a knife and the evidence did not show in that case that the police officers could have foreseen his sudden collapse or had failed to respond adequately to his condition.

Where two police officers had no reason to believe a suspect might be armed, they were not at fault for failing to seek further information or calling for reinforcement before proceeding to the arrest which turned fatally violent.[76]

(iii) Action lawfully taken for the purpose of quelling a riot (Art.2, para.2(c))

II–665 There is no Convention definition of a riot. Where a 13–year-old boy died from a plastic bullet striking his head and the applicant denied that there was a riot situation, the Commission considered that, while definitions of what constituted a riot might differ between various jurisdictions, 150 people throwing missiles at a patrol of soldiers such that they risked serious injury did fall within the term. As to the justification for the firing of the bullet, it had regard to the continuous public disturbances which had given rise to loss of life in Northern Ireland, where such events were often used as cover for sniper attacks. Notwithstanding the arguments raised by the applicant as to the known risk to life from baton rounds, it concluded, given the threat facing the soldiers and the fact that the soldier's aim was disturbed when he fired, that the death resulted from the use of force no more than absolutely necessary for the purpose of quelling a riot.[77]

In *Gülec v Turkey*, the Court for the first time considered this limb of Art.2 where the applicant's 15–year-old son had been killed by a bullet fired by gendarmes during a demonstration which had turned unruly. While it accepted that the use of force might be justified under para.2(c), it was axiomatic that the response by State agents had to use proportionate means. Despite the fact that the region was subject to disorder, the gendarmes had only machine guns to cope with the crowd, no truncheons, riot shields, water cannons, tear gas or rubber bullets were available which the Court found incomprehensible and unacceptable. Unconvinced that armed terrorists had been amongst the crowd, the Court found the level of force used was not "absolutely necessary". Where officers fired on a crowd killing 17 people without first having recourse to less life-threatening methods, in finding the use of force was not absolutely necessary, the Court also emphasised the lack of centralised command and proper training of the officers as key *lacunae*.[78]

(e) Planning and control of the use of lethal force

II–666 The State has the responsibility in the planning and executing of operations to take steps to minimise the need for the use of lethal force. The Court has also referred to its role in evaluating whether the authorities were negligent in their choice of action.[79] Thus, in *McCann and Others*, even though it was found that the soldiers' own actions did not contravene Art.2, the lack of care in evaluating and providing adequate information to the soldiers and the failure to allow for other contingencies were identified, in the context of using soldiers trained to shoot to kill, as not

[76] *Ramsahai v Netherlands*, May 15, 2007, ECHR 2007–. . . , paras 282 and 288.
[77] See fn.53 above.
[78] *Simsek v Turkey*, July 26, 2005, paras 109–110. See also *Evrim Oktem*, fn.38 above, where the Court criticised the training and response of officers faced with an alleged violent mob situation, who, instead of waiting for support, launched an ill-considered attempt to arrest suspects and alleged, in vague terms, that they had to open fire to save their own lives.
[79] *Andronicou and Constantinou v Cyprus*, October 9, 1997, R.J.D. 1997–VII, No.52, 25 E.H.R.R. 491, para.181.

conforming with this standard. In *Andronicou and Constantinou v Cyprus*, the use of special teams, trained to kill, armed with sub-machine guns to intervene in a domestic dispute between a young couple was found by the Commission to increase the risk of injury and death. The Court, differing,[80] held that the decision to use the special team was considered one of last resort and did not disclose any lack of care, given that Andronicou was known to be armed and with a capacity for violence and that Elsie Constantinou had been screaming repeatedly that he was going to kill her. The Court saw no problem in the carrying of machine guns, since, inter alia, clear instructions had been issued as to their use and Andronicou was armed with a shotgun. It did not find that the officers had been supplied with misleading information as in *McCann and Others*.[81]

Conversely, in *Ogur v Turkey*, where the security officers were operating in fog without means of communicating between themselves and without any loudhailers, gross negligence was disclosed by the situation in which a night watchman was shot dead when mistaken for the escaping suspect, without any warning or warning shot being given. Failure of proper communication, where a police arrest team were not informed of the presence of a television camera crew, which led to the accidental shooting of a journalist, also fell short of Art.2 requirements.[82]

Agents of the State have to be trained to react with the degree of caution to be expected of law enforcement officers in a democratic society. Over-reaction was therefore a factor in finding a violation in *McCann and Others*, where the suspects were shot repeatedly at close range and, in the opinion of the Commission, in *Andronicou and Constantinou* where officers reacted to two shots by a rate of firing which rendered almost inevitable the death of the hostage they were seeking to rescue.[83]

Absence of clear rules as to the use of weapons by the police and insufficient training founded a violation where an officer, disobeying his superior, approached a violent and armed suspect, placing himself at risk and then drew his weapon, which then misfired, with fatal consequences, in a struggle with the suspect.[84]

Where operations take place in the vicinity of civilian populations, necessary steps must also be taken to avert the risk of inadvertent death or injury in any ensuing clash. In *Ergi v Turkey*, where the security forces set up an ambush for the PKK at the entrance to a village, and a clash ensued with firing across the houses resulting in the death of a young mother, the Court agreed with the Commission's findings that, in the absence of direct evidence by the State authorities on the planning and conduct of the ambush, it could reasonably be inferred that insufficient precautions had been taken to protect the lives of the civilian population. In *Isayeva v Russia*, there was a failure to take sufficient precautions to protect fleeing civilian refugees

[80] However, it found no violation by a narrow margin of five votes to four.

[81] See also *Bubbins*, fn.59 above, paras 141–151, where the police gave ample opportunities for the apparent gun man to surrender and took no precipitate action, the Court did not consider they could be held liable, due to public safety considerations, for positioning officers close to the rear of the flats (which put them in danger if he rushed out) or for not bringing in a special negotiator (though this last was regrettable); and *Huohvanainen v Finland*, March 13, 2007, where the siege was monitored, controlled and reviewed by senior officers, with their primary concern being to break the deadlock by persuasion.

[82] *Trevalec v Belgium*, fn. 42 above, paras 75–87.

[83] See, however, *Brady v UK*, fn.59 above, where an unarmed man was killed during a robbery, the Court found the ambush planned by the police did not render lethal force inevitable or highly probable and that although it could have perhaps been more efficiently executed, errors of judgement or mistaken assessments would not per se entail responsibility under Art.2.

[84] *Celniku v Greece*, July 5, 2007.

from military air and artillery strikes on armed insurgents.[85] Even if aerial bombardments may be justified against an insurgent threat, the Court required that the authorities make some effort to avoid civilian casualties, whether through pinpoint targeting or attempts at evacuation; it criticised very heavily the use of high explosive fragmentation bombs in a settlement in which many civilians were resident.[86]

A distinction can be drawn between cases in which the armed forces had to react spontaneously to a fast-developing situation and those where an operation had been pre-planned. In the latter, the Court applies a more rigorous examination to verify that the planning of the operation had due regard to reducing the risk to life to the minimum.[87] In a less clear-cut situation of rioting over most of a city, the Court showed a pragmatic attitude, noting the fluid nature of the situation, in which sudden, unpredictable flurries of violence occurred. In such circumstances, where thousands of police had to be brought in, it was not prepared to impose unrealistic standards as regarded the level of training or experience of all those involved, the types of vehicles used and the level of communications between the different units. Thus the fact that a young, inexperienced and injured police officer was allowed to keep his gun, which he fired when his unprotected jeep came under attack by rioters en route to the hospital, did not disclose any failure in planning or control.[88]

(c) *Special contexts*

(I) Death in custody

II–667 States are under a duty to protect detainees who are in a vulnerable position and have to account for injuries caused in custody. A particularly stringent obligation lies on the authorities to account for deaths in custody and strong presumptions of fact will arise in respect of injuries and fatalities occurring during detention.[89] Where the authorities therefore fail to satisfy the burden of proof lying on them to provide a satisfactory and convincing explanation, a violation of Art.2 arises, as in *Salman v Turkey* where the applicant's husband, with no prior history of heart disease, died in police custody, inter alia, with a broken sternum and bruising and swelling to the sole and ankle of the left foot indicative of the torture practice of *falaka*. In *Tanli v Turkey*, where the 22–year-old, in prior good health, died during interrogation in police custody, the Court refused to accept the Government's assertion that he died of natural causes as providing a plausible or satisfactory explanation for his death, as the domestic post mortem was defective in fundamental respects and failed to establish the cause of death.[90] Where a 20–year-old Roma was taken into custody

[85] *Isayeva v Russia*, February 24, 2005, paras 179–201. See also *Isayeva, Yusupova and Bazayeva v Russia*, February 24, 2005, paras 174–200.

[86] *Kerimov v Russia*, May 3, 2011, paras 245–258.

[87] e.g. *Mansuroglu v Turkey*, fn.50 above, paras 85–89, where the Government failed to provide a convincing explanation for the deaths of three suspects under a hail of bullets, one with wounds all to the back, during a planned arrest operation.

[88] *Giuliani and Gaggio*, fn.54 above, paras 252–262.

[89] *Salman v Turkey*, June 27, 2000, ECHR 2000–VII, para.99.

[90] *Tanli v Turkey*, fn.89 above, paras 143–147. Also *Aktas*, fn.49 above, paras 292–294, where there were signs consistent with mechanical asphyxia; *Avsar v Turkey*, July 10, 2001, ECHR 2001–VII, paras 410–416, where the victim's body was found dead in a field after he had been taken into a gendarme station;

and died of a pistol shot fired during interrogation, the Court noted that whether or not the suspect had forcibly removed the interrogator's gun as alleged, the police had failed to take basic precautions to protect his health and welfare: no explanation had been forthcoming as to why the interrogator had been armed or failed to keep his weapon secure.[91]

Where a detainee dies as a result of a health problem, the State must also offer an explanation as to the cause of death and the treatment administered to the person concerned prior to their death.[92] Defective medical care of a prisoner which led to his death from post-operative complications disclosed a violation of Art.2 where the prison hospital had no blood transfusion facilities.[93]

However, although there is an obligation to give medical or emergency assistance where a detainee or arrestee collapses, the Court has hesitated in imposing too heavy a burden on the authorities. Where a young man collapsed and later died, it was sufficient that the police officers placed him in the recovery position and called promptly for medical assistance without attempting themselves to resuscitate him.[94] An absence of any steps or precautions is more problematic. In *Tais v France*, where an AIDS sufferer placed in a cell in a state of inebriation was found dead, the Court found that the police had shown gross shortcomings in their inertia, omitting to check his condition, or to provide for any medical examination, during the night.[95] Similarly where a handicapped person who had reportedly fallen downstairs was taken into custody and subsequently died of skull fractures, the Court criticised the failure to carry out a prompt medical examination to verify his condition, a duty all the more necessary where the police had been informed of his vulnerable, handicapped status.[96]

As regards the obligation on the authorities to protect detainees from other inmates or their own attempts to commit suicide, see further below (sub-s.4(a)).

(ii) Disappearances

The disappearance of a person in custody is not sufficient in itself to found a violation of Art.2 of the Convention.[97] The Court generally requires concrete evidence supporting the conclusion that the person has, beyond reasonable doubt, II–668

Velikova v Bulgaria, May 18, 2000, ECHR 2000–VI, paras 71–74; *Anguelova v Bulgaria*, June 13, 2002, ECHR 2002–IV, paras 112–121, where the Court rejected as implausible the Government's claims that the fatal injuries were received before the deceased's arrest or from falling at the police station; *Ognyanova and Choban v Bulgaria*, February 23, 2006, para.101, where the Government did not account "comprehensively" for the death and injuries of a detained suspect who fell, handcuffed, from a window; *Mojsiejew v Poland*, March 24, 2009, where the applicant died from asphyxiation, bearing signs of neck injuries, while detained in a sobering-up centre, without a plausible explanation; contrast *Fonseca Mendes v Spain*, (43991/02) (Dec.) February 1, 2005, the deceased's good health prior to arrest could not in itself support a finding of responsibility, where, although the cause of death remained obscure, there had been a thorough investigation and were no other reliable indications of foul play.

[91] *Mizigarova v Slovakia*, December 14, 2010, 2005, paras 87–90.

[92] *Slimani v France*, July 27, 2004, ECHR 2004–VII, para.27.

[93] *Tarariyeva v Russia*, December 14, 2006.

[94] *Scavuzzo-Hager*, fn.74 above, paras 67–68.

[95] *Tais v France*, June 1, 2006.

[96] *Jasinkis v Lavia*, December 21, 2010, paras 59–68, there had been an assumption that the deceased had been drunk.

[97] See *Kurt v Turkey*, May 25, 1998, R.J.D. 1998–III, No.74, paras 107–108.

been killed by the authorities, though this can be provided by sufficient circumstantial evidence based on concrete elements, as first found in *Cakici v Turkey*, where the applicant's brother was established as having been the victim of serious ill-treatment while in unacknowledged detention and the authorities later claimed that he was dead as his identity card had been found, in unverified circumstances, on the body of an alleged terrorist after a clash.[98] The length of time over which the person has disappeared is a significant factor, though it has not yet been found sufficient in itself.[99] The Court acknowledges that with the passage of time the likelihood of death becomes stronger and that can influence the weight to be attached to circumstantial elements.[100] Particular features of the unacknowledged detention may show that it is life-threatening.[101] The general context may also be sufficient to give strong grounds for believing that unacknowledged detention would be life-threatening and thus in breach of Art.2, as in southeast Turkey in the early-to mid-1990s when there was an atmosphere of impunity[102] and in the Chechen region during periods of conflict after 2000.[103]

In the cases concerning disappearances in the Chechen Republic, it has been sufficient to establish that the victims were taken by security forces where family members and other witnesses have put forward generally consistent accounts identifying the perpetrators as dressed, and acting, as State armed forces, with military methods of operation and carrying out official actions such as verifying identities, as well as being able to travel freely at night through official road blocks. These elements have also been strengthened by presumptions as to the veracity of the applicants' accounts drawn from the failure of the Government to provide documentary evidence to counter the applicants' prima facie case.[104]

[98] *Cakici v Turkey*, July 8, 1999, ECHR 1999–IV, 31 E.H.R.R. 5, paras 85–87. Also *Ertak v Turkey*, May 9, 2000, paras 131–132, witness evidence that the applicant's son had been tortured and last seen dead or dying in detention; *Tas v Turkey*, November 14, 2000, paras 65–66, strong inferences drawn from the lack of documentary evidence from the authorities as to the location of the applicant's son after his acknowledged arrest and no satisfactory explanation for what had happened to him (the story of an escape while assisting a military operation was lacking in credibility and was unsubstantiated by any reliable evidence); *Orhan v Turkey*, June 18, 2002, the men, missing for eight years after their arrest, had been wanted by the security forces. Contrast *Tekdag v Turkey*, January 15, 2004, paras 64–68, insufficient evidence to corroborate the applicant's assertion that her husband was taken away in the street by police in plain clothes: an alleged eyewitness did not appear to give evidence before the Court delegates.

[99] *Timurtas v Turkey*, June 13, 2000, paras 84–86, where the Court laid emphasis on the six-year period as longer than the four-year disappearance in *Kurt*, fn.97 above: however, other elements included the fact that the disappeared person was wanted as a terrorist and that the authorities had taken steps to conceal his apprehension and detention, as well as findings in other Turkish cases on the lack of accountability of the security services in the region at that time. See also strong inferences drawn from lapse of over seven years in *Akdeniz v Turkey*, May 31, 2001, paras 87–88, other inferences drawn from lack of custody records and the Government's inability to account for what had happened to missing detainees; *Cicek v Turkey*, February 27, 2001, paras 146–147 and *Ipek v Turkey*, February 17, 2004, ECHR 2004–II, where there was very little by way of "concrete elements" beyond the respective six- and nine-year lapse of time.

[100] *Bilgin v Turkey*, November 16, 2000, para.139, more than six-and-a-half years had passed: the Court drew very strong inferences from witness evidence that the applicant's brother had been ill-treated and in a bad physical state in custody.

[101] e.g. *Bazorkina v Russia*, July 27, 2006, where there was evidence that an officer ordered the execution of a purported rebel fighter.

[102] *Ipek*, fn.99 above, para.167.

[103] e.g. *Betayev and Betayeva v Russia*, fn.18 above, para.72, referring to the well-known phenomenon of disappearances during the conflict in the Chechen Republic.

[104] e.g. *Betayev and Betayeva*, fn.18 above, paras 68–69.

Where men had disappeared during an international armed conflict, the Court did not require specific proof that each was last seen in the actual custody of the opposing forces. It took a broader approach, noting that in that context there were wider obligations to account for prisoners of war, care for the wounded and provide for burial of those killed, such that, whatever the individual fate of the missing person, the State left in control of the particular area where the person was last seen was under an obligation for them one way or another.[105]

The procedural obligation to investigate disappearances applies largely as outlined in cases of unlawful killings (see sub-s.3(c) below). However the requirement for the authorities to act promptly takes on crucial urgency since it is in the very early moments after the disappearance that it is most likely that traces of the victim's whereabouts can be followed up effectively and his or her safety secured. The Court has commented adversely on even a delay of a few days in launching an investigation.[106]

(c) *Procedural requirements*

While it may be permissible for a State to use lethal force in certain limited circumstances, the *McCann* case established that there must some form of effective official investigation. Otherwise the protection offered by Art.2 would be rendered nugatory if there was no form of open and objective oversight into the circumstances of a killing.[107] The nature and degree of the scrutiny which will satisfy the minimum threshold of effectiveness depends on the circumstances, some cases being undisputed and requiring a minimum formality, whereas in others the facts might be unclear or the situation suspicious.[108] The emphasis is on effective accountability and transparency to ensure respect for the rule of law and maintain public confidence.[109] **II–669**

The Court has refrained from specifying the exact form or procedures that should be involved.[110] However, cases from Turkey and Northern Ireland in particular have identified particular features necessary to an effective investigation.

- The onus is on the authorities to launch the investigation without relying on a complaint being made by a relative.[111] The availability of civil proceedings, undertaken at the initiative of the next-of-kin and not involving the identification or punishment of the perpetrator of an unlawful killing, cannot be taken into account.[112]

[105] *Varnava v Turkey*, fn.4 above, paras 185–186.
[106] *Betayev and Betayeva*, fn.18 above, para.85, delay of five days.
[107] *McCann and Others v UK*, September 27, 1995, Series A, No.324, 21 E.H.R.R. 97, para.161.
[108] e.g. *Velikova*, fn.90 above, para.80..
[109] *Avsar*, fn.90 above, para.393; *Gül*, fn.62 above, para.90, lack of accountability for use of weapons; *Ramsahai*, fn.76 above, para.325, "what is at stake is the nothing less than public confidence in the state's monopoly on the use of force".
[110] e.g. *McKerr v UK*, fn.14 above, para.159, where the Court rejected the applicant's arguments in favour of a Scottish model of inquiry instead of a system splitting the tasks of fact-finding, investigation and prosecution between various authorities.
[111] *Ergi v Turkey*, July 28, 1998, R.J.D., 1998–IV, No.81, 32 E.H.R.R. 388, paras 82–83; *Tanrikulu v Turkey*, July 8, 1999, ECHR 1999–IV, para.103; also *Tanli*, fn.90 above, para.152, where onus was on the public prosecutor, not the family, to obtain a full autopsy; *Nachova*, fn.55 above, para.131.
[112] *Hugh Jordan v UK*, May 4, 2001, para.141.

- The investigation should be conducted by an officer or body independent from those implicated in events, in a hierarchical, institutional and practical sense.[113] It is not enough for the investigating body, if not independent, to be supervised by one that is.[114] Even a short period of control of the investigation by the police force whose members have carried out the shooting is enough to disclose a breach.[115] Where the prosecution service is hierarchically separate from the police, it was not fatal that the local prosecutor decided on whether or not to prosecute local police officers, although the Court commented that problems could arise if in practice there was a close working relationship between a prosecutor and a particular police force.[116] Where it was the chief prosecutor himself who was allegedly implicated in unlawful acts leading up to the murder of a high-ranking prosecutor with whom he was in conflict, the Court found that the investigation into the death could not be regarded as impartial and independent as the chief prosecutor had remained in effective charge throughout.[117]
- The notion of effectiveness requires that the investigation be capable of leading to a determination of whether the force used was justified and to the identification and punishment of those responsible.[118] The Court has specified that this is an obligation of means, not result.[119] Lack of prosecution or conviction will therefore not be decisive, as long as the authorities have taken reasonable steps to secure the evidence concerning the incident, including, inter alia, eyewitness and forensic evidence[120]; and where

[113] e.g. *Ogur v Turkey*, May 20, 1999, ECHR 1999–III, 31 E.H.R.R. 912, paras 91–82, administrative councils lacking independence from governor, also head of the security forces; *McKerr v UK*, fn.14 above, para.127 and *Hugh Jordan*, fn.112 above, para.120, lack of independence of RUC and ICPC investigations into shootings by RUC officers; *Kelly v UK*, fn.68 above, para.114; *McShane v UK*, May 28, 2000, paras 111–112, RUC officers investigating deaths caused by soldiers were connected, albeit indirectly, with the operation; *Shanaghan v UK*, May 4, 2001, ECHR 2001–III, para.104, and *Finucane v UK*, July 1, 2003, para.76, RUC investigators connected with those under suspicion of collusion; *Soare*, fn.57 above, paras 151–157, military prosecutor part of same hierarchy as officers under investigation.

[114] e.g. *McKerr*, fn.14 above, para.128.

[115] *Ramsahai*, fn.76 above, paras 333–341, where it took about 15 hours for the State Criminal Investigation Department to take over from the local police; see also *Kamil Uzun v Turkey*, May 10, 2007, paras 57–59, where in the first months the military authorities, rather than the civilian prosecutors, investigated the purported firing of a military mortar on a village and signally failed to carry out the most elementary steps in the necessary gathering of evidence; *Celniku*, fn.84 above, where investigating officers were in the same department as those implicated in the shooting and the officer who fired the lethal shot was involved in such steps as searching the body.

[116] *Ramsahai*, fn.76 above, paras 342–346.

[117] *Kolevi v Bulgaria*, November 5, 2009, paras 196–215.

[118] e.g. *Ogur*, fn.113 above, para.88; *Aktas*, fn.49 above, paras 301–307.

[119] *Avsar*, fn.90 above, paras 394 and 404; see, e.g. *Douglas-Williams*, fn.75 above, where all the relevant evidence and arguments had been aired at the inquest at which the family were represented, the fact that the jury reached a verdict of accidental, not unlawful death, did not deprive the procedure of its effectiveness.

[120] e.g. *Güleç v Turkey*, July 27, 1998, R.J.D., 1998–IV, No.80, 28 E.H.R.R. 121, para.79, failure to obtain witness evidence; *Tanrikulu*, fn.19 above, paras 104–107 and *Gül*, fn.62 above, para.89, superficial scene investigation and inadequate forensic testing; *Velikova*, fn.108, paras 78–84, failure to collect key evidence; *Makaratzis*, fn.52 above, para.76, failure to identify all police officers involved in the car chase or secure and identify the bullets fired; *Perk*, fn.11 above, para.79, failure to draw up a detailed plan of the scene or a reconstruction of events; *Celniku*, fn.84 above, para.67, failure to secure the crime scene; *Mizigarova*, fn.91 above, para.102, failure to test for powder residues. See *Ramsahai*, fn.76 above, paras

appropriate, an autopsy providing a complete and accurate record of injuries and an objective analysis of clinical findings including the cause of death[121]; as well as having reached conclusions supported by a careful analysis of the facts and all relevant elements.[122] Thus, any defect in the investigation which undermines its ability to establish the cause of death or person responsible risks falling short of this standard.[123] Where after a thorough ventilation of the evidence, a judicial officer directed a jury that the only verdict could be lawful death, this did not deprive the procedure of effectiveness.[124]

Even if a prosecution is brought and suspects stand trial, the Court will examine whether this is a meaningful or serious exercise with any realistic prospect of bringing the perpetrators to account.[125] Violations have been found where the trial has dragged on unduly,[126] where the penalties imposed on the convicted officers have never been executed,[127] where the trials ended by prescription or amnesty allowing the accused perpetrators to escape accountability,[128] and where the investigation failed to address whether the use of lethal force by police officers on the occupants of a car had been proportionate or the way in which the operation had

326–332, where the majority took a very demanding approach in finding that failures in testing the police officers' hands for residue, lack of reconstruction of events, etc disclosed a violation, while the minority noted that, since there was no real dispute as to who killed the victim, and in what circumstances, these shortcomings did not undermine the adequacy of the investigation.

[121] *Kaya*, fn.2 above, para.89, perfunctory autopsy; *Ogur*, fn.113 above, para.89; *Salman*, fn.89 above, paras 106–107, defects in the autopsy investigation (e.g. lack of proper forensic photographs, dissection and analysis of marks and injuries); *Tanli*, fn.90 above, where procedures were not carried out by forensic experts; *Musayev and Others v Russia*, July 26, 2007, paras 160–162, where the investigative efforts were so sporadic and half-hearted that the Court could perceived no attempt to create a comprehensive picture of the circumstances of a mass killing of civilians. Contrast *Guiliani and Gaggio*, fn.54 above, paras 316–319, where an autopsy showed no serious deficiencies, only an omission to remove a bullet fragment capable of shedding a limited light on the events: this was not considered a crucial oversight.

[122] *Nachova*, fn.55 above, para.116, where the prosecutors ignored highly relevant facts, e.g. the location of cartridges, use of a machine gun on automatic mode and that one victim was hit in the chest (impliedly while trying to surrender); *Kolevi*, fn.117, paras 201–215, where the chief prosecutor was implicated in the death of a fellow prosecutor but could not, effectively, be charged, suspended or even investigated, the investigation into the death failed to carry out an objective analysis of an obvious line of inquiry.

[123] e.g. *Yasa*, fn.37 above, paras 105–107, exclusion from investigation of any consideration of security force responsibility; *Cakici*, fn.98 above, para.80, general inertia; *Bilgin v Turkey*, fn.100, para.144, inability of investigator to access police premises or obtain information about police officers; *Kiliç v Turkey*, March 28, 2000, ECHR 2000–III, paras 82–83, limited scope of investigation excluding possible collusion by security forces; *Akdeniz*, fn.99 above, para.92, lack of serious effort to investigate and repeated jurisdictional transfers of file; *Tanli*, fn.90 above, para.153, lack of proper autopsy findings led to acquittal of police officers; *Avsar*, fn.90 above, paras 404–408, failure to investigate effectively alleged security force suspect. See, conversely, *Sabutekin v Turkey*, March 19, 2002, paras 100–104, where the investigation was adequate and the lack of promptness in one aspect did not deprive it of effectiveness.

[124] *Bubbins v UK*, fn.59 above, para.163, the coroner's direction was subject to judicial review.

[125] e.g. *Akkum*, fn.8 above, para.231, no meaningful effort to identify those who killed the villagers, question those indicted somewhat randomly or seriously consider the evidence; *Juozaitiene and Bikulcius*, fn.71 above, where the inquiry blatantly restricted itself to the account of the police officers, without seeking to elucidate events further, question any gaps or resolve any inconsistencies.

[126] e.g. *Fatma Kaçar v Turkey*, July 15, 2005, para.79.

[127] e.g. *Teren Aksakal*, fn.11 above, para.99, nor had the officers ever been suspended.

[128] e.g. *Ali and Ayse Duran v Turkey*, April 4, 2008, para.69; *Association 21 December 1989 v Romania*, May 24, 2011, para.144.

been planned and executed.[129] However, the mere fact that two soldiers, convicted of killing the applicant's husband, were allowed to rejoin their units after six years in prison was not a flagrant rejection of the criminal conviction or cynical and retrospective approbation of the soldiers' conduct which could be regarded as capable of undermining the efficacy of the earlier criminal proceedings in providing the appropriate deterrent and retribution. The Court considered that any general policy issues concerning standards of conduct or recruitment were matters for public and political debate.[130]

- The investigation must commence promptly[131] and be conducted with reasonable expedition to maintain public confidence in the rule of law and to prevent any appearance of collusion or tolerance of unlawful acts.[132] It is for the State to organise its judicial system so that it can deal with these cases with due expedition; the fact that a particular case is of considerable political and public sensitivity is less an excuse for delay than a further reason for prompt action to avoid any appearance of a cover-up.[133]
- Public confidence and appearances also require sufficient public scrutiny of the investigation and its results, the extent of which may vary from case to case.[134] There is no automatic requirement that families have access to police files or any information that they demand, or that they are kept informed throughout the investigation.[135] However, in all cases, the next of kin must be involved in the procedure to the extent necessary to safeguard their legitimate interests.[136] This appears to require that they are provided with a basic minimum of information, and are given an opportunity to put forward

[129] *Wasilewska and Kalucka v Poland*, fn.63 above, paras 62–63.
[130] *McBride v UK*, (1396/06) (Dec.) May 9, 2006.
[131] Delays in commencing inquests, e.g. 25 months in *Hugh Jordan*, fn.112 above; over a four-year delay in re-opening the inquest in *McKerr*, fn.14 above, eight years in *Kelly*, four-and-a-half years in *Shanaghan*, fn.113 above. Ten-year delay in opening inquiry in *Finucane*, fn.113 above, para.80. Outside the UK context, see *Musayev*, fn.121 above, para. 60, one-month delay in opening investigation into dozens of civilian deaths during a military operation was found unacceptable.
[132] e.g. *Timurtas v Turkey*, fn.99 above, para.89, delay in taking statements; *Mahmut Kaya v Turkey*, March 28, 2000, ECHR 2000–III, paras 106–107, delays in seeking statements and inactivity not excused by burden of work on public prosecutors as it was incumbent on authorities to respond actively and with reasonable expedition; *Avsar*, fn.90 above, paras 405–408, dilatoriness in investigating security force suspect; *McKerr*, fn.14 above, paras 152–155, frequent and lengthy adjournments in inquest; *Kamil Uzun*, fn.115 above, para.62, investigation and trial dragged out over 12 years; *Teren Aksakal*, fn.11 above, procedures lasted an overall 22 years, which would have been difficult to justify by any explanation, marred by numerous lacunae and errors in the investigation and court procedures.
[133] e.g. *Sandru*, fn.11 above, paras 73–80.
[134] e.g. *Hugh Jordan*, fn.112 above, paras 122–124, lack of reasons by the D.P.P. for decisions not to prosecute the killing of an unarmed man provided insufficient scrutiny and explanation to family; *McKerr*, fn.14 above, para.141, reports from the independent police inquiry were not published; *Kelly*, fn.113 above, para.118, no reasons given for no prosecution where nine men, at least two unarmed and one unconnected with the IRA, were shot, and the situation cried out for an explanation; *Finucane*, fn.113 above, paras 82–83, no public explanation of decisions not to prosecute. See, however, *McShane*, fn.113 above, paras 117–119, where the D.P.P. gave brief reasons and the applicant could have taken judicial review proceedings challenging their adequacy, it was not a problem that the family had to request the reasons.
[135] e.g. *Hugh Jordan*, fn.112 above, para.121, as long as requisite access to information is provided at another stage of the investigative procedure; *Ramsahai*, fn.76 above, paras 347–350.
[136] e.g. *Ogur*, fn.113 above, para.92, lack of any access by family to case file or to administrative council proceedings.

their version of events and to be informed of the investigative conclusions and the key decisions taken by the investigative and prosecuting authorities, including reasons for not prosecuting.

An investigation followed by a criminal trial with an adversarial procedure before an independent and impartial judge is generally regarded as furnishing the strongest safeguards and most effective procedure for the finding of facts and attribution of responsibility.[137] There may, however, be circumstances where issues arise that were not or could not be addressed in the trial or where the aims of reassuring the public and the family were not met adequately due to subsequent doubts as to the effectiveness of the original investigation, as in *McKerr v UK*, where it transpired that there had been deliberate concealment of evidence and wider concerns arose about an alleged shoot-to-kill policy.[138] Thus, where new evidence comes to light, there may be an obligation on the authorities to pursue further investigations; although the scope of the obligation may well differ from that applicable at the time of the original events, particularly if there has been a considerable lapse of time.[139] Furthermore, an investigation which deals only with individual criminal responsibility of the state agents immediately involved may not be sufficient. Narrow focus of an investigation into an alleged death by drowning resulting from ill-treatment in army custody in Iraq offended, since Art.2 required examination of the broader issues of State responsibility for the death, including the instructions, training and supervision given to soldiers.[140]

Where a life-threatening disappearance is concerned, the State remains under a continuing obligation to provide an effective investigation, even where considerable time has elapsed since events occurred.[141]

In the context of Northern Ireland, the Court found problems arising from the inquest procedure into deaths implicating the security forces. The limited scope of the enquiry which, as the jury was restricted to the immediate facts surrounding the death and could not give any verdict as to the lawfulness or otherwise, was found to prevent the inquest from playing an effective role in the identification or prosecution of any criminal offences.[142] The inability to compel the security force personnel to give evidence also detracted from the inquest's capacity to establish the facts[143] as did the use of public interest immunity certificates to exclude certain potentially

[137] e.g. *McKerr*, fn.14 above, para.134; also *Green v UK*, (28079/04) (Dec.) May 19, 2005, where the police officer had been tried in criminal proceedings, the applicant could not complain about any alleged defects in subsequent disciplinary procedures.

[138] See also *Gül*, fn.62 above, para.94, where reliance on a flawed security force report effectively deprived the court of the ability to decide the factual and legal issues.

[139] *Hackett v UK*, fn.34 above; the Court adverted to the difficulty of revisiting historical crimes in Northern Ireland and was not prepared to find the authorities' ongoing examination of new evidence an inadequate response at that stage. See also *Brecknell*, fn.32 above, paras 73–75.

[140] *Al-Skeini v UK*, July 7, 2011, para.174.

[141] *Cyprus v Turkey*, May 10, 2001, ECHR 2000–IV, paras 135–136.

[142] *Hugh Jordan*, fn.112 above, paras 129–130; see also *Shanaghan*, fn.113 above, paras 111–113, where the Coroner excluded evidence relevant to alleged RUC collusion in the targeting of the victim; *Finucane*, fn.113 above, para.78, no examination of collusion issues at inquest.

[143] *McKerr*, fn. 14 above, para.144; *Kelly*, fn.113 above, para.121. Granting anonymity did not cause problems where the officers could be questioned, behind screens, by the applicants' counsel: *Bubbins*, fn.59 above, paras 157–158.

relevant evidence.[144] Non-disclosure of statements and evidence to the relatives of the deceased also showed failure to respect their interests.[145]

4. Protection from violence or risks from other sources

(a) *Extent of obligation to protect from other threats to life*

(i) General considerations

II–670 The Court has stated under Art.2, as in other contexts, that it must be careful not to impose obligations in such a way as to impose an impossible or disproportionate burden on authorities. It has referred to the difficulties that arise in policing and issues of priorities and resources, as well as the need to respect other rights, in particular a respect for due process, the right to liberty and rights under Art.8 of the Convention.[146] However, it has gone on to develop its case-law in this area quite extensively and, in some cases, quite rigorously, influenced, it seems, by the importance of the right which is at stake even where it might be considered as intervening pro-actively in areas of executive and administrative policy and decision-making.

In the earliest statements on the point, the Court held that Art.2 must be interpreted as requiring the State not only to refrain from taking life in unjustified circumstances but also to take appropriate steps to safeguard lives with its jurisdiction and that positive obligations might arise to protect an applicant from third persons or other threats to life.[147] This, firstly, includes a primary duty to secure the right to life by putting in place effective criminal law provisions to deter offences against the person together with machinery for the prevention, suppression and sanctioning of such measures.[148] A proper regulatory framework also appears to be required in other areas, such as dangerous activities, where the authorities may be held responsible[149] and in the area of health care and hospitals.[150] Secondly, where the authorities know, or should know, of a risk to life, they may come under an operational obligation to take reasonable steps to diminish that particular risk. Thirdly, as under the so-called procedural obligation, there may be an obligation to carry out an investigation into the incident of loss of life.

There are some difficulties in applying this framework of positive obligations which have been extended piecemeal from cases concerning violence from third persons through a gamut of other activities and situations where loss of life has arisen. In particular, the first head of responsibility has been extended beyond the provision of a legal system geared to enforce the law and regulate the activity in

[144] *McKerr*, fn.14 above, paras 150–151.

[145] *Hugh Jordan*, fn.112 above, para.134; *Kelly*, fn.113 above, para.128. Contrast *Bubbins*, fn.59, para.161, where some non-disclosure of materials on the decision of the Coroner, not the police, did not prevent the inquest shedding the necessary light on events.

[146] *Osman*, fn.37 above, para.116.

[147] (9438/81) (Dec.) February 28, 1983, 32 D.R. 190.

[148] *Osman*, fn.37 above, para.115. See also *Mastromatteo v Italy*, October 24, 2002, ECHR 2002–VIII, paras 72–73, where the Court examined whether the penal system provided sufficient protective measures when re-integrating prisoners into society; *Maiorano v Italy*, December 15, 2009, the prisoner release system was found to be sufficiently protective (paras 108 and 112).

[149] *Öneryildiz v Turkey*, November 30, 2004, ECHR 2004–XI, para.90.

[150] *Byrzykowski v Poland*, June 27, 2006, para.104.

question to a somewhat detailed examination of the extent to which the legal or regulatory system functioned in practice, including notions of promptness and expedition which would appear identical to issues of length of proceedings ordinarily examined under Art.6.[151] It echoes what Art.6 specifically guarantees, namely, that judicial systems should function without undue delay, and with expedition where the subject-matter of the dispute requires it. Reaching a finding of delay in procedures under Art.2 might, perhaps, be considered as underlining the importance of judicial efficiency where the right to life is at stake. Indeed, in some cases, there are findings of delay under Arts 2 and 6, the Court seemingly considering different purposes are served by findings under both provisions.[152] In other cases, the Court has declined to reach separate findings under both and opted for examining the complaints under one provision only.[153] Bearing in mind that the positive obligation now covers cases of death by negligence, in contexts such as road traffic accidents, matters commonly dealt with in the civil and administrative courts, without any of the controversial or pressing public concerns that arise in cases of the use of lethal force by the State, it might nonetheless be regarded as somewhat diluting the purpose and impact of Art.2 to use it routinely in these contexts.

There is also an overlap between the first and third aspects of positive obligation. When the first aspect is interpreted as requiring an examination of how the legal and judicial system operated in regulating the "dangerous activity" under consideration, the analysis sometimes strays into matters which are also examined under the compliance with the obligation to carry out an effective investigation into the loss of life concerned.[154] The categories are somewhat fuzzily applied. The first aspect could perhaps be interpreted as applying to systemic failings and not concern the deficiencies disclosed by the authorities' practical handling of the case, but this is not borne out by the varying lines of case-law. Conversely, the view might be taken that these two aspects are often so closely entangled that they should be regarded as one, and dealt with as such rather than being split up in an artificial manner.

Furthermore, where the third aspect—the obligation to investigate—is concerned, it has not assisted matters that the case-law, often transposed without explanation, originated under the negative obligation, namely concerning killings and extra-judicial executions by State agents, in which context the requisite investigation was generally geared towards criminal prosecution. However, where the other situations of loss of life are concerned, it is not at all obvious that a criminal investigation is the appropriate response. Confusion has arisen at least partly from the varying ways in which the domestic systems of the Contracting States view the role of the criminal law and public prosecutors; most differ from the common law approach of the United Kingdom. In many countries, private individuals commonly rely on prosecutors to gather evidence and join the criminal

[151] See Part IIA, s.17: Length of proceedings.

[152] See *Oyal v Turkey*, fn.25 above, breaches of Arts 2 and 6 for delay in compensation proceedings, no explanation as to why it was "appropriate" to examine the problem under both provisions (para.78); *Dvoracek and Dvorackova v Slovakia*, July 28, 2009, breaches of Arts 2 and 6 for undue length of civil compensation proceedings for alleged medical negligence leading to death.

[153] *Kalender v Turkey*, December 15, 2009, paras 56–67, the issue of length of compensation proceedings was dealt with under Art.6 (under Art.2 the Court only examined substantive responsibility and the issue of effective accountability in criminal proceedings); *Florea Pop*, fn.25 above, the length of the civil compensation proceedings for the death from negligent medical treatment in prison was examined under Art.6 only.

[154] *Furdik v Slovakia*, (42994/05) (Dec.) December 2, 2008.

proceedings as civil parties in preference to taking on the thankless task of mounting and pursuing their own civil case. In some contexts, where the judicial system has effectively ceased to function, it may indeed be impossible for a private citizen to take on, for example, the army in the courts and the only effective avenue of redress is through the state-sponsored criminal prosecution service. However the principles adopted in these kind of cases have seeped through into other areas and a surprising emphasis on the provision of effective criminal-type investigations appears in cases of negligence and breach of official and administrative duty. Nonetheless, criminal prosecutions cannot always be required in situations of loss of life.

As can be seen below, the positive obligation has been applied in a large number of contexts where the respondent State was not directly responsible for the death. The positive obligation does not yet go so far as to require protection in every sphere of life capable of engendering fatal risk though there are some cases which might seem to tend that way. Other cases do indicate a recognition by the Court that the mere fact someone has died, although a tragic event, cannot be enough to trigger Art.2. There is no right to absolute security of person, even in the prison context where the authorities have a special obligation to ensure the welfare of their detainees. Thus, the mere fact that there were faults in a prison electrical system was not enough to attract responsibility, the Court noting that the light fitting had worked for some twenty years without incident and that no-one could have predicted the prisoner would have tried to change the socket in the way that he did; thus he was primarily responsible for electrocuting himself.[155] In a case where a young boy had a fatal fall from a handball net on which he and a friend were swinging, the Court was not prepared to find the school authorities or teachers responsible for an accident caused by the improper use of the sporting equipment, noting that there could not be a general guarantee of protection wherever there might be a possible risk to life.[156] To impose a positive obligation to protect villagers, even children, from stray dogs would also have gone too far, where the fatal attack by a dog on a nine-year-old was the result of a tragic but random occurrence, rather than a matter for which the authorities could be held responsible.[157]

(II) PROTECTION FROM CRIMINAL VIOLENCE OF OTHERS

II–671 In early cases concerning Northern Ireland, where persons complained that the State had failed to protect them from terrorists, the Commission was not prepared to hold that a State was under an obligation to exclude all possible occurrence of violence, nor to examine in detail whether the United Kingdom had adopted appropriate and efficient measures to combat terrorism. It was sufficient that there were 10,500 soldiers in the area and that hundreds of them had lost their lives in the conflict; it did not consider that the State had been obliged to take any further steps to protect the applicant and her family. Where, however, in southeast Turkey there were serious allegations of collusion in counter-terrorist targeting of alleged PKK

155 *Koseva v Bulgaria*, (6414/02) (Dec.) June 22, 2010.
156 *Molie v Romania*, (13754/02) (Dec.) September 9, 2009.
157 *Beru v Turkey*, January 11, 2011, paras 47–49. Contrast, however, *Georgel and Georgeta Stoiescu v Romania*, July 26, 2011, failure to take protective measures against roaming packs of wild dogs in Bucharest breached Art.8 (protection of physical and psychological integrity) where the elderly applicant was attacked and bitten.

supporters, a failure in the system to hold security forces properly accountable for the use of force played a role in finding the Government responsible for a number of so-called 'unknown perpetrator' killings.[158]

A positive obligation to take preventive operational measures to protect life from the criminal acts of another may arise in certain well-defined circumstances. In *Osman v UK*, where the applicants' family was subject to a murderous attack by a school teacher whose behaviour had been increasingly bizarre and threatening, the Court held that failure to comply with such an obligation would be disclosed where the authorities had not done all that could be reasonably expected of them to avoid a real and immediate risk to life of which they knew or ought to have had knowledge. However, on the facts of the case, the Court found that in the absence of any clear threat of serious violence or any evidence that would have supported arrest on reasonable suspicion of criminal offences or detention on mental health grounds, the police could not have known that the applicant family were at real and immediate risk and did not fail to take reasonable steps in that regard.[159] Where the authorities were aware that death threats had been made against a journalist by ultra-nationalists and been informed of the likely instigators, the failure to take any steps to protect him from assassination breached the positive obligation—it was no excuse that the journalist had not himself asked for protection.[160]

Where there has been a known history of violence by a family member on others, a failure by the police to take appropriate steps in response may disclose a violation. In *Kontrova v Slovakia*, where the wife had complained to the police about assault by her husband and family members had reported threats by the husband to kill the children, the Court noted that the police had not even registered the criminal complaints, kept proper records of the calls or passed on information as well as not searching for the reported shotgun in the husband's possession; these failings had been found by the domestic courts to lead as a direct consequence to the death of the children at their father's hands and, as such, disclosed a breach of Art.2.[161] Where there had been escalating violence by the applicant's husband against herself and her mother over a number of years, incidents which were known to the authorities, the Court considered that they should have been able to foresee the lethal attack on the mother. While it was uncertain as to whether matters would have turned out differently if the authorities had reacted more vigorously, it held

[158] e.g. *Kiliç*, fn.123 above, paras 71–77, *Mahmut Kaya*, fn.132 above, paras 94–99, and *Akkoç v Turkey*, October 10, 2000, where the victims had been threatened before their death to the knowledge of the authorities, the Court, in finding the Government responsible under Art.2, took into account defects undermining the effectiveness of the criminal justice system in the southeast and the protection of the rule of law (e.g. limitation on the public prosecutor's ability to investigate offences by State officials, the role of non-judicial bodies in investigations, the inadequate investigations generally and the lack of independence of the State Security Courts).

[159] *Osman v UK*, fn.37 above, paras 115–122. Also *Dawn Bromiley v UK*, (33747/96) (Dec.) November 23, 1999, where the applicant's daughter was killed by a prisoner on home leave, there was no evidence that the authorities should have been aware that he was likely to commit a violent crime or that the daughter was at any risk; *Mastromatteo*, fn.148 above, where the authorities could not have reasonably suspected that the release of two prisoners would lead to the death of the applicant's son during a robbery. Cf. *Kiliç*, fn.123 above, para.76, where the journalist had informed the authorities of threats to his life and requested protection but the authorities failed to take any steps; *Maiorano*, fn.147 above, where a released prisoner with a history of violence, had renewed links with criminals and breached other terms of parole, and, according to an informer, was planning a murder, but this information was either not passed on or disregarded by the supervising magistrates.

[160] *Dink v Turkey*, September 14, 2010, paras 66–75.

[161] *Kontrova v Slovakia*, May 31, 2007.

that a failure to take reasonable measures which had a real prospect of altering the outcome or mitigating the harm was sufficient to engage the responsibility of the State.[162] In the context of domestic violence, the Court has also underlined that the authorities cannot remain passive, or be dismissive as to the family nature of the dispute, relying on the victim's attitude as dispensing them from action. Thus, even though an applicant and her mother had on occasion withdrawn their complaints about various incidents of alleged assault, the Court noted that the authorities had not queried the motives for the withdrawals (namely, due to threats by the perpetrator) nor, despite the seriousness of the physical violence, had they considered that action should be taken nonetheless to protect the lives of the applicant and her mother.[163] Psychiatric treatment of a compulsory nature may also be one of the measures that should be available to diminish the risks from a person with a known mental disorder; and, where treatment is ordered by a court, there should be clear guidelines and provision for enforcement.[164]

In the context of prisoners, where the authorities have in any case a duty to protect their welfare, the positive obligation will apply as regards threats of violence from other detainees. In *Paul and Aubrey Edwards v UK*, the failures in communication and proper medical screening on entry to prison which resulted in a seriously disturbed prisoner being placed in the cell of the applicant's son, who was then battered to death, led the Court to find that the authorities had failed to take reasonable steps to protect him from a man who should have been identified as a real and serious risk to others.

In the context of trafficking and exploitation of women as sex workers, the Court did not consider that conditions were such that their lives must be regarded at risk in a general sense. Thus, where the police handed an absconding Russian cabaret dancer back to the manager who was responsible for her and she later died falling from the balcony of his apartment in suspicious circumstances, the Court found no concrete element in the particular case indicating that the police should have realised her life was at risk.[165]

(iii) Disappearances

II–672 Where a victim has gone missing in life-threatening circumstances in which State officials are not implicated or proved to be involved, there is still an obligation on the authorities to react in order to protect the life of the missing person.

What is expected by way of reaction of the authorities will vary in the circumstances. In *Osmanoglu v Turkey*, the disappearance of the applicant's son in southeast Turkey was life-threatening given its similarity with numerous others incidents where missing persons were later found dead. The Court found a failure to protect the son's life where the authorities failed to react promptly to the incident in the crucial early days following the abduction and merely checked the custody register and put the name on a missing list; they had failed to take any active

[162] *Opuz v Turkey*, June 9, 2009.
[163] *Opuz v Turkey*, fn.162 above, paras 137–149 and 153.
[164] *Branko Tomasic v Croatia*, January 15, 2009, paras 55–61, in this case, where the partner of the applicant's daughter had, before killing her and their child, been sentenced for threats to kill, psychiatric treatment had been ordered during a prison sentence but not carried out and there was no legal provision for such treatment once he had been released.
[165] *Rantsev v Cyprus and Russia*, January 7, 2010, paras 222–223.

preventive measures such as inspecting premises where the son was last seen, taking statements, seeking eyewitnesses or alerting the official roadblocks in the region.[166]

In *Dodov*, where an old lady suffering from Alzheimers wandered off from a nursing home, the Court were not prepared to find the police at fault for not launching an intensive search, given the central city location of the home and the fact that the nursing home staff who knew the patient had already scoured the immediate area.[167]

(iv) Dangerous situations

A positive obligation has also been construed under Art.2 as applying in the context of any activity, whether public or not, in which the right to life may be at stake.[168] **II–673**

In *Öneryildiz v Turkey*, there was for the first time a breach of Art.2 for deaths not caused directly by agents of the State, where the Court found Government responsibility for the deaths of people killed by a methane explosion at a waste tip, where the risks had been known and the authorities had tolerated the shanty town that had grown up in the vicinity without taking any measures to avert the catastrophe.

This has been extended to life-threatening situations stemming from natural sources. In *Budayeva v Russia*, the risk of mudslides to a town was well known and there had been prior warnings as to the possibility of a large-scale incident, including warnings by the competent agency about the need to repair a protective dam. The Court found that the authorities could have reasonably been expected to be aware of the risk and to inform the civilians and make provision for emergency evacuation, including setting up temporary observation posts to permit early warning. Their failure to do so was causally linked to the loss of life and injury that followed the disastrous mudslide and disclosed a breach of the positive obligation to establish an effective framework to minimise threats to life.[169]

The Court has also stated that the State's duty to safeguard the right to life must also extend to the provision of emergency services where it has been brought to the notice of the authorities that the life or health of an individual is at risk on account of injuries sustained as a result of an accident. Depending on the circumstances, this duty may go beyond the provision of essential emergency services such as fire-brigades and ambulances and include the provision of air-mountain or air-sea rescue facilities to assist those in distress. This is subject to the proviso of not placing an undue burden on the authorities. Thus, in *Furdik v Slovakia*, where the applicant's daughter was injured while mountain climbing and died as the rescue services were just reaching her, some four hours later, the Court examined whether the State had set up an appropriate regulatory framework for rescuing persons in distress which worked effectively and whether there was an effective independent judicial system such that an alleged deficient response to an emergency resulting in the death of the person in distress could be the subject of scrutiny and, as appropriate, those found to

[166] *Osmanoglu v Turkey*, January 24, 2008, paras 70–84. See also *Medov v Russia*, January 15, 2009, violation where armed abductors and their victim were brought in for questioning from a roadblock by law enforcement officers, but then released after the officers had failed properly to verify the purported official identities of the abductors and to copy and record their documents.

[167] *Dodov*, fn.45 above, para.102.

[168] *Öneryildiz*, fn.149 above, para.71.

[169] *Budayeva*, fn.43 above, paras 147–160.

be responsible would be held accountable for their acts or omission. The Court looked in some detail at the regulatory framework and found it adequate; the Court was not prepared, as urged by the applicant, to find that the failure to impose a minimum emergency response time (he proposed 10–15 minutes) was in breach of the State's obligation, given all the variables, such as weather conditions and terrain that could come into play.[170]

(v) Road traffic accidents, boats and trains

II–674 This appears to be an area of State responsibility for public safety to which the Court considers Art.2 applies.

Where the applicant's husband died in a collision with two other vehicles, it was held, without explanation, that the principles set out in the public health sphere also extended to deaths on the road. The Court noted that there was nothing to indicate that there was not an adequate legislative and regulatory framework protecting road users and that in the absence of intentional infliction of harm criminal proceedings might not be required. On the facts of the case, there was no failure either to provide for criminal and civil proceedings to deal with the responsibility of the other drivers or to make available compensation. It did not find that the length of time, over seven years, taken to convict one driver was problematic, nor the failure to trace the driver of the third car.[171] In later cases, inadequate investigations into road accident deaths have disclosed procedural violations of Art.2.[172]

Boats and trains are covered, apparently irrespective of whether a State-run enterprise is concerned. Where a boat sank in French waters, the Court found nothing lacking in the regulatory framework or the rescue operation, relying largely on the domestic procedures into the tragedy.[173] Where a teenager was killed after exiting a train on the wrong side, the Court emphasised that the primary cause of the tragedy was his own conduct and was not prepared to hold the authorities at fault for not requiring an automatic door locking system.[174] In contrast, in a Turkish case, where two people were killed alighting on the wrong side of a train at a station lacking proper platforms, adequate lighting and information or guidance to passengers, the Court held the State accountable for the proper regulation of the railway system which was hazardous activity. While noting that the State could not be liable for all imprudences of passengers, it considered the number of deficiencies in proper enforcement of safety regulations was such as to disclose a breach of the positive obligation to safeguard life.[175]

(vi) Public places

II–675 The Court has gone so far as to state that the State's duty to safeguard the right to life must also be considered to involve the taking of reasonable measures to ensure the safety of individuals in public places and, in the event of serious injury or death, having in place an effective independent judicial system securing the availability of

170 (42994/05) (Dec.) December 2, 2008.
171 *Rajkowska v Poland*, (37393/02) (Dec.) November 27, 2007.
172 e.g. *Railean v Moldova*, January 5, 2010, paras 25–35.
173 *Leray v France*, (44617/98) (Dec.) January 16, 2001.
174 *Bone v France*, (69869/01) (Dec.) March 1, 2005.
175 *Kalender v Turkey*, fn.153 above.

legal means capable of establishing the facts, holding accountable those at fault and providing appropriate redress to the victim.[176]

Thus where the applicant's husband was killed by a fallen tree in a municipal park, Art.2 was found applicable. There was a breach as the domestic legal system failed effectively to establish any liability for the death of her husband and to provide appropriate civil redress due to a combination of dilatoriness in the criminal proceedings brought against the municipal officer responsible for trees and the rejection by the criminal court of the civil claim without giving reasons.[177]

(vii) Workplace

Safety of workers attracts Art.2 protection also. The death of a worker on a building site, due to an apparent breach of safety regulations, required effective procedural protection through court procedures.[178] II–676

(viii) Landmines

Where the authorities placed a minefield near a village to protect a gendarme station, the Court had no difficulty in finding a breach of the obligation to take sufficient measures of protection when a child was able to stray through the fence and was severely injured.[179] However, the approach to the problem of mines has varied in following cases. In one case, where a 14–year-old had been found by the domestic authorities to have knowingly taken the risk of seeking livestock in a mined military area, the complaint was rejected for non-exhaustion as it was sufficient that the family could have sought compensation in administrative proceedings.[180] However, in a later case, the Court took the view that the deaths from mines, known to cause a disproportionate amount of injury in children, had to be regarded as akin to the deliberate use of force by the armed services in respect of which the appropriate remedy was a criminal investigation rather than a no-fault indemnity procedure.[181] II–677

(ix) Protection against suicide

Obligation to take precautions where the risk to the person derives from self-harm has been found to arise principally as regards prisoners who are under the total control of the authorities and in a vulnerable position, and latterly, in respect of conscripts who are subjected to a stressful environment and are also under the control of the State in its military guise. II–678

However, while special duties are owed by the authorities to protect the lives of prisoners from harm, including self-harm, the Court noted that the measures imposed should take into account principles of dignity and self-determination, indicating that oppressive security measures may go too far.[182] It has also rejected

[176] *Ciechonska v Poland*, June 14, 2011, para.67.
[177] *Ciechonska*, fn.176 above, paras 68–79.
[178] *Henriques Pereira v Luxembourg*, May 9, 2006.
[179] See *Pasa and Erkan Erol v Turkey*, December 12, 2006.
[180] *Uca v Turkey*, (3743/06) (Dec.) April 29, 2008.
[181] *Alkin v Turkey*, October 13, 2009.
[182] *Keenan v UK*, April 3, 2001, ECHR 2001–III, para.91.

the argument that every prisoner should be regarded as being at such risk: this would pose a disproportionate burden on the authorities and unnecessary and inappropriate restrictions on prisoners.[183]

The approach concentrates on the facts of each particular case and avoids reliance on hindsight. Thus in *Keenan v UK*, where the applicant's son committed suicide in his cell, the Court found that the prison authorities were aware of his mental problems but had taken reasonable steps by placing him in hospital care and under close watch when he showed signs of suicidal tendencies. There had been no reason on the day of the incident for the authorities to suspect that an attempt was likely.[184] A more rigorous line was adopted by the Court in a later case, where a prisoner, who had already tried to harm himself and was apparently suffering from a more extreme psychotic condition, committed suicide despite receiving medical supervision and treatment. It was no answer that there had been no immediate indication before the suicide that such an attempt was likely, since his state indicated self-harm was a real risk. The Court found a failure to protect his right to life, commenting strongly on the fact that the prison authorities and medical staff had maintained the prisoner in the general population rather than transferring him to a hospital setting for full medical supervision and that they had entrusted the prisoner with taking the medication which was essential to suppress hallucinatory tendencies. The decision shortly before the suicide to punish the prisoner with 45 days of solitary confinement also did not sufficiently take into account his troubled mental condition.[185] A deteriorating psychological state, with only one verbalised indication of suicidal tendencies, was regarded as enough to put the prison on notice that a young disturbed prisoner might be at risk of suicide; in that case, there was a failure to protect life by proper and effective medical supervision as the prisoner had managed to save up his medication and kill himself with an overdose; it was no excuse that the prisoner must have dissembled by hiding the pills under his tongue as the administering nurse should have checked.[186]

Similar considerations apply in the context of military service, the authorities being under an obligation to take special care as regards conscripts who carry weapons and to take necessary measures where they show psychological problems. This involves not only properly checking the physical and mental health of conscripts on taking up military service, but ensuring a practical and effective protection through the applicable regulations and military medical services as well as taking concrete measures to adapt duties and conditions to those with psychological difficulties. Where a conscript suicide had been hospitalised briefly due to mental disturbance and was then placed on guard duty with a weapon by his unit, which was uninformed of his problem, a failure in this obligation arose[187] in that the military allowed a conscript, with known psychological difficulties and who was under treatment for depression, to continue to carry out duties with an armed weapon.[188] Even in the absence of a psychiatric history, oppressive behaviour by a

[183] *Younger v UK*, (57420/00) (Dec.) January 7, 2003, ECHR 2003–I.

[184] Also *Younger*, fn.182 above, where the applicant's son hung himself in his cell, the Court found no evidence that his conduct, despite some signs of distress on remand in custody, should have alerted the authorities to a real and imminent risk of suicide; *Trubnikov v Russia*, July 5, 2005, where the suicide was not reasonably foreseeable on his medical or recent history.

[185] *Renolde v France*, October 16, 2008, paras 95–110, the autopsy revealed that the prisoner had not in fact been taking his medication for several days prior to the suicide.

[186] *Jasinska v Poland*, June 1, 2010, paras 67–79.

[187] *Ataman v Turkey*, April 27, 2006, paras 58–62.

[188] *Lüfti Demirci v Turkey*, March 2, 2010, paras 35–36.

superior which provokes a spontaneous desperate act may lead to State responsibility under Art.2. In *Abdullah Yilmaz v Turkey*, the Court found that the system of appointment and training of special sergeants was defective where one such sergeant, with a problematic record, had been in charge of conscripts and through his incompetent and unprofessional conduct provoked one of his charges to shoot himself.[189]

As events within military installations may be regarded as under the exclusive control of the authorities and thus within their exclusive knowledge, the burden will often be on the State to provide a plausible explanation for deaths which occur. Thus, where a soldier allegedly shot himself, the Court closely scrutinised the account given by the Government; it found that the investigation into the incident was careless and left many questions unanswered, in particular since there were four sergeants in the room with the victim at the time who all claimed not to have seen anything, there had been no forensic tests on the gun used which had not belonged to the victim and the official conclusion as to the manner in which the deceased had shot himself defied logic: the State therefore bore responsibility for the death.[190]

In other situations, outside the direct knowledge and control of the authorities, State responsibility may perhaps be less likely to attach. In a case where the police, probably unlawfully, were threatening to evict the applicant's family and his wife set herself on fire in protest, the Court noted that this had not been a foreseeable response to the eviction, even regarding a vulnerable sector of the population such as refugees or internally displaced people.[191]

(x) Medical services

The extent to which a State is under an obligation to protect a person's state of health is increasingly raised. It trespasses on an area of State health policy in which matters of finance and policy are sensitive and controversial. II–679

Concerning complaints that the vaccination of children was causing severe brain damage and even death, the Commission held that States were under an obligation to take adequate measures to protect life and that this might raise issues in the area of medical care.[192] However, in that case, it noted that there was no evidence that the vaccinations were administered poorly or that proper and adequate steps were not taken to avoid the risks of damage and death materialising. It appears to have given weight to the number of vaccinations which pursued the purpose of avoiding serious illness in comparison to the relatively few adverse reactions. It concluded that overall the system of supervision and control of those administering the vaccinations was sufficient to comply with the obligation.

The Court has adopted the Commission's view that Art.2 applied in the public health sphere,[193] although no breach has yet to be found in a substantive, as opposed

[189] *Abdullah Yilmaz v Turkey*, June 17, 2008, paras 64–70.

[190] *Beker v Turkey*, March 24, 2009, paras 45–53, ". . . no meaningful investigation was conducted at the domestic level capable of establishing the true facts surrounding the death. . ."

[191] *Mikayil Mammadov v Azerbaijan*, December 17, 2009, para.111, nor was it possible to establish from the facts whether during the operation the police should have been able to act to prevent the self-immolation. The Court was not prepared to draw inferences and impose responsibility as in cases of deaths in custody. The lack of comprehensive factual picture emerging from the domestic investigation led to a finding of a procedural breach.

[192] (7154/75) (Dec.) July 12, 1978, 14 D.R. 31.

[193] *Calvelli and Ciglio v Italy*, January 17, 2002, ECHR 2002–I, paras 49–50; *Byrzykowski*, fn.150 above, para.104.

to a procedural, aspect outside a prison setting where the authorities are under a particular responsibility to ensure the provision of adequate medical treatment to those under their immediate care. Some link between the defective, or lack of, treatment and the death is necessary, but despite application of a strict causal test in some early cases,[194] an approach taking into account more indirect or merely contributory factors seems to be applied. In *Tarariyeva v Russia*, the applicant died of post-operative complications where the prison infirmary did not have the necessary blood transfusion facilities and drug therapy,[195] while in *Dzieciak v Poland*, the applicant died of a heart attack during detention on remand, after several appointments for surgery had been inexplicably cancelled and he had been certified as unfit for detention.[196]

The Court has stated in cases about medical malpractice that the State's positive obligation under Art.2 to protect life includes the requirement to have regulations for the protection of patients' lives and to provide an independent judicial system which can determine the cause of death of patients in the care of the medical profession, whether in the public or the private sector, and hold accountable those responsible: if it has done so, it is not accountable for errors of judgment by doctors or negligent co-ordination between health administrators.[197] In *Calvelli and Ciglio v Italy*, it found no violation arising from the failure to prosecute a doctor who allegedly had caused the death of the applicant's newborn baby through negligence, considering that the civil proceedings would serve to elucidate the issues of responsibility that arose.[198]

However, the Court's statement in *Calvelli and Ciglio* that the domestic system must not only exist in theory but must also operate effectively in practice has been interpreted as requiring a detailed examination of the procedure applied in the particular case to identify any deficiencies or shortcomings. The principles established in judgments concerning investigations into deaths by violence have been treated as transferring to this context in a somewhat blanket fashion. Consequently, there have been a number of cases where the Court has adopted the approach of examining whether the procedures following the death, whether criminal, civil or administrative, were conducted without unnecessary delay. Indeed, the Court has stated that a prompt examination of such cases is required not only due to the interests of the individual but as it was essential where deaths occurred in a hospital setting for the facts and possible errors to be speedily examined to prevent repetition of mistakes and safeguard all users of the health service.[199] Thus, in *Bryzkowski v Poland*, although the State had provided a framework of criminal, civil and disciplinary procedures, there was undue delay in the reaching of any final decision in these proceedings for over seven years and the failure to provide an effective

[194] See *McGlinchey v UK*, April 29, 2003, ECHR 2003–V and *Keenan*, fn.182 above, where the prisoners died of drug withdrawal complications and suicide respectively, but it was not proved that they would not have died but for the lack of proper monitoring and care—a breach of Art.3 arose instead.

[195] *Tarariyeva v Russia*, December 14, 2006.

[196] *Dzieciak v Poland*, December 9, 2008.

[197] *Powell v UK*, (45305/99) (Dec.) April 5, 2000, ECHR 2000–IV; *Byrzykowski*, fn.150 above, para.104.

[198] e.g. *Calvelli and Ciglio*, fn.193 above, para.49. See also *Karchen v France*, (5722/04) (Dec.) March 4, 2008, the Court rejected complaints by an AIDS sufferer contaminated by the blood bank that no criminal penalty for the resulting injuries had been imposed on those responsible, noting that the courts had found, without arbitrariness, no intentional infliction of harm, that remedies of damages had been available and that persons involved had been convicted on lesser charges relating to contamination of the blood supplies.

[199] *Byrzykowski*, fn.150 above, para.117.

examination of the circumstances of the death of the applicant's wife in childbirth disclosed a breach of Art.2.[200] In *Silih v Slovenia*, a procedural violation arose for delay of 13 years in a medical malpractice case.[201]

So far the Court has refrained from embarking on its own examination of the substantive issues of cause of death due to negligence or malpractice in general health care, although it has not excluded that the acts and omissions of the authorities in the realm of public health might engage their responsibility for a death.[202] To date only in the more administrative context of the contamination and use of infected blood supplies has it examined whether there was substantive responsibility for the life-threatening infection of an applicant. In *GN and Others v Italy*, it addressed the question whether the Italian health authorities knew or should have known of the risks of infection from blood products before 1988, and was content to rely on the domestic courts' conclusions excluding responsibility for that period as being neither manifestly arbitrary or unreasonable.[203] Other failings in the judicial system which render it incapable of properly elucidating in a convincing, thorough and objective manner the cause of death may also offend, as in *Eugenia Lazar v Romania*, where the superior forensic legal medical institute was able to refuse requests by the courts for elucidation of its report on the death of the applicant's son in hospital, and where the superior institute had overruled the opinions of the body that had direct involvement in the case without giving any detailed, scientific reasoning to support that conclusion or to resolve any conflicts of opinion.[204]

The Court also commented in *Cyprus v Turkey* that an issue could arise under Art.2 where it is shown that the authorities put an individual's life at risk through the denial of health care which they have undertaken to make available to the population generally.[205] No obligation arose on the authorities to refund the full price of life-saving drugs, where the applicant had had access to medical treatment and facilities under the Polish health service.[206]

In the absence of any real or immediate risk to life, it is unlikely that complaints about general standards or denial of medical care would be found to raise any

[200] *Byrzykowski*, fn.150 above, paras 197–210, e.g. the civil case was stayed pending a criminal investigation, frequent change of judges, applications challenging venue and bias of judges. See also violation for nine-year procedure in *Oyal v Turkey*, fn.25 above, concerning proceedings for compensation due to the applicant having been given HIV-infected blood at birth; *GN v Italy*, December 1, 2009, proceedings against health ministers for use of contaminated blood supplies over six, eight and ten years respectively did not disclose the required "rapid" response; *Eugenia Lazar v Romania*, February 16, 2010, paras 73–75, four-and-a-half years for an investigation into an alleged failure in communication between doctors that led to a fatally delayed emergency treatment was not sufficiently prompt.

[201] *Silih v Slovenia*, fn.7 above.

[202] *Eugenia Lazar*, fn.200 above, para.68, lack of communication between hospital services had led to an emergency tracheotomy being fatally delayed: the Court examined rather whether the avenues of redress enabled the course of events and those accountable to be established and the matter subjected to public scrutiny (paras 70–71).

[203] *GN v Italy*, fn.200 above, paras 85–95.

[204] *Eugenia Lazar*, fn.200 above.

[205] *Cyprus v Turkey*, fn.141 above, para.219, it was not established that the minorities in northern Cyprus had been denied access to hospital or that any lives had been put at risk by the alleged delay in requests for treatment in the south.

[206] *Nitecki v Polani,d* (65653/01) (Dec.) March 21, 2002. See also *Georghe v Romania*, (19215/04) (Dec.) September 22, 2005, where the applicant had access to hospital services for any health problems linked to his haemophilia, no failure to respect his Art.2 rights flowed from the lack of availability of free, preventive therapy.

issues.[207] In the case brought by the parents of children killed and injured by the nurse Beverley Allitt, the applicants sought to attack the system of national health as a whole. It was argued, inter alia, that the financial cutbacks and organisation of the local health services had led to the situation in which an untrained and dangerous individual could be allowed to care unsupervised for children. The Commission did not consider that Art.2 extended to an examination of national health policy and practice in general. It was sufficient that Allitt had been prosecuted, that the applicants could sue the health authorities for negligence and that an inquiry had been held which had made public its findings with regard to the procedures at fault in the hospital in question.[208]

(xi) Protection of the vulnerable

II–680 In a rather anomalous case, *Dodov v Bulgaria*, there was State responsibility under Art.2 for the presumed death of an old lady, suffering from Alzheimer's who disappeared from a closed part of a nursing home, as there was found to be a direct link between staff failures in supervision and the disappearance. Since the legal system had failed over some ten years to either hold those responsible criminal or civilly responsible or even provide a disciplinary response, due in part to lack of proper regulation of the duties of nursing home staff, a violation was found.[209] Responsibility appears to have been extended on the same basis as in the medical and hospital context.

(b) Procedural requirements

II–681 The obligation to carry out an effective investigation extends not only to those deaths in which security forces are implicated but also to killings by use of force generally, and arguably any unlawful or suspicious death.[210] It also covers deaths from dangerous activities or public dangers for which the authorities bear responsibility[211] and suicides of persons in the care or custody of the authorities[212] as well as requiring an investigation into failures by the security forces to protect life where there are positive obligations to take steps to prevent specific risks of criminal violence has arisen.[213] What form of investigation will achieve the purposes required

[207] e.g. *Pentiacova v Poland*, (14462/03) (Dec.) January 4, 2005, ECHR 2005–. . . , where the applicants, suffering from chronic renal failure, had not shown their lives were at risk from allegedly insufficient haemodialysis, etc; also (6839/74) (Dec.) October 4, 1974, 7 D.R. 78, where a mother complained of the denial of a medical card to her severely disabled daughter, the Commission found, whether Art.2 would apply or not, on the facts the daughter had been receiving medical assistance and her life had not been endangered.

[208] (23412/94) (Dec.) August 30, 1994, 79–A D.R. 127.

[209] *Dodov v Bulgaria*, fn.45 above.

[210] *Paul and Aubrey Edwards v UK*, March 14, 2002, ECHR 2002–II, killing of a prisoner by another detainee. See *Henriques Pereira v Luxembourg*, fn.178 above, where the death of a worker on a building site was apparently regarded as suspicious (apparent breach of safety regulations) to attract the procedural obligation; *Angelova and Iliev v Bulgaria*, July 26, 2007, procedural obligation applied to lethal attack on a Roma victim by a mob of teenagers.

[211] *Öneryildiz*, fn.149 above, paras 93–94, breach of Art.2 due to lack of proper investigation concerning accountability for deaths from an explosion at an unregulated waste tip (the fining of two mayors for negligence in their duties was not sufficient). See also sub-s.4(c): Medical services, for deaths in hospital.

[212] *Trubnikov*, fn.184 above, para.89.

[213] *Dink*, fn.160, paras 82–91.

by Art.2 will again depend on the circumstances.[214] Special vigour is required where there is a suspicion of racial motivation[215] although prosecution does not require special charges related to racial hatred or explicit penalty enhancing provisions as long as the domestic system provides a means of taking the racial motivation into account.[216] Where the authorities prosecute and convict the perpetrators, this will generally show compliance with the requirements of Art.2 in relation to the unlawful use of force.[217]

The requirements of independence, effectiveness, promptness and expedition,[218] and access to the public and relatives[219] apply equally as in cases under the negative obligation discussed above. Thus, in *Trubnikov v Russia*, the investigation into a prison suicide was defective where the prison governor in charge was not independent and the family were not given the status of victims in later proceedings which would have allowed them to participate.[220] In *Paul and Aubrey Edwards v UK*, the lack of power of inquiry into a death in prison to compel prison officers to give evidence diminished its effectiveness. The holding of the inquiry in private and the inability of the parents of the deceased to attend also failed to comply with the procedural requirements of Art.2.[221] In *Rantsev v Cyprus and Russia*, there were procedural defects where the investigation failed thoroughly to investigate the circumstances of the victim's fall from a balcony, either by seeking the necessary evidence or to resolve inconsistencies in the evidence; it also failed properly to involve the family of the victim who were not informed of the inquest or its finding until some fifteen months later.[222] Similar requirements to investigate thoroughly and establish a comprehensive picture of events has also been applied to a case of self-harm allegedly provoked by official actions.[223] However, a failure to cover every aspect will not necessarily be fatal, if the element is not considered crucial for the

214 *Paul and Aubrey Edwards*, fn.210 above, para.69.

215 *Menson v UK*, (47916/99) (Dec.) May 6, 2003, emphasis on impartial, effective investigations into racially motivated killings, inter alia to maintain confidence of minorities in the ability of the authorities to protect them from racist violence; *Nachova*, fn.55 above, paras 157–158.

216 *Angelova and Iliev*, fn.210 above.

217 *Menson*, fn.215 above, where the deceased's family complained about institutional racism in the investigation, the Court noted that nonetheless the perpetrators had been tried and convicted and that Art.2 did not guarantee, as such, a remedy in respect of alleged defects in the authorities' discharge of their obligations under that provision.

218 *Velcea and Mazare*, fn.10 above, para.115, where the investigation lasted more than 11 years.

219 *Velcea and Mazare*, fn.10 above, paras 113–114, the family could not claim access to all police reports as they were issued but it was sufficient that the prosecutor made them available at later stages; it was not acceptable that the family were not informed of all the decisions of *non-lieu* or, in one case, not given reasons, which prevented any effective challenge on their part and proper public scrutiny. Contrast *Koseva v Bulgaria*, fn.155 above, where there was sufficient respect for the applicant mother's interests as the investigation took some steps that she requested in gathering evidence and although it was regrettable that when reviewing the autopsy's findings at her request no reasons were given for concluding that no amendments were said to need to be made, this was not found to invalidate the findings in the circumstances.

220 *Trubnikov*, fn.184 above, paras 89–95.

221 Contrast (23412/94), fn.208 above, where an inquiry was held into a series of murders by a nurse, Beverly Allitt, in a hospital, the Commission had not found it incompatible with Art.2 that the enquiry was not open to the public and its membership not wholly independent from the health authorities.

222 *Rantsev v Cyprus and Russia*, fn.165 above.

223 *Mikayil Mammadov*, fn.191 above, paras 122–133, including a failure to clarify factual circumstances, sketchy findings of facts, failure to properly question eyewitnesses leading to vague testimony, failure to tackle major discrepancies in evidence leading to the inability to produce a complete and detailed factual picture of the incident.

elucidation of the cause of death, as in *Koseva v Bulgaria*, where the investigation omitted to identify the exact time of death but had otherwise convincingly concluded that the prisoner had died from electrocution while trying to change a light fitting, rather than as a victim of murder as alleged by the applicant.

In systems where the family of victims must gain formal status in order to participate in the investigation, delays in according such status will show a failure to protect their interests.[224]

It will not always be sufficient that criminal proceedings are brought against the perpetrator of the unlawful violence, if there is no provision for examining any responsibility of State officials for the events that occurred. Thus, in *Maiorano v Italy*, the Court found a procedural shortcoming since, even though the released prisoner who committed the murder was convicted and sentenced to life, the disciplinary procedures concerning the handling of the case by the authorities did not touch on the failure of the prosecuting authorities to pass on information about the prisoner's breach of parole conditions to the tribunal, which would have been able to order his recall.[225]

Generally, the obligation to investigate falls on the State where the death takes place. Where this is a cross-border element, the State may be required to make use of mechanisms to obtain evidence from another State, which equally would be under an obligation to co-operate in providing such evidence.[226]

Where State officials or bodies are implicated in fatal incidents arising out of dangerous activities, the Court has indicated the criminal proceedings may be required. However, this is only where it is established that the negligence attributable to State officials or bodies goes beyond an error of judgment or carelessness, in that the authorities in question, fully realising the likely consequences and disregarding the powers vested in them, failed to take measures that were necessary and sufficient to avert the risks inherent in a dangerous activity.[227] Thus, in *Öneryildiz v Turkey*, where local officials had allowed people to settle in housing close to a dangerous tip which later exploded, the Court considered that as the criminal proceedings only sought to sanction the mayors for negligence in their duty, and imposing minimum fines, rather than examine their accountability for serious loss of life it could not be said that the Turkish criminal justice system had secured the full accountability of State officials or authorities or the effective implementation of provisions of domestic law guaranteeing respect for the right to life, in particular the deterrent function of the criminal law. The same approach was adopted in case involving a fatal accident on a railway line where the Court found that authorities, in only examining the individual criminal responsibility of the conductor of the train rather than the possible liability of the railway authority itself for faulty safety precautions, were lacking in compliance with the obligation to investigate.[228]

[224] *Mikayil Mammadov*, fn.191 above, para.132; see also the Russian cases about Chechen disappearances, e.g. *Estamirov v Russia*, October 12, 2006, para.92, where there was no indication that involvement of the family was ensured by other means.

[225] *Maiorano v Italy*, fn. 148 above, paras 130–131.

[226] *Rantsev*, fn.165 above, paras 241 and 245, Cyprus was found in breach as it made no attempt to obtain evidence from Russia, where the applicant had been brought through trafficking; Russia was not found in breach, as the authorities had expressed their willingness to co-operate if any such request for evidence was forthcoming; they apparently did not have to act on their own motion.

[227] *Öneryildiz*, fn.149 above, para.116.

[228] *Kalender*, fn.153 above, paras 56–58.

It will not be in every tragic occurrence that special steps by way of investigation or enquiry will be required. In contexts such as medical negligence it may be sufficient that the relatives have the opportunity to take civil proceedings or that disciplinary proceedings are taken.[229] In *Mastromatteo v Italy*, where the applicant's son was killed by two men released from prison, it was sufficient that the State had tried and punished the two men and that the applicant could take civil proceedings against the State alleging gross negligence. Article 2 does not require that the State provide compensation on the basis of strict liability.[230] In the context of emergency services, when there is an allegation of failure promptly to take action to save life, the Court will look at whether the available legal remedies, taken together, as provided in law and applied in practice, could be said to have secured legal means capable of establishing the facts, holding accountable those at fault and providing appropriate redress to the victim. Thus in *Furdik*, there was no deficiency in the legal system, as the prosecution examined the case and found that it did not disclose a criminal offence and it had been open to the applicant to file for civil damages for damage caused by the delay in responding to the emergency.[231]

As concerns promptness and expedition, in the medical context there is an apparently rigorous standard (see above) due to the perceptions of the need to avoid repetition of life-threatening mistakes. In the road traffic sphere, it seems that the standard is less exacting: over seven years was not sufficient to cause problems,[232] whereas in a medical negligence case, the same period disclosed a breach.[233]

The procedural obligation does not extend to requiring a general, wide-ranging enquiry into the structural and policy defects that may be background to the case.[234]

Cross-reference

Part IIB, s.1: Abortion.
Part IIB, s.16: Euthanasia.
Part IIB, s.18: Extradition, sub-s.2(b): Death penalty.
Part IIB, s.46: Torture, inhuman and degrading treatment (in particular, sub-s.5: Matters of proof and causation, dealing with the standard of proof and relevance of domestic fact-finding).

[229] *Calvelli and Ciglio*, fn.193 above, para.51, concerning allegations that a doctor's negligence caused the death of the applicants' baby.

[230] See also *Vo v France*, July 8, 2004, where it was sufficient, under Art.2, that the applicant could sue for negligence in the administrative court and apply for damages in respect of a medical mistake that terminated her pregnancy.

[231] *Furdik*, fn.154 above.

[232] *Rajkowska*, fn.171 above.

[233] *Byrzykowski*, fn.150 above.

[234] See (23412/94), fn.208 above, where the authorities prosecuted the nurse for poisoning the applicants' children and there was the possibility to bring civil proceedings against the hospital for negligence, the Commission considered that Art.2 did not additionally require an enquiry into the funding and hiring flaws of the national health system.

44. Surveillance and secret files

Key provision:

II–682 Article 8 (private life).

Key case-law:

Klass v Germany, September 6, 1978, Series A, No.28, 2 E.H.R.R. 214; *Leander v Sweden*, March 26, 1987, Series A, No.116, 9 E.H.R.R. 433; *Amann v Switzerland*, February 16, 2000, ECHR 2000–II, 30 E.H.R.R. 843; *Rotaru v Romania*, May 4, 2000, ECHR 2000–V; *Khan v UK*, May 12, 2000, ECHR 2000–V, 31 E.H.R.R. 1016; *Bykov v Russia*, March 10, 2009.

1. General considerations

II–683 Under this section, the clandestine process of information-gathering and storing by democratic States is considered. While surveillance techniques will frequently involve interception of communications, this receives separate treatment under the Convention due to the specific protection of correspondence. Surveillance and intelligence gathering is a much wider and potentially unlimited field of activity. Many similar factors however come into play. The need for information gathering and storage is generally not questioned where it is in the context of police investigation or security, the legitimacy of the aims and the necessity of which is undoubted.[1] The concentration has been on lawfulness and procedural aspects to prevent arbitrariness or abuse.

2. Private life

II–684 Besides direct interception of phone and mail, there is a myriad of methods, from the use of listening devices or bugs in privately owned houses[2]; radio-transmitter devices[3]; indirect information from intercepts in place on other persons[4]; collection of press reports, data from surveillance by Special Branch, photographs (usually from passport applications)[5]; long-range cameras, drilling holes in wall[6]; and installation of a GPS device in a car.[7] Though doubt has been expressed whether the gathering of publicly accessible information or information relating to matters in the public

[1] *Leander v Sweden*, March 26, 1987, Series A, No.116, 9 E.H.R.R. 433, para.49; even where the surveillance subjects are perhaps surprising as in *Hewitt and Harman v UK (No.1)*, (12175/86) (Rep.) May 9, 1989, 67 D.R. 88; civil rights lawyers and Labour Party members or Campbell Christie, the trade union leader: (21482/93) (Dec.) June 27, 1994 78–A D.R.119. See, however, the concurring opinion in *Rotaru v Romania*, May 4, 2000, ECHR 2000–V, which stated that the Court would have been entitled to find that unlawful and arbitrary collection and storage of information on the applicant's activities going back 50 years did not pursue a legitimate aim.

[2] *Redgrave v UK*, (20271/92) (Dec.) September 1, 1993.

[3] *Bykov v Russia*, March 10, 2009, para.79.

[4] *Hewitt and Harman (No.1)*, fn.1 above.

[5] *Hewitt and Harman*, fn.1 above.

[6] *Govell v UK*, (27327/95) (Rep.) January 14, 1998.

[7] *Uzun v Germany*, September 2, 2010, paras 49–53.

domain (for example, press cutting files or criminal records) concern private life,[8] the Court has held that public information can fall within the scope of private life where it is systematically collected and stored in files held by the authorities, particularly where such information concerns a person's distant past or where it is false and likely to injure reputation.[9] While information about movement obtained by GPS tracking device was less intrusive as not revealing a person's conduct, opinion or feelings, the collation of data over a period to draw up a pattern of movements and the processing and use of that data amounted to an interference with private life.[10] So did collection of data about a human right activist's movements.[11] The Court has also stated that Art.8 corresponds with the Council of Europe's Data Protection Convention whose purpose is to secure for every individual his right to privacy with regards to the automatic processing of personal data relating to him and such personal data being defined as "any information relating to an identified or identifiable individual."[12]

A security check per se was not objectionable for the Commission which held in *Hilton v UK* that issues only arose where the check was based on information about a person's private affairs.[13]

3. State surveillance: establlishing an interference

While *Klass v Germany* concerned interception of communications in particular, it also referred to "surveillance measures" in more general terms. The Court stated that it was enough for there to be in existence a system permitting the use of such measures for Art.8, para.1 to be invoked by applicants as constituting an interference with private life. The Commission added a gloss in *Hilton v UK*, adopted later by the Court,[14] to the effect that it could not be open to anyone in the country to complain that they were subject to violations due to the activities of secret service activities: an individual had to show that there was a reasonable likelihood that he had been subject to such measures or was in a category of persons likely to be targeted. Once an applicant is in that category, it is not necessary to show that the information compiled and stored has been applied to his detriment. There seems however to be a return to the *Klass* position, as a Bulgarian human rights association was found to have victim status to complain about surveillance legislation without itself claiming to have been subject to measures. The Court distinguished the *Hilton* approach which was considered to apply only where the applicant claimed to have been affected personally by measures.[15] II–685

[8] e.g. Judge Bonello's dissent in *Rotaru*, fn.1 above. See *Zdanoka v Latvia* (GC), March 16, 2006, 45 E.H.R.R. 17, where information about the applicant contained in public archives and public knowledge about her activities was considered information about her public, not private, life.

[9] *Rotaru*, fn.1 above, paras 43–44.

[10] *Uzun*, fn.7 above, paras 49–53.

[11] *Shimovolos v Russia*, June 21, 2011, para.66.

[12] Convention for the Protection of Individuals with regard to the Automatic Processing of Personal Data, January 28, 1981, in force on October 1, 1985: *Amann v Switzerland*, February 16, 2000, ECHR 2000–II, 30 E.H.R.R. 843, para.65; *Rotaru*, fn.1 above, para.43.

[13] (12015/86) (Dec.) July 6, 1988, 57 D.R.108; also *N v UK*, (12327/86) (Rep.) May 9, 1989, 67 D.R. 123. For example, a security check might involve scrutiny only of the materials given by the person in the application or reference to files where no entries exist.

[14] *Halford v UK*, June 25, 1997, R.J.D. 1997–III, No.39.

[15] *Association for European Integration and Human Rights and Ekimdliev v Bulgaria*, June 28, 2007, para.59. See also *Weber and Saravia v Germany*, (54934/00) (Dec.) June 29, 2006, para.78; *Iordachi v Moldova*, February 10, 2009, it was enough that the applicants were at risk of measures or fell within the ambit of the legislation.

In *Hilton*, the applicant did not establish a reasonable likelihood. It was only shown that the BBC had materials submitted in the context of her job application and that the Security Service objected due to her membership of a particular society. There was no indication that it had or continued to retain any information of a personal character about her. In *Hewitt and Harman v UK (No.1)*, where an MI5 operative made revelations in an affidavit, a reasonable likelihood that secret surveillance occurred and files compiled was established. While in *N v UK*, where the applicant was offered a post connected with an electronic warfare department working on defence projects, subject to "enquiries" which he was later told were not satisfactory, the Commission found there was a reasonable inference that he had been subject to security checks.[16]

The nature of an applicant's own activities may also render it reasonably probable that surveillance had been carried out and information gathered in secret files, as in the case of Vanessa Redgrave who found a bug on her premises which she alleged had been placed by the Government. The Commission noted that she was well-known for her involvement in a revolutionary party and controversial political causes, as well as evidence from documents showing US security interest over a considerable period of time.[17]

Once a file has been in existence, it is also likely that it will be presumed to exist at a later date, in the absence of rules for destruction.[18]

4. "In accordance with law"[19]

II–686 The basic principles have received significant examination in the area of interception of communications. It is established that the lawfulness criterion refers to the existence of a basis for the interference in domestic law, and the quality of the law, which must be accessible and render measures reasonably foreseeable, thus providing protection against arbitrariness. The requirement of foreseeability however is affected by the special context of secret controls concerning national security. Thus in *Leander v Sweden* an individual did not have to be able to foresee precisely what checks would be made by the Swedish special police service. Nevertheless in a system applicable to citizens generally the law had to be sufficiently clear in its terms to give an adequate indication as to the circumstances in which and the conditions on which public authorities are empowered to resort to secret and potentially dangerous interference with private life.[20]

[16] Also *Esbester v UK*, (18601/91) (Dec.) April 2, 1993, *D, E and F v UK*, (18600–2) (Dec.) October 12, 1992, concerning applicants who applied unsuccessfully for civil service posts—the Commission accepted the Government's submissions that, for two applicants, their residence abroad rendered a satisfactory security clearance impossible so that their applications were not checked; for the third, offered a post subject to enquiries which were unsatisfactory, the Commission found it was a reasonable inference that a security check had been carried out involving reference to recorded information falling within the sphere of private life.

[17] *Redgrave*, fn.2 above.

[18] *Hewitt and Harman v UK (No.2)*, (20317/92) (Dec.) September 9, 1993, the Government ceded an interference for these applicants, in respect of whom files had already been found to have existed years before.

[19] See also Pt I, s.C: Convention Approach, para.I–066 on lawfulness.

[20] e.g. *Rotaru*, fn.1 above, paras 56–63, where the law provided no explicit, detailed provision concerning the persons authorised to consult the secret files or the use to be made of the files, nor did the system provide supervisory safeguards against abuse; *Amann*, fn.12 above, paras 75–80, where the creation and storage of a card with information on the applicant lawyer from telephone interceptions of the Soviet embassy was not carried out under a law specifying the conditions in which the card could be created or the circumstances in which the information could be stored.

Lack of a proper basis in domestic law for the activities of the security service disclosed a violation in *Hewitt and Harman v UK (No.1)*, where there was only a 1952 Home Secretary directive, which though published did not have the force of law. A similar violation arose in *Govell v UK*, where there was no statutory system regulating the use of covert listening devices.[21] Where surveillance was governed by a ministerial decree not published or accessible to the public, this criterion was not fulfilled.[22] While use of a radio transmitting device recording conversations found by the domestic authorities not to be covered by the statutory regulations led the Court to hold that such "operative experiments" were, in the absence of specific and detailed rules about the use of this surveillance technique, lacking in adequate safeguards against abuses and open to arbitrariness.[23]

In assessing the quality of the law, the Court may take into account instructions and administrative practices without status of substantive law.[24] However, the system must, provide as a minimum, a definition of the categories of people liable to be monitored; a limit on the duration of monitoring; the procedure to be followed for examining, using and storing the data obtained; the precautions to be taken when communicating the data to other parties; and the circumstances in which records may or must be destroyed.[25]

Though in *Leander* there was a wide discretion as to what information could be entered, there were also significant limitations, e.g. no entry on the basis of expression of political opinion, detailed rules on how information on the register could be used and the system was subject to the necessity of measures for the purposes of national security. However the requisite standard of protection was not met where the law defining the tasks of the Dutch Military Intelligence Services did not state the limits to be respected in carrying out their activities and there was no definition of categories of persons liable to be subject to measures of secret surveillance or the circumstances in which measures could be employed or the means to be employed.[26]

The provision of independent scrutiny of measures and rules governing the use, and destruction of material is required, as well as, apparently, provision for the subject of the measure to be notified when this will no longer jeopardise the purpose of the surveillance.[27]

Provisions do not have to be subject to comprehensive definition. In *Esbester v UK* the Commission rejected the complaint that the phrase "in the interests of national security" was only partially defined since the subject was inevitably couched in terms which had to be flexible and developed through practice. It was enough that there were express limits, in particular that the information could only be used where necessary to fulfil the specified functions. In *Hewitt and Harman (No.2)*, the Commission was not impressed that other systems limited powers more narrowly,

[21] *Govell v UK*, fn.6 above, paras 61–63, the Home Office Guidelines were neither legally binding on the police or publicly accessible.
[22] *Shimovolos*, fn.11 above, para.69.
[23] *Bykov*, fn.3 above, paras 80–83.
[24] Thus in *Leander*, fn.1 above, there was no problem since, even though there was only one administrative instruction, it was public.
[25] See, mutatis mutandis, *Association for European Integration and Human Rights*, fn.14 above, para.76; *Weber*, fn.15 above, para.95.
[26] (14084/88) (Rep.) December 3, 1991.
[27] See mutatis mutandis, concerning interception of communications, *Association of European Integration and Human Rights* case, fn.15 above.

for example, to those who advocated the use of force, as opposed to a definition which potentially covered actions intended to overthrow parliamentary democracy by non-violent means.[28]

A less rigorous standard of statutory regulation is apparently applicable to some surveillance measures than others. A GPS tracking device limited to information about movement by car in public places was regarded as less intrusive of private life than interception of communication methods. The Court did not check for the specific statutory limitations which case-law had laid down for the latter; it applied the general approach of verifying adequate safeguards against abuse.[29]

5. Necessity and procedural safeguards

II–687 Regarding the necessity of measures, there is a wide margin of appreciation accorded to Contracting States in choosing the means of protecting national security.[30] The fact that a person finds himself subject to security checks which bar him from employment or is subject to secret surveillance is not enough to disclose a violation, whether justified on the facts or not.[31] The scrutiny of the Convention organs has concentrated rather on the existence of procedural safeguards, since the grant of such powers poses a risk of undermining, even destroying democracy on the ground of defending it. There must therefore be adequate and effective guarantees against abuse, and where these exist, there may be no violation. A pragmatic and not overly demanding approach, requiring an adequate framework of safeguards of a minimum level of protection, has been adopted.

In the context of procedural safeguards, the Court has referred to direct and regular control as constituting a major safeguard against abuse. It appears impressed by the involvement of judicial or parliamentarian bodies which can provide independent scrutiny of measures. In *Leander*, the safeguards which were found sufficient included the presence of parliamentarians on the National Police Board who participated in all decisions as to whether information should be released to a requesting authority and supervision by the Parliamentary Ombudsman and the Chancellor of Justice.

Following *Klass*, no problem arises as such from the failure to notify subjects of surveillance measures since it is the absence of communication which ensures at least partly the efficacy of the control procedure. It appears however that there should be some provision made for subsequent notification to the subject of the measure as and when this becomes possible.[32]

In *Esbester v UK*, where the applicant attacked the system set up under the Security Service Act 1989, the Commission found references to systems in other jurisdictions of limited relevance. While other arrangements might be more liberal, its role was to see if the system under examination in the concrete case passed the

[28] *Hewitt and Harman (No.2)*, fn.18 above.

[29] *Uzun*, fn.7 above, paras 65–67.

[30] *Leander*, fn.1 above, para.59.

[31] (35099/94) (Dec.) April 5, 1995, 81–A D.R. 136, where the Northern Irish applicant, living in Geneva, was subject to allegedly unjustified police surveillance but could only gain limited access to the files to refute their contents. Procedural safeguards were sufficient.

[32] *Weber and Saravia*, fn.15 above, para.136, citing German legislative safeguards with approval. This aspect has also been dealt with in the context of "lawfulness": see *Association of European Integration and Human Rights* case, fn.15 above.

threshold imposed by Convention guarantees.[33] As a whole the 1989 Act provided adequate safeguards against abuse—an independent tribunal with lawyers of 10 years' experience and a Commissioner of high judicial office who made annual reports to Parliament and recommendations to the Secretary of State. It did not therefore consider that the inability of the Commissioner to make binding decisions, or the limited scope of the tribunal's review and its inability to verify or correct information recorded were decisive. In the absence of any indication that the system was not functioning as required by domestic law, it considered that the framework of safeguards achieved a compromise between the requirements of defending democratic society and the rights of the individual. When further complaint was made in *Hewitt and Harman v UK (No.2)*, the Commission, in examining the Commissioner's reports, found that he was fulfilling his role actively and authoritatively, and therefore saw no reason to depart from its reasoning in *Esbester*, namely, the system functioned properly. The complaints, inter alia, that the tribunal did not hear witnesses on oath, that its decisions were brief and that Commissioner could not order the destruction of records where he found it unreasonable to retain them, were not given weight.[34]

Prior approval of measures by a judge or court is not required, as long as there is an effective court review of any complaints *ex post facto*.[35]

Regarding any right to consult data held on files, for example to correct any erroneous entries, the cases do not indicate that this can be derived from Art.8 as yet. Though a right of consultation, even limited is commented on favourably in assessing the procedural safeguards available, no violation has yet been founded upon its absence as such.[36] In *Brinks v Netherlands*, where provision was made for disclosure and judicial scrutiny of non-disclosed material, it was found proportionate to limit the applicant's access to the information held on him by the intelligence service to outdated information which did not contain personal data relating to a third party and which could not give an insight into sources, working methods and current level of knowledge, as such might undermine the security of the State.[37] Further, in *Turek v Slovakia*, there was a violation due to the lack of a procedure by which the applicant could seek effective protection of his right to respect for his private life. The Court did not express its views as to whether a problem could have arisen if he had enjoyed a proper procedure and still been refused access. It also distinguished this case, concerning lustration and information gathered under previous communist regime, from current intelligence files relevant to the ongoing security of the State.[38]

Authorities should consider whether less intrusive measures are practicable. Intensive surveillance, by different agencies, was regarded as a serious interference

[33] *Esbester v UK*, fn.16 above. See also *Hewitt and Harman (No.2)*, fn.18 above, comparison with other systems (Canadian and Australian) might indicate that the Government incorrectly assumed that other methods were not practicable but that did not assist in determining whether the concrete case passed the threshold.

[34] *Hewitt and Harman v UK (No.2)*, fn.18 above.

[35] *Uzun*, fn.7 above, paras 71–73.

[36] This point was raised unsuccessfully by *D, E, and F*, fn.16 above, and the lack of any possibility to amend errors was referred to in *Hewitt and Harman (No.1)*, fn.1 above. See also *Leander*, fn.1 above, para.48, where the inability to check contents was part of the interference; (35099/94), fn.24 above, where complete access was not necessary.

[37] *Brinks v Netherlands*, April 5, 2005.

[38] *Turek v Slovakia*, February 14, 2006, paras 116–117.

but justified due to the seriousness of the terrorist offence under investigation, the short period of the measures and the fact other lesser measures had been tried and failed. Where total and comprehensive surveillance is concerned, the Court would seem likely to impose more rigorous requirements.[39]

6. Use of material in court

II–688 The fact that material was obtained unlawfully or in breach of lawfulness requirements in Art.8 does not per se require its exclusion as use in evidence. The overriding consideration is fairness under Art.6. If the applicant has due opportunity in adversarial procedure to challenge the reliability of the evidence, no failure to respect the rights of the defence may be disclosed. Issues may however arise if the material involves a breach of the applicant's right not to incriminate himself or involves entrapment. Where the applicant's conversations with an informer were recorded on his own property, the Court detected no elements of coercion or oppression, the applicant free to avoid or not to talk to the informer if he wished. Further, as the recording played only a limited role in the proceedings, no breach of Art.6 was found.[40]

7. Surveillance by private individuals

II–689 Where the surveillance is not conducted by the State, the approach adopted by the Court has a different emphasis. It examines whether the State has complied with any positive obligation to balance the competing interests. Sufficient protection of private life may be given by effective court scrutiny without the existence of a specific statutory system of protection. Where in order to uncover a dishonest employee, a supermarket conducted video surveillance of the applicant cashier, the Court considered the domestic courts properly balanced the interests of the employer against the private life interference of the employee; the lack of statutory regulation of such surveillance by private individuals was not problematic.[41]

Cross-reference

Part IIB, s.30: Interception of communications.
Part IIB, s.37: Private Life.

[39] *Uzun*, fn.7 above, paras 77–81.

[40] *Bykov*, fn.3 above, paras 94–105. See also Part IIB, s.30: Interception of Communication, sub-s.6: Use of material in court proceedings

[41] *Kropke v Germany*, (420/07) (Dec.) October 5, 2010, due weight had been given by the courts to the brevity of the surveillance: considering the ineffectiveness of other means of discovering the thief and the property rights of the supermarket. There was a heavy hint that for more intrusive types of surveillance a different result might have been reached.

45. Tax

Key provisions:

Articles 5, para.1 (right to liberty), 6 (access to court and fair trial) and Art.1 of Protocol No.1 (right to property). II–690

Key case-law:

Darby v Sweden, October 23, 1990, Series A, No.187, 13 E.H.R.R. 774; *Bendenoun v France*, February 24, 1994, Series A, No.284, 18 E.H.R.R. 54; *Gasus Dosier GmbH v Netherlands*, February 23, 1995, Series A, No.306–B, 20 E.H.R.R. 403; *Benham v UK*, June 10, 1996, R.J.D. 1996–III, No.10, 20 E.H.R.R. 293; *National & Provincial Building Society v UK*, October 23, 1997, R.J.D. 1997–VII, No.55, 25 E.H.R.R. 127; *Ferrazzini v Italy*, July 12, 2001, ECHR 2001–VII; *Jokela v Finland*, May 21, 2002, ECHR 2002–IV; *Janosevic v Sweden*, July 23, 2002, ECHR 2002–VII; *Jussila v Finland*, November 23, 2006, ECHR 2006–XIII.

1. General considerations

Tax receives special treatment under the Convention. Not surprisingly, in drafting the Convention, the Contracting States did not intend to undermine the basis on which their financing depends. An individual's right to enjoyment of his property is accordingly subject to the State's right to assess, levy and enforce contributions by way of tax under the second paragraph of Art.1 of the First Protocol. The provision is to be interpreted in light of the underlying principle in the first sentence of the first paragraph of Protocol No.1, namely, to achieve a fair balance between the general interest of the community and the protection of the fundamental rights of the individual.[1] II–691

There are few significant cases concerning the way in which States choose to tax or the levels of taxation. Where issues arise the ubiquitous margin of appreciation is present and wide. Arguable complaints arise more frequently in peripheral areas, as regards access to court and fairness of proceedings in tax-related matters. Peripheral issues may also arise where there is apparent discrimination in tax matters.

2. Imposition of tax: assessment and levels

It is for national authorities to decide in the first place what kind of taxes or contributions are to be collected and the methods by which they are collected, such decisions commonly involving the appreciation of political, economic and societal questions which the Convention leaves within the competence of the Contracting States which enjoy a wide margin of appreciation.[2] The Commission found no problems arising as regards the imposition on employers of the costly PAYE system,[3] the increase of contributions on certain categories of persons to benefit II–692

[1] *Sporrong and Llonroth v Sweden*, September 23, 1982, Series A No.52, para.69.

[2] (11036/84) (Dec.) December 2, 1985, 45 D.R. 211; *Spacek SRO v Czech Republic*, November 9, 1999, para.41.

[3] (7427/76) (Dec.) September 27, 1976, 7 D.R. 148.

others[4] and the imposition of retrospective tax measures;[5] while the Court dismissed complaints against a rise in a licence fee for running gaming machines[6] and against a high wealth tax rate of 85% imposed on the excessively rich.[7]

But there may be limits. The Commission stated that the imposition of tax would not generally be incompatible with Art.1 of Protocol No.1 unless it amounted to a de facto confiscation of some part of the taxpayer's possessions.[8] A financial liability might conceivably raise problems if it placed an excessive burden on the person concerned or fundamentally undermined with his financial position.[9] Reference is also made in cases to whether the imposition of a tax is disproportionate or an abuse of the State's power.[10] The cases indicate that gross arbitrariness or misuse of powers would be required for the Convention organs to find any violation. In *Jokela v Finland*, for example, the Court found a violation where the authorities, in levying inheritance tax on land, had given insufficient explanation for the highly inflated market value used in reaching the assessment, which was glaringly inconsistent with the low value placed on the property for the purposes of expropriation. There was also a failure to strike a fair balance where, due to the unjustified and excessive delays in paying compensation for expropriated land, the sums finally paid became subject to a new and significant tax, thereby imposing an excessive burden on the applicant.[11]

3. Rebates and refunds

II–693 Where a taxpayer fulfills the criteria in domestic law for repayment of tax or compensation for overpaid tax, the Court has found that a repeated failure, without any apparent reason, to confirm the amounts due to enable recovery placed an excessive burden on the applicant contrary to Art.1 of Protocol No.1.[12] A failure by the authorities to provide for the repayment of VAT paid by companies which had been exonerated by an EU directive similarly failed to strike the fair balance between the individual and public interest.[13] Refusing a business the right to deduct

[4] (7995/77) (Dec.) July 11, 1978, 15 D.R. 198, where the imposition of additional N.I. contributions on some self-employed fell within of Art.1, para.2 of Protocol No.1 as justified in the general interest for financing the social security system for lower earners.

[5] (8531/79) (Dec.) March 10, 1981, 23 D.R. 203, concerning retrospective legislation to prevent deliberate trading losses to set off against tax—the measure was not excessive: tax liabilities for the previous year had not yet been settled and the losses were artificial.

[6] *Orion-Breclav, SRO v Czech Republic*, (43783/98) (Dec.) January 13, 2004.

[7] *Imbert de Tremiolles v France*, (25834/05) and (27815/05) (Dec.) January 4, 2008, the applicants' allegations that the tax imposed exceeded their income was not made out in the circumstances.

[8] (9908/82) (Dec.) May 4, 1983, 32 D.R. 266, where the tax authorities upped the applicant's tax, regarding large investments in companies as income unless shown to derive from capital or a gift. See mutatis mutandis, *Mamidakis v Greece*, January 11, 2007, where the size of administrative fines (over €3 million) was so large as to amount to confiscation of the applicant's property.

[9] e.g. *Buffalo SRL in liquidation v Italy*, July 3, 2003, para.32; *Orion Breclav SRO v Czech Republic*, rejecting complaints about a 300 per cent rise in licencing fees on gaming machines, fn.6 above.

[10] (13013/87) (Dec.) December 14, 1988, 58 D.R. 163, concerning a 7 per cent wealth tax on life assurance companies, the Commission noted the measure was introduced to tackle the budget deficit and inflation: it referred to the "sovereign power" of the State and found no lack of proportionality or abuse.

[11] *Di Belmonte v Italy*, March 16, 2010, paras 43–47.

[12] *Intersplav v Ukraine*, January 9, 2007.

[13] *Aon Conseil and Courtage SA v France*, January 25, 2007; see also *Dangeville SA v France*, April 16, 2002, ECHR 2002–III, paras 52–61, and *Buffalo SRL*, fn.9 above, where there was undue delay and uncertainty in the repayment of tax credits and the payment of simple interest was not sufficient compensation for the situation.

VAT due to the lack of payment by its suppliers did not strike a fair balance: while the authorities could claim a public interest in enforcing VAT regulations, the penalisation of a fully compliant business who had no control or knowledge of defaults further up the chain went too far.[14]

4. Measures in enforcement of taxation and duties

Measures taken to ensure the payment of taxes or prevent defaulting are generally found compatible with the second paragraph of Art.1 of Protocol No.1. There is perhaps not as close a scrutiny as under other provisions, as this area is recognised as concerning the hard core of public law prerogatives. Nonetheless issues of unlawfulness, arbitrariness and manifest lack of proportionality can still arise. II–694

Consideration is given to whether the measure is of such a kind that it can reasonably be regarded as necessary for the purpose and whether its application is grossly disproportionate.[15] The imposition of a mortgage on a defaulter in favour of the authorities to ensure payments was not disproportionate[16] and the prevention of the removal of property from the country by a person with outstanding tax liabilities fell within the second paragraph of Art.1.[17] The seizure by the tax authorities of a concrete mixer over which the vendor applicant had retained title was not a deprivation of property within the meaning of the first paragraph but a measure to secure the payment of taxes. In the circumstances the applicant company was involved in a commercial venture, which by its very nature involved an element of risk. Proportionality was satisfied since it could have taken measures of protection, such as stipulating payment in advance, which the tax authorities were not in a position to do in respect of defaulters, and the applicant was not without a measure of protection since it enjoyed priority over other creditors and an adequate review procedure before the courts.[18]

It was not regarded as particularly excessive to put an applicant's television under seal for failure to pay his licence fees.[19]

5. Penalties and fines: failure to comply with tax authorities

Where a person is penalised for failure to comply with tax regulations, issues may arise where the sanction falls within the scope of "criminal charge" for the purposes of Art.6, para.1.[20] In *Bendenoun v France*, where a taxpayer, accused of not acting in good faith in relation to declared business receipts, was subject to tax surcharges (almost half a million francs) the Court agreed with the Commission that the tax surcharges concerned a "criminal charge" rendering the Art.6 guarantees applicable. It noted the charges were imposed under the Tax Code which applied to everyone; II–695

[14] *Bulves AD v Bulgaria*, January 22, 2009, paras 62–71.

[15] (7287/75) (Dec.) March 3, 1978, 13 D.R. 27, the duties, fines and forfeiture were not so disproportionate in this case since the judge could have regard to the applicant's economic means and, though very severe, they were not excessive.

[16] (9889/82) (Dec.) October 6, 1982, 31 D.R. 237.

[17] (10653/83) (Dec.) May 6, 1985, 42 D.R. 224.

[18] *Gasus Dosier GmbH v Netherlands*.

[19] *Faccio v Italy*, (33/04) (Dec.) March 3, 2009.

[20] See, e.g. *Janosevic* and *Vastaberga Taxi Aktiebolag v Sweden*, July 23, 2002, where penalty surcharges were imposed on the applicants in addition to the amount of unpaid tax.

were not intended as pecuniary compensation for damage but essentially as a punishment to deter reoffending; were posed under a general rule whose purpose was deterrent and punitive; and there was liability of committal to prison for non-payment. However, tax surcharges may be regarded as a "criminal penalty" even where there is no risk of committal to prison, if they are nonetheless punitive and deterrent in character.[21] The Court has recently clarified that the mere fact that the surcharge is a small amount will not be enough to remove it from the criminal sphere; the purpose of the surcharge as deterrent and punitive is the decisive criterion.[22] Once Art.6 is applicable, the usual guarantees concerning effective access to court and fairness of procedures apply, but may be tailored to the special nature of the proceedings. Thus, in *Jussila v Finland*, the Court found that an oral hearing was not required in the interests of fairness due to the nature of the issues which could be adequately dealt with on the basis of written submissions.[23]

Where a person is committed for failure to pay tax, this may constitute detention compatible with Art.5, para.1(b) as lawful arrest or detention in order to secure the fulfilment of an obligation prescribed by law. Issues have arisen in the context of poll tax, as to whether magistrates have complied with lawfulness criteria in exercising the power to commit defaulters.[24]

6. Civil rights

II–696 Art.6 does not apply to proceedings relating to the assessment or imposition of tax, including the consequences of a change in tax legislation.[25]

In *Ferrazzini v Italy*, the Court emphasised that tax matters still formed part of the hard core of public authority prerogatives. The fact that pecuniary interests of the tax payer might be at stake was not sufficient to remove tax from the public law sphere.[26]

In *National & Provincial Building Society v UK*, where the applicants were claiming restitution of monies paid under invalid tax regulations however, the Convention organs found that Art.6 applied. The restitution proceedings were regarded as private law actions decisive for private law rights to quantifiable sums of money and the judicial review proceedings were closely related to them.[27]

7. Retrospectivity

II–697 There is no express prohibition on retrospective legislation outside the criminal sphere. However, in respect of a retrospective removal of tax relief aimed at preventing tax avoidance, the Commission held that a retrospective measure

[21] *Janosevic*, fn.20 above, para.68.

[22] *Jussila v Finland*, November 23, 2006, ECHR 2006–XIII, para.38: a surcharge of €308.80 was nonetheless criminal in nature.

[23] *Jussila*, fn.22 above, para.47, no issues of credibility or necessity for cross-examination of witnesses; close connection with the assessment of tax which itself was outside the scope of Art.6. See also *Barsom and Varli v Sweden*, (407766/06) and (40831/06) (Dec.) December 4, 2008, where legal aid for representation was not required where businessmen were challenging the imposition of a tax surcharge, such not being indispensable for them to adequately put forward their defence.

[24] *Benham v UK*, June 10, 1996, R.J.D. 1996–III, No.10, 20 E.H.R.R. 293. See Pt IIB, s.9: Deprivation of liberty, sub-s.5: In accordance with a procedure prescribed by law.

[25] *Joubert v France*, July 23, 2009, paras 30–32.

[26] *Ferrazzini v Italy*, July 12, 2001, ECHR 2001–VII, paras 28–31, where the Court confirmed, tacitly, Commission case-law. However, where criminal charges relate to tax matters, Art.6 in its criminal head will apply, albeit not necessarily in full force: see Part IIA, s.1b: Civil rights and obligations.

[27] Also *Editions Periscope v France*, March 26, 1992, Series A No.234–B, para.40.

imposing a liability or removing a relief must be regarded as more severe due to the uncertainty which it engenders, in particular since it prevents a taxpayer arranging his affairs to mitigate new liabilities. On the facts of that particular case however, the measure was not excessive.[28]

Where claims are made for tax rebates, retrospective legislation which interferes with the ongoing litigation may interfere excessively with legitimate expectations protected by Art.1 of Protocol No. 1.[29]

8. Other types of contributions

Requirements to pay child support payments have been found to fall within this part of Art.1 of Protocol No. 1. Thus, discrimination issues have arisen in respect of unjustified differences in such obligations as between gay couples and heterosexual couples.[30] II–698

Requirement to pay court fees in proceedings challenging the amount of compensation for expropriated land were regarded as "contributions" in *Perdigao v Portugal* but as the issue concerned the fact that the fees swallowed up the entire amount of compensation, it was examined as an interference with right to peaceful enjoyment of possessions under the first sentence of Art.1 of Protocol No. 1. The minority dissenters pointed out that previously excessive court fees had been regarded under Art.6 as an access to court problem, and warned that the finding that the imposition of the court fees infringed Art.1 of Protocol No. 1 as being excessive was an undesirable abandonment of the principle that the imposition of taxes and contributions should not as a rule be challengeable under that provision.[31]

Compulsory contributions imposed on insurance companies to help fund emergency services and prevent road accidents were not a problem, there being nothing to indicate that such a levy was prohibitive, oppressive or disproportionate.[32]

9. Discrimination

Differences in treatment of persons in relevantly similar positions may raise issues under Art.14 in conjunction with Art.1 of Protocol No.1 since matters of taxation fall within the scope of that provision. The Commission considered that a wider margin of appreciation would apply in this area than in others, since taxation systems inevitably differentiate between groups of taxpayers and the implementation of any system creates marginal situations. It noted that attitudes and goals in taxation will change and a government may need to strike a balance between the need to raise revenue and to reflect other social objectives, the authorities being best placed to assess those requirements and the moment when it was appropriate to amend the tax system. Where the applicant was complaining of the inequal effect of II–699

[28] (8531/79), fn.5 above.

[29] e.g. *Joubert v France*, fn.25 above, retrospective legislation impinging on recovery of tax rebates was a disproportionate interference not justified by any pressing state interest, mere avoidance of financial liability not being enough. See also Part IIB, s.38: Property, sub-s.2(d): Debts and claims.

[30] *JM v UK*, September 28, 2010.

[31] *Perdigao v Portugal*, November 16, 2010. See also *Hoare v UK*, (16261/08) (Dec.) April 12, 2011, order to pay costs of opposing party regarded as an interference with possessions, not the imposition of "contributions".

[32] *Allianz-Slovenska poistovna, AS v Slovakia*, (19276/05) (Dec.) November 9, 2010.

taxation depending on whether the husband or the wife was the principal earner and pointed to the pending proposal to render the position of spouses identical, the Commission found that the anomaly resulted from measures of positive discrimination in favour of married women to encourage them into the job market and was proportionate and within the margin of appreciation. It also considered that for taxation purposes married and unmarried couples were not in comparable positions, marriage constituting a regime which attracted specific rights and obligations.[33]

Different tax rates can be justified by the consideration of avoiding too high a burden on lower earners.[34] Differences applied to taxpayers who live abroad may be justified, as in the case where civil servants working abroad were liable to pay Austrian tax on part of their salary but were unable to claim a single breadwinner's allowance. The Commission, having regard to the margin of appreciation, found that the difference could be justified since it was difficult for the Austrian authorities to verify what happpened outside their borders.[35] However in *Darby v Sweden* where the applicant was liable to pay church tax in Sweden even though he was not resident in the country but could not, unlike residents, apply for an exemption, the Court found no objective or reasonable justification in the alleged administrative difficulties that eligibility to non-residents would engender.

Cross-reference

Part IIA, s.1: General principles: fairness.
Part IIA, s.1a: Criminal charge.
Part IIA, s.1b: Civil rights and obligations.
Part IIB, s.12: Discrimination.
Part IIB, s.38: Property.

[33] (11089/84) (Dec.) November 11, 1986, 49 D.R. 181. See further, Part IIB, s.12: Discrmination, sub-s.7(a): Sex.
[34] (7995/77), fn.4 above.
[35] (12560/86) (Dec.) March 16,1989, 60 D.R. 194.

46. Torture, inhuman and degrading treatment

Key provision:

Article 3 (prohibition on torture, inhuman and degrading treatment or punishment). II–700

Key case-law:

Ireland v UK, January 18, 1978, Series A, No.25, 2 E.H.R.R. 25; *Tyrer v UK*, April 25, 1978, Series A, No.26, 2 E.H.R.R. 1: *Soering v UK*, July 7, 1989, Series A, No.161, 11 E.H.R.R. 169; *Tomasi v France*, August 27, 1992, Series A, No.241–A, 15 E.H.R.R 1; *Herczegfalvy v Austria*, September 24, 1992, Series A, No.244, 15 E.H.R.R. 437; *Costello-Roberts v UK*, March 25, 1993 Series A, No.247–C, 19 E.H.R.R. 112; *Ribitsch v Austria*, December 4, 1995, Series A, No.336, 21 E.H.R.R. 573; *Chahal v UK*, November 15, 1996, R.J.D. 1996–V, No.22, 23 E.H.R.R. 413; *Aksoy v Turkey*, December 18, 1996, R.J.D. 1996–VI, No.26, 23 E.H.R.R. 553; *Aydin v Turkey*, September 25, 1997, 1997–VI, No.50; *Raninen v Finland*, December 16, 1997, R.J.D. 1997–VIII, No.60, 26 E.H.R.R. 563; *A v UK*, September 23, 1998, 1998–VI, No.90, 27 E.H.R.R. 611; *Assenov v Bulgaria*, October 28, 1998, R.J.D. 1998–VII, No.96; *Selmouni v France*, July 28, 1999, ECHR 1999–V, 29 E.H.R.R. 403; *Ilhan v Turkey*, June 27, 2000, ECHR 2000–VII; *Keenan v UK*, April 3, 2001, ECHR 2001–III; *Z v UK*, May 10, 2001, ECHR 2001–V; *Kalashnikov v Russia*, July 15, 2002, ECHR 2002–VI; *Ocalan v Turkey*, May 12, 2005, ECHR 2005–IV; *MC v Bulgaria*, December 4, 2003, ECHR 2003–XII; *Nevmerzhitsky v Ukraine*, April 5, 2005, ECHR 2005–II; *Jalloh v Germany*, July 11, 2006, ECHR 2006–IX; *Gäfgen v Germany*, June 10, 2010, ECHR 2010–. . . ; *M.S.S. v Greece and Belgium*, January 21, 2011, ECHR 2011–. . .

1. General approach

Article 3 sets an absolute prohibition. There are no stated exceptions and no derogation is possible under Art.15. The Court has said that it enshrines one of the fundamental values of the democratic societies making up the Council of Europe[1] and calls for heightened vigilance.[2] It applies irrespective of the victim's conduct or whether life is at stake.[3] II–701

That said, however, and perhaps as a result, the threshold for treatment falling within the scope of Art.3 was initially set high by the Convention organs. The

[1] *Soering v UK*, July 7, 1989, Series A, No.161, 11 E.H.R.R. 169, para.88.

[2] *Ribitsch v Austria*, December 4, 1995, Series A, No.336, 21 E.H.R.R. 573, para.32.

[3] Governments have argued that in certain circumstances Art.3 does not have full effect. In *Chahal v UK*, November 15, 1996, R.J.D. 1996–V, No.22, 23 E.H.R.R. 413, the Court rejected the argument that the expulsion of the alleged Sikh terrorist to India was justified due to the security threat posed to the UK if he stayed; in *Tomasi v France*, August 27, 1992, Series A, No.241–A, 15 E.H.R.R 1, that it was relevant that the applicant was a terrorist and involved in a violent crime was smartly rejected by the Court which held that the fight against crime and difficulties with regard to terrorism could not justify limits on the protection to be afforded to the physical integrity of individuals (para.115). Even where the threat of torture was applied to obtain information to save a kidnapped child's life, the Court held that this was not an exception or justifying circumstance: *Gäfgen v Germany*, June 10, 2010, ECHR 2010–. . . , para.107.

Commission in the Greek Inter-State case distinguished acts prohibited by Art.3 from a "certain roughness of treatment", which might take the form of slaps or blows of the hand on the face or head.[4] The Court distinguished between the use of violence which is to be condemned on moral grounds and also in most cases under the domestic law of the Contracting States but which does not fall within Art.3.[5] The test established by the Court is that of attaining a certain minimum level of severity. The basic approach is:

> ". . . ill-treatment must attain a minimum level of severity if it is to fall within the scope of Article 3. The assessment of this minimum is, in the nature of things, relative; it depends on all the circumstances of the case, such as the duration of the treatment, its physical and mental effects and, in some cases, the sex, age and state of health of the victim."[6]

While in the early years of the Convention system there was perhaps a sentiment that to find a State in violation of this provision was particularly serious and not to be undertaken lightly, there has, since the new Court, been an evolution in the application of that minimum level and a more rigorous standard is now considered appropriate,[7] though it still describes itself as attentive to the seriousness that attaches to a ruling that a Contracting State has violated fundamental rights.[8] A certain trend may perhaps be appearing in the case-law which focusses on the maintenance of proper and humane standards of conduct by the authorities rather than the actual impact on the applicant or any concrete indications of significant harm or suffering.[9]

The Convention system has received, and continues to receive, many complaints of grave, distressing situations in which Art.3 is invoked. However, expulsion or extradition per se (without any risk to life or limb being involved), the taking into care and adoption of a person's children, the imposition of long sentences of imprisonment, while they may all entail significant personal distress are not such as to fall within Art.3, particularly where the distress is a collateral effect of measures primarily aimed at achieving other legitimate aims.[10] There would have to be special elements or circumstances bringing the case beyond the "usual" effect that the

[4] *The Greek Case*, (3321–3/67) and (3344/67), 11th Yearbook of the ECHR, (Rep.) November 5, 1969, (1969), 501. More controversially, it commented that this was tolerated, even taken for granted by the detainees and that the point up to which people accepted physical violence as being neither cruel nor excessive depended on societies and the different sections within them: see also the Commission in *Ireland v UK*, January 18, 1978, Series A, No.25, 2 E.H.R.R. 25, in respect of conditions in holding centres, i.e. no bedding, compulsory "military drill" type exercises, even though some detainees were old and in poor condition this was harsh, even illegal, and a practice that was reprehensible but not contrary to Art.3.

[5] *Ireland v UK*, fn.4 above, para.167.

[6] *Ireland v UK*, fn.4 above, para.162.

[7] See *Selmouni v France*, July 28, 1999, ECHR 1999–V, 29 E.H.R.R. 403, para.101, and the cases on prison conditions below.

[8] e.g. *Nachova v Bulgaria*, July 6, 2005, ECHR 2005–VII, para.147.

[9] See, e.g. standards of care of prisoners (sub-s.4(e): Illness and access to medical treatment) and standards of treatment applied to asylum-seekers (sub-s.6(b): Obligation to prevent ill-treatment).

[10] e.g. *V v UK*, December 16, 1999, ECHR 1999–IX, para.71. See also *D v UK*, (38000/05) (Dec.) March 4, 2008, where the applicant parents were mistakenly suspected of abusing their child who had suffered an unexplained injury, this error was not enough in itself to disclose Art.3 treatment, even if causing distress and humiliation; some factor apart from the normal implementation of child protection duties had to be present.

measure inevitably entails, such as discrimination based on racial grounds which degrade and stigmatise[11] or perhaps where the execution of the measure is unnecessarily and unjustifiably distressful.[12]

The principal Art.3 treatment cases have risen in the context of physical ill-treatment inflicted by the authorities or agents of the State—the archetypal police or prison brutality type case. This is gradually being extended to risk of severe physical or psychological harm where a State takes steps which may lead to a person being exposed to such harm, or even to the imposition of a positive obligation, to take steps to avoid such risk occurring. This is in the context of expulsion and extradition particularly but has been raised also in the context of punishment of children[13] and increasingly as regards the medical treatment and facilities available for prisoners (see further below (3e): Illness and access to medical treatment).

Only individuals can invoke Art.3, not legal persons.[14] And as death extinguishes the human identity it does not apply to mutilation or ill-treatment of dead bodies as such, however cruel.[15]

The importance of Art.3 is also reflected in the development of a procedural obligation requiring States to investigate effectively incidents of alleged ill-treatment (see further below). As in the context of Art.2, these have led to certain implications for admissiblity criteria, namely, the application of the rule on exhaustion of domestic remedies and the circumstances in which an applicant may lose victim status.

2. Admissibility issues—victim status and remedies

Where an applicant alleges ill-treatment at the hands of State officers, there must be an acknowledgement, expressly or in substance, or the breach and redress must be afforded before victim status is lost. A finding by the courts that unlawful ill-treatment has occurred will generally satisfy the first. However, for redress it appears to be required, firstly, to avoid abuse of rights with impunity, that there has been an effective investigation capable of leading to the identification and punishment of those responsible and, secondly, an award of compensation must be available, where appropriate, or the possibility of seeking such. An investigation II–702

[11] *East African Asians case*, (4403/70) etc. (Rep.) December 14, 1973, 78–A D.R. 5; however, see *Abdulaziz v UK*, May 28, 1985, Series A, No.94, para.91, where the difference in treatment in immigration matters did not denote any contempt or lack of respect for the personality of the applicants, but was intended solely to achieve the aims of protection of employment, the economy and immigration control.

[12] e.g. (19579–82/92), April 4, 1993, the Orkney childcare cases were communicated under Art.3 in relation to the dawn raid, the complete separation from families and familiar objects, and intensive "interrogations"; the question would possibly have arisen whether these were accepted practices and without any therapeutic basis (applications later withdrawn); *V v UK*, fn.10 above, para.79, where the traumatic effects of the murder trial on the 11–year-old defendant did not cause, to a significant degree, suffering going beyond what would inevitably have been engendered by an attempt by the authorities to deal with him after the offence.

[13] e.g. *Soering*, fn.1 above; *Chahal*, fn.3 above; *D v UK*, May 2, 1997, R.J.D. 1997–III, No.37 (expulsion cases); as regards corporal punishment of children in school *Costello-Roberts v UK*, March 25, 1993 Series A, No.247–C, 19 E.H.R.R. 112, and *A v UK*, September 23, 1998, 1998–VI, No.90, 27 E.H.R.R. 611 (see Part IIB, s.7: Corporal punishment).

[14] (11921/86) (Dec.) October 12, 1988, 57 D.R. 81.

[15] *Akpinar and Altun v Turkey*, February 27, 2007, suffering amounting to Art.3 treatment was found, however, as regarded the presentation of the mutilated bodies to close relatives.

leading to a criminal trial and conviction will not be sufficiently effective if the penalty imposed is not sufficiently deterrent and does not reflect the gravity of the act. The test is whether there is a manifest disproportion between the breach of the core right and the punishment. In *Gäfgen v Germany*, where police officers threatened a suspect with torture and were punished by suspended fines of small amounts, the Court considered that this raised serious doubts as to the authorities' reaction reflecting the seriousness of what was involved.[16] In cases of acts of more serious brutality, it would appear that the imposition of enforceable prison sentences would be appropriate.[17] The examination of whether the authorities have properly reacted to the seriousness of the breach also covers disciplinary proceedings and sanctions. Officers charged with ill-treatment should, the Court seems quite categorical on the point, be suspended from duty pending investigation and dismissed if convicted.[18] This does not seem to leave much leeway for authorities to take into account mitigating or other special circumstances.

Where the civil remedies prove ineffective, either due to undue delay,[19] or due to the fact that the amount of compensation is regarded as inadequate,[20] a victim will also retain victim status. The issue as to whether redress for ill-treatment applied by police officers to obtain confessions would require the evidence to be held inadmissible has been left open for the moment.[21]

The above factors also take on relevance as regards exhaustion of domestic remedies. Civil remedies which drag on or which cannot provide non-pecuniary damage of an adequate amount will not apparently be regarded as effective, nor those which, in systems in which victims can join criminal proceedings as civil parties, are undermined by inadequacies in the criminal investigation or criminal justice system. Further, the Court has taken to applying the principle that effective deterrence against ill-treatment by State officials, where fundamental values are at stake, requires efficient criminal-law provisions and that civil remedies, aimed at awarding damages rather than identifying and punishing those responsible, are not sufficient in that context: thus, in continental systems an applicant is frequently found to have complied with the requirements of exhaustion by merely bringing the ill-treatment to the attention of the prosecuting authorities.[22]

Where the domestic system provides an effective mechanism whereby those with criminal or civil responsibility may be held answerable, wider questions raised by the background of the incident or as to the policy measures apt to prevent any

[16] *Gäfgen v Germany*, fn.3 above, paras 120–125.

[17] *Gäfgen*, fn.3 above, para.124, citing *Nikolova and Velichkova v Bulgaria*, December 20, 2007, para.63 and *Ali and Ayse Duran v Turkey*, April 8, 2008, paras 67–72, Art.2 killing cases where the officers received a minimum and suspended prison sentence considered inadequate to the seriousness of what was at stake: procedural violations.

[18] *Gäfgen*, fn.3 above, para.125, the Court frowned at the fact one police officer even seemed to have been promoted.

[19] *Gäfgen*, fn.3 above, para.127.

[20] *Ciorap v Moldova (No.2)*, July 20, 2010, paras 24–26, the amount awarded by the domestic court for inhuman treatment was €600, which was considerably below what the Court considered it had awarded in previous cases, citing examples of awards of €6,000. It in fact awarded €4,000 itself.

[21] *Gäfgen*, fn.3 above, paras 128–129. See the minority opinion of Judges Tulken, Ziemele and Bianku who considered that exclusion of the evidence was the most appropriate redress and that sentencing should be left for the domestic courts, particularly since the deterrent effects of prison was open to doubt, and sentencing was a delicate and difficult task requiring knowledge and proximity to the facts: imprisonment, for them, should always be a last resort.

[22] e.g. *Mader v Croatia*, June 21, 2011, para.90.

recurrence in the future are matters for public and political debate which fall outside the scope of Art.3 of the Convention.[23]

3. Different categories of ill-treatment

Consideration is given to the particular circumstances of each case. Relevant factors include the manner and method of execution of the punishment; the nature and context of the punishment[24]; premeditation and systematic organisation; age[25]; sex[26]; duration[27]; effect on health[28]; state of health at the time[29]; public nature of the punishment[30]; whether alternative courses were open to the authorities[31] and the necessity and proportionality of measures taken for security or crime detection reasons.[32] The Court also appears to give weight to the unlawful nature of a measure as exacerbating the mental anguish.[33] II–703

While a certain seriousness of effects, whether physical or mental, has usually been required for findings of treatment incompatible with Art.3, together with substantiation or medical evidence of some kind, this approach was applied more

[23] *Banks v UK*, (21387/05) (Dec.) February 6, 2007, where the applicants claimed a public enquiry should have been held concerning wide-scale abuse at a particular prison.

[24] e.g. *Costello-Roberts*, fn.13 above.

[25] Youth was an important element in *Soering*, fn.1 above, concerning extradition to possible death penalty and detention on death row the Court noted that the ICCPR and the American Convention on Human Rights prohibited the death penalty for those who commit the offence under the age of 18; *Hussein v UK*, February 21, 1996, R.J.D. 1996–I, No.4, para.61, mandatory life sentences were not acceptable as punishment for children; *Mubilanzila Mayeka and Kaniki Mitunga v Belgium*, October 12, 2006, inappropriate detention conditions of five-year-old child pending expulsion. Advanced old age was a factor in *Henaf v France*, November 27, 2003, where the 75–year-old prisoner was chained to a hospital bed; and decisive in *Tastan v Turkey*, March 4, 2008 for imposition of conscription on a 71–year-old.

[26] e.g. *Menesheva v Russia*, March 9, 2006, para.61, the fact that the applicant was 19 and a girl in the hands of several male police officers was an aggravating factors.

[27] The wait on death row (six to eight years), "anguish and mounting tension" and long exposure to the stringent conditions on death row was a significant factor in *Soering*, fn.1 above; mutatis mutandis, the short cooling-off period in which prison officers confined a teenage drug addict in her cell did not disclose inhuman or degrading treatment in *Bollan v UK*, (42117/98) (Dec.) May 4, 2000, even though during this period she committed suicide.

[28] See, e.g. *Aerts v Belgium*, July 30, 1998 (1998–V), where the applicant, suffering from mental illness, was detained in a prison wing criticised as below acceptable standards by the CPT, the Court found no breach of Art.3 as he could not point to any serious effects on his mental health; *Ebbinge v Netherlands*, (47240/99) (Dec.) March 14, 2000, ECHR 2000–IV, where the Court criticised an interrogation technique (involving the use of photographs of the murder victim and the applicant's own family), but did not find it established that use of the method resulted in mental pain or suffering attaining a minimum level of severity.

[29] *Soering*, fn.1 above, was suffering mental abnormality when he committed the murders, which was relevant to the acceptability of the "death row phenomenon"; *Keenan v UK*, April 3, 2001, ECHR 2001–III, para.115, punishment imposed on prisoner who was mentally fragile and a suicide risk; *Aliyeva v Russia*, February 18, 2010, paras 82–88, where a handicapped victim was dragged outside at night.

[30] See *Tyrer v UK*, April 25, 1978, Series A, No.26, 2 E.H.R.R. 1.

[31] In *Soering*, the Court took into account the possibility of obtaining the applicant's trial for serious crimes in Germany instead of the US. In *Chahal*, fn.3 above, in response to the Government's allegations that he was a dangerous terrorist, it noted that it was open to the authorities to try him themselves for any offences committed, while in *Jalloh v Germany*, July 11, 2006, ECHR 2006–IX, the authorities could have waited for the swallowed drugs to pass through the suspect's system without using emetics.

[32] e.g. *Henaf*, fn.25 above, para.56, chaining of 75–year-old prisoner to a hospital bed was disproportionate to alleged security risk; *Jalloh*, fn.31 above, para.71.

[33] e.g. *Mader v Croatia*, fn.22 above, paras 108–110, also an apparent lack of food and drink during that period.

noticeably in the past. The current approach sets the bar for offending treatment somewhat lower, on occasion focussing more on the unacceptability of the authorities' conduct than on its concrete effects. Thus, there was inhuman treatment for depriving a suspect of sleep for two days, without any reference to physical or mental ill-effects or medical evidence[34]; deprivation of a person's spectacles was regarded as degrading[35]; and where witnesses were kept overnight in a police station without food and drink, this was considered as degrading rather than merely callous and inconsiderate.[36]

Article 3 requires domestic legal systems to offer protection against ill-treatment and serious injury through their laws and regulations governing the use of force by security forces. Where domestic rules permitted the use of firearms to wound and arrest suspects merely due to their failure to respond to a warning and did not take into account the danger presented by the suspect or the offence in issue, this failed to provide the legal protection required by Art.3.[37]

(a) Torture

II–704 The Court in *Ireland v UK* held that torture involves suffering of a particular intensity and cruelty, attaching a "special stigma to deliberate inhuman treatment causing very serious and cruel suffering". It saw support in a resolution of the UN General Assembly referring to torture as an "aggravated and deliberate form of cruel, inhuman or degrading treatment of punishment". It found, overruling the Commission, that the five interrogation techniques used in holding centres in Northern Ireland did not constitute torture but inhuman and degrading treatment. The techniques involved keeping detainees' heads covered by a hood; submitting the detainees to continuous and monotonous noise of a volume calculated to isolate them from communication; deprivation of sleep; deprivation of food and water other than one round of bread and a pint of water every six hours; and making the detainees stand legs apart with their hands up against a wall for long periods. This was systematic but not sufficiently severe to be torture.

The Commission's approach attached weight to the character of the pressure involved, whether it intended to break or eliminate the will and the premeditated, systematic nature of the treatment.[38] In *Ireland v UK* it found that the five techniques caused some physical pain which stopped when the treatment ceased, exhaustion and a number of acute psychiatric symptoms, which it could not be excluded continued to exist for some time afterwards (anxiety, disorientation, isolation, etc.) While separately some of the techniques might not have fallen within Art.3, the techniques applied together were designed to impose severe mental and physical stress and suffering on a person in order to obtain information from him, which constituted torture.

[34] e.g. *Fedotov v Russia*, October 25, 2005, para.68.

[35] e.g. *Slyusarev v Russia*, April 20, 2010, paras 43–44, there was no evidence of impairment to eyes caused by the delayed replacement and he could move around and look after himself without difficulty. The principal effect was that he could not read or write normally.

[36] e.g. *Soare v Romania*, February 22, 2011, paras 221–223.

[37] *Fahriye Caliskan v Turkey*, October 2, 2007, para.43.

[38] *Ireland v UK*, (Rep.) January 25, 1976, p.402; *The Greek Case*, 12/1 Yearbook of the ECHR 461, where torture for the Commission implied inhuman treatment which had a purpose such as the obtaining of information or confessions or the infliction of punishment.

In the subsequent findings of torture in Turkish cases, the Commission in particular emphasised the element of punishment or coercion.[39] In *Aksoy v Turkey*, the infliction of Palestinian hanging in interrogation which left the applicant partially paralysed was, without discussion, torture. Electric shocks and beatings,[40] falaka[41] and palestinian hanging[42] have all qualified.

Rape is an especially cruel act amounting to torture. In *Aydin v Turkey*, where a 17–year-old girl was raped in gendarme custody, the Commision found rape was found to be ill-treatment of an especially severe kind, "inherently debasing" striking at the heart of physical and moral integrity, aggravated by the fact that it was committed by person in authority and involving acute physical and psychological suffering in a punitive and coercive context.[43]

The new Court revised the applicable standard in *Selmouni v France*. Re-iterating the principle that the Convention was a living instrument which had to be interpreted in the light of present-day conditions, it stated that an increasingly high standard was required in the area of human rights and that certain acts classified in the past as "inhuman and degrading treatment" as opposed to "torture" could be classified differently in future. It found in that particular case, where the applicant was assaulted and humiliated by police over a number of days with a view to inducing him to confess to the offence of which he was suspected, that the physical and mental violence was particularly serious and cruel and must be regarded as acts of torture.[44] The gratuitous, punitive beating of prisoners with truncheons for allegedly minor acts of disobedience was regarded as torture.[45] Where however ill-treatment was inflicted on the applicant in *Egmez v Cyprus* over a short period of heightened emotions and there was some doubt as to the gravity of the injuries caused by the police officers and no indication of long-term consequences, the Court found that the ill-treatment could not be qualified as torture but was serious enough to be considered inhuman.[46]

Force-feeding which is not medically necessary has been found to constitute torture.[47]

Non-physical torture may also be possible, namely the infliction of mental suffering by creating a state of anguish and stress by other than bodily means.[48]

[39] e.g. in *Yagiz v Turkey* (Rep.) May 16, R.J.D. 1996–III, No.13, it cited the UN Convention against Torture which in Art.1 includes elements of deliberateness for specific purposes of obtaining information or punishing or intimidating or coercing.

[40] *Cakici v Turkey*, July 8, 1999, ECHR 1999–IV; see also *Dikme v Turkey*, July 11, 2000, ECHR 2000–VIII, severe beatings over lengthy interrogation, exacerbated by blindfolding.

[41] *Salman v Turkey*, June 27, 2000, ECHR 2000–VII, falaka and bruising to the chest.

[42] *Aktas v Turkey*, April 24, 2003.

[43] *Aydin v Turkey*, (Rep.) September 25, 1997, 1997–VI, No.50, para.189. The Court also found torture separately for other aspects of ill-treatment, e.g. blindfolding, being kept naked, beaten and pummelled with high pressure water (paras 82–86); *Maslova and Nalbandov v Russia*, January 24, 2008, para.105, finding of torture for rape in police custody.

[44] Also *Ilhan v Turkey*, June 27, 2000, ECHR 2000–VII, where the severity of the beating and the delay in obtaining treatment for brain damage was considered torture; *Bati v Turkey*, June 3, 2004, ECHR 2004–VI, duration and intensity of ill-treatment, especially given the vulnerability of young applicants and a pregnant woman, attained the level of torture.

[45] *Dedovskiy Russia*, May 15, 2008, paras 82–86.

[46] *Egmez v Cyprus*, December 21, 2000, ECHR 2000–XII, paras 78–79. See also, pre-*Selmouni*, *Tekin v Turkey*, June 9, 1998, R.J.D. 1998–IV, No.78, where treatment in police custody leaving wounds and bruises was regarded only as inhuman and degrading treatment.

[47] *Nevmerzhitsky v Ukraine*, April 5, 2005, ECHR 2005–II, para.98.

[48] *The Greek Case*, fn.4 above, pp.86 and 461; *Akkoç v Turkey*, October 10, 2000, ECHR 2000–X, para.116, reference to intense fear caused by threats to children.

However, where coercion by means of verbal threats of torture was applied to obtain information as to the location of a kidnapped child, the Court noted that the treatment lasted only ten minutes before the applicant gave in and did not reach the level of cruelty amounting to torture itself.[49]

(b) Inhuman treatment and punishment

II–705 Inhuman treatment covers at least such treatment as deliberately causes severe mental and physical suffering.[50] The physical injuries in *Ireland v UK* fell within this notion (where individual detainees had been beaten and kicked by the security forces causing, for example, massive, substantial bruising, cuts to the head, a broken cheekbone, gross swelling) as did the injuries in *Tomasi v France*, in which medical reports indicated a large number of blows of sufficiently serious intensity (abrasions on face, chest and arms, haematoma on left ear) and their intensity. In *Ribitsch v Austria*, the applicant received bruises and haematomas on the arm caused while in police custody and there was a medical report that he was suffering from cervical syndrome, vomiting, violent headache and a temperature, after the applicant had allegedly been punched repeatedly, kicked, and his head banged on the floor. The physical injuries and considerable psychological trauma constituted inhuman and degrading treatment. The Court added a very strong statement that in respect of a person deprived of liberty any recourse to physical force which has not been made strictly necessary by his own conduct diminishes human dignity and is in principle an infringement of the right in Art.3.

The use of force in the context of arrest, although resulting in injury, may fall outside Art.3, particularly if it resulted from the conduct of the applicant. Force may only be used however if it is indispensable[51] and a burden rests on the Government to show the use of force was not excessive.[52] In *Klaas v Germany*, where police officers used force to arrest a 48–year-old woman, who suffered a bruise to the temple, concussion, contusion of the left shoulder joint, in circumstances where the police alleged that she had tried to run away, the Court found nothing to lead it to depart from findings of fact of the national courts who had found the use of force not excessive and not unlikely to have been caused in her struggles.[53] Similarly in *Hurtado v Switzerland*, where the applicant received cracked ribs from the officer kneeling on him, the Commission accepted that the force used in the circumstances of the arrest did not contravene Art.3.[54] Where serious injury is inflicted during an arrest however, the Government will be required to furnish credible and convincing

[49] *Gäfgen*, fn.3 above, paras 94–108.

[50] e.g. the Commission in *The Greek Case*, fn.4 above, and *Ireland v UK*, fn.4 above, and the Court in *Ireland v UK*; as regards mental suffering see, e.g. the village destruction cases at sub-s.4(g) and the disappearance cases at sub-s.4(h); *Mubilanzila Mayeka and Kaniki Mitunga*, fn.25 above, mother's anguish at lack of information and uncertainty about her child detained in transit.

[51] *Ivan Vasilev v Bulgaria*, April 2, 2007, para.63.

[52] *Rehbock v Slovenia*, November 28, 2000, ECHR 2000–XII, para.72.

[53] *Klaas v Germany*, September 22, 1993, Series A No.269; *Caloc v France*, July 20, 2009, ECHR 2000–IX, where there was nothing to call into question regarding domestic findings as to the justified level of force used on the applicant, who had tried to run away; *Berlinski v Poland*, June 20, 2002, paras 62–64, where the applicant bodybuilders, resisted the legitimate actions of the police, making recourse to physical force necessary by their own conduct.

[54] *Hurtado v Switzerland*, (Rep.) July 8, 1993, Series A, No.280–A (settled before the Court), the arrest took place during a planned police operation breaking into a drug ring: there was reason to believe the suspects were dangerous.

arguments to justify the degree of force and a violation will ensue if none is forthcoming, as in *Rehbock v Slovenia*, where the police accounts of how the applicant, unarmed and unresisting, came to suffer a double fracture were inconsistent and vague.[55] Mere assertion that an applicant resisted arrest was not sufficient to justify as indispensable the use of force involving a blow to the head by police officers seeking to disperse a demonstration.[56] Nor was it a justification, as a police officer claimed, that the female applicant had slapped his face, he could have been expected to react with restraint: the injuries which she had suffered in retaliation, including a blow to the head, were disproportionate and not shown to be strictly necessary.[57] Use of imobilisation techniques may be justified by the violence of the suspect[58] but if maintained for too long, without medical intervention the resulting death may fall under the responsibility of the authorities.[59]

Medical treatment of injuries suffered on arrest and detention must be promptly forthcoming or issues of treatment contrary to Art.3 may arise.[60] Refusal to carry out an examination where the applicant, injured in the head while in custody, was unable to pay for treatment disclosed a violation.[61]

Treatment was not sufficiently severe in consequences in *Tyrer v UK*, where three strokes of the birch raised but did not break the skin; and in the context of school corporal punishment, three smacks from a shoe on the bottom through shorts causing no visible injury was not inhuman.[62] The Commission did find inhuman and degrading treatment in *Y v UK*[63] where the punishment resulted in four weals on the bottom from a cane, while in *A v UK* the corporal punishment inflicted by the stepfather of repeated caning causing significant bruising also reached this level. A small cut near a child's eye caused by a thrown tile was not sufficiently severe to bring Art.3 into play.[64]

In the military context, the Court has found that imposing physical disciplinary punishments which endanger health and well-being of soldiers is incompatible with Art.3. Thus, where as a punishment, a conscript, with known knee and spine problems, was ordered to perform 350 kneebends, resulting in his collapse and permanent physical injury, there was a finding of inhuman punishment.[65]

[55] *Rehbock v Slovenia*, fn.52 above, paras 74–78. See also *RL and M-JD v France*, May 19, 2004, the extent of bruising on two restaurant owners disclosed excessive force given the age, build and non-violent history of the arrestees, the Court was not convinced by the police version that their "agitation" necessitated such a degree of force.
[56] *Tsekov v Bulgaria*, February 23, 2006, paras 53–54 and 66. See also *Umar Karatepe v Turkey*, October 12, 2010, paras 59–63, head injury suffered during altercation in court building not shown to have been justified by the applicant's conduct or level of resistance.
[57] *Fahriye Caliskan v Turkey*, October 2, 2007, para.43.
[58] *Douglas-Williams v UK*, (56413/00) (Dec.) January 8, 1002, use of positional restraint techniques was found justified by the applicant's violence, even though he later died from asphyxia.
[59] *Saoud v France*, October 9, 2007, paras 98–104, Art.2 breached where the violent suspect was pinned to the ground for over 30 minutes, leading to his death by asphyxia; the Court seemed influenced by the authorities' failure to have given any guidance to police over the risks of this type of restraint, and the length of time the suspect was immobilised without medical treatment being provided.
[60] *Ilhan*, fn.44 above.
[61] *Umar Karatepe v Turkey*, fn.56 above, paras 66–74, refusal of the test was enough; there is no indication that this had subsequent repercussions on his condition.
[62] *Costello-Roberts*, fn.13 above.
[63] *Y v UK*, (Rep.) October 8, 1991, Series A, No.247–A, settled before the Court.
[64] *Tonchev v Bulgaria*, November 19, 2009, paras 40–42.
[65] *Chember v Russia*, July 3, 2008, paras 52–57.

(c) Degrading treatment or punishment

II–706 This consists of treatment or punishment which grossly humiliates a person or drives him to act against his will or conscience.[66] The five techniques in *Ireland v UK* were found to be degrading as well as inhuman since they were such as to arouse in their victims feelings of fear, anguish, and inferiority capable of humiliating and debasing them and possibly breaking their physical and moral resistance.[67] The purpose of the authority is particularly relevant, in the sense whether the measure denotes contempt or lack of respect for the personality of the person subjected to it and whether it is designed to humiliate or debase, instead of other aims. However the absence of such a purpose does not conclusively rule out a finding of degrading treatment or punishment.[68]

In *Tyrer v UK*, to distinguish between punishment which is generally humiliating to adults and degrading punishment within Art.3, the Court held that the humiliation or debasement involved must attain a particular level, beyond the usual element. This will depend on the circumstances of the case, in particular, the nature and context of the punishment, the manner and method of execution. While the public nature of the punishment might be relevant, its absence is not fatal, since a person may be sufficiently humiliated in his own eyes even if not in the eyes of others.[69] For the Court in *Tyrer*, it was "institutionalised violence" of the birching that was the crucial element, where the applicant was treated as an object in the power of the authorities and subjected to an assault on his personal dignity and physical integrity. There was the element of delay, leading to the mental anguish of anticipation; the official aura attending the procedure and infliction of the punishment by strangers. The factor that the punishment entailed the stripping of clothes was only one aggravating element.

Where an applicant claimed that he had defecated on arrest, attributable to the use of a stun grenade, and had been unable to change clothes until the next day at the earliest, the Commission found that the wearing of soiled clothes for one day, during a hearing before a judge and on various journeys, due to the failure of the authorities to take the most elementary hygiene measures in making available clean clothes, was humiliating and debasing and therefore degrading.[70]

Humiliating circumstances of a sexual nature rendered the infliction on a teenage girl of corporal punishment by a male teacher in the presence of another male teacher degrading treatment though the severity of the punishment was not such as to render it inhuman.[71] In *Valasinas v Lithuania*,[72] requiring a male prisoner to strip naked in the presence of a female prison officer and touching his sexual organs and food with bare hands during a strip search diminished human dignity and was degrading. The imposition of strip searches, without any security justification, may

[66] *The Greek Case*, fn.4 above, p.186.

[67] *Ireland v UK*, fn.4 above, para.67.

[68] *V v UK*, fn.10 above, para.71; *Peers v Greece*, April 19, 2001, ECHR 2001–III, para.74, violation where the exceedingly hot conditions or open toilet in the cell were not in any sense intended to humiliate or debase.

[69] *Tyrer v UK*, fn.30, para.32. See also *Yankov v Bulgaria*, December 11, 2003, paras 112–122, the visible and public stigma of head-shaving a prisoner for arbitrary punitive reasons.

[70] *Hurtado*, fn.54 above.

[71] (9471/81) (Rep.) July 18, 1986, 60 D.R. 5, the applicant was caned on the hand.

[72] *Valasinas v Lithuania*, July 24, 2001, ECHR 2001–VIII, para.117.

also humiliate and debase contrary to Art.3,[73] as will systematic and repeated searches of prisoners requiring special precautions which err on the excessive.[74] Where the female applicant was forcibly undressed by male personnel at a sobering-up centre when she refused to put on a gown and then restrained on a bed with belts for about ten hours, the Court found that this was degrading treatment.[75] Seeking to conduct a gynaecological examination on a prisoner, who remained handcuffed, while male prison officers remained in the room, albeit behind screens, was found to humiliate and undermine personal dignity, even though, due to her protests, the examination was not in the end carried out.[76] Where a remand prisoner was required, for over a year, to wear a cagoule covering his face when leaving his cell, the Court considered that this caused him anguish and feelings of debasement; it took into account the lack of legal basis for the measure and that the purported reasons—to protect him from public violence and to safeguard ongoing investigations—did not explain why the measure applied even within the prison and when seeing his family and lawyer and therefore had a strong punitive flavour.[77]

The imposition of conscription on a 71–year-old man was found to disclose degrading treatment given that he was required to follow a regime and training geared to young men, which must have caused him considerable suffering and loss of dignity.[78]

The suffering of relatives presented with the mutilated corpse of a family member disclosed degrading treatment.[79]

Forced prostitution is regarded as contrary to human dignity, and would likely found a breach of Art.3. Where an applicant claimed that she could not quit prostitution and was being forced to continue to earn money through prostitution due to the heavy demands for social insurance contributions from the State, the Court rejected her complaints on the facts since even if she was placed in a difficult situation, the State authorities could not be said to requiring her to earn the money by prostitution and she had not shown that she could not have sought to earn the money another way.[80]

[73] e.g. *Iwanczuk v Poland*, November 15, 2001, where to use the prison voting facilities the applicant had to strip for a body search before four guards who ridiculed him; *Wieser v Austria*, February 22, 2007, a forcible strip search on arrest in the applicant's home was degrading, not justified by the aim of looking for weapons rather than drugs or small items; *Frerot v France*, June 12, 2007, systematic body searches involving visual anal inspection went beyond what could be regarded as inevitable humiliation attaching to such measures; see also *Khider v France*, July 9, 2009, systematic searches not justified by security concerns.

[74] *El Shennawy v France*, January 20, 2011, paras 39–46, searches up to six times per day, exacerbated by the fact that the officers wore balaclavas and the searches were filmed.

[75] *Wiktorko v Poland*, March 31, 2009, even if her conduct may have necessitated initial restraint, the Court found no explanation for the length of time over which she was held immobilised.

[76] *Filiz Uyan v Turkey*, January 8, 2009, paras 32–35, the precautions were not justified for her conviction for terrorist offences. Contrast *Juhnke v Turkey*, May 13, 2008, no breach of Art.3 as the prisoner was persuaded by the doctor to consent to the gynaecological examination; there was breach of Art.8, however, as the examination, to prevent her claiming sexual assault by gendarme officers (she had not made any such complaint), was not in accordance with law or justified since the Court was not persuaded that she had given free and informed consent.

[77] *Petyo Petkov v Bulgaria*, January 7, 2010, paras 41–46.

[78] *Tastan*, fn.25 above, paras 32–33.

[79] *Akpinar*, fn.15 above. See Art.3 violation due to suffering from the dismemberment of the applicants' sons, such that they had never been able properly to bury them: *Khadzhialiyev v Russia*, November 6, 2008, para.122.

[80] *Tremblay v France*, September 11, 2007.

Discrimination based on race, or membership of a national minority may be sufficiently severe to disclose degrading treatment.[81]

4. Particular contexts

(a) *Handcuffing, police control and security measures*

II–707 The early case-law showed a certain reluctance to find handcuffing sufficiently serious to breach Art.3 of the Convention.[82] Where the measure has been justified by security concerns or duration and exposure to public view was limited, no problems have arisen.[83] However, in *Erdogan Yagiz v Turkey*, where a doctor was publicly manacled, in front of family, neighbours and colleagues, the Court found that the intention was deliberately to humiliate and break his spirit, which together with the mental problems flowing from the incident, disclosed degrading treatment.[84] Nor has the handcuffing of a defendant in a public court room been found justified by security or administration of justice concerns[85] or the seating of an accused in a metal cage during his trial.[86] Systematic handcuffing of a life prisoner every time he quit his cell constituted degrading treatment when endured over more than 13 years in the absence of any escape attempt.[87] Handcuffing of a mentally ill patient while kept in his cell for seven days, purportedly to prevent him injuring himself or others, disclosed a breach of Art.3 since he was alone in his cell and the measure, imposed without pyschiatric medical advice, in fact caused him injuries to his wrists which had not been treated.[88] Restraint immobilising an individual to a bed may disclose degrading treatment, particularly if its duration is not convincingly justified.[89]

Use of a pepper spray in dispersing demonstrators, where no significant physical effects transpired, was not inhuman.[90] However, minor acts of disobedience in prison

[81] *East African Asians case*, fn.11 above; *Cyprus v Turkey*, May 21, 2001, ECHR 2001–IV, paras 305–311; *Moldovan v Romania (No.2)*, July 12, 2005, para.113, concerning Roma villagers burnt out of their homes with connivance of State officials, kept in poor living conditions, blocked from redress and abused.

[82] *Raninen v Finland*, December 16, 1997, R.J.D. 1997–VIII, No.60, 26 E.H.R.R. 563, the Commission found degrading treatment where a conscientious objector was handcuffed publicly when unlawfully arrested by military police but, notwithstanding the unjustified nature of the measure, the Court noted a lack of mental and physical effects on the applicant and found the treatment did not attain the required level of severity.

[83] *Ocalan v Turkey*, May 12, 2005, ECHR 2005–IV, para.184, where the applicant was handcuffed and blindfolded on his arrest and transfer from Kenya to Turkey, the Court found that this justified for security reasons; it did not go beyond the usual degree of humiliation inherent in arrest and detention; *Wieser*, fn.54 above, four hours' handcuffing not in public view: no violation.

[84] *Erdogan Yagiz v Turkey*, March 6, 2007. See also handcuffing of prisoners while in hospital, fn.90 below, which disclosed inhuman and degrading treatment.

[85] *Gorodnichev v Russia*, May 24, 2007, where the Government had not been able to explain the need for the measure. See also *Ramishvili and Kokhriedze v Georgia*, January 27, 2009, paras 97–102.

[86] *Ashot Harutyunyan v Armenia*, June 15, 2010, paras 125–29, the applicant's conduct and record not showing any security risk, the use of the cage was seen as humiliating and likely to impinge on his concentration and alertness during the trial.

[87] *Kashavelov v Bulgaria*, January 20, 2011, paras 38–40.

[88] *Kucheruk v Ukraine*, September 6, 2007, paras 142–145, handcuffing was also not a normal method of restraint for mentally ill persons.

[89] *Wiktorko*, fn.75 above, over ten hours immobilised in a sobering up centre was not shown to be necessary.

[90] *Ciloglu v Turkey*, March 6, 2007, nor did minor bruising resulting from tussles with the police during the demonstration. See also *Oya Ataman v Turkey*, December 5, 2006, no ill-effects from spray substantiated.

did not justify use of truncheons by special forces.[91] Use of force in penal institutions indeed must only be resorted to where indispensable and not go beyond what is necessary: the use of truncheons to enforce an order for prisoners to leave their cell was not shown to be necessary in general or on the applicant in particular, and certainly not the continued beating after the prisoners had been taken from the cell.[92]

Strip searches, inherently degrading, require justification. They cannot be imposed on prisoners without due security justification or in an insulting and offensive manner. Even a prisoner requiring special security measures should not be excessively subjected to such measures. Factors such as the presence of women officers for male prisoners and vice versa, the participation of officers wearing cagoules and the unregulated filming of the search are aggravating features.[93]

(b) Punishment, length of sentence and place of detention

Matters of length of sentence are generally outside the scope of this provision.[94] However elements of shocking disproportionality could raise an exception. In *Weeks v UK*, where the applicant aged 17 received a life sentence for robbery of 35 pence, the Court commented, in finding that discretionary life sentences attracted the right to review of lawfulness of continued detention, that otherwise a life sentence for such a minor crime by a young person would have been doubtfully compatible with Art.3.[95] It has also stated that issues might arise from the imposition of an irreducible life sentence on an adult, but where an applicant had the hope of release, the fact that he served an exceptionally lengthy sentence (41 years before release) did not disclose an extraordinary ordeal capable of attaining the severity of Art.3 treatment.[96] Where a mandatory life sentence had no system of remission but the President, with the agreement of the Attorney-General could commute or remit, the Court noted that prospects of release were limited but could not be said to be de facto or de iure irreducible.[97] No system of release on licence is required; the availability of a pardon or commutation of sentence will suffice although the Court appears likely to verify whether release is in fact available by this method.[98] II–708

[91] *Dedovskiy*, fn.45 above, para.83.

[92] *Vladimir Romanov v Russia*, July 24, 2008, paras 65–68. See also use of truncheons unjustified on agitated prisoner where no evidence that he was posing a threat to guards or other prisoners: *Kucheruk v Ukraine*, fn.88 above, para.132.

[93] See in particular *El Shennawy v France*, fn.74 above, paras 39–46, searches up to six times per day, exacerbated by the fact that the officers wore balaclavas and the searches were filmed; see cases cited at fnn.72–74 and 129.

[94] e.g. (5871/72) (Dec.) September 30, 1974, 1 D.R. 54; also (11653/85) (Dec.) March 3, 1986, 41 D.R. 231, where a drastic change in parole policy, which dashed hopes of imminent release and increased effective length to be served, was not covered; nor, in *Kafkaris v Cyprus*, February 12, 2008, para.106, did the disappointment engendered by a change in prospects of early release reach the level of severity infringing Art.3.

[95] *Weeks v UK*, March 2, 1987, Series A, No.114, para.47. See also *Kafkaris*, fn.94 above, para.97, stating, "The imposition of a sentence of life imprisonment on an *adult* offender is not in itself prohibited by or incompatible with Art.3 of any other Article. . . " (emphasis added).

[96] *Leger v France*, April 11, 2006, case later struck out before the Grand Chamber.

[97] *Kafkaris*, fn.94 above, paras 102–108. See also *Garagin v Italy*, (33290/07) (Dec.) April 29, 2008, life sentence also subject to possible early release.

[98] *Iorgov v Bulgaria (No.2)*, September 2, 2010, paras 48–60, no pardon was possible before 20 years were served; very few prisoners had reached this stage so the Court was not prepared to draw any conclusion, in practice no-one was ever released this way.

Where an applicant had AIDS with a life expectancy of two years and his sentence was extended two years, the Court noted that he was receiving treatment and could apply for release if his situation deteriorated; it did not seem to consider the hope of release was minimal.[99]

Extreme old age is not a bar as such to detention or imprisonment though the Court has not excluded that issues could arise and examines the individual circumstances of each case.[100] Detaining a severely disabled person, without requisite provision for their needs, may raise problems, as in *Price v UK*, where the applicant, a four limb deficient thalidomide victim with numerous health problems, including defective kidneys was committed to prison for contempt.[101]

Where a fifteen-year-old was placed in an adult prison, the Court did not state this per se was in breach of Art.3 though it noted that it was against domestic and international norms. It found that this factor, along with duration of the placement for five years, the lack of proper medical care and attention for his ensuing serious psychological and health problems, including numerous suicide attempts, disclosed inhuman and degrading treatment.[102]

Mentally ill persons should not be kept in ordinary prisons which do not cater for their conditions. Degrading treatment may be found where such an applicant is thereby caused acute hardship and distress or adversity of an intensity exceeding the unavoidable level of suffering inherent in detention.[103] Placement of mentally prisoners in disciplinary cells has offended in a number of cases where suicide followed, the Court stressing that such penalties are not compatible with humane treatment of the mentally fragile who may require special measures to ensure conditions meet the standards of Art.3 in their regard.[104]

Detention of prisoners for long periods in facilities geared for short stays may also disclose degrading treatment.[105]

[99] *Ceku v Germany*, (41559/06) (Dec.) March 13, 2007.

[100] e.g. *Papon v France*, (64666/01) (Dec.) June 7, 2001, ECHR 2001–VI, where the applicant was 90 years old with serious heart problems, the Court found that he was under regular medical supervision no indication that the inconveniences or constraints caused by the imprisonment were sufficiently severe to breach Art.3; *Sawoniuk v UK*, (63716/00) (Dec.) May 29, 2001, ECHR 2001–VI, no problem per se from the imposition of a life sentence at 78.

[101] *Price v UK*, July 10, 2001, ECHR 2001–VII, the cell was cold, without a bed which she could use and she suffered, inter alia, from problems with fluid intake and had to be lifted on and off the toilet by male officers. See the separate opinion of Judge Bratza, who noted that the prison authorities did the best they could and laid responsibility on the judicial authorities for imposing detention on a severely handicapped person without at least verifying the existence of adequate facilities. See *Huseyin Yildirim v Turkey*, May 3, 2007, following an accident, the applicant's health was such that the courts and medical bodies had considered him unfit for incarceration: violation for three years in a regime unsuited for his condition.

[102] *Güveç v Turkey*, January 20, 2009, ECHR 2009–. . .

[103] *Rivière v France*, July 11, 2006. See also Pt IIB, s.36: Prisoners' rights, sub-s.3(d): Nature of place of detention.

[104] *Renolde v France*, October 16, 2008, ECHR 2008–. . . , where the disturbed prisoner with a history of suicide attempts was sentenced to 45 days; see also *Keenan*, fn.29 above, mentally ill prisoner sentenced to seven days' segregation and had prison term extended by a month; *Dybeku v Albania*, December 18, 2007, conditions in Albanian prisons for chronically mentally ill were not appropriate; *Slavomir Musial v Poland*, January 20, 2009, paras 90–96, failure to treat the mentally ill prisoner any differently than other prisoners although they were more vulnerable; there was a lack of supervision and appropriate care.

[105] *Kaja v Greece*, July 27, 2006. See also *Shchebet v Russia*, June 12, 2008, where the applicant was held for more than 30 days in an airport transport administrative holding cell designed for short-term stays of a few hours, thus it was lacking in basic needs as to space, natural lighting, privacy, hygiene, access to exercise, etc.

(c) *Compulsory medical treatment*

Previously, where compulsory medical treatment, including force feeding, being strapped down, compulsory administration of drugs, constituted a therapeutic necessity in line with current medical practice, it could not in principle disclose inhuman or degrading treatment—so said the Court in *Herczegfalvy v Austria*. This was notwithstanding the "worrying" length of time that the applicant was handcuffed and restrained in a security bed. The Commission had found a violation, imposing the additional requirement that the manner of the application of the treatment must be compatible with Art.3. It found the timing and the use of massive force and the long term fettering were not so compatible.[106] However, the Court will now verify that there is a convincing medical necessity for force feeding in order to save life, that the procedural guarantees as to its implementation are fulfilled and that the manner of its implementation is not of such a nature as to disclose inhuman and degrading treatment. Where in *Nevmerzhitsky v Ukraine* the Government failed to show that the force feeding, four days into a hunger strike, was medically necessary, this breached Art.3 as did the manner of administering the treatment, which the applicant had resisted, to a degree constituting torture.[107] II–709

Compulsory gynaecological examinations on female detainees may disclose Art.3 treatment, where carried out, or even threatened, in conditions undermining of dignity, such as while being handcuffed and with the presence in the room, albeit behind a screen, of male officers.[108]

While the Court has not ruled out that forcible medical intervention for investigative purposes might be compatible with the Convention, it found that compulsory administration of an emetic to induce a suspect to regurgitate swallowed drugs constituted inhuman treatment. It took into account the risks to health, the fact that most other countries refrained from such measures, the brutal and humiliating nature of the intervention and the fact that the authorities could have waited for the small package to exit the suspect's system naturally.[109] Where the authorities operated to remove a drug package from the applicant without his consent, it was evident that this was undertaken to save his life, as the package had split, threatening to poison him: no violation arose.[110]

(d) *Conditions of detention*

Until relatively recently, conditions of imprisonment had not been found to breach the requirements of Art.3. The early Commission cases, in particular, accepted significant levels of hardship, an approach reflecting an implicit acceptance that II–710

[106] *Herczegfalvy v Austria*, September 24, 1992, Series A, No.244, 15 E.H.R.R. 437, paras 82–83; (Rep.) paras 247–254: See Pt IIB, s.36: Prisoners' rights, sub-s.5: Medical treatment.

[107] See also *Ciorap v Moldova*, June 19, 2007, the forced-feeding was not prompted by valid medical reasons, but to end the applicant's protests; its implementation caused great pain and humiliation: there was also reference to a possible alternative method of an intravenous drip.

[108] *Filiz Uyan*, fn.76 above, the examination did not take place as the applicant refused, but the mere threat appears to have been sufficiently humiliating for the majority to find a breach of Art.3. The dissenting minority noted that similar complaints had been rejected in *Devrim Turan v Turkey*, March 2, 2006, paras 17–22, the applicant had refused consent and no examinations took place there were no other aggravating features mentioned as in *Uyan*.

[109] *Jalloh*, fn.31 above.

[110] *Bogumil v Portugal*, October 7, 2008, paras 77–82.

prison regimes require rigid discipline and severe restrictions on personal freedom. Any reluctance to criticise the conditions in which prisoners are held has now disappeared, though the Court continues to emphasise that issues only arise where the measures subject the prisoner to distress or hardship exceeding the unavoidable level of suffering inherent in detention.[111] Where a violation has been found, the Court has tended to categorise the treatment as degrading, rather than inhuman. It has had regard in particular to the length of time over which the prisoner has been obliged to endure the conditions[112] and taken account of the cumulative effects of the conditions, as well as specific shortcomings.[113] However, even short periods of detention may disclose a violation may disclose inhuman treatment, as in a 22–hour stay in a police station cell unfit for an overnight stay, without food, water or access to a toilet[114] and conditions on transfer in a prison van to and from court.[115] Other offending features have included serious overcrowding, insufficient sanitary and sleeping facilities,[116] open unpartitioned toilets in shared cells,[117] high temperatures in unventilated cells[118]; insufficient natural light and rundown conditions[119]; lack of running water, insufficient and repulsive food, lack of bedding and prisoners' having to pay to repair and furnish cell[120]; prisoners having to provide for own food[121]; pest infestation linked with recurring skin diseases and fungal infections[122]; and insanitary and crowded conditions leading to infection and disease.[123]

Passive smoking is a new relevant factor. Where an applicant enjoyed a single cell and only had to put up with smoking of others in one communal space, this factor was not regarded as reaching Art.3 level.[124] Where however, an applicant, with chronic health conditions and a medical note recommending the avoidance of

[111] *Kudla v Poland*, October 26, 2000, ECHR 2000–XI, paras 93–94; *Valasinas*, fn.72 above, para.102, where the general conditions of detention were found, after a visit, not to attain the minimum level of severity, though an atmosphere of boredom due to lack of work and educational facilities and some regrettable shortcomings in toilet facilities was noted.

[112] *Dougoz v Greece*, March 6, 2001, para.48; *Peers*, fn.68 above, para.75; *Kalashnikov v Russia*, July 15, 2002, ECHR 2002–VI, para.102; while in *Valasinas*, fn.72 above, para.108, the absence of toilet partitions was noted to have been temporary.

[113] *Dougoz*, fn.112 above, para.46; *Kalashnikov*, fn.112 above, para.95.

[114] *Fedotov*, fn.34 above, para.68, administrative detention cells which often contained only a bench (para.55).

[115] *Khudoyorov v Russia*, November 8, 2005, paras 116–120, citing CPT recommendations on transport conditions; also *Yakovenko v Ukraine*, October 25, 2007, paras 103–113, finding cramped space in prison vans and prison train carriages as well as a lack of lighting and provision of food infringed Art.3 with reliance on CPT reports and recommendations; *Moiseyev v Russia*, paras 133–136, inadequate space, ventilation and lighting in the van in which the prisoner travelled several hours a day to and from court, deleterious to the concentration and alertness the prisoner would have needed for his court appearances.

[116] *Dougoz*, fn.67 above; also severe overcrowding in *Kalashnikov*, fn.112 above, where the applicant shared his bed on a rota with two others; *Novoselov v Russia*, June 2, 2005, severe overcrowding (less than $1m^2$ per detainee in cell). See also Pt IIB, s.36: Prisoners' rights, sub-s.3(c): Cell conditions.

[117] *Peers*, fn.68 above, para.75; *Kalashnikov*, fn.112 above, para.99.

[118] *Peers*, fn.68 above.

[119] *Payet v France*, January 20, 2011, paras 80–85.

[120] *Modarca v Moldova*, May 10, 2007, paras 65–69.

[121] *Ramishvili and Kokhriedze*, fn.85 above, para.87, e.g. food parcels from family did not dispense Government from providing for basic needs of prisoners.

[122] *Kalashnikov*, fn.112 above, para.100, where it was also a concern that the applicant was detained with persons suffering from syphilis and TB.

[123] *Nevmerzhitsky*, fn.47 above, para.87, where the insanitary conditions were linked with skin diseases; *Melnik v Ukraine*, March 28, 2006, where the applicant appeared to contract TB in prison (also failure to promptly diagnose and provide proper treatment).

[124] *Aparicio Benito v Espagne*, (36150/03) (Dec.) November 3, 2006.

cigarettes, was confined almost all day in seriously over-crowded cells where occupants smoked and even the hospital ward was not non-smoking, the passive smoking element was relevant in the finding of conditions incompatible with Art.3.[125] The Court has stated that the State is under an obligation to take measures to protect prisoners from passive smoking where their state of health so requires.[126]

Given the present-day rejection of capital punishment by European countries, the Court took a rigorous approach to the complaints of death row prisoners in Ukraine and found that the anxiety and uncertainty as to the effectiveness of the moratorium on executions together with, inter alia, the confinement 24 hours a day in a restricted cell space without natural light and little or no exercise or activities caused the applicants considerable mental suffering, diminishing their human dignity and disclosing degrading treatment contrary to Art.3.[127]

Special security regimes sometimes raise concerns about social or sensory isolation. The Court has generally not taken issue with the domestic authorities' assessment of the need for stringent precautions against escape in these cases and found acceptable quite serious limitations of visits and association with other prisoners.[128] In *Van Der Ven v Netherlands*, concerning the Extra-Security Institution (EBI), it was the almost automatic weekly strip search of the applicant over a three-and-a-half year period that appeared to tip the balance over the threshold of acceptable treatment.[129] Two years in a special security regime of solitary isolation was found inhuman and degrading, where the Court noted no substantive reasons for its application to the applicant had been given, giving an appearance of arbitrariness and where there were only very restricted opportunities for exercise outdoors and visitors, and constant handcuffing whenever the prisoner left his cell.[130] Frequent transfers from prison to prison on security grounds have been found to inflict excessive suffering and anxiety on prisoners, where the automatic policy was unjustified by considerations of prevention of disorder and transfers not carried out in response to a

[125] *Florea v Romania*, September 14, 2010, paras 57–65.

[126] *Elefteriadis v Romania*, January 25, 2011, paras 48–55, where the prisoner, suffering from a chronic pulmonary condition, had to share a cell with two smokers, as well as being held on occasion in court waiting rooms in which prisoners smoked.

[127] *Poltoraskiy v Ukraine*, April 29, 2003, ECHR 2003–V, paras 134–149; also judgments of the same date: *Kuznetzov*, paras 124–129, *Khokhlich*, paras 167–182, *Dankevich*, paras 125–145; *Aliov*, paras 133–152; *Nazarenko*, paras 128–145. Contrast *Iorgov v Bulgaria*, March 11, 2004, where there was no such uncertainty concerning a moratorium on executions, but the stringent regime, lasting some eight years with minimum social contact, went too far.

[128] *Van der Ven v Netherlands*, February 4, 2003, ECHR 2003–II, para.55; see *Messina v Italy*, (25498/94) (Dec.) June 8, 1999, ECHR 1999–V, no violation of Art.3 concerning the special regime for mafia prisoners: severe restrictions on contacts with other detainees and prohibition from communal recreation were justified by security requirements, the social isolation was not absolute and there had been no physically or psychologically damaging effects; similar reasoning in *Bastone v Italy*, (59638/00) (Dec.) January 18, 2005, ECHR 2005–II, and concerning restrictive regime for terrorist suspects: *Sotiropoulou v Greece*, (40225/02) (Dec.) January 18, 2007.

[129] *Van Der Ven v Netherlands*, fn.128 above, paras 52–63; also *Lorse v Netherlands*, February 4, 2003, where the applicant was subjected to the regime for over six years. There was also evidence in both cases of some mental side-effects over time under these severe restrictions and a report from the CPT expressing considerable concern that the regime was having a harmful psychological effect on the detainees. Concerning solitary confinement, see Pt IIB, s.36: Prisoners' rights, sub-s.3(a): Solitary confinement.

[130] *Csullog v Hungary*, June, 7, 2011, paras 32–38.

particular problem or need in individual cases[131]; where the prisoner concerned had a history of escape attempts and organising escapes, no violation was found.[132]

Where asylum-seekers or immigrants are concerned, the Court has found it impermissible to abandon them in limbo in transit zones, without taking responsibility for ensuring their essential needs, such zones not catering for more than very transitory travellers.[133] Poor conditions at asylum or frontier holding centres have also fallen short, where there has been no possibility of exercise, and shortage of basic amenities such as bedding, hygiene and telephone access to the outside world.[134] Even short periods of four days or a week in conditions of overcrowding and lack of basic amenities is sufficient to disclose treatment contrary to Art.3[135]; two days where a minor of fifteen years was concerned.[136] Detaining children in closed asylum centres not designed to cater for their needs has also infringed Art.3.[137]

Lack of resources or economic problems cannot in principle justify prison conditions which offend the standards of Art.3.[138]

(e) Illness and access to medical treatment in prison

II–711 Article 3 imposes an obligation on the State to ensure the health and well-being of persons deprived of their liberty, including providing them with the requisite medical assistance.[139] The Court has stopped short of adopting the CPT principle of equivalence of health care in prisons with the outside world, acknowledging that prison medical facilities could be limited compared with civilian clinics. The standard of care thus is flexible one, requiring compatibility with human dignity while taking into account the prison context.[140] Responsibility may also arise where a prisoner enters prison healthy and later proves to have developed a serious illness; in those circumstances, the authorities may be held liable unless they come up with a plausible explanation.[141]

Serious ill-health does not necessarily render imprisonment incompatible with Art.3, where there is evidence that the prison authorities are providing appropriate care. It would generally appear to require evidence of an identifiable shortcoming or defect in the treatment attaining a sufficient level of severity for the Court to find a

[131] *Khider v France*, July 9, 2009, such frequent transfers disrupted family visits and psychological treatment while imposing the stress of constant adaptation to new surroundings.
[132] *Payet v France*, fn.119 above, paras 57–64, 26 transfers in over five years.
[133] *Riad and Idiab v Belgium*, January 24, 2008, paras 97–111, finding of inhuman and degrading treatment where the applicants were stranded for more than ten days.
[134] *SD v Greece*, June 11, 2009, paras 51–54.
[135] *M.S.S. v Greece and Belgium*, January 21, 2011, ECHR 2011–. . . , paras 216–234, serious overcrowding, lack of ventilation in unbearably hot conditions, not enough bedding, restricted access to sanitation facilities, and no outdoor exercise.
[136] *Rahimi v Greece*, April 5, 2011, paras 81–86.
[137] See *Mubilanzila Mayeka et Kaniki Mitunga*, fn.25 above, where the child was held alone, without a parent; *Muskhadzhiyeva v Belgium*, January 19, 2010, paras 55–63.
[138] e.g. *Poltoratskiy*, fn.127 above, para.148, where the Court noted the serious socio-economic problems in the Ukraine.
[139] *Kudla*, fn.111 above, para.94.
[140] See *Aleksanyan v Russia*, December 22, 2008, paras 139–140.
[141] *Dobri v Romania*, December 14, 2010, paras 45–56, the applicant developed TB after entering prison; the Court criticised the lack of screening of incoming prisoners to prevent the spread of infection.

violation in this respect.[142] It is not necessary for the lack of treatment to lead to medical emergency or even severe or prolonged pain, the Court appearing to consider the denial of necessary treatment may of itself cause anguish and suffering contrary to Art.3.[143]

In *McGlinchey v UK*, there was a failure by prison medical staff to monitor properly the state of the applicant who was vomiting repeatedly under withdrawal symptoms and dehydrated to the point of collapsing with multiple organ failure.[144] Lack of treatment for skin diseases contracted in prison, together with lack of appropriate treatment or monitoring of health during and after a hunger strike disclosed degrading treatment.[145] A failure to monitor effectively prisoners with mental problems may also disclose degrading treatment but there is no obligation as such for automatic and regular examinations by specialised psychiatric personnel.[146] Failure to provide a schizophrenic with proper psychiatric medical care and supervision in prison and delay in transferring him to hospital disclosed a breach where there was a clear medical recommendation to that effect from the relevant authorities.[147] Thus, where a prisoner's state is so serious that he requires care in a specialised hospital, continuing detention in a prison setting, even in the prison hospital, will show an insufficiency of medical care contrary to Art.3 standards.[148]

Though due allowance is made for the practical exigencies of imprisonment, the strain imposed on an ill prisoner may attain the prohibited level of severity. In *Mouisel v France*,[149] the Court found objectionable the way in which the applicant, suffering from cancer, had to be transferred to and from the prison to obtain external treatment, handcuffed throughout, which caused him suffering beyond that inevitably associated with either imprisonment or chemotherapy. The pyschological and neurological deficiencies flowing from Wernicke-Korsakoff syndrome were also found to render an applicant's condition unfit for imprisonment.[150] The conditions of

[142] No failure to comply with necessary standards was found in *Kudla*, fn.111 above, prison staff's failure to supply pain-killing medication on several occasions was insufficiently serious in *Rehbock*, fn.52 above, para.80; *Reggiani Martinelli v Italy*, (22682/02) (Dec.) June 16, 2005, suffering of prisoner due to after-effects of a brain operation before his detention was adequately dealt with in prison; *Prencipe v Monaco*, July 16, 2009, no violation where the applicant benefitted from over 200 external medical visits, with no convincing medical evidence of incompatibility of prison for her condition.

[143] *Ashot Harutyunyan v Armenia*, June 15, 2010, paras 114–116.

[144] *McGlinchey v UK*, April 29, 2003, ECHR 2003–V, paras 57–58.

[145] *Nevmerzhitsky*, fn.47 above, paras 102–106; see also *Popov v Russia*, July13, 2006, where the applicant, suffering from cancer, was not given the necessary examinations and information; *Yakovenko*, fn.115 above, paras 90–102, where the applicant, who was suffering from HIV and TB, did not receive timely or adequate medical care; *Kaprykowski v Poland*, February 3, 2009, paras 74–75, where the applicant with serious neurological conditions, including epilepsy, was not under constant medical supervision and the remand centre doctors changed the prescription made by specialised doctors causing an increase in fits; *Ghavatdze v Georgia*, March 3, 2009, where diagnosis and treatment of hepatitis and TB was delayed by unexplained transfers from hospital to prison and the prisoner's condition deteriorated due to appalling conditions.

[146] *Rohde v Denmark*, July 21, 2005, para.108, monitoring was effective in the circumstances; contrast *Keenan*, fn.29 above, where the lack of effective monitoring and informed psychiatric input into the treatment of the mentally ill applicant, combined with a disciplinary punishment following which he committed suicide, was incompatible with the standard of treatment required for such a person.

[147] *Kucheruk*, fn.88 above, paras 147–152.

[148] *Aleksanyan*, fn.140, paras 151–158.

[149] *Mouisel v France*, November 14, 2002, ECHR 2002–IX, inhuman and degrading treatment. See also inhuman treatment disclosed by handcuffing of a post-operative prisoner to his bed where there was no risk of absconding or security issues in *Tarariyeva v Russia*, December 14, 2006.

[150] *Tekin Yildiz v Turkey*, November 10, 2005. See also *Farbtuhs v Latvia*, December 2, 2004, where the applicant's age (81) and severe incapacities were not compatible with detention.

transfer of a sick prisoner, transported over 100km to and from hospital, in an ordinary van were found inhuman.[151] Where a partially paralysed prisoner was kept in cramped, overcrowded, insanitary and unhygienic conditions incompatible with medical recommendations regarding his condition, the cumulative effect over several years reached a level of intensity beyond the inevitable level of suffering flowing from detention and disclosed degrading treatment.[152]

Misconduct on a prisoner's part furnishes no justification for delaying medical treatment.[153] Nor can the authorities rely on the fact that other prisoners are able to provide assistance to a sick prisoner.[154] Medical treatment prescribed by doctors should not be overruled or ignored by prison authorities; decisions as to the necessity of further medical examinations should also be taken by medically-qualified personnel, the Court disapproving strongly of medical examinations of a multiple sclerosis sufferer having to be approved by a prosecutor.[155] Government argument as to the high cost on the prison administration of providing special drugs to a prisoner was rejected, the Court noting such drugs were available free to people in public hospitals.[156]

Failure over a number of years to provide a prisoner, who had lost most of his teeth, with dentures was found to breach Art.3, although there was no finding that this had caused him health difficulties.[157] Removal of the applicant's glasses and failure to replace them for five months was also found incompatible with Art.3 as degrading treatment, the Court noting that it would have aroused feelings of insecurity and helplessness, and rendered him unable to read and write.[158]

Minor deficiencies may not disclose a problem. Where a prisoner was diagnosed with TB but did not receive the appropriate treatment for 14 days until his release, the Court did not find a violation of Art.3.[159]

(f) *Expulsion and extradition*

II–712 The Convention organs, in *Soering v UK*, established that it would not be compatible with the fundamental principles underlying the Convention if a Contracting State were knowingly to surrender a fugitive to another State where he would be at risk of torture however heinous a crime he might have committed. This has since been extended to measures of expulsion generally and a potential breach of Art.3 will be found where there are substantial grounds for believing that an applicant faces a real risk of being subjected to torture or to inhuman and degrading treatment or punishment if expelled (see Pt IIB, Extradition; Immigration and expulsion).

[151] *Tarariyeva*, fn.149 above.
[152] *Flaminzeanu v Romania*, April 12, 2011, paras 82–100, spinal and renal problems, in particular requiring constant use of a catheter.
[153] *Iorgov*, fn.127 above, para.85.
[154] *Kaprykowski*, fn.145, para.74, lack of medical care was not compensated for when an epileptic prisoner was kept in a cell where the other detainees knew how to deal with fits.
[155] *Grori v Albania*, July 7, 2009, paras 120 and 131.
[156] *Grori*, fn.155 above, para.131, epileptic prisoner was kept in a cell where his fellow detainees knew how to deal with his fits.
[157] *VD v Romania*, February 16, 2010, the prison authorities claimed that he would have to pay for the treatment himself, although the prisoner was impecunious; however, even when, by law, medical coverage extended such treatment to prisoners, the treatment was still not carried out.
[158] *Slyusarev v Russia*, fn.35 above, paras 33–34, contrast loss of glasses for a few days which was not considered problematic in the Commission cases cited therein.
[159] *Gavrilita v Romania*, June 22, 2010, paras 34–35.

(g) *Village destruction*

The traumatic events alleged when Turkish security forces burnt houses in the south-east region, rendering villagers homeless and destitute, were found by the Commission to be sufficiently severe in their effects to constitute inhuman treatment, in particular where the applicants had been present, laying stress on the inherently violent nature of the experience and the anguish and distress caused in the process.[160] Although the Court showed an initial reluctance to find such breaches,[161] it found the circumstances in *Selçuk and Asker v Turkey* sufficiently traumatic to fall within the scope of Art.3 (namely, the burning was carried out without regard to the safety of the elderly applicants who witnessed the destruction of their home and all their possessions and were provided with no assistance afterwards).[162] The destruction of Roma housing, leaving the applicants in poor living conditions together with the general attitude of the authorities to their complaints, disclosed degrading treatment.[163] II–713

(h) *Disappearance*

The Court has rejected argument that the fact of a forced disappearance per se disclosed treatment for the victim contrary to Art.3.[164] In the absence of evidence of ill-treatment, it has so far declined to make any presumptions.[165] In special circumstances, the situation of uncertainty inflicted on the relative of the disappeared person may render him or her a victim of treatment contrary to Art.3.[166] The Court has given weight to the parent-child bond, to whether the relative witnessed the incident in which the victim was taken away, to the extent of the attempts by the relative to obtain information and the way in which the authorities have responded to those inquiries.[167] It has stated that the essence of the violation does not lie as such in the disappearance of the family member but rather the authorities' II–714

160 e.g. *Mentes v Turkey*, (23186/94) (Rep.) March 7, 1996, R.J.D. 1998–VIII, No.59, where children were present and left without clothing and threats of physical force were made. The Court found it unnecessary to decide in view of the breach of Art.8.

161 e.g. *Akdivar v Turkey*, September 16, 1996, R.J.D. 1996–IV, No.15.

162 *Selçuk and Asker v Turkey*, April 24, 1998, R.J.D. 1998–II, No.71; also *Bilgin v Turkey*, November 16, 2000; *Dulas v Turkey*, January 30, 2001, para.54.

163 *Moldovan (No.2)*, fn.81 above.

164 *Kurt v Turkey*, May 25, 1998, R.J.D. 1998–III, No.74, para.116; *Çiçek v Turkey*, February 27, 2001, paras 155–157.

165 cf. *Cakici v Turkey*, fn.40 above, paras 91–92, and *Akdeniz v Turkey*, May 31, 2001, where there was eyewitness evidence of ill-treatment of the disappeared persons; *Aliyeva v Russia*, fn.29 above, paras 82–88, where eyewitnesses saw the missing person, who was handicapped with only one leg, dragged outside in his underwear at night in late October.

166 *Cakici*, fn.40 above, paras 97–99, the Court held that the finding of an Art.3 violation on the part of the mother in the earlier case of *Kurt*, fn.164 above, did not establish any general principle and referred to the need for "special features".

167 e.g. *Kurt*, fn.164 above, paras 133–134, *Çiçek*, fn.164 above, paras 173–174; *Timurtas v Turkey*, June 13, 2000, paras 96–97 and *Tas v Turkey*, November 14, 2000, ECHR 2000–XI, para.80, where, respectively, mothers or fathers of disappeared persons were victim of the authorities' complacency or callous disregard in the face of their anguish; *Cyprus v Turkey*, fn.81 above, para.157; *Tanis v Turkey*, August 2, 2005, para.220, family blocked from access to information; *Bazorkina v Russia*, July 27, 2006, where mother saw video of son apparently being taken for execution; *Luluyev v Russia*, November 9, 2006, paras 94–101, lack of information and delay in granting victim status to relatives which gave procedural rights in criminal proceedings.

reactions and attitudes in respect of which a relative may claim directly to be a victim.[168] Thus, where some eleven members of the disappeared person's close and extended family claimed violations of Art.3, the Court distinguished between those who participated in the search and contacts with the authorities and those who, although doubtless distressed by the disappearance, had not been so involved, finding a violation only for the former three.[169]

Other circumstances attached to a disappearance of a short nature not of itself reaching the threshold of Art.3 may impose suffering of a nature and degree as to disclose a violation. In a case where the applicants' sons were forcibly abducted and their bodies found some four days later, the fact that the remains were incomplete and scattered due to the use of explosives meant that the applicants had never been able properly to bury their loved ones, causing them suffering beyond that inevitably flowing from a serious human rights violation.[170]

(i) *Witnessing the death of relatives*

II–715 The fact that a relative has been unlawfully and violently killed, however distressing, does not give rise to a separate violation of Article 3 as regards the bereaved. An exception to this general rule appears in one case where a father witnessed the death of his wife and two children under an army bombardment, sending him into deep shock and causing short term amnesia.[171]

5. **Matters of proof and causation**

(a) *Standard of proof*

II–716 The Convention organs have adopted an approach of the free assessment of evidence, without any formal burden of proof on either party. The Court in *Ireland v UK* stated that it must examine all the material before it and may obtain evidence *proprio motu*. To assess this evidence it adopts, as the Commission did in *The Greek case*, the standard "beyond reasonable doubt".[172] Such proof may also follow from the coexistence of sufficiently strong clear and concordant inferences or of similar unrebutted presumptions of fact. In this context the conduct of the parties when evidence is being obtained has to be taken into account.[173]

In *Ireland v UK*, following complaints by the Irish Government that the United Kingdom had not afforded on occasion the necessary facilities for the effective conduct of the investigation, the Court considered this regrettable but this appeared

[168] *Cakici*, fn.40 above, paras 98–99; *Ipek v Turkey*, February 17, 2004, para.183; amongst many Chechen disappearance cases, *Gekhayeva v Russia*, May 29, 2008, paras 117–121; *Varnava v Turkey*, September 18, 2009, ECHR 2009–. . . , paras 200–202, referring to officialdom's attitude of indifference to the relatives' acute anxiety.

[169] *Musikhanova v Russia*, December 4, 2008, paras 81–83. Also, *Cakici*, fn.40, para.99, no violation in respect of the brother of the victim, who had neither witnessed the disappearance or been particularly involved in abortive contacts with the authorities; *Akdeniz*, fn.93 above, para.102, no special features were found to exist.

[170] *Khadzhialiyev*, fn.79 above, para.121.

[171] *Esmukhambetov v Russia*, March 29, 2011, paras 185–190.

[172] A reasonable doubt means not a doubt based on a mere theoretical possibility, but a doubt for which reasons can be drawn from the facts presented: *Ribitsch*, fn.2 above, (Rep.) para.104.

[173] *Ireland v UK*, fn.5 above, para.161.

to have no backlash on the assessment of the facts. However, a failure to produce relevant documents or witnesses has since been taken into account in drawing inferences and assessing facts in a number of cases.[174]

(b) Injuries in custody

As persons in custody are in a vulnerable position, the authorities are under a duty to protect them and to provide a plausible explanation for any injuries received.[175] Where a person held in custody suffers injury, there is accordingly a strong inference as to causation. This was applied by the Commission in *Ireland v UK*, where there was medical evidence of injuries received by detainees while under the responsibility of the security forces, with no other credible explanation, beyond vague, unsubstantiated references to the possibilities of fights or riots. In *Tomasi v France*, where the injuries clearly dated from the period in detention and the Government acknowledged that it could give no other explanation, the authorities were regarded as responsible.[176] II–717

This presumption may be dislodged if there is sufficient explanation by the authorities. In *Diaz Ruano v Spain*,[177] concerning the shooting of the applicant's son while in police custody, the Commission accepted that the police officer shot when attacked and in self-defence. Although marks on the body supported the allegations of ill-treatment, there was no firm opinion as to timing from pathologists and the Commission did not find it established beyond reasonable doubt that injuries had been caused in police custody.[178] However, the Court has since shifted the burden still further onto the Government. Where injuries are discovered on a prisoner in custody and the reports equivocal as to whether they were inflicted before arrest, the Court places a certain onus on the Government to substantiate that this is the case; it is for the authorities in particular to carry out a proper medical examination on a person entering custody which duly records the existence of any prior injuries and accurately records their state of health.[179] Similarly, after a prison incident in which inmates were injured, it was for the authorities promptly to carry out medical examinations of those involved; in the absence of such, the Government could not rely on an absence of recorded injuries to rebut prisoners' claims of assaults.[180]

[174] e.g. *Aydin v Turkey*, (Rep.) September 25, 1997, 1997–VI, No.50, , where failure to provide a full plan of the custody area was found significant; *Mikheyev v Russia*, January 26, 2006, a refusal to provide documents from the investigation file was taken into account in finding a violation where the applicant claimed to have leapt from a high window to escape torture.

[175] *Selmouni*, fn.7 above, para.87; *Salman*, fn.41 above, para.99; *Berktay v Turkey*, March 1, 2001, para.167, where the applicant fell from a balcony while in the custody of six police officers; *Anguelova v Bulgaria*, June 13, 2002, ECHR 2002–IV, para.149, where the victim received injuries including a skull fracture in police custody; *Mikheyev*, fn.174 above, lack of plausible explanation as to why the applicant would have jumped, handcuffed, out of a high window during questioning.

[176] See also *Aksoy v Turkey*, December 18, 1996, R.J.D. 1996–VI, No.26, 23 E.H.R.R. 553, where the injuries were alleged to have been received while in custody, and must have occurred at about that time but the Government gave no convincing explanation for their cause or what might have happened in the brief delay between release and the receipt of medical treatment.

[177] *Diaz Ruano v Spain*, (Rep.) August 31, 1993, Series A, No.285–B, settled before the Court.

[178] Also *Klaas, Berlinski, Caloç*, fn.53 above.

[179] See e.g. *Mammadov v Azerbaijan*, January 11, 2007; *Akkurt v Turkey*, May 4, 2006, paras 34–38; see also *Toma v Romania*, February 24, 2009, where after several days in custody a brief note by a doctor "clinically healthy" was not sufficient to contradict the applicant's claim that he had been ill-treated during that time.

[180] *Dedovskiy*, fn.45 above, para. 90.

(c) Prison conditions

II–718 Where the capacity for proving the reality of prison conditions lies in the hands of the authorities, the Court has said it will not make rigorous application of the principle "*affirmanti incumbit probatio*" (he who alleges something must prove that allegation) giving a certain benefit of the doubt to prisoners and requiring the authorities to rebut arguable complaints.[181] The existence of CPT or other reports on conditions of detention are frequently used to support and substantiate prisoners' allegations.[182]

See more generally, Pt IC, Convention Principles and Approach, 16. Convention approach to the evidence and burdens of proof.

(d) Relevance of domestic fact-finding

II–719 While the Convention organs have always denied acting as a court of appeal or that they should substitute their opinion on the merits, they have not regarded themselves as bound by domestic courts' findings in any formal sense. Indeed, the Court has stated that in cases concerning allegations under Arts 2 and 3 it must apply a particularly thorough scrutiny.[183] The fact therefore that a domestic court has tried and acquitted an official concerning the same allegations will not prevent the Court finding a breach, as criminal law liability is distinct from international law responsibility under the Convention.[184]

Thus, in *Ribitsch*, the Commission and Court both found a violation of Art.3 in respect of the injuries suffered by the applicant in police custody although in the domestic proceedings the police officer's conviction was quashed on appeal and this decision was upheld at third instance. The Court proceeded to re-assess the evidence, giving significance to the existence of injuries, the fact that the injuries were not all explained by the policeman's story of a fall, the discrepancies in the police officer's versions of events and the lack of any other witness to the fall. It relied on the findings of the first instance court as to credibility and impliedly criticised the second instance's inadequate reasoning, inter alia, its references to the applicant's lack of credibility due to his past criminal record and personal extravagance, which the Court found irrelevant to events while he was in police custody.[185]

[181] e.g. *Khudoyorov v Russia*, February 22, 2005, para.113, Government failed to provide specifications/ occupancy details of prison transport vans; *Ogica v Romania*, May 27, 2010, para.45, Government failure to provide documents on occupancy, hygiene and conditions in the cells.

[182] e.g. concerning conditions of detention for asylum seekers in Greece, see *M.S.S v Greece and Belgium*, January 21, 2011, ECHR 2011–. . .

[183] *Ribitsch*, fn.2 above, para.32.

[184] *Avsar v Turkey*, July 10, 2001, para.284, the Court is dealing with the responsibility of the State, under the Convention, for the acts of its organs and agents, which is not the same as issues of individual criminal responsibility, or concerned with findings of guilt or innocence in that sense.

[185] In the Commission Report, see the then Mr. Bratza's separate opinion, stating that while he did not question the domestic decision to give the police officer the benefit of the doubt, the Government had not discharged the burden on them of providing a sufficiently convincing alternative explanation as to how the applicant came by his injuries. See also *Rivas v France*, April 1, 2004, where a police officer was acquitted of assault, the Court rejected the appellate court's finding that kneeing the minor in the testicles had been legitimate self-defence and took into account the history of complaints of violence against the officer (even though he had never been convicted before).

6. Positive and procedural obligations on the State

(a) *The obligation to investigate*

In order to render effective the fundamental safeguards enshrined in Art.3, the Court has, following its approach in Art.2, interpreted the provision as requiring an effective, official investigation where an individual raises an arguable claim that he has been seriously ill-treated by the authorities[186] or by private individuals.[187] The investigation should be thorough and diligent, disclosing a serious attempt to find out what happened and should not rely on hasty or ill-founded conclusions to close the file or as the basis of their decisions.[188] It should be capable of leading to the identification and punishment of those responsible, and requires appropriate independence, public scrutiny, promptness and expedition.[189] Thus in *Assenov v Bulgaria*, the cursory and defective investigation into allegations that police officers had beaten the 14–year-old applicant disclosed a breach of Art.3. The Court had found it impossible to establish from the evidence on the substantive complaints whether or not the boy's injuries had been caused by the police as alleged.[190] Systemic defects which prevent applicants obtaining independent and effective investigation of their allegations may also found procedural breaches.[191] However the mere fact a prosecution is not brought where there are credible assertions of ill-treatment is not decisive, if that independent and objective investigation has II–720

[186] *Assenov v Bulgaria*, October 28, 1998, R.J.D. 1998–VII, No.96, para.102, citing Art.2 cases, in particular *McCann v UK*, September 27, 1995, Series A, No.324, para.161. See also *Stepuleac v Moldova*, November 6, 2007, even though there was insufficient evidence to show that the applicant had in fact been intimidated in solitary confinement, the Court considered that the procedural obligation to investigate arose given the dubious reasons for his confinement, his vulnerable position and the potential for abuse flowing from the fact that the detention centre was run by the authority also responsible for prosecuting him.

[187] e.g. *Secic v Croatia*, May 31, 2007, where the applicant Roma was assaulted by skinhead extremists; *Denis Vasilyev v Russia*, December 17, 2009, paras 101–104, assault in the street.

[188] see, e.g. *Mikheyev*, fn.174, para.108; *Chitayev and Chitayev v Russia*, January 18, 2007, paras 163–166; *Maslova and Nalbandov*, fn.43 above, where proceedings against police officers accused of rape were discontinued as, due to procedural failings, the evidence against them was ruled inadmissible, the "manifest incompetence" of the prosecution disclosed a procedural breach; *Cobzaru v Romania*, July 26, 2007, where the prosecutors relied solely on police officers' statements, ignoring other eyewitness testimony or inconsistencies in the official account; *Stoica v Romania*, March 4, 2008, the prosecutors limited themselves to exonerating the police, giving no reasons as to why they considered only police evidence credible.

[189] See, e.g. *Mikheyev*, fn.174 above, paras 107–116; *Menesheva*, fn.26 above, paras 67–71, where the competent authorities had to act with "exemplary diligence and promptness"; *Denis Vasilyev*, fn.187 above, crucial failure to launch immediate investigation leading to loss of evidence.

[190] See also *Labita v Italy*, April 6, 2000, ECHR 2000–IV, where the lack of records and access by the prisoner to means of proving the assault by prison officers also resulted in the Court finding insufficient evidence to disclose ill-treatment contrary to Art.3—instead it found a procedural breach arising out of the tardy, inactive investigation into the applicant's complaints; *Poltoratskiy*, fn.127 above, paras 121–128, where there was insufficient evidence before the Court that the applicant had been beaten by prison guards, but the prosecutor's investigation into the allegations had been perfunctory and superficial in breach of Art.3.

[191] See *Macovei v Romania*, June 21, 2007, paras 43–57, where the prosecutors had a monopoly, unchallengeable, as to the characterisation of offences going before the courts, which had led in that case to the dismissal of complaints of serious bodily harm.

thoroughly established the facts and identified that any failings fall short of criminal responsibility.[192]

The requirements of effectiveness also extend past the stage of preliminary investigation to the examination of the complaints before the courts, which are required to carry out a careful scrutiny ensuring the deterrent effect of the judicial system and upholding the prohibition of ill-treatment. Thus, where court proceedings become time-barred for undue delay and the facts never established by a competent court, a procedural breach arose.[193]

In *Ilhan v Turkey*, the Court noted however that this approach might lead to an unnecessary overlap with Art.13 of the Convention, which requires an effective remedy for arguable breaches of the Convention and would generally impose the necessary procedural safeguards against abuse and the possibility of redress. It considered that Art.2 differed significantly, both in the terms in which it was framed and in the problems with which it dealt; the procedural obligation could not be automatically transplanted to Art.3.[194] Whether or not it was appropriate or necessary to find a procedural breach of Art.3 would depend on the circumstances, impliedly where the authorities' cursoriness or passivity, as in *Assenov*, hindered any possibility of making conclusive findings on the facts.[195] This distinction is, however, no longer drawn in the now common and often summary dual findings of substantive and procedural breaches of Art.3, with no separate examination of Art. 13 being undertaken.[196]

Thus, notwithstanding the differences between Arts 2 and 3, in substance and form, the procedural guarantees required under the former have been transferred lock, stock and barrel under the latter, flowing presumably from the Court's concern to ensure the effective implementation of anti-torture guarantees.

It may be noted that, where there were numerous complaints of ill-treatment in Wandsworth prison, the Court doubted that any procedural obligation arose under Art.3 in respect of allegations of systemic negligence as there had been no lack of investigative procedures into the allegations as such. However, even if Art.3 rather than Art.13 applied, the Court was not persuaded that there was any obligation to hold a public inquiry into the incidents as a whole where there had been investigations, prosecutions, convictions and disciplinary sanctions arising out of individual cases, sufficient to show that there was no lack of accountability.[197]

The obligation was interpreted in *MC v Bulgaria* as requiring the proper investigation and punishment of rape. The failure of the prosecuting authorities to investigate the surrounding circumstances of the alleged rape of the applicant by two men on a date accordingly disclosed breaches of both Arts 3 and 8.

[192] See *Van Melle v Netherlands*, (19221/08) (Dec.) September 29, 2009, concerning a fire in an asylum refuge leading to many casualties; the independent committee report was exhaustive, identified various administrative failings and led to the resignation of two ministers, but did not find any breach of duty of a criminal nature.

[193] See *Beganovic v Croatia*, June 25, 2009.

[194] *Ilhan*, fn.44 above, paras 91–92.

[195] See also *Khashiyev and Akiyeva v Russia*, February 24, 2005, paras 189–190, where lack of forensic measures or questioning of witnesses made it impossible to assess whether the applicants' relatives had been tortured before death; *Filip v Romania*, December 14, 2006, para.45, where the Court examined whether the lack of effective investigation into alleged ill-treatment on a psychiatric ward prevented finding of substantive breach. In *Ilhan*, fn.44 above, where the Court was able to find a breach of Art.3 in the beating of the victim with a rifle butt: it dealt with procedural matters under Art.13.

[196] e.g. *Fedotov*, fn.34 above, paras 63 and 70.

[197] *Banks v UK*, (21387/05) (Dec.) February 6, 2007.

The system must also apparently allow some way in which applicants can challenge the decision of the prosecutor as to how alleged ill-treatment is categorised for pursuit before the courts.[198]

(b) The obligation to prevent ill-treatment

Article 3 has also been interpreted, in conjunction, with Art.1, to require States to take measures designed to ensure that individuals within their jurisdiction are not subjected to torture or to inhuman or degrading treatment or punishment.[199] This positive obligation to take protective measures applies particularly to children, or other vulnerable individuals,[200] including women subjected to domestic violence.[201] II–721

Positive obligations have been found to arise concerning children, where the local authority had failed to protect children from serious abuse or neglect of which it knew or should have known.[202] Issues of school discipline, including protection from threats and injuries from bullying, apparently fall under Art.3.[203] Positive obligations arise concerning prisoners, where the risk of harm came either from other prisoners or from the applicant's own vulnerable mental or health condition.[204] Structural shortcomings due to lack of facilities and resources are no answer to failure of the State to adequately secure the well-being of prisoners, including the risk of attack from other inmates.[205] Outside the prison context, failure to take steps to protect the applicant, a Hare Krishna member, from frequent and predictable attacks, founded a violation together with ongoing investigative failures by the authorities which were largely passive and disinterested.[206]

Article 3 has also been interpreted as requiring that adequate protection against severe ill-treatment exists in domestic law, such as protecting children from corporal punishment[207]; ensuring appropriate procedures are followed when a child is subject

[198] *Macovei v Romania*, June 21, 2007, where the prosecutor had total discretion as to how the brutal attack on the applicants was dealt with: this system was seen as likely to undermine public confidence in the judicial system and adherence to the rule of law.

[199] *A v UK*, fn.13 above, para.22; *Al-Adsani v UK*, November 21, 2001, paras 38–40, where the ill-treatment took place in Kuwait without any causal connection to the UK and thus no positive obligation arose on the State to hold Kuwait to account in UK courts.

[200] *A v UK*, fn.13 above, para.22.

[201] *Opuz v Turkey*, June 9, 2009, para.160.

[202] *Z v UK*, May 10, 2001, ECHR 2001–V, para.74, where the local authority failed to take effective steps, including removal, to protect the children from four and a half years of "appalling neglect" and physical and psychological injury; *E v UK*, November 26, 2002, paras 89–101, where the local authority failed to take effective measures which might have prevented the convicted abuser of the children of the family from returning to the home to continue sexual and physical abuse; conversely, *DP and JC v UK*, October 10, 2002, paras 110–114, where it was not established that the local authority had, or should have had, any suspicion of the long term abuse of the applicants by their stepfather.

[203] *Durdevic v Croatia*, July 19, 2011, paras 104 and 108–119, however, the applicants' allegations were too lacking in detail and specificity to trigger Art.3 in the actual case.

[204] *Keenan*, fn.29 above, para.115, lack of monitoring of suicide risk; *Pantea v Romania*, June 3, 2003, ECHR 2003–VI, paras 188–196, where the prison authorities failed to monitor the situation of the applicant, who had paranoid tendencies, or intervene effectively when he was suffering attacks from other detainees.

[205] *Rodic v Bosnia-Herzegovina*, May 27, 2008, paras 68–73, where the Bosnian-Serb prisoners convicted of war crimes against Bosnian Muslims were held in the general population and assaulted by other prisoners, the Government claim that there was no room to hold them in segregation was not a defence.

[206] *Milanovic v Serbia*, December 14, 2010, paras 87–91, the apparently religiously-motivated attacks, suffered over many years, had occurred around major orthodox holidays.

[207] *A v UK*, fn.13 above, paras 23–24.

to police investigation[208]; providing an effective criminal law system punishing all forms of rape and sexual abuse;[209] and ensuring effective steps are taken to deter domestic violence offenders and protect their victims, without placing the onus on the victims to maintain and prosecute complaints in their vulnerable situation.[210]

Failure of police officers to respond appropriately in giving due assistance to persons in need will also raise issues, as in a case where two police officers found the applicant injured and unconscious in the street after an assault and merely moved him from the road before leaving for other apparently more pressing duties.[211] Issues may also arise where domestic courts appear to allow ill-treatment with impunity. Where the prison sentence imposed on police officers for beating a child was suspended and no disciplinary consequences followed the conviction, the Court found that the domestic system had not shown the necessary rigour and failed to ensure proper accountability.[212]

Article 3 may also require that steps be taken to protect the individual against harm from third persons.[213] Taking the test applied in Art.2 positive obligation cases, the Court has held that the authorities should take reasonable steps to prevent ill-treatment of which they had or ought to have had knowledge.[214] The scope of positive obligations must not, however, be interpreted in such a way as to impose an impossible or disproportionate burden on the authorities and also should be compatible with the other rights and freedoms under the Convention.[215] Due respect is given to the authorities' assessment of the needs of the situation, particularly where there is a volatile and unpredictable public order situation as in Northern Ireland where to require the police to seek to end forcibly all violent protests would have been disproportionate and risk escalation.[216] On the other hand, the test does not require it to be shown that 'but for' the failing or omission of the public authority the ill-treatment would not have occurred. State responsibility is also engaged by a failure to take reasonably available measures which could have had a real prospect of altering the outcome or mitigating the harm.[217]

[208] *Okkali v Turkey*, fn.128 above, October 17, 2006, paras 69–70, where a minor was accused of theft and taken into police custody without prior notice to parent or the provision of a lawyer and was not questioned by a prosecutor instead of the police.
[209] *MC v Bulgaria*, December 4, 2003, ECHR 2003–XII, para.182, undue emphasis in domestic law on the element of "resistance" in proving rape.
[210] *Opuz*, fn.201, paras 166–176, the prosecutors had not pursued matters concerning serious assaults on the applicant when she withdrew her complaints (allegedly under duress from her husband), nor did they make use of the other protective measures available to them, while the domestic court only imposed a fine for a multiple stabbing; see also *ES v Slovakia*, September 15, 2009, failure to provide effective protection from abusive father and husband due to inability to exclude him from the matrimonial home.
[211] *Denis Vasilyev v Russia*, December 17, 2009, paras 115–122.
[212] *Okkali*, fn.128 above, paras 71–78, proceedings against security officials for torture or ill-treatment should not end due to prescription, amnesty or pardon (the cases cited in para.76 in fact concern findings of ineffective remedies contrary to Art.13 where such measures intervened).
[213] *Z v UK*, fn.202 above, para.73.
[214] *Z v UK*, fn.202 above, para.73, citing *Osman v UK*, October 28, 1998, Reports 1998–VIII, No.95, para.116.
[215] *Keenan*, fn.29 above, paras 89–91, for example, there is a limit on the steps that can be taken, consistently with Arts 5 or 8 for example, to protect a person against deliberate self-harm.
[216] *PF and EF v UK*, (28326/09) (Dec.) November 23, 2010, where Catholic children for several months ran the gauntlet of abusive loyalist protest on the way to school: the police had provided a shield of officers, who had taken injuries themselves but had prevented physical injury to any child. The Court accepted that the authorities had reasonably assessed the best steps to take in this situation, and that it was for them to weigh the varying dangers and difficulties.
[217] *E v UK*, fn.202 above, para.99.

That there is a certain overlap between obligations to protect and to investigate may be seen where the Court found a violation of Art.3 for the failure of the authorities to intervene to prevent attacks by fanatical Orthodox believers on a congregation of Jehovah's Witnesses and properly to investigate the incident afterwards, their attitude effectively undermining the effectiveness of any available remedies.[218]

As to whether any positive obligation could extend to protect individuals from the effects of poverty or homelessness, the Court has not ruled out that a wholly insufficient amount of pension and social benefits may raise an issue under Art.3 of the Convention and that State responsibility for "treatment" could arise where an applicant, wholly dependent on State support faced official indifference when in a situation of serious deprivation or want incompatible with human dignity. However, while the complaint of an applicant that her pension was insufficient to support her basic needs was not ruled outside the scope of the Convention, the Court found, on her own account, she received enough to cover her accommodation and food, and also benefited from free medical care: she had not shown therefore that she was in a plight contrary to human dignity.[219] A special category appears to exist however as regards asylum-seekers who are a particularly vulnerable group and in respect of which Contracting States are under international obligations with respect to their welfare. Thus, leaving an asylum seeker to fend for himself on the street for over a year, without provision for shelter, food or other needs, breached Art. 3 in *M.S.S. v Greece and Belgium*. A violation also arose where the authorities released an unaccompanied 15–year-old asylum seeker without making any provision for support, assistance or accommodation.[220] In *M.S.S.*, the Court was not convinced by the Greek Government's arguments that the applicant adult had not made the most of the opportunities available to him, but appears squarely to have put the duty on the authorities to take the initiative by way of furnishing information and giving access to facilities and support. The judgment emphasises the factual and legal situation of asylum seekers, who have frequently no knowledge of the language or country, are in a fragile psychological state with no family or friends.[221] It remains to be seen whether the positive obligation would be further developed to require pro-active steps by the State as regards other vulnerable groups or individuals.

7. Relationship with Art.2

Since Art.2 provides for judicial execution, the Court in *Soering* found that Art.3 could not be interpreted as containing a general prohibition against the death penalty as inhuman punishment, though the manner of an execution, the personal circumstances of the condemned person or the disproportionality to the offence II–722

[218] *97 Members of the Gldani Congregation of Jehovah's Witnesses and 4 others v Georgia*, May 3, 2007.

[219] *Budina v Russia*, (45603/05) (Dec.) June 18, 2009, ECHR 2009–. . . Contrast *O'Rourke v UK*, (39022/97) (Dec.) June 26, 2001, where the applicant, living on the street had been eligible for state assistance but had refused offers of accommodation.

[220] *Rahimi*, fn.136 above, paras 87–94, the minor was given shelter after two days by a voluntary organisation; no reference to whether in fact he claimed to have suffered particular distress or difficulty during this period; the "abandonment" and "passivity" of the authorities in his regard appears to have been the essential consideration.

[221] *M.S.S.*, fn.135 above, paras 249–264, no emphasis was put on the actual harm or suffering of the applicant asylum seeker in the case; his general situation of uncertainty and vulnerability was apparently enough.

committed as well as conditions of detention while awaiting execution could be capable of bringing the treatment within Art.3. The length of time spent on death row, in the constant shadow of execution, is also relevant in that context, as well as the legitimacy of the sentence.[222] Since then the ratification by almost all member states of Protocol No.6, which bans the death penalty save in time of war, has led the Court in *Ocalan v Turkey* to consider that there has arguably been an abrogation or modification of Art.2 and that capital punishment may be regarded as an unacceptable, if not inhuman, form of punishment which is no longer permissible under that provision. It did not reach any firm conclusion on this point as, in any event, it found on the facts of the individual case that there had been a breach of Art.3 in imposing the death penalty in a trial which failed to comply with Art.6. It referred to the fear and uncertainty as to possible enforcement, which anguish could not be dissociated from the unfairness of the proceedings.

Where accidental harm is the consequence of a use of force which complies with the requirements of Art.2, para.2, no issue arises under Art.3.[223]

Cross-reference

Part IIB, s.7: Corporal punishment.
Part IIB, s.18: Extradition.
Part IIB, s.29: Immigration and expulsion.
Part IIB, s.36: Prisoners' rights.

[222] See also *Ilascu v Moldova and Russia*, July 8, 2004, ECHR 2004–VII, paras 435–436, the applicant was held on death row over seven years, the sentence imposed arbitrarily by authorities outside a recognised constitutional framework in a breakaway republic.
[223] *Stewart v UK*, (10044/82) (Dec.) July 10, 1984, 39 D.R. 162.

47. Transsexuals

Key provisions:

Articles 8 (respect for private and family life), 12 (right to marry) and 14 (prohibition on discrimination). II–723

Key case-law:

Rees v UK, October 17, 1986, Series A, No.106, 9 E.H.R.R. 56; *Cossey v UK*, September 27, 1990, Series A, No.184, 13 E.H.R.R. 622; *B v France*, March 25, 1992, Series A, No.232–C, 16 E.H.R.R. 622; *X, Y and Z v UK*, April 22, 1997, R.J.D. 1997–II, 24 E.H.R.R. 143; *Christine Goodwin v UK*, July 11, 2002, ECHR 2002–VI; *I v UK*, July 11, ECHR 2002–VI; *Van Kuck v Germany*, June 12, 2003, ECHR 2003–VII; *L v Lithuania*, September 11, 2007.

1. General considerations

The problems facing transsexuals in obtaining legal recognition of their change of gender and the consequences on their enjoyment of the rights guaranteed under the Convention was an area disclosing a marked divergence between the Commission and old Court as to the application of the principles of the Convention. For the old Court the matter raised legal, scientific, medical, social and ethical issues of a controversial nature, and in the absence of any clear consensus in Contracting States it accorded them a wide margin of appreciation.[1] Since it is an area in which applicants tend to require States to take steps to ensure their rights, their complaints also concern positive obligations by States, where the Court is generally more reluctant to impose stringent requirements.[2] The recent cases of *Christine Goodwin* and *I* show that the balancing exercise has at last tipped in favour of individual rights and away from presumed public interests militating against change to the existing status quo. There is an emerging emphasis on the right to personal development and self-determination.[3] II–724

2. Ability to change name and official documents

Inability to change name and amend official documents after a change of gender disclosed a breach of Art.8 in *B v France*, where the applicant (male to female transsexual) was unable to obtain a rectification of the civil status register, with her masculine first name unchanged and recorded on all official identity papers, sometimes accompanied by the indication that she was of the male sex. These included documents which were in frequent use (e.g. cheque books, national II–725

[1] *Rees v UK*, October 17, 1986, Series A, No.106, 9 E.H.R.R. 56, para.44; *Cossey v UK*, September 27, 1990, Series A, No.184, 13 E.H.R.R. 622, para.40; *X, Y and Z v UK*, April 22, 1997, R.J.D. 1997–II, 24 E.H.R.R. 143, para.44.

[2] See Pt IIB, s.37: Private life, sub-s.3: State obligations and Pt I, s.C: Convention principles, sub-s.12: Positive obligations.

[3] *Christine Goodwin v UK*, July 11, 2002, ECHR 2002–VI, para.90; *Van Kuck v Germany*, June 12, 2003, ECHR 2003–VII, para.78.

insurance number, driving licence, voting card, etc.) and placed the applicant in an embarrassing and humiliating situation on a daily basis which the Court considered incompatible with the respect due to her private life.

3. Change of birth certificate

II–726 The right to respect for private life was held in *Rees v UK* and *Cossey v UK* not to require that the national birth register amend birth certificates to record a transsexual's gender re-assignment.[4] In balancing the general interest of the community with the interests of individual transsexuals, the latter were given little weight since they had been able to change first names and official documents, which was at the time a situation more favourable than in some countries. On the other side of the scale, the Court considered that the United Kingdom could not be required to alter its entire birth registration system to a record of civil status as found in other Contracting States. It accepted the Government's argument that amendments to the register were not possible, save in the cases of clerical or medical mistake, since the system was based on recording facts at the time they occurred and that any subsequent changes would amount to a falsification of the record. It also accepted that measures protecting transsexuals from disclosure of gender re-assignment would have adverse effects, namely, an alleged risk of confusion and complication in family and succession matters, as well as apparently depriving third parties and government bodies of information which they might have a legitimate interest to receive.

This position, taken by the old Court, is not expressly overruled by the new Court's findings in *Christine Goodwin* and *I*. The UK Government was there found in breach of Art.8 for failing to accord legal recognition to the applicants' change of gender without the Court specifying what means should be employed to bestow such recognition.[5]

4. The right to legal recognition

II–727 A post-operative transsexual may now claim a right to official, legal recognition of his/her change of gender. While the failure to accord such recognition in the United Kingdom did not cause the daily humiliation suffered in *B v France*, the Court overturned its cautious approach to the subject in *Christine Goodwin* and *I*. It was in particular influenced by the fact that the applicant had undergone gender re-assignment surgery recommended, and carried out, by the national health services and found the general international recognition of the condition and of the need for the treatment was more significant than the lack of any clear scientific explanation as to the causes of the condition. Having regard also to the clear consensus in Contracting States to granting legal recognition, if not the means of achieving it, and the continuing international trend in that direction outside Europe (particular references to Australia and New Zealand), the Court found no detriment to the public interest which could outweigh the interest of the individual.[6]

[4] The Registrar adopted the biological approach as assessed at the time of birth without regard to later surgical intervention, as in *Corbett v Corbett* [1971] P.83.

[5] *Christine Goodwin*, fn.3 above, para.93, though the Court noted that providing for exceptions to the historic basis of the birth register had not been shown as likely to produce such a disastrous impact as previously assumed and that in any event the Government were proposing to introduce an ongoing civil registration system in the future (paras 86–88).

[6] *Christine Goodwin*, fn.3 above, paras 76–93. See also *Grant v UK*, May 23, 2005, concerning the non-retrospective nature of breaches.

5. Right to marry

The old cases took the view that an individual who had received gender re-assignment could not derive a right from Art.12 to marry a person of the biological sex opposite to that with which he or she was attributed at birth.[7] In *Christine Goodwin* and *I*, the Court expressly departed from the reasoning in those cases. It rejected the argument that Art.12 was to be interpreted as the traditional marriage between persons of opposite biological sex due to the reference in the same provision to the founding of a family, pointing out that the modern right to marry could not sensibly be held to be conditional on the capacity or intention to have children. Nor could the reference to "men and women" any longer be regarded as referring to the determination of gender by purely biological criteria. While the exercise of the right was subject to the national laws of Contracting States, the Court considered that the legal impediment imposed on post-operative transsexuals from marrying persons of the sex opposite to their assigned sex impinged upon the essence of the right to marry and could not be compatible with Art.12. The Court however phrased its conclusion in terms which appear to leave a considerable margin of appreciation to national legal systems as regards the formalities and conditions that can be imposed, inter alia, regarding the information to be provided to the intended spouse and the means by which a transsexual establishes that gender re-assignment has been effected.[8] II–728

Where however a State does provide for legal recognition of change of gender, including for the purposes of marriage, a transsexual cannot complain under Art.12 of the resulting inability to marry a person of the same legal sex,[9] or to remain married to such a person,[10] where national law does not permit same-sex marriages.

6. Family life

In *X, Y and Z v UK*, the Court agreed with the Commission that de facto family life falling within the scope of Art.8 existed where X (a female to male transsexual) had been in a stable relationship with a woman Y for over 15 years and Y, with his support and involvement, had undergone artificial insemination by donor (AID) treatment which resulted in the birth of a daughter Z. However, while the inability of X under domestic law to have his name registered as the child's father was found by the Commission to disclose a lack of respect for their family life, emphasising the interests of the child and the family unit to security and legal protection, against which it saw no convincing countervailing public interest, the Court differed. It seemed influenced by what it perceived to be the controversial nature of the AID treatment and found that, while it had not been established that legal recognition would harm any public interest, it had neither been established that it was in the interests of the child. Since the applicants were able to live together as a family, the elements of practical detriment arising from the lack of legal relationship between X II–729

[7] *Rees*, fn.1 above; *Cossey*, fn.1 above.

[8] e.g. *Christine Goodwin*, fn.3 above, para.103.

[9] (14573/89) (Dec.) November 9, 1989, Sweden did recognise changed gender but in this case the transsexual (male to female) wanted to marry another female. The Commission found that Swedish law was not lacking in respect for the right to marry since both persons were of the same sex and Art.12 covered only the right to marry someone of the opposite sex.

[10] See *Parry v UK*, (42971/05) November 11, 2006; *R and F v UK*, (35748/05) November 28, 2006.

and the child Z, such as succession rights, rights of support, transmission of nationality or tenancy, were not considered to be significant, since they were either not relevant or steps could be taken to counteract any detriment.[11]

The *X, Y and Z* judgment was given by the old Court, some five years before the recent findings in *Christine Goodwin* and *I* that transsexuals could claim, under Art.8, a right to legal recognition of their change of gender. It would appear likely that the consequent changes brought about by the UK Government to comply with these judgments will meet some of the difficulties experienced by a family in which one parent is a transsexual. It remains to be seen whether any residual differences in status will remain that would be found to cause sufficient concrete prejudice to breach the family life aspect of Art.8.

7. Legislative provision for gender-assignment surgery

II–730 It appears that treatment must be made legally available. A legislative gap disclosed a breach of Art.8 where the applicant, who had undergone partial surgery, had been left in a distressing state of uncertainty as to when his re-assignment could be completed. The Court considered that budgetary constraints could not justify the continued delay in regulating what was a right under domestic law, robustly holding that if subsidiary legislation did not within three months make the surgery available, the Government should pay EUR 40,000 to fund his operation abroad.[12]

8. Reimbursement of medical expenses

II–731 Failure to give proper and appropriate consideration to a transsexual's condition in the context of a dispute with a private insurance company for reimbursement of her gender re-assignment surgery disclosed violations of both Arts 6 and 8 in *Van Kuck v Germany*. The Court purportedly did not make any finding about an entitlement to such expenses but found that the domestic courts' approach in requiring the applicant to prove the necessity of surgery and the "genuine nature" of her condition was disproportionate, inappropriate and in conflict with her right to self-determination.[13] The Court also found it problematic in *Schlumpf v Switzerland* where the courts upheld a refusal to reimburse the surgery of the applicant on the ground that she had not waited for a two-year period after the diagnosis of transsexualism. Since this criterion was only relevant in the context of ensuring the correctness of the diagnosis and no real doubt had been raised as to the diagnosis in the case, the reliance on this element without taking into account the personal circumstances of the applicant, who was of an advanced age and who had delayed taking medical steps due to her concerns for the children and spouse of her former marriage, disclosed a breach of Art.8.[14]

[11] Concerning the lack of legal recognition of relationships between parents and children born out of wedlock, the ability to make inter vivos dispositions, etc. was not considered to remedy the disadvantages, e.g. *Johnston v Ireland*, December 18, 1986, Series A No.112, 9 E.H.H.R 203.

[12] *L v Lithuania*, September 11, 2007, the estimated cost was some €47,000.

[13] The Court did not make a pecuniary award but, for non-pecuniary damage, happened to award a figure slightly above the amount of the claimed medical expenses.

[14] *Schlumpf v Switzerland*, June 8, 2009, there were also breaches of Art.6 due to the refusal of the court to hear the applicant's expert witnesses and to give her a public hearing. The applicant claimed the cost of the operation, €28,000 under the head of non-pecuniary damage: the Court awarded only €15,000, this time stating that it could not speculate as to what would have happened if there had not been breaches of the Convention in the proceedings.

9. Discrimination

It is doubtful whether many issues will be found to arise here. If a violation is established under substantive provisions, such as Art.8, no separate issue is likely under Art.14 (as in *Christine Goodwin*). Conversely, if there is no lack of respect under Art.8, it is likely that any difference in treatment will be found to be based on objective and reasonable justification. Where there is perhaps most scope for complaints by transsexuals of a difference in treatment, e.g. employment, access to services, such matters will fall outside the scope of the provision if they do not concern substantive Convention rights. II–732

However, if a person's status as a transsexual is the determining reason in a decision which adversely affects their rights, Art.14 may well come into play. Where a male-to-female transsexual undergoing gender re-assignment found her access visits to her child curtailed on application by the mother, the Court found no discrimination since the domestic courts had based themselves not on the gender re-assignment as such but the emotional instability of the applicant attested to by expert reports; the measure was also proportionate, not depriving the applicant of parental responsibility or terminating access rights altogether.[15]

Cross-reference

Part IIB, s.12: Discrimination.
Part IIB, s.31: Marriage and founding a family.
Part IIB, s.37: Private life.

15 *PV v Spain*, November 30, 2010, paras 30–37.

48. Welfare benefits

Key provisions:

II–733 Article 6, para.1 (fair hearing guarantees); Art.1 of Protocol No.1 (right to property) and Art.14 (prohibition against discrimination).

Key case-law:

Feldbrugge v Netherlands, May 29, 1986, Series A, No.99, 8 E.H.R.R. 425; *Deumeland v Germany*, May 29, 1986, Series A, No.100, 8 E.H.R.R. 448; *Salesi v Italy*, February 26, 1993, Series A, No.257–E; *Schuler-Zgraggen v Switzerland*, June 24, 1993, Series A, No.263, 16 E.H.R.R. 432; *Schouten and Meldrum v Netherlands*, December 9, 1994, Series A, No.304, 19 E.H.R.R. 432; *Gaygusuz v Austria*, September 16, 1996, R.J.D. 1996–IV, No.14, 23 E.H.R.R. 364; *Duclos v France*, December 17, 1996, R.J.D. 1996–VI, 32 E.H.R.R. 86; *Van Raalte v Netherlands*, February 21, 1997, R.J.D. 1997–I, No.29, 24 E.H.R.R. 503; *Mennitto v Italy*, October 5, 2000, ECHR 2000–X; *Willis v UK*, June 11, 2002; *Koua Poirrez v France*, September 30, 2003, ECHR 2003–X.

1. General considerations

II–734 The omission of social and economic-type rights from the Convention gave the initial impression at least that complaints about welfare benefits fell outside the scope of the Convention. Gradually, however, the developing case-law on the scope of civil rights under Art.6, para.1 and the approach to property rights under Art.1 of Protocol No.1 in conjunction with Art.14 (discrimination) have eroded the validity of this assumption. Generally, a complaint that a welfare benefit is not granted or that it is of a particular level will not be considered by the Court. However, as soon as eligibility criteria appear to single out persons unjustifiably on grounds of status (sex, nationality) or the proceedings dealing with disputes of entitlement show failure to conform to Art.6 requirements, the picture becomes problematic.

2. Applicability of Art.6

II–735 To attract the procedural guarantees of Art.6, there must be a dispute about a civil right or obligation. Whether a claim to a particular benefit or concerning levels of contributions concerns such right or obligation depends on a consideration of the nature and characteristics of the benefit concerned.

The Convention organs initially gave particular consideration to the public and private law features of the benefit. In that context, the categorisation of the right in domestic law was only a starting point and not conclusive unless corroborated by other factors.[1] In a number of cases, the Commission rejected claims based on benefits which it considered to be essentially public law in character, in particular where based on a scheme wholly paid out of State funds without direct contributions from the workforce.[2]

[1] *Feldbrugge v Netherlands*, May 29, 1986, Series A, No.99, 8 E.H.R.R. 425

[2] (10855/84) (Dec.) March 3, 1988, 55 D.R. 51; also (8341/78) (Dec.) July 9, 1980, 20 D.R. 161, where the payment of "military insurance" to soldiers injured on duty was regarded as a purely unilateral initiative, with no payments from the beneficiaries; (11450/85) (Dec.) March 8, 1988, 55 D.R. 142, where a claim for higher level sickness benefit was found to fall outside Art.6 since the the connection with employment was remote and assessment and collection operated in the same legal framework as tax.

Disputes concerning entitlement to benefits were first found to fall within the scope of "civil rights" in *Feldbrugge v Netherlands* and *Deumeland v Germany*. Since those cases, the existence of public law features (e.g. the character of the legislation; the compulsory nature of the social security scheme and the assumption by the State or other public institution of full or partial responsibility for ensuring social protection) has tended not to be decisive and have been outweighed by private law features, including the individual, personal and economic nature of the right; the link between social insurance schemes and the contract of employment; and affinities with private insurance.

The fact that in *Feldbrugge* the State intervened to regulate health insurance and the scheme was compulsory was not enough in itself to bring the matter within the sphere of public law. The Court noted that other types of insurance (e.g. car or housing) were compulsory but the entitlement to benefits could not be qualified as public law. It also found an analogy between contributions to social security schemes and premiums for compulsory insurance.[3] In *Schouten and Meldrum v Netherlands* it noted that private insurance covering largely the same risks was available in the Netherlands to those not compulsorily affiliated to or entitled to benefit from those schemes primarily intended to benefit those likely to find private insurance beyond their means. In that case it was also not relevant that rules governing the deduction and payment of contributions corresponded to those governing the deduction of tax from wages, as it was inevitable that means used by government agencies to ensure payment bore such a resemblance.

Although the insurance scheme in *Feldbrugge* derived from statute and not from a contract, the Court considered that the provisions were effectively grafted onto the contract and formed part of the relationship between employer and employee. Insofar as the private and economic nature of the right is concerned, the Court has regard to whether there has been an interference with a means of subsistence and whether the applicant is claiming a right flowing from specific rules laid down by the legislation in force.[4] In *Feldbrugge* it found that it was of crucial importance where the employee, unable to work, had no other source of income and that the right was "personal, economic and individual". In *Mennitto v Italy*, where a non-discretionary statutory entitlement to an invalid carer's allowance was concerned, the Court referred merely to the economic nature of the right in finding Art.6 applicable.

In *Schuler-Zgraggen*, where the Government pointed out that sickness benefit did not derive from a contract of employment since affiliation was compulsory also for self-employed and unemployed, that the amount of pension depended entirely on degree of incapacity with no relation to amount paid in or level of income and that the Swiss system operated on a mixture of pay as you go, solidarity and drawing on tax revenues, the Court emphasised that State intervention was not decisive but that the most important consideration was that the applicant suffered an interference with her means of subsistence and was claiming an individual, economic right flowing from specific rules laid down in a statute. It found no distinction therefore between the applicant's right to an invalidity pension and the rights to social insurance benefits claimed by Mrs Feldbrugge and Mr Deumeland.

The Court has generally taken the approach that the State has been intervening in an area of private law allied closely to employment and acting as a form of

[3] *Schouten and Meldrum v Netherlands*, December 9, 1994, Series A, No.304, 19 E.H.R.R. 432, para.53.
[4] e.g. *Feldbrugge*, fn.1 above, para.37.

insurance company.[5] In light of statements in *Schuler-Zgraggen* and *Salesi v Italy* and the emphasis given to the effect on subsistence, it would appear likely that Art.6, para.1 will be found to apply to most key benefits.[6] In *Duclos v France*, there was no dispute that it applied to the applicant's various disputes with the social security authority about the daily allowance for his disablement benefit; with an insurance company UAP about a disablement insurance policy his former employer had taken out with it; and with the family allowance body as to whether his drop in his earnings on unemployment should affect the calculation of the allowance.

As regards contributions to social security schemes, in *Schouten and Meldrum v Netherlands*, the Court found the approach would not necessarily be the same since in previous cases concerning claims to benefits the most important consideration had been the fact that the applicant had suffered "an interference with her means of subsistence" and was claiming an individual economic right, which did not apply automatically to disputes about contributions.[7] Also the fact that the obligation was "pecuniary" in nature would not be of the same decisiveness since pecuniary obligations exist vis-à-vis the State in public law, as taxes or part of other civic duties.

3. Application of the procedural guarantees under Art.6

II–736 Once Art.6, para.1 is applicable, in theory the usual guarantees as to, for example, independence and impartiality, length[8] and fairness[9] apply, as well as a requirement for effective enforcement of awards.[10] The application of procedural guarantees may however be affected by the nature of social security proceedings.

In *Schuler-Zgraggen*, an exception appears to have been established to the general principle of providing a hearing. The Court found that the applicant could have asked for a hearing and since she did not, she waived her right unequivocally. As

[5] Art.6 was applicable in *Feldbrugge,* fn.1 above, a dispute as to entitlement to sickness allowance: insurance was compulsory for persons bound by contracts of employment and, in cases of unfitness, entitlement flowed from a statute, as a substitute for salary; *Deumeland v Germany*, May 29, 1986, Series A, No.100, 8 E.H.R.R. 448, claim by a widow for pension on the death of her husband who was covered by compulsory industrial accidents insurance: closely linked to his status as an employee and an extension of his salary under the contract; *Salesi v Italy*, February 26, 1993, Series A, No.257–E, a refusal of disability allowance, a benefit funded entirely by the Government but under the jurisdiction of the labour magistrates' court; *Schuler-Zgraggen v Switzerland*, June 24, 1993, Series A, No.263; 16 E.H.R.R. 432, cancellation of invalidity pension following birth of child; *Schouten and Meldrum*, fn.3 above, dispute about payment of contributions under health/unemployment insurance schemes covering employees.

[6] It is less apparent whether the considerations adverted to would apply to auxiliary benefits, such as mobility allowances, attendance allowances, etc.

[7] *Schuler-Zgraggen*, fn.5 above, para.46.

[8] e.g. *Deumeland*, fn.5 above, (over 11 years) the Court considered that particular diligence was required in social security cases (para.90); *Duclos v France*, December 17, 1996, R.J.D. 1996–VI; 32 E.H.R.R. 86, where the Government argued that the distinctive features of social security cases in the French system had to be taken into account (i.e. tribunals had no power to give directions, the parties had full control over the proceedings), the Court noted that tribunals were subject to the same code of procedure as civil cases and the reasonableness of the time taken was to be judged as before civil courts—there was no mention of special diligence however—and periods of over eight and nine years disclosed a violation. In *Koua Poirrez v France*, September 30, 2003, ECHR 2003–X, para.62, over seven years was acceptable where the applicant had meanwhile received an alternative benefit.

[9] e.g. *Feldbrugge*, fn.1 above, where the procedure did not allow the applicant proper participation, e.g. the President of the Appeals Board neither heard the applicant nor gave her the opportunity to consult the evidence in the case file and to submit written pleadings.

[10] e.g. *Poznakhirina v Russia*, February 24, 2005.

regarded whether nonetheless the nature of the proceedings required an hearing before a court, it found that the highly technical nature of the issues rendered proceedings in writing more effective and it was legitimate for national authorities to have regard to demands of efficiency, economy and the need for particular diligence in social security cases, in which context systematic oral hearings would be an obstacle.

4. Property rights

There is no right as such that a State provide a particular type or amount of benefit.[11] However, despite early case-law distinctions between contributory and non-contributory benefits, the Court has now stated that, given the fact that many people in Contracting States are dependent, for at least part of their lives on benefits, and given the variety of funding methods, where a Contracting State has in force legislation providing for the payment as of right of a welfare benefit—whether conditional or not on the prior payment of contributions—that legislation must be regarded as generating a proprietary interest falling within the ambit of Art.1 of Protocol No.1 for persons satisfying its requirements.[12] II–737

In *Gaygusuz v Austria*, benefits were treated for the first time as falling within the scope of Art.1 of Protocol No.1. While this was only in the context of Art.14, nonetheless the Court found that the right to emergency assistance was pecuniary in nature and linked to the payment of contributions to the unemployment insurance fund, which brought it within the scope of Art.1 of Protocol No.1. The Court has more recently held that a claim for a disabled adult's allowance, a non-contributory benefit, concerned a pecuniary right for the purposes of Art.1 of Protocol No.1. The reasoning appears based on the fact that the applicant fulfilled the statutory criteria for the benefit, save for the element of nationality which discriminatory factor was in issue under Art.14.[13] Reduced earnings allowance, a non-contributory benefit, has been found to fall within the scope of property rights,[14] as have the right to family allowances payable to security force personnel.[15]

Where the amount of a benefit is reduced, or discontinued, this appears to constitute an interference with possession that requires justification in the general interest and be duly proportionate, without imposing "an individual and excessive burden". Thus, where legislative reform totally removed a disability pension which the applicant fisherman had received for some 20 years, the Court found that, notwithstanding genuine need to overhaul the system, it had a disproportionate effect on a small group of people, including the applicant.[16] Changes to entitlements to reflect new social trends may well be acceptable however; for example, a

[11] *Stec v UK*, (65731/01) and (65900/01) (Dec.) July 6, 2006 para.54; earlier Commission precedent, e.g. (10671/83) (Dec.) March 4, 1985, 42 D.R. 229.

[12] *Stec*, fn.11 above, para.54. See description of earlier approaches in paras 43–46.

[13] *Koua Poirrez*, fn.8 above, paras 37–42, the Court's reasoning for this extension is somewhat thin, holding that the fact that the benefit in *Gaygusuz v Austria*, September 16, 1996, R.J.D. 1996–IV, No.14; 23 E.H.R.R. 364, was contributory did not mean, by converse implication, that non-contributory benefits did not qualify. See Judge Mularoni's dissent.

[14] *Stec*, fn.11 above, paras 54–55.

[15] (44792/98) (Dec.) September 26, 2002, ECHR 2002–VIII.

[16] *Kjartan Asmundsson v Iceland*, October 12, 2004, ECHR 2004–IX. Contrast partial forfeiture of a policeman's pension for serious criminal misconduct in *Banfield v UK*, (6223/04) (Dec.) October 18, 2004, complaint manifestly ill-founded.

reduction to take into account a widow's alternative source of income from her cohabitee was not disproportionate even if it had an impact on the applicant's standard of living.[17]

5. Discrimination

II–738 Differences in entitlements or in obligations to pay contributions may disclose discrimination in conjunction with either Art.6 or Art.1 of Protocol No.1. Where there is a complaint under Art.14 in conjunction with Art.1 of Protocol No.1 that the applicant has been denied all or part of a particular benefit on a discriminatory ground covered by Art.14, the test is whether, but for the condition of entitlement about which the applicant complains, he or she would have had a right, enforceable under domestic law, to receive the benefit in question. Even if Protocol No. 1 does not include the right to receive a social security payment of any kind, if a State does decide to create a benefits scheme, it must do so in a manner which is compatible with Art.14.[18]

Differences based on sex require very weighty reasons by way of justification in light of the importance of the goal of equality of the sexes. In *Schuler-Zgraggen*, such reasons were not discerned by the Court where a decision as to entitlement of sickness pension was based on the assumption that in general women gave up work when they had children. A violation was found in conjunction with Art.6, apparently on the basis that matters concerning the assessment and weight given to evidence fell within the scope of Art.6.

In *Van Raalte v Netherlands*, the obligation on the applicant, a man over 45, to pay a contribution to a child benefits scheme was discriminatory where women over 45 were not so obliged. The obligation to pay contributions to the social security system was found to fall within the scope of Art.1 of Protocol No.1 as part of the right of the State to "secure the payment of taxes or other contributions". In *Willis v UK*, discrimination arose where the applicant widower was unable to obtain benefits (Widow's Payment and Widowed Mother's Allowance) enjoyed by a woman in the same position. However, the continued differences in various pension and benefit entitlements or contributions flowing from the differing ages of retirement for men and women, during a long transitional period, have been found to fall within the margin of appreciation due to the serious financial and social implications of equalising ages.[19]

Refusal of benefits where the applicant would have qualified but for his status as a foreigner may also disclose discrimination. In *Gaygusuz v Austria*, as the applicant, of Turkish nationality, was lawfully resident in Austria and had worked and paid contributions on the same basis as Austrian nationals, there was no objective and reasonable justification to refuse emergency assistance exclusively on the fact of his nationality. Nor was the lack of French citizenship or any reciprocal agreement with the Ivory Coast found to justify the refusal of an allowance to the applicant in *Koua Poirrez v France*, where he was resident in France and son of a French citizen working in France. Discrimination can also arise where a foreigner is excluded from even

[17] *C. Goudswaard-Van der Lans v Netherlands*, (75255/01) (Dec.) September 22, 2005, there was no evidence that the benefit was needed to safeguard the applicant from poverty.

[18] *Stec*, fn.11 above, para.55.

[19] *Stec v UK*, April 12, 2006, ECHR 2006–. . . ; *Pearson v UK*, *Barrow v UK* and *Walker v UK*, August 22, 2006.

affiliating to a social insurance scheme, as in a case where a Frenchman working as a farmer in Poland was excluded from the the farmers' social insurance scheme due to his foreign citizenship.[20]

Cross-reference

Part IIA, s.1b: Civil rights and obligations.
Part IIB, s.12: Discrimination.
Part IIB, s.33: Pensions.

[20] *Luzcak v Poland*, November 27, 2007.

PART III: JUST SATISFACTION

A. GENERAL PRINCIPLES

Key sources: Art.41 (awards of just satisfaction); Practice Direction on Just Satisfaction Claims. III–001

The grant of just satisfaction under Art.41 of the Convention[1] is dependent on the finding of a violation and the absence of total reparation in domestic law. When only partial reparation is given, as in *Barbera, Messegué and Jabardo v Spain*, where the domestic courts quashed the applicants' convictions, the Court may still award just satisfaction.[2]

Just satisfaction is generally awarded at the same time as the finding of a violation. Where, however, difficult questions of assessment arise, it may be adjourned for further consideration.[3] When just satisfaction is adjourned and the parties reach agreement as to the damages to be paid, the Court will verify that the settlement has been reached on the basis of respect for human rights and, if it is acceptable, it will strike the case out.[4] Just satisfaction issues may also be adjourned where an applicant happens to be pursuing redress at a domestic level which could provide compensation for the violation of the Convention, the Court sometimes preferring to see the outcome of those proceedings before ruling itself.[5] An applicant cannot however be required to institute further domestic proceedings in order to obtain just satisfaction after the Court's finding of a violation[6] and the fact that he might be able to obtain damages in later domestic proceedings does not prevent the Court making an award.[7]

Just satisfaction cannot be claimed by an applicant as a right: just satisfaction is only to be granted if necessary and the matter falls to be determined by the Court at its discretion, having regard to what is equitable.[8] The Court will also not raise any just satisfaction issue of its own motion.[9]

[1] Formerly Art.50.

[2] *Barbera, Messegué and Jabardo v Spain* (Art.50), June 13, 1994, Series A, No.285-C. The Court rejected the Government's arguments that the quashing was total reparation since it did not compensate for the damage suffered from real loss of opportunity to defend themselves at the original trial.

[3] e.g. where large pecuniary losses are involved with disputed value assessments as in *Papamichalopoulos v Greece*, June 24, 1993, Series A, No.260-B; (Art.50), October 31, 1995, Series A, No.330-B. Parties may be requested to nominate experts for a valuation report, e.g. *Belvedere Albighiera Srl v Italy (just satisfaction)*, October 30, 2003.

[4] rr.62(3) and 43(2). See e.g. *Maurice v France*, June 21, 2006.

[5] e.g. *Salah v Netherlands*, July 6, 2006, paras 66–82.

[6] e.g. *Dogan v Turkey*, July 13, 2006, para.50, just satisfaction.

[7] *Mikheyev v Russia*, January 26, 2006, para.155.

[8] e.g. *Sunday Times v UK (No.1) (Art.50)*, November 6, 1980, Series A, No.38; see *X v UK (Art.50)*, October 18, 1982, Series A, No.55, where the applicant died, while noting that he may have suffered distress from a breach of Art.5, para.4, the Court found that it was not necessary to award a sum to his estate as it would not advance the cause of justice (para.19).

[9] e.g. *Francesco Lombardo v Italy*, November 26, 1992, Series A, No.249-B, para.25.

Concrete measures

III–002 The Court has no express jurisdiction under Art.41 to issue directions to Contracting States on the measures or steps which they should take to rectify violations. Nor can it examine complaints that a State had failed to comply with its obligations under a judgment.[10] However, while it acknowledges that responsibility for supervising the execution of judgments lies with the Committee of Ministers under Art.46 of the Convention,[11] it increasingly has taken on a role of specifying concrete measures that should be taken in cases of a particular gravity or urgency. It continues to decline to impose any particular requirements in more run-of-the-mill cases, or cases which do not lend themselves to identifying specific steps or actions or where it does not appear useful or appropriate to underline the State's duties as regards compliance with a particular judgment.[12] For example, it has declined, where finding a breach of Art.2 for lack of an effective investigation, to order that a fresh investigation should be held, noting that where there has been a lapse of time, it cannot be assumed that the evidence or witnesses would be available for that to be a satisfactory or useful response.[13] It refused to indicate any measures which an applicant who had suffered breaches of Arts 3, 5, paras 1 and 4 requested with a view to future trial procedures, stating that these had nothing to do with remedying past breaches but were with a view to preventing future breaches which had to be regarded as speculative.[14]

Examples of indications of concrete measures include the following. In cases concerning issues of detention or medical urgency Art.3, the Court has directed that a prisoner, held in arbitrary and unlawful detention be released at the earliest possible date[15]; that detention on remand be ended of a prisoner, ill with HIV and other serious conditions[16]; that a prisoner detained for over six years and six months be brought to trial as soon as possible or released[17]; that a newspaper editor locked up in violation of freedom of expression be released immediately[18]; that as a matter of urgency adequate prison conditions and necessary medical treatment be provided to a prisoner with a chronic mental health illness[19]; that a prisoner suffering from hepatitis C and pulmonary tuberculosis be transferred to a specialised medical

[10] e.g. *Komanicky v Slovakia*, March 1, 2005; *Haase and Others v Germany*, (34499/04) (Dec.) February 12, 2008.

[11] e.g. *Finucane v UK*, July 1, 2003, ECHR 2003-VIII, para.89; *Maestri v Italy*, February 17, 2004, ECHR 2004-I, para.47.

[12] e.g. *DH and Others v Czech Republic* (GC), November 13, 2007, para.216, the Court noted the offending legislation had already been repealed and recommendations made to Governments by the Committee of Ministers on the subject of education of Roma children; *De Clerck v Belgium*, September 25, 2007, para.101, the Court declined to direct the State to put an end to a criminal procedure that had been unreasonably long.

[13] e.g. *Finucane v UK,* fn.11 above; see also *Varnava v Turkey*, September 18, 2009, para.222, the Court declined to specify the procedures to be adopted to provide an effective investigation into disappearances. Contrast *Abuyeva v Russia*, December 10, 2010, paras 240-243, where a direction to hold an effective investigation into loss of life in a village during a counter-terrorist operation was issued exceptionally, as the incident had already been subject of a judgment by the Court, the authorities had conducted a second investigation undermined by the same flaws and data and evidence had been collected but awaited proper, objective and independent examination.

[14] e.g. *Khordokovskiy v Russia,* May 31, 2011, paras 269–271.

[15] *Assanidze v Georgia*, April 4, 2004.

[16] *Aleksanyan v Russia*, December 22, 2008, para.240.

[17] *Yakisan v Turkey*, March 6, 2007, para.49.

[18] *Fatullayev v Azerbaijan*, April 22, 2010, para.177.

[19] *Dybeku v Albania*, December 18, 2007, para.64.

establishment[20]; that all possible steps be taken to obtain assurances that prisoners transferred by the British army to the Iraqi authorities would not face the death penalty.[21]

Directions have been given to amend legislation found in breach of the Convention: to pass subsidiary legislation on gender reassignment of transsexuals[22]; to bring the school system and domestic legislation concerning religious education into compliance with Art.2 of Protocol No.1[23]; to enact appropriate legislation to regulate the situation of individual applicants erased from the citizenship register.[24]

Other directions include: to provide full and free medical cover to the applicant for his lifetime[25]; for the authorities to support the applicant's efforts to rebuild his relationship with his daughter and to take the initiative[26]; and for the State to ensure effective contact between the applicant and his daughter at a time compatible with his working hours and on suitable premises.[27]

The Court had long refused to issue any directions in fair trial cases, for example, requiring the quashing a conviction[28] but has more recently given indications that the most appropriate form of redress in cases of breaches of Art.6 would be, where the applicant so requests, to grant a retrial or to re-open the proceedings without undue delay[29] although it has declined to give guidance as to the form or procedures such retrials should adopt.[30] It has also indicated where a civil case was discontinued due to failure to pay court fees that the discontinuance be lifted and the case re-opened.[31] In cases of non-enforcement of final judgments, the Court has frequently indicated that the judgment should be executed.[32] Where an applicant was deprived of the benefit of a more lenient summary procedure in breach of Art.7, the Court directed that the sentence of life imprisonment be replaced by a penalty consistent with that procedure.[33]

Where there are systemic or structural problems, the Court will, under Art.46, identify weaknesses or dysfunctions and indicate, in appropriate cases, general and/

[20] *Ghavatdze v Georgia*, March 3, 2009, paras 104–106. See also *Slavomir Musial v Poland*, January 20, 2009.

[21] *Al-Saadoon and Al-Mufdhi v UK*, March 2, 2010, para.171

[22] *L v Lithuania*, September 11, 2007, para.74, time-limit of within three months; see also *Tan v Turkey*, July 3, 2007, para.35, law on opening of prisoners' correspondence to be rendered in conformity with Art.8.

[23] *Hasan and Zengin v Turkey*, October 9, 2007, para.84.

[24] *Kuric v Slovenia*, July 13, 2010, 2007, para.407.

[25] *Oyal v Turkey*, March 23, 2010, para.102, where the applicant had been infected at birth with HIV due to contaminated blood.

[26] *Amanalachioai v Romania*, May 26, 2009, para.107.

[27] *Gluhakovic v Croatia*, April 12, 2011, para.89.

[28] e.g. *Schmautzer v Austria*, October 23, 1995, Series A, No.328-A, para.44; *Oberschlick v Austria (No.1)*, May 23, 1991, Series A, No.204, (violation of Art.10 for defamation) request for a judgment to be set aside; *Vocaturo v Italy*, May 24, 1991, Series A, No.206, a request for a judgment to be published in the Official Gazette; *Idrocalce v Italy*, February 27, 1992, Series A, No.229-F, request for a declaration that State should adopt legislative measures to protect the human rights violated in the case.

[29] e.g. where the applicant was convicted *in absentia*: *Somogyi v Italy*, May 18, 2004; where applicants have been tried by courts lacking independence and impartiality, e.g. *Gençel v Turkey*, October 23, 2004; where a conviction was based on fundamentally flawed evidence in *Laska and Lika v Albania*, April 20, 2010, paras 74–77. See statements of principle in *Sejdovic v Italy* (GC), March 1, 2006, ECHR 2006-II, paras 119–126.

[30] *Sejdovic*, fn.29 above, para.127.

[31] *Mehmet and Suna Yigit v Turkey*, July 17, 2007, para.47.

[32] *Nitescu v Romania*, March 23, 2009, para.48; *Karanovic v Bosnia-Herzegovina*, November 20, 2007, para.30.

[33] *Scoppola v Italy (No.2)*, September 17, 2009.

or individual measures that should be adopted in the domestic legal order to put an end to the violation found and to redress its effects.[34] Where the structural problem has spawned a series of cases, the Court may make use of the pilot judgment procedure: examining the problem in a chosen case or cases and issuing a detailed judgment setting out the problems and the measures, general and individual that should be adopted,[35] in particular the provision of proper and effective remedies so that the problems may be solved on the domestic level for the future.[36] Time-limits for the remedies to be enacted or drawn up may be imposed.[37] The remaining cases may be struck off or rejected for non-exhaustion once the remedial measures have been put in place.[38]

In property cases where there has been an interference infringing principles of legality (see below), it has stated that the return of the property would constitute restitutio in integrum although in the absence of restitution it has provided for a monetary award.[39] In certain cases, disclosing flagrant unlawfulness or arbitrariness in detention, the Court has found that the nature of the violation left no choice in the measure required and held that the State should secure the applicants' release at the earliest possible date.[40]

The Government may also be directed to take steps to facilitate the execution of an award of just satisfaction, as in a case where the applicant had been expelled to Uzbekistan in breach of Art.3 and the Court directed the Government to assist in locating and contacting the applicant with a view to ensuring the payment of the award.[41]

[34] *Broniowski v Poland*, June 22, 2004 ECHR 2004-V, paras 189-194 and September 28, 2005, approving the general and individual measures in the context of a friendly settlement. See also *Lukenda v Slovenia*, October 6, 2005, State encouraged to provide remedies for length of proceedings problems; *Tekin Yildiz v Turkey*, November 10, 2005, measures to remedy defects in the official system of forensic medical reports; *Hutten-Czapska v Poland*, June 19, 2006, ECHR 2006-. . . , concerning malfunctioning of housing legislation imposing excessive restrictions on landlords, *Burdov v Russia (No.2)*, January 15, 2009, concerning remedies for non-enforcement of judgments against the State.

[35] See Art.46 indications in overcrowded prison conditions cases: *Orchowski v Poland*, October 22, 2009, paras 147–154; implementing fair disciplinary procedures in prisons: *Gülmez v Turkey*, May 20, 2008, para.63.

[36] See requirements to provide effective remedies in non-enforcement of final judgment cases: *Burdov v Russia (No.2)*, January 15, 2009; expropriated property cases: *Viasu v Romania*, December 9, 2008; length of proceedings cases: *Martins Castro and Alves Correia de Castro v Portugal*, June 10, 2008, paras 61–66 and *Rumpf v Germany*, September 2, 2010, para.73; setting a time-limit of one year to provide the remedy or remedies.

[37] See *Sekerovic and Pasalic v Bosnia-Herzegovina*, March 8, 2011, the Government was given six months to amend legislation; *Kharchenko v Ukraine*, February 10, 2011, para.101, the Government was given six months to submit a reform strategy; *Greens and M.T. v UK*, November 23, 2010, para.115, legislative proposals to be introduced within six months.

[38] See e.g. *Demopoulos v Turkey* (GC), (46223/99) et al (Dec.) March 1, 2010, cases rejected for non-exhaustion in light of a remedy provided for owners of property in the occupied "TRNC" area of Cyprus; *Association of Real Property Owners in Lodz v Poland*, (3485/02) (Dec.) March 8, 2011, strike-out decision; closing the pilot judgment procedure in *Hutten-Czapska v Poland*, fn.33 above.

[39] *Papamichalopoulos*, fn.3 above; *Hentrich v France*, September 22, 1994, Series A, No.296, para.71. See *Scordino v Italy (No.3)*, March 6, 2007, distinguishing cases where the expropriation had a legal basis but failed to strike the right balance as concerning the amount of compensation.

[40] *Assanidze v Georgia*, fn.15 above, paras 203–204; *Ilaşcu v Moldova and Russia*, July 8, 2004, para.490. See also *Yakisan v Turkey*, March 6, 2007, where the applicant had been in pre-trial detention for more than 11 years, the Court indicated that the trial should end swiftly or that he should be released to put an end to the violation.

[41] *Muminov v Russia*, November 4, 2010, para.19.

Monetary awards

Just satisfaction is awarded under three heads: pecuniary loss, non-pecuniary loss, and costs and expenses. The governing principle under all three heads is the notion of "equity". III–003

An applicant must detail his claims: the Court will not examine possible damage of its own motion.[42] The Court has not proved unduly generous in its approach to awarding compensation under any head. The emphasis is not on providing a mechanism for enriching successful applicants but rather on the Court's role in making public and binding findings of applicable human rights standards.[43] Where there are large groups of cases of the same kind, the Court has, for the same reason, adopted an expedited approach to just satisfaction, applying a uniform lump sum for pecuniary and non-pecuniary damage to each applicant, rather than seek to compensate losses minutely and exhaustively.[44]

Although the Court has stated awards of just satisfaction should be exempt from attachment by the authorities since this would, for example, frustrate the purpose of compensation for non-pecuniary damage and costs awards for ill-treatment under Art.3, it has stated that it has no jurisdiction to make any order or direction in that regard, leaving it to the State's discretion.[45]

Since 2002, all awards are made in Euros to enable direct comparison between cases from different countries.

[42] e.g. *Kostovski v Netherlands*, November 20, 1989, Series A, No.166, 12 E.H.R.R. 434, para.46; *Huvig v France*, April 24, 1990, Series A, No.176-B, para.37.
[43] *Varnava v Turkey* (GC), September 18, 2009, paras 224–225.
[44] e.g. *Ryabov and 151 privileged pensioners v Russia*, December 17, 2009, para.21.
[45] *Selmouni v France*, July 28, 1999, ECHR 1999-V, para.133.

B. DIFFERENT TYPES OF LOSS

1. Pecuniary loss

III–004 There must be a causal link between the violation and the loss. Where the nature of the breach allows of restitutio in integrum, it is for the State to effect it but if this does not occur the Court will award just satisfaction.[1] Loss must have been actually incurred.[2] While an applicant is generally expected to substantiate the pecuniary loss flowing from a breach,[3] the Court acknowledges that in some cases a precise calculation, in particular of future losses, may not be possible and makes an equitable assessment.[4] There must, however, be at least some basis for a claim of financial dependence to obtain an award reflecting loss of financial support flowing from the death of a relative.[5] Where the data allowing precise calculation of pecuniary loss are in the hands of the authorities and are not made available in the Strasbourg proceedings, the Court will give the applicant the benefit of the doubt where the claims are prima facie reasonable.[6]

In cases of interference with property rights, a distinction is drawn between cases of lawful and unlawful deprivations or dispossession. Where the breach results from inadequate compensation or procedural flaws, less than a full measure of compensation may be called for,[7] particularly where the taking of property is linked to fundamental changes in the constitution or pursues economic reform and social justice[8] or preservation of the environment or heritage sites.[9] In such cases, the Court may consider it appropriate to fix a sum "reasonably related" to the value of the property and which would have been found acceptable had the State compensated the applicants, or otherwise find an appropriate, equitable basis for compensation.[10] Where, however, there is "manifest unlawfulness" in the deprivation or dispossession, full restitution of losses is generally awarded.[11] In cases of

[1] In *Papamichalopoulos v Greece* (Art.50), June 24, 1993, Series A, No.260–B, paras 38–39, the Court held that the return of the expropriated land with award for loss of enjoyment would constitute restitutio in integrum, but if the land was not returned within six months the State was to pay the value of the land; similarly in *Brumarescu v Romania*, January 23, 2001, ECHR 2001-I, paras 19–20, just satisfaction.

[2] e.g. *Öztürk v Germany* (Art.50), October 23, 1985, Series A, No.85, para.8, there had been a breach of Art.6, para.3(e), but the applicant's insurance company had paid the interpretation fees.

[3] e.g. *Metin Turan v Turkey*, November 14, 2006, no award made for costs flowing from a punitive transfer of the applicant civil servant due to trade union membership as not properly substantiated.

[4] *Smith and Grady v UK (just satisfaction)*, July 25, 2000, ECHR 2000-IX, paras 8–9; *Oneryildiz v Turkey*, November 30, 2004, ECHR 2004-IX, paras 168–170, approximate calculations of lost financial support of dead family members and value of destroyed house and contents.

[5] *Akkum v Turkey*, March 24, 2005, paras 282 and 284; *Simsek v Turkey*, July 26, 2005, para.138; *Osmanoglu v Turkey*, January 24, 2008, para.123; *Gelayevy v Russia*, July 15, 2010, para.169, elderly parents could claim that they would have received support from disappeared son.

[6] See *Dacia Srl v Moldova (just satisfaction)*, February 24, 2009, para.47.

[7] See *Dacia Srl v Moldova (just satisfaction)*, February 24, 2009, para.47.

[8] e.g. *The Former King of Greece v Greece (just satisfaction)*, November 11, 2002; *James v UK*, February 21, 1986, Series A, No.98.

[9] e.g. *Kozacioglu v Turkey*, February 19, 2009, 1986, para.82; *Turgut v Turkey*, October 13, 2009, paras 15-19.

[10] e.g. *The Former King of Greece*, fn.12 above; *Beyeler v Italy (just satisfaction)*, May 28, 2002; *Sovtransavto Holding v Ukraine (just satisfaction)*, October 2, 2003.

[11] *Iatridis v Greece (just satisfaction)*, October 19, 2000, ECHR 2000-XI, para.35; see also *Belvedere Albighiera Srl (just satisfaction)*, October 30, 2003. See also *Guiso-Gallisay v Italy (just satisfaction)* (GC), December 22, 2009, paras 102–106.

constructive expropriation, akin to a form of expedited public interest procedure, a modified approach is taken—the date of value of property is not the date of the Court's judgment but the date of loss of ownership and the value of the public works built on the land is not taken into account.[12] Where possible, the Court also considers that property, seized unlawfully or arbitrarily, should be returned where possible but has yet to give a direction of restitution without the alternative of pecuniary damages, essentially leaving it to the State to decide whether to return the property.[13]

Where Art.6 violations are concerned, it is rare that a procedural failing is seen as causative of pecuniary loss following upon the subsequent conviction or from the decision affecting civil rights or obligations.[14] The Court usually finds itself unable to speculate on the outcome if the breach had not occurred. In rare cases, it may find that there has nonetheless been a real loss of opportunity which requires an award. In *Barbera, Messegué and Jabardo v Spain*, following a finding of a violation of Art.6 in a criminal trial in a number of fundamental aspects, the Court considered that there was a real loss of opportunity for the applicants to defend themselves in accordance with the requirements of Art.6 and thus a clear causal connection between the damage claimed and the violation. It did not, however, accept the calculations of loss of earnings and career prospects during their period of detention, awarding a sum on an equitable basis together with non-pecuniary damage.[15] Where a property owner had been unable to regain possession of his flat for a long time due to lack of police enforcement, the Court found that the losses from interference with property rights flowed primarily from the tenant's unlawful behaviour while the State's violation under Art.6 was procedural in nature. As domestic law provided for the possibility of suing the tenant, the Court made no award for pecuniary damage.[16]

In cases of unreasonable length of proceedings, pecuniary loss may be granted where it is attributable to the delay rather than the fact that the proceedings were instituted or brought.[17]

Fines imposed and costs incurred in domestic proceedings directly linked to the violation are covered.[18]

[12] *Guiso-Gallisay v Italy*, fn.15 above, paras 102–107.

[13] *Dacia Srl v Moldova (just satisfaction)*, February 24, 2009, paras 37–57; *Guiso-Gallisay*, fn.15 above, paras 90–97.

[14] e.g. claims were unsuccessful in *Findlay v UK*, February 25, 1997, R.J.D. 1997-I, No.30, (lack of independent and impartial court martial) claim for loss of salary/pension following army discharge; *Saunders v UK*, December 17, 1996, R.J.D. 1996-VI, No.24, (breach of privilege against self-incrimination) claim of over £3 million for loss of salary; access to court cases where no causal link found with loss of trade, fees, etc., e.g. *Tre Traktorer v Sweden*, July 7, 1989, Series A, No.159, revocation of license to sell alcohol; *Fredin v Sweden*, February 18, 1991, Series A, No.192, revocation of permit to exploit gravel pit.

[15] *Barbera, Messegué and Jabardo v Spain* (Art.50), June 13, 1994, Series A, No.285-C, it accepted the original claim which was based on the minimum salary in their respective fields of employment for the period held in closed prison plus one million pesetas for loss of career prospects, plus increase by retail price index. It rejected the later claim based on daily rates awarded by Spanish courts for incapacity to work. Pecuniary awards also made in *Teixiera de Castro v Portugal*, June 9, 1998, R.J.D. 1998-IV, No.77; *Pelissier and Sassi v France*, March 23, 1999, ECHR 1999-II.

[16] *Mascolo v Italy*, December 16, 2004.

[17] e.g. *Laine v France*, January 17, 2002, para.41.

[18] e.g. where journalists were fined, required to pay costs or incur costs of publishing in defamation proceedings found in breach of Art.10: *Lingens v Austria*, July 8, 1986, Series A, No.103; *De Haes and Gijsels v Belgium*, February 24, 1997, R.J.D. 1997-I, No.30; *Association Ekin v France*, July 17, 2001, ECHR 2001-VIII; *Nikula v Finland*, March 21, 2002, ECHR 2002-II.

Interest can be claimed from the dates on which each recoverable element of past pecuniary damage accrued.[19]

Applicants cannot be required to exhaust domestic remedies to obtain compensation for pecuniary loss in light of the Court's judgment since this would prolong the procedure before the Convention organs in a manner incompatible with the effective protection of human rights.[20] Conversely, where independent of the proceedings before the Court, a finding of material loss has been made by the domestic courts, the Court may decline to make an award, referring the applicant to the relevant domestic organs to recoup his damages.[21]

[19] e.g. *Smith and Grady*, fn.8 above, para.24.

[20] e.g. *Papamichalopoulos* (Art.50), fn.5 above, para.40; *Barbera (Art.50)*, fn.19 above, para.17.

[21] e.g. *Paudicio v Italy*, May 24, 2007, paras 57–59.

Examples of Court findings of pecuniary loss

III–005

Main issues	Case	Just satisfaction awards
ARTICLE 2		
Deaths for which the State is responsible	*Nachova v Bulgaria*	€25,000 and €20,000 respectively, for loss of support of relatives shot by police
	Akkum v Turkey	€57,300 loss of financial support from relative killed during a military operation
	Eskmukhambetov v Russia	€1,000–€3,000 burial expenses (one to three relatives)
	Osmanoglu v Turkey	€60,000 loss of support from disappeared son who helped in family shop
	Gelayevy v Russia	€18,000 elderly parents' claim for support from son
Failure to protect life	*Oyal v Turkey*	€300,000 medical costs for child contaminated with HIV from blood bank
Disappearance	*Akdeniz v Turkey*	£10,000–£80,0000 for loss of earnings from farming activities; including sums for loss of a minor's contribution to work on farm and loss of service pension
	Akhmadova and Sadulayeva v Russia	€15,000 loss of earnings
ARTICLE 3		
Failure to protect children from abuse	*Z v UK*	£8,000; £100,000; £80,000; £4,000. Sums to cover future counselling and psychotherapy and for two boys, sums to reflect damage to future wage-earning capacity. Based on medical reports of damage. The Court rejected statistical claims as to future mental illness
	E v UK	£16,000–£32,000 pecuniary and non-pecuniary together, to reflect some loss of future earning capacity. Took into account an award made by the Criminal Injuries Compensation Board

Main issues	Case	Just satisfaction awards
Prison conditions/lack of medical care	*Nevmerzhitsky v Ukraine, Koval v Ukraine*	€1,000 medical expenses to mitigate conditions and the effect on the prisoner's health
Torture inducing suicide attempt	*Mikheyev v Russia*	€130,000 for future medical treatment and loss of working capacity
Ill-treatment in police custody	*Calisir v Turkey*	€700 absence from work for ten days
ARTICLE 5		
Deprivation of liberty	*Assanidze v Georgia*	€150,000 loss of working opportunity and non-pecuniary damage for over three years' detention
	Ilascu v Moldova and Russia	€180,000 each for breaches of Art.3 and Art.5 para.1 (arbitrary detention for three–six years), including element of lost salaries, allowances, etc
	Lloyd v UK	€3,000 36 days loss of working opportunity
	Paladi v Moldova	€2,080 loss of earnings during illegal detention
Procedural defects, etc	*Baranowski v Poland, Jecius v Lithuania, Storck v Germany*	Loss of earnings/pecuniary loss rejected due to lack of causal link with breach
ARTICLE 6		
Lack of fair trial (criminal)	*Kreps v Poland*	No earnings award as no causal link between breach and detention
Legislative intervention in pension proceedings	*Maggio v Italy*	€20,000 and €50,000 for loss of real opportunities
Length of proceedings	*Probstmeier v Germany, Pammell v Germany*	15,000 DEM for real loss of opportunity from the effect of delay on applicability of rent provisions
	Union Alimentaria v Spain	award for depreciation of the value of the debt during the excessively long proceedings
Lack of free interpretation	*Isyar v Bulgaria*	Costs of interpretation reimbursed.
Effect of liquidation proceedings	*Laine v France*	€50,155, e.g. destruction of property

Main issues	Case	Just satisfaction awards
ARTICLE 7		
Retrospective criminal offence	*Pessino v France*	Repayment of fine
ARTICLE 8		
Gays in the army: investigation and dismissal based on sexual orientation	*Smith and Grady v UK, Lustig-Prean and Becket v UK (Just Satisfaction)*	Loss of past earnings: £30,000–£34,000 loss of future earnings: £7,000–£25,000 loss of benefit of non-contributory service pension: £14,000–£30,000
Lack of recognition of change of gender	*Grant v UK*	€1,700 loss of pension
Turkish village destruction cases	*Akdivar (Art.50); Mentes, Selcuk and Asker (Art.50); Bilgin; Dulas; Ayder; Ozkan*	Awards between £12,000–€97,000 in light of findings that homes were destroyed but taking into account lack of independent or decisive evidence about their property or previous income, sums awarded, e.g. for home, possessions, foodstuffs, fuel, costs of alternative accommodation, livestock, loss of income from land. No awards for land itself as it was not expropriated
Chechen home destruction cases	*Eskhambutov and Others v Russia* *Khamidov v Russia*	€20,000 for the house; €18,000 for household possessions, €3,000 €157,000 for damage to home and possessions from occupation by armed forces
ARTICLE 9		
Dismissal as teacher due to beliefs	*Ivanova v Bulgaria*	€589 for loss of salary (6 months)
ARTICLE 10		
Prohibition of counselling service	*Open Door Counselling v Ireland*	£25,000 IR loss of earnings on equitable basis
Unjustified defamation liability for publishing article	*Lombardo v Malta*	€1,460 for damages award imposed
Unjustified conviction for defamation	*July and SARL Liberation v France*	€7,000 for fine and damages imposed.

Main issues	Case	Just satisfaction awards
Prohibition of counselling service	*Open Door Counselling v Ireland*	£25,000 IR loss of earnings on equitable basis
Restriction on journalist entering Davos to report on G8	*Gsell v Switzerland*	€1026 loss of salary and wasted travel expenses
Ban of sales of book	*Association Ekin v France*	250,000 FRF though speculative, some undoubted losses
Injunction against publication	*Verlagsgruppe News GmbH v Austria (No.2)*	Award to cover the costs paid to the plaintiff in the domestic proceedings
Closure of newspaper	*Kommersant Moldovy v Moldova*	€8,000 loss of profits
ARTICLE 11		
Dismissal due to closed shop	*Young, James and Webster v UK*	£17,626, £45,215 and £8,706 for loss of earnings and travel privileges
Failure to protect association from violence	*Ouranio Toxo v Greece*	€2,000 for damage to property
Refusal of registration of political party	*Linkov v Czech Republic*	€150 return of registration fee
ARTICLE 14 in conjunction with ARTICLE 1 of Protocol No.1		
Denial of legal standing to pursue proceedings to protect property	*Canea Catholic Church v Greece*	5 million GRD losses incurred in dismissal of action
Liability to pay church tax	*Darby v Sweden*	8,000 SEK for tax paid plus interest
Racial discrimination in eligibility for unemployment assistance	*Gaygusuz v Austria*	200,000 ATS
Invalid planning permission	*Pine Valley v Ireland (Art.50)*	£1.2 million IRL in respect of value of the land if it had been immediately developed, taking into account reduction for rental value and uncertainties in land development
Sexual discrimination in obligation to pay welfare contributions	*Van Raalte v Netherlands*	finding did not entitle the applicant to retrospective exemption of contributions
Difference in levels of benefits due to national origin	*Koua Poirrez v France*	€20,000 pecuniary and non-pecuniary

Main issues	Case	Just satisfaction awards
Lack of survivor's pension for Roma widow:	*Munoz Diaz v Spain*	€70,000 for loss of benefits/ non-pecuniary damage together
Discrimination in family benefits to non-national	*Zeibek v Greece*	€8,455 for unpaid benefits
Discrimination in pension regime for non-national farmer	*Luczak v Poland*	€5,000 loss of opportunity and non-pecuniary together
Discrimination in inheritance rights to child born out of wedlock	*Mazurek v France*	376,000 FRF difference between sum inherited and that which he would have received if "legitimate"
	Merger and Cros v France	€612,145 the difference between the sum that the applicant actually received and the share of her father's estate that she would have received if "legitimate"
Lack of eligibility for benefits on death of wife	*Willis v UK*	£25,000, for sums which would have been paid to bereaved widow, including interest
In conjunction with ARTICLE 4		
Obligation on men to pay fire levy	*Karl-Heinz Schmidt v Germany*	225 DEM for levy paid over two years
In conjunction with ARTICLE 8		
Lack of rights for child born out of wedlock	*Vermeire v Belgium*	22,192 BEF for loss of inheritance to which applicant would have been entitled if legitimate
Discrmination in family benefits to non-national	*Fawzie v Greece*	€13,190 for unpaid benefits
ARTICLE 1 of Protocol No.1		
Expropriation: deficient compensation for historical site	*Kozacioglu v Turkey*	€75,000
Deprivation of rights over land designated as State forest	*Turgut and Others v Turkey*	€1,350,000
Planning: designation of land for roads without compensation	*Bugajny and Others v Poland*	€247,000 (value of land if expropriated by the authorities)

Main issues	Case	Just satisfaction awards
Planning: imposition of environmental building restrictions	*Consorts Richet et Le Ber v France*	€700,000 and €800,000 respectively for financial losses
Quashing of final judgments (also breach of Art.6)	*Tarnopolskaya and Others v Russia*	Awards for unpaid pension up to the date of the quashing; no awards for future, speculative amounts of pensions
Suppression of pension on conviction	*Apostolakis v Greece*	€23,327.64 for shortfall in pension received
Wrongful revocation of child invalidity benefit	*Moskal v Poland*	€15,000 pecuniary and non-pecuniary
Failure to implement restitution of property rights:	*Viasu v Romania* *Hirshchorn v Romania* *Dokic v Bosnia-Herzegovina*	€115,000 pecuniary and non-pecuniary together €200,000 loss of earnings; €1,900,000 value of property €60,000 for failure to return pre-war flat
Retrospective amendment to fiscal regulations	*Joubert v France*	no award; applicants acknowledged their error in their tax returns,and could not complain of fiscal action taken to redress this.
Oppressive system of court fees	*Perdigao v Portugal*	€190,000 pecuniary and non-pecuniary (sum largely covering the fees which had wiped out the applicant's judgment award)
Oppressive system of VAT imposition	*Bulves AD v Bulgaria*	€1,851 covering the amount of input VAT the company had been required to pay due to the default of other persons
Non-recognition of inheritance rights	*Nacaryan and Deryan v Turkey*	€250,000 based on market value of property
Confiscation by customs	*Ismayilov v Russia* *Bowler International v France*	€20,000 for confiscated foreign currency €15,000 for confiscated sale goods in lorry carrying drugs
Lack of indemnisation for failure to return property seized in criminal proceedings	*Tendam v Spain*	€200,000

Main issues	Case	Just satisfaction awards
Inadequate interest on delayed expropriation award	*Yetis and Others v Turkey*	€16,000
Pre-emption on purchase of painting	*Beyeler v Italy*	€1.3 million as breach flowed from unfair procedures, award was not based on value of painting
Failure to provide proper/fair procedure to protect property rights	*Sovtransavto Holdings v Ukraine (just satisfaction)*	€500,000 based not on loss of value of shares but on real loss of opportunities
ARTICLE 2 of Protocol No.1		
Suspension from school	*Campbell and Cosans v UK*	£3,000 for pecuniary/non-pecuniary the Court accepted some effect on loss of education and job prospects
ARTICLE 3 of Protocol No.1		
Disqualification as MP	*Lykourezos v Greece* *Paschalidis v Greece*	€20,000 loss of salary, etc €119,613, €78,298 and €142,532 for loss of salary for over two years, with other alternative sources of income deducted
ARTICLE 2 of Protocol No.4		
Travel ban	*Gochev v Bulgaria*	Claim of businessman for loss of profits due to inability to travel rejected as speculative

2. Non-pecuniary loss

An award for non-pecuniary damage may be made in respect of pain and suffering and physical or mental injury, including feelings of anxiety, helplessness or frustration, where such can be regarded as causally linked to the breach. The latter has led to damages in childcare cases for example but not in respect of many procedural breaches of Arts 5 and 6 cases or where terrorist suspects have been involved.[22] The Court makes awards on an equitable basis, generally without any explanation of its quantification or more than brief reasoning. It often appears to take a moral stance, as in the cases of terrorist suspects and reacts with evidently more sympathy to certain applicants or where there has been a clearly arbitrary use of power. Context can therefore be significant even in cases of loss of life or **III–006**

22 See Art.8, childcare cases below. Terrorist cases: see *McCann and Others v UK*, September 27, 1995, Series A, No.324 (breach of Art.2); *Brogan v UK (Art.50)*, May 30, 1989, Series A, No.152–B (Art.5, para.3); *Fox, Campbell and Hartley v UK (Art.50)*, March 27, 1990, Series A, No.190–B (Art.5, para.1(c)). Art.5: general principle that award made only in respect of damage resulting from a deprivation of liberty that the applicant would not have suffered if he or she had had the benefit of applicable guarantees: *HL v UK*, October 5, 2004, ECHR 2004–IX, para.148.

deprivation of liberty: where detained terrorist suspects were subject to discrimination as non-nationals, the Court reduced awards having regard to the good faith of the Government acting to protect the population from terrorist attacks and the fact that the suspects would in any event have been subject to a form of restriction on liberty of some form.[23]

In length of proceedings cases, it awards standard sums reflecting to some degree the length of the delay, but may on occasion show some regard to significant hardship or effect on employment or career.[24]

The Court does not make very large awards by UK standards, rarely going above £100,000 even in cases of death or torture and has declined invitations to impose exemplary or punitive damages.[25]

The Court also considers whether there has been a real loss of opportunity from a breach, in the absence of any strict causal link, for example, lack of access to court in childcare cases where it could not be established that an application for custody would have been successful but the loss of opportunity to apply is given weight. It has in certain cases referred to the effect on reputation or damage to career.[26]

Where there are large numbers of applicants, this may have the effect of bringing down the amount of individual awards. In length of proceedings cases, the Court has noted that applicants who have been parties together in the same case will have shared the emotional as well as financial burden; it thus reduces the awards to take this into account.[27]

In the absence of any of the above features, the Court may find that a finding of a violation in itself constitutes just satisfaction. It may award a sum in respect of pecuniary and non-pecuniary loss together, on an equitable basis, without distinguishing respective proportions.[28] Although it initially expressed doubts that a company or organisation could suffer non-pecuniary damage,[29] it has stated that it may make awards taking into account effects on a company's reputation, uncertainty in decision-planning, disruption in the management of the company and the anxiety and inconvenience caused to the members of the management team.[30] Similarly an award for inconvenience and prolonged uncertainty has been made to a

[23] *A and Others v UK*, February 19, 2009, paras 251–253.

[24] e.g. *Triggiani v Italy*, February 19, 1991, Series A, No.197–B.

[25] e.g. *Akdivar v Turkey (Art.50)*, April 4, 1998, R.J.D. 1998–II, No.69, para.38; *Orhan v Turkey*, June 18, 2002, para.448; *Varnava v Turkey*, September 18, 2009, para.223.

[26] e.g. *Darnell v UK*, October 26, 1993, Series A, No.272 (length case), £5,000 for damage to career during the long legal battle; *Helmers v Sweden*, October 29, 1991, Series A, No.212–A, where the applicant university lecturer's claims of discrimination and defamation were rejected but he nonetheless received 25,000 Kroner for a lack of public hearing.

[27] *Arvanitaki-Roboti v Greece* (GC), February 15, 2008, paras 26–37. See also *Selahattin Cetinkaya v Turkey*, October 20, 2009, paras 31–38, where the applicants were heirs of the original party in the proceedings, they shared an award jointly, no individual awards made.

[28] As in *Allenet de Ribemont v France*, where the applicant and the Commission unsuccessfully sought interpretation of the Court's judgment awarding two million Francs for both heads. It was relevant to the applicant's claims in domestic proceedings that the award was immune from attachment in respect of other liabilities. The Court explained that it did not feel bound to identify proportions in making aggregate awards and that it was often difficult or impossible to make distinctions: August 7, 1996, R.J.D. 1996–III, No.12.

[29] *Manifattura v Italy*, February 27, 1992, Series A, No.230–B.

[30] *Comingersoll SA v Portugal*, April 6, 2000, ECHR 2000–IV, paras 35–36; award also made in *Sovtransavto Holding v Ukraine* (just satisfaction), October 2, 2003, paras 79–82.

religious institution[31] and for frustration at an annulment of a collective agreement to a trade union.[32]

Even where Court judgments are binding on domestic courts, an applicant cannot be expected to bring new proceedings for compensation on the basis of a judgment finding a violation. The Court thus awarded non-pecuniary damage in *Philis v Greece (No.2)* for length of proceedings, notwithstanding the Government argument that the applicant could apply for compensation to the domestic courts on the basis of the Court's finding of a violation.[33]

The Court has declined to give detailed guidelines on the calculation of non-pecuniary awards in length of proceedings or other cases although has indicated the factors tending to increase or decrease awards.[34] The awards also are geared to some extent to cost of living index in Member States, awards being adjusted downwards for those countries at the lower end of the scale. The Court recently revised its internal scales seeking to render them more consistent after fifty years of varying practices. The sums awarded since 2009 therefore in some types of cases are markedly higher than in previous years. There is also a noticeable decrease in the occasions on which the Court finds that no monetary award for non-pecuniary damage is appropriate.

[31] *Beneficio Cappella Paolini v San Marino*, July 13, 2004, ECHR 2004–VII, para.38. See also *Metropolitan Church of Bessarabia v Moldova*, December 113, 2001, ECHR 2001–XII.

[32] *Demir and Baykara v Turkey*, November 12, 2008, paras 180–181.

[33] *Philis v Greece (No.2)*, February 27, 1997, R.J.D. 1997–IV, No.40, para.59. See, however, *Clooth v Belgium*, December 12, 1991, Series A, No.225, where the Court reserved Art.50 as it wished to take into account the award that the applicant might receive in domestic proceedings for the breach of Art.5, para.3 and (Art.50), March 5, 1998, R.J.D. 1998–I, No.66, where it found the domestic court award of non-pecuniary damage provided just reparation.

[34] *Ernestina Zullo v Italy* (GC), March 29, 2006. See also the approach disclosed by the Chamber judgment of November 10, 2004.

Court findings of non-pecuniary loss

III–007 **(FOVIS: finding of violation was just satisfaction in the circumstances of the case)**

Principal issues	Case	Findings
ARTICLE 2		
Excessive use of force on arrest	*McCann and Others v UK* *Evrim Oktem v Turkey* *Wasilewska and Kalucka v Poland*	No damages appropriate (IRA suspects killed while on bombing mission) €16,000 victim shot (not killed) €20,000 victim killed in arrest operation
Killings during security operations	*Abuyeva and Others v Russia*	€60,000 one relative killed €80,000 two relatives kiled €120,000 four relatives killed €30,000 injuries, still alive €90,000 one relative killed and injuries suffered
Killings/life-threatening injury during prison riot	*Perisan and Others v Turkey* *Peker v Turkey (No.2)*	€60, 000 to heirs of deceased €36,000 to the seriously injured applicants €18,000 to the injured applicant
Death in police custody	*Mizigarova v Slovakia* *Jasinkis v Latvia*	€45,000 €50,000
Death in prison	*Bekirski v Bulgaria*	€75,000 death in prison, plus breaches of Art.3 for beating and lack of medical care
Death in army barracks	*Beker v Turkey*	€20,000 to widow, €5,000 to siblings
Lack of protection for life	*Opuz v Turkey* *Branko Tomasic v Croatia* *Dink and Others v Turkey* *Oyal v Turkey* *Maiorano v Italy*	€30,000 failure to protect from domestic violence €40,000 failure to protect from domestic violence €100,000 failure to protect journalist from nationalist extremists (substantive and procedural breaches, plus breaches of Arts 10 and 13) €78,0000 HIV contamination of child at birth from blood bank €5,000–€10,000 failure to protect from prisoner released on parole

Principal issues	Case	Findings
	Jasinka v Poland	€16,000 failure to protect mentally ill prisoner from suicide
Disappearances	*Varnava v Turkey*	€12,000 failure to investigate disappearances
	Osmanoglu v Turkey	€20,000 for victim of disappearance and his family €10,000 for the applicant, father of the victim
	Magomadova and others v Russia	€35,000 disappearance in Chechnya, substantive and procedural breach of Art.2
	Gelayevy v Russia	€78,000 as above
Lack of investigation	*Agache v Romania*	€20,000 killings during anti-communist demonstrations
	Ceichonska v Poland	€20,000 death from falling tree
	Anna Todorova v Bulgaria	€8,000 road accident
	Dodov v Bulgaria	€8,000 old person missing from nursing home
	Eugenia Lazar v Romania	€20,000 medical negligence
	Dvoracek and Dvorackova v Slovakia	€10,000 medical negligence
ARTICLE 3		
Ill-treatment by police	*Umar Karatepe v Turkey*	€12,000 beating, lack of medical care (plus breach of Art.5, para.1)
	Firat Can v Turkey	€23,400 torture (plus breaches of Art.5, paras 3 and 4)
	Safak v Turkey	€25,000 ill-treatment of minor (substantive and procedural breach)
Conditions of detention	*Payet v France*	€9,000 security cell confinement
	Kashavelov v Bulgaria	€7,000 conditions, plus breach of Art.3 due to handcuffing, plus breaches of Arts 6 and 13
	Slavomir Musial v Poland	€10,000 inadequate care and conditions for mentally ill prisoner
	Ashot Harutyunyan v Armenia	€16,000 inadequate care in detention, use of metal cage at trial (plus breaches of Art.6, paras 1 and 2)

Principal issues	Case	Findings
	Flaminzeanu v Romania	€10,000 overcrowding, inadequate facilities for medical condition
	Dobri v Romania	€12,000 prisoner developed TB, inadequate conditions
	Eleftheriadis v Romania	€4,000 prisoner with health problems kept in cells with smokers
Other aspects of detention	*El Shennawy v France*	€8,000 systematic body searches
	Khider v France	€12,000 frequent transfers, body searches, security restrictions (plus breach of Art.13)
Threat of expulsion/ expulsion/asylum detention	*Ben Khemais v Italy*	€10,000 expulsion to Tunisia
	M.S.S. v Belgium and Greece	€24,900 against Belgium (plus breach of Art.13 for expulsion to Greece
	Rahimi v Greece	€15,000 conditions of asylum detention/failure to ensure proper supervised release of minor (plus breaches of Arts 5 and 13)
	Mubilanzila Mayeka and Kaniki Mitunga v Belgium	€10,000 to mother of child held in asylum €25,000 to child in detention (also breaches of Arts 5, 8, and 13)
	Muskhadzhiyeva v Belgium	€17,000 children held inadequate asylum detention facilities
Medical context	*R.R. v Poland*	€45,000 humiliating treatment by doctors; lack of proper access to treatment and abortion where foetus gravely handicapped (also breach of Art.8)
Failure to protect from others	*Milanovic v Serbia*	€10,000 failure to protect from religious extremist
Other	*Tastan v Turkey*	€5,000 71 year old required to do military service
	Ocalan v Turkey	(FOVJS) imposition of death sentence after unfair trial

Principal issues	Case	Findings
ARTICLE 4		
	Rantsev v Cyprus and Russia	€40,000 against Cyprus: failure to protect from trafficking (plus procedural breach of Art.2, breach of Art.5) €2,000 against Russia: failure to protect from trafficking
ARTICLE 5 **General principle: just satisfaction awarded only in respect of damage resulting from a deprivation of liberty that the applicant would not have suffered if he or she had had the benefit of the guarantees of Art.5.**[36]		
	M v Germany	€50,000 lack of lawfulness for prolongation of preventive detention (plus breach of Art.7)
	Medvedyev v France	€5,000 arrest and detention on the high seas
	Pulatli v Turkey	€9,000 seven days' arrest of soldier
	Ichin v Ukraine	€6,000 lack of lawfulness for detention of juveniles over a month
	Ogica v Romania	€7,000 lack of lawfulness of several days pre-trial detention (plus breach of Art.3 for conditions)
	Kolevi v Bulgaria	€30,000 over two months' unlawful pre trial detention (plus breach of Art.5, paras 3 and 4)
	Nasrulloyev v Russia	€40,000 arbitrary detention pending extradition (plus breach of Art.5, para.4)
	Iskandarov v Russia	€30,000 arbitrary arrest to carry out extra-legal extradition (plus breach of Art.3 for expulsion
	Al-Jedda v UK	€25,000 internment of suspect by army in Iraq
	Mikolenko v Latvia	€2,000 detention pending expulsion, lack of valid basis.

[35] *Nikolova v Bulgaria,* March 25, 1999, ECHR 1999–II, para.148.

Principal issues	Case	Findings
	CB v Romania	€20,000 unjustified psychiatric internment for fourteen days (also breach of Art.5, para.4)
Reasons for detention	*Saadi v UK*	FOVJS no reasons for detention pending expulsion
Pre-trial detention	*Ignatenco v Moldova* *Stoican v Romania* *Moulin v France* *Prencipe v Monaco* *Jarkiewicz v Poland* *Yigitdogan v Turkey* *Miroslaw Garlicki v Poland*	€2,000 lack of reasons given €2,000 over four days before brought before a judge; lack of reasons for continued detention €6,000 over four days before brought before a judge €6,000 almost four years' pre-trial detention €2,500 two and a half years' pre-trial detention €11,000 over nine years pre-trial detention (plus breach of Art.5, para.4 €6,000 lack of "judicial" officer
Review of detention (Art.5, para.4)	*Mooren v Germany* *Allen v UK* *Castravet v Moldova* *STS v Netherlands*	€5,000 lack of speediness/ lack of access to case file €1,000 lack of hearing on bail appeal €2,500 lack of confidential consultation with lawyer (plus breach of Art.5, para.3 for lack of diligence) €2,000 lack of speed and effectiveness
Right to compensation for unlawful detention	*Ciulla v Italy; Brogan v UK Fox; Campbell and Hartley v UK; Thynne, Gunnell and Wilson v UK; Hood, Stephen Jordan v UK; SBC v UK; O'Hara v UK* *Danev v Bulgaria*	Previously no awards made €1,000 lack of right to compensation for irregular pre-trial detention
ARTICLE 6		
Lack of fairness	*Olujic v Croatia*	€5,000 lack of independence, inequality of arms delay in proceedings, exclusion of public etc

Principal issues	Case	Findings
	Buijen v Germany	€5,000 failure to abide by prosecutor's undertaking on transfer of sentence to home country
Access to court	*Cudak v Lithuania*	€10,000 pecuniary and non-pecuniary together
	Sabeh El Leil v France	€60,000 as above
	Lawyer Partners S.S. v Slovakia	€10,000 loss of opportunities
	Chatellier v France	€15,000
	Zylkov v Russia	€1,500
	Ligue du monde islamique et Organisation islamique mondiale du secours islamique v France	FOVJS
	Kohlhofer and Minarik v Czech Republic	FOVJS
	Suda v Czech Republice	FOVJS
Double jeopardy	*Zolotukhin v Russia*	€1,500
	Ruotsilainen v Finland	€1,500
Entrapment	*Malininas v Lithuania*	FOVJS
Equality of arms	*Uzukauskas v Lithuania*	€3,500
	Zhuk v Ukraine	€1,200
Evidence issues	*Laska and Lika v Albania*	€4,800
Independence and impartiality	*Micallef v Malta*	FOVJS
	Savino v Italy	FOVJS
	Henryk and Ryszard Urban v Poland	FOVJS
Jury verdict: insufficient safeguards	*Taxquet v Belgium*	€4,000
Lack of legal certainty	*Iordan Iordanov v Bulgaria*	€4,000–€4,500
	Stefanica v Romania	€3,000
Legal representation issues	*Sakhnovskiy v Russia*	€2,000 also lack of participation by applicant
	Kulikowski v Poland	€3,000 also breach of Art.5, para.3
	Bakan v Turkey	€7,500 to widow and children
	Salduz v Turkey	€1,000
	Adamkiewicz v Poland	€10,000 lack of lawyer after arrest, use of confession at trial, plus breach of independence criterion

Principal issues	Case	Findings
	Aleksandr Zaichenko v Russia	€3,000 lack of lawyer when charged; plus breach of privilege against self-incrimination
	Pishchalnikov v Russia	€5,500 lack of lawyer, plus breach of length
Lack of presence at hearing	*Sobolewski v Poland*	€1,500
Lack of public hearing	*Udorovic v Italy*	€5,000 plus breach for inexact reasoning
Legislative intervention	*Maggio and Others v Italy*	€12,000
Length of proceedings UK Civil	*Richard Anderson v UK*	€1,500
	Bhandari v UK	€7,000 eight years, two months
UK Criminal	*Blake v UK*	€5,000 nine years, two months
	King v UK (+13 years)	FOVJS more than 13 years, tax surcharge proceedings drawn out by applicant
Other	*Gorou v Greece (No.2)*	€4,000 four years, three months
	McFarlane v Ireland	€5,500 plus breach of Art.13
Right to silence	*Brusco v France*	€5,000
Witness issues	*Orhan Cacan v Turkey*	€1,800
	Balsyte-Lideikiene v Lithuania	€2,000
ARTICLE 6, para.2 breach of presumption of innocence		
	Konstas v Greece	€12,000 plus breach of Art.13
	Vassilios Stavropoulos v Greece	€10,000
	Klouvi v France	€8,000
	Poncelet v Belgium	€5,000
ARTICLE 7		
	Kafkaris v Cyprus	FOVJS quality of law lacking as regards the meaning of "life imprisonment"
	Sud Fondi Srl v Italy	€10,000 quality of law lacking concerning penalties for planning violations
	Liivik v Estonia	€5,000 quality of law lacking for offence of abuse of office
	Scoppola v Italy (No.2)	€10,000 removal of benefit of more lenient summary procedure for serious offences

Principal issues	Case	Findings
	Gurguchiani v Spain	€5,000 imposition of heavier penalty on non-national
	Welch v UK; Jamil v France; Pessino v France	FOVJS retrospective penalties
ARTICLE 8		
Childcare issues	*A.D. and O.D. v UK*	€15,000 child placed in care
	R.K. and A.K. v UK	€10,000 child placed in care
	Gluhakovic v Croatia	€15,000 failure effectively to implement father's contact with child
	Iordache v Romania	€9,000 deprivation of parental rights
	Stochlak v Poland	€7,000 failure to enforce return of custody
	Eberhard and M v Slovenia	€7,500 failure to enforce contact rights
	Kurochkin v Ukraine	€6,000 annulment of adoption of a child
	Mustafa and Armagan Akin v Turkey	€15,000 lack of contact by father and two jointly children together
	Clemeno v Italy	€30,000 lack of contact by parents and sibling with fourth applicant; to place for adoption
	Moretti and Benedetti v Italy	€10,000 failure to consider properly foster parents' application to adopt
	Saviny v Ukraine	€5,000 insufficient reasons for removal of children into care
	Tsourlakis v Greece	€5,000 lack of access to report in care proceedings
Other family and private life issues	*X v Croatia*	€8,000 mother divested of capacity in proceedings for adoption of her child
	Emonet v Switzerland	€5,000 loss of parental link on adoption of an adult child by the parent's partner
	Dadouch v Malta	€3,000 two year delay in registering marriage with a foreigner
	A, B and C v Ireland	€15,000 lack of proper legal regulation of abortion
Environment issues	*Taskin and Others v Turkey*	€3,000 failure to enforce closure of mine

Principal issues	Case	Findings
	Lemke v Turkey	€3,000 lack of procedural protection in grant of licence to mine
	Branduse v Romania	€8,000 smells from tip invading prison cell, plus breach of Art.3 for overcrowding
	Mileva v Bulgaria	€6,000–€8,000 noise nuisance from unauthorised activities in block of flats
	Dees v Hungary	€6,000 nuisance from road congestion
Home cases	*McCann v UK*	€2,000 lack of procedural protection from
	Cosic v Croatia	summary eviction from council housing
	Zehentner v Austria	€30,000 lack of procedural protection from forced judicial sale of a flat
	Khamidov v Russia	€15,000 damage to home and possessions due to occupation by armed Forces, also breaches of Art.1 of Protocol No.1 and Art.6
	Andre v France	€5,000 search and seizure
	H.M. v Turkey	€1,000 lack of procedural protection and investigation into offences against property
Interception and surveillance	*Bykov v Russia*	€1,000 lack of safeguards on surveillance measures (also breach of Art.5, para.3)
	Liberty v UK	FOVJS lack of "lawfulness" in too broad discretion
	Association 21 December 1989 v Romania	€6,000 lack of safeguards concerning files based on past interception and surveillance
ARTICLE 9		
	Bayatyan v Armenia	€10,000 conviction for refusal to do military service
	Alexandridis v Greece	€2,000 requirement to disclose religious affiliation on being sworn in as a lawyer
	Dimitras v Greece	€3,000 requirement to take oath in court
	Religionsgemeinschaft der Zeugen Jehovas v Austria	€10,000 delay in granting legal personality to a church, also breaches of Arts 6 and 13

Principal issues	Case	Findings
	Kimyla v Russia	€5,000 15-year rule on legal registration of "new" religious groups
	Jehovah's Witnesses of Moscow v Russia	€20,000 jointly dissolution of community and refusal to re-register, also breach of Arts 6 and 11
	Mirolubovs v Latvia	€4,000 State intervention in churches' dispute
	Holy Synod of the Bulgarian Orthodox Church (Metropolitan Inokentiy) v Bulgaria	€50,000 State intervention to impose church leader
	Ahmad Arslan v Turkey	FOVJS prohibition on wearing certain religious dress in public
	Masaev v Moldova	€1,500 conviction for religious service conducted in private premises
	Jakobski v Poland	€3,000 lack of vegetarian diet for Buddhist prisoner
	Barankevich v Russia	€6,000 ban on religious open air service
ARTICLE 10		
Sanctions imposed on, inter alia, journalists, politicians, e.g. injunctions, convictions	*Goodwin v UK, Oberschlick v Austria; Castells v Spain; Weber v Switzerland, Jersild v Denmark; De Haes and Gijssels v Belgium; Vereinigung demokraticher soldaten v Austria; Piermont v France; Grigoriades v Greece; Lopes Gomes da Silva v Portugal; Du Roy and Lemaurie v France; Jerusalem v Austria; Thoma v Luxembourg; Maronek v Slovakia; Perna v Italy; Lehideux and Isorni v France; News Verlags Gmbh and Cokg v Austria; Krone Verlag v Austria, Cumpana and Mazare v Romania; Damman v Switzerland* (breach of official secrets); *Karhuvaara and Italehti v Finland*	FOVJS
Prosecution for leaflets about electoral candidates	*Bowman v UK*	FOVJS
	Women on Waves v Portugal	€2,000 ban on protest ship entering national waters

Principal issues	Case	Findings
	Orban v France	FOVJS conviction for book allegedly condoning Algerian war crimes
	Vajnai v Hungary	FOVJS prosecution for wearing a red star
	Urper v Turkey	€1,800 suspension of newspaper
	Saygili and Bilgic v Turkey	€9,000 jointly seizure of newspaper
	Bodrozic v Serbia	€500 conviction of journalist for defamation
	Lepojic v Serbia	€3,000 conviction for article
	Artun and Guvener v Turkey	€6,000 jointly conviction for insulting the President
	Otegi Mondragon v Spain	€20,000 conviction for insulting the King
	Fatullayev v Azerbaijan	€25,000 two convictions for articles (two years spent in prison, plus breaches of Art.6, paras 1 and 2)
	July and SARL Liberation v France	FOVJS conviction for defamation
	Obukhova v Russia	€1,000 injunction against journalist reporting on an incident
	Manole v Moldova	€2,000 State censorship imposed on media journalists
	Guja v Moldova	€10,000 for pecuniary and non-pecuniary, dismissal of whistleblower
	Tillack v Belgium	€10,000 search and seizures at journalist's home and work
	Gsell v Switzerland	FOVJS bar on journalist entering Davos for G8
	Cox v Turkey	€12,000 bar on foreign academic re-entering the country
	Lombardi Vallauri v Italy	€10,000 failure to renew academic's teaching contract at Catholic university due to his views
ARTICLE 11		
	Demir and Baykara v Turkey	€20,000 annulment of collective agreement
	Zhchev v Bulgaria	FOVJS refusal to register an association

Principal issues	Case	Findings
	Bozgan v Romania, Bekir-Ousta v Greece, Koretskyy v Ukraine	€1,500 refusal to register an association
	Church of Scientology v Russia	€10,000 refusal to re-register an association
	Tebieti Mühafize Cemiyyeti and Israfilov v Azerbaijan	€8,000 dissolution of an association
	Association of Citizens Radko and Paunkovksi v FYROM	€5,000 dissolution of an association
	Ouranio Toxo v Greece	€30,000 failure to protect association from violent attack
	Alekseyev v Russia	€12,000 ban on Gay Pride march in Moscow (also breach of Arts 13 and 14)
	Bukta v Hungary	FOVJS dispersal of peaceful demonstration
	Patyi v Hungary	FOVJS ban on peaceful assembly
	Samut Karabulut v Turkey	€3,000 arrest during demonstration (also breach of Art.3 for use of excessive force)
	Sergey Kuznetsov v Russia	€1,500 fine for picketing
	Galstyan v Armenia	€3,000 administrative detention for demonstrating (also breaches of Art.6 and Art.2, Protocol No.7
ARTICLE 12		
	B and L v UK	FOVJS ban on marriage parent-in-law and child-in-law
	Frasik v Poland	€5,000 refusal to allow prisoner to marry
	O'Donoghue v UK	€8,500 restrictive rules on marriage of persons subject to immigration control (also breach of Art.14
ARTICLE 13		
	Chahal v UK, Valsamis v Greece (no substantive breach); *Camenzind v Switzerland* (no substantive breach); *Khan v UK; Jabari v Turkey; Messina v Italy (No.2); Hatton v UK* (no substantive breach)	FOVJS
	Hamiyet Kaplan v Turkey	€1,000 no remedy for deaths in police raid
	Devim Turan v Turkey	€1,500 no remedy for ill-treatment in police custody

Principal issues	Case	Findings
	Soysal v Turkey	€500 no remedy for transfers of civil servants due to political opinions/trade union membership
	Konstas v Greece	€12,000 no remedy for statements presuming guilt by public figures (plus breach of Art.6, para.2)
ARTICLE 14		
In conjunction with ARTICLE 2		
	GN v Italy	€39,000 lack of compensation for blood contamination, also Art.2 procedural breach
In conjunction with ARTICLE 5		
	Clift v UK	€10,000 discriminatory Parole Board rules on release
In conjunction with ARTICLE 6		
	Schuler-Zgraggen v Switzerland	FOVJS sex discrimination in access to court
	Paraskeva Todorova v Bulgaria	€5,000 racist sentencing statement
	Paroisse Greco Catholique Sâmbata Bihor v Romania	€15,000 bar on access to court
In conjunction with ARTICLE 8		
	Kiyutin v Russia	€15,000 rejection of residence permit due to HIV status
	Losonic Rose and Rose v Switzerland	€15,000 discrimination in use of names by married couples
	Fawsie v Greece	€1,500 discrimination in family benefits for non-nationals
	Bigaeva v Greece	€7,000 refusal to allow non-national to sit bar exam
	E.B. v France	€10,000 refusal of adoption by gay couple
In conjunction with ARTICLE 9		
	Savez Crkava "Rijec Zibota" and Others v Croatia	€9,000 inability to furnish religious education in schools etc
	Loffelman v Austria	€4,000 no exemption from military service for Jehovah's Witness

Principal issues	Case	Findings
	Grzelik v Poland	FOVJS prejudicial absence of mark in school report for child not attending Catholic classes
In conjunction with ARTICLE 1 of Protocol No.1		
	J.M. v UK	€3,000 discrimination in child support calculation
	Zeibek v Greece	€5,000 discrimination in family allowance
In conjunction with ARTICLE 2 of Protocol No. 1		
	DH and Others v Slovakia	€4,000 racial segregation of Roma in schools
	Orsus and Others v Croatia	€4,500 as above
	Sampanis v Greece	€6,000 exclusion of Roma from local school
ARTICLE 34		
	Al-Saadoon and Mufdhi v UK	FOVJS failure to comply with interim measure preventing handover of suspects by UK army to Iraqi authorities
	Nurmagomedov v Russia	€500 restriction on prisoner's correspondence with Court
	Buldakov v Russia	€3,000 prison misplacing of prisoner's application
	Kamaliyevy v Russia	€9,000 failure to comply with interim measure suspending expulsion to Uzbekistan
ARTICLE 1 of Protocol No. 1		
	Turgut v Turkey	FOVJS deprivation of land designated as State forest
	Kozacioglu v Turkey	FOVJS deficient compensation for expropriation of historical site
	Ryabov and 151 other privileged pensioners v Russia	€2,000 quashing of final judgments on pension entitlements: group award of fixed sums
	Apostolakis v Greece	€1,000 removal of pension on conviction
	Burdov v Russia (No.2)	€6,000 failure to enforce judgments against the State, exacerbated by State practice of non-enforcement

Principal issues	Case	Findings
	Hirschhorn v Romania	€10,000 failure to enforce judgement restoring possession of property
	Dokic v Bosnia-Herzegovina	€5,000 failure to restore pre-war flat
	Suljagic v Bosnia-Herzegovina	€5,000 deficient legislation on repayment of frozen foreign bank assets
	Kiladze v Georgia	€4,000 deficient legislation on compensation victims of communist repression
	Bulves A.D. v Bulgaria	FOVJS unjustified imposition of VAT due to default of others.
	Yetis v Turkey	FOVJS insufficient interest rates applied to delayed payment of expropriation compensation
	Ismayilov v Russia	€5,000 confiscation of foreign currency
ARTICLE 2 of Protocol No. 1		
	Folgero v Norway	FOVJS inability for exemption of children from religious course
	Hasan and Eylem Zengin v Turkey	FOVJS failure to respect rights of Alevi parents in school religious studies
	Irfan Temel v Turkey	€1,500 disciplinary suspension at university
ARTICLE 3 of Protocol No.1		
	Hirst v UK (No.2)	FOVJS prisoner's inability to vote
	Kovach v Ukraine	€8,000 electoral irregularities/ loss of seat as MP
	Grosaru v Romania	€5,000 as above
	Namat Aliyev v Azerbaijan	€7,500 as above
	Paschalidis v Greece	FOVJS disqualification of MPs—loss of seats for over two years
	Adamsons v Lithuania	€10,000 ineligibility to stand as MP due to lustration
	Georgian Labour Party v Georgia	FOVJS irregularities during election
	Petkov v Bulgaria	FOVJS failure to enforce decision on electoral lists
	Seyidzade v Azerbaijan	€7,500 disqualification from standing for MP

Principal issues	Case	Findings
	Sejdic and Finci v Bosnia-Herzegovina	FOVJS inability to stand as MP due to constitutional arrangements excluding minorities
	Paksas v Lithuania	FOVJS bar on standing as MP due to impeachment as President
ARTICLE 2 of Protocol No.4		
	Villa v Italy	FOVJS five months' delay in lifting restriction following court order
	Gochev v Bulgaria	€5,000 over six years' restriction on travel abroad
	Nalbantski v Bulgaria	€6,500 over three years'' restriction (with breach of Arts 6 and 13 length of proceedings)

3. Legal costs and expenses

This head potentially covers not only the cost of proceedings before the Court but expenses incurred in domestic proceedings in order to prevent the violation or to obtain redress.[36] In *Le Compte v Belgium (Art.50)*, where the appeal proceedings against the disciplinary sanctions were not part of a procedure to obtain redress for the lack of public hearing, these costs were not awarded whereas the applicants' application to the Court of Cassation where the lawyers pleaded the Convention as part of the process of exhaustion of domestic remedies was taken into account and costs awarded.[37] The Court applies the test whether the costs and expenses were actually[38] and necessarily incurred in order to prevent, or obtain redress for the matter found to constitute a violation of the Convention and were reasonable as to quantum.[39] The Court does not consider itself bound by domestic scales and practices in assessing what is reasonable by way of fees, although it may derive **III–008**

[36] See, e.g. award made in *ASLEF v UK*, February 27, 2007. However in *Sunday Times v UK (No.1) (Art.50)*, November 6, 1980, No.38, where the parties in the domestic proceedings agreed to pay their own costs, the Court made no award in this respect; and in *Keegan v UK*, July 18, 2006, where the applicants claimed that they were liable in theory to reimburse legal aid funding of their domestic action for damage, the Court accepted the Government's argument that these costs had not been actually incurred and stated that the applicants could re-apply to the Court if this situation changed.

[37] *Le Compte v Belgium (Art.50)*, October 18, 1982, Series A, No.54.

[38] Fees to be paid on a contingency basis have been discounted as they were not legally enforceable, e.g. *Dudgeon v UK (Art.50)*, February 24, 1983, Series A, No.59; also *McCann Farnell and Savage v UK*, September 27, 1995, Series A, No.324, where legal representatives acted free of charge at an inquest, the applicants could not claim to be under any obligation to pay the solicitor and the inquest costs could not be said to be "actually" incurred. Nor when legal aid had funded domestic proceedings could the applicant's representatives use the Court proceedings to charge higher fees retrospectively: *Hirst v UK (No.2)*, October 6, 2005, ECHR 2005–IX, paras 97–98.

[39] e.g. *Sunday Times v UK (No.1)* (Art.50), fn.36 above, para.23.

assistance from them.[40] It resisted the invitation by the Commission to impose a uniform approach to the assessment of fees since there is too great a disparity between the rates applicable in Contracting States.[41] Claim by an applicant for legal costs of 20% of the sums awarded for damages was refused.[42]

Where the Court finds one or more of the applicant's complaints of violation unfounded, it may reduce the amount of costs awarded.[43] It will not do so where a violation is found on the principal matter in issue as in *Soering v UK*, where the essential concern and bulk of the argument was on Art.3, although complaints under Art.6, paras 3(c) and 13 were rejected.[44] Where an applicant's claims for pecuniary and non-pecuniary damage are rejected in Art.41 proceedings, the legal costs for that part may not be granted.[45] However the Court rejected in *Sunday Times v UK (No.1) (Art.50)* the Government argument that amounts should be reduced due to the fact that not all submissions under Art.10 were successful, i.e. criticising the length and detail of the applicant's case. The Court noted that a lawyer must present his case as fully as he is able and may not anticipate what arguments will convince.

While an applicant is not required to agree to joint legal representation with other applicants before the Court, the Court will reduce claims that fail to take sufficient account of the similarity of cases or the potential for efficient co-ordination between the various representatives.[46] An applicant is not required to instruct counsel within his own country but may use lawyers from another Contracting State even if this has the result of increasing legal expenses.[47]

Awards are made subject to deduction of any sums granted by way of legal aid from the Council of Europe, unless stated otherwise.

The UK Government is active in querying fees which exceed domestic norms or which appear excessive. The Court has shown itself responsive to its objections to the level of fees or hours claimed, or to the number of representatives involved.[48] In *Young, James and Webster v UK*, the Court noted high litigation costs might themselves constitute an impediment to effective human rights protection and considered it wrong to give encouragement to such a situation in costs awards under

[40] e.g. *Silver v UK* (Art.50), October 24, 1983, Series A, No.67, para.20. See also *Abdulaziz v UK*, May 28, 1985, Series A, No.94, where the Government contested the rate of fees for junior counsel as higher than the domestic rate but the Court found the amount reasonable as to quantum; *Hadjianstassiou v Greece*, December 16, 1993, Series A, No.252, where the Court discounted the Government's complaints that fees claimed exceeded domestic rates.

[41] *Tolstoy v UK*, July 13, 1995, Series A, No.316–B, para.77.

[42] *Adam v Romania*, November 3, 2009, para.47.

[43] e.g. *Le Compte*, fn.37 above, award reduced where most of the complaints were rejected; reductions also in *Tolstoy*, fn.41 above where claims only partly successful; *Glass v UK*, March 9, 2004, ECHR 2004–III, where one complaint was declared admissible.

[44] *Soering v UK*, July 7, 1989, Series A, No.161. Also *Observer and Guardian v UK* and *Sunday Times (No.2)*, November 26, 1991, Series A, No.216, where there was no reduction despite no findings of violations of Arts 13 and 14 since the bulk of the argument had been on Art.10; *Grant v UK*, May 23, 2005, no reduction as the Art.8 complaint had been central throughout.

[45] *Welch v UK* (Art.50), February 26, 1996, R.J.D. 1996–II, No.5.

[46] e.g. *IJL v UK* (just satisfaction), September 25, 2001, para.19.

[47] e.g. *Kurt v Turkey*, May 25, 1998, R.J.D. 1998–III, No.74, para.179, where the applicant instructed UK lawyers with expertise in international human rights.

[48] e.g. the Court accepted the Government objections to hourly rates in *Fox, Campbell and Hartley v UK* (Art.50), March 27, 1991, Series A, No.190–B, and *Gaskin v UK*, July 7, 1989, Series A, No.160; reduction of counsel's fees by 25 per cent in *Connors v UK*, May 27, 2004.

Art.41.[49] High costs claims have almost always been subject to reductions. The highest awards for awards in UK proceedings have been in the *Observer and Guardian, Sunday Times (No.2), Saunders* and *Tolstoy* cases (see below). In cases concerning length of proceedings or following a lead judgment, the Court is likely to reduce any high costs claims as unjustified by the issues or procedures and to make relatively small awards.[50]

Failure to itemise costs properly may lead to no award being made, or to a reduction in the award.[51] An applicant representing himself cannot claim to have incurred legal fees but may be paid costs of postage, photocopying, etc.[52] In some cases the Court does not appear to require an applicant to provide detailed substantiation of personal costs but accepts some may have been incurred, making a small award.[53]

Where UK lawyers have represented applicants in other countries, the Court has been amenable, on request, to ordering the respondent Government to pay costs and expenses directly to their bank account rather than to their client abroad with the rest of the award of just satisfaction.[54]

[49] The Court awarded the £65,000 proposed by the Government, finding the applicant's claims for additional representation by a French legal firm debatable and criticising the applicant's refusal of the Government's offer to have the costs taxed domestically.

[50] e.g. telephone tapping, court martial. See table below.

[51] See r.60(2), e.g. *Zubani v Italy*, June 16, 1999, para.23, no award; *Wood v UK*, November 16, 2004, €10,000 fee for counsel disallowed for lack of invoice; *Wilson v UK*, July 2, 2002, ECHR 2002–V, reduction in award.

[52] e.g. *Foley v UK*, October 22, 2002.

[53] e.g. *Hirst v UK (No.2)*, fn.42 above, award to prisoner applicant of €200.

[54] e.g. *Ocalan v Turkey*, May 12, 2005, ECHR 2005–V, para.217.

Awards of legal costs and expenses

Recent selected UK cases

III–009

Case	Court Awards (A: applicant; G: government; Ct: court)
Al-Skeini	A: claimed £119,928
	G: objected that counsel hourly rates too high; too many lawyers:
	Ct: awarded €50,000
Al-Jeddah	A: claimed £85,946
	Gov: objected rates too high, too many lawyers instructed
	Ct: awarded €40,000
Clift	A: claimed £12,592 for Strasbourg proceedings
	Gov: objected to lack of itemisation
	Ct: awarded €7,150
Al-Saadoon and Mufdhi	A: claimed £48,131
	Gov: time claimed and hourly rates excessive
	Ct: awarded €40,000
A.D and O.D.	As: claimed £20,000
	Gov: objected as excessive
	Ct: awarded €10,000
Gillan and Quinton	As: claimed £40,652
	Gov: objected as excessive
	Ct: awarded €35,000
A and Others	As: claimed £144,752
	Gov: objected to hours and rates claimed
	Ct: awarded €60,000
S. and Marper	As: claimed £52,066
	Gov: claimed excessive and no more than £20,000 appropriate
	Ct: awarded €42,000
McCann	A: claimed £75,570 for domestic and Strasbourg proceedings
	Gov: objected, proposed no more than £51,000
	Ct: awarded €75,000

Case	**Court Awards (A: applicant; G: government; Ct: court)**
Repetitive/simple cases *Telephone tapping/ covert surveillance* *Taylor-Sabori* *Chalkley,* *Elahi*	 Ct: awarded €4,800 €6,000
Court martial *Thompson v UK* *GW* *Bell* *Martin*	 €5,000 €2,900 €2,500 €9,000 (three rounds of written pleadings)
Prison disciplinary *Black* *Young*	 €2,500 €3,500
Length cases *Blake* *Obasa*	 A: claimed £3,000 Ct: awarded €2,000 A: claimed over £92,000 Ct: awarded €5,000
Mitchell and Holloway	A: claimed over £58,000 Ct: awarded €15,000
Massey	Ct: awarded €4,000

4. Default interest

Interest in default of payment of awards after three months from the date of delivery of judgment is set, since 2002, to reflect the use of the euro as reference currency, namely, at three percentage points above the marginal lending rate of the European Central Bank.[55] **III–010**

[55] See *Christine Goodwin v UK*, July 11, 2002, ECHR 2002–VI, para.124.

APPENDICES

APPENDIX 1

The 1950 European Convention for the Protection of Human Rights and Fundamental Freedoms, as amended by Protocols Nos 11 and 14, (Arts 1–49) and Protocols Nos 1, 4, 6 and 7

The governments signatory hereto, being Members of the Council of Europe, **A–001**

Considering the Universal Declaration of Human Rights proclaimed by the General Assembly of the United Nations on December 10, 1948;

Considering that this Declaration aims at securing the universal and effective recognition and observance of the rights therein declared;

Considering that the aim of the Council of Europe is the achievement of greater unity between its Members and that one of the methods by which that aim is to be pursued is the maintenance and further realisation of human rights and fundamental freedoms;

Reaffirming their profound belief in those fundamental freedoms which are the foundation of justice and peace in the world and are best maintained on the one hand by an effective political democracy and on the other by a common understanding and observance of the Human Rights upon which they depend;

Being resolved, as the governments of European countries which are like-minded and have a common heritage of political traditions, ideals, freedom and the rule of law, to take the first steps for the collective enforcement of certain of the rights stated in the Universal Declaration;

Article 1—Obligation to respect Human Rights

The High Contracting Parties shall secure to everyone within their jurisdiction the rights and freedoms defined in Section I of this Convention.

SECTION I

Article 2—Right to life

1. Everyone's right to life shall be protected by law. No one shall be deprived of his life intentionally save in the execution of a sentence of a court following his conviction of a crime for which this penalty is provided by law.

2. Deprivation of life shall not be regarded as inflicted in contravention of this Article when it results from the use of force which is no more than absolutely necessary:

(a) in defence of any person from unlawful violence;
(b) in order to effect a lawful arrest or to prevent the escape of a person lawfully detained;
(c) in action lawfully taken for the purpose of quelling a riot or insurrection.

Article 3—Prohibition of torture

No one shall be subjected to torture or to inhuman or degrading treatment or punishment.

Article 4—Prohibition of slavery and forced labour

1. No one shall be held in slavery or servitude.

2. No one shall be required to perform forced or compulsory labour.

3. For the purpose of this Article the term "forced or compulsory labour" shall not include:

(a) any work required to be done in the ordinary course of detention imposed according to the provisions of Article 5 of this Convention or during conditional release from such detention;
(b) any service of a military character or, in case of conscientious objectors in countries where they are recognised, service exacted instead of compulsory military service;
(c) any service exacted in case of an emergency or calamity threatening the life or well-being of the community;
(d) any work or service which forms part of normal civic obligations.

Article 5—Right to liberty and security

1. Everyone has the right to liberty and security of person. No one shall be deprived of his liberty save in the following cases and in accordance with a procedure prescribed by law:

(a) the lawful detention of a person after conviction by a competent court;
(b) the lawful arrest or detention of a person for non-compliance with the lawful order of a court or in order to secure the fulfilment of any obligation prescribed by law;
(c) the lawful arrest or detention of a person effected for the purpose of bringing him before the competent legal authority on reasonable suspicion of having committed an offence or when it is reasonably considered necessary to prevent his committing an offence or fleeing after having done so;
(d) the detention of a minor by lawful order for the purpose of educational supervision or his lawful detention for the purpose of bringing him before the competent legal authority;
(e) the lawful detention of persons for the prevention of the spreading of infectious diseases, of persons of unsound mind, alcoholics or drug addicts or vagrants;
(f) the lawful arrest or detention of a person to prevent his effecting an unauthorised entry into the country or of a person against whom action is being taken with a view to deportation or extradition.

2. Everyone who is arrested shall be informed promptly, in a language which he understands, of the reasons for his arrest and of any charge against him.

3. Everyone arrested or detained in accordance with the provisions of paragraph 1(c) of this Article shall be brought promptly before a judge or other officer authorised by law to exercise judicial power and shall be entitled to trial within a reasonable time or to release pending trial. Release may be conditioned by guarantees to appear for trial.

4. Everyone who is deprived of his liberty by arrest or detention shall be entitled to take proceedings by which the lawfulness of his detention shall be decided speedily by a court and his release ordered if the detention is not lawful.

5. Everyone who has been the victim of arrest or detention in contravention of the provisions of this Article shall have an enforceable right to compensation.

Article 6—Right to a fair trial

1. In the determination of his civil rights and obligations or of any criminal charge against him, everyone is entitled to a fair and public hearing within a reasonable time by an independent and impartial tribunal established by law. Judgment shall be pronounced publicly but the press and public may be excluded from all or part of the trial in the interests of morals, public order or national security in a democratic society, where the interests of juveniles or the protection of the private life of the parties so require, or to the extent strictly necessary in the opinion of the court in special circumstances where publicity would prejudice the interests of justice.

2. Everyone charged with a criminal offence shall be presumed innocent until proved guilty according to law.

3. Everyone charged with a criminal offence has the following minimum rights:

(a) to be informed promptly, in a language which he understands and in detail, of the nature and cause of the accusation against him;
(b) to have adequate time and facilities for the preparation of his defence;
(c) to defend himself in person or through legal assistance of his own choosing or, if he has not sufficient means to pay for legal assistance, to be given it free when the interests of justice so require;
(d) to examine or have examined witnesses against him and to obtain the attendance and examination of witnesses on his behalf under the same conditions as witnesses against him;
(e) to have the free assistance of an interpreter if he cannot understand or speak the language used in court.

Article 7—No punishment without law

1. No one shall be held guilty of any criminal offence on account of any act or omission which did not constitute a criminal offence under national or international law at the time when it was committed. Nor shall a heavier penalty be imposed than the one that was applicable at the time the criminal offence was committed.

2. This Article shall not prejudice the trial and punishment of any person for any act or omission which, at the time when it was committed, was criminal according to the general principles of law recognised by civilised nations.

Article 8—Right to respect for private and family life

1. Everyone has the right to respect for his private and family life, his home and his correspondence.

2. There shall be no interference by a public authority with the exercise of this right except such as is in accordance with the law and is necessary in a democratic society in the interests of national security, public safety or the economic well-being of the country, for the prevention of disorder or crime, for the protection of health or morals, or for the protection of the rights and freedoms of others.

Article 9—Freedom of thought, conscience and religion

1. Everyone has the right to freedom of thought, conscience and religion; this right includes freedom to change his religion or belief and freedom, either alone or in community with others and in public or private, to manifest his religion or belief, in worship, teaching, practice and observance.

2. Freedom to manifest one's religion or beliefs shall be subject only to such limitations as are prescribed by law and are necessary in a democratic society in the interests of public safety, for the protection of public order, health or morals, or for the protection of the rights and freedoms of others.

Article 10—Freedom of expression

1. Everyone has the right to freedom of expression. This right shall include freedom to hold opinions and to receive and impart information and ideas without interference by public authority and regardless of frontiers. This Article shall not prevent States from requiring the licensing of broadcasting, television or cinema enterprises.

2. The exercise of these freedoms, since it carries with it duties and responsibilities, may be subject to such formalities, conditions, restrictions or penalties as are prescribed by law and are necessary in a democratic society, in the interests of national security, territorial integrity or public safety, for the prevention of disorder or crime, for the protection of health or morals, for the protection of the reputation or rights of others, for preventing the disclosure of information received in confidence, or for maintaining the authority and impartiality of the judiciary.

Article 11—Freedom of assembly and association

1. Everyone has the right to freedom of peaceful assembly and to freedom of association with others, including the right to form and to join trade unions for the protection of his interests.

2. No restrictions shall be placed on the exercise of these rights other than such as are prescribed by law and are necessary in a democratic society in the interests of national security or public safety, for the prevention of disorder or crime, for the protection of health or morals or for the protection of the rights and freedoms of others. This Article shall not prevent the imposition of lawful restrictions on the exercise of these rights by members of the armed forces, of the police or of the administration of the State.

Article 12—Right to marry

Men and women of marriageable age have the right to marry and to found a family, according to the national laws governing the exercise of this right.

Article 13—Right to effective remedy

Everyone whose rights and freedoms as set forth in this Convention are violated shall have an effective remedy before a national authority notwithstanding that the violation has been committed by persons acting in an official capacity.

Article 14—Prohibition of discrimination

The enjoyment of the rights and freedoms set forth in this Convention shall be secured without discrimination on any ground such as sex, race, colour, language, religion, political or other opinion, national or social origin, association with a national minority, property, birth or other status.

Article 15—Derogation in time of emergency

1. In time of war or other public emergency threatening the life of the nation any High Contracting Party may take measures derogating from its obligations under this Convention to the extent strictly required by the exigencies of the situation, provided that such measures are not inconsistent with its other obligations under international law.

2. No derogation from Article 2, except in respect of deaths resulting from lawful acts of war, or from Articles 3, 4 § 1 and 7 shall be made under this provision.

3. Any High Contracting Party availing itself of this right of derogation shall keep the Secretary General of the Council of Europe fully informed of the measures which it has taken and the reasons therefore. It shall also inform the Secretary General of the Council of Europe when such measures have ceased to operate and the provisions of the Convention are again being fully executed.

Article 16—Restrictions of political activity of aliens

Nothing in Articles 10, 11 and 14 shall be regarded as preventing the High Contracting Parties from imposing restrictions on the political activity of aliens.

Article 17—Prohibition of abuse of rights

Nothing in this Convention may be interpreted as implying for any State, group or person any right to engage in any activity or perform any act aimed at the destruction of any of the rights and freedoms set forth herein or at their limitation to a greater extent than is provided for in the Convention.

Article 18—Limitation on use of restrictions on rights

The restrictions permitted under this Convention to the said rights and freedoms shall not be applied for any purpose other than those for which they have been prescribed.

SECTION II

Article 19—Establishment of the court

To ensure the observance of the engagements undertaken by the High Contracting Parties in the Convention and the Protocols thereto, there shall be set up a European Court of Human Rights, hereinafter referred to as "the Court". It shall function on a permanent basis.

Article 20—Number of judges

The Court shall consist of a number of judges equal to that of the High Contracting Parties.

Article 21—Criteria for office

1. The judges shall be of high moral character and must either possess the qualifications required for appointment to high judicial office or be juris consults of recognised competence.

2. The judges shall sit on the Court in their individual capacity.

3. During their term of office the judges shall not engage in any activity which is incompatible with their independence, impartiality or with the demands of a full-time office; all questions arising from the application of this paragraph shall be decided by the Court.

Article 22—Election of judges

The judges shall be elected by the Parliamentary Assembly with respect to each High Contracting Party by a majority of votes cast from a list of three candidates nominated by the High Contracting Party.

Article 23—Terms of office and dismissal

1. The judges shall be elected for a period of nine years. They may not be re-elected.

2. The terms of office of judges shall expire when they reach the age of 70.

3. The judges shall hold office until replaced. They shall, however, continue to deal with such cases as they already have under consideration.

4. No judge may be dismissed from office unless the other judges decide by a majority of two-thirds that that judge has ceased to fulfil the required conditions.

Article 24—Registry and rapporteurs

1. The Court shall have a Registry, the functions and organisation of which shall be laid down in the rules of the Court.

2. When sitting in a single-judge formation, the Court shall be assisted by *rapporteurs* who shall function under the authority of the President of the Court.

They shall form part of the Court's Registry.

Article 25—Plenary Court

The plenary Court shall

(a) elect its President and one or two Vice-Presidents for a period of three years; they may be re-elected;
(b) set up Chambers, constituted for a fixed period of time;
(c) elect the Presidents of the Chambers of the Court; they may be re-elected;
(d) adopt the rules of the Court;
(e) elect the Registrar and one or more Deputy Registrars;
(f) make any request under Article 26 § 2.

Article 26—Single-judge formation, Committees, Chambers and Grand Chamber

1. To consider cases brought before it, the Court shall sit in a single-judge formation, in Committees of three judges, in Chambers of seven judges and in a

Grand Chamber of seventeen judges. The Court's Chambers shall set up Committees for a fixed period of time.

2. At the request of the plenary Court, the Committee of Ministers may, by a unanimous decision and for a fixed period, reduce to five the number of judges of the Chambers.

3. When sitting as a single judge, a judge shall not examine any application against the High Contracting Party in respect of which that judge has been elected.

4. There shall sit as an ex officio member of the Chamber and the Grand Chamber the judge elected in respect of the High Contracting Party concerned. If there is none or if that judge is unable to sit, a person chosen by the President of the Court from a list submitted in advance by that Party shall sit in the capacity of judge.

5. The Grand Chamber shall also include the President of the Court, the Vice-Presidents, the Presidents of the Chambers and other judges chosen in accordance with the rules of the Court. When a case is referred to the Grand Chamber under Article 43, no judge from the Chamber which rendered the judgment shall sit in the Grand Chamber, with the exception of the President of the Chamber and the judge who sat in respect of the High Contracting Party concerned.

Article 27—Competence of single judges

1. A single judge may declare inadmissible or strike out of the Court's list of cases an application submitted under Article 34, where such a decision can be taken without further examination.

2. The decision shall be final.

3. If the single judge does not declare an application inadmissible or strike it out, that judge shall forward it to a Committee or to a Chamber for further examination.

Article 28—Competence of Committees

1. In respect of an application submitted under Article 34, a Committee may, by a unanimous vote,

(a) declare it inadmissible or strike it out of its list of cases, where such can be taken without further examination; or
(b) declare it admissible and render at the same time a judgment on the merits, if the underlying question in the case, concerning the interpretation or the application of the Convention or the Protocols thereto, is already the subject of well-established case-law of the Court.

2. Decisions and judgments under paragraph 1 shall be final.

3. If the judge elected in respect of the High Contracting Party concerned is not a member of the Committee, the Committee may at any stage of the proceedings invite that judge to take the place of one of the members of the Committee, having regard to all relevant factors, including whether that Party has contested the application of the procedure under paragraph 1 (b).

Article 29—Decisions by Chambers on admissibility and merits

1. If no decision is taken under Article27 or 28, or no judgment rendered under Article 28, a Chamber shall decide on the admissibility and merits of individual

applications submitted under Article 34. The decision on admissibility may be taken separately.

2. A Chamber shall decide on the admissibility and merits of inter-State applications submitted under Article 33. The decision on admissibility shall be taken separately unless the Court, in exceptional cases, decides otherwise.

Article 30—Relinquishment of jurisdiction to the Grand Chamber

Where a case pending before a Chamber raises a serious question affecting the interpretation of the Convention or the Protocols thereto, or where the resolution of a question before the Chamber might have a result inconsistent with a judgment previously delivered by the Court, the Chamber may, at any time before it has rendered its judgment, relinquish jurisdiction in favour of the Grand Chamber, unless one of the parties to the case objects.

Article 31—Powers of the Grand Chamber

The Grand Chamber shall

(a) determine applications submitted either under Article 33 or Article 34 when a Chamber has relinquished jurisdiction under Article 30 or when the case has been referred to it under Article 43;
(b) decide on issues referred to the Court by the Committee of Ministers in accordance with Article 46 § 4; and
(c) consider requests for advisory opinions submitted under Article 47.

Article 32—Jurisdiction of the Court

1. The jurisdiction of the Court shall extend to all matters concerning the interpretation and application of the Convention and the Protocols thereto which are referred to it as provided in Articles 33, 34, 46 and 47.

2. In the event of dispute as to whether the Court has jurisdiction, the Court shall decide.

Article 33—Inter-State cases

Any High Contracting Party may refer to the Court any alleged breach of the provisions of the Convention and the Protocols thereto by another High Contracting Party.

Article 34—Individual applications

The Court may receive applications from any person, non-governmental organisation or group of individuals claiming to be the victim of a violation by one of the High Contracting Parties of the rights set forth in the Convention or the Protocols thereto. The High Contracting Parties undertake not to hinder in any way the effective exercise of this right.

Article 35—Admissibility criteria

1. The Court may only deal with the matter after all domestic remedies have been exhausted, according to the generally recognised rules of inter-national law, and within a period of six months from the date on which the final decision was taken.

2. The Court shall not deal with any application submitted under Article 34 that

(a) is anonymous; or
(b) is substantially the same as a matter that has already been examined by the Court or has already been submitted to another procedure of international investigation or settlement and contains no relevant new information.

3. The Court shall declare inadmissible any individual application submitted under Article 34 if it considers that:

(a) the application is incompatible with the provisions of the Convention or the Protocols thereto, manifestly ill-founded, or an abuse of the right of individual application; or
(b) the applicant has not suffered a significant disadvantage, unless respect for human rights as defined in the Convention and the Protocols thereto requires an examination of the application on the merits and provided that no case may be rejected on this ground which has not been duly considered by a domestic tribunal.

4. The Court shall reject any application which it considers inadmissible under this Article. It may do so at any stage of the proceedings.

Article 36—Third party intervention

1. In all cases before a Chamber or the Grand Chamber, a High Contracting Party one of whose nationals is an applicant shall have the right to submit written comments and to take part in hearings.

2. The President of the Court may, in the interest of the proper administration of justice, invite any High Contracting Party which is not a party to the proceedings or any person concerned who is not the applicant to submit written comments or take part in hearings.

3. In all cases before a Chamber or the Grand Chamber, the Council of Europe Commissioner for Human Rights may submit written comments and take part in hearings.

Article 37—Striking out applications

1. The Court may at any stage of the proceedings decide to strike an application out of its list of cases where the circumstances lead to the conclusion that

(a) the applicant does not intend to pursue his application; or
(b) the matter has been resolved; or
(c) for any other reason established by the Court, it is no longer justified to continue the examination of the application.

However, the Court shall continue the examination of the application if respect for human rights as defined in the Convention and the Protocols thereto so requires.

2. The Court may decide to restore an application to its list of cases if it considers that the circumstances justify such a course.

Article 38—Examination of the case

The Court shall examine the case together with the representatives of the parties and, if need be, undertake an investigation, for the effective conduct of which the High Contracting Parties concerned shall furnish all necessary facilities.

Article 39—Friendly settlements

1. At any stage of the proceedings, the Court may place itself at the disposal of the parties concerned with a view to securing a friendly settlement of the matter on the basis of respect for human rights as defined in the Convention and the Protocols thereto.

2. Proceedings conducted under paragraph 1 shall be confidential.

3. If a friendly settlement is effected, the Court shall strike the case out of its list by means of a decision which shall be confined to a brief statement of the facts and of the solution reached.

4. This decision shall be transmitted to the Committee of Ministers, which shall supervise the execution of the terms of the friendly settlement as set out in the decision.

Article 40—Public hearings and access to documents

1. Hearings shall be in public unless the Court in exceptional circumstances decides otherwise.

2. Documents deposited with the Registrar shall be accessible to the public unless the President of the Court decides otherwise.

Article 41—Just satisfaction

If the Court finds that there has been a violation of the Convention or the Protocols thereto, and if the internal law of the High Contracting Party concerned allows only partial reparation to be made, the Court shall, if necessary, afford just satisfaction to the injured party.

Article 42—Judgments of Chambers

Judgments of Chambers shall become final in accordance with the provisions of Article 44 § 2.

Article 43—Referral to the Grand Chamber

1. Within a period of three months from the date of the judgment of the Chamber, any party to the case may, in exceptional cases, request that the case be referred to the Grand Chamber.

2. A panel of five judges of the Grand Chamber shall accept the request if the case raises a serious question affecting the interpretation or application of the Convention or the Protocols thereto, or a serious issue of general importance.

3. If the panel accepts the request, the Grand Chamber shall decide the case by means of a judgment.

Article 44—Final judgments

1. The judgment of the Grand Chamber shall be final.

2. The judgment of a Chamber shall become final

(a) when the parties declare that they will not request that the case be referred to the Grand Chamber; or
(b) three months after the date of the judgment, if reference of the case to the Grand Chamber has not been requested; or
(c) when the panel of the Grand Chamber rejects the request to refer under Article 43.

3. The final judgment shall be published.

Article 45—Reasons for judgments and decisions

1. Reasons shall be given for judgments as well as for decisions declaring applications admissible or inadmissible.

2. If a judgment does not represent, in whole or in part, the unanimous opinion of the judges, any judge shall be entitled to deliver a separate opinion.

Article 46—Binding force and execution of judgments

1. The High Contracting Parties under-take to abide by the final judgment of the Court in any case to which they are parties.

2. The final judgment of the Court shall be transmitted to the Committee of Ministers, which shall supervise its execution.

3. If the Committee of Ministers considers that the supervision of the execution of a final judgment is hindered by a problem of interpretation of the judgment, it may refer the matter to the Court for a ruling on the question of interpretation. A referral decision shall require a majority vote of two thirds of the representatives entitled to sit on the Committee.

4. If the Committee of Ministers considers that a High Contracting Party refuses to abide by a final judgment in a case to which it is a party, it may, after serving formal notice on that Party and by decision adopted by a majority vote of two-thirds of the representatives entitled to sit on the Committee, refer to the Court the question whether that Party has failed to fulfil its obligation under paragraph 1.

5. If the Court finds a violation of paragraph 1, it shall refer the case to the Committee of Ministers for consideration of the measures to be taken. If the Court finds no violation of paragraph 1, it shall refer the case to the Committee of Ministers, which shall close its examination of the case.

Article 47—Advisory opinions

1. The Court may, at the request of the Committee of Ministers, give advisory opinions on legal questions concerning the interpretation of the Convention and the Protocols thereto.

2. Such opinions shall not deal with any question relating to the content or scope of the rights or freedoms defined in Section I of the Convention and the Protocols thereto, or with any other question which the Court or the Committee of Ministers

might have to consider in consequence of any such proceedings as could be instituted in accordance with the Convention.

3. Decisions of the Committee of Ministers to request an advisory opinion of the Court shall require a majority vote of the representatives entitled to sit on the Committee.

Article 48—Advisory jurisdiction of the Court

The Court shall decide whether a request for an advisory opinion submitted by the Committee of Ministers is within its competence as defined in Article 47.

Article 49—Reasons for advisory opinions

1. Reasons shall be given for advisory opinions of the Court.

2. If the advisory opinion does not represent, in whole or in part, the unanimous opinion of the judges, any judge shall be entitled to deliver a separate opinion.

3. Advisory opinions of the Court shall be communicated to the Committee of Ministers.

The Substantive Protocols to the Convention

PROTOCOL No. 1
MARCH 20, 1952

The Governments signatory hereto, being Members of the Council of Europe,

Being resolved to take steps to ensure the collective enforcement of certain rights and freedoms other than those already included in section 1 of the Convention for the Protection of Human Rights and Fundamental Freedoms signed at Rome on November 4, 1950 (hereinafter referred to as "the Convention"),

Have agreed as follows:

Article 1

Every natural or legal person is entitled to the peaceful enjoyment of his possessions. No one shall be deprived of his possessions except in the public interest and subject to the conditions provided for by law and by the general principles of international law.

The preceding provisions shall not, however, in any way impair the right of a State to enforce such laws as it deems necessary to control the use of property in accordance with the general interest or to secure the payment of taxes or other contributions or penalties.

Article 2

No person shall be denied the right to education. In the exercise of any functions which it assumes in relation to education and to teaching, the State shall respect the right of parents to ensure such education and teaching in conformity with their own religious and philosophical convictions.

Article 3

The High Contracting Parties undertake to hold free elections at reasonable intervals by secret ballot, under conditions which will ensure the free expression of the opinion of the people in the choice of the legislature.

PROTOCOL No. 4
SEPTEMBER 16, 1963

The Governments signatory hereto, being Members of the Council of Europe,

Being resolved to take steps to ensure the collective enforcement of certain rights and freedoms other than those already included in Section I of the Convention for the Protection of Human Rights and Fundamental Freedoms signed at Rome on November 4, 1950 (hereinafter referred to as "the Convention") and in Articles 1 to 3 of the First Protocol to the Convention, signed at Paris on March 20, 1952,

Have agreed as follows:

Article 1

No one shall be deprived of his liberty merely on the ground of inability to fulfil a contractual obligation.

Article 2

1. Everyone lawfully within the territory of a State shall, within that territory, have the right to liberty of movement and freedom to choose his residence.

2. Everyone shall be freed to leave any country, including his own.

3. No restriction shall be placed on the exercise of these rights other than such as are in accordance with law and are necessary in a democratic society in the interests of national security or public safety, for the maintenance of ordre public, for the prevention of crime, for the protection of health or morals, or for the protection of the rights and freedoms of others.

4. The rights set forth in paragraph 1 may also be subject, in particular areas, to restrictions imposed in accordance with law and justified by the public interest in a democratic society.

Article 3

1. No one shall be expelled, by means either of an individual or of a collective measure, from the territory of the State of which he is a national.

2. No one shall be deprived of the right to enter the territory of the State of which he is a national.

Article 4

Collective expulsion of aliens is prohibited.

PROTOCOL No. 6
APRIL 28, 1983

The Member States of the Council of Europe, signatory to this Protocol to the Convention for the Protection of Human Rights and Fundamental Freedoms, signed at Rome on November 4, 1950 (hereinafter referred to as "the Convention"),

Considering that the evolution that has occurred in several Member States of the Council of Europe expresses a general tendency in favour of abolition of the death penalty,

Have agreed as follows:

Article 1

The death penalty shall be abolished. No one shall be condemned to such penalty or executed.

Article 2

A State may make provision in its law for the death penalty in respect of acts committed in time of war or of imminent threat of war; such penalty shall be applied only in the instances laid down in the law and in accordance with its provisions. The State shall communicate to the Secretary General of the Council of Europe the relevant provisions of that law.

PROTOCOL No. 7
NOVEMBER 22, 1984

The Member States of the Council of Europe signatory hereto,

Being resolved to take further steps to ensure the collective enforcement of certain rights and freedoms by means of the Convention for the Protection of Human Rights and Fundamental Freedoms signed at Rome on November 4, 1950 (hereinafter referred to as "the Convention").

Have agreed as follows:

Article 1

1. An alien lawfully resident in the territory of a State shall not be expelled therefrom except in pursuance of a decision reached in accordance with law and shall be allowed:

(a) to submit reasons against his expulsion,
(b) to have his case reviewed, and
(c) to be represented for these purposes before the competent authority or a person or persons designated by that authority.

2. An alien may be expelled before the exercise of his rights under paragraph 1(a), (b) and (c) of this Article, when such expulsion is necessary in the interests of public order or is grounded on reasons of national security.

Article 2

1. Everyone convicted of a criminal offence by a tribunal shall have the right to have his conviction or sentence reviewed by a higher tribunal. The exercise of this right, including the grounds on which it may be exercised, shall be governed by law.

2. This right may be subject to exceptions in regard to offences of a minor character, as prescribed by law, or in cases in which the person concerned was tried

in the first instance by the highest tribunal or was convicted following an appeal against acquittal.

Article 3

When a person has by a final decision been convicted of a criminal offence and when subsequently his conviction has been reversed, or he has been pardoned, on the ground that a new or newly discovered fact shows conclusively that there has been a miscarriage of justice, the person who has suffered punishment as a result of such conviction shall be compensated according to the law or the practice of the State concerned, unless it is proved that the non-disclosure of the unknown fact in time is wholly or partly attributable to him.

Article 4

1. No one shall be liable to be tried or punished again in criminal proceedings under the jurisdiction of the same State for an offence for which he has already been finally acquitted or convicted in accordance with the law and penal procedure of that State.

2. The provisions of the preceding paragraph shall not prevent the reopening of the case in accordance with the law and penal procedure of the State concerned, if there is evidence of new or newly discovered facts, or if there has been a fundamental defect in the previous proceedings, which could affect the outcome of the case.

3. No derogation from this Article shall be made under Article 15 of the Convention.

Article 5

Spouses shall enjoy equality of rights and responsibilities of a private law character between them, and in their relations with their children, as to marriage, during marriage and in the event of its dissolution. This Article shall not prevent States from taking such measures as are necessary in the interests of the children.

APPENDIX 2

Dates of entry into force

A–002

States	Convention CETS 005	Protocol No. 1 CETS 009	Protocol No. 4 CETS 046	Protocol No. 6 CETS 114	Protocol No. 7 CETS 117	Protocol No. 13 CETS 187
Albania	02/10/96	02/10/96	02/10/96	01/10/00	01/01/97	—
Andorra	22/01/96	—	—	01/02/96	—	01/07/03
Armenia	26/04/02	26/04/02	26/04/02	01/10/03	01/07/02	—
Austria	03/09/58	03/09/58	18/09/69	01/03/85	01/11/88	01/05/04
Azerbaijan	15/04/02	15/04/02	15/04/02	01/05/02	01/07/02	—
Belgium	14/06/55	14/06/55	21/09/70	01/01/99	—	01/10/03
Bosnia and Herzegovina	12/07/02	12/07/02	12/07/02	01/08/02	01/10/02	01/11/03
Bulgaria	07/09/92	07/09/92	04/11/00	01/10/99	01/02/01	01/07/03
Croatia	05/11/97	05/11/97	05/11/97	01/12/97	01/02/98	01/07/03
Cyprus	06/10/62	06/10/62	03/10/89	01/02/00	01/12/00	01/07/03
Czech Republic	01/01/93	01/01/93	01/01/93	01/01/93	01/01/93	—
Denmark	03/09/53	18/05/54	02/05/68	01/03/85	01/11/88	01/07/03
Estonia	16/04/96	16/04/96	16/04/96	01/05/98	01/07/96	01/06/04
Finland	10/05/90	10/05/90	10/05/90	01/06/90	01/08/90	—
France	03/05/74	03/05/74	03/05/74	01/03/86	01/11/88	—
Georgia	20/05/99	07/06/02	13/04/00	01/05/00	01/07/00	01/09/03
Germany	03/09/53	13/02/57	01/06/68	01/08/89	—	—
Greece	28/11/74	28/11/74	—	01/10/98	01/11/88	—
Hungary	05/11/92	05/11/92	05/11/92	01/12/92	01/02/93	01/11/03
Iceland	03/09/53	18/05/54	02/05/68	01/06/87	01/11/88	—
Ireland	03/09/53	18/05/54	29/10/68	01/07/94	01/11/01	01/07/03
Italy	26/10/55	26/10/55	27/05/82	01/01/89	01/02/92	—
Latvia	27/06/97	27/06/97	27/06/97	01/06/99	01/09/97	—
Liechtenstein	08/09/82	14/11/95	—	01/12/90	—	01/07/03
Lithuania	20/06/95	24/05/96	20/06/95	01/08/99	01/09/95	—
Luxembourg	03/09/53	18/05/54	02/05/68	01/03/85	01/07/89	—
Malta	23/01/67	23/01/67	05/06/02	01/04/91	01/04/03	01/07/03
Moldova	12/09/97	12/09/97	12/09/97	01/10/97	01/12/97	—
Netherlands	31/08/54	31/08/54	23/06/82	01/05/86	—	—
Norway	03/09/53	18/05/54	02/05/68	01/11/88	01/01/89	—
Poland	19/01/93	10/10/94	10/10/94	01/11/00	01/03/03	—
Portugal	09/11/78	09/11/78	09/11/78	01/11/86	—	01/02/04
Romania	20/06/94	20/06/94	20/06/94	01/07/94	01/09/94	01/08/03
Russia	05/05/98	05/05/98	05/05/98	—	01/08/98	—
San Marino	22/03/89	22/03/89	22/03/89	01/04/89	01/06/89	01/08/03
Serbia and Montenegro	03/03/04	03/03/04	03/03/04	01/04/04	01/06/04	01/07/04
Slovakia	01/01/93	01/01/93	01/01/93	01/01/93	01/01/93	—
Slovenia	28/06/94	28/06/94	28/06/94	01/07/94	01/09/94	01/04/04
Spain	04/10/79	27/11/90	—	01/03/85	—	—
Sweden	03/09/53	18/05/54	02/05/68	01/03/85	01/11/88	01/08/03
Switzerland	28/11/74	—	—	01/11/87	01/11/88	01/07/03
the former Yugoslav Republic of Macedonia	10/04/97	10/04/97	10/04/97	01/05/97	01/07/97	—
Turkey	18/05/54	18/05/54	—	01/12/03	—	—
Ukraine	11/09/97	11/09/97	11/09/97	01/05/00	01/12/97	01/07/03
UK	03/09/53	18/05/54	—	01/06/99	—	01/02/04

APPENDIX 3

Article 63 Declaration

United Kingdom:

Declarations contained in a letter from the Permanent Representative of the United Kingdom, dated 31 March 2004, registered at the Secretariat General on 1 April 2004—Or. Engl.

The Government of the United Kingdom declares that it extends the Convention to the Sovereign Base Areas of Akrotiri and Dhekelia in Cyprus, being a territory for whose international relations the United Kingdom is responsible. A–003

The Government of the United Kingdom declares on behalf of the above territory that the Government accepts the competence of the Court to receive applications as provided by Article 34 of the Convention.

[**Note by the Secretariat**: In accordance with the letter from the Permanent Representative of the United Kingdom, dated 21 February 2006, registered at the Secretariat General on 23 February 2006—Or. Engl.—the current situation of territories for whose international relations the United Kingdom is responsible is the following:

1. Application of the Convention:

Anguilla, Bermuda, British Virgin Islands, Cayman Islands, Falkland Islands, Gibraltar, the Bailiwick of Guernsey, Isle of Man, the Bailiwick of Jersey, Montserrat, St Helena, St Helena Dependencies, South Georgia and South Sandwich Islands, Sovereign Base Areas of Akrotiri and Dhekelia in Cyprus, Turks and Caicos Islands.

2. Recognition of the right of individual petition before the European Court of Human Rights:

Territorial extension renewed for a period of *five years as from 14 January 2006*: Anguilla, Bermuda, Montserrat, St Helena, St Helena Dependencies, Turks and Caicos Islands.

Territorial extension accepted *on a permanent basis as from 14 January 2001*: Bailiwick of Jersey.

Territorial extension accepted *on a permanent basis as from 1 June 2003*: Isle of Man.

Territorial extension accepted *on a permanent basis as from 1 May 2004*: Sovereign Base Areas of Akrotiri and Dhekelia in Cyprus.

Territorial extension accepted *on a permanent basis as from 14 January 2006*: Falkland Islands, Gibraltar, South Georgia and South Sandwich Islands.

Territorial extension accepted *on a permanent basis as from 23 February 2006*: Bailiwick of Guernsey, Cayman Islands.

Period covered: 1/5/2004—

APPENDIX 4

Voir Notice explicati
See Explanatory Not

A–004 COMMISSION EUROPÉENNE DE DROITS DE L'HOMME
EUROPEAN COMMISSION OF HUMAN RIGHTS

Conseil de l'Europe — *Council of Europe*
Strasbourg, France

REQUÊTE
APPLICATION

présentée en application de l'article 25 de la Convention européenne des Droits de l'Homme, ainsi que des articles 43 et 44 du Règlement intérieur de la Commission

under Article 25 of the European Convention on Human Rights and Rules 43 and 44 of the Rules of Procedure of the Commission

IMPORTANT: La présente requête est un document juridique et peut affecter vos droits et obligations.
This application is a formal legal document and may affect your rights and obligations.

APPENDIX 4

I— LES PARTIES
THE PARTIES

A. LE REQUÉRANT
THE APPLICANT
(Renseignements à fournir concernant le requérant et son représentant éventuel)
(*Fill in the following details of the applicant and any representative*)

1. Nom de famille .... 2. Prénom(s) ....
Name of applicant *First name(s)*

3. Nationalité .... 4. Profession ....
Nationality *Occupation*

5. Date et lieu de naissance ....
Date and place of birth

6. Domicile ....
Permanent address

.... 7. Tel. No ....

8. Adresse actuelle ....
At present at

....

Le cas échéant, (*if any*)

9. Nom et prénom du représentant* ....
*Name of representative**

10. Profession du représentant ....
Occupation of representative

11. Adresse du représentant ....
Address of representative

.... 12. Tel. No ....

A. LA HAUTE PARTIE CONTRACTANTE
THE HIGH CONTRACTING PARTY

(Indiquer ci-après le nom de l'Etat contre lequel le requête est dirigée)
(*Fill in the name of the Country against which the application is directed*)

13. ....

---

* Si le requérant est représenté, joindre une procuration signée par le requérant en faveur du représentant.
A form of authority signed by the applicant should be submitted if a representative is appointed.

II— EXPOSÉ DES FAITS
STATEMENT OF THE FACTS

(Voir chapitre II de la note explicative)
(*See Part II of the Explanatory Note*)

14.

III— EXPOSÉ DE LA OU DES VIOLATION(S) DE LA CONVENTION ALLÉGUÉE(S) PAR LE REQUÉRANT, AINSI QUE DES ARGUMENTS À L'APPUI
STATEMENT OF ALLEGED VIOLATION(S) OF THE CONVENTION AND OF RELEVANT ARGUMENTS

A. (Voir chapitre II de la note explicative)
See Part III of the Explanatory Note

15.

Si nécessaire, continuer sur une feuille séparée
Continue on a separate sheet if necessary

IV— EXPOSÉ RELATIF AUX PRESCRIPTIONS DE L'ARTICLES 26 DE LA CONVENTION
STATEMENT RELATIVE TO ARTICLE 26 OF THE CONVENTION

(Voir chapitre IV de la note explicative. Donner pour chaque grief, et au besoin sur une feuille séparée, les renseignements demandés sous ch. 16 à 18 ci-après)
(See Part IV of the Explanatory Note. If necessary, give the details mentioned below under points 16 to 18 on a separate sheet for each separate complaint)

16. Décision interne définitive (date et nature de la décision, organe — judiciaire ou autre — l'ayant rendue)
Final decision (date, court or authority and nature of decision)

17. Autres décisions (énumérées dans l'ordre chronologique en indiquant, pour chaque décision, sa date, sa nature et l'organe — judiciaire ou autre — l'ayant rendue)
Other decisions (list in chronological order, giving date, court or authority and nature of decision for each one)

18. Le requérant disposait-il d'un recours qu'il n'a pas exercé? Si oui, lequel et pour quel motif n'a-t-il pas été exercé?
Is any other appeal or remedy available which you have not used? If so, explain why you have not used it.

V— EXPOSÉ DE LA REQUÊTE
STATEMENT OF THE OBJECT OF THE APPLICATION

(Voir chapitre V de la note explicative)
(*See Part V of the Explanatory Note*)

19.

VI— AUTRES INSTANCES INTERNATIONALES TRAITANT OU AYANT TRAITÉ L'AFFAIRE
STATEMENT CONCERNING OTHER INTERNATIONAL PROCEEDINGS

(Voir chapitre VI de la note explicative)
(*See Part VI of the Explanatory Note*)

20. Le requérant a-t-il soumis à une autre instance internationale d'enquête ou de règlement les griefs énoncés dans la présente requête? Si oui, fournir des indications détaillées à ce sujet.
Have you submitted the above complaints to any other procedure of international investigation or settlement? If so, give full details.

VII— PIÈCES ANNEXÉES
LIST OF DOCUMENTS

(PAS D'ORIGINAUX, UNIQUEMENT DES COPIES)
(*NO ORIGINAL DOCUMENTS ONLY PHOTOCOPIES*)

(Voir chapitre VII de la note explicative. Joindre copie de toutes les décisions mentionnées sous ch. IV et VI ci-avant. Se procurer, au besoin, les copies nécessaires, et, en cas d'impossibilité, expliquer pourquoi celles-ci ne peuvent pas être obtenues. Ces documents ne vous seront pas retournés.)
(*See Part VII of the Explanatory Note. Include copies of all decisions referred to in Parts IV and VI above. If you do not have copies, you should obtain them. If you cannot obtain them, explain why not. No document will be returned to you.*)

21. a) ....

b) ....

c) ....

Si nécessaire, continuer sur une feuille séparée
Continue on a separate sheet if necessary

VIII— LANGUE DE PROCÉDURE SOUHAITÉE
STATEMENT OF PREFERRED LANGUAGE

(Voir chapitre VIII de la note explicative)
(*See Part VIII of the Explanatory Note*)

22. Je préfère recevoir la décision de la Commission en:
I prefer to receive the Commission's decision in:

anglais/français*
*English/French**

IX— DÉCLARATION ET SIGNATURE
DECLARATION AND SIGNATURE

(Voir chapitre IX de la note explicative)
(*See Part IX of the Explanatory Note*)

23. Je déclare en toute conscience et loyauté que les renseignements qui figurent sur la présente formule de requête sont exacts et je m'engage à respecter la caractère confidentiel de la procédure de la Commission.
I hereby declare that, to the best of my knowledge and belief, the information I have given in the application is correct and that I will respect the confidentiality of the Commission's proceedings.

24. S'il n'est pas indiqué clairement ci-après que le requérant désire garder l'anonymat à l'égard du public, il sera considéré qu'il n'a pas d'objection à ce que son identité soit révélée:
It will be assumed that there is no objection to the identity of the applicant being disclosed unless it is stated here in unambiguous terms that the applicant does object:

Lieu/*Place* .... *Date/Date* ....

....
(Signature du requérant ou du représentant)
(*Signature of the applicant or of the representative*)

* Biffer ce qui ne convient pas.
Delete as appropriate.

APPENDIX 5

CONSEIL DE L'EUROPE — COUNCIL OF EUROPE

COUR EUROPÉENNE DES DROITS DE L'HOMME
EUROPEAN COURT OF HUMAN RIGHTS

Legal aid rates

A–005 A. FEES AND EXPENSES — Lump sum per case

Preparation of the case

- Filing written pleadings at the request of the Court on the admissibility or merits of the case
- Supplementary observations at the request of the Court (on the admissibility or merits of the case at whatever stage of the proceedings)
- Submissions on just satisfaction or friendly settlement[1]
- Normal secretarial expenses (for example telephone, postage, photocopies)

} €850

B. OTHER

1. Appearance at an oral hearing before the Court or attending the hearing of witnesses (including preparation) €300
2. Assisting in friendly settlement negotiations[2] €200
3. Travelling costs incurred in connection with appearance at an oral hearing or hearing of witnesses or with friendly-settlement negotiations .... according to receipts
4. Subsistence allowance in connection with appearance at an oral hearing or hearing of witnesses or with friendly-settlement negotiations .... €175 per diem

[1] The lump sum covers all written exchanges on the subject.
[2] This involves taking part in a meeting organised by the Registry and attended by the parties and Registry staff (one or more judges may also attend) with a view to reaching a friendly settlement.

APPENDIX 6

A. Practice Direction

Requests for interim measures

(Rule 39 of the Rules of Court) A–006

By virtue of Rule 39 of the Rules of Court, the Court may issue interim measures which are binding on the State concerned. Interim measures are only applied in exceptional cases.

The Court will only issue an interim measure against a Member State where, having reviewed all the relevant information, it considers that the applicant faces a real risk of serious, irreversible harm if the measure is not applied.

Applicants or their legal representatives who make a request for an interim measure pursuant to Rule 39 of the Rules of Court should comply with the requirements set out below.

I. Accompanying information

Any request lodged with the Court must state *reasons*. The applicant must in particular specify in detail the grounds on which his or her particular fears are based, the nature of the alleged risks and the Convention provisions alleged to have been violated.

A mere reference to submissions in other documents or domestic proceedings is not sufficient. It is essential that requests be accompanied by all necessary supporting documents, *in particular relevant domestic court, tribunal or other decisions*, together with any other material which is considered to substantiate the applicant's allegations.

The Court will not necessarily contact applicants whose request for interim measures is incomplete, and requests which do not include the information necessary to make a decision will not normally be submitted for a decision.

Where the case is already pending before the Court, reference should be made to the application number allocated to it.

In cases concerning extradition or deportation, details should be provided of the expected *date and time* of the removal, the applicant's address or place of detention and his or her official case-reference number. The Court must be notified of any change to those details (date and time of removal, address etc.) as soon as possible.

The Court may decide to take a decision on the admissibility of the case at the same time as considering the request for interim measures.

II. Requests to be made by facsimile or letter

Requests for interim measures under Rule 39 should be sent *by facsimile or by post. The Court will not deal with requests sent by e-mail*. The request should, where possible, be in one of the official languages of the Contracting Parties. All requests should be marked as follows in bold on the face of the request:

Rule 39—Urgent
Person to contact: {name and contact details}

[In deportation or extradition cases]

Date and time of removal and destination: {date and time}

III. Making requests in good time

Requests for interim measures should normally be received *as soon as possible* after the final domestic decision has been taken, in order to enable the Court and its Registry to have sufficient time to examine the matter. The Court may not be able to deal with requests in removal cases received less than a working day before the planned time of removal.

Where the final domestic decision is imminent and there is a risk of immediate enforcement, especially in extradition or deportation cases, applicants and their representatives should submit the request for interim measures without waiting for that decision, indicating clearly the date on which it will be taken and that the request is subject to the final domestic decision being negative.

IV. Domestic measures with suspensive effect

The Court is not an appeal tribunal from domestic tribunals, and applicants in extradition and expulsion cases should pursue domestic avenues which are capable of suspending removal before applying to the Court for interim measures. Where it remains open to an applicant to pursue domestic remedies which have suspensive effect, the Court will not apply Rule 39 to prevent removal.

V. Follow-up

Applicants who apply for an interim measure under Rule 39 should ensure that they reply to correspondence from the Court's Registry. In particular, where a measure has been refused, they should inform the Court whether they wish to pursue the application. Where a measure has been applied, they must keep the Court regularly and promptly informed about the state of any continuing domestic proceedings. Failure to do so may lead to the case being struck out of the Court's list of cases.

B. Institution of proceedings

(Individual applications under Article 34 of the Convention)

I. General

1. An application under Article 34 of the Convention must be submitted in writing. No application may be made by telephone.

2. An application must be sent to the following address:

The Registrar
European Court of Human Rights
Council of Europe
F-67075 Strasbourg Cedex

3. An application should normally be made on the form3 referred to in Rule 47 § 1 of the Rules of Court and be accompanied by the documents and decisions mentioned in Rule 47 § 1(h).

Where an applicant introduces his or her application in a letter, such letter must set out, at least in summary form, the subject matter of the application in order to interrupt the running of the six-month rule contained in Article 35 § 1 of the Convention.

4. If an application has not been submitted on the official form or an introductory letter does not contain all the information referred to in Rule 47, the applicant may be required to submit a duly completed form. It must be despatched within eight weeks from the date of the Registry's letter requesting the applicant to complete and return the form.

Failure to comply with this time-limit will have implications for the date of introduction of the application and may therefore affect the applicant's compliance with the six-month rule contained in Article 35 § 1 of the Convention.

5. Applicants may file an application by sending it by fax. However, they must despatch the signed original by post within eight weeks from the date of the Registry's letter referred to in paragraph 4 above.

6. Where, within six months of being asked to do so, an applicant has not returned a duly completed application form, the file will be destroyed.

7. On receipt of the first communication setting out the subject-matter of the case, the Registry will open a file, whose number must be mentioned in all subsequent correspondence. Applicants will be informed thereof by letter. They may also be asked for further information or documents.

8. (a) An applicant should be diligent in conducting correspondence with the Court's Registry.
(b) A delay in replying or failure to reply may be regarded as a sign that the applicant is no longer interested in pursuing his or her application.

9. Failure to provide further information or documents at the Registry's request (see paragraph 7) may result in the application not being examined by the Court or being declared inadmissible or struck out of the Court's list of cases.

II. Form and contents

10. An application should be written legibly and, preferably, typed.

11. Where, exceptionally, an application exceeds ten pages (excluding annexes listing documents), an applicant must also file a short summary.

12. Where applicants produce documents in support of the application, they should not submit original copies. The documents should be listed in order by date, numbered consecutively and given a concise description (e.g., letter, order, judgment, appeal, etc.).

13. An applicant who already has an application pending before the Court must inform the Registry accordingly, stating the application number.

14. (a) Where an applicant does not wish to have his or her identity disclosed, he or she should state the reasons for his or her request in writing, pursuant to Rule 47 § 3.

(b) The applicant should also state whether, in the event of anonymity being authorised by the President of the Chamber, he or she wishes to be designated by his or her initials or by a single letter (e.g., "X", "Y", "Z", etc.)

C. Written pleadings

I. Filing of pleadings

General

1. A pleading must be filed with the Registry within the time-limit fixed in accordance with Rule 38 and in the manner described in paragraph 2 of that Rule.

2. The date on which a pleading or other document is received at the Court's Registry will be recorded on that document by a receipt stamp.

3. With the exception of pleadings and documents for which a system of secured electronic filing has been set up, all other pleadings, as well as all documents annexed thereto, should be submitted to the Court's Registry in 3 copies sent by post or in 1 copy by facsimile ("fax"), followed by 3 copies sent by post.

4. Pleadings or other documents submitted by electronic mail shall not be accepted.

5. Secret documents should be filed by registered post.

6. Unsolicited pleadings shall not be admitted to the case file unless the President of the Chamber decides otherwise (see Rule 38 § 1).

Filing by facsimile

7. A party may file pleadings or other documents with the Court by sending them by fax.

8. The name of the person signing a pleading must also be printed on it so that he or she can be identified.

Secured electronic filing

9. The Court may authorise the Government of a Contracting State to file pleadings and other documents electronically through a secured server. In such cases, the practice directions on written pleadings shall apply in conjunction with the practice directions on secured electronic filing.

II. Form and contents

Form

10. A pleading should include:

(a) the application number and the name of the case;
(b) a title indicating the nature of the content (e.g. observations on admissibility [and the merits]; reply to the Government's/the applicant's observations on admissibility [and the merits]; observations on the merits; additional observations on admissibility [and the merits]; memorial etc.).

11. A pleading should normally in addition
(a) be on A4 page format having a margin of not less than 3.5 cm wide;
(b) be typed and wholly legible, the text appearing in at least 12 pt in the body and 10 pt in the footnotes, with one-and-a-half line spacing;
(c) have all numbers expressed as figures;
(d) have pages numbered consecutively;
(e) be divided into numbered paragraphs;
(f) be divided into chapters and/or headings corresponding to the form and style of the Court's decisions and judgments ("Facts"/"Domestic law [and practice]"/"Complaints"/"Law"; the latter chapter should be followed by headings entitled "Preliminary objection on . . ."; "Alleged violation of Article . . ." as the case may be);
(g) place any answer to a question by the Court or to the other party's arguments under a separate heading;
(h) give a reference to every document or piece of evidence mentioned in the pleading and annexed thereto;
(i) if sent by post, the text of a pleading must appear on one side of the page only and pages and attachments must be placed together in such a way as to enable them to be easily separated (they must not be glued or stapled).

12. If a pleading exceptionally exceeds 30 pages, a short summary should also be filed with it.

13. Where a party produces documents and/or other exhibits together with a pleading, every piece of evidence should be listed in a separate annex.

Contents

14. The parties' pleadings following communication of the application should include:
(a) any comments they wish to make on the facts of the case; however,
(i) if a party does not contest the facts as set out in the statement of facts prepared by the Registry, it should limit its observations to a brief statement to that effect;
(ii) if a party contests only part of the facts as set out by the Registry, or wishes to supplement them, it should limit its observations to those specific points;
(iii) if a party objects to the facts or part of the facts as presented by the other party, it should state clearly which facts are uncontested and limit its observations to the points in dispute;
(b) legal arguments relating first to admissibility and, secondly, to the merits of the case; however,
(i) if specific questions on a factual or legal point were put to a party, it should, without prejudice to Rule 55, limit its arguments to such questions;

(ii) if a pleading replies to arguments of the other party, submissions should refer to the specific arguments in the order prescribed above.

15. (a) The parties' pleadings following the admission of the application should include:

(i) a short statement confirming a party's position on the facts of the case as established in the decision on admissibility;
(ii) legal arguments relating to the merits of the case;
(iii) a reply to any specific questions on a factual or legal point put by the Court.

(b) An applicant party submitting claims for just satisfaction at the same time should do so in the manner described in the practice direction on filing just satisfaction claims.

16. In view of the confidentiality of friendly-settlement proceedings (see Article 38 § 2 of the Convention and Rule 62 § 2), all submissions and documents filed within the framework of the attempt to secure a friendly settlement should be submitted separately from the written pleadings.

17. No reference to offers, concessions or other statements submitted in connection with the friendly settlement may be made in the pleadings filed in the contentious proceedings.

III. Time-limits

General

18.It is the responsibility of each party to ensure that pleadings and any accompanying documents or evidence are delivered to the Court's Registry in time.

Extension of time-limits

19. A time-limit set under Rule 38 may be extended on request from a party.

20. A party seeking an extension of the time allowed for submission of a pleading must make a request as soon as it has become aware of the circumstances justifying such an extension and, in any event, before the expiry of the time-limit. It should state the reason for the delay.

21. If an extension is granted, it shall apply to all parties for which the relevant time-limit is running, including those which have not asked for it.

IV. Failure to comply with requirements for pleadings

22. Where a pleading has not been filed in accordance with the requirements set out in paragraphs 8-15 of this practice direction, the President of the Chamber may request the party concerned to resubmit the pleading in compliance with those requirements.

23. A failure to satisfy the conditions listed above may result in the pleading being considered not to have been properly lodged (see Rule 38 § 1 of the Rules of Court).

INDEX

LEGAL TAXONOMY
FROM SWEET & MAXWELL

This index has been prepared using Sweet and Maxwell's Legal Taxonomy. Main index entries conform to keywords provided by the Legal Taxonomy except where references to specific documents or non-standard terms (denoted by quotation marks) have been included. These keywords provide a means of identifying similar concepts in other Sweet & Maxwell publications and online services to which keywords from the Legal Taxonomy have been applied. Readers may find some minor differences between terms used in the text and those which appear in the index. Suggestions to *sweetandmaxwell.taxonomy@thomson.com*.

All references are to paragraph numbers